THE SOURCEBOOK FOR
POLITICAL COMMUNICATION RESEARCH

The Sourcebook for Political Communication Research offers a comprehensive resource for current research methods, measures, and analytical techniques. The contents herein cover the major analytical techniques used in political communication research, including surveys, experiments, content analysis, discourse analysis (focus groups and textual analysis), network and deliberation analysis, comparative study designs, statistical analysis, and measurement issues. It also includes such innovations as the use of advanced statistical techniques, and addresses digital media as a means through which to disseminate as well as study political communication. It considers the use of methods adapted from other disciplines, such as psychology, sociology, and neuroscience.

With contributions from many of the brightest scholars working in the area today, the *Sourcebook* is a benchmark volume for research, presenting analytical techniques and investigative frameworks for researching political communication. As such, it is a must-have resource for students and researchers working and studying activity in the political sphere.

Erik P. Bucy is the Marshall and Sharleen Formby Regents Professor of Strategic Communication in the Department of Advertising at Texas Tech University.

R. Lance Holbert is an Associate Professor in the School of Communication at The Ohio State University.

ROUTLEDGE COMMUNICATION SERIES
Jennings Bryant/Dolf Zillmann, Series Editors

Selected titles include:

- Frey: *Group Communication in Context: Studies of Bona Fide Groups, Second Edition*
- Bucy/Holbert: *The Sourcebook for Political Communication Research*
- Heath/Bryant: *Human Communication Theory and Research, Second Edition*
- Stacks/Salwen: *An Integrated Approach to Communication Theory and Research, Second Edition*
- Rubin et al: *Communication Research Measures II*
- Frey/Cissna: *Routledge Handbook of Applied Communication Research*
- Hollingshead/Poole: *Research Methods for Studying Groups and Teams*

THE SOURCEBOOK FOR POLITICAL COMMUNICATION RESEARCH

Methods, Measures, and Analytical Techniques

Edited by

Erik P. Bucy
Texas Tech University

R. Lance Holbert
The Ohio State University

NEW YORK AND LONDON

First published in paperback 2013

First published 2011
by Routledge
711 Third Avenue, New York, NY 10017

Simultaneously published in the UK
by Routledge
2 Park Square, Milton Park, Abingdon, Oxon OX14 4RN

Routledge is an imprint of the Taylor & Francis Group, an informa business

© 2011, 2013 Taylor & Francis

Library of Congress Cataloging-in-Publication Data
    Bucy, E. Page, 1963–
    Sourcebook for political communication research : methods, measures, and
    analytical techniques / Erik P. Bucy, R. Lance Holbert.
    p. cm.
    Includes bibliographical references.
    1. Communication in politics–Research. I. Holbert, R. Lance. II. Title.
    JA86.B74 2010
320.01'4--dc22   2010018104

ISBN 13: 978–0–415–96495–1 (hbk)
ISBN 13: 978–0–415–88497–6 (pbk)
ISBN 13: 978–0–203–93866–9 (ebk)

Typeset in Times New Roman
by Keystroke, Station Road, Codsall, Wolverhampton

Printed and bound in the United States of America by Publishers Graphics,
LLC on sustainably sourced paper.

Dedicated to the memory of Michael Pfau—scholar, mentor, friend.

Contents

Preface   xi

Contributors   xiii

INTRODUCTION

1. Advancing Methods and Measurement: Supporting Theory and Keeping Pace
   with the Modern Political Communication Environment   3
   R. Lance Holbert, The Ohio State University, and Erik P. Bucy, Texas Tech University

I. SURVEY METHODOLOGY

2. Challenges and Opportunities of Panel Designs   19
   *William P. Eveland, Jr., The Ohio State University, and Alyssa C. Morey,
   The Ohio State University*

3. The Rolling Cross-Section: Design and Utility for Political Research   34
   *Kate Kenski, University of Arizona, Jeffrey A. Gottfried, University of
   Pennsylvania, and Kathleen Hall Jamieson, University of Pennsylvania*

4. Political Communication Survey Research: Challenges, Trends, and Opportunities   55
   *Lindsay H. Hoffman, University of Delaware, and Dannagal Goldthwaite Young,
   University of Delaware*

II. SECONDARY ANALYSIS AND META-ANALYSIS

5. Secondary Analysis in Political Communication Viewed as a Creative Act   81
   *R. Lance Holbert, The Ohio State University, and Jay D. Hmielowski,
   The Ohio State University*

6. Comparing the ANES and NAES for Political Communication Research   96
   Michael W. Wagner, University of Nebraska–Lincoln

7. The Implications and Consequences of Using Meta-Analysis for Political
   Communication   114
   *Mike Allen, University of Wisconsin–Milwaukee, David D'Alessio, University
   of Connecticut–Stamford, and Nancy Burrell, University of Wisconsin–Milwaukee*

III. EXPERIMENTAL METHODS

8. Experimental Designs for Political Communication Research: Using New
    Technology and Online Participant Pools to Overcome the Problem of
    Generalizability   129
    Shanto Iyengar, Stanford University

9. Expressing versus Revealing Preferences in Experimental Research   149
    Yanna Krupnikov, Indiana University, and Adam Seth Levine, Vanderbilt University

10. The Face as a Focus of Political Communication: Evolutionary Perspectives
    and the Ethological Method   165
    *Patrick A. Stewart, University of Arkansas, Frank K. Salter, Max Planck Research
    Group, and Marc Mehu, University of Geneva*

11. Multi-Stage Experimental Designs in Political Communication Research   194
    *Glenn J. Hansen, University of Oklahoma, and Michael Pfau, University of
    Oklahoma*

IV. CONTENT ANALYSIS

12. Image Bite Analysis of Political Visuals: Understanding the Visual Framing
    Process in Election News   209
    Maria Elizabeth Grabe, Indiana University, and Erik P. Bucy, Texas Tech University

13. Identifying Frames in Political News   238
    *Dennis Chong, Northwestern University, and James N. Druckman, Northwestern
    University*

14. Content Analysis in Political Communication   268
    William L. Benoit, Ohio University

V. DISCOURSE ANALYSIS

15. The Use of Focus Groups in Political Communication Research   283
    Sharon E. Jarvis, University of Texas–Austin

16. Genealogy of Myth in Presidential Rhetoric   300
    Robert L. Ivie, Indiana University, and Oscar Giner, Arizona State University

VI. NETWORK AND DELIBERATION ANALYSIS

17. Methods for Analyzing and Measuring Group Deliberation   323
    *Laura W. Black, Ohio University, Stephanie Burkhalter, Humboldt State
    University, John Gastil, University of Washington, and Jennifer Stromer-Galley,
    University of Albany–SUNY*

18. Porous Networks and Overlapping Contexts: Methodological Challenges in the
    Study of Social Communication and Political Behavior   346
    Scott D. McClurg, Southern Illinois University

VII. COMPARATIVE POLITICAL COMMUNICATION

19. Mediatization of Politics: Toward a Conceptual Framework for Comparative
    Research   367
    Jesper Strömbäck, Mid Sweden University

20. International Applications of Agenda-Setting Theory's Acapulco Typology   383
    *Maxwell E. McCombs, University of Texas–Austin, Salma Ghanem, Central
    Michigan University, Federico Rey Lennon, Catholic University, Argentina,
    R. Warwick Blood, University of Canberra, Australia, Yi-Ning (Katherine) Chen,
    National Chengchi University, Taiwan, and Hyun Ban, University of Incheon*

21. Political Communication across the World: Methodological Issues Involved in
    International Comparisons   395
    *Christina Holtz-Bacha, University of Erlangen-Nürnberg, Germany, and
    Lynda Lee Kaid, University of Florida*

VIII. STATISTICAL TECHNIQUES

22. Expanding the Use of Structural Equation Modeling (SEM) in Political
    Communication   419
    *R. Lance Holbert, The Ohio State University, and Heather L. LaMarre,
    University of Minnesota*

23. Mediation and the Estimation of Indirect Effects in Political Communication
    Research   434
    *Andrew F. Hayes, The Ohio State University, Kristopher J. Preacher,
    University of Kansas, and Teresa A. Myers, The Ohio State University*

24. Time Series Analysis and the Study of Political Communication   466
    Jennifer Jerit, Florida State University, and Adam F. Simon, Yale University

IX. MEASUREMENT

25. Concept Explication in the Internet Age: The Case of Political Interactivity   485
    *S. Shyam Sundar, The Pennsylvania State University, and Saraswathi Bellur,
    The Pennsylvania State University*

26. Beyond Self-Report: Using Latency to Respond to Model the Question Answering
    Process on Web-Based Public Opinion Surveys   505
    John E. Newhagen, University of Maryland

27. What the Body Can Tell Us About Politics: The Use of Psychophysiological
Measures in Political Communication Research   525
Erik P. Bucy, Texas Tech University, and Samuel D. Bradley, Texas Tech University

CONCLUSION

28. Looking Back and Looking Forward: Observations on the Role of Research
Methods in the Rapidly Evolving Field of Political Communication   543
*Gerald M. Kosicki, The Ohio State University, Douglas M. McLeod, University of
Wisconsin–Madison, and Jack M. McLeod, University of Wisconsin–Madison*

Index   570

Preface

As serendipity would have it, the idea for this *Sourcebook* arose in the wake of a well-received talk Holbert gave on political communication and structural equation modeling to the Colloquium on Political Communication Research at Indiana University, organized by Bucy in the spring of 2006. As Holbert suggested at the time, his visit and talk should mark the beginning of an ongoing dialogue rather than represent an isolated experience. The resulting scholarly dialogue is reflected in the chapters that constitute this *Sourcebook*.

Written by leading researchers, the chapters assembled here represent a diverse set of topics covering both cutting-edge and time-honored methods, measures, and analytical techniques in political communication research. Since any project of this size and scope depends on the diligence of its contributors to produce consistently high-quality chapters, we would like to express our gratitude foremost to each contributor for sharing our vision of advancing the field through methodological innovation and analytical inventiveness.

Regardless of approach, the emphasis throughout is on innovation. As with the field itself, the topics covered are wide-ranging and reflect the dynamism of current research trends. The *Sourcebook* opens with Part I on survey methodology, including chapters on panel and rolling cross-sectional designs, followed by a set of chapters in Part II that explicate secondary analyses and meta-analysis. From there, issues in experimental methods are interrogated in Part III, with chapters examining multi-stage designs and techniques for overcoming the problem of generalizability.

The time-honored technique of content analysis is extended into the areas of visual analysis and framing research in Part IV, with contributions on image bite analysis of political visuals and the identification of frames in political news. Discourse analysis receives attention in Part V, with chapters on focus group research and "genealogical" methods for analyzing presidential rhetoric. The growing popularity of network and deliberation analysis is reflected in two chapters in Part VI addressing the challenges associated with studying social communication, group deliberation, and political behavior.

Because political communication research is a truly global phenomenon, Part VII engages issues in comparative research, including the mediatization of politics, agenda-setting in different national contexts, and methodological issues that arise when making transnational comparisons. The final two sections illuminate important issues in statistical analysis and concept measurement. Chapters in Part VIII on statistical analysis make the case for expanding the use of structural equation modeling in political communication, explain mediation analysis and the estimation of indirect effects, and review the issues involved in time series analysis.

The final group of chapters, in Part IX on measurement, address how latency measures can be used to model the question answering process in Web-based public opinion surveys and what the body can tell us about politics through the use of psychophysiological measures in political communication research. A concept explication of political interactivity—a phenomenon of central relevance in our networked media era—is also offered as a case study in the conceptualization of technology-related research and touches on issues of scale construction and validation.

A thoughtful concluding chapter ties together seemingly disparate elements of the preceding sections with observations on political communication as a rapidly evolving field of study.

Although labeled a *Sourcebook*, the spirit of this project is similar to a foundational early volume edited by Chaffee (1975) titled *Political Communication: Issues and Strategies for Research*, which helped establish political communication as a recognized area of research. The similarity in our approaches resides in the bringing together of diverse perspectives and methodologies to the study of political communication as a multilayered enterprise. As Chaffee noted then, "the study of political communication needs to be approached from fresh intellectual perspectives, and with new tools. [The] goal is not the achievement of positive certitude about human behavior; it is the more pragmatic aim of developing vigorous and challenging fields of inquiry" (1975, p. 15).

The contributors to this *Sourcebook* advance this tradition by recognizing how methodological innovation and analytical refinement not only sustain vigorous fields of inquiry but also extend the boundaries of knowledge about political communication—and, by extension, communication processes more generally.

The editors would like to extend our sincere thanks to Linda Bathgate, our editor at Routledge, who was a champion of this project from the outset. Beyond advancing the cause of political communication research by shepherding this *Sourcebook* through the editorial process, Linda has performed invaluable service to the field of communication over the past 15 years by signing scores of authors at both Routledge and Lawrence Erlbaum Associates, where she began her editorial career. We greatly value her enthusiasm, advice, and—that most divine of editorial virtues—patience throughout the writing and editing process. Sarah Stone, our production editor at Routledge, was also marvelously professional in overseeing the production aspects of the project, as was Sarah Enticknap, our diligent copy editor, Rictor Norton, our able proof-reader, and Maggie Lindsey-Jones, project manager extraordinaire.

Throughout the vicissitudes of soliciting and editing chapters, both editors contributed equally to the work involved; the authorship order is alphabetical. The editing of this work was truly a collaborative effort, one we hope readers of this *Sourcebook* will find to have produced valuable results based on the insights offered in the chapters that follow.

Finally, we would like to pay special tribute to Professor Michael Pfau, to whom this volume is dedicated. Michael enjoyed a storied career that touched the lives of many at Augustana College, the University of Wisconsin–Madison, and the University of Oklahoma. We salute his legacy as a scholar, teacher, and mentor. Although Michael's academic work spanned many subfields within communication, political communication remained one of his constant fascinations. He will be missed within and beyond the discipline.

Erik P. Bucy
R. Lance Holbert

REFERENCE

Chaffee, S. H. (Ed.) (1975). *Political communication: Issues and strategies for research*. Beverly Hills: Sage.

Contributors

Mike Allen (PhD, Michigan State University, 1987) is Professor and Director of Graduate Studies in the Department of Communication at the University of Wisconsin–Milwaukee. His work primarily involves the application of meta-analysis to issues in social influence and he has published more than 100 meta-analyses examining such issues as negative political advertising, fairness of presidential media coverage, and self selection of media coverage. He is the current editor of *Communication Monographs.*

Hyun Ban (PhD, University of Texas–Austin, 1999) is an Associate Professor in the Department of Mass Communication, University of Incheon, Korea. His research interests include journalism theories (agenda-setting, framing), political communication, online journalism, and new media research, including blogs, portal news, and user-generated content (UGC). Ban's recent research has examined agenda-setting in the 2007 Korean presidential election, media framing effects of the North Korean nuclear crisis in the U.S. and South Korea, and innovation among UGC users in the U.S. and South Korea.

Saraswathi Bellur (MS, Iowa State University, 2006) is a PhD student in the Mass Communication doctoral program and coordinator of the Media Effects Research Laboratory in the College of Communications at Penn State University. Her research interests include the examination of psychological and physiological effects of communication technology. Situated in the broad area of the media effects paradigm, her studies focus on the effects of structural features of new media on user attention, perception, and evaluation, especially as they pertain to persuasive and interpersonal-communication outcomes.

William L. Benoit (PhD, Wayne State University, 1979) is a Professor of Communication Studies at the Ohio University. His research interests include political campaign messages and image restoration discourse. His most recent book is *Communication in Political Campaigns.* He has published in a variety of journals including *Communication Monographs, Journal of Communication, Human Communication Research, Journalism and Mass Communication Quarterly*, and *Political Communication.*

Laura Black (PhD, University of Washington, 2006) is an Assistant Professor in the School of Communication Studies at Ohio University. Her research interests include conflict management, storytelling, dialogue, and decision making in deliberative groups. She has authored or co-authored studies of online forums, juries, organizational training, and public meetings. In 2007 she received the Laura Crowell Thesis/Dissertation Award from the group division of the National Communication Association for her work on how members of deliberative groups use stories to help them manage conflict.

R. Warwick Blood (PhD, Syracuse University, 1981) is Professor of Communication on the Faculty of Communication and International Studies, University of Canberra, Australia. His research interests are risk theory, risk communication theory and practice, and public opinion processes. His recent research has examined the news reporting of suicide and mental illness and of war and terrorism.

Samuel D. Bradley (PhD, Indiana University–Bloomington, 2005) is an Associate Professor of Advertising at Texas Tech University. Bradley's research employs psychophysiological measures to assess responses to mediated messages and computational modeling of underlying cognitive processes. Bradley is the co-author of *Advertising and Public Relations Research* (M. E. Sharpe, 2010). He serves on the editorial boards of the *Journal of Applied Communication Research* and *Southwest Mass Communication Journal*. Bradley's research has been published in a variety of scholarly journals, including the *Journal of Advertising, Journal of Consumer Psychology, Human Communication Research*, and *Media Psychology*. A former reporter and section editor for the Las Cruces (NM) *Sun-News*, Bradley also served as a copy editor for the *Albuquerque Journal* and *Modesto Bee*. Bradley won the 2006 Indiana University Outstanding Dissertation Award from the program in cognitive science.

Erik P. Bucy (PhD, University of Maryland–College Park, 1998) is the Marshall and Sharleen Formby Regents Professor of Strategic Communication in the Department of Advertising at Texas Tech University. Bucy is the editor of *Politics and the Life Sciences*, and author, with Maria Grabe, of *Image Bite Politics: News and the Visual Framing of Elections* (Oxford, 2009), winner of the 2010 ICA Outstanding Book Award. Bucy serves on the editorial boards of *Human Communication Research, The Information Society*, and *Mass Communication and Society*. He has held visiting and research appointments at the University of Michigan and Dartmouth College.

Stephanie Burkhalter (PhD, University of Washington, 2007) is an Assistant Professor in the Department of Politics at Humboldt State University. Her current research focuses on communication and deliberation in the U.S. Congress. In addition, her work has addressed political deliberation in small groups, specifically the challenge of translating normative concepts derived from democratic theory into empirical measures of actual citizen-based deliberation.

Nancy Burrell (PhD, Michigan State University, 1987) is Professor and Chair in the Department of Communication at the University of Wisconsin–Milwaukee where she also is Director of the Campus Mediation Center. Her published work focuses on analyzing the discourse of conflict in interpersonal and organizational settings and has been published in such journals as *Human Communication Research, Communication Research*, and *Conflict Resolution Quarterly*. She has been recognized as the Dick Ringler Distinguished Peace Educator for her work with public schools.

***Yi-Ning Chen* (Katherine)** (PhD, University of Texas–Austin, 1999) is an Associate Professor in the Department of Advertising and Co-chair of the Chinese Communication research group at National Chengchi University, Taiwan. Her research interests include political communication, science communication, and public relations online.

Dennis Chong (PhD, University of California–Berkeley, 1987) is the John D. and Catherine T. MacArthur Professor of Political Science at Northwestern University. He specializes in the study of choice and decision-making and is the co-editor of the Cambridge University Press book series, *Studies in Public Opinion and Political Psychology*. He has written extensively on political ideology, rationality, tolerance, political activism, and related subjects, and is the author of *Collective Action and the Civil Rights Movement* and *Rational Lives: Norms and Values in Politics and Society*.

David D'Alessio (PhD, Michigan State University, 1997) is an Associate Professor in the Department of Communication at the University of Connecticut–Stamford. His work considers the issues of political communication dealing with agenda setting, political advertising, and the perceptions of the media images. His work has been published in journals such as *Human Communication Research, Journal of Communication*, and *Political Communication.*

James N. Druckman (PhD, University of California–San Diego, 1999) is the Payson S. Wild Professor of Political Science and Faculty Fellow at the Institute for Policy Research at Northwestern University. He also is an Honorary Professor of Political Science at Aarhus University in Denmark. His research focuses on political preference formation and communication. He has published articles in the *American Political Science Review, American Journal of Political Science*, the *Journal of Politics*, and other political science, communication, economic, and psychology journals. He is currently editor of *Public Opinion Quarterly*.

William P. Eveland, Jr. (PhD, University of Wisconsin–Madison, 1997) is a Professor in the School of Communication and Department of Political Science at The Ohio State University. His research interests center on the role of the news media and political conversations in producing an informed and participatory citizenry. He considers individual motivations and information processing, as well as social network characteristics, news content variations across media markets, and news form differences across modalities, as important in the communication effects process.

John Gastil (PhD, University of Wisconsin–Madison, 1994) is a Professor in the Department of Communication at the University of Washington. He is the author of two Sage volumes, *Political Communication and Deliberation* (2008) and *The Group in Society* (2010). He is co-editor, with Peter Levine, of *The Deliberative Democracy Handbook* (Jossey-Bass, 2005) and has authored *By Popular Demand* (University of California, 2000) and *Democracy in Small Groups* (New Society, 1993), along with numerous articles on small groups, deliberation, civic engagement, political communication, culture, public opinion, and related topics.

Salma Ghanem (PhD, University of Texas–Austin, 1996) is Dean of the College of Communication and Fine Arts at Central Michigan University. Her research interests include political communication, the first and second levels of agenda-setting theory, and news coverage of the Middle East.

Oscar Giner (DFA, Yale University School of Drama, 1987) is a Professor in the Department of Theatre and Film of the Katherine K. Herberger College of the Arts, Arizona State University. His research interests include myth, ritual, performance, and Native American ceremonials. His produced plays include *Nosferatu* and *Stories from the Conquest of the Kingdom of New Mexico*. He has recently completed the manuscript of a forthcoming book, *Performing Scarface: In Praise of Shakespearean Villains, Cuban Gangsters and Hip-Hop Myths*.

Jeffrey A. Gottfried (MA, University of Pennsylvania, 2009) is a doctoral candidate at the Annenberg School of Communication of the University of Pennsylvania. His research interests include political communication and presidential and judicial elections. He is a senior researcher at the Annenberg Public Policy Center and is member of both the National Annenberg Election Survey (2004, 2008) and the National Annenberg Judicial Election Survey.

Maria Elizabeth Grabe (PhD, Temple University, 1995) is a Professor in the Department of Telecommunications at Indiana University–Bloomington. Her research interests include experimental studies of information processing and content analysis of news narratives and election visuals. Her research has appeared in numerous leading scholarly journals in communication, journalism studies, and media research. She is the lead author, with Erik Bucy, of *Image Bite Politics: News and the Visual Framing of Elections* (Oxford, 2009), winner of the 2010 ICA Outstanding Book Award. Her research has been funded by the Shorenstein Center on the Press,

Politics, and Public Policy at Harvard University, the Lilly Foundation, and the Ford Foundation, and she is a recipient of the South African Human Research Council's Prestige Fellowship for Foreign Research. A former chair of the Journalism Studies Division of the International Communication Association, Grabe serves on the editorial boards of *Ecquid Novi*, the *Web Journal of Mass Communication Research*, and the *Journal of Broadcasting & Electronic Media*. She began her career as a documentary news producer for the South African Broadcasting Corporation in Johannesburg, South Africa.

Glenn J. Hansen (PhD, University of Missouri, 2004) is an Assistant Professor and Director of the Political Communication Center in the Department of Communication at the University of Oklahoma. Hansen's scholarship focuses on the content and effect of mediated and non-mediated sources of information in a political campaign context. Hansen's research has been published in *Mass Media & Society, Human Communication Research, Southern Communication Journal*, and a number of other venues. He was recently awarded the John Hunter Meta-Analysis Award by the Information Systems Division of the International Communication Association.

Andrew F. Hayes (PhD, Cornell University, 1996) is an Associate Professor in the School of Communication, The Ohio State University. He is the author of *Statistical Methods for Communication Science* (Lawrence Erlbaum Associates, 2005), coeditor of the *Sage Sourcebook of Advanced Data Analysis Methods for Communication Research*, and has authored over 40 articles in the areas of public opinion, political communication, social psychology, and statistical methods. He also serves as editor-in-chief of *Communication Methods and Measures*.

Jay D. Hmielowski (MA, Washington State University, 2007) is a doctoral student in the School of Communication at The Ohio State University. His research interests include the study of political communication, news influence, and the role of media in generating political campaign effects.

Lindsay H. Hoffman (PhD, University of Wisconsin–Madison, 2000) is an Associate Professor in the School of Communication at The Ohio State University. Her research is grounded in public opinion, media effects, and political communication theory. Her work emphasizes the social and media contexts that influence individual political and communication behaviors. She has published in *Journalism & Mass Communication Quarterly, Journal of Broadcasting and Electronic Media, Howard Journal of Communications*, and the *International Journal of Public Opinion Research*.

R. Lance Holbert (PhD, University of Wisconsin–Madison, 2000) is an Associate Professor and Director of Graduate Studies in the School of Communication at The Ohio State University. He is the author of several articles on the use of structural equation modeling in the communication sciences. His most recent research has appeared in *Journal of Communication, Communication Research, Communication Monographs*, and *Media Psychology*. He serves on many editorial boards, including *Journal of Communication, Communication Monographs*, and the *Journal of Broadcasting & Electronic Media*.

Christina Holtz-Bacha (PhD, University of Münster, 1978) is Professor of Communication at the University of Erlangen-Nürnberg, Germany. She received her postdoctoral dissertation (Habilitation) in Hannover and taught at the universities of Munich, Bochum, and Mainz. She has published widely in the area of political communication and media policy. Among the most recent publications are *Frauen, Politik und Medien* [*Women, Politics and Media*], *The Encyclopedia of Political Communication, The Sage Handbook of Political Advertising*, and *Medienpolitik für Europa* [*Media policy for Europe*].

Robert L. Ivie (PhD, Washington State University, 1972) is a Professor in the Department of Communication & Culture at Indiana University, Bloomington. His research interests focus on rhetoric as a mode of political critique and cultural production, with particular emphasis on democracy and the problem of war. His work on U.S. presidential rhetoric appears in journals such as *Presidential Studies Quarterly, Rhetoric & Public Affairs*, and *Quarterly Journal of Speech*. His two most recent books are *Dissent from War* (2007) and *Democracy and America's War on Terror* (2005).

Shanto Iyengar (PhD, University of Iowa, 1973) holds the Harry and Norman Chandler Chair in Communication at Stanford University where he is also Professor of Political Science. His current research focuses on cross-national differences in the content of news, knowledge gaps, and the role of racial cues in political perception.

Kathleen Hall Jamieson (PhD, University of Wisconsin–Madison, 1972) is the Elizabeth Ware Packard Professor of Communication at the Annenberg School for Communication at the University of Pennsylvania and director of its Annenberg Public Policy Center. She has authored and co-authored 15 books and over 90 articles in the areas of presidential discourse, political argumentation, media framing, gender and sexism, and adolescent mental health.

Sharon E. Jarvis (PhD, University of Texas–Austin, 2000) is an Associate Professor of Communication Studies and Government and Associate Director of the Annette Strauss Institute for Civic Participation at the University of Texas at Austin. Her research focuses on the intersection of language use, politics, and persuasion. She is the author of *The Talk of the Party: Political Labels, Symbolic Capital & American Life* (Rowman & Littlefield) and a co-author of *Political Keywords: Using Language that Uses Us* (Oxford University Press). Her research has also appeared in *Journal of Communication, Political Psychology, Political Communication, Communication Quarterly, Communication Studies*, and *Journal of Computer Mediated Communication*.

Jennifer Jerit (PhD, University of Illinois–Urbana-Champaign, 2002) is Assistant Professor in Political Science at Florida State University. Her research examines the rhetorical strategies of political elites as well as the influence of the mass media on political knowledge and awareness. Dr. Jerit's work has appeared in the *American Journal of Political Science, Journal of Politics, Political Behavior, Political Psychology, Public Opinion Quarterly, Harvard International Journal of Press/Politics*, and *Journal of Communication*.

Lynda Lee Kaid (PhD, Southern Illinois University, 1974) is Professor of Telecommunication at the University of Florida. She previously served as the Director of the Political Communication Center and supervised the Political Commercial Archive at the University of Oklahoma. Her research specialties include political advertising and news coverage of political events. A Fulbright Scholar, she has also done work on political television in several European countries. She is the author/editor of more than 25 books, including *The Encyclopedia of Political Communication, The Handbook of Political Communication Research, The Sage Handbook of Political Advertising, The Handbook of Election News Coverage Around the World, Videostyle in Presidential Campaigns, Civic Dialogue in the 1996 Campaign*, and *Mediated Politics in Two Cultures*. She has also written over 150 journal articles and book chapters on various aspects of political communication and has received over $2 million in external grant funds for her research efforts, including support from the Federal Election Assistance Commission, U.S. Department of Commerce, the U.S. Department of Education, the National Endowment for the Humanities, and the National Science Foundation.

Kate Kenski (PhD, University of Pennsylvania, 2006) is an Assistant Professor in the Department of Communication at the University of Arizona, where she teaches political communication, research methods, and statistics. She was a member of the National Annenberg Election Survey team at the Annenberg Public Policy Center of the University of Pennsylvania in 2000, 2004, and 2008. Her research interests include presidential campaigns, public opinion, research methods and statistics, and gender and politics.

Gerald M. Kosicki (PhD, University of Wisconsin–Madison, 1987) is an Associate Professor in the School of Communication at The Ohio State University. He manages the university's Graduate Interdisciplinary Specialization in Survey Research, a 23-hour interdisciplinary minor available to any graduate student at Ohio State. Most of his research involves the framing and media priming of political issues in public opinion contexts.

Yanna Krupnikov (PhD, University of Michigan, 2009) is an Assistant Professor in the Department of Political Science at Indiana University. Her research focuses on the conditions under which strategic communication can alter political decision making and political behavior. Her work has been published in the *National Tax Journal* and *Political Communication*.

Heather L. LaMarre (PhD, The Ohio State University, 2009) is an Assistant Professor in the School of Journalism and Mass Communication at the University of Minnesota. Her recent research has appeared in the *International Journal of Press/Politics*, *Communication Research*, and *Mass Communication & Society*. Her research interests include the study of entertainment media and politics, strategic communication, and persuasion.

Federico Rey Lennon (PhD, University of Navarra, Spain, 1996) is a Professor at the Argentine Catholic University. His research interests include agenda setting and corporate communications. His most recent books are *Reflexiones sobre el management de la comunicación* and *Edward Bernays. El día en que se inventaron las relaciones públicas*.

Adam Seth Levine (PhD, University of Michigan, 2010) is a research fellow at the Center for the Study of Democratic Institutions at Vanderbilt University. His research examines how people decide to participate in politics (such as donating money and volunteering time) and when requests for participation are persuasive. His research is grounded in political science, psychology, marketing, and economics. He has published in *Political Analysis*, *Perspectives on Politics*, and the *National Tax Journal*.

Scott D. McClurg (PhD, Washington University, 2000) is an Associate Professor in the Department of Political Science at Southern Illinois University. His research centers on the study of political mobilization in America, particularly as a function of social and political context. His recent work focuses on the political geography of turnout in American elections, the consequences of political expertise in social networks for political behavior, and how social context contributes to quality voting decisions. His research appears in the *American Journal of Political Science*, *Political Research Quarterly*, *American Politics Research*, and *Political Behavior*.

Maxwell E. McCombs (PhD, Stanford University, 1966) holds the Jesse H. Jones Centennial Chair in the School of Journalism at the University of Texas at Austin. A co-founder of agenda-setting theory, his research is focused on the explication of this theory and other aspects of political communication.

Douglas M. McLeod (PhD, University of Minnesota, 1989) is a Professor in the School of Journalism and Mass Communication at the University of Wisconsin–Madison. He has published more than 90 journal articles and book chapters in the areas of political communication, public opinion, social conflict, terrorism, and the media.

Jack M. McLeod (PhD, University of Michigan, 1962) is Maier-Bascom Professor Emeritus at the University of Wisconsin–Madison. He most recently co-authored chapters: "Communication and education: Creating competence for socialization into public life"; "Levels of analysis"; and "Social networks, public discussion, and civic engagement: A socialization perspective."

Marc Mehu (PhD, University of Liverpool, 2007) is a postdoctoral researcher in the Swiss Centre for Affective Sciences at the University of Geneva. His main research interests lie in the function of emotional communication with a particular focus on facial expression. He is the author of several articles on the function of smiling in social interactions. He is also part of the European Network of Excellence on Social Signal Processing dedicated to the advancement of automatic analysis of nonverbal behavior.

Alyssa C. Morey (BA, University of Wisconsin–Madison, 2007) is a graduate student in the School of Communication at The Ohio State University. Her research interests include the study of social networks and the role of political discussion in the democratic process, the importance of political entertainment media in fostering engaged citizens, emotional reactions to political advertising, and also the correlates and measurement of political tolerance.

Teresa A. Myers (PhD, The Ohio State University, 2010) is a postdoctoral research associate in the School of Communication at The Ohio State University. Her research interests focus on communication, public opinion, and collective action. Recent work has examined public opinion, the Iraq war, issue advocacy groups, and environmental concerns. She is also interested in statistical methods.

John E. Newhagen (PhD, Stanford University, 1990) is an Associate Professor in the Phillip Merrill College of Journalism at the University of Maryland. He worked as a foreign correspondent in Central America and the Caribbean for nearly 10 years. He served as bureau chief in San Salvador, regional correspondent in Mexico City, and foreign editor in Washington, DC for United Press International during the 1980s. Newhagen's research on the effects of emotion in television and on the Internet has been published widely in a number of leading academic journals.

Michael Pfau (PhD, University of Arizona, 1987) was Professor and Chair of the Department of Communication at the University of Oklahoma and an active scholar in communication. He passed away on March 12, 2009, and this sourcebook is dedicated in his honor. Pfau's research and writing focuses on the influence of the mass media in a variety of contexts and on uses of the inoculation strategy to confer resistance to influence. Pfau authored more than one hundred monographs and book chapters that have appeared in most of the leading journals in communication, including *Communication Monographs*, *Communication Research*, *Human Communication Research*, *Journal of Communication*, and *Journal of Broadcasting & Electronic Media*. Pfau served as editor of the *Journal of Communication*. He co-authored/co-edited six books, most recently the *Handbook of Persuasion* (2002) and *With Malice toward All? The Media and Public Confidence in Democratic Institutions* (2001).

Kristopher J. Preacher (PhD, The Ohio State University, 2003) is Assistant Professor in the Department of Psychology at the University of Kansas. Much of his work involves finding ways to improve upon and refine the application of common multivariate techniques. His research focuses primarily on the use of factor analysis, structural equation modeling, and multilevel modeling to analyze longitudinal and correlational data. Other interests include developing strategies to test mediation and moderation hypotheses, bridging the gap between theory and practice, and studying model evaluation and model selection in the application of multivariate methods to social science questions.

Frank K. Salter (PhD, Griffith University, Brisbane, Australia, 1990) is an independent scholar and management consultant based at the Max Planck Research Group for Human Ethology in Andechs, Germany. He studies politics, including organizations and ethnicity, using the methods and findings of behavioral biology in addition to conventional approaches. His first monograph was an observational study of interpersonal communications within hierarchies (*Emotions in Command: Biology, Bureaucracy, and Cultural Evolution*, Transaction edition, 2008). He has also published on the relationship between ethnic signaling and solidarity and its impact on welfare rights and collective risk-taking, including suicide terrorism. He is presently researching a quantitative model of elite ethnic group influence in the United States and dominance strategies used in work organizations.

Adam F. Simon (PhD, University of California–Los Angeles, 1997) was a National Science Foundation Graduate Fellow. His current work is *Mass Informed Consent: Upgrading Democracy with Polls and New Media*. This hybrid popular/academic work popularizes polling and public opinion research by introducing social scientific techniques in three empirical studies—partial birth abortion, the Harry and Louise ads, and the Iraq War—that relate media to polling results. His first book, *The Winning Message: Candidate Behavior, Campaign Discourse and Democracy*, broke new ground in investigating candidate behavior in American electoral campaigns. This project brought together normative and empirical methods as well as formal (game) theory to address the issue of campaign quality. His work has also appeared in the *American Political Science Review* and the *Journal of Communication* as well as other scholarly journals. He is a member of the American Political Science Association and the International Communication Association.

Patrick A. Stewart (PhD, Northern Illinois University, 1998) is an Assistant Professor of political science at the University of Arkansas. From 2000 to 2008 he was Director of Arkansas State University's Masters of Public Administration (MPA) program and co-Director/Creator of ASU's Center for Social Research. His current research emphasis is on the role of emotions in decision making, focusing on nonverbal communication, with publications on this topic appearing in *Motivation and Emotion, Political Psychology, Harvard International Journal of Press/Politics*, and *Politics and the Life Sciences*.

Jesper Strömbäck (PhD, Stockholm University, 2001) is Lubbe Nordström-Professor and Chair in Journalism at Mid Sweden University, where he is also research director at the Centre for Political Communication Research. He has published more than 25 articles in various communication and political science journals. Among his most recent books are *Global Political Marketing* (co-edited with Jennifer Lees-Marshment and Chris Rudd, Routledge, 2010) and *Handbook of Election News Coverage Around the World* (co-edited with Lynda Lee Kaid, Routledge, 2008).

Jennifer Stromer-Galley (PhD, University of Pennsylvania, 2002) is an Associate Professor in the Department of Communication at the University at Albany, SUNY. Her research interests include the political uses and effects of new communication technology, including campaigning through the Internet, organic citizen's political talk, and formal political deliberations.

S. Shyam Sundar (PhD, Stanford University, 1995) is Distinguished Professor and founding director of the Media Effects Research Laboratory at Penn State University's College of Communications. His research investigates the effects of technological variables related to modality, agency, interactivity, and navigability upon individuals' perceptions and processing of online content. Sundar has been identified as the most published author of Internet-related research in the field of communication during the medium's first decade. He served as chair of the Communication and Technology division of the International Communication Association, 2008–2010, and has held a visiting appointment at Sungkyunkwan University in Seoul, South Korea, as a WCU (World Class University) Professor of Interaction Science.

Michael W. Wagner (PhD, Indiana University–Bloomington, 2006) is an Assistant Professor in the Political Science Department at the University of Nebraska–Lincoln. His research interests include framing, political communication, political psychology, partisan polarization, and biology and politics. He is published in the *Annual Review of Political Science, American Politics Research, The Forum, State Politics and Policy Quarterly*, and several edited volumes. He is currently completing two co-authored book projects: one explores public attitudes about Congress while the other focuses on ideological heterogeneity and partisan polarization in the American electorate.

Dannagal Goldthwaite Young (PhD, University of Pennsylvania, 2007) is an Assistant Professor in the Department of Communication at the University of Delaware. Her research interests include political media effects, public opinion, political satire, and the psychology of political humor. Her work on the role and effects of late-night comedy in the changing political environment has been published in numerous journals including *Media Psychology, Political Communication, International Journal of Press/Politics, Journal of Broadcasting and Electronic Media*, and *Mass Media and Society*.

INTRODUCTION

1

Advancing Methods and Measurement

Supporting Theory and Keeping Pace with the Modern Political Communication Environment

R. Lance Holbert
School of Communication
The Ohio State University

Erik P. Bucy
Department of Advertising
Texas Tech University

The job of the political communication scholar is to improve and enhance our understanding of a complex set of communicative dynamics that influence political outcomes, both as means and as ends. The political outcomes studied within the field represent the spectrum of effects, from the most basic matters of exposure and attention (e.g., news use and reliance) to more advanced outcomes like political behaviors (e.g., voting and other forms of participation) or post-behavior cognitive integration (e.g., perceptions of campaign legitimacy, perceptions of vote count accuracy). The communication theories developed to study a broad range of phenomena continue to expand and evolve, and these theoretical developments are taking place within the context of an ever-changing communication landscape (Bimber, 2003; Campus, Pasquino, & Vaccari, 2008; Holbert & Benoit, 2009; Prior, 2009; Scheufele, 1999).

The evolving nature of the communication environment has caused the field to engage in a debate about which conceptual frameworks are the most useful in assessing communicative influence in politics (see Bennett & Iyengar, 2008, 2010; Holbert, Garrett, & Gleason, 2010). This debate has centered on how the field's research can remain accessible, or "interpretable, cumulative, and socially significant" (Bennett & Iyengar, 2008, p. 709), to relevant audiences. The long-running debate over how to properly conceptualize the past, present, and future of the effects traditions in political communication is beyond the scope of this *Sourcebook* (but see Bucy & D'Angelo, 1999, 2004). However, within this project's purview is a detailed examination and explication of the advanced methods employed by political communication scholars to analyze theoretical propositions and measure communication dynamics at play at the media–politics interface.

On one level, methods represent a constant within the field of political communication. Communication is a variable field (Paisley, 1984), so the use of a wide range of methods has been standard practice since the field's inception (see Chaffee, 1975; Nimmo & Sanders, 1981). In addition, communication straddles the boundary (somewhat artificially constructed at times) between the humanities and the social sciences. Thus, methods commonly employed across both of these much broader epistemological foundations are treated as common within the interdisciplinary field of political communication. In short, methodological diversity has been an integral part of the field for many years and all signs indicate that this will remain the case for the foreseeable future.

However, on another level, the foundational methods commonly employed in political communication (e.g., survey research, experimentation, content analysis) are continually progressing, and it is becoming the informal duty of every political communication scholar to maintain a firm understanding of the latest advancements in method to enable the most rigorous analysis of the core questions driving individual research agendas. Toward this end, this *Sourcebook* serves as a vehicle by which to introduce political communication researchers to some of the latest advances in methods, measurement, and analytical techniques. The broad range of methods commonly employed in the field are well represented in this volume, but many of the topics covered represent innovations and novel applications of existing techniques that together are pushing and advancing research. For intellectual vibrancy it is important that political communication scholars remain ever vigilant in advancing and refining the varied methodological tools at their disposal. Indeed, the advancement of method is a necessary condition enabling the field to progress and remain "interpretable, cumulative, and socially significant" over the long haul.

Survey methods remain a dominant methodological tool for political communication analysis. A recent content analysis conducted by Evans and Bucy (2010) of peer-reviewed articles appearing in two of political communication's primary journals, *Political Communication* and the *International Journal of Press/Politics*, revealed that more than a quarter of the articles published in these outlets over the past decade retained some type of survey method as their primary analytical tool. As many scholars have observed, the study of communication is about the study of process, and advanced survey designs allow for ever more precise ways to assess communication influences. The traditional cross-sectional survey design, which claims a long and storied history within the field, retains several distinct *dis*advantages that prevent political communication researchers from truly understanding processes and effects that unfold over time (Holbert & Stephenson, 2008). The persistent use and deployment of cross-sectional survey designs to this point has left many core causal questions unresolved. Through the use of more advanced longitudinal and panel designs, political communication scholars are beginning to wrestle with some of the field's most basic causal issues (e.g., Eveland, Hayes, Shah, & Kwak, 2005), of which there are many.

ORGANIZATION OF THE *SOURCEBOOK*

The first section in this volume examines important developments in survey research. Two chapters in particular address how political communication researchers should approach multistage survey designs that, for the most part, overcome the limitations of cross-sectional designs. In Chapter 2, Eveland and Morey spell out in detail the value of panel designs in addressing empirical questions posed by political communication scholars. In addition, they offer a series of examples to illustrate the appropriate use of panel data. Most importantly, they stress that an advanced methodological design means little without a solid theoretical foundation. For example, these researchers argue that the answers to basic panel design issues (e.g., What time lags should be used between different phases of data collection?) can only be addressed in a valid and reliable way through the use of theory. Theoretical considerations should guide the decision as to whether the time lag between the data collected at Time 1 and Time 2 should be an hour, a day, a week, a month, or a year. Even the most sophisticated analytical technique can't make up for a lack of theory or weak conceptualization, and a given methodological tool is best utilized when given solid conceptual grounding. These principles guide the topics covered throughout this *Sourcebook*.

In Chapter 3, Kenski, Gottfried, and Jamieson summarize the use of the rolling cross-sectional survey design to enhance our understanding of political communication processes within the election context. The rolling cross-sectional design serves as the foundation for the National Annenberg Election Studies (NAES), and Wagner (in Chapter 6, this volume) highlights the key strengths and weakness of the Annenberg approach compared to the American National Election Studies (ANES) surveys, which were long conducted through the University of Michigan's Institute for Social Research and now involves a collaboration between Stanford University and Michigan. Kenski and colleagues review several of the fundamental issues involved in designing a rolling cross-sectional survey, highlighting the four primary steps to constructing such a design: determination of the total number of target interviews, creation of replicates, establishment of time intervals between replicates, and equal treatment of all subsamples. In addition, these authors discuss the choices researchers need to make relative to the resources available and how, again, theory should inform key design decisions, including the total number of target interviews or establishment of proper time intervals. The strengths and weaknesses of rolling cross-sectional designs are also compared against the use of other more advanced survey designs, such as repeated cross-sectional designs and panel designs.

Discussion of more advanced survey design issues does not mean that political communication researchers should gloss over other important considerations, including the measurement of core concepts, the use of the "don't know" response, and minimizing response biases and response errors. In Chapter 4, Hoffman and Young emphasize the need for political communication scholars to remain focused on the basics, even while pushing the boundaries of survey research through the use of more advanced designs. Foundational concepts such as media use, voting, political knowledge, and sophistication are often the most difficult to operationalize in research, and Hoffman and Young perform a valuable service by addressing the strengths and weaknesses of various survey-based approaches used in the literature to measure these constructs. Even the most sophisticated of survey designs is likely to remain ineffective if proper attention is not given to core concerns, a point which Hoffman and Young make abundantly clear.

Another insight revealed by a systematic review of political communication journals is the prevalence of secondary analysis in the field (Evans & Bucy, 2010). With cross-sectional or "one-shot" survey designs, secondary analyses are just about on par with the use of primary data by political communication researchers. With panel data, secondary analyses far outweigh the use of primary data. This is understandable given the additional resources of time, money, and research effort needed to collect panel data. Regardless, a reasonable conclusion can be reached that secondary analyses, given their abundance in the field, provide some utility in addressing a broad range of political communication inquiries. Consequently, the field should give secondary analysis its due as a legitimate method, much like the credit it receives in political science, and continue to focus on refining analytical techniques for the analysis of existing data sources.

On this point, Holbert and Hmielowski make an argument in Chapter 5 that secondary analysis should be viewed as a creative act. A common criticism of secondary analysis is that it is not as original or intellectually creative as doing primary research where the researcher is in full control of design, measurement, and analysis (see Kiecolt & Nathan, 1985). This criticism is addressed by Holbert and Hmielowski with a nine-part typology consisting of three stages of secondary analysis (choice of data, variable creation, and data analysis) and three dimensions of creativity (novelty, effectiveness, and authenticity), as detailed by Averill (2002). Nine studies that reflect a specific mix of secondary analysis stages and creative dimensions are highlighted in Holbert and Hmielowski's examination in support of the argument that performing secondary analysis represents something original and inventive.

Interdisciplinary Considerations

The field of political communication not only cuts across multiple levels of analysis and a wide range of epistemological foci, but it is also unique in terms of straddling two well-established disciplines, communication and political science. Indeed, discussions of how the two fields of study approach the topic of political communication have been given careful consideration in recent years (see Benoit & Holbert, 2010; Bucy & D'Angelo, 2004; Graber & Smith, 2005). In Chapter 6, Wagner highlights how the widely influential (and older) ANES and important (but newer) NAES embody the differences between the approach political scientists and communication scholars take in studying election campaigns. Distinct in design, the ANES and NAES data present some unique opportunities and definitive advantages while maintaining their own idiosyncratic limitations, although they both remain amenable to periodic change and inclusion of new items (e.g., extended panel designs across election cycles, off-year pilot study designs). Choosing a suitable dataset is a foundational task for those engaging in secondary analysis and Wagner's chapter provides political communication scholars with an informative framework for deciding how to utilize the unique qualities of both the ANES and NAES.

The field of political communication has reached a point in its development where well-defined bodies of evidence are being amassed in relation to several core questions driving the discipline (e.g., the relationship between news use and knowledge gain, or the influence of political advertising on voting intentions). As a result, there is ample opportunity for conducting meta-analyses of existing studies to determine broader patterns of political communication processes and effects. In Chapter 7, Allen, D'Alessio, and Burrell provide a summary of the unique epistemological value of conducting a meta-analysis. As the field of political communication continues to expand, one would expect meta-analysis to grow in popularity as an analytical technique. And, indeed, it appears that we are beginning to see an increase in the number of published meta-analyses in our journals (e.g., Benoit, Hansen, & Verser, 2003; D'Alessio & Allen, 2007; Hansen & Benoit, 2007). Equally important from a methodological standpoint is for research to continually refine the procedures involved in meta-analysis. With increased utilization, a broader group of scholars will be able to gain a more comprehensive understanding of a core set of relationships deemed important. Allen, D'Alessio, and Burrell go a long way toward aiding scholars in achieving this goal.

At the individual level, political communication has always embraced the use of experimentation (Simon & Iyengar, 1995). Compared to early experimental studies, the designs employed in current research have become significantly more nuanced and complex. In addition, a new level of creativity is being demonstrated in the manner by which experiments are being conducted. In Chapter 8, Iyengar details how political communication scholars can employ new media software and Web-based platforms to better address research questions that call for the causal inference that experimentation allows while at the same time reaching a probability sample of subjects. With hybrid survey-experimental designs and computer software that enables participants to take part in a study within a familiar setting and at their convenience, a new era of experimentation has arrived. As a result, our understanding of political communication processes stands to benefit enormously. As shown by some of Iyengar's own work conducted within his Political Communication Lab at Stanford (http://pcl.stanford.edu), as well as by pioneering research funded by the Time-sharing Experiments for the Social Sciences (TESS) program sponsored by the National Science Foundation (http://tess.experimentcentral.org), new media are offering considerably expanded opportunities for experimental and hybrid survey-experimental research.

Many of the core research questions driving the study of political communication focus on behaviors. However, there is a clear conceptual distinction between behavorial intention on the one hand and actual behavior on the other. In Chapter 9, Krupnikov and Levine explicate the difference between expressing behavioral preferences (i.e., intentions) and revealing preferences (i.e., performing actual behaviors of interest), detailing how various political communication research projects have focused on the former at the expense of verifying what amounts to behavioral promises. In addition, these authors review the comparative advantages of various experimental designs suitable for measuring each type of preference. Most importantly, Krupnikov and Levine provide a series of remedies for maximizing the strengths and minimizing the weaknesses of analytical techniques when examining expressed versus revealed preferences in experimental research.

Building on the experimental study of political behavior, Stewart, Salter, and Mehu in Chapter 10 synthesize the interesting and sometimes overlooked experimental literature on nonverbal communication, focusing in particular on televised leader displays. A broad theoretical argument, grounded in ethology, is offered that speaks to the importance of nonverbal communication in different political contexts, including elections, international crises, and governance. A series of advances in the experimental study of viewer responses to televised leader displays is then detailed. Stewart and colleagues link the study of nonverbal political communication to several core areas of political communication scholarship, including leadership, emotion, source perceptions, and audience responsiveness. It is worth repeating that methodological advances are best employed within the context of a well-grounded theoretical framework. Stewart, Salter, and Mehu illustrate this point by offering a solid conceptual foundation for investigating a series of questions that will require the field to employ innovative methods and pioneering techniques to study political leaders and other news sources as nonverbal communicators.

Scholars of all stripes, not just political communication, commonly associate the use of experimentation with the identification of "short-term" effects. However, more elaborate designs currently allow for the assessment of long-term effects within the controlled environment of the experimental setting. Theoretical arguments that predict the unfolding of a specific effect over time (e.g., a sleeper effect in persuasion, or long-term memory gain in information processing) call for longitudinal experimental designs. In Chapter 11, Hansen and Pfau detail the strengths and pitfalls associated with conducting political communication experiments that involve multiple contacts with participants over periods of time that could span days, weeks, or months. This chapter should be seen as a corollary to the Eveland and Morey contribution on panel designs. Despite addressing different methodologies, Chapters 2 and 11 examine similar opportunities and limitations, with insights offered by each author team that speak to the uniqueness of survey research compared to experimentation. Most importantly, political communication scholars need to step away from associating experimental research with studying only those effects that are immediately measurable. Experimentation has the ability to assess long-term effects, as long as researchers develop an appreciation for more complex design issues and the delayed or follow-up data collections that are necessary to show long-term effects.

Content and Discourse Analysis

The first three sections of this *Sourcebook* address the central methodologies employed in the study of political communication: survey and experimentation. Another important element of political communication methodology is content analysis. Three chapters are devoted to this method of determining patterns in message content, beginning with an examination of political visuals. The study of visuals has long presented a conundrum for political communication researchers. Although recognized as influential, political visuals (especially full motion video with audio) have proven difficult to systematically quantify and reliably measure. The field's ability to nail down specific empirical insights as to how and when visual effects take place, and the magnitude of visual effects in terms of political influence, has been hindered by this lack of reliable measures with which to assess the visual landscape. In Chapter 12, Grabe and Bucy address this need by summarizing how to empirically study visuals within the context of televised election coverage, following their "image bites" approach to broadcast news analysis (see Grabe & Bucy, 2009; Bucy & Grabe, 2007, 2008). By providing a foundation for the study of political visuals in any televised setting, they open this essential element of political communication research to more systematic study and analysis.

Content analysis as a methodology dovetails with theory in the context of framing, one of the central theoretical pillars of political communication research (along with agenda setting and priming). Much intellectual effort has been expended in recent years explaining how framing as a mode of analysis interfaces with agenda setting, its variants, and related concepts (see Scheufele, 2000; Schuefele & Tewksbury, 2007). As a research team, Chong and Druckman (2007a, 2007b, 2007c) have been doing as much as anyone to advance the study of framing, both in terms of theory development and in terms of methodology. In Chapter 13, on identifying frames in political news, they explicate some of the fundamental methodological issues associated with the study of frames. The methodological principles addressed in this chapter build on themes introduced in their earlier work. For example, Chong and Druckman stress that a frame can only be identified in relation to a given attitude object that is the focus of the frame, whether this object in a political context is a candidate, event, or issue. Their chapter also addresses many of the fundamental assumptions associated with the study of political media frames and how many framing studies work within a competitive framework through an analysis of the influence of competing frames (e.g., episodic versus thematic). The study of framing remains a conceptually diverse area of research and Chong and Druckman bring methodological clarity to this important line of inquiry.

The final chapter in this section, authored by Benoit, provides an overview of the myriad ways in which political communication researchers set about the task of conducting content analyses. The basics of content analysis (e.g., identification of a sampling frame, development of content categories) are spelled out in some detail. In addition, attention is devoted to the matters of reliability and validity, which are vitally important to conducting quality research using this method. Benoit stresses the need for the proper assessment of intercoder reliability in any content analysis and provides classic arguments for why this should be the case. Far too many content analyses in political communication do not give proper attention to the issue of intercoder reliability, and the Benoit chapter serves as a not-so-gentle reminder that this issue should not be overlooked. Finally, Benoit offers a comparative assessment of the strengths and weaknesses of conducting content analyses using human coders versus an ever-expanding range of software packages that allow for automated coding of texts. Recent advancements in these software packages have made computer-aided coding a viable option for a broader range of research projects, so it is important for political communication scholars to have some sense of what these programs offer in terms of research possibilities (for a counter view on automated coding procedures, see Grabe & Bucy, Chapter 12, this volume).

At the heart of any communication process or event is discourse, and a dominant method for the study of discourse involves the use of focus groups. As highlighted by Jarvis in Chapter 15, focus groups are widely used within the practical realm of politics. Political campaigns, political consultants, and many news organizations use focus group-oriented activities to test message strategies, understand why selected voters hold a particular view on a given public policy issue, or gauge initial reactions to how competing candidates fared in a debate. However, as noted in the study by Evans and Bucy (2010), political communication scholars do not frequently employ focus group research in our peer-reviewed journals. There certainly are landmark studies in political communication that have utilized focus groups as a central methodology (see Graber, 1988; Just et al., 1996), but for the most part they remain underutilized within the field. Jarvis offers a general summary of the types of knowledge produced by focus groups, what constitutes a successful focus group, the potential pitfalls of conducting a focus group, and how to go about analyzing focus group data. We hope the inclusion of a chapter specifically on focus group research will lead to greater awareness of the attributes of this important methodology—and spur increased use of focus groups by political communication scholars.

Political discourse does not occur only among citizens at an individual level; it is also practiced on a daily basis by political elites through the news media at what might be called a macro-social level. In Chapter 16, Ivie and Giner focus on such issues as national myths, demonization, and the use of metaphor in political language. The language we use in our national debates shapes our consciousness and influences the interpretive frames we use when approaching the major issues affecting our daily lives. In particular, Ivie and Giner present a method of genealogical interpretation for studying political rhetoric. This method is described by the authors as a "distinctly generative approach to the critique of political culture, which bridges the artificial divide between the theory and use of rhetoric while enriching the social imaginary for the purpose of enhancing human relations." Since discourse occurs at multiple levels of communication, it is important for political communication scholars to remain attentive to how citizens and politicians (speaking on behalf of nations) communicate political understandings and intentions. Whether analyzed at the individual or macro-social level, the study of discourse offers a rich and varied discursive topography through which to understand politics and analyze political machinations and processes.

One area of research within political communication that is clearly on the rise involves the study of deliberation. In Chapter 17, Black, Burkhalter, Gastil, and Stromer-Galley define deliberation within small groups as those instances when citizens come together, engage in issue discussion, and then take part in a series of communicative acts that are grounded in egalitarian norms of mutual respect and consideration. Indeed, deliberation is distinct from everyday political talk—it is a special kind of political discussion that requires unique methods to properly assess. Black and colleagues detail the boundary conditions of what makes deliberation distinct from everyday political talk and outline a method of analyzing small group deliberation that has become well defined in the political communication literature. In addition, attention is given to the different ways in which researchers have gone about measuring deliberation, both directly and indirectly. It seems apparent that the study of deliberation will continue to expand in the coming decades, as well it should, and this chapter provides useful insights on how to approach this area of study methodologically.

Linked with the study of deliberation is the analysis of social networks, although one area of research need not entail the other. As with deliberation, the study of networks is increasing exponentially within political communication. In Chapter 18, on social communication and political behavior, McClurg begins by distinguishing between the study of social networks and the study of contextual research, with the former focused on interpersonal communication and the latter focused on the relationships that exist between people within a given network. McClurg argues for more clearly delineated boundaries within this area of research and devotes significant attention to methodological issues concerning the selection of cases, appropriate units of analysis, and study designs that enable defensible assessments of causality. Proper explication, both in terms of conceptual development and variable operationalization, needs to become a hallmark of this area of research if network analysis, i.e., the role of social communication in political behavior, is to develop a solid foundation of benchmark findings.

Internationalization of the Field

Certainly by now the study of political communication has become a global endeavor. In terms of method, a broad range of issues arise when researchers engage in the study of intercultural political communication, communication influences across distinct political cultures, or comparisons of how a single phenomenon is studied differently within specific cultural contexts. In Chapter 19, Strömbäck focuses on the concept of mediatization in offering a systematic approach for conducting comparative political communication research. As greater reciprocity in shared expertise increases between scholars located in different parts of the world, opportunities for conducting comparative research will likely grow over time. However, as has been well documented, there are many methodological barriers and hurdles involved in this type of work (see Esser & Pfestch, 2004). Under the rubric of mediatization, Strömbäck offers a broad conceptual framework for approaching issues in comparative research, and from this theoretical foundation he outlines the myriad methodological issues that come to the fore in multinational research efforts. Central concepts reviewed in his chapter include media dependency, media logic, and political logic. In the end, Strömbäck offers a four-part conceptualization of the mediatization of politics, including information source, media autonomy, media practices, and political practices, that represents a foundation for engaging in the comparative research enterprise.

Agenda setting remains *the* core theory of political communication—it is clearly the most cited theory in the field (see Bennett & Iyengar, 2008) and recent arguments have advanced the case that agenda setting is the foundation from which one should approach media influence in politics (see Benoit & Holbert, 2010). The four-part Acapulco Typology introduced by McCombs more than two decades ago organizes the four primary methodological approaches used to study agenda setting. The typology is a 2×2 matrix that categorizes various methods by the nature of the data collected (individual versus aggregate) and the focus of attention (single agenda item versus entire news agenda). Given agenda setting's international influence, McCombs and colleagues in Chapter 20 review the prevalence of the four different approaches as they are being employed in different parts of the world. In addition to a summary of North American research, this author team surveys extant agenda-setting research in Western Europe, Eurasia and Africa, Australia, South America, and East Asia. As becomes readily apparent, different methodologies tend to dominate in different regions of the world. Only through the use of a diverse range of approaches can we gain a full understanding of the salience transfer process as outlined in agenda setting theory. The summary of the Acapulco Typology offered in their chapter reveals several gaps in agenda setting research spanning continents, suggesting opportunities for future research studies far and wide.

Finally, in relation to the international study of political communication, Holtz-Bacha and Kaid in Chapter 21 offer a systematic assessment of the major issues involved across a wide range of subspecialties located within the broad tent of interdisciplinary research that is political communication. The specific areas of research examined by Holtz-Bacha and Kaid include news exposure and news coverage, public opinion, political advertising, and political debates. Each area of study has received a plethora of research attention around the world, yet gaining a firm sense of the strength and generalizability of our theories and findings requires direct comparisons of influence processes across unique political and cultural contexts (i.e., nations). However, this worthy endeavor is fraught with perils and Holtz-Bacha and Kaid identify some of the major concerns when beginning to make assessments of political communication influence across different political cultures.

Statistical Analysis and Measurement

The sections of the *Sourcebook* discussed thus far largely focus on methodological design and the linking of design considerations to core concepts and theories that are central to the study of political communication. However, we would be remiss if this volume did not also address two additional aspects of method: statistical analysis and measurement. The analytical acumen of the field has grown by leaps and bounds over the past decade and the section on statistical techniques showcases some of the more advanced analytical tools being used by political communication researchers today.

In Chapter 22, Holbert and LaMarre assert that the multivariate analytical tool of structural equation modeling (SEM) remains underutilized within the field and offer a series of prescriptive remedies for how to better employ this technique to maximize its potential to illuminate relationships central to communication influence. Particular attention is given to the use of SEM as a means by which to assess measurement. Measurement-related topics discussed in the chapter include the evaluation of higher-order factor structures, multitrait-multimethod matrix (MTMM) models, and the use of dichotomous variables in confirmatory factor analysis. In terms of examining structural relations between variables, Holbert and LaMarre break down this process into three steps: specification, estimation, and evaluation. Topics covered in these areas include power estimation, specifying interaction terms, replication, and the decomposition of effects. By providing this explication of SEM research, Holbert and LaMarre point the way toward the next steps that need to be taken by political communication researchers to make more effective use of this versatile analytical tool.

Building on the importance of analyzing the decomposition of effects as highlighted in the previous chapter, Hayes, Preacher, and Myers in Chapter 23 offer a more detailed assessment of how political communication scholars should approach the analytical assessment of mediation and indirect effects. Once again, the study of communication is about the study of process. Thus, mediation and the analysis of indirect effects should be central to political communication research. Hayes and colleagues argue that the field needs to step away from the purely conceptual framework of studying mediation as outlined by Baron and Kenny (1986) and move more toward the direct empirical assessment of the role of mediating variables. Bootstrapping procedures become paramount in the approach to mediation outlined by Hayes, Preacher, and Myers and details are offered in their chapter on the resources that are available to political communication scholars for the application of bootstrapping in mediation analysis. The shift toward increased use of bootstrapping procedures, not just for the assessment of mediation, represents a distinct advancement for the field, allowing a new level of precision that reflects the uniqueness of each dataset analyzed to assess processes involving mediation.

Finally, in relation to statistical analysis, Jerit and Simon in Chapter 24 provide a summary of how to gainfully employ time-series analysis (TSA) in political communication research. Building on the earlier design themes of studying processes of influence as they unfold across time (see Eveland & Morey, Chapter 2; Hansen & Pfau, Chapter 11), TSA enables the assessment of long-term and persistent communication effects while retaining the specific strengths and weaknesses of individual analytical techniques. Jerit and Simon offer a detailed examination of time series techniques and ground their observations with examples of different outcomes of interest that can be studied through the use of TSA. For example, these authors explain how TSA is suitable for analyzing the cumulative effects of competing campaign message strategies across time on such outcome variables as political knowledge, attitudes, and behaviors. Jerit and Simon also assess how this analytical tool has been used by political communication researchers to date and provide suggestions for how researchers can continue to innovate and best utilize the technique. Mirroring the comments of Holbert and LaMarre in relation to SEM, Jerit and Simon feel TSA is vastly underutilized within the field.

Perhaps no scholarly activity focused on measurement can have much lasting value without a proper explication of the concept being measured (Chaffee, 1991). However, full explications of the field's major concepts are rarely found in our peer-reviewed journal articles. Research arguably suffers when there is an insufficient or anemic explication of concepts, stalling amidst a lack of clearly defined terms and a multitude of competing operationalizations for key concepts within the literature (see Bucy, 2004; Holbert, 2005). In Chapter 25, Sundar and Bellur perform a careful explication of the concept of interactivity, which has grown in importance across virtually all communication subfields in recent years. In particular, the chapter focuses on a discussion of where interactivity resides—whether in the source, the medium, or the message. In addition, consideration is given to whether researchers should focus on concrete representations of interactivity or assess audience perceptions of interactivity regardless of where the concept is located for research purposes. Finally, Sundar and Bellur discuss the ways in which political communication researchers can devise experimental manipulations involving different degrees of political interactivity and how to specifically measure perceived interactivity. Although this chapter is focused on a single concept, it serves as a useful model or exemplar for how to explicate any concept of interest to political communication scholars.

Moving beyond the creation of valid and reliable measures and dealing with the broader issue of referential realism, Newhagen in Chapter 26 makes the case for the value of measuring response latency (i.e., the time it takes for research participants to respond to a stimulus or requested task). Response latency can provide valuable insights concerning the types of psychological processes that are at the heart of many of the field's cognitive-based theories of political communication influence. Newhagen brings this matter to our attention at a time when the use of Web-based surveys is becoming increasingly common. The use of the Web for experimental purposes, for survey-based research, and for hybrid survey-experimental designs (see Iyengar, Chapter 8), allows researchers to measure response latency with an ease not realized through the use of other experimental and survey procedures. In particular, Newhagen discusses the potential benefits of measuring response latency in relation to self-reported voting behavior, a democratic outcome variable with a well-understood social desirability bias. As with Iyengar's chapter in this volume, Newhagen urges political communication researchers not to overlook the use of new technology to maximize their data collection efforts and, more importantly, to better address some of the field's core research questions in a more valid and reliable fashion than what has been produced by extant methods.

Another new measurement technique beginning to infiltrate the field is psychophysiology. In Chapter 27, on the use of psychophysiological measurement in political communication research, Bucy and Bradley explore what the body can tell us about televised politics. Depending on the research question, there are two general advantages to using physiology—biological measures such as heart rate, skin conductance, and facial EMG—over other outcome measures, particularly self-reports. The first is the ability to capture viewer or participant responses in real time, and with a high degree of precision. Since the body's signals are sampled electronically (20 or more times per second), researchers are able to pinpoint exactly when an effect occurred—what particular aspect of a politician's message, expressive display, or delivery impacted potential voters. Readings of participant responses are taken during exposure rather than being reconstructed by participants afterwards, in a post hoc fashion. The second advantage is the indirect nature of these measures. Since they do not rely on participant self-reflections, they are not subject to social desirability biasing and prior attitudes—what participants feel they *should* say, or efforts to maintain cognitive consistency. If an effect occurs that physiological measures detect, it generally happens outside conscious awareness and without the interference of ideological orientation. Because physiological responses occur with millisecond accuracy and before reports of opinions and preferences can be formulated, they are arguably more reliable evidence of message influence than self-reports, at least in the short term. Physiological measurement thus has great relevance to political communication, where close elections often turn on the assessments of candidate qualities received through audiovisual media rather than close scrutiny of policy positions.

Summary Considerations

The closing chapter of this *Sourcebook* features the venerable author team of Kosicki, McLeod, and McLeod, who together have generated some of the more valuable insights about communication generally (e.g., McLeod, Kosicki, & McLeod, 2010) and political communication particularly (e.g., McLeod, Kosicki, & McLeod, 2002) in their conceptual pieces over the years. These authors turn their attention to offering some summary judgments on the status of method within the field of political communication—whether the field has been doing well or poorly of late, what roadblocks or possible landmines await the field, and what directions the field should be moving in to enable further insights on the role of communication in politics.

Among other recommendations, Kosicki, McLeod, and McLeod devote attention to the need for multilevel research, and rightfully so. Various political communication researchers remain mired in single levels of analysis, and, as a result, the field sometimes has difficulty in bringing together multiple lines of research on the same topic into a coherent whole (Hayes, 2006). These authors consider several of the analytical advancements made by the field in recent years, singling out such techniques as SEM and the assessment of mediation (covered by Holbert & LaMarre, Chapter 22, and Hayes, Preacher, & Myers, Chapter 23, respectively), but caution researchers not to become too mesmerized by analytical tools, lest we lose sight of theory development and testing. This is an appropriate cautionary message. Kosicki and colleagues also stress the need for more systematic employment of replication and the need for researchers to be more willing to share insights unearthed through their many research efforts—including those efforts that fly beneath the radar and do not result in peer-reviewed journal publications, books, or conference presentations. In as much as political communication reflects a community of scholarship, the most effective way for individual researchers to gain a thorough appreciation of the role of communication in the context of politics is to conduct research with a current, and preferably broad, understanding of the work of others.

Indeed, the community of scholars that represents the field of political communication continues to expand the use of advanced methodological designs. New areas of research, such as empirical studies of political deliberation, social network analysis, and visual analysis, are increasing in popularity. And with these emerging areas come new methodological considerations and challenges. The study of political communication continues to proliferate around the globe, and this increase in the volume and scope of research should be seen as inherently beneficial. However, the movement toward international research means that political communication scholars will need to become better versed in cross-cultural and comparative research methods. In addition, it is becoming increasingly apparent to many working in this vital area that it is no longer desirable, or perhaps even viable, to work with a stagnant skill set when it comes to statistical analysis. New tools that hold great promise for the field are being forged and existing univariate and multivariate tools are constantly being improved upon. From our perspective, it is advantageous to anticipate change and embrace these new advancements. But striving for methodological progress must be balanced with ample attention to the foundations of theory and research. The chapters that follow address each of these topics and areas of inquiry in an insightful manner, explaining the myriad ways in which political communication researchers are pushing the methodological envelope, while outlining a series of paths that will allow scholars to advance our understanding of the role of communication in politics for many years to come.

REFERENCES

Averill, J. R. (2002). Emotional creativity: Toward "spiritualizing the passion." In C. R. Snyder & S. J. Lopez (Eds.), *Handbook of positive psychology* (pp. 172–185). Oxford: Oxford University Press.

Baron, R. M., & Kenny, D. A. (1986). The moderator-mediator variable distinction in social psychological research: Conceptual, strategic, and statistical considerations. *Journal of Personality and Social Psychology, 51*, 1173–1182.

Bennett, W. L., & Iyengar, S. (2008). A new era of minimal effects? The changing foundations of political communication. *Journal of Communication, 58*, 707–731.

Bennett, W. L., & Iyengar, S. (2010). The shifting foundations of political communication: Responding to a defense of the media effects paradigm. *Journal of Communication, 60*(1), 35–39.

Benoit, W. L., Hansen, G. J., & Verser, R. M. (2003). A meta-analysis of the effects of viewing U.S. presidential debates. *Communication Monographs, 70*, 335–350.

Benoit, W. L., & Holbert, R. L. (2010). Political communication. In C. R. Berger, M. E. Roloff, & D. Roskos-Ewoldsen (Eds.), *Handbook of communication science, 2nd ed.* (pp. 437–452). Thousand Oaks, CA: Sage.

Bimber, B. (2003). *Information and American democracy: Technology in the evolution of political power.* Cambridge: Cambridge University Press.

Bucy, E. P. (2004). Interactivity in society: Locating an elusive concept. *The Information Society, 20*(5), 375–385.

Bucy, E. P., & D'Angelo, P. (1999). The crisis of political communication: Normative critiques of news and democratic processes. *Communication Yearbook, 22*, 301–339.

Bucy, E. P., & D'Angelo, P. (2004). Democratic realism, neoconservatism, and the normative underpinnings of political communication research. *Mass Communication and Society, 7*(1), 3–28.

Bucy, E. P., & Grabe, M. E. (2007). Taking television seriously: A sound and image bite analysis of presidential campaign coverage, 1992–2004. *Journal of Communication, 57*, 652–675.

Bucy, E. P., & Grabe, M. E. (2008). "Happy warriors" revisited: Hedonic and agonic display repertoires of presidential candidates on the evening news. *Politics and the Life Sciences, 27*(1), 24–44.

Campus, D., Pasquino, G., & Vaccari, C. (2008). Social networks, political discussion, and voting in Italy: A study of the 2006 election. *Political Communication, 25*, 423–444.

Chaffee, S. H. (Ed.). (1975). *Political communication: Issues and strategies for research.* Beverly Hills, CA: Sage.

Chaffee, S. H. (1991). *Communication concepts 1: Explication.* Newbury Park, CA: Sage.

Chong, D., & Druckman, J. N. (2007a). A theory of framing and opinion formation in competitive elite environments. *Journal of Communication, 57*(1), 99–118.

Chong, D., & Druckman, J. N. (2007b). Framing public opinion in competitive democracies. *American Political Science Review, 101*(4), 637–655.

Chong, D., & Druckman, J. N. (2007c). Framing theory. *Annual Review of Political Science, 10*(1), 103–126.

D'Alessio, D., & Allen, M. (2007). The selective exposure hypothesis and media choice processes. In R. Preiss, B. Gayle, N. Burrell, M. Allen, & J. Bryant, J. (Eds.), *Mass media effects research: Advances through meta-analysis* (pp. 103–118). Mahwah, NJ: Lawrence Erlbaum.

Esser, F., & Pfestch, B. (2004). *Comparing political communication: Theories, cases, and challenges.* Cambridge: Cambridge University Press.

Evans, H. K., & Bucy, E. P. (2010). The representation of women in publication: An analysis of *Political Communication* and the *International Journal of Press/Politics. PS: Political Science & Politics, 43*(2), 295–301.

Eveland, W. P., Hayes, A. F., Shah, D. V., & Kwak, N. (2005). Understanding the relationship between communication and political knowledge: A model comparison approach using panel data. *Political Communication, 22*, 423–446.

Grabe, M. E., & Bucy, E. P. (2009). *Image bite politics: News and the visual framing of elections.* New York: Oxford University Press.

Graber, D. A. (1988). *Processing the news: How people tame the information tide* (2nd ed.). New York: Longman.

Graber, D. A., & Smith, J. M. (2005). Political communication faces the 21st Century. *Journal of Communication, 55*, 479–507.

Hansen, G. J., & Benoit, W. L. (2007). Communication forms as predictors of issue knowledge in presidential campaigns: A meta-analytic assessment. *Mass Communication & Society, 10*, 189–210.

Hayes, A. F. (2006). A primer on multilevel modeling. *Human Communication Research, 32*, 385–410.

Holbert, R. L. (2005). Back to basics: Revisiting, resolving, and expanding some of the fundamental issues of political communication research. *Political Communication, 22*, 511–514.

Holbert, R. L., & Benoit, W. L. (2009). A theory of political campaign media connectedness. *Communication Monographs, 76*, 303–332.

Holbert, R. L., Garrett, R. K., & Gleason, L. S. (2010). A new era of minimal effects? A response to Bennett and Iyengar. *Journal of Communication, 60*(1), 15–34.

Holbert, R. L., & Stephenson, M. T. (2008). Commentary on the uses and misuses of structural equation modeling in communication research. In A. F. Hayes, M. D. Slater, & L. B. Snyder (Eds.), *The Sage handbook of advanced data analysis methods for communication research* (pp. 185–218). Thousand Oaks, CA; Sage.

Just, M. R., Crigler, A. N., Alger, D. E., Cook, T. E., Kern, M., & West. D. M. (1996). *Crosstalk: Citizens, candidates, and the media in a presidential campaign*. Chicago: Chicago University Press.

Kiecolt, K. J., & Nathan, L. E. (1985). *Secondary analysis of survey data*. Beverly Hills, CA: Sage Publications.

McLeod, J. M., Kosicki, G. M., & McLeod, D. M. (2010). Levels of analysis and communication science. In C. Berger, M. Roloff, & D. Roskos-Ewoldsen (Eds.), *The handbook of communication science* (2nd ed., pp. 183–200). Thousand Oaks, CA: Sage.

McLeod, D. M., Kosicki, G. M., & McLeod, J. M. (2002). Resurveying the boundaries of political communication effects. In J. Bryant & D. Zillmann (Eds.), *Media effects: Advances in theory and research* (2nd ed., pp. 215–267). Hillsdale, NJ: Lawrence Erlbaum.

Nimmo, D., & Sanders, K. R. (Eds.). (1981). *Handbook of political communication*. Beverly Hills, CA: Sage.

Paisley, W. (1984). Communication in the communication sciences. In B. Dervin & M. Voigt (Eds.), *Progress in the communication sciences* (Vol. 5, pp. 1–43). Norwood, NJ: Ablex.

Prior, M. (2009). The immensely inflated news audience: Assessing bias in self-reported news exposure. *Public Opinion Quarterly, 73*, 130–143.

Scheufele, D. A. (1999). Framing as a theory of media effects. *Journal of Communication, 49*, 103–122.

Scheufele, D. A. (2000). Agenda-setting, priming, and framing revisited: Another look at cognitive effects of political communication. *Mass Communication & Society, 3*, 297–316.

Schuefele, D. A., & Tewksbury, D. (2007). Framing, agenda setting, and priming: The evolution of three media effects models. *Journal of Communication, 57*, 9–20.

Simon, A. F., & Iyengar, S. (1995). Toward theory-based research in political communication. *PS: Political Science and Politics, 29*, 29–33.

I
SURVEY METHODOLOGY

2

Challenges and Opportunities of Panel Designs

William P. Eveland, Jr.
School of Communication
The Ohio State University

Alyssa C. Morey
School of Communication
The Ohio State University

Panel studies are studies in which data are gathered regarding the same individuals at multiple points in time. They can be contrasted with cross-sectional studies, in which data are gathered at a single point in time, and with longitudinal studies more generally, in which data are gathered at multiple points in time, but *not necessarily* on the same individuals at multiple points in time (e.g., a repeated cross-sectional study or a rolling cross-sectional study). Panel studies have particular advantages for the study of political communication—most prominent of which is their greater ability to address issues of causality and change—and in the past decade or so data from panel studies have become much more prominent in the political communication literature. However, as with any study design, panel studies have limitations and must be properly designed for the particular research goal at hand to provide the highest return on the considerable investment required to conduct them.

This chapter will examine the use of panel survey designs in political communication research. We place particular emphasis on the challenge of aligning central theoretical considerations with the particular design of the panel study. Panel studies are most effective when researchers consider critical design factors, including the lag between waves, the timing of the waves themselves, the appropriate selection of questions, and the specific wording of survey items. We will discuss the results of an informal content analysis of the use of panel studies in political communication in recent years, as well as make reference to specific political communication panel studies in order to identify typical approaches in the field and potential areas for improvement. Pragmatic issues related to panel designs—including cost, sample attrition, sensitization, and the limitations of using secondary panel data—are considered in detail. The increasing application of consumer mail panels and online panels, as well as more traditional face-to-face and telephone panel surveys, will also be addressed. The complexity of panel data analysis requires that we leave such topics for more thorough treatments. We refer the reader to relevant overviews of the analysis of panel data, including Cole and Maxwell (2003), Finkel (1995), and Henry and Slater (2008).

THE PAST AND PRESENT OF PANEL DESIGNS IN POLITICAL COMMUNICATION RESEARCH

Panel designs have an important place in the origin of empirical political communication research, most prominently in Lazarsfeld, Berelson, and Gaudet's *The People's Choice* (1944). They conducted a seven-wave panel study using a probability sample of Erie County, Ohio, residents during the course of the 1940 presidential election campaign. Panel respondents were interviewed once each month from May through November 1940. The study also included "control groups" interviewed only once at important points in the campaign, allowing the researchers to assess the impact of repeated interviewing and increase sample sizes at those key times. Some of the Columbia group's later studies also employed the panel study method, although in a much less ambitious form (e.g., Katz & Lazarsfeld, 1955).

In addition, the American National Election Study (ANES) has conducted nationally representative two-wave panel studies during every presidential election year since 1948, as well as some panel studies that extend beyond a single election year (e.g., the 1972–1974–1976 panel). The ANES has been a major source of data for the study of political communication, although as a panel study it has serious limitations we will discuss later.

To effectively summarize the current use of panel studies in political communication research, we conducted an informal content analysis of articles from 1992 through 2006 that we were able to identify through a search using the Web of Science database.[1] Immediately apparent is that the number of articles reporting panel data has increased dramatically in the past several years.[2] During most of the decade from 1992 to 2001, an average of fewer than two articles reporting panel studies were published in any given year. However, in the five-year time span from 2002 through 2006, at least 46 political communication articles employing panel studies were published, for an average of over nine per year (see Figure 2.1, top panel). Clearly, the use of panel studies has increased dramatically during this decade.

Also interesting is that the majority (68%) of panel analyses in these articles were based on only two waves of data (see Figure 2.1, bottom panel),[3] with the percentage employing either two or three waves of data accounting for about 82% of all panel studies. Most of the remaining panel study analyses employed four or five waves. We will return to other findings of our informal content analysis later as they become more directly relevant to points we make about issues of panel lags, attrition, and related matters.

THE VALUE OF PANEL STUDIES

Causal processes and individual-level change are of particular interest to political communication researchers. Do campaigns inform voters? How do vote preferences develop and change during an election campaign? Does exposure to negative news produce political cynicism or political participation (or both)? Unfortunately, much of the data employed in political communication studies offer limited ability to address these types of questions. Limitations of historically popular research methods may underlie the growing use of panel studies in the past decade (see Chapter 3, this volume). While all research designs and methods are subject to drawbacks and inherent restrictions, well-designed panel studies offer a unique opportunity to combine some of the strengths of cross-sectional surveys, time-series studies, and laboratory experiments in an effort to produce evidence of causality and individual-level change.

The major purpose for gathering panel data rather than cross-sectional or longitudinal data, and thus the major advantage of panel designs, is the analysis of change and causality at the

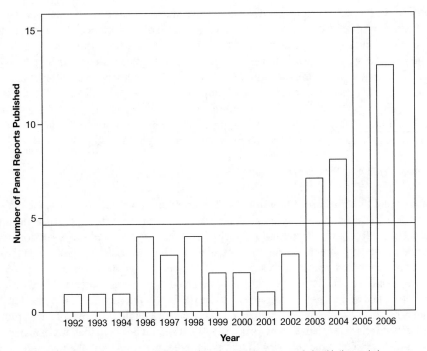

The reference line is the mean number of published panel studies per year during this time period

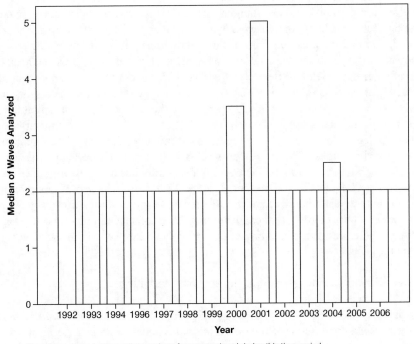

The reference line is the median number of waves analyzed during this time period

FIGURE 2.1 Relationship between year of publication and number of panel studies (top panel) and number of waves employed (bottom panel).

individual level. Properly designed, a two-wave panel study can produce estimates of population change, correlates of individual change, and better evidence of the factors causing the change than a cross-sectional or non-panel longitudinal study. However, two-wave panel studies themselves are limited in how well they can address change. Panel designs with three or more waves have even greater strengths, including distinguishing between measurement error and true change over time (Bartels, 1993), assessing causal mediation processes (Cole & Maxwell, 2003), examining reinforcing spirals (Slater, 2007), and determining whether change is linear or nonlinear over time (Singer & Willett, 2003). Below, we briefly discuss two cases in which the use of panel data helped to advance an area of political communication research.

The Case of Rallying 'Round the Flag

The "rally-round-the-flag" effect describes the tendency for Americans to cast aside their differences in times of international political crisis and come together in support of the president (Mueller, 1973). Research on the rally effect often employs repeated cross-sectional data. If presidential approval is higher during or immediately after the crisis than before, support for a rally effect is claimed. Increases in presidential support at the aggregate level may indeed provide evidence of a rally effect. However, analysis of repeated cross-sectional data offers little insight about the theoretical process underlying the rally effect. Mueller (1973) suggested that an overwhelming patriotic sentiment compels citizens to stand behind the president, appropriately labeled the "patriotism" explanation by Brody (1991). It should be noted that this explanation does not distinguish among Americans with different predispositions or characteristics. Rather, patriotic fervor is held to escalate among all U.S. citizens.

In contrast to research using cross-sectional surveys, Edwards and Swenson (1997) studied the rally effect using panel data. They found no support for the patriotism explanation, but instead demonstrated that individuals otherwise predisposed to support the president are the citizens most likely to rally behind the president in times of international crisis. In the absence of repeated measurement of the same individuals over time—that is, panel data—this important disconfirmation of a key explanation of the rally effect would have less credence. Moreover, the panel data allowed Edwards and Swenson (1997) to evaluate two plausible mechanisms, one direct and one indirect, by which the news media may perpetuate the rally effect. First, opinion leadership in the news media may garner support for the president. If the valence of commentary by political leaders concerning the event is positive (as it was at the time), citizens should respond to this discourse by finding the president's performance more worthy of approval. Alternatively, by covering certain issues, the news media may influence individuals to rely on those issues in the formation of overall evaluations of political leaders. There was evidence of this priming effect, with a significant interaction between news attention and support for the president's handling of foreign policy. In other words, news exposure may have influenced individuals to weight their attitudes toward the president's handling of foreign policy more heavily in their overall evaluations of the president.

The Case of Political Knowledge and Intramedia Mediation

News media use effects on political knowledge have primarily been studied from a cross-sectional perspective. Despite the absence of time-ordering of variables or control for prior levels of the outcome measure, most researchers have assumed that news media influence political knowledge (rather than political knowledge driving exposure to news). Moreover, much of this research pits various forms of news media use against one another to assess their unique, direct contributions to knowledge. Two papers published in *Political Communication*, which used panel data to address the issue of causality in these relationships, as well as the possibility of mediation, illustrate the point. Eveland and colleagues (2005b) employed two-wave panel data from the 2000 presidential election to test competing models of the causal process between news media use, discussion of politics, and political knowledge. Their findings confirmed that the best-fitting causal model included synchronous paths from news media use and discussion to change in political knowledge compared to a series of theoretically derived alternative causal models that included the possibility of reverse causality. In the same issue of that journal, Holbert (2005) used the National Annenberg Election Survey panel data to demonstrate that television viewing and newspaper use have not only direct, but also indirect effects through one another on political knowledge. The panel data were an important advance over prior research that typically examined only a single direction of mediation through these two variables. In a follow-up study, Eveland, Hayes, Shah, and Kwak (2005a) extended the intramedia mediation hypothesis to the context of news media and political discussion, finding that the clearest mediation is of discussion effects through news use to political knowledge.

ISSUES FOR CONSIDERATION IN THE DESIGN OF PANEL STUDIES

The ability of a panel study to maximize its advantages over other forms of data collection is highly dependent on time-related design considerations that might often be overlooked in cross-sectional surveys. Since cross-sectional surveys cannot directly address issues of time order or causal process in the same manner as panel surveys, researchers experienced only in the design of cross-sectional surveys may inadvertently fail to attend to some of the most important aspects of panel design. These major considerations in the design of panel studies include (1) the time necessary for causal processes to occur; (2) decay time for outcome variables; (3) the timing of occurrence of external stimuli, including campaigns; (4) the timeframe referenced in survey questions; (5) repeated measurement; and (6) measurement of states versus traits.

Timing of Causal Processes

The length of time necessary for a cause to produce an effect may be the most central concern in the design of a panel study. For instance, exposure to information in a given newscast could, almost immediately, produce a learning effect. Thus, the time to produce a causal effect would be incredibly short. By contrast, the effect of that same newscast on motivating engagement in some participatory behavior, such as attending a rally or campaign event, could take days, weeks, or even months. Part of this delay could result from the production of a potential (e.g., motivation) that must wait for an opportunity to be realized. Even if news exposure generates the motivation to vote, this effect cannot be manifested until Election Day. Alternatively, cumulative exposure to multiple newscasts may be required to produce any effect on motivation (or, for instance, cynicism). Or it could be that persuasive effects can occur based on a single negative advertisement, but in order for them to manifest themselves a time delay is necessary for the association between the low credibility source of the ad and the content of the message to decay (i.e., the classic "sleeper effect").

These considerations are crucial for the design of panel studies, as they should inform the time lag between waves. If the time necessary for a causal effect to manifest itself is substantially longer than the lag between waves, the research will likely infer an absence of effects when they might in fact be present. Similarly, if the time for a causal effect to manifest itself is considerably shorter than the lag between waves, decay of the causal effects (addressed next) could lead to inferences of weaker or non-existent effects. As Cole and Maxwell (2003, p. 564) note, "the practical effect of timing [of survey waves] can be remarkable."

An important example of this might be the production of knowledge gaps on the basis of media campaigns. The original knowledge gap hypothesis suggested that over time, gaps between high and low socioeconomic groups would increase as media information entered the system (Tichenor, Donohue, & Olien, 1970). Evidence regarding whether gaps increased, decreased, or remained the same over time, however, was mixed. Moore (1987, specifically Figure 2.2) made the cogent argument that, from a diffusion perspective, initial gaps might widen at first, but then proceed to shrink. Thus, the timing of waves—both the timing of the initial wave, and also the lag between waves—could lead to entirely different conclusions about the operation of the exact same theoretical process.

Decay Time for Outcome Variables

Many outcome variables decay, or are susceptible to subsequent change, over time (e.g., Watt, Mazza, & Snyder, 1993). Although the effect of reading a newspaper on voting behavior in a presidential election cannot be altered or rescinded once the vote is cast, information learned from a newspaper can be forgotten, and attitude activation by a political advertisement can decay in relatively short periods of time. Moreover, the effect of media content on attitudes is thought to diminish over time (e.g., Fan, 1988). Thus, an important consideration in the determination of the lag between waves of a panel study is to assess the dependent variable within a range of time in which the effect of the independent variable will still be manifested. Failure to do so could lead to inferences of no effects when the real issue is that the effects occurred, but dissipated prior to the collection of data assessing them.

Imagine, for instance, a two-wave panel study with the goal of assessing the impact of eating on hunger. Wave I is conducted on Monday evening with an independent variable of estimated caloric consumption on that day. Wave II is conducted on Thursday evening with an independent variable of felt hunger. The absence of a correlation between these measures does not mean that caloric intake does not reduce hunger—because the effect of Monday's caloric intake has dissipated by Thursday. Any observed relationship between Monday's caloric intake and Thursday's hunger is likely produced by relatively stable individual differences in caloric intake over time, meaning that Monday's caloric intake would at best be a proxy for Thursday's caloric intake, which should have an impact on felt hunger on Thursday.

This issue of a lack of fit between survey waves and the decay of effects may be most apparent in panel research on media priming effects. According to research in cognitive psychology, when a concept is primed, the "temporary accessibility" of this concept is increased. Temporary accessibility increases the likelihood that a concept will be used in subsequent judgments (Iyengar & Kinder, 1987). However, the accessibility of the concept (due to the prime) decays rapidly—typically within an hour or at most a day (Srull & Wyer, 1979). Thus, panel studies of priming effects that employ survey lags of months (Krosnick & Brannon, 1993) or even a year (Pan & Kosicki, 1997) seem inappropriate to test priming effects produced through a process of temporary accessibility (see Roskos-Ewoldsen, Roskos-Ewoldsen, & Carpentier, 2002, for a discussion). It is true that repeated priming of a concept can make it "chronically accessible"—that is, accessible for lengthy periods without significant decay. However, most panel studies of the media priming effect address neither the amount of exposure required to make an issue chronically accessible, nor how chronically accessible concepts decay in their accessibility—nor how long it takes for this to occur.

Timing of Occurrence of External Stimuli

Panel studies are often designed to serve as quasi-experiments, with at least a subset of respondents being exposed to some stimulus between the waves of data collection. If all respondents are exposed to the stimulus, these designs are effectively the same as a one-group pretest-posttest design. If exposure to the stimulus is somehow measured (likely in the posttest) but not randomly distributed, such designs might also be considered a nonequivalent control group design (see Campbell & Stanley, 1963).

In many studies of political communication effects, this stimulus is broadly conceived, as in an entire election campaign, or perhaps some aspect of the campaign, such as news coverage or political advertising. Used for this purpose, panel waves must be timed so that the first wave captures a baseline *prior* to any exposure to the stimulus. For instance, if the stimulus is the campaign period, the first wave of data must be gathered before the presidential campaigning begins. However, the larger and more diffuse the conceived stimulus (and presumably the lag between panel waves), the greater the concern about history and maturation effects—that is, that changes across panel waves resulting from factors other than the presumed stimulus (Campbell & Stanley, 1963). Arguments for effects are strengthened if exposure to the stimulus is a measured variable rather than assumed, but then concerns about nonrandom differences in exposure (i.e., selection effects) come into play. In any case, the more general issue is that studies designed to serve as quasi-experiments must carefully choose the timing of waves to not only account for the time it takes for causal effects to occur and decay, but also to tightly bracket the presumed natural stimulus. And, the better the "stimulus" can be described, the more clearly the causal inferences that may be derived from the panel study. We discuss this matter further in the section on linking external data to panel studies.

Time Frames Referenced in Survey Questions

Many survey questions about communication or political behaviors reference specific time frames. For instance, respondents might be asked about the frequency of their television news viewing in the past week, during a campaign, or during a "typical week." Or they might be asked whether they engaged in any political activities during the prior year. Choosing appropriate time frames for such questions involves multiple considerations.

First, researchers must consider whether respondents can accurately recall and report various behaviors during specific time frames (see Chang & Krosnick, 2003). Second, from a logical standpoint, these time frames must be coordinated with the design of the panel study, including the timing of lags as they relate to the timing of external stimuli. For instance, suppose we conduct a panel study to examine the influence of news use on political participation. This relationship is analyzed using news use questions asked in the first wave of the survey (say, September), and political participation gauged in the second wave of data collection (say, November). However, if the post-election wave of the survey asks respondents about their political participation during the full prior year, but the news questions gauge media behaviors in the prior week or month, the time order of variables undermines the value of the panel data. Obviously, news use during September cannot predict political behavior in the summer, spring, or winter of the previous year. In other words, the dependent variable (participation) is measured over a one-year time span that not only includes, but in large part precedes, the time frame of the independent variable of news media use. Thus, the time-order benefits of the panel design are lost. A better approach might be to frame dependent variable time frames in the second wave to refer to the lag between waves.

Repeated Measurement

Sensitization caused by repeated measurement is a major concern of pre–post experimental designs. That is, the act of measuring some variable during the first wave may affect measurement of this same variable (or some other variable) during the second wave (Campbell & Stanley, 1963). In panel survey designs, this has been labeled "time-in-sample-bias" or "panel conditioning" (Trivellato, 1999).

This can be a particular problem in the measurement of a variable such as political knowledge. Asking specific knowledge questions in the first wave can make respondents more sensitive to this or related information when they encounter it later. Thus, learning would be greater among those interviewed in the first wave than comparable individuals who were not. This would confound any inference of learning across waves. One potentially better approach would be to produce equivalent forms of a measure (Cronbach, 1960), with one form administered during the first wave and the equivalent form administered during the second wave (see Eveland, Hayes, Shah, & Kwak, 2005a, for a more thorough discussion). Ideally, of course, there should be external evidence for the equivalence of the two forms.

Similarly, the absence of repeated measurement of some dependent variables across waves would be a significant limitation that would fail to take full advantage of the analytic strengths of panel designs. That is, for many variables, such as opinions toward political issues or candidates, repeated measurement *is* the specific advantage of the panel design. In those cases, designs that fail to measure—using identical wording—the same variables repeatedly are problematic. Absence of prior measures of dependent variables is also a significant limitation for most causal analyses, including tests of mediation (Cole & Maxwell, 2003).

Measurement of States vs. Traits

By definition, variables vary. However, some vary only between individuals (e.g., gender, race), and so these variables need only be measured once in any study, and it does not matter in what wave the measurement occurs. Other variables vary both between individuals and within individuals over time. Here, the distinction between state variables and trait variables becomes relevant. Traits are stable differences across individuals that persist over relatively long time periods. For instance, personality traits vary little over time and so measuring them repeatedly within weeks or months—or possibly even years—would seem to have little value. Additionally, whether the variable is measured in the first wave or a subsequent wave would seem to have little theoretical import if the trait assumption is indeed accurate.

By contrast, state variables measure characteristics that change within an individual over relatively short time periods. This variation within individuals over time can be visualized as the oscillation of sound waves. Some variables, such as visual attention or the accessibility of a concept in memory, oscillate very quickly within individuals. Others, such as values or habits, oscillate very slowly within individuals. Moreover, the amount of variation (i.e., amplitude, in sound wave terminology) could be relatively small or relatively large. The timing of changes for any given variable should affect not only the decisions about whether to measure the variable repeatedly, but also the wording of the timeframe for the variable and the lag between waves if there is repeated measurement.

More generally, this raises questions about certain variables and their stability over time. Variables that represent highly stable individual differences over time are probably not good choices for inclusion in panel studies designed to assess change over time. An exception would be when the study includes a strong change agent (i.e., the quasi-experimental stimulus) that will likely disrupt a normally stable variable. For instance, the progression of election campaigns appears to influence the mean level of attention to campaign news. However, this influence is of the sort "a rising tide lifts all ships." That is, individual differences in campaign attention are stable even as the average amount of campaign attention increases over time (Eveland, Shah, & Kwak, 2003). These sorts of factors should be carefully considered in the design of panel studies.

INTEGRATION OF PANEL DATA WITH OTHER DATA SOURCES

Researchers using panel study designs as quasi-experiments must carefully integrate individual-level panel survey data with data addressing the presence of relevant information in the environment, which serves as the stimulus in the quasi-experiment. The simplest approach would be to identify an event—an election campaign, a televised presidential debate, a State of the Union address—and note its occurrence between waves of data collection. However, more sophisticated approaches would seek to integrate media content analyses or other macro-level data into the design and analysis.

For example, during the 2006 senate and gubernatorial campaigns in Ohio, our colleagues in Ohio State University's Communication and Political Science departments conducted a three-wave—September, October, and post-election—panel study of an RDD (random digit dial) sample of Ohio adults. Among other questions, respondents were asked to report the specific newspaper they read and the local television news program they typically watched (if any). Simultaneously, the researchers recorded local television newscasts in the three largest media markets in Ohio (Cleveland, Columbus, and Cincinnati) and gathered content from over a dozen electronically archived newspapers from throughout the state. In various projects that use these data, we are linking variations in media coverage across communities and over time to changes in political knowledge and opinions throughout the campaign. Our ability to have temporally tied media content data—essentially, a panel study of media content over time—and linked individual-level panel survey data, with observed variation across geographical space—increases the strength of causal inferences about media effects that we can make relative to the panel data alone.

Another strategy is to gather other macro-level data not directly tied to media content. For instance, one could gather data about over-time changes in the economy, the competitiveness of a political race, the number of campaign visits in a locale, or any number of politically relevant variables. These data could then be integrated with the panel data to increase the strength of causal inference beyond a simple reference to the occurrence of a campaign or some abstract stimulus in the environment. As with individual-level data, it is important to consider theoretical time lags for effects of the macro-level variables, and also the decay of these effects over time.

INHERENT LIMITATIONS OF PANEL STUDIES

Despite potential advantages, panel studies have some inherent (or nearly inherent) drawbacks. The time required to gather multiple waves of data—especially when lags between waves are lengthy—is necessarily longer than for an otherwise identical cross-sectional study. The cost of collecting panel data is considerably higher than the cost of gathering cross-sectional data, especially when employing interviewer-administered as opposed to self-administered surveys. These costs are not only attributable to the time necessary to interview individuals repeatedly; the longer the lag between waves, the more difficult it is to locate and recontact panel members due to residential mobility and other changes in contact information (Trivellato, 1999). Additionally, the more waves of data collection and the longer the lag between those waves, the greater the likelihood that participants will drop out of the panel.

This points to a major concern about many panel studies—panel attrition, or the nonresponse problem of losing first-wave respondents in subsequent waves (Foster & Fang, 2004). Panel attrition does not just reduce sample sizes and statistical power. As panel attrition increases, questions about the representativeness of the sample increase because rarely is panel attrition completely random. Just as important are questions regarding whether the characteristics that predict dropping out versus remaining as part of the panel—presuming this is nonrandom—are in some way related to the goals of the research.

Our content analysis of panel studies found that panel attrition is a significant issue for most studies. On average, about one-third of the respondents to the first wave of panel studies in our content analysis dropped out prior to the second wave. Attrition ranged from as little as 8% to as much as 63% across the various studies. In general, the longer the lag between the first and second waves, the greater the attrition ($r = .48, p < .01, n = 47$; see Figure 2.2, top panel). However, this only holds when analyzing all studies, including those with lags of one year or more. Among only those studies with lags of less than 12 months, the correlation between lag length and attrition was nonsignificant ($r = .22, n = 36$; see Figure 2.2, bottom panel). Attrition from the second wave to the third wave was lower on average, but attrition was still another 25% of respondents, with a range from 5% to 45%. Interestingly, the correlation between the Wave 2–Wave 3 lag and attrition in Wave 3 is actually negative ($r = -.67, p < .01, n = 17$). But, when the parametric correlations are recalculated as rank-order correlations (due to the small sample size and skew), the relationship becomes nonsignificant (Spearman's *rho* $= -.35, p = .17, n = 17$).

There are no simple answers to solving the problem of panel attrition that we can address in the space available here (but see Foster & Fang, 2004). However, the effort to keep panel attrition as low as possible is yet another factor that leads panel studies to be considerably more expensive than cross-sectional studies.

STRENGTHS AND WEAKNESSES OF PUBLICLY AVAILABLE PANEL DATA

Our content analysis of recent political communication articles employing panel studies suggests that most panel data are gathered by individuals or small groups of investigators. Additionally, these panel studies are generally designed to address specific research questions. We hope researchers implementing their own panel studies can benefit from our suggestions above regarding optimizing the design of the panel study in order to provide the strongest evidence for hypothesis testing.

However, a substantial number of published reports employ some sort of publicly available panel data, most frequently the ANES. This section devotes particular attention to the strengths and weaknesses of the ANES panel design for political communication research because, for most political communication scholars, the ability to fund, design, and gather their own panel data may be rare. Thus, publicly available panel data sources such as the ANES may be the only viable option for many researchers interested in panel analysis.

In general, the ANES incorporates two different panel designs. The first, and most common, began in 1948 with a pre-election and post-election wave of data collection. This pre–post panel design has been repeated during every presidential election since 1948. For instance, the ANES also intermittently extends its panel data collection beyond a single election year. For instance, a panel was created based on the 2000, 2002, and 2004 election studies, producing a subset of respondents interviewed in five waves beginning prior to Election Day 2000 and ending after

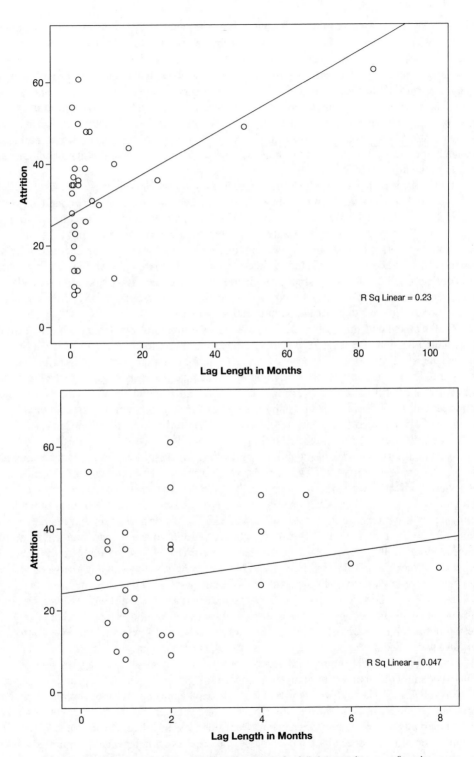

FIGURE 2.2 Relationship of lag length with attrition for full data set (top panel) and limited to studies with lag of less than one year (bottom panel).

Election Day 2004. An ever more ambitious multiwave panel study conducted online was fielded by the ANES in 2008–2009. For purposes of this chapter, we will focus on the traditional pre–post election panel study, which takes a similar form each presidential election year.

Recall from our previous discussion that if researchers strive to maximize the benefits of a panel study, they must allow their particular theoretical considerations to inform the design of the study, including repeated measurement, timing, lag between waves, and so forth. Unfortunately, but unsurprisingly, because sources of secondary panel data such as the ANES are designed in advance by committee to meet the needs of a large body of researchers with myriad interests and diverse research goals, they have significant drawbacks when applied to most political communication questions requiring panel data.

Generally speaking, the ANES begins interviewing for the pre-election wave after the Labor Day weekend, at what has been called the start of the general presidential election campaign—although this clearly is not the case today when campaigns begin long before Labor Day (Patterson, 2002, p. 121). Interviews are conducted from early September until the day before Election Day—effectively spanning two months. Post-election interviews begin the day after Election Day and continue until mid- to late-December. The strengths of this design are that it employs a probability sampling strategy with good response rates at the first wave and relatively low rates of attrition. Moreover, the available variables allow researchers to address a multitude of questions of interest to political communication scholars.

On the other hand, this design itself imposes many limitations. First, many of the most important communication effects may have taken place prior to the first interview because advertising campaigns, candidate visits, and news coverage have been occurring for months prior to the first interview. Thus, in many ways the "stimulus" of the campaign began long before the pre-election survey began. For instance, in 2004 about 60% of ANES respondents who voted for president reported having made up their minds by the end of the summer nominating conventions, and almost half of those report not knowing "all along"—that is, they were open-minded at some point but made their decision *prior* to the ANES pre-election wave.

Another limitation of the design is the lengthy time necessary for data collection, particularly during the pre–election wave. The cumulative information environment for the individuals interviewed in early September is dramatically different from that experienced by individuals interviewed in late October. Additionally, the time span between the culmination of the campaign and the post-test interview for those interviewed early in the post-election wave is rather small, but could be more than a month for those interviewed late in the second wave. This presents significant difficulties for measurement because the time delay since the election—and thus accuracy of recall—will vary by individuals. More importantly, the actual lag between waves of the ANES is highly variable across respondents. For instance, in 2004 when the Election Day was November 2, the shortest pre–post lag for a respondent was only eight days (November 1 until November 9) and the longest lag was over three months (September 8 until December 15). This design limitation can seriously limit causal inference, especially when the timing of interviews within a wave, and the length of lag between waves, is not random.

This problem of the timing of the interviews within waves and the lag between waves is compounded by the phrasing of many of the questions. For instance, in the post-election survey in 2004, the ANES asked "How many days *in the past week* did you talk about politics with family or friends?" (emphasis added). Given that this question is asked only in the post-election survey, and this survey could be administered in mid-December, it is not clear why this specific timeframe should be employed, especially if this variable was used as an independent variable predicting, say, participation in the campaign, vote choice, or any other variable that would have been "affected" during the campaign.

This provides an important segue into another design concern of the ANES, namely, the relative lack of repeated measurement of key variables employed by political communication scholars—and the waves in which these questions are asked. Most communication variables are asked only in one wave, or the wording of the measures is substantively different across waves. For instance, in 2004, exposure to local television news was measured only in the pre-election wave, whereas exposure to network news was measured in both waves—but the wording was different across waves.[4] This eliminates any ability to track change over time for these variables or to control prior levels of a dependent variable when assessing effects of some other variable on the post-election measure.

There are more limitations particular to the ANES, or other public panel studies, that we could address here. However, the major point is simply that, even more so than for cross-sectional research, the limitations of public panel designs for the specific research purposes of political communication scholars are considerable. This is through no inherent flaw in the individuals who have designed them, but instead is based on the great importance of designing panel studies to link closely to specific causal processes of specific variables. This is generally not something that lends itself well to secondary analysis of publicly available data, which is probably why the ANES and other public panel studies are used less often than we might expect to address panel-related theoretical issues compared to its use for cross-sectional analyses that ignore the panel design.

NON-PROBABILITY PANEL DESIGNS

In recent years, a number of scholars have generated and published panel data based on some form of consumer mail panel (e.g., Eveland & Thomson, 2006; Ridout, Shah, Goldstein, & Franz, 2004) or other non-probability sampling method. With regard to cost and ease of data collection, these designs have important benefits. Mail or Web-based surveys are generally less expensive than surveys involving actual interviewers (e.g., in-person or telephone interviews), and data tend to be gathered more quickly. This means that the cost of a non-probability panel survey may be on par with the price of a probability cross-sectional survey. Moreover, employing a generally representative (although non-probability) sample of first-wave respondents who have preemptively agreed to repeated surveying, in return for some sort of incentive, reduces panel attrition across waves. Finally, the speed of data collection reduces problems such as those discussed for the in-person ANES, including large variations in the timing of the interviews and the lag between waves across respondents.

However, a non-probability survey should not technically be analyzed using parametric statistics. Moreover, such a study cannot be formally generalized to any specific population. Many scholars will reject these sorts of panel studies as inherently invalid on these grounds. Others may acknowledge the limitations of these data, but recognize that response biases due to low response rates and high attrition in many probability panel surveys make many of them—including those from pre-recruited probability Web panel surveys—susceptible to many of the same critiques (see Lee, 2006). Scholars considering a panel study must decide whether benefits of non-probability panel designs outweigh the limitations.

CONCLUSION

Since the outset of the empirical study of political communication, scholars have employed panel studies to answer important research questions. Yet, recent years have witnessed a striking growth in the use of panel data in political communication studies. This suggests that the time to carefully reconsider the strengths and weaknesses of panel studies is upon us. Panel studies offer significant logical and empirical advantages over cross-sectional studies for making inferences about change and causality. However, there are also many limitations—some of which can be addressed by careful consideration of design issues in advance of data collection—that suggest caution in any headstrong rush toward panel studies as a panacea for the field.

NOTES

1. This search likely underestimates the total number of articles employing panel studies. The Web of Science is not an exhaustive index of published work on political communication, and even within this index we were more likely to identify articles that made explicit mention of employing panel data in their titles or abstracts due to our selection of search terms. Also, since this was an informal content analysis, we simply made judgment calls regarding whether or not a paper addressed "political communication." Thus, these data are meant to merely describe rough trends over time in the use of panel data in the broad area of political communication research.
2. Because a few published studies have analyzed data from more than one panel study, and many panel studies are analyzed in multiple published articles, here we consider the report of a panel study in a published article as the unit. That is, a study reporting the results of two separate panel studies will appear twice in the data—once for each panel study. And a single panel data set analyzed in two different articles will also appear twice in these summaries.
3. It is important to note here that although often articles would report that more waves of data had been collected, we report the number of waves upon which the analyses are based, not the number of waves of data collected. For instance, the mean number of waves of data collected in these studies was 3.38, but the mean number of waves analyzed was 2.65. Forty-nine percent of the studies reported *gathering* 3 or more waves of data, but only about 32% reported *analyzing* 3 or more waves of data.
4. In the pre-election wave, the question asked ". . . did you watch the NATIONAL network news on TV?" whereas in the post-election wave the question asked "did you watch the news on TV?" The corresponding attention measures had the same change across waves.

REFERENCES

Bartels, L. M. (1993). Messages received: The political impact of media exposure. *American Political Science Review, 87*, 267–285.

Brody, R. A. (1991). *Assessing the president: The media, elite opinion, and public support*. Stanford, CA: Stanford University Press.

Campbell, D., & Stanley, J. (1963). *Experimental and quasi-experimental designs for research*. Chicago: Rand McNally.

Chang, L., & Krosnick, J. A. (2003). Measuring the frequency of regular behaviors: Comparing the "typical week" to the "past week." *Sociological Methodology, 33*, 55–80.

Cole, D. A., & Maxwell, S. E. (2003). Testing mediational models with longitudinal data: Questions and tips in the use of structural equation modeling. *Journal of Abnormal Psychology, 112*, 558–577.

Cronbach, L. J. (1960). *Essentials of psychological testing* (2nd ed.). New York: Harper & Brothers.

Edwards, G. C., & Swenson, T. (1997). Who rallies? The anatomy of a rally event. *Journal of Politics, 59*, 200–212.

Eveland, W. P., Jr., Hayes, A. F., Shah, D. V., & Kwak, N. (2005a). Observations on estimation of communication effects on political knowledge and a test of intracommunication mediation. *Political Communication, 22*, 505–509.

Eveland, W. P., Jr., Hayes, A. F., Shah, D. V., & Kwak, N. (2005b). Understanding the relationship between communication and political knowledge: A model comparison approach using panel data. *Political Communication, 22*, 423–446.

Eveland, W. P., Jr., & Thomson, T. (2006). Is it talking, thinking, or both? A lagged dependent variable model of discussion effects on political knowledge. *Journal of Communication, 56*, 523–542.

Eveland, W. P., Jr., Shah, D. V., & Kwak, N. (2003). Assessing causality in the cognitive mediation model: A panel study of motivations, information processing, and learning during campaign 2000. *Communication Research, 30*, 359–386.

Fan, D. P. (1988). *Predictions of public opinion from the mass media: Computer content analysis and mathematical modeling*. New York: Greenwood Press.

Finkel, S. E. (1995). *Causal analysis with panel data*. Thousand Oaks, CA: Sage.

Foster, E. M., & Fang, G. Y. (2004). Alternative methods for handling attrition: An illustration using data from the Fast Track Evaluation. *Evaluation Review, 28*, 434–464.

Henry, K. L., & Slater, M. D. (2008). Assessing change and intraindividual variation: Longitudinal multilevel and structural equation modeling. In A. F. Hayes, M. D. Slater, & L. B. Snyder (Eds.), *The Sage sourcebook of advanced data analysis methods for communication research* (pp. 55–87). Los Angeles, CA: Sage.

Holbert, R. L. (2005). Intramedia mediation: The cumulative and complementary effects of news media use. *Political Communication, 22*, 447–461.

Iyengar, S., & Kinder, D. R. (1987). *News that matters: Television and American opinion*. Chicago: University of Chicago Press.

Katz, E., & Lazarsfeld, P. F. (1955). *Personal influence: The part played by people in the flow of mass communications*. Glencoe, IL: Free Press.

Krosnick, J. A., & Brannon, L. A. (1993). The impact of the Gulf War on the ingredients of presidential evaluations: Multidimensional effects of political involvement. *American Political Science Review, 87*, 963–975.

Lazarsfeld, P. F., Berelson, B., & Gaudet, H. (1944). *The people's choice: How the voter makes up his mind in a presidential campaign*. New York: Columbia University Press.

Lee, S. (2006). An evaluation of nonresponse and coverage errors in a prerecruited probability Web panel survey. *Social Science Computer Review, 24*, 460–475.

Moore, D. W. (1987). Political campaigns and the knowledge-gap hypothesis. *Public Opinion Quarterly, 51*, 186–200.

Mueller, J. (1973). *War, presidents and public opinion*. New York: Wiley.

Pan, Z., & Kosicki, G. M. (1997). Priming and media impact on the evaluations of the president's performance. *Communication Research, 24*, 3–30.

Patterson, T. E. (2002). *The vanishing voter: Public involvement in an age of uncertainty*. New York: Alfred A. Knopf.

Ridout, T. N., Shah, D. V., Goldstein, K. M., & Franz, M. M. (2004). Evaluating measures of campaign advertising exposure on political learning. *Political Behavior, 26*, 201–225.

Roskos-Ewoldsen, D. R., Roskos-Ewoldsen, B., & Carpentier, F. R. D. (2002). Media priming: A synthesis. In J. Bryant & D. Zillmann (Eds.), *Media effects: Advances in theory and research* (2nd ed., pp. 97–120). Mahwah, NJ: Erlbaum.

Singer, J. D., & Willett, J. B. (2003). *Applied longitudinal data analysis: Modeling change and event occurrence*. Oxford: Oxford University Press.

Slater, M. D. (2007). Reinforcing spirals: The mutual influence of media selectivity and media effects and their impact on individual behavior and social identity. *Communication Theory, 17*, 281–303.

Srull, T. K., & Wyer, R. S., Jr. (1979). The role of category accessibility in the interpretation of information about persons: Some determinants and implications. *Journal of Personality and Social Psychology, 37*, 1660–1672.

Tichenor, P. J., Donohue, G. A., & Olien, C. N. (1970). Mass media flow and differential growth in knowledge. *Public Opinion Quarterly, 34*, 159–170.

Trivellato, U. (1999). Issues in the design and analysis of panel studies: A cursory review. *Quality & Quantity, 33*, 339–352.

Watt, J. H., Mazza, M., & Snyder, L. (1993). Agenda-setting effects of television news coverage and the effects decay curve. *Communication Research, 20*, 408–435.

3

The Rolling Cross-Section
Design and Utility for Political Research

Kate Kenski
Department of Communication
University of Arizona

Jeffrey A. Gottfried
The Annenberg School for Communication
University of Pennsylvania

Kathleen Hall Jamieson
The Annenberg School for Communication
University of Pennsylvania

Cross-sectional surveys have been a mainstay of scholarly work in political communication. These surveys constitute a snapshot of public opinion. A cross-section refers to data that have been collected at a single point in time. When there is no reason to believe that the attitudes, beliefs, and/or knowledge of sampled respondents differ from day to day, this means of knowing invites plausible inferences. Communication scholars, however, are often interested in the changes that take place in attitudes, beliefs, and/or knowledge from exposure to messages. For political communication scholars studying campaigns and their potential effects, exposure to campaign messages often takes place over a period of time, and the dissemination of those messages across that period of time often varies in intensity. Consequently, traditional cross-sectional surveys are unable to capture the dynamic nature of campaign messages and their potential effects on the electorate. The rolling cross-section method (RCS), however, is predicated on the assumption that time matters.

Cross-sectional surveys have been used to test numerous theories in mass and political communication, theories that emerged to explain dynamic, real world phenomena. For example, one of the most well-known theories in mass communication research is agenda setting, which argues that the public's evaluations of issue salience are affected by the prominence and intensity of issue coverage in the media. Behr and Iyengar (1985) comment:

> The cross-sectional sample survey favored by most researchers is hardly a powerful means of testing a dynamic process such as agenda setting. A more appropriate strategy is to search for media effects over time, as news coverage and public concern evolve. (p. 39)

Researchers looking for the effects of ads, debates, or news routinely make the assumption that effects can take place from day to day. Political scholars in search of communication effects often find cross-sectional data inadequate as a result.[1] Single cross-sections are a limited research tool for political communication scholars because they can only reveal correlations. For causation to be inferred with some confidence, a design should include time as a factor. Consequently, when the Annenberg Public Policy Center of the University of Pennsylvania launched its National Annenberg Election Survey (NAES) in 2000, it adopted an RCS design. In this chapter we explain the RCS methodology, its use within the NAES, and the advantages and challenges that it offers communication scholars.

The RCS design was introduced to the field in the 1984 American National Election Study (ANES). The ANES also included an RCS component in its study of the Super Tuesday primaries of 1988. The RCS design attracted serious scholarly notice when it was adopted as the central model for the 1988 Canadian Election Study (CES); the same model was in place for the 1992–93 and 1997 CES. The RCS design was also implemented by the 1996 New Zealand Election Study and the 2000, 2004, and 2008 National Annenberg Election Surveys.

The fundamental objective of the RCS design is to capture campaign dynamics and their corresponding effects by taking a series of cross-sections of a target population across time. "The rolling cross-section (RCS) is a design that facilitates detailed exploration of campaign dynamics. Its essence is to take a one-shot cross-section and distribute interviewing in a controlled way over time" (Johnston & Brady 2002, p. 283). By employing the RCS design, political communication researchers are able to identify when attitude changes happened and map those changes against the time line of events that occurred during a campaign. As a result, researchers are able to make stronger causal inferences about actual campaign messages and their consequences on the electorate than they can with other designs.[2]

ROLLING CROSS-SECTION METHODOLOGY

The deployment of a sample to the field and the structured way in which pieces of a sample are treated after being released into the field are what make the RCS design unique compared to other research methodologies. There are four main steps in the implementation of the RCS methodology.[3] First, the total target number of interviews to be completed over the entire course of the study is established. For a telephone survey, a list is composed of random numbers from which telephone numbers are made, taking into account current response rates. Second, the total sample from the master list is then divided into multiple "replicates." A replicate can be thought of as a "miniature" of the total sample (Johnston & Brady 2002, p. 284), whereby each replicate is a smaller random sample from the list of the larger total sample. For a telephone survey, a replicate is a random subsample of telephone numbers derived from the master list of telephone numbers to be targeted for the entire study.

Third, specified replicates are released into the field at specific intervals of time. The assignment of any given replicate to a specified release date is completely random. The length of the time intervals varies from study to study. The interval was one week for the 1984 American National Election Study. The 1988 Canadian Election Study was the first RCS survey to implement a daily interval. The National Annenberg Election Survey also uses a daily interval release of replicates. The advantage of having a smaller interval for the release of replicates is that the resulting data are more sensitive to changes in the environment and thus better equipped to capture the dynamics of the specified period of evaluation. It should be noted, however, that as the length of the interval decreases, the management costs of the study may rise because releasing fresh replicates into the field each day and monitoring the response rate process can be a time-intensive endeavor for the organization collecting the data.[4]

Due to the nature of response rates with telephone interviewing, it is unlikely that all of the telephone numbers in a given replicate will yield completed interviews on the first day of the replicate's release into the field. Figures 3.1 and 3.2 show the number of attempted calls made and their corresponding percentages of completion in the 2000 and 2004 NAES. The graphs show that more than 25 percent of the interviews were completed on the first call attempt. It can take many days for a replicate to become exhausted, which means that additional call attempts to telephone numbers in the replicate that have not yet yielded completed interviews are futile and should therefore be abandoned.

In the RCS approach, a new replicate is introduced into the field before an older replicate is exhausted. Consequently, there is overlap between subsamples released into the field. Once the first rounds of replicates have been completed, however, any given day will be composed of approximately the same percentage of first-call-attempt numbers, second-call-attempt numbers, and so on. This is important, because respondents who answer their telephone on the first call may be systematically different from those who do not answer until several attempts have been made. Because of the overlap of replicates, a daily sample will include both those respondents who answered the telephone immediately on the day that the replicate was released into the field, as well as those from previous days' replicates for whom multiple attempts have been required. The data collected at the beginning of the survey should be used with caution as they will contain a

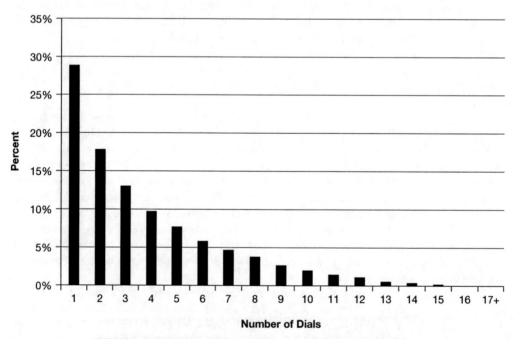

FIGURE 3.1 Percentage of completed interviews in the national rolling cross-section by the number of dials made in 2000.

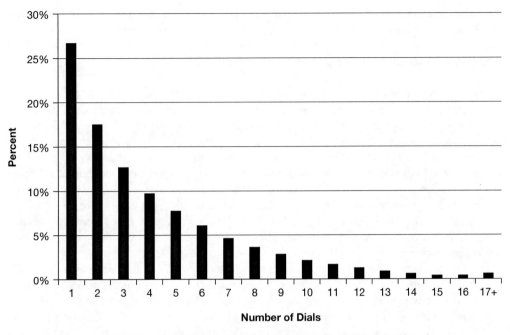

FIGURE 3.2 Percentage of completed interviews in the national rolling
cross-section by the number of dials made in 2004.

higher percentage of first-call attempts than data collected after the first round of subsamples released into the field have been exhausted.

The number of random subsamples of telephone numbers released into the field at each time interval is at the discretion of the researcher and will depend on the sample size goals and response rates achieved. The extent to which the researcher is obtaining his or her target sample size for a given interval will determine whether more or less replicates are released into the field at the following interval. When a period of time is of particular interest to the researcher, the number of replicates released can be increased to enhance the sample's power and thus ability to capture campaign effects. During the 2000 and 2004 National Annenberg Election Surveys, for example, additional subsamples of telephone numbers were released during the primaries, debates, and the general election period in order to obtain a higher overall sample size around those events.

A final element of the RCS approach is that all subsamples of telephone numbers must be treated in the same manner when released into the field. To ensure that each replicate is treated the same way, a research team should construct a consistent schedule of callbacks for all numbers. A set length of time for a telephone number to be active in the field should be determined before the study begins. Each telephone number should be given the same opportunity for completion as every other telephone number in the study. Telephone numbers released to the field on a Monday should not be treated differently from telephone numbers released to the field on a Saturday.

OTHER LONGITUDINAL METHODS

Two other longitudinal methods for capturing campaign effects deserve consideration when adopting a dynamic campaign survey methodology: repeated cross-section and panel studies. The

RCS has some advantages over these approaches. As will be explained in the next section, the panel study design also has some strengths that the RCS design does not have.

Repeated Cross-Section Designs

The RCS approach is a specific type of repeated cross-section design. In repeated cross-section studies, samples of the same population are gathered at two or more time points. Each sample (or cross-section) contains an independent set of respondents. Unlike the RCS design, which requires specific time intervals for each cross-section collected, the repeated cross-section design "does not specify how far apart in time the waves of cross-sections should be conducted" (Kenski, 2006a, p. 59). Unlike the panel design, repeated cross-section respondents interviewed at Time 1 are not re-interviewed at Time 2. During an election, the cross-sections will often take place around key campaign events. This design is best used when "the goal is to determine whether a population has changed over time" (Schutt, 2006, p. 185). The purpose of repeated cross-section studies is to determine if a change has taken place in sample responses when the two or more time periods are compared.

A disadvantage of the general repeated cross-section approach when compared to the RCS is that the former may fail to capture unexpected events if the focus is solely on key predictable events that determine the timing of the cross-section placement. Because the data are not necessarily released in a controlled way within a given cross-section, they cannot be used to examine changes that may have occurred within the timeframe in which the cross-section was conducted. The RCS design, however, can capture unexpected events because of the controlled way in which numbers are released into the field.

During election campaigns, media outlets and polling firms often conduct tracking polls, which are a type of repeated cross-section design. Tracking polls may take the form of the repeated cross-section design or the RCS design, depending on how the researchers release the sample to the field. Although published in multiple venues, such as newspapers, magazines, and websites, media polls are not vetted through an anonymous peer-review process prior to publication and are not often accompanied by details about their sampling protocols. Polling organizations working for private clients have no obligation to release the details of their protocols either, even when their numbers appear in media reports. It is possible that such organizations use strict sampling protocols, but if they do, that information is often not available to news audiences. It is reasonable to conclude, however, that because the standards for publication in media outlets are different from those in academic publications and because media and private organizations often need to generate polls quickly, structured sample release and clearance are probably not a priority.[5]

Rasmussen Reports and Gallup, for example, conduct daily tracking polls during the general election. It does not appear that these tracking polls employ the sampling protocols of the RCS designs. In its release of top-line data of the standings of the presidential candidates, Rasmussen Reports states that the daily tracking poll is based on nightly telephone interviews with 1,000 likely voters that are released as three-day rolling averages.[6] Such tracking polls are popular in the media. Because there is no daily census available to which the tracking polls (or the RCS for that matter) could be compared, it is not known how well these polls capture reality. The potential problem is that daily sample sizes could contain different proportions of first-call attempts, second-call attempts, and so on if the sampling release has not been systematized so that the daily samples contain approximately the sample proportions of call attempts across time. Differences in call attempt proportions across time are only a problem if people who answer surveys after the first or second call attempt differ systematically from people who answer the survey after additional contact attempts; this is unfortunately not easy to determine in advance of conducting a study.

Panel Designs

In a panel study, the same individuals are interviewed at two or more points in time. This method allows the researcher to capture changes in individuals over time. In RCS and repeated cross-section studies, individuals are not monitored across time, as each sample is made up of different individuals at the different time points. Because the same individuals are sampled at two or more points in time, panel designs are better than cross-sectional designs for establishing causal inferences (Schutt, 2006, p. 186). While the RCS and repeated cross-section designs can make inferences about groups, the panel design can make inferences about changes in behavior at the individual level.

For example, suppose one wanted to argue that party conventions are persuasive events and that watching convention coverage increases people's preference for the nominee of the party holding the convention. A researcher with repeated cross-section data could do two things to argue that a convention had increased a candidate's favorability ratings. First, she could compare favorability ratings from the cross-section collected before the convention to favorability ratings from the cross-section collected after the convention. Second, if respondents in the second cross-section were asked whether or not they had watched the convention, she could check to see if convention watchers gave the candidate higher ratings than did non-watchers. If both tests yield support for the hypothesis, then the researcher could conclude that she has empirical support for the claim that convention watching increases the favorability ratings of the candidate from the party holding the convention.

The problem, however, is that even if the researcher has demonstrated that favorability ratings increased from Time 1 to Time 2 and she has shown that convention viewers gave a candidate higher favorability ratings than non-viewers, there are some compelling alternative hypotheses that will not have been addressed by the design. How do we know that it was the convention that brought about the changes in people's favorability ratings and not something else, such as advertising or favorable news coverage? How do we know that convention watchers were not already the kinds of people favorably disposed toward the candidate around whom the convention was centered? In this instance, a panel design would be able to address these counterarguments by offering empirical support that the individuals who reported watching the convention had actually changed their favorability ratings from Time 1 to Time 2.

When conducting a study over long periods of time, such as the length of a presidential campaign, the panel design has some limitations. First, the cost is too high to be able to realistically track the same respondents over the course of an entire campaign season, especially if the time interval between each wave of data collection is small. Second, panel mortality (or attrition) is often a problem. Panel mortality refers to "the loss of panel members as a result of the difficulty of reaching the same person for two or more contacts or because of the respondent's refusal of continuous cooperation" (Miller & Salkind, 2002, p. 320). As panel mortality increases, potentially more bias is introduced into the sample, and the less generalizable the study becomes. Those who drop out of a study may be systematically different from those who remain in the study. For example, in the 2000 NAES panel around the first presidential debate, Kenski (2006a) reported that panel participants were more likely to report being older, married, educated, and interested in politics than individuals who were interviewed just once for the RCS.

Third, interviewing the same individuals repeatedly may sensitize them to the concepts and methods of the study, and even allow for respondents to provide stock answers. This is often called re-interviewing bias, which refers to "the effect of repeated discussions on certain topics on the respondent's behavior or attitude towards these very topics" (Miller & Salkind, 2002, p. 320). For example, a respondent who has been asked questions about current events or candidate issue positions may become more attuned to the campaign environment and therefore have an easier time answering these questions when interviewed the second time around; it is therefore difficult to parse out who learned the information because of natural campaign events exposure and who learned the information because they were primed to pay attention to campaign events after having been interviewed about those topics.[7] As respondents become more sensitized to a panel's design, the results could become less generalizable.

THE NATIONAL ANNENBERG ELECTION SURVEY

The National Annenberg Election Survey, which is funded by and administered through the Annenberg Public Policy Center of the University of Pennsylvania, was created to study the 2000 presidential campaign.[8] The NAES is primarily a national RCS survey, but it also has incorporated panel and cross-sectional side studies. During the primary seasons, oversample RCS surveys were conducted in New Hampshire (2000 and 2004), the Super Tuesday states (2000), and the Second Tuesday states (2000), demonstrating that RCS data can be collected in smaller geographic locations than the nation as a whole.[9] For the national RCS, replicates are released daily because an election campaign can be unexpectedly volatile. Consequently, it is more useful and revealing to have a smaller interval for the release of the replicates than it is to use longer intervals. As explained earlier, the smaller the interval for the release of the replicates, the more sensitive the data are to capturing campaign dynamics. A set schedule was established for callbacks to telephone numbers that were not answered on the first attempt.[10]

For the 2000 NAES, the national RCS began in December 1999 and ended in January 2001. A total of 373,016 numbers were called with 58,373 completed interviews (about a 6:1 ratio of attempted to completed interviews). The mean number of call attempts per each completed interviews was 3.71. As seen in Figure 3.3, in July 2000 the total number of daily completed

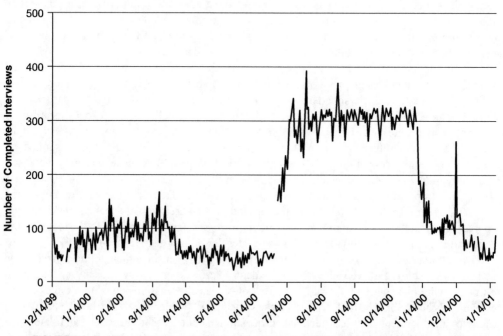

FIGURE 3.3 Number of interview completions by day in the 2000 national rolling cross-section.

interviews increased from previous periods of the campaign, which was accomplished by increasing the total number of replicates that were released into the field each day. In 2000, it was determined that the period between July and November was the critical period of campaigning for the general election. After the general election in November 2000, the number of replicates was decreased. Between 50 and 300 interviews were completed daily, with a higher average number of interviews from July through November than the remaining months.

The 2004 NAES national RCS began in October 2003 and concluded in November 2004. A total of 761,089 numbers were called, producing a total of 81,422 completed interviews (about a 9:1 ratio of attempted calls to completed interviews). The mean number of attempted calls per completed interview was 4.07. The 2004 NAES release of the replicates followed the same protocol as that in 2000. The graph of total number of completed interviews for 2004 is presented in Figure 3.4. The average daily number of completed interviews varied between 60 and 360. General election campaigning began earlier in 2004 than in 2000, in part due to an upsurge of advertising from 527 independent expenditure groups.[11] Thus, the target number of interviews completed per day was increased earlier in the year in 2004 than in 2000.

Panels for both the 2000 and 2004 NAES were conducted around key campaign events: primaries, conventions, debates, and the general election. Repeated cross-sections were also conducted around the primaries in 2000 and President Bush's second inauguration for the 2004 NAES.[12]

The 2008 National Annenberg Election Survey contains the usual telephone RCS and a new Internet study component.[13] The national telephone survey contains over 57,000 interviews with American adults collected between December 2007 and November 2008. The Internet study is a novel addition to the 2008 NAES; this study combines the RCS and panel design. Approximately 100,000 interviews had been conducted when the 2008 Internet NAES was completed. Participants in the Internet study were interviewed five times over the course of the presidential

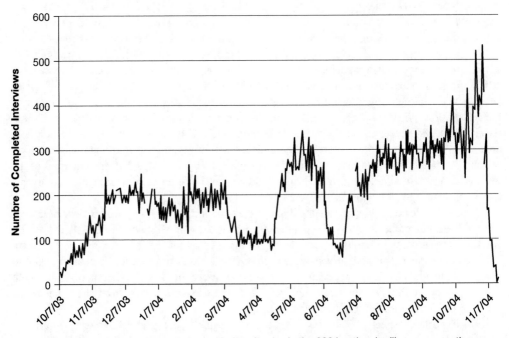

FIGURE 3.4 Number of interview completions by day in the 2004 national rolling cross-section.

campaign. Within each wave, contacts were made with study participants based on a subsample release process; interviews within the time period of the wave can be treated as an RCS.

ADVANTAGES TO THE RCS DESIGN

The RCS design has many advantages. First, it incorporates temporal heterogeneity into the methodology. Instead of treating time as a problem, the study design employs time as an opportunity for capturing effects. Second, the RCS design is able to capture unexpected campaign events. Third, by tracking phenomena across time, scholars can potentially avoid misattributing outcomes to the wrong events. Fourth, data collected with the RCS can be segmented into different time periods for analysis. The design is flexible, allowing data to be utilized as single cross-sections, repeated cross-section, or aggregated into time series. Fifth, if the RCS study is large, small subpopulations can be analyzed. Sixth, because respondents are interviewed once, there is minimal conditioning of study participant responses.

Incorporation of Temporal Heterogeneity

The RCS design is particularly useful for studying a population across an extended period of time, making it valuable for analyzing election campaigns. A criticism of alternative methodologies is that temporal heterogeneity is an inherent flaw in their designs. The samples in a repeated cross-section study are taken over a specified period of time (although the length of the interval in one cross-section need not necessarily be the same as the length in another cross-section). The design assumes that no meaningful variation will take place within the sampling period of each collection. Let us assume, for example, that a cross-section over a period of three days was taken from September 10–12, 2001. Individuals would have answered questions about politics very differently on September 12, 2001 than they would have on September 10, 2001. Unfortunately for the design, one would not be able to compare respondents from September 12 to those from September 10, because the interviews within the cross-section were not randomly distributed across days.

Because of the constant release of replicates over the period of study, the RCS design takes advantage of temporal heterogeneity by incorporating it as the driving force behind the method. "By being self-conscious about release and clearance of the sample, we could convert temporal heterogeneity into an object of study" (Brady & Johnston, 2006, p. 284). Because the design focuses on capturing change across an extended period of time, the data can be placed into a time-series format. By presenting the data in this fashion, one is able to more accurately track across time such variables as vote preference, candidate favorability, approval ratings, and the like. Placing the data into a time series format allows for an advanced analysis of the dynamics of the set period, thus allowing for more facility in making causal inferences between campaign events and opinion change (Johnston & Brady, 2002).

Figure 3.5, for example, shows the dynamics of support for the Iraq War between October 21, 2003 and November 1, 2004. Respondents from the 2004 NAES were asked, "All in all, do you think the situation in Iraq was worth going to war over, or not?" After the capture of Saddam Hussein, the support for the war was at its highest level, but as time went on, support began to decline as the outlook of the war became less favorable. When the Abu Ghraib prison photos were exposed, support for the war declined even further. But support rose from the time of the Democratic Convention up until the election.

An important aspect of studying election campaigns is being able to track opinions of candidate traits across time. Figure 3.6 presents candidate trait ratings of "strong leader" for

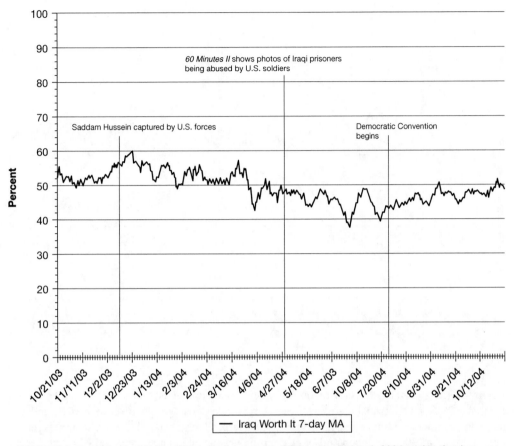

FIGURE 3.5 Percentage of U.S. adults from October 21, 2003 to November 1, 2004 stating that Iraq was worth it (MA, moving average). Reprinted from Kenski, 2006a, p. 59.

Democratic presidential nominee John Kerry from January 2, 2004 through November 1, 2004. Respondents were asked, "On a scale of zero to 10, how well does 'strong leader' apply to John Kerry? Zero means it does not apply at all, and 10 means it applies extremely well." An analysis of this graph can be advanced by focusing on the month of August. After the Democratic Convention was held July 26–29, John Kerry had his highest level of being viewed as a strong leader since February. The "Swift Boat Veterans for Truth," which was a 527 group attacking John Kerry's Vietnam service (and thus attacking Kerry as a "strong leader"), released their ads on August 4. As seen in the graph, Kerry being viewed as a strong leader took a sharp turn downwards. When the data are depicted in this fashion, it becomes much easier to see the link between events and opinion.

Capturing Unexpected Campaign Events

Most of the events that were referenced previously were not traditional campaign events that could have been predicted at the start of the campaign season. No one could have pinpointed the date when Saddam Hussein was going to be captured (if at all), foreseen that photos would have surfaced of American soldiers abusing Iraqi prisoners, or expected that an independently financed

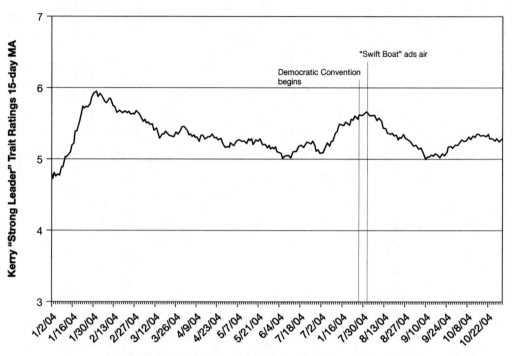

FIGURE 3.6 John Kerry "strong leader" trait ratings across 2004.

group would have attacked Kerry on his Vietnam service in August. Other unanticipated events from the 2004 election included the elementary school hostage situation in Beslan and the surfacing of another Osama Bin Laden tape right before the general election. Such unexpected events from the 2000 election included the controversy surrounding the repatriation of the Cuban boy Elian Gonzalez, the Clinton administration's decision to release oil from the petroleum reserve, and reports about George W. Bush's decades-old DUI. In 2007, no one predicted that the 2008 Democratic presidential primary would offer a highly competitive contest between Senator Hillary Clinton and Senator Barack Obama that would not be decided until June.

A timeline of events that occurred during the 2000 and 2004 elections, or any campaign for that matter, reveals that many of the significant events that occur during a campaign season are not scheduled campaign events. (For a 2000 election timeline, see Jamieson & Waldman, 2001, pp. 10–11; for a 2004 election timeline, see Jamieson, 2006, pp. 8–10.) A repeated cross-section or panel design, which focuses primarily on traditional campaign events, is likely to miss these unexpected events. Because the survey is continuously being administered in an RCS design, inferences can be made about the relationship between unexpected campaign events and public opinion.

Prevention of False Attribution

Because the repeated cross-section and panel designs focus on scheduled events, they can mistakenly attribute opinion change to the wrong event as unexpected events intervene between scheduled ones. A comparison of a repeated cross-section study to an RCS study of the debates regarding the 2000 presidential election (using NAES data) reveals this problem of false attribution. One of the questions asked in the survey included a feeling thermometer that rated the candidate trait of honesty. Honesty was a trait of particular importance in the 2000 election, because the downfall of the Gore campaign was attributed to a slip in character perception (Johnston, Hagen, & Jamieson, 2004).

As portrayed in Figure 3.7, the rating of honesty for Gore declines before the debate and continues after the first debate; it becomes even lower after the second debate. Typically, researchers using repeated cross-sectional data before and after an event compare the mean differences between the two time periods with a *t*-test or the percentages between the two time periods with a proportions test. Had researchers conducted an analysis of repeated cross-sections before and after the first debate, they would have concluded that the debates perhaps *caused* the perception of Gore's honesty to decline.

The data collected using an RCS design present a different picture from those of the repeated cross-section. In Figure 3.7, it is still true that perceptions of Gore's honesty decline after the first debate and decline even further after the second debate. But what is further explained by this graph that is missing in the repeated cross-section approach is that the perception of Gore being honest was on a decline well before the first debate ever took place. The decline started two weeks prior to the first debate.

While a repeated cross-section study set around the debates would have captured the pre–post debate difference, it would not have been able to demonstrate that the decline took place *well before* the dates. Consequently, depending on a repeated cross-section study might have led one to falsely attribute this change in opinion to the debates.

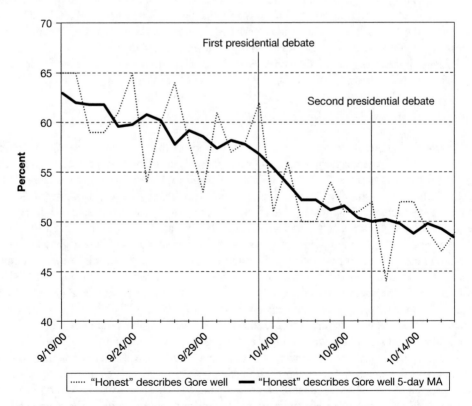

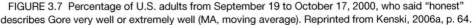

FIGURE 3.7 Percentage of U.S. adults from September 19 to October 17, 2000, who said "honest" describes Gore very well or extremely well (MA, moving average). Reprinted from Kenski, 2006a, p. 64.

Flexibility in Breaking Down Data

The RCS design allows data to be sliced or aggregated in different ways. Smaller subsets of data can be taken from the larger dataset and used as a single cross-section or repeated cross-sections. Because the date of interview is a random event, the data can be divided into various time periods. With a repeated cross-section or panel design, the data cannot be sliced up into smaller time periods within a given cross-section or panel wave because the date of interview is not a random event. Because people who respond to a survey immediately may be different from those respondents who require several contact attempts before an interview is completed, one cannot simply split a single cross-section into smaller time units. If a cross-section is conducted over a month's time, then the entire month's sample should be used in the analysis.

For an election study, one may wish to focus on the primary season, the period leading up to the election, or the period after the election. The RCS design allows researchers to slice the data into these larger units of time. For example, Winneg, Kenski, and Jamieson (2005) studied the reception of deceptive advertising about the presumptive presidential nominees that was prevalent in March and April of 2004 using NAES data collected between April 19 and May 2 of that year. They concluded that several deceptive claims about President George W. Bush and Senator John Kerry were believed by a majority of citizens, consistent with the ads being aired.

The data can also be used for time series purposes. To do so, the researcher need merely screen the data for the dates he or she wishes to use in the analyses and then aggregate responses to whatever unit of analysis needed for the time series. Figures 3.3 through 3.10 in this chapter use NAES data to create aggregated estimations of public opinions across time. Stroud and Kenski (2007) used the NAES data tracking daily changes in refusal rates to investigate nonresponse patterns in random digit dialing telephone surveys. Times series were created to show variables visually, and time series statistical techniques were used to uncover patterns not visible to the naked eye (for more on time series, see Chapter 24, this volume).

Facility in Studying Populations and Subpopulations

As numerous replicates are released over the set period for the study in large RCS collection efforts like the NAES, the aggregate number of interviews becomes very large. There were a total of 58,373 interviews in the 2000 NAES national RCS and 81,422 interviews in the 2004 NAES national RCS. Large numbers of respondents were made possible by the length of time in the field and the constant release of replicates. Even though each replicate comprises a smaller number of interviews completed each day, the collective sample from the RCS can become substantial.

Because the NAES sample size is large, researchers can use the data to make generalizations about both large and small populations. The sample size allows for the unique study of small subgroups. A large random sample will include subgroups that it would not be possible to study with samples in the mere hundreds. Studies conducted from the NAES data on small sub-samples include whether Native Americans were offended by the Washington Redskin's name (Annenberg Public Policy Center, Sept. 24, 2004), Hispanic voting behavior (Kenski & Tisinger, 2006), and news consumption and late-night comedy consumption among young people (Young & Tisinger, 2006). Further, these subpopulations potentially can be tracked across time to analyze group dynamics.[14] For example, Kenski (2007) tracked gender and voting decision across the span of the 2000 presidential campaign, and Winneg and Stroud (2005) conducted a study on Internet users versus non-Internet users' information acquisition about presidential candidates during the 2004 election.

Minimal Conditioning

In an RCS design, replicates are never re-interviewed throughout the entire period of the study, although some RCS designs incorporate a panel design into them. For the initial RCS respondents, there is minimal conditioning (Brady & Johnston, 2006, p. 173). Each respondent is fresh to the interviewing process. Respondent conditioning is a problem that has plagued much panel research and potentially hurts the internal validity of the data collected from the panel design.

CHALLENGES FOR THE RCS

Although the RCS design has a number of advantages, there are also challenges inherent in the design that are important to address. With all methodological designs, there are limitations which other designs may better handle. First, the RCS is not able to capture individual change and thus make generalizations about individual-level attitudes and behavior change. Second, because interviews are dispersed across a given time period, there can be difficulty studying individual days, because of issues pertaining to sample size. Third, researchers conducting time series analyses often use smoothing techniques to reveal dynamics visually; these smoothing techniques make assumptions that may not be able to disentangle "real" movement from sampling error. Fourth, because of the strict protocols employed to pieces of sample released to the field, response rates may potentially be lower than in other types of designs.

Inability to Capture Individual-Level Change

The RCS design contains fresh respondents in each replicate released to the field. Individuals are never interviewed more than once. Thus, this methodology cannot be used if the purpose of a study is to track individual change across time (Brady & Johnston, 2006; Kenski, 2006a). A panel design is better suited for capturing individual-level changes (see Chapter 2, this volume).

It is inappropriate to make generalizations about individuals from data that are group aggregated. Performing generalizations about individuals from group-level data constitutes the *ecological fallacy*: "The conclusions may or may not be correct, but we must recognize that group-level data do not necessarily reflect solely individual-level processes" (Schutt, 2006, p. 170). The inability of the RCS design to capture individual change is also a problem with repeated cross-section studies generally because interviews with individuals in the samples are not repeated.

The Difficulty of Studying Individual Days

Because the RCS is based on a relatively small number of interviews aggregated over a period of time, trying to analyze an individual interval of replicate release can be problematic as the sample size may be too small. This problem, of course, can be alleviated if funding permits the researcher to increase the number of completed interviews for each interval. Even with the 2004 NAES, in which some days had as many as 360 interviews, many desired analyses of the individual interval cannot be performed on account of such a small daily sample size. A single day's worth of data may not yield a sample size that has the power to detect specific associations.

Introducing Bias with Smoothing

Time series created from RCS data can be used to reveal campaign dynamics through visual inspection.[15] When graphically portraying RCS data in a time series format, the data often look "noisy" because of sampling error. The lower the sample size, the higher the sampling error. A common method to alleviate this problem is smoothing out the data lines with moving averages, which pool data across days. Information is averaged across days so that noise from the sampling error is reduced by capitalizing on samples from nearby days. There are numerous ways that days could be pooled to create daily estimates. The smoothing technique employed will contain assumptions that may or may not match up with the reality being estimated. Therefore, bias potentially enters into the picture with the introduction of smoothing.

Figure 3.8 shows the percentage of adults who said that the U.S. is ready to elect a black president during the summer of 2008. The dotted line on the graph represents the daily percentage of respondents who said that the U.S. was ready. The solid line is a 5-day centered moving average of the percentages. A centered moving average for a particular day is created from that day's value averaged with specified values before and after it. For example, the 5-day centered moving average in Figure 3.8 took the value of a particular day and averaged it with the values from the two preceding days and the two subsequent days. When one pools information across days, sampling variance is reduced. In formulas for sampling variance, sample size is the factor in the denominator. Assuming that daily sample sizes are equal, when one pools data across several days, the sampling variance is reduced accordingly. In a 5-day centered moving average, the sampling variance should be reduced to one-fifth of the daily sampling variance, if the daily sample sizes are equal and the daily sampling variances were otherwise equal to each other. The results from 5-day centered moving averages are drawn more closely to the center than the day-to-day samples, which contain more volatile swings (higher and lower extremes).

As shown in Figure 3.9, as the intervals of the moving averages increase, the noise in the curve decreases; the 7-day moving average is smoother than the daily average, and the 15-day moving average is smoother than the 7-day average. Smoothing the data using the centered

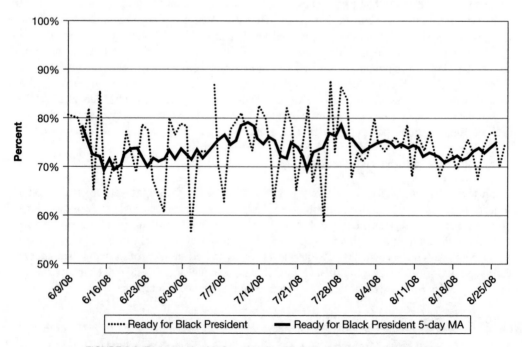

FIGURE 3.8 Percentage of U.S. adults from June 9, 2008 to August 27, 2008
who said the U.S. is ready to elect a black president (MA, moving average).

moving average technique reveals that knowledge increased before the Republican Convention and after the Democratic Convention, but it was level *between* the Republican Convention and the Democratic Convention, suggesting that the Republican Convention did not facilitate learning of candidate issue positions.

Smoothing data, however, introduces potential bias into the analytical process (Brady & Johnston, 2006). This bias did not exist in the data prior to the smoothing because the mean is an unbiased estimator of the population parameter. Johnston, Blais, Brady, and Crète (1992) note that pooling data has a disadvantage if figures in the actual population are changing. "[W]here the true percentage is shifting, mixing values together from different days can mask the shift" (p. 26). As the interval of the moving average increases, so does the potential bias. A way to prevent having to smooth the data is to increase the sample sizes for each day. As a sample size increases, sampling error decreases.

Different smoothing techniques can result in different conclusions about when important events occurred. Consequently, the assumptions that one makes about the dynamics being studied can affect the conclusions reached from the data. Among the many ways that one could calculate moving averages, two general approaches are often employed: the centered moving average and the prior moving average. Figure 3.10 illustrates the differences between them visually. The graph presents data collected from the 2008 NAES on campaign attention. Adults in the study were

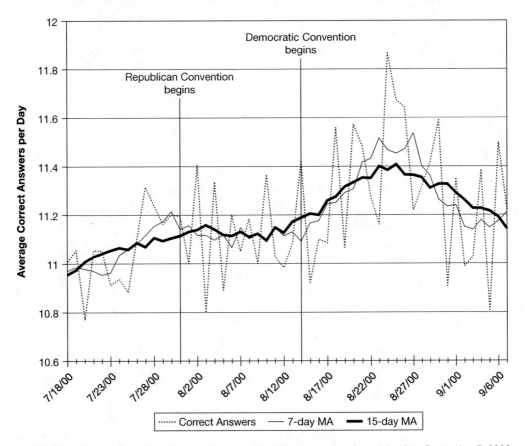

FIGURE 3.9 Knowledge index of major party candidate issue positions from July 18 to September 7, 2000 (MA, moving average). Reprint from Kenski, 2006c, p. 112.

asked how closely they were following the presidential campaign. The percentage of adults reporting that they were following the campaign "very closely" is presented in Figure 3.10. Notice that the movement in prior moving average occurs a week after movement takes place in the centered moving average. A problem with the centered moving average is that it will reflect the change before a change has actually occurred in the population because a given time interval's estimate includes data from subsequent days when real changes are taking place. If interested in locating the exact moment that is a turning point, notice how a different conclusion is reached using the centered moving average than when using the prior moving average.

Response Rate Tradeoff

There is a response rate tradeoff that occurs when one decides to follow strict protocols for the treatment of telephone numbers rather than to target aggressively some telephone numbers at a later point in time.[16] By treating all numbers in exactly the same way, one avoids misattributing changes in the times series to campaign events instead of protocol fluctuations. If telephone numbers are not treated with the same protocols and changes appear in the data, the researcher will not know if the changes should be attributed to campaign events or changes in the protocols that resulted in a different type of sample composition. The disadvantage of following RCS protocols, however, is that by allowing numbers into the field for only a specified duration, one misses out on the opportunity to increase the study's response rate by doing follow-up calls at a later point in time with telephone numbers that have not resulted in a completed interview and have not been dismissed as ineligible numbers (e.g., business numbers, numbers no longer in service). For example, a potential respondent whose number was being called may not have had the opportunity to participate in the survey during the time that her number was active in the field

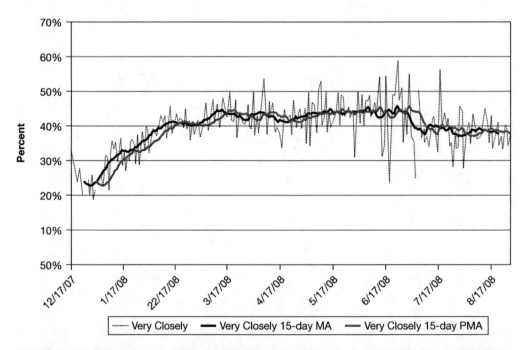

FIGURE 3.10 Percentage of U.S. adults from December 17, 2007, to August 27, 2008, who report following the campaign for president "very closely" (MA, moving average; PMA, prior moving average).

because she was on vacation. If she were called a month later, the follow-up call might have resulted in a completed interview, thus increasing the study's response rate.

Toward the end of an RCS study, new replicates will be released to the field, even though the researcher has no intention of making follow-up contacts if the numbers have not resulted in completed interviews. From the researcher's point of view, it is more important to have each interval of time contain data with similar proportions of cases derived from first-call attempts, second-call attempts, and on down the line, than to complete all numbers in the replicates at the end of the study. Consequently, RCS response rates will be somewhat lower in general than single cross-section designs that are conducted over a longer period of time.[17]

CONCLUSION

The RCS design is predicated on the assumption that campaigns matter and that their effects can be captured by an approach that capitalizes on time as a unit of analysis. Single cross-sections are a limited research tool for political communication scholars because while they can reveal correlations, they lack the time element required to make strong inferences about causality. Repeated cross-sections and panel designs improve upon the single cross-section design by incorporating time as a feature, but they do not utilize time as extensively as the RCS design.

The RCS design, however, is able to fully incorporate time as a variable in the study. By doing so, the RCS is able to capture unexpected events and prevent misattributing effects to campaign events by monitoring trends before and after the events have occurred. Although data in the RCS design are collected with potential time series analyses in mind, the data are flexible, so that if the researcher decides that he or she is interested in static factors rather than dynamic processes, the data can easily be used as single cross-sections. Large RCS surveys, such as the NAES, allow researchers to analyze small groups. Nevertheless, one need not necessarily have an extra-ordinarily large sample to conduct an RCS. Any regular cross-section conducted over a period of time can employ RCS techniques to potentially capture changes across time. Because respondents are only interviewed once with the RCS design, moreover, minimal conditioning is involved.

As with all research designs, the RCS design does have some disadvantages in comparison to other longitudinal designs in trying to establish causality of campaign outcomes. One limitation is that, unlike the panel design, the RCS cannot capture changes at the individual level. While the design can capture changes across time, the dispersal of sample across specific intervals of time means that it is often problematic to use only the data captured with a single time interval because sample size is small. While RCS data can be aggregated into a time series and presented in appealing visual formats that may be more intuitive for audiences to understand than formal statistics, using smoothing techniques to reduce sampling error may introduce bias into the analytical process. Another potential challenge to the RCS design is that its strict sampling protocols may slightly reduce response rates in an effort to keep the proportion of callbacks stable across sampling intervals. Similar to other longitudinal methodologies that are employed in natural settings, the RCS design is not able to determine causality as effectively as laboratory experiments, but it is strongly suited for detecting real campaign dynamics in real time.

The RCS design is a more recent innovation to campaign methodologies than single cross-section, repeated cross-section, and panel study designs. Consequently, the number of times that it has been employed is rather small in comparison to other approaches. While it is currently being used for large-scale studies, such as the National Annenberg Election Survey, it should be considered by researchers who are planning to do cross-sectional work if dynamic changes are possible within the timeframe of the cross-section's collection. The tradeoffs between the costs and potential benefits suggest that if the researchers have the management capacity, much can be gained from employing the RCS design. The utilization of such designs need not only apply to national election studies. Much could be learned from studying dynamic processes at many levels of government.

NOTES

1. Gelman and King (1993) use election polls across campaigns to evaluate models from political science that have often suggested that presidential campaigns do not matter because the outcomes of elections can be predicted from factors months in advance versus media assumptions that election outcomes are influenced by campaign events as evidenced by the variability of election polls. They argue that news media can influence campaign outcomes by enlightening voter preferences through the dissemination of information about candidate issue positions. Although models emphasizing the supremacy of indicators independent from campaign events have dominated the political science literature, Holbrook (1996) argues that campaign events can influence outcomes by analyzing shifts in opinion. He states, "Only by expanding the analysis to include studying the dynamics of public opinion during the campaign period can one gain an appreciation for the effect of the campaign" (p. 46).
2. Experiments are considered the best general method for establishing causality. Their drawbacks are that they require advanced planning and often do not look as realistic as natural or observational approaches.
3. For other explanations of the RCS design, see Brady and Johnston (2006), Johnston and Brady (2002), and Kenski (2006b).
4. Brady and Johnston (2006) contend that, "The cost of a rolling cross-section is only marginally more than any other telephone cross-section with correspondingly aggressive clearance. Somewhat more management overhead is dictated by the need to monitor the process every day" (p. 172).
5. In their haste to make results available as quickly as possible, media organizations often conduct one-night studies of citizen responses collected immediately after the presidential debates, even though response rates to such studies may be low. Consequently, the samples will contain more easy-to-get respondents than surveys that contact potential respondents multiple times over the course of several days.
6. See http://www.rasmussenreports.com.
7. Researchers can gauge the effects of being interviewed at Time 1 and the interview's potential interaction with the stimulus by employing what is called the Soloman four-group design.
8. Pilot tests of the RCS design were conducted by researchers at the Annenberg Public Policy Center in 1998. The pilot tests were based on data collected in Chicago and San Francisco during general election gubernatorial campaigns. The telephone protocol for the NAES was refined during these pilot tests.
9. Further demonstrating that the RCS design can be applied to smaller geographical locations than the nation, Karp and Garland (2007) analyzed RCS data collected in the 19th congressional district in Texas to test competing explanations of ticket-splitting. They concluded that the likelihood of ticket splitting increases when media exposure contributes to ambiguity over the candidates' ideological positions.
10. For the first four days of the release of a replicate, each number was attempted twice daily. For the next ten days, each number was attempted once daily. If a respondent refused to be interviewed within the first six days of the telephone number's release into the field, then the person was asked to participate again four days after the initial date of refusal. If a respondent refused within the seventh through ninth days of a telephone number's release, the person was called back on the tenth day of the replicate. If a respondent refused within ten to thirteen days of the telephone number's release into the field, then the person was called back the next day. If the person refused on the fourteenth day, s/he was called back for conversion that day. If a person was not reached after a telephone number had been in the field fourteen days, the telephone number was no longer dialed.
11. A 527 group is an organization that is allowed to spend unlimited amounts of soft money during a campaign because it does not officially represent a party or candidate. The number 527 refers to the

section of the IRS tax code that contains the loophole for these groups, exempting them from campaign finance restrictions.

12. For a detailed explanation of the methodology of the panels and repeated cross-section studies of the 2000 and 2004 NAES, see Romer, Kenski, Winneg, Adasiewicz, and Jamieson, (2006).

13. The telephone survey was conducted by Schulman, Ronca, and Bucuvalas, Inc. The Internet survey was conducted by Knowledge Networks.

14. The smaller the group being studied, the more difficult analyses between groups over time become. It would not be possible, for example, to conduct a time series analysis of Native Americans at the daily unit of analysis because of power limitations from sample size.

15. Johnston and Brady (2002) argue that "RCS data require—and also repay—intense graphical treatment. Indeed, informal, nonparametric, visual analysis is often necessary prior to formal, statistical effort" (p. 284).

16. In their study of the University of Michigan's Survey of Consumer Attitudes, Curtin, Presser, and Singer (2005) demonstrate that survey response rates declined between 1979 and 2003. The rate of the decline has been more precipitous in recent years.

17. The response rates for the National Annenberg Election Survey were 25 percent in 2000 and 22 percent in 2004 (using the American Association for Public Opinion Research's Response Rate 1 formula). The Response Rate 1 formula is the most conservative calculation for response rates of those published as standard definitions by the American Association for Public Opinion Research. The calculation involves making the assumption that all telephone numbers of unknown eligibility are eligible numbers.

REFERENCES

Annenberg Public Policy Center. (2004, September 24). Most Indians say name of Washington "Redskins" is acceptable while 9 percent call it offensive, Annenberg data show. Retrieved November 9, 2007, from http://www.annenbergpublicpolicycenter.org.

Behr, R. L., & Iyengar, S. (1985). Television news, real-world cues, and changes in the public agenda. *Public Opinion Quarterly, 49*, 38–57.

Brady, H. E. & Johnston, R. (2006). The rolling-cross section and causal attribution. In H. E. Brady & R. Johnston (Eds.), *Capturing campaign effects* (pp. 164–195). Ann Arbor: University of Michigan Press.

Curtin, R., Presser, S., & Singer, E. (2005). Changes in telephone survey nonresponse over the past quarter century. *Public Opinion Quarterly, 69*, 87–98.

Gelman, A., & King, G. (1993). Why are American presidential election campaign polls so variable when votes are so predictable? *British Journal of Political Science, 23*, 409–451.

Holbrook, T. M. (1996). *Do campaigns matter?* Thousand Oaks, CA: Sage.

Jamieson, K. H., & Waldman, P. (2001). *Electing the president 2000: The insiders' view.* Philadelphia: University of Pennsylvania Press.

Jamieson, K. H. (2006). *Electing the president 2004: The insiders' view.* Philadelphia: University of Pennsylvania Press.

Johnston, R., Blais, A., Brady, H. E., & Crète, J. (1992). *Letting the people decide: Dynamics of a Canadian election.* Stanford, CA: Stanford University Press.

Johnston, R., & Brady, H. E. (2002). The rolling cross-section design. *Electoral Studies, 21*, 283–295.

Johnston, R., Hagen, M. G., & Jamieson, K. H. (2004). *The 2000 presidential election and the foundations of party politics.* Cambridge: Cambridge University Press.

Karp, J. A., & Garland, M. W. (2007). Ideological ambiguity and split ticket voting. *Political Research Quarterly, 60*, 722–732.

Kenski, K. (2006a). Research designs concepts for understanding the rolling cross-section approach. In D. Romer, K. Kenski, K. Winneg, C. Adasiewicz, & K. H. Jamieson (Eds.), *Capturing campaign dynamics 2000 & 2004* (pp. 43–67). Philadelphia: University of Pennsylvania Press.

Kenski, K. (2006b). The rolling cross-section design. In D. Romer, K. Kenski, K. Winneg, C. Adasiewicz, & K. H. Jamieson (Eds.), *Capturing campaign dynamics 2000 & 2004* (pp. 68–78). Philadelphia: University of Pennsylvania Press.

Kenski, K. (2006c). Visualizing data across the campaign. In D. Romer, K. Kenski, K. Winneg, C. Adasiewicz, & K. H. Jamieson (Eds.), *Capturing campaign dynamics 2000 & 2004* (pp. 104–120). Philadelphia: University of Pennsylvania Press.

Kenski, K. (2007). Gender and time of voting decision: Decision certainty during the 2000 presidential campaign. *Journal of Political Marketing, 6*(1), 1–22.

Kenski, K., & Tisinger, R. (2006). Hispanic voters in the 2000 and 2004 presidential general elections. *Presidential Studies Quarterly, 36,* 189–202.

Miller, D. C., & Salkind, N. J. (2002). *Handbook of research design and social measurement.* Thousand Oaks, CA: Sage.

Romer, D., Kenski, K., Winneg, K., Adasiewicz, C., & Jamieson, K. H. (2006). *Capturing campaign dynamics 2000 & 2004.* Philadelphia: University of Pennsylvania Press.

Schutt, R. K. (2006). *Investigating the social world: The process and practice of research* (5th ed.). Thousand Oaks, CA: Sage.

Stroud, N. J., & Kenski, K. (2007). From agenda setting to refusal setting: Survey nonresponse as a function of media coverage across the 2004 election cycle. *Public Opinion Quarterly, 71,* 539–559.

Winneg, K., Kenski, K., & Jamieson, K. H. (2005). Detecting the effects of deceptive presidential advertisements in the spring of 2004. *American Behavioral Scientist, 49*(1), 114–129.

Winneg, K., & Stroud, N. J. (2005, May). *Using the internet to learn about the presidential candidates and issue positions in the 2004 presidential primary and general election campaigns.* Paper presented to the 60th annual meeting of the American Association for Public Opinion Research, Miami Beach, FL.

Young, D. G., & Tisinger, R. M. (2006). Dispelling late-night myths: News consumption among late-night comedy viewers and the predictors of exposure to various late-night shows. *Harvard International Journal of Press/Politics, 11*(3), 113–134.

4

Political Communication Survey Research

Challenges, Trends, and Opportunities

Lindsay H. Hoffman
Department of Communication
University of Delaware

Dannagal Goldthwaite Young
Department of Communication
University of Delaware

The cognitive revolution of the 1970s and 1980s led to an increased focus on the construction of cognitions in social science research. During this time, researchers made many methodological advances in how they designed studies and obtained data. One area of such innovation was in survey methodology—particularly in respect to questionnaire wording and design. Fairly simple models of the response process evolved into stage models outlining the cognitive tasks and motivations underlying responses.

Political communication scholars employ survey research as a primary tool for assessing attitudes, cognitions, and behaviors relevant to both politics and communication. Yet the measurement of these variables presents several challenges, requiring scholars to be familiar with the psychology of the response process, particularly the processes involved in answering attitude questions and the ubiquitous presence of "nonattitudes." This chapter will discuss these issues as they pertain to research in political communication and related fields. There are numerous options for survey researchers to employ when considering mode and format: telephone, mail, face-to-face, and the Internet. This chapter will outline both the benefits and drawbacks for political communication scholars in employing these various modes.

Every measure of attitudes or behaviors presents its own set of complications in survey research. We first address the issues associated with attitude measurement, providing a brief history of how scholars have attempted to measure attitudes, followed by a discussion of behavioral measures. We also examine current issues in survey research, such as the increasing number of cell-phone-only households and the ubiquity of Web surveys. Finally, we provide suggestions to political communication researchers for reducing measurement and response error.

THE EVOLUTION OF RESEARCH ON ATTITUDES VERSUS "NONATTITUDES"

For years, survey methodologists presumed that respondents had fixed, pre-existing attitudes that were readily accessible when answering a survey question. This model has been referred to as the "file-drawer" model because, as the metaphor suggests, respondents need only search for the appropriate answer (or "file") in their memory. The model has been labeled by some as normatively biased, suggesting that all citizens *should* have attitudes about those topics that are of importance to the country and perhaps more importantly, to the researcher.

The file-drawer model corresponds to the "memory-based" perspective of memory retrieval, which was assumed to be the dominant method by which respondents answered attitude questions, particularly those associated with political attitudes (Hastie & Park, 1986). This model suggests that respondents form evaluations about an attitude object each time new information is encountered. When asked for their attitude about the object, the respondent is presumed to compute how many positive and negative evaluations they have of a candidate, issue, or other item of interest. The resulting computation is the attitude.

The memory-based perspective assumes that respondents have accessible and preformed attitudes to a given question. Yet respondents are often incapable of presenting all the reasons they have for holding certain attitudes, such as why they favor or oppose a particular candidate. If respondents are indeed relying on the memory-based model, they should be able to recount the different considerations that informed their final attitude. The fact that individuals are often unable to account for *why* they hold a particular attitude exposes a logical flaw in the memory-based model. Because of these issues, scholars have suggested that respondents are more likely to use "online based" memory retrieval, where they simply refer to what has been recently recalled in order to report their attitude (Tourangeau, Rips, & Rasinksi, 2000).

The file-drawer model was prominent until Converse (1964) and others began to question respondents' abilities to consistently answer attitude questions. Scholars discovered that subjects' responses were often inconsistent over time and respondents did not exhibit readily accessible attitudes when asked survey questions. Converse (1964) and other scholars (e.g., Bishop, 2005; Schuman & Presser, 1996; Zaller, 1992; Zaller & Feldman, 1992) have demonstrated that respondents sometimes respond to attitude questions even when they do not have attitudes about an object—resulting in a construct referred to as a "nonattitude." Perhaps the best demonstration of these nonattitudes lies in studies of responses to fictitious and obscure objects. Bishop, Oldendick, Tuchfarber, and Bennett (1980) found that 30 to 40% of respondents offered opinions on whether the fictitious Public Affairs Act of 1975 should be repealed. Schuman and Presser (1996) revealed that 25 to 30% of respondents offered their opinions on highly obscure legislation—the Agricultural Trade Act of 1978 and the Monetary Control Bill of 1979.

In early literature on attitudes, Allport (1935) argued that an attitude is a mental or neural state, suggesting that an attitude was a *cognitive* construct. Later, Petty and Cacioppo (1981) defined attitudes as enduring feelings about an attitude object, calling attention to the *affective* nature of attitudes. Eagly and Chaiken (1993) suggest that an attitude is a "psychological tendency" that includes cognitive, affective, and behavioral components. Current literature identifies attitudes as the evaluative judgments that integrate these components (Crano & Prislin, 2006), and develop from one's general beliefs and values, but are more specific to objects.

This definition of attitudes makes it perhaps easier to understand how Converse and others viewed attitudes as either consistent or inconsistent. Respondents were perceived to either have stable attitudes, or none at all. He suggested that inconsistent respondents provided essentially random answers in order to avoid looking ignorant. Since then, scholars have debated what it is that leads people to express nonattitudes or to be "floaters" (those who vacillate between response options when filters are included in the question). Evidence suggests these responses can either result from individual traits, such as educational level (i.e., the "trait model"), or that there is something about the survey itself that encourages respondents to provide nonattitudes ("threshold model") (Schuman & Presser, 1996). But Converse was admittedly driven by the normative assumption that respondents *should* have responses to attitude questions, and ultimately placed the blame on respondents rather than on the survey design. It wasn't until the cognitive revolution in psychology and related disciplines that scholars began to examine questionnaires with more precision (Weisberg, 2005). Both the trait and threshold models, while ideally mutually exclusive, appear to offer complementary explanations for nonattitudes and floaters, although the trait model offers somewhat less conclusive evidence (Shuman & Presser, 1996). This is perhaps one reason why researchers focus so much attention on survey design.

Because of the prevalence of nonattitudes, scholars like Bishop (2005) and Zaller (1992) have echoed the possible repercussions of relying on survey research to obtain a representative view of public attitudes. Bishop defined a nonattitude as a response to a question that appears genuine but really has no basis; he has gone so far as to describe public opinion as "illusory." Both Bishop and Zaller claim that nonattitudes are prevalent on surveys. In fact, Zaller and Feldman (1992) reported that nearly 50% of questions asked on surveys over repeated interviews six months apart were answered differently by the *same* respondents.

If respondents are willing to give an answer to something they clearly know nothing about or one that is completely fictitious, what is the likelihood they will respond to issues with which they have some familiarity, but about which they have no opinion? This concern is clearly a central one for political communication scholars, who often rely on responses to attitude questions to test theory. Fortunately, there are some precautions (presented later in this chapter) that can be taken in order to reduce nonattitudes, but researchers should be aware that they will always be present in some form.

An additional component in the discussion of nonattitudes is the normative structure of the interview process. Grice's (1975) conversational maxims serve as guidelines for many conversations and have also been shown to influence responses to survey questions. One rule in Grice's theory is that of being truthful; not only do interviewers expect—or at least hope—that respondents are being truthful in their responses, but respondents also assume that interviewers have honest motivations for asking certain questions. As many of Bishop's studies have concluded, respondents will provide opinions on issues that are not well known or do not exist. Yet part of this error may result from this truthfulness maxim, meaning that respondents simply assume that researchers will not ask about fictitious issues.

The debate continues over whether there are true attitudes or whether surveys are simply creating attitudes through the process of measuring them. However, Zaller and Feldman (1992) suggested that the solution to this debate is more complicated than it might appear. These authors argued that our democracy is fraught with contradictions and issues that contain multiple dimensions—where equality is valued but discrimination persists; where we demand better government services alongside lower taxes; and where polls show poor evaluations of Congress yet incumbents are regularly reelected (Zaller & Feldman, 1992). Thus, it is no surprise that respondents consider one of these conflicting dimensions in answering a survey question. This suggests that perhaps we are not giving respondents enough credit; they might simply be accessing different dimensions of an issue from survey to survey. The current perspective on the response process—Tourangeau's four-stage model—provides some support for this conclusion in outlining the complex processes that underlie survey response.

APPLYING MODELS OF THE SURVEY RESPONSE PROCESS

Tourangeau and colleagues (2000) credit Cannell, Miller, and Oksenberg (1981) as well as Strack and Martin (1987) for their development of the dual-mode processing models specific to the survey response process. The Cannell model examined how respondents provide answers, suggesting that they take the "high road" or the "low road"—that is, they either answer completely or superficially. Similarly, Strack and Martin suggested that respondents either develop new judgments based upon the parameters of the survey question or rely on retrieval of prior judgments. However, these original models were underdeveloped, and applied generally to the final stage of the process: reporting an answer (Tourangeau et al., 2000).

The four-stage model applies not only to the reporting of a response, but addresses the stages of comprehension, retrieval, and judgment before assessing how respondents report or map their answers. *Comprehension* refers to the respondent's initial understanding of a question, including the understanding of both language and meaning. *Retrieval* refers to the stage after which respondents have comprehended both the language and inferred meaning of the question and must retrieve a response from memory. The retrieval process is important when asking about behaviors, but it also plays an important role in responses to attitude questions. For example, when asked about one's opinion on military spending, a respondent might retrieve her husband's opinion on the issue and her general values underlying federal spending. If she is asked the same question at a different time (or in a different part of the survey), it is possible she might retrieve very different objects from memory, such as recent events in the Iraq war.

The third stage, *judgment,* is particularly prone to the use of shortcuts and biases. Here, the respondent will judge how they feel about the attitude object based upon any number of attributes of their memory retrieval (see Tversky & Kahneman, 1973). For example, if the attitude were recalled with little difficulty, the respondent might assume that he feels strongly about this attitude (the *availability heuristic*). If the respondent is not motivated to search through her memory, but instead answers with the most recently recalled and relevant attitude, she is demonstrating the *accessibility bias*. When asked about a specific person, a respondent might place that person in a broader category, such as "Republicans," and make a judgment based upon that category (the *representativeness heuristic*). Finally, Tourangeau and colleagues adapted the *reporting* or *mapping* state from Cannell, Strack and Martin. Because respondents must translate their retrieved and judged attitude onto the scale provided by the survey researcher, they can often be biased by the response scale. If the respondent is unsure about his attitude, he might rely on the *anchor-and-adjustment heuristic*, selecting the middle point or the extreme ends of the scale as anchor points and map his judgment from there. Respondents are not always biased by the wording, but they must work within the parameters provided by the response scale. It is here where vague response options (e.g., what exactly is the difference between "slightly" and "somewhat?") can result in inaccurate response mapping. (See Table 4.1.)

Perhaps most importantly, Tourangeau et al.'s (2000) model of the response process is less biased against the respondent than previous conceptions and acknowledges that the survey itself can create error. Each of the four stages should be considered by scholars as they develop survey items—particularly those about attitudes. We refer the reader to Tourangeau et al. (2000) and Weisberg (2005) for comprehensive resources on the response process.

The satisficing model, developed by Krosnick and colleagues (see Krosnick, 1999), is closely related to the dual-mode cognitive models. However, this model was developed specifically for the context of survey response and refers to motivational rather than cognitive processes as

TABLE 4.1
Components of the Response Process

Component of the Response Process	Processes Undertaken
Comprehension	Attend to questions and instructions
	Represent logical form of question
	Identify question focus (information sought)
	Link key terms to relevant concepts
Retrieval	Generate retrieval strategy and cues
	Retrieve specific, generic memories
	Fill in missing details
Judgment	Assess completeness and relevance of memories
	Draw inferences based on accessibility
	Integrate material retrieved
	Make estimate based on partial retrieval
Response	Map judgment onto response category
	Edit response

Note: From Tourangeau, Rips, and Rasinksi (2000), p. 8

underlying which "track" a respondent takes. This model also maps directly onto Tourangeau's four-stage process model.

According to Krosnick's (1999) model, *satisficing* can be considered the "low road" while *optimizing* can be considered the "high road." Krosnick also differentiates between weak and strong satisficing. Weak satisficing describes the lack of motivation to complete all four stages of Tourangeau's process model. For example, the respondent may not pay close attention to the question, look for the most recently activated attitude, judge that one to be relevant, and anchor his or her response based upon the middle response option. Strong satisficing is a more extreme route, where the respondent skips the retrieval and judgment stages altogether. In this way, the respondent only comprehends the question and selects a response.

As opposed to the original dual-mode theories, the satisficing model exists along a continuum from strong satisficing to optimizing. The respondent might answer questions with the same motivation during the length of the survey, or slide from one position to another on the continuum as new questions are posed. This depends on characteristics of both the individual and the survey. If a respondent is in a bad mood or is not interested in the topic of the survey—as we must admit is sometimes the case with political communication research—he or she might be motivated to satisfice throughout the questionnaire. On the other hand, if a survey question is vague or includes abstract language, an otherwise optimizing respondent might satisfice on that particular question simply because it is difficult to understand. Thus, it is crucial that survey questions are easily understood by all respondents. If researchers wish to get the most optimized responses, they should focus on pretesting survey questions through think-alouds or cognitive interviewing, where respondents might be asked to report strategies for arriving at their conclusions (i.e., Did they fully understand the question before answering? Did they anchor on the middle response option?). Simply, scholars should take precautions to discourage respondents from satisficing based solely upon the instrument itself.

MEASURING KEY CONSTRUCTS IN POLITICAL COMMUNICATION RESEARCH: VOTING BEHAVIOR, POLITICAL KNOWLEDGE, AND MEDIA USE

So how do these assessments of attitudes and the response process apply to issues of interest to political communication scholars? In this section, we examine several variables that appear frequently in our surveys: voting intention and behavior, political knowledge, and media use. Our goals here are to (1) discuss the conceptual and operational definitions of these constructs, (2) highlight several common problems inherent in obtaining self-reported estimates from survey participants, and (3) provide some useful tactics and strategies for maximizing accuracy while minimizing bias and error.

Voting Intention and Behavior

Voting behavior is often a key dependent variable in political communication research. While vote choice is the logical behavioral extension of one's attitude toward political candidates, voting behavior and intention are both central to democratic theory. When using a survey to obtain measures of voting behavior, the first goal should be to minimize frustration of those respondents who do not vote. While most researchers know to screen for citizenship and voter registration before asking if a participant actually voted, an increasing issue facing survey researchers concerns the prevalence of absentee and early voting. Voting doesn't just happen on Election Day. Data from the National Annenberg Election Survey (NAES) (Romer et al., 2006), for example, show that as early as 15 days before Election Day in 2004, 5% of the population had already voted. This observation should give pause to survey researchers who are interested in tracing "vote intention" up until Election Day. Just as being a citizen or being registered to vote should precede vote intention or vote choice items, so should early voting behavior prompt a skip pattern to avoid asking individuals who have already voted, whom they "intend to vote for."

A second, equally serious issue in measuring voting behavior concerns the prevalence of over-reported estimates of past voting behavior, which, by some accounts have reached as high as 20% in recent elections (Martinez, 2003; McDonald, 2003). The highest rates of voting over-report occur among those respondents who *look like* those people who actually *did* vote, both socio-demographically and in terms of their political attitudes. For example, research by Bernstein, Chadha, and Montjoy (2001) found that those most likely to overreport past voting behavior were more educated, more strongly partisan, and more invested in the outcome of the election than people who accurately reported their past voting behavior. This phenomenon likely results from both internal factors like the social desirability bias—driven by acts of "intentional deception" and "motivated misremembering" (Belli, Traugott, & Beckmann, 2001)—as well as external factors like public mood and campaign coverage (Leshner & Thorson, 2000).

For years, the American National Election Studies (ANES) have tried to minimize the problem of overreporting with a question script designed to make respondents feel more comfortable admitting they did not vote: "In talking to people about elections, we often find that a lot of people were not able to vote because they weren't registered, they were sick, or they didn't have time. How about you? Did you vote in the elections this November?" Research involving costly voter validation studies (comparing survey obtained self-reported behavior with actual voter records) has indicated that even with the introductory text, the likelihood of overreported socially desirable responses remains high (Belli, Traugott, & Beckmann, 2001).

As a result of continued concerns, in 2000 the ANES added new response options (instead of simply yes/no) designed to allow respondents to "save face" when talking with the interviewer. Following the same introductory text described above, respondents were asked, "Which of the following statements best describes you: 1) I did not vote (in the election this November); 2) I thought about voting this time but didn't; 3) I usually vote but didn't this time; 4) I am sure I voted." In an experiment comparing the effects of the additional response options to the effects of the original item on reported voting behavior, Duff, Hanmer, Park, and White (2007) found that the addition of "excuses" to the response options succeeded in significantly reducing overestimates of turnout by 8%. These findings suggest that if resources are scarce, rather than obtaining validated voter records, more accurate estimates of past voting behavior can be obtained by simply including multiple response options that provide respondents with acceptable excuses for their socially "undesirable" behaviors.

Political Knowledge

In the past several decades, as information processing has become the dominant paradigm in which to explore political media effects, the role of political knowledge has become increasingly important (Delli-Carpini & Keeter, 1996). Political knowledge is examined as both a predictor and an effect of exposure to political information, as well as moderator of political communication effects (see Eveland, Hayes, Shah, & Kwak, 2005; McGuire, 1968, 1972; Zaller, 1992). Yet knowledge as a construct can take many different forms. What operationalization of political knowledge a researcher will choose depends on the conceptual role thought to be played by this construct in the proposed theoretical models.

For example, the political knowledge scale proposed by Delli-Carpini and Keeter (1996), often referred to as "civics knowledge," consists of items that capture an individual's familiarity with the American system of government (i.e., "Do you happen to know what job or political office is now held by Joe Biden?"; "Whose responsibility is it to determine if a law is constitutional or not—the president, the Congress, or the Supreme Court?"; "How much of a majority is required for the U.S. Senate and House to override a presidential veto?"; "Do you happen to know which party has the most members in the House of Representatives in Washington?"). While this scale is important for its stability and reflection of a keen understanding of how American politics work, it would *not* be an ideal dependent variable to capture increases in knowledge as a function of time or media exposure. Increases in knowledge witnessed over the course of a political campaign, for example, would be more pronounced and quantifiable by assessing citizens' knowledge of candidates' issue positions or biographies, not knowledge of electoral structures and practices. The civics knowledge scale should be thought of as a fairly stable characteristic and should be conceptualized as an exogenous construct that can help tease out self-selection biases in models of political media effects.

When examining political knowledge as an *outcome* of exposure to mass media, interpersonal communication, or campaign information, it would be appropriate to employ a measure designed to capture more accessible, recently acquired information. More suitable measurements of this form of political knowledge might be more akin to the "information awareness" scale employed by Patterson and McClure (1976) to capture participants' knowledge of issues raised in the campaign. Other options include quizzes on candidate policy or biography. A straightforward policy position quiz would require respondents to choose which political candidate supports or opposes a particular policy. A quiz on candidate knowledge would ask respondents specific questions about biographical information—such as which candidate is a senator from Illinois or which candidate was a prisoner of war in Vietnam.

Additionally, given the prevalence of scholarly research on nontraditional forms of political socialization and information, it would be useful to consider some "new" forms of knowledge explored in the context of soft news. Baum (2003) argues for an expanded conceptualization of political knowledge when assessing the impact of media exposure on the concept of "learning." He points out that learning includes not only "increasing the volume of factual political knowledge" but also cognitive outcomes such as the construction and reinforcement of heuristic pathways that people may use to foster efficient and logical political judgment formation (p. 174). Hence, when considering how information might enhance participants' cognitive processing capabilities or the complexity of their mental models about the political world, alternative methods to the traditional political knowledge assessments might be more appropriate. These include assessments of construct salience and thought listings to capture the breadth and depth of linkages between political concepts. Thought listings allow respondents to indicate concepts, beliefs, events, and emotions associated with a given stimulus, without the constraints posed by closed-ended items. Such measures facilitate the creation of coding schemes post hoc to begin to cluster thought content into mental networks and to recognize salient constructs. In so doing, scholars can begin to capture a sense of the accessibility, organization, and depth of knowledge of structures in working and long-term memory, rather than a more unidimensional notion of information recall.

An additional issue to consider when measuring political knowledge through survey research is the role of context effects. Where scholars choose to place the political knowledge batteries within a questionnaire depends first and foremost on how political knowledge is hypothesized to function in one's theoretical model. For example, political knowledge that is hypothesized to be an outcome of media exposure or political discussion should be placed at the *beginning* of a survey to minimize the likelihood that parameter estimates have been affected by other questions in the survey. As a rule of thumb, placing key endogenous variables (those variables explained by the theoretical model) up front is an easy way to increase one's confidence in the sanctity of the dependent measures. In this way, those variables of interest will likely be less influenced by questions throughout the survey.

Finally, while a positivist might argue that political knowledge items are either right or wrong, there are those items designed to tap into a more nuanced political understanding than our statistical software packages have the capacity to infer. For example, when asked which party is "more conservative at the national level" (see Delli-Carpini & Keeter, 1996), a politically savvy participant who considers both parties to be in the hands of special interests might answer, "neither." For this participant, the question designed to capture knowledge may be better described as an attitude item. While not necessarily ideal as a measure of information recall, such items might be used, in tandem with open-ended items, to indirectly capture attitude and a unique form of political sophistication.

Media Use

Of all the measures used by political communication researchers, the one that is bound to be used most often that is of greatest theoretical significance in political communication models is media use. Whether we call it exposure or consumption, viewing or using, the central predictive mechanisms in many—if not most—of our analyses in this field demand that we find a way to capture an accurate, unbiased, and reliable estimate of the extent to which an individual is in the flow of mediated information. While there are numerous conceptual and methodological issues to consider when measuring media use through survey research, in this section we focus on the following: (1) attention versus exposure measures, (2) the importance of measurement specificity, and (3) recent recommendations for measurement.

Scholars have long abandoned measures of general television exposure as a central media use variable due to its poor predictive power (Pfau et al., 1997). Instead, logic and experience dictated that measures of exposure to specific programming content performed better in models predicting politically relevant constructs, including cultivation effects (Potter & Chang, 1990). In the 1980s, Chaffee and Schleuder (1986) proposed that media effects researchers include a hybrid measure that combined both exposure *and* attention to media content. Since then, numerous studies have indicated that integrating attention to political content into a measure of media use increases this item's predictive power when examining outcomes ranging from information acquisition (Drew & Weaver, 1990; Zhao & Bleske, 1995) to political interest (Drew & Weaver, 1998) and voter turnout (Norris, 1996). For example, to capture mere exposure to 24-hour cable news networks, a researcher might ask, "How many times in the past week did you tune into a 24-hour cable news network such as CNN, MSNBC, or Fox News?" To tap into attention paid to campaign news within the genre, a follow-up item might take the form, "How much attention do you pay to news about the presidential campaign on 24-hour cable news networks?"

However, given the increasing scholarly attention being paid to nontraditional sources of political information and influence (Baum, 2003, 2005; Delli-Carpini & Williams, 2001; Holbert et al., 2003; Young, 2006, 2008), and the subtle mechanisms thought to operate in some of these models, measuring attention to political content within entertainment programs such as *The Daily Show* with Jon Stewart, or even *South Park* might not always make sense. When attempting to capture incidental exposure (see Baum, 2005), drawing a participant's focus to the specific portion of political content to which he or she is *incidentally* exposed may undermine the theoretical model under investigation. This is especially true given the kinds of people who might be more likely to report paying attention to political aspects of entertainment programming, regardless of the actual attention being paid. Perhaps it is better to think of the "attention to political content in programming" as a construct that captures the kind of programming that one deems an appropriate source of political information. This assessment is likely correlated with many other important constructs, key among them, education and age.

In an important contribution to the field, Prior (2005, 2006, 2007) has conducted numerous analyses to better understand the validity and utility of self-reported media exposure. Using Nielsen ratings data to validate self-reported media exposure measures, he finds startlingly low correlations between what people *say* they watch and what they are *actually* watching. In addition, analyses indicate a trend of overreported news consumption, indicative of a social desirability or motivated-misremembering bias (Prior, 2007). If attempting to identify audiences who attend to specific genres, Prior's work suggests that exposure might be appropriate. However, if trying to quantify the extent to which individuals were exposed to specific messages in order to later assess the impact of those very messages, his work should—at the very least—give media scholars pause when extrapolating findings from self-reported exposure measures.

The second issue worthy of attention is the specificity of the media use measures in question. As indicated above, political communication scholars have long abandoned "general television exposure" as a predictive construct to account for political effects. Recognizing the need for specificity, many political survey organizations, including the Pew Research Center for the People & the Press, the ANES, and the NAES, have integrated separate measures of exposure to national news, cable news, local news, political talk radio, newspapers, and online news, along with occasional items to capture which specific program within the genre the respondent consumes most often. In addition, these organizations have sought to integrate exposure to nontraditional forms of political information like late-night comedy programs. The NAES has even integrated specific items to capture exposure and attention to particular media events such as individual debates and specific speeches given during presidential conventions (Romer et al., 2006). Recent research has also examined exposure to specific content instead of genre or medium, concluding that these specific measures are more likely to result in significant effects with behavioral outcomes (Annenberg Media Exposure Research Group, 2008). Moreover, although open-ended measures generate higher predictive power in content recall, closed-ended measures perform equally well when focused on specific topics (Romantan et al., 2008). This research suggests that scholars should rely on specific media exposure items for optimum reliability and validity.

Given the evolving digital media landscape, researchers must also consider whether the "mode" or platform of content delivery matters given the theoretical mechanism proposed. For example, participants will need to be offered a distinction between "reading the newspaper" and "reading the newspaper online" if and only if the mode of delivery matters given the goals of the analysis. At present, almost all content that can be delivered through the television can also be delivered via the Internet: cable news stories, local news segments, and national news broadcasts, for example. Even clips from *Saturday Night Live*, *The Daily Show* or *The Colbert Report* are available through streaming video within hours of their original broadcast. Deciding whether to incorporate the "viewed *online*" distinction should be contingent upon time, resources, and most importantly, theory. We raise the point here simply to compel scholars to have these conversations in advance of survey construction.

In addition to specificity of program, mode, and content is the issue of specificity of usage. As recommended by Althaus and Tewksbury (2007), by standardizing exposure and use items into "days in a typical week," one avoids issues of noninterval estimates posed by response categories such as "often," "regularly," and "rarely." Scholars can also seek to maximize measurement specificity by not conflating exposure, attention, and learning. By operationalizing media use in a way that demands respondents account for their *own* sources of learning, we run the risk of increased measurement error and social desirability bias. People are notoriously bad at recalling the sources of their political information. The more time that passes between information acquisition and being called upon to cite the source of that information, the worse the recall (Mares, 1996; Yegiyan & Grabe, 2007). Given these findings, we should be cautious when interpreting parameter estimates from media use items such as "How often, if ever, do you learn something about the presidential campaign or the candidates from [insert media source here]." If used to measure "rates of learning about the campaign from particular sources," items such as this, used by the Pew Research Center for the People & the Press (2004), invite spurious correlations between individual characteristics and media "learning" estimates. For example, when capturing consumption of nontraditional political programming, such as comedy shows, countless individual characteristics would render a respondent more or less likely to see comedy shows as an *appropriate* source of "learning something about the presidential campaign." For instance, older people might see comedy shows as inappropriate sources of political information, while younger people might see such programs as legitimate and credible sources. Hence, individuals' self-reported estimates of learning from these shows may be a better reflection of their own evaluations of these sources of political content, rather than estimates of information actually gleaned from such programs.

Finally, we focus here on several broad recommendations for measurement. Althaus and Tewksbury (2007), in a report to the American National Election Studies Board of Overseers, urged political researchers to recognize and methodologically embrace the evolving media landscape by integrating items that reflect a more accurate depiction of how people are currently experiencing their political world, including online sources. They also proposed that survey items integrate contemporary theories of cognitive psychology and information processing through the introduction of psychological scales capturing decisiveness, closed-mindedness, and need for cognition. Such items could play a key role in moderating effects of exposure or attention on various political outcomes. (See Chapter 6 of this volume for a more detailed discussion of ANES and NAES media measures.)

SUGGESTIONS FOR REDUCING RESPONSE ERROR

Bishop (2005) has suggested that the public opinion process, as a whole, is illusory. In his argument and in the statements of some other scholars, attitudes are simply constructions made on the spot, or "top-of-the-head" responses (Zaller, 1992). Although many survey methodologists agree that nonattitudes and top-of-the-head responses are a problem, few are ready to throw in the towel. This optimism is due in large part to the advances made in research that has come out of the cognitive revolution. Survey methodologists are now able to identify response processes and the factors that lead respondents to be more or less motivated to answer questions. In this section, we outline some of those advances and how they apply to political communication research.

Question Wording

There are a number of checklists and guidelines regarding "good" and "bad" survey questions. We refer readers to Converse and Presser (1986), Bradburn, Sudman, and Wansink (2004), as well as Sudman, Bradburn, and Schwarz (1996), for user-friendly guides. In addition, Dillman (2007) has provided explicit directions regarding how to maintain flow and aid comprehension of self-administered questionnaires. Many of these checklists suggest avoiding vague or complicated words and jargon, as well as reducing the number of syllables and words to aid respondents in comprehension. There are also guidelines based upon the mode of the survey, since telephone surveys are more prone to a recency effect (giving the most recent response) while face-to-face surveys are more likely to exhibit primacy effects (giving the first response). Some of these authors have encouraged survey designers to place the least desirable option either first or last, depending on the mode of presentation.

Krosnick and his colleagues continue to test whether simple changes in wording affect responses over time and between respondents of different education levels and backgrounds. For example, while those respondents of lower education are more likely to offer "don't know" responses, they do not appear to be affected by the form of the survey (Krosnick & Abelson, 1992). Considering the influence that a "don't know" option has on the reduction of nonattitudes, we generally encourage the inclusion of this option. It can be phrased in terms of knowledge, interest, or opinion. That is, the question might end with "or don't you know enough about this issue to respond?", "or are you not interested in this issue?", or "or don't you have an opinion on this issue?" Recall that Bishop et al.'s (1980) study examining responses to the fictitious Public Affairs Act garnered opinions from up to 40% of respondents. When the question included the phrase, "or haven't you thought much about this issue?" the proportion expressing an opinion dropped to 4%. The implication is that such wording reduces the likelihood of obtaining nonattitudes.

There is also the closely related issue of a neutral or middle category. Schwarz and colleagues (Schwarz et al., 1985; Schwarz & Hippler, 1995) argued that respondents infer that the middle response option represents the *typical* value of an *average* person. An "assimilation effect" can result from this inference, because respondents base answers on vague impressions and rely on the middle response option as a starting point for their answer (Tourangeau et al., 2000). Krosnick (1991) has argued against the inclusion of such categories as they invite satisficing. Yet the inclusion of a middle or neutral category may be warranted if "conceptually demanded" (Krosnick & Fabrigar, 1997, p. 148). In general, scholars are using such response categories less and less frequently as concerns about satisficing increase (Weisberg, 2005).

Another problem that respondents encounter in survey response is simple forgetting: either the failure to retrieve a memory, an inaccurate reconstruction of a memory, or the retrieval of a generic memory (Groves et al., 2004). Particularly with questions about past behaviors, respondents must search their memory and map what they've retrieved onto the given response options. Many political communication researchers rely on self-reported estimates of media exposure. However, such questions ask respondents to retrieve information that may not be readily available. When events are not distinctive (e.g., watching *ABC News* versus *CBS News*), or there are a lot of them (e.g., multiple days or weeks of viewing), or they didn't make an impression to begin with, questions about past behaviors can be difficult to answer (Groves et al., 2004). Unfortunately for us, respondents often fill in missing information by using cues, schemas, or scripts.

Respondents also have difficulty remembering reference periods, and are susceptible to *forward telescoping* (remembering events as having taken place more recently) and *backward telescoping* (remembering events as having happened longer ago) (Tourangeau et al., 2000). Scholars can prevent some of these problems by limiting the reference period (Althaus & Tewksbury, 2007, recommend "days per week") and by providing specific content and media categories, such as national network news on television *and* national network news online, to discourage reliance on scripts and schemas. Choice of response categories should be specific to researchers' questions of interest.

But there are some scenarios in which even the most carefully written questions could result in error, whether they ask about attitudes, cognitions, or behaviors. For instance, older respondents are more error-prone in recognizing exposure to media, instead relying more on "gist-like fuzzy traces" (i.e., memory focused on the meaning of the experience rather than specific attribute details) than younger ones (Southwell & Langteau, 2008, p. 103). In addition, research has demonstrated that women are more likely than men to give "don't know" responses to political knowledge questions, while men are more likely to guess (Kenski & Jamieson, 2000; Mondak & Canache, 2004). Given that the process of guessing at least offers a chance of getting the correct answer, political knowledge scales that treat "don't know" responses as incorrect (as many do, according to Mondak & Canache, 2004) will tend to show inflated gaps in knowledge between men and women (Kenski, 2000; Pew Research Center, 2007). Moreover, since most knowledge scales are constructed in a way that treats a "don't know" response as equivalent to an incorrect response, both answers receive scores of zero. As such, "don't know" and incorrect responses each are presumed to indicate an absence of knowledge. Controlling for guessing propensity is one solution to this problem; Mondak and Canache (2004), for example, use the formula *incorrect responses/(incorrect responses + "don't know" responses)* and use it as a control for the tendency to guess. This value calculates the proportion of times the lack of information is indicated by a wrong answer compared to a don't know response.

Some researchers have turned to cognitive experiments, group evaluations, and "think-alouds" to guide them in developing the best questions (Bradburn, Sudman, & Wansink, 2004; Sudman, Bradburn, & Schwarz, 1996). Generally, these pilot tests involve two phases with a suitable sample size ranging from 25 to 75 people (Converse & Presser, 1986). In this process, respondents provide the reasons and processes they go through to get an answer, and these responses are coded by researchers with objective coding schemes (Tourangeau et al., 2000). Some questions researchers might ask in this process are "How did you get to that opinion?" or "How strongly do you feel about that opinion?"

Asking about attitude strength is essential for understanding attitudes and identifying non-attitudes. In addition to the direction of an attitude (agree *versus* disagree), researchers should also ask whether respondents feel strongly about that opinion or not. If they do not feel strongly at all, this is likely to be a nonattitude. Moreover, attitude strength can influence cognitions and behaviors

(Krosnick & Abelson, 1992). Krosnick and Abelson suggested that *extremity* and *intensity* are the most frequently studied dimensions of strength; the feeling about the attitude is the *intensity*, while *extremity* is simply the deviation from the middle or neutral response on the scale. This latter option may be desirable when time or space is of concern. This type of question is particularly relevant when asking about perceptions of others' opinions, because respondents are already prone to projection (i.e., self-generating a consensus for one's own opinion; Orive, 1988). If a person feels strongly about his or her own opinion, this projection is stronger (Krosnick & Abelson, 1992). Thus, at least for this area of research, it is important to also gauge attitude strength.

Closely related to the measurement of attitude strength is that of ambivalence. In general, ambivalence is defined as conflicting opinions about certain issues (Zaller & Feldman, 1992), but many social psychologists identify it as both positive and negative evaluations of an attitude object (McGraw, Hasecke, & Conger, 2003; Priester & Petty, 1996). Suffice it to say that, when it comes to politics, many respondents have ambivalent attitudes. One person could evaluate a candidate for president positively on personal characteristics, for example, but negatively on policy preferences. So when this person is asked, "What is your opinion of candidate X?" we can't be certain which evaluation will surface in the response.

Researchers generally employ one of three strategies for evaluating ambivalence. The first is to assess the respondents' emotional state either in an interview setting or through coding of open-ended responses (as in Zaller & Feldman, 1992). Second, researchers can develop self-evaluation measures for participants by asking them if they have both positive and negative feelings about the attitude object (McGraw, Hasecke, & Conger, 2003; Priester & Petty, 1996). Finally, researchers can solicit positive and negative evaluations from respondents about various components of an attitude object and combine those into a continuous measure of ambivalence (McGraw, Hasecke, & Conger, 2003).

A similar measurement strategy, the "mushiness index," has been proposed by Yankelovich (1991) and others, aimed at assessing the volatility of respondents' attitudes. The four-item index includes how much the respondent thinks the issue affects him or her personally; how well informed the respondent feels on the issue; how much the respondent has discussed the issue with others; and how likely the respondent thinks it is that his or her views on the issue would change (Bishop, 2005). This index enables researchers to more accurately assess opinions on issues that are likely to generate nonattitudes by providing insight into how "mushy" or "firm" a respondent's opinion is. For complex or less well-known issues, such as stem cell research, genetically engineered food, or various policies related to "going green," a mushiness index could substantially reduce the frequency of nonattitude reportage.

There are also a number of techniques that can be employed to encourage respondents to provide the most truthful answers. The "bogus pipeline" procedure is intended to encourage respondents to give the most accurate responses by suggesting that inaccurate answers can be detected (e.g., with physiological devices that can detect "true feelings" or by asking permission to cross-check official documents, such as voting records, Weisberg, 2005, p. 87). In addition, the Randomized Response Technique asks respondents to answer one of two questions, one of which is sensitive and the other of which is not. This technique is specific to sensitive questions, such as sexual or risky behaviors, and is most often used in a face-to-face context (although it can be used on the phone by asking respondents to flip a coin).

Questionnaire Design

Scholars who employ survey research must contend with the fact that attitude questions themselves are always context-dependent (Weisberg, 2005). That is, respondents will look to the order, form, and structure of questions for cues on how to respond to them and this ultimately produces some error. In order to reduce context effects, surveys can be designed to provide questions in random—yet comprehensible—order. This can apply to the questions themselves, components of the questions, or the response scales. Questions that are likely to influence those around them (i.e., those of related content) might be distributed randomly to reduce context effects. One component of the question can also be randomly switched in order to reduce acquiescence or social desirability biases. For example, questions on perceptions of public opinion may influence responses if they are systematically phrased in either "favor" or "oppose" language. By randomizing, for instance, "how many people in your community do you think are [in favor of/opposed to] this issue?" that systematic bias can be reduced (Gunther, 1998; Gunther & Christen, 1999; Hoffman et al., 2007). The response scales themselves should be thoughtfully constructed with attention to primacy and recency effects as dependent on mode of administration. If the responses are in a list, survey designers might wish to randomize them to reduce context effects. Perhaps the best method is to pretest the items, including multiple question wordings rather than relying on one single wording.

Many surveys also include both specific and general questions on, for example, political interest. A general question should almost always precede a specific question because respondents are likely to infer that, if the first question asked about interest in a current political campaign, and the second question asked about political interest in general, that second question must mean to *exclude* interest in the current campaign. Some scholars have provided lists of guidelines as great as 50 or so, while others provide succinct lists of 10. Our suggestion, in brief, is to be as understandable, clear, and concise as possible.

Based upon this collection of recommendations, we encourage scholars who want to obtain the most accurate answers to their political communication surveys to keep in mind the four stages of Tourangeau et al.'s (2000) model. For each question in one's survey, as well as for the entire questionnaire, scholars should ideally be able to affirmatively answer four questions: (1) Can the question be comprehended easily? (2) Does the question wording ensure that the respondent can adequately retrieve a response from memory? (3) Have possible biases in judgment, such as accessibility or availability, been accounted for? And, finally, (4) can respondents accurately map their responses onto the scale provided? If the survey—as well as the questions therein—is short and easy to understand, measures attitude strength, and includes "don't know" or neutral response categories when appropriate, scholars should be sufficiently confident they have made an honest effort to minimize survey error.

ISSUES OF SURVEY MODE

Political communication researchers have several modes from which they can choose to conduct surveys. The choice of mode depends on numerous factors, such as cost, convenience, need for representativeness, and time. Importantly, there is no perfect mode that combines all the features researchers need for their surveys. Here, we outline a few of the major differences, and discuss some pressing issues associated with two newer technologies: cell phones and the Internet.

Self-Administered Surveys

Each survey environment has its own benefits and drawbacks. Notorious for having very low response rates, mail surveys are self-administered and require a good portion of motivation on the part of the recipient. Because this format provides respondents with more control, it inherently reduces the amount of control on the part of the survey designer. Mail or strict paper-and-pencil surveys are also "static," meaning the flow of the survey cannot be easily controlled by the researcher (Weisberg, 2005). This can often result in complicated designs, where respondents are required to answer "If no, skip the next 10 questions" type items, further reducing motivation to complete the survey.

Mail surveys also lack the presence of an interviewer, which can facilitate respondent understanding and completion of the survey. However, this absence of an interviewer can produce fewer socially desirable or acquiescent responses (Smyth, Dillman, & Christian, 2006). Yet an additional drawback of mail survey design is the presence of context effects, since respondents are able to refer back to previous questions, which could influence subsequent answers. The cost and administration of mail surveys can also have negative consequences for researchers and their budgets.[1]

Face-to-Face and Telephone Surveys

Face-to-face surveys generally have higher response rates than telephone surveys, which have higher response rates than mail surveys, although some of that difference reflects the number of contact attempts (Groves et al., 2004). This pattern is repeated when it comes to item nonresponse (Weisberg, 2005), mainly because the content of a mail survey is revealed to a respondent before he or she decides to take part (Groves et al., 2004). But the primary advantage of telephone or face-to-face surveys over other modes is the presence of the interviewer. The interviewer can probe unclear or inadequate answers and encourage completion of the survey. The presence of an interviewer in a respondents' home also elicits a "guest script" in the mind of the respondent, whereby the interviewer is treated as a guest in one's home (Weisberg, 2005). Nonverbal cues, such as eye contact and nodding, can facilitate the response process in a face-to-face context; as such, these surveys may also have higher response rates because of greater credibility afforded to interviewers (Groves et al., 2004). On the telephone, however, respondents may employ a "solicitation script," in which they feel as if they are being sold a product, and it can be difficult to keep respondents engaged in the survey without visual or nonverbal cues (Weisberg, 2005). In both phone and face-to-face modes, the possibility of interviewer error is always present.

Context and response-option effects plague these interviewer-assisted survey modes just as in self-administered surveys. For instance, if questions are not randomly asked, respondents may use previous questions to assist them in answering questions, either assimilating toward or contrasting from some standard of comparison (Smyth, Dillman, & Christian, 2006). Moreover, an adherence to conversational rules in the "guest" or "solicitation" script can evoke cultural norms like politeness, consistency, and nonredundancy in respondents.

As such, both self-administered and interview-administered survey modes have their benefits and drawbacks in regard to measurement error. Political communication scholars should be particularly attentive to issues of social desirability—as in responses to media use or voting behavior—and employ interviewer-free designs in order to discourage overreporting. But researchers should also consider issues of representativeness and coverage error, particularly when it comes to the increasing number of cell phone-only households.

Cell Phones, Cell Phones, Everywhere

Fueled in part by the democratizing flow of discourse from digital media like websites and blogs, pollsters and political scholars have found themselves responding to questions and allegations regarding the legitimacy of public opinion data (Blumenthal, 2005). During the 2004 general election campaign, critics such as Arianna Huffington and Michael Moore, as well as the progressive online group, MoveOn.org, used digital and traditional media to pose questions about the validity of the results reported by large polling firms including Gallup and Zogby International.

One criticism of public opinion polls concerned a phenomenon that had already become a growing thorn in the side of many public opinion researchers: the increasing number of individuals whose only telephone is a cell phone—hence excluding them from telephone-based public opinion polls. As Michael Moore (2004) wrote on his blog, "they [pollsters] are not polling people who use their cell phone as their primary phone . . . That means they are not talking to young people."

The implications of excluding cell phone-only (CPO) individuals from a sampling frame depend on how and to what extent that excluded population is systematically different from those individuals who are included in that sample. In 2004, Michael Moore suggested that a lack of CPOs—largely owned by young, liberal people—would introduce a systematic Republican bias into polling results. While these allegations were influenced by his own political leanings, the broader premise of his argument is certainly fair: Does the exclusion of CPO individuals from telephone surveys systematically bias a sampling frame? If so, how significant is this effect, and what are the practical implications for the estimates we, as political communication researchers, obtain? Recent estimates place the percentage of adult Americans whose only working telephone is a cell phone at 12.8% (Blumberg & Luke, 2007). But these numbers are changing rapidly. As recently as 2005, that percentage was 7.7%, up from 2.9% in early 2003 (Blumberg & Luke, 2007).

Because of the structure and regulation of the American telephone industry, most telephone survey research in the U.S. has continued to involve landlines only (see Kuusela, Callegaro, & Vehovar, 2008). Among other hurdles, the Telephone Consumer Protection Act of 1991 prohibits the use of automated dialing devices for unsolicited calls to cell phones. Plus, most U.S. cell phone plans place the cost of airtime (for both outgoing and incoming calls) on the subscriber. Hence, including cellular phone numbers in a sampling frame increases the need for time (to manually dial the numbers) and resources to (a) fund the labor-intensive calling procedure, which cannot be automated, and (b) financially reimburse respondents who are reached via cell phone to offset the cost of airtime. The headaches involved in accessing cell phone numbers and the lower response rate through cell phone contacts (Tuckel, Daniels, & Feinberg, 2006) have rendered many researchers hesitant to venture into telephone surveys for CPO individuals.

But as the adoption of the CPO "lifestyle" (Ehlen & Ehlen, 2007) has increased, so has its potential role in biasing parameter estimates. Unfortunately, consistent with murmurings from 2004, the CPO lifestyle is being adopted at a faster rate among young people. For instance, in early 2007, between 28 and 31% of 18- to 29-year-olds were only reachable by cell phone, according to the National Health Interview Survey (NHIS) (see Blumberg & Luke, 2007).

While age is the strongest socio-demographic correlate of a CPO lifestyle, it is certainly not the only one. The NHIS found CPO lifestyle adoption highest among renters, men, adults living in poverty, non-Hispanic black adults, and Hispanics. And, among young people, evidence suggests that important qualitative differences separate those young CPO-lifestyle adopters from their young landline counterparts. A series of studies by Keeter, Kennedy, Clark, Tompson, and Mokrzycki (2007) found statistically significant differences between young people (ages 18 to 25) reachable by landline versus those reachable only by cell phone in the context of politically relevant attitude and behavioral items, including religiosity, social attitudes, and conservatism. For example, comparing CPO individuals to those reachable by landline among only 18–25 year olds, Keeter et al. (2007) found that half of those young respondents reachable by landline reported living with their parents, compared to only 19% of the CPO group. Those young people reachable only by cell phone were also more likely to report drinking alcohol in the past seven days, more likely to say it is okay for people to smoke pot, less likely to attend religious services, and less likely to believe that homosexuality should be discouraged when compared to their landline owning counterparts.

At present, the significant differences in parameter estimates found between young CPO respondents versus young landline respondents have failed to substantively affect survey results when included in a sample of adults over the age of 18. However, if (a) focusing specifically on young people, (b) exploring political phenomena as a function of age, or (c) examining age as a conditional variable that may moderate media effects, it would pay to be mindful of the potential biases introduced by excluding this growing segment of CPO-lifestyle adopters.

In addition to the labor- and cost-intensive process of including CPO lifestyle adopters, there are several methodological solutions. The typical recommendation—weighting—would involve using sociodemographic variables as statistical correlates of the CPO lifestyle and creating weights to account for the existing coverage bias. However, as Ehlen and Ehlen (2007) suggest, because the nature of this CPO population is rapidly in flux, using weights based on previously obtained estimates is like trying to chase a moving target. Instead, they suggest using a model to forecast the CPO population based on a behavioral process defined as the "rate of habit retention," a trend that can be estimated from prior wireless lifestyle adoption (see Ehlen & Ehlen, 2007, for details).

Internet Surveys

Internet surveys reduce a number of the problems associated with both mail and phone surveys, but they are not error-free. To understand the pluses and minuses of Web surveys, researchers must examine when these surveys resemble phone surveys in order to take advantage of that format and avoid its pitfalls, as well as when they are more similar to mail surveys. For instance, presenting questions page-by-page online is more like a phone survey, but putting the questions all on one page resembles a mail survey. The advantage of Internet surveys is that we as researchers can use what we know about both mail and phone surveys to create a survey with reduced measurement error.

There are a number of interactive components of Web surveys that can enhance the accuracy of results. Progress indicators, such as a percent-completed bar on each page, not only provide users with information about how long the survey is, but also where the respondent is in terms of completion. Internet surveys can also utilize a number of tools that require respondents to answer certain questions in specific order. However, it is important that both directions and the error messages respondents receive are as clear as possible to reduce drop-out (Christian, Dillman, & Smyth, 2007). Because Internet surveys can produce response order effects similar to those of mail surveys, researchers are encouraged to utilize randomization of response options (Smyth, Dillman, & Christian, 2006). Randomization of the questions themselves can also prevent context effects.

Issues of space and time—often limited by budgets—are less problematic in Internet surveys than in mail or phone surveys, but this does not mean that scholars should ask every question possible. Respondents are still free to opt out of Web surveys and will do so if they perceive it to be too long (Ganassali, 2008). Researchers can also incorporate images or graphical elements to aid respondents' understanding. However, Couper, Conrad, and Tourangeau (2007) discovered that in some circumstances, images can prime certain responses and should be carefully considered before being included. Yet images can do more than simply aid understanding; images can be utilized to differentiate among the most important constructs in our discipline. For instance, Prior (2008) measured both visual and verbal political knowledge and found that the knowledge gender gap essentially disappeared for respondents to the visual measures. He echoes sentiments of Graber (2001) and others, claiming that "relying exclusively on verbal measures of political knowledge biases assessments of knowledge for some people more than others" (p. 2). Web surveys allow scholars to expand current notions of traditional measures and explore new operationalizations.

Although the digital divide is declining—at least within the U.S.—scholars are still presented with issues of coverage error. Several market-research organizations are working to reduce this error by offering free Internet access to respondents obtained through a random-digit dialing sampling procedure (Weisberg, 2005). One such organization is Knowledge Networks (2008), which utilizes a representative online panel. Other organizations, such as Harris Interactive, supplement Web-based surveys with traditional telephone, face-to-face, and mail surveys, then weight the sample with "propensity score weighting," or the respondents' likelihood to be online (Harris Interactive, 2008). Dever, Rafferty and Valliant (2008) also outline several statistical adjustments, which can potentially reduce coverage bias in Internet surveys.

The best Internet surveys will use the most effective aspects of telephone surveys—randomization, page-by-page survey construction, and representativeness—as well as those superior elements of paper-and-pencil surveys, such as increased perceptions of confidentiality. Although we have primarily addressed questionnaire design issues across these modes, researchers must also consider a variety of issues regarding sampling, outlined in a number of books such as Weisberg (2005) and Dillman (2007). We refer readers to these sources and encourage scholars to consider the possibility of mixed-mode surveys, which employ a combination of face-to-face, self-administered, and telephone modes, and can reduce coverage error while increasing representativeness.

CONCLUSION

The issues to consider when engaging in survey research in the context of political communication are numerous. They include fundamental conceptual issues regarding what constitutes an "attitude," and what survey response processing model we embrace as we approach our theoretical questions. They also include issues of unbiased sampling frames and how evolving technologies like cell phones and the Internet affect our methodological decisions. They include issues of measurement as we seek to maximize accuracy and minimize the effects of social desirability and bias. Yet, in spite of the many challenges associated with capturing attitudes, cognitions, and behaviors through survey research, these measures are essential to advance our understanding of political communication and effects processes in our field. We need not accept the flawed methods of the past or ignore these challenges in the hopes that they pose no substantial problem. Instead, political communication scholars owe it to the scientific merit of their work to develop a sharpened understanding of the cognitive and motivational processes underlying how participants engage in the process of responding to surveys. In so doing, we as a discipline benefit from a shared body of knowledge based on the most unbiased and accurate data obtainable at any given moment.

Pretesting, randomized techniques and questioning, and the inclusion of attitude strength questions are all solutions that can reduce the number of nonattitudes reported. Taking time to consider the theoretical role(s) hypothesized to be played by key constructs, such as political knowledge, media use, and voting behavior, will help inform our choices not only of survey placement, but of wording and response-option selection as well. Acknowledging and embracing the true complex nature of our ever-evolving digital media landscape by extending measures of media use will help capture the many portals through which citizens may be interacting with their political environment, thereby empirically reflecting a more accurate representation of our postmodern world.

As social scientists, our object of inquiry—whether it is the individual or society—is an ever-moving target. Just as environmental scientists must contend with an ever-changing global climate, so too must we acknowledge and accommodate the evolving nature of our world. However, our field gets to contend with the additional frustration of studying a subject with free will. Although the universe may seem a daunting object to study because of its size, also daunting are human beings, who make our task difficult because they have pride or shame; may be contrary or want to please; may be apathetic or over-eager; engage in selective perception; and are blessed with a flawed notion of just how accurately they are able to know exactly what is going on in their own heads.

Yet, these admittedly maddening characteristics are what render the field of political communication so rife with opportunity. At each pass, we may answer one question, only to open the door to four other questions that need to be addressed. For instance, how do we differentiate political cynicism from skepticism, and how do these constructs map onto trust? When is the content in the media to which respondents attend political and when is it entertainment or something else; or can they exist simultaneously? And how can we assess political knowledge over time with context-specific questions that ensure their ecological validity while maintaining their usefulness?

Often, it seems that the many advances in our understanding of how information is delivered, encountered, cognitively processed, stored, and retrieved simply complicate the strategies we must use when designing surveys for political communication research. However, these improvements, while logistically cumbersome at times, may indeed bring us closer to some "real," measurable constructs than have yet been created. All the while, we must see our work in the same light as cognitive psychologists who reconceptualized attitudes decades ago; just as an attitude is best viewed as a process rather than a fixed entity, so too is our discipline. We encourage readers to seize these challenges of survey research and grow from them, furthering our shared understanding of the concepts and theories underlying political communication research.

NOTE

1. The cost differences between telephone and mail surveys are generally 1.2 to 1.7:1 (Groves et al., 2004), but mail surveys can be significantly more expensive than Internet surveys.

REFERENCES

Allport, G. (1935). Attitudes. In C. A. Murchison (Ed.), *A handbook of social psychology* (pp. 798–844). Worchester, MA: Clark University Press.

Althaus, S. L. & Tewksbury, D. H. (2007, May 2). Toward a new generation of media use measures for the ANES. A report to the board of overseers American National Election Studies. Retrieved April 15, 2008, from http://www.electionstudies.org/resources/papers/Pilot2006/nes011903.pdf.

Annenberg Media Exposure Research Group. (2008). Linking measures of media exposure to sexual cognitions and behaviors. *Communication Methods and Measures, 2*, 23–42.

Baum, M. A. (2003). *Soft news goes to war.* Princeton, NJ: Princeton University Press.

Baum, M. A. (2005). Talking the vote: What happens when presidential candidates hit the talk show circuit? *American Journal of Political Science, 49*, 213–234.

Belli, R. F., Traugott, M. W., & Beckmann, M. N. (2001). What leads to voting overreports? Contrasts of overreporters to validated voters and admitted nonvoters in the American National Election Studies. *Journal of Official Statistics, 17*, 479–498.

Bernstein, R. Chadha, A. & Montjoy, R. (2001). Overreporting voting: Why it happens and why it matters. *Public Opinion Quarterly, 65*, 22–44.

Bishop, G. F. (2005). *The illusion of public opinion.* Lanham, MD: Rowman & Littlefield.

Bishop, G. F., Oldendick. R. W., Tuchfarber, A. J., & Bennett, S. E. (1980). Pseudo-opinions on public affairs. *Public Opinion Quarterly, 44*, 198–209.

Blumberg, S. J., & Luke, J. V. (2007). Coverage bias in traditional telephone surveys of low-income and young adults. *Public Opinion Quarterly, 71*, 734–749.

Blumenthal, M. M. (2005). The methods and accuracy of polling: Towards an open-source methodology. What we can learn from the blogosphere. *Public Opinion Quarterly, 69*, 655–669.

Bradburn, N., Sudman, S., & Wansink, B. (2004). *Asking questions: The definitive guide to questionnaire design for market research, political polls, and social and health questionnaires.* San Francisco, CA: Jossey-Bass.

Cannell, C., Miller, P., & Oksenberg, L. (1981). Research on interviewing techniques. In S. Leinhardt (Ed.), *Sociological methodology 1981* (pp. 389–437). San Francisco: Jossey-Bass.

Chaffee, S. H., & Schleuder, J. (1986). Measurement and effects of attention to media news. *Human Communication Research, 13*, 76–107.

Christian, L. M., Dillman, D. A., & Smyth, J. D. (2007). Helping respondents get it right the first time: The influence of words, symbols, and graphics in web surveys. *Public Opinion Quarterly, 71*, 113–146.

Converse, J. M., & Presser, S. (1986). *Survey questions: Handcrafting the standardized questionnaire.* Thousand Oaks, CA: Sage.

Converse, P. E. (1964). The nature of belief systems in mass publics. In D. Apter (Ed.), *Ideology and discontent* (pp. 202–261). New York: John Wiley.

Couper, M. P., Conrad, F. G., & Tourangeau, R. (2007). Visual context effects in web surveys. *Public Opinion Quarterly, 71*, 623–634.

Crano, W. D., & Prislin, R. (2006). Attitudes and persuasion. *Annual Review of Psychology, 57*, 345–374.

Delli-Carpini, M. X., & Keeter, S. (1996). *What Americans know about politics and why it matters.* New Haven, CT: Yale University Press.

Delli-Carpini, M. X., & Williams, B. (2001). Let us entertain you: Politics in the new media environment. In L. Bennett and R. Entman (Eds.), *Mediated politics: Communication in the future of democracy* (pp. 160–191). New York: Cambridge University Press.

Dever, J. A., Rafferty, A., & Valliant, R. (2008). Internet surveys: Can statistical adjustments eliminate coverage bias? *Survey Research Methods, 2*, 47–60.

Dillman, D. (2007). *Mail and Internet surveys: The tailored design method* (2nd ed.). New York: John Wiley & Sons.

Drew, D., & Weaver, D. (1990). Media attention, media exposure, and media effects. *Journalism Quarterly, 67*, 740–748.

Drew, D., & Weaver, D. (1998). Voter learning in the 1996 presidential election: Did the media matter? *Journalism & Mass Communication Quarterly, 75*, 292–301.

Duff, B., Hanmer, M. J., Park, W., & White, I. K. (2007). Good excuses: Understanding who votes with an improved turnout question. *Public Opinion Quarterly, 71*, 67–90.

Eagly, A. H., & Chaiken, S. (1993). *The psychology of attitudes.* Fort Worth, TX: Harcourt Brace Jovanovich.

Ehlen, J., & Ehlen, P. (2007). Cellular-only substitution in the United States as a lifestyle adoption: Implications for telephone survey coverage. *Public Opinion Quarterly, 71*, 717–733.

Eveland, W. P., Jr., Hayes, A. F., Shah, D. V., & Kwak, N. (2005). Understanding the relationship between communication and political knowledge: A model comparison approach using panel data. *Political Communication, 22*, 423–446.

Ganassali, S. (2008). The influence of the design of web survey questionnaires on the quality of responses. *Survey Research Methods, 2*, 21–32.

Graber, D. A. (2001). *Processing politics: Learning from television in the Internet age.* Chicago: University of Chicago Press.

Grice, H. P. (1975). Logic and conversation. In P. Cole & J. L. Morgan (Eds.), *Syntax and Semantics, 3* (pp. 41–58). New York: Academic Press.

Groves, R.M., Fowler, F. J., Couper, M. P., Lepkowski, J. M., Singer, E., & Tourangeau, R. (2004). *Survey Methodology.* Hoboken, NJ: John Wiley & Sons.

Gunther, A. C. (1998). The persuasive press inference: Effects of mass media on perceived public opinion. *Communication Research, 25,* 486–504.

Gunther A. C. & Christen, C. T. (1999). Effects of news slant and base rate information on perceived public opinion. *Journalism and Mass Communication Quarterly, 76,* 277–292.

Harris Interactive. (2008). Online methodology. Retrieved June 23, 2008, from http://www.harrisinteractive.com/partner/methodology.asp.

Hastie, R., & Park, B. (1986). The relationship between memory and judgment depends on whether the judgment is memory-based or on-line. *Psychological Review, 93,* 258–268.

Hoffman, L. H., Glynn, C. J., Huge, M. E., Thomson, T., & Seitman, R. B. (2007). The role of communication in public opinion processes: Understanding the impacts of individual, media, and social filters. *International Journal of Public Opinion Research, 19*(3), 287–312.

Holbert, R. L., Pillion, W., Tschida, D. A., Armfield, G. G., Kinder, K., Cherry, D. L., et al. (2003). *The West Wing* as endorsement of the U.S. presidency: Expanding the bounds of priming in political communication. *Journal of Communication, 53,* 427–447.

Keeter, S., Kennedy, C., Clark, A., Tompson, T., & Mokrzycki, M. (2007). What's missing from national landline RDD surveys? The impact of the growing cell-only population. *Public Opinion Quarterly, 71,* 772–792.

Kenski, K. (2000). Women and political knowledge during the 2000 primaries. *Annals of the American Academy of Political and Social Science, 572,* 26–28.

Kenski, K., & Jamieson, K. H. (2000). The gender gap in political knowledge: Are women less knowledgeable than men about politics? In K. H. Jamieson, *Everything you think you know about politics . . . and why you're wrong* (pp. 83–92). New York: Basic Books.

Knowledge Networks. (2008). Overview. Retrieved June 23, 2008, from http://www.knowledgenetworks.com/knpanel/index.html

Krosnick, J. A. (1991). Response strategies for coping with the cognitive demands of attitude measures in surveys. *Applied Cognitive Psychology, 5,* 213–236.

Krosnick, J. A. (1999). Survey research. *Annual Review of Psychology, 50,* 537–567.

Krosnick, J. A., & Abelson, R. P. (1992). The case for measuring attitude strength in surveys. In J. M. Tanur (Ed.), *Questions about questions: Inquiries into the cognitive basis of surveys* (pp. 177–195). New York: Russell Sage Foundation.

Krosnick, J. A., & Fabrigar, L. R. (1997). Designing rating scales for effective measurement in surveys. In L. Lyberg et al. (Eds.), *Survey measurement and process quality.* New York: John Wiley & Sons.

Kuusela, V., Callegaro, M., & Vehovar, V. (2008). The influence of mobile telephones on telephone surveys. In J. M. Lepkowski, C. Tucker, J. M. Brick, E. D. de Leeuw, L. Japec, P. J. Lavrakas, M. W. Link, & R. L. Sangster (Eds.), *Advances in telephone survey methodology* (pp. 87–112). New York: John Wiley & Sons.

Leshner, G., & Thorson, E. (2000). Overreporting voting: Campaign media, public mood, and the vote. *Political Communication, 17,* 263–278.

Mares, M. L. (1996). The role of source confusions in television's cultivation of social reality judgments. *Human Communication Research, 23,* 278–297.

Martinez, M. D. (2003). Comment on "Voter Turnout and the National Election Studies." *Political Analysis, 11,* 187–92.

McDonald, M. P. (2003). On the overreport bias of the National Election Study turnout rate, *Political Analysis, 7,* 180–186.

McGraw, K. M., Hasecke, E., & Conger, K. (2003). Ambivalence, uncertainty, and processes of candidate evaluation. *Political Psychology, 24,* 421–448.

McGuire, W. J. (1968). Personality and susceptibility to social influence. In E. F. Borgatta and W. W. Lambert (Eds.), *Handbook of personality theory and research* (pp. 1130–1187). Chicago: Rand McNally.

McGuire, W. J. (1972). Attitude change: The information-processing paradigm. In C. G. McClintock (Ed.), *Experimental social psychology* (pp. 108–141). New York: Holt, Rinehart, and Winston.

Mondak, J. J., & Canache, D. (2004). Knowledge variables in cross-national social inquiry. *Social Science Quarterly, 85,* 539–559.

Moore, M. (2004, September 20). Put away your hankies ... A message from Michael Moore. Retrieved February 20, 2008, from http://www.michaelmoore.com/words/message/index.php?messageDate=2004-09-20.

Norris, P. (1996). Does television erode social capital? A reply to Putnam. *PS: Political Science and Politics, 29,* 474–480.

Orive, R. (1988). Social projection and social comparison of opinions. *Journal of Personality and Social Psychology, 54,* 953–964.

Patterson, T. E., & McClure, R. D. (1976). *The unseeing eye: The myth of television power in national politics.* New York: G. P. Putnam's Sons.

Petty, R. E., & Cacioppo, J. T. (1981). *Attitudes and persuasion: Classic and contemporary approaches.* Dubuque, IA: William C. Brown.

Pew Research Center for the People & the Press. (2004). Cable and Internet loom large in fragmented political news universe. Retrieved July 3, 2008, from http://people-press.org/report/?pageid=776.

Pew Research Center for the People & the Press. (2007). Public knowledge of current affairs little changed by news and information revolutions. Retrieved June 23, 2008, from http://people-press.org/report/319/public-knowledge-of-current-affairs-little-changed-by-news-and-information-revolutions.

Pfau, M., Kendall, K. E., Reichert, T., Hellweg, S. A., Lee, W., Tusing, K. J., & Prosise, T. O. (1997). Influence of communication during the distant phase of the 1996 Republican presidential primary campaign. *Journal of Communication, 47,* 6–26.

Potter, W. J., & Chang, I. C. (1990). Television exposure measures and the cultivation hypothesis. *Journal of Broadcasting & Electronic Media, 34,* 313–333.

Priester, J. R., & Petty, R. E. (1996). The gradual threshold model of ambivalence: Relating the positive and negative bases of attitudes to subjective ambivalence. *Journal of Personality and Social Psychology, 71,* 431–449.

Prior, M. (2005, September). Warning: Use of media exposure measures may cause serious side effects, or, The pitfalls of self-reported news exposure. Paper presented at the annual meeting of the American Political Science Association, Washington, DC.

Prior, M. (2006, September). The pitfalls of self-reported news exposure (part 2): Can anything be done to make it more accurate? Paper presented at the annual meeting of the American Political Science Association, Philadelphia, PA.

Prior, M. (2007). *Post-broadcast democracy: How media choice increases inequality in political involvement and polarizes elections.* New York: Cambridge University Press.

Prior, M. (2008, April). Using visuals to measure political knowledge. Paper presented at the annual meeting of the Midwest Political Science Association, Chicago, IL.

Romantan, A., Hornik, R., Price, V., Cappella, J., & Viswanath, K. (2008). A comparative analysis of the performance of alternative measures of exposure. *Communication Methods and Measures, 2,* 80–99.

Romer, D., Kenski, K., Winneg, K., Adasiewicz, C., & Jamieson, K. H. (2006). *Capturing campaign dynamics 2000 & 2004: The National Annenberg Election Survey.* Philadelphia: University of Pennsylvania Press.

Schuman, H., & Presser, S. (1996). *Questions and answers in attitude surveys: Experiments on question form, wording, and context.* New York: Academic Press.

Schwarz, N., & Hippler, H. (1995). Subsequent questions may influence answers to preceding questions in mail surveys. *Public Opinion Quarterly, 59,* 93–97.

Schwarz, N., Hippler, H., Deutsch, B., & Strack, F. (1985). Response categories: Effects on behavioral reports and comparative judgments. *Public Opinion Quarterly, 59,* 93–97.

Smyth, J. D., Dillman, D. A., & Christian, L. M. (2006). Context effects in Internet surveys: New issues and evidence. Retrieved April 23, 2008, from http://www.sesrc.wsu.edu/dillman/papers.htm.

Southwell, B. G., & Langteau, R. (2008). Age, memory changes, and the varying utility of recognition as a media effects pathway. *Communication Methods and Measures, 2,* 100–114.

Strack, F., & Martin, L. L. (1987). Thinking, judging, and communicating: A process account of context effects in attitude surveys. In H. P. Hippler, N. Schwarz, and S. Sudman (Eds.), *Cognitive aspects of survey methodology* (pp. 123–148). New York: Springer.

Sudman, S., Bradburn, M., & Schwarz, N. (1996). *Thinking about answers: The application of cognitive processes to survey methodology.* San Francisco: Jossey-Bass.

Tourangeau, R., Rips, L. J., & Rasinski, K. (2000). *The psychology of survey response.* Cambridge: Cambridge University Press.

Tuckel, P., Daniels, S., & Feinberg, G. (2006, May). *Ownership and usage patterns of cell phones: 2000–2006.* Paper presented at the annual meeting of the American Association for Public Opinion Research, Montréal, Canada.

Tversky, A., & Kahneman, D. (1973). Availability: Heuristic for judging frequency and probability. *Cognitive Psychology, 5,* 207–232.

Weisberg, H. F. (2005). *The total survey error approach: A guide to the new science of survey research.* Chicago: University of Chicago Press.

Yankelovich, D. (1991). *Coming to public judgment: Making democracy work in a complex world.* Syracuse, NY: Syracuse University Press.

Yegiyan, N., & Grabe, M. E. (2007). An experimental investigation of source confusion in televised political messages: News versus advertisements. *Human Communication Research, 33,* 379–395.

Young, D. G. (2006). Late-night comedy and the salience of the candidates' caricatured traits in the 2000 election. *Mass Communication and Society, 9,* 339–366.

Young, D. G. (2008). The privileged role of the late-night joke: Exploring humor's role in disrupting argument scrutiny. *Media Psychology, 11,* 119–142.

Zaller, J. (1992). *The nature and origin of mass opinion.* New York: Cambridge University Press.

Zaller, J., & Feldman, S. (1992). A simple theory of the survey response: Answering questions versus revealing preferences. *American Journal of Political Science, 36,* 579–616.

Zhao, X., & Bleske, C. L. (1995). Measurement effects in comparing voter learning from television news and campaign advertisements. *Journalism & Mass Communication Quarterly, 72,* 72–83.

II

SECONDARY ANALYSIS
AND META-ANALYSIS

5

Secondary Analysis in Political Communication Viewed as a Creative Act

R. Lance Holbert
School of Communication
The Ohio State University

Jay D. Hmielowski
School of Communication
The Ohio State University

The employment of previously existing data collected by other researchers for use in a current research project has been in practice for as long as there has been a field of political communication. Political communication scholars frequently engage in secondary analyses in order to address a wide range of research questions. Some recent examples of secondary analyses include Kiousis and McCombs' (2004) use of American National Election Study (ANES) data to assess the ability of attitude strength to serve as a mediator of the traditional salience transfer process outlined in agenda setting theory, Feldman and Young's (2008) use of National Annenberg Election Study (NAES) data to better understand the influence of late-night comedy television viewing on traditional TV news consumption (i.e., Baum's gateway hypothesis), and Putnam's (2000) use of DDB-Needham Lifestyle Study data to update his discussion of the present state of social capital in American society. Additional data collected by the Pew Charitable Trusts (e.g., Christie, 2007), the Wisconsin Media Analysis Group (e.g., Shah, Cho, et al., 2007), and the General Social Survey (e.g., Robinson, Rivers, & Brecht, 2006) have been used by political communication and public opinion scholars alike to tackle a wide range of research questions, issues, and agendas.

The potential upsides and downsides of conducting secondary analyses have been outlined in previous texts (e.g., Boruch, 1978; Carter, 2003; Hakim, 1982), and will be briefly summarized in this chapter. However, Kiecolt and Nathan (1985) have raised a unique potential pitfall of secondary analysis when they argue that research of this kind can cause a "possible inhibition of creativity" (p. 14). In contrast to Kiecolt and Nathan, we devote our efforts here to making an argument that political communication scholars have been extremely creative in their use of secondary data as a means by which to move the discipline forward. In fact, we wish to argue that a researcher's creative energy is a necessary, but not sufficient condition for the conduct of a quality secondary analysis.

This chapter outlines the basics of conducting a secondary analysis—the major stages involved in this type of research and the key issues a researcher must be cognizant of when conducting a secondary analysis. Space will then be devoted to summarizing the present state of secondary analysis in the field—how much of our research can be classified as secondary analysis and in what specialties within political communication this type of work can be found. We will then give attention to the study of creativity using work from the field of positive psychology (see Simonton, 2002, for a summary). Creativity will be shown to consist of three dimensions: novelty, effectiveness, and authenticity (Averill, 2002). The three creativity dimensions will be placed alongside three important components of a secondary analysis: choice of dataset, variable creation, and data analysis. A resulting nine-part, creativity-by-secondary analysis typology will be utilized to show how political communication scholarship has been highly creative in its engagement of secondary analyses. Recently published political communication articles will be plugged into each area of the typology to detail and reinforce our argument that conducting a secondary analysis (if done well) is an inherently creative act. The chapter will close with thoughts on how researchers should approach secondary analyses and the research possibilities which exist for this method.

SECONDARY ANALYSIS

Secondary analysis, as defined by Hyman (1972), is "the extraction of knowledge on topics other than those which were the focus of the original surveys" (p. 3). This definition does not describe a process, but instead touches upon the goal of secondary analysis (i.e., to extract knowledge). There are a number of benefits and limitations a scholarly community receives from engaging in secondary analyses. Carter (2003) outlines several basic positive qualities of using secondary data for a specific research project. First, scholars save time and money when they use data collected by others. Second, as Bryman (2001) has noted, the quality of a publicly available secondary dataset (e.g., ANES, NAES) is likely to exceed anything that one researcher or a small group of researchers with limited resources could achieve by doing primary research. Clearly, the research assistants and the funds available for the collection of national datasets, which were conceived with an eye toward public use, far exceed the resources available to any single research team. Third, another benefit derived from secondary analyses is that the secondary datasets most commonly used by social scientific researchers are often large enough in size to allow scholars to conduct meaningful subgroup analyses (Bryman, 2001).

Several of the benefits derived from secondary analyses exist not just at the individual researcher level, but can also be found at the community-of-scholarship macro level. Hyman (1972) brought up a prophetic point when he stated that the various polling firms, research organizations, and independent academic researchers tapping the public to respond to a host of different issues have overwhelmed citizens. In the years since this statement was offered, this point has grown to become all the more relevant. Many of today's political communication scholars have felt the public's reaction to this increased poking and prodding through higher rejection rates in their surveys. Just imagine the additional number of studies that would be in the field, especially around the time of political elections, if political communication scholars could not draw upon a wealth of quality publicly available secondary data. Secondary data allows the field to stem the tide of oversampling, at least to some small degree.

The limitations inherent to any secondary analysis may be well known or at least intuitive to many political communication scholars. One often-mentioned limitation is having little to no control over the quality of the data. For example, in its quest to be all things to all people, a large national survey may ask a series of dichotomous questions whereas an individual researcher would most often desire that the data collection organization had used operationalizations that reflect higher measurement levels (i.e., ordinal, interval, or ratio). Bryman (2001) also notes that datasets may exclude key variables. Many scholars have cursed the research gods for offering a dataset that contains a majority of the items needed to test a particular hypothesis or research question, except for a single, central variable of interest. In addition, it is often difficult to understand the techniques used to clean and organize the data. Researchers who lack a certain degree of familiarity with a particular dataset can become bogged down with trying to decipher how the primary researchers constructed specific variables and whether missing data should be understood as systematic (e.g., decisions to use split-sampling techniques) versus random. Inexperience with a particular dataset opens the door to researchers producing fundamentally flawed work. It is essential for political communication scholars conducting secondary analyses to know their datasets. When data are presented to researchers with such ease, it is often tempting to jump right into various analyses. However, researchers must make themselves fully aware of the potential fatal missteps that come with such a ripe piece of fruit.

Now that the basic strengths and weaknesses of secondary analysis have been outlined, space can be devoted to the steps involved in conducting an analysis of secondary data. Carter (2003) has outlined a five-step process that encapsulates a secondary analysis from start to finish. The first step of a secondary analysis, as with any research endeavor, is to identify a research question. It is imperative that research questions come before the data—a secondary analysis does not involve researchers first finding a dataset, then seeking to generate research questions from that dataset (based on what questions were asked). This type of research lacks proper theory development and often leads to results that are unlikely to be replicated in subsequent studies. Once the researcher identifies a research question, they can search for and secure appropriate data to address their research question. This can often be a laborious, time-consuming, and frustrating process. However, casting a wide net when searching for a particular set of items within existing data often produces worthwhile results. Reliance on only the most often used datasets (e.g., ANES data for the study of political communication) can create severe limitations concerning the types of research questions that can be asked. Third, a research design is outlined, isolating a particular set of items from the secondary dataset and the analytical procedures appropriate to test the proposed research questions or hypotheses. These first three steps represent the foundation for any solid secondary analysis.

Carter (2003) insists that scholars must complete the final two steps (i.e., formal preparation of data and data analysis) with the utmost caution and diligence. Preparing the data requires generating a list of variables stemming from one's theoretical foundation, identifying the key items in the secondary data which will be used to form those variables, performing the necessary transformations to format the data for proper use, and selecting a target sample if one is doing some type of subgroup analysis. The data analysis phase works much like any other research project, but Carter (2003) stresses the importance of replicating results using multiple secondary datasets if they are available.

With secondary analysis defined and its basic process outlined, including the strengths and weaknesses inherent to the method, it is important to gain a sense of the state of secondary analysis in today's political communication research landscape.

SECONDARY ANALYSIS IN CURRENT POLITICAL COMMUNICATION RESEARCH

Political communication is a vast area of research that comprises a wide range of topic areas. The field includes the study of political campaigns, news and public affairs media, public opinion, new media, entertainment media, and audience analyses (to name just a few examples). Secondary analyses can be found relative to each of these research areas. However, the one area of political communication research that has seen more than its fair share of secondary analyses is the study of political campaign effects. This phenomenon is logical given that the major national politically relevant datasets collected and made publicly available to advance scholarship—the American National Election Study (ANES) and the National Annenberg Election Study (NAES)—are designed in coordination with national elections. One area of research that is rich with analyses of secondary data focuses on political debate influence. For example, Holbert, LaMarre, and Landreville (2009) analyzed 2004 Annenberg data to assess the role of debate viewing as partisan reinforcement and the effects of this partisan reinforcement on post-election perceptions of personal vote count accuracy. Kenski and Stroud (2005) also used Annenberg data to better understand who among the electorate gravitates toward greater consumption of nationally televised presidential debates. Holbert (2005a) used 2000 and 2004 ANES data to assess the role of debate viewing on strength of vote choice and the role of debate viewing as a mediator of the relationship between traditional television news use and vote choice as political behavior. These works are just a few recent examples of secondary analyses conducted in relation to the study of elections in general and political debates in particular.

Secondary analyses are also used in the study of news as political communication. For example, Kiousis and McCombs (2004) used ANES data to assess the influence of attitude strength as a potential mediator of the relationship between news media salience and public salience of major political figures. Dalrymple and Scheufele (2007) used ANES data to compare the influence of traditional news sources to new media news sources on citizens' political knowledge structures. Similarly, Liu and Eveland (2005) employed ANES data to introduce added nuance to the study of news effects on the often-studied knowledge gap. Finally, Holbert (2005b) used ANES data to study how news influences public perceptions of the proper size of government, and where government should be spending its money in terms of social programs.

In terms of public opinion research, secondary analyses are plentiful. *Public Opinion Quarterly* (*POQ*) regularly offers a "Poll Trends" feature that allows researchers to compile data from multiple secondary sources, collected across multiple years, focusing on a single topic. All trends studies of this kind are examples of secondary analyses. In addition to the individual trends pieces, one can find secondary analyses strewn throughout the rest of *POQ*. For example, Haider-Markel and Joslyn (2008) used Pew data to look at public perceptions concerning homosexuality. Hetherington and Smith (2007) used GSS data to look at public opinion of the U.S. Supreme Court in relation to issue preferences within the American public over time. McDonald (2007) used a variety of data sources (e.g., Current Population Survey) to look at the present state of the American electorate and current trends in political behavior. In short, the study of public opinion is saturated with secondary analyses using a variety of popular and widely available data sources.

Beyond the more traditional studies of political debates, news, and various matters of public opinion, several emerging areas of political communication research have embraced secondary analysis as a means by which to address a variety of research questions. The study of new media is one area of research that has used a variety of secondary datasets to creatively address research questions. For example, Wu and Bechtel (2002) analyzed data collected by the research department of the *New York Times* online to obtain click-on rates for the major news Web sites to study the relationship between online behavior and the content being offered on a news-based website.

Shah, Kwak, and Holbert (2001) used DDB-Needham Lifestyle data to look at the predictive value of a variety of individual-difference variables with regard to general Internet use and the relationship between Internet use and social capital. These are just two examples of studies using secondary data to look at new media within the context of politically related issues.

Like the study of new media, the study of entertainment media has grown in stature in the field of political communication. For example, there are several studies by Danna Young and colleagues (Feldman & Young, 2008; Young & Tisinger, 2006) using secondary analyses to address some central questions related to how late-night television news use affects various democratic processes and outcomes. Holbert, Shah, and Kwak (2003, 2004) used DDB-Needham Lifestyle data to address a series of relationships between various forms of entertainment-based media use and public opinion concerning a range of public policy issues (e.g., the environment, women's rights, handguns, the death penalty; see also, Holbert, Kwak, & Shah, 2003). Much of the work by Baum (2003) has also used secondary analysis to look at a variety of effects of soft news on democratic outcomes. In short, the study of entertainment media and politics is replete with secondary analyses.

With the use of secondary data across the field clearly in evidence, just how prevalent is reliance on secondary data by political communication scholars? Graber (2005) conducted a content analysis of flagship communication and political science journals in order to gain an understanding of the prevalence of political communication-related research in these academic outlets. Her study revealed a higher proportion of space in communication journals devoted to political communication research compared to our subfield's research efforts in political science journals.

Given the short supply of political communication-related research in political science journals, we decided to focus on three communication-based journals identified by Graber, *Communication Research* (*CR*), *Journalism & Mass Communication Quarterly* (*J&MCQ*), and *Journal of Communication* (*JoC*), for our own brief content analysis. We isolated all available issues of these three journals for 2003–2008 (only the first two issues of 2008 for *J&MCQ* were available at the time of this writing), isolated all published articles dealing with a topic related to the study of political communication, and made a dichotomous determination (yes/no) as to whether the article contained any secondary analysis activity. Our analyses revealed that 32 of the 89 (36%) political communication articles that appeared in these three journals over the course of the six-year span can be classified as secondary analyses. This is a healthy percentage, and this statistic reveals that secondary analysis is a robust methodological technique used by today's political communication researchers. We wish to add a quick note that this percentage would have been much higher had the sole focus been on audience- and effects-based research efforts, at the exclusion of content-based research. A large number of political communication-oriented content analyses, a vast majority of which appear in *J&MCQ*, did not involve the use of secondary analysis. A focus on just audience and effects work would have yielded a percentage much closer to 50%, signaling even greater use of secondary analysis by political communication scholars.

The conclusion that can be reached from this brief overview of the current state of secondary analysis in political communication research is that no area of the field is devoid of this method. All types of political communication scholars have embraced secondary analysis as a legitimate tool for addressing their research agendas (and rightfully so). Secondary analyses have been around as long as the field, and there is every indication that secondary analyses will remain prevalent for years to come. However, what is needed is a proper recognition of what a secondary analysis represents as a research activity. In addition, there needs to be a well-rounded appreciation of what goes into a solidly conducted secondary analysis. In particular, we wish to call attention to the fact that good secondary analyses represent fundamentally creative activities, and that researchers who conduct strong secondary analyses are engaging in creative acts which serve to advance the discipline.

CREATIVITY

Creativity as a concept has been the focus of much research in the field of psychology (e.g., Campbell, 1960; James, 1880; Kohler, 1925; Simon, 1986). Creativity has also received a great deal of attention in several related fields, including education (Kim, 2008), business (e.g., Dahlen, Rosengren, & Torn, 2008), and sociology (e.g., Murayama, 2003; Uzzi & Spiro, 2005), to name just a few examples. Indeed, there are entire academic journals devoted to the concept, including the *Journal of Creative Behavior* and the *Creativity Research Journal*.

As identified by Simonton (2002), a majority of scholarly works on the concept of creativity can be placed into one of three bins. First, there is a great deal of research conducted on creativity as an individual-difference variable and on how people can be trained to be more creative in the tasks they perform. The question of whether creativity is a trait or something that can be acquired over time speaks to a nature–nurture issue, and studies of this kind wrestle with this issue. Second, there are studies of creativity that tend to focus on an outcome or product. Judgments are made in these works as to what exhibits the qualities of being (or not being) creative. Third, there are several lines of creativity research that tend to focus on the creative process itself, not so much the individuals who are engaging in the activity or the actual final products that come out of various processes. Some recent work by Sawyer (2006) would fit within this last area of creativity research. This work on creativity focuses on how some commonalities exist within the creative processes of well-known individuals who have been recognized as innovators in the arts, business, and the sciences (Sawyer, 2006). These three areas of creativity research are not wholly unidimensional, but they do represent different foci for research conducted on this important concept.

The focus of this chapter will not be on the levels of creativity retained by political communication scholars who have engaged in the use of secondary analysis. Instead, attention will be paid to the creative products produced by political communication scholars in the form of published secondary analysis articles. In addition, attention is paid to secondary analysis as a creative process. In particular, the analysis focuses on creativity related to choice of data, variable creation, and data analysis, which are the core stages of secondary data analysis. Creativity can exist at any or all of these three stages of a secondary analysis, and there could be considerable debate as to whether all three stages should be treated as equally influential when judging the overall creativity of a secondary analysis. However, the purpose of this chapter is not to engage in such a debate. Instead, the focus is on making the case that some level of creativity is evident in the secondary analyses being produced by political communication scholars.

As with any important concept, there is considerable debate concerning how to conceptualize and operationalize creativity. The conceptualization chosen for our purposes envisions creativity as consisting of three elements: novelty, effectiveness, and authenticity (Averill, 2002). Novelty focuses on the newness of the product or the part of the process used to create the product. Averill notes that this dimension is "a relative concept" (p. 176) in that an inherently comparative judgment is made between the product in question and what came before the product in question. In short, novelty is akin to originality.

However, in the long term, novelty for the sake of being novel will not hold much weight. As Sawyer's (2006) work on creativity has revealed, there is always a *purpose* driving individuals engaged in creative acts. As a result, we need to judge the overall *effectiveness* of a creative act in order to determine whether the creative act served to achieve some goal. For this essay, a central question stemming from this dimension of creativity is whether the secondary analysis research produced valid and reliable results that propelled the field forward.

Finally, there is authenticity. The focus here is on the degree to which a secondary analysis is authentic to the field of political communication and what this area of social scientific research represents within the larger social science community. There are distinct elements of political communication research—the types of research questions we ask, the independent and dependent variables we focus on, and the processes that command our attention—that allow us to stand out relative to other disciplines. Our secondary analyses can reflect who we are as political communication scholars and this aspect of our work should be part of our judgment of the creativity inherent within any given secondary analysis.

In the end, our assessment of the existence of creativity in the secondary analyses performed by political communication scholars is not a creativity that exists without specific boundaries. The choice of a particularly novel dataset, the use of a unique operationalization of a particular variable, or the choice of a relatively rare analytical technique needs to be assessed alongside whether the field has been effective as a result of engaging in these bits of originality and whether what is novel about our secondary analyses remains authentic to the field. It is only through the combined assessment of all three dimensions (novelty, effectiveness, and authenticity) that we can gain a full sense of the degree of creativity within the secondary analyses being conducted within political communication.

SECONDARY ANALYSIS-BY-CREATIVITY TYPOLOGY

All too often scholars characterize secondary analysis as research on the cheap, or the lazy way of doing research. In fact, the use of high-quality data collected by someone else in order to address some of your own hypotheses or research questions is not as easy as it may first appear. Engaging in such a research effort often requires a researcher to be exceedingly inventive. It is clear from our survey of the political communication landscape that a case can be made for secondary analysis being a truly creative act. For this chapter we have isolated nine separate works by renowned political communication scholars within a secondary analysis-by-creativity typology to bring this point to its full light (see Figure 5.1). The typology has three elements of a secondary analysis (choice of data, variable creation, and data analysis) on its vertical axis and three dimensions of creativity (novelty, effectiveness, and authenticity) on its horizontal axis. The next section

	Novelty	Effectiveness	Authenticity
Secondary Analysis Creativity			
Choice of Data	Nisbet (2006)	Price & Czilli (1996)	Moy et al. (2005)
Variable Creation	Nir (2005)	Cappella et al. (2002)	Eveland & Scheufele (2000)
Data Analysis	Holbert (2005c)	Feldman & Young (2008)	Fan & Tims (1989)

FIGURE 5.1 Nine-part secondary analysis-by-creativity typology.

is devoted to detailing how these published works embody creative acts within the context of conducting secondary analyses.

TYPOLOGY APPLIED TO RECENT POLITICAL COMMUNICATION SCHOLARSHIP

Novelty

Data Source.   The article we have chosen for this section of our typology is "The Engagement Model of Opinion Leadership: Testing Validity within a European Context" by Erik Nisbet (2006). This article tests the engagement model of opinion leadership across 15 European countries using the European Social Survey (ESS), a biennial face-to-face survey conducted in 22 European nations.

Nisbet's use of the ESS is novel compared to most recent political communication peer-reviewed journal articles using secondary data. As we have already discussed, the two main sources of secondary data for political communication scholarship are the American National Election Survey and the National Annenberg Election Survey. These sources are dominant because of their large, representative samples, their inclusion of commonly used political communication measures, their consistency of measurement over time, especially with regard to the ANES, and questions addressing unpredicted campaign events, a feature of the NAES (see Chapter 6, this volume).

Despite their quality, overuse of the ANES and NAES constricts political communication research because their samples only include people living in the United States. The use of international secondary datasets, such as the ESS, allows scholars to answer alternative research questions and determine the validity and generalizability of theories and models outside the United States. As Nisbet's (2006) article has shown, the engagement model works best in Western European countries that share cultural and structural similarities with the United States, but runs into problems in countries that do not share similar features.

Variable Creation.   Next, we focus on a novel example of variable creation from a secondary data analysis. Secondary data papers require scholars to use existing items to create measures for their variables of interest. Sometimes this act requires little work, such as creating a measure of political knowledge; other times this requires more than a bit of creativity. An example of creatively constructed variables comes from "Ambivalent Social Networks and the Consequences for Participation" by Lilach Nir (2005). This article examines the relationship between individual-level ambivalence and perceived network-level ambivalence on political participation and preference for presidential candidates.

To test her hypotheses, Nir created two measures of ambivalence using existing items from the 2000 ANES. To build her measure of individual-level ambivalence, Nir put respondents' feeling thermometer ratings of George W. Bush and Al Gore into a formula that calculated an individual's level of ambivalence toward the two candidates. To create a measure of perceived network ambivalence, Nir (2005) first created a measure of network size by adding up the number of people in a respondent's discussion network. Next, Nir calculated the number of people with similar and dissimilar preferences for president in a person's network and put these numbers into the same formula used to measure individual-level ambivalence. This gave Nir a measure of network-level ambivalence.

Nir's measures are excellent examples of the novel creation of variables from existing data. These variables are novel because she takes existing survey items and uses them in a unique way to create two measures of ambivalence. In addition, Nir's (2005) findings that individual-level ambivalence, and not the network-level measure, predicted less engagement with the political process and putting off deciding who to support in the 2000 presidential election served to advance the discipline.

Data Analysis.   Scholars often need to be creative when analyzing secondary data sets. For this section of our typology, we analyze the article "Intramedia Mediation: The Cumulative and Complementary Effects of News Media Use" by R. Lance Holbert (2005c), which examines the indirect and cumulative effects of television and newspaper use on political knowledge. Using NAES data, Holbert (2005c) engaged in the use of a unique variant of structural equation modeling, latent composite modeling, that is not often seen in the field of communication (Holbert & Stephenson, 2002). A latent composite model "constructs a latent variable model by specifying a given composite as a single observable variable loading on its respective latent construct, and fixing the error variance of this composite to (1-reliability) times the variance of the indicator" (Holbert, 2005c, p. 453; see also Matsunaga, 2008).

In this case, the use of latent-composite modeling yielded some interesting findings. Holbert's (2005c) results indicated a "cumulative and complementary function" of television and newspaper use over time (p. 447). That is, there was a greater effect of media on political knowledge when accounting for the relationship between television *and* newspaper use. Considering that latent-composite modeling is a data analysis technique uncommon in the field of political communication and that the results added to the literature on media effects reveals that a researcher's creativity in analyzing secondary data can produce results capable of moving the field forward.

Effectiveness

Data Source.   We begin by looking at an effective choice of data in the article "Modeling Patterns of News Recognition and Recall" by Vincent Price and Edward Czilli (1996). Price and Czilli (1996) used items from a 1989 ANES pilot study that asked respondents recognition and recall questions about various news stories. To measure recognition, they used an item that presented respondents with a list of stories and asked them to identify the ones they recognized. If they recognized a story, the survey then asked whether they could recall any details about the story. For example, if a respondent recognized a story about the conflict in Gaza between the Palestinians and Israelis, the respondent was asked to provide any information that could be recalled, such as the reason for Israel's attacks on the Palestinians. To determine if the recall information was accurate, Price and Czilli (1996) also content analyzed stories that appeared in the news at the time of the ANES survey.

These researchers' results indicated this was an effective use of secondary data. Their first logistic regression model estimating story recognition successfully classified 81% of respondents, a 58% improvement over a chance model (Price & Czilli, 1996). Similarly, their second logistic regression model estimating recall of a news story successfully classified 80% of respondents, which is 61% above the success rate of a chance model. The success of their models to predict news recognition and recall indicates this was appropriate data for their study. Stated succinctly, this secondary data set was highly effective in addressing the scholars' research questions.

Variable Creation.   "Reliable and Valid Measure of Opinion Quality: Electronic Dialogue During Campaign 2000," by Joseph Cappella, Vincent Price, and Lilach Nir (2002) has been selected as a piece of secondary analysis scholarship representative of highly effective variable creation. In this article, the authors introduced and evaluated a new measure of opinion quality they called "argument repertoire" (AR).

Cappella and colleagues (2002) defined AR as consisting of two dimensions: the relevant reasons for your own opinion and the relevant reasons for the opinion of others. These relevant reasons for an opinion must be "acknowledged in public discourse as a plausible reason" for supporting a political party or public policy (p. 77). For example, a Republican may say they support the Republican Party because they believe in small government and lower taxes, and that Democrats disagree with Republicans because they support labor unions and a woman's right to choose (Cappella et al., 2002).

To create a measure of AR, Cappella and colleagues (2002) used data from the Electronic Dialogue 2000 project. They used favorability ratings of three politically relevant topics: the two political parties, the presidential candidates' tax plans, and the Supreme Court's decision to stop the recount of votes in Florida. After providing favorability ratings, the survey asked respondents to list the reasons for their favorable or unfavorable opinions and the reasons for others' favorable or unfavorable opinions. The authors coded these open-ended responses and assigned values for skipped questions, irrelevant answers, vague statements, and substantive answers. After obtaining reliability for their coding scheme, they added up the values for each individual's statements and created indexes for one's own opinion and the opinion of others. Reliability was assessed for these two measures, with alpha scores of .77 and .80, respectively.

Cappella and colleagues (2002) tested AR for convergent and predictive validity. For convergent validity, they predicted—and their results showed—that those with higher AR tended to be more interested and knowledgeable about politics, and were more likely to pay attention to political news and read the newspaper. To test for predictive validity, they looked at whether AR could predict certain behaviors of participants. Results of regression models showed that individuals with higher AR were more likely to both attend and contribute to online discussion groups. With these results, the authors concluded that their measure of AR met the threshold for convergent and predictive validity.

We put this study by Cappella and colleagues in the effective creation of variable category of our typology for several reasons. First, the study takes measures from an existing dataset to create a new measure of AR. In addition, their tests for reliability and convergent and predictive validity reveal that their measure of AR is both reliable and valid. Finally, their research on AR adds a new measure of opinion quality to the field of political communication.

Data Analysis. "Late-Night Comedy as a Gateway to Traditional News: An Analysis of Time Trends in News Attention Among Late-Night Comedy Viewers During the 2004 Presidential Primaries" by Lauren Feldman and Dannagal Goldthwaite Young (2008) is an example of the use of effective data analysis within the context of conducting a secondary analysis. These scholars looked at the relationship between watching late-night comedy shows and attention to campaign news during the 2004 presidential primaries.

To test their hypotheses, Feldman and Young (2008) employed 2004 NAES data. Two variables were of primary interest. The first was viewing of late-night comedy shows, which they measured with items asking respondents how many times they watched late-night comedy shows in the past week and which show they watched most often. The second was attention to news, which they measured using a single item asking respondents their level of attention to news stories about the presidential campaign.

To determine the relationship between viewing late-night comedy shows and attention to political news, Feldman and Young (2008) used a combination of OLS regression and time series analysis. First, Feldman and Young used OLS regression to establish a relationship between watching late-night comedy shows and attention to news. Next, they used time series analysis to show that viewing late-night comedy led to higher levels of attention to news stories about the presidential campaign.

The use of time series analysis makes this work an excellent example for the effective data analysis category of our typology. The article fits well here because the time series analysis revealed robust findings that viewing late-night comedy leads to an increase in attention to campaign news. These results also added to the growing body of literature looking at the effects of entertainment media on political communication outcome variables.

Authenticity

Data Source. We now address the final characteristic of creativity: authenticity. The first article, entitled "Priming Effects of Late-Night Comedy" by Patricia Moy, Michael Xenos, and Verena Hess (2005), represents the use of an authentic data source. In their study, Moy and colleagues examined the extent to which late-night comedy viewing influenced people's evaluations of candidates after appearing on these shows during the 2000 presidential election.

The authors employed 2000 NAES data, and, for their measure of favorability, they used feeling thermometer ratings of the two presidential candidates: George W. Bush and Al Gore. They also used measures of candidate personality characteristics, which asked respondents to describe how well various traits such as honesty applied to the respective candidates. They then took an item that asked respondents how frequently they watched late-night comedy shows in the past week to create a binary variable to indicate whether a person watched late-night comedy shows.

This use of the NAES is an authentic choice of data for the field of political communication for a couple of reasons: (1) NAES is run by the Annenberg Public Policy Center at the University of Pennsylvania—which has ties to their school of communication—by Kathleen Hall Jamieson and Diana Mutz, two distinguished political communication scholars, and (2) the NAES contains a large number of items that do a better job than the ANES of measuring key communication concepts. Wagner (Chapter 6, this volume) supports this second point. He argues that the NAES does a better job of measuring exposure to specific types of media, with questions asking respondents about their sources of media content. For example, the NAES asks respondents to provide their sources of network and cable news, the newspaper they rely on for news, and whether they watch late-night comedy shows. This goes beyond media use measures included in the ANES. This greater emphasis on measuring communication makes the NAES more authentic to the field of communication. Because of the survey's affiliation with a school for communication and emphasis on communication measures, we believe it represents an authentic choice of data for the field of political communication.

Variable Creation. The next article creates an authentic communication variable from secondary data. The article is "Communication, Context, and Community: An Exploration of Print, Broadcast, and Internet Influences" by William P. Eveland, Jr. and Dietram Scheufele (2000). Using data from the 1996 ANES, the authors examined whether media use affects the gaps in political knowledge and participation between people with higher and lower levels of education.

For their analysis, Eveland and Scheufele (2000) constructed measures of media use for television news and newspapers using existing measures from the ANES. The measure of television use was a four-item index consisting of two media exposure items that asked respondents how often they watched local and national news, and two items asking participants their level of attention to the campaign in local and national news. Their newspaper use measure used similar items that asked respondents about exposure to newspapers and their level of attention to the campaign in newspapers. Both measures were shown to be reliable, with alpha scores of .81 and .71, respectfully.

These measures get at two latent components—exposure and attention—that, when combined, produce a better measure of media use than a simple measure of exposure alone. This call for a measure of media use comes from a study by Chaffee and Schleuder (1986), which found that combining exposure and attention accounted for more variance when looking at gains in knowledge from the media than exposure alone. These results support Chaffee and Schleuder's contention that communication scholars need to go beyond measures of media exposure when looking at media effects. For a measure to be authentic, it must have roots in the field of communication. The media use measure created by Eveland and Scheufele (2000) meets this requirement because it was developed in communication and by communication scholars.

Data Analysis.   We conclude with a data analysis technique authentic to the field of political communication. For this section of our typography, we picked the article "The Impact of the News Media on Public Opinion: American Presidential Election 1987–1988" by David Fan and Albert Tims (1989). The authors tested how well the ideodynamic model, created by Fan, predicted public opinion of the two presidential candidates—George H. W. Bush and Michael Dukakis—during the 1988 presidential election.

Many steps were involved in creating and testing the ideodynamic model. Fan and Tims (1989) built their model by collecting a random sample of articles from the AP wire and pulling out all the stories related to George H. W. Bush and Michael Dukakis. From these stories, they removed paragraphs that did not refer to Bush or Dukakis and content analyzed the remaining paragraphs for positive and negative information about the two candidates. Fan and Tims added up the amount of positive and negative information for each candidate and put the totals into an equation that approximated public opinion toward Bush and Dukakis during the campaign. To examine the accuracy of their model, they compared their approximation of public opinion to actual public opinion polls collected during the election. Results indicated that their model came close to matching public opinion polls. On average, their model was within 2.7 points of the polls.

We believe this article fits into the authentic data analysis portion of our typology. The reasons are, first, that Fan is an affiliated faculty member of the School of Journalism and Mass Communication at the University of Minnesota, making this a technique rooted in political communication. In addition, the data analysis technique focused on political communication variables. The independent variable, news coverage of political candidates, and the dependent variable, public opinion toward presidential candidates, are of central interest to political communication scholars.

CONCLUSION

The typology we have offered provides a framework for showing how political communication scholars have been creative in conducting secondary analysis. There are many potential downsides to conducting secondary analyses relative to conducting primary research, but one point we wish to stress is that the creative energy of a researcher has the potential to overcome many of these weaknesses. A researcher seeking out a data set that has already been collected for the purposes of addressing a specific research question cannot create something out of nothing (e.g., make a specific item materialize that was not collected). However, with some creative thinking researchers can create explanatory variables from existing items (sometimes even seemingly disparate items) and employ unique data analytic techniques in order to address a given research agenda with an existing dataset. Researchers also need to use their creativity to seek out alternative sources of existing data and not remain tied to only those datasets most commonly used in the field. As we argued earlier, creativity is a necessary, but not sufficient condition for conducting a quality secondary analysis.

As a result, secondary analyses should be given proper credit as a form of social scientific exploration which is every bit as valid as primary research. Secondary analyses should be treated no differently than primary research, especially when it comes to making judgments of what type of work ultimately advances the discipline. Solid research is solid research, and whether a given scholar has collected his or her own data or sought out the use of an already existing dataset should matter little during the publication review process. Yes, scholars who conduct secondary analyses are able to bypass the design, data collection, data entry, and data cleaning phases associated with primary research, but this does not mean that it is the lazy scholar's means for conducting research. Quite the contrary, as an enormous amount of time and intellectual energy is required to conduct a solid secondary analysis. It is our hope that the field of political communication recognizes this simple fact.

We also wish to encourage formal training in secondary analysis within the field of political communication. Fledgling scholars should be trained on how to approach a secondary analysis, what will be required in the course of this research effort, and the difficulties they can expect to encounter over the course of the various stages of a secondary analysis. Ambitious graduate students seeking to make a name for themselves and address a given set of research questions with very little research funds in hand may turn to secondary data as a means by which to pursue publication and find answers to the queries which led them to want to become academics in the first place. Any scholars seeking to conduct a secondary analysis for the first time would be well served to take a brief look at any of several textbooks on the topic (see the list of references to secondary analysis texts and chapters offered at the beginning of this chapter), and also talk with well traveled scholars who have experience conducting secondary analyses in the past and have learned much along the way. Secondary analysis is not something that one should just jump into head first—all political communication scholars should recognize that the demands of conducting secondary analyses requires a certain skill set and solid training for studies of this kind to be done well. Most of all, conducting a strong secondary analysis requires that a researcher be creative within the project from start to finish. Recent secondary analyses in political communication have demonstrated this point full well.

REFERENCES

Averill, J. R. (2002). Emotional creativity: Toward "spiritualizing the passion." In C. R. Snyder & S. J. Lopez (Eds.), *Handbook of positive psychology* (pp. 172–185). Oxford: Oxford University Press.

Baum, M. A. (2003). *Soft news goes to war*. Princeton, NJ: Princeton University Press.

Boruch, R. F. (1978). *Secondary analysis*. San Fancisco: Jossey-Bass.

Bryman, A. (2001). *Social research methods*. New York: Oxford University Press.

Campbell, D. T. (1960). Blind variation and selective retention in creative thought as in other knowledge processes. *Psychological Review, 67*, 380–400.

Cappella, J. N., Price, V., & Nir, L. (2002). Argument repertoire as a reliable and valid measure of opinion quality: Electronic dialogue during campaign 2000. *Political Communication, 19*, 73–93.

Carter, D. F. (2003). Secondary analysis of data. In F. K. Stage & K Manning (Eds.), *Research in the college context: Approaches and methods* (pp. 153–168). New York: Brunner-Routledge.

Chaffee, S. H. & Scheuder, J. (1986). Measurement and effects of attention to media use. *Human Communication Research, 13*(1), 76–107.

Christie, T. B. (2007). The role of values in predicting talk radio listening: A model of value equivalence. *Journal of Radio Studies, 14*, 20–36.

Dahlen, M., Rosengren, S., & Torn, T. (2008). Advertising creativity matters. *Journal of Advertising Research, 48*, 392–403.

Dalrymple, K. E., & Scheufele, D. A. (2007). Finally informing the electorate? How the Internet got people thinking about presidential politics in 2004. *Harvard International Journal of Press/Politics, 12*, 96–111.

Eveland, W. P., Jr. & Scheufele, D. A. (2000). Connecting news media use with gaps in knowledge and participation. *Political Communication, 17,* 215–237.

Fan, D. P., & Tims, A. (1989). The impact of news media on public opinion: American presidential elections 1987–1988. *International Journal of Public Opinion Research, 1*(2), 151–163.

Feldman, L., & Young, D. G. (2008). Late-night comedy as a gateway to traditional news: An analysis of time trends in news attention among late-night comedy viewers during the 2004 presidential primaries. *Political Communication, 25,* 401–422.

Graber, D. A. (2005). Political communication faces the 21st century. *Journal of Communication, 55,* 479–507.

Haider-Markel, D. P., & Joslyn, M. R. (2008). Beliefs about the origins of homosexuality and support for gay rights. *Public Opinion Quarterly, 72,* 291–310.

Hakim, C. (1982). *Secondary analysis in social research: A guide to data sources and methods with examples.* London: George Allen & Sons.

Hetherington, M. J., & Smith, J. L. (2007). Issue preferences and evaluations of the U.S. Supreme Court. *Public Opinion Quarterly, 71,* 40–66.

Holbert, R. L. (2005a). Debate viewing as mediator and partisan reinforcement in the relationship between news use and vote choice. *Journal of Communication, 55,* 85–102.

Holbert, R. L. (2005b). Television news viewing, governmental scope, and postmaterialist spending: Assessing partisan differences in mediation-based processes of influence. *Journal of Broadcasting & Electronic Media, 49,* 416–434.

Holbert, R. L. (2005c). Intramedia mediation: The cumulative and complementary effects of news media use. *Political Communication, 22,* 447–461.

Holbert, R. L., Kwak, N., & Shah, D. V. (2003). Environmental concern, patterns of television viewing, and pro-environmental behaviors: Integrating models of media consumption and effects. *Journal of Broadcasting & Electronic Media, 47,* 177–196.

Holbert, R. L., LaMarre, H., & Landreville, K. (2009). Fanning the flames of a partisan divide: The role of debate viewing in the formation of partisan-driven post-election evaluations of personal vote count accuracy. *Communication Research, 36,* 155–177.

Holbert, R. L., Shah, D. V., & Kwak, N. (2003). Political implications of prime-time drama and sitcom use: Genres of representation and opinions concerning women's rights. *Journal of Communication, 53,* 45–60.

Holbert, R. L., Shah, D. V., & Kwak, N. (2004). Fear, authority, and justice: The influence of TV news, police reality, and crime drama viewing on endorsements of capital punishment and gun ownership. *Journalism & Mass Communication Quarterly, 81,* 343–363.

Holbert, R. L. & Stephenson, M. T. (2002). Structural equation modeling in the communication sciences, 1995–2000. *Human Communication Research, 28,* 531–551.

Hyman, H. H. (1972). *Secondary analysis of sample surveys: Principles, procedures, and potentialities.* New York: Wiley & Sons.

James, W. (1880, October). Great men, great thoughts, and the environment. *Atlantic Monthly, 46,* 441–459.

Kenski, K., & Stroud, N. J. (2005). Who watches presidential debates? A comparative analysis of presidential debate viewing in 2000 and 2004. *American Behavioral Scientist, 49,* 213–228.

Kiecolt, K. J., & Nathan, L. E. (1985). *Secondary analysis of survey data.* Beverly Hills, CA: Sage Publications.

Kim, K. H. (2008). Underachievement and creativity: Are gifted underachievers highly creative? *Creativity Research Journal, 20,* 234–242.

Kiousis, S., & McCombs, M. (2004). Agenda-setting effects and attitude strength: Political figures during the 1996 presidential election. *Communication Research, 31,* 36–57.

Kohler, W. (1925). *The mentality of apes.* New York. Harcourt, Brace.

Liu, Y., & Eveland, Jr., W. P. (2005). Education, need for cognition, and campaign interest as moderators of news effects on political knowledge: An analysis of the knowledge gap. *Journalism & Mass Communication Quarterly, 82,* 910–929.

Matsunaga, M. (2008). Item parceling in structural equation modeling: A primer. *Communication Methods and Measures, 2,* 260–293.

McDonald, M. P. (2007). The true electorate. *Public Opinion Quarterly, 71*, 588–602.

Moy, P., Xenos, M. A., & Hess, V. K. (2005). Priming effects of late-night comedy. *International Journal of Public Opinion Research, 18*(2), 198–210.

Murayama, M. (2003). Causal loops, interaction, and creativity. *International Review of Sociology, 13*, 607–628.

Nir, L. (2005). Ambivalent social networks and their consequences for participation. *International Journal of Public Opinion Research, 17*(4), 422–442.

Nisbet, E. C. (2006). The engagement model of opinion leadership: Testing validity within a European context. *International Journal of Public Opinion Research, 18*(1), 3–30.

Price, V., & Czilli, E. J. (1996). Modeling patterns of news recognition and recall. *Journal of Communication, 46*(2), 55–78.

Putnam, R. D. (2000). *Bowling alone: The collapse and revival of American community.* New York: Simon & Schuster.

Robinson, J. P., Rivers, W. P., & Brecht, R. D. (2006). Demographic and sociopolitical predictors of American attitudes towards foreign language policy. *Language Policy, 5*, 421–442.

Sawyer, R. K. (2006). *Explaining creativity: The science of human innovation.* Oxford: Oxford University Press.

Shah, D. V., Cho, J., Nah, S., Gotlieb, M. R., Hwang, H., Lee, N., Scholl, R. M., & McLeod, D. M. (2007). Campaign ads, online messaging, and participation: Extending the communication mediation model. *Journal of Communication, 57*, 676–703.

Shah, D. V., Kwak, N., & Holbert, R. L. (2001). "Connecting" and "disconnecting" with civic life: The effects of Internet use on the production of social capital. *Political Communication, 18*, 141–162.

Simon, H. A. (1986). What we know about the creative process. In R. L. Kuhn (Ed.), *Frontiers in creative and innovative management* (pp. 3–20). Cambridge, MA: Ballinger.

Simonton, D. K. (2002). Creativity. In C. R. Snyder & S. J. Lopez (Eds.), *Handbook of positive psychology* (pp. 189–201). Oxford: Oxford University Press.

Uzzi, B., & Spiro, J. (2005). Collaboration and creativity: The small world problem. *American Journal of Sociology, 111*, 447–504.

Wu, H. D., & Bechtel, A. (2002). Website use and news topic and type. *Journalism & Mass Communication Quarterly, 79*, 73–86.

Young, D. G., & Tisinger, R. M. (2006). Dispelling late-night myths: News consumption among late-night comedy viewers and the predictors of exposure to various late-night shows. *Harvard International Journal of Press/Politics, 11*(3), 113–134.

6

Comparing the ANES and NAES for Political Communication Research

Michael W. Wagner
Department of Political Science
University of Nebraska–Lincoln

In the ongoing pursuit to better understand how politics works, scholars regularly explore how the process citizens use to seek, learn, and retain information improves our understanding of why people think, reason, feel, and behave in the ways they do with respect to political choices and outcomes. At its heart, this quest is about political communication: the study of the transmission of information between political actors, the news media, and the public. While social scientists regularly examine why people vote the way they do, their communicative process of decision-making, and how they make sense of politics in an increasingly mediated world, it is equally important to understand the advantages and disadvantages of the sources of information scholars use to answer these important questions.

In the spirit of comparative evaluation, this chapter closely scrutinizes two of the most prominent measures of the democratic blood flow, the American National Election Studies (ANES) and National Annenberg Election Survey (NAES).[1] On the one hand, both the ANES and NAES are overlapping treasure troves of invaluable data for political communication research. On the other hand, each project's central mission, depth, breadth, and overall design have particular strengths and limitations that scholars should be mindful of when undertaking scholarly analysis.[2]

It is tempting to think of the ANES as "political science data" and the NAES as "communication studies data" given the traditional differences in scholarly focus between the two disciplines. Yet when considering political science's historical focus on the constrained use of power (Goodin & Klingemann, 1996) and "who gets what, when and how" (Lasswell, 1950) and the focus of communication research on how people use different messages to engender meanings both within and across a variety of media, cultures, and contexts,[3] both the ANES and NAES concomitantly serve political science, communication research, and related social science disciplines in useful and important ways. While the two surveys have different missions, instruments, and research designs, a comparison of the ANES and NAES suggests that the complementary and even synthetic, use of each of these unique resources is a productive way to advance political communication scholarship.

This chapter proceeds as follows: first, I sketch the history of both the ANES and NAES; second, I explore the most crucial elements of each survey's research design; third, I examine each survey in the context of its utility in uncovering both traditional and new questions in political communication research; and lastly, I make some brief comparisons of the ANES and NAES to other prominent secondary data sources and offer some recommendations for future iterations of each survey. Together and individually, the ANES and NAES cast a great deal of light on the influence of political communication on public preferences, political behavior, and political outcomes.

ORIGINS OF THE ANES AND NAES

Before the National Science Foundation officially launched the National Election Studies in 1977, two centers housed within the Institute for Social Research at the University of Michigan— the Survey Research Center and Center for Political Studies—had conducted an unbroken series of national election surveys from 1952 to 1976 focusing on presidential and midterm elections. Presidential election years always include a pre- and post-election survey while the midterm election surveys occur only after the votes have been cast. Regularly, the ANES conducts panel surveys over three-election periods, interviewing the same respondents at different points in time in order to more precisely explore change and continuity in public opinion and political behavior.

Originally and most famously reported by Campbell, Converse, Miller, and Stokes (1960) in *The American Voter*, the ANES' genesis comes from a study led by Campbell and Kahn during the 1948 election (Carmines & Huckfeldt, 1996). The website of the Interuniversity Consortium for Political and Social Research (ICPSR) lists the scope of study for the ANES as:

> a time-series collection of national surveys fielded continuously since 1952. The election studies are designed to present data on Americans' social backgrounds, enduring political predispositions, social and political values, perceptions and evaluations of groups and candidates, opinions on questions of public policy, and participation in political life.

The mission of the ANES is to provide a wide swath of data from individual interviews, which allows researchers to explore a variety of hypotheses seeking to explain election outcomes across individuals, varying contexts, and time.[4] The formal establishment of the ANES by the NSF allowed the survey's designers to move beyond merely extending the time-series into the realm of pursuing better measures and methodological innovations. In 2006, the ANES did not conduct a midterm election survey, though a pilot study was conducted to test new questions and examine innovative survey methods. Thus, the ANES' presidential time-series remains unbroken, while the midterm election time-series unfortunately has stopped.[5] Current principal investigators are Jon Krosnick of Stanford University and Arthur Lupia of the University of Michigan.

Beginning in 2000, the National Annenberg Election Survey (NAES) challenged Holbrook's (1996) assertion that presidential campaigns have minimal (at most) effects on election outcomes by following the guiding assumption that "understanding campaign dynamics is important because campaigns do matter" (Jamieson & Kenski, 2006, p. 1). Housed at the Annenberg Public Policy Center of the University of Pennsylvania, the survey's co-directors for 2008 were Kathleen Hall Jamieson, Richard Johnston, and Diana Mutz. The ambitious design of the NAES is meant to allow for systematic analysis of particular events that occur at unpredictable times during an election cycle by providing public opinion data (from national telephone surveys in 2000 and 2004; from phone and Web surveys in 2008) for each day of the race for the White House. For example, the 2004 NAES began telephone interviews on October 7, 2003 and ended them on November 16, 2004. Rather than merely drawing a single sample in the fall of an election year, the NAES begins several months earlier, combining a rolling cross-section (RCS) and several smaller panel studies—usually around presidential debates and key primaries—from the beginning of the election season through a few days after the election (see Chapter 3, this volume). As is currently the case for the ANES, the NAES is only concerned with presidential election years, an unfortunate limitation preventing scholars from examining nonpresidential-year political communication, and nonelection-centric political communication more generally.[6]

ELEMENTS OF RESEARCH DESIGN: CONVERGENCE AND DIVERGENCE

ANES Research Design

After the survey instrument is designed, the American National Election Studies' examination of public attitudes begins with a pretest of about 30 respondents who are administered the penultimate draft of the survey.[7] The pretests are recorded so that ANES interviewers can hear examples of problems that can come up during the interview process such as an interviewer departing from the question text or a respondent giving a nonresponsive answer to a question. An extensive debriefing of these respondents informs the principal investigators of problems with question order effects, confusing wordings, and respondent fatigue.

With a completed survey instrument in hand, the ANES implementation process proceeds in three phases: drawing the sample, conducting the interviews, and readying the data for dissemination.

While simple random sampling is the classic, most representative way to assess public opinion, the ANES engages in a multi-stage area probability design. Step one of such a process is to divide the country into four geographic regions, each of which contains a number of randomly selected counties and standard metropolitan statistical areas for analysis (Erikson & Tedin, 2007). The second step is to select the area that will be sampled (i.e., subsampled places of Census Enumeration Districts).[8] This leads to the third step, randomly sampling a specific housing unit, and the fourth step, randomly selecting an eligible member of the household for the interview.

ANES interviews are conducted face-to-face. From the 1940s to the 1990s respondents completed interview booklets. Beginning in 1996 the ANES began using Computer Assisted Personal Interviewing (CAPI), which allows face-to-face interviewers to take advantage of similar Computer Assisted Telephone Interviewing (CATI) techniques on a laptop computer. In-person interviewing has the advantage of a high response rate, which for the ANES has never fallen below 59.8%.

Each ANES survey includes special themes or new topics, many of which are particularly useful for political communication scholars. In 1974, media use patterns were carefully explored for the first time; in 1976, questions sought to examine how the media and presidential debates affected political learning. Social network questions were added in 1980, as were survey items gauging public policy preferences and perceptions of leadership. Questions allowing for the integration of political communication and political psychology perspectives have been regularly added to the ANES as well. Measures of individualism and egalitarianism were added in 1984; additional questions concerning political knowledge and values came along in 1986; a racial stereotypes battery was added in 1992; while the 2000 survey brought with it more questions about social trust, networks, and cognitive style. Typically, new measures of this kind are added to the ANES after being established elsewhere.

ANES survey instruments are developed by its principal investigators and diverse Board of Overseers as well as the ANES community, broadly construed.[9] The research agendas of the board and other cutting-edge work in the discipline often leads to the addition (or subtraction, as scholars leave the board) of particular questions. Typically, the Board of Overseers is made up of political scientists, though the 2005–2009 board included those with a joint appointment in departments of political science and communication, a psychologist, sociologists, and economists.

Recently, the ANES added an "Online Commons" where social scientists and interested citizens can propose questions that they would like included on the ANES instrument. Indeed, in order for a question to be added to the ANES, it must now be posted on the Online Commons. For example, the use of the Online Commons resulted in a new battery of media use questions, which are described below. It should be noted that this process requires significant commitment from the scholars seeking to improve the ANES instrument as proposed questions must win the competition to be pilot tested, actually get pilot tested and analyzed, and only then are added to the survey instrument. Over 600 scholars have participated in the process and, thus, the construction of the 2008 ANES, including (as an example) a special competition that was held to develop questions to gauge public attitudes about terrorism and homeland security.[10] The introduction of the Online Commons should help the ANES to quickly and transparently respond to suggestions for modifications to the main survey, which has historically been constrained by its mission and efforts to preserve measures over time.

Prior to this innovation, the ANES began including several questions about Congress into the "core" instrument in 1978. Many questions, mostly dealing with the amount of contact respondents had with their representatives and congressional candidates, were discontinued in 1994, but other questions relating to congressional approval, recall of one's representative in the House, and candidate likes and dislikes have remained in subsequent years.

A notable innovation in the 2008 ANES is the decision to record respondents' response times. Response latency measures have long been used in psychology (Fazio, 1990) and political science (Huckfeldt, Sprague, & Levine, 2000). With the measurement of response times, the ANES will open a new door for political communication scholars to measure the accessibility of knowledge, communicative processes, issue preferences, and political choices. The addition of the Online Commons makes it more likely that theoretical and methodological innovations will take less time to find their way into the ANES.

ANES Panel Data

While the central purpose of the ANES is to allow scholars to explore the reasons why a particular election season turned out the way that it did, many important trends in American politics can only be uncovered with the use of panel data involving the reinterviewing of the same respondents at different points in time (see Chapter 2, this volume). While panels naturally suffer from attrition (the 2000–2002–2004 ANES panel interviewed 1,807 respondents in 2000, 1,187 in 2002, and 840 in 2004), they have the ability to explore changes over time on topics including abortion, affirmative action, party identification, candidate evaluations, political knowledge, and evaluations of Congress. Panel data that include media measures, such as the 2000–2002–2004 ANES panel, are especially useful for political communication scholars, as they afford the opportunity to explore the stability of news viewing, whether respondents have seen campaign ads in presidential and congressional elections, and how media use and attention affect other attitudes, behaviors, and group identities over time (see Carsey & Layman, 2006). In 2008, the

ANES conducted a six-wave, random-digit-dialing-recruited, panel study administered on the Internet. The panel remained in the field after the election to provide scholars with the ability to investigate public perceptions of the beginning of a new American presidency.

NAES Research Design

While the ANES typically relies on in-person interviewing during short periods from Labor Day to Election Day and from after the election to late December or early January, the NAES design consists of the largest academic telephone surveys ever administered in the United States. Whereas the ANES Cumulative File includes data from approximately 45,000 participants from 1948–2004, the NAES contains data from upwards of 200,000 respondents (in some form or another) for just 2000 and 2004 alone.

The major differences between the NAES and ANES begin with the mode of interviewing. The NAES is conducted via the telephone using numbers generated by random digit dialing.[11] As such, the NAES questionnaire, while lengthy, is much shorter than the ANES survey instrument, since it is quite difficult to keep respondents on the phone for more than half an hour. To maximize the number of questions asked of respondents, the NAES often engages in "split sample" interviews, where selected questions are asked of some respondents but not others. Typically, this is done randomly. Split samples are most often used to ask additional questions, conduct survey experiments, and test question wording effects. The split sample gives scholars access to more information to analyze; of course, sample size suffers from carving respondents out of particular question batteries.

Keeping up with the range and timing of the NAES sample splits requires careful attention. For example, a standard election season question, such as "How would you rate economic conditions in this country today—would you say they are excellent, good, fair, or poor?" was asked of every respondent from October 7, 2003 to October 29, 2004. The question was then asked of a random half of the samples drawn from October 30 to November 1, 2004 and was asked of all respondents again until November 16, 2004. Other questions, such as whether respondents would favor repealing tax cuts for the wealthy to pay for health insurance, are asked for a shorter period of time (e.g., February 19 to May 25, 2004) *and* of a smaller, random set of each day's respondents (one-third of all respondents in this case). Investigators must pay attention to issues of statistical power when running multivariate analyses with a high number of variables containing randomly assigned split samples (Zaller, 2002), although in most cases this problem should be offset by the size of the NAES sample.

When it comes to standard variables of interest to the political communication scholar, far fewer questions are asked of split samples. The core media use battery, for example (which is discussed below), is asked of all participants on all dates of the survey. When the sample is split, it is typically to test the wording of the question at hand, as is the case when the NAES splits the sample in half for a question about the frequency with which presidential campaign information was accessed or read online. Standard political discussion questions are also present on all dates for all respondents, while others, such as whether respondents tried to influence the votes of others, are asked at intermittent points during the election season to one-third of a given day's sample.

The centerpiece of the NAES is an RCS design, which was in the field from December 1999 through January 2001 for the 2000 election and from October 2003 through mid-November 2004 for the contest between George W. Bush and John Kerry.[12] During the primary season and the summer before the election, the NAES conducts about 100 random-digit-dialed interviews per day, tripling that number during the final months of the campaign. The number of interviews can pick up day-to-day changes, allowing for the actual testing of the oft-stated proposition that "overnight is a lifetime in politics." The response rate for the NAES in 2004 ranged between 25 and 31%, falling well short of the ANES rate, which averages well over 60%,[13] while the cooperation rate—the rate at which people agreed to be surveyed upon being reached—was a much more respectable 53%.

Because each iteration of the NAES spans a period of well over a year, some survey questions are dropped from the instrument over time while others are added, reflecting the ebbs and flows of issues, salient candidate traits, and information present in the campaign environment. There are advantages and disadvantages to this approach. On the one hand, the NAES' strategy provides maximum flexibility with respect to the kinds of information gathered during the campaign. On the other hand, dropping and adding questions prevents scholars from uncovering long-term within-campaign effects for questions that are not asked on all dates. Perhaps the most prominent example of information lost occurred with the NAES' 2004 campaign advertising battery, which asked respondents if they had seen and learned anything from political ads that season. The NAES asked the most useful portions of the television advertising battery from April to May 2004,[14] stopping long before most voters started tuning in and paying attention to the race for the White House—and long before candidates, political action committees, and special interest groups saturated swing states with commercials![15]

To its credit, the 2004 NAES did return to questions about advertising in August with items about the "Swift Boat" ads against John Kerry. The unique flexibility of the NAES' design allows for the inclusion of questions as issues like the "swift-boating" of John Kerry come up; at the same time, the last NAES questions about the "Swift Boat" issue or other campaign advertising-related issues were asked in August, long before Election Day.

The Wisconsin Advertising Project has coded political television advertisements for the U.S. House, Senate, and gubernatorial races for 1996, 2000, 2002, and 2004 (http://wiscadproject. wisc.edu/project.php). Given the data gathered by the Wisconsin Advertising Project, which tracks finely grained information about campaign advertisements such as advertisement tone, content, and placement (i.e., when an ad aired), cutting off the advertising battery in May is a missed opportunity, especially when coupled with the NAES' lack of any questions about congressional campaign ads. Since the NAES' sample size is so large, many congressional districts receive enough coverage to investigate how campaign ads influence congressional vote choice, roll-off, political knowledge, split-ticket voting, and other questions relevant to political behavior.

On the upside, the rolling cross-sectional design of the NAES allows investigators to capture the potential effects of campaign-relevant events that pop up briefly well before Election Day that would otherwise be lost. Take the following examples: the NAES asked respondents for a week in April 2004 whether they watched Condoleezza Rice's 9/11 Commission testimony; early in the primary season, the NAES asked which Democratic candidate was proposing universal health care; and, the Annenberg team fielded a variety of questions after each presidential debate in the 2004 general election between Bush and Kerry, providing the opportunity for scholars to assess what impact these campaign dynamics had at the time they occurred and whether there were any lingering effects on the campaign's outcome.

NAES Panel Data

The ANES' panel data afford scholars the opportunity to investigate change and continuity among respondents over several election years. The NAES includes several panels in its research design that allow for the exploration of short-term effects on respondents during a *single* election cycle. Particularly impressive is the sheer number of respondents in NAES' panel studies. In 2000, between 1,500 and 6,500 respondents were sampled in panels before and after the Iowa caucuses, the New Hampshire primary, Super Tuesday, the South Carolina and Michigan primaries, each party's convention, each presidential debate, and throughout the primary and general election season (from January to December).

In 2004, fewer panels were fielded and these focused on the conventions and a presidential debate, and tracked voter support of candidates throughout the election season—from July to December (Romer et al., 2006). Indeed, the availability of these data presents an auspicious opportunity for political communication scholars to conduct media content analyses of these events to facilitate fine-grained examinations of potential media effects at a variety of important stages in a campaign. For example, Hershey (1992) has shown how the news media "constructs" explanations for why candidates won presidential elections. With content analysis of debate coverage coupled with the NAES panels, scholars could compare evaluations of the presidential candidates immediately following a debate to evaluations after media constructions (should they develop) of who won the debate and why. Even though the NAES has only been in existence for three presidential elections, the rolling cross-sectional design allows for the widespread use of time-series analysis (see Chapter 3, this volume; Chapter 24, this volume).

The 2008 NAES is especially innovative. Included in the rolling cross-sectional design is a five-wave panel with over 19,000 respondents and data points covering the entire duration of the 2008 campaign season, complete with surprising wins, the rise and fall of Rudy Giuliani, a misty-eyed Hillary Clinton before New Hampshire, the Obama–Rev. Jeremiah Wright controversy, Sen. McCain's Sunni/Shiite gaffe overseas, and so forth. Given the NAES' willingness to add questions as campaign events unfold (e.g., gaffes, dramatic results, and feeding frenzies), the enormous panel size is an extraordinarily useful feature of the NAES. While the ANES' traditional pre- and post-election survey design gives scholars some leverage to explore media effects like agenda-setting (Kiousis & McCombs, 2004; McCombs & Shaw, 1972), framing (Brewer, 2003; Druckman, 2004), and priming (Iyengar & Kinder, 1987), the NAES' rolling cross-sectional design—including panels in 2000 and 2004 and a five-wave panel in 2008—allow for uniquely precise analyses that can shed new light on the conditions under which these recognized media effects are present in presidential electoral politics. The 2008 NAES also interviews a considerable number of respondents online, enabling comparisons of web-based and CATI survey responses (see Johnston, 2008, for complete details of the NAES' move to Web-based surveys of campaign dynamics).[16]

SURVEY INSTRUMENTATION:
UNCOVERING SHORT- AND LONG-TERM MEDIA EFFECTS

Media Use

Of crucial importance to the political communication scholar is the prevalence of media use questions present in any survey dataset. At the same time, as Price and Zaller (1993) argue, "students of political communication would do well in many cases to abandon their normal reliance on self-reported levels of news media exposure and look instead to prior political knowledge as the preferred general indicator of news reception" (p. 160). Impressively, Price and Zaller base their conclusions on analyses of the 1989 ANES Pilot Study, which included a wider variety of media exposure questions than are normally present in the "core" survey instrument. Putting this important insight aside for the moment, it is still valuable to inspect the ANES media use offerings, compare them to the NAES media exposure and opinion battery, and scrutinize some proposed innovations to both survey instruments.

The ANES' contemporary battery of media exposure questions has its roots in the 1980 and 1984 studies; thus, they are comparable for about three decades of over-time analysis. Several additional media use questions are present in the 1989 pilot study, tapping differences in respondents' use of national, local, and "infotainment"-type news programs (such as *Good Morning America*) in national and local settings. Unfortunately, no set of media use questions have been consistently asked throughout the entire lifespan of the ANES cumulative file (1948–2004), making ANES-based analyses of media use over time exceptionally limited and challenging. A battery of questions became consistent starting in 1984, with the addition of a media trust question in 1996. Additionally, some media use questions are only asked in presidential years, making comparisons to midterm elections impossible. Perhaps more frustrating for the longitudinally-minded investigator, some political communication measures are included in seemingly random ways. For example, the ANES asked respondents whether they watched presidential debates in 1976, 1980, 1984, 1996, and 2000 but did not ask the same debate question in 1988, 1992, and 2004.

These are not the only problems with the ANES media exposure questions. As items were added at different points in time, little effort was made to make questions comparable across different media. For instance, as Althaus and Tewksbury (2007) have pointed out, the ANES asks respondents to report the number of days in the past week they watched national television news and, separately, the number of days in the past week they read a newspaper; these are both interval-level measures. By contrast, the talk radio item simply asks whether the respondent listened to political talk radio, which is a nominal-level measurement. Thus, precise comparisons between the number of days voters might have watched television news or listened to political talk radio are not possible. Moreover, those who listened to radio news in a non-talk format (e.g., listeners of National Public Radio or local all-news AM stations) have no way of conveying that information to the ANES interviewer. Furthermore, the ANES is behind in measuring how, in the contemporary media landscape, citizens now acquire their political news, lacking a question, for instance, that gauges regular consumption of political news on the Internet (see Althaus & Tewksbury, 2007; ANES, 2004).[17]

Having comparable measures of the changing information environment is important for another reason. Prior (2007) demonstrates that as political information becomes increasingly available via the Internet, cable news channels and other information sources, including soft news and entertainment programs, are much more likely to be offered at the same time as traditional hard news program, easily allowing politically disinterested citizens to "opt-out" of watching or listening to the news (choosing, for example, a rerun of *Seinfeld* over the *NBC Nightly News with Brian Williams*). In his analyses, Prior demonstrates that the array of media choices that encapsulates contemporary political communication, a condition he refers to as "post-broadcast" democracy, increases political inequality and fosters partisan polarization due to the fact that those who opt out of political viewing subsequently know less about politics and participate less in political activities than those who voraciously consume political information.

Fortuitously, the 2006 ANES Pilot Study incorporated new measures that are yielding promising results. Indeed, the new measures included in the pilot address the lack of comparability between the previous media use questions about television and newspapers to items measuring talk radio exposure and Internet use. Simply changing the response set to include the number of days per week a respondent listens to radio news and surfs for information on the Internet should vastly improve our knowledge of the political information consumption habits of Americans. Interestingly, these four forms of media use found in the 2006 Pilot Study are not strongly predicted by demographic variables, partisan identification, or political knowledge (Althaus & Tewksbury, 2007).

The 2006 pilot data illustrate that, while citizens are consumers of multiple forms of media, they do pick favorites. Reliance on multiple sources of news is particularly consequential: regular use of three of the four news sources on the battery of questions is positively correlated with political knowledge (Althaus & Tewksbury, 2007). Indeed, this finding is interesting when juxtaposed with analysis of both cable and network television coverage of the 2006 congressional elections,[18] which showed that television news users were more likely to vote for congressional Republican candidates while politically knowledgeable television viewers were more likely to vote for Democratic candidates for Congress (Carmines, Gerrity, & Wagner, 2008).

Even more promising is the inclusion of psychological measures that, when combined with improved media use measures, will help scholars understand how citizens *process* the information they receive about politics. Taking seriously developments in social psychology, such as the Need for Cognition scale (Cacioppo & Petty, 1982) in the 2004 ANES instrument and the Need for Closure scale (Kruglanski, Webster, & Klem, 1993) in the 2006 ANES pilot, Althaus and Tewksbury (2007) chart a reasonable, yet exciting course for the future of measuring information consumption, retention, and processing. Crucially, Althaus and Tewksbury's (2007) proposal keeps the traditional "number of days" question for both television and newspapers,[19] providing much needed continuity for over-time analyses. If these or similar suggestions are not adopted by the ANES, the problems with the current media use battery outlined above will become even more pronounced as media technology continues to alter the ways in which citizens gather political information and participate in democratic processes (see Bucy & Gregson, 2001).

The media exposure battery on the NAES instrument represents a distinct advantage over nearly every iteration of the ANES. In addition to asking the network news and newspaper use questions, the NAES asks *which* network news program and newspaper respondents used the most. Nor does the NAES ignore the growth of cable news, asking identically worded questions about respondents' cable news viewing and most-watched cable news station. The NAES also uses its enormous sample to its advantage, asking if respondents watched Spanish language news or BET (Black Entertainment Television), listened to NPR (National Public Radio) or other talk radio shows (and *which* talk radio program was listened to the most), or viewed late-night comedy programs (along with the *most-watched* program). As noted above, the NAES also asks respondents if they have access to the Internet and whether they use the Web to stay current with political information. While sharing the ANES' inability to directly compare radio use to network and cable television as well as newspaper use, the NAES' battery is a marked improvement over what is typically found in the ANES.

Not surprisingly given its communication lineage, the NAES also asks questions regarding opinions about the news media and whether respondents saw particular salient episodes in the race for the White House. These kinds of questions are good examples of how the NAES measures public perceptions of the communicative process, something not found in the ANES. For example, for about eight weeks at the end of 2003 and beginning of 2004, the NAES asked if respondents believed that the news media were responsible for deciding the Democratic frontrunner. Cleverly, the NAES also asked who respondents thought that "media created" frontrunner was. Additionally, in the days directly after each presidential and vice presidential debate, the NAES asked whether the respondents watched the debate and, if so, on which channel?

A short trip from these media use items is each survey's questions measuring the influence of one's social communication networks on political beliefs and behavior. In the 2000 ANES survey, respondents were asked for the names of people with whom they discussed "important matters," a desirable way to measure political discussion within social networks as it increases the likelihood that respondents will name people with whom they both agree and disagree politically (Huckfeldt, Johnson, & Sprague, 2004). From an interpersonal communication perspective, the

ANES always asks whether the respondent tried to persuade someone else how that person "should vote" in the upcoming election. A useful wrinkle in the NAES instrument is a measure of the prevalence with which respondents chat about politics online.

In the main, the NAES asked more and better media use questions than the ANES in 2000 and 2004, but the 2006 ANES Pilot Study fixed some old problems while adding additional questions, opening the door to new conceptual and empirical development with respect to information exposure and processing. A distinct advantage of using NAES data is the ability (via the rolling cross-section design) to determine *when* people started paying attention to the race and whether time of attention influences vote choice, partisan attitudes, political knowledge, and other outcomes of interest. That said, the ANES' 2008 panel study will enable researchers to explore the times at which voters started attending to the election (or not) in much the same way as the NAES. Finally, users of both studies must remain mindful of issues including causal direction (e.g., does watching Fox News cause one to vote Republican or do Republicans just like watching Fox News?), measurement scales of different sizes, and selection bias since exposure to particular media outlets is not random (see Barabas, 2008).

Issues and Evaluations

For all their utility, media exposure items may not be the most effective way for political communication scholars to test the influence of the mass media on public opinion and political behavior. Zaller (1996) uses a measure of political awareness to revive the idea that the news media have a substantial effect on public opinion. Both the ANES and NAES ask half a dozen or more political knowledge questions. The ANES asks general questions that are comparable over decades while the NAES presents an inventory of knowledge questions as well as more detailed explorations of what specific candidates for president support. With respect to traditional political knowledge measures, both surveys provide adequate data for most political communication research questions,[20] with the ANES holding an advantage for analysis over time and the NAES providing sharper measures of presidential campaign-related knowledge, including questions about which candidate is proposing to cut taxes.

Among other reasons, measures of media use and political awareness are important because scholars seeking to test hypotheses regarding agenda-setting, framing, priming, political learning, turnout, partisan attitudes, and voter choice require them as control variables. But what kinds of specific issues and respondent evaluations and attitudes do the ANES and NAES provide scholars the opportunity to scrutinize?

The NAES offers dozens of ways for respondents to evaluate presidential candidates (and their running mates) during both the general election and primary season. The NAES selects potentially relevant trait attributions and evaluative question topics that are consistent with media coverage of the campaign. In 2004, for example, respondents were asked whether George W. Bush or John Kerry was reckless, steady, knowledgeable, easy to like, trustworthy, prone to changing his mind, out of touch, and so forth.[21] Unfortunately, many of these questions were not asked at all points of the election season, making analyses of whether and how media coverage affected general public preferences and judgments about the candidates challenging to disentangle.

While generally exploring fewer specific traits of candidates for office than the NAES, the ANES asks several "feeling thermometer"[22] questions about candidates, political parties, organized interests, ethnic groups, religious groups, and the like. Feeling thermometer questions about major political parties and religious groups are consistently included in the ANES while measurements of feelings toward other kinds of groups such as young people and Independents are taken inconsistently. The ANES also routinely asks respondents to list their "likes and dislikes" for candidates and political parties and whether there are important differences between the two major parties.

One distinct advantage of using the ANES is the ability to explore with identically worded questions attitudes over time on issues as diverse as government aid to blacks, abortion, women's rights, health care, and whether the government should guarantee that its citizens have jobs.[23] Consistently available for two decades or more of inspection are questions concerning civil rights, school busing, government spending on social services, gay rights, affirmative action, and school prayer. Availability of attitude data about a wide variety of issues has facilitated systematic examination of the media's role in the stability of public opinion (Page & Shapiro, 1992), conflict extension (Carsey & Layman, 2006), and issue ownership (Petrocik, 1996), to name a few. Political communication scholars willing to content analyze media coverage or campaign advertising relating to these issues have decades of data to work with.

The NAES asks dozens of issue-related questions, but only a few (e.g., about the most important problems facing the nation, the state of the economy, war in Iraq) are used for all dates of the survey. Indeed, many issue questions are not present during the major portion of the general election, August through November. Some particularly unique questions that were asked for at least a few months during the 2004 election cycle included whether respondents had "personally benefited" from President Bush's tax cuts, or favored the Medicare prescription drug law passed during President Bush's first term, even in the face of counterarguments.

Institutions

By design, the NAES does not devote much attention to the legislative and judicial branches of government. General attitudes of favorability toward Congress and the judicial branch (including, but not limited to the Supreme Court) are measured for brief periods of time (October, 2003–April 2004), as is congressional vote choice. The ANES asks a wider variety of questions relating to respondents' evaluations of congressional candidates, leaders, and partisans. Of course, given the NAES' large N, political communication scholars can don a spelunker's hat and dig deep into the data across different kinds of districts (competitive, uncontested, rural, urban) to explore a variety of questions with respect to what people know about Congress and how the information environment influences congressional approval and vote choice. Even though the NAES has a much shorter history than the ANES, the 2000 and 2004 studies already allow for pre- and post-redistricting comparisons of the ways in which voters receive information about Congress when redistricting affects how media markets overlap congressional districts (Engstrom, 2005; Winburn & Wagner, 2010).

From 1978 to 1994, the ANES asked respondents a battery of questions regarding citizens' contact with and evaluations of their congressional representatives and challengers for seats in Congress, resulting in work on the "grateful electorate" (Yiannakis, 1981), the public's view that congressional casework is increasingly partisan (Wagner, 2007b), and debates regarding the existence of legislator benefits gained by congressional communication with constituents (Johannes & McAdams, 1981). In his analysis of information and voting in congressional elections, Althaus (2001) used ANES data to construct a new dependent variable in political communication research: voting estimates of a "fully informed" population, which views political communication as something that can happen from the "bottom up" (from citizens to political actors) as easily as it does from the "top down" (elite actors and the mass media to citizens). The current designs of the NAES and ANES make it difficult to find appropriate data to build on these kinds of political communication investigations about Congress.

Summary

A decided advantage for scholars using the ANES is the ability to examine political communication questions across decades. Indeed, as it gets easier to gather and code news coverage and political advertising data thanks to sources such as Lexis-Nexis,[24] the Vanderbilt Television News Archive,[25] Video Monitoring Service,[26] and the Wisconsin Advertising Project, scholars are increasingly engaging in ambitious coding projects that can be merged with NAES and ANES datasets to ask more complex and precise questions about how news coverage and the content of political advertising affect public preferences and political behavior. Here, the ANES has had a 50-year head start. Studies such as Kellstedt's (2003) examination of how the mass media's framing of racial issues affected the dynamics of racial attitudes and more recent work on how the partisan framing of issues affected public awareness of elite differences on abortion and tax policy (Wagner, 2007a) rely on ANES and General Social Survey (GSS) public opinion data (see also Chapter 13, this volume, on identifying frames in political communication research). Disadvantages include problematic measures of media use, changes in question wording, the current lack of a midterm congressional survey, and a comparatively small N, which can make uncovering media effects especially challenging (see Chapter 24, this volume).

For its part, the NAES earns high marks for the length of time the survey instrument (or portions of it) is in the field, its nimbleness in reacting to events as they happen, inclusion of multiple panels, coverage of a wide variety of issue and knowledge questions asked at various points of the campaign season, and the large sample size. The statistical power afforded by the sample size alone could play a transformative role in helping to uncover small, but real media effects that are hidden from data sets containing too few respondents (Zaller, 2002). Additionally, the NAES should be praised for mailing free copies of University of Pennsylvania Press books with its data (and CDs of the data!) to members of political communication sections of prominent scholarly associations such as the American Political Science Association and International Communication Association.

ALTERNATIVE DATA SOURCES

Unfortunately, one of the ANES' major advantages over the NAES—namely, midterm studies, which allow for political communication scholarship relating to Congress, congressional campaigns, and comparing these races to presidential races—is a thing of the past now that the ANES will only occur during presidential election years. Fortunately, the midterm elections of 2006 were systematically investigated by a few key alternative research consortia, including the Cooperative Congressional Elections Study (CCES) and the Congressional Elections Study (CES) sponsored by the Center on Congress at Indiana University. The CES study includes a pre- and post-election telephone survey of over 1,100 respondents at each point in time. One innovation of the CES instrument relative to the ANES designs was to not only ask about issue preferences but also how *important* each issue was to respondents. The approximately 800-member panel allows for explorations of agenda setting that do not rely on the "most important problem" measure. The CES, which over-samples competitive congressional districts, also includes several questions about public attitudes toward Congress, knowledge of the legislative branch, congressional behavior, and congressional elections. In terms of media usage, the CES asks respondents how often they consume newspapers, national television news, and local television news; it also includes an extensive battery of social network questions. In addition, the CES measures the "big five" personality traits[27] and contains some embedded experiments gauged at estimating a variety of potential campaign effects.

The Cooperative Congressional Elections Study from Polimetrix is a Web-based survey of about 30,000 respondents from which scholars can purchase the use of 1,000 respondents (or buy more by sharing costs with co-authors, etc.) for the administering of about 120 questions.[28] The CCES features about 60 "common content" questions, counting the pre- and post-election surveys. These questions do not contain media use measures but do include measures of political knowledge (Price & Zaller, 1993; Zaller, 1996). The CCES, which is scheduled to run at least through 2010, completed surveys in 2006 and 2007 and fielded a 2008 survey with 37 participating research teams.[29]

Also through Polimetrix, in 2008 the Cooperative Campaign Analysis Project (CCAP) conducted a six-wave, Web-based panel study of 20,000 respondents containing an over-sample of battleground and early primary states. As is the case with the CCES, CCAP participants purchase time to be included beyond the common content available to all coinvestigators. For those political communication scholars unwilling to embrace Zaller's (1996) suggestion to use political knowledge measures as a proxy for gauging media effects or purchase time on the surveys themselves, this common content would not be enough to do a great deal of political communication research.

Aside from data sources that are built around election cycles, there are many other resources available to the political communication scholar, including the General Social Survey and the data archives at the Roper Center (http://www.ropercenter.uconn.edu/), which provide a vast amount and wide array of survey data containing information about public attitudes, media use, social behavior, political behavior, and the like. Additionally, the Time Shared Experiments for the Social Sciences (TESS, http://www.experimentcenter.org), which has its roots in survey experiments conducted by Paul Sniderman (Sniderman & Carmines, 1997), allows scholars to propose survey experiments that, if funded, are run on a national survey via the Internet and Web TV, helping to synthesize the generalizability of surveys with the ability to isolate causation afforded by experiments.

THE FUTURE OF THE ANES AND NAES: POTENTIAL INNOVATIONS

As the ANES and NAES further refine their research designs, one area to consider is the growing applications of biology, psychophysiology, and cognitive neuroscience to politics (Alford, Funk, & Hibbing, 2005; Hibbing & Smith, 2007; Lieberman, Schreiber, & Ochsner, 2003). While it would be impractical for the ANES and NAES to conduct physiological data collection or magnetic resonance imaging, the ANES could, given its face-to-face interviewing, collect genetic material (e.g., human cells drawn from a respondent's cheek via a Q-tip) for analysis. While drawing blood is the best (and longest-lasting) way of collecting DNA, it can also be quite obtrusive and off-putting to respondents, driving down the ANES' traditionally high response rate. Rather than giving blood, ANES respondents could simply consent to having their cheek swabbed to provide enough DNA for genetic analysis. As DNA-gathering technology improves, it is quite possible that relevant information from the respondent's genetic material could be instantly downloaded onto the interviewer's laptop, solving the problem of the shorter DNA "shelf life" of saliva samples compared to blood cells.

Of course, adding this measure would first require a sea change in the thinking of the ANES and the political science community more generally. Although "biopolitics" has existed as a recognized subfield for over two decades (Alford & Hibbing, 2008), with its own journal (*Politics and the Life Sciences*) and professional association, the biopolitical approach has not (as yet) achieved mainstream status. Most behavioral genetics studies rely on samples of convenience, such as twins (Neale & Cardon, 1992; Segal, 1993). With its multistage area probability design, the ANES could open doors for collaborations with behavioral geneticists and genetic scientists more generally to explore how particular political traits are represented in the population—and how these traits predict political dispositions, attitudes, and behaviors.

Adding questions from the Need for Cognition and Decisiveness scales will expand the ANES' psychological reach, though measures of other established cognitive perspectives, such as motivated reasoning, Bayesian updating, and online processing, remain absent from the ANES instrument (Barabas, 2008). Opening other information processing vistas, the NAES could employ response-latency timers on its CATI data. On the NAES' Web-based survey instrument, Implicit Association Test (IAT) technology could also be employed to study a wide array of political attitudes. The IAT is a technique used to induce people to reveal their implicit preferences about attitude objects (political views, racial/ethnic groups, etc.) that they may be unwilling or unable to intentionally reveal (see http://implicit.harvard.edu for demonstrations of IATs). Of course, such innovations are both financially expensive and costly in terms of respondent time, but their potential to generate new knowledge could be well worth the investment of both money and time.

Perhaps more affordable innovations could include the introduction of more survey-based (or "hybrid") experiments, as described by Iyengar (see Chapter 8, this volume). Examples include experiments that come in list form (Sniderman & Carmines, 1997), by varying whether issue frames are administered sans-label or with a partisan label (Sniderman & Theriault, 2004), and so forth. As the scholarship that has come out of the TESS project has illustrated, hybrid studies that incorporate probability sampling with experimental control can teach us a great deal about how citizens learn and use information in complex information environments.

Of course, both surveys should seek to introduce (NAES) or add to (ANES) psychological measures relating to how people process information. Now that a mountain of evidence demonstrates the existence and influence of the "big five" personality factors, the previously intermittent attention political scientists and communication scholars paid personality is no longer justified (Mondak & Halperin, 2008). Given that variations in human personality affect a wide variety of attitudes and that there is considerable variation with respect to the ways in which humans engage in the political world, it is crucial to better understand whether there are "personality-based" antecedents to political behavior. A new cottage industry of work examining the role of personality, political preferences (Hibbing, Theiss-Morse, & Whitaker, 2008), and political behavior (Mondak & Halperin, 2008) provides the ANES and NAES with useful measures of personality and clues as to how future scholars may combine political psychological approaches with political communication research (see Crigler, 1998).

In the end, the ANES and NAES are extraordinarily valuable, but often frustrating, data resources, each with their share of strengths and limitations. Both datasets provide scholars with the opportunity to estimate effects of communication processes on political preferences, behaviors, and outcomes. While the ANES asks more "political" questions and the NAES includes more media- and communication-related measures, both surveys provide ample opportunities to examine campaign dynamics as well as the political preferences, values, and civic participation of citizens.

Large research undertakings such as the NAES and ANES are fertile ground for collaborations and interdisciplinary projects, as they each generate data across a wide range of political variables, including candidate evaluations, political behavior, knowledge, psychology, and communication. Following Herrnson (1995) and King's (1995) call for greater replication in the social sciences, scholars can fruitfully employ the measures offered in the ANES and NAES to pursue the most important questions animating political communication research. With the NAES' emphasis on communication and electoral processes and the ANES' greater focus on political outcomes, scholars would do well to use these data resources in concert with each other to further uncover media effects, improve the generalizability of findings, and examine how variables present in one dataset but not the other bear on questions important to political communication research. While the health of the measures tracing the body politic has been uneven at times, longstanding practices and recent innovations from both the "classic" (ANES) and "up and coming" (NAES) data sources bode well for the future of political communication research.

NOTES

1. I am grateful to R. Lance Holbert and Erik Bucy for their helpful, detailed comments and suggestions. I am also thankful to Diana Mutz for providing information on the 2008 NAES study. All interpretations of the ANES and NAES in this chapter and any remaining errors are solely my own responsibility.
2. The General Social Survey (GSS) is another prominent, over-time data source for scholars interested in political communication, though the survey construction has a more sociological orientation.
3. See http://www.natcomorg/nca and http://www.natcom.org/nca/files/ccLibraryFiles/FILENAME/000 000000181/NRC—Presentation%20Version%202.ppt#284,2,Communication Research.
4. The sample universe for the ANES is all U.S. households in the "lower 48" states and the District of Columbia. Presently, the ANES uses a multistage area probability design (Erikson & Tedin, 2007). For more information, see http://www.electionstudies.org/overview/overview.htm.
5. During the 2006 midterm elections, several other survey studies (most notably the 2006 Congressional Elections Study) sought to keep particularly important elements of the midterm time-series alive. In the interest of full disclosure, I was the project director for the 2006 CES at the Center on Congress at Indiana University. Ted Carmines was principal investigator. Co-PIs included Robert Huckfeldt, Jeff Mondak, John Hibbing, Walt Stone, Herb Weisberg, and Gary Jacobson.
6. The length of time that the NAES is in the field gives scholars interested in issues of political communication that are unrelated to elections plenty of data to analyze that is gathered 6 to 9 months before a federal election.
7. Available online: http://www.electionstudies.org/overview/implement.htm.
8. Census Enumeration Districts are specific geographic areas assigned to a census taker. Typically, an "ED" is simply a part of a town or county.
9. As of this writing, the Board of Overseers includes political scientists John Aldrich, Stephen Ansolabehere, Henry Brady, Brandice-Canes Wrone, Kenneth Goldstein, Donald Green, John Mark Hansen (Chair), Vincent Hutchings, Paula McClain, Kathleen McGraw, Walter Mebane, Vincent Price, Gary Segura, Daron Shaw, and Paul Sniderman. It also includes sociologists Karen Cook and Lynn Smith-Lovin; social psychologist Richard Petty; and economists Catherine Eckel, Randy Olsen, and V. Kerry Smith.
10. Thanks to Arthur Lupia for this information about the 2008 ANES. The Online Commons Web address (registration required) is http://www.electionstudies.org/onlinecommons.htm.
11. Web interviews were added to the 2008 research design.
12. The Canadian National Election Studies pioneered the RCS in 1988 and 1993 (Johnston et al., 2004).
13. Face-to-face interviews typically have a higher response rate than telephone surveys.
14. Questions relating to direct mail and voter contact were included from January to March 2004.
15. In August 2004, a few questions were added about the "Swift Boat" ads, although they were asked for only a few days.
16. Bowers, Burns, Ensley, and Kinder (2005) and Bowers and Ensley (2003) discuss important differences in the results from the ANES' RDD and CAPI respondents in 2000, suggesting that the mode of interviewing is important when it comes to comparing results across years. Indeed, NAES project director Richard Johnston expects respondents to be "franker" in the NAES Web-based surveys as compared to telephone surveys (http://www.annenbergpublicpolicycenter.org/Downloads/OnTheRecords/Onthe Record2_final_sept2007.pdf).
17. The 2008 ANES survey instrument included the 2006 Althaus/Tewksbury battery as a split sample with the traditional ANES media battery, allowing scholars to directly compare the two.

18. This study used survey data from the 2006 Congressional Elections Study, which is referenced later in this chapter.
19. The instrument also includes "number of days" questions for use of the Internet and talk radio.
20. See Mondak, Carmines, Huckfeldt, Mitchell, and Schraufnagel (2007) for analyses showing how institution-specific questions—in this case about Congress—can improve our understanding of relevant political knowledge.
21. See Hayes (2005) for an analysis using the ANES measures of different traits from 1980–2004 and how they are ascribed to particular parties by voters.
22. Feeling thermometers measure favorable and unfavorable evaluations of attitude objects by asking respondents to rate their feelings about the attitude object (e.g., a candidate or political party); a temperature of 0 degrees represents very cool or negative feelings, 50 degrees represents moderate or lukewarm feelings, and 100 degrees represents very warm or positive feelings.
23. Unfortunately, the ANES' abortion question changed its wording in 1980.
24. Lexis-Nexis enables searches of news coverage from a wide variety of newspaper and magazine sources, along with national television news program transcripts. Scholars can search the full text of newspaper stories, television transcripts, congressional testimony, and the like.
25. The Vanderbilt Television News Archive contains video copies and news summaries of major network newscasts (ABC, CBS, and NBC) from 1968 to the present, CNN from 1995 to the present, and Fox News from 2004 to the present.
26. The Video Monitoring Service provides abstracts from local television newscasts in media markets throughout the country. The abstracts typically contain information on the subject and length of the story, the issues discussed, and sources interviewed.
27. The "big five" personality dimensions include openness, conscientiousness, extraversion, agreeableness, and neuroticism.
28. For information on "matching" a random sample to the population of Polimetrix respondents, see http://web.mit.edu/polisci/portl/cces/sampledesign.html.
29. Thanks to Stephen Ansolabehere for this information.

REFERENCES

Alford, J. R., Funk, C. L., & Hibbing, J. R. (2005). Are political orientations genetically transmitted? *American Political Science Review, 99*(2): 153–68.

Alford, J. R., & Hibbing, J. R. (2008). The new empirical biopolitics. *Annual Review of Political Science, 11*, 183–203.

Althaus, S. L. (2001). Who's voted in when the people tune out? Information effects in congressional elections. In R. P. Hart & D. Shaw (Eds.) *Communication in U.S. elections: New agendas*. Lanhan, MD: Rowman and Littlefield Publishers.

Althaus, S. L., & Tewksbury, D. H. (2007). "Toward a new generation of media use measures for the ANES." Report to the Board of Overseers for the American National Election Studies, ANES Pilot Study Report, No. nes011903.

American National Election Studies. (2004). *The 2004 national election study*. Ann Arbor, MI: University of Michigan, Center for Political Studies, http://www.electionstudies.org

Barabas, J. (2008). "Measuring media exposure in the 2006 ANES pilot study and beyond," in *Political Communication Report*, http://www.jour.unr.edu/pcr/1801_2008_winter/index.html.

Bowers, J., Burns, N., Ensley, M. J., & Kinder, D. R. (2005). Analyzing the 2000 National Election Study, *Political Analysis, 13*, 109–111.

Bowers, J., & Ensley, M. J. (2003). Issues in analyzing data from the dual mode 2000 American National Election Study. *National Election Studies Technical Report* (available at http://www.umich.edu/~nes).

Brewer, P. R. (2003). Values, political knowledge, and public opinion about gay rights: A framing-based account, *Public Opinion Quarterly, 67*, 173–201.

Bucy, E. P., & Gregson, K. S. (2001). Media participation: A legitimizing mechanism of mass democracy, *New Media and Society*, 3(3), 359–382.

Cacioppo, J. T., & Petty, R. E. (1982). The need for cognition, *Journal of Personality and Social Psychology*, 42,116–131.

Campbell, A., Converse, P., Miller, W., & Stokes, D. (1960). *The American Voter*. New York: Wiley.

Carmines, E. G., Gerrity, J. C., & Wagner, M. W. (2008). Did the media do it? The influence of news coverage on the 2006 congressional elections. In J. J. Mondak & D.-G. Mitchell (Eds.), *Fault lines: Why the Republicans lost Congress*. London: Routledge.

Carmines, E. G. & Huckfeldt, R. (1996). Political behavior: An overview. In R. E. Goodin & H.-D. Klingermann (Eds.), *A new handbook of political science* (pp. 223–254). Oxford: Oxford University Press.

Carsey, T. M., & Layman, G. C. (2006). Changing sides or changing minds? Party identification and policy preferences in the American electorate. *American Journal of Political Science*, 50(2), 464–477.

Crigler, A. (Ed.). (1998). *The psychology of political communication*. Ann Arbor: University of Michigan Press.

Druckman, J. N. (2004). Political preference formation: Competition, deliberation, and the (ir)relevance of framing effects. *American Political Science Review*, 98(4), 671–686.

Engstrom, R. N. (2005). District geography and voters. In P. F. Galderisis (Ed.), *Redistricting in the new millennium* (pp. 65–84). Lanham, MD: Lexington Books.

Erikson, R. S. & Tedin, K. L. (2007). *American public opinion: Its origins, content, and impact* (7th ed.). Boston: Allyn and Bacon.

Fazio, R. H. (1990). A practical guide to the use of response latency in social psychological research. In C. Hendrick & M. S. Clark (Eds.), *Review of personality and social psychology: Vol. 11. Research methods in personality and social psychology* (pp. 74–97). Newbury Park, CA: Sage.

Goodin, R. E. & Klingemann, H.-D. (1996). *A new handbook of political science*. New York: Oxford University Press.

Hayes, D. (2005). Candidate qualities through a partisan lens: A theory of trait ownership. *American Journal of Political Science*, 49, 908–923.

Herrnson, P. S. (1995). Replication, verification, secondary analysis, and data collection in political science. *PS: Political Science and Politics*, 28, 452–455.

Hershey, M. R. (1992). The constructed explanation: Interpreting election results in the 1984 presidential race. *Journal of Politics*, 54(4):944–976.

Hibbing, J. R. & Smith, K. B. (2007). The biology of political behavior: An introduction. *The Annals of the American Academy of Political and Social Sciences*, 614, 6–14.

Hibbing, J. R., Theiss-Morse, E., & Whitaker, E. (2008). Americans' perceptions of the nature of governing. In Jeffrey J. Mondak & Dona-Gene Mitchell (Eds.), *Fault lines: Why the Republicans lost Congress*. London: Routledge.

Holbrook, T. M. (1996). *Do campaigns matter?* Thousand Oaks, CA: Sage.

Huckfeldt, R., Johnson, P. E., & Sprague, J. (2004). *Political disagreement: The survival of diverse opinions within communication networks*. New York: Cambridge University Press.

Huckfeldt, R., Sprague, J., & Levine, J. (2000). The dynamics of collective deliberation in the 1996 election: Campaign effects on accessibility, certainty, and accuracy. *American Political Science Review*, 94(3), 641–651.

Iyengar, S., & Kinder, D. R. (1987). *News that matters*. Chicago: University of Chicago Press.

Jamieson, K. H. & Kenski, K. (2006). Why the National Annenberg Election Survey? In D. Romer, K. Kenski, K. Winneg, Christopher Adasiewicz, & Kathleen Hall Jamieson, *Capturing campaign dynamics 2000 and 2004*. Philadelphia: University of Pennsylvania Press.

Johannes, J. R. & McAdams, J. C. (1981). Does casework matter? A reply to Professor Fiorina. *American Journal of Political Science*, 25, 581–604.

Johnston, R., Hagan, M., & Jamieson, K. H. (2004). *The 2000 presidential election and the foundations of party politics*. New York: Cambridge University Press.

Johnston, R. (2008). Modeling campaign dynamics on the web in the 2008 National Annenberg Election Study. *Journal of Elections, Public Opinion, and Parties*, 18(4), 401–412.

Kellstedt, P. M. (2003). *The mass media and the dynamics of American racial attitudes*. Cambridge: Cambridge University Press.

King, G. (1995). Replication, replication. *PS: Political Science and Politics, 28*, 444–452.

Kiousis, S., & McCombs, M. (2004). Agenda setting effects and attitude strength: Political figures during the 1996 presidential election. *Communication Research, 31*, 36–57.

Kruglanski, A. W., Webster, D. M., & Klem, A. (1993). Motivated resistance and openness to persuasion in the presence or absence of prior information. *Journal of Personality and Social Psychology, 65*, 861–876.

Lasswell, H. (1950). *Politics: Who gets what, when, how*. New York: P. Smith.

Lieberman, M. D., Schreiber, D., & Ochsner, K. N. (2003). Is political thinking like riding a bicycle? How cognitive neuroscience can inform research on political thinking. *Political Psychology, 24*, 681–704

McCombs, M. E., & Shaw, D. L. (1972). The agenda-setting function of the mass media. *Public Opinion Quarterly, 36*, 176–187.

Mondak, J. J., Carmines, E. G., Huckfeldt, R., Mitchell, D.-G., & Schraufnagel, S. (2007). Does familiarity breed contempt?: The impact of information on mass attitudes toward Congress. *American Journal of Political Science, 51*, 34–48.

Mondak, J. J., & Halperin, K. D. (2008). A framework for the study of personality and political behavior. *British Journal of Political Science, 38*(2): 335–362.

Neale, M.C., & Cardon, L. R. (1992). *Methodology for genetic studies of twins and families*. Dordrecht, The Netherlands: Kluwer Academic Press.

Page, B. I., & Shapiro, R. Y. (1992). *The rational public: Fifty years of trends in Americans' policy preferences*. Chicago: University of Chicago Press.

Petrocik, J. R. (1996). Issue ownership in presidential elections, with a 1980 case study. *American Journal of Political Science, 40*(3), 825–850.

Price, V., & Zaller, J. (1993). Who gets the news? Alternative measures of news reception and their implications for research. *Public Opinion Quarterly, 57*(2), 133–164.

Prior, M. (2007). *Post-broadcast democracy: How media choice increases inequality in political involvement and polarizes elections*. New York: Cambridge University Press.

Romer, D., Kenski, K., Winneg, K., Adasiewicz, C., & Jamieson, K. H. (2006). *Capturing campaign dynamics, 2000 and 2004: The National Annenberg Election Survey*. Philadelphia: University of Pennsylvania Press.

Segal, N. L. (1993). Twin, sibling, and adoption methods. *American Psychologist, 48*(9), 943–956.

Sniderman, P. M., & Carmines, E. G. (1997). *Reaching beyond race*. Cambridge, MA: Harvard University Press.

Sniderman, P. M., & Theriault, S. M. (2004). The structure of political argument and the logic of issue framing. In W. E. Saris & P. M. Sniderman (Eds.), *Studies in public opinion*. Princeton, NJ: Princeton University Press.

Wagner, M. W. (2007a). The utility of staying on message: Competing partisan frames and public awareness of elite differences on political issues. *The Forum, 5*(3), 1–18.

Wagner, M. W. (2007b). Beyond policy representation in the U.S. House: partisanship, polarization, and citizens' attitudes about casework. *American Politics Research, 35*, 771–789.

Winburn, J. C., & Wagner, M. W. (2010). Carving voters out: Redistricting's influence on political information, turnout, and voting behavior. *Political Research Quarterly, 63*(2), 373–386.

Yiannakis, D. E. (1981). The grateful electorate: Casework and congressional elections. *American Journal of Political Science, 25*(3), 568–580.

Zaller, J. R. (1996). The myth of massive media impact revived: New support for a discredited idea. In D. C. Mutz, P. M. Sniderman, & R. A. Brody (Eds.), *Political persuasion and attitude change*. Ann Arbor: University of Michigan Press.

Zaller, J. R. (2002). The statistical power of election studies to detect media exposure effects in political campaigns. *Electoral Studies, 21*, 297–329.

7

The Implications and Consequences of Using Meta-Analysis for Political Communication

Mike Allen
Department of Communication
University of Wisconsin–Milwaukee

David D'Alessio
Department of Communication
University of Connecticut–Stamford

Nancy Burrell
Department of Communication
University of Wisconsin–Milwaukee

The impact of the application of meta-analysis within the social sciences is only beginning to be realized. Meta-analysis provides a means of aggregating existing data to investigate and resolve apparent and real empirical inconsistencies. When combined with sophisticated theoretical model building and testing, the procedure permits the full assessment of existing and proposed theories. Meta-analysis, rather than a single technique, represents a cluster of various procedures used to identify and eliminate existing statistical artifacts.

This chapter provides a description of the technique, some examples of application, and the future implications and applications of meta-analysis research. The implications for political communication are interesting because of the connection to fundamental views about the First Amendment and political participation. A necessary part of the discussion of any scientific finding for political communication concerns the implications for ongoing election practices. Arguments about the impact of media or a particular communication strategy receive evaluation against the existing evidence and require careful consideration.

DESCRIPTION OF THE TECHNIQUE

Basic Practices

Meta-analysis constitutes a literature review designed to quantitatively summarize existing data. The primary goal involves the generation of average estimates that have the sampling error properties of the combined sample size across the number of studies. The two challenges facing probabilistic research relying on the significance test are Type I (false positive) and Type II error (false negative). Type I error, or alpha error, is set typically at 5%. The level of Type II error represents a combination of three factors (level of Type I error, size of the effect, and size of the sample). The general expectation is that Type II error (based on a Type I error rate of 5%, average sample size of about 80, and average size of effect, $d = .20$, see Hedges, 1987, for the basis of this assumption) is about 50%, meaning that the reliability of the nonsignificant finding is the same as flipping a coin in terms of accurately estimating the existence of a relationship. When flipping a coin is as accurate as relying on research findings to make a decision, there is need for improvement. Type II error is reduced in meta-analysis because the size of sampling error reduces as the sample size increases. A scholar combining 200 investigations that average 100 participants generates results based on the combined sample of 20,000 of a negligible level of Type II error.

The typical process in a meta-analysis involves the following steps: (a) literature search, (b) conversion of information to a common metric as well as artifact corrections, (c) estimating an average and assessment of variability, and (d) testing potential moderating variables and/or other theoretical models. At each step the goal of a report should be sufficient to provide detail to permit others to replicate the meta-analysis and verify the conclusion. Meta-analysis should provide for an explicit and replicable means of establishing findings.

The literature search should be explained in some detail. Determining which investigations become included (as well as the reasons for inclusion or exclusion) should be stated. The critical determination is whether another scholar given the same manuscripts and the same rules could replicate the decision-making processes. The difference in definitions and applications can play some part in making conclusions as well as differences in statistical procedure (for a good example, see the disagreement on whether one-sided or two-sided messages are more persuasive; Allen, 1991, 1993; Allen et al., 1990; O'Keefe, 1993, 1999).

After obtaining manuscripts, the available information is converted to a common metric. The underlying assumption of meta-analysis is that statistical information as represented either in a significance test or as a size of relationship is convertible from one form to another. What this means is that in a strict mathematical sense the choice of statistic is arbitrary. The most common forms are d and z (difference between means or groups expressed in standard units), or r (correlation). Theoretically, a meta-analysis could be conducted in any metric, although some of the formulas for some metrics might be very complicated.

The estimation of an average involves weighting by the sample size and assessment of the variability in the sample of the effects. Generally, there is consensus on most aspects of meta-analysis (i.e., conversion, correction, variability assessment). Differences between approaches usually address issues concerning the impact and appropriateness of some decision rules (see Hunter & Schmidt, 2002, for discussion of some of these), but the impact seldom influences the average effect size. Usually the difference in procedures is over the estimation and evaluation of the observed variability in effects, the requirements for independence of estimates, or whether any particular transformation or correction is warranted. In particular, the tests for homogeneity of estimates serve as a point of disagreement or discussion (Aguinis, Sturman, & Pierce, 2008).

The only real consensus seems to be that random effects models should be avoided when fixed model analysis is possible (see discussions of this in Cook et al., 1990; Cooper & Hedges, 1994; Hedges & Olkin, 1985; Hunter & Schmidt, 2002; Petitti, 2000). The problem with random models is that the more forgiving homogeneity tests are gained by sacrificing interpretability of the findings. As a result, virtually all analysts recommend using a fixed effect form of analysis initially and using random effects models later if a fixed procedure fails to produce a satisfactory solution (Johnson et al., 2008).

Advanced Practices

The next evolution of meta-analysis involves the use of data compilations for tests of extended propositions or complete theoretical systems, essentially, the application of path analysis, ANOVA, multiple regression, or some other statistical test using data derived from meta-analysis involves the testing of more extended theoretical systems of argument. A simple correlation may provide evidence for some fundamental proposition or point to some important outcome but most theoretical statements provide more comprehensive systems requiring more sophisticated tests.

Consider a simple structural equation model (SEM) that has variable A causes variable B causes variable C. The model requires data about the relationships between each variable (a total of three). To test the model one could generate average correlations using a meta-analysis for each of the three estimates and use the averages to test the model. If one expands the system to four variables, the number of meta-analyses required goes up (to six) and for five variables the number of analyses continues to expand (to ten). What this indicates is that even for relatively simple theoretical model testing the number of meta-analyses that have to be conducted can quickly become very large. The development (Cheung & Chan, 2005; Stanley & Jarrell, 1989; Viswesvaran & Ones, 1995) and application (Dindia & Allen, 1992; Emmers-Sommer & Allen, 1999) of meta analysis techniques continues to receive attention. The distinction between moderating and mediating variables and understanding variability in outcomes also remains an important topic (Muller, Judd, & Yzerbyt, 2005; Rosenthal & DiMatteo, 2001). The continued development and evolution of statistical procedures for more advanced applications of meta-analysis increases the utility of this technique.

LIMITATIONS OF META-ANALYSIS

The authors view five principal limitations of meta-analysis: (a) ethnographic trap, (b) lack of full diversity in the existing data, (c) differing values for analysis, (d) inappropriate application of social data to clinical issues, and (e) ability to make multiple interpretations of any finding. These issues should be viewed as limitations to the application or conclusions drawn by the technique rather than flaws of the technique. The distinction is between something that makes the technique inherently subject to error as opposed to something that simply provides a boundary on what can be obtained or concluded. The inaccurate interpretation or belief in application without consideration of possible limitations provides the basis for the possibility of error.

Ethnographic Trap. The ethnographic trap is the problem of taking the results from any meta-analysis that seems to provide clear advice and translating that into action. Consider that for fear appeals, various meta-analyses (e.g., Boster & Mongeau, 1984; Witte & Allen, 2000) find that high-fear messages are more persuasive than low-fear messages. The implication is clear: if you are constructing a fear appeal, the more fear generated, the greater the level of behavioral adoption.

The problem is that, while understanding that for persuasive messages based on fear appeals increases the persuasiveness of the message, the meta-analysis does not define fear. No meta-analysis provides the "equipment for living" that is required for practical application. Different audiences and cultures have different fears and any particular audience requires precise language to increase fear. The meta-analysis provides the value of a strategy but does not indicate the means by which to construct the actions required. Within the individual fear appeals studies, there exists an unarticulated understanding of the message and the audience. The scholars conducting the original studies possessed that necessary knowledge to generate the messages in their investigations. The application of any meta-analysis to a particular situation requires the appropriate cultural understanding to articulate this abstract knowledge into practice.

The reason for the ethnographic trap is that the underlying assumptions or practices necessary for understanding application cannot be articulated or measured in a strict scientific sense. The knowledge exists within a dynamic set of cultural assumptions and practices to which a person (study participant) responds. To view the process as fixed or unchanging misunderstands the under-lying nature of culture. The impact of the underlying construct of fear does not change but the manifestation of what is fearful does change. A meta-analysis cannot capture or craft that manifestation within the scientific model.

Lack of Diversity in Existing Data.   A meta-analysis provides a systematic and comprehensive summary of existing data. The problem of generalization is the degree to which the sample of estimates is typical of the population of possible values that the researcher wishes to generalize to.

Consider an example of a meta-analysis of 100 or more studies on the impact of campaign contributions on electoral outcomes. Even if a consistent and homogeneous finding is generated, if the studies were all conducted in the eastern United States, the finding may not generalize to the rest of the country and may similarly be problematic for electoral situations and conditions outside the United States.

This is not an indictment of the particulars of the meta-analysis; the meta-analysis could be perfect. The limitation of the meta-analysis reflects the limits of the existing available data, which may or may not generalize to conditions not existing in the current data. Unfortunately, there exists an infinite set of possible conditions (including temporal aspects) that cannot provide universal generalizability. Instead, the argument against generalizing should invoke a set of theoretical arguments that provide a basis for the limitation.

Differing Values for Analysis.   This limitation considers the impact of various features of the studies that may exist in small quantities for examination. Suppose that a meta-analysis finds a consistent finding for newspaper coverage bias in elections. The sample of studies, even if large, may consist of a mixture of presidential (50%), senate (30%), congressional (15%), and other state-level races (5%). The limitation in this case is that even though there exist some investigations for elections to offices like state attorney general, that pool of studies may be very small. The limited pool of available studies may make broad generalization claims unwarranted.

The claims for presidential elections may contain enough data both in terms of diversity and quantity that claims about the generalization of the data become reasonable. The same may be true for senatorial elections. When the particular combinations have very small amounts of available data, even when the effects appear homogeneous and there is no reason to doubt the possibility of generalization, the evidence for generalization remains weak. This assessment requires an examina-tion of the size of cells for particular moderator combinations. While the overall meta-analysis may contain enough data for consistent findings, individual claims need to be assessed against the available data. The problem remains the inability to generate an infinite set of conditions or contexts that could satisfy all possible combinations for generalization. Instead, the outcome is argumentative: Does the data provide a reasonable case for generalization given all the circumstances?

Inappropriate Application of Social Data to Clinical Issues.   Social science applications refer generally to a mass or class of individuals and have limited applicability to isolated cases. For example, while a meta-analysis might indicate that form A of advertising is generally more effective than form B, that does not mean in all cases that the relationship holds true. There might be a variety of individual cases where there is no observed difference between the impact of a choice between form A and form B of advertising.

Social science deals with general or average tendencies such that as variable 1 changes there will be a predictable change in the level of variable 2. That statement, when supported by an adequate database or meta-analysis, holds true for the relationship, but for any individual case the outcome is only a probability. Numerous counterexamples will exist when considering a true relationship with an average correlation of .10. One can argue, for example, that the media has a liberal bias, but that does not mean on any particular issue that the bias must exist. Arguing for the existence of bias in a particular case from a meta-analysis is an inappropriate application. The question of application to a particular case is a clinical application based on the context and circumstances of that particular situation.

What this provides is a technique that becomes more useful at understanding the big picture and the formulation of theory. At the same time, the technique should be viewed as permitting numerous counterexamples to exist without undermining the general principle. The view is analogous to medicine, which involves an application of scientific information that makes the practice an art, not a science.

Possibility of Multiple Interpretations.   A fact must be interpreted and applied before it becomes useful. Any particular set of outcomes may imply an infinite set of possible actions or implications. An attempt to reason from the meta-analysis to any particular justification is possible but no such justification should be viewed as inevitably warranted on the basis of the meta-analysis alone.

There always exists the capacity for various policy alternatives to square with the facts. The focus should be on what facts the meta-analysis establishes and to what degree various policy alternatives are consistent with those facts rather than reasoning from the fact to the inevitability of some particular action. The danger of reasoning from a meta-analysis is that various alternatives that may exist that are not fully considered because different theoretical interpretations may provide contexts for different understandings of the relationships expressed in the meta-analysis.

The argument for "evidence based" policy analysis and use of science can become a process of misapplication when considering the implications of meta-analysis. The problem is that deriving an "ought" in terms of action from a fact that "is" may seem an easy and inevitable process, but the derivation depends on a variety of assumptions that may or may not be warranted. Meta-analysis creates the danger of a false sense of confidence in the justification for an action that *may be* warranted but is not *necessarily* warranted. The bottom line is that the evidence from a meta-analysis may provide *sufficient* information for some policy decisions but not always provide the *necessary* information that justifies an action. This does not mean that meta-analyses should be ignored as a basis for action; clearly, a properly conducted series of meta-analyses can provide the basis for clear and convincing (as well as beneficial) action.

APPLICATION OF META-ANALYSIS IN POLITICAL COMMUNICATION

The first meta-analyses in an area of social science typically examine underlying disputes or arguments about the existence or nature of some relationship or outcome. For example, does negative political advertising provide a benefit to those using it, or whether political debates influence the choice of voters. Essentially, the reviewers examine arguments about the empirical effectiveness of differing message strategies or the impact of using various campaign tactics. The application to the study of political communication has been varied and, not surprisingly, filled with insightful conclusions.

Political Debates

Debates between candidates probably provide the most fundamental method of direct comparison of candidates. Political debates occur between candidates at virtually all levels, but most of the scholarship has focused on the presidential debates, which are the most documented and covered.

The question is whether the main outcome sought by the campaign—improved knowledge of the positions taken by candidates—has in fact been met; also of interest are whether political debates assist in establishing the views of those who watch and increase the understanding of the differences between the candidates. The effective management of election activities remains a concern of candidates, accentuating the positive and minimizing the consequences of poor choices or performance. Benoit, Hansen, and Verser (2003) summarize the effect of viewing presidential debates. Viewers demonstrated that the debates increased their knowledge of issue position (*average r* = .256), have an agenda setting effect (*average r* = .291), impact the perception of the character of the candidates (*average r* = .266), and influence the preference for voting (*average r* = .149). What this set of studies indicates is that presidential debates serve the intended goal of improving knowledge about candidate issue positions and candidate character, set the agenda for the campaign, and, perhaps most importantly, influence the potential balloting. The argument for continuing or changing debate formats should consider the evidence from previous elections about the importance of this endeavor.

Political News Coverage

Political news coverage deals with representations by the news media of political parties, candidates, or events. The general focus of political coverage research is on whether the media "fairly" cover the candidates or events in question. The problem is that fairness is usually associated with the notion of "objective" reporting. However, no standard exists to provide a sense of what would constitute objectivity; instead, the standard really is that of fairness, allowing the major candidates or parties (usually defined as two) to present the argument or case for their conclusion.

D'Alessio and Allen (2000) report the level of bias in media coverage of presidential elections from 132 studies comparing Republican and Democrat candidates. The findings indicate no significant differences when considering gatekeeping bias (number of stories) or coverage bias (amount or valence). The lack of difference did not occur when breaking this coverage down on the basis of television, newspapers, or news magazines. The overall findings illustrate that studies of the media indicate that news coverage has been remarkably neutral. However, when D'Alessio and Allen (2007) examined the coverage of newspapers at the individual level, there was evidence of pro-Republican bias on the part of newspapers, perhaps reflecting the views of the ownership.

Given the decline of newspapers in favor of electronic media and online sources of information, this bias may play less importance in the future.

This focus on coverage does not consider or include the "bias" in editorial or opinion columns. The editorial page of a newspaper is supposed to provide an opinion and therefore supports particular candidates or positions. Political pundits like Bill O'Reilly, Rush Limbaugh, or Bill Marr make no pretense at objectivity and therefore cannot be considered biased in terms of this view. Bias comes from the failure of a news source to retain what is represented as an objective opinion. What this implies is that if Fox News or CNN provides an analysis that is considered "biased," then the analysis should be viewed as journalistically unfair, not because of the slant of the coverage but because the standard claim of objectivity (or fairness) was not met by the organization.

Another problem with bias research is the institutional bias of various news sources that come from national or other ideological views. For example, no U.S. mainstream media source would have represented the 9/11 hijackers as anything other than homicidal terrorists. Mainstream media outlets characterized the hijackers as persons committing a cowardly or terroristic act that killed thousands of innocent victims.

What this indicates is that any meta-analysis of objectivity must establish a standard for objectivity and therefore define objectivity. Defining equal treatment of political candidates as the number of column inches in a newspaper or amount of television air time allotted to a candidate usually is predicated as a comparison of Republican and Democrat candidates. Yet, almost all elections involve more than the two candidates from the major political parties. Defining fairness in terms of those parties means that other parties may not receive any coverage and therefore ignoring those candidates is considered "fair."

Another impact of political coverage is the effect on political participation. Miron and Bryant (2007) found for three studies that political exposure via television reduces the level of voter turnout (*average r* = −.09) but exposure to newspaper coverage increases voter turnout (*average r* = .19). Hollander (2007) found similar results when considering the relationship of general political involvement with television news (*average r* = −.05) and newspaper exposure with political involvement (*average r* = .33). This set of findings starts to suggest a general relationship that is stronger with newspapers than television. However, given the decline of newspapers and the rise of electronic journalism, it is unclear what changes will take place in political fortunes as media platforms evolve. The necessity for studying this change and subsequent meta-analyses to summarize and compare this research promises a rich future research agenda.

Political Advertising

Advertising by political candidates makes no pretense at fairness or objectivity. The goal of an advertising message is to provide reasons to support a particular candidate or position. The central issues are whether the practices of the advertisers are ethical and whether the sheer amount of information in advertisements can predetermine the results of the election.

If the electorate is only aware of one candidate, then the ability of any other candidate to win an election becomes difficult. But citizen awareness, while constituting a necessary condition for election, does not provide a sufficient condition for a candidate to win. Awareness must also translate into desirability and motivate the individual supporters to participate in a campaign and vote for the candidate.

One area of analysis is the impact of negative political advertising on election campaigns. At least two different meta-analyses have examined the impact of negative political advertising (Allen & Burrell, 2002; Lau & Sigelman, 1999). Both meta-analyses agree about the impact of negative political campaign ads. Despite prevailing assumptions, the available scientific evidence would indicate that negative political advertising has relatively little impact on voters. The findings are supported by an updated analysis by Lau, Sigelman, and Rovner (2007) that replicates the original finding of little impact, even considering studies of recent elections.

The problem with these empirical findings about negative political campaign ads is that they lack resonance with the experience of those in campaigns. Clearly, the "Swift Boat" ads were perceived as effective against Democratic presidential candidate John Kerry in reducing his credibility on national security. The history of campaigning is filled with effective negative political material that undermined a candidate and helped elect an opponent. There exists a bit of disconnect between the world of academic research and the lived reality of those engaged in the practice of political campaigning where the strategies represent useful and successful tactics.

There is the gap, then, between empirical research design and actual practical application in the middle of a campaign. This problem is not uncommon in persuasion. Consider the meta-analysis that demonstrates that statistical evidence is more persuasive than narrative evidence (Allen et al., 2000; Allen & Preiss, 1997); at the same time there exists a base-rate fallacy (Allen, Preiss, & Gayle, 2006) that indicates message receivers are unable to apply statistical information in the presence of a counterexample. This demonstrates a paradox between the general findings of research and the actual application of this finding to an ongoing set of messages.

The more fundamental issue for understanding research is that general message strategies are usually targeted at understanding single message exposures about specific topics (HIV infection, second-hand smoke dangers, etc.). An election campaign consists of a set of messages that are dynamic where information comes from a multitude of sources obtained in a variety of manners. The ability of controlled experiments to replicate this kind of information environment in an authentic manner remains difficult.

Political Perceptions

Researching political perceptions about issues and their relationship to various economic, ideological, or other electoral considerations involves understanding how political issues ebb and flow as a result of public pressure and media coverage. Various political perceptions or processes have been examined, such as the third-person perception (Paul, Salwen, & Dupagne, 2007), the spiral of silence (Glynn, Hayes, & Shanahan, 1997; Shanahan, Glynn, & Hayes, 2007), connection of information acquisition and issues knowledge (Hansen & Benoit, 2007), and selective exposure (D'Alessio & Allen, 2002). The findings of these meta-analyses indicate how message receivers choose, process, or react to messages. Similarly, the news industry, in an effort to maintain readership or viewership, will adapt to these political discourses to maximize their relevance. Meta-analysis provides the potential for understanding the dynamic nature of political communication by indicating how various communication practices change over time or impact subsequent decisions. Political communication implies more than simply what happens during an election and includes an array of issues concerning how developments including disasters, war, economics, racial bias, and education are presented and covered.

What these findings provide is a basis for understanding how media coverage of political events and outcomes impacts public perception. This research can be expanded to consider not only news coverage but also material provided for and by a campaign. As the type and function of media changes, the agendas of research—as well as research designs—must adapt to keep pace with real-world practices. One challenging question has always been whether shifts in media use generate different impacts compared to previous media. For example, the shift from newspapers to radio, to television, and now to the Web represents both generational and technological change.

The impact of new technologies and message strategies can be assessed over time with meta-analysis to determine whether changes are taking place.

As important as political perceptions is the impact of media coverage on the motivation of the population to seek out or desire additional information about some event. News coverage has still an element of popularity measured by ratings or sales on the part of the public that drives the sense of "newsworthiness" of a story. The capacity of circumstances or political operatives to provide a good storyline that will generate interest motivates the public to follow a drama over time as it unfolds.

The question of which parts of society should be permitted entry into policy debates and how much power or control of the process they should have constitutes a broader question about political participation. Understanding how lobbyists, corporate donors, special interest groups, and other organized bodies influence the process of perception and participation in decision-making provides a reference point for understanding political communication that goes beyond the issues of elections and campaigning.

FUTURE IMPLICATIONS

Locating Knowledge

The traditional literature review involves finding a group of studies and then classifying or representing the outcomes and using that conclusion to justify a theoretical model or some empirical investigation. The problem with this research approach is the reliance on a limited set of studies or "favorite" studies without considering the entire historical scope of data. Traditional narrative review of the literature therefore provides a relatively inefficient method of incorporating or utilizing information for conducting the literature search.

The challenge for the reviewer is to find relevant meta-analyses, understand the implication of individual designs as prototypical examples, and then provide a web of interrelated findings to serve as the basis for a knowledge claim. Meta-analysis provides the ability to determine whether there is a pattern of change over time or between elections. Of considerable interest is whether a particular election or elections represent a departure from "normal" expectations or practice. The anomalous or unique case should serve as the basis for enlarging and expanding theoretical argument. Meta-analysis permits an examination that can identify an outlier. Whether such an outlier is simply a random occurrence or represents some important departure can be the basis of additional empirical consideration.

A meta-analysis provides a systematic way of taking a large body of existing literature and then combining and translating that morass into a standardized set of outcomes that summarize previous efforts. What this mode of analysis does is shift the focus on individual studies or the latest research to the accumulated body of findings thought of as a series of replications.

Model Evaluation and Testing

The focus of future meta-analyses should involve the development and testing of more sophisticated theoretical models. The current meta-analyses provide an empirical foundation to examine how various changes take place over time as well as across political systems. A comparison of data collected primarily in the United States with democratic elections in other countries can begin to examine the comparative influence of media coverage and its influence on political processes internationally.

The trajectory of technological and other social changes can be mapped onto elections at both the local, regional, and national level. The influence of changing political practices can be viewed historically to determine if the parameters are influenced by changes over time. What may have been a vital source of influence 100 years ago in elections may play a limited or no role in current elections. Changes in technology and the structure of the election process provide a dynamic set of influences in a constantly changing society. Political campaigns learn from one another and adapt to successful efforts by winning teams. For instance one campaign successfully obtains money from the Internet and other campaigns quickly copy that process in order to increase available resources.

The impact of legal changes can also be assessed by comparing the outcomes of studies examining the process (see below). Essentially, a meta-analysis can provide the means of examining a process longitudinally without requiring an individual researcher to conduct the analysis. A comparison of outcomes can be conducted even though data were collected by different persons in different jurisdictions under different conditions. Meta-analysis creates the possibility for the whole to be greater than the sum of the parts by providing techniques that permit analysis that go beyond the limitations of any particular dataset.

APPLICATIONS BY ADMINISTRATIVE, JUDICIAL, AND LEGISLATIVE BRANCHES

Scientific knowledge about some event or process provides information relevant to advising various policymaking bodies. Clearly, the legislative branch can consider research findings if supported by appropriate empirical evidence as a means for making determinations about legislative issues. The partisan nature of any decision carries more value than scientific evidence, but for lobbying and public interest groups the ability to marshal evidence and create public pressure holds persuasive potential over the long term. The assumption is that the vagaries of the political process are always subject to the current controversy but over the long run the assumption of democracy is that free and open debate will improve decision-making.

Administrative bodies can consider scientific evidence and use that as a basis for rule-making or other decisions. A good meta-analysis can become part of the evidence and that process. The basis for any regulation or set of advice usually involves some assumptions about the facts. The administrative bodies can provide a means of translating those findings into some type of policy regulation intended to further particular outcomes sought by the society.

The problem with any meta-analysis is that in the world of politics, a result can be spun. A fundamental limitation of meta-analysis is that multiple interpretations are always possible, so any agency, legislature, or political organization can reinterpret or recast a finding. The prognosis is that meta-analysis provides a justification and some scientific evidence for action but that, ultimately, the translation from knowledge to application requires an interpretive theory to provide that bridge between fact and policy. The dynamic nature of the communication environment means that any regulatory attempt simply provides a new set of rules to be interpreted and applied. The ability of campaigns, agencies, or organizations to find loopholes or alternatives creates a footrace that the regulatory body probably cannot win.

The goal of election campaigns is to provide an electorate with information (within a system of rules for this process) that permits a choice among options. The question of fairness is dependent on the ability of the electorate to access information that is accurate and reliable. The challenge of understanding the differences between competing policy options can be balanced if information is readily available and public. The utilization of meta-analysis in policy debates may or may not be permitted by regulatory bodies based on whether the technique is viewed as promoting a fair choice among competing options. A meta-analysis may provide information about some aspect of the process but cannot provide clear guidance on the preference for any regulatory action. The meta-analysis may indicate some outcomes for regulation; whether such outcomes are viewed as desirable depends in part on policymakers' faith in the findings.

CONCLUSION

As with any scientific advance, the implications for practice take time to fully comprehend and implement. Meta-analysis changes social science research by permitting the comprehensive and systematic analysis of enormous amounts of data collected over a long period of time using a plethora of different methods and techniques. Increasing the diversity of the methods and techniques analyzed is that the ability to generalize the findings also increases.

European countries have begun to implement as part of the political discourse, "evidence based" policymaking analysis. The focus for legislative or administrative bodies has begun to turn to the ability (or inability) to assemble evidence evaluating the effectiveness of various policies. The goal becomes the application of scientific data to improve the decision-making practices of the deliberative and judicial bodies. The challenge remains whether the limitations of the approaches to empirical knowledge and the obvious pitfalls of inappropriate or incorrect application of scientific knowledge can be avoided. Any view that takes the position that policy action may be obvious based on scientific data misunderstands the implications of scientific data for practice. A meta-analysis can provide information that may serve as a basis for a choice among options, but a meta-analysis mandates no particular action.

Meta-analysis provides the ability to evaluate the impact of various processes over time. As laws, technology, or other practices are changed, the impact of those changes can be tracked and compared to determine whether such changes impact the decision or information gathering practices of the electorate. A fundamental change can be identified, threats potentially understood, and solutions to particular problems, as well as the costs and implications, evaluated.

Meta-analysis constitutes a process that looks back in time to ascertain, with some sense of increased certainty, the current state of knowledge. The application of meta-analysis represents the challenge of taking a technique framed in understanding the history of practice and forecasting or understanding that history in a projective application to the future for the purposes of improving practice. Not surprisingly, there exists an inherent gap between that understanding of history, no matter how complete or accurate, and the ability to translate that knowledge into a fair and complete set of advice for future circumstances. While it is true that those who forget the past may be doomed to repeat it, the challenge of using knowledge is the assumption that the future is not simply predetermined by the past but susceptible to change based on current actions. As with any analytical tool, meta-analysis represents a source of scientific knowledge that provides improved understanding of processes and outcomes.

Ultimately, any enterprise involving an application of meta-analysis to improve practice will require an ethics of practice. For example, establishing that newspaper editorials influence election results does not indicate anything about the suitability of the practice. Clearly, newspaper endorsements are intentionally provided to influence election outcomes; meta-analysis only establishes whether such endorsements are effective. Understanding the occurrence of this outcome unfortunately provides little information about whether such practices are justified or should be permitted.

Meta-analysis should play an important role is assessing the impact of various practices related to politics. However, it is only when such knowledge is combined with an understanding of what constitutes desirable and/or ethical practice that the full benefits of the technique can be realized. Meta-analysis should not be done to distract or detract from debates over the ethics or the desirability of practices; instead, the impact of meta-analysis should be to increase the importance and urgency of such discussions. Meta-analysis takes such debates from the realm of the hypothetical and possible, and makes them part of the reality of practice with direct implications for the political process. A consistent body of empirical research demonstrating a consistent outcome in political communication paired with an accurate interpretation of that relationship provides a basis for application.

REFERENCES

Aguinis, H., Sturman, M. C., & Pierce, C. A. (2008). Comparison of three meta-analytic procedures for estimating moderating effects of categorical variables. *Organizational Research Methods, 11,* 9–34.

Allen, M. (1991). Meta-analysis comparing effectiveness of one and two-sided messages. *Western Journal of Speech Communication, 55,* 390–404.

Allen, M. (1993). Determining the persuasiveness of message sidedness: A prudent note about utilizing research summaries. *Western Journal of Communication, 57,* 98–103.

Allen, M., Bruflat, R., Fucilla, R, Kramer, M., McKellips, S., Ryan, D., & Spiegelhoff, M. (2000). Testing the persuasiveness of evidence: Combining narrative and statistical evidence. *Communication Research Reports, 17,* 331–336.

Allen, M., & Burrell, N. (2002). The negativity effect in political advertising: A meta-analysis. In J. Dillard and M. Pfau (Eds.), *The persuasion handbook: Developments in theory and practice* (pp. 83–98). Thousand Oaks, CA: Sage.

Allen, M., Hale, J., Mongeau, P., Berkowitz-Stafford, S., Stafford, S., Shanahan, W., Agee, P., Dillon, K., Jackson, R., & Ray, C. (1990). Testing a model of message sidedness: Three replications. *Communication Monographs, 57,* 275–291.

Allen, M., & Preiss, R. (1997). Comparing the persuasiveness of narrative and statistical evidence using meta-analysis. *Communication Research Reports, 14,* 125–131.

Allen, M., Preiss, R. W., & Gayle, B. M. (2006). Meta-analytic examination of the base-rate fallacy. *Communication Research Reports, 23,* 1–7.

Benoit, W. L., Hansen, G. J., & Verser, R. M. (2003). A meta-analysis of the effects of viewing U.S. presidential debates. *Communication Monographs, 70,* 335–350.

Boster, F. J., & Mongeau, P. (1984). Fear-arousing persuasive messages. In R. Bostrom (Ed.), *Communication Yearbook 8* (pp. 330–375). Newbury Park, CA: Sage.

Cheung, M. W. L., & Chan, W. (2005). Meta-analytic structural equation modeling: A two-stage approach. *Psychological Methods, 10,* 40–64.

Cook, T. D., et al. (Eds.). (1990). *Meta-analysis for explanation: A casebook.* New York: Russell Sage Foundation.

Cooper, H., & Hedges, L. V. (Eds.). (1994). *Handbook of research synthesis.* New York: Russell Sage Foundation.

D'Alessio, D., & Allen, M. (2000). Media bias in presidential elections: A meta-analysis, *Journal of Communication, 50,* 133–156.

D'Alessio, D., & Allen, M. (2002). Selective exposure and dissonance after decisions. *Psychological Reports, 91,* 527–532.

D'Alessio, D., & Allen, M. (2007). On the role of newspaper ownership on bias in presidential campaign coverage by newspapers. In R. Preiss, B. Gayle, N. Burrell, M. Allen, & J. Bryant, J. (Eds.), *Mass media effects research: Advances through meta-analysis* (pp. 429–454). Mahwah, NJ: Lawrence Erlbaum.

Dindia, K., & Allen, M. (1992). Sex differences in self-disclosure: A meta-analysis. *Psychological Bulletin, 112,* 106–124.

Emmers-Sommer, T., & Allen, M. (1999). Variables related to sexual coercion: A path model. *Journal of Social and Personal Relationships, 16*, 659–678.

Glynn, C. J., Hayes, A. F., & Shanahan, J. (1997). Perceived support for one's opinion and willingness to speak out: A meta-analysis of survey studies of the "spiral of silence." *Public Opinion Quarterly, 61*, 452–463.

Hansen, G. J., & Benoit, W. L. (2007). Communication forms as predictors of issue knowledge in presidential campaigns: A meta-analytic assessment. *Mass Communication & Society, 10*(2), 1–22.

Hedges, L. V. (1987). How hard is hard science and how soft is soft science? The empirical cumulativeness of research. *American Psychologist, 42*, 443–445.

Hedges, L. V., & Olkin, I. (1985). *Statistical methods for meta-analysis.* Orlando, FL: Academic Press.

Hollander, B. A. (2007). Media use and political turnout. In R. Preiss, B. Gayle, N. Burrell, M. Allen, & J. Bryant, J. (Eds.), *Mass media effects research: Advances through meta-analysis* (pp. 377–390). Mahwah, NJ: Lawrence Erlbaum.

Hunter, J. E., & Schmidt, F. (2002). *Methods of meta-analysis: Correcting for artifact and bias in research findings* (2nd ed.). Newbury Park, CA: Sage.

Johnson, B. T., Scott-Sheldon, L. A., Synder, L. A., Noar, S. M., & Huedo-Medina, T. B. (2008). Contemporary approaches to meta-analysis in communication research. In A. Hayes, M. Slater, & L. Synder (Eds.), *Advanced data analysis methods for communication research* (pp. 311–348). Thousand Oaks, CA: Sage.

Lau, R., & Sigelman, L. (1999). The effects of negative political advertisements: A meta-analytical assessment. *American Political Science Review, 93*, 851–875.

Lau, R., Sigelman, L., & Rovner, I. B. (2007). The effects of negative political campaigns: A meta-analytic reassessment. *Journal of Politics, 69*, 1176–1209.

Miron, D., & Bryant, J. (2007). Mass media and voter turnout. In R. Preiss, B. Gayle, N. Burrell, M. Allen, & J. Bryant (Eds.), *Mass media effects research: Advances through meta-analysis* (pp. 391–414). Mahwah, NJ: Lawrence Erlbaum.

Muller, D., Judd, C. M., & Yzerbyt, V. Y. (2005). When moderation is mediated and mediation is moderated. *Journal of Personality and Social Psychology, 89*, 853–863.

O'Keefe, D. (1993). The persuasive effects of message sidedness variations: A cautionary note concerning Allen's (1991) meta-analysis. *Western Journal of Communication, 57*, 87–97.

O'Keefe, D. (1999). How to handle opposing arguments in persuasive messages: A meta-analytic review of the effects of one-sided and two-sided messages. In M. Roloff (Ed.), *Communication Yearbook 22* (pp. 209–250). Thousand Oaks, CA: Sage.

Paul, B., Salwen, M. B., & Dupagne, M. (2007). The third-person effect: A meta-analysis of the perceptual hypothesis. In R. Preiss, B. Gayle, N. Burrell, M. Allen, & J. Bryant (Eds.), *Mass media effects research: Advances through meta-analysis* (pp. 81–102). Mahwah, NJ: Lawrence Erlbaum.

Petitti, D. (2000). *Meta-analysis, decision analysis, and cost effectiveness analysis.* New York: Oxford University Press.

Rosenthal, R., & DiMatteo, M. R. (2001). Meta-analysis: Recent developments in quantitative methods for literature reviews. *Annual Review of Psychology, 52*, 59–82.

Shanahan, J., Gynn, C., & Hayes, A. (2007). The spiral of silence: A meta-analysis and its impact. In R. Preiss, B. Gayle, N. Burrell, M. Allen, & J. Bryant (Eds.), *Mass media effects research: Advances through meta-analysis* (pp. 415–428.). Mahwah: Lawrence Erlbaum.

Stanley, T. D., & Jarrell, S. B. (1989). Meta-regression analysis: A quantitative method of literature surveys. *Journal of Economic Surveys, 19*, 299–308.

Viswesvaran, C., & Ones, D. S. (1995). Theory testing: Combining psychometric meta-analysis and structural equation modeling. *Personnel Psychology, 48*, 865–885.

Witte, K., & Allen, M. (2000). A meta-analysis of fear appeals: Implications for effective health campaigns. *Health Education & Behavior, 27*, 591–615.

III
EXPERIMENTAL METHODS

8

Experimental Designs for Political Communication Research

Using New Technology and Online Participant Pools to Overcome the Problem of Generalizability

Shanto Iyengar
Department of Communication
Political Communication Lab
Stanford University

As recently as three decades ago, the use of experimental methods was a rarity in the disciplines of political science, sociology, and communications. Beginning in the early 1980s, a surge of interest in the interdisciplinary field of political psychology set in motion a trickle of experimental methods into several subfields of political science, including political communication. But despite the increased interest, longstanding concerns over the artificiality of experimental settings, the unrepresentativeness of experimental subject pools, and the questionable generalizability of experimental findings has continued to impede the further diffusion of experimental methods.

In this chapter I describe the inherent strengths of the experiment as a basis for causal inference, using recent examples from political communication research. I argue that the technological advances associated with the rapid diffusion of the Internet have already gone a long way toward neutralizing the traditional weaknesses of experimentation for two reasons. First, experiments administered online can prove just as realistic as conventional experiments. Second, issues of sampling bias—previously endemic to experiments—can be overcome through the greater "reach" of online experiments and, in addition, by the application of standard probability sampling techniques to the recruitment of online experimental participants. These developments significantly alleviate concerns over the generalizability of experimental research and, as a result, experiments now represent a dominant methodology for political communication.

CAUSAL INFERENCE: THE STRENGTH OF EXPERIMENTS

In the field of political communication, the principal advantage of the experiment over the survey— and the focus of the discussion that follows—is the researcher's ability to isolate and test the effects of specific components of political messages. Consider the case of political campaigns. At the aggregate level, campaigns encompass a concatenation of messages, channels, and sources, all of which may influence the audience, often in inconsistent directions. The researcher's task is to identify specific causal factors and delineate the range of their relevant attributes. Even at the relatively narrow level of campaign advertisements, for instance, there is virtually an infinite number of potential causal factors, both verbal and visual. What was it about the infamous "Willie Horton" advertisement that is thought to have moved so many American voters away from Michael Dukakis during the 1988 presidential campaign? Was it, as widely alleged, Mr. Horton's race? Or was it the violent and brutal nature of his described behavior, the fact that he was a convict, the race of his victim, or something else entirely? Experiments make it possible to isolate the explanation, whether it be verbally based or in the form of audiovisual cues. Surveys, on the other hand, can only provide indirect evidence on self-reported exposure to the causal variable in question.

Of course, experiments not only shed light on treatment effects but also enable researchers to test more elaborate hypotheses concerning the interaction of message factors with individual difference variables. Not all individuals are equally susceptible to incoming messages. Perhaps Democrats with a weak party affiliation and strong sense of racial prejudice were especially likely to sour on Governor Dukakis in the aftermath of exposure to the Horton advertisement.

The weaknesses of survey design for isolating the effects of mass communication have been amply documented. In a widely cited paper, Hovland (1959) identified several problematic artifacts of survey research including unreliable measures of media exposure. Clearly, exposure is a necessary precondition for media influence, but self-reported exposure to media coverage is hardly equivalent to actual exposure. People have notoriously weak memories for political experiences (see, for instance, Bradburn, Rips, & Shevell, 1987; Pierce & Lovrich, 1982). In the Ansolabehere and Iyengar experiments on campaign advertising (which spanned the 1990, 1992, and 1994 election cycles), over 50% of the participants who were exposed to a political advertisement were unable, *some 30 minutes later*, to recall having seen the advertisement (Ansolabehere, 2006). In a more recent example, Vavreck found that nearly half of a control group *not* shown a public service message responded either that they couldn't remember or that they *had* seen it (Vavreck, 2007; also see Prior, 2003). Errors of memory also compromise recall-based measures of exposure to particular news stories (see Gunther, 1987) or news sources (see Price & Zaller, 1993). Of course, the scale of the error in self-reports necessarily attenuates survey-based estimates of the effects of political campaigns (see Bartels, 1993, 1996; Prior, 2003).

An even more serious obstacle to causal inference in the survey context is that self-reported media exposure is typically endogenous to a host of political attitudes researchers seek to explain, including candidate preference. That is, those who claim to read newspapers or watch television news on a regular basis differ systematically (in ways that matter to their vote choice) from those who do not. This problem has become more acute in the aftermath of the revolution in information technology since the rise of the Internet. In 1968, approximately 75% of the adult viewing audience watched one of the three network evening newscasts (ABC, CBS, or NBC), but by 2008 the combined audience for network news was less than 35% of the viewing audience. In 2008, the only people watching the news were those with a keen interest in politics; almost everyone else had migrated to more entertaining, nonpolitical programming alternatives (see Prior, 2007).

The endogeneity issue has multiple ramifications for political communication research. First, consider those instances where self-reported exposure is correlated with political predispositions but actual exposure is not. This is generally the case with televised political advertising. Most voters encounter political ads unintentionally, in the course of watching their preferred television programs in which the commercial breaks contain a heavy dose of political messages. Thus, actual exposure is idiosyncratic (based on the viewer's preference for particular programs), while self-reported exposure is often based on political predispositions.

The divergence in the antecedents of self-reported exposure has predictable consequences for "effects" research. In experiments that manipulated the tone of campaign advertising, Ansolabehere and Iyengar (1995) found that *actual exposure* to negative messages "demobilized" voters, i.e., discouraged turnout. However, on the basis of *self-reports*, survey researchers concluded that exposure to negative campaign advertising stimulated turnout (Wattenberg & Brians, 1999). Was it recalled exposure to negative advertising that prompted turnout, or was greater interest in campaigns among likely voters responsible for their higher level of recall? When recall of advertising in the same survey was treated as endogenous to vote intention and the effects reestimated using appropriate two-stage methods, the sign of the coefficient for recall was reversed: those who recalled negative advertisements were *less* likely to express an intention to vote (see Ansolabehere, Iyengar, & Simon, 1999). Unfortunately, most survey-based analyses fail to disentangle the reciprocal effects of self-reported exposure to the campaign and partisan attitudes and behaviors. As this example suggests, in cases where actual exposure is less selective than reported exposure, self-reports may prove especially biased.

In other scenarios, the tables may be turned and the experimental researcher may be at a disadvantage. Actual exposure to political messages in the real world is typically not analogous to random assignment. Unlike advertisements, news coverage of political events can be avoided by choice, meaning that exposure is limited to the politically engaged. Thus, as Hovland (1959) pointed out, manipulational control actually weakens the ability to generalize to the real world where exposure to politics is typically voluntary. In these cases, as noted below, it is important for the researcher to use designs that combine manipulation with self-selected exposure.

In summary, the fundamental advantage of the experimental approach is the ability to isolate causal variables, which remain the basis for experimental manipulations. In the next section, I describe manipulations designed to isolate the effects of negative advertising campaigns, racial cues in television news coverage of crime, and the physical similarity of candidates to voters.

Negativity in Campaign Advertising

At the very least, establishing the effects of negativity in campaign advertising on voters' attitudes requires varying the tone of a campaign advertisement while holding all other attributes of the message constant. Despite the significant increase in scholarly attention to negative advertising, few studies live up to this minimal threshold of control (for exceptions, see Biocca, 1991; Brader, 2006; for examples of survey-based analyses see, Finkel & Geer, 1998; Freedman & Goldstein, 1999; Kahn & Kenney, 1999).

A series of experiments conducted by Ansolabehere and Iyengar manipulated negativity by varying the content of the verbal channel (soundtrack) of an advertisement while preserving the visual backdrop. The negative version of the message typically placed the sponsoring candidate on the unpopular side of some salient policy issue. During the 1990 gubernatorial campaign between Pete Wilson (Republican) and Dianne Feinstein (Democrat), the treatment ads positioned the candidates either as opponents or proponents of offshore oil drilling and thus as either friends or foes of the environment. This manipulation was implemented by simply substituting the word "yes" for the word "no." In the positive conditions, the script began as follows: "When federal bureaucrats asked for permission to drill for oil off the coast of California, [Pete Wilson or Dianne Feinstein] said no . . ." In the negative conditions, we substituted "said yes" for "said no." An additional substitution was written into the end of the ad when the announcer stated that the candidate in question would either work to "preserve" or "destroy" California's natural beauty. Given the consensual nature of the issue, negativity could be attributed to candidates who claimed their opponent was soft on polluters.[1]

The results from these studies (which featured mayoral, gubernatorial, senatorial, and presidential candidates) indicated that participants exposed to negative rather than positive advertisements were less likely to express an intention to vote. The demobilizing effects of exposure to negative advertising were especially prominent among viewers who did not identify with either of the two political parties (see Ansolabehere & Iyengar, 1995).

Racial Cues in Local News Coverage of Crime

As any regular viewer of television will attest, crime is a frequent topic in broadcast news. In response to market pressures, television stations have adopted a formulaic approach to covering crime, an approach designed to attract and maintain the highest degree of audience interest. This "crime script" suggests that crime is invariably violent and those who perpetrate crime are disproportionately nonwhite. Because the crime script is encountered so frequently (several times each day in many cities) in the course of watching local news, it has attained the status of common knowledge. Just as we know full well what happens when one walks into a restaurant, we also know—or at least think we know—what happens when a crime occurs (Gilliam & Iyengar, 2000).

In a series of recent experiments, researchers have documented the effects of both the race and violence elements of the crime script on audience attitudes (see Gilliam, Iyengar, Simon, & Wright, 1996; Gilliam, Valentino, & Beckman, 2002). For illustrative purposes, I focus here on the race element. In essence, these studies were designed to manipulate the race/ethnicity of the principal suspect depicted in a news report while maintaining all other visual characteristics. The original stimulus consisted of a typical local news report, which included a close-up still "mug shot" of the suspect. The picture was digitized, "painted" to alter the perpetrator's skin color, and then re-edited into the news report. As shown in Figure 8.1, beginning with two different perpetrators (a white male and a black male), we were able through the use of technology to produce altered versions of each individual in which their race was reversed, but all other features remained identical. Participants who watched the news report in which the suspect was thought to be non-white expressed greater support for "punitive" policies, e.g., imposition of "three strikes and you're out" remedies, treatment of juveniles as adults, and support for the death penalty. Given the precision of the design, these differences in the responses of the subjects exposed to the white or black perpetrators could only be attributed to the perpetrator's race (see Gilliam & Iyengar, 2000).

Facial Similarity as a Political Cue

A consistent finding in the political science literature is that voters gravitate to candidates who most resemble themselves on questions of political ideology, public policies, and party affiliation. But what about physical resemblance: Are voters also attracted to candidates who look like them?

Several lines of research suggest that physical similarity in general, and facial similarity in particular, is a relevant criterion for choosing between candidates. Thus, frequency of exposure to any stimulus–including faces– induces a preference for that stimulus over other, less familiar stimuli (Zajonc, 2001). Moreover, evolutionary psychologists argue that physical similarity is a kinship cue and there is considerable evidence that humans are motivated to treat their kin preferentially (see, for instance, Burnstein, Crandall, & Kitayama, 1994; Nelson, 2001).

In order to isolate the effects of facial similarity on voting preferences, researchers obtained digital photographs of 172 registered voters selected at random from a national Internet panel (for

FIGURE 8.1 Race of suspect manipulation.

details on the methodology, see Bailenson, Iyengar, Yee, & Collins 2008). Participants were asked to provide their photographs approximately three weeks in advance of the 2004 presidential election. One week before the election, these same participants were asked to participate in an online survey of political attitudes that included a variety of questions about the presidential candidates (George W. Bush and John Kerry). The computer screens on which these candidate questions appeared also included photographs of the two candidates displayed side by side. Within this split-panel presentation, participants had their own face morphed with either Bush or Kerry at a ratio of 60% of the candidate and 40% of themselves.[2] Figure 8.2 shows two of the morphs used in this study.

The results of the face morphing study revealed a significant interaction between facial similarity and strength of the participant's party affiliation. Among strong partisans, the similarity manipulation had no effect; these voters were already convinced of their vote choice. But weak partisans and independents, whose voting preferences were not as entrenched, moved in the direction of the more similar candidate (see Bailenson, Iyengar, Yee, & Collins, 2008). Thus, the evidence suggests that nonverbal cues can influence voting, even in the most visible and contested of political campaigns.[3]

In short, as these examples indicate, the experimental method provides unequivocal causal evidence because the researcher is able to isolate the causal factor in question, manipulate its presence or absence, and hold other potential causes constant. With carefully controlled experimental studies, then, any observed differences between experimental and control groups can be attributed to the factor that was manipulated.

FIGURE 8.2 Facial similarity manipulation.

IMPROVED MEASURES OF AUDIENCE RESPONSE

The ability to launch experiments online further strengthens the ability of communication researchers to draw causal inferences by providing more precisely calibrated indicators of audience reactions to media messages. In addition to the qualities of conventional experimental studies, online experiments permit observation of information-seeking behavior as well as user reactions to visual, verbal, and audiovisual stimuli *and* enable finely grained, longitudinal indicators of voter response to campaign advertisements.

Behavioral Indicators of Selective Exposure

Researchers have long assumed that people possess an innate preference for attitude-consistent messages or sources of information. According to this "selective exposure" hypothesis, voters seek to avoid information that clashes with their preexisting beliefs (e.g., Festinger, 1957) and instead put themselves in the path of information they expect to agree with. As Lazarsfeld, Berelson, and Gaudet (1948) pointed out, biased exposure to information has clear implications for the exercise of informed citizenship: "In recent years there has been a good deal of talk by men of good will about the desirability and necessity of guaranteeing the free exchange of ideas in the market place of public opinion. Such talk has centered upon the problem of keeping free the channels of expression and communication. Now we find that the consumers of ideas, if they have made a decision on the issue, themselves erect high tariff walls against alien notions" (p. 89).

Given the practical difficulties of delivering large quantities of information, the typical study on selective exposure provides participants with only a limited range of choice. Indeed, Cotton (1985) observed that the selective exposure literature had failed to address "how people actively seek and avoid information on their own" (p. 29) in naturalistic settings. Digital technology now makes it possible to deliver voluminous quantities of information in a compact and easy-to-navigate format.

In a study of selective exposure during the 2000 presidential campaign, researchers provided a representative sample of registered voters with a multimedia CD containing extensive information about candidates Bush and Gore—including text of all of their stump speeches delivered between July 1 and October 7, a full set of televised ads, and the texts of the Democratic and Republican party platforms. The CD also included the soundtrack and transcripts of the candidates' nomination acceptance speeches as well as the first televised debate. All told, the information amounted to over 600 pages of text and two hours of multimedia (see Iyengar et al., 2008).

The campaign CD was delivered to a representative sample of American adult Internet users two weeks before Election Day. Participants were informed in advance that their use of the CD would be examined by the researchers (and they were asked not to share the CD with members of their family or friends). As the user navigated through the CD offerings, a built-in tracking feature recorded every visited page (in the order of visit), the number of total times the CD was accessed, and the length of each browsing session in a log file on the user's hard drive. Upon completing a post-election questionnaire, participants were given instructions for finding and uploading their log-files. From these files, we were able to monitor the degree to which CD users gravitated to information provided by the candidate they preferred. The findings revealed only partial evidence of selective exposure based on partisanship; Republicans (and conservatives) showed a lopsided preference for information concerning Bush, but Democrats (and liberals) proved more evenhanded in their information-seeking behavior.

The tendency for partisans on the right to show greater avoidance of attitude-discrepant information is attributable to both dispositional and contextual factors. In comparison with liberals, conservatives may have a more intense sense of group identity, thus heightening their need to avoid dissonance. On the other hand, the greater selectivity among Republicans may reflect habituation over time. Since the launch of the Fox News network in 1996, Republicans have enjoyed easy access to television news with a pro-Republican tilt. The tendency to avoid attitude-discrepant information encouraged by Fox News may have promoted similar information-seeking behaviors in a non-news context.

Continuous Tracking of Viewers' Reactions to Campaign Ads

Campaign advertising is the major source of information for voters in nonpresidential elections. Understanding voters' reactions to ads is thus fundamental to understanding the effectiveness of campaigns. Most researchers who investigate the effectiveness of ad campaigns typically rely on verbal measures to gauge the influence of ads. Viewers might be asked if they agreed or disagreed with the ad in question, or if the ad elicited positive or negative feelings concerning the sponsoring candidate. These measures ask respondents to provide a post hoc summary or "averaged" assessment of their reaction to the content and imagery of ads.

With the diffusion of digital technology, it is possible to monitor viewer response to advertising on a continuous basis, over the entire playing of the ad (see Iyengar, Jackman, & Hahn, 2007). Rather than asking for a summary assessment *after* viewers have watched the ad, researchers can use an online "dialing" (or sliding scale) procedure that synchronizes viewers' self-reported feelings concerning the soundtrack and visual imagery they encounter at any given moment *during* the playing of the ad.

This dial meter/sliding scale methodology was implemented online in a study of the 2006 senate elections in six battleground states. A sample of approximately 1,900 registered voters with Internet access was selected at random from a nationwide online panel. Participants were instructed (and given a practice task) online on how to move a slider located immediately below the video in accordance with their feelings about the content of the ad. The specific instruction was: "If what you see or hear makes you feel good, or you agree with the speaker, indicate this by moving the slider towards the green end. If, however, your reaction is negative, and you dislike what you see or hear, then move the slider to the red zone."

Special Javascript-based software recorded the position of the slider once a second by evenly dividing the range of dial positions into 100 intervals, with zero indicating the left or negative end of the dial, and 100 the right or positive end. Thus, as the ad played, we could monitor voters' reactions in real time from beginning to end. At the start of each ad, the slider was positioned at the neutral or "50" position, and this was the first dial value recorded for each ad view. Figure 8.3 displays a pair of screen shots from one of the Tennessee conditions featuring the race between Republican Bob Corker and Democrat Harold Ford Jr., with two hypothetical settings of the dial (the top one negative, the bottom one positive).

The results from this study indicated that most ads polarize partisan viewers; over the course of viewing ads, Democrats and Republicans inevitably move in opposite directions (see Figure 8.4). This pattern is consistent with prior research showing that exposure to campaign ads strengthens viewers' partisan predispositions (Ansolabehere & Iyengar, 1995). While partisans responded rapidly to the content of advertising, Independents were typically unmoved, remaining lukewarm over the entire playing of the ad.

A further finding from this study was that the rate of polarization proved variable across the partisanship of the sponsoring candidate. Democrats consistently converged (arrived at their stable end point) faster in response to Democratic ads than did Republicans in response to Republican ads. In effect, Democratic ads resonated more powerfully with Democrats than Republican ads did with Republicans. Perhaps this effect was due to the partisan appeal of the ads' messages. Democratic ads, which tended to highlight the state of the war in Iraq and the fallout from the Abramoff ethics scandal linking the Republican candidate with President Bush, mobilized the Democratic base more effectively than generic Republican appeals on national security, immigration, and taxes.

THE ISSUE OF GENERALIZABILITY

The problem of limited generalizability, long the bane of experimental design, is manifested in three different contexts: the realism of the experimental setting, the representativeness of the participant pool, and the discrepancy between experimental control and self-selected exposure to media presentations.

Mundane Realism

Because of the need for tightly controlled stimuli, the setting in which the typical laboratory experiment occurs is often quite dissimilar from the setting in which subjects ordinarily experience the "target" phenomenon, or media message. Concern over the artificial properties of laboratory experiments has given rise to an increased use of so-called field experiments in which the procedures and settings more closely reflect ordinary life.[4]

A common strategy in field experiments is the reliance on interventions with which subjects are familiar. The Ansolabehere/Iyengar campaign experiments, conducted in the Los Angeles area

FIGURE 8.3 Screen shots from online dials.
Note: As the ad played, participants could move the slider to indicate their feelings
about the content of the ad, with the position of the dial recorded once a second.

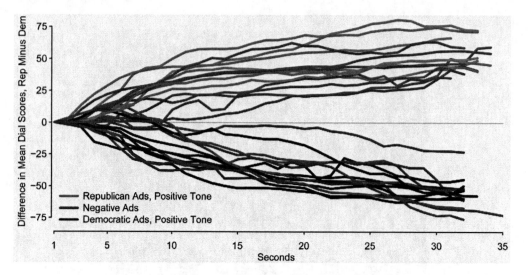

FIGURE 8.4 Partisan polarization in dial scores.

in the early 1990s, were realistic in the sense that they occurred during ongoing campaigns characterized by heavy levels of televised advertising (see Ansolabehere & Iyengar, 1995). The presence of political advertisements in a local newscast (the vehicle used to convey the manipulation) was hardly unusual or unexpected since candidates advertise most heavily during news programs. The advertisements featured real candidates—Democrats and Republicans, liberals and conservatives, males and females, incumbents and challengers—as the sponsors. The material that made up the experimental stimuli were selected either from actual advertisements used by the candidates during the campaign, or were produced to emulate typical campaign advertisements. In the case of the latter, the researchers spliced together footage from actual advertisements or news reports, editing the treatment ads to be representative of the genre. (The need for experimental control made it necessary for our stimulus ads to differ from actual political ads along several important attributes, including the absence of music and appearance of the sponsoring candidate.)

Realism also depends upon the physical setting in which the experiment is administered. Asking subjects to report to a location on a university campus may suit the researcher but may make the experience of watching television for the participant equivalent to visiting the doctor. A more realistic strategy is to provide subjects with a milieu that closely matches the setting of their living room or den. To that end, the Ansolabehere/Iyengar experimental "laboratory" was designed to resemble, as closely as possible, the natural "habitat" of the television viewer.[5] Comfortable couches and chairs were arranged in front of a television set, with houseplants and wall hangings placed around the room. Respondents also had access to refreshments and reading material (newspapers and magazines) during the viewing sessions. In most cases, a family member or friend took part in the experiment at the same time, so that subjects did not find themselves sitting next to a stranger while viewing the target advertisements.

A further step toward realism concerns the power of the manipulation (also referred to as experimental realism). Of course, the researcher would like the manipulation to have an effect. At the same time, it is important that the required task or stimulus not overwhelm the subject (as in the Milgram obedience studies, where the task of administering an electric shock to a fellow participant proved overpowering and ethically suspect). In the case of our campaign advertising experiments, we resolved the experimental realism versus mundane realism tradeoff by embedding the manipulation in a commercial break of a local newscast. For each treatment condition, the stimulus ad appeared with other nonpolitical ads, and because subjects were led to believe that the study was about "selective perception of news," they had no incentive to pay particular attention to ads. Overall, the manipulation was relatively small, amounting to 30 seconds of a 15-minute videotape.

In general, there is a significant tradeoff between experimental realism and manipulational control. In the advertising studies described above, the fact that subjects were exposed to the treatments in the company of others meant that their level of familiarity with fellow subjects was subject to unknown variation. And producing experimental ads that more closely emulated actual ads (e.g., by including a soundtrack and featuring the sponsoring candidate) would have necessarily introduced a series of confounding variables associated with the appearance and voice of the sponsor. Despite these tradeoffs, however, it is still possible to achieve a high degree of experimental control with stimuli that closely resemble the "naturally occurring" phenomenon of interest.

Sampling Bias

The most widely cited limitation of experiments concerns the composition of the subject pool (Sears, 1986). Typically, laboratory experiments are administered upon "captive" populations— college students who must serve as guinea pigs in order to gain course credit. College sophomores may be a convenient subject population for academic researchers, but are they comparable to "real people"?

In conventional experimental research, it is possible to broaden the participant pool but at considerable cost and effort. Locating experimental facilities at public locations and enticing a quasi-representative sample to participate proves both cost- and labor-intensive. Typical costs include rental fees for an experimental facility in a public area (such as a shopping mall), recruitment of participants, and training and compensation of research staff to administer the experiments. In our local news experiments conducted in Los Angeles in the summer and fall of 1999, the total costs per subject amounted to approximately $45. Fortunately, as described below, technology has both enlarged the pool of potential participants and reduced the per capita cost of administering an experimental study.

Today, traditional experimental methods can be rigorously and far more efficiently administered using an online platform. Utilizing the Internet as the experimental "site" provides several advantages over conventional locales, including the ability to reach diverse populations without geographic limitations. Advances in multimedia have made it possible to bring video presentations to the computer screen with relative ease. Indeed, it is now standard for candidates to feature their televised ads on their websites, and access to video reports from a variety of online sources is growing. The technology is sufficiently user friendly that most Web users can now "self-administer" experimental manipulations. Compared with conventional shopping mall studies, therefore, the costs of online experiments are minimal. Moreover, with ever-increasing use of the Internet, not only are online samples becoming more diverse but the setting in which participants encounter the manipulation (surfing the Web on their own) is also becoming more realistic and common.

"Drop-in" Samples

The Political Communication Laboratory at Stanford University has been administering experiments over the Internet for nearly a decade. One of the Lab's more popular online experiments is "whack-a-pol" (http://pcl.stanford.edu/exp/whack/polm), modeled on the well-known whack-a-mole arcade game (see Figure 8.5). Ostensibly, the game provides participants with the opportunity to "bash" well-known political figures. Before playing the game, participants complete a consent form and brief pretest survey. After playing the game, they self-administer the post-test survey. Since the game imposes severe time and attention constraints (players see five different moving faces, each hittable for a period of between two and three seconds), the whacking task provides an unobtrusive measure of group identity. That is, we expect subjects to target "out-group" figures (defined on the basis of party identification, i.e., Democrats should target Republicans and vice-versa) for more extensive whacking. Party affiliation is the most salient basis for political choice, although one could replicate this design with other groupings such as gender or ethnicity.

Since going live in 2001, over 2,000 visitors have played whack-a-pol. These "drop in" subjects found the PCL site on their own initiative. How does this group compare with a representative sample of adult Americans with home access to the Internet and a representative sample of all voting-age adults? We can use two different baselines to assess this. First, we gauge the degree of online self-selection; that is, the degree of divergence between drop-in participants and typical Internet users. The second comparison indicates the degree of discrepancy between self-selected online samples and all voting-age adults (from a sample drawn in 2000).

The results of these comparisons showed two broad patterns. The more surprising of the two was that participants in the online experiments reasonably approximated the online user population. However, as described below, there is evidence of a nagging digital divide in that major categories of the population remain underrepresented in online studies.

The match between our drop-in experimental subjects and the typical Internet user was closest with respect to race/ethnicity and education. The predominance (over 80%) of whites and

FIGURE 8.5 Whack-a-pol screenshot.

college-educated (50%) users in the online participant pool was approximately the same as among all Internet users. The key background variable of party identification also proved consistent across our online participants and the user community at large. Among whack-a-pol players, Republicans were the largest group (37%), followed by Democrats and Independents. Although the participant pool was somewhat less Democratic (and more Republican) than the broader online population, it appears that party identification is not a significant predictor of the decision to participate in online experiments with political content.

The clearest evidence of selection bias vis-à-vis the online population emerged with age and gender. The mean age of our drop-in study participants was 31 (it was 41 for the wider online sample); participants were also more likely to be male (65%) than the typical online user (52%). The sharp divergence in age between the drop-in and online subject pools may be attributed to the general "surfing" proclivities of younger users and the fact that our studies were launched from an academic server that is more likely to be encountered by college students. The gender gap is more puzzling and may reflect differences in political interest. Our studies are explicitly political in focus, which may act as a disincentive to potential female subjects, who express less interest in politics than male subjects.

In summary, if the population of interest is limited to American Internet users, the results of our online experiments can at least be generalized with respect to race, education, and party affiliation. Experimental participants deviate from the online population on the attributes of gender and age, drawing disproportionately male and younger participants.

Turning to the comparisons between online participants and the population at large (the digital divide question), it is clear that the technology access threshold remains a strong liability for online research. In relation to the broader adult population, our experimental participants were younger, more educated, more likely to be white males, and less apt to identify as a Democrat. With the exception of age and gender, these differences were just as stark when comparisons were made between the offline and online populations (for evidence of the scale of differences between Internet users and nonusers, see Papadakis, 2000; Pew Internet and American Life Project, 2005).

Although these data suggest that people who participate in online media experiments are no microcosm of the adult population overall, the fundamental advantage of online over conventional field experiments cannot be overlooked. Conventional experiments recruit subjects from particular locales; online experiments draw subjects from across the country— and from around the world. The Ansolabehere/Iyengar campaign advertising experiments, for example, recruited subjects from a particular area of southern California (greater Los Angeles). Our online experiments, in contrast, attracted a sample of subjects from 30 different American states and several countries.

Expanding the Pool of Online Participants

One way to broaden the online subject pool is by recruiting participants from more well-known and frequently visited websites. News sites that cater to political junkies, for example, may be motivated to increase their "circulation" by collaborating with scholars whose research studies focus on controversial issues. While the researcher obtains data which may be used for scholarly purposes, the news organization gains a form of "interactivity" through which the audience may be engaged. Playing an arcade game or watching a brief video clip that doubles as an experimental stimulus may pique participants' interest, thus encouraging them to return to the site and boosting the news organization's online traffic.

In recent years, PCL has partnered with Washingtonpost.com to expand the reach of online experiments. Studies designed by PCL—focusing on topics of interest to people who read

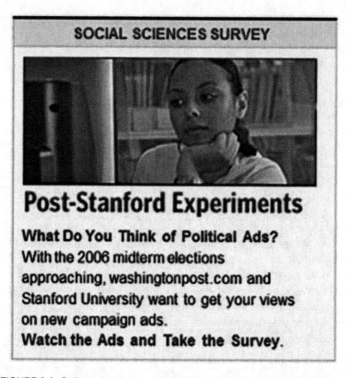

FIGURE 8.6 Online advertisement for the Washingtonpost.com experiment.

Washingtonpost.com—are advertised on the website's "Politics" section (see Figure 8.6). Readers who click on a link advertising the study in question are sent directly to the PCL site, where they complete the study, and are then returned to Washingtonpost.com. The results from these experiments are then described in a newspaper story and online column. In cases where the results were especially topical (e.g., a study of news preferences described below showing that Republicans avoided CNN and NPR in favor of Fox News), a correspondent from Washingtonpost.com hosted an online "chat" session to discuss the results and answer questions.

The development of cable television and explosion of media outlets on the Internet have created a fragmented information environment in which cable news, talk radio, and online news outlets compete for audience attention. Given this dramatic increase in the number of available news outlets, it is not surprising that media choices increasingly reflect partisan considerations. In the new media environment, there is growing evidence that partisans gravitate to sources perceived as more congenial to their preferences (see Pfau, Houston, & Semmler, 2007).

A PCL-Washingtonpost.com experiment was designed to investigate the relationship between political predispositions and news preferences, namely, the extent to which partisans on the right treated Fox News as a preferred provider. To explore this idea, the study assessed whether attention to an identical news story increased or decreased when the story was attributed to Fox News, NPR, CNN, or the BBC.

Using the MSNBC daily news feed (which includes news reports from a variety of sources), news reports were randomly assigned to one of the four above-named sources. Participants were provided a brief headline accompanied by the logo of the news organization and asked to indicate which of the four reports displayed on the screen they would like to read. (They could also click a "can't say" box, as shown in Figure 8.7.) They repeated this task across six different news

FIGURE 8.7 Screenshot from news preference experiment.

categories: American politics, the war in Iraq, "race in America," crime, travel, and sports. We also included a baseline or control condition in which all source logos were deleted; here, participants could only choose between the reports based on the headline content. All other aspects of the presentation were equalized across the different news organizations. For instance, the placement of a particular story or source on the screen was randomized so that no particular news source gained by its placement (e.g., first or last) on the screen.

The results from this news preference experiment revealed that the effects of the source manipulation on news story selection were strongest for political topics where partisan divisions are intense. Thus, Republicans gravitated to Fox reports on politics and Iraq, while Democrats avoided Fox in favor of CNN or NPR. Even though the partisan divide was bigger for hard news, it did not disappear entirely for nonpolitical subjects. Republicans continued to show a preference for Fox News, even when reading about the NBA or possible vacation destinations (for details, see Iyengar & Hahn, 2009).

Since 2006, PCL and Washingtonpost.com have undertaken eight joint studies with an average sample size of 1,300—a relatively large N, at least by the standards of experimental research. Experiments on especially controversial or newsworthy subjects attracted a high volume of traffic (on some days exceeding 500). In other cases, the rate of participation slowed to a trickle, resulting in a longer period of time to gather the data.

Sampling from Online Research Panels

Even though drop-in online samples provide more diversity than the typical "college sophomore" sample, they are obviously biased in several important respects. Participants from Washington post.com, for instance, included very few conservatives or Republicans. Fortunately, it is now possible to overcome issues of sampling bias (assuming the researcher has access to funding) by administering online experiments to representative samples. In this sense, the lack of generalizability associated with experimental designs can be largely overcome.

Two market research firms have pioneered the use of Web-based experiments with fully representative samples. Not surprisingly, both firms are located in the heart of Silicon Valley. The first is Knowledge Networks based in Menlo Park, and the second is Polimetrix (recently purchased by the UK polling company of YouGov) based in Palo Alto.

Knowledge Networks has overcome the problem of selection bias inherent to online surveys, which reach only that proportion of the population that is both online and inclined to participate in research studies, by recruiting a nationwide panel through standard telephone methods. This representative panel, including over 150,000 Americans between the ages of 16 and 85, is provided free access to the Internet via WebTV. In exchange, panel members agree to participate (on a regular basis) in research studies being conducted by Knowledge Networks. The surveys are administered over the panelist's WebTV. Thus, in theory Knowledge Networks can deliver samples that meet the highest standards of probabilistic sampling. In practice, because their panelists have an obligation to participate, Knowledge Networks also provides artificially high response rates (Dennis, Li, & Chatt, 2004).

Polimetrix uses a novel "matching" approach to the sampling problem. In essence, they extract a quasi-representative sample from large panels of online volunteers. The process works as follows. First, Polimetrix assembles a very large pool of opt-in participants by offering small incentives for study participation (e.g., the chance of winning an iPod). As of November 2007, the number of Polimetrix panelists exceeded 1.5 million Americans.

To extract a representative sample from this pool of self-selected panelists, Polimetrix uses a two-step sampling procedure. First, they draw a conventional random sample from the target population of interest (i.e., registered voters). Second, for each member of the target sample, Polimetrix substitutes a member of the opt-in panel who is similar to the corresponding member of the target sample on a set of demographic characteristics such as gender, age, and education. In this sense, the matched sample consists of respondents who "represent" the respondents in the target sample. Rivers (2006) describes the conditions under which the matched sample approximates a true random sample.

The Polimetrix samples have achieved impressive rates of predictive validity, thus bolstering the claims that matched samples emulate random samples. In the 2005 California special election, Polimetrix accurately predicted the public's acceptance or rejection of all seven propositions (a record matched by only one other conventional polling organization), with an average error rate comparable to what would be expected given random sampling (Rivers, n.d.).

DISCUSSION

The standard comparison of experiments and surveys favors the former on the grounds of precise causal inference and the latter on the grounds of greater generalizability. As I have suggested, however, traditional experimental methods can be effectively and just as rigorously replicated using online strategies which have the advantage of reaching a participant pool that is more far-flung and diverse than the pool relied on by conventional experimentalists. Online techniques also permit a more precise "targeting" of recruitment procedures so as to enhance participant diversity. Banner ads publicizing the study and the financial incentives for study participants can be placed in portals or sites that are known to attract underrepresented groups. Female subjects or African-Americans, for instance, could be attracted by ads placed in sites tailored to their interests. Most recently, the development of online research panels makes it possible to administer experiments on broad cross-sections of the American population. As technology diffuses still further, the generalizability gap between experimental and survey methods will continue to close.

Although information technology has clearly advanced the conduct of experimental research, there are challenges ahead. The most notable concerns the increasingly self-selected nature of media audiences. Since there is a much wider range of media choices than ever before, providing greater variability of available information, people uninterested in politics can avoid news programming altogether while political junkies can exercise discretionary or selective exposure to political information.

The self-selected composition of audiences has important consequences for political communication research. In a recent study, for example, young voters in California were mailed a CD featuring the candidates contesting the 2002 gubernatorial election (see Iyengar & Jackman, 2003). The researchers found that actual turnout among young voters who used the CD was 11 percentage points higher than among young voters in the control group (who did not receive the CD). This observed difference could be attributed not only to the treatment, but also to the *ex ante* level of political interest among participants who chose to use the CD. When exposure to the experimental treatment is based on choice, it becomes necessary to estimate the average treatment effect after adjusting for self-selection. In the CD experiment, 78% of those assigned to the treatment group ignored the CD, due to general disinterest in the subject matter, insufficient time, or other such factors. Those who did accept the treatment were drawn disproportionately from the ranks of those interested in politics. Thus, exposure to the treatment was nonrandom and correlated with key outcome variables of interest.

Fortunately, in recent years there has been considerable progress in estimating treatment effects in nonrandomized experimental or observational settings. Recent reviews include Imbens (2004), Angrist and Krueger (2000), and Heckman, Ichimura, and Todd (1998). The general idea is straightforward: although respondents have self-selected into a particular treatment or experimental condition, after the researcher controls for factors that predispose assignees to accept or refuse treatment, the outcomes of interest and treatment are no longer confounded. Given the availability of variables (covariates) known to motivate participation, the researcher can overcome the failure of random assignment and recover an unbiased estimate of the treatment effect. In particular, it is possible to carry out *matched comparisons* of treated and control participants (matching on the covariates); averaging over these matched comparisons generally produces an unbiased estimate of the causal effect of treatment (see Rosenbaum & Rubin, 1983).

In the youth CD study, the researchers were able to match the treatment and control groups for previous voting history, propensity to participate in surveys, and socioeconomic indicators related to political participation (i.e., age, marital status, and education). In comparison with non-participants, CD users were older, more frequent survey takers, more educated, and had higher incomes. After adjusting for these motivational biases, the effects of CD use on actual turnout was 5%, a substantial reduction from the original estimate of 11%.

In summary, the use of digital technology in experimental research represents a double-edged sword. While researchers are in a position to administer precisely controlled manipulations to an increasingly diverse subject pool, thus increasing generalizability, they face a radically altered media environment in which exposure to political content is driven by choice (see Bennett & Iyengar, 2008). As a result, assignment to treatments in political communication-related experiments will inevitably depend on the participant's political preferences and estimating treatment effects will require the use of more powerful statistical tools.

NOTES

1. Of course, this approach assumes a one-sided distribution of policy preferences and that the tone manipulation would be reversed for experimental participants who actually favored offshore drilling.
2. We settled on the 60:40 ratio after a pretest study indicated that this level of blending was insufficient for participants to detect traces of themselves in the morph, but sufficient to move evaluations of the target candidate.
3. Facial similarity is necessarily confounded with familiarity—people are familiar with their own faces. There is considerable evidence (see Zajonc, 2001) that people prefer familiar to unfamiliar stimuli. An alternative interpretation of these results, accordingly, is that participants were more inclined to support the more familiar-looking candidate.
4. Psychologists typically use this term to describe experiments administered in naturalistic public settings such as elevators, subway cars, or shopping malls (see Snyder, Grather, & Keller, 1974).
5. On the other hand, it is possible for the experimental setting to be *too* realistic. During the initial implementation of our campaign experiments, we provided subjects with access to a remote control device, only to discover that a subject used it to fast-forward the tape during the commercial breaks where the experimental manipulation was embedded.

   The number of participants per experimental session ranged from one to four. In most cases, sessions with multiple participants consisted of people who scheduled the session together (i.e., members of the same family or work group). It is possible that the social atmosphere of the viewing sessions (watching with people you know, watching with strangers, or watching alone) may have interacted with the manipulations, but we had no *a priori* basis for expecting the effects of advertising tone on political attitudes to be conditioned by the sociability of the viewing experience.

REFERENCES

Angrist, J., & Krueger, A. (2000). Empirical strategies in labor economics. In O. Ashenfelter and D. Card (Eds.), *Handbook of labor economics:* Vol. 3 (pp. 1277–1366). New York: Elsevier Science.

Ansolabehere, S. (2006). The paradox of minimal effects. In H. Brady and R. Johnston (Eds.), *Capturing campaign effects* (pp. 29–44). Ann Arbor: University of Michigan Press.

Ansolabehere, S., & Iyengar, S. (1995). *Going negative: How political ads shrink and polarize the electorate.* New York: Free Press.

Ansolabehere, S., Iyengar, S., & Simon, A. (1999). Replicating experiments using aggregate and survey data. *American Political Science Review, 93,* 901–910.

Bailenson, J., Iyengar, S., Yee, N., & Collins, N. (2008). Facial similarity between voters and candidates causes influence. *Public Opinion Quarterly, 72,* 935–961.

Bartels, L. (1993). Messages received: The political impact of media exposure. *American Political Science Review,* 87, 267–285.

Bartels, L. M. (1996). Uninformed votes: Information effects in presidential elections. *American Journal of Political Science, 40*(1), 194–230.

Bennett, W. L., & Iyengar, S. (2008). A new era of minimal effects? The changing foundations of political communication. *Journal of Communication,* 58(4), 707–731.

Biocca, F. (Ed.). (1991). *Television and political advertising, vol. 1: Psychological processes.* Hillsdale, NJ: Lawrence Erlbaum Associates.

Bradburn, N., Rips, L., & Shevell, S. (1987, April). Answering autobiographical questions: The impact of memory and inference in surveys. *Science, 236,* 157–161.

Brader, T. (2006). *Campaigning for hearts and minds: How emotional appeals in political ads work.* Chicago: University of Chicago Press.

Burnstein, E., Crandall, C., & Kitayama, S. (1994). Some neo-Darwinian decision rules for altruism: Weighing cues for inclusive fitness as a function of the biological importance of the decision. *Journal of Personality and Social Psychology, 67,* 773–789.

Cotton, J. (1985) Cognitive dissonance in selective exposure. In D. Zillman and J. Bryant (Eds.), *Selective exposure to communication* (pp. 11–33). Hillsdale, NJ: Lawrence Erlbaum.

Dennis, J. M., Li, R., & Chatt, C. (2004, February). Benchmarking Knowledge Networks' Web-enabled panel survey of selected GSS questions against GSS in-person interviews. Knowledge Networks Technical Report.

Festinger, L. (1957). *A theory of cognitive dissonance.* New York: John Wiley.

Finkel, S., & Geer, J. (1998) A spot check: Casting doubt on the demobilizing effect of attack advertising. *American Journal of Political Science, 42,* 573–595.

Freedman, P., & Goldstein, K. (1999). Measuring media exposure and the effects of negative campaign ads. *American Journal of Political Science, 43,* 1189–1208.

Gilliam, F., Jr., & Iyengar, S. (2000). Prime suspects: The influence of local television news on the viewing public. *American Journal of Political Science, 44,* 560–573.

Gilliam, F., Jr., Iyengar, S., Simon, A., & Wright, O. (1996). Crime in black and white: The violent, scary world of local news. *Harvard International Journal of Press/Politics, 1,* 6–23.

Gilliam, F., Jr., Valentino, N., & Beckman, M. (2002). Where you live and what you watch: The impact of racial proximity and local television news on attitudes about race and crime. *Political Research Quarterly, 55,* 755–780.

Gunther, B. (1987). *Poor reception: Misunderstanding and forgetting broadcast news.* Hillsdale, NJ: Lawrence Erlbaum.

Heckman, J., Ichimura, H., & Todd, P. (1998). Matching as an econometric evaluation estimator. *Review of Economic Studies, 65,* 261–294.

Hovland, C. (1959). Reconciling conflicting results derived from experimental and survey studies of attitude change. *American Psychologist, 14,* 8–17.

Imbens, G. (2004). Semiparametric estimation of average treatment effects under exogeneity: A review. *Review of Economics and Statistics, 86,* 4–29.

Iyengar, S., & Hahn, K. (2009). Red media, blue media: Evidence of ideological selectivity in media use. *Journal of Communication, 59*(1), 19–39.

Iyengar, S., Hahn, K., Krosnick, J., & Walker, J. (2008). Selective exposure to campaign communication: The role of anticipated agreement and issue public membership. *Journal of Politics, 70,* 186–200.

Iyengar, S., & Jackman, S. (2003). Can Information technology energize voters? Evidence from the 2000 and 2002 campaigns. Paper presented at the annual meeting of the American Political Science Association, Philadelphia, PA.

Iyengar, S., Jackman, S., & Hahn, K. (2007). Polarization in less than thirty seconds: Continuous monitoring of voter response to campaign advertising. Paper presented to the annual meeting of the Midwest Political Science Association, Chicago, IL.

Kahn, K., & Kenney, P. (1999). Do negative campaigns mobilize or suppress turnout? Clarifying the relationship between negativity and participation. *American Political Science Review, 93,* 877–890.

Lazarsfeld, P., Berelson, B., & Gaudet, H. (1948). *The people's choice.* New York: Columbia University Press.

Nelson, C. (2001). The development and neural bases of face recognition: Reply to critiques. *Infant and Child Development, 10,* 3–18.

Papadakis, M. (2000, March). *Complex picture of computer use in the home emerges.* National Science Foundation Issue Brief.

Pew Internet and American Life Project. (2005). *Digital divisions.* Retrieved from, http://www.pewinternet.org/pdfs/PIP_Digital_Divisions_Oct_5_2005.pdf.

Pfau, M., Houston, B., & Semmler, S. (2007). *Mediating the vote: The changing media landscape in U.S. presidential campaigns.* Lanham, MD: Rowman and Littlefield.

Pierce, J., & Lovrich, N. (1982). Survey measurement of political participation: Selective effects of recall in petition signing. *Social Science Quarterly, 63,* 164–171.

Price, V., & Zaller, J. (1993). Who gets the news? Alternative measures of news reception and their implications for research. *Public Opinion Quarterly, 57,* 133–164.

Prior, M. (2003). Any good news in soft news? The impact of soft news preference on political knowledge. *Political Communication, 20,* 149–172.

Prior, M. (2007). *Post-broadcast democracy: How media choice increases inequality in political involvement and polarizes elections.* New York: Cambridge University Press.

Rivers, D. (2006). *Sample matching: Representative sampling from Internet panels.* Retrieved from http://www.polimetrix.com/documents/Polimetrix_Whitepaper_Sample Matching.pdf.

Rivers, D. (n.d.). *Scientific sampling for online research.* Retrieved from http://www.polimetrix.com/documents/Polimetrix_Sampling.pdf.

Rosenbaum, P., & Rubin, D. (1983, January). The central role of the propensity score in observational studies for causal effects. *Biometrika, 70,* 41–55.

Sears, D. (1986). College sophomores in the laboratory: Influences of a narrow database on the social psychology view of human nature. *Journal of Personality and Social Psychology, 51,* 515–530.

Snyder, M., Grather, J., & Keller, K. (1974). Staring and compliance: A field experiment on hitchhiking. *Journal of Applied Social Psychology, 4,* 165–170.

Vavreck, L. (2007). The exaggerated effects of advertising on turnout: The dangers of self-reports. *Quarterly Journal of Political Science, 2,* 325–343.

Wattenberg, M., & Brians, C. (1999). Negative campaign advertising: Demobilizer or mobilizer? *American Political Science Review, 93,* 891–900.

Zajonc, R. (2001). Mere exposure: A gateway to the subliminal. *Current Directions in Psychological Science, 10,* 224–228.

9

Expressing versus Revealing Preferences in Experimental Research

Yanna Krupnikov
Department of Political Science
Indiana University

Adam Seth Levine
Center for the Study of Democratic Institutions
Vanderbilt University

Over the past several decades, numerous scholars have sought to identify the conditions under which political communication can affect various forms of political behavior. Research has focused on such behaviors as voter turnout, volunteerism, information acquisition, and more recently, small campaign donations. Many advancements in this area have been due to the use of experiments. The use of experiments has allowed researchers to isolate focal relationships by measuring individual responses immediately after exposure to strategic communication (Brader, 2005; Kinder & Palfrey, 1993). In many ways, the experimental approach has proven to be ideally suited to analyzing the effects of political communication.

At the same time, however, studying the relationship between political communication and political behavior in an experimental setting brings a unique challenge. While experiments allow scholars to better isolate the effect of a particular stimulus, any inferences drawn from these experiments depend upon the precision with which they can measure people's willingness to act in response to that stimulus. This leads to a central question: When considering the effect of political communication on political action, should scholars ask people to *express* their preferences for action or should they ask people to *reveal* them? Expressing preferences means that people report how likely or willing they are to engage in certain types of activity, either now or sometime in the future. Revealing preferences, on the other hand, means that people actually engage in the activity.

Here we discuss the use of expressed and revealed preference questions in several parts. First, we discuss the use of expressed preference measures in experiments. This is the most commonly used approach to measuring propensity for political action. In this section we review the various ways of measuring expressed preferences for action and then discuss difficulties that arise when relying upon expressed preferences alone. Second, we consider measures of revealed preferences. While this approach is often more difficult to employ in an experimental setting and is, as a result, less frequent in studies of political communication, we consider the conditions under which revealed preferences offer a more valid measure of propensity for action. In the final section, we offer a compromise between the two approaches and discuss how small modifications in experimental design may strengthen our understanding of the relationship between political communication and political behavior.

EXPRESSED PREFERENCES FOR ACTION

When people are asked to *express* their preferences, they state how likely they are to engage in certain types of activities, either now or sometime in the future.[1] This is a popular strategy for examining how various forms of political communication affect people's willingness to act. Moreover, it is often the only means of studying action, given that it is impossible for scholars to create experimental situations in which individuals may actually engage in certain forms of political behavior. Here we consider various forms of expressed preference measures and discuss both the advantages and disadvantages of this approach.

Examples of Expressed Preferences

One of the focal areas in which experimental design necessitates the use of expressed preference measures is the study of how various forms of strategic communication affect voter turnout. Typical expressed preference questions of voter turnout range from measures that focus on an individual's likelihood of voting in a *particular* election to broader questions that try to gauge more general attitudes toward voting.

Ansolabehere and Iyengar (1995) provide an example of the first kind of question. Relying on experiments to consider how differences in advertising tone affect propensity to vote in an actual campaign, Ansolabehere and Iyengar measured expressed preferences by asking individuals if they were registered to vote and then if they intended to turn out and vote in the upcoming election (p. 177). This is a basic measure of expressed preferences as individuals answer by thinking through their likelihood of engaging in a political action in the future.

Valentino, Beckmann, and Buhr (2001) relied on a similar question to measure expressed preferences for turnout when considering the way news frames affect voter turnout and other important political outcomes such as efficacy and trust in government. To consider propensity for action, the authors asked individuals to express their preferences using the following question: "Looking forward to the November election, do you intend to vote?" (p. 356). In general, this type of question is both basic and frequently used (Brooks & Geer, 2007; Clinton & Lapinksi, 2004; Min, 2004), although it is difficult to rely on such a question during off-election years, when experimental stimuli cannot include actual candidates running for office.

While the studies above focused on a real, upcoming election, often experimental designs necessitate the use of fictitious candidates and elections. Krupnikov (2009), for example, analyzed how differences in the timing of exposure to campaign advertisements affect voter turnout; in her experiments, she relied on appeals that featured fictitious candidates. To ensure that experimental subjects thought about the two fictitious candidates in expressing their turnout preferences, Krupnikov utilized the following intent question:

> Suppose on the day of the election, you find out that your local polling place is closed due to an electrical outage. If Candidate A and Candidate B are the only candidates on the ballot, how much effort would you put into going to another polling location?

This question directly focused subjects' attention on the two candidates mentioned in the experimental campaign appeals.

Finally, Glynn, Huge, and Lunney (2009) provide an example of gauging more general attitudes toward voting. In their study about the effect of communication of social norms on college students' propensity to vote, they asked individuals to either agree or disagree with the following statement: "I plan to vote as often as possible in the future" (p. 54). Unlike either of the two previous questions, this question does not focus attention on a particular election (real or imaginary).

Despite the differences in wording, however, the goal of all these questions is similar: after exposure to some form of political communication, each experimental participant must consider how they would behave when the opportunity to turn out and vote presents itself in the future.

In addition to studies of voter turnout, measures of expressed preferences figure prominently in other studies of political communication and action. For example, in a study of deliberation effectiveness, Stromer-Galley and Muhlberger (2009) rely on these types of questions. Although the substance of this question is different, their structure is similar to the voter turnout questions we discussed in the last section because they ask people to consider the likelihood of future action. Stromer-Galley and Muhlberger (2009) asked all participants to respond to the following statement: "I would be willing to work with this group on other projects in the future." This type of question is similar to the broadest type of voter intent question: it asks individuals how they might behave in the future, without providing any information about concrete opportunities to take such actions.

Expressed Preferences: Advantages and Disadvantages

Keeping these examples of expressed preference questions in mind, in this section we turn to the advantages and disadvantages of this approach. First, considering the advantages, expressed preferences are often the most practical means of examining political behavior in an experimental setting. In order to maintain control and create a precise stimulus, scholars must often rely on fictitious candidates and doctored news articles. When doing so, the best way to measure behavior is to simply ask individuals how they may behave in the future. Measuring expressed preferences may help capture some behavioral patterns even when an individual may never actually have the opportunity to take part in a particular political activity.

At the same time, however, the very factors that make these measures useful may also make them troublesome. When individuals are asked if they would be willing to undertake an action in the future, giving an affirmative answer is costless. It is simple for experimental participants to report, for example, that they will turn out to vote, sign up for a listserv, or participate in a deliberative exercise in the future if they know that they will never actually have to do any of these things. Put another way, because expressing preferences for action is a relatively costless activity, individuals may say that they'll do something that they would not do if confronted with the actual, costly, task. Kroes and Sheldon (1988) put the concern most succinctly: "The significant disadvantage is that people may not necessarily do what they say" (p. 13). In short, expressed preferences may lead individuals to overstate actual willingness to take political action.

The question becomes whether this overreporting is really a problem for the inferences that scholars wish to draw. We certainly know that it can be a significant problem in nonexperimental studies. In this arena scholars have long suggested that individuals generally have a tendency to overreport their turnout in past elections (Traugott & Katosh, 1979), likely turnout in the future (Pinkleton, Austin, & Fortman, 1998), and their intent to engage in other forms of political action such as contacting one's congressperson (Keeter et al., 2002). Indeed, the trouble with self-reported political behavior—be it actual or intended voter turnout, media use, or volunteerism—has been so well documented that some have suggested the errors of self-reports are too great to identify the effect of political communication on political behavior (Vavreck, 2007).[2]

But is this tendency to overreport as problematic in an experimental setting? After all, experimentalists might argue that as long as people are equally willing to overreport in all conditions, the mere fact that they do overreport is not problematic (see Valentino et al., 2001, for a discussion of this argument). Such an argument, however, makes a key assumption that the stimuli of interest do not interact with the tendency to overreport. This assumption will not always hold. In some cases, one treatment level may be more likely to affect overreporting than another treatment level. In other cases, both treatments may have an impact on an individual's tendency to overreport, but have little effect on the tendency to act. Relying on expressed preferences, then, may mean that scholars are identifying the effect of a stimulus on overreporting, rather than on the key variable of interest, willingness to act. As a result, it becomes unclear whether we observe group differences because one level of the treatment made individuals more or less likely to overreport a willingness to act, or we observe group differences because a stimulus has a causal effect on people's willingness to take political actions we care about.

A study by Leshner and Thorson (2000) vividly illustrates this concern. The authors considered whether positive or negative political attitudes are better at predicting actual political behavior or self-reported behavior. Their results are striking. Positive impressions of politics are positively related to people's *self-reported* willingness to vote but do not predict their actual vote behavior. On the other hand, negative attitudes do not explain patterns in self-reported intent to vote, but work well to explain *actual* voting behavior. In short, Leshner and Thorson's study shows positive and negative impressions about politics can have divergent effects on people's expressed and revealed preferences. Indeed, one implication of their result is that an experimental design which compares positive and negative political communication may limit a scholar's ability to make inferences: it would be difficult to tell if group differences were due to a theoretically interesting relationship between communication and behavior, or whether the effect is due to the fact that one level of the experimental treatment was less likely to lead individuals to form a positive impression of politics and thus lead them to overreport their expressed preferences.[3]

REVEALED PREFERENCES

One way to overcome the disadvantages of expressed preference measures is to ask individuals to reveal their preferences. When people are asked to *reveal* their preferences, they are given the opportunity to actually engage in some form of political action—for example, asking people to donate real money or to add their real names and addresses to an organization's mailing list (e.g., Fowler, 2006; Fowler & Kam, 2007). Fowler (2006) argues that revealed preferences are superior measures because "respondents actually experience a cost in order to give a benefit to [a group]" (p. 676). Although this approach has not been utilized as frequently as the expressed measures approach, recently more scholars have turned to revealed preference measures to analyze how various forms of political communication affect political behavior.

Examples of Revealed Preferences

A focus on revealed preferences begins with studies that ask individuals to distribute real funds between themselves and a partner. Fowler and Kam (2007), for example, posit that one reason people participate in politics is to help other people, whether these other people are everyone in a society or members of a particular social or political group. They measured such other-regardingness by asking individuals to reveal their preference for helping others. They did so by asking subjects to engage in a "dictator game" in which subjects are first provided with real money and then the opportunity to give some of that money away. What is unique about Fowler and Kam's study is the information that they provided subjects about the recipient of the donation—in some cases the recipient was just an anonymous individual, whereas in other cases the recipient was a member of a political in- or out-group (using partisan affiliation). The decision was particularly costly because subjects kept whatever money they did not give away.

Recently, other scholars have adopted this revealed preference approach to consider how strategic communication from political groups affects people's willingness to make campaign donations. Levine (2009), for example, focused on how differences in the content of donation solicitations affects an individual's propensity to donate money. In his study, Levine conducted dictator game experiments in which subjects received a small sum of money and were then randomly assigned to receive different requests for money from US PIRG, a nonpartisan organization active on many college campuses. He then instructed subjects to give away as much of their money to US PIRG as they would like, with the understanding that they got to keep whatever they did not donate for themselves. Levine's approach allowed subjects to directly reveal their preferences for donating by incurring actual costs to do so.

Another example considers how much time people would be willing to spend to obtain information about a campaign. To this end, Lau and Redlawsk (2006) used a *dynamic information board* to present political information to experimental participants. This board allowed them to create an environment in which information about political candidates was constantly changing and new information was constantly available. When a participant opted to focus on a particular piece of information, he did so at the expense of other incoming information, much like in a real campaign media environment. Relying on this board, Lau and Redlawsk could then trace how individuals allocated their attention and selected which information they would like to learn about the candidates. Given that participants had to make actual informational choices—rather than simply report which types of information they might be interested in—the dynamic information board served as a measure of revealed informational preferences.

Translating this approach to new media, Valentino et al. (2008) considered how an individual's emotional state during a campaign affects the way she seeks information about candidates. To measure revealed preferences for information acquisition, the authors gave participants the chance to visit candidates' websites. The websites created specifically for the study blocked individuals from going to other Internet sites and allowed the researchers to track which links participants followed, how participants searched for information, and exactly how much time participants spent on each candidate's website. Providing individuals with the opportunity to search for candidate information—rather than simply asking individuals to express how interested they were in various aspects of the candidates—allowed participants to reveal their preferences for information acquisition.

Finally, recent work has broadened the use of revealed preferences to incorporate a wider range of political behaviors. In an experiment conducted by Braden, Valentino, and Suhay (2008), experimental participants were given the opportunity to actually request that a letter concerning immigration be sent to Congress on their behalf. Given that this meant that participants' names would be included in a real letter to a Congressperson, deciding whether such a letter should be sent meant that individuals had to reveal their preferences. In another study, Levine (2009) asked individuals whether they would be willing to sign up to hear about volunteer opportunities with US PIRG. He compared how different types of strategic communications from US PIRG affected an individual's willingness to volunteer with the organization. To measure willingness to volunteer, he asked individuals to reveal their preferences by providing their full name and e-mail address on US PIRG's actual volunteer sign-up website. In doing so, individuals were aware that US PIRG would add their names to a listserv and contact them for future volunteer opportunities. In this way, the costs of volunteering were made much more salient than if individuals had simply been asked how likely they would be to volunteer in the future.

Revealed Preferences: Advantages and Disadvantages

As the above discussion suggests, in an ideal world all studies would ask individuals to reveal their preferences because it is those revealed preferences that interest most scholars of political communication and political behavior.[4] Moreover, revealed preferences make the costs of action salient and as a result are less likely to produce an overreporting of behavioral intent. If scholars observe group differences using revealed preferences, then they can be more certain that these differences are a function of key stimuli affecting political behavior, rather than certain treatments having differential effects on people's willingness to overreport behavioral intent. In short, revealed preferences can increase the precision with which scholars identify relationships between political communication and political behavior.

At the same time, however, we recognize that it is often impractical, if not impossible, to measure revealed preferences under certain experimental conditions. Experimental participants cannot actually engage in numerous forms of political action while in the laboratory—a strong disadvantage of the revealed preference approach.

Given the measurement disadvantages of expressed preferences and the practical disadvantages of revealed preferences, below we consider two additional experimental approaches to evaluate the effect of political communication on political behavior. The first approach stems from behavioral economics and relies on applying tangible costs to expressed preference measures. The second relies on the psychological theory of scripts and creates conditions under which individuals will consider the costs of action before expressing their preferences. We propose that scripts will foster experimental conditions such that people's expressed preferences will match their revealed ones. Although the first approach can be beneficial, here we suggest that the script method is more practical and has wider applicability in political communication research.

BEHAVIORAL INTENT: NEW MEASURES

In the majority of experimental studies that ask individuals to express their preferences for political action, this expression of preferences is costless. When subjects are asked, "How likely is it that you would turn out and vote for [a candidate]?" they do not actually have to turn out and vote. Reporting that they are highly likely to turn out and vote for this candidate does not mean that they will actually take time out of their day and stand in line to vote on Election Day, for example. In the same way, replying affirmatively to the statement "I would be willing to work with this group on other projects in the future" is equally costless: participants are likely aware or at least believe that they will never actually have to work with this group in the future. In short, when people express their preferences, they do not have to consider the costs associated with action. Following arguments made by Camerer (2003), when people can ignore the costs of action, they overreport their willingness to take that action. Given that this is the case, and that discreetly asking participants to reveal their preferences is often impractical, in this section we consider measures of behavioral intent that attempt to overcome the basic problem of overreporting by making the costs of action salient. These measures leverage the practicality of expressed preference measures with the cost-salient nature of revealed preference measures. Below, we discuss the logic of two types of measures: costs for preferences and scripts. Following this discussion, we advocate for the scripts measure as a particularly advantageous means of measuring the effect of various forms of communication on behavioral intent.

Behavioral Intent: Costs for Expressed Preferences

If expressed preferences lead to overreporting because individuals do not consider the costs associated with action, one way to address this problem and produce more valid measures is to simply add a cost for expressing a preference. For example, in order to express a preference for voting versus not, an experimenter could require the individual to incur actual costs (either in real money or experimental points that then get converted to real money).

Ahn, Huckfeldt, and Ryan (2007) relied on this measure in experiments that provided subjects with the opportunity to pay a tangible cost to obtain certain types of political information. Arguing that some political information is relatively high cost (reading a newspaper article about a complex policy issue) and other information is relatively low cost (talking to a friend about a campaign), Ahn et al. designed experiments where subjects were given the task of selecting between two candidates; these experiments instructed subjects that their goal was to make the best selection possible. To make this selection, experimental participants had to rely on information about the candidates, but different political information came at a different cost to participants. While participants were not required to pay for information that was "public," obtaining private information of higher quality meant that they had to pay points to the experimenters. This approach added a tangible cost to an expressed preference for information because the points that subjects did not spend over the course of the experiment were translated into real money that they took home.

This addition of costs has also often been applied in experimental studies of voter turnout—an expressed preference that is notoriously difficult to measure accurately. To consider whether media projections of presidential election outcomes in Eastern time zone states affect voter turnout in Western time zone states, Battaglini, Morton, and Palfrey (2007) designed an experiment that required participants to pay a set fee for the opportunity to vote. The cost of voting added a layer of tension to participant decision-making, given that abstaining in this particular setting was costless. In a similar manner, Krupnikov (2009) considered the effect of campaign negativity on voter turnout by creating an experimental setting where voting was costly. The goal of this study was to identify whether exposure to campaign negativity makes individuals less likely to pay the costs of voting in a laboratory setting. In both of these cases, subjects have an incentive to pay the cost if they believe that doing so will lead to an outcome with a higher ultimate payoff.

Adding a tangible cost to measures of behavior alters their costless nature in the most direct way: if study participants want to respond affirmatively, they actually have to pay a cost. While this approach may work well to reduce overreporting, its usefulness in analyzing the relationship between political communication and political action may be more tenuous. The costs associated with specific political behaviors are often more complex and less tangible than the very direct costs (for example, "1 point" per piece of information or "25 cents" per vote) applied to these behaviors in the lab. If the goal is to understand how certain types of political communication affect individuals' propensity to act, it may be problematic if the costs individuals are weighing in the laboratory are profoundly different from the costs they will weigh in the real world. While in Krupnikov's study, for example, negativity may make experimental participants less likely to pay 10 points and vote, in a real campaign setting negative campaigning may interact with perceptions of voting costs (time, effort) in a more complex way. In short, while adding direct tangible costs is one method of introducing disincentives for overreporting, this approach may not always clarify how political communication affects political behavior.

Behavioral Intent: Scripts for Expressed Preferences

How may scholars use measures of expressed preferences that make salient the costs that people incur in the real world? Here we propose a theory of scripts. The theory of scripts is based on research in psychology and marketing that asks individuals to imagine taking certain actions or being part of certain events. Here we use the term *script* to describe vignettes that individuals are asked to read that help them imagine actually taking action or envision the occurrence of event.

Researchers have shown that when people are asked to read a script that describes a particular event they come to believe that the event is more likely to happen (Gregory, Burroughs, & Ainslie, 1985; Gregory, Cialdini, & Carpenter, 1982; Petrova & Cialdini, 2005; Sherman et al., 1985). This effect occurs by increasing the availability of the event in people's minds (Tversky & Kahneman, 1973). As an example of this mechanism at work, Bone and Ellen (1992) conducted a series of studies in which individuals were asked to imagine either themselves or someone else eating popcorn. Individuals who were asked to imagine themselves eating popcorn were significantly more likely to report that they would probably have a chance to eat popcorn in the future. In another example, Carroll (1978) asked subjects to imagine themselves on the Tuesday of Election Day (1976) and on the Wednesday following it. Then, he asked participants to imagine reading or watching different political scenarios: some subjects were assigned to scripts where Ford won the election, others to scripts where Carter won the election. In all cases, subjects were asked to imagine these events as if they were "present on Tuesday and Wednesday, watching some of the news on television, perhaps staying up late, or checking the early morning news by television or newspaper" (p. 91). The outcome of the study showcased the power of scripts: participants grew to believe that the candidate in their script had a stronger chance of winning the election. Carroll replicated this same study with scripts about football teams.

By making an individual believe that an event is more likely to occur, scripts also change the way the costs of action are viewed. Once an individual believes that a given event is more likely to occur, the costs associated with taking part in that event also become more salient. Indeed, as Petrova and Cialdini (2008) write, "imagining an action and the actual production of the action rely upon common neural structures" (p. 509). This point is important for understanding how we measure people's willingness to engage in political action. By making costs salient, scripts bring to mind the same considerations that are brought to mind when people have to reveal their preferences. As a result, people's expressed preferences following a script should match their revealed preferences. Relying on scripts is also helpful for clarifying a relationship between political communication and political action in experimental settings: because the script brings to mind the types of costs that may be associated with taking a specific action in the real world, scholars can incorporate a script prior to an expressed preference question, yet still achieve high levels of internal validity from the experimental setting.

Consider the following example. A scholar is interested in how different forms of communication (ads, direct mail, personal requests, etc.) affect people's willingness to volunteer their time for a political organization. Her dependent variable of interest is whether study participants would be willing to sign up for a listserv to hear about volunteer opportunities. The costs here concern the likelihood and frequency with which one will be asked to volunteer, as well as the time associated with volunteering. If people are only asked whether they would be willing to sign up, then the costs are not necessarily made salient and there may be a tendency to overstate their willingness to sign up. If people are instead given the opportunity to actually join, then these costs will immediately become salient and people will be less willing to sign up. Yet, when people are asked whether they would be willing to sign up but are first asked to imagine what it would be like to be a member of the listserv, then here too the costs will be immediately salient. The script leads people to take the costs into account as if they were actually asked to reveal their preferences.

Experimental Test.   A brief experimental test clarifies the power of scripts by considering how scripts affect expressed preference measures. Our goal here was to show how scripts lead people to take the costs of action into consideration. In our brief study ($N = 58$)[5] we asked adult individuals to consider whether they would be willing to sign up and receive information about the American Cancer Society Cancer Action Network (ACS CAN), a nonprofit, nonpartisan political organization that pursues public policy goals.[6] In this small study, all subjects first received basic information about the ACS CAN. This information briefly described the ACS CAN's purpose and was obtained from the organization's official website:

> In a moment you will receive information describing the mission and activities of the American Cancer Society Cancer Action Network. This organization is a nonprofit, nonpartisan affiliate of the American Cancer Society. Its primary mission is to advocate to legislators on issues related to the detection and treatment of cancer.

Following this information, the control group received information about the critical work that volunteers perform for this organization as follows:

> This organization has built up a large mailing list of individuals from across the country. Members of this mailing list receive periodic communications from the organization about current cancer-related legislation before their Member of Congress and their state legislators. The organization contacts members of the mailing list with requests that these individuals write letters to their representatives to let them know how they feel about upcoming legislation affecting the detection and treatment of cancer. The organization also contacts members of the mailing list asking them to volunteer in their regional offices. Overall, volunteers are absolutely essential for ensuring that legislators hear the voices of people who are committed to finding a cure for cancer.

The treatment group received similar information, in the form of a script. Here, participants were asked to imagine what it would be like to be a volunteer for this organization:

> As you read the following paragraph, imagine what it would be like to be on this organization's mailing list. As a member of the mailing list, you would receive periodic communication regarding current cancer-related legislation before your Member of Congress and your state legislators. Imagine now that you sit down to check your email and find that this organization has contacted you with a request that you write a letter to your representative about upcoming legislation related to the detection and treatment of cancer. Now imagine that you are checking your email again

several days later. As you open your email program and log in, you find that this organization has contacted you again, asking you to volunteer in its regional office. Overall, volunteers like you would be absolutely essential for ensuring that legislators hear the voices of people who are committed to finding a cure for cancer.

This script brought to mind the considerable costs associated with joining a listserv. In particular, it reminded participants that the communications they would receive from ACS CAN would likely be frequent and that many of these communications would be asking individuals for their time (e.g., volunteering, contacting legislators). We did so because, as Levine (2009) finds, these are the costs that individuals think about when considering whether to join such a list. In short, while control group members were informed that the ACS CAN contacts its listserv members and asks them to volunteer, treatment group members received a script that asked individuals to *imagine themselves* receiving these communications (i.e., "imagine that you are checking your email again. . .").

Following the information provided about ACS CAN, subjects were asked whether they would be willing to sign up for a listserv to hear about volunteer opportunities with the organization. To consider a participant's likelihood of signing up for the organization, we asked the following question:

> Suppose that you were asked to sign up for the American Cancer Society's Cancer Action Network. This would entail putting your email and/or phone number on a list of people who are interested in volunteering with the organization. How likely would you be to sign up?

Participants were then provided with a horizontal scale with 1 meaning "very slightly likely" to sign up and 23 meaning "extremely likely" to sign up. This question is quite similar to the types of expressed preference questions we discussed earlier: it asks participants how likely they would be to sign up for ACS CAN but does not give participants the chance to actually sign up for the listserv.

The results are striking. Participants in the script condition—who had been asked to imagine the costs associated with signing up for the ACS CAN listserv—were significantly less likely to report that they would sign up for the listserv (see Figure 9.1).[7]

Moreover, a content coding of the thoughts that people listed after their decision revealed that the imagination script led people to directly consider the costs associated with being on the email listserv. Participants in both groups generally used the open-ended answers to note that they believed ACS CAN was a useful organization. However, participants randomly assigned to the script condition were much more likely to follow their complimentary description of the ACS CAN with mentions about how much they did not like receiving numerous emails from organizations and how they would feel overwhelmed by such communication. In contrast, control group members were far less likely to mention these costs. In short, including a basic script changed the nature of considerations individuals brought to bear on their expressed preferences.[8]

Experimental Scripts.   In an experimental setting, a script may be applied in any number of ways. In the example above, the script simply serves to document what happens to people's expressed preferences when costs of action are made salient. In cases where the goal is to identify the effect of political communication on people's willingness to act, rather than just measure the effectiveness of a script, a script may be incorporated directly into expressed preference questions. This will induce individuals to think through the costs of action as they determine how likely they are to act, similar to what they would do if they were revealing their preferences.

Scripts need not be complex or lengthy, but simply need to ask individuals to imagine the costs associated with the action of interest, whether these costs are affiliated with future behavior

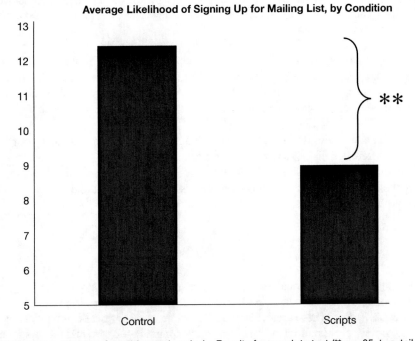

FIGURE 9.1 Results of experimental analysis. Results from scripts text (**$p <.$ 05, two-tailed test) show that people who were asked to imagine being a volunteer on the listserv (the experimental group) were less willing to sign up than those who were just provided information about the listener.

or those that affected past behavior.[9] This application will also work to maintain the internal and external validity of the experimental study.

We developed the script in our brief study about signing up for the ACS CAN listerv based on pretests and interviews with individuals who indicated that the frequency of messages is a high cost of listserv membership. In a similar manner, scripts could be applied to studies about other forms of political action. As an example, consider measures of voter turnout. Research has shown that some of the key costs individuals consider when deciding whether to turn out and vote are time and convenience (Berinksy, Burns, & Traugott, 2001). By considering a script that makes these costs salient, we can extrapolate from Houston and Doan's (1999) expressed preference measures of turnout. In an experimental study, the authors measured turnout intent in four parts. In each of the four parts, the authors set up a specific voting situation and then asked experimental participants how likely or unlikely they would be to turn out under these different conditions. The four situations began with one where voting would be relatively easy: "The polling place is on your way to work; the line is short and quick-moving; the weather is warm and sunny" (p. 198). The conditions, however, become more costly such that in the fourth and final voting situation, the most common costs of voting are made clear: "The polling place is out of your way; the line is long and slow; it is raining" (p. 198). While the measure in its current form may prompt individuals to respond in the same manner to each of the four situations in order to appear consistent (Cialdini & De Nicholas, 1989), encouraging individuals to imagine the fourth—and most costly—situation may bring responses closest to a revealed preference measure:

Imagine now that it is Election Day. Imagine that it is raining and you are running late for work [or class], the polling place is out of your way. Imagine now that you've been informed that the line is long and slow.

The use of scripts, of course, is not without its limitations. The first limitation is the need for precise knowledge about the appropriate content of a script. A script will not have its intended effect if it does not remind people about the costs of action as they see them. Pretests and cognitive interviews are a way to address this potential limitation, so long as the costs are reasonably similar across subjects.

The second potential limitation is the need to lengthen questions by adding a script prior to the measure of interest. This need not be a significant limitation, as the script does not have to be lengthy in order to have its intended effect. Indeed, in the above examples the script is quite short. Once these limitations are met, however, scripts provide a useful and practical alternative to revealed preference measures.

CONCLUSIONS

The relationship between political communication and political behavior has long been of interest to scholars. In recent years, this topic has only become more important. As Iyengar and Simon (2000) write, "These are heady times for students of political communication. To an extent not previously seen, politicians' use—even manipulation—of the mass media to promote political objectives is now not only standard practice but in fact essential to survival" (p. 150). Moreover, the rise of the Internet, arguably the most accessible medium yet, has led to increases in the sheer volume of available political communication (Bimber, 2001; Bimber & Davis, 2003; Druckman, Kifer, & Parkin, 2007). As citizens receive an increasing number of political communications, understanding how, when, and if they have behavioral consequences is crucial.

Experiments are particularly well suited to analyzing the effect of political communication. Only in an experimental setting can scholars control the incoming communication *and* measure its effect immediately after exposure (or in real time). Leveraging the power of experiments to isolate the specific causal effect of a stimulus, however, depends on the ability to measure the key dependent variable: political behavior.

In this chapter we have considered various ways to measure people's willingness to take political actions. In doing so, we identified four basic techniques for measuring propensity to act in an experimental setting (as shown in Table 9.1). The first, expressed preferences, is often the most practical approach in an experiment—though it is an approach with several disadvantages. In particular, it is often unclear if and how participants' tendency to overreport their intention to act interacts with experimental stimuli, thereby threatening internally valid conclusions.

The next approach, revealed preferences, asks individuals to actually take the action rather than simply report how likely they are to do so in the future. This is a more direct measure of political behavior, but unfortunately this measure is often impractical in a laboratory setting: while individuals can engage in some forms of political action while in the lab, it is virtually impossible in engage in others.

As a next step, we assessed how best to overcome the disadvantages of standard expressed and revealed preference measures. One solution simply added tangible costs to expressed preference measures to make expressions of behavioral intent more costly in the most direct way.

TABLE 9.1
Typology of Behavioral Intent

Measure	Definition	Question Examples	References
Expressed Preferences	Respondent states how likely they are to engage in a particular action	"I plan to vote as often as possible in the future." "I would be willing to work with this group on other projects in the future."	Glynn, Huge, & Lunney (2009) Stromer-Galley & Muhlberger (2009)
Revealed Preferences	Respondent is given the opportunity to actually engage in some form of political action during a study	Giving away real money during an experiment Sending a real letter to their Congress member	Fowler & Kam (2007) Brader, Valentino, & Suhay (2008)
Costs added to Expressed Preferences	Respondent must pay a tangible fee or cost created by the experimenter if she chooses to respond affirmatively to an expressed preference measure	Participants pay financial fee to cast vote Participants pay point fee for high quality information	Battaglini, Morton, & Palfrey (2007) Ahn, Huckfeldt, & Ryan (2007)
Scripts added to Expressed Preferences	Respondent is asked to imagine the real-world costs associated with taking an action, prior to being asked an expressed preference measure	Reminding subjects of frequency of email contact, prior to asking question about willingness to sign up for listserv Asking subject to imagine time it takes to cast ballot, prior to expressing preference for future voter turnout	Krupnikov & Levine (2010)

While this approach is well suited to the issue of overreporting that is usually associated with expressed preferences, it is less helpful if the goal is to identify key relationships between political communication and political action. In a real-world setting the costs associated with action are often more complex than the tangible costs in the experimental setting. Thus, even if these measures involve less overreporting, it is still unclear how stimuli affect the real-world behavior of interest.

A second solution relies on the psychological theory of scripts. In this case, a researcher can include a script that increases the saliency of the costs of action. In this way, measuring behavioral intent with a script can bring expressed preferences in line with revealed preferences. By adding scripts to experimental measures of behavioral intent, scholars can combine the practicality of expressed measures with the costs-focused nature of revealed preferences.

Turning to scripts is a relatively small adjustment, but one with a potentially high payoff. In making the costs of action salient, scripts allow scholars to measure behavioral intent more precisely, leading to stronger (and in some cases more valid) inferences about the relationship between political communication and action. Moreover, if individuals are instructed to consider the same costs of action in an experimental setting that they would consider if they actually thought about taking this action, inferences will be more generalizeable. In sum, we suggest that using scripts can be highly beneficial for analyzing political behavior with greater precision, thus leveraging the experimental setting to clarify the behavioral consequences of political communication.

NOTES

1. Expressing a preference has also been called "stated" preference (Kroes & Sheldon, 1988).
2. Research has tied the problem of overreporting to social desirability, as well as basic forgetfulness of past behavior (Belli et al., 1999).
3. While this would certainly be an interesting finding in itself, it does not help to clarify the relationship between political communication and political behavior.
4. Although studies have certainly focussed on the likelihood of future action, in most cases the goal is to consider how a particular stimulus affects action, rather than an individual's belief about how they may act in the future.
5. This sample size provides enough participants to observe group differences of $d = 1$ with a β of .90 and an α of .05.
6. We selected the ACS CAN because it is an organization that pursues policy goals and depends upon the support of individual citizens for volunteers and donations. It is exactly the type of organization that scholars of political behavior may be interested in studying.
7. The control group had an average score of 12.44; the treatment group had an average score of 9. This difference is significant at $p < .05$, two-tailed test.
8. Other control variables, including partisanship and an individual's familiarity with the ACS CAN, had no effect on group differences.
9. These costs, moreover, can be ascertained based on pretests such as cognitive interviews.

REFERENCES

Ahn, T. K, Huckfeldt, R., & Ryan, J. B. (2007). Political expertise, shared biases, and patterns of political communication. Paper presented at the annual meeting of the Midwest Political Science Association, Chicago IL.

Ansolabehere, S., & Iyengar, S. (1995). *Going negative: How political advertisements shrink and polarize the electorate.* New York: Simon & Schuster.

Battaglini, M., Morton, R., & Palfrey, T. (2007). Efficiency, equity, and timing of voting mechanisms. *American Political Science Review, 101,* 409–424.

Belli, R., Traugott, M., & Beckmann, M. (2001). What leads to voting overreports? Contrasts of overreports to validated voters and admitted nonvoters in the American National Election Studies, *Journal of Official Statistics, 17,* 479–498.

Berinsky, A. J., Burns, N., & Traugott, M. W. (2001). Who votes by mail? *Public Opinion Quarterly, 65,* 178–197.

Bimber, B. (2001). Information and political engagement in America: The search for effects of information technology at the individual level. *Political Research Quarterly, 54,* 53–67.

Bimber, B., & Davis, R. (2003). *Campaigning online: The Internet in U.S. elections.* New York: Oxford University Press.

Bone, P. F., & Scholder Ellen, P. (1992). The generation and consequences of communication-evoked imagery. *Journal of Consumer Research, 19,* 93–104.

Brader, T. (2005). Striking a responsive chord: How political ads motivate and persuade voters by appealing to emotions. *American Journal of Political Science, 49,* 388–405.

Brader, T., Valentino, N., & Suhay, E. (2008). What triggers public opposition to immigration? Anxiety, group cues, and immigration threat. *American Journal of Political Science, 52,* 959–978.

Brooks, D. J., & Geer, J. G. (2007). Beyond negativity: The effects of incivility on the electorate. *American Journal of Political Science, 51,* 1–16.

Camerer, C. (2003). *Behavioral game theory.* Princeton, NJ: Princeton University Press.

Carroll, J. S. (1978). The effect of imagining an event on expectations for the event: an interpretation in terms of the availability heuristic. *Journal of Experimental Social Psychology, 14,* 88–96.

Cialdini, R. B., & De Nicholas, M. E. (1989). Self-presentation by association. *Journal of Personality and Social Psychology, 57*, 626–631.

Clinton, J. D., & Lapinksi, J. S. (2004). 'Targeted' advertising and voter turnout: An experimental study of the 2000 presidential election. *Journal of Politics, 66*, 69–96.

Druckman, J., Kifer, M. J., & Parkin, M. (2007). The technological development of congressional candidate Web sites. *Social Science Computer Review, 25*, 425–442.

Fowler, J. H. (2006). Altruism and turnout. *Journal of Politics, 68*, 674–683.

Fowler, J. H., & Kam, C. D. (2007). Beyond the self: Altruism, social identity, and political participation. *Journal of Politics, 69*, 813–827.

Glynn, C., Huge, M., & Lunney, C. (2009). The influence of perceived social norms on college students' intention to vote. *Political Communication, 26*, 48–64.

Gregory, W. L., Burroughs, W. J., & Ainslie, F. M. (1985). Self-relevant scenarios as an indirect means of attitude change. *Personality and Social Psychology Bulletin, 11*, 435–444.

Gregory, W. L., Cialdini, R. B., & Carpenter, K. M. (1982). Self-relevant scenarios as mediators of likelihood estimates and compliance: Does imagining make it so? *Journal of Personality and Social Psychology, 43*, 89–99.

Houston, D. A., & Doan, K. (1999). Can you back that up? Evidence (or lack thereof) for the effects of negative and positive political communication. *Media Psychology, 1*, 191–206.

Iyengar, S., & Simon, A. F. (2000). New Perspectives and evidence on political communication and campaign effects. *Annual Review of Psychology, 51*, 149–169.

Keeter, S., Zukin, C., Andolina, M., & Jenkins, K. (2002). *The civic and political health of the nation: A generational portrait.* Center for Information and Research on Civic Learning and Engagement. Retrieved July 15, 2010, from http://www.civicyouth.org/?page_id=151.

Kinder, D. R., & Palfrey, T. R. (1993). On behalf of an experimental political science. In D. R. Kinder & T. R. Palfrey (Eds.), *Experimental foundations in political science* (pp. 1–39). Ann Arbor: University of Michigan Press.

Kroes, E. P., & Sheldon, R. J. (1988). Stated preference methods: An introduction. *Journal of Transport Economics and Policy, 22*, 11–25.

Krupnikov, Y. (2009). *Who votes? How and when negative campaign advertisements affect voter turnout.* Unpublished doctoral dissertation, Department of Political Science, University of Michigan, Ann Arbor.

Krupnikov, Y., & Levine, A. S. (2010). How likely are you to act? The psychology of measuring willingness to engage in political action. Paper presented at the annual meeting of the Midwest Political Science Association, Chicago, IL.

Lau, R., & Redlawsk, D. (2006). *How voters decide.* New York: Cambridge University Press.

Leshner, G., & Thorson, E. (2000). Overreporting voting: Campaign media, public mood, and the vote. *Political Communication, 17*, 263–278.

Levine, A. S. (2009). *Why common candidate rhetoric can backfire in requests for political donations.* Paper presented at the annual meeting of the Midwest Political Science Association, Chicago IL.

Min, Y. (2004). Turnout and candidate preference news coverage of negative political campaigns: An experiment of negative campaign effects on turnout and candidate preference. *Harvard International Journal of Press/Politics, 9*, 95–111.

Petrova, P. K., & Cialdini, R. B. (2005). Fluency of consumption imagery and the backfire effects of imagery appeals. *Journal of Consumer Research, 32*, 442–452.

Petrova, P. K., & Cialdini, R. B. (2008). Evoking the imagination as a strategy of influence. In C. P. Haugtvedt, P. M. Herr, & F. R. Kardes (Eds.), *Handbook of consumer psychology* (pp. 505–524), London: Taylor and Francis Group.

Pinkleton, B. E., Austin, E. W., & Fortman, K. K. J. (1998). Relationships of media use and political disaffection to political efficacy and voting behavior. *Journal of Broadcasting & Electronic Media, 42*, 34–49.

Sherman, S., Cialdini, R. B., Schwartzman, D. F., & Reynolds, K. D. (1985). Imagining can heighten or lower the perceived likelihood of contracting a disease: The mediating effect of ease of imagery. *Personality and Social Psychology Bulletin, 11*, 118–127.

Stromer-Galley, J., & Muhlberger, P. (2009). Agreement and disagreement in group deliberation: Effects on deliberation satisfaction, future engagement, and decision legitimacy. *Political Communication, 26,* 173–192.

Traugott, M. W., & Katosh, J. P. (1979). Response validity in surveys of voting behavior. *Public Opinion Quarterly, 43,* 359–377.

Tversky, A., & Kahneman, D. (1973). Availability: A heuristic for judging frequency and probability. *Cognitive Psychology, 5,* 207–232.

Valentino, N. A., Beckmann, M. N., & Buhr, T. A. (2001). A spiral of cynicism for some: The contingent effects of campaign news frames on participation and confidence in government. *Political Communication, 18,* 347–367.

Valentino, N. A., Hutchings, V., Banks, A., & Davis, A. (2008). Is a worried citizen a good citizen? Emotions, political information seeking and learning via the Internet. *Political Psychology, 29,* 247–273.

Vavreck, L. (2007). The exaggerated effects of advertising on turnout: The dangers of self-reports. *Quarterly Journal of Political Science, 2,* 287–305.

10

The Face as a Focus of Political Communication

Evolutionary Perspectives and the Ethological Method

Patrick A. Stewart
Department of Political Science
University of Arkansas

Frank K. Salter
Max Planck Research Group for Human Ethology
Andechs, Germany

Marc Mehu
Swiss Centre for Affective Sciences
University of Geneva
Geneva, Switzerland

The significance of the face for political communication has long been appreciated by practitioners and commentators alike, with the face expressing not just immediate emotional experience and behavioral intent but also reflecting an individual's character as well. Individuals compete for positions of power and then exert influence largely due to their ability to communicate non-verbally, chiefly through the face. Nonverbal communication signals that leaders possess the requisite qualities for group members to cede control to them and that they have the capacity to lead the group in effectively confronting obstacles. For their part, the mass media operates as an intermediary between a political leader and his or her presumed followers by offering virtual face-to-face contact that hearkens back to the evolutionary roots of small group decision making.

The importance of leaders provoking the passions of followers has been known since at least Aristotle (Arnhart, 1981), while the systematic study of the face and how it communicates emotional intent has been carried out since Charles Darwin's time (Darwin, 1872/1998). However, the systematic experimental research of the potential for faces to affect political communication traces its roots back to just over a quarter of a century ago with studies by Friedman and colleagues analyzing the impact of newscaster facial expressions while discussing presidential candidates during political campaigns (Friedman, DiMatteo, & Mertz, 1980; Friedman, Mertz, & DiMatteo, 1980) and its influence on electoral outcomes (Mullen et al., 1986). During this same period, the Committee for the Experimental Study of Social and Political Behavior at Dartmouth College (hereafter, the "Dartmouth group") through their systematic research agenda considered how viewers respond to the facial expressions of political leaders in a series of experiments taking place over more than a decade (Masters, 1989a; Masters, Sullivan, Lanzetta, McHugo, & Englis, 1986; McHugo, Lanzetta, Sullivan, Masters, & Englis, 1985; Sullivan & Masters, 1988). Likewise, Ellyson and Dovidio's edited book (1985) provides an early reference for understanding how to approach the study of nonverbal political communication by considering how nonverbal display behavior correlates with dominance and power across cultures, ages, and species.

A major indicator of a politician's status as a serious candidate is the attention, or "face time," he or she obtains from the mass media. This visual dominance is well established as an indicator of status not only with humans, but with any animal species in which there is a hierarchical social structure (Chance, 1967; De Waal, 1982; Eibl-Eibesfeldt, 1989; Mazur, 2005; Salter, 1995; Turner, 1997). In order to be chosen as a leader, one must look and act like a viable leader; this, in turn, is preconditioned on having other individuals paying attention. Visual dominance is key for candidates to nonverbally communicate their capacity for leadership to the public, with nonverbal delivery more likely to affect the emotional response of viewers than the same information provided via audio only, in a written format, or covered in a news report (Exline, 1985; Patterson, Churchill, Burger, & Powell, 1992; Schubert, 1998).[1]

The face is an especially important source of information not just due to its being the location where smell, taste, sight, and hearing stimuli are received, but also due to it being always visible and providing information, be it verbal or nonverbal, even in repose. The face provides information through different properties.[2] The first property, *morphological structure*, is static, as the size, shape, location of facial features, and their contours provide information about the identity and attractiveness of an individual. Morphological structure is affected by *slow signs* such as wrinkles and bags, that provide information about age, and *artificial signs*, such as cosmetics, tattoos, piercings, and plastic surgery, that attempt to alter the slow signs. The final, focal property for this chapter is that of *rapid signs*, in which changes in muscle tonus, blood flow, and skin temperature affect the facial displays that communicate emotional state and behavioral intent (Cohn & Ekman, 2005; Schmidt & Cohn, 2001).[3]

Therefore, this chapter focuses on the face as the key component of political communication, emphasizing displays that are flexible and momentary and that may signal behavioral intent, by taking an ethological perspective. Specifically, we consider the major theoretical framework for understanding dominance relationships between leaders and followers and how nonverbal communication plays a role in it. Particularly, we focus on key categories of facial display behavior. We next analyze an extended selection of published experimental studies considering the influence of nonverbal behavior by politicians on research subjects in terms of stimuli, measures, and subject pool. We follow this with suggestions for future research, again, in terms of stimuli, measures, and subjects before offering concluding comments.

EVOLUTIONARY QUESTIONS AND METHODS

Key in the early political communication studies concerning facial displays, and the developments inspired by them, was an appreciation for the importance of evolutionary theory to understanding commonalities in political behavior and an interdisciplinarity that drew extensively upon the natural sciences. Non-human mammalian, especially primate, species provided insight, and still present models of behavior for human political activities. This biobehavioral perspective draws heavily from classical ethology, and differs from traditional perspectives that focus solely on proximal influences on political behavior by considering four different types of questions. These questions are separate, yet not mutually exclusive, and consider not just proximal causation by looking at the behavior of individuals, but also ultimate causation, which considers both individual and population-level behavior (Lehner, 1996).

These four types of questions about behavior were posited by ethologist Niko Tinbergen in his seminal 1963 paper and concern proximate causation, ontogenetic development, phylogenetic roots, and ultimate causation (Barrett, Dunbar, & Lycett, 2002; Lehner, 1996; Tinbergen, 1963). The first two consider proximal causes of individual behavior. *Proximate causation* considers what motivates an individual to behave in a particular manner at a specific moment in time, asking questions concerning mechanisms that produce different types of behavior. *Ontogenetic development* looks at the roots of and development of behavior over an individual's lifetime; in other words, whether there are innate tendencies in upbringing or development of an individual over his or her lifespan that trigger particular behaviors. Both environmental and internal factors are considered in ontogeny, although both are intertwined and difficult to separate, especially as ontogeny occurs over an individual's lifespan (albeit with greater development occurring earlier in life).

The last two questions address ultimate causal factors with the understanding that questions answered at one level of analysis may not provide a valid basis for generalization to another level (Peterson & Somit, 1982). The third question considers how behavior develops in a species over its history and analyzes its *phylogenetic roots* by considering differences in behavior amongst several closely related species. *Ultimate causation* considers the functional cause of a behavior in terms of how it promotes the passing of an individual's genes to future generations (Barrett et al., 2002; Lehner, 1996; Tinbergen, 1963).[4]

METHODOLOGICAL ISSUES

The ability to answer each of these four questions posed is limited to the tools that may be employed in terms of research design and measurements employed. Be this as it may, a necessary first step in understanding human behavior is observing and measuring it. As stated by Tinbergen "[C]ontempt for simple observation is a lethal trait in any science . . ." (1963, p. 412). Following from that is experimentation to test whether changes in parameters can influence the occurrence of particular types of behavior. Both of these approaches have limitations. These include the effect of observation on behavior, whether in the field or laboratory, knowing what to measure and employing the proper metric, choosing a sample with adequate numbers, and observing behavior over a sufficient amount of time and settings to address recurrently occurring events and environments that might influence outcomes (Peterson & Somit, 1982).

Further difficulties lie in ethical limitations when experimenting on humans. Because a major endeavor of research is to ascertain a "human nature" allowing for inferences to be drawn to all humans, "true" experiments that alter "human behavior" are rare.[5] Instead, the great majority of experiments attempt to alter contextual/environmental information. In addition, while issues of internal validity, based upon how a research design is set up and carried out, are always points of concern, the major criticism of experimental studies is their external validity (Barrett et al., 2002; Hansen & Pfau, this volume); in other words, can the findings be applied to "the real world" with confidence? Specific questions concern whether people will do what they state during interviews or note on questionnaires and whether the behavior is universal enough for inferences to be drawn from a homogenous sample or whether the pool of subjects is diverse enough to reflect differences. This can play havoc with the external validity of findings.

Therefore, most research, predominantly experimental, considers proximal causation to understand why people make the decisions they do. However, both observational studies and experimental research considering developmental changes across an individual's lifespan (onto-genetic) and cross-species comparisons (phylogenetic), especially with social primates genetically related to humans, are highly useful in understanding behavior. In the former case there is an understanding of how individuals interact with their environment and change in developmental manner (Panksepp, 1998). In the latter, social primates such as bonobos (*Pan paniscus*) and chimpanzees (*Pan troglodytes*) are seen as closely related species that give insight into behavior that may have been inherited from a common ancestor (Chance, 1967; De Waal, 1982; Eibl-Eibesfeldt, 1989; Parr, Waller, & Fugate, 2005; Preushoft & Van Hooff, 1997; Van Hooff & Preushoft, 2003; Waller & Dunbar, 2005).

ETHOLOGICAL APPROACH TO FACIAL DISPLAYS OF EMOTION

Humans are a socially labile species in which individuals exhibit a strong desire to attain social dominance over others, yet will give up this chance for the sake of preventing others from dominating them. Therefore, while strong hierarchical dominance relationships in which leaders exert coercive power to produce submissiveness from the rank-and-file do become established (Somit & Peterson, 1997), there also seems to be a countervailing impetus toward an "anti-hierarchy" in which egalitarianism reigns (Boehm, 1999). Specifically, there is a wariness of leaders who would overstep their boundaries of control and a series of group social sanctions in response to leaders who would attempt to exert their authority beyond group norms (Boehm, 1999). Those who wish to become leaders must communicate the "absence of arrogance, overbearingness, boastfulness, and personal aloofness" (p. 69) and "espouse a combination of unaggressiveness, generosity, and friendly emotions" (p. 234).

Therefore, potential leaders must exhibit not just the ability to dominate others, whether in response to internal threats to the group's peace or external threats to its well-being, but also the ability to affiliate with group members. Facial display behavior of leaders, and those who hope to wear the mantle of leadership, therefore must be able to communicate both agonistic and hedonic intent. However, circumstances determine which type of display behavior is appropriate and should predominate (Bucy, 2000; Bucy & Bradley, 2004; Bucy & Grabe, 2008; Bucy & Newhagen, 1999).

Ethological research regarding political figures carried out by the Dartmouth group (Lanzetta et al., 1985; Masters, 1989b; Masters, Sullivan, Lanzetta, McHugo, & Englis, 1986) and elaborated upon by Salter (1995), suggest a typology of emotional display based upon whether the social circumstance is competitive or non-competitive and the rank held by the displayer. Specifically, dominant individuals are expected to display anger/threatening behavior in agonistic/competitive situations, whereas submissive individuals are expected to show they are fearful and will submit. The ability to signal threat and submissiveness by the respective parties benefits both by ensuring social order and the lack of danger from serious injury or death that would occur to either or both parties if the display behavior was not successfully encoded or interpreted. In those non-competitive situations in which individuals affiliate in the group, dominant individuals are expected to display higher rates of happiness/reassurance, whereas lower-status group members avoid potential conflict and/or social interaction by displaying higher rates of sadness/appeasement behavior, both against a background of neutral affect (Salter, 2007/1995, p. 145). Such display behavior benefits group members by strengthening coalitions through shared displays of non-competitiveness and personal affinity. However, to the extent that leaders or competitors for leadership positions exhibit submissiveness or appeasement, there will be a concomitant weakening of attributions of status (Bucy & Bradley, 2004; Bucy & Grabe, 2008).

An attractive feature of ethological and other evolutionary approaches is their emphasis on behavioral universals. This improves the prospects for discovering principles of communication that pertain to all cultures. Salter (2007/1995) makes this point when defining observational categories of nonverbal behavior for his study of command hierarchies. For instance, dominance has often been associated with smooth, relaxed movements (e.g., Knipe & Maclay, 1972). But there are exceptions, and the association of dominance with both jerky and smooth, aggressive and affiliative displays suggests that leadership might require skill in combining or blending different gestural cues in a functional manner. In particular, leaders appear socially skilled at selecting appropriate nonverbal behaviors in agonistic and affiliative encounters (de Waal, 1982; Sapolsky, 1990; Tiedens & Fragale, 2003).

Along these lines, Palagi and colleagues have carried out extensive observational research with bonobos (Palagi, Paoli, & Tarli, 2004), lemurs (Palagi, Paoli, & Tarli, 2005), chimpanzees (Palagi, Cordoni, & Tarli, 2004), and gorillas (Cordoni, Palagi, & Tarli, 2006), highlighting the importance of post-conflict reconciliation and consolation for group cohesion and harmony. Agonistic behavior is typically followed by affiliative encounters to maintain group order. Although this research focused on broadly defined behavior, facial displays by primates are recognized as being "highly conserved," that is, constant across species, albeit with differences in social function, since at least Darwin's (1872/1998) *The Expression of the Emotions in Man and Animals* (see also, De Marco, Petit, & Visalberghi, 2008; Preuschoft & van Hooff, 1997; van Hooff & Preuschoft, 2003; Visalberghi, Valenzano, & Preuschoft, 2006). Cross-species comparisons have been further enhanced by the development of ChimpFACS, a standardized observational tool allowing direct structural comparison of human and chimpanzee facial display behavior based on facial musculature (Parr et al., 2007; Parr, Waller, & Fugate, 2005; Parr, Waller, & Vick, 2007; Vick et al., 2007).

The face, then, is a premier communication site that has universal features. Across human populations, there appears to be a consensus concerning the emotional meaning attributed to particular facial expressions (Ekman & Oster, 1979), with the muscle movements underlying these emotionally meaningful configurations present in most individuals (Waller, Cray, & Burrows, 2008). While there are cultural differences in display rules, when a prototypical facial configuration is displayed it has a similar meaning across cultures (Marsh, Anger-Elfenbein, & Ambady, 2003). Scherer and Grandjean (2008) have recently suggested that this effect could be due to the fact that emotion words (as well as emotion components) are more readily available to make categorical judgments about faces than other kinds of categories like social motives and action tendencies. Of the six basic emotions identified by Ekman and colleagues (Ekman & Friesen, 2003) as occurring in prototypical facial displays (surprise, fear, disgust, anger, happiness, and sadness), four are closely tied to dominance relationships, whether affiliative (happiness–reassurance and sadness–appeasement) or agonistic (anger–threat and fear–evasion).

However, the precise meaning of a facial expression often depends on context. For example, a smile can express dominance as well as submission and function as a greeting or invitation to play or interact socially. A smile can also be used instrumentally to communicate these meanings even though the sender is not feeling happiness. The meaning of a smile or other facial expression depends on the interactants' relationship and the social setting. A leader's smile can function to reassure a subordinate that punishment is not pending. From a subordinate, a smile is more likely to signal willingness to cooperate (Salter, 2007/1995; Salter, Grammer, & Rikowski, 2005). Subtle changes in smiles may also be linked to different meanings, such as affiliation with peers or yielding to those with greater dominance, depending on the context (Mehu, Grammer, & Dunbar, 2007; Mehu & Dunbar, 2008a). In the next section we revisit Salter's (2007/1995) elaboration on the Dartmouth group's typology (Masters et al., 1986) of facial display behavior, which has been used as observational categories for field studies, media content analyses, and experiments assessing the influence of leader displays.

AFFILIATIVE FACIAL EXPRESSIONS

Primate Comparisons

Across primate species affiliative mood is signaled by variable posture and gaze while body movements are smooth (van Hooff, 1973; de Waal, 1982). The head is often tilted or translated to one side in happy mood. However, the facial displays are crucial in primate societies for signaling behavioral intentions, thus shaping interactions and relationships of affiliation, attachment, and appeasement. Three facial patterns stand out as being used most often in affiliative encounters in primates: lip-smacking, relaxed open mouth, and, with variation discussed later, the silent bared teeth display. The first display, lip-smacking, is most closely associated with greeting and consists of (1) eyebrows lifted; (2) eyelids lifted (or not lowered with chimpanzees); (3) gaze averted or unfixed; (4) mouth not fixed but varied between open and closed; (5) lips relaxed and showing at least some teeth; (6) mouth corners variable; (7) head tilted up; and (8) smooth body motions (De Marco et al., 2008; van Hooff, 1969; Visalberghi et al., 2006).

The relaxed open mouth and silent bared teeth displays, while separate in some non-human primates, are seen to have converged in humans to serve affiliative functions, although recent research suggests higher levels of conservation of these two displays in social behavior. Specifically, the relaxed open mouth display, in which the lip corners are stretched and the mouth is open, is seen across a range of primate species and is used as an indicator of willingness to play (De Marco et al., 2008 Preuschoft & van Hooff, 1997; van Hooff & Preuschoft, 2003; Visalberghi et al., 2006; Waller & Dunbar, 2005) and, in Tonkin macaques (Preuschoft & van Hooff, 1997), tufted capuchins (De Marco et al., 2008), and chimpanzees (Waller & Dunbar, 2005), affiliative behavior. The silent bared teeth display, which is also associated with submissive/appeasement behavior, is used with the initiation of contact and other affiliative behavior and is indicated by the mouth corners being pulled back to show upper and lower teeth in a closed position (De Marco et al., 2008 Preuschoft & van Hooff, 1997; van Hooff & Preuschoft, 2003; Visalberghi et al., 2006; Waller & Dunbar, 2005).

Happiness/Reassurance

In human happiness/reassurance displays, non-threatening gestures are combined with reassuring facial actions such as smiles and raised eyebrows (Eibl-Eibesfeldt, 1989; Kleinke, 1986). These behaviors follow the general pattern with primates. A smiling face can induce a similar expression and corresponding mood in the observer and alleviate the impulse to flee. Hence, a smile may act to neutralize aggression and function as an effective greeting. Morris (1977) observed that the human recognition response consists of a smile, eyebrow flash (lasting approximately one sixth of a second), head tilt, hail, wave, and intentional embrace. The first three are almost always present and occur simultaneously, while the last three are more variable between situations and cultures. Eibl-Eibesfeldt (1979) identified salient features of greeting displays as initial eye contact followed by the head toss and eyebrow flash, followed by one or more nods. The smile is usually, but not always, present. The eyebrow flash communicates agreement in various contexts, including agreement to social contact. Grammer, Shiefenhovel, Schleidt, Lorenz, and Eibl-Eibesfeldt, (1988) have described smiles as a "social-marking" tool used to emphasize the meaning of other facial, gestural, and verbal signals. The nature of greeting displays is consistent with Darwin's (1998/1872, Chapter 2) principle of antithesis, with the greeter exhibiting the opposite of agonistic, anger/threat behavior.

The mouth is an important indicator of affiliative intent through the happiness/reassurance display of the smile. However, there are many different types of smiles that can be distinguished by varying mouth movements (Brannigan & Humphries, 1972), or by the coactivation of the orbicularis occuli, a ring of muscles surrounding the eye that produce cheek raise and crow's feet wrinkles when stimulated (Duchenne de Boulogne, 1862; Ekman & Friesen, 1982). Another affiliative display that involves the mouth is the relaxed open mouth display, which is mainly observed in playful interactions and promotes affiliative relationships (Preushoft & van Hooff, 1997; van Hooff & Preushoft, 2003; Waller & Dunbar, 2005). The co-occurrence of relaxed open-mouth and silent bared teeth displays (evident during laughter) is particularly salient in egalitarian relationships where these behaviors function to strengthen social bonds.

In addition, recent research suggests that different types of smiles have different functions in social interactions (Mehu & Dunbar, 2008a), in that emotion-based smiles can function to regulate cooperative relationships through the advertisement of altruistic intentions (Brown, Palameta, & Moore, 2003, Mehu et al., 2007; Mehu, Little & Dunbar 2007). This functional emancipation of the silent bared teeth display is thought to stem from selection pressures imposed by increasingly complex social organization (Parr, Waller, & Fugate, 2005; Preuschoft & van Hooff, 1997). Hierarchical relationships are based on the ability to signal one's social position in the hierarchy and therefore avoid potentially damaging conflicts. In this case, it is important to have explicit signals of power and submission that are distinct from affiliative and cooperative signals. In egalitarian relationships, the need for distinct signals for power, submission, and affiliation is considerably diminished because payoffs depend heavily on collaborative effort, hence on the strength of the social bond. This explains why smiling and laughter are used interchangeably in egalitarian relationships whereas both displays are used separately in hierarchical contexts (Mehu & Dunbar, 2008b; Preuschoft & van Hooff, 1997).

Sadness/Appeasement

Sadness has been interpreted to serve the function of a yielding behavior which appeases an aggressor, reducing the risk of further attack and allowing the defeated individual to remain in the group. The former function has been traced to separation distress in infants by Plutchik (1980, pp. 322–326; also see Darwin, 1998/1872, Chapter 6). Price and Sloman's (1987) yielding hypothesis interprets the sad individual's behavior as reassuring adversaries that he is incapable of "making a comeback" (Schjelderup-Ebbe 1935) and therefore is deserving of caring and concern.[6] With rare exceptions, displaying sadness is behavior not acceptable from our leaders. For instance, Senator Edmund Muskie, front-runner for the 1972 Democratic party presidential nomination, found his campaign derailed by appearing to cry in response to an attack on his wife. On the other hand, President George W. Bush's apparent sadness during his nationally televised speeches in the wake of the September 11, 2001 terrorist attacks were deemed appropriately empathetic.

Descriptions of sadness are in strong agreement. In addition to downturned mouth corners, the sad face features the inner eyebrows being raised and pulled together, forming an inverted "U" shaped wrinkle at the center of the forehead. The eyes are distinguished by the inner upper eyelid being drawn up and the lower eyelid appearing raised (Darwin, 1998/1872, pp. 177–178; Ekman & Friesen, 2003, p. 117). Darwin considered the eyebrows and the horizontal forehead furrows to be the major signalers of sadness or grief, calling the responsible muscles the "grief muscles" (1998/1872, p. 179) and concluded from cross-cultural evidence that the latter display was universal. While sadness is relatively well recognized across cultures, the precision afforded researchers by electromyographic detection of muscle activity allows a more rigorous analysis of emotional expressiveness than visible expressions. Notably, in the case of sadness/appeasement, the corrugator muscle, lying laterally above and on either side of the nose, is generally associated with expressions of sadness, grief and pain and is reliably activated by depressed mood.

AGONISTIC FACIAL EXPRESSIONS

Primate Comparisons

Common features of the anger–threat display in nonhuman primates, the open-mouth threat face, were categorized by van Hooff (1969) and include fixed direction of gaze (at or away from others) and tense mouth, with lowered eyebrows in apes. In general, agonistic behavior is marked by greater body tension than in happiness–reassurance. In anger–threat displays, dominant primates bend the head forward with the transition to attack being achieved with jerky or sudden movements. These displays tended to be used instrumentally in conjunction with agonist behavior against lower-ranking members to elicit submissive displays (Visalberghi, Valenzano, & Preuschoft, 2006), although in tufted capuchins the open-mouth threat face display is often met with the same response (De Marco, Petit, & Visalberghi, 2008). However, this display is not met with play or affiliative behavior (De Marco et al., 2008; Visalberghi et al., 2006).

Displays uniquely identified with submission include averted gaze, head oriented away from the dominant, and closed eyelids (Marler, 1965, p. 571). Common primate characteristics of the fear-submission display, the silent bared teeth display, include, as discussed above, open mouth, lips retracted vertically to expose most of the teeth, and corners of mouth completely retracted (De Marco et al., 2008; Preuschoft 1992; Visalberghi et al., 2006). This display is flexible, being seen used to indicate appeasement in Rhesus and long-tailed macaques, Barbary macaques, Tonkin macaques, chimpanzees, and humans (Preushoft & van Hooff, 1997); however, this display is context-dependent, with this display not associated with submissive behavior or in response to aggression in tufted macaques (De Marco et al., 2008) or tufted capuchin monkeys (Visalberghi et al., 2006). Specifically, as posited by Van Hooff and Preuschoft, the intent of this display is flexible based upon the social context, in this case how hierarchical or egalitarian a species or social grouping is (Preuschoft & van Hooff, 1997; van Hooff & Preuschoft, 2003).

Anger/Threat

In humans, anger/threat is a relatively unambiguous and readily decoded emotional display, as emphasized by Ekman's description of the lowered-brow anger expression (see Box 10.1) is applicable across human cultures (Ekman, Friesen, & Ellsworth, 1972). Based on extensive cross-cultural observations, Eibl-Eibesfeldt (1989, pp. 370–371) described the human threat display as a fixed stare unaccompanied by signs of reassurance, with brows raised or lowered. The psychological literature supports the view that stares become especially threatening when unaccompanied by dynamics associated with smiles or physical attractiveness (Kleinke, 1986). Social psychologists have long documented how dominant individuals stare more than others in competitive situations

(Dovidio & Ellyson, 1985; Exline, Ellyson, & Long, 1975). The stare is most threatening, measured by arousal levels, when the eyes are in a horizontal plane. Thus, a wide-eyed horizontal stare is characteristic of threat and seems to project anger (Morris, 1967, pp. 162–163).

In addition to (and likely because of) communicating threat, aggressive behaviors attract attention. Dominant individuals are more adept at and enjoy greater freedom to deploy aggressive gestures and tactics as a means of holding the floor. And dominance, once attained, is attention-getting in its own right. Visual attentiveness signals social power such that the greater the amount of visual attention given to an individual, the lower the observer's status relative to the focus of attention (Hold-Cavell, 1992). Likewise, experiments find that dominant individuals look more at their audience or conversational partner while speaking but less when listening to lower-status individuals (Dovidio & Ellyson 1985; Exline et al., 1975).

Fear/Submission

From an evolutionary perspective encounters between strangers are expected to elicit signals of fear–submission since humans are adapted to function in small, intimate groups. This prediction is supported by physiological evidence that indicated increased anxiety in participants approached by strangers (McBride, King, & James, 1965). One observational study found that in over 90% of observed interactions between strangers, individuals displayed combinations of gaze avoidance, lip compression and lip-bite; tongue show and tongue-in-cheek; hand-to-face, hand-to-hand, and hand-to-body manipulations; and postures involving flexion and abduction of the upper limbs (Givens 1981, p. 222). These self-directed "displacement activities" serve as behavioral measures of social stress in humans and non-human primates (Troisi, 2002).

Ekman's description of the facial signals of fear has the eyelids in a similar configuration to that of anger, leaving the combination of raised eyebrows and the horizontally stretched mouth as the main distinguishing feature of fearful facial expressions (Ekman & Friesen, 2003). Several mouth configurations are consistent with Ekman's description of horizontally stretched lips. For instance, the compressed mouth display has been associated with anxiety in interactions with strangers and other unpleasant social interactions (Givens, 1981; Grant, 1969; Smith, Chase, & Lieblich, 1974; Stern & Bender, 1974). And smiles, as mentioned earlier, can express appeasement (Eibl-Eibesfeldt, 1989, pp. 466–467; Ekman, Friesen, & Ancoli, 1980; Ekman, Friesen, & O'Sullivan 1988; Mehu & Dunbar, 2008b; Waller & Dunbar, 2005).

Since submissive or fearful expressions involve the lowered brow similar to anger displays, albeit with a furrowed appearance, additional signals of head orientation and gaze add important contextual cues. In contrast to anger, the chin is lowered and gaze is averted, as can be seen cross-culturally with children (Konner, 1972; McGrew, 1972; Stern & Bender, 1974). The aversion of gaze may be used to reduce stress. Indeed, research has linked increased arousal with gaze from strangers in threatening situations (Kleinke, 1986). While continuous gaze is disliked, those who avert gaze during conversation are judged to be defensive, evasive, nervous, or lacking in confidence (Kraut & Poe, 1980).

VIEWER RESPONSES TO NONVERBAL LEADER DISPLAYS

Studies investigating the nonverbal display behavior of political leaders have applied these and other display categories in longitudinal content analyses of election campaigns as well as experimental research that continues to inform our understanding of politics and leadership. Over time, the methods and measures of investigation have become more sophisticated and have achieved greater ecological validity. Specifically, research carried out since the mid-1980s has become more externally valid in terms of stimuli employed, more savvy in measuring viewer responses, and more cognizant of the need to test a range of participants. The following section reviews published studies carried out over the past quarter century that focus on viewer responses to nonverbal leader displays. Attention is given to how the stimulus of the face is presented in experimental research, how the dependent variables are measured, and who the experimental participants for the studies are (see Table 10.1).

As pointed out by Masters et al. (1986, p. 323), research concerning facial display behavior leads to three different questions: (1) whether the actor actually *feels* the emotion displayed—in other words, whether the display is genuine; (2) whether observers ascribe intent to the actor in terms of how the displayer plans to act; and (3) whether displays reliably elicit emotional responses in observers. While the first question may only be inferred, as politicians likely have mastered the ability to mask their internal state while presenting the socially appropriate displays, the latter two may be empirically interrogated through experimental research. Therefore, the study of facial display behavior is not limited to just assessing the emotional state of the actor (Fridlund, 1994, 1997) but to the social dynamic of communication that may occur with or without conscious awareness on the part of the observer.

The Face as Experimental Stimulus

Analysis of the influence of nonverbal leader displays on viewers can be grouped into two categories. The first grouping considers the influence of presidential candidate nonverbal behavior during televised debates.[7] Exline's (1985) analysis of nonverbal stress cues by President Gerald Ford and Governor Jimmy Carter during their first 1976 debate and Patterson et al.'s (1992) investigation of the second Reagan–Mondale debate found that movements that reflect tension or stress affect how favorably the candidates in their respective debates are evaluated. These nonverbal indicators of stress include eye blinks, gaze shift and direction, lip moistening, awkward speech, head nods, body sway, and hand gestures, and along with affective gestures such as brow movements and smiles were shown to have an influence on participant perceptions of the presidential candidates.

The second approach, used by the Dartmouth group and subsequent researchers, takes the more theoretically driven approach discussed above using cross-cultural, developmental, and cross-species studies to derive three prototypic facial displays: happiness/reassurance, anger/threat, and fear/evasion, as well as a neutral display as a reference point. Whereas early studies focused on the influence of the prototypic displays (Masters & Sullivan, 1989; McHugo et al., 1985; Sullivan & Masters, 1988), later studies considered intensity and valence of display

TABLE 10.1
Emotional Displays in the Context of Rank

		BEHAVIOR AND PHYSIOLOGY	
		Agonistic (competitive)	*Affiliative (noncompetitive)*
RANK	Dominant	**Anger–threat**	**Happiness–reassurance**
	Submissive	**Fear–submission**	**Sadness–appeasement**

Source: Modified from Masters et al. (1986) with the addition of sadness–appeasement. From Salter, 1995, p. 144.

behavior (Bucy, 2000; Bucy & Bradley, 2004; Bucy & Newhagen, 1999; McHugo, Lanzetta, & Bush, 1991), and moved from focusing solely on leader expressions to studying facial displays in relation to specific news story contexts, particularly national crisis news (Bucy, 2000, 2003; Bucy & Bradley, 2004; Bucy & Newhagen, 1999; Sullivan & Masters, 1994), giving the experimental research greater external validity.

The selection of treatment stimuli from evening newscasts and other publicly accessible sources can be seen as contributing to the external validity of these studies. Nationally known political figures represent highly salient stimuli due to their public visibility and the ability of these figures, once in office, to influence policy outcomes through their leadership.

As noted by Masters (1989a), context matters in the interpretation and power of the stimuli. Politicians presented in a competitive situation, such as in a debate, are viewed differently than when presented alone. Likewise, politicians who are not presently holding political office will have less salience for the viewer than those currently serving and exerting influence (Way & Masters, 1996a, 1996b).

With the exception of Exline's 9- and 10-minute sequences from presidential debates (1985), the duration of experimental treatments featuring dynamic facial displays generally lasts between 30 and 75 seconds. Mapping the prevalence and influence of nonverbal cues present in news takes into consideration an explicit understanding of the structure of television news stories and how they are presented (see Grabe & Bucy, 2009). In addition to candidate displays, the influence of newscaster expressions have been investigated. Early work by Friedman and colleagues examined the perceived "bias" of network newscaster facial expressions toward presidential candidates Gerald Ford and Jimmy Carter during the 1976 election. Of five network news anchorpersons analyzed, one (John Chancellor) showed greater judged facial positivity toward Gerald Ford and three (Walter Cronkite, David Brinkley, and Harry Reasoner) showed greater facial positivity toward Jimmy Carter. The fifth anchor (Barbara Walters) did not exhibit significant differences. With just one anchorperson exhibiting greater positivity when the verbal content of the news stories was considered (toward Ford), media "bias" may be perceived more accurately in the facial expressiveness of newscasters than in the semantic content of their story narratives (Friedman, DiMatteo, & Mertz, 1980; Friedman, Mertz, & DiMatteo, 1980). Subsequent work by Mullen and colleagues found that newscaster expressions may have played a role in shaping voting behavior, with the ABC network news anchor Peter Jennings exhibiting strong bias in favor of Ronald Reagan over Walter Mondale in his facial display behavior when reporting news stories. When a subsequent telephone survey of four media markets was carried out, there was a significant difference in voting patterns with those respondents watching ABC more likely to vote for Reagan (Mullen et al., 1986).

An interesting finding from this research is that the effect of leader displays can be modified via a priming effect by visuals that immediately precede the target stimulus. Viewer sensitivity to subtle, if not subliminal,[8] emotionally relevant cues of 33 milliseconds before viewing multiple political figures was documented in experimental studies by Way and Masters (1996a, 1996b) who found that these brief stimuli only affected participants when viewing Democratic President Bill Clinton when compared with less salient Democrats (Earnest Hollings, Reubin Askew, and Walter Mondale), suggesting higher levels of attentiveness to leaders. A study investigating "micro-expressions" of emotion in the face of President George H. W. Bush during his 1991 speech to the American public declaring his intent to attack Iraq in response to its invasion of Kuwait found that several inappropriate facial displays of less than 1 second each led to dampened emotional response in viewers, reinforcing the sensitivity of viewers to thin slices of problematic nonverbal behavior by leaders in times of crisis (Stewart, Waller, & Schubert, 2009).

Measures

While most studies in both groupings employed self-report items and scales to assess experimental effects, the use of psychophysiological measures and latency in response was also seen in several of the studies considered in this review, suggesting the importance of multiple methods in measuring viewer responses. Complementary measures allow investigators to confirm patterns of response from multiple vantage points, whether to determine the signal value or meaning of leader displays as perceived by observers or the cognitive, emotional, or physiological responses that observers have to political display behavior (Masters et al., 1986). Studies have also examined viewer evaluations of politicians more generally, typically in the form of feeling thermometers, and have employed trait evaluations including measures of competence, honesty, trustworthiness, attractiveness, leadership ability and likeability, among others. By utilizing multiple measures researchers are able to address concerns over measurement validity and reliability.

Politician Evaluation

When viewer evaluations, including both affective ratings and trait attributions, have been subjected to factor analysis, two distinct yet theoretically congruent factors emerge: reassurance and dominance. In a cross-cultural study comparing responses to leaders in the United States (Ronald Reagan) and France (Jacques Chirac and Laurent Fabius), the first factor extracted was reassurance, with negative loadings for the emotion terms comforting and joyful, and positive loadings for angry and disgusted (Masters & Sullivan, 1989). The second factor, dominance, likewise emerged for all three politicians, with positive loadings for strong and interested, and negative loadings for confused and fearful.[9] An administration of the study in the United States (Sullivan & Masters, 1994) found reassurance to be denoted by positive loadings for warm, competent, inspiring, and moral, and a negative loading for evasive. Likewise, in the U.S.-only study, trait attributions of confident and aggressive led to the extraction of a dominance factor.

Emotional Response

Self-reports of emotional response to the facial displays of leaders were widely employed in the Dartmouth group studies, reflecting an appreciation for the role of emotion in decision making.[10] While a number of studies consider single measures of emotion (Bucy, 2000, 2003; McHugo et al., 1985; Stewart et al., 2009) or summary variables based upon theoretical rationales (Bucy & Bradley, 2004; Masters, 1994; McHugo et al., 1991; Sullivan & Masters, 1988; Warnecke, Masters, & Kempter, 1992; Way & Masters, 1996a, 1996b), when factor analysis of multiple measures of emotion are carried out, two factors are generally extracted. These two factors reproduce the circumplex model of emotion seen in national opinion survey research (Abelson et al., 1982; Marcus, Neuman, & MacKuen, 2000) where two orthogonal dimensions of affect are extracted. These two factors have been referred to as emotional valence and arousal (Bucy, 2000), behavioral approach and behavioral inhibition (Gray, 1987), or, as described in the political psychology literature, as enthusiasm and anxiety, representing the emotional disposition and surveillance systems (Marcus et al., 2000). In the ethological literature, these dimensions are labeled as hedonic and agonic behavioral styles, respectively, and have been used as overarching themes to cluster specific emotional cues (Masters et al., 1986, p. 322). When tested through factor analysis, the two factors are extracted in direct response leader displays of emotion (Lanzetta et al., 1985; Masters & Sullivan, 1989) or from reflections on emotional experience in the days following experimental treatment (Masters & Carlotti, 1994; Sullivan & Masters, 1994).

Psychophysiological responses were analyzed in a select number of studies and provide insight into not just the response itself, but also the process by which participants consider politicians. Specifically, in three studies reviewed here (Bucy & Bradley 2004; McHugo et al., 1991, 1985), skin conductance, heart rate, and facial electromyographic (EMG) measures were used to assess participant response to leader displays. In this research, skin conductance is employed as an indicator of arousal, heart rate as an indicator of viewer attention, and facial EMG as an indicator of emotional valence. Skin conductance increased in response to anger/threat display behavior (McHugo et al., 1985) and upon viewing inappropriate leader displays (Bucy & Bradley, 2004). Heart rate in one early study increased as a result of both agonic expressions of anger/threat and fear/evasion, especially when compared with happiness/reassurance (McHugo et al., 1985). Bucy and Bradley (2004) found heart rate initially *decreased* (signaling attentional focus) upon exposure to high-intensity displays of President Clinton that followed negative news images, suggesting increased attention to agonic display behavior by the president.

With facial electromyography, electrodes placed over the corrugator muscles are used to measure frowning or negative affect, while recording of zygomatic muscle activity, which is implicated in smiling, are used to measure smiling or positive affect. Both have been successfully employed to measure facial feedback, whether empathetic or counterempathetic, in response to politician display behavior (Bucy & Bradley, 2004; McHugo et al., 1991, 1985). On the other hand, the obicularis oris, which is used to control the opening of the mouth (i.e., the lips) did not show significant effects in the one study in which it was used. In this study, the authors concluded that participant response to the experimental stimuli was primarily affective, whereas the obicularis oris could indicate the depth of information processing (i.e., cognitive response) through subvocal argumentation (McHugo et al., 1991, pp. 32–33).

Bucy and colleagues have used some of the more novel approaches to analyze information processing and emotional experience. Bucy and Newhagen (1999) considered thought elaboration by asking participants to write down their thoughts after each news-story-leader display stimulus, then content analyzed viewer responses for number of thoughts and type of evaluation made. They also employed recognition latency to measure depth of processing, assessed by how quickly participants identified short video segments as being from the experimental stimuli they saw or from distractor material; finally, they considered cued recall of information from the news narrative through multiple choice identification of audio information as part of the exit questionnaire. In addition to the facial EMG and psychophysiological measures reported above, Bucy and Bradley (2004) asked participants to rate their subjective emotional experience by using the Self-Assessment Manikin (SAM) scales, which consist of a series of pictorial indices along the three emotional dimensions of valence (negative–positive), arousal (calm–excited), and dominance (in control–not in control), finding increased arousal for negative and high-intensity news images and leader displays, and lower dominance for increased intensity in both news images and leader displays.

Experimental Participants

Not unexpectedly, the great majority of studies considered here used undergraduates as research participants. The reliance on the stereotypical college sophomore has come under fire for being too narrow a database. Notably, Sears (1986) has argued that the portrayal of human nature might be biased as a result of using a predominantly undergraduate research base that is more likely to be socially compliant, especially to authority figures, and that is more likely to be mercurial in their attitudes due to a lack of self-knowledge. At the same time, Sears observed that the "use of relatively well-educated subjects, selected for their superior cognitive skills, along with research sites, procedures, and tasks that promote dispassionate, academic-like information processing, should help produce empirical evidence that portrays humans as dominated by cognitive processes, rather than by strong evaluative predispositions" (Sears, 1986, p. 526; see also Stewart, 2008).

Interestingly, this might give greater credence to the work on nonverbal communication presented here, as the findings suggest robust affective results in spite of the presumed bias toward cognitive processing by college students (Sears, 1986, p. 527). Despite this, the findings considered here may to some extent be tempered by lingering questions about ecological validity (i.e., approximation of real-life situations) and generalizability. Specifically, the studies are predominantly populated by convenience or opportunity samples of undergraduates, samples which in the case of the Dartmouth group's work (at an elite Ivy League campus) represent highly accomplished young scholars. In terms of interest in and understanding of political information, as well as (at times) close proximity to political events, particularly during the New Hampshire primaries, such a sample population can be expected to not entirely approximate the general population. It is worth noting, however, that some scholars have convincingly argued that basic information processing and emotional responding, particularly processes recorded with psychophysiological measures, may not be completely affected by prior learning (Lang, 1988).

In later studies, the problem of ecological validity was taken into account with research comparing viewer responses across different cultures (Masters & Sullivan, 1989), different ethnicities within the United States (Masters, 1994), and adult, non-student participant pools (Bucy, 2000, exp. 1; Bucy, 2003; Bucy & Newhagen, 1999; Warnecke et al., 1992). While adult populations enhance the external validity of findings, the systematic analysis of data considering the influence of lifecycle effects remains to be explored.[11]

FUTURE RESEARCH DIRECTIONS

Future analysis of the affect of politician facial display behavior necessarily will be presaged by what has come before, in terms of treatment, measurement, and subjects. Furthermore, it will be affected by advancements in technology that allows for replication and progression with the research agenda started almost 30 years ago. However, at the same time a continued appreciation for the guiding principles of evolutionary theory and ethological methods, namely through Tinbergen's four questions (1963), will guide hypothesis generation and testing. Below we consider technological and theoretical advances in recent years that likely will affect future political communication research concerning facial display behavior of political figures.

Observation and Measurement

One of the significant lessons learned is the importance of joining experimentation with observation for understanding the behavior of politicians and concomitant news media coverage of them. Understanding how facial behavior influences viewer perceptions is an important first step; understanding how a politician is presented to the public is likewise salient for researchers hoping to understand the influence of the media on public opinion. Findings suggest that media coverage of facial display behavior varies both in terms of frequency and type of facial display on the basis of campaign phase (Bucy & Grabe, 2008; Masters et al., 1987), candidate status (Bucy & Grabe, 2008; Masters et al., 1987; Masters, Frey & Bente, 1991), and culture (Masters et al., 1991)

While content analysis of news coverage of political candidates over time has been carried out, both over single primary elections (Masters et al., 1987) and over multiple general elections

(Bucy & Grabe, 2008) and have provided extensive insight into media coverage of the electoral process, little research has considered how individuals change in their response to politicians' facial displays of emotion over an extended period of time. Specifically, with the exception of the Dartmouth group's comparison group design in which candidate's fortunes are mapped out at different points during the electoral season by separate samples of individuals (Sullivan & Masters, 1988 [1984 presidential election]; Masters, 1994 [1988 presidential election]; Masters & Carlotti, 1994 [1992 presidential election]) and with their panel design asking subjects to evaluate candidates a day later (Sullivan & Masters, 1994), there is the potential to map an individual's emotional and cognitive response to single (or multiple) politicians over a period of time.

One of the criticisms that may be made concerning research by the Dartmouth group and Bucy is the reliance on interpretation of stereotyped patterns of facial displays such as anger, fear, happiness, and sadness, and the level of precision afforded by coding focusing on movements of specific facial muscles. Specifically, the advent and ascendance of the Facial Action Coding System (FACS) (Box 10.1), an observer-based system in which 41 facial action units (if one excludes head and eye movements) are coded, has provided greater accuracy in the coding of facial displays. Since this system makes a distinction between anatomically based facial movements and inferences about what they mean, it allows a much greater accuracy in the description of facial behavior and does not commit investigators to any theoretical position. The relatively exhaustive character of FACS also allows the description of complex facial configurations that result from the additional effect of individual facial action units (Cohn, Ambadar, & Ekman, 2007).

While the accuracy of Ekman & Friesen's (2003) FACS is not disputed, its frame-by-frame analysis is not well suited for dynamic facial activity (Nusseck, Cunningham, Wallraven, & Bulthoff, 2008) and is prohibitively time expensive when the coding of video segments is required. With each relevant frame demanding an average of 10 minutes to code, the research investment can jump from the estimated 5 minutes non-verbal coding time per event per coder to an hour and a half per event. Therefore the gain in coding precision can be heavily outweighed by the cost in time and energy put into the research. However, new developments in computer vision allows for automatic extraction of facial movements with good levels of accuracy on a number of action units (Cohn & Kanade, 2007; Valstar & Pantic, 2006), which promises to simplify the research process.

Experimentation

A key problem to be addressed by future research concerns how specific nonverbal cues are communicated and processed. Specifically, signals from the eyes and mouth may be communicated as separate components of the face, or as a configuration of these cues. In the latter case, stereotypical facial expressions are seen as readouts of basic emotional states (happiness, sadness, anger, fear, disgust, surprise). While these expressions may be masked, modified through display rules, or mixed to express more nuanced emotional states (Ekman & Friesen, 2003), the key starting point is that of reflecting the core emotional state of an individual.

On the other hand, facial movements may reflect behavioral intent based upon the social context (Fridlund, 1994, 1997; Russell et al., 2003). Since emotion can be said to reflect behavioral tendencies (Frijda, 1986) and result from cognitive evaluation of external events (Scherer, 2001), emotional expression could be used to predict future behavior in a particular situation. With this approach, individual facial action units are assumed to reflect the outcome of cognitive appraisal checks of a particular event, for example the event's relevance to the individual or the capacity of

BOX 10.1 FACIAL ACTION CODING SYSTEM

Ekman and Friesen's (1977) Facial Action Coding System (FACS), an elaboration of Hjortsjö's (1969) pioneering analysis, is the most exhaustive system of facial assessment available. FACS is designed to analyze expressions at the level of muscular contractions. A description of eyebrow movements is pertinent to affiliative and other facial displays since the eyebrow is one of the most salient facial features. Lowered eyebrows have been identified with aggressive faces (Keating et al., 1981).

The three single actions and four combinations exhaust the known repertoire of eyebrow expressions. Neither disgust nor happiness expressions involve eyebrow actions (Ekman, 1979, p. 181). Happiness–reassurance is best decoded from actions of the cheeks and mouth (98% reliability) and from combined actions of eyes, eyelids, cheeks, and mouth (99% reliability) (Boucher & Ekman, 1975). Ekman describes sadness, surprise, fear, and anger thus:

> In *sadness*, either Action Unit 1 or the combination 1+4 occurs, together with the relaxation of the upper eyelid (probably *levator palpebralis superioris*), sometimes a pulling in of the skin around the eye and slight raising of the cheeks (*orbicularis oculi, pars orbitalis* and *zygomatic minor*), a slight depression of the angle of the mouth (*triangularis*), sometimes also a pushing up of the chin (*mentalis*) and lowering of the lower lip (*depressor labii inferioris*). In the distress cry some of the facial actions change. Action Unit 4 is most important in the eyebrows, with less evidence of Action Unit 1. This is joined by the inner and outer portions of *orbicularis oculi*, raising the cheeks, pulling in skin towards the eyes, and tightening the eyelids. Around the mouth the actions described for sadness are joined by horizontal stretching of the lips (*risorius* and/or *platysma*), lowering of the mandible, lowering of the lower lip (*depressor labii inferioris*), and raising of the upper lip (*levator labii superioris*).
>
> In *surprise*, the combination 1+2 is accompanied by raising the upper eyelid (*levator palpebralis*) and dropping the jaw (relaxation of the *masseter*).
>
> In *fear*, the combination 1+2+4 is accompanied by raising the upper eyelid and tightening the lower eyelids (*orbicularis oculi, pars palpebralis*), and by horizontal stretching of the lips (*risorius* and/or *platysma*).
>
> In *anger*, Action Unit 4 without any brow raising is accompanied by the same actions around the eyes as described for fear, with the lips either pressed firmly together (*orbicularis oris* and perhaps *mentalis*), or squared and tightened (some combination of *orbicularis oris, levator labii superiouris quadratus*, and *depressor labii inferioris*).

For two emotions—disgust and happiness—no specific eyebrow actions are recruited (Ekman, 1979, pp. 180–181, some emphases added).

Ekman (1979) found that eyebrow actions 1+2 and 4 are used more frequently than the others. Consistent with Darwin's antithesis principle, they are the most easily recognized and performed actions. Fear (1+2+4) and anger (4) are best predicted from eye and eyelid actions (67% reliability) (Boucher & Ekman, 1975). This indicates that agonistic and submissive eyebrow displays are the most readily distinguished.

the individual to cope with that event (Kaiser & Wehrle, 2001; Scherer, 2001; Scherer & Ellgring, 2007). In other words, the influence of nonverbal behavior might occur through processing of separate components of the face, namely the eyes and the mouth. Therefore, due to the subtle nature of nonverbal communication, in which individual cues may indicate behavioral intent, we consider nonverbal displays in the mouth and the eyes separately.

The Mouth and Eyes as Separate Stimuli

The mouth is an important indicator of affiliative intent through the happiness/reassurance display of the smile. However, there are many different types of smiles that can be distinguished by various degrees of mouth opening (Brannigan & Humphries, 1972) or by the coactivation of the orbicularis occuli, a ring of muscles surrounding the eye and producing cheek raise and crows feet wrinkles when stimulated (Duchenne de Boulogne, 1862; Ekman & Friesen, 1982). Another affiliative display that involves the mouth is the relaxed open mouth display, which is mainly observed in playful interactions and promotes affiliative relationships (Preushoft & van Hooff, 1997; van Hooff & Preushoft, 2003; Waller & Dunbar, 2005). The co-occurrence of relaxed-open-mouth and silent bared teeth displays (evident in the laughter display) is particularly salient in egalitarian relationships where these behaviors function to strengthen social bonds.

The idea that different types of smiles have different social functions was formalized in the *power asymmetry hypothesis* (Preushoft & van Hooff, 1997; van Hooff & Preushoft, 2003), which suggests that strong hierarchical relationships elicit different patterns of facial displays from those seen in more egalitarian relationships. Specifically, the power asymmetry hypothesis proposed that the pattern of occurrence of these different types of affiliative displays will depend on the kind of power relationship between the interactants. This hypothesis found support in recent research that showed that men were displaying disproportionally higher rates of deliberate smiles in comparison to laughter when they were interacting with older, and presumably higher status, individuals. This effect was not found for spontaneous smiles, indicating that some types of smiles could be relevant to hierarchical contexts and other types of smiles to affiliative contexts (Mehu & Dunbar, 2008a). The extension of meaning associated with lip corner rise is likely to be the reason why the Masters (1989a) and Salter (1995) political ethology frameworks indicate this display in both fear/submission and happiness/reassurance categories See Table 10.2 for an outline of the criteria for classifying facial expressions.

The Eyes

Research concerning processing of facial display behavior suggests that while the mouth plays an important signaling role, especially when indicating happiness/reassurance (Nusseck et al., 2008; Smith et al., 2007), the mouth does not play as significant a role in the identification of core and complex mental states as do the eyes (Adolphs et al., 2005; Ambadar, Schooler, & Cohn, 2005; Baron-Cohen, Wheelwright, & Joliffe, 1997; Nusseck et al., 2008; Smith et al., 2007). From birth, social mammals tend to focus their attention on the eyes (Adolphs et al., 2005; Goossens et al., 2008). The wide-eyed expressions of fear and surprise, in which the schlera (whites) of the eye are accentuated, are processed pre-cognitively through the amygdala (Whalen et al., 2004). Furthermore, direction of eye gaze, especially in anger/threat and fear/submission displays, can alter amygdala response, as greater ambiguity in the gaze can lead to the perception of a potential threat, with resultant increased physiological and emotional response and concomitant focusing of cognitive efforts on response (Adams et al., 2003; Goossens et al., 2008).

TABLE 10.2
Criteria for Classifying Facial Expressions

	Anger–Threat	Fear–Submission	Happiness–Reassurance	Sadness–Appeasement
Eyebrows	Lowered	Lowered and furrowed	Raised	Inner corners raised
Eyelids	Open wide	Upper raised/lower tightened	Open wide, normal, or slightly closed	Lower raised
Eye orientation	Staring	Averted	Focused, then cut off	Averted
Mouth corners	Forward or lowered	Pulled back or normal	Pulled back or raised	Lowered
Teeth showing	Lower	Variable or none	Upper or both	Variable or none
Head motion: lateral	None	Side-to-side	Side-to-side	Away from the source
Head motion: vertical	None	Up-down	Up-down	Down
Head orientation to body	Forward from trunk	Turned down from vertical	Normal to trunk	Turned down
Head orientation: Angle to vertical	Down	Down	Up	Down

Source: Modified from Masters et al. (1986) with the addition of sadness–appeasement from Salter (2007/1995).

Facial Attractiveness

A caveat must be noted as individual characteristics of the politicians used as stimuli are likely to influence individual response. Although politicians as a whole must have a modicum of charisma to be successful, some politicians are more charismatic than others. Arguably, Ronald Reagan, who has provided the majority of stimuli for the Dartmouth group's research, has been one of the most telegenic presidents in U.S. history, due in great part to his extensive training and experience as an actor. Likewise, Bill Clinton exhibited (and still exhibits) a great deal of public (and private) charisma while possessing a level of physical attractiveness (Keating, Randall, & Kendrick, 1999) that enhanced his ability to communicate with the public. On the other hand, both the Dartmouth group (Sullivan & Masters, 1988) and Patterson et al. (1992) note that, in comparison with Ronald Reagan, the 1984 Democratic presidential candidate Walter Mondale was found lacking in both expressiveness and attractiveness, factors that likely played no small part in his loss.

With President Clinton, as well as other political candidates, the face is seen as reflecting character, thus encapsulating what they have done and what they are likely to do. Therefore, the choice of a leader may be the result of their fitting the model of what a successful candidate looks like—in other words, they might be just more attractive, dominant, and healthy looking than other candidates.[12] Research considering the influence of facial attractiveness on electoral success suggests automaticity in the choice of those who would be our leaders. Todorov and colleagues found that even with only a second to evaluate candidate faces, subjects were able to predict U.S. congressional electoral winners with a high rate of accuracy (Todorov, Mandisodza, Goren, & Hall, 2005). Benjamin and Shapiro (2009) likewise found support for this at the state level as naïve participant evaluation of 10-second video clips of candidates accounted for 20% of the variance in gubernatorial election predictions.

These results have been found across different cultures. James Schubert's research found cross-cultural support for facial attractiveness playing a role in whether a candidate was deemed a viable candidate or not, as facial attractiveness correlated strongly with electability ratings in the 1996 Romanian election outcomes (Schubert, Curran, & Strungaru, 1998). Likewise, Antonakis and Dalgas (2009) found Swiss children and adults appear to use similar cues to judge competence from facial appearance when choosing winners in a 2002 French parliamentary election, suggesting not just cross-cultural effects (albeit small with neighboring nations), but also a degree of age-invariance.

Little et al. (2007) found not only that facial appearance was strongly related to the winning of elections in four countries (Australia, New Zealand, United Kingdom, United States), but that there are preferences for different faces based upon the environmental context. Specifically, faces with masculine characteristics are favored during time of war, whereas more forgiving and feminine features are preferred during peace-time. Traits perceived in faces might reflect dimensions of reassurance and dominance seen in facial displays. In their factor analysis of trait attributions to 66 natural faces and 200 computer generated faces, Todorov, Said, Engell, and Oosterhof (2008) found a two-factor solution, with dimensions suggesting a potential interaction of trait qualities and state behavior. As stated by Todorov et al. "subtle resemblance of neutral faces to expressions that signal whether a person should be avoided (anger) or approached (happiness) serves as the basis of valence evaluation. Cues for physical strength such as facial maturity and masculinity serve as the basis of dominance evaluation and are generalized to attributions of related dispositions" (2008, p. 458).

In summary, future experimentation should consider not only the degree of variance in facial displays and their impact on communicating behavioral intent (as in McHugo, Lanzetta, & Bush, 1991), but also consider the interactive effect of facial characteristics on such displays. For instance, some politicians' faces might be better configured to communicate specific emotions and behavioral intent that others (Waller, Cray, & Burrows, 2008), in turn affecting both their competitiveness for office and leadership style when in office. Furthermore, as suggested by the research reviewed here, contextual information might affect citizen preferences, shaping future research.

Measures

Research concerning nonverbal facial display behavior by politicians has been at the forefront of experimental research by utilizing not just self-reports, but also affective response and cognitive processing. Self-reports can be expected to remain a mainstay of experimental research, whether done using paper-and-pencil or on computer, and have been effectively used to extract under-lying factors, albeit with greater conceptual clarity as structural equation model (SEM) becomes incorporated (see Holbert, Chapter 22). Analysis of cognitive processes through response time, thought elaboration, and information recall, has built upon self-reports and provided a more complete and sophisticated understanding how subjects respond to facial display behavior, especially that nested within news stories (Bucy & Newhagen, 1999). The continued use of such measures, especially latency, has the potential to provide insight into the automatic processing of information (Newhagen, Chapter 26), including that of the level of comfort with a particular leader, with high levels of support likely leading to quicker response times due to lower levels of anxiety.

Likewise, physiological measures of heart rate and skin conductance and facial display behavior in the corrugators and zygomatic muscle have been used to effectively measure affective response to politician display behavior (see Bucy & Bradley, Chapter 27). However, while EMG measurement of facial display behavior has been effectively used to detect even minute subject response to politician facial displays, they are arguably highly intrusive, reducing the "mundane" and "psychological realism" of experiments, as having measurement devices on the face and body is not likely to occur in the "real world" and as a result might affect everyday psychological processes (see Chapter 11, this volume). Perhaps a less intrusive measure and one not used in the studies reviewed here (with the exception of EMG facial measures), is video analysis of nonverbal reactions by subjects. While this approach is time intensive, especially if FACS is used, advances in automated analysis of facial behavior (see above and Box 10.2), make this approach more accessible when carrying out political communication research. At the very least, it has long been suggested that ". . . modifications in blinking rate are more significant of emotional states than is the GSR" (galvanic skin response) (Peterson & Allison in Exline, 1985, p. 190).

BOX 10.2 AUTOMATIC EXTRACTION OF FACIAL EXPRESSION

Automatic analysis of facial behavior typically occurs in three steps (Pantic & Rothkrantz, 2000). First the face has to be localized in a video scene, then facial movements have to be detected and tracked, and finally the detected changes have to be classified in appropriate categories. To achieve reliable detection of a face in a scene, the system has to tackle a number of problems including changes in size and orientation provoked by movements of the subject or the camera, or the presence of facial hair and glasses. Once these problems are resolved, the system needs to detect and extract information relative to the position and movement of the facial features that are relevant to facial behavior (e.g., mouth, eyes, eyebrows). Several approaches are used to achieve this step, such as optical flow, Gabor wavelets, multistate models, and generative model fitting (Cohn & Kanade, 2007). The efficiency of these approaches depends on the type of movement to be detected. The final step involves the transformation of the extracted features into a set of parameters that will be used to identify facial movements. The categories used for this identification differ between research teams as some choose to use general emotional categories like anger, happiness, or fear, while others prefer to use FACS-based facial action units to categorize the detected changes (Bartlett, Hager, Ekman, & Sejnowski, 1999; Cohn & Kanade, 2007; Valstar & Pantic, 2006). Because the latter does not assume a relationship between particular facial configurations and emotional categories, this method is seen as more rigorous and internally valid.

Subjects

The importance of moving beyond the "college sophomore" as the research subject of choice was duly noted and acted on as the research of the Dartmouth group progressed and in the work of Bucy and colleagues (see above). Findings concerning African-American college subjects (Masters, 1994) and European subjects (Masters & Sullivan, 1989; Warnecke et al., 1992) and their differential response to political figure display behavior suggests that while there might be a modicum of agreement as to what the basic displays of emotions are, there is variance in what is perceived as appropriate and how they are processed cognitively (Anger-Elfenbein & Ambady, 2002; Fridlund, 1994; Russell & Fernandez-Dols, 1997; Scherer & Ellgring, 2007). For instance, as suggested by experimental research by Marsh, Anger-Elfenbein, and Ambady (2003) considering decoding pictorial presentations of facial displays in two cultures (Japanese nationals and Japanese-Americans), there might be nonverbal "accents" in which case subtle differences in nonverbal behavior indicate the culture of the person displaying, in turn potentially affecting observer perception, interpretation, and response. Therefore, drawing from a more diverse subject pool to tease out the differences in both encoding of facial display behavior by politicians and response to it is suggested.

Although the recruitment of subjects beyond the opportunity sample afforded by college students can be difficult to organize, the saturation of Internet technology and its accessibility, at least in the United States and Western Europe, provides the opportunity to draw from a broader sample of subjects and to follow up with them over a period of time (Iyengar, Chapter 8; Stewart, 2008; Box 10.3). Furthermore, studies involving the Internet might prove to be more naturalistic than laboratory studies (see Chapters 8 and 11, this volume), in which subjects are placed in unnatural surroundings, a constraint appreciated by political scientists using the experimental method (e.g., Brader, 2006).

BOX 10.3 INTERNET SUBJECT RECRUITING

While most academic studies rely on college students as research subjects (Sears, 1985), with concomitant research biases that may result, the Alkami Research Subject Volunteer Program (RSVP) allows investigators to connect with participants who can more closely represent their study's target population. As of August 2010, the RSVP had a membership of over 7,400 registered volunteers who range in age from 18 to 90. As part of the program's prescreening process, members provide responses to a selection of standardized survey questions as well as customized questionnaires that individual researchers can request to best select participants for the unique needs of their research protocol.

In addition to subject recruitment, screening, and tracking for on-site protocols, the RSVP obtains survey and behavioral experiment participants for Web-based studies at universities worldwide including Harvard University, the University of California at Berkeley, the University of California at San Francisco, Universität Göttingen (Germany), University College London (England), and the University of Oxford (England).

The RSVP began in 2006 as part of a research project at the University of California at Berkeley and is a now a service provided by the nonprofit Alkami Biobehavioral Institute (ABI). To learn more about the Alkami RSVP, please visit http://rsvp.alkami.org.

CONCLUSIONS

Although the importance of visual representations of political leaders has long been appreciated, as reflected by the research programs considered here, new developments only serve to underscore the importance of understanding the influence of facial display behavior. Not only have politicians become increasingly savvy in their media strategies, hitting the talk show circuit to better showcase their likeability to individuals with lower levels of political interest and motivation (Baum, 2005), viewing technology has changed with television screens becoming larger visually, richer aurally, and higher in resolution. Looking forward, television is likely to become ever more realistic with heightened clarity and more lifelike, if not *larger than life*, presentations. In the case of the latter, we know from existing research that the perception of proximity in political dialogue leads to higher levels of arousal, with concomitant effects on attitudes towards and memory of politicians and the legitimacy of their policy positions (Mutz, 2007). Furthermore, the easy accessibility of recordings from a range of media sources, whether television, online news pages, or video uploaded directly by viewers to file-sharing sites like YouTube upon witnessing events, is greatly expanding public scrutiny of political figures.

With this in mind, research considering viewer responses to ubiquitous, cross-platform recordings of memorable moments in televised politics becomes a pressing concern, especially in light of the accumulated findings reported here. Recent findings that media bias does exist, albeit in visual form and contrary to popular understandings (Grabe & Bucy, 2009), underscores the importance of fully understanding a rapidly advancing and proliferating technology that influences individuals on multiple levels. By coupling theoretical insights from ethology with the research design lessons from studies reviewed here, a fuller, more detailed understanding of human political behavior should emerge.

NOTES

1. This is not to say that the audio channel doesn't convey nonverbal information. Specifically, vocalic information such as tone, intensity, and pitch influences emotional response and has been studied in political contexts such as city council meetings and the U.S. Supreme Court by James N. Schubert and colleagues (Schubert, 1988; Schubert et al., 1992).
2. Not everything that conveys information is a signal. The word "signal" is reserved to entities (such as morphological structures, or behaviors) that were selected because they influenced the behavior of receivers to the advantage of the sender. This doesn't always imply that some information is communicated (see, for instance, Dawkins & Krebs, 1978). A sign or a cue is a structure or behavior from which a receiver can infer some information, but which hasn't necessarily evolved to convey information. For example, body size can be a good indicator of physical strength, but it hasn't evolved because of its effect on the receiver.
3. It is expected that the four signal systems will interact to influence the quality and content of signals. For instance, markers of age and experience, such as eye glasses, lend gravitas to individuals, but may detract from perceptions of vitality, whereas botox treatments might give a youthful visage, but also inhibit the expression of emotions through the eyes and eye brows.
4. Examples may be drawn from the topic of humor and laughter. A question considering the proximate causation of laughter and the humor that provokes it could consider the social bonds built by laughter, both between the joke teller and the audience and among the audience members themselves. For instance, when considering the topic of humor and the production of laughter, in terms of ontogenetic causation one might consider when an individual starts laughing (~3.5–4 months; Provine, 2000, p. 112), when joking and laughter become a prominent part of social life (5–6 years; Provine, 2000, p. 93) and its diminishing as one ages. When analyzing the phylogenetic roots of laughter one might consider the production of homologous signals and social uses in a range of species, including rats (Panksepp, 1998, 2007) and non-human primates (Preushoft & van Hooff, 1997; van Hooff & Preushoft, 2003), and how it compares with human uses. In terms of ultimate causation, one could consider how engaging in laughter and laughter-eliciting behavior might benefit the behaving individual or group/species engaging in it in terms of obtaining and defending resources, which in turn affects rates of reproduction (Preushoft & van Hooff, 1997).
5. True experiments can use the strategy of considering variations of the assumed normal "human nature" and then assess differences between "normals" and this "experimental" group. Examples of such an approach include Damasio's extensive work with brain damaged individuals (1994) and studies that consider "blind" individuals' facial display behavior, including a recent study comparing spontaneous facial expressions of congenitally and noncongenitally blind athletes with sighted athletes after winning/losing high-level matches (Matsumoto & Willingham, 2009).
6. Price and Sloman (1987) cite the observation of dominance in fowls by Schjelderup-Ebbe to argue that sadness is sequenced by a "yielding subroutine": "If a certain a-bird loses in the fight and has to take refuge in flight, its behavior becomes entirely changed. Deeply depressed in spirit, humble, with

drooping wings and head in the dust, it is—at any rate, directly upon being vanquished overcome with paralysis, although one cannot detect any physical injury" (Schjelderup-Ebbe, 1935, p. 966).

7. Another experimental study was carried out in 1981 and analyzed viewer response to the 1976 vice-presidential debate between Robert Dole and Walter Mondale in light of different content presented (audio-visual, video only, transcript, and content-filtered, in which speech was unintelligible, but reflected paralinguistic qualities). However, there was no direct coding of nonverbal facial behavior (Krauss et al., 1981), and hence is not used here.

8. Studies presenting facial expressions near or below the threshold of conscious awareness demonstrate that facial displays of emotions such as anger, fear, and happiness impact an individual's emotional response without their awareness (Masters & Way, 1996; Stewart et al., 2009).

9. When this data was analyzed on the basis of response to specific facial display behavior, three factors were extracted, with Happiness/Reassurance displays leading to a factor comprised of the terms strong, joyful, comforting, and interested; Anger/Threat leading to a factor made up of the terms angry and disgusted; and Fear/Evasion leading to the terms fearful, confused, and evasive loading onto a factor (Lanzetta et al., 1985).

10. The separability of emotion and cognition, and which has primacy, is one of the core debates in psychology with productive debate between Zajonc (1980, 1982) and Lazarus (1982) bringing this discussion to the forefront of research agendas in the early 1980s. It is, however, beyond the scope of this paper (see Ekman & Davidson, 1994 for an excellent discussion of the fundamental questions over the nature of emotion).

11. Additionally, the effect of personality may need to be considered as well, especially in light of a recent online study testing and expanding upon Sears' (1986) assertions, using a nearly 10,000-participant database ($N > 9,800$) to compare undergraduates and a broad community sample, which found significant and strong differences between the samples (Stewart, 2008). While Stewart notes personality is a complex phenomenon changing as a result of life experiences and physiological age, she also recognizes an element of self-selection for higher education that may play a role in influencing the effects of experimental studies such as discussed here.

12. Facial attractiveness plays a major role in whether an individual is considered as a leadership candidate because facial attractiveness affects inferences of competence and honesty in the workforce, politics, and life generally (Mazur, 2005).

REFERENCES

Abelson, R. P., Kinder, D. R, Peters, M. D., Fiske, S. T. (1982). Affective and semantic components in political personal perception. *Journal of Personality and Social Psychology, 42,* 619–630.

Adams, R. B. J., Gordon, H. L., Baird, A. A., Ambady, N., & Kleck, R. E. (2003). Effects of gaze on amygdale sensitivity to anger and fear faces. *Science, 300,* 1536–1537.

Adolphs, R., Gosselin, F., Buchanan, T. W., Tranel, D., Schyns, P., & Damasio, A. R. (2005, January 6). A mechanism for impaired fear recognition after amygdala damage. *Nature, 433*(7021), 68–72.

Ambadar, Z., Schooler, J. W., Cohn, J. F. (2005). Deciphering the enigmatic face: The importance of facial dynamics in interpreting subtle facial expressions. *Psychological Science, 16,* 403–410.

Anger-Elfenbein, H., Ambady, N. (2002). On the universality and cultural specificity of emotion recognition: A meta-analysis. *Psychological Bulletin, 128,* 203–235.

Antonakis, J., & Dalgas, O. (2009, February 27). Predicting elections: Child's play! *Science, 323,* 1183.

Arnhart, L. (1981). *Aristotle on political reasoning: A commentary on the "Rhetoric."* DeKalb, IL: Northern Illinois University Press.

Baron-Cohen, S., Wheelwright, S., & Joliffe, T. (1997). Is there a "language of the eyes"? Evidence from normal adults, and adults with autism or Asperger Syndrome. *Visual Cognition, 4,* 311–331.

Barrett, L., Dunbar, R., & Lycett, J. (2002). *Human evolutionary psychology.* New York: Palgrave.

Bartlett, M. S., Hager, J. C., Ekman, P., & Sejnowski, T. J. (1999). Measuring facial expressions by computer image analysis. *Psychophysiology, 36,* 253–263.

Baum, M. A. (2005). Talking the vote: Why presidential candidates hit the talk show circuit. *American Journal of Political Science, 49*, 213–234.

Benjamin, D. J., & J. M. Shapiro. (2009). Thin-slice forecasts of gubernatorial elections. *Review of Economies and Statistics, 91*(3), 523–536.

Boehm, C. (1999). *Hierarchy in the forest: The evolution of egalitarian behavior.* Cambridge, MA: Harvard University Press.

Brader, T. (2006). *Campaigning for hearts and minds: How emotional appeals in political ads work.* Chicago, IL: University of Chicago Press.

Brannigan, C. R., Humphries, D. A. (1972). Human nonverbal behavior, a means of communication. In N. Blurton-Jones (Ed.), *Ethological studies of child behavior* (pp. 37–64). Cambridge: Cambridge University Press.

Brown, W. M., Palameta, B., & Moore, C. (2003). Are there nonverbal cues to commitment? An exploratory study using the zero-acquaintance video presentation paradigm. *Evolutionary Psychology, 1*, 42–69.

Bucy, E. P. (2000). Emotional and evaluative consequences of inappropriate leader displays. *Communication Research, 27*(2), 194–226.

Bucy, E. P. (2003). Emotion, presidential communication, and traumatic news. *Harvard International Journal of Press/Politics, 8*, 76–96.

Bucy, E. P. & Bradley, S. D. (2004). Presidential expressions and viewer emotion: Counterempathic responses to televised leader displays. *Social Science Information, 43*(1), 59–94.

Bucy, E. P., & Grabe, M. E. (2008). "Happy warriors" revisited: Hedonic and agonic display repertoires of presidential candidates on the evening news. *Politics and the Life Sciences, 27*(1), 24–44.

Bucy, E. P., & Newhagen, J. E. (1999). The emotional appropriateness heuristic: Processing televised presidential reactions to the news. *Journal of Communication,* 59–79.

Chance, M. R. A. (1967). Attention structure as the basis of primate rank orders. *Man, 2*, 503–518.

Cohn, J. F., Ambadar, Z., & Ekman, P. (2007). Obersver-bsased measurement of facial expression with the Facial Action Coding System. In J. A. Coan & J. B. Allen (Eds.), *The handbook of emotion elicitation and assessment* (pp. 222–238). New York: Oxford University Press.

Cohn, J. F. & Ekman, P. (2005). Measuring facial action. In J. A. Harrigan, R. Rosenthal, & K. R. Scherer (Eds.), *The new handbook of methods in nonverbal behavior research* (pp. 9–64). New York: Oxford University Press.

Cohn, J. F., & Kanade, T. (2007). Use of automated facial image analysis for measurement of emotion expression. In J. A. Coan & J. J. B. Allen (Eds.), *The handbook of emotion elicitation and assessment* (pp. 222–238). New York: Oxford University Press.

Cordoni, G., Palagi, E., & Tarli, S. B. (2006). Reconciliation and consolation in captive western gorillas. *International Journal of Primatology, 27*, 1365–1382.

Damasio, A. R. (1994). *Descartes' error: Emotion, reason and the human brain.* New York: Avon Books.

Darwin, C. (1998). *The expression of the emotions in man and animals* (3rd ed.). New York, Oxford University Press.

Dawkins, R., & Krebs, J. R. (1978). Animal signals: Information or manipulation? In J. R. Krebs & N. B. Davies (Eds.), *Behavioral ecology: An evolutionary approach* (pp. 282–309). Oxford: Blackwell.

De Marco, A., Petit, O., & Visalberghi, E. (2008). The repertoire and social function of facial displays in *Cebus capucinus. International Journal of Primatology, 29*, 469–486.

De Waal, F. B. M. (1982). *Chimpanzee politics: Power and sex among apes.* Baltimore, MD: The Johns Hopkins University Press.

Dovidio, J. F., & Ellyson, S. L. (1985). Patterns of visual dominance behavior in humans. In S. L. Ellyson & J. F. Dovidio (Eds.), *Power, dominance, and nonverbal behavior* (pp. 129–149). New York: Springer-Verlag.

Duchenne de Bologne, G. B. (1862). *The mechanisms of human facial expression* (R. A. Cuthbertson, trans.). New York: Cambridge University Press.

Eibl-Eibesfeldt, I. (1979). Ritual and ritualization from a biological perspective. In M. V. Cranach, K. Foppa, W. Lepenies, & E. Klinghammer (Eds.), *Human ethology* (pp. 3–55). New York: Cambridge University Press.

Eibl-Eibesfeldt, I. (1989). *Human ethology.* New York: Aldine de Gruyter.

Ekman, P., & Davidson, R. J. (Eds.). (1994). *The nature of emotion: Fundamental questions.* New York: Oxford University Press.

Ekman, P., & Friesen, W. V. (1977). *Manual for the Facial Action Coding System.* Palo Alto, CA: Consulting Psychologists.

Ekman, P., & Friesen, W. V. (1982). Felt, false and miserable smiles. *Journal of Nonverbal Behavior, 6,* 238–252.

Ekman, P., & Friesen, W. V. (2003). *Unmasking the Face.* Cambridge, MA: Malor Books.

Ekman, P., Friesen, W. V., & Ancoli, S. (1980). Facial signs of emotional expression. *Journal of Personality and Social Psychology, 39,* 1125–1134.

Ekman, P., Friesen, W. V., & Ellsworth, P. (1972). *Emotion in the human face: Guidelines for research and an integration of findings.* New York: Pergamon Press.

Ekman, P., Friesen, W. V., & O'Sullivan, M. (1988). Smiles when lying. *Journal of Personality and Social Psychology, 54,* 414–420.

Ekman, P., & Oster, H. (1979). Facial expressions of emotion. *Annual Review of Psychology, 30,* 527–554.

Ellyson, S. L., & Dovidio, J. F. (Eds.). (1985). *Power, dominance, and nonverbal behavior.* New York: Springer-Verlag.

Exline, R. V. (1985). Multichannel transmission of nonverbal behavior and the perception of powerful men: The presidential debates of 1976. In S. L. Ellyson & J. F. Dovidio (Eds.), *Power, dominance, and nonverbal behavior.* New York: Springer-Verlag.

Exline, R. V., Ellyson, S. L., & Long, B. (1975). Visual behavior as an aspect of power role relationships. In P. Pliner, L. Krames, & T. Alloway (Eds.), *Nonverbal communication of aggression* (pp. 79–114). New York: Plenum Press.

Fridja, N. H. (1986). *The emotions.* New York: Cambridge University Press.

Fridlund, A. J. (1994). *Human facial expression: An evolutionary view.* San Diego, CA: Academic Press.

Fridlund, A. J. (1997). The new ethology of human facial expressions. In J. A. Russell and J. M. Fernandez-Dols (Eds.), *The psychology of facial expression* (pp. 103–129). London: Cambridge University Press.

Friedman, H. S., DiMatteo, M. R., & Mertz, T. I. (1980). Nonverbal communication on television news: The facial expressions of broadcasters during coverage of a presidential election campaign. *Personality and Social Psychology Bulletin, 6,* 427–435.

Friedman, H. S., Mertz, T. I., & DiMatteo, M. R. (1980). Perceived bias in the facial expressions of television news broadcasters. *Journal of Communication, 30,* 103–111.

Givens, D. (1981). Greeting a stranger: Some commonly used nonverbal signals of aversiveness. In T. A. Sebeok & J. Umiker-Sebeok (Eds.), *Nonverbal communication, interaction, and gesture* (pp. 219–235). New York: Mouton.

Goossens, B. M. A., Dekleva, M., Reader, S. M., Sterck, E. H. M., & Bolhuis, J. J. (2008). Gaze following in monkeys is modulated by observed facial expression. *Animal Behaviour, 75,* 1673–1681.

Grabe, M. E., & Bucy, E. P. (2009). *Image bite politics: News and the visual framing of elections.* New York: Oxford University Press.

Grammer, K., Shiefenhovel, W., Schleidt, M., Lorenz, B., & Eibl-Eibesfeldt, I. (1988). Patterns on the face: The eyebrow flash in crosscultural comparison. *Ethology, 77,* 279–299.

Grant, E. (1969). Human facial expression. *Man,* 525–536.

Gray, J. A. (1987). *The psychology of fear and stress.* New York: Cambridge University Press.

Hjortsjö, C. H. (1969). *Man's face and mimic language.* Lund, Sweden: Studentlitteratur.

Hold-Cavell, B. C. L. (1992). Showing-off and aggression in young children. *Aggressive Behavior, 11,* 303–314.

Kaiser, S., & Wehrle, T. (2001). Facial expressions as indicators of appraisal processes. In K. R.Scherer, A. Schorr, & T. Johnstone (Eds.), *Appraisal processes in emotion: Theory, methods, research* (pp. 285–300). New York: Oxford University Press.

Keating, C. F., Randall, D., Kendrick, T. (1999). Presidential physiognomies: Altered images, altered perceptions. *Political Psychology, 20*(3), 593–610.

Kleinke, C. L. (1986). Gaze and eye contact: A research review. *Psychological Bulletin, 100*, 78–100.

Knipe, H., & Mclay, G. (1972). *The dominant man.* London, England: Collins.

Konner, M. (1972). Infants of a foraging people. In N. G. Blurton-Jones (Ed.), *Ethological studies of child behavior* (pp. 285–304). New York: Cambridge University Press.

Krauss, R. M., Apple, W., Morency, N., Wenzel, C., & Winton, W. (1981). Verbal, vocal, and visible factors in judgements of another's affect. *Journal of Personality and Social Psychology, 40*, 312–320.

Kraut, R. E., & Poe, D. (1980). Behavioral roots of person perceptions: The deception judgments of customs inspectors and laymen. *Journal of Personality and Social Psychology, 39*, 784–798.

Lang, P. J. (1988). What are the data of emotion? In V. Hamilton, G. H. Bower, & N. H Frijda (Eds.), *Cognitive perspectives on emotion and motivation* (pp. 173–191). Boston, MA: Kluwer Academic Publishers.

Lanzetta, J. T., Sullivan, D. G., Masters, R. D., & McHugo, G. J. (1985). Emotional and cognitive responses to televised images of political leaders. In S. Kraus & R. Perloff (Eds.), *Mass media and political thought* (pp. 85–116). Beverly Hills, CA: Sage.

Lazarus, R. S. (1982). Thoughts on the relation between emotion and cognition. *American Psychologist, 37*, 1019–1024.

Lehner, P. N. (1996). *Handbook of ethological methods* (2nd ed.). New York: Cambridge University Press.

Little, A. C., Burriss, R. P., Jones, B. C., & Roberts, S. C. (2007). Facial appearance affects voting decisions. *Evolution and Human Behavior, 28*, 18–27.

Marcus, G. E., Neuman, W. R., & Mackuen, M. (2000). *Affective intelligence and political judgment.* Chicago, IL: University of Chicago Press.

Marler, P. (1965). Communication in monkeys and apes. In I. DeVore (Ed.), *Primate behavior* (pp. 544–584). New York: Holt, Rinehart, and Winston.

Marsh, A. A., Anger-Elfenbein, H., & Ambady, N. (2003). Nonverbal "accents": Cultural differences in facial expressions of emotion. *Psychological Science, 14*, 373–376.

Masters, R. D. (1989a). *The nature of politics.* New Haven, CT: Yale University Press.

Masters, R. D. (1989b). Gender and political cognition: Integrating evolutionary biology and political science. *Politics and the Life Sciences, 8*, 3–26.

Masters, R. D. (1994). Differences in responses of blacks and whites to American leaders. *Politics and the Life Sciences, 13*, 183–194.

Masters, R. D., & Carlotti, S. J., Jr. (1994). Gender differences in response to political leaders. In L. Ellis (Ed.), *Social stratification and socioeconomic inequality* (Vol. 2, pp. 13–35). Boulder, CO: Praeger.

Masters, R. D., Frey, S., & Bente, G. (1991). Dominance and attention: Images of leaders in German, French and American TV news. *Polity, 23*, 373–394.

Masters, R. D., & Sullivan, D. G. (1989). Nonverbal displays and political leadership in France and the United States. *Political Behavior, 11*, 121–130.

Masters, R. D., Sullivan, D. G., Feola, A., & McHugo, G. J. (1987). Television coverage of candidates' display behavior during the 1984 Democratic primaries in the United States. *International Political Science Review, 8*, 121–130.

Masters, R. D., Sullivan, D. G., Lanzetta, J. T., McHugo, G. J., & Englis, B.G. (1986). The facial displays of leaders: Toward an ethology of human politics. *Journal of Social and Biological Structures, 9*, 319–343.

Masters, R. D., & Way, B. M. (1996). Experimental methods and attitudes toward leaders: Nonverbal displays, emotion, and cognition. In S. Peterson & A. Somit (Eds.), *Research in Biopolitics, Vol. 4* (pp. 61–98). Greenwich, CT: JAI Press.

Matsumoto, D., & Willingham, B. (2009). Spontaneous facial expressions of emotion of congenitally and noncongenitally blind individuals. *Journal of Personality and Social Psychology, 96*, 1–10.

Mazur, A. (2005). *Biosociology of dominance and deference.* Rowman & Littlefield Publishers.

McBride, G., King, M., & James, J. (1965). Social proximity effects on GSR in adult humans. *Journal of Psychology, 61*, 153–157.

McGrew, W. (1972). Aspects of social development in nursery school children with emphasis on introduction to the group. In N. Blurton-Jones (Ed.), *Ethological studies of child behavior* (pp. 129–156). New York: Cambridge University Press.

McHugo, G. J., Lanzetta, J. T., & Bush, L. K. (1991). The effect of attitudes on emotional reactions to expressive displays of political leaders. *Journal of Nonverbal Behavior, 15*, 19–41.

McHugo, G. J., Lanzetta, J. T., Sullivan, D. G., Masters, R. D., & Englis, B. G. (1985). Emotional reactions to a political leader's expressive displays. *Journal of Personality and Social Psychology, 49*, 1513–1529.

Mehu, M., & Dunbar, R. I. M. (2008a). Naturalistic observations of smiling and laughter in human group interactions. *Behaviour, 145*, 1747–1780.

Mehu, M., & Dunbar, R. I. M. (2008b). Relationship between smiling and laughter in humans (*Homo sapiens*): Testing the power asymmetry hypothesis. *Folia Primatologica, 79*, 269–280.

Mehu, M., Grammer, K., & Dunbar, R. I. M. (2007). Smiles when sharing. *Evolution and Human Behavior, 28*, 415–422.

Mehu, M., Little, A. C., & Dunbar, R. I. M. (2007). Duchenne smiles and the perception of generosity and sociability in faces. *Journal of Evolutionary Psychology, 5*, 133–146.

Morris, D. (1967). *The naked ape*. London: Jonathan Cape.

Morris, D. (1977). *Manwatching: A field guide to human behavior*. New York: Abrams.

Mullen, B., Futrell, D., Stairs, D., Tice, D. M., Dawson, K. E, Riordan, C.A., Kennedy, J. G., Baumeister, R. F., Radloff, C. E., Goethals, G. R., & Rosenfield. P. (1986). Newscasters' facial expressions and voting behavior of viewers: Can a smile elect a president? *Journal of Personality and Social Psychology, 51*, 291–295.

Mutz, D. C. (2007). Effects of "in-your-face" television discourse on perceptions of legitimate opposition. *American Political Science Review, 101*, 621–635.

Nusseck, M., Cunningham, D. W., Wallraven, C., & Bulthoff, H. H. (2008). The contribution of different facial regions to the recognition of conversational expressions. *Journal of Vision, 8*, 1–23.

Palagi, E., Cordoni, G., Tarli, S.B. (2004). Possible roles of consolation in captive chimpanzees (*Pan troglodytes*). *American Journal of Physical Anthropology, 129*, 105–111.

Palagi, E., Paoli, T., & Tarli, S. B. (2004). Reconciliation and consolation in captive bonobos (*Pan paniscus*). *American Journal of Primatology, 62*, 15–30.

Palagi, E., Paoli, T., & Tarli, S. B. (2005). Aggression and reconciliation in two captive groups of *Lemur catta*. *International Journal of Primatology, 26*, 279–294.

Panksepp, J. (1998). *Affective neuroscience: The foundation of human and animal emotions*. New York: Oxford University Press.

Panksepp, J. (2007). Neuroevolutionary sources of laughter and social joy: Modeling primal human laughter in laboratory rats. *Behavioral Brain Research, 182*, 231–244.

Pantic, M., & Rothkrantz, L. J. M. (2000). Automatic analysis of facial expressions: The state of the art. *IEEE Transactions on Pattern Analysis and Machine Intelligence, 22*, 1424–1445.

Parr, L. A., Waller, B. M., & Vick, S. J. (2007). New developments in understanding emotional facial signals in chimpanzees. *Current Directions in Psychological Science, 16*, 117–122.

Parr, L. A., Waller, B. M., Vick, S. J., & Bard, K. A. (2007). Classifying chimpanzee facial expressions using muscle action. *Emotion, 7*, 172–181.

Parr, L. A., Waller, B. M., & Fugate, J. (2005). Emotional communication in primates: Implications for neurobiology. *Current Opinion in Neurobiology, 15*, 716–720.

Patterson, M. L., Churchill, M. E., Burger, G. K., & Powell, J. L. (1992). Verbal and nonverbal modality effects on impressions of political candidates: Analysis from the 1984 presidential debates. *Communication Monographs, 59*, 231–242.

Peterson, S.A., & Somit, A. (1982). Methodological problems associated with a biologically oriented social science. In T. C. Wiegele (Ed.), *Biology and the social sciences: An emerging revolution* (pp. 349–366). Boulder, CO: Westview Press.

Plutchik, R. (1980). *Emotion: A psychoevolutionary synthesis*. New York: Harper and Row.

Preuschoft, S. (1992). "Laughter" and "smile" in Barbary macaques (*Macaca sylvanus*). *Ethology, 91*, 220–236.

Preuschoft, S., van Hooff, J. A. R. A. M. (1997). The social function of "smile" and "laughter": Variations across primate species and societies. In U. Segerstrale & P. Molnar (Eds), *Nonverbal communication: Where nature meets culture* (pp. 171–189). Mahwah, NJ: Lawrence Erlbaum.

Price, J. S. & Sloman, L. (1987). Depression as yielding behavior: An animal model based on Schjelderup-Ebbe's pecking order. *Ethology and Sociobiology, 8*, 85S–98S.

Provine, R. R. (2000). *Laughter: A scientific investigation*. New York: Penguin Books.

Russell, J. A., Bachorowski, J. A., & Fernandez-Dols, J. M. (2003). Facial and vocal expressions of emotion. *Annual Review of Psychology, 54*, 329–349.

Russell, J. A., & Fernandez-Dols, J. M. (1997). What does a facial expression mean? In J. A. Russell & J. M. Fernandez-Dols (Eds.), *The psychology of facial expressions* (pp. 3–30). New York: Cambridge University Press.

Salter, F. K. (2007/1995). *Emotions in command: Biology, bureaucracy, and cultural evolution*. New York: Transaction.

Salter, F. K., Grammer, K., & Rikowski, A. (2005). Sex differences in negotiating with powerful males: An ethological analysis of approaches to nightclub doormen. *Human Nature: An Interdisciplinary Biosocial Perspective, 16*, 306–321.

Sapolsky, R. M. (1990). Stress in the wild. *Scientific American, 262*, 106–113.

Scherer, K. R. (2001). Appraisal considered as a process of multi-level sequential checking. In Scherer, K. R., Schorr, A., & Johnstone, T. (Eds.), *Appraisal processes in emotion: Theory, methods, research* (pp. 92–120). New York: Oxford University Press.

Scherer, K. R., & Ellgring, H. (2007). Are facial expressions of emotion produced by categorical affect programs or dynamically driven by appraisal? *Emotion, 7*, 113–130.

Scherer, K. & Grandjean, D. (2008). Facial expressions allow inference of both emotions and their components. *Cognition and Emotion, 22*, 789–801.

Schjelderup-Ebbe, T. (1935). Social behavior of birds. In C. A. Murchinson (Ed.), *A handbook of social psychology* (pp. 947–972). Worchester, MA: Clark University Press.

Schmidt, K. L., & Cohn, J. F. (2001). Human facial expressions as adaptations: evolutionary questions in facial expression research. *Yearbook of Physical Anthropology, 44*, 3–24.

Schubert, J. N. (1988). Age and active-passive leadership style. *American Political Science Review, 82*, 763–772.

Schubert, J. N. (1998). The role of sex and emotional response in indoctrinability: Experimental evidence on the "rally 'round the flag" effect. In I. Eibl-Ebbesfelt & F. Salter (Eds.), *Indoctrinability, warfare and ideology* (pp. 241–262). Oxford, England: Berghahan Books.

Schubert, J., Curran, M., & Stungaru, C. (1998, August). Male/female differences in leadership appraisal. Paper presented to the 14th biennial conference of the International Society for Human Ethology. Burnaby, Canada.

Schubert, J. N., Peterson, S. A., Schubert, G., & Wasby, S. (1992). Observing Supreme Court oral argument: A biosocial approach. *Politics and the Life Sciences, 11*, 35–51.

Sears, D. O. (1986). College sophomores in the laboratory: Influences of a narrow database on social psychology's view of human nature. *Journal of Personality and Social Psychology, 51*, 515–530.

Smith, J., Chase, J., & Lieblich, A. (1974). Tongue showing. *Semiotica, 11*, 210–236.

Smith, K., Larimer, C. W., Littvay, L., & Hibbing, J. R. (2007). Evolutionary theory and political leadership: Why certain people do not trust decision makers. *Journal of Politics, 69*, 285–299.

Somit, A., & Peterson, S. A. (1997). *Darwinism, dominance, and democracy: The biological bases of authoritarianism*. Westport, CT: Praeger Press.

Stern, D., & Bender, E. (1974). An ethological study of children approaching a strange adult. In R. C. Friedman, R. M. Richart, & R. L. Va de Wiele (Eds.), *Sex differences in behavior* (pp. 233–258). New York: John Wiley & Sons.

Stewart L. E. (2008). *College students as research subjects: Are study results generalizable?* Poster presented at the PsyPAG Annual Conference 2008, University of Manchester, Manchester, UK.

Stewart, P. A., Waller, B. M., & Schubert, J. N. (2009). Presidential speechmaking style: Emotional response to micro-expressions of facial affect. *Motivation and Emotion, 33*, 125–135.

Sullivan, D. G., & Masters, R. D. (1988). Happy warriors: Leaders' facial displays, viewers' emotions, and political support. *American Journal of Political Science, 32*, 345–368.

Sullivan, D. G., & Masters, R. D. (1994). Biopolitics, the media, and leadership: Nonverbal cues, emotions, and trait attributions in the evaluation of leaders. In A. Somit & S. A. Peterson (Eds.), *Research in Biopolitics* (Vol. 2, pp. 237–273). New York: JAI Press.

Tiedens, L. Z. (2001). Anger and advancement versus sadness and subjugation: The effect of negative emotion expressions on social status conferral. *Journal of Personality and Social Psychology, 80,* 86–94.

Tiedens, L. Z., & Fragale, A. R. (2003). Power moves: Complementarity in dominant and submissive nonverbal behavior. *Journal of Personality and Social Psychology, 84,* 558–568.

Tinbergen, N. (1963). On aims and methods of ethology. *Zeitschrift fur Tierpsycholgie, 20,* 410–433.

Todorov, A., Mandisodza, A. N., Goren, A., & Hall, C. C. (2005). Inferences of competence from faces predict election outcomes. *Science, 308,* 1623–1626.

Todorov, A., Said, C. P., Engell, A. D., & Oosterhof, N. N. (2008). Understanding evaluation of faces on social dimensions. *Trends in Cognitive Sciences, 12,* 455–460.

Troisi, A. (2002). Displacement activities as a behavioral measure of stress in nonhuman primates and human subjects. *Stress, 5,* 47–54.

Turner, J. H. (1997). The evolution of emotions: The nonverbal basis of human social organization. In U. Segerstråle & P. Molnár (Eds.), *Nonverbal communication: Where nature meets culture* (pp. 211–223). Mahwah, NJ: Lawrence Erlbaum.

Van Hooff, J. A. R. A. M. (1969). The facial displays of the catarrhine monkeys and apes. In D. Morris (Ed.), *Primate ethology* (pp. 9–98). New York: Academic Press.

Van Hooff, J. A. R. A. M. (1973). A structural analysis of the social behavior of a semi-captive group of chimpanzees. In M. Cranach & I. Vine (Eds.), *Social communication and movement* (pp. 75–162). New York: Academic Press.

Van Hooff, J. A. R. A. M., & Preushoft, S. (2003). Laughter and smiling: The intertwining of nature and culture. In F. B. M. de Waal & P. L. Tyack (Eds.), *Animal social complexity: Intelligence, culture, and individualized societies* (pp. 260–292). Cambridge, MA: Harvard University Press.

Vick, S.-J., Waller, B. M., Parr, L. A., Smith Pasqualini, M. C., & Bard, K. A. (2007). A cross-species comparison of facial morphology and movement in humans and chimpanzees using the facial action coding system (FACS). *Journal of Nonverbal Behavior, 31,* 1–20.

Visalberghi, E., Valenzano, D. R., & Preuschoft, S. (2006). Facial displays in *Cebus apella. International Journal of Primatology, 27,* 1689–1707.

Waller, B. M., Cray, J .J., & Burrows, A. M. (2008). Selection for universal facial emotion. *Emotion, 8,* 435–439.

Waller, B. M., & Dunbar, R. I. M. (2005). Differential behavioral effects of silent bared teeth display and relaxed open mouth display in chimpanzees (*Pan troglodytes*). *Ethology, 111,* 129–142.

Warnecke, A. M., Masters, R. D., & Kempter, G. (1992). The roots of nationalism: Nonverbal behavior and xenophobia. *Ethology and Sociobiology, 13,* 267–282.

Way, B. M., & Masters, R. D. (1996b). Emotion and cognition in political information processing. *Journal of Communication, 46,* 48–65.

Way, B. M., & Masters, R. D. (1996b). Political attitudes: Interactions of cognition and affect. *Motivation and Emotion, 20*(3), 205–236.

Whalen, P. J., et al., (2004, December 17). Human amygdala responsivity to masked fearful eye whites. *Science, 306,* 2061.

Zajonc, R. B. (1980). Feeling and thinking: Preferences need no inferences. *American Psychologist, 35,* 151–175.

Zajonc, R. B. (1982). On the primacy of affect. *American Psychologist, 39,* 117–123.

11

Multi-Stage Experimental Designs in Political Communication Research

Glenn J. Hansen
Department of Communication
University of Oklahoma

Michael Pfau
Department of Communication
University of Oklahoma

Political communication experimentalists rely heavily on single-shot outcomes as opposed to longer-term effects. This is unfortunate given the instability of political attitudes. More than 50 years ago Converse (1964) argued that most people's political attitudes are superficial and, hence, unstable. As a result, their responses vary when asked the same questions at two or more points in time. Converse (1964) coined the term, "nonattitudes" to characterize the political beliefs of most American adults. Asher maintains that "the presence of nonattitudes is one of the . . . most perplexing problems in public opinion polling" (1998, p. 26). The problem of instability in people's responses to queries about their preferences among candidates or their attitudes about issues has vexed public opinion scholars for decades and explains the seeming volatility found in public opinion poll results (Asher, 1998; Bishop, 1990; Erickson, Luttbeg, & Tedin, 1980). The problem may stem from the fact that most people do not have stable beliefs about political issues, which is Converse's position. It may stem from measurement error, which is an intrinsic shortcoming for many social science measurements, as Achen (1975) argues. Or, the problem may be a product of both considerations. Zaller (1994) provides an explanation based on "ambivalence." Even if people possess "meaningful beliefs" about political issues, they respond to questionnaires based on "top of the head considerations" and, therefore, our instruments only capture part of their beliefs (1994, pp. 278, 280).

Regardless of the cause, the problem of response instability to queries about political attitudes is a conundrum for political communication scholars, who assume that respondent answers are, in fact, meaningful reflections of what respondents think and feel. This problem is magnified by reliance on single-shot data collection, which typifies political communication research. Obviously, the questions posed in a study dictate design, data collection, and analysis strategies employed in an investigation and, sometimes, the questions a researcher seeks to answer warrant multi-stage data collection. However, above and beyond this, we maintain that multi-stage data collections are superior to isolated snapshots of political beliefs, feelings, and attitudes due to the instability of citizen responses.

In this chapter we seek to encourage more multi-stage experimental designs in political communication research (we also urge more longitudinal survey designs; see Chapter 2, this volume). In the next section, we articulate several approaches to multi-stage experiments and illustrate them with examples drawn from political communication scholarship. Then, we examine two important issues in experimental research: realism (mundane, experimental, and psychological) and external validity. We close with a summary of our major arguments and observations.

APPROACHES TO MULTI-STAGE EXPERIMENTAL RESEARCH

Our first task is to articulate several different approaches to multi-stage experimental designs. At the outset, we want to differentiate the term *approaches* from the phrase *experimental design*. As is the case with many terms, "design," "research design," or "experimental design" are defined differently by different authors (Pedhazur & Pedhazur Schmelkin, 1991); therefore, we cannot rely on a single previous definition of these concepts. Generally, the phrase *experimental design* refers to a particular experimental configuration that is employed. For instance, an experiment could utilize a Solomon four-group design or a posttest-only control group design; see Campbell and Stanley (1963) for their detailed description of 16 different experimental/quasi-experimental designs. Our use of the term *experimental approach* differs from *experimental design*. We prefer to use approaches for two reasons. First, experimental approaches should be considered prior to the design determination. Second, regardless of what decision is made at the approach level, the researcher still has the entire array of experimental designs to choose from. For example, say a researcher determines that at the approach level she wants to utilize a multi-stage data collection with a randomized component (defined below); a decision must still be made about which specific experimental design (e.g., pretest-posttest, posttest-only) to use.

We derive four experimental approaches from the literatures of experimental methodology, political communication, and political science. The four approaches include (1) multi-stage data collection with randomization, (2) sequential implementation, (3) the cascading outcome approach, and (4) a reinforcing spirals system approach. It should be noted that these considerations are not necessarily mutually exclusive. A single study could incorporate both a multi-stage data collection with randomization and sequential implementation. The articulation of these approaches should provide researchers with useful options to consider during the planning phase of their research.

The first approach is rather straightforward and seems to be the most frequently used in political communication research. We refer to this approach as *multi-stage with a randomized component*. Of course, without randomly assigning participants to different experimental conditions, this would not be considered an experimental study (depending on the particulars, it may be considered a quasi-experiment; see Campbell & Stanley, 1963). By randomly assigning participants to different experimental conditions, this approach meets the classic criteria for an experimental study (Campbell & Stanley, 1963). The objective of this particular approach is to allow the researcher to assess the impact of the manipulation after some period; in other words, to manipulate the cause and assess the effect at some point in the future. In contrast, the single-shot experiment has no interest in this longitudinal dimension. Depending on the investigation, the interval between manipulation and assessment could be measured in milliseconds (e.g., Lodge & Taber, 2005; Morris, Squires, Taber, & Lodge, 2003), days (e.g., An & Pfau, 2004; Iyengar &

Kinder, 1987; Prior & Lupia, 2008), or even weeks (e.g., Gerber, Green, & Larimer, 2008). For example, research exploring the priming effect of a subliminal political stimulus may examine the effect within a millisecond of manipulation and then again after a few minutes have elapsed (as opposed to only immediate measurement after the stimulus is applied). Likewise, research examining the effects of viewing a political debate might examine the effects several days after the debate was viewed (again, as opposed to only measuring the effect of the debate within minutes of viewing it). In many cases, compared with the single-shot approach (e.g., exposure to a political debate followed immediately by measurement of the effect), the multi-stage approach with randomization should be theoretically appealing to political communication experimentalists.

An example of research that employs a multi-stage approach with a randomized component is Iyengar and Kinder's (1987) classic work, *News that Matters*. As a part of their experimental approach, Iyengar and Kinder recruited participants to view manipulated television news for several successive days. The researchers edited the newscasts to insert certain news content (i.e., stories about investigate defense, pollution, and the economy) and remove unwanted content. Participant responses were collected at the beginning and end of the study. Iyengar and Kinder's objective was to experimentally investigate the agenda-setting hypothesis from a cognitive portrait perspective (see Chapter 20, this volume) and to examine priming effects in a political communication context. Their work stands, two decades following its publication, as a model of political communication research. Their studies employ a multi-stage approach with a randomized component. A significant strength of this research, and an obvious goal built into the project, is enhanced external validity. That is, to a large degree, the experimental situation that Iyengar and Kinder created reflected how news is consumed on an everyday basis.

A second multi-stage experimental approach is what we refer to as *sequential implementation*. There is an important difference between this and the approach just outlined. Specifically, the reason to employ sequential implementation is to fully implement the manipulation. In a sequential implementation, the manipulation cannot be effectively carried out in a single setting; therefore, the manipulation is introduced over an extended period. This differs from the multi-stage with a randomized component approach in that the former included the multi-stage component only to examine the impact of the manipulation *after* a period of time. By contrast, the sequential implementation approach has a multi-stage component because it is the best or only valid means of manipulating certain conditions.

Pfau's inoculation research illustrates the sequential implementation approach. His study of inoculation in politics suggests the efficacy of the inoculation strategy to foster resistance to the influence of candidate-sponsored or third party-sponsored political attack advertising (Pfau & Burgoon, 1988; Pfau, Holbert, Szabo, & Kaminski, 2002; Pfau, Kenski, Nitz, & Sorenson, 1990), the influence of print and television news reports (Pfau et al., 2006; Pfau et al., 2008), or the insidious impact of the spiral of silence (Lin & Pfau, 2007). Inoculation research requires an experimental design coupled with sequential implementation over a period of days, if not weeks or months. An and Pfau's (2004) investigation into use of inoculation in televised political debates illustrates this approach.

The An and Pfau (2004) study was conducted in three phases over a one-month period. The first phase of the study was necessary to collect initial candidate preferences. The initial measures allowed the researchers to randomly assign participants to treatment conditions and, more importantly, to stratify the sample based on preferences (this ensures that assignment was random with regards to initial attitudes). The second phase featured the experimental manipulation, specifically, the inoculation against the influence of attacks on the candidate the viewer supported versus a no-inoculation control condition. This phase also allowed for assessing threat, a key theoretical component in the inoculation process. The third phase of the study was carried out several weeks after the participants had been inoculated. During this phase, all participants viewed a televised debate with candidates who were the subject of the inoculation message. After viewing the debate, all participants completed a questionnaire designed to assess their attitudes toward the candidates in the debates.

Logistically, it would be possible to conduct the same study in a single setting; however, this approach would have significantly lower levels of internal validity. First, by stratifying the sample this study achieved higher levels of internal validity (i.e., we can be more confident that the manipulation was responsible for the outcome; that the outcome was not due to the groups being unequal prior to the manipulation). Stratification might be possible in a single experimental setting, but it seems like the logistics of trying to accomplish this would raise suspicion with participants, threatening internal validity. Second, and most importantly, this study demonstrated that the inoculation was still effective several weeks after it was induced. This long-term effectiveness speaks to the validity of the study and would not have been possible with a single-shot experiment.

A third approach is what we are referring to as the *cascading outcome approach*. The objective here is to determine how a stimulus influences some future outcome. For example, the framing of a news story can be manipulated (e.g., episodic or thematic) and then the effect of framing can be assessed relative to consumption and interpretation of news content across different media channels. The objective with this approach is to replicate naturalistic behavior. In this example, it is reasonable to conclude that newspaper content is not consumed in a vacuum and would be consumed along with other forms of communication. In theory, this cascading progression could continue across any number of effects, which then become a cause. However, in application, the number of progressions is limited by practical considerations (e.g., participant fatigue, logistical support).

A published example will illuminate this particular experimental approach. Holbert, Hansen, Caplan, and Mortensen (2007) use a cascading outcome approach in their investigation of Michael Moore's *Fahrenheit 9/11* documentary and how exposure to it subsequently influenced viewing of a presidential debate that featured George W. Bush (the subject of the film) and John F. Kerry. At phase one of the study, a set of initial measures were gathered to stratify the sample. The second phase of the study involved the manipulation (i.e., film or no film) and a second collection of data. The final phase had participants view a live presidential debate and complete another data collection. Of interest to these researchers was how participants' emotional reactions to the film (joy and anger) influenced confidence in the candidates after viewing the debate. While the specific results for this study are not of interest to the current discussion, the cascading outcome approach seems to have clear utility when compared to a simple one-shot design.

A fourth, and final, experimental approach involves a *reinforcing spirals system*. Slater (2007) details the theoretical logic associated with this particular approach, which involves media use influencing some outcome variable and then that outcome influencing additional media use. As Slater (2007) posits, "some type of media use influences corresponding beliefs or behaviors . . . that belief or behavior in turn increases that type of media use . . . then the process should be mutually reinforcing over time" (pp. 284–285). There is similarity between the reinforcing spirals system and cascading outcome approach. However, there is a key distinction. This distinction concerns the reinforcing nature of the spiral system. In the spiral system, media use influences the outcome and that outcome influences media use. The spiral system can lead either to more media use (upward spiral system) or less media use (downward spiral system). Eveland, Shah, and Kwak's (2003) study of media use and issue knowledge in the 2000 presidential campaign illustrates the spiral system approach. In this study, the researchers found that news attention at time 1 predicted issue knowledge at time 2. They further reported that the reverse was also the case. That is, issue knowledge at time 1 predicted news attention at time 2. In short, media use affected levels of issue knowledge and prior issue knowledge influenced subsequent media use. To date, the reinforcing spirals system approach has not been prominent in political communication experiments. However, as Slater (2007) maintains, this design holds promise, particularly for political communication scholars.

REALISM IN MULTI-STAGE EXPERIMENTS

Regardless of the experimental approach, design concerns may arise about the realism of political communication research. Compared to a one-shot experiment, realism takes on additional significance in a multi-stage study. This stems from the multi-staged nature of the research and the need to make the protracted encounter as realistic as possible for all participants. Experimental methodologists (e.g., Aronson & Carlsmith, 1968; Aronson et al., 1994, 1998) distinguish between three types of realism—experimental, mundane, and psychological. According to Aronson and Carlsmith (1968) *experimental realism* is achieved if the study is involving to participants, that is, if they take the study seriously and the study has an impact on them. A second type of realism is *mundane*. Experimental studies evidence mundane realism to the degree that "events occurring in a laboratory setting are likely to occur in the 'real world'" (p. 22). A third form is *psychological realism* (Aronson et al., 1994, 1998). Psychological realism concerns "how well an experiment captures the psychological processes like those occurring in everyday life" (Aronson et al., 1994, p. 58). Aronson and Carlsmith (1968) argue that these forms of realism are not mutually exclusive concepts. A study could manifest all three, or show a high degree of one type and a low amount of the other two. The goal for political communication experimentalists should be to maximize all three forms of realism.

There are several parallels between realism and experimental validity; given these parallels, it is important to distinguish between these concepts. First, Campbell (1957) maintains that the validity of an experimental study can be evaluated using two criteria: internal and external validity.[1] Internal validity addresses the question of whether the experimental manipulation produced the outcome in question. Stated differently, a study is internally valid to the extent that one is certain that the manipulation of the cause or stimulus led to the changes in the criterion—or outcome—measure. On the other hand, external validity concerns representativeness or generalizability (Campbell, 1957). The question here is whether the results of a particular experimental study can be generalized to other populations or settings.

What are the parallels between the three types of realism (experimental, mundane, and psychological) and criteria for validity? First, internal validity is *sine qua non* for an experiment to be at all meaningful (Aronson & Carlsmith, 1968; Campbell & Stanley, 1963; Pedhazur & Pedhazur Schmelkin, 1991). If a study is not internally valid, then it makes no sense to even consider the degree to which it is realistic. In other words, if we have no confidence that the manipulation of the independent variable led to changes in the dependent variable why, then, would the realism of the study matter? A clear parallel between realism and validity is that the internal validity of a study can be addressed by attending to issues related to realism (Aronson & Carlsmith, 1968). For example, Campbell and Stanley (1963) articulated several factors that could jeopardize the internal validity of a study. One of these factors, particularly relevant to a multi-stage experiment, is "experimental mortality" (i.e., attrition, or the differential loss of participants from experimental/control groups). In this case, the researcher cannot be certain that the change in the dependent variable is produced by the manipulation of the independent variable or because participants from, for example, the experimental condition quit the study and those who dropped out differ in some significant way from those who remained. It is quite plausible to suspect that the realism of a study could impact experimental mortality. Specifically, high levels of experimental realism would likely impact levels of attrition. If the study is involving to the participant, if the study convinces participants to take the task and setting seriously, and if the study has meaning for the participant, one could predict that there would be less attrition than if none of these qualities were present.

To understand the distinction between the types of realism in longitudinal experimental research, we further examine Iyengar and Kinder's (1987) experimental work as an example of a well implemented multi-stage experimental study. First, the study scores high on experimental realism. This type of realism concerns the participants' involvement and engagement in the experiment. Sustaining levels of involvement over time can be a challenge. Iyengar and Kinder achieve experimental realism by exposing participants to actual newscasts that were originally aired on the evening before participants saw them. Compare the level of realism here with a study that chose to assemble the weeks' worth of news prior to a study commencing (that is to say, the news could be a week or more old). This would be akin to using political advertisements as stimulus material in fictitious campaigns (campaigns in which either the candidates or the electoral context is artificial to study participants, which has been the case in too many studies of political advertising's influence). This study also achieves experimental realism by having participants view newscasts that have been "unobtrusively altered" so that they would not stand out as being experimentally manipulated. Clearly, if the newscasts had seemed contrived, they may have proven to be a distraction to participants, thereby diminishing experimental realism.

Next, turning to mundane realism, the Iyengar and Kinder study has lower levels of this form of realism. As a reminder, mundane realism concerns the extent to which the events of the study would occur in the real world. Certainly, some of the participants of this investigation likely watched at least some national news in a given week. The question here is to what degree the experimental news viewing experience parallels actual news viewing outside the study. It is unlikely that all participants would watch the news for five consecutive days or sit through the entire newscast when they do watch news.[2] Instead, participants who do watch nightly news probably do so while also doing other things (e.g., helping children with homework, performing household chores). Finally, it is unlikely that the participants would watch the nightly news with a group of strangers in a relatively unfamiliar setting. All of these factors lead to questions about the levels of mundane realism in this study.

The third type of realism, psychological, can also be examined vis-à-vis the Iyengar and Kinder research. Psychological realism concerns how well the study captures psychological processes similar to those occurring in everyday life. The psychological effects that Iyengar and Kinder were concerned with are those related to agenda setting and priming. Given what we know, or do not know, about the psychological mechanisms involved with these two theories, it is difficult to be certain about assessing the psychological realism of this work. One reaction is that any agenda setting and priming effects should psychologically work the same in the confines of this study as they do in real life. However, another reaction, related to the concerns with mundane realism, is that psychologically these participants were in a much different place than they would be normally. The bottom line here is that arguments could be made for or against optimal levels of psychological realism.

We encourage experimentalists doing multi-stage work to take the realism of their experimental undertaking seriously. Specifically, researchers need to assess the three types of realism that we have addressed experimental, mundane, and psychological. In designing a study, researchers should try to maximize the three types of realism. However, they need to recognize that there may be trade-offs. A given study may be able to achieve high levels of experimental and psychological realism, but less than ideal levels of mundane realism. Our advice is that, if levels of realism are less than ideal, researchers need to replicate findings (see Campbell & Jackson, 1979; Rosenthal, 1991, for the importance of replication research in the social sciences). A goal for the replication research should be to address the low levels of realism of the original studies. But in doing so, there may be diminished realism for one of the other criteria. However, if all of the studies are considered together, a better understanding of the process in question should be achieved.

EXTERNAL VALIDITY AND MULTI-STAGE EXPERIMENTS

As mentioned above, external validity concerns the extent to which a particular experimental study can be generalized to other populations or settings. The argument we want to make is that, for some experimental studies (long or short in duration), undue emphasis may be placed on issues related to external validity. Baxter and Babbie (2004) offer a caveat about experimental research, namely that "communication processes that occur in a laboratory setting might not necessarily occur in more natural social settings" (p. 228). Additionally, Brader (2006) observes that, "Establishing causality is the hallmark strength of experiments. Failing to inspire confidence in the generality of the results is their notorious weakness" (p. 181). We do not claim that generalizability of results is unimportant. There are times when multi-stage experimentalists need to place emphasis on the external validity of their work; however, this is not always the case. The reasons for this are discussed next.

In considering the generalizability of experimental results, it is advantageous to first examine the specific threats to external validity. Campbell and Stanley (1963) articulate four factors that jeopardize external validity. The first is a reactive effect to a test. In other words, a pretest could enhance or reduce a respondent's sensitivity to a stimulus. Abnormal sensitivity can make responses to an experimental variable unrepresentative of what an untested group's reaction would be. Another threat concerns how an unrepresentative sample could lead to biased results. This threat is probably cited most frequently with research that involves college students. Sometimes manipulations are intricate and are best tested with undergraduate students. The issue here is not whether college students generalize to the broader population of potential voters (obviously, they do not), but whether the process or effects revealed by the manipulation generalizes to the theory being tested. If the research is focused on testing theory, and if the study in other respects meets conditions of realism, described previously, then external validity issues are less of a concern. Third, if participants react in a certain way to the *experimental arrangement*, the induced effect may not hold for persons exposed to the stimulus in a nonexperimental study. Finally, Campbell and Stanley argue that the external validity of an experimental study may suffer because of interference caused by multiple treatments. That is, the effect of an initial treatment cannot be erased when a second treatment is applied; therefore, any interpretation of results needs to take the multiple treatments into consideration. We do not take issue with these threats that Campbell and Stanley outline. Indeed, in those circumstances in which external validity (i.e., generalizability) is the goal of the research, these threats warrant serious consideration.[3] Our argument is that, depending on the goals of the research, there are instances where the external validity of the study is less relevant.

Mook (1983) and Aronson et al. (1998) address this issue, noting goals for experimental research in addition to external validity. In what follows we discuss these goals in the specific context of multi-stage experimental research.

First, the researcher may be asking *can something happen*, rather than *does something typically happen* (Mook, 1983). Whether a stimulus elicits a given outcome is a much different question than whether a stimulus produces a generalizable result. If the goal of the research is the former, then the external validity of the study is less of a concern. The goal here is to test a theory or hypothesized relationship. Without question, programmatic research should in time address issues related to external validity; however, at least initially, this does not have to be the case. For instance, little is known about how the changing presentation of news via the Internet affects traditional political communication theory (e.g., agenda setting). It is now common on news media websites to be able to provide feedback to a given news story. In many cases, this user-generated content is accessible to anyone who wants to view it. The question is, *can* this public feedback change the dynamics of agenda setting theory? Our goal here would be to test theory. A multi-stage experiment could be designed with this theory-testing in mind. The manipulated measure could be the tone of the user-generated content or feedback (e.g., supportive of the particular news story, opposed to the story, and mixed). If the goal of the study is answering the question—*can* these comments influence the traditional agenda-setting relationship?—then criticisms related to external validity are misplaced. Researchers, of course, need to be clear about their goals (e.g., theory testing) and they should not over-claim the external validity of their results.

A long-term experimental study may also wish to produce conditions that do not have an analog in real life, where generalizing to the real world would have no meaning (Aronson et al., 1998; Mook, 1983). An example here are Milgram's (1974) notorious obedience to authority experiments. It seems unlikely that the laboratory setting (e.g., sterile room, a fake shock generator, white coated scientists) in much of Milgram's work would generalize to any real-world setting. For instance, would Milgram's lab setting generalize to the crimes committed in concentration camps by German soldiers or to the humilations of the Abu Ghraib prison? It does not seem likely. Milgram's participants were asked to deliver "shocks" to strangers who performed poorly on a memory test—does this generalize to what German soldiers faced? Does it generalize to what took place in the Iraqi prison with American soldiers? Again, it does not seem likely. However, are the findings, then, of no value? This also seems unlikely.

Another example of research that does not have an analogue in real life would be the "assemblage experiments" that Iyengar and Kinder (1987) did as part of their agenda-setting examination. In the assemblage experiments, the researchers had participants view six television news stories, one right after the other, all relating to defense, energy, or inflation. This does not mirror the news viewing experience. Both the Milgram and Iyengar and Kinder examples were performed in a setting that does not replicate "the real world"; however, both of these studies produced influential findings. Milgram's work, despite the artificiality, helped us to understand how, when people step out of their standard routine, they are willing to violate normal rules and conventions to the point of harming a complete stranger because an authority figure tells them to. The Iyengar and Kinder studies gave us a better understanding of agenda setting through a more "precise calibration" of the treatment conditions—news stories shown to viewers—than had previously been the case (Iyengar & Kinder, 1987, p. 21).

Experimental work is often subject to criticism for what Mook (1983) calls the checklist approach, which consists of examining a given experimental study and checking off the differences between the "real world" and the "experimental world." In the end, the experiment is deemed to be invalid if there are more differences than similarities. Some multi-stage experimental studies are particularly susceptible to this criticism, given the prolonged contact that participants have with the experimental situation. As we have suggested, these criticism are, at times, overstated. Clearly, if researchers claim that their results are externally valid, these types of criticisms are warranted. However, as we have indicated, this may not be the objective of the research. Nevertheless, there does seem to be much confusion among researchers (and reviewers) in this area.

In part, we think this confusion about research objectives stems from misunderstanding the differences between problem-oriented versus process-oriented research (Aronson et al., 1998). Problem-oriented research is similar to *applied* research or what Zanna and Fazio (1982) refer to as "is questions" (e.g., *is* there an effect or *is* there a phenomenon). Aronson et al. (1998) indicate that problem-oriented researchers are mainly interested in studying a phenomenon that they want to understand and possibly change. This type of research more likely has external validity as its goal, even more so after initial studies have been conducted.[4] Once it has been determined that there is an effect, the generalizability of the effect is more important than replicating results that have already been determined.

Process-oriented research, by contrast, has as its goal the underlying mechanisms responsible for a phenomenon (Aronson et al., 1998). Zanna and Fazio (1982) indicate that these goals often relate to "when" questions (i.e., questions related to moderation) or "how" questions (i.e., questions related to mediation). Process-oriented research would be similar to *basic* research. With basic research, researchers are looking for the "best answers to questions of why people behave the way they do, purely for reasons of intellectual curiosity" (Aronson et al., 1998, p. 106) or future application. Generally, those doing basic research do not have a direct interest in solving social problems (Aronson et al., 1998). In our view, experimental research that is focused on a process can justify forgoing goals of external validity. At this juncture political communication needs to move more towards a focus on process than problem-oriented research. Zanna and Fazio (1982) characterize this shift as a move from first- and second-generation research to a third generation of process-oriented discovery. Holbert and Stephenson (2003) make a similar argument for more process-oriented media effects investigations.

In summary, we are not suggesting that internally invalid results should be the goal for political communication experimentalists. To the contrary, we maintain that political communication scholars should be clear about their goals. If the goal of the research is generalizability, then, by all means, the researcher needs to take steps in an effort to realize this goal. However, if the research is focused on a process, with the goal of understanding how or whether something happens, then theory building should be the goal, not generalizability. Given the need to conduct political communication research that is focused on process, we would gladly forgo, at least initially, external validity for the understanding of the processes that take place in the domain of political communication.

CONCLUSION

We want to reiterate our belief that multi-stage data collections are superior to isolated snapshots of people's political beliefs, feelings, and attitudes because of the instability of their responses. It is important to get beyond many of the one-shot experimental studies that political communication scholars have relied on in the past. A goal here has been to encourage more multi-stage experimental designs in political communication research. We hope that the information provided in this chapter will help researchers to achieve that goal. Experimentalists should first consider the appropriate experimental approach for their study before contemplating a specific design. We also see a need to consider issues related to the realism of the multi-stage studies and have discussed three dimensions of realism that are of particular concern. Finally, regarding external validity, it is important for political communication researchers to carefully consider the objectives of their research and to make certain that these objectives align with any possible criticisms.

NOTES

1. Cook and Campbell (1979) and Shadish, Cook, and Campbell (2002) discuss two additional types of validity assessment. Statistical conclusion validity, as suggested by the name, concerns the validity of the statistical conclusions drawn for a particular study. Issues concerning statistical power, restrictions of range, and error rate inflation are examples of threats to this type of validity. The second additional type of validity assessment that Cook and colleagues added was construct validity. Construct validity concerns the findings that researchers report and how they square with the constructs measured.
2. In support of this claim, the 1984 American National Election Studies data indicates that 60 percent of the public watch television news fewer than five days per week and that 50 percent of the public indicate that they only pay "some" attention to television news when they do watch.
3. Shadish et al. (2002) present a slightly different set of threats to external validity; however, their version of threats generally matches the Campbell and Stanley (1963) typology, so we determined that it was clearest to present the version that is likely most familiar. In any case, the overall argument we make is not contingent on specific threats.
4. See our above discussion about the research objective being *can something happen* versus external validity. At first glance, this statement about problem-focused research more likely having goals of external validity may seem at variance with our discussion of research having the objective of testing whether *can something happen*. The key here is that when doing problem-oriented research, once the *can something happen* is affirmed, future research should have a goal of external validity.

REFERENCES

Achen, C. H. (1975). Mass political attitudes and the survey response. *American Political Science Review*, *69*, 1218–1231.

An, C., & Pfau, M. (2004). The efficacy of inoculation in televised political debates. *Journal of Communication*, *54*, 421–436.

Aronson, E., & Carlsmith, J. M. (1968). Experimentation in social psychology. In G. Lindzey & E. Aronson (Eds.), *The handbook of social psychology* (Vol. 2, 2nd ed., pp. 1–79). Reading, MA: Addison-Wesley.

Aronson, E., Wilson, T. D., & Akert, R. M. (1994). *Social psychology: The heart and the mind.* New York: Harper Collins.

Aronson, E., Wilson, T. D., & Brewer, M. B. (1998). Experimentation in social psychology. In D. T. Gilbert, S. T. Fiske, & G. Lindzey (Eds.), *The handbook of social psychology* (Vol. I, pp. 99–142). New York: McGraw-Hill.

Asher, H. (1998). *Polling and the public: What every citizen should know* (4th ed.). Washington, DC: CQ Press.

Baxter, L. A., & Babbie, E. (2004). *The basics of communication research.* Belmont, CA: Wadsworth.

Bishop, G. F. (1990). Issue involvement and response effects in public opinion surveys. *Public Opinion Quarterly*, *54*, 209–218.

Brader, T. (2006). *Campaigning for hearts and minds: How emotional appeals in political ads work.* Chicago: University of Chicago Press.

Campbell, D. T. (1957). Factors relevant to the validity of experiments in social settings. *Psychological Bulletin*, *54*, 297–311.

Campbell, D. T., & Stanley, J. C. (1963). *Experimental and quasi-experimental designs for research.* Boston: Houghton Mifflin.

Campbell, K. E., & Jackson, T. T. (1979). The role and need for replication research in social psychology. *Replications in Social Psychology, 1*, 3–14.

Converse, P. E. (1964). The nature of belief systems in mass politics. In D. A. Apter (Ed.), *Ideology and discontent* (pp. 206–261). New York: Free Press.

Cook, T. D., & Campbell, D. T. (1979). *Quasi-experimentation: Design and analysis issues for field settings.* Chicago: Rand McNally College Publishing.

Erikson, R. S., Luttbeg, N. R., & Tedin, K. L. (1980). *American public opinion: Its origins, content, and impact.* New York: Wiley.

Eveland, W. P., Jr., Shah, D. V., & Kwak, N. (2003). Assessing causality in the cognitive mediation model: A panel study of motivation, information processing, and learning during campaign 2000. *Communication Research, 30*, 359–386.

Gerber, A. S., Green, D. P., & Larimer, C. W. (2008). Social pressure and voter turnout: Evidence from a large-scale field experiment. *American Political Science Review, 102*, 33–48.

Holbert, R. L., Hansen, G. J., Caplan, S. E., & Mortensen, S. (2007). Presidential debate viewing and Michael Moore's *Fahrenheit 9/11*: A study of affect-as-transfer and passionate reasoning. *Media Psychology, 9*, 673–694.

Holbert, R. L., & Stephenson, M. T. (2003). The importance of indirect effects in media effects research: Testing for mediation in structural equation modeling. *Journal of Broadcasting & Electronic Media, 47*, 556–572.

Iyengar, S., & Kinder, D. R. (1987). *News that matters: Television and American opinion.* Chicago: University of Chicago Press.

Lin, W.-K., & Pfau, M. (2007). Can inoculation work against the spiral of silence? A study of public opinion on the future of Taiwan. *International Journal of Public Opinion Research, 19*, 155–172.

Lodge, M. & Taber, C. S. (2005). The automaticity of affect for political leaders, groups, and issues: An experimental test of the hot cognition hypothesis. *Political Psychology, 26*, 455–482.

Milgram, S. (1974). *Obedience to authority.* New York: Harper & Row.

Mook, D. G. (1983). In defense of external invalidity. *American Psychologist, 38*, 379–388.

Morris, J. P., Squires, N. K., Taber, C. S., & Lodge, M. (2003). Activation of political attitudes: A psychophysiological examination of the hot cognition hypothesis. *Political Psychology, 24*, 727–745.

Pedhazur, E. J., & Pedhazur Schmelkin, L. (1991). *Measurement, design, and analysis: An integrated approach.* Hillsdale, NJ: Lawrence Erlbaum Associates.

Pfau, M., & Burgoon, M. (1988). Inoculation in political campaign communication. *Human Communication Research, 15*, 91–111.

Pfau, M., Holbert, R. L., Szabo, E. A., & Kaminski, K. (2002). Issue-advocacy versus candidate advertising: Effects on candidate preferences and democratic process. *Journal of Communication, 52*, 301–315.

Pfau, M., Kenski, H. C., Nitz, M., & Sorenson, J. (1990). Efficacy of inoculation strategies in promoting resistance to political attack messages: Application to direct mail. *Communication Monographs, 57*, 25–43.

Pfau, M., et al. (2006). The effects of print news photographs of the casualties of war. *Journalism & Mass Communication Quarterly, 83*, 150–168.

Pfau, M., et al. (2008). The influence of television news depictions of the images of war on viewers. *Journal of Broadcasting & Electronic Media, 52*(2), 303–322.

Prior, M., & Lupia, A. (2008). Money, time, and political knowledge: Distinguishing quick recall and political learning skills. *American Journal of Political Science, 52*, 169–183.

Rosenthal, R. (1991). Replication in behavioral research. In J. W. Neuliep (Ed.), *Replication in the social sciences* (pp. 1–30). Newbury Park, CA: Sage.

Shadish, W. R., Cook, T. D., & Campbell, D. T. (2002). *Experimental and quasi-experimental designs for generalized causal inference.* Boston: Houghton Mifflin.

Slater, M. D. (2007). Reinforcing spirals: The mutual influence of media selectivity and media effects and their impact on individual behavior and social identity. *Communication Theory, 17*, 281–303.

Zaller, J. (1994). Positive constructs of public opinion. *Critical Studies in Mass Communication, 11,* 276–287.

Zanna, M. P. & Fazio, R. H. (1982). The attitude-behavior relation: Moving toward a third generation of research. In M. P. Zanna, E. T. Higgins, & C. P. Herman (Eds.), *Consistency in social behavior: The Ontario symposium.* (Vol. 2, pp. 283–302). Hillsdale, NJ: Lawrence Erlbaum Associates.

IV
CONTENT ANALYSIS

12

Image Bite Analysis of Political Visuals

Understanding the Visual Framing Process in Election News

Maria Elizabeth Grabe
Department of Telecommunications
Indiana University

Erik P. Bucy
Department of Advertising
Texas Tech University

This chapter makes the case for the importance of analyzing audiovisual messages in political communication research and presents a content analysis methodology for reliable assessment of visual content in televised coverage of presidential elections. Despite repeated calls for increased consideration of televised images, the visual aspect of broadcast, cable, and now online news remains under-researched. As we have noted elsewhere (see Bucy & Grabe, 2007; Grabe & Bucy, 2009), this is due in part to a normative, social-scientific bias against image-based media and a tendency to dismiss television as a superficial or entertainment medium that lacks the seriousness of print. "The belief that audiovisuals are poor carriers of important political information has become so ingrained in conventional wisdom that it has throttled research," Graber (2001, p. 93) has observed. Although various coding schemes have been proposed over the years for evaluating the content of news visuals, including Graber's (1996, 2001) "gestalt coding" procedure and detailed categories for camera presentation techniques (see Kepplinger, 1991), none have caught on in a significant way.

Our approach to the systematic analysis of political visuals, which is based on presidential election news coverage by the major broadcast networks (ABC, CBS, and NBC), has been presented in the book *Image Bite Politics: News and the Visual Framing of Elections* (Grabe & Bucy, 2009), several refereed journal articles (Bucy & Grabe, 2007, 2008; Grabe, 1996), and a series of research presentations at scholarly venues and conferences. Our "image bite" analyses of audiovisual segments in which candidates are shown but not necessarily heard employ detailed measurement of candidate depictions, structural features of newscasts such as camera angles, shot lengths, and durations, and visual framing of candidates to document and explain the information value that news visuals have for viewers. These categories, beyond having a descriptive and documentary purpose, have predictive value in experimental and survey-based research (see Bucy, 2010; Grabe & Bucy, 2009, Chapter 6). In this chapter we explicate and track the prevalence of three prominent visual frames in election news—the ideal candidate, populist campaigner, and sure loser—and report their visual manifestation across four presidential election cycles. Throughout the analysis we also offer methodological observations on how to conduct image-based research.

APPLICATIONS OF THE "IMAGE BITES" APPROACH

The utility of analyzing television news visually can be appreciated by considering different applications of our approach. First, the packaging of election coverage can be analyzed using categories to detect *visual bias* in the form of some two dozen camera and editing techniques (see Grabe, 1996; Grabe & Bucy, 2009, Chapter 5). One example of visual bias involves the use of a camera viewpoint that purposefully scrutinizes politicians to reveal or emphasize peculiar physical characteristics or emotional expressions. Indications of nervousness, tension, and unflattering physical qualities of political candidates are revealed through an under-distanced or overly tightly framed camera viewpoint. Close-up camera shots or zoom-in lens movements can emphasize sweat on the upper lip, a twitching eye, bad complexion, double chin, and other unappealing qualities. Moreover, a cutaway shot of nervous hand movements—a technique commonly employed by television news magazine programs such as *60 Minutes*—may visually contradict the verbal assertiveness of an office seeker.

Visual bias may subtly but significantly alter the relationship between viewers and political figures, highlight appealing or unappealing personal attributes and communicative behaviors of candidates, and result in a type of visual distortion that undermines one candidate while favoring another—all without saying a word.

Second, newscasts can be analyzed for the manner in which news organizations depict the candidates' *nonverbal behavior*. Using principles drawn from behavioral biology and primate ethology (animal behavior), the facial expressions and display behavior of political candidates can be categorized according to four prominent display types: anger/threat, fear/evasion, happiness/ reassurance, and sadness/appeasement (Bucy & Grabe, 2008; Stewart, Salter, & Mehu, Chapter 10, this volume). These display categories, readily evident in television news coverage of political campaigns, index the affective state and behavioral intention of the communicator while transmitting important social signals to observers. While displays of dominance are associated with anger and aggression, signs of fear or evasion indicate subordination. Bonding expressions, on the other hand, including displays of gladness or sadness, typically convey reassurance or appeasement.

The political value of such display behavior is widely evident. Candidates and office holders adept at projecting displays of dominance (e.g., Ronald Reagan) and bonding (e.g., Bill Clinton) are viewed as effective communicators, while politicians who reveal signs of subordination (e.g., Jimmy Carter) or who are unable to convey reassurance (e.g., Al Gore) do not last long on the national political stage. The prevalence of these display types may then be correlated with political success or failure in the form of tracking poll data or presidential approval ratings (see Grabe & Bucy, 2009). In addition, the appropriateness of candidate reactions to the news context can be analyzed. Deviations from audience expectations regarding the appropriateness of political acts to their settings may signal ineptitude and generate doubt (Bucy, 2000; Edelman, 1964)—a concern, certainly, among undecided voters in recent presidential elections.

Third, newscasts can be analyzed for the quality and frequency of *candidate image frames* employed by television journalists. News frames have been defined as the salient story emphasis of election coverage that provides media audiences with visual and verbal cues to make sense of unfolding events. Frames consist of, among other things, recurring characteristics verbally assigned by journalists to leading candidates in news accounts of campaigns—and consistent visual portrayals of candidates and office holders in television news. Framing, according to Entman (1993), is an interpretive process by which some aspects of a candidate's character or governing ability are emphasized over others in such a way as to promote a particular under-standing or evaluation. The extent to which candidates are visually depicted as having ideal attributes, mass appeal, or losing qualities often determines their ability to either surface from a field of relative unknowns or be winnowed from the pool of frontrunners. Visual framing is thus one of the mechanisms through which media power is wielded.

The frame construction process is not entirely one-sided, however. Political advisors, mindful of the capacity of visual images to form impressions, routinely stage photo opportunities to highlight campaign themes, taking pains to manufacture positive imagery; for example, a sea of waving flags to convey patriotism, or candidate appearances before enthusiastic crowds to convey popularity. Perfected by Ronald Reagan's campaign organizers in the 1980s, such image-based messaging is now routinely employed on both sides of the political aisle by Democratic and Republican politicians alike and was utilized to brilliant effect by the 2008 Obama campaign team, as with his triumphant summer speech in Berlin. Our approach to analyzing the visual framing process thus identifies (a) salient candidate image frames used in television coverage of presidential elections, (b) the constituent elements of those frames, and (c) the political dynamics associated with the promotion and appearance of specific frames in broadcast news. This chapter in particular explicates the three aforementioned visual frames—the ideal candidate, populist campaigner, and sure loser—then reports on their visual manifestation across election years and offers methodological observations on how to conduct image-based analysis.

The Struggle for Frame Control

According to classic arguments about the press, the news media should serve as the public's eyes and ears, reporting and analyzing political events while acting as an unbiased conduit of infor-mation (Chaffee & Hochheimer, 1985). Through image orchestration, employed with increasing sophistication since the Kennedy era, politicians and their advisors continually battle journalists for control over news story framing—what the public ultimately sees and hears about the campaign. This battle for frame control is not an esoteric academic perspective of what goes on—journalists and image handlers do, in fact, battle it out on the campaign trail. As Joe Lockhart, former Clinton White House press secretary and senior advisor to John Kerry's 2004 presidential campaign, summed it up, the process involves "pretty skilled manipulators, manipulating people who are very well aware of being manipulated" (quoted in Jamieson, 2006, p. 141). The struggle for frame control is captured in Entman's (1993) description of a news frame as an "imprint of power—it registers the identity of actors or interests that competed to dominate the text" (p. 53). Of course, the "text" may be verbal, visual, or a combination of both presentation modalities.

In the contentious climate of the modern campaign, neither the press nor political candidates want to be controlled by the other (Blumler & Gurevitch, 1995; Swanson, 1992; Zaller, 1998). Political journalists employ a variety of measures to ward off attempts by political campaigns to manipulate them into serving as the candidate's mouthpiece, particularly by reporting on campaign strategy, while campaigns accuse the press of distorting the message that candidates want conveyed to voters (Blumler & Gurevitch, 1995). Despite this antagonism, the two sides are compelled to cooperate with each election cycle to address their mutual needs; indeed, election news is created through the *joint* efforts of political journalists and candidates (Blumler & Gurevitch, 1995). As Swanson (1992) has observed, "politicians cannot succeed without access to the media, just as reporters cannot succeed without access to political leaders" (p. 399).

In plying their craft, political consultants (whom we refer to as image handlers) take a rather formulaic approach to crafting candidate images. Typically, polling is used to identify salient issues on the minds of voters. The next step is to assess which of these issues play to their client's advantage. A campaign strategy is then devised to prime the audience on those issues, deploying images, symbols, and phrases that will connect the candidate to those issues in the minds of voters (Farrell, Kolodny, & Medvic, 2001). By exercising editorial autonomy during political campaigns, journalists do exercise message control through the selection, investigation, interpretation, framing, and regulation of election stories and candidates (Zaller, 1998). The press may thus construct frames for candidates that convey a message *different* from that desired by campaigns as a way of exercising their control over media content and demonstrating their independence from campaign influence. Voters integrate these filtered campaign messages, in conjunction with other campaign information (e.g., political advertising) and their own experiences and discussion networks, to construct a personalized candidate image (Moriarty & Garramone, 1986; Trent & Trent, 1997). Perceptions of candidates thus arise from the interaction between campaign-supplied images, news filtering, and the feelings and cognitions voters have about those running for office.

VISUAL SIGNS OF CANDIDATE CHARACTER

Despite the tendency to define political campaigns on the basis of policy positions and issue stands, candidate character traits are of central interest to voters, image handlers, and journalists alike (Graber, 1997; Patterson, 1980). Research has also convincingly demonstrated that voters attend to candidate images in addition to their statements on issues to extrapolate underlying evaluations that form the basis of voting decisions (Graber, 1987; Kinder, 1986; Lau, 1986). As a medium that traffics in images, television is ideally suited to convey character information. Indeed, most news stories may be too short to do anything *except* present information about the candidate's character and personality (Graber, 1987). Studying the visual representation of candidates during elections may therefore forecast what news consumers infer about candidates from media appearances.

Most academic insights about framing and its effects, however, are derived from verbal aspects of media coverage (see Gamson, 1992; Reese, Gandy, & Grant, 2001). These studies serve an important function in that they evaluate how well journalism delivers on one of its most grandiose commitments to society: to provide fair and balanced information that will empower citizens to make informed decisions when they elect political leaders. Yet, because it largely ignores visual information, research in this area has limited value. Despite the fact that voters rely most on television to acquire political information, the visual framing process remains under-studied. Instead, the bastions of elite print media such as the *New York Times* and *Washington Post* are regarded as more worthy of investigation. We suspect that the assumption driving this approach is that detecting frames or even biases in these venerated news outlets might be more harmful to the democratic process than the transgressions of broadcast journalists. Evidence documenting the role of television news generally, and political visuals specifically, in contributing to political learning, candidate impression formation, and voter decision-making makes this insistence on exclusively studying the written or spoken word at best misdirected (see Grabe & Bucy, 2009, Chapter 7).

Research on visual framing has received only sporadic attention and overlooks specific character-related dimensions of candidate images. Instead, the few visual framing studies that have been conducted tend to construct broad "valence frames" that cast election coverage as either favorable or unfavorable to particular candidates and parties (Coleman & Banning, 2006; Moriarty & Garramone, 1986; Moriarty & Popovich, 1991; Waldman & Devitt, 1998). While these analyses provide an important foundation for improving our understanding of the visual framing process, they offer little insight into specific aspects of television news coverage that influence voter evaluations; neither do they present categories of coverage that can be compared with the image-construction strategies of campaigns.

Another limitation of coding visuals in simple valence terms as either favorable or unfavorable concerns the interpretation of image valence. Although an image bite—television footage in which a candidate is shown but not necessarily heard—might have all the markings of positive representation, for instance a shot of candidate interaction with well-wishers at a rally, a particular candidate's comfort in executing this behavior might make the image all *but* positive. Al Gore, for example, was widely described as appearing stiff and aloof during the 2000 campaign (Sella, 2000). Images of an uncomfortable Gore mingling with crowds should hardly count as positive visual framing but would count as such under a simple valence approach. Another problem here concerns automated (computer-assisted) coding procedures of news transcripts, which are simply incapable of analyzing visual content or assessing the visual context in which candidates are depicted to millions of viewers on a nightly basis during campaigns.

Visual analyses need to move beyond crude positive versus negative index measures and investigate more specific and nuanced elements of character frames. Our goal here, therefore, is to identify enduring character frames and examine the visual manifestations of these frames in election news. In support of this effort we draw from research on journalistic (i.e., verbal) framing of candidate character dimensions, valence studies of visual framing, and experimental research on the impact that televised character portrayals have on audience perceptions. From this literature a coding instrument was devised to measure visual framing of three enduring character frames: the ideal candidate, populist campaigner, and sure loser. A detailed justification for each of these visual frames follows.

The Ideal Candidate

Research has shown that voters hold a mental picture of specific characteristics that an ideal presidential candidate should have (Hellweg, 1979; Trent & Trent, 1997). Early studies found that voters valued such candidate qualities as physical appeal, personality, firm issue stands, personal background and beliefs, and character traits including leadership ability, honesty, and intelligence (Nimmo & Savage, 1976). Other voter perception studies have identified similar traits, including compassion, sincerity, integrity, and warmth, as important evaluative criteria (Nimmo & Savage, 1976; Waterman, Wright & St. Clair, 1999). Assessments of job performance, including decisiveness, executive experience, competence, and speaking style, also receive mention (Nimmo, 1976; Nimmo & Savage, 1976; Waterman, Wright, & St. Clair, 1999). From these qualities, the ideal candidate frame seems to coalesce around two major character themes: statesmanship (a job performance dimension) and likeability (Nimmo & Savage, 1976; Trent & Trent, 1997). In fact, Kinder (1986) reports that statesman-like traits (competence, leadership ability, integrity) and compassion (empathy) form the basis of how voters evaluate candidates. Consequently, we examine the statesman and likeability subdimensions separately.

Statesmanship. Visual manifestations of statesmanship signal the mythic proportions of the presidency, projecting authority, power, and control. To measure these character qualities visually, two television production techniques deserve consideration: associational juxtaposition and *mise-en-scène*. These packaging strategies also inform our explication of the populist campaigner and loser frames in subsequent sections.

Associational juxtaposition is an editing device by which qualities of one object of attention are transferred to another via sequential depiction (Messaris, 1994). Implicit analogy often results when two unrelated scenes are brought into direct association, as when a shot of the American flag juxtaposed with a shot of a political candidate evokes a sense of patriotism (Messaris, Eckman & Gumpert, 1979). The *mise-en-scène*, or environmental context of portrayed objects, may also transfer symbolic meaning to a political candidate. Environmental transfer happens in television news, for example, when symbols of progress, such as a new fuel-efficient car or alternative energy source, are clearly visible within the candidate's visual environment.

Using Messaris' (1994) conceptualization of associational juxtaposition and the notion of symbolic transfer through visual context, statesmanship framing can be observed in network news coverage by measuring the occurrence of specific portrayals. Visual associations with high-ranking peers, for instance, serve as implied endorsements of candidates and cultivate perceptions of competence and credibility (Grabe, 1996; Rudd, 1986). Appearances at ceremonies or campaign visits to symbolic venues such as war memorials or locations associated with economic authority (e.g., Wall Street, trade union meetings) or technological advancement (e.g., NASA flight centers, high tech manufacturing plants) play on cherished societal principles and buttress the myth of the statesman as a symbol of patriotism and shepherd of cultural norms and progress (Bennett, 2007; Erickson, 2000; Glassman & Kenney, 1994; Grabe, 1996; Lee, Ryan, Wanta, & Chang, 2004; Sabato, 1981; Waldman & Devitt, 1998). Figure 12.1, a screen capture from general election news coverage of Bob Dole's 1996 presidential campaign, illustrates the symbolic transfer of patriotism with a small-town "Americana" sign and flag image clearly evident in the background.

The celebratory pomp and ceremony of political spectacle provoke emotional and aesthetic responses that include pleasure, joy, awe, and wonderment (Erickson, 2000; Sabato, 1981). Linking candidates to celebratory displays such as large entourages, parades, and rallies with campaign paraphernalia and confetti showers authenticate and reference the grandeur and authority of a presidential candidate as a potential chief executive. Such visual signals of statesmanship have been employed as categories in visual content analyses of candidates in newspaper photographs (Glassman & Kenney, 1994; Lee et al., 2004). Figure 12.2, a screen capture from news coverage of Al Gore's 2000 campaign, demonstrates the visual linkage between campaign paraphernalia and candidate support.

Performing the role of statesman, as Sarah Palin's 2008 vice-presidential nomination colorfully illustrated, also requires the use of an appropriate wardrobe. Moriarty and Popovich (1991) have distinguished between "dignified" attire (e.g., suit and tie) and casual clothing (e.g., sportswear, shirtsleeves) in coding the valence of candidate appearances. Kaid and Davidson (1986) include a formal dress code in conceptualizing an "incumbent videostyle" compared to informal dress, which they denote as a challenger style (p. 199). Although not articulated directly, both of these coding systems can be interpreted as drawing a distinction between a suited statesman and more casual populist campaigner (see Trebay, 2007).

Compassion. Voters apparently look for evidence that candidates are compassionate (Nimmo, 1995; Nimmo & Savage, 1976). Candidates address this expectation by running as warm and benevolent people, despite their campaign maneuverings (Keeter, 1987; see also Bennett, 1995). Compassion finds visual expression in candidate behavior towards symbols that are culturally revered, such as children and families. In ethological research, these expressive behaviors are referred to as affinity displays and may include embraces, reassuring hand signals, or similar gestures (see Bucy & Grabe, 2008; Stewart, Salter, & Mehu, Chapter 10, this volume).

FIGURE 12.1 Bob Dole, 1996: Linked to patriotic symbols.

FIGURE 12.2 Al Gore, 2000: Linked to campaign paraphernalia.

The political candidate's embrace of a supporter's baby involves perhaps the most clichéd construction of compassion on the campaign trail (Erickson, 2000; Rudd, 1986; Sherr, 1999). Presidential candidates also have a history of surrounding themselves with their own children and grandchildren for public demonstrations of family friendliness (Sabato, 1981; Sherr, 1999). During war and in times of economic hardship children are featured more prominently in campaigns to emphasize the softer side of a candidate; the implication is that decisions about war and the economy will be made with consideration of the most vulnerable among us (Glassman & Kenney, 1994; Sabato, 1981; Sherr, 1999).

Visual linkages to children also reinforce the mythology of family, a dominant value in American culture (Nimmo & Combs, 1980; Rudd, 1986). In a patriarchal social environment, protection of women and children as well as honoring family (and God), evoke framing of the candidate as an idealized surrogate father for the nation: a protector, provider, and moral compass (Glassman & Kenney, 1994; Parry-Giles & Parry Giles, 2002; Sabato, 1981). Numerous visual analyses have utilized symbolic linkages to family to assess candidate image construction (Coleman & Banning, 2006; Glassman & Kenney, 1994; Lee et al., 2004; Moriarty & Garramone, 1986; Moriarty & Popovich, 1991). Figures 12.3 and 12.4, screen captures from news coverage of Bill Clinton's 1996 reelection campaign, illustrate political compassion through the visual association of Clinton with children and admiring female supporters. Compassion and benevolence are also behaviorally signaled through personal interaction with voters and nonverbal affinity gestures, including waving, shaking hands, and giving the thumbs-up sign (Glassman & Kenney, 1994; Lee et al., 2004; Moriarty & Garramone, 1986; Moriarty & Popovich, 1991; Waldman & Devitt, 1998). Figure 12.5, showing George W. Bush posing for a photograph with his arms around a supporter in 2004 as others look on admiringly, illustrates the social bonding that affinity gestures promote. Figure 12.6 shows another example of social bonding from 2004, this time between John Kerry and a supporter along the rope lines.

FIGURE 12.3 Bill Clinton, 1996: Linked to children.

FIGURE 12.4 Bill Clinton, 1996: Linked to women.

FIGURE 12.5 George Bush, 2004: Physical contact, affinity

FIGURE 12.6 John Kerry, 2004: Compassion display.

The Populist Campaigner

Populist narratives are built on the idea that ordinary people, a noble but humble troupe, stand in opposition to undemocratic and self-serving elites (Kazin, 1995; Spragens, 2007). The populist frame visually depicting the candidate as "one with the people" is achieved through displays of an ordinary appearance and popularity among the masses (Denton, 2002; Erickson, 2000). Below we examine these two subdimensions of the populist frames: mass appeal and ordinariness.

Mass Appeal. Celebrities, as symbols of populist worship, transfer their cultural appeal to political candidates by lending their prestige through joint appearances and endorsements (Sabato, 1981). Mass appeal in television news coverage also finds visual expression through linkages to large and approving crowds (Glassman & Kenney, 1994; Lee et al., 2004; Moriarty & Garramone, 1986; Moriarty & Popovich, 1991). The allure of these portrayals is based in part on the idea of a mass movement coalescing around the candidate. On account of such popular appeal, all should join the bandwagon in support (Grabe, 1996). Indeed, speakers who are surrounded by an audience that responds positively through affirmative head nodding, smiles, and attentive nonverbal responses may boost their authority ratings and character dynamism compared to those shown with a disapproving audience exhibiting frowns, inattentiveness, and other signs of obvious disapproval (Hylton, 1971). Favorable audience reaction shots can also make featured speakers appear more interesting and popular (Duck & Baggaley, 1975). A screen capture of an attentive and approving audience visually linked to George W. Bush in 2004 campaign coverage is shown in Figure 12.7.

Ordinariness. This second dimension of the populist campaigner frame finds expression in visual appearances with regular folks, displays of physical labor or athletic ability, and the style of dress that candidates wear. During the 1992, 1996, and 2000 presidential campaigns, Bill

FIGURE 12.7 George Bush, 2004: Approving audience.

Clinton and Al Gore often campaigned in a suit, but without a jacket and with their shirtsleeves rolled up. This slightly casual style loosened the formality of their on-stage appearances at public rallies and contributed to their image as "young guns," as a *Newsweek* cover described the Clinton–Gore candidacy the week of the 1992 Democratic National Convention (Thomas, 2008; see also Kaid & Davidson, 1986). Their style of dress also suggested that the candidates were subverting the formality and ceremoniousness of proper political attire. Casual and sports clothing, including jeans, sports shirts, and shorts, visually suggest that a candidate is an everyday person. Coupled with athletic activities or depictions of physical work, populist framing establishes empathy with common folk and represents the candidate as "one of us"—a man (or woman) of the people (Kazin, 1995; Rudd, 1986; Sabato, 1981). In Figure 12.8 John Kerry rolls up his shirt sleeve to demonstrate his ordinariness, a visual aspect of populism that became institutionalized in Democratic presidential campaigning during the 2000 and 2004 elections.

Certain athletic and work-related activities may be better suited for advancing an image of populism than others. George H. W. Bush, for example, was strongly advised by his image handlers to quit indulging in "manic rounds of his favorite elitist pastimes, golf and boating," as those recreational appearances were thought to "reinforce the image of an aristocratic president out of touch with the common man" (Glassman & Kenney, 1994, p. 6). In 2004 John Kerry arguably undermined his populist frame-building efforts by windsurfing, snowboarding, and skiing—sports also considered elitist. Not surprisingly, when George W. Bush's 2004 campaign sought to portray John Kerry negatively in advertising, they exploited his image as a windsurfer in a devastating ad titled "Windsurfing" that depicted Kerry as a flip-flopper on the question of the Iraq War, seemingly directionless as the prevailing winds (see http://www.livingroom candidate.org/commercials/2004).

FIGURE 12.8 John Kerry, 2004: Casual dress, ordinary.

The Sure Loser

The underlying theme of the sure loser frame is that the American political system remains open and accessible; anyone can dream of being president, no matter how unattainable that dream might actually be. Losers fall from grace, become branded, and are identified as no longer viable for various reasons, among them their own (at times, ill-advised) actions, media disfavor, and opposition attacks. Indeed, political performances can backfire and expose campaigners to interpretive framing by journalists and opponents in ways that cultivate doubt and mistrust (Erickson, 2000).

Visual manifestations of the loser frame often surface in opposition to some of the traits associated with the other two frames. Disapproving, inattentive, and small crowds at public rallies, for example, link the candidate to lack of support (Grabe, 1996; Graber, 1987; Moriarty & Popovich, 1991). Being surrounded by an audience that responds in a disapproving way (e.g., with head shaking, frowns, boredom, or inattentiveness) may also erode a speaker's authority and character dynamism (Hylton, 1971). Negative audience reaction shots can also make a speaker appear less interesting and popular—and at the same time confusing, shallow, and inexpert (Duck & Baggaley, 1975; Wiegman, 1987). An example of audience disapproval is presented in Figure 12.9, a screen capture from coverage of George H. W. Bush showing a protest sign at a rally during the 1992 election. Visual displays of physical weakness, defiance, and inappropriate behavior have also all been shown to erode perceptions of leadership potential (Bucy, 2000; Masters & Sullivan, 1989) as visually demonstrated in Figure 12.10. Bob Dole's displays of anger during the 1996 campaign made him appear sour and unfit for leadership.

Coding categories were developed to measure the visual manifestations of the three character frames described here. Their prevalence in network news coverage was then examined across four presidential campaigns to assess the extent of visual framing—and frame elements—in

FIGURE 12.9 George Bush, 1992: Disapproving audience.

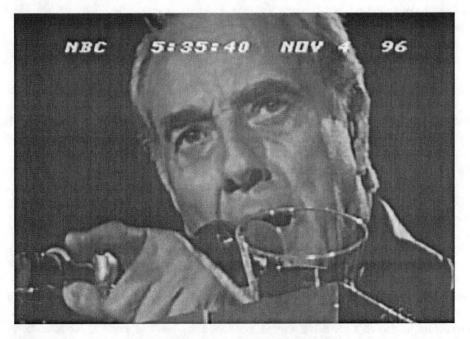

FIGURE 12.10 Bob Dole, 1996: Anger display.

election news. Before reporting the results of our analysis, we explain our sampling strategy, coding categories, and methodology.

SAMPLING PROCEDURES

The categories presented below were derived from a detailed content analysis of network news coverage of the 1992, 1996, 2000, and 2004 elections (Grabe & Bucy, 2009). The sampling frame stretched from Labor Day to Election Day for each election year. This time period is routinely used in content analyses of presidential elections as it spans the traditional start of the general election campaign (Labor Day) to the day voters go to the polls. Moreover, the general election is the most closely watched phase of the campaign when the largest number of viewers is paying attention to the election (Moriarty & Popovich, 1991; Waldman & Devitt, 1998).

For each election year, composite weeks of the three over-the-air evening newscasts were constructed, with a different, randomly selected network recorded each weekday: one from ABC, CBS, or NBC (see Hallin, 1992, for a similar sampling strategy).[1] The sample contained a total of 178 newscasts—42 each for 1992 and 2004, and 47 for 1996 and 2000. During data collection we focused on the visual content of all candidates who received coverage during the four election cycles analyzed. Because the frequencies for independent candidates were quite low, only results for the major party nominees are reported.

Three separate coding instruments, each representing a different unit of analysis, were designed. Coding sheet 1 used the individual news broadcast as the unit of analysis, addressing matters related to the volume or overall amount of coverage. Coding sheet 2 employed the individual campaign story as the unit of analysis and featured categories related to journalists and story-specific dimensions. Coding sheet 3 entailed the most detailed categories, focusing on the individual candidate as the unit of analysis. Together, these different foci enabled comprehensive examinations of network news content across the different players in the election drama, both in the press and among political contenders.

Two primary coders who received extensive training collected the data for this study while two secondary coders (the authors) served as reliability checks for the pretest. The testing of categories and training of coders extended over several weeks. During this time, refinements were made to the coding instrument. Overall, the pretest produced a reliable level of agreement (Krippendorff's alpha = .84) between all four coders. For the categories related to the individual news program as the unit of analysis, the reliability figure was .82, whereas for categories related to the individual campaign story the figure was .85. For categories related to the individual candidate as the unit of analysis, the figure was .84. Although the pretest produced acceptable reliability figures, more training, specifically on how to accurately measure durations, ensued before the beginning of data collection.

Table 12.1 summarizes the study sample as a whole, including the candidates featured, time periods analyzed, and number of individual stories by network for each year in the sample.

CODING OF VISUAL FRAMES

Using the individual candidate as the unit of analysis, visual framing was assessed for each of the three character frames. The presence (value = 1) or absence (value = 0) of a visual category was coded for each candidate per news story and collapsed by news program to produce scores for each party per newscast. Several instances of a variable could be in play for a candidate within a

TABLE 12.1
Summary of the Study Sample

	Election Year			
	1992	*1996*	*2000*	*2004*
Candidates				
Democrat	Bill Clinton	Bill Clinton	Al Gore	John Kerry
Republican	George H.W. Bush	Bob Dole	George W. Bush	George W. Bush
Network campaign stories				
ABC	$n = 54$ (35.8%)	$n = 30$ (31.9%)	$n = 38$ (39.2%)	$n = 36$ (38.7%)
CBS	$n = 51$ (33.8%)	$n = 40$ (42.6%)	$n = 31$ (32.0%)	$n = 29$ (31.2%)
NBC	$n = 46$ (30.5%)	$n = 24$ (25.5%)	$n = 28$ (28.9%)	$n = 28$ (30.1%)
Total	$N = 151$	$N = 94$	$N = 97$	$N = 93$
Campaign stages				
Stage 1	Sept. 7–Oct. 9	Sept. 2–Oct. 4	Sept. 4–Oct. 3	Sept. 6–Sept. 30
Stage 2	Oct. 12–Oct. 21	Oct. 7–Oct. 18	Oct. 4–Oct. 19	Oct. 1–Oct. 15
Stage 3	Oct. 22–Nov. 3	Oct. 21–Nov. 5	Oct. 20–Nov. 7	Oct. 18–Nov. 2

single news story. Yet, only one instance of a given variable had to be present to be counted. Although this coding procedure does not assess the relative strength of a frame, it provides a conservative quantitative measure of the presence of frames within a story for each Democratic and Republican candidate. Coders were instructed to consider the foreground and backgrounds of televised scenes in which candidates appeared and to scrutinize shots adjacent (before and after) to those of the candidate for associational juxtaposition.

The Ideal Candidate   The ideal candidate frame was measured as visual manifestations of statesmanship and compassion, using the following categories:

Statesmanship

- Appearances with elected officials or influentials—people with power, status, and/or money—on the national or local level. Examples include prominent members of the business community, former presidents, and other well-known politicians but excludes military dignitaries.
- Visual linkages to patriotic symbols, including monuments, memorials, statues, the American flag, paintings and photos of patriots, military machinery, and living "heroes" such as Colin Powell or Norman Schwartzkopf.
- Visual linkages to symbols of progress and prosperity, such as Wall Street banks, NASA flight centers, or high technology manufacturing plants.
- Portrayal of an entourage, including security attachments, aides, reporters, motorcades, a campaign caravan, or police vehicles.
- Campaign paraphernalia such as posters, banners, buttons, signs, and other political adornments or clothing.
- Political hoopla, including raining confetti, streamers, balloons, and related props.

- Formal attire, namely a dress suit in its full range from tuxedo and black tie to a conventional business suit.

Compassion

- Visual linkages to children, especially interactions with young children and the holding, kissing, or touching of babies.
- Visual linkages to family symbols, either through direct appearances with family members or indirectly via photographic references.
- Visual linkages to admiring women, including expressions of awe, wonder, excitement, and approval through cheering and waving.
- Visual linkages to religious symbolism, including places of worship, religious figures, or symbols such as crosses, candles, or religious scriptures.

Three behavioral display categories were used to measure compassion, as follows:

- Affinity gestures without physical contact, including waving, thumbs-up, fanning the crowd, George W. Bush's three-finger "W" sign, a "V" for victory or peace, informal salutes, winks to the audience or camera, and tipping or waving a hat.
- Individual interactions with supporters not involving physical contact, in other words, engaging and giving individual attention to people but not embracing them.
- Individual interactions with adult supporters involving physical contact, including hugging, embracing, shaking hands, and kissing.

The Populist Campaigner.   The candidate's visual association with the plight of common people was coded in terms of mass appeal and ordinariness. In all, nine categories were used.

Mass Appeal

- Visual linkages with celebrities, including movie stars, athletes, television personalities, and other well-known cultural figures.
- Visual linkages with large audiences, including images of supporters tightly packed into an event space, the candidate appearing amidst a sea of admiring faces, or portrayals of mass attendance at rallies.
- Visual linkages to approving audiences, expressed by applauding, waving, cheering, whistling, laughing, nodding approvingly, or toting/displaying campaign paraphernalia.
- Portrayals of interactions with crowds, including rope-line greetings, handshakes, grips, or touches without individualized attention or paused engagement with anyone in particular.

Ordinariness

- Portrayals of candidates in informal attire, including a shirt and tie without a jacket, or the candidate's shirtsleeves rolled up.
- Portrayals of candidates in casual dress, including khaki pants, slacks, jeans with a long- or short-sleeved shirt or sport coat, sweater, or wind-breaker.

- Portrayals of candidates in athletic clothing, including shorts, jogging gear, skiwear, golf slacks and shirt, a wetsuit, or other athletic attire.
- Visual linkages with ordinary people, such as visits to working-class communities or manufacturing plants.
- Portrayals of physical exertion, including athletic activities or physical work: chopping wood, serving meals at a homeless shelter, hunting, and so on. Expensive sports such as yachting, golf, and windsurfing were excluded because they suggest more elitist pastimes.

The Sure Loser. This frame was measured with the following categories:

- Visual linkages to small audiences where few people are scattered around at campaign events, spaces are sparsely filled, and empty chairs are shown.
- Visual linkages to disapproving audiences, including instances of obvious jeering, booing, disapproving gestures such as thumbs down, posters with disapproving comments, protesting, frowning, or nodding off.
- Visual depictions of weakness, including illness, clumsiness (tripping, falling, stumbling), or displaying lack of coordination.
- Portrayals of defiant nonverbal gestures, including finger pointing or shaking, raising a fist in defiance, pounding on a podium, or similar displays.
- Visual depictions of inappropriate displays, including facial expressions and gestures that are incongruent with the associated news context.

RESULTS

Overview of 1992 Campaign Dynamics

The Bush Camp.   According to Klein (2006), George H.W. Bush embraced a strong populist frame during the 1988 election—as "more American" than Democratic nominee Michael Dukakis, a lover of pork rinds and country music—but he governed after the election as an aristocrat. Fundamentally, Bush struggled to show that he cared about people, awkwardly verbalizing his sentiments to the media by reading directly off a campaign advisor's note card: "Message: I care" (Rosenthal, 1992, p. 14).

Several blunders during the 1992 campaign illustrated that Bush was out of touch with ordinary Americans. At a grocers' convention, Bush revealed he was not aware that scanners were widely used at checkout lines, a technology that had been operational for 20 years (Kurtz, 1992). Moreover, he tried too hard, and awkwardly so, to use the language of common folk. In reference to Gore he once said: "He is way out, far out. Far out, man!" (Glad, 1995, p. 23). If anything, these awkward attempts to connect with voters undermined his populist efforts, giving it a spurious quality.

Bush went on the attack, escalating with a "daily fax attack" on Clinton–Gore, a peppery verbal hit on the Democratic candidates sent to national news media every day of the general election season. The first one contained the following line: "Bill Clinton is the Pinocchio of the political season" (Kranish, 1992, p. 1). While incumbents and challengers typically stay above the fray and send out surrogates to do the dirty work of politics, Bush joined in the mudslinging, bucking the conventional wisdom that an incumbent rarely wins by direct negative campaigning (Bennett, 1995; Wayne, 1996).

The Clinton Camp.   Clinton also embraced populist framing in 1992—as an Arkansan, lover of fast food, and pick-up truck owner with Astroturf in the bed—with a strong focus on compassion and empathy for ordinary people (Bennett, 1995; Klein, 2006). When Clinton won the Democratic nomination and found himself behind Bush and Perot in the polls, his image handlers responded with a political "Manhattan Project" to overcome the image of a privileged Rhodes scholar who had evaded the draft during Vietnam and experimented with marijuana (Bennett, 1995; Klein, 2006). The campaign re-introduced Clinton as a man of the people from a town called Hope—the hard-working son of a poor single mother (Bennett, 1995; Parry-Giles & Parry-Giles, 2002).

Clinton also hit the talk show circuit, including appearances on *The Arsenio Hall Show*, *Oprah*, *Larry King Live*, and MTV to talk about his small-town roots, alcoholic father, and experience of poverty. So enamored were Clinton's image handlers with talk shows that their candidate appeared on these popular formats every time his poll numbers dipped from February 1992 to Election Day in November (Bennett, 1995). When the campaign turned nasty, Clinton's surrogates and image handlers did the attacking, leaving their candidate to perfect his famous handshake (which entailed a warm smile and direct eye contact while steadying the voter's elbow with his free hand) on the rope lines.

Given the image handling efforts of the Bush and Clinton teams, we expected both candidates to be framed in a populist light, perhaps with Bush showing up as a loser more often than Clinton. There were no strong indications of ideal candidate frame building on either side. Yet, given that compassion developed into a strategic theme for Clinton during the campaign, one would expect that dimension of the ideal candidate frame to appear in news coverage. Clearly, these expectations are built on the assumption that image handlers succeeded in efforts to bypass journalistic frame control.

Findings.   Our analysis revealed a fairly persistent pattern of Bush appearing more statesmanlike than Clinton (see Table 12.2). In the case of visual linkages to patriotic symbols, this difference was statistically significant, $t(79) = -2.77$, $p = .007$, perhaps indicating the campaign strategy to present Bush as a "patriot" in contrast to Clinton, the "draft dodger." Associations with technological and economic progress approached significance, $t(79) = -1.74$, $p = .086$, with Bush at higher levels. Overall, Bush had a higher composite statesmanship score while Clinton outscored Bush on the compassion dimension of the ideal candidate frame. In particular, Clinton's physical contact with supporters, $t(79) = 1.83$, $p = .072$, and attention to children, $t(79) = 1.92$, $p = .05$, achieved visual distinction in the news.

Clinton's compassion also found visual traction in the populist frame, where his signature technique of working the crowds showed up significantly more than for Bush, $t(79) = 3.12$, $p = .003$. Table 12.2 shows a persistent pattern of Clinton's mass appeal surfacing. In fact, of all the presidential candidates in our four-election sample, Clinton was shown with the highest level of mass appeal. Campaigning in a tie, no jacket, and rolled-up sleeves added to his populist image, at significantly higher levels than for Bush, $t(79) = 2.79$, $p = .007$. Clinton also appeared more ordinary and populist overall than Bush but not at statistically significant levels, perhaps revealing a close race between the two campaigns' image handling teams, who consciously strove to craft a populist image for their clients.

Although there were no significant differences between Bush and Clinton in terms of loser framing, Bush was shown significantly more often among disapproving crowds, $t(79) = -2.24$, $p = .028$. He also exhibited more defiance than Clinton.

Overview of 1996 Campaign Dynamics

The Clinton Camp.   Early in 1996 Clinton was generating powerful visual images on the campaign trail: energetic speeches, gregarious working of rope lines, and an event-filled bus tour. But his pollsters did not see these images translate into high approval numbers. Consequently, his

TABLE 12.2
Means for Individual Variables and Visual Frames by Party and Election Year

Variables/frames	Election year and political party									
	1992		1996		2000		2004		Overall	
	D	R	D	R	D	R	D	R	D	R
Ideal candidate	7.60	7.70	5.79	7.79*	7.11	6.47	7.75	8.13	7.07	7.49
Statesmanship	4.83	5.39	3.33	4.71*	4.32	3.70	5.38	5.39	4.47	4.78
Linked, influentials	.68	.54	.31	.34	.66	.53	.43	.64	.52	.52
Linked, patriotism	.63	1.15*	.56	.82	.59	.47	1.53	1.62	.82	1.00+
Linked, progress	.05	.17+	.05	.08	.20	.19	.15	.15	.12	.15
Linked, entourage	.33	.39	.62	.87	.32	.21	.43	.44	.41	.47
Campaign paraphernalia	.98	.98	.49	.97*	.84	.60	.98	.89	.82	.86
Confetti shower	.08	.15	.00	.05	.14	.16	.18	.05	.10	.11
Wearing a suit	2.10	2.02	1.31	1.58	1.57	1.53	1.70	1.60	1.67	1.68
Compassion	2.78	2.32	2.46	3.08	2.80	2.77	2.38	2.74	2.61	2.72
Linked, children	.40	.15*	.21	.34	.23	.40	.23	.28	.26	.29
Linked, family	.20	.15	.05	.08	.52	.35	.15	.54*	.24	.28
Linked, women	.43	.41	.49	.66	.32	.37	.30	.33	.38	.44
Linked, religion	.05	.00	.00	.00	.00	.00	.03	.05	.02	.01
Affinity gestures	.96	.73	.59	.89*	1.02	.93	1.18	1.13	.88	.96
Individual interaction	.25	.34	.46	.39	.34	.30	.23	.21	.32	.31
Physical contact	.73	.39+	.67	.71	.36	.42	.28	.21	.50	.43
Populist campaigner	4.75	3.83	2.69	2.95	4.41	3.00*	4.73	4.76	4.16	3.62+
Mass appeal	3.65	2.98	1.90	2.34	2.93	2.19	2.78	2.69	2.82	2.55
Linked, celebrities	.10	.12	.10	.16	.27	.19	.43	.51	.23	.24
Large audience	1.18	1.17	.69	.82	.75	.47+	.33	.36	.74	.70
Approving audience	1.35	1.17	.69	.86	1.20	.98	1.20	1.18	1.12	1.05
Crowd interaction	1.03	.51*	.41	.50	.70	.56	.83	.64	.74	.55*
Ordinariness	1.10	.85	.79	.61	1.48	.81*	1.95	2.05	1.34	1.07+
Casual dress	.20	.22	.15	.05	.64	.26*	.85	1.03	.47	.38
Sports clothing	.08	.10	.13	.00*	.05	.02	.10	.15	.09	.07
Rolled sleeves	.45	.15*	.00	.00	.64	.33+	.75	.58	.47	2.62*
Linked, ordinary people	.28	.29	.41	.53	.09	.16	.08	.10	.21	.27
Physically active	.10	.10	.10	.03	.07	.05	.18	.23	.11	.10
Sure loser	.65	.95	.44	1.45*	.73	.21*	.74	.49+	.64	.76
Disapproving audience	.03	.17*	.03	.03	.07	.00+	.03	.03	.04	.06
Small audience	.18	.15	.26	.42	.02	.02	.00	.00	.11	.14
Physical weakness	.05	.02	.00	.42*	.00	.00	.00	.00	.01	.11*
Defiant behavior	.38	.59	.13	.58*	.64	.14*	.73	.46*	.47	.43
Inappropriate behavior	.03	.02	.03	.00	.00	.05	.00	.00	.01	.02

Note: *Statistically significant between parties; +approaching statistical significance. D = Democrat, R = Republican.

advisors took him back to govern in Washington as an above-the-fray incumbent rather than a hard-driving campaigner (Klein, 2006). Bill-signing ceremonies were orchestrated to project the image of a statesman who brought legislative issues through the Republican-controlled Congress to a successful conclusion (Thomas, Rosenberg, Kaufman, & Murr, 1997). Consultant Dick Morris convinced Clinton that the more he spent on advertising, the less he had to appear on the hustings. Thus, Clinton was absent from the campaign trail for much of the 1996 election.

Throughout the lackluster 1996 general election, polls identified traditional social values, specifically, crime, drugs, and violence in the media, as salient voter issues (Klein, 2006; Thomas et al., 1997). As long as Clinton stood tough on these issues and emphasized economic prosperity, his image handlers argued, voters would forgive his personal indiscretions. Incidentally, these issues were exactly what Bob Dole ran on. In essence, the Clinton team was able to co-opt traditionally Republican issues (Ceaser & Busch, 1997; Thomas et al., 1997). Lewis (1997) compared Clinton and Dole to *Time* and *Newsweek*, observing that "no matter how much they claim to differ, they still run the same covers week after week" (p. 161).

The Dole Camp.   Among insiders there is little disagreement that the Dole campaign of 1996 was a fiasco (Lichter, Noyes, & Kaid, 1999; Ponnuru, 1996). Among the most destructive elements were the dysfunctional inner workings of the campaign staff, lack of a clear message, and Dole's weakness as a national campaigner. The Dole campaign was characterized as a "floundering exercise in muddled messages, riven by conflict and dulled by low morale" (Thomas et al., 1997, p. 4). Within the campaign there were multiple camps, with battles erupting between those who advocated for professional advice—focus groups and polling—against those who wanted the campaign to run on instinct and bold speeches (Seelye, 1996).

If the Dole campaign had an over-arching strategy, it could be loosely characterized as securing endorsements from influentials and promoting a conservative brand of social populism while engaging in attacks on Clinton's "liberalism." Despite the campaign's disarray, Dole was surrounded by the Republican Party establishment, who showed up at his side in public (Lewis, 1997; Ponnuru, 1996). Dole's populist appeals derived most noticeably from references to his poor upbringing in small town America, his long and painful recovery from a serious war injury, and (self-defeatingly) his resentment for people who had not suffered like he had (Ponnuru, 1996).

More than any other candidate in our sample, Dole refused to be image-handled, turning down teleprompters and speechwriters and refusing to stay on message. Many sources have described Dole that year as an incoherent speaker who referred to himself in the third person, spoke in incomplete sentences, and delivered speeches with no main point (Lewis, 1997; Ponnuru, 1996; Thomas et al., 1997). Although he received the same advice as Clinton—that the election was going to be won on social values—Dole disliked sermonizing and thought values were too personal a foundation on which to campaign (Thomas et al., 1997). By the end of the campaign Dole went negative in character attacks on Clinton. As with Bush in 1992, he came off as sour, grim, and desperate (Dowd, 1996; Lewis, 1997).

Given these campaign strategies (or lack thereof) during the 1996 general election, we expected Clinton to receive consistent ideal candidate framing in network news coverage while Bob Dole was expected to appear in the populist frame more often than Clinton—unlessjournalistic frame control intervened.

Findings.   Ironically, Dole was visually portrayed significantly more statesman-like, $t(75) = -2.48$, $p = .015$, and as having more ideal qualities overall, $t(75) = -2.22$, $p = .029$, than Clinton (see Table 12.2). In fact, Dole was portrayed as more compassionate in network news coverage of the elections than any other candidate in our sample period. Dole's image handlers were clearly fond of campaign paraphernalia, $t(75) = -3.34$, $p = .001$, perhaps something they could agree on. Overall, these findings do not line up with the strategies of the two campaigns, suggesting journalistic frame control.

Of all the major party nominees examined in this study, Dole was also visually portrayed as the most loser-like, $t(75) = -5.09$, $p = .001$. Images of physical weakness, $t(75) = -4.39$, $p = .001$, and defiance, $t(75) = -3.68$, $p = .001$, were statistically higher for Dole than for Clinton. This pattern perhaps reflects the anger and frustration of a politician who was not a major optimist to begin with and whose image handlers were unable to modify his affect (although his appearances in post-election ads for Pepsi and other companies softened his image quite a bit).

Interestingly, Clinton's trademark compassion did not show up visually as strongly as it did during the 1992 campaign. His efforts to pose as a statesman also did not make it into the news very clearly; neither did his attempts at populism. Clinton did appear in athletic attire more often than Dole, mainly from his televised jogging performances, $t(75) = 2.33$, $p = .022$. Not surprisingly, given his war injury, Dole was never seen in sports clothing.

Overview of 2000 Campaign Dynamics

The Gore Camp.   Democratic consultant Bob Shrum engineered Al Gore's presidential campaign of 2000. Regardless of candidate, Shrum's trademark frame was economic populism, with an emphasis on healthcare, jobs, and Social Security (Auletta, 2004; Glasser, 2000; Klein, 2006). Throughout the campaign season of 2000, Gore embraced a populist campaign slogan, "The People versus the Powerful," and followed a strict market-tested approach to campaigning. This obsession with market testing backfired, however, and is widely cited as a key reason for why Gore appeared unbelievable—and unlikable. As Klein (2006) put it, Gore "shoe-horned himself inside the Message Box that had been created for him—because he had been polledand focus-grouped and dial-grouped and market-tested *literally* to the point of distraction" (p. 158).

Gore's public persona was marked by inexplicable moments of awkwardness, followed by panicked reactions after the fact. Klein (2006, p. 139) described this peculiar behavior as an odd oxymoron—a "panicky robot" mode of campaigning. After extensive coaching and image handling, Gore gradually became frustrated with his coterie of consultants and resentful toward his critics. In preparation for the debates, identical studio sets were built and Gore's practice performances were taped and taken to dial groups to assess which answers were favorably received (Klein, 2006). Gore resisted this style of preparation and people close to him viewed his disastrous performance in the debates as a purposeful rebellion against his image handlers. During debate practice Gore's advisors pointed out that his tendency to sigh came across as arrogant and urged him to keep his aggressive nonverbal behavior in check. They even drew a line on the set and made him practice not crossing it. But during the televised debates Gore sighed often and physically approached Bush. He also did not stay in rehearsed character: "Three different Gores showed up: the lion, the lamb, and the stalker" (Klein, 2006, p. 156). Bush showed up as Bush—in a simplistic but coherent way.

The Bush Camp.   While Gore's image handlers focus-grouped policy ideas, cerebrally strategizing that the candidate's character would emerge from complicated policy proposals, Bush's image handlers worked on framing a social populist character for their candidate. In particular, Bush was to be presented as a Republican who cared about people—in the famous phrase of Karl Rove, as a "compassionate conservative" (Klein, 2006; Marshall, 2000). The Bush campaign gauged Gore's public demeanor and built their populist frame in antithesis to it: compassionate, plain speaking, and trustworthy. What followed were consistently sharp attacks on Gore's character and reputation (Von Drehle, 2000).

The half-truths that Gore uttered when he was caught in panicky robot mode were used to attack another character weakness—questions about his honesty—which the Bush camp used to link him with Clinton. Gore's verbal blunders included references to himself as "the father of the Internet" and claims that he and his wife Tipper were the Harvard couple on which *Love Story* was based. These and other false assertions were publicly disproved at Gore's expense. In stark contrast, Bush's advisors promoted their candidate as someone who would restore honor, trust, and respect to the White House (Marshall, 2000).

Given these image-handling approaches and challenges, we expected both Gore and Bush to receive populist framing during the 2000 campaign. Given Gore's stiffness, we further expected his compassion scores to be lower than Bush's, since Bush ran on a theme of compassionate conservatism. The lack of strong evidence of ideal candidate framing by campaign image handlers also led us to expect low scores for both candidates, especially for the statesman dimension of the frame.

Findings. Unexpectedly, Bush and Gore received noticeable and similar amounts of ideal candidate framing. Closer inspection of the two ideal candidate subframes did not reveal significant differences: Gore was visually represented as more statesmanlike than Bush on all variables, except for confetti showers (see Table 12.2). Bush, running as a compassionate conservative, had a slight edge on Gore for the compassion subframe. Interestingly, Gore was shown interacting with people more than Bush, but his stiffness surfaced in less physical contact with supporters. However, these differences were not statistically significant.

The populist campaigner and sure loser frames, by contrast, brought significant differences to light. Gore was visually represented as more populist, $t(85) = -2.00$, $p = .048$, than Bush. The Shrum strategy to transform a stiff candidate into a people's politician did surface in network news coverage. In fact, Gore outscored Bush on all mass appeal variables with linkage to large crowds at a near-significant level, $t(85) = 1.68$, $p = .096$. Gore also appeared visually more ordinary, $t(85) = 2.13$, $p = .036$, than Bush. Dress variables accounted for most of this difference. Gore was featured more often in casual clothing, $t(85) = 2.46$, $p = .016$, and with a tie, no jacket, and sleeves rolled up, $t(85) = 1.76$, $p = .081$, than Bush. The then-Texas governor was linked to ordinary people more often than Gore, but not at significant levels.

The analysis also revealed scattered signs of Gore's panicky robot mode that Klein (2006) described, particularly in the form of aggressive and defiant gestures. Gore was shown exhibiting significantly more aggression and defiance than Bush, $t(85) = 4.42$, $p = .001$. These gestures, in conjunction with visual linkages to disapproving crowds, $t(85) = 1.75$, $p = .083$, attached Gore to the loser frame at statistically higher levels than Bush, $t(85) = 3.62$, $p = .001$.

Overview of 2004 Campaign Dynamics

The Bush Camp. In the Rove tradition, the Bush campaign seemed to be more focused on John Kerry in 2004 than on their own candidate. They had polling evidence that the American people knew the president—flaws included—but thought he was a strong leader. Bush's team pursued a two-pronged attack on Kerry's character: to portray him as an elitist and a flip-flopper (McKinnon, quoted in Jamieson, 2006). The 2004 race cast voter trust of candidates in moral terms (Klein 2006; Mellman, quoted in Jamieson, 2006). The Bush line that, "You may not always agree with me but you'll always know where I stand," characterized the president as a strong and honest man in contrast to a purportedly elusive and indecisive Kerry (Devenish, quoted in Jamieson, 2006, p. 151; Klein, 2006). The line also confirmed the straightforward populist message that the Bush team promoted, meandering into fear-invoking 9/11 territory. In Liz

Cheney's words, Bush was not running "a feel-good campaign. He wasn't saying it's morning [again] in America" (quoted in Jamieson, 2006, p. 127). Instead, he was straight and honest with voters that the country was at war and that he was going to keep them safe.

The post-9/11 straight talk motif also cast the president as a family man and foregrounded his concern for his larger family, the nation. This meant higher visibility for the first family (Dowd, quoted in The Institute of Politics, 2006). Republican pollsters determined that the image of the president as protector of the nation-family resonated with voters (Castellanos, quoted in Jamieson, 2006), a campaign message poignantly reinforced by the infamous "Ashley's Story" advertisement sponsored by the Progress for America Voter Fund (see http://www.livingroomcandidate. org/commercials/2004).

The Kerry Camp.   As with Al Gore's presidential run, Bob Shrum's strategy for Kerry was to rely on time-honored populist issues, including health care, education, and jobs (Donilon, quoted in Jamieson, 2006). Shrum's commitment to the populist frame persisted despite Bush campaign attacks on Kerry's military and voting record. In fact, Kerry was initially advised not to defend his character but rather to stick to the central message of his campaign, of fighting for middle America—the same mistake Michael Dukakis made against George H. W. Bush in 1988. Images of Kerry engaging in expensive and elitist sports—windsurfing, snow boarding, and skiing—did not bring credibility or visual coherence to his "fighting for the middle class" message, however (The Institute of Politics, 2006).

Against this backdrop of insider information about both campaign efforts, we expected the populist frame to appear prominently for both Bush and Kerry in 2004. If the Bush camp succeeded in turning negative attention on Kerry, one would also expect to see more loser framing of Kerry than Bush. At the same time, Bush's ability to connect with people on a personal level was expected to surface in the compassion dimension of the ideal candidate frame.

Findings.   From Table 12.2 it is clear that Bush and Kerry received similar visual treatment in terms of ideal candidate framing. A closer look at the composite subthemes of this frame reveals that Bush was portrayed noticeably more statesman-like and compassionate than Kerry—but not at a statistically significant level. As for visual linkages to family, the Bush campaign's emphasis on the president as a family man did make it onto the evening news at statistically higher levels than for Kerry, $t(77) = -3.32, p = .001$.

The Kerry campaign devoted considerably more resources on pomp and spectacle (e.g., confetti showers and campaign paraphernalia) than the Bush re-election team. Or at least, these images found their way onto network news more often than for Bush. Perhaps the Bush campaign felt that the sober message of the president, that freedom was under attack and America was at war and needed a strong leader, made celebratory images in a post-9/11 election seem inappropriate. Instead, the campaign worked at developing a linkage between their candidate and political influentials (see Table 12.2).

In terms of populist framing, the two candidates were visually depicted with almost the same amount of mass appeal and ordinariness. Given this parity, the crucial matter seems to be which candidate wore this visual frame more comfortably.

The results for the loser frame further highlight the relative successes of the two campaigns. Rove and associates indeed managed to control defiant nonverbal behavior in Bush while their relentless attacks on Kerry as a flip-flopper probably sent Kerry into a defensive mode, observable in our analysis through statistically higher defiance scores than for Bush, $t(77) = 1.96, p = .05$. These scores also drove a near-significant difference, $t(77) = 1.83, p = .072$, in loser framing for Kerry. In closing, it must be noted that of all eight major party nominees examined in our sample, no one was portrayed more prominently as an ideal candidate or populist campaigner than Bush in 2004.

General Findings

Considering overall framing scores for all years collapsed, we found that Democratic presidential candidates received more populist framing overall than Republicans at a near-significant level, $t(321) = 1.73$, $p = .085$ (see Table 12.2). Images of Democratic candidates working the crowds have assumed signature status in presidential election coverage, distinguishing their visual portrayals from Republicans, $t(321) = 2.41$, $p = .016$. Democrats also signaled their ordinariness more clearly than Republicans, $t(321) = 1.80$, $p = .073$, especially by way of dress. Campaigning in a tie, no jacket, and with shirtsleeves rolled up has become a Democratic candidate trademark, $t(321) = 2.72$, $p = .007$.

During our sampling period, Republicans were more often portrayed in an ideal candidate frame, with linkages to patriotic symbols, than Democrats, $t(322) = -1.84$, $p = .067$. Republicans also appeared more often as sure losers, but not at statistically significant levels, and this finding was probably driven by Bob Dole's fall from a stage on the campaign trail in 1996. The physical weakness scores for Dole in that election drove an overall statistically higher score for Republicans than Democrats, $t(322) = -3.28$, $p = .007$.

These results do not provide evidence of systematic visual bias against candidates of either party—there was no consistent pattern of favoring either side over the four election cycles analyzed (although other visual variables did reveal consistent favoritism by the networks to the benefit of Republicans, see Grabe & Bucy, 2009, Chapter 5). Favorable visual representation, such as ideal candidate and populist framing, characterized Republican and Democratic candidates during different election years. Sure loser framing was also evident in coverage of both parties' candidates across election years: George H. W. Bush in 1992, Bob Dole in 1996, Al Gore in 2000, and John Kerry in 2004.

DISCUSSION

Our analysis suggests that visual frame construction of presidential candidates is richer and more nuanced than typically acknowledged in conventional framing research. Consideration of campaign efforts to engage in specific frame-building strategies provides a rich context for analysis and informs assessments about the role of image handlers in shaping news coverage. The struggle for frame control between journalists and image handlers—two key players in the election drama—is greatly under-documented. Instead, researchers seem to be set on analyzing news texts as the product of journalistic storytelling without regard for the influence of political message shapers and without regard for the visual dimensions of news. What we report here is certainly not offered as evidence of causal relationships between image handler strategies and news output. Yet, our data do provide some insight into how well image handler strategies match the visual outcome of candidate portrayals on the evening news.

The hard reality is that in every election one side will lose. Information from within campaigns and the data we report here point to a clean standard for success: an unambiguous message backed by a character frame that becomes the candidate. Populism represented a good fit for Clinton in 1992, who embraced his role as an ordinary guy from Hope, Arkansas. The populist frame certainly seemed to be a more authentic match for Clinton than for George H. W. Bush, who campaigned as a people's president in 1988 but had a full term in office to remind voters that he was something other than what his campaign image suggested. Pursuing populism again in 1992 was not a good decision for Bush. Even though we found evidence of visual linkages to the statesman subframe in our analysis, the Bush campaign ran on a populist theme, miscasting the incumbent president in an ill-fitting role. Indeed, the notion of "frame fit" is an important consideration to emerge from our analysis.

Clinton's 1996 campaign translated into an unremarkable but safe visual show on network news, particularly in comparison to Dole's haphazard election bid. Reinforcing these findings, a study of newspaper photographs found that Dole received more visual coverage in the *New York Times* than Clinton in 1996 (Lee et al., 2004). The Clinton campaign strategy that year was to keep the president in Washington as much as possible, showing that he could govern on a soft social-populist platform, thereby inoculating him from Republican attacks. In that election, Clinton emerged as a winner perhaps more as a result of Dole's incoherent campaign strategy and loser depictions than his own impressiveness on the campaign trail.

The 2000 and 2004 campaigns represented consecutive match-ups between strategists Bob Shrum and Karl Rove for successful populist image framing. From insider accounts, the Republican campaigns those election years were highly disciplined, coherent, and focused on attacking the opponent's character. Consistent with this assessment, our analysis shows that the strategy of promoting Bush's populism while attacking Kerry's character was visually evident in network news coverage of the 2004 campaign. In both elections, populist framing was employed prominently in news coverage of Bush, who was shown reassuring largely favorable crowds with his ordinariness. In conjunction with the coverage Bush received as a compassionate candidate, the populist frame fit Bush comfortably. At the same time, Democrats were pegged in the loser frame after failing in their efforts to construct—and wear—an ill-fitting populist frame of their own. Insiders who have observed Rove describe him as a hired gun who wages psychological warfare on his opponents, attacking their character and unnerving them to the extent that they drift into defensiveness and, ultimately, into a losing position. Our findings, while not providing definitive evidence with respect to the Gore and Kerry campaigns, nevertheless support this observation.

This is not to say that Shrum's efforts at populist frame-building did not surface in network news coverage of the 2000 and 2004 presidential elections. Indeed, in some ways Shrum's efforts were even more evident than Rove's. But the Democrats' doggedness in pursuing populist images had awkward and counter-productive outcomes for both Gore and Kerry. In essence, Shrum tried to "out-Rove" the Bush campaign over two consecutive elections by force-fitting two brainy aristocrats into a populist frame. On a broader level there was no over-arching narrative to convince voters that Gore and Kerry were anything other than opportunistic populists (Castellanos, quoted in Jamieson, 2006, p. 137). As Marty Kaplan, a former speechwriter for Walter Mondale, observed: "Gore's populism seemed more poll-generated than organic to his history and character," adding that "if populism did not quite fit Al Gore, it doesn't fit the patrician John Kerry in the least" (quoted in Auletta, 2004, p. 75).

Shrum also underestimated the power of visual awkwardness by assuming that patrician candidates could suddenly come off as convincing commoners. From the perspective of visual analysis, a candidate's nonverbal behavior is clearly capable of signaling inauthenticity and, when captured by the unforgiving eye of a camera, is closely scrutinized by an audience equipped with skills that evolved over millions of years to recognize visual signs of leadership (see Grabe & Bucy, 2009, Chapter 1). In 2000 and again in 2004, viewers did not fail to notice that both Al Gore and John Kerry were uncomfortable populists. As Edelman (1964) observed in his classic analysis of the symbolic uses of politics, inauthentic political performances create ambivalence and skepticism, perhaps enough to scuttle an election. And, importantly, visual inauthenticity may interfere with a candidate's verbal message. In the words of one image handler, "if someone doesn't come across as real . . . they're not going to be believable in their content either" (Carrick, quoted in Trebay, 2007).

The individual variables and frames employed in this analysis may be readily adapted to other campaign contexts and election settings. Given that this chapter has made the case for a more detailed and systematic approach to studying political visuals, it should come as no surprise that we endorse analyses that rely on the care and precision of human coders to gather data from image bite content. Conway (2006) has demonstrated irreconcilable differences between human and computer coding in a careful application of these two modes of data collection to election coverage. In particular, he notes that while computer-assisted coding allows large amounts of text to be analyzed quickly, automated content analyses struggle to detect the emotional tone of coverage, recognize nuances in news reporting, especially between different candidates within the same story, and often fail to link specific attributes to particular candidates. As for coding visuals, computer systems are even less helpful, although some advanced facial recognition software programs may be useful in analyzing the faces of politicians in still photographs.

There is much to be gained from visual analysis of political news, and we hope the categories we have outlined here and in *Image Bite Politics* are widely employed. But work in this area, for now at least, should proceed with the perceptiveness and subtlety and that only human coding can afford.

NOTE

1 . Although the national news networks have been losing viewership to local, cable, and online news outlets (Iyengar & McGrady, 2007), our analyses focus on network news coverage for two reasons. First, it was the most widely used source of presidential campaign information over the course of the elections analyzed. Despite declines in network viewership, neither cable nor local television news has nearly the audience of network news. At the time of this data collection and analysis, the audience size of the three networks combined was double that of cable news and Fox combined (Project for Excellence in Journalism, 2004). Second, network news has been stable in popularity among those who are likely voters (Pew Research Center, 2000), namely, older adults.

REFERENCES

Auletta, K. (2004, Sept. 20). Kerry's brain; annals of communications. *The New Yorker*, 64–79.
Bennett, W. L. (1995). The cueless public: Bill Clinton meets the new American voter in Campaign '92. In S. A. Renshon (Ed.), *The Clinton presidency: Campaigning, governing, and the psychology of leadership* (pp. 91–112). Boulder, CO: Westview Press.
Bennett, W. L. (2007). *News: The politics of illusion* (7th ed.). New York: Pearson Longman.
Blumler, J., & Gurevitch, M. (1995). *The crisis of public communication*. London: Routledge.
Bucy, E. P. (2000). Emotional and evaluative consequences of inappropriate leader displays. *Communication Research*, 27(2), 194–226.
Bucy, E. P. (in press). Nonverbal communication, emotion, and political evaluation. In E. Konijn, K. Koveling, & C. von Scheve (Eds.), *Handbook of emotions and mass media*. New York: Routledge.
Bucy, E. P., & Grabe, M. E. (2007). Taking television seriously: A sound and image bite analysis of presidential campaign coverage, 1992–2004. *Journal of Communication*, 57, 652–675.
Bucy, E. P., & Grabe, M. E. (2008). "Happy warriors" revisited: Hedonic and agonic display repertoires of presidential candidates on the evening news. *Politics and the Life Sciences*, 27(1), 24–44.
Ceaser, J. W., & Busch, A. E. (1997). *Losing to win: The 1996 elections and American politics*. Lanham, MD: Rowman & Littlefield.

Chaffee, S. H., & Hochheimer, J. L. (1985). The beginnings of political communication research in the United States: Origins of the "limited effects" model. In E. M. Rogers & F. Balle (Eds.), *The media revolution in America and Western Europe* (pp. 267–296). Norwood, NJ: Ablex.

Coleman, R., & Banning, S. (2006). Network TV news' affective framing of the presidential candidates: Evidence for a second level agenda-setting effect through visual framing. *Journalism & Mass Communication Quarterly, 83*(2), 313–328.

Conway, M. T. (2006). The subjective precision of computers: A methodological comparison with human coding. *Journalism & Mass Communication Quarterly, 83*(1), 186–200.

Denton, R. E. (2002). The form and content of political communication. In C. J. Nelson, D. A. Dulio, & S. K. Medvic (Eds.), *Shades of gray: Perspectives on campaign ethics* (pp. 185–214). Washington, DC: Brookings.

Dowd, M. (1996, Oct. 10). Bill be limbo. *New York Times*. Retrieved from http://www.nytimes.com.

Duck, S. W., & Baggaley, J. (1975). Audience reaction and its effect on perceived expertise. *Communication Research, 2*(1), 79–85.

Edelman, M. J. (1964). *The symbolic uses of politics*. Urbana, IL: University of Illinois Press.

Entman, R. M. (1993). Framing: Toward clarification of a fractured paradigm. *Journal of Communication, 43*(4), 51–58.

Erickson, K. V. (2000). Presidential rhetoric's visual turn: Performance fragments and the politics of illusionism. *Communication Monographs, 67*(2), 138–157.

Farrell, D. M., Kolodny, R., & Medvic, S. (2001). Parties and campaign professionals in a digital age. *Harvard International Journal of Press Politics, 6*(4), 11–30.

Gamson, W. A. (1992). *Talking politics*. New York: Cambridge University Press.

Glad, B. (1995). How George Bush lost the presidential election of 1992. In S. A. Renshon (Ed.), *The Clinton presidency: Campaigning, governing, and the psychology of leadership* (pp. 11–35). Boulder, CO: Westview Press.

Glasser, S. B. (2000, May 1). Winning a stake in a losing race; ad commissions enriched strategists. *The Washington Post*, p. A1.

Glassman, C., & Kenney, K. (1994). Myths and presidential campaign photographs. *Visual Communication Quarterly, 49*(10), 4–7.

Grabe, M. E. (1996). The SABC's coverage of the 1987 and 1989 elections: The matter of visual bias. *Journal of Broadcasting & Electronic Media, 40*(1), 1–27.

Grabe, M. E., & Bucy, E. P. (2009). *Image bite politics: News and the visual framing of elections*. New York: Oxford University Press.

Graber, D. A. (1987). Kind pictures and harsh words: How television presents the candidates. In K. L. Schlozman (Ed.), *Elections in America* (pp. 115–141). Boston: Allen & Unwin.

Graber, D. A. (1996). Say it with pictures. *The Annals of the American Academy of Political and Social Science, 546*(1), 85–96.

Graber, D. A. (1997). *Mass media and American politics* (5th ed.). Washington, DC: Congressional Quarterly Press.

Graber, D. A. (2001). *Processing politics: Learning from television in the Internet age*. Chicago: University of Chicago Press.

Hallin, D. C. (1992). Sound bite news: Television coverage of elections, 1968–1988. *Journal of Communication, 42*(2), 5–24.

Hellweg, S. (1979). An examination of voter conceptualizations of the ideal political candidate. *Southern Speech Communication Journal, 44*(4), 373–385.

Hylton, C. (1971). Intra-audience effects: Observable audience response. *Journal of Communication, 21*(3), 253–265.

The Institute of Politics, John F. Kennedy School of Government, Harvard University. (2006). *Campaign for president: The managers look at 2004*. Lanham, MD: Rowman & Littlefield.

Iyengar, S., & McGrady, J. A. (2007). *Media politics: A citizen's guide*. New York: W. W. Norton & Company.

Jamieson, K. H. (Ed.). (2006). *Electing the president 2004: The insiders' view*. Philadelphia: University of Pennsylvania Press.

Kaid, L. L., & Davidson, D. K. (1986). Elements of videostyle. In L. L. Kaid, D. Nimmo, & K. R. Sanders (Eds.), *New perspectives on political advertising* (pp. 184–209). Carbondale: Southern Illinois University Press.

Kazin, M. (1995). *The populist persuasion.* New York: Basic Books.

Keeter, S. (1987). The illusion of intimacy: Television and the role of candidate personal qualities in voter choice. *Public Opinion Quarterly, 51*(3), 344–358.

Kepplinger, H. M. (1991). The impact of presentation techniques: Theoretical aspects and empirical findings. In F. Biocca (Ed.), *Television and political advertising: Psychological processes, Vol. 1* (pp. 173–194). Hillsdale, NJ: Lawrence Erlbaum.

Kinder, D. R. (1986). Presidential character revisited. In R. R. Lau & D. O. Sears (Eds.), *Political cognition: The 19th annual Carnegie symposium on cognition* (pp. 233–256). Hillsdale, NJ: Lawrence Erlbaum.

Klein, J. (2006). *Politics lost: How American democracy was trivialized by people who think you're stupid.* New York: Doubleday.

Kranish, M. (1992, July 30). Bush campaign is riven by debate over new strategy, economic plan. *The Boston Globe*, p. 1.

Kurtz, H. (1992, Feb. 19). The story that just won't check out. *The Washington Post*, p. C1.

Lau, R. R. (1986). Political schema, candidate evaluations, and voting behavior. In R. R Lau & D. O. Sears (Eds.), *Political cognition: The 19th annual Carnegie symposium on cognition* (pp. 95–126). Hillsdale, NJ: Lawrence Erlbaum.

Lee, T. T., Ryan, W. E., Wanta, W., & Chang, K. K. (2004). Looking presidential: A comparison of newspaper photographs of candidates in the United States and Taiwan. *Asian Journal of Communication, 14*(2), 121–139.

Lewis, M. (1997). *Trail fever.* New York: Knopf.

Lichter, S. R., Noyes, R., & Kaid, L. L. (1999). New news or negative news: How the networks nixed the 1996 campaign. In L. L. Kaid & D. G. Bystrom (Eds.), *The electronic election: Perspectives on the 1996 campaign communication* (pp. 3–13). Hillsdale, NJ: Lawrence Erlbaum.

Marshall, J. M. (2000, April 25). *Al Gore's campaign stagnates.* Retrieved from http://archive.salon.com/politics2000/feature/2000/04/25/quiet/index.html.

Masters, R. D., & Sullivan, D. G. (1989). Nonverbal displays and political leadership in France and the United States. *Political Behavior, 11*, 121–153.

Messaris, P. (1994). *Visual literacy: Image, mind, and reality.* Boulder, CO: Westview Press.

Messaris, P., Eckman, B., & Gumpert, G. (1979). Editing structure in the televised versions of the 1976 presidential debates. *Journal of Broadcasting, 23*(3), 359–369.

Moriarty, S. E., & Garramone, G. M. (1986). A study of newsmagazine photographs of the 1984 presidential campaign. *Journalism Quarterly, 63*(4), 728–734.

Moriarty, S. E. & Popovich, M. N. (1991). Newsmagazine visuals and the 1988 presidential election. *Journalism Quarterly, 68*(3), 371–380.

Nimmo, D. (1976). Political image makers and the mass media. *Annals of the American Academy of Political and Social Science, 427*(1), 33–44.

Nimmo, D. (1995). The formation of candidate images during presidential campaigns. In K. Hacker (Ed.), *Candidate images in presidential elections* (pp. 51–63). Westport, CT: Praeger.

Nimmo, D. & Combs, J. E. (1980). *Subliminal politics: Myths and myth-makers in America.* Englewood Cliffs, NJ: Prentice-Hall.

Nimmo, D., & Savage, R. (1976). *Candidates and their images: Concepts, methods, and findings.* Pacific Palisades, CA: Goodyear Publishing.

Parry-Giles, S. J., & Parry-Giles, T. (2002). *Constructing Clinton: Hyperreality and presidential image-making in postmodern politics.* New York: Peter Lang.

Patterson, T. E. (1980). *The mass media election: How Americans choose their president.* New York: Praeger.

The Pew Research Center for the People and the Press. (2000, February 5). *The tough job of communicating with voters.* Retrieved from http://peoplepress.org/reports/display.php3?PageID=242.

Ponnuru, R. (1996, March 25). Doledrums. *National Review*. Retrieved from http://findarticles.com/p/articles/mi_m1282/is_n5_v48/ai_18141530.

Project for Excellence in Journalism (2004). *The state of the news media 2004*. Retrieved from http://www.stateofthenewsmedia.org/narrative_networktv_audience.asp?cat=3&media=4.

Reese, S. D., Gandy, O. H., & Grant, A. E. (Eds.). (2001). *Framing public life: Perspectives on media and our understanding of the social world*. Mahwah, NJ: Lawrence Erlbaum.

Rosenthal, A. (1992, January 24). The 1992 campaign: White House leader and salesman; Bush turns to power of incumbency and tries to defuse revolt in party. *New York Times*, p. A14.

Rudd, R. (1986). Issues as image in political campaign commercials. *Western Journal of Speech Communication, 50*(1), 102–118.

Sabato, L. J. (1981). *The rise of political consultants: New ways of winning elections*. New York: Basic Books.

Seelye, K. Q. (1996, February 27). With Dole campaign off track, he puts two advisers off the team. *New York Times*, p. A1.

Sella, M. (2000, September 24). The stiff guy vs. the dumb guy. *New York Times Magazine*, p. 72.

Sherr, S. A. (1999). Scenes from the political playground: An analysis of the symbolic use of children in presidential campaign advertising. *Political Communication, 16*(1), 45–59.

Spragens, T. A. (2007). Populist perfectionism: The other American liberalism. *Social Philosophy and Policy, 24*, 141–163.

Swanson, D. (1992). The political-media complex. *Communication Monographs, 59*, 397–400.

Thomas, E. (2008, February 25). A perennial press opera. The roots of the Clinton-media tension. *Newsweek*. Retrieved from http://www.newsweek.com/id/112842.

Thomas, E., Rosenberg, D., Kaufman L., & Murr, A. (1997). *Back from the dead: How Clinton survived the Republican revolution*. New York: Atlantic Monthly Press.

Trebay, G. (2007, July 22). Campaign chic: Not too cool, never ever hot. *New York Times*. Retrieved from http://www.nytimes.com/2007/07/22/fashion/22candidates.html.

Trent, J. S., & Trent, J. D. (1997). The ideal candidate revisited. *American Behavioral Scientist, 40*(8), 1001–1020.

Von Drehle, D. (2000). Lee Atwater, the specter of South Carolina. *The Washington Post*, p. C1.

Waldman, P., & Devitt, J. (1998). Newspaper photographs and the 1996 presidential election: The question of bias. *Journalism & Mass Communication Quarterly, 75*(2), 302–311.

Waterman, R., Wright, R., & St. Clair, G. (1999). *The image-is-everything presidency*. Boulder, CO: Westview Press.

Wayne, S. J. (1996). *The road to the White House 1996: The politics of presidential elections*. New York: St. Martin's Press.

Wiegman, O. (1987). Attitude change in a realistic experiment: The effect of party membership and audience reaction during an interview with a Dutch politician. *Journal of Applied Social Psychology, 17*, 37–49.

Zaller, J. (1998). The rule of product substitution in presidential campaign news. *The Annals of the American Academy of Political and Social Science, 560*(1), 111–128.

13

Identifying Frames in Political News

Dennis Chong
Department of Political Science
Northwestern University

James N. Druckman
Department of Political Science
Northwestern University

In a democracy, a strong and independent public voice depends on the existence of a free media that represents the diversity of viewpoints in society. Citizens learn about politics through personal experiences and conversations with others, but most of what happens in the world is viewed indirectly through the reporting of the mass media. More than any other source of communication, the news media shape the considerations that people use to understand and evaluate political events and conditions (Iyengar & Kinder, 1987).

The study of public opinion, therefore, is linked inextricably to analyzing how the news media frame their coverage of politics and how the public uses this information. A media frame is an interpretation or evaluation of an issue, event, or person that emphasizes certain of its features or consequences. Scholars have examined the mass media's treatment of issues and candidates and shown that public opinion can shift as the balance of stories changes to favor one side or the other (e.g., Chong & Druckman, 2007c). If one side dominates public discussion of a subject, its framing of the issue will shape public opinion.

Consider, for example, two of the most significant domestic and foreign policies of the George W. Bush administration: the tax cuts of 2001 and 2003, and the decision to go to war in Iraq in 2003. On both issues, the administration influenced the media's framing of its news coverage, leading to increased public support for the administration's policies. Public discussion of the tax cuts in the media emphasized the savings that would accrue to taxpayers while ignoring the likely negative consequences for government spending on social programs (Bartels, 2005; Hacker & Piereson, 2005). The administration built support through the media for invading Iraq by linking the regime of Saddam Hussein to the events of 9/11 and making the invasion an integral part of its larger war on terror (Gershkoff & Kushner, 2005). Therefore, despite the substantial impact that each of these policies has had on the American public, debate over their merits was surprisingly skewed.

In this chapter, we describe and apply methods for analyzing how information and arguments are framed in media coverage of political news. Our focus is on frames in the news rather than frame-building or frame-setting processes (see de Vreese, 2005; Scheufele, 1999). We begin by defining the meaning of "frames" and linking "framing" to the psychology of attitudes. After describing an approach to identifying frames in the mass media, we outline a theory of how such frames influence popular interpretations of politics. In contrast to the focus of most prior work, which emphasizes the frequency with which frames are used, a novel feature of our theory is its identification of contextual features of frames that are predicted to affect opinions. We illustrate how these details of frames can be identified in a content analysis of fourteen distinct national, state, and local issues, examined over time. The results of our analysis highlight the usefulness of taking a longitudinal approach to studying the frequency, balance, and interaction of frames.

WHAT IS FRAMING?[1]

The major premise of framing theory is that an issue can be viewed from multiple perspectives and evaluated on different bases, not all of which will yield the same attitude toward the issue. Framing refers to a process by which citizens learn to construe and evaluate an issue by focusing on certain "frames"—i.e., certain features and implications of the issue—rather than others. In this chapter, we will focus on the media's role in influencing the frames that citizens use to evaluate political issues that are discussed and debated in the news.

A more precise definition of framing starts with a conventional expectancy value model of an individual's attitude (e.g., Ajzen & Fishbein, 1980; Nelson, Oxley, & Clawson, 1997). An attitude toward an object, in this view, is the weighted sum of a series of evaluative beliefs about that object. Specifically, $Attitude = \Sigma v_i * w_i$, where v_i is the evaluation of the object on attribute i, and w_i is the salience weight ($\Sigma w_i = 1$) associated with that attribute.

For example, one's overall attitude, A, toward a tax cut might consist of a combination of negative and positive evaluations, v_i, of the policy on different dimensions i. An individual may believe that the tax cut will have favorable implications for her pocketbook ($i = 1$) but also cause the elimination of various social programs ($i = 2$). If she values both her financial status and these social programs, then v_1 is positive and v_2 is negative and her attitude toward the tax cut will depend on the relative magnitudes of v_1 and v_2 discounted by the relative weights (w_1 and w_2) assigned to each attribute, respectively (Nelson & Oxley, 1999).

The conventional expectancy model is an idealized conception of an attitude as a summary of a definable set of beliefs that an individual holds about an object. Nonetheless, the expectancy value model's general assumption that different emphases can be placed on various considerations about the object is a useful abstraction for discussing the psychology of framing.[2] The set of dimensions that affect an evaluation constitute an individual's "frame in thought." For example, if one believes that free speech dominates all other considerations in deciding whether a hate group has the right to rally, that person's frame in thought is free speech. If, instead, one gives consideration to free speech, public safety, and the effect of the rally on the community's reputation, then one's frame in thought consists of this mix of considerations.

Obviously, an individual's frame in thought can have a marked impact on her overall opinion (e.g., a free speech frame inclines one to support the group's right to rally). For this reason, political elites attempt to mobilize voters in support of their policies by encouraging them to think about those policies along particular lines. This is accomplished by highlighting or repeatedly mentioning certain features of the policy, such as its likely effects or its relationship to important values (e.g., Jacoby, 2000, p. 751). In so doing, the speaker invokes a "frame in communication" that is a candidate for adoption by others (on the distinction between frames in thought and frames in communication, also see Brewer, 2003; Druckman, 2001; Kinder & Sanders, 1996; Scheufele, 1999). When, for example, a speaker argues that a hate group's planned rally is "a First Amendment issue," she makes a case for the relevance of free speech (this is a frame in communication because it is part of a speech act). Standardized guidelines on how to identify (or even define more precisely) a frame in communication do not exist. In the next section, we review previous work on identifying frames in communication, and we put forth an inductive approach to gathering data.

IDENTIFYING FRAMES IN COMMUNICATION

Over the past decade, the identification of frames in communication—that is, the key considerations emphasized in a media message—has become a virtual cottage industry. Scholars track frames to identify trends in issue definitions, compare coverage across media outlets, and examine variations across different types of media (e.g., Semetko & Valkenburg, 2000). While uniform measurement standards are not available, the most compelling studies tend to take the following steps to identify frames (see, e.g., Boydstun, 2006; de Vreese, 2004; Gamson & Modigliani, 1987, p. 143, 1989; Shah, Watts, Domke, & Fan, 2002, p. 343; Tuchman, 1978, p. 193).

First, an issue, person, or event is selected (Entman, 2004, pp. 23–24). A frame in communication can be defined only in relation to a specific issue, event, or political actor. For example, the frames for Social Security reform differ from the frames for immigration reform. Even the same issue at different times may invoke alternative frames; as we show below, the frames used in media coverage of Social Security reform in 1997–2000 tended to be more positive than those invoked in 2003–2005. Also the frames appeared with varying frequencies in these two time periods with, for example, the "outcome" frame appearing signficantly more often in the second time period.

Second, if the goal is to understand how frames in communication affect public opinion, then the researcher needs to isolate a specific attitude. For example, one could focus on overall attitudes toward welfare reform or, alternatively, on attributions of reasons why people are on welfare. Different frames may underlie each of these attitudes. The frame-defining attitudes toward welfare reform may include considerations of economic costs, humanitarianism, and individualism (Feldman & Zaller, 1992). Causal attributions relevant to welfare might employ an episodic frame, such as an individual's work ethic, or a thematic frame, such as the economic opportunities available in society (Iyengar, 1991).[3]

Third, an initial set of frames for an issue is identified inductively to create a coding scheme. Prior work in the academic and popular literatures serves as a good starting point; for example, the book, *Framing the Social Security Debate* (Arnold, Graetz, & Munnell, 1998), would be an obvious source for gathering contemporary Social Security frames. Gamson and Modigliani (1987, p. 144; 1989, p. 7) suggest going further by examining the frames produced by various elite actors and organizations on both sides of the issue in court opinions and briefs, editorial writings, and the publications of interest groups or social movements (also see Brewer, 2003). Such in-depth analysis provides the set of "culturally available frames" in elite discourse (Gamson & Modigliani, 1987, p. 144). Elite sources can be complemented by asking samples of individuals to record the considerations that come to mind on a given issue, using open-ended questions (see Chong & Druckman, 2007b, for a discussion).

Fourth, once an initial set of frames is identified, the next step is to select sources for content analysis. These might include communications that advocate particular positions (e.g., communications from social movements) but more typically scholars analyze mass media sources, including major newspapers, magazines, websites, or television broadcasts (although see Tewksbury, Jones, Peske, Raymond, & Vig, 2000). The choice of specific news outlets depends on the researcher's intent; for example, the goal of a study might be to capture general trends in coverage, or to compare specific types of coverage across media. Articles or stories are identified via searches (such as keyword searches in electronic databases) (cf. Dimitrova, Kaid, Williams, & Trammell, 2005; Tankard, 2001, p. 101). Coders then analyze a sample, identifying the presence or absence of predefined frames in the story or article. Coders can also separately analyze distinct parts of the article, such as headlines, photos, and informative graphics (de Vreese, 2004, p. 54).

Prior to coding, it is necessary to specify how any particular frame can be identified. When researchers rely on computerized searches to analyze large volumes of text, they must identify the universe of words that mark the presence of a frame. For example, in his study of public attitudes toward governmental efforts to promote racial equality, Kellstedt (2000, 2003) tracked the use of two media frames over time: individualism and egalitarianism. He created a dictionary of words and phrases that indicated the presence of each of these broad, thematic frames (e.g., mentions of "fairness" and "equal protection of the laws" denoted the egalitarianism frame) and then used content analysis software to analyze more than 4,000 *Newsweek* articles and 2,500 *New York Times* articles. Shah et al. (2002) used a similar approach to examine how the Clinton–Lewinsky scandal was framed in nearly 20,000 news articles (for another computer-based approach, see Simon & Xenos, 2004).

In contrast to machine coding, manual or human coding guided by prototypes instead of exact terminology allows greater flexibility to discover new frames that were not identified in the initial coding scheme. This added flexibility, however, comes with a potential cost of lower reliability and smaller samples. In general, checks for intercoder reliability are imperative when manual coding is used (for a mixed hand-computer coding method, see Hopkins & King, 2007; see also Chapters 12 and 14, this volume).

There are copious examples of research on frames in communication using approaches similar to those outlined above, including analyses of affirmative action (e.g., Gamson & Modigliani, 1987), support for war (e.g., Dimitrova et al., 2005), opinions about stem cell research (Nisbet, Brossard, & Kroepsch, 2003, p. 48), cynicism toward government (Brewer & Sigelman, 2002), and attributions of responsibility for the obesity epidemic (Lawrence, 2004).

These framing analyses provide insight into cultural shifts (Richardson & Lancendorfer, 2004, p. 75; Schudson, 1995), media biases (Entman, 2007; Tankard, 2001), public understanding (Berinsky & Kinder, 2006), and opinion formation (Chong & Druckman, 2007c). They also demonstrate that framing is best conceptualized as a process that evolves over time. The passage of time allows new issues to be separated from previously debated issues that are familiar to those who pay attention to politics. Although new issues are often variants of existing issues that have been in the news, they are distinguished by the absence of general agreement among elites and the public about how to construe them. Older issues, by contrast, have a defined structure and elicit more routine considerations.

EFFECTS OF FRAMES IN COMMUNICATION

Frames in communication matter—they affect the attitudes and behaviors of their audiences (Druckman, 2001). The bulk of attention in the political science and communication literatures has been on how frames in the communications of elites (e.g., politicians, media outlets, interest groups) influence citizens' frames and attitudes. This process is typically called a "framing effect."[4]

Scholars have demonstrated framing effects with experiments, surveys, and case studies across a range of issues, including government spending (Jacoby, 2000), campaign finance (Grant & Rudolph, 2003), support for the Supreme Court (Nicholson & Howard, 2003), evaluations of foreign nations (Brewer, Graf, & Willnat, 2003), and many others. In these cases, a journalist, politician, or commentator may introduce a frame in communication (e.g., representing a hate group rally as a free speech issue) that increases the weight (w_j) an individual attaches to a certain dimension or consideration (i) (e.g., free speech considerations), thereby shaping the person's overall opinion (e.g., increasing support for the right to rally).

In other work, we suggest a three-step process of the psychological mechanisms of framing (Chong & Druckman, 2007a). First, a given consideration—say free speech in the evaluation of a hate group's right to rally—needs to be stored in memory to be *available* for retrieval and use. If, for example, an individual does not understand the concept of free speech, then free speech is not an available consideration, and she will be unaffected by a free speech frame. Second, the consideration must be *accessible* (Price & Tewksbury, 1997), meaning its activation potential exceeds a certain threshold level, above which knowledge is available for use (e.g., the consideration may be retrieved from long-term memory). One way to increase accessibility of a consideration is through frequent or recent exposure to a communication frame that emphasizes it.

Third, under some conditions, an individual will consciously evaluate the *applicability* of accessible considerations.[5] The perceived applicability of a given communication frame (and thus the likelihood it will affect an individual's opinion) increases with perceptions of its strength or relevance (Eagly & Chaiken, 1993, p. 330). Strength or relevance, in turn, depends on *semantic and rhetorical features of the frame* such as whether the frame is culturally resonant, is refuted, includes statistical information (i.e., the explicit citation of a statistic, such as the percentage of people favoring the privatization of Social Security), includes episodic information (i.e., reference to a particular case or person as an example, such as a story of someone who relies on Social Security), is endorsed by a credible source, and so on. An implication of these effects— supported by experimental evidence (Chong & Druckman, 2007b)—is that the volume or frequency of messages is not the only factor affecting public opinion. Under competitive circumstances, applicable or strong frames can defeat frames that are more prevalent (i.e., available and accessible) but less applicable or weaker.

Evaluations of the applicability of a frame also depend critically on the *mix of frames* an individual encounters. For example, opposing strong frames may offset the effects of one another; alternatively, weak frames may backfire when countered by strong opposing frames if the strong frames accentuate the inapplicability of the weak frames (see Chong & Druckman, 2007a, 2007b). In short, it is necessary to account for the relative strength and frequency of each side's frames to gauge framing effects in competitive political environments.

When encountering a series of frames over time (Chong & Druckman, in press), the order of the frames influences the magnitude of framing effects, but individuals vary in the degree to which they favor either earlier or later arguments. Individuals who process information online, by using a running tally that is updated following exposure to each piece of information, show stronger primacy effects; in other words, their opinions correspond more closely to the *early* frames they encounter. Individuals who rely more heavily on memory-based information processing are affected to a greater degree by recent frames because they base their opinions more on immediate considerations. This finding accentuates the importance of understanding more generally how frames are represented over time in media coverage—something largely ignored in the literature (exceptions include de Vreese, 2004; Druckman & Nelson, 2003; Tewksbury et al., 2000).

THEORETICAL ASSUMPTIONS OF MEDIA CONTENT ANALYSIS

Past work analyzing frames in media content concentrates attention almost exclusively on the prevalence of frames as the vehicle of framing effects. It does this by recording whether a frame is present or absent in an article and then reporting frequencies with which different frames appear, sometimes charting frequencies over time (e.g., de Vreese, Peter, & Semetko, 2001; Edy & Meirick, 2007; Gamson & Modigliani 1987, 1989; Gross & Goldman, 2005; Kellstedt, 2005; Miller & Riechert, 2001; Porto, 2007; Schnell & Callaghan, 2005; Schuck & de Vreese, 2006).[6]

The focus on frequency stems from assumptions common in the literature. For example, Zaller's (1992) RAS (Receive-Accept-Sample) model suggests that the considerations a person holds about an issue depend on the volume of messages received and accepted on either side. Few dimensions of these messages are considered relevant; only their direction and whether they provide partisan or ideological cues to the audience are considered. Politically sophisticated individuals are more likely to accept frames from partisan sources, but public opinion in general responds primarily to the relative intensity of opposing messages.[7] Simply put, prevalent frames prevail, as citizens "are blown about by whatever current of information manages to develop with greatest intensity" (Zaller, 1992, p. 311; see also, Cappella & Jamieson, 1997, pp. 81–82; Domke, Shah, & Wackman, 1998, p. 53; Iyengar, 1991, pp. 130–136; Pan & Kosicki, 1997, pp. 9–11; Riker, 1990, p. 49).

The framing theory described above suggests that framing depends on factors other than the intensity or volume of messages, which tends to affect the availability and accessibility of relevant considerations. Framing effects also depend on the relative applicability or strength of frames, the combination of frames encountered (which may or may not be balanced), and the sequence of frames over time. Experimental research confirms these factors are relevant (Chong & Druckman, 2007b), but this research has been limited by designs that test only a few simple competitive contexts (e.g., one-sided framing, dual framing, balanced debate).

In practice, competition between frames can take many alternative forms, particularly on issues that are debated over extended periods. Current experimental studies typically employ only one or two frames to represent media coverage of an issue when in practice there are likely to be multiple competing and complementary frames. Future research on the effects of different forms of competition therefore would benefit from empirical studies evaluating how frames are represented in actual media coverage of salient political issues. This is the task we set for ourselves in the remainder of the chapter. Using the content analysis methodology outlined earlier, we will code how a variety of national, state, and local political issues have been framed in the news media. We will calculate the frequency with which different frames appear in news stories and the prevalence of debate involving opposing frames. We will note when frames are refuted and when they employ statistical or episodic information, as these features may be related to the applicability of a frame. Because media coverage of each issue is extended over time, we also will examine changes in the number, balance, and presentation of frames. We expect to find that, in contrast to the usual simplified design of framing experiments, real-world debate will involve numerous frames representing both sides of the issues and that competition between opposing positions will be commonplace but rarely balanced.

ANALYZING COMPETING FRAMES

Selecting Issues and Attitudes

Moving beyond coverage of a single issue to studying how news media cover political issues generally presents the additional methodological problem of deciding which issues to select for analysis. When there is no well-defined population of issues from which to draw a representative sample, it is unclear whether the concept of a sampling frame is meaningful (i.e., what constitutes the universe of media-covered issues?). Perhaps the closest analogy is selecting a small-N data sample from a large, incompletely specified population.

An alternative to drawing a representative sample when the population is vaguely defined is to select a set of issues that vary in some specific, identifiable respects. Political issues vary first and foremost in their substance or content: foreign versus domestic policy, social or cultural (including race and religion) versus economic concerns, and so on. Party platforms are readily located along these broad dimensions, as are the attitudes of voting groups in the electorate (Carmines & Layman, 1997). Individual attitudes within a given policy domain also are likely to display enough consistency to indicate that such subdivisions of the "issue space" are meaningful to politicians and voters alike.

As noted earlier, issues also vary in their age or political longevity. Health care and Social Security, for example, have been debated continually in recent decades, whereas controversy over permissible methods for interrogating terrorism suspects is a relatively new topic of public debate. However, the distinction between old and new is often fuzzy. Conflicts over the place of religion in the education system, for example, have focused at different times on school prayer, the reading of the Bible, the posting of the Ten Commandments in classrooms, and the teaching of evolution, among other controversies. The latest iteration of debate on this issue (e.g., intelligent design) may introduce new tactics and arguments but is also likely to resurrect familiar claims that reflect longstanding cleavages in society.

Many ostensibly new issues are new only in their latest manifestation, whereas enduring issues are frequently updated or refitted with new considerations. Traditional issues can therefore potentially be transformed into "new" issues by reframing. In the 1980s and 1990s, for example, proponents of hate speech regulations on college campuses made considerable headway by drawing a parallel between racial harassment in the university and sexual harassment in the workplace (Chong, 2006). By arguing that hate speech was not a traditional First Amendment concern, they shifted the value dimension of the issue and reframed the debate in terms of whether hate speech violated the civil rights of women and racial and ethnic minorities (Delgado, 1982, 1991; MacKinnon, 1993; Matsuda, 1989).

The rationale behind separating new and enduring issues is that attitudes toward new issues tend to be weaker and, therefore, individuals should be more susceptible to persuasion and framing effects on these issues. In this sense, the key distinction across issues is the relative difficulty or ease with which citizens can relate the issue to their existing attitudes and beliefs.

Issues also vary in their salience to the public. The more salient an issue is, the more likely citizens will know something about the issue, hold prior opinions related to it, and be motivated to evaluate new information about the issue. Knowledge, prior attitudes, and motivation are all expected to influence how people process information about issues (Chong & Druckman, 2007a).

For our analyses here, we define salience on the basis of substantive media coverage. Although the volume of media attention does not necessarily mean that an issue will become personally important to any individual citizen, it increases the likelihood of issue awareness and exposure to information about the issue that can affect one's opinions and attitudes.

The set of issues we analyze (see Table 13.1) have enjoyed varying durations on the public agenda (i.e., they vary in terms of age) and include both issues that fall clearly within one substantive domain and others that cut across domains (i.e., they vary in terms of content). The ongoing discussion of ways to shore up the Social Security program falls squarely in the economic realm and has been a subject of debate for a relatively long period of time (at least periodically). The debate over gay marriage and the teaching of evolution and intelligent design are prominent

TABLE 13.1
Coding Details

Issue or Event	Attitude	Time Period	Rationale for Time Period	Source	Keywords	Number of Articles Coded
Patriot Act	Support (pro) or oppose (con) the Patriot Act and its restrictions	9/12/01–12/31/05	Debate about security restrictions began immediately after 9/11/01.	New York Times	"Patriot Act" IN "headline," OR "lead paragraph," OR "terms"	122
Global warming	Support or oppose efforts to control global warming (e.g., Kyoto Accord)	1/1/00–12/31/04	The Kyoto Accord was agreed upon in 12/97 and entered force in 2/05. This is an ongoing issue, and we focus our analysis on the Bush administration, which, during the period coded, opposed global efforts including the accord.	New York Times	"Global warming" OR "Kyoto Treaty" IN "headline"	82
Intelligent design	Support or oppose intelligent design as a viable alternative to evolution (and its teaching in schools)	11/1/04–12/31/05	The most recent debate traces its origins to a campaign launched by the Discovery Institute starting in 1990 (see New York Times 8/05 series). It took several years, however, for the Institute to generate a public debate which began in earnest in early spring of 2005 (New York Times) with numerous school boards taking up the issue.[a]	New York Times	"intelligent design" AND "evolution" IN "headline," "lead paragraph," OR "terms"	58
Same-sex marriage in the U.S.	Support or oppose the right to same-sex marriage (and constitutional amendments pertaining to it)	8/1/03–12/31/05	The Massachusetts Supreme Court ruled on the issue in 11/03 (and then again on 2/3/04).[b]	New York Times	"Gay marriage" OR "same-sex marriage" OR "civil union" IN "headline" OR "lead paragraph" OR "terms" AND "constitutional amendment" IN "full text"	139
Same-sex marriage in Canada	Support or oppose the right to same-sex marriage	8/1/03–12/31/05	We used the same time period as in the U.S. for a point of comparison. During this time period, the issue received extensive coverage in Canada. Numerous provinces legalized gay marriage and, on 12/9/04, the Supreme court of Canada ruled that same-sex marriage is constitutional (and on 6/20/04, the Civil Marriage Act legalized same-sex marriage through Canada).	Globe and Mail	"gay marriage" OR "same-sex marriage" OR "civil union" IN "headline/lead paragraph"	139

TABLE 13.1 continued
Coding Details

Issue or Event Coded	Attitude	Time Period	Rationale for Time Period	Source	Keywords	Number of Articles
Social Security 1	Support or oppose privatization or radical change/reform	6/1/97– 6/31/00	Cook (2005) suggests that key years over two presidential terms were 1998 and 1999 (starting with Clinton's 1997 reform proposals) and 2004–2005 (once Bush won his second term and began pushing for privatization).	New York Times	"Social security" IN "headline" AND "reform" OR "overhaul" OR "privatization" IN "full text"	40
Social Security 2	Support or oppose privatization or radical change/reform	1/1/04– 12/31/05	See Social Security 1 rationale.	New York Times	"Social security" IN "headline" AND "reform" OR "overhaul" OR "privatization" IN "full text"	92
Bush v. Gore	Support or challenge the Election Day election outcome (favoring Bush)	11/9/00– 12/13/00	This began the day after the 2000 election and continued until the final Court decision.	New York Times	"Bush" AND "Gore" AND "Recount AND "Ballot" IN "headline" OR "lead paragraph" OR "terms"	134
Abu Ghraib controversy	Support or criticize the administration, government, and/or military (attributions)	3/20/04– 9/30/04	Charges of alleged abuse were made on 3/20/04. Media coverage and discussion began with the publication of photos on 4/28/04. Coverage subsided by fall of 2004, with the trials ongoing.	New York Times	"Abu Ghraib AND abuse OR torture" IN "Headline, Lead Paragraph, Terms"	159
California immigration initiative (Prop. 187)	Support or oppose Proposition 187, which would bar illegal immigrants from receiving various basic public services	11/1/93– 12/31/98	Efforts to put the initiative on the 1994 ballot began in late 1993. Debate persisted after the initiative passed due to court appeals. Most of the coverage subsided by 1997.	San Francisco Chronicle	"187" AND "immigration" IN "Headline, Lead Paragraph, or Terms"	80

Nazi rally	Support or oppose the right of a hate group rally	1/1/78–12/31/78	Time period covers debate before and after 7/9/78 march at Marquette Park, Chicago.	*Chicago Tribune*	"Nazi" AND "rally" AND "Marquette park" OR "Skokie"	36
Penn. Ku Klux Klan rally	Support or oppose the right of a hate group rally	8/1/01–9/31/01	Time period covers debate before and after aborted 9/8/01 rally in Lancaster.	*Lancaster New Era*	"Ku Klux Klan" IN "Headline/Lead Paragraph/Terms"	23
Tenn. Ku Klux Klan rally	Support or oppose the right of a hate group rally	1/1/98–2/28/98	Time period covers debate before and after 1/17/98 rally in Memphis.	*The Commercial Appeal*	"Ku Klux Klan" IN "Headline/Lead Paragraph/Terms"	29
2006 casino proposal in Illinois	Support or oppose the proposal for a state owned casino	8/24/06–11/7/06 (Election Day)	The proposal was put forward by candidate Topinka on 8/23/06 as a major part of her campaign agenda. Our ending time constitutes the end of the campaign.	*Chicago Tribune*	"gubernatorial," "Topinka," and/or "Blagojevich," AND "Casino"	20

Notes:

[a] There is a long history dating at least to the 1925 Scopes trial and the 1982 *McClean v. Arkansas Board of Education* decision. The idea of intelligent design was first introduced in 1802 (Morowitz, Hazen, & Trefil, 2005, p. B7).

[b] The issue remained contentious through the 2004 election and after, as groups continued to organize to place ballot initiatives on the issue before voters.

examples of social or cultural issues; both of these issues can be best seen as relatively new in terms of specifics but quite similar to other issues that have generated debate for years. The discussion of global warming in the context of the Kyoto Treaty combines elements of foreign policy with domestic economic considerations. This is a topic that has become increasingly prominent in recent years.

Another increasingly controversial issue is immigration; we follow media reporting on immigration at the national level and coverage at the state level on Proposition 187 in California. Immigration is a multidimensional issue that can be framed in racial or economic terms while it also introduces considerations of security and civil rights. The Patriot Act is a new issue that poses old questions about civil liberties and the tradeoffs between individual liberty and security. The same civil liberties and human rights considerations are raised in the Abu Ghraib controversy involving the abuse of foreign prisoners by American soldiers. The unique *Bush v. Gore* controversy in the 2000 presidential election raised issues of voting rights and electoral laws that were intensely debated but quickly resolved. For added variation, we also coded coverage of proposed hate group rallies in three distinct locations at three different points in time, as well as a short-lived proposal for a publicly funded casino that received attention during the 2006 gubernatorial campaign in Illinois.

Selecting Time Periods

Given our focus on *salient* issues, we chose a timeframe for each issue in which there was active debate or discussion of the issue in the news, usually stimulated by an event such as a policy proposal, election, or change of policy that brought attention to the issue and prompted news coverage. In Downsian (1972) terms, we examined roughly the middle phases of the issue-attention cycle between discovery, enthusiastic discussion, and gradual subsiding of public interest. These are the periods when public opinion is most likely to be affected by media framing of the issue.

In most instances we used a focal event to center the time frame of the content analysis. We set the starting point for our analysis a few months prior to the event and continued the analysis for a few months afterward to monitor changes in coverage over the course of this peak period of attention.

For each issue, we identified the public attitude (pro or con) that was most clearly affected by media coverage of the issue. The relevant attitudes corresponding to these issues appear in the second column of Table 13.1. Notice that each attitude has a *pro* position—generally supportive of the issue—and a *con* position that opposes it (e.g., opposition to the Patriot Act, Kyoto Accord, intelligent design, same-sex marriage, or Social Security privatization).

All coding, with the exception of the 2006 casino proposal, was completed by December 2005, so we do not examine media coverage beyond that period. The specific time periods for each issue are listed in the third column of Table 13.1. The fourth column of the table offers more detailed rationales for the time periods. We code Social Security during two distinct time periods when it received considerable attention (i.e., 1997–2000 and 2004–2005), thereby allowing for comparative analyses. We also code three proposed hate group rallies, allowing for comparison across these cases.

Selecting Sources and Articles

The aim of our study is to capture and explain how information about political issues is represented to mass audiences. Although people can obtain information on issues from a variety of sources (e.g., friends, Internet sites, talk shows, magazines), television and newspapers continue to be the primary sources through which individuals receive information (e.g., Fridkin & Kenney, 2005). Therefore, we concentrate our analysis on the information that is available through the mass media. This approach follows others who analyze how issues are framed (e.g., Entman, 2004; Gilens, 1999; Gross & Goldman, 2005; Jerit, 2008; Jones & Baumgartner, 2005; Kellstedt, 2003; Patterson, 1993).[8]

In terms of specific sources, past work has analyzed a variety of sources, including newsmagazines such as *Newsweek* (Gilens, 1999; Kellstedt, 2000, 2003), television news transcripts (Entman, 2004), the AP wire (Jerit, 2008), the *New York Times* (Baumgartner, De Boef, & Boydstun, 2008; Boydstun, 2006; Jones & Baumgartner, 2005; Patterson, 1993), and other newspapers (Gross & Goldman, 2005).[9] For national level issues, we examine the *New York Times*, often regarded as the national newspaper of record in the United States and an agenda-setter for other newspapers and mass media. For the local issues—hate group rallies, Proposition 187, and the casino proposal—we analyzed relevant local papers.[10] We also include an analysis of the same-sex marriage issue in Canada using the major national Canadian paper, the *Globe and Mail*. Coding the *Globe and Mail*'s treatment of same-sex marriage offers an interesting cross-national comparison with coverage of the same issue in the *New York Times*. The specific sources used for each issue are listed in the fifth column of Table 13.1.

Articles for each issue were drawn from the Lexis/Nexis database; Factiva or ProQuest was used for supplemental searches on some local issues when local newspapers were only available through these databases. On each issue, the optimal set of keywords was determined by experimenting with alternative word combinations and locations (e.g., in the headline or lead paragraph of the article) and reading a sample of articles generated by each combination to ensure that all major articles were captured. The keywords used for each issue are listed in the sixth column of Table 13.1.

A simple count of the number of articles published in each month during the interval studied confirms that media attention to each issue increased and, in some cases, declined toward the end of our coding period. Therefore, the analysis tracks how the issue is discussed in the media as it becomes more salient to the public.

In cases where our search procedure resulted in more articles than we could feasibly code,[11] a random sample of articles was drawn from the total population of articles without regard for their placement in the paper.

In terms of visual content, photographs accompanying the articles were not coded because they could not be obtained from the search engines used to sample relevant articles. (Coding photographs would have required a painstaking manual search though microfilm.) The inaccessibility of photographs is a drawback insofar as pictures may reinforce or contradict the text (Messaris & Abraham, 2001). Visual frames also may have effects that are distinct from the text, which will not be captured in our coding. Neither does Lexis/Nexis define the place on a page that an article appears; thus, while we will have the page number for each article, we were not able to determine if it was a lead article.

Identifying Frames in Communication

To identify the set of frames used in discussion of each issue, we consulted prior academic and popular literature (e.g., Cook, 2005, on Social Security; Price, Nir, & Cappella, 2005, on gay marriage), interest group publications, and past news coverage of the issues. This approach yielded a set of initial frames. In many cases, frames were added after coding began, reflecting the flexibility available with human coding of news text.

For each issue, we constructed a detailed coding document that explained the frame and offered examples of how the frame might be invoked in the news stories. Each frame was defined by its emphasis on a certain aspect of the issue, usually (but not always) a rationale for either supporting or opposing one side of the issue. Thus, we do not rely merely on the presence or absence of certain keywords to define a frame (e.g., Kellstedt, 2003), but rather use keywords to search for relevant articles. An example of our frame identification instructions on intelligent design is provided in Appendix 13.1.

Our decision to use human coding to identify news frames (and other features) assumed that most articles would have a complex structure, containing multiple frames that would often be interlocked or overlapping, reinforcing or refuting one another. This juxtaposition of frames precludes estimating the number of lines devoted to any particular frame because the boundaries of frames are often unclear. Because attempts to count lines proved highly unreliable, articles were coded simply for the presence or absence of various frames, as well as other features discussed below. The general disorderliness of actual frames in news contrasts with the small number of clearly defined frames typically employed as stimuli in the experimental literature on framing.

The set of frames for each issue appears in Appendix 13.2 (note that this list only includes frames that actually appeared; codes for a few frames that were never invoked are not listed in the appendix, but are available from the authors). In many cases, there are clear evaluative consequences of a given frame. For example, emphasizing civil rights in discussions of the Patriot Act is usually an opposition frame. In other cases, the evaluative implications of the frame are less clear. Emphasizing the partisan divide in debates on the Patriot Act, for instance, could be a frame used by either side in accusing opponents of hindering a resolution by "politicizing" the issue.

We sampled approximately 25% of coded articles and had a second coder code them for reliability. Using the Kappa statistic, we find reliability statistics equal or above .80 for the presence or absence of frames (correcting for chance), and statistics near or above .70 for all other features on which we report here (see below). The details of how we assessed the reliability of our coding as well as more detailed results of our reliability analyses appear in Appendix 13.3.

Coding Frames in News

All coders were undergraduate students who were trained in content analysis in a 10-week undergraduate seminar course on the concept of framing in politics. Each coder completed the content analysis of a political issue as a class assignment for course credit. As part of their training, all coders worked on several practice articles until they understood how to properly apply the defined codes.

To identify frames, each coder proceeded by reading the entire article carefully (multiple times if necessary) to ensure he or she understood the article. Coders were encouraged to make notes directly on the article or on a separate note page as they coded for the following features:

Frames.   For each issue, coders referred to the set of defined frames listed on a "frame sheet" (or code book) accompanied by concrete examples of each frame (see Appendix 13.1). Each frame in communication invoked a specific consideration (such as a value, principle, or consequence) that typically established the stakes surrounding the issue. If coders encountered a frame that was not listed in the code book, they placed it in the residual "other frame" category and described the consideration raised by the frame. When the "other frame" appeared multiple times, the set of defined frames was updated to include the new frame.[12] Coders accounted for the presence or absence of each frame in each article.

Frame Position.   Each frame may or may not be clearly linked to an *overall position* on a given issue, either in support or opposition to the issue attitude described in Table 13.1. Coders evaluated whether the frame reflected a position (either pro or con or no position) and recorded the context in which the frame was used. While this introduces obvious subjectivity, we found an impressive amount of reliability on frame position, with agreement (correcting for chance) reaching nearly 0.90 (see Appendix 13.3). As expected, many frames were marshaled exclusively on only one side of the issue, but there also were other frames that were invoked by both sides.

Other Frame Features. A number of semantic or rhetorical features may influence the applicability of a given frame. As mentioned, this is an area in need of substantial development and future study (and thus we simply explore whether the features appear or not). We identified three general features, based on persuasion research on "message factors," that may affect applicability in specific circumstances (see also Arceneaux, 2008; Petersen, 2008). First, coders noted when a frame was put forth and then was explicitly *argued against* or *refuted* in the same article. For example, "some say urban sprawl will hurt the environment, but that is not the case." When refutation occurred, the counter-frame was noted (if one existed). Refutation is orthogonal to the position codes—a frame may take a pro, con, or no position and still be criticized or refuted. Coders also noted whether support for a frame was buttressed by a reference to *statistical* or numerical data or whether frames were supported with *episodic* evidence pertaining to individual cases or experiences.[13]

These three features—refutation and references to statistical or episodic evidence—have been shown to affect the strength of messages on different issues in various ways; the precise impact of each may depend on other characteristics of the news story and of the particular issue under consideration (see O'Keefe, 1999, 2002). Experimental research on how these semantic or rhetorical features affect framing is needed if we are to isolate effects.[14]

A final aspect of the frames we coded was whether, in the case of multiple frames, the frames were presented *simultaneously* (i.e., both frames were raised at the same point in the articles and discussed in conjunction with each other), or *sequentially* (i.e., multiple frames were presented one after the other without overlap). An example of simultaneous presentation would be: "The proposed KKK rally raises conflicts between concerns for free speech and public safety. Free speech advocates defend the rally on First Amendment grounds, while opponents of the rally argue that the threat of violence should take priority over free speech." Sequential presentation would be: "The proposed KKK rally has elicited a range of reactions. Some commentators have argued that the rally falls squarely within the scope of the First Amendment. Critics emphasize the threats to public safety that are posed by the rally." Such juxtaposition of frames is worth exploring because it may affect how people process information, as individuals typically have less difficulty understanding sequential presentations (e.g., Rahn, Aldrich, & Borgida, 1994).

RESULTS

As mentioned, most studies of media frames focus on the frequencies with which different frames appear. This is certainly important information and we report these frequencies for each issue in tables that appear in Appendix 13.2. The tables show that, across issues, some frames rarely appear whereas others are used with great frequency. While there are some interesting trends on specific issues, we focus on four dimensions of media framing that typically get little or no attention. These include (1) assessing the number of different frames in the news environment, (2) the direction of those frames relative to the issue, (3) over-time changes in number and direction, and (4) the juxtaposition of frames in media coverage.

Table 13.2 reports the number of articles coded for each issue (recall that for several issues, random samples were drawn), the total number of frames identified across all articles, and the

TABLE 13.2
Number and Direction of Frames

Issue or Event	Number of articles coded	Total frames identified	Average number of frames per article (std. dev.)	Total effective number of frames	Frame direction (% Pro minus % Con)	Over time change in effective no. of frames (Time 2 no. minus Time 1 no.)	Over time change in frame direction (Time 2% minus Time 1%)
Patriot Act	122	279	2.29 (1.50)	5.76	-10.55%	0.21	-62.75%
Global warming	82	175	2.13 (1.18)	4.96	-4.00%	-0.44	-29.29%
Intelligent design	58	115	1.98 (1.78)	4.6	-87.83%	-0.43	-14.63%
Same-sex marriage in U.S.	139	251	1.81 (1.40)	5.41	-18.37%	1.53	19.48%
Same-sex marriage in Canada	139	388	2.79 (1.78)	6.19	-14.43%	-0.03	-32.99%
Social Security 1	40	97	2.43 (1.20)	5.37	-4.17%	-1.74	-5.50%
Social Security 2	92	204	2.22 (2.26)	5.84	-43.84%	1.6	21.00%
Bush v. Gore	134	261	1.95 (1.55)	5.51	2.70%	-0.38	-38.49%
Abu Ghraib controversy	159	286	1.81 (1.36)	6.9	-68.31%	-1.44	-4.43%
California immigration initiative (Prop. 187)	80	183	2.29 (1.50)	6.74	-86.44%	-2.21	-14.63%
Nazi rally	36	64	1.78 (1.04)	3.52	-41.94%	0.11	-21.54%
Penn. Ku Klux Klan rally	23	26	1.13 (0.69)	3.22	-100.00%	-1.27	0.00%
Tenn. Ku Klux Klan rally	29	43	1.48 (0.87)	3.03	-95.35%	-1.58	50.00%
Illinois casino proposal	20	29	1.45 (0.89)	4.25		-0.74	
Total/average across issues	1153	2401	1.97 (0.42)	5.09 (1.19)	-44.04%	-0.49	-10.29%

average number of frames per article. Overall, 1,153 articles were coded and 2,401 total frames identified. Across all issues, the average article contained nearly two frames, a reality at odds with the typical experimental manipulation using single-frame stories or reports. There is some variance in frames per article across issues; of note is that stories about same-sex marriage in the U.S. contained an average of 1.81 frames per article while, in the *Globe and Mail*, they contained 2.79. It is unclear whether these differences reflect differences in the nature of media reporting across news sources (i.e., the *New York Times* versus the *Globe and Mail*) or variation in the substance of the issue in the two countries. Table 13.3 shows more clearly the distribution of frames by article. Over 35% of the articles contained more than two frames, contrasting even more sharply with current experimental designs.

Aside from the number of frames in each article, we were interested in the total number of frames that were discussed regularly—that is, the number that set the terms of the debate. As mentioned, experimental work on framing typically assumes that one or, at most, two frames inform debate in any given news story. To assess the extent to which this deviates from actual media coverage, we calculated the "effective number" of frames per issue based on the number of unique frames appearing in news stories and the relative frequency with which each frame is used. Our specific measure used for this purpose borrows from Laakso and Taagepera's (1979) measure of the effective number of parties (also see Rae, 1971). Specifically, if there are T unique frames on an issue and p_i ($i = 1$ to T) is the proportion of times that frame i is used relative to other frames, then the effective number of frames can be expressed as $N_F = 1/\Sigma p^2_i$. This approach assigns a weight to each frame based on its relative frequency of use. For example, if two frames appeared in equal proportion, the index would generate two effective frames. If instead, one of the frames occurs two-thirds of the time and the other one-third of the time, the index computes 1.84 effective frames.[15] This number therefore reflects the actual number of frames that are salient in the debate.

The effective number of frames for each issue appears in the fifth column of Table 13.2. Without exception, the effective number of frames used in the discussion of the issue substantially exceeds 1 or 2, and in some cases, approaches 7. Clearly, this stands in sharp contrast to the controlled experimental environment in which there is a focus on just one or two frames. In reality, audiences are exposed *to multiple frames per article and to an even greater number of distinct frames across a series of articles*. How individuals deal with this large mix of frames when forming opinions is unclear and demands further study.

The large number of effective frames undoubtedly reflects each side of an issue putting forth various alternative ways of defining the issue. As mentioned, some scholars suggest that competition between frames will be balanced and, therefore, neither side will gain a significant advantage (e.g., Jackman & Sniderman, 2006; Sniderman & Theriault, 2004; Wittman, 1995).

TABLE 13.3
Frame Frequencies in Articles

Number of frames	Article frequency	Percentage of articles
0	153	13%
1	306	27%
2	285	25%
3	223	19%
4 or more	186	16%
Total	1,153	100%

There are two meanings of balance here: balance in the relative strength of opposing frames, and balance in the relative frequency of opposing frames. The relative strengths of the frames identified for the various issues we analyzed will have to be assessed in a subsequent study, so we cannot say whether opposing sides on these issues employed equally strong frames. But we can determine whether directional balance occurs because we coded the direction of each frame used in the article. In essence, we can evaluate Zaller's (1996, p. 20) claim that because "the mass media routinely carry competing political messages . . . members of the public who are heavily exposed to one message tend to be heavily exposed to its opposite as well."[16]

To assess this proposition, we computed the percentage of frames used in a pro direction and the percentage used in a con direction (with pro and con defined relative to the attitude of interest for each issue in Table 13.1). We then subtracted the percentage con from the percentage pro to yield an overall measure of directional bias; for example, if the number of pro and con frames were identical (i.e., balanced), the result would be 0. If con frames exceeded pro frames, the percentage would be negative. The results, reported in the sixth column of Table 13.2, reveal a stark negative bias. In only three cases (global warming, Social Security phase I, and *Bush v. Gore*) is the index within 5% on either side of 0, which can be regarded as roughly balanced coverage. However, *balance is not the norm*: on average, negative frames greatly exceeded positive frames by 44%. The largest negative biases emerge on the trio of right-wing rallies (which overall show similar trends with one another), immigration, intelligent design, Abu Ghraib, and Social Security phase II. Moderate negative biases (between −10% and −20%) occurred in coverage of the renewal of the Patriot Act and same-sex marriage in both the United States and Canada.

While these results are consistent with the general *negativity bias* noted in other realms of political discussion (e.g., Geer, 2006; Lau, 1989), an equally compelling possibility is that it reflects the *dominance of liberal frames* expressed in opposition to the KKK and Nazis, teaching intelligent design in public schools, denying illegal immigrants access to public benefits under Proposition 187, the government and military's treatment of prisoners in Abu Ghraib, and the privatization of Social Security (see Entman, 2007, on using frames to study media bias).

One final point revealed by these data is how an issue can change over time. In the case of Social Security, our second time period (2004–2005) displayed much greater negativity than the first (1997–2000). To capture potential changes of coverage corresponding to changes in the salience of the issue, we analyzed the number and direction of frames before and after the midpoint in the time series on each issue. We computed the effective number of frames and the directional bias of frames for each time period and then calculated the difference between times 1 and 2. Negative numbers thus reflect shrinkage in the number of frames and a change in directional bias in a negative direction.

The seventh column of Table 13.2 indicates that the number of effective frames declines over time, on average dropping by nearly half of a frame per story. There are exceptions, as in the case of same-sex marriage in the U.S. and Social Security (from 2004–2005), but there appears to be a general tendency over time toward reduction in the number of effective frames. This presumably reflects a process where opposing sides on an issue, after learning which frames resonate best with the public, choose to promote those frames and cause them to dominate media coverage.

There is a similar trend over time in the directional bias of media coverage. Although there are some exceptions, the evidence shows a general movement toward increasingly negative coverage, with the average issue exhibiting 10% more negativity later in the issue cycle compared to earlier. These over-time trends provide guidance as scholars begin to explore over-time effects. As mentioned, with few exceptions, this is an unexplored area. The results of this analysis suggest that further research in this area should look at how *over-time trends in the number and balance of frames* affects public opinion.

Our final set of coding categories concerns specific features of the frames. Frames were mentioned and refuted 13% (314/2,380) of the time; statistics were cited 7% (168/2,374) of the time; and episodic references to personal examples were included 13% (312/2,372) of the time.[17] As explained, several of these characteristics could influence the applicability of a frame and warrant further study of framing effects on public opinion, despite the limited appearance of these features in the issues included in this investigation.

Finally, we coded how frames appear in relation to one another in the context of a news report (i.e., simultaneously or sequentially with another frame). A frame is *simultaneous* with another if the two frames are conjoined in the text with no clear division. Frames are *sequential* if they appear in succession in the text without being explicitly connected.[18] Both simultaneous and sequential frames appeared regularly in news articles: 46% (1,089/2,356) of frames appeared simultaneously with another frame, and 40% (936/2,349) of frames were presented sequentially to one another.

CONCLUSION

A realistic study of opinion formation during political campaigns needs to first develop a conceptual framework for characterizing the context in which opinions are formed (Druckman & Lupia, 2005). With this goal in mind, we outlined in this chapter a methodology for content analyzing media frames of political issues that takes account of the substance, competitive balance, and interaction of media frames during periods when issues are salient on the public agenda. Our results suggest that studies of media frames should pay greater attention to the variety of competitive contexts in which the public receives information. We found that in the life cycle of a salient political issue, each side uses many frames to advance its position. There are varying degrees of direct engagement between opposing arguments, and media coverage rarely presents balanced coverage of each side's frames. Because news stories typically contain *more* than one or two effective frames, readers rarely encounter a scenario—common in experimental studies— in which they are restricted to a single monolithic frame of the issue. Thus, framing effects that occur outside controlled experimental settings are not well understood.

We suggest that the next step in this program of research should be to empirically examine how these additional features of media frames affect public opinion. This research agenda is consistent with a large literature on decision-making that shows the influence of context on how the public processes information (e.g., Payne, Bettman, & Johnson, 1993; see also Mueller, 1973; Zaller, 1992). Our own experimental research has found that direct competition between frames increases the motivation of individuals to assess the strength or applicability of frames. The limited scope of our experiments, however, did not permit us to explore which other aspects of media coverage may make a frame more or less persuasive. Future studies, therefore, should examine the impact of exposure to more realistic news scenarios to understand how the relative balance and interaction of multiple frames over time affect their availability, accessibility, and applicability in public opinion.

APPENDIX 13.1

INTELLIGENT DESIGN FRAMES

Intelligent Design (ID)

This page reports the set of "intelligent design" frames. The specific frames are in **bold** with representative quotes/examples following. In some cases a given example would be coded as including multiple frames. This is explained in the examples. In many cases, frames may be invoked simultaneously.

These examples are not exhaustive—a frame can be invoked using related language. Also recall that frames can be added and/or merged if your coding experience suggests doing so.

Positions

Pro = Support the right to teach intelligent design in school and/or support intelligent design as a viable alternative to evolution.

Con = Oppose the right to teach intelligent design in school and/or oppose intelligent design as a viable alternative to evolution.

Note that "science" will be commonly invoked with all the frames. We have a "scientific theory" frame that refers specifically to the substance of science (i.e., a scientific theory) and/or scientists; this would not *include teaching science, education science standards, or vague references to science.*

Education/teaching—ID is about the appropriate way to educate/teach and decisions about ID revolve around what one thinks of education.

- Supporters of ID have had an insidious influence on the teaching of science in local schools.
- Voters came to their senses in voting out school board members opposed to the teaching of evolution.
- School boards have gutted science standards.
- Teaching ID is a matter of academic freedom.

Scientific theory/scientists—ID is about science and what appropriate scientific theory is. Often science and culture will be invoked simultaneously. This can be done by proponents saying ID is valid science even if it is consistent with religion, or opponents saying ID is not valid science and it is just religion. Code for both frames if both are invoked.

- Intelligent design is "supernatural science."
- Only a tiny minority of scientists support ID.
- *[ID is a religious belief,]* masquerading as science—*the bracketed part invokes a culture/religion frame. Thus, this sentence would be coded as two frames.*
- *[ID is a cultural issue,]* not a scientific one—*the bracketed part invokes a culture/religion frame. Thus, this sentence would be coded as two frames.*
- *[Attacks on intelligent design are veiled cultural attacks against religion—part of a move to devalue the beliefs of religious people in this country]; therefore defense of ID as a scientific theory is needed to defend religious believers in this country—the bracketed portion invokes a culture/religion frame. Thus, this sentence would be coded as two frames.*
- Scientific arguments for evolution cannot resolve a debate between *[opposing sides in a cultural debate.]—the bracketed part invokes a culture/religion frame. Thus, this sentence would be coded as two frames.*

Culture/Religion—ID is a cultural or religious issue. Often science and culture will be invoked simultaneously. This can be done by proponents saying ID is valid science even if it is consistent with religion, or opponents saying ID is not valid science and that it is just religion. Code for both frames if both are invoked.

- ID is a religious belief, *[masquerading as science]—the bracketed part invokes a scientific theory frame. Thus, this sentence would be coded as two frames.*
- ID is a cultural issue, *[not a scientific one]—the bracketed part invokes a scientific theory frame. Thus, this sentence would be coded as two frames.*
- ID is part of the cluster of issues including anti-abortion, anti gay rights, Christian symbols.
- One cannot present a religious viewpoint as the other side in a debate with evolution.
- Attacks on intelligent design are veiled cultural attacks against religion—part of a move to devalue the beliefs of religious people in this country; *[therefore defense of ID as a scientific theory is needed to defend religious believers in this country.]—the bracketed part invokes a scientific theory frame. Thus, this sentence would be coded as two frames.*
- *[Scientific arguments for evolution cannot resolve a debate between]* opposing sides in a cultural debate—*the bracketed part invokes a scientific theory frame. Thus, this sentence would be coded as two frames.*

Tolerance/Free Speech—ID is about the right to speak freely and be tolerant of other views, and/or about censorship. If there is a discussion of religious intolerance, code as both tolerance and culture/religion.

- Opponents of ID are fanning the flames of intolerance.
- Opposition to discussing ID amounts to a suppression of free speech (Discovery Institute frame).
- Both sides ought to be taught (George W. Bush frame). People should be exposed to different ideas.
- Defense of ID is a defense of freedom of inquiry and free speech, given the attacks on scientists who experience recriminations for departing from Darwinian orthodoxy.
- The influence of ID has been achieved through back-door pressure on textbook publishers, resulting in censorship of references to evolution in textbooks.

Other Frame—portraying the issue in terms that that do not fit into one of the other frames.

APPENDIX 13.2

FRAMES AND FRAME FREQUENCIES[a]

Patriot Act	Number	Percentage
Civil liberties	74	26.52%
Terrorism	65	23.30%
Implementation/process	28	10.04%
Enactment/renewal	18	6.45%
Politics	37	13.26%
Ambivalence/balance	6	2.15%
Expanded/excessive government power	36	12.90%
Other	15	5.38%
Total	279	100%

Global warming		
Environmental problems/evidence of specific environmental problems	41	23.43%
Health/human rights	15	8.57%
Economy	28	16.00%

Global warming (cont.)	Number	Percentage
Treaties/rules to control global warming	55	31.43%
Ethics	10	5.71%
Market	19	10.86%
Other	7	4.0%
Total	175	100%

Intelligent design		
Education/teaching	20	17.39%
Scientific theory/scientists	41	35.65%
Culture/religion	28	24.35%
Tolerance/free speech	3	2.61%
Other	23	20.00%
Total	115	100%

Same-sex marriage in the U.S.		
Equal/civil rights	36	14.34%
Freedom/tolerance	21	8.37%
Special rights	5	1.99%
Religious/cultural values	28	11.16%
Family	32	12.75%
Business	5	1.99%
Politics/strategy	77	30.68%
Federalism	46	18.33%
Other	1	0.40%
Total	251	100%

Same-sex marriage in Canada	Number	Percentage
Equal/civil rights	62	15.98%
Freedom/tolerance	5	1.29%
Special rights	1	0.26%
Religious/cultural values	89	22.94%
Family	55	14.18%
Politics/strategy	95	24.48%
Federalism	10	2.58%
Anti-U.S.	7	1.80%
Human rights	12	3.09%
Other	52	15.00%
Total	388	100%

Social Security I		
Beneficiary/victim	14	14.43%
Security (in old age)	6	6.19%
Individual choice	9	9.28%
Outcome (results of radical change, results of no change, sustainability)	15	15.46%
Political strategy	26	26.80%
Exaggeration/real problem	3	3.09%
Forecasting	23	23.71%
Other	1	1.03%
Total	97	100%

Social Security II	Number	Percentage
Beneficiary/victim	32	15.69%
Security (in old age)	25	12.25%
Individual choice	22	10.78%
Outcome (results of radical change, results of no change, sustainability)	54	26.47%
Political strategy	40	19.61%
Fairness/equality	6	2.94%
Exaggeration/real problem	21	10.29%
Other	4	1.96%
Total	204	100%

Bush v. Gore	Number	Percentage
Expected winner	32	12.26%
Electoral system	4	1.53%
Democratic process	33	12.64%
Constitution/court	52	19.92%
Political motives	36	13.79%
Framing political motives	3	1.15%
International repercussions	3	1.15%
Election equipment/counting	78	29.89%
Specific voter groups	5	1.92%
Federalism/states rights	10	3.83%
Other	5	1.92%
Total	261	100%

Abu Ghraib controversy	Number	Percentage
Military responsibility	47	16.43%
Administration responsibility	52	18.18%
Individual responsibility	53	18.53%
Military commander responsibility	53	18.53%
Other responsibility	5	1.75%
Negative international relations consequences	29	10.14%
Positive international relations consequences	5	1.75%
Negative domestic consequences	8	2.80%
Positive domestic consequences	1	0.35%
Justification	19	6.64%
Other	14	4.90%
Total	286	100%

California immigration initiative (Prop. 187)[b]	Number	Percentage
Democratic process	14	7.65%
Political strategy	24	13.11%
Characterizations of the illegal immigrant	10	5.46%
Causes of the increasing number of illegal immigrants	7	3.83%
Effectiveness of measures to deter illegal immigration	13	7.10%
Legality of 187's provisions	33	18.03%
Consequences	50	27.32%
Legal vs. illegal immigrants	8	4.37%
Police state/excessive state authority	15	8.20%
Other	9	4.92%
Total	183	100%

Nazi rally	*Number*	*Percentage*
Public safety	23	35.94%
Free speech	21	32.81%
Broader implications (e.g., of not allowing the rally)	4	6.25%
Reputation	3	4.69%
Opposing racism and prejudice	13	20.31%
Total	64	100%

Pennsylvania KKK rally		
Public safety	5	19.23%
Free speech	4	15.38%
Opposing racism and prejudice	13	50.00%
Other	4	15.38%
Total	26	100%

Tennessee KKK rally		
Public safety	22	51.16%
Free speech	9	20.93%
Broader implications (e.g., of not allowing the rally)	2	4.65%
Reputation	4	9.30%
Opposing racism and prejudice	5	11.63%
Other	1	2.33%
Total	43	100%

Illinois casino proposal		
Public schools/education	9	31.03%
Tax relief	10	34.48%
Job creation	3	10.34%
Economic development help	2	6.90%
Other budgetary relief from casino	1	3.45%
Social costs (addiction, suicide, family impact)	1	3.45%
Effects on poor	1	3.45%
Need for other political support (from state legislature and/or Mayor Daley)	1	3.45%
Other	1	3.45%
Total	29	100%

[a] We only list frames that appeared at least once in the coverage. We coded for some other frames that were never invoked (e.g., reputation in the Pennsylvania KKK rally).

[b] Much of the debate about Prop. 187 revolved around race and economics. References to race and/or economics occur with various different frames. We thus coded, along with each specific frame, whether there was a reference to race and/or economics. These data are available from the authors.

APPENDIX 13.3

CODING RELIABILITY

We assessed the reliability of our coding by taking a random sample of 25% of the articles for each issue. A separate trained coder then coded the subsample and we compared the results between this reliability coder and the main coders. Our key variables denote the absence or presence of a frame in a given article, and the position taken by a given frame. Since both of these variables are nominal, the appropriate reliability statistics are the percentage agreement between the two coders and the percentage of agreement correcting for the possibility of agreement by chance. To account for chance agreement, we used the Kappa statistic. In a given article (e.g., on the Patriot Act), we analyzed whether the two coders agreed on the presence or absence of each frame (e.g., civil liberties). Kappa corrects for the fact that the coders would sometimes arrive at the same coding decision by chance (especially since they only have two options: present or absent). Then, for each frame that is present, we examined agreement between the coders on the positional direction of the frame (i.e., whether it was pro or con).

Overall, we find that our data are reliable with frame percentage agreement of 93% and a Kappa of .80 (standard error = .02).[19] Our percentage agreement and Kappa for frame direction are, respectively, 91% and .88 (.03). These statistics meet or exceed typical standards of reliability (see, e.g., Neuendorf, 2001, p. 143; Riffe, Lacy, & Fico 1998, p. 131). The specific reliability statistics for each issue appear in the table below. (We merge the three hate group rallies, each of which had the same set of frames, so as to increase the number of cases). In all cases, the Kappas are highly significant with $p \leq .01$ for two-tailed tests. Note that the Kappa values are considerably lower on average than the percent agreement.

Our reliability statistics for the other measures—including refutation, statistics, and episodes—are just as high, with respective Kappas of .95 (.08), .84 (.11), and .86 (.07). The simultaneous and sequential coding was less reliable with respective Kappas of .71 (.13) and .67 (.15).

Issue or event	Presence of frame: Percent agreement	Presence of frame: Kappa	Direction: Percent agreement (std. error)	Direction: Kappa (std. error)
Patriot Act	93%	.84 (.07)	93%	.91 (.07)
Global warming	94%	.85 (.08)	94%	.90 (.12)
Intelligent design	96%	.91 (.14)	100%	1.00 (.15)
Same-sex marriage in the U.S.	95%	.84 (.07)	86%	.82 (.10)
Same-sex marriage in Canada	93%	.78 (.05)	96%	.95 (.07)
Social Security I	89%	.76 (.12)	86%	.79 (.16)
Social Security II	95%	.78 (.09)	88%	.84 (.13)
Bush v. Gore	92%	.72 (.05)	95%	.83 (.09)
Abu Ghraib controversy	92%	.73 (.05)	89%	.85 (.08)
California immigration initiative (Prop. 187)	95%	.86 (.07)	73%	.62 (.08)
Hate group rallies	92%	.79 (.10)	100%	1.00 (.22)
Casino proposal	93%	.84 (.15)	92%	.81 (.20)
Total across issues	93%	.80 (.02)	91%	.88 (.03)

NOTES

1. Parts of this section come from Chong and Druckman (2007c).
2. This conceptualization can apply to any object of evaluation, including candidates as well as attributions of responsibility (see Chong & Druckman, 2007a, for a discussion). Also, without loss of generality, we can think of i as a dimension (Riker, 1990), a consideration (Zaller, 1992), a value (Sniderman, 1993), or a belief (Ajzen& Fishbein, 1980).
3. de Vreese et al. (2001, pp. 108–109; 2004) distinguish issue-specific from generic frames. The former pertain to "specific topics or news events [while the latter are] broadly applicable to a range of different news topics, some even over time, and potentially, in different cultural contexts." Examples of generic frames include episodic and thematic frames, conflict frames, or strategic frames. We agree that some frames apply across

issues and are more general descriptions of news; however, we prefer to link a frame explicitly to an issue and an evaluation (also see Entman, 2004). This obviates the need to specify when a frame is sufficiently general to be classified as generic. For example, is an economic frame a generic frame? De Vreese et al. (2001) suggest it is, but it also serves as a specific issue frame for welfare reform, according to Shen and Edwards (2005). Also, if there is a feature in the communication such as conflict that is not connected to an issue and evaluation, we suggest using a term other than frame (Entman suggests "script").

4. Others explore how politicians or the media adopt frames (e.g., Carragee & Roefs, 2004; Druckman, Jacobs, & Ostermeier, 2004; Entman, 2004; Fridkin & Kenney, 2005; Scheufele, 1999, p. 109) or how citizens adopt frames based on discussions with other citizens (e.g., Druckman & Nelson, 2003; Gamson, 1992; Walsh, 2004).

5. See Chong and Druckman (2007a, 2007b) for a discussion of the conditions that stimulate applicability evaluations.

6. Jerit's (2008) research on the debate over passage of the Clinton health care policy is an exception. Jerit examines each side's arguments and the effect on public opinion of proponents' engaging opposition arguments. She finds that engagement appears to increase aggregate public support for the policy. Another exception is Baumgartner et al. (2008), who offer an impressively detailed analysis of death penalty coverage.

7. In our terms, the RAS model largely focuses on accessibility and ignores applicability.

8. Other sources one could use include congressional testimony, presidential statements, interest group statements, campaign advertisements, and so on. We obviously endorse the use of multiple sources (and comparisons between them), with the rationale of maximizing ecological validity (i.e., what the information environment actually looks like), whether from elite- or to citizen-based discourse. Woolley (2000) suggests that different media lead to very different portrayals of coverage; but given our focus on the dynamics of coverage (e.g., presence, absence, over-time sequence of multiple frames) rather than the actual percentages of specific frame use, we suspect the *New York Times* will provide a fairly accurate picture of general media dynamics along these lines.

9. See Althaus, Edy, and Phalen (2001) and Edy, Althaus, and Phalen (2005) on using news abstracts.

10. We monitor coverage of Proposition 187 through the *San Francisco Chronicle* rather than the *Los Angeles Times* because the latter is not available on major databases.

11. Given the size and capacities of our coding team, we drew samples for any issue on which we found substantially more than 150 articles. The analysis excluded letters to the editor.

12. For example, in our analysis of proposals for reforming Social Security between 1997 and 2000, coders regularly encountered discussion of how evaluations of reform proposals depend on uncertain future forecasts; therefore, we added a forecasting frame to the initial set of frames.

13. This is related to but distinct from Iyengar's (1991) purely episodic or thematic frames; for us, these are specific aspects or subdimensions of issue frames.

14. For this project, we also coded for various items that we do not analyze here. We recorded the identity of any source cited or quoted in connection with the frame, because credible sources can increase the applicability of a frame. (We do not analyze this code here because we are continuing to work on its operationalization.) Additionally, we recorded whether a given frame was "primary," meaning that it was the most prominent in the article (e.g., received the most space), or "secondary," meaning it was mentioned more in passing (a frame could only be secondary if there was another frame that was primary). We also coded whether the article, overall, was pro or con (regardless of the frames), and whether a frame was evident in the title of the article. Coders also estimated the percentage of the article that was "unframed." Non-framed material included transitions, facts, background material, and general text that did not put forth one of the frames.

We considered including other message factors, but additional story features either did not clearly apply to specific frames (e.g., fear appeals may appear in news stories but did not seem to occur as parts of frames *per se*) or did not surface in our preliminary assessments.

15. The index is a variation of the Herfindahl–Hirschman concentration index, which is simply $\Sigma p2i$. While some have suggested alternative weighting schemes (e.g., Molinar, 1991), this is clearly the most accepted index (see, e.g., Lijphart, 1994).

16. Jackman and Sniderman (2006, p. 272) make an analogous claim about the balance of frame quality,

stating that a "commonly satisfied" condition in politics is that "arguments on opposing sides of an issue are of equal quality" (also see Brewer & Gross, 2005; Hansen, 2007; Sniderman & Theriault, 2004).

17. Most but not all coders recorded these features; thus, our number of observations is lower here.
18. An example of simultaneous frames, on the intelligent design issue, would be a sentence such as "Intelligent design is a religious belief, masquerading as science." This frames the issue in terms of culture/religion and science. It would be sequential if the article presented religious and scientific portrayals completely separately (e.g., in distinct paragraphs with no mixing).
19. In checking reliability, we excluded "other" frames.

REFERENCES

Ajzen, I., & Fishbein, M. (1980). *Understanding attitudes and predicting social behavior.* Englewood Cliffs, NJ: Prentice-Hall.

Althaus, S., Edy, J. A., & Phalen, P. (2001). Differences in knowledge acquisition among readers of the paper and online versions of a national newspaper. *Journalism & Mass Communication Quarterly, 77*(3), 457–479.

Arceneaux, K. (2008). *Cognitive biases and the strength of political arguments.* Unpublished manuscript. Temple University, Philadelphia PA.

Arnold, R. D., Graetz, M. J., & Munnell, A. H. (1998). *Framing the Social Security debate: Values, politics, and economics.* Washington, DC: National Academy of Social Insurance Conference.

Bartels, L. M. (2005). Homer gets a tax cut: Inequality and public policy in the American mind. *Perspectives on Politics, 3*(1), 15–31.

Baumgartner, F. R., De Boef, S. L., & Boydstun, A. E. (2008). *The decline of the death penalty and the discovery of innocence.* New York: Cambridge University Press.

Berinsky, A. J., & Kinder, D. R. (2006). Making sense of issues through media frames: Understanding the Kosovo crisis. *Journal of Politics, 68*(3), 640–656.

Boydstun, A. E. (2006). Agenda-setting and issue-framing dynamics in front-page news. Paper presented at the annual meeting of the American Political Science Association, Philadelphia, PA.

Brewer, P. R. (2003). Values, political knowledge, and public opinion about gay rights. *Public Opinion Quarterly, 67*(2), 173–201.

Brewer, P. R., Graf, J., & Willnat, L. (2003). Priming or framing: Media influence on attitudes toward foreign countries. *International Journal for Communication Studies, 65*(6), 493–508.

Brewer, P. R., & Gross, K. (2005). Values, framing, and citizens' thoughts about policy issues: Effects on content and quantity. *Political Psychology, 26*(6), 929–948.

Brewer, P. R., & Sigelman, L. (2002). Political scientists as color commentators: Framing and expert commentary in media campaign coverage. *Harvard International Journal of Press/Politics, 7*(1), 23–35.

Cappella, J. N., & Jamieson, K. H. (1997). *Spiral of cynicism: The press and the public good.* New York: Oxford University Press.

Carmines, E. G., & Layman, G. C. (1997). Issue evolution in postwar American politics: Old certainties and fresh tensions. In B. E. Shafer (Ed.), *Present discontents: American politics in the very late twentieth century* (pp. 89–134). Chatham, NJ: Chatham House Publishers.

Carragee, K. M., & Roefs, W. (2004). The neglect of power in recent framing research. *Journal of Communication, 54*(2), 214–233.

Chong, D. (2006). Free speech and multiculturalism in and out of the academy. *Political Psychology, 27*(1), 29–54.

Chong, D., & Druckman, J. N. (2007a). A theory of framing and opinion formation in competitive elite environments. *Journal of Communication, 57*(1), 99–118.

Chong, D., & Druckman, J. N. (2007b). Framing public opinion in competitive democracies. *American Political Science Review, 101*(4), 637–655.

Chong, D., & Druckman, J. N. (2007c). Framing theory. *Annual Review of Political Science, 10*(1), 103–126.

Chong, D., & Druckman, J. N. (in press). Dynamic public opinion. Communication effects over time. *American Political Science Review*.

Cook, F. L. (2005). Navigating pension policy in the United States: From the politics of consensus to the politics of dissensus about Social Security. *Tocqueville Review, 26*(2), 37–66.

de Vreese, C. H. (2004). Primed by the Euro: The impact of a referendum campaign on public opinion and evaluations of government and political leaders. *Scandinavian Political Studies 27*(1), 45–65.

de Vreese, C. H. (2005). News framing: Theory and typology. *Information Design Journal, 13*, 51–62.

de Vreese, C. H., Peter, J., & Semetko, H. A. (2001). Framing politics at the launch of the euro: A cross-national comparative study of frames in the news. *Political Communication, 18*(2), 107–122.

Delgado, R. (1982). Words that wound: A tort action for racial insults, epithets and name calling. *Harvard Civil Rights-Civil Liberties Law Review, 17*, 133–181.

Delgado, R. (1991). Campus antiracism rules: Constitutional narratives in collision. *Northwestern University Law Review, 85*(2), 343–387.

Dimitrova, D. V., Kaid, L. L., Williams, A. P., & Trammell, K. D. (2005). War on the Web: The immediate news framing of Gulf War II. *Harvard International Journal of Press/Politics, 10*(1), 22–44.

Domke, D., Shah, D. V., & Wackman, D. B. (1998). "Moral referendums": Values, news media, and the process of candidate choice. *Political Communication, 15*, 301–321.

Downs, A. (1972). Up and down with ecology: The issue-attention cycle. *The Public Interest, 28*, 38–50.

Druckman, J. N. (2001). The implications of framing effects for citizen competence. *Political Behavior, 23*(3), 225–256.

Druckman, J. N., Jacobs, L. R., & Ostermeier, E. (2004). Candidate strategies to prime issues and image. *Journal of Politics, 66*(4), 1205–1227.

Druckman, J. N., & Lupia, A. (2005). Mind, will, and choice: Lessons from experiments in contextual variation. In C. Tilly & R. E. Goodin (Eds.), *The Oxford handbook on contextual political analysis* (pp. 97–113). Oxford University Press.

Druckman, J. N., & Nelson, K. R. (2003). Framing and deliberation: How citizens' conversations limit elite influence. *American Journal of Political Science, 47*(4), 729–745.

Eagly, A. H., & Chaiken, S. (1993). *The psychology of attitudes*. Fort Worth: Harcourt Brace Jovanovich College Publishers.

Edy, J. A., Althaus, S., & Phalen, P. (2005). Using news abstracts to represent news agendas. *Journalism & Mass Communication Quarterly, 82*(2), 434–446.

Edy, J. A., & Meirick, P. C. (2007). Wanted, dead or alive: Media frames, frame adoption, and support for the war in Afghanistan. *Journal of Communication, 57*, 119–141.

Entman, R. M. (2004). *Projections of power: Framing news, public opinion, and U.S. foreign policy*. Chicago: University of Chicago Press.

Entman, R. M. (2007). Framing bias: Media in the distribution of power. *Journal of Communication, 57*(1), 163–173.

Feldman, S., & Zaller, J. (1992). The political culture of ambivalence: Ideological responses to the welfare state. *American Journal of Political Science, 36*(1), 268–307.

Fridkin, K. L., & Kenney, P. J. (2005). Campaign frames: Can candidates influence media coverage? In K. Callaghan & F. Schnell (Eds.), *Framing American politics* (pp. 54–75). Pittsburgh, PA: University of Pittsburgh Press.

Gamson, W. A. (1992). *Talking politics*. New York: Cambridge University Press.

Gamson, W. A., & Modigliani, A. (1987). The changing culture of affirmative action. In R. Braungart (Ed.), *Research in political sociology* (Vol. 3, pp. 137–177). Greenwich: JAI Press.

Gamson, W. A., & Modigliani, A. (1989). Media discourse and public opinion on nuclear power: A constructionist approach. *American Journal of Sociology, 95*(1), 1–37.

Geer, J. G. (2006). *In defense of negativity: Attack ads in presidential campaigns*. Chicago: University of Chicago Press.

Gershkoff, A., & Kushner, S. (2005). Shaping public opinion: The 9/11-Iraq connection in the Bush administration's rhetoric. *Perspectives on Politics, 3*, 525–537.

Gilens, M. (1999). *Why Americans hate welfare: Race, media, and the politics of antipoverty policy.* Chicago: University of Chicago Press.

Grant, J. T., & Rudolph, T. J. (2003). Value conflict, group affect, and the issue of campaign finance. *American Journal of Political Science, 47*(3), 453–469.

Gross, K., & Goldman, S. (2005). Framing hate: *A comparison of media coverage of anti-gay hate crime in the Washington Post, New York Times and Washington Blade.* Unpublished manuscript. George Washington University, Washington DC.

Hacker, J. S., & Pierson, P. (2005). *Off center: The Republican revolution and the erosion of American democracy.* New Haven: Yale University Press.

Hansen, K. M. (2007). The sophisticated public: The effect of competing frames on public opinion. *Scandinavian Political Studies, 30*(3), 377–396.

Hopkins, D. & King, G. (2007). *Extracting systematic social science meaning from text.* Unpublished manuscript. Center for the Study of American Politics, Yale University, New Haven, CT.

Iyengar, S. (1991). *Is anyone responsible? How television frames political issues.* Chicago: University of Chicago Press.

Iyengar, S., & Kinder, D. R. (1987). *News that matters: Television and American opinion.* Chicago: University of Chicago Press.

Jackman, S., & Sniderman, P. M. (2006). The limits of deliberative discussion: A model of everyday political arguments. *Journal of Politics, 68*(2), 272–283.

Jacoby, W. G. (2000). Issue framing and public opinion on government spending. *American Journal of Political Science, 44*(4), 750–767.

Jerit, J. (2008). Issue framing and engagement: Rhetorical strategy in public policy debates. *Political Behavior, 30*(1), 1–24.

Jones, B. D., & Baumgartner, F. R. (2005). A model of choice for public policy. *Journal of Public Administration Research and Theory, 15*(3), 325–351.

Kellstedt, P. M. (2000). Media framing and the dynamics of racial policy preferences. *American Journal of Political Science, 44*(2), 239–255.

Kellstedt, P. M. (2003). *The mass media and the dynamics of American racial attitudes.* New York: Cambridge University Press.

Kellstedt, P. M. (2005). Media frames, core values, and the dynamics of racial policy preferences. In K. Callaghan & F. Schnell (Eds.), *Framing American politics* (pp. 167–178). Pittsburgh, PA: University of Pittsburgh Press.

Kinder, D. R., & Sanders, L. M. (1996). *Divided by color: Racial politics and democratic ideals.* Chicago: University of Chicago Press.

Laakso, M., & Taagepera, R. (1979). Effective number of parties: A measure with application to West Europe. *Comparative Political Science, 12*(1), 3–27.

Lau, R. R. (1989). Construct accessibility and electoral choice. *Political Behavior, 11*(1), 5–32.

Lawrence, R. G. (2004). Framing obesity: The evolution of news discourse on a public health issue. *Harvard International Journal of Press/Politics, 9*(3), 56–75.

Lijphart, A. (1994). *Electoral systems and party systems: A study of twenty-seven democracies, 1945–1990.* Oxford: Oxford University Press.

MacKinnon, C. A. (1993). *Only words.* Cambridge: Harvard University Press.

Matsuda, M. J. (1989). Public response to racist speech: Considering the victim's story. *Michigan Law Review, 87*(8), 2320–2381.

Messaris, P., & Abraham, L. (2001). The role of images in framing news stories. In S. D. Reese, O. H. Gandy Jr., & A. E. Grant (Eds.), *Framing public life: Perspectives on media and our understanding of the social world* (pp. 215–226). Mahwah, NJ: Lawrence Erlbaum.

Miller, M. M., & Riechert, B. P. (2001). The spiral of opportunity and frame resonance: Mapping the issue cycle in news and public discourse. In S. D. Reese, O. H. Gandy Jr., & A. E. Grant (Eds.), *Framing public life: Perspectives on media and our understanding of the social world* (pp. 107–121). Mahwah, NJ: Lawrence Erlbaum.

Molinar, J. (1991). Counting the number of parties: An alternative index. *American Political Science Review, 85*(4), 1383–1391.

Morowitz, H., Hazen, R., & Trefil, J. (2005, September 2). Intelligent design has no place in the science curriculum. *The Chronicle of Higher Education*, p. B6.

Mueller, J. E. (1973). *War, presidents, and public opinion*. New York: John Wiley & Sons.

Nelson, T. E., & Oxley, Z. M. (1999). Issue framing effects on belief importance and opinion. *Journal of Politics, 61*(4), 1040–1067.

Nelson, T. E., Oxley, Z. M., & Clawson, R. A. (1997). Toward a psychology of framing effects. *Political Behavior, 19*(3), 221–246.

Neuendorf, K. A. (2001). *The content analysis guidebook*. Thousand Oaks: Sage.

Nicholson, S. P., & Howard, R. M. (2003). Framing support for the Supreme Court in the aftermath of *Bush v. Gore. Journal of Politics, 65*(3), 676–695.

Nisbet, M. C., Brossard D., & Kroepsch, A. (2003). Framing science: The stem cell controversy in an age of press/politics. *Harvard International Journal of Press/Politics, 8*(2), 36–70.

O'Keefe, D. J. (1999). How to handle opposing arguments in persuasive messages: A meta-analytic review of the effects of one-sided and two-sided messages. *Communication Yearbook, 22*, 209–249.

O'Keefe, D. J. (2002). *Persuasion: Theory and research*. Thousand Oaks: Sage.

Pan, Z., & Kosicki, G. M. (1997). Talk show exposure as an opinion activity. *Political Communication, 14*(3), 371–388.

Patterson, T. E. (1993). *Out of order*. New York: Alfred A. Knopf.

Payne, J. W., Bettman, J. R., & Johnson, E. J. (1993). *The adaptive decision maker*. New York: Cambridge University Press.

Petersen, M. B. (2008). *Causes of political affect: Investigating the interaction between political cognitions and evolved emotions*. Unpublished manuscript. University of Aarhus, Denmark.

Porto, M. P. (2007). Framing controversies: Television and the 2002 presidential election in Brazil. *Political Communication, 24*(1), 19–36.

Price, V., Nir, L., & Cappella, J. N. (2005). Framing public discussion of gay civil unions. *Public Opinion Quarterly, 69*(2), 179–212.

Price, V., & Tewksbury, D. (1997). News values and public opinion. In G. A. Barnett & F. J. Boster (Eds.), *Progress in communication sciences* (Vol. 13, pp. 173–212). Greenwich, CT: Ablex Publishing Corporation.

Rae, D. W. (1971). *The political consequences of electoral laws*. New Haven: Yale University Press.

Rahn, W. M., Aldrich, J. H, & Borgida, E. (1994). Individual and contextual variations in political candidate appraisal. *American Journal of Political Science, 88*, 193–199.

Richardson, J. D., & Lancendorfer, K. M. (2004). Framing affirmative action: The influence of race on newspaper editorial responses to the University of Michigan cases. *Harvard International Journal of Press/Politics, 9*(4), 74–94.

Riffe, D., Lacy, S., & Fico, F. G. (1998). *Analyzing media messages*. Mahwah, NJ: Lawrence Erlbaum.

Riker, W. H. (1990). Heresthetic and rhetoric in the spatial model. In J. Enelow & M. Hinich (Eds.), *Advances in the spatial theory of voting* (pp. 46–65). Cambridge, MA: Cambridge University Press.

Scheufele, D. A. (1999). Framing as a theory of media effects. *Journal of Communication, 49*(1), 103–122.

Schnell, F., & Callaghan, K. (2005). Terrorism, media frames, and framing effects: A macro- and microlevel analysis. In K. Callaghan & F. Schnell (Eds.), *Framing American politics* (pp. 123–147). Pittsburgh, PA: University of Pittsburgh Press.

Schuck, A. R. T., & de Vreese, C. H. (2006). Between risk and opportunity: News framing and its effects on public support for EU enlargement. *European Journal of Communication, 21*(1), 5–32.

Schudson, M. (1995). *The power of news*. Cambridge, MA: Harvard University Press.

Semetko, H. A., & Valkenburg, P. M. (2000). Framing European politics: A content analysis of press and television news. *Journal of Communication, 50*(2), 93–109.

Shah, D. V., Watts, M. D., Domke, D., & Fan, D. P. (2002). News framing and cueing of issue regimes. *Public Opinion Quarterly, 66*(3), 339–370.

Shen, F., & Edwards, H. H. (2005). Economic individualism, humanitarianism, and welfare reform: A value-based account of framing effects. *Journal of Communication, 55*, 795–809.

Simon, A. F., & Xenos, M. (2004). Dimensional reduction of word-frequency data as a substitute for intersubjective content analysis. *Political Analysis, 12*(1), 63–75.

Sniderman, P. M. (1993). The new look in public opinion research. In A. Finifter (Ed.), *Political science: The state of the discipline* (pp. 219–246). Washington, DC: American Political Science Association.

Sniderman, P. M., & Theriault, S. M. (2004). The structure of political argument and the logic of issue framing. In W. E. Saris & P. M. Sniderman (Eds.), *Studies in public opinion* (pp. 133–165). Princeton, NJ: Princeton University Press.

Tankard Jr., J. W. (2001). The empirical approach to the study of media framing. In S. D. Reese, O. H. Gandy Jr., & A. E. Grant (Eds.), *Framing public life: Perspectives on media and our understanding of the social world* (pp. 95–106). Mahwah, NJ: Lawrence Erlbaum.

Tewksbury, D., Jones, J., Peske, M. W., Raymond, A., & Vig, W. (2000). The interaction of news and advocate frames: Manipulating audience perceptions of a local public policy issue. *Journalism and Mass Communication Quarterly, 77*(4), 804–829.

Tuchman, G. (1978). *Making news: A study in the construction of reality.* New York: Free Press.

Walsh, K. C. (2004). *Talking about politics: Informal groups and social identity in American life.* Chicago: University of Chicago Press.

Wittman, D. A. (1995). *The myth of democratic failure: Why political institutions are efficient.* Chicago: University of Chicago Press.

Woolley, J. T. (2000). Using media-based data in studies of politics. *American Journal of Political Science, 44*, 156–173.

Zaller, J. (1992). *The nature and origins of mass opinion.* New York: Cambridge University Press.

Zaller, J. (1996). The myth of massive media impact revived. In D. C. Mutz, P. M. Sniderman, & R. A. Brody (Eds.), *Political persuasion and attitude change* (pp. 17–78). Ann Arbor, MI: University of Michigan Press.

14

Content Analysis in Political Communication

William L. Benoit
School of Communication Studies
Ohio University

Content analysis is an extremely important method for research into political communication. Although other methods for understanding texts are available—qualitative (see, e.g., Berg, 2006; Creswell, 2007; Denzin & Lincoln, 2005; Lindlof & Taylor, 2002) and critical (see, e.g., Burgchardt, 2005; Foss, 2008; Hart & Daughton, 2005)—content analysis is a means of measuring or quantifying dimensions of the content of messages. Lombard, Snyder-Duch, and Bracken (2002) explain that the method of content analysis "is specifically appropriate and necessary for (arguably) the central work of communication scholars, in particular those who study mass communication: the analysis of messages." In fact, they appropriately observe that this method is "fundamental to communication research (and thus theory)" (p. 587).

Not surprisingly, content analysis has been used widely to describe the content of political communication messages (see, e.g., Benoit, 2007; Kaid & Johnston, 2001). Content analysis is also frequently employed with other methods. For example, the quintessential study of agenda-setting combines content analysis of news media content with surveys of news consumers (see, e.g., McCombs, 2004; McCombs & Shaw, 1972) to investigate relationships between news content and the attitudes of news consumers. The importance of this method to communication theory and research is difficult to underestimate. Furthermore, unlike other research methods, content analysis emerged in the communication discipline (e.g., quantitative research developed largely in agricultural research [Wright, 1921]; much of the early qualitative work was conducted in anthropology and sociology [Vidich & Lyman, 1998]). This chapter will discuss the basics of content analysis—the definition of "content analysis," categories for content analysis, sampling texts, the process of coding, reliability and validity—and then contrast human and computer content analysis.

DEFINITIONS OF "CONTENT ANALYSIS"

Scholars have worked to define this research method for over half a century (for discussions of the history of content analysis, see Krippendorff, 2004; Neuendorf, 2002). I will comment on some of the important definitions in the literature before offering my own contribution. Berelson (1952) stated that "content analysis is a research technique for the objective, systematic, and quantitative description of the manifest content of communication" (p. 18). Content analysis strives for objectivity but practitioners are human beings who attribute meaning to the numbers produced by this process, so I am reluctant to call content analysis objective. Discussions of objectivity in the news (and public journalism) stress the important idea that we can stress objectivity in the *process* independent of the results of that process (see, e.g., Holbert & Zubric, 2000; Westerstahl, 1983).

Another commonly cited definition was proposed by Holsti (1969): "Content analysis is any technique for making inferences by objectively and systematically identifying specified characteristics of messages" (p. 14). Again, objectivity is probably better viewed as a goal than an essential characteristic of this method. Krippendorff (2004) declared that "Content analysis is a research technique for making replicable and valid inferences from texts (or other meaningful matter) to the contexts of their use" (p. 18, emphasis omitted). This definition is important for stressing the context of content analysis. I would also say that, of course, we do not want to report results of invalid content analysis; however, validity is probably best considered to exist on a continuum, which means including validity as part of the definition would require drawing a contrast between valid and invalid inferences. Another perspective on the nature of content analysis is provided by Riffe, Lacy, and Fico (2005, p.25):

> Quantitative content analysis is the systematic and replicable examination of symbols of communication, which have been assigned numeric values according to valid measurement rules and the analysis of relationships involving those values using statistical methods, to describe the communication, draw inferences about its meaning, or infer from the communication to its context, both of production and consumption.

This definition incorporates many of the ideas already mentioned (systematic, replicable, valid, inferences about the context) along with two new ideas. First, they note that "statistical methods" are employed in content analysis. As long as this phrase can include measures of central tendency, such as means, I agree. Much content analysis uses inferential statistics (e.g., tests of difference or association), of course, but I do not believe it is necessary to go beyond descriptive statistics for a study to qualify as content analysis. Their definition also explicitly notes that one can derive inferences about production and consumption (reception) of messages, which is an important observation. Taking these ideas into consideration, I offer the following definition of "content analysis":

> The measurement of dimensions of the content of a message or message in a context. Content analysis can be employed to describe a group of related messages, draw inferences about the sources who produced those messages, or draw inferences about the reception of those messages by their audience.

I take for granted that the process is a systematic research technique and that the researcher strives for objectivity, validity, and reliability. I want to note that content analysis generally can take two broad approaches: classifying texts into a set of two or more categories and rating texts on a scale of, say, 1–7, representing a quality of a text. This chapter focuses on the first approach but I want to acknowledge that content analysis sometimes uses a "rating" approach.

Drawing particularly on the ideas from Krippendorff (2004) and Riffe, Lacy, and Fico (2005), I offer a multidimensional perspective on the role of content analysis of communication (see Figure 14.1). Content analysis quantifies dimensions (variables) of content in message texts.

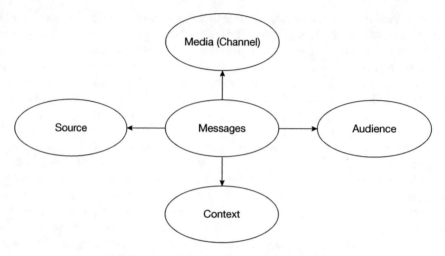

FIGURE 14.1 Content analysis of communication.

Coupled with other data, one can draw various inferences. For example, content analysis of American general election presidential debates according to *topic* (policy, character) shows that 75% of statements concern policy and 25% character. However, if political campaign messages are grouped according to whether their sources are Democrats or Republicans, one can discover that Democrats tend to emphasize policy more (77%, 72%), and character less (23%, 27%), than Republicans.

If the researcher looks at context (and expands the sample to include primary debates), it becomes clear that general election debates in the U.S. discuss policy more (75%, 64%), and character less (28%, 36%), than primary debates. If one looks at media (and constitutes the sample to be American presidential TV spots and debates from the general election campaign), one can see that debates emphasize policy more (75%, 62%), and character less (25%, 38%), than television spots. Finally, if one considers the audience, we learn that candidates who stress policy more, and character less, are more persuasive with voters; that is, they are more likely to win elections (all data from Benoit, 2007). So, content analysis quantifies dimensions of the content of messages. However, when other variables—source, context, media, and audience—are included in the analysis, one can draw other kinds of conclusions from the data created from content analysis.

Content analysis most commonly focuses on verbal elements of messages—words and ideas expressed in words: arguments, claims, themes. This emphasis on analyzing the verbal dimensions of messages is probably in part a matter of convenience: We write (publish) and teach primarily through words. It is telling that we talk about "aids." This phrase suggests that the verbal is primary and visual elements are supplementary ("aids"). Nevertheless, the visual elements of messages, often referred to as images, are important, as are nonverbal sound elements such as music, sound effects, paralanguage. For work on analyzing political images, see Grabe and Bucy (2009), Grabe (1996), Kepplinger (1991), or Kepplinger and Donsbach (1987), as well as Chapter 12, this volume.

CATEGORIES FOR CONTENT ANALYSIS

The categories employed in content analysis are vitally important. Quantitative content analysis requires a set of categories that coders use to assign numeric values to dimensions of messages.

For example, many agenda setting studies (e.g., McCombs, 2004) identify a set of issues—such as employment, education, crime, or taxes—and count the number of times these issues occur in a sample of news stories. The research typically begins by identifying a set of categories to measure the content of messages. These categories should meet three important criteria. Categories for content analysis must be exhaustive, mutually exclusive, and relevant. The categories should be exhaustive so that important parts of the content are not overlooked. Categories should be mutually exclusive so that the part of the text being coded can be placed in only one category (this assumption is particularly important for statistical analysis). Finally, the categories must be relevant to the purpose (research questions or hypotheses) of the study.

Categories can be derived in two ways, deductively or inductively. A researcher may find a set of categories in the literature which are relevant to the study at hand (e.g., Verser & Wicks, 2006). Preferably these categories should be derived from theory, which should help understand the data that arise from application of these categories to texts. However, if no theoretically based categories can be derived, one may rely on categories found in previous research. Both of these approaches are deductive: The researcher begins with a set of categories and applies those categories through content analysis to a group of texts. In contrast, researchers may also develop their own categories inductively. This can be done via a preliminary reading of texts to produce a list of the topics or types of content (categories) found in the text. An alternative approach is to use a systematic approach to generate a list of categories, as with grounded theory. Benoit and McHale (2003) used the method of constant comparison (Glaser & Strauss, 1967) to develop a list of the categories used in presidential television spots to describe candidates' personal qualities. The authors developed a list of four general dimensions (morality, drive, sincerity, and empathy) and generated search terms for each dimension. Once the categories had been developed inductively, computer content analysis was employed to determine the relative frequency of these dimensions. It is also possible to produce categories that are ordinal (e.g., less complex, more complex; less vicious, more vicious), interval (e.g., assign a textual element a value from 1 to 7 to represent degree of quality or beauty), or ratio (e.g., length of message in seconds). Frequency data is probably the most common level of measurement in content analysis.

SAMPLING TEXTS

Content analysis is used to measure dimensions of content of groups of messages, so a study must identify a sample of texts. Scholars list a variety of types of sampling (e.g., Krippendorff, 2004; Riffe, Lacy, & Fico, 2005). Five methods are most commonly distinguished. A census sample includes all members of a population. Given the fact that most populations of texts will in all likelihood continue to accumulate members (e.g., American presidential debates), the best one can usually claim is a census up through the time the sample is collected; relatively few studies use a true or complete census. However, in some cases a census sample is possible (e.g., content analysis of all of the episodes of a television show that has ceased production, such as *The West Wing* or the short-lived drama, *Commander in Chief*, starring Geena Davis).

Arguably one of the most desirable approaches is a random sample of the population. This method of sampling means that one need not analyze every member of the population (a census). Furthermore, because each member of the population by definition has an equal probability of being included in the sample, the conclusions drawn from content analysis of random samples of texts are more likely to generalize to the population than conclusions based on purposive forms of sampling. Ferris and colleagues (2007) developed their sample of reality TV shows in two ways. First, they randomly recorded programming from 18 channels, selecting reality shows from that sample of various types of programming. Second, they randomly sampled additional programs from a sample limited to reality shows. Random samples of texts or shows may be stratified, which means that the population is subdivided into groups and each group (or strata) is randomly sampled. Depending on which strata are selected, stratified random sampling ensures that certain groups within the population are represented in the sample.

One of the most common sampling techniques is the convenience sample, which consists of texts that are easily (conveniently) available to the researcher (e.g., Robertson, et al., 1999). Obviously, one cannot be sure that the conclusions derived from this kind of sample will generalize to the population. Unfortunately, the populations of some kinds of political texts (e.g., mayoral television spots, debates for state representative, face-to-face discussions among citizens) are simply not available for sampling; other populations may be difficult to sample. The argument for convenience samples is that they provide better insights into the communication phenomenon under investigation than no sample. Of course, we must be careful about the conclusions that are drawn from research employing convenience samples.

Another type of sampling, purposive sampling, involves the selection of texts for analysis with a particular goal (purpose) in mind. For example, studies of news might want to focus on the three major broadcast networks—ABC, CBS, and NBC—rather than randomly sample all networks. Similarly, rather than sample all newspapers, or even all newspapers with a national circulation, a study may decide just to study texts from the *New York Times*, arguing that this is the single most influential newspaper.

THE PROCESS OF CODING TEXTS

Once the researcher has a set of categories and a sample of texts, the actual analysis of content can proceed. It is important to develop a codebook, sometimes referred to as protocols, and to train coders in the process of coding. The codebook should specify key concepts, such as the coding unit, which specifies the part of the text to be coded (e.g., words, sentences, paragraphs, camera shot) as well as the context unit, which specifies the larger part of the text used to interpret a given coding unit. The codebook should also describe the process of coding, including what steps to follow when multiple variables are coded, provide definitions and examples of each category, and offer coding rules needed to guide the application of categories to texts from the sample. The codebook must be developed with the research purpose (research questions or hypotheses) in mind. The point of developing the codebook is to specify procedures that will allow the researcher to accomplish the purpose envisioned for the study.

With the coding process now standardized, coders should then be trained and they should practice coding texts similar to those in the sample to make sure they are applying the codebook as the researcher intends. It is possible to train coders using texts from the sample collected for the study, but then the research must decide which coding is "correct" and suitable to use for the data reported in the study; this question does not arise when separate texts are used for training. As any experienced analyst knows, it can be frustrating to have coders analyze texts, check intercoder reliability when they are finished, and discover that they disagree so much that one cannot be confident in the data produced. Although codebooks can be developed to specify the procedures employed in developing a set of categories inductively, they are more commonly used for deductive content analysis. Coders should carefully examine each coding unit in the text, making the decisions called for in the codebook and record the resulting findings as specified.

RELIABILITY AND VALIDITY

Content analytic research can be evaluated with two concepts: reliability and validity. Reliability is the extent to which two or more coders agree in their analysis of a common pool of texts: Is the variable (dimension of content) being measured *consistently*? Reliability is measured numerically. When two (or more) coders disagree about how to categorize a text or coding unit, we have no way of knowing which interpretation to accept. When two coders agree, we do not have to choose between two different readings of a text and can be more confident that we are not relying on an idiosyncratic interpretation of the texts. Given that texts are produced—and consumed—by human beings, some ambiguity, and hence some disagreement, between coders can be expected and should be tolerated. However, when coders consistently disagree about the meaning of a text, we cannot be confident in the data produced. So, content analytic studies should measure intercoder reliability, try correct low reliability (by refining the codebook and/or retraining coders), and report reliability.

It should be noted that coders can agree by chance, and with two categories one might expect that 50% agreement could occur just by chance. Consequently, content analysis studies should report reliability statistics that control for agreement by chance (e.g., Cohen's [1960] *kappa*, Krippendorff's [2004] *alpha*, Scott's [1955] *pi*). Simple agreement between coders (e.g., North, et al., 1963) is less suitable for assessing reliability than statistics that control for agreement by chance. I also want to note that intercoder reliability ought to be calculated on *variables* not *categories*. So, for example, one ought to report reliability for *topic* of political campaign messages (comprised of two categories, say, policy and character) rather than on the presence/absence of policy and the presence/absence of character. Criteria for evaluating categories are relevant to research purpose, exhaustiveness, and mutual exclusivity. Furthermore, reliability should be reported for each variable rather than as an average, which can mask low levels of reliability for some variables, or even a range. For interpretations of the acceptability of various levels of reliability, see Fleiss (1981) or Landis and Koch (1977).[1]

It is fairly common in content analysis to distinguish between manifest and latent content (see Riffe, Lacy, & Fico, 2005). Manifest content is the obvious, explicit, surface, or denotative nature of texts. Identifying the sources cited in a news story—whether a quotation is from a government official, a corporate officer, an academic expert, or citizen—is an example of analysis of manifest content. The issue addressed in a campaign message—such as the war in Iraq, unemployment, health care, or education—can be another instance of manifest content. On the other hand, subtle, implicit, connotative aspects of the text illustrate latent content, requiring inference or judgment about the nature of the content—evaluation as opposed to identification of content. For example, identifying which emotion (e.g., fear, hope, anger, pride) is expressed in a message can be considered latent content. Satire or irony are other examples of latent content: The meaning intended by the source can be the opposite of the literal (manifest) content of the words expressed.

Rating the quality of a text, such as assigning a numeric value to message features like how harsh, useful, or pertinent, a given text is, constitutes another example of latent content. Analysis of the manifest content ("surface") features of the text, as opposed to latent content, meanings based more on inference than observation of political messages, is likely to be more reliable. But content analysis of latent content can also be useful and important. Content in this sense lies on a continuum—latent and manifest content are not a mutually exclusive dichotomy—and so it is impossible to always draw a sharp contrast between these two poles. Communication scholars probably conduct more content analyses that gravitate toward the manifest end of the content continuum because dealing with latent content (and attempting to achieve high reliability with such analyses) is more difficult than investigating manifest content.

Validity, in contrast, is the extent to which the data measure what the content analysis is designed to measure (see Krippendorff, 2004; Riffe, Lacy, & Fico, 2005). This criterion for evaluating content analytic data is more difficult to measure than reliability: Some studies using content analysis fail to report reliability, but even more studies fail to discuss validity. Most content analytic studies implicitly offer face validity, the idea that the categories make sense upon simple reflection about the nature of the categories. Validity can also be demonstrated with correlation. When two studies analyze the same basic kind of content with different content analytic procedures, the two sets of data can be correlated. If there is a strong relationship between the two sets of data produced, that provides support for the validity of each set of procedures. Thus, Geer (2006, p. 36) argues for the validity of his content analysis of presidential television advertising based on comparisons with the results of other analyses of these texts:

> Before we accept the measure of negativity [in presidential TV spots] reported . . . as sound, it is important to compare my results to other measures of negativity over the same time period. . . . My measure, for example, correlates 0.78 with Jamieson's, an impressive 0.93 with Kaid and Johnston's, and a staggering 0.97 with Benoit's.

Geer concludes that "given the strong correlation between our measures, I am confident that our data are tracking what we want quite well" (2006, pp. 37–38). Predictive validity trades on the assumption that the message variable being quantified via content analysis is empirically related to some effect on the audience. If such an effect can be measured, say with survey data, and relates as expected to the results of the content analysis, this relationship can serve as evidence of validity for the content analysis. In this way, for example, when an agenda setting study finds the predicted relationship between the content of news and audience attitudes, that finding tends to shore up the validity of the content analysis.

HUMAN VERSUS COMPUTER CONTENT ANALYSIS

Several texts discuss computer content analysis (Krippendorff, 2004; Neuendorf, 2002; Riffe, Lacy, & Fico, 2005; West, 2001a, 2001b; see also webpages such as Janda, 2008; Klein, 2008). Because human and computer content analysis use the same basic research method—content analysis—they share the need for a conceptual rationale, reliable categories, an appropriate sample, and so forth. However, there are several places in which these two approaches depart. First, computer content analysis requires computer files of texts in the sample. (Most computer content analysis still investigates textual data, but as face recognition software and other visual techniques become more sophisticated, surely we will see analysis of more than text files.) As the world becomes ever more digital, the availability of computer text files is increasing rapidly. Lexis-Nexis is a particularly useful resource for computer content analysis. It is also possible to scan printed texts into computer files—and the technology for doing so is improving in quality (scanned texts probably still need to be examined with word processing software to correct errors in converting the printed text into electronic files). Furthermore, some content analysis software has particular file requirements (e.g., files must be saved as *.txt files before Concordance can analyze them). The fact that computer content analysis requires digital files has implications for content analysis of nontextual materials (e.g., images). Still, it may not be possible or practical to employ computer content analysis on some texts. The researcher who is considering using computer content analysis must determine whether suitable computer files are available or can be created for the purpose of the study.

Computer content analysis has two important advantages over human coding. First, it is reliable. Given the same parameters (e.g., identical search term lists and procedures), computer content analysis will unvaryingly produce the same results on a given sample of texts. Human coders, as discussed in relation to reliability, are likely to disagree on some coding decisions. Unlike human coding, a study does not need to calculate intercoder reliability when using computer content analysis. A second advantage of computer content analysis is that computers can analyze texts significantly (exponentially) faster than humans. This means the coding task can be completed sooner or that a larger sample of texts can be processed with computer than human coding.

On the other hand, unlike reliability, the question of validity arises with both human and computer content analysis. Human coders can attribute meaning to texts, whereas computers cannot. This may mean that humans can better deal with vague, awkwardly worded, or ambiguous texts: Texts are created by and for humans, so human coders may be able to see nuances in the text not evident to a software program. Some research has compared human and computer content analysis with mixed results (Conway, 2006; Nacos et al., 1991); it seems inevitable that these two approaches would have similar levels of reliability on some research questions but varying validity on others. In general, computers are better suited for studies that analyze texts for content dimensions that are more manifest; humans are better suited for analyzing texts for latent dimensions.

A researcher who contemplates using computer content analysis should ask: Is a content analysis program available that will be able to test the hypothesis or answer the research questions posited in the research? Computer content analysis has advantages as well as limitations. Riffe, Lacy, and Fico (2005, p. 208) identify seven common forms of computer content analysis: Word counts, key-word-in-context (KWIC) and concordances, dictionaries, language structure, readability, artificial intelligence, and dynamic content analysis (J. Bryant, personal communication; Franzosi, 1995; Holsti, 1969; Krippendorff, 2004; Weber, 1990).

Word counts, as the name implies, quantify the number of times a particular word appears in a given text. Key-word-in-context programs list all the occurrences of a word (or words) along with the context (words before and after the target word). This seems most useful as an aid to interpreting the text: by looking at the immediate context, one can determine, for example, whether the word "drugs" is used to discuss crime (illegal drugs) or health care (prescription drugs). Dictionaries go a step beyond word counts, quantifying the number of instances of a list of words representing a common feature, quality, or topic. Language structure content analysis is designed to identify grammatical features of texts. Readability concerns how easy it is to comprehend a text (clarity, simplicity) and such software often identifies the school grade level for which a text is appropriate. Finally, dynamic content analysis seems to be more of a program to analyze data where researchers input their coding of visual texts and the computer searches for relationships among the data.

I would like to highlight two content analysis programs (see Skalski [2002] for a list), to illustrate how they can be used in research. Petrocik, Benoit, and Hansen (2003–04) employed Concordance (Watt, 2004) to investigate the issue content of presidential candidate nomination acceptance addresses and TV spots. Petrocik's (1996) "issue ownership" theory includes a prediction that candidates from the Democratic and Republican parties will exhibit a tendency to emphasize and express familiarity with different sets of issues. Different issues are said to be "owned" by the two parties: most people think Democrats can do a better job handling education, Social Security, and health care, whereas most believe Republicans can do a better job dealing with national security, crime, and taxation.

For the Petrocik et al. (2003–04) study, Concordance was first used to produce a list of every word that appeared in presidential ads from 1952 to 2000 (called a "full concordance"). These words were then grouped by coders into Democratic- and Republican-owned issues, such as national defense, employment, health care, and education (words for personal qualities, such as honesty or strength, were ignored). Second, these issue term lists were applied by Concordance to the texts of acceptance addresses and TV spots to determine the relative frequency with which these issues (as measured by the frequency of words on the issue lists) occurred in these texts. They found that, in fact, Democratic candidates discussed "Democratic" issues more than Republicans, and vice versa. This research exemplifies an approach to computer content analysis which falls on the manifest end of the content continuum.

Hart's (2005) Diction program represents the dictionary approach to computer content analysis. Hart has developed lists of words that represent qualities of discourse, such as certainty, optimism, activity, and realism. These dictionaries are in turn based on other dictionaries. For example, "certainty" is defined by Hart (1984, p. 16) as:

> Statements indicating resoluteness, inflexibility, and completeness. Leveling terms (all, everyone), collective nouns (bureau, department), and rigid verbs (will, shall) make for assured statements, while qualifying terms (almost, might), specificity (e.g., numerical citations), and first-person pronouns signaled an individual's refusal to speak *ex cathedra*.

In turn, the major dictionaries are created through combinations of subdictionaries. Certainty is calculated with this formula: [rigidity + leveling + collectives + power factor] − [numerical frequency + qualification + self-reference + variety] (Hart, 1984, p. 293). These categories were applied using Diction to identify the rhetorical styles of every president from Truman through Reagan. Other computer content analysis programs have been developed, with unique applications and customized abilities, so these examples are more illustrative of how content analysis can be employed in political communication research rather them exhaustive. The above studies exemplify the use of computer content analysis to investigate content which lies more on the latent end of the continuum (see Diction, 2008).

CONCLUSION

Content analysis of texts will undoubtedly continue to be a staple in political communication research. Given that scholars approach research questions with different purposes, we can expect both human and computer content analysis to occupy important places in this work. Political communication research places texts and their content in the forefront of theory and research. Content analysis is not the only way to grapple with texts, but it is a well-established and important technique quantifying dimensions of the content of political messages.

If I had to identify areas in which content analysis of communication texts has the most potential for progress, it would be the analysis of visual and audio texts. There can be no question that these elements of texts are fundamentally important: These aspects of texts can reinforce the verbal message (e.g., a candidate declaring his or her patriotism with the American flag in the background), contradict the verbal message (irony or sarcasm indicated by tone of voice), or even send a different message (e.g., subtle cues of racism amid protestations of the importance of equal opportunity). The fact that Google for example, allows one to search for images as well as text strings is a potentially promising development. However, computer content analysis must develop entirely new approaches to analyzing texts that do not consist of word strings (I suspect the importance of word-processing via computer, and the ready accessibility of text files, facilitates the development of verbal content analysis programs).

Content analysis was developed explicitly as a research tool for investigating the nature of communication generally, as well as mass communication. This method is vitally important for theory and research in political communication. As a field, we have developed this method, considering both reliability and validity, and the quality of research employing content analysis is steadily improving (e.g., reporting of intercoder reliability controlling for agreement by chance; development of codebooks or protocols for coders). Use of computers for content analysis has clear advantages, although limitations must be acknowledged.

NOTE

1. Some research reports reliability as a correlation coefficient (e.g., Pearson's r) representing the relationship between the data produced by two coders for the same group of texts. This approach to reliability is better suited for the kinds of content analytic research described here as evaluative "rating" studies, in which a text is assigned a value on a scale (e.g., 1–7) depending on the extent to which it possesses or exemplifies a quality, rather than for research that assigns texts to discrete categories. However, even there the problem is that reliability concerns the question of whether coders assign the same category to each coding unit; correlational statistics answer the different question of whether two variables covary (so it is possible to have large correlations without identical coding decisions).

REFERENCES

Benoit, W. L. (2007). *Communication in political campaigns*. New York: Peter Lang.

Benoit, W. L., & McHale, J. P. (2003). Presidential candidates' television spots and personal qualities. *Southern Communication Journal, 68*, 319–334.

Berelson, B. R. (1952). *Content analysis in communication research*. New York: Free Press.

Berg, B. L. (2006). *Qualitative research methods for the social sciences* (6th ed.). Boston, MA: Allyn & Bacon.

Burgchardt, C. R. (2005). *Readings in rhetorical criticism* (3rd ed.). State College, PA: Strata Publishing.

Cohen, J. (1960). A coefficient of agreement for nominal scales. *Educational and Psychological Measurement, 20*, 37–46.

Conway, M.T. (2006). The subjective precision of computers: A methodological comparison with human coding. *Journalism & Mass Communication Quarterly, 83*(1), 186–200.

Creswell, J. W. (2007). *Qualitative inquiry and research design: Choosing among five traditions* (2nd ed.). Thousand Oaks, CA: Sage.

Denzin, N. K., & Lincoln, Y. S. (2005). *The Sage handbook of qualitative research*. Thousand Oaks, CA: Sage.

Diction. (2008). *Diction 5.0*. Retrieved June 3, 2008, from http://www.dictionsoftware.com.

Ferris, A. L., Smith, S. W., Greenberg, B. S., & Smith, S. L. (2007). The content of reality dating shows and viewer perceptions of dating. *Journal of Communication, 57*, 490–510.

Fleiss, J. L. (1981). *Statistical methods for ratios and proportions*. New York: John Wiley & Sons.

Foss, S. K. (2008). *Rhetorical criticism: Exploration and practice* (4th ed.). Long Grove, IL: Waveland Press.

Franzosi, R. (1995). Computer-assisted content analysis of newspapers: Can we make an expensive research tool more efficient? *Quality & Quantity, 29*, 157–172.

Geer, J. G. (2006). *In defense of negativity: Attack ads in presidential campaigns*. Chicago: University of Chicago Press.

Glaser, B. G., & Strauss, A. L. (1967). *The discovery of grounded theory: Strategies for qualitative research.* Chicago: Aldine.

Grabe, M. E. (1996). The SABC's coverage of 1987 and 1989 elections: The matter of visual bias. *Journal of Broadcasting & Electronic Media, 40*, 1–27.

Grabe, M. E., & Bucy, E. P. (2009). *Image bite politics: News and the visual framing of elections.* New York: Oxford University Press.

Hart, R. P. (1984). *Verbal style and the presidency: A computer-based analysis.* New York: Academic Press.

Hart, R. P. (2005). Diction. Retrieved May 1, 2008, from http://www.dictionsoftware.com/.

Hart, R. P., & Daughton, S. (2005). *Modern rhetorical criticism* (3rd ed.). Boston, MA: Pearson Education.

Holbert, R. L., & Zubric, S. J. (2000). A comparative analysis: Objective and public journalism techniques. *Newspaper Research Journal, 21*, 50–67.

Holsti, R. R. (1969). *Content analysis for the social sciences and humanities.* Reading, MA: Addison-Wesley.

Janda, K. (2008). *Content analysis programs and references.* Retrieved February 12, 2008, from http://janda.org/workshop/content%20analysis/programs.htm.

Kaid, L. L., & Johnston, A. (2001). *Videostyle in presidential campaigns: Style and content of televised political advertising.* Westport, CT: Praeger.

Kepplinger, H. M. (1991). The impact of presentation techniques: Theoretical aspects and empirical findings. In F. Biocca (Ed.), *Television and political advertising: Psychological processes* (vol. 1, pp. 173–194). Hillsdale, NJ: Lawrence Erlbaum.

Kepplinger, H. M., & Donsbach, W. (1987). The influence of camera perspective on the perception of a politician by supporters, opponents, and neutral viewers. In D. Paletz (Ed.), *Political communication research: Approaches, studies, assessments* (pp. 63–71). Norwood, NJ: Ablex.

Klein, H. (2008). *Text analysis info page.* Retrieved February 12, 2008, from http://www.textanalysis.info/.

Krippendorff, K. (2004). *Content analysis: An introduction to its methodology* (2nd ed.). Thousand Oaks, CA: Sage.

Landis, J. R., & Koch, G. G. (1977). The measurement of observer agreement for categorical data. *Biometrica, 33*, 159–174.

Lindlof, T., & Taylor, B. C. (2002). *Qualitative communication research methods* (2nd ed.). Thousand Oaks, CA: Sage.

Lombard, M., Snyder-Duch, J., & Bracken, C. C. (2002). Content analysis in mass communication: Assessment and reporting of intercoder reliability. *Human Communication Research, 28*, 587–604.

McCombs, M. (2004). *Setting the agenda: The mass media and public opinion.* Cambridge: Polity.

McCombs, M. E., & Shaw, D. L. (1972). The agenda setting function of the mass media. *Public Opinion Quarterly, 36*, 176–187.

Nacos, B. L., Shapiro, R. Y., Young, J. T., Fan, D. P., Kjellstrand, T., & McCaa, C. (1991). Content analysis of news reports: Comparing human coding and a computer-assisted method. *Communication, 12*, 111–128.

Neuendorf, K. A. (2002). *The content analysis guidebook.* Thousand Oaks, CA: Sage.

North, R. C., Holsti, O., Zaninovich, M. G., & Zinnes, D. A. (1963). *Content analysis: A handbook with applications for the study of international crisis.* Evanston, IL: Northwestern University Press.

Petrocik, J. R. (1996). Issue ownership in presidential elections, with a 1980 case study. *American Journal of Political Science, 40*, 825–850.

Petrocik, J. R., Benoit, W. L., & Hansen, G. J. (2003–04). Issue ownership and presidential campaigning, 1952–2000. *Political Science Quarterly, 118*, 599–626.

Riffe, D., Lacy, S., & Fico, F. G. (2005). *Analyzing media messages: Using quantitative content analysis in research* (2nd ed.). Mahwah, NJ: Lawrence Erlbaum.

Robertson, T., Froemling, K., Wells, S., & McCraw, S. (1999). Sex, lies, and videotape: An analysis of gender in campaign advertisements. *Communication Quarterly, 47*, 333–341.

Scott, W. A. (1955). Reliability of content analysis: The case of nominal scale coding. *Public Opinion Quarterly, 19*, 321–325.

Skalski, P. D. (2002). Computer content analysis software. In K. A. Neuendorf (Ed.), *The content analysis guidebook* (pp. 225–239). Thousand Oaks, CA: Sage.

Verser, R., & Wicks, R. H. (2006). Managing voter impressions: The use of images on presidential candidate websites during the 2000 campaign. *Journal of Communication, 56,* 178–197.

Vidich, A. J., & Lyman, S. M. (1998). Qualitative methods: Their history in sociology and anthropology. In N. K. Denzin & Y. S. Lincoln (Eds.), *The landscape of qualitative research: Theories and issues* (pp. 41–110). Thousand Oaks, CA: Sage.

Watt, R. (2004). Concordance. Retrieved May 1, 2008, from http://www.dundee.ac.uk/english/wics/wics.htm.

Weber, R. P. (1990). *Basic content analysis* (2nd ed.). Newbury Park, CA: Sage.

West, M. D. (Ed.). (2001a). *Applications of computer content analysis.* Westport, CT: Ablex.

West, M. D. (Ed.). (2001b). *Theory, method, and practice in computer content analysis.* Westport, CT: Ablex.

Westerstahl, J. (1983). Objective news reporting: General premises. *Communication Research, 10,* 403–424.

Wright, S. (1921). Correlation and causation. *Journal of Agriculture Research, 20,* 557–585.

V
DISCOURSE ANALYSIS

15

The Use of Focus Groups in Political Communication Research

Sharon E. Jarvis

Department of Communication Studies
University of Texas–Austin

> When I die, I want to come back with real power. I want to come back as a member of a focus group.
> —Roger Ailes (cited in Luntz, 1994)

> It's not what you say. It is what they hear.
> —Frank Luntz (1994)

Since the 1980s, focus groups have enjoyed considerable attention in political communication. In *electoral politics*, for instance, focus groups have helped candidates both to refine their own messages and to sharpen strategies to attack their opponents (Kolbert, 1992; Luntz, 1994, 2006; Moyers, 1989; Sypher, 1994). In *political news coverage*, focus groups have emerged as a story in and of themselves as news outlets use them to gauge audience responses to campaign advertisements and debate performances (Bedard & Kaplan, 2004; Mundy, 2000; "The pulse of the voters," 1996). And, in *academic research*, focus groups have become increasingly prevalent across the social sciences (see Morgan, 1996) and in political communication research particularly (see Graber, 2004; Johnson-Cartee, & Copeland, 1997).

This chapter provides an introduction to focus group methodology, reviews its history and uses, compares it to related methods, addresses its strengths and limitations, and considers ethical concerns. Throughout, examples from published work in political communication are provided to show how and why researchers have used this approach. These scholarly projects have much in common with the comments of Roger Ailes and Frank Luntz that open this chapter. Indeed, focus groups provide insight into how individuals make sense of messages and form social opinions in the contemporary over-communicated environment.

DEFINITION AND OVERVIEW

Focus groups are a qualitative research method in which a trained moderator conducts a collective interview of a set of participants (Barbour & Kitzinger, 1999; Greenbaum, 1998, 2000; Krueger,

1998a, 1998b; Morgan, 1988, 1998; Wheelan, 2005). These group interviews create lines of communication across individuals and rely on the interaction between the participants to yield data that would be impossible to gather in individual interviews (in which participants are responding individually to a set of items) or participant observation (in which participants are engaged in normal routines, but may or may not be interacting to address a researcher's scholarly interest). This approach has been credited with providing special insight into research participants, as it uncovers how people *really think* as opposed to how they are *supposed to think* (Mischler, 1986). The focus group method has also been praised for helping scholars better understand the entire research process, offering (1) richer insight into topics of inquiry, (2) a way to make sense of discrepancies between anticipated and actual effects as well as discrepancies between prevailing effects and deviant cases, and (3) clues to the complicated process of social influence (Merton & Kendall, 1946).

As a unique methodology, focus groups possess a set of distinct characteristics. Specifically:

1. They are truly *group interviews*. Group interaction is regarded as a hallmark of this method. Because individuals do not form "opinions in isolation," researchers use focus groups to "glimpse the complex process of social interaction that is involved in opinion formation" (Krueger, 1998a, 1998b, p. 142).
2. They are *contextual*. As Hollander (2004) observes, these group conversations are influenced by *associational concerns* (the common characteristic(s) bringing the participants together), *social status* (relative positions in local, societal or cultural hierarchies), and *conversational factors* (norms and expectations emerging in dialogue).
3. They are *relational*. Research participants create an audience for one another as they ask questions, exchange anecdotes and comment on each others' experiences and points of view (Barbour & Kitzinger, 1999). Accordingly, groups are influenced by the presence or absence of intimacy across participants (Gamson, 1992; Hollander, 2004), as individuals come together to explore socially shared knowledge (Markova, Linell, Grossen, & Orvig, 2007).
4. They are *dialogic*. As Glick (1999) details, the focus group "places people in the position of talking with each other, of convincing or disagreeing with each other" and of using their most powerful arguments to convince others in the group (p. 116). Through conversation, "people often invoke powerful images which to them make the point about why their opinion and way of thinking is correct" (p. 117).
5. They are tied to *meaning*. Focus groups should not be used to answer the research questions of "how many" or "how much" (Wimmer & Dominick, 2000, p. 120). Rather, they are a means of answering the research questions "how" and "why" and help to uncover the "particular over the general" (Morgan, 1997, p. 18).
6. They are *heuristic*. Unanticipated and inconsistent views often emerge in focus groups (Delli-Carpini & Williams, 1994). Scholars should anticipate surprises (Glick, 1999) and have a tolerance for disorder while making sense of focus group data (Luntz, 1994).
7. They are *revelatory*. First used by Merton and Lazarsfeld in the 1940s to "provide some basis for interpreting statistically significant effects of mass communications" (Merton & Kendall, 1946, p. 542), focus groups help researchers and marketers learn how people regard, use, and alter messages and products. So much faith had Merton on the virtues of "focused" discussion on a topic that he wrote, "when subjects are led to describe their reactions in minute detail, there is less prospect that they will, intentionally or unwittingly, conceal the actual character of their responses; apparent inconsistencies will be revealed; and, finally, a clear picture of the total response emerges" (Merton & Kendall, 1946, p. 542).

8. They are *democratic*. Group conversations can give participants power and voice (Morgan, 1997) and possibly provide a "new politics of knowledge" (Barbour & Kitzinger, 1999, p. 18) by challenging previously held beliefs of the academic community. These group conversations represent "an appreciation of the interest and value of entering into people's lives and in trying to understand their reality from the inside . . . of the hopes and fears of real people" (Glick, 1999, p. 121).

Focus groups are a relatively inexpensive and seemingly transparent means of scholarship. These characteristics are regarded as both a strength and a weakness of this approach. On the one hand, many applaud the method for its accessibility; on the other, many worry that it is easy to approach the method too casually (Lunt & Livingstone, 1996; Merton, 1987; Morrison, 1998). Advocates of rigor in focus group research stress that there are important concerns regarding group size, composition, segmentation, and saturation that influence the rigor of this method (Fern, 2001; Morrison, 1998)

There is a general agreement in the published work about focus groups that the ideal number of participants is between seven and twelve individuals (with eight to ten being the most popular number, see Glick, 1999; Luntz, 1994; Kern & Just, 1995; Krueger, 1998a, 1998b; Morgan, 1988, 1997, 1998). Morgan (1997), however, resists hard and fast rules as to how many participants officially constitute a group and prefers to view group interviewing in an inclusive way, deferring to researchers to decide how many individuals comprise a meaningful group (see also Krueger, 1998b; Morgan, 1997). Concerning large groups, most practitioners warn that if the group grows to over ten participants, it can be difficult to control (Morrison, 1998). And, on the topic of smaller groups, some scholars have argued that even three participants can constitute an effective group (Gamson, 1992; Mindich, 2005; Wimmer & Dominick, 2000).

In an analysis of the bases for determining group size, Morgan (1997) contends that smaller groups may be more appropriate for "emotionally charged topics that generate high levels of participant involvement," while larger groups work better with more "neutral topics" that generate "lower levels of involvement" (p. 146). In political communication studies, scholars have elected to conduct groups with as few as two and three (Mindich, 2005), four to six (Gamson, 1992), four to seven (Bucy & Newhagen, 1999), and six to twelve (Stevens et al., 2006) members per group. It has been more common, however, for groups to be composed of eight to twelve members (Carlin & McKinney, 1994; Just et al., 1996; Kaid, McKinney, & Tedesco, 2000; Kern & Just, 1995; Mickiewicz, 2005).

There is also agreement that participants should be selected for focus groups because of a shared characteristic of interest to the researcher (Krueger, 1998a; Morgan, 1997; Morrison, 1998). As Morgan (1997) explains, "the group composition should ensure that participants in each group have something to say about the topic and feel comfortable saying it to each other" (p. 36). The goal here, he continues, is to provide homogeneity in background and experience so that participants are able to speak to the issue at hand and feel comfortable asking and answering questions of each other. Researchers should not get too carried away when recruiting for homogeneity, though. While participants should share a common background to facilitate conversation, recruiting a sample with "virtually identical perspectives" on the researcher's topic of interest would lead to a "flat, unproductive discussion" (Morgan, 1997, p. 26). In political communication research, groups have been segmented by gender, race, social class and education levels (Bucy & Newhagen, 1999; Gamson, 1992; Kolbert, 1992; Mickiewicz, 2005), ideology and partisanship (Kern & Just, 1995), geographic region (Carlin & McKinney, 1994; Jamieson, 1993), urban versus rural areas (Stevens et al., 2006), nationality (Beom, Carlin, & Silver, 2005), ethnicity (Chiu & Knight, 1999; Hughes & Dumont, 1993), occupation (Jarvis, Barberena, & Davis, 2007), and age (Apker & Voss, 1994).

Academic projects employing the focus group method should also be prepared to conduct a *set* of groups to increase the validity of their project. While the exact number of groups necessary to run can vary, the "rule of thumb is to continue conducting interviews until little new information is provided" (Krueger, 1988b, p. 97). Three to six groups per project is standard and practitioners and researchers know that they can stop conducting groups when they "can anticipate what will be said next by a group" or "the additional data collected no longer generates new understanding" (Morgan, 1997, p. 43; see also Fern, 2001).

This notion of *saturation* (see Glaser & Strauss, 1967) is easier to reach with homogenous groups. As Morgan (1997) details, "projects that bring together more heterogeneous participants will typically need more total groups because the diversity in the group often makes it more difficult to sort out coherent sets of opinions and experiences" (p. 44). In the field of political communication research, published studies have reported conducting two (Kaid, McKinney, & Tedesco, 2000; Kern & Just, 1995), four (Beom, Carlin, & Silver, 2005; Bucy & Newhagen, 1999), seven (Stephens et al., 2006), nine (Delli-Carpini & Williams, 1994), twelve (Kaid, McKinney, & Tedesco, 2000), sixteen (Just et al., 1996; Mickiewicz, 2005), thirty-seven (Gamson, 1992), and sixty-two (Carlin & McKinney, 1994) groups.

HISTORY AND USES

Focus groups first appeared in academic research in the 1920s. At that time, group interviews were used in the early stages of psychological measurement and survey development (Krueger& Casey, 2000; Morgan, 1988). In the 1940s, sociologists Robert Merton and Paul Lazarsfeld used focus groups to study the social and psychological effects of radio, print, and film communications during World War II (see Lunt & Livingstone, 1996; Merton, 1987; Merton & Kendall, 1946; Morgan, 1988). Merton, particularly, is credited as the founder of the "focused interview" in academic research. As outlined in his seminal pieces (with Kendall, 1946, and with Fiske and Kendall, 1956), and in his address to the American Association of Public Opinion Research in 1986 entitled "How Did We Get from Focused Interviews to Focus Groups?" Merton (1987) employed group interview settings to help interpret experimental findings and to listen for interaction between group members, particularly as they built on, questioned, and interpreted each other's responses.

Between the 1950s and early 1980s, focus groups became increasingly prominent in marketing practices (and, curiously, were rarely found in academic research). Marketers began to refer to them as "group depth interviews" in which professionals trained in probing unconscious sources of behavior could work to uncover customers' psychological motivations. By the late 1980s, focus groups had become more prominent in scholarly circles (Morgan, 1997). This renewed attention was due both to work conducted by social marketers researching public health concerns and by scholarly books emerging on focus groups as a method (see Krueger & Casey, 2000; Morgan, 1988).

Focus groups continue to play a central role in marketing practices and have been embraced by political communication researchers (Greenbaum, 1998; 2000; Krueger & Casey, 2000; Luntz, 1994). This methodological approach allows marketers to learn more about basic concerns, including:

- how consumers feel, respond and think about ideas or products;
- how often or deeply they feel or think about ideas or products;
- how, when, and in what instances their thoughts and feelings actually lead to behaviors;

- when complicated or contradictory thoughts and behaviors emerge in response to topics or products; and
- how diverse groups view a specific idea or product.

More practically, marketers value how these group interviews shed light on how "consumers name products, improve old ones and reinvent needs for others" (Sypher, 1994, p. 39). This type of data would be impossible to gather through closed-ended survey items and very difficult to collect in individual interviews which lack the sharing and comparing process of group conversations.

Campaign strategists, too, employ group interviews to solicit reactions to candidate images, messages, and policies (Glick, 1999; Luntz, 1994; Sypher, 1994). At the presidential level, group interviews have aided in the development of candidate strategies, including the construction of Ronald Reagan's power phrases in 1980 and 1984 (e.g., shifting references to the Strategic Arms Initiative to "Star Wars"), Bill Clinton's responses to attacks on his character in 1992, and George W. Bush's plainspoken style in campaigns 2000 and 2004 (Carney & Dickerson, 2000; Luntz, 2006; Moyers, 1989). Group interviews have also helped consultants refine negative campaigning strategies, as they did in 1988, helping the George H. W. Bush team learn that a litany of attacks against Michael Dukakis was more persuasive than individual charges, and in 2004, aiding the George W. Bush team fine-tune allegations that John Kerry was a flip-flopper (Luntz, 2006; Stewart, Shamdasani, & Rook, 2007). Additionally, focus groups have been employed for more broad-based campaign strategies, as they were by Frank Luntz in 1994 when he provided Republican U.S. House candidates with a "Language for the 21st Century" via the "Contract with America" talking points (Lemann, 2000).

In political communication research, focus groups are a good fit for several paths of inquiry. Scholars interested in political language can benefit from this approach in at least three ways. First, group interviews allow scholars to "capture the comments or language of a target population" (Krueger & Casey, 2000, p. 24). Second, they help researchers learn more about how points of view are expressed. Third, they convey how "knowledge, ideas, storytelling, self-presentation and linguistic exchanges operate within a given cultural context" (Barbour & Kitzinger, 1999, p. 5). Two notable book projects provide examples of how listening to the language choices in group interviews can help scholars answer their research questions. Specifically, in *Talking Politics*, Gamson (1992) conducted thirty-seven peer group conversations among 188 participants to explore how people talk about mediated portrayals of four key issues (troubled industry, affirmative action, nuclear power, and the Arab-Israeli conflict). Focusing specifically on a sample of "working people" (p. 14) in the Boston area, Gamson's data challenge the conventional wisdom that most political issues and events do not make much sense to most everyday citizens. Instead, Gamson was struck by the deliberative and insightful quality of citizen conversations about these complex issues.

In *Tuned Out*, Mindich (2005) conducted over twenty-five individual and group interviews to learn more about why young people are less likely to follow the news. Listening to group conversations allowed him to avoid the simplistic but tempting strategy of offering soft news presentations in order to lure a larger youth audience. Instead, his group interviews with young people helped him see "how social and societal factors play important roles in how we value news" (p. 39). From his sessions, he identified two of the most powerful reasons why young people follow news: (1) to feel like they are part of a community; and (2) to learn information that they can use, particularly in conversation (p. 37). Consequently, he argued that the real challenge for bringing young people back to the news is not to soften it, but to help youth see how information can help them in their daily lives.

Researchers who embrace a constructivist approach have employed focus groups to observe the social construction of meaning (Kern & Just, 1995) and to listen to how groups interpret new information in light of their own attitudes and values (Gamson, 1992; Just et al., 1996). One example can be found in Just and colleagues' (1996) *Crosstalk* project, an ambitious study of how the "meaning of an election is forged in the discourse of a campaign" (p. 3) between candidates, journalists, and citizens. These scholars conducted sixteen focus groups at three points during the primary and general election phases of the 1992 campaign. They found that their focus group participants used personal knowledge and experience to actively interpret news stories and candidate advertisements (p. 152). Intriguingly, this process only increased over the course of the campaign as people "drew more on their own experiences—both direct and indirect—to evaluate campaign information" as the election neared (p. 166).

Because focus groups provide insight into the process of social influence, they have been a valuable tool for projects examining voter information processing. In *Dirty Politics*, for instance, Jamieson (1993) reported data from 106 focus group participants in nine states to share how voters made sense of the strategic frame in news coverage of campaign 1988. Her findings show how a focus on strategy in news encouraged people to "see themselves not as voters but as spectators evaluating the performances of those bent on cynical manipulation" (p. 10). In their analysis of how different media formats influence evaluations of candidates, Bucy and Newhagen (1999) report on the results of four focus sessions. During these sessions, participants watched televised clips of a town hall meeting featuring a conversation between Bill Clinton and a student questioner (fifty-seven seconds in length), a close-up interview of Clinton (thirty-five seconds), and a Democratic advertisement (twenty-three seconds). After coding the transcripts, Bucy and Newhagen found that their focus group participants processed the "media formats featuring close-ups in terms of individual candidate attributes" and the "political advertising and televised town meetings with multiple actors (candidate, audience members, and journalists) as contextualized social phenomena" (p. 193).

Additionally, in speaking to advancements in research on emotion in politics, McDermott (2007) observes that the key to successful measurement in studies "lies in its effective manipulation" (p. 383) particularly because political stimuli (and people's reactions to them) are influenced both by properties of the messages as well as the predispositions of audiences. Focus groups are helpful in two respects, here: first, they can be conducted *prior* to experimental work to pretest and refine the experimental stimulus; and, second, they can be used *after* experimental work to "provide some basis for *interpreting* statistically significant effects" relating to audience processing of political discourse (Merton & Kendall, 1946, p. 542; see also Lunt & Livingstone, 1996).

Researchers interested in re-examining fundamental questions have also opted for this method. For instance, in *Processing Politics*, Graber (2001) employed focus group data to assess "how well or ill-suited to effective citizenship is Americans' actual knowledge about politics?" (p. 53). In doing so, she coded the transcripts of twenty-one focus groups for levels of cognitive complexity in political discussions. Her analyses led her to argue that participants "possess reasonably sophisticated, politically useful knowledge about current problems that confront them and that the issue areas covered by this knowledge are generally quite well suited to carrying out the actual tasks of citizenship that most citizens perform" (p. 64).

In their project challenging the dominant metaphors of citizens as consumers and media content as hypodermic injections of political information, Delli-Carpini and Williams (1994) conducted nine groups. They were particularly interested in when and how citizens contest media content. Their findings show that viewers have a "surprising awareness of (and concern for) their dependence on the media" and have a "real but limited autonomy" in identifying and sometimes rejecting television's "ideological biases" (p. 792).

Research projects examining new populations (such as young voters, immigrants, bilingual communities, and so on) can benefit from focus group methodology, particularly because this approach allows scholars to refine measures for them and see how they compare to previously studied populations (Merton & Kendall, 1946). Indeed, scholars have conducted groups with children (Green & Hart, 1999), college students (Apker & Voss, 1994), international students (Beom, Carlin, & Silver, 2005), minority groups (Chiu & Knight, 1999; Hughes & Dumont, 1993), and new neighborhood associations (Krueger & King, 1998; Waterton & Wynne, 1999).

Additionally, researchers exploring public problems have utilized focus groups to gather rich data on campaign communications, target populations and public policy outcomes. In their book examining candidate, media, and public voices in campaign 1996, Kaid, McKinney, and Tedesco (2000) conducted twelve focus groups in addition to a set of experiments and a comprehensive content analysis of media discourse. Their findings led to a set of recommendations for future candidates, the media, and the public. Their focus group data were central to their recommendations for the public, where they called for citizens to (1) organize citizen discussion groups and promote political efficacy, (2) embrace a positive view of the interaction of public, media, and candidate voices, and (3) take control by initiating their own television spots. In their examination of what and how viewers learn from debates, Carlin and McKinney (1994) oversaw sixty-two focus groups in campaign 1992. Their data led them to advance their own set of recommendations, including calling for multiple formats for debates in each election year, diverse questioners, citizen discussion groups following the debates, and questions that call for "clash" or direct encounters between the candidates (a reform that may be resisted by candidates). Additionally, focus groups have been employed in externally funded projects geared toward reform, examining what types of content citizens want to hear from political candidates and in media coverage (Lipsitz et al., 2005) and how civic education can be improved to better prepare high school students for political life (Jarvis, Barberena, & Davis, 2007).

FOCUS GROUPS AND RELATED METHODS

Focus groups most closely resemble two other qualitative methods: open-ended interviewing and participant observation (Bloor et al., 2001; Fern, 2001). As with open-ended interviews, focus group moderators approach groups with a protocol of questions and encourage participants to focus on an identified topic. Unlike open-ended interviews, however, moderators do not gather in-depth information from individuals and they can be flexible with how the questions are asked (Kitzinger & Barbour, 1999; Morgan, 1988, 1998). In explaining why he selected focus groups over individual interviews for his project, Gamson (1992) observed that "to talk about issues with others, people search for a common basis of discourse . . . a working frame that can be shared with the other participants" (pp. 191–192). Uncovering how individuals discussed these issues allowed Gamson to understand how working citizens made sense of political topics.

Like participant observation, focus groups afford interaction among individuals and require that moderators surrender some power, at least, to the group; however, moderators need to be mindful of domineering personalities (Wimmer & Dominick, 2000). Unlike participant observation, though, focus groups produce large amounts of data on a specific topic in a short period of time and researchers do not get to watch how things unfold organically in their natural contexts. Two criteria, then, help researchers discern if focus groups are a good methodological choice for them compared to individual interviews and participant observation: (1) Would the research project be better off with the individual level data acquired from interviews rather than the group-level conversational data generated from focus groups? (2) Would the contextual information afforded by naturally occurring events witnessed during participant observation be preferable over the focused, yet less naturalistic, data gathered during a focus group conversation?

Focus groups appear in many multi-method projects at various stages of these endeavors. While Merton and Kendall (1946) observed that the "primary purpose" of the focused interview was to provide some basis for interpreting empirical effects (p. 542), they also noted that focus groups can precede the experimental or statistical study in order to develop hypotheses for future testing (p. 557). Consider the following examples of how researchers have employed groups before and after other analyses:

- In her analysis of teen-aged girls, Mitchell (1999) conducted focus groups first (and in-depth interviews second) to assess how issues of status encouraged some girls to speak in front of their peers whereas others stayed silent.
- A study of community views of nuclear risks employed focus groups to unpack the data offered by an initial survey (Waterton & Wynne, 1999). These steps led the authors to conclude that their survey constructed a "misleadingly simple" and "impoverished view" (p. 127) of attitudes and feelings on this issue.
- In the *Crosstalk* project, focus groups, in-depth interviews, and surveys were conducted over the course of the 1992 presidential campaign to assess how citizens make sense of politics as a campaign unfolds (Just et al., 1996).
- In their analysis of campaign communication from 1996, Kaid, McKinney, and Tedesco (2000) conducted focus groups after experiments to help interpret the effects of political ads and debates.

PRACTICAL CONCERNS IN CONDUCTING FOCUS GROUPS

Several thorough and accessible guides have been published which should be consulted before any group session to prepare researchers for the practical and logistical concerns of conducting focus groups. Recommended works include *Focus Groups: A Practical Guide for Applied Research* (Sage, 2000) by Kreuger and Casey and *The Focus Group Kit* (Sage, 1998), a six-volume set by Morgan, Kruegar, and King.

Briefly stated, though, focus group preparation involves the following steps. First, researchers must decide what kind of people should be studied and how many groups should be conducted. Second, researchers should select a moderator and ensure that the moderator is not of an age, ethnic background, gender, education level, or social class that might prevent group members from participating fully in the conversation. Third, researchers should decide upon the desired level of structure for the group and on the scope of the actual focus group questions—also called a protocol, questioning route, or topic guide (discussed in greater detail below and in the Appendices).

Fourth, basic logistical issues of recruitment and compensation must be considered, selecting participants on a variable of interest and in such a way that they will not disrupt the contexts of the group (see Hollander, 2004). Screener questions can be employed to identify individuals who might have attitudes or background experiences that could intimidate other group members or hamper the group discussion. Researchers can also attempt to over-recruit participants for each group and then, after the participants have arrived to the location, selectively tell potentially problematic group members that the group is over-enrolled (and thank such members and send them home with any promised compensation). While it might seem wasteful to pay an individual for not participating in the group, it can be far more costly to keep that individual in the group if there is a risk that he or she will threaten the group dynamics.

Fifth, moderators should heed the best practices of facilitating the session as outlined in practical guides (see Morgan, 1988; Morgan & Scannell, 1998). A few tips here bear mentioning. Sessions should be held around a round (or rectangular) table. The moderator should be in a position to see all participants to help control the flow and content of the conversation, and if the session is being video recorded, the recording device should be behind the moderator. Name cards (with first names only) can be placed around the table to assign the participants to specific places and to facilitate the recognition of names through the conversation and during transcription. Additionally, the moderator must remain sensitive to the reality that participants will have varying levels of comfort in speaking in front of the group and should be mindful of his or her own nonverbal behaviors.

Scholars should pay special attention to the creation of their protocols. The overall logic of a protocol is to imagine guiding the group through five types of questions (Krueger, 1998a). The conversation should start with *opening questions* to help participants become comfortable in the group setting. The group interview should then move to *introductory questions* to begin discussion on the topic of interest. The focus group can then shift to *transition questions* to gather basic data on the specific topic of inquiry. Krueger (1998a) then advises launching into the *key questions* to directly answer the study's research questions. Here, he encourages researchers to ensure that they have translated their academic concerns into conversational questions that can really tap their hypotheses or research objectives. The group then should close with *ending questions* to conclude the discussion and to see if the participants wish to comment on points that are important to them. Appendix 15.1 features a sample protocol on the topic of political socialization that could be asked of a set of differently segmented groups (e.g., individuals of higher and lower political sophistication, older and younger citizens, men and women). This questioning guide serves as an applied example of Krueger's (1998a) question types.

Appendix 15.2 provides another example of a focus group protocol, this one from an aforementioned study on how media formats influence viewer evaluations and political judgments (Bucy & Newhagen, 1999). This appendix shares Bucy and Newhagen's research topic, hypotheses, focus group protocol, and key findings to show how all of these elements of a study are interrelated. Their focus group began with opening questions, then showed a political communication stimulus to participants, and shifted to key questions. The process was repeated by showing a second political stimulus, moving through the same key questions, and then sharing a third and fourth political stimulus, followed by a last round of questions.

DATA ANALYSIS

Focus group data can be analyzed different ways, and the standards vary between those employed in marketing practices and campaign research to those preferred by academic communities. Most of the focus group analysis in the field of marketing is impressionistic and focuses on explaining the motivations behind people's attitudes, responses, and feelings. It is common for marketers to employ tape-based coding (taking notes from audio or videotapes, searching for preestablished themes), note-based coding (relying on field notes from the actual groups), and memory-based coding (drawing on recollections from the group conversations). In each instance, practitioners typically focus on the actual group discussion as their data (rather than a typed transcript), placing particular attention on the group process and making distinctions between what participants spent the most time discussing and their most important statements (Morgan, 1998).

Scholarly research advances stricter and more systematic approaches to analyzing data than most marketing practices (Bloor et al., 2001; Fern, 2001; Morrison, 1998). Full transcription of the group conversation is regarded as central to valid analyses in academic research (Bloor et al., 2001; Fern, 2001). Once the group interview has been transcribed, scholars may engage in diverse analytic approaches. Many political communication scholars opt to read their transcripts closely and report themes, as well as departures from those themes, in their data (see Beom, Carlin, & Silver, 2005; Carlin & McKinney, 1994; Jamieson, 1993; Kaid, McKinney, & Tedesco, 2000; Mickiewicz, 2005).

Others have conducted content analyses on their transcripts. In doing so, researchers have employed various units of analysis and content analytic variables. Units of analysis range from the line of the transcript (Delli-Carpini & Williams, 1994), to the conversational turn (or "an individual's single uninterrupted utterance," see Bucy & Newhagen, 1999, p. 200; Graber, 2001), to conversational exchanges (between at least two or more people on a given subject; see Just et al., 1996). Content analytic categories stem from the research questions of particular projects. Notably, Just and colleagues (1996) searched for the personal experiences, political knowledge, and media sources that individuals mentioned in conversation as well as references that participants made to the verbal, visual, and verbal/visual aspects of the messages they were presented with. Graber (2001) coded transcripts for levels of cognitive complexity (starting with five levels of complexity and collapsing the analysis to two levels). Bucy and Newhagen (1999) coded for candidate identification, audience identification, emotional valence, and perceived interactivity (all on 1–7 Likert-type scales, see pp. 201–202).

Less common in the area of political communication are prominent qualitative techniques such as grounded theory (Corbin & Strauss, 1990), emergent category designation (Erlandson et al., 1993), analytic induction (sometimes also known as deviant case analysis; see Denzin, 1978; Frankland & Bloor, 1999; Gilgun, 1995; Patton, 2002), and conversation and discourse analysis (Myers & Macnaghten, 1999). These approaches are more common in sociological studies and cultural (and critical cultural) work (see Barbour & Kitzinger, 1999; Morgan, 1996; Morrison, 1998).

Several computer software packages created for qualitative researchers are emerging as an option to help scholars with their analyses. Software packages are constantly being developed, but have three general properties: they can serve as text retrievers, code-and-retrieve packages, and theory builders (see Patton, 2002). Three packages currently used by scholars include NVivo (www.qsrinternational.com), Ethnograph (www.qualisresearch.com), and Atlas (www.atlasti.com).

In their analysis of metaphors inspired by television, for instance, Delli-Carpini and Williams (1994) employed the Ethnograph software package to "ease transcript management, allowing more systematic and in-depth examination" (p. 792) of their data. These scholars were very clear, however, that their trained coders—*and not the software*—made coding decisions on a line-by-line basis. While Ethnograph might have been a good choice for this study since Delli-Carpini and Williams searched for the presence and absence of patterns *line by line*, many scholars employ the conversation as a unit of analysis for coding. In such instances, all data must be pre-sorted into message units (or conversational exchanges) prior to submission to the program. Because the message unit and conversational exchange are the most common units of analysis for focus group data, the use of software packages that conduct aggregate analyses—often disregarding and dismantling context—should be justified in detail if employed (Fern, 2001; Morrison, 1998).

Assessments of validity in focus group analysis have been addressed in two ways. First, researchers note the value of conducting multiple groups. Most authors agree that focus group research requires somewhere between four and six groups (Fern, 2001, p. 123); two groups is regarded as a minimum number to yield valid results (Kern & Just, 1995). Second, scholars stress that the integrity of the focus group transcripts and recordings are crucial to capturing the dialogic nature of the group interview. Accordingly, Bloor and colleagues (2001) offer the following advice for transcription of group sessions: (1) all recorded speech should be transcribed—even, and especially, when more than one person is talking, when participants interrupt each other, and when they trail off; (2) speech should be transcribed "as is" and not tidied up; (3) nonverbal communication such as laughter should be noted; and (4) all efforts should be made to accurately (but anonymously) identify the speakers in the transcripts (p. 60).

Focus group methodologists address concerns of generalizability differently than do most empirical researchers (see Fern, 2001; Patton, 2002). As Krueger and Casey (2000) outline, focus group research *can* be regarded as social scientific, as it represents "a process of disciplined inquiry that is systematic and verifiable" (p. 198); it is not, however, an approach that is *intended* to generalize. They write:

> Our goal is to go in depth into a topic, and therefore, we spend a sizable amount of time conducting research with a small number of people. Other research methods, by contrast, do not go "in depth" but are closed-ended questions with limited response choices that offer breadth instead of depth. The studies that offer breadth are the ones used to make generalizations . . . what we suggest is the concept of *transferability*. That is, when a person wants to use the results, he or she should think about whether the findings can transfer into another environment. What we suggest is that you consider the methods, procedures and audience and then decide the degree to which these results fit the situation you face. (p. 203)

For many focus group methodologists, then, the emphasis is placed not on the generalizability of a project, but on the generable credibility of the work. This credibility is similar to Lincoln and Guba's (1985) goal of assessing trustworthiness in naturalistic inquiry, asking not if a study's findings can be generalized to another population but "how can one establish confidence in the truth of the findings of a particular inquiry for the subjects (participants) with which, and the context in which, the inquiry was carried out?" (p. 290).

STRENGTHS AND LIMITATIONS

As with all methods, focus groups have both strengths and limitations. Strengths of this approach include how groups provide for exploration and discovery, context and depth, and rich interpretation of data (Merton & Kendall, 1946; Morgan, 1998). Scholars argue that the group interview format yields more complete and less inhibited responses than individual interviews since participants have the opportunity to ask questions of each other, build upon each other's statements, and support their positions in a group setting (Merton & Kendall, 1946; Wimmer & Dominick, 2000). Focus groups are also relatively inexpensive (as compared to surveys and experiments), can be conducted quickly, and offer the moderator and researcher some flexibility in question design and follow-up (Wimmer & Dominick, 2000, p. 119).

The limitations of focus groups are similar to those of other qualitative methods. This approach has been criticized for: relying on small samples that are not selected on a probability basis and that therefore cannot yield generalizable findings; allowing researchers and moderators the flexibility to make adjustments to the protocol during the group session such that questions are not asked the same way each time with regard to ordering or phrasing; and, not standardizing the unit of analysis in making sense of the data—scholars have freedom to employ the statement or conversational turn as their coding unit, which raises questions about the independence versus interdependence of the data analyzed.

Given these limitations, focus groups are clearly not appropriate for all projects. Group interviews should be avoided when participants are not comfortable with each other or the topic, when a project requires generalizable statistical data, when consensus or emotionally charged information is desired, or when confidentiality cannot be ensured (see, Fern, 2001; Morgan, 1988; Morrison, 1998). These concerns noted, Morrison (1998), Morgan (1998), and Fern (2001) maintain that informed choices and detailed reporting techniques protect the integrity of focus group analyses.

ETHICAL CONSIDERATIONS

Several ethical considerations arise with focus group research. Because focus groups resemble interviews and participant observation, moderators must be conscious of the ethical concerns of both interpersonal questioning and group observation. One issue arises during the recruiting process. Morrison (1998) argues that "it is wrong not to tell the participants what the subject is for conversation" (p. 25). If researchers are overly vague or give the wrong impression during the recruiting process, they may face uncomfortable or even hostile group members. A second concern involves considering whether participants are exposed to any risk. Here, researchers can protect participants by providing them with a statement of informed consent, clarifying that they are adults and that they are willingly participating in a study and may opt out at any time (Morgan, 1998).

A third risk regards attending to basic privacy issues. Researchers can protect the privacy of participants by restricting access to information that reveals their identities. Strategies for this step include referring to participants by first names or pseudonyms only, limiting access to the transcripts and tapes of the focus groups (and destroying the recordings after a period of time), removing or modifying identifying information on transcripts, and reminding participants not to over-disclose personal information during group discussions (Morgan, 1998; Morrison, 1998).

A fourth issue includes the discussion of potentially stressful topics. Researchers can protect participants against stress by emphasizing how participation is voluntary and by reminding them that they are free to take a break at any time—and they do not have to offer an explanation for taking one (Kreuger & Casey, 2000; Morgan, 1998).

Researchers should observe that there are also ethical concerns in the reporting of focus group data to the academic community. As Morrison (1998) notes, "the focus group is very much a private act. It is not open to critical inspection to the same extent as the survey questionnaire" (p. 249). Because most institutional review boards (university groups that approve research with human subjects) forbid the sharing of the recordings of focus group sessions with other researchers, Morrison regards it an ethical responsibility for researchers to offer sufficient documentation from their focus group data to support the claims they advance in their scholarly reports.

CONCLUSION

Focus groups have enjoyed increased visibility of late in public and academic circles. The acclaim can be attributed to both a desire to understand how individuals understand political life as well as to increased media attention to this method in political campaigns. As Luntz (1994) has stated, "most pollsters know what voters think, but too few understand how they feel." Because there is a goodness of fit between focus groups and research questions in political communication, both in terms of unpacking the meaning(s) of empirical effects and interpreting mixed findings, it is intriguing that this method—long regarded as impressionistic and unscientific—may contribute to the validity and programmatic growth of our subfield in the years to come.

APPENDIX 15.1

Sample Protocol for a Study on Political Socialization

Research Question: What are the patterns of *political socialization* for different demographic groups?

Opening: Please share your name, your age, and where you were born.

Introduction

- What is your first memory of your parents (when you were young)?
- What is your first television memory?
- What is your first political memory?

Transition

- Tell us about the types of television you would watch with your family when you were growing up?
- Tell us about the types of conversations you might have had with your family when you were growing up?
- Tell us about the types of political conversations you might have had with your family when you were growing up?

Key

- How often did you watch political television programming with your parents? (probe: news, Sunday shows, cable, etc.)
- How politically active would you say your family was when you were growing up?
- How involved with political parties would you say your family was when you were growing up?
- Tell us about the types of political candidates that impressed your family when you were growing up?
- Can you remember your parents getting upset while talking about politics? If so, what did they get upset about?
- Can you recall your parents getting upset with political candidates or elected officials while you were growing up? If so, what did they get upset about?

Ending

- If you have a pivotal (or most vivid) political memory, what would that be?
- Is there anything you would like to add on the topic of political memories?

Note: Protocol derived from Krueger's (1998a) question types.

APPENDIX 15.2

Sample Protocol and Research Summary

Research Topic: This study examines whether the social context and production features of different political communication formats affect the ways viewers assess and evaluate a candidate on television.

Hypotheses

H1: Audience viewing of the microdrama [up-close camera perspective] format will induce higher levels of identification with the candidate than the televised town meeting or political spot formats.

H2: Televised town meeting formats featuring audiences in first-order space [the foreground] will induce higher levels of audience identification than the microdrama or political spot formats.

H3: The microdrama represented by the close-up interview will produce more positive evaluations than either the televised town meeting or political spot formats.

H4: Exposure to televised town meeting formats will result in higher levels of perceived interactivity than either the microdrama or political spot formats.

Focus Group Protocol

• Would someone like to describe what this clip was about?

A general question sequence followed, entailing approximately 15 to 20 minutes of discussion for each clip:

• What did you like or dislike about this clip?
• Do you think this clip is an example of good or bad political communication?
• What do you think this clip tells us about politics?
• Do you feel like you were part of what was going on in the clip?
• Do you think that the candidate is credible or trustworthy?
• Does the split-screen add anything or detract anything from this clip?
• Do you think anyone in this clip represents you?
• Is this clip memorable for you?
• Is there anything that stood out in the clip that we haven't discussed yet?

Findings Summary: "Viewers process media formats featuring close-ups in terms of individual candidate attributes, while they regard political advertising and televised town meetings with multiple actors (candidate, audience members, and journalists) as contextualized social phenomena. Production techniques . . . can either associate candidates with other elements on the media stage, or disassociate them from externals while focusing on (the candidate's) persona" (Bucy & Newhagen, 1999, p. 193).

Note: Protocol and research summary derived from Bucy and Newhagen (1999).

REFERENCES

Apker, J., & Voss, C. R.W. (1994). The student voter. In D. Carlin and M. McKinney (Eds.), *The 1992 presidential debates in focus* (pp. 187–204). Westport, CT: Praeger.

Barbour, R.S., & Kitzinger, J. (Eds.). (1999). *Developing focus group research: Politics, theory and practice.* Thousand Oaks, CA: Sage.

Bedard, P., & Kaplan, D. E. (2004, May 10). When TV spots beat the real deal. *U.S. News and World Report, 136*(16), 4.

Beom, K., Carlin, D. B., & Silver, M. D. (2005). The world was watching and talking: International perspectives on the 2004 presidential debates. *American Behavioral Scientist, 49*(2), 243–264.

Bloor, M., Frankland, J., Thomas, M., & Robson, K. (2001). *Focus groups in social research.* Thousand Oaks, CA: Sage.

Bucy, E. P., & Newhagen, J. E. (1999). The micro- and macrodrama of politics on television: Effects of media format on candidate evaluations. *Journal of Broadcasting & Electronic Media, 43*(2), 193–210.

Carlin, D., & McKinney, M. (1994). *The 1992 presidential debates in focus.* Westport, CT: Praeger.

Carney, J., & Dickerson, J. F. (2000, October 9). Polling for the perfect pitch. *Time, 156*(15), 58.

Chiu, L. F., & Knight, D. (1999). How useful are focus groups for obtaining the views of minority groups? In R. S. Barbour & J. Kitzinger (Eds.), *Developing focus group research: Politics, theory and practice* (pp. 199–112). Thousand Oaks, CA: Sage.

Corbin, J., & Strauss, A. (1990). Grounded theory research: Procedures, canons, and evaluative criteria. *Qualitative Sociology, 13*(1), 3–21.

Delli-Carpini, M. X., & Williams, B. (1994). Methods, metaphors and media messages: The uses of television in conversations about the environment. *Communication Research,* 21, 780–812.

Denzin, N. (1978). *The research act: A theoretical introduction to sociological methods.* New York: McGraw-Hill.

Erlandson, D. A., Harris, E. L., Skipper, B. L., & Allen, S. D. (1993). *Doing naturalistic inquiry: A guide to methods.* Thousand Oaks, CA: Sage.

Fern, E. F. (2001). *Advanced focus group research.* Thousand Oaks, CA: Sage.

Frankland, J., & Bloor, M. (1999). Some issues arising in the systematic analysis of focus group materials. In R. S. Barbour & J. Kitzinger (Eds.), *Developing focus group research: Politics, theory and practice* (pp. 144–155). Thousand Oaks, CA: Sage.

Gamson, W. (1992). *Talking politics.* Cambridge: Cambridge University Press.

Gilgun, J. F. (1995). We shared something special: The moral discourse of incest perpetrators. *Journal of Marriage and the Family, 57,* 265–281.

Glaser, B., & Strauss, A. (1967). *The discovery of grounded theory.* Chicago: Aldine.

Glick, J. A. (1999). Focus groups in political campaigns. In D. D. Perlmuttter (Ed.), *The Manship School guide to political communication* (pp. 114–121). Baton Rouge: University of Louisiana Press.

Graber, D. (2001). *Processing politics: Learning from television in the Internet age.* Chicago: University of Chicago Press.

Graber, D. (2004). Methodological developments in political communication research. In L. L. Kaid (Ed.), *Handbook of political communication* (pp. 45–67). Mahwah, NJ: Lawrence Erlbaum.

Green, J., & Hart, L. (1999). The impact of context on data. In R. S. Barbour & J. Kitzinger (Eds.), *Developing focus group research: Politics, theory and practice* (pp. 21–35). Thousand Oaks, CA: Sage.

Greenbaum, T. L. (1998). *The handbook for focus group research* (2nd ed.). Thousand Oaks, CA: Sage.

Greenbaum, T. L. (2000). *Moderating focus groups: A practical guide for group facilitation.* Thousand Oaks, CA: Sage.

Hollander, B. (2004). The social contexts of focus groups. *Journal of Contemporary Ethnography, 33,* 602–637.

Hughes, D., & Dumont, K. (1993). Using focus groups to facilitate culturally anchored research. *American Journal of Community Psychology, 21*(6), 775–806.

Jamieson, K. H. (1993). *Dirty politics: Deception, distraction and democracy.* New York: Oxford University Press.

Jarvis, S., Barberena, L., & Davis, A. (2007). *Civics, not Government: Redirecting social studies in the nation's schools.* Austin, TX: The Annette Strauss Institute for Civic Participation. Retrieved March 15, 2007, from http://communication.utexas.edu/strauss/pdf/gates_report.pdf.

Johnson-Cartee, K. S., & Copeland, G. A. (1997). *Inside political campaigns: Theory and practice.* Westport, CT: Praeger.

Just, M. R., Crigler, A. N., Alger, D. E., Cook, T. E., Kern, M., & West, D. M. (1996). *Crosstalk: Citizens, candidates and the media in a presidential campaign.* Chicago: University of Chicago Press.

Kaid, L. L., McKinney, M., & Tedesco, J. (2000). *Civic dialogue in the 1996 presidential campaign: Candidate, media, and public voices.* Cresskill, NJ: Hampton Press.

Kern, M., & Just, M. (1995). The focus group method, political advertising, campaign news and the construction of candidate images. *Political Communication, 12,* 127–145.

Kitzinger, J., & Barbour, R. S. (1999). Introduction: The challenge and promise of focus groups. In R. S. Barbour & J. Kitzinger (Eds.), *Developing focus group research: Politics, theory and practice* (pp. 1–20). Thousand Oaks, CA: Sage.

Kolbert, E. (1992, August 30). Bypassing the press helps candidates; Does it also serve the public interest? *New York Times Magazine,* pp. 18–21, 60, 68, 72–73.

Krueger, R. A. (1998a). *Developing questions for focus groups: Focus group kit 3.* Thousand Oaks, CA: Sage.

Krueger, R. A. (1998b). *Moderating focus groups: Focus group kit 4.* Thousand Oaks, CA: Sage.

Krueger, R. A., & Casey, M. A. (2000). *Focus groups: A practical guide for applied research* (3rd ed.). Thousand Oaks, CA: Sage.

Krueger, R. A., & King, J. A. (1998). *Involving community members in focus groups: Focus group kit 5.* Thousand Oaks, CA: Sage.

Lemann, N. (2000, October 16). The word lab: The mad scientist behind what the candidates say. *New Yorker, 79*(11), 100–108.

Lincoln, Y. S., & Guba, E. G. (1985). *Naturalistic inquiry.* Newbury Park, CA: Sage.

Lipsitz, K., Trost, C., Grossman, M., & Sides, J. (2005). What voters want from political campaign communication. *Political Communication, 22,* 337–354.

Lunt, P. & Livingstone, S. (1996). Rethinking the focus group in media and communication research. *Journal of Communication, 46*(2), 79–98.

Luntz, F. (1994, May 16). Focus group research in American politics. *Polling Report.* Retrieved July 15, 2010, from http://www.pollingreport.com/focus.htm.

Luntz, F. (2006). *Words that work: It's not what you say, it's what people hear.* New York: Hyperion.

Markova, I., Linell, P., Grossen, M., & Orvig, A. (2007). *Dialogue in focus groups: Exploring socially shared knowledge.* London: Equinox.

McDermott, R. (2007). Cognitive neuroscience and politics: Next steps. In W. R. Neuman, G. E. Marcus, A. N. Crigler, & M. Mackuen (Eds.), *The affect effect: Dynamics of emotion in political thinking and behavior* (pp. 375–398). Chicago: University of Chicago Press.

Merton, R. (1987). The focused interview and focus groups: Continuities and discontinuities. *Public Opinion Quarterly, 51,* 550–556.

Merton, R., Fiske, M., & Kendall, P. (1956). *The focused interview.* New York: The Free Press.

Merton, R., & Kendall, P. (1946). The focused interview. *American Journal of Sociology, 51,* 541–557.

Mickiewicz, E. (2005). Excavating concealed tradeoffs: How Russians watch the news. *Political Communication, 22,* 355–380.

Mindich, D. (2005). *Tuned out: Why Americans under 40 don't follow the news.* New York: Oxford University Press.

Mischler, E. G. (1986). *Research interviewing: Context and narrative.* Cambridge, MA: Harvard University Press.

Mitchell, L. (1999). Combining focus groups and interviews: Telling how it is; telling how it feels. In R. S. Barbour & J. Kitzinger (Eds.), *Developing focus group research: Politics, theory and practice* (pp. 36–46). Thousand Oaks, CA: Sage.

Morgan, D. L. (1988). *Focus groups as qualitative research*. Newbury Park, CA: Sage.

Morgan, D. L. (1996). Focus groups. *Annual Review of Sociology, 22*, 129–152.

Morgan, D. L. (1997). *Focus groups as qualitative research* (2nd ed.). Thousand Oaks, CA: Sage.

Morgan, D. L. (1998). *The focus group guidebook: Focus group kit 1*. Thousand Oaks, CA: Sage.

Morgan, D. L., & Scannell, A. U. (1998). *Planning focus groups: Focus group kit 2*. Thousand Oaks, CA: Sage.

Morrison, D. E. (1998). *The search for a method: Focus groups and the development of mass communication research*. Luton: University of Luton Press.

Moyers, B. (1989). *Leading questions (The public mind: Image and reality in America)*. Videorecording. A presentation of WNET/New York and WETA/Washington. Alexandria, VA: PBS.

Mundy, A. (2000). Pollster yields must-see TV. *Media Week, 10*(26), 14–16.

Myers, G., & Macnaghten, P. (1999). Can focus groups be analysed as talk? In R. S. Barbour & J. Kitzinger (Eds.), *Developing focus group research: Politics, theory and practice* (pp. 173–185). Thousand Oaks, CA: Sage.

Patton, M. Q. (2002). *Qualitative research & evaluation methods* (3rd ed.). Thousand Oaks, CA: Sage.

Stephens, D., Alger, D., Allen, B., & Sullivan, J. L. (2006). Local news coverage in a social capital capital: Election 2000 on Minnesota's local news stations. *Political Communication, 23*, 61–83.

Stewart, D.W., Shamdasani, P.N., & Rook, D.W. (2007). *Focus groups: Theory and practice* (2nd ed.). Thousand Oaks: Sage Publications.

Sypher, B. (1994). The focus group as a research tool. In D. Carlin and M. McKinney (Eds.), *The 1992 presidential debates in focus* (pp. 37–54). Westport, CT: Praeger.

The pulse of the voters, minute by minute. (1996, October 14). *Newsweek, 128*(16), 32–34.

Waterton, C., & Wynne, B. (1999). Can focus groups access community views? In R. S. Barbour & J. Kitzinger (Eds.), *Developing focus group research: Politics, theory and practice* (pp. 127–143). Thousand Oaks, CA: Sage.

Wheelan, S. A. (Ed.). (2005). *The handbook for focus group research*. Thousand Oak, CA: Sage.

Wimmer, R. D,. & Dominick, J. R. (2000). *Mass media research: An introduction* (6th ed.). Belmont, CA: Wadsworth Publishing.

16

Genealogy of Myth in Presidential Rhetoric

Robert L. Ivie
Department of Communication and Culture
Indiana University

Oscar Giner
School of Theatre and Film
Arizona State University

> They think me mad—Starbuck does; but I'm demoniac, I am madness maddened! That wild madness that's only calm to comprehend itself! The prophecy was that I should be dismembered; and—Aye! I lost this leg. I now prophesy that I will dismember my dismemberer.
>
> —Ahab in Melville's *Moby Dick*

> We're fighting evil, and we cannot let it stand.
>
> —George W. Bush, October 11, 2001

Herman Melville's *Moby Dick* is at once mythopoeic and prosaic, an epic tale of good and evil that unites primal metaphor with narrative realism. This convergence of "the factual and the fanciful" (Arvin, 1957, p. v)—the literal and the symbolic—is an American prototype of allegorical realism that transcends the peculiarities of time and place and crosses the border between literary and political genres. As such, it typifies the practical operation of myth in contemporary political persuasion—including the presidential rhetoric of George W. Bush, which continued the tradition of articulating national identity and insecurity in terms of that which is alien, evil, and subversive (Campell, 1998, p. 3). As analogs of sacred myths, political myths are accepted by the public as essentially valid, "especially those established over long periods of time" that purport to convey in myriad forms "a true account of past, present, or predicted political events" (Flood, 2002, pp. 41, 44). These plastic images are the cultural DNA of national identity (O'Shaughnessy, 2004, pp. 87–89, 94–97).

National myths, such as myths of American exceptionalism and innocence, Hughes (2003, pp. 2–8) argues, function largely at an unconscious level to define and legitimize a people and their state. Thus, foundational images of a chosen people and millennial nation, deeply embedded in the American creed, are constitutive myths in the sense of being necessary fictions (Von Hendy, 2002, p. 304), fictions that construct boundaries of national identity that are always in some degree of flux between self and other, good and evil (Campbell, 1998, pp. 116–118). By conflating Indians with witchcraft and Devil worship, as Campbell (1998, pp. 107–133) observes, the Puritans practiced an "evangelism of fear," which produced a potent "myth of America" that has since been written into contemporary American foreign policy texts by substituting one marginal group after another in the position of the Antichrist.

Our purpose is to analyze this mythos, which weakens the nation's egalitarian inclinations and diminishes its democratic impulse to make peace with others (Ivie, 2005a, pp. 195–198), by exploring the presence of the myth from the perspective of its past or, in Rosenau's (1992, p. xi) terms, by producing a "history of the present that looks to the past for insight." Our method is genealogy—what Condit and Lucaites (1993, p. xvii) have termed "rhetorical history." Our focus is on myth and metaphor as rhetorical *topoi* and foundational narratives within U.S. political culture, with particular attention given to the mythos of evil and the projected image of the Devil. Our goal is to illustrate a critical method of analyzing political rhetoric for historical analogs relevant to engaging the demonizing projections of today. Thus, we discuss myth's constitutive function in political persuasion as it can be revealed by genealogical means in the living analog of the Salem witch hunt.

As a method of rhetorical critique, this genealogical investigation of foundational myths in political persuasion is distinctively concerned with disclosing problematic articulations of living collective memory (Hasian, 1998, p. 99; Hussein, 2002, p. 7), especially articulations of normative regimes of collective memory that diminish the democratic order (Brown, 2000, pp. 215, 220–221) and its peace-building potential. We acknowledge, along with Ono and Sloop (1992) and others (Prado, 2000, pp. 41–49), that critique is engaged scholarship necessarily positioned by perspective and purpose. The *telos* of critical historiography, or rhetorical genealogy, is in the present instance the enrichment of democratic culture. "To use genealogy to study articulation," as Stormer (2004, p. 276) argues, "is a way to make historiography of rhetoric more effective by highlighting the power issues involved in the maintenance of one form of rhetoric over others"— in this case, for the purpose of promoting democratic rhetoric over its coercive and violent alternatives.

CONSTITUTIVE MYTH IN POLITICAL PERSUASION

Myth and Political Piety

The great insight of Giambattista Vico (1668–1744), who was obscure in his own day but now "bestrides the modern social sciences and humanities like a colossus" (Grafton, 1999, p. xi; see also Fish, 1995, p. 209), was that we cannot understand the human world—especially the world of nations, political affairs, and civil institutions—without grasping its constitutive myths (Mali, 1992, p. 13). Appreciating such foundational narratives is to see "history and society as human productions" (Bové, 1995, p. 55). Myths stem from the poetic tradition, and poetic wisdom, Vico understood, is the essence of common sense, the expression of political sensibility, and the origin of conceptual and critical language. Metaphorical or symbolic language—often literalized in public discourse beyond immediate recognition as figure and fable—suffuses the vernacular language of everyday life and the commonplaces of politics. The archetypal myths of modern public culture are the imaginative agents of collective mind and political will. In this way, Vico deciphered the "mythopoeic constitution of humanity," revealing civilization's logos or sense of reason and rationality, which evolves "in and through and out of mythos," i.e., out of a culture's foundational stories (Mali, 1992, pp. 5, 129, 151). Reading Vico's *New Science* teaches us to see myth and to appreciate the continuing influence of embedded political symbolism.

Presidential rhetoric, no more or less than other constituent elements of political culture, manifests such a "poetic logic," in which metaphor operates as a myth in miniature and, thus, as a master trope for conferring sense and sensibility on the political world (Vico, 1744/1999, p. 159, paragraph 404). "Archetypal metaphors," as Osborn (1967, p. 116) has observed, "are characterized by their prominence in rhetoric, their tendency to occupy important positions within speeches, and their especial significance within the most significant speeches of a society." Rhetoric, as the vehicle of poetic wisdom and the source of political stability as well as cultural change, plays a managerial role in civic affairs, where knowledge is necessarily contingent and constructed (Hobbs, 2002, pp. 65, 78, 85; Schaeffer, 1990, pp. 100, 151, 159).

Moreover, political leadership, whether exercised by monarchs or presidents, is grounded in the authority of archetypal myths. Archetypes constitute the symbolic essence of myths, which engender "our common knowledge of what is certain," and such knowledge is made certain in the sense that it is imaginatively defined and conventionally understood by myth makers. The certitude of this authority of archetypal myths carries the day when judgment is required in the political realm of the contingent, that is, the "unreflecting judgment" of the social order that Vico calls common sense (Vico, 1744/1999, pp. 20–25, 79–80, 93, 130, paragraphs 29–34, 141–142, 209, 350). The sublime wisdom of such myths yields political authority (Vico, 1744/1999, p. 407, paragraph 942). Accordingly, political authority is less a matter of *who* governs than how the mythic means of governance are *rhetorically managed* (Mali, 1992, p. 241, 245).

To manage the archetypal myths of governing authority in political discourse is to engage in a secular sacrament that has spiritual roots and carries moral overtones. Vico's genealogy of political culture grounds these civilizing myths of poetic logic in their sacred origins. It is the "terrifying thought of some deity" or higher order that reduces savagery to civilized, dutiful behavior (Vico, 1744/1999, p. 124, paragraph 338) and leads to what Foucault calls the "disciplinary and regulatory apparatuses of governmentality" (Venn, 2007, p. 113). The human mind and morality, as the foundation of nations, is known through "divine reason" and is derived "from the knowledge of God" by the divining of myth (Vico, 1744/1999, pp. 207–209, 409, paragraphs 503–503, 506, 948). Thus, as White notes, piety is for Vico "the basis of any sound commonwealth," the lack thereof leading to decline, decadence, and dissolution and the cyclical need for renewal. The bestial, White continues, "exists in the human in the same way that the human exists in the bestial" and in the same way that "savagery is contained in civilization and civilization in savagery" (White, 1976, pp., 68, 85). "Unless one is pious, one cannot be truly wise," Vico concluded, and "if peoples lose their religion [that is, their civilizing piety], nothing remains to keep them living in society" (Vico, 1744/1999, pp. 490–491, paragraphs 1109, 1112). The civilizing bond of the nation is its divining of, and devotion to, founding myths.

Critiquing the Mythos of Evil

Given myth's constitutive role in public culture, two important purposes are served by identifying foundational myths and tracking governing metaphors (miniature myths) that are embedded in political rhetoric but usually are not overtly perceived as such by modern minds. First, the discovery of buried myth exposes the architecture of political authority. Presidential rhetoric, not unlike the discourse of other cultural agents and institutions, exhibits the nation's reigning worldview. Charting the "conceptual dictionary" (Vico, 1744/1999, pp. 25, 80, 84, 131, paragraphs 35, 145, 162, 355) of generative images enables us to denote basic "mytho-logical patterns of thought" that incite and constrain contemporary political thought and action (Mali, 1992, pp. 259, 270). A polity's commonplaces (*topoi*), extracted from the traces of embedded myths found on the "etymological surface" of political discourse, are sources of rhetorical invention past and present that operate as modes of *ingenium*—which is Vico's term for the "ingenious generation of novel meanings or insights" (Daniel, 1990, p. 129).

Second, in addition to revealing sources of political authority and piety in the civil world— a world Vico insists "*is certainly the creation of humankind*" as a function of the divining of myths (Vico, 1744/1999, p. 119, paragraph 331, emphasis in original)—constructing a genealogy of myth operating more or less covertly within presidential rhetoric serves the important purpose of performing political critique without succumbing to the "barbarism" of critical reflection, i.e., sans the negativity of factional strife and calculated malice (Vico, 1744/1999, p. 488, paragraph 1106). While criticism can make the collective mind "more exact" and "rational," it lacks a necessary and proper degree of "ingenuity" without the benefit of generative *topoi* or tropes of similitude (Vico, 1774/1999, p. 203, paragraph 498). Invention, criticism, and judgment are necessarily intertwined in Vico's view of social history and civic affairs. Rational consciousness itself is an "outcropping" of metaphor, myth, and the faculty of *ingenium*, which constitute the *sensus communis* from which critical reason emerges (Hobbs, 2002, pp. 66–68, 72, 75–76). Even critics are rhetorical poets and cultural workers.

By Vico's calculation, Daniel (1990, pp. 133–134) observes, "humanity is characterized primarily not in terms of its rationality but in terms of its communal procedures for creative problem solving," which entails the articulation of similarities more than differences. Thus, it is useful not only to observe that archetypal myths have been articulated within presidential rhetoric to express, for instance, the conventional wisdom of war but also to consider that they might be redeployed to construct an alternative wisdom for making peace. In this sense, productive political critique operates from the same source of *ingenium*—the same poetic dictionary of archetypal symbols—as the discourse it analyzes and evaluates. In Vico's (1744/1999, p. 203, paragraphs 497–498) words, topics are the means by which we come "to know a subject well and completely"; thus "providence directed human affairs wisely by causing the human mind to conceive the art of topics before that of criticism, for we must be familiar with things before we can judge them."

Consistent with these general observations about the mythic constitution of political culture, and by way of illustration of this rhetorical method of productive critique, our purpose is to examine a particular archetypal image that haunts presidential war rhetoric and casts its shadow onto the face of the nation's adversaries. Such an undertaking raises two important questions. First, how are we to gauge the cultural authority and grasp the poetic logic of a presidential discourse of terror, especially if we wish to turn away from war-making and toward peace-building? And, second, how are we to confront the debilitating myth that terrorism is a mortal threat to liberal democracy, and the corresponding rhetoric of evil that "externalizes the danger and thus serves to hide a much more endemic and structural threat" (Curtis, 2004, p. 141) to America's democratic institutions—the abuse of freedom itself? Valuable perspective on these questions can be found in the nation's Puritan origins and the ancestral struggle of these "strangers in a strange land" to sustain their pious perception of a savage New World, that is, to make order out of chaos by conquering evil.

The articulation of evil and the demonizing of enemies are distinctive marks of presidential war rhetoric and an enduring dynamic of American political culture (Ivie & Giner, 2007). Their rhetorical formulation and cultural immanence have codified mythic undertones into a ritual of national redemption that spans time and circumstances. Just as George W. Bush called upon the nation to destroy "evildoers" in a global war on terrorism, Ronald Reagan rallied Americans to defeat an "evil empire" in the long Cold War against the Soviet Union. Each president drew rhetorically on a constitutive myth of the Devil that is deeply embedded in U.S. history—a shadow figure that can be traced back to the Salem witch trials in colonial America, which was manifest in an outburst of witch hunting during the vicious era of McCarthyism and has metamorphosed in the modern age into the ubiquitous image of diabolical enemies. Indeed, the convergence of seemingly distinct moments of public exorcism (separated in time by more than two and a half centuries) in the production of Arthur Miller's (1953) play, *The Crucible*—and the play's film adaptation over four decades later at the beginning of the post-Cold War era (Hytner, 1996)—signifies the enduring influence of demonology in its various iterations on the nation's political conscience.

Tracing the genealogy of this demonology not only exposes its mythic presence in American political culture but also helps us to understand the impetus of presidential war rhetoric. Hunting the Devil, that is, reveals the archetypal myth conjured in sacrificial rituals of redemptive violence. Although sometimes momentarily arrested, the deadly projection is never fully exorcised from the body politic. Thus, our guiding concern is to find the Devil in modern disguise—to unmask the myth of evil savagery posing as political rationality and stark realism even as it projects its shadow outward in a recurring exercise of the hostile imagination—so that this projection might be better recognized for what it is and eventually retrieved and integrated into the nation's collective self.

Toward this end, mythic dynamics can be rendered transparent by placing presidential rhetoric in its broader historical and cultural context. The Bush administration's investment in the language of evil after the trauma of 9/11, employed to rationalize an open-ended war on terror, was as blatant as its rhetorical clout was difficult to explain. Understood, however, as a mythic rite of redemptive violence (Ivie, 2007b), a presidential rhetoric of evil imbued with the language of savagery translates into a cyclical quest for salvation. The rhetorical image of savagery drives a chosen people and exceptional nation to the imperial defense of civilization (Ivie, 2005b), for the beast, as noted by Umberto Eco (2007, pp. 90–104), is the legendary sign of the presence of the Devil.

Rhetorical Genealogy

As a method of cultural investigation, charting the genealogy of constitutive myths derives direction and heuristic value from its critical orientation rather than from any narrowly prescribed procedure. Genealogy requires no single reading or closed archive (Wendt, 1996, p. 252) because it is itself a performance—a critical interpretation of reigning mythic constructions. The performance of genealogy, Fenske (2007, p. 57) observes, approaches "the culture of the present as a complex puzzle whose scattered pieces contain fragments of images, words, thoughts, and actions, which, once assembled, create a picture of cultural memory." For example, Arntfield (2008) advances a genealogical interrogation of the disciplinary nomenclature of Western police forces. Unlike content analysis or other quantitative methods that operate within preset categories and definitions, genealogical inquiry sets out to confound governing classifications and to render their established boundaries more permeable in order to open a space for critical reflection (Owen, 1999, pp. 30–37; Ransom, 1997, pp. 78–100). It "tropes" or turns pivotal terms within naturalized hierarchies of political discourse to put them productively in play again (Brown, 2000, pp. 210–211, 214; Mills, 2003, pp. 78–79, 91–92; Prado, 2000, p. 49; Schrift, 1990, p. 93).

An interpretive genealogical study of rhetorical discourse proceeds through key cases to construct mutable typologies of social action (Alasuutari, 1995, pp. 4, 130–31) and thus helps to reveal enduring but changeable discursive patterns or formations of social knowledge (Kendall & Wickham, 1999, pp. 29–31, 41–42). We can achieve "a strong sense of discourse as an enduring flow" by tracing its genealogy "as a series of events existing as transformations of one another" (Bové, 1995, p. 54, referencing Foucault, 1977). By examining texts closely "within a specific historical juncture" for their "constitutive cultural codes" (Turner, 1996, pp. 12–16, 30), we seek to identify conventions of representation, or signifying systems and practices, that construct cultural meaning (Clifford, 2001, p. 21). As a system of relations, discourse "establishes categories and makes distinctions through networks of difference and similarity" (Turner, 1996, p. 14). As a set of culturally recognized rules, a signifying code produces meaning and guides interpretation (Edgar & Sedgwick, 1999, p. 69) to bring into existence, for example, the social reality of evil. Genealogy recognizes that social knowledge and power constitute a "circular dynamic," in which truth and power are so thoroughly enmeshed that they are interdependent to the point of producing one another (Dreyfus & Rabinow, 1983, pp. 105–106; Han, 2002, p. 107).

Such an approach to critical inquiry is especially revealing when it brings into focus precursors of cultural mutation. Cultural heritage is itself, as Foucault (1984, p. 82) argues, "an unstable assemblage." Unlike a traditional historical method that searches for "fixed truths, laws, finalities, or origins," genealogy is alert to discontinuities among recurrences and to the dynamism of interconnections as it "seeks to problematize and overturn the primacy of origins and the reification of truths" (Wendt, 1996, p. 257). As such, rhetorical genealogy "can illuminate contradictions, controversies, and conflicts surrounding [the] authority and use" of pivotal terms within particular discursive formations (Ziegler, 2007, p. 422) for the purpose of producing "a space of reflexivity" about the supposed origin of things and thus questioning "the taken-for-granted concepts or categories of existence that condition consciousness" (Berry, 2006, p. 13–14; see also Clifford, 2001, p. 20; Mills, 2003, pp. 64, 76–77; Visker, 1995, pp. 48–49). Seeing the strangeness of the past helps us to see the strangeness of the present (Mills, 2003, p. 24). De-literalizing the mythos of today's rhetoric of evil can be accomplished by probing from a genealogical perspective the complex form of its cultural production. Evil, as Nietzsche understood, is an artifact of an ethical system that articulates not free-standing realities but "the interests of particular social groups" that are "produced by social and historical processes" and can be grasped as a cultural category by tracing its genealogy (Edgar & Sedgwick, 1999, p. 159).

Genealogy itself, in Foucault's (1984, p. 76) words, is "grey, meticulous, and patiently documentary," requiring a "knowledge of details." It is alert to lines of development from past to present and fascinated by "recurrence and repetition" but skeptical of grand narratives of progress and naturalized logics of the linear unfolding of events inevitably toward present conditions or future outcomes (Dreyfus & Rabinow, 1983, pp. 118–125; Johnson et al., 2004; pp. 131–132). Genealogy thus "does not map the destiny of a people" or reveal an "uninterrupted continuity" (Foucault, 1984, pp. 81, 83). History as heritage is not determined but is instead subject to a combination of discipline and transformation. Rather than revealing the origin or "inviolable identity" of something like evil, genealogy instead uncovers dissension, derision, and irony, teaching us "how to laugh at the solemnities" of an origin—divine or not—by cultivating the "details and accidents that accompany every beginning" (Foucault, 1984, pp. 79–80; see also p. 93).

In Foucault's apt analogy, dispelling the "chimera" of a troubled origin is akin to exorcising the "shadow" of a pious man's soul (Foucault, 1984, p. 80). Rather than attempting to represent a constitutive myth, a genealogical "interpretation of interpretations" serves productively to disfigure and transgress the myth's legitimizing historical formulation (LaFountain, 1989, pp. 124–125). Indeed, genealogy is a method of coming to terms with a troublesome formation of living memory within the collective self for the purpose of escaping its debilitating grasp on the present (Clifford, 2001, pp. 5–12, 151–153; Dreyfus & Rabinow, 1983, pp. xxvi–xxvii, 103; Simons, 1995, pp. 20–22; Wendt, 1996, p. 257). Accordingly, genealogical interpretation "opens towards a politics of memory" (Venn, 2007, p. 123).

Genealogy, in this sense of the critical interpretation of public memory, is much like a process of writing what Condit and Lucaites (1993, p. xvii) call "rhetorical history," which produces a record of malleable foundations of political culture that change meanings within "changing times." Unlike genealogies that reflect back primarily on theoretical meta-categories, including concepts such as power and hegemony (Venn, 2007), the public sphere (Splichal, 2006), publics (Dayan, 2005), social capital (Coole, 2009), or embodied rhetoric (Hawhee, 2006), culturally grounded rhetorical history charts the changing meaning of terms like *equality* "as a foundation of American political life" by interrogating its "continuing, dynamic genealogy within American public discourse" (Condit & Lucaites, 1993, p. xvii). Such a history describes various usages of equality by which Americans have constituted and reconstituted national identity. Current variations on this "ideographic" approach to the critical analysis of rhetorical formations in public culture—an approach that defines an ideograph as "a culturally biased, abstract word or phrase, drawn from ordinary language, which serves as a constitutional value for a historically situated collectivity" (Condit & Lucaites, 1993, p. xii)—include, for example, interrogations on disciplining gender (Sloop, 2004), the construction of enemies in debates over immigration (Ono & Sloop, 2002), and terrorism as a problematic linguistic marker of American identity (Winkler, 2006).

As we turn now to an examination of the Devil's crucible, our approach to rhetorical history focuses on the plasticity of a particular archetypal myth, tracing its genealogy to Salem so that we might better understand its residual contours as a cultural code and thereby demonstrate the method of our critical practice, which is to circle back in order to see a way forward. Myth is the cultural category and constitutive code under genealogical scrutiny here, whereas Condit and Lucaites (1993, p. xii) and others work within the theoretical framework of critical rhetoric to focus on ideographs as "central, organizing" elements of public culture. Ideographs are condensed, normative representations such as "liberty," "property," "privacy," "law and order," and "equality" (Condit & Lucaites, 1993, pp. xii–xiii). Yet, political culture encompasses many rhetorical forms other than ideographs within its symbolic boundaries, as Condit and Lucaites note, including most importantly myths, metaphors, *topoi*, narratives, and related tropes of similitude. These additional rhetorical forms are the archetypal sources of poetic wisdom and engines of cultural production that are especially operative in constructing categories of good and evil, which makes them powerful heuristics for recognizing the changing face of the Devil and thus the focus of our critical genealogy.

THE DEVIL AND ARTHUR MILLER: SEEKING A METAPHOR

Arthur Miller went to Salem in search of a metaphor. The times—Cold War America during the early 1950s—were out of joint. Unsettling developments were threatening a United States flush with the arrogance of its own power after World War II: there was "the recent Red victory in China, the Russian demonstration of the atomic bomb, and the expansion of Soviet territory into Eastern Europe" (Miller, 1987, p. 329). The Washington hearings of the House Un-American Activities Committee and the cultural eruption of McCarthyism were terrorizing the nation into becoming a "philosophical monolith," and if—Miller (1987, p. 330) believed—"the current degeneration of discourse continued . . . we could no longer be a democracy, a system that requires a certain basic trust in order to exist."

Marion Starkey's (1949/1989) classic book on the Salem witch hunt, *The Devil in Massachusetts*, had fallen into Miller's hands "as though it had been ordained" (Miller, 1987, p. 330). In 1952 he had given a copy of Starkey's book to Elia Kazan—the director of *All My Sons* and *Death of a Salesman*. "It's all here . . . every scene," he commented to Kazan, for he was contemplating writing a new play (Kazan, 1988, p. 449). Miller had sensed disturbing parallels between his situation and Salem and between Salem—across the breach of time—and contemporary Washington.

Before leaving on a research trip to what was then "a town dribbling away, half forsaken," Miller stopped, at Kazan's request, for a visit at Kazan's Connecticut home. In a fateful conversation in the woods that recalls Goodman Brown's conversation with the Devil in Nathaniel Hawthorne's story,[1] Kazan told Miller that he had decided to co-operate with HUAC—to confess his past and tenuous connections to the Communist Party, and to publicly reveal the names of former associates. Miller loved Kazan like a brother, but he could not get past the sum conclusion: "Had I been of his generation, he would have had to sacrifice me as well" (Miller, 1987, p. 333). As Miller said goodbye, he mentioned that he was on his way to Salem. Understanding the implication of Miller's journey (Kazan, 1988, pp. 460–461; Miller, 1987, pp. 332–335), Kazan's wife, Molly, exclaimed: "You're not going to equate witches with this!"[2] Miller (1987, p. 335) wrote that while driving up to Salem, "The gray rain on my windshield was falling on my soul." He was aware that he was "moving inward as well as north" (Miller, 1987, p. 332).

Symbolizing Otherness

Tituba was a woman, a slave, an immigrant, and a foreigner to Puritan society—a perfect symbol of Otherness for seventeenth-century Massachusetts and for our own time. Had she not been sold by Barbados merchants and bought by Samuel Parris (parish minister of Salem Village in 1692) in the West Indies, she would also have been considered illegal. In all probability she was an Arawak Indian, from the region of the mouth of the Orinoco River in South America (Breslaw, 1996, pp. 3–20). In the Salem documents she is repeatedly called *titibe an Indian Woman*, or more simply, *Tituba Indian* (Boyer & Nissenbaum, 1977, pp. 745, 756). In their resort to these descriptive phrases, Salem folk insisted she was separate, apart from them, ominously related to the American Indian tribes that besieged their community of "saints."

The Other, once defined, becomes a receptacle for fresh projections of Otherness. Over time, Tituba's features have been colored by our own projections. Starkey (1949/1989, p. 29) describes her as "half Carib and half Negro." In *The Crucible*, Miller (1953, p. 8) describes her as a "Negro slave," and so she was portrayed in Nicholas Hytner's 1996 film of the play. Caribbean novelist Maryse Condé (1992) titled her contemporary novel on the Salem slave *I, Tituba, Black Witch of Salem*.

Tituba was married to John Indian, the second of Parris' West Indian slaves. John appears frequently in the original documents, but only sporadically in later accounts of the Salem trials. In his nineteenth-century classic history of the witch hunt, Charles W. Upham (1867/1971, Vol. 2, p. 2) writes that "these two persons may have originated the 'Salem witchcraft.'" Together John and Tituba were thought to exert a psychic and spiritual manipulation of the Salem inhabitants, which resulted in persecution, death, and the implosion of their community.

On March 1, 1692, Sarah Good, Sarah Osborne, and Tituba were examined at Salem Village (now Danvers, Massachusetts) for suspicion of witchcraft by Jonathan Corwin and John Hathorne (a forefather of Nathaniel Hawthorne), Assistants to the General Court of the Massachusetts Bay Colony. The women were accused of Devil worship and of sending their spectral shapes to torment a group of afflicted children. Over the next few days, Good, Osborne, and Tituba were interrogated by the magistrates and confronted by a chorus of howling, disturbed adolescents and their relatives, in front of a large gathering of spectators and covenanted church members. Sarah Good denied tormenting the children and blamed Osborne for their ills. Sarah Osborne denied having made a contract with the Devil and claimed that instead of being a witch she was probably bewitched herself (Boyer & Nissenbaum, 1977, Vol. 2. p. 611). Tituba, examined next, had been beaten and abused by her slave master, Reverend Parris, in order to make her confess and accuse others of witchcraft. At first she too refused to admit hurting the children and denied familiarity with evil spirits, but eventually she began to speak the myth that would energize the witch hunt.

Tituba said that several weeks before, when the children had first fallen ill, "one like a man Just as I was goeing to sleep Came to me . . . he sayd he would kill the Children & she would never be well, and he Sayd if I would nott Serve him he would do soe to mee." This man, who came from Boston, "Tell me he god." He wore "black Cloaths Some times, Some times Searge Coat of other Couler, a Tall man w'th white hayr, I think." The man asked Tituba to write her name in his book:

Q. did you write?
A. yes once I made a marke in the Booke & made itt with red Bloud
Q. did he gett itt out of your Body?
A. he Said he must gett itt out the Next time he Come againe, he give me a pin tyed in a stick to doe itt w'th, butt he noe Lett me bloud w'th itt as yett butt Intended another time when he Come againe. (Boyer & Nissenbaum, 1977, Vol. 3, pp. 750–755)

The Tall Man in Black often appeared in the company of the shapes of Sarah Good and Goody Osborne, and those of two other women from Boston who also dressed in dark colors and sober fabrics. On one occasion, the Tall Man and the four women had appeared to Tituba at her master's house: "The man stand behind mee & take hold of mee to make mee stand still in the hall." The spectral shapes had forced Tituba to pinch and hurt the children of the household—Betty Parris and Abigail Williams. The man, who was "very strong," had also made Tituba ride "upon a stick or poale & Good & Osburne behind me we Ride takeing hold of one another." They had traveled to Thomas Putnam's house, so the story went, to kill his young daughter with a knife. On the same pole, Tituba and the Tall Man in Black had ridden through the air but had come back to Salem Village without reaching Boston. She had seen "noe trees, noe Towne" (Boyer & Nissenbaum, 1977, Vol. 3, pp. 750–55).

Tituba's was the first documented confession by a Salem "witch." The sexual metaphors in her language—later picked up and repeated by the Salem accusers in their depositions—readily identify the Tall Man from Boston as a Medieval incubus. In subsequent examinations, the image of the Tall Man in Black would recur as an obsessive concern in the questions of prosecutors, in the hallucinations of the afflicted children, and in the relations of confessed witches (the signing of one's name in blood to a contract with the Devil is a story as old as the legend of Dr. Faustus). Religious officials and Salem citizens feared the presence in their midst of a conspiracy of witches led by a Grand Wizard. George Burroughs, former minister of Salem, was tried and hung on August 19, 1692, based on evidence that held him to be the "minister with a black coat," or the "little black beard man . . . in blackish apparil" who was the "Cheife of all the persons accused for witchcraft or the Ring Leader of them" (Boyer & Nissenbaum, 1977, Vol. 1, pp. 167, 170, 176–177). Tituba's man with "black Cloaths," whose spectral shape tormented victims into signing the Devil's book, had become the "dreadfull wizzard" who sounded the "Trumpett" for the "generall meeting of the Witches in the feild near Mr. Parrisse's house," and who presided over their "sacramental meeting" where they ate "Red Bread" and drank "Red Wine like Blood" in a devilish inversion of the Supper ritual (Boyer & Nissenbaum, 1977, Vol. 1, pp. 172–174; Vol. 2, p. 423).

What the Salem folk did not perceive—what Arthur Miller sensed, but did not discover—was that a momentous shift had occurred in Tituba's discourse during her interrogation. Pressed by the magistrates, the disturbed children, and the menacing congregation, Tituba had withdrawn into her own dream world. The forces that the Puritans believed to be at work in Salem (God and the Devil; angels and familiar spirits; witches and saints) existed in different forms in Tituba's native mythology—a mythology that was organic to the Americas and that did not partake of the moral Manichaeism of Christianity.

The Arawak tribes of the South American continent first immigrated to the Caribbean Islands between 500 BC and AD 600. In the centuries between AD 1200 and AD 1500, the Taíno culture— formed by successive waves of Arawak migrations, which combined with early pre-agricultural settlers on the islands—flourished in western Cuba, Española (today Haiti and the Dominican Republic), and eastern Puerto Rico. The Taíno language was a branch of the Proto-Arawakan languages. In AD 1500 it was closely related to the Island/Carib language of the Lesser Antilles, and to the Arawak/Lokono language of the continent (Granberry & Vascelius, 2004, pp. 14–15; Rouse, 1992, pp. 39–42). In the Caribbean Islands, the Taínos encountered Christopher Columbus and his caravels in 1492. Facing the need to communicate with native tribes, Columbus entrusted Fray Ramón Pané—a Catalonian hermit who came to the New World during the second voyage— with the task of living among the Indians of Española in order to "know and understand the beliefs and idolatries of the Indians, and how they venerate their gods" (Pané, 1988, p. 3). Pané recorded his findings in a document entitled *Relación de las antiguedades de los indios*, which is today an invaluable source for the study of the language, myths, and ceremonies of the Caribbean Taínos. Pané's brief manuscript, dating from 1498, was the first book written in the New World.

Breslaw (1996) has noted that the name of a young slave, *Tattuba*, appears on two slave inventories of plantations from Barbados in 1676. She suggests that this was the same slave bought by Parris in the mid-1670s, and points out that the name "Tituba or Tattuba denoted an Arawak Indian tribe in South America—the Tetebetana" (Breslaw, 1996, pp. 24–25, 30). Coincidentally, we find in Pané's *Relación* (1988, pp. 16–17) the myth of a woman called *Itiba Cahubaba* who dies giving birth to four sons. One of them was the sacred trickster figure of Taíno mythology, Deminán Caracaracolero, who brings about the cosmogonic origin of the sea by smashing the treasured pumpkin of an Old Chieftain. As Itiba Cahubaba gave birth to the Taíno trickster figure and his identical brothers, so Tituba became the mother of the trickster rhetoric and mythology that cast the "great delusion of Satan" upon New England (Upham, 1867/1971, Vol. 2, p. 510).

We learn from the *Relación* that the Taínos believed in an Other World of spirits—or as Salem folk would call them, *shapes*—which communicated freely with human beings. At night, the spirits of the dead (*opías*) would eat of the fruit of the guava tree, celebrate dances, and come to the world to make love to the living (Pané, 1988, pp. 22–23). The House of the Dead (Coaybay) was ruled by a dark lord, called Maquetaurie Guayaba (Pané, 1988, pp. 21–22). They believed that the living spirit of human beings could appear to others in the shapes "of father, mother, brothers or relatives, and in other shapes" (Pané, 1988, pp. 23–24).

The parallels between the Salem narratives—first framed and colored by Tituba's coerced confession—and the *Relación* are striking in their similarity of detail. Ghostly apparitions by the spirits of dead relatives were recorded by Ann Putnam, Sr. in Salem:

> Immediatly their did appere to me: six children in winding sheets which called me aunt: which did most greviously affright me: and they tould me that they ware my sisters Bakers children of Boston and that goody Nurs and Mistris Cary of Charlstown and an old deaft woman att Boston had murthered them. (Boyer & Nissenbaum, 1977, Vol. 2, p. 601)

Salem girls were "tortored" by specters; men were suffocated by familiar spirits in their houses at night (Boyer & Nissenbaum, 1977, Vol. 2, p. 572). Tituba's Tall Man in Black from Boston, who appeared along with other spectral shapes, has his counterpart in the semblance of Maquetaurie Guayaba, Ruler of Coaybay. Her flight with the Tall Man upon a "stick or poale" is an apt metaphor for nocturnal love-making. Like an *opía*, the Man in Black would instantly disappear after his adventures: "They hall me and make me pinch Betty . . . and then quickly went away altogether" (Boyer & Nissenbaum, 1977, Vol. 2, p. 753).

The breadth of incidence in Salem of Tituba's original Arawak-based story is remarkable. The shapes, for instance, of some of the familiar spirits that Tituba identified in her confession can be found among Taíno *cemíes* (carved stone, wood or cotton sculptures of deities and animal figures). The "hairy Imp" as well—which she described as "a thing all over hairy, all the face hayry & a long nose & I don't know how to tell how the face looks w'th two Leggs, itt goeth upright & is about two or three foot high & goeth upright like a man" (Boyer & Nissenbaum, 1977, Vol. 3, p. 752)—can be recognized in the wooden sculpture of *Opiyelguobirán*, the doglike cemí of the cacique Sabananiobabo, which always escaped to the rain forests at night (Lamarche, 2005, p. 95).

Otherwise powerless before the Salem Magistrates, the slave Tituba allowed—by mythological translation and adaptation—her own demi-gods and spirits to assume the masks of the cast of characters of the Salem Christian Passion play of Good and Evil. Forty years after his original research for *The Crucible*, Arthur Miller commented that the Salem Puritans gave Tituba "inadvertently the power to destroy them by investing her with this mysterious power from hell" and "then proceeded to destroy each other, once that was let loose among them" (Hytner & Miller, 2004). Thus, Tituba created the mythos that informed and compelled the witch hunt. Her graphic syncretization of mythological images invigorated the threats that the Puritans perceived and exacerbated their fears. Thus was the fury of the witch hunt unleashed upon Salem.

If Tituba gave birth to the demons that tormented Salem and sparked the witch hunt, then her husband, John Indian, became the instigator who whipped them into shape and fanned the flames. John and Tituba had baked the witch-cake (a mixture of rye meal and urine from the afflicted children) that had raised the Devil in Salem.[3] Ever since that time, according to Samuel Parris in his rebuke of Mary Sibley at the village church on March 25, 1692, "apparitions have been plenty." The Devil's "rage is vehement and terrible; and, when he shall be silenced, the Lord only knows" (Upham 1867/1971, Vol. 2, p. 95).

Soon after Tituba's testimony, John Indian joined the ranks of the bewitched. In a complaint lodged against John Proctor in April of 1692, he appears in the role of accuser:

> Then John [Indian] cryed out to the Dog under the Table to come away for Goodm: Proctor was upon his back, then he cryed out of Goody Cloyse, O you old Witch, & fell immediately into a violent fit that 3 men & the Marshall could not without exceeding difficulty hold him. (Boyer & Nissenbaum, 1977, Vol. 2, p. 677)

From Nathaniel Cary's account of the examination of his wife Mary, it is clear that by May of 1692 John had crafted his convulsions into a masterful performance:

> The Indian before mentioned, was also brought in to be one of her Accusers: being come in, he now (when before the Justices) fell down and tumbled about like a Hog, but said nothing. The Justices asked the Girls, who afflicted the Indian? they answered she (meaning my wife) and now lay upon him; the Justices ordered her to touch him, in order to his cure . . . but the Indian took hold on her hand, and pulled her down on the Floor, in a barbarous manner; then his hand was taken off, and her hand put on his, and the cure was quickly wrought. (Calef, 1866/1970, Vol. 3, pp. 23–24; original in italics)

There is a precedent for John Indian's "fits" in Pané's *Relación*. His gambols and mountebank behavior were part of the ceremonial practices of the Taíno *behiques*—medicine men who were known to speak to the gods and to the dead. Both the "touch test" applied in the case of Mary Cary, and John Indian's pulling of Mrs. Cary to the floor, existed among the healing rituals of the *behiques* (Pané, 1988, pp. 27–28). John Indian inflamed the witch hunt by the simple tactic of affirming the Puritan narratives that the witch hunters wanted to hear.

Projecting the Shadow

It is difficult today, at our remove in time, to prove conclusively that Tituba's mythology and John Indian's ritual behavior in Salem were based directly on the practices of the Taínos, who were Antillean Arawaks. Some of the parallels between the peoples of the Caribbean and practices among the slaves of Salem can be attributed more broadly to the fact that visionary cultures—societies that acknowledge and are conversant with spiritual worlds—construct comparable visual images and ritual practices. Upham's account of the Salem witch trials, dating to the nineteenth century, contended that Tituba and John Indian contributed to the witch hunt by borrowing from Indian culture "the wild and strange superstitions prevalent among their native tribes" (Upham, 1867/1971, Vol. 2, p. 2). In such a setting, pregnant with suspicion, their rhetorical performances "added to the commonly received notions on such subjects, heightened the infatuation of the times, and inflamed still more the imaginations of the credulous" (Upham, 1867/1971, Vol. 2, p. 2). Moreover, many of the stories and images that flourished in Salem, Upham (1867/1971, Vol. 2, p. 2) concludes, can be found in "the systems of demonology" of other native cultures in the Americas.

Upham reminds us of what Cotton Mather discovered in the seventeenth century: "the *Black Man*" (shades of Maquetaurie Guayaba) is what "the Witches call the Devil; and they generally say he resembles an *Indian*" (Mather, 1866/1970, Vol. 1, p. 150; italics in the original). Behind the mask of the archetypal devil in Salem there was always the face of the American Indian—natural and mysterious, alien and threatening, a projection of Otherness, and a constant symbol of violence, danger, and distance from the American landscape.

The synchretic crystallization of images that combined the contours of the European Devil with the substance of American Indian divinities had a previous history in the Americas (Pané, 1988, pp. 26, 33). Puzzled by the mysteries of an unknown natural environment and anxious over the loss of familiar spiritual and social contexts, European colonizers tried to comprehend the New World through their own inherited images. Massachusetts Puritans, "flying from the depravations of Europe," had come to an American "Indian wilderness" to live and celebrate the "Wonders of the Christian Religion" (Cotton Mather, quoted in Vaughan & Clark, 1981, p. 135). When the strange landscape proved threatening and harmful, they projected onto it, for safety and recognition, their own mental constructs.

If the New England Puritans are to be remembered for the Salem witch hunt, they must also be remembered for the efforts that brought the witch hunt to a halt. To the extent that the violence and zealotry that characterized the witch hunters serves as a warning against the excesses of ideological fundamentalism in the present era, we must remember that it was also the Puritans who found strength in their faith and bravely resisted tyranny, delusion, and the dominion of folly in Salem. Roberts-Miller (1999, p. 19) has noted the presence of a monologic discourse in Puritan rhetoric that "imagined only two possible identities in an audience: the reprobate and the elect."[4] Puritanism, she argues, thus "*required* a degree of dissent that it could not manage" (Roberts-Miller, 1999, p. 137). That is, it contained within its repressed self an unmanageable impulse to dialogism. On one hand, "Puritans were dissenters in search of religious freedom who treated their own dissenters with no mercy and forbad religious freedom to everyone else" (Roberts-Miller, 1999, p. 136). But their very reliance on dualities produced an indeterminacy rather than a hegemony in the sense that "true piety" in this fallen world of apparent but irresolvable paradoxes required, almost against their will, "a balancing of competing demands," which was ultimately achieved by "hear[ing] the voices from both sides" (Roberts-Miller, 1999, p, 140). Those cast in the role of reprobate by their accusers could only take comfort in the belief that affliction was a path to salvation.

The threat was felt by all. The Devil was a culturally inherited image with deep moral and religious associations (Russell, 2001, p. 122); the New World landscape was a perpetual source of threat and vague, unnamable dangers; armed conflicts with Indian tribes and their French allies were regular occurrences in the colonists' lives. Around the time of the witch trials, Salem children and adult victims were palpably sick—most of the accused did not deny the veracity of the sufferings of the bewitched.[5] The region's livestock and farm animals were distempered as if with a plague. The Salem folk, Miller (1953, p. 7) observed, found in the witch hunt an outlet for communal anxiety as well as an "opportunity for everybody so inclined to express publicly his guilt and sins, under the cover of accusations against the victims."

The Devil/Indian avatar that Tituba unleashed was an aggregate of living terrors, a crystallized antagonist which signified disparate threats, a literalized metaphor that obsessed both accused and witch hunters alike (Von Franz, 1968, p. 175). Tituba and John Indian led the Salem folk to believe that the Devil lived among them. Such psychoanalytical projections occur, according to Von Franz (1991, p. 15), when an "image which has been 'radiated' outward onto another object is 'bent back' and returns to oneself." Projections of the shadow side of the collective self, when reflected back upon the subject, never at first reveal the enemy within to be among us, but always elsewhere—among our neighbors. When the works of the Devil were discovered in Salem, the blame was fixed upon those who were tinged with Otherness.

Combating the Literalization of Metaphors

There are lessons to be found in this troubled and dissentient precursor of contemporary political culture's struggle to suppress and purge the satanic forces of terrorism—lessons about listening to dissenting voices and about the limited possibilities of retrieving a projected shadow given such strong tendencies to deflect blame onto "others" inside and outside the community. The people of Salem did not accept communal responsibility for an acknowledged error. Instead, the protests, professions of innocence, and admonitions of the condemned, the petitions of loved ones, neighbors, and moral figures within the community, and especially the calamity of the rich and powerful who eventually became ensnared in the growing web of accusations had the collective effect of prompting those involved to play the role of victim of an evil deceit. The category of evil—the presence of the Evil One—remained untouched by the acknowledged and lamented tragedy of the witch hunt, just as it continues to rent American politics today in the form of opposing religious and secular fundamentalisms (Wallis, 2005, p. 7) and in self-sustaining and self-righteous rites of redemptive violence (Ivie, 2007a, pp. 62–67; Wink, 1998, pp. 42–62) in the wake of disenchantment over the Iraq War.

How to combat the literalization of metaphors, or to acknowledge and retrieve mythic projections of the archetypal shadow? Salem Puritans struggled mightily against the witch hunt from different perspectives. First came the resolute denials of the victims. There was Martha Corey, for instance, proclaiming before her accusers that she was a "Gosple-woman" (Boyer & Nissenbaum, 1977, Vol. 1, p. 248). Her husband, Giles Corey, was pressed to death for refusing to answer the charges of witchcraft. In the face of howling accusations, Rebecca Nurse declared:

"I am as innocent as the child unborn" (Boyer & Nissenbaum, 1977, Vol. 2, p. 585). Elizabeth Proctor warned her accusers: "There is another judgment, dear child" (Boyer & Nissenbaum, 1977, Vol. 2, p. 660). At Gallows Hill, moments before his death on August 19, 1692, George Burroughs repeated the Lord's Prayer without fault and spoke so fervently that the gathered crowd almost turned against the witch hunters, save for a timely oration delivered by Cotton Mather on a horse.

Not only the condemned resisted or tried to pierce the clouds of fear that oppressed Salem. In the cases against John and Elizabeth Proctor, thirty-one neighbors signed a petition of protest, declaring "upon o'r Consciences we Judge them Innocent of the crime objected" (Boyer & Nissenbaum, 1977, Vol. 2, p. 682). Margaret Jacobs recanted her confession (Boyer & Nissenbaum, 1977, Vol. 2, pp. 491–492). A deposition submitted in favor of Mary Bradbury of Salisbury (ancestor of science fiction writer Ray Bradbury) contained the signatures of ninety-three of her neighbors. When petitions did not move the court, Puritans took stronger and more direct action. Thomas Bradbury and supporters orchestrated the escape of his wife from jail and kept her in hiding.

On July 23, John Proctor sent a petition to several Boston ministers alleging that the confessions of witches were being obtained through torture ("Popish Cruelties") (Boyer & Nissenbaum, 1977, Vol. 2, p. 690). After reviewing Proctor's letter, Increase Mather and other Boston ministers declared unanimously against one of the key assumptions of the trials, holding that the Devil could appear in the shape of an innocent person, even though they qualified this statement by admitting that such instances were "rare and extraordinary" (Starkey, 1949/1989, p. 191).[6] At a conference of ministers in Cambridge, Mather later warned in sterner tones against spectral evidence and denounced the "touch" test (Starkey, 1949/1989, p. 214).[7] Starkey (1949/1989, p. 214) reports that numerous preachers came to the defense of individual parishioners.

Still the witch hunt raged, and the witch hunters continued down their cruel path. The Kingdom of Satan had descended in great wrath, legions of the Devil's servants were torturing the minds and bodies of the faithful, a score of condemned persons had been executed on Gallows Hill, and the jails were filled with confessed witches and wizards. As Von Franz (1968, p. 182) observed, sometimes "a passionate drive within the shadowy part" of the self is so impervious to reason that it requires a bitter experience, "a brick, so to speak," to "drop on one's head" in order to stop such impulses. Such a "brick," such an irreconcilable chasm between delusion and reality, such a personal calling to account for the consequences of unexamined projections of evil, was to fall squarely on the head of the Reverend John Hale.

In October of 1692, Mary Herrick of Wenham complained of being tormented by Mrs. Sarah Hale. When accusations "came so near to himself," the reverend shifted his attitude and maintained that he was "fully satisfied of his Wife's sincere Christianity" (Calef, 1866/1970, p. 48). There were others who were spared and protected from accusations, including Mrs. Thatcher of Boston, who was the mother-in-law of Jonathan Corwin, one of the judges and chief witch hunters of the trials (Thomas Brattle in Hill, 2000, p. 92). When the Revered Samuel Willard (who made efforts to oppose the witch hunt), one of the most distinguished ministers in Boston, was accused, the judges rejected the charges outright (Starkey, 1949/1989, p. 168).

When the relatives of the rich, eminent, and powerful became the object of accusations, the doubts that had gnawed at the poor and defenseless were finally entertained, and the witch hunt promptly came to an end. By comparison, prosecuting a few sacrificial soldiers for the sins of the Abu Ghraib prisoner abuse scandal in Iraq was not the bitter, mind-clearing experience of a brick falling on the head of the politically powerful. (Indicting the Secretary of Defense or the President himself for violating international law, however, might have been a brick of sufficient force to halt the projection of evil.)

Modern psychoanalysis holds that "the withdrawal of a projection . . . is almost always a moral shock" (Von Franz, 1991, p. 17). Once error had been perceived, once the conviction of delusion had been gained, the Puritans of Salem reacted with humble apologies, public confessions, and rituals of reconciliation to the horror of the witch hunt. In 1696 the General Court of Massachusetts Bay proclaimed a "Day of Prayer, with Fasting throughout this Province," so that "whatever mistakes on either hand have been fallen into . . . referring to the Late Tragedy . . . he would humble us therefore and pardon all the Errors of his Servants and People . . ." (Calef, 1866/1970, Vol. 3, pp. 132–133). On the day of the Fast, January 14, 1697, Judge Samuel Sewall, lamenting the "reiterated strokes of God upon himself and family" because of his "Guilt contracted" during the Salem Trials, stood in the South Meeting House of Boston while the Reverend Samuel Willard read an apology and expressed his desire "to take the Blame & Shame of it, Asking pardon of Men, And especially desiring prayers that God who has an Unlimited Authority, would pardon that Sin, and all other his Sins" (quoted in Francis, 2005, p. 181). Jury members of the Salem trials, fearing that they had brought upon the "People of the Lord" the "Guilt of Innocent Blood," released a public document which stated, "We justly fear that we were sadly deluded and mistaken, for which we are much disquieted and distressed in our minds; and do therefore humbly beg forgiveness, first of God for Christ's sake for this our Error" (Calef, 1866/1970, Vol. 3, pp. 134–135). Troubled by the episode, John Hale (1702/1973, p. 9) wrote his book, *A Modest Enquiry into the Nature of Witchcraft*, to "at least give some light to them which come after, to shun those Rocks by which we were bruised, and narrowly escaped Shipwreck upon."

Puritan theology foreclosed on the realization that the Devil they feared was within themselves; that whatever else he may be he was also a formal manifestation of the shadow archetype; that he was the alternate face of the Puritan coin; that he was their dark brother—an artful representation of the shadow side of their self with which their belief system countenanced no compromises. Lacking acquaintance with modern theories of the self, Puritan identity in 1692 would have been characterized by Jung as *archaic*, "one in which [man] saw all psychic processes in an 'outside'—his good and evil thoughts as spirits, his affects as gods (Ares, Cupid) and so on" (Von Franz, 1991, p. 14). Ann Putnam, Jr. was characteristic of others in assigning blame for her actions to the Devil she battled as a child and renounced as an adult: "What I did was ignorantly, being deluded of Satan" (Hill, 2000, p. 108). The General Court proclaimed that the witch hunt had been "raised among us by Satan and his Instruments, thro the awful Judgment of God" (Calef, 1866/1970, pp. 132–133). The Jurors of the Salem trials also blamed their mistakes on the Devil: "We confess that we ourselves were not capable to understand, nor able to withstand the mysterious delusions of the Powers of Darkness, and Prince of the Air" (Calef, 1866/1970, p. 134). Samuel Parris, in his grudging apology to his mutinous parishioners in 1694, was convinced that "God . . . has suffered the evil angels to delude us on both hands . . ." (Hill, 2000, p. 156).

The very Devil they had fought had tricked them, outsmarted them, but the Devil—and their belief in him—remained very much alive.

SEEING METAPHORICALLY A WAY FORWARD

Projections that are withdrawn, but which cannot be integrated into the conscious personality, will be "transferred" to other "concrete persons and situations" (Jung, 1959, p. 401). Detached unconscious contents are projected again, thus repeatedly creating new threats and fears. When the Devil was no longer to be found among witches, he was found among American Indians. At a later time in history (what Arthur Miller revealed in *The Crucible*), when Indians, like witches, were no longer a threat, the Devil was found to exist among Communists, as he is found existing in the image of evil terrorists today. Like Massachusetts Puritans, we have yet to see the Devil metaphorically as a projection of our own darkness. We prefer to fancy him as sheer evil in the form of a living, breathing, external enemy, such as Adolph Hitler, Joseph Stalin, Osama bin Laden, Saddam Hussein, or Mahmoud Ahmadinejad.

Indeed, Eco (2007, p. 185) notes that the growing tendency of the modern world is to assign satanic features to the foreign Other and thus literally "demonize the enemy." Andersen's (2006) recent study of media over the last century of American war propaganda confirms Eco's basic observation and affirms the continuing relevance of Lasswell's (1927/1971, p. 77) post-World War I insight about the theme of "Satanism" as a pervasive instrument of public persuasion. Conquering the "Evil One" is glorified in this modern "cult of evil," Lasswell (1927/1971, p. 96) concluded. As a continuation of the dehumanizing fantasy of enmity, which O'Shaugnessy (2004, p. vii) identifies as the essence of contemporary war rhetoric, President Bush in the wake of the September 11 terrorist attacks quickly branded Osama bin Laden the "Evil One" (Andersen, 2006, p. 202)—a satanic mark that remained evident five years later in the discourse of the 2008 presidential campaign (Ivie & Giner, 2009), including the hardcore rhetoric of John McCain, who vowed to pursue Osama bin Laden all the way "to the gates of hell."

During one of Arthur Miller's last days in Salem, he observed several framed etchings of the witch trials on the walls of the Salem Historical Society. In a flash of recognition, Miller recalled his own childhood memories of devout followers praying in a New York synagogue and instantly knew "what the connection was: the moral intensity of the Jews and the clan's defensiveness against pollution from outside the ranks. Yes, I understood Salem in that flash, it was suddenly my own inheritance" (Miller, 1987, p. 338). *The Crucible* is an artistic metaphor that represents a terror created by the outburst of a latent myth. It is an aesthetic evocation of a spiritual vision, a harmonic conjuring of a reigning narrative. The presence of that myth in society, its latency in collective consciousness, allows for a "subjective reality" to be raised to the level of a "holy resonance" by a precise, semiotic manipulation of its contents (Arthur Miller, quoted in Budick, 1999, p. 96). Hence the value of a portentous play.

The Crucible serves as both a warning and reminder of how the better angels of our nature can become demonic—perhaps they were demons to begin with—without us noticing. "One of the incidental consequences for me," Miller (1987, p. 342) professed, "was a changed view of the Greek tragedies; they must have had their therapeutic effect by raising to conscious awareness the clan's capacity for brutal and unredeemed violence so that it could be sublimated and contained by new institutions, like the law Athena brings to tame the primordial, chainlike vendetta." *The Crucible* is a prescient dramatization that fuses separate moments in time, separate corners of consciousness, separate stages in the spiral ascent of our mythical history. It is a Vichean trope of similitude, a seeing of similarities, a metaphor that expresses the discomforting analogue between hunting the Devil then and demonizing enemies now.

Grasping a historical analogue of the archetypal shadow projected so readily in post-9/11 presidential rhetoric constitutes an opportunity to integrate otherwise detached and demonizing projections into the nation's democratically troubled consciousness (Ivie, 2005a). This, it would appear, is a way forward from domineering and self-destructive rhetorical rituals, of spiraling toward peace-building discourses, of bridging the human divide, of addressing the great challenge of pluralistic democracy (Mouffe, 2000, 2005), and of preventing necessarily agonistic political relations from deteriorating so readily into violent confrontations between absolute good and sheer evil. It is a method of rhetorical critique that Rushing and Frentz (1995, pp. 47–49) characterize as probing public dreams to reveal the troubled condition of the cultural unconscious and thus to show "how we might change that condition" through a therapeutic practice of "listening and conversing." Interpreting myth as a mode of critical inquiry engages the whole self, they argue, more than using "any set of pre-established critical operations"; it is a project undertaken for the purpose of *withdrawing* projections and replacing old tropes with new observations (Rushing & Frentz, 1995, pp. 50–51). Just as their close examination of the frontier hunter myth reveals the dehumanizing effects of technology in contemporary films such as *The Deer Hunter,* our genealogy of Salem's Devil myth exposes the continuing presence of the shadow in today's political constructions of the evil other.

Such rhetorical histories, or genealogical excavations, produce practical knowledge of foundational myths in public culture—that is, knowledge of cultural formations which otherwise operate below the threshold of critical consciousness, thereby remaining immune to resistance and beyond the reach of constructive change (Russell, 2001, p. 125). Unlike conventional histories or other standard methodologies in search of (or aiming to approximate) universal truths, immutable laws, and static causes, the genealogical scrutiny of archetypal myths postulates malleable rhetorical origins, which—operating as tropes of similitude—are considered to be potential precursors of transformation within a problematic political culture inclined toward coercion and violence.

As a rhetorical method of interpretation, the genealogical investigation of political myth engages the scholarly critic in a purposefully productive project of articulating democratic values and formulating alternatives to hostile projections (Ivie, 2001). It is a distinctly generative approach to the critique of political culture which bridges the artificial divide between the theory and use of rhetoric while enriching the social imaginary for the purpose of enhancing human relations. Thus, it is a productive rather than reductive method of scholarship that cultivates democratic culture by addressing the problem of the scapegoat, or demonized Other, as an unreflective rite of projection and detrimental ritual of victimization. Rhetorical genealogy is, in the end, a way of mining a troubled political culture for its renewable archetypal tropes so that they might be put to a better—that is, less hateful and fearful—use than the terrorizing Devil myth of presidential persuasion.

NOTES

1. The character Goodman Brown in Hawthorne's (1835/1946) short story, "Young Goodman Brown," leaves his home for a walk, at which point the Devil appears to him, and they engage in a lengthy conversation while walking together through the woods.
2. In Kazan's (1988, pp. 460–461) retelling, this conversation took place before his decision to cooperate with HUAC; in Miller's (1987, pp. 332–335) version, Kazan had already testified.
3. At the behest of Mary Sibley, the witch cake was fed to a village dog in order to discover the culprit Witch who was disturbing the children (Hale, 1702/1973, 23–24).
4. Roberts-Miller (1999, p. 123) defines monologic discourse as "a form of public argumentation that purports to get audiences to adopt the right course of action through clearly stating and logically demonstrating true propositions."
5. Carlson (1999) has advanced the intriguing notion that the ailments in Salem were caused by an epidemic of *encephalitis lethargica* or sleeping sickness—a disease for which there is no cure even today.
6. The Salem witch hunters believed that the Devil could only appear in the likeness of those under his rule.
7. The accused were asked to "touch" the persons with fits at the hearings. If their fits disappeared at that moment, the evil was thought to have returned to the witch.

REFERENCES

Alasuutgari, P. (1995). *Researching culture: Qualitative method and cultural studies*. London: Sage Publications.

Andersen, R. (2006). *A century of media, a century of war*. New York: Peter Lang.

Arntfield, M. (2008). Hegemonic shorthand: Technology and metonymy in modern policing. *Communication Review, 11*(1), 76–97.

Arvin, N. (1957). Introduction to *Moby Dick*. In Herman Melville, *Moby Dick or the whale*. New York: Holt, Rinehart and Winston.

Berry, D. (2006). Radical mass media criticism: An introduction. In D. Berry and J. Theobald (Eds.), *Radical mass media criticism: A cultural genealogy* (pp. 1–16). Montreal: Black Rose Books.

Bové, P. A. (1995). Discourse. In F. Lentricchia & T. McLaughlin (Eds.), *Critical terms for literary study* (pp. 50–65). Chicago: University of Chicago Press.

Boyer, P., & Nissenbaum, S. (Eds.). (1977). *The Salem witchcraft papers* (Vols. 1–3). New York: Da Capo Press.

Breslaw, E. G. (1996). *Tituba, reluctant witch of Salem*. New York: New York University Press.

Brown, W. (2000). Nietzsche for politics. In A. D. Schrift (Ed.), *Why Nietzsche still? Reflections on drama, culture, and politics* (pp. 205–223). Berkeley: University of California Press.

Budick, E. M. (1999). History and other spectres in Arthur Miller's *The Crucible*. In H. Bloom (Ed.), *Arthur Miller's the crucible* (pp. 21–39). Philadelphia: Chelsea House Publishers.

Calef, R. (1866/1970). More wonders of the invisible world. In S. G. Drake (Ed.), *The witchcraft delusion in New England* (Vol. 3, pp. 3–167). New York: Burt Franklin.

Campbell, D. (1998). *Writing security: United States foreign policy and the politics of identity* (Rev. ed.). Minneapolis: University of Minnesota Press.

Carlson, L. W. (1999). *A fever in Salem*. Chicago: Ivan R. Dee.

Clifford, M. (2001). *Political genealogy after Foucault: Savage identities*. New York: Routledge.

Condé, M. (1992). *I, Tituba, black witch of Salem*. Charlottesville, VA: University Press of Virginia.

Condit, C. M., & Lucaites, J. L. (1993). *Crafting equality: America's Anglo-African word*. Chicago: University of Chicago Press.

Coole, D. (2009). Repairing civil society and experimenting with power: A genealogy of social capital. *Political Studies, 37*(2), 374–396.

Curtis, N. (2004). Nihilism, liberalism and terror. *Theory, Culture & Society, 21*(3), 141–157.

Daniel, S. H. (1990). *Myth and modern philosophy*. Philadelphia: Temple University Press.

Dayan, D. (2005). Paying attention to attention: Audiences, publics, thresholds and genealogies. *Journal of Media Practice, 6*(1), 9–18.

Dreyfus, H. L,. & Rabinow, P. (1983). *Michel Foucault: Beyond structuralism and hermeneutics* (2nd ed.). Chicago: University of Chicago Press.

Eco, U. (Ed.). (2007). *On ugliness* (A. McEwen, Trans.). New York: Rizzoli.

Edgar, A., & Sedgwick, P. (1999). *Cultural theory: The key concepts*. London: Routledge.

Fenske, M. (2007). Movement and resistance: (Tattooed) bodies and performance. *Communication and Critical/Cultural Studies, 4*(1), 51–73.

Fish, S. (1995). Rhetoric. In F. Lentricchia & T. McLaughlin (Eds.), *Critical terms for literary study*. Chicago: University of Chicago Press.

Flood, C. G. (2002). *Political myth*. New York: Routledge.

Foucault, M. (1977). *Discipline and punish: The birth of the prison* (A. Sheridan, Trans.). New York: Pantheon.

Foucault, M. (1984). Nietzsche, genealogy, history. In P. Rabinow (Ed.), *The Foucault reader* (pp. 76–100). New York: Pantheon.

Francis, R. (2005). *Judge Sewall's apology: The Salem witch trials and the forming of an American conscience*. New York: Harper Collins.

Giner, O., & Ivie, R. L. (2009). More good, less evil: Contesting the mythos of national insecurity in the 2008 presidential primaries. *Rhetoric & Public Affairs, 12*(1), 279–302.

Grafton, A. (1999). Introduction. In Giambattista Vico, *New science* (D. Marsh, Trans.) (pp. xi–xxxiii). London: Penguin Books.

Granberry, J., & Vescelius, G. S. (2004). *Languages of the pre-Columbian Antilles*. Tuscaloosa: University of Alabama Press.

Hale, J. (1702/1973). *A modest enquiry into the nature of witchcraft*. Bainbridge, NY: York-Mail Print.

Han, B. (2002). *Foucault's critical project: Between the transcendental and the historical* (E. Pile, Trans.). Stanford, CA: Stanford University Press.

Hasian, M. A. (1998). Intercultural histories and mass-mediated identities: The re-imagining of the Arab–Israeli conflict. In J. N. Martin, T. K. Nakayama, & L. A. Flores (Ed.), *Readings in cultural contexts* (pp. 97–104). Mountain View, CA: Mayfield Publishing Co.

Hawhee, D. (2006). Language as sensuous action: Sir Richard Paget, Kenneth Burke, and gesture-speech theory. *Quarterly Journal of Speech, 92*(4), 331–354.

Hawthorne, N. (1835/1946). *Short stories*. New York: Vintage Books.

Hill, F. (2000). *The Salem witch trials reader*. Cambridge, MA: Da Capo Press.

Hobbs, C. L. (2002). *Rhetoric on the margins of modernity: Vico, Condillac, Monboddo*. Carbondale, IL: Southern Illinois University Press.

Hughes, R. T. (2003). *Myths America lives by*. Urbana: University of Illinois Press.

Hussein, A. A. (2002). *Edward Said: Criticism and society*. London: Verso.

Hytner, N. Director. (1996). *The crucible*. 20th Century Fox.

Hytner, N., & Miller, A. (2004). Commentary. *The crucible*, DVD: Twentieth Century Fox Entertainment.

Ivie, R. L. (2001). Productive criticism then and now. *American Communication Journal, 4*(3). Available online at http://acjournal.org/holdings/vol4/iss3/special/ivie.htm.

Ivie, R. L. (2005a). *Democracy and America's war on terror*. Tuscaloosa: University of Alabama Press.

Ivie, R. L. (2005b). Savagery in democracy's empire. *Third World Quarterly, 26*(1), 55–65.

Ivie, R. L. (2007a). *Dissent from war*. Bloomfield, CT: Kumarian Press.

Ivie, R. L. (2007b). Fighting terror by rite of redemption and reconciliation. *Rhetoric & Public Affairs, 10*(2), 221–48.

Ivie, R. L., & Giner, O. (2007). Hunting the devil: Democracy's rhetorical impulse to war. *Presidential Studies Quarterly, 37*(4), 580–98.

Johnson, R., Chambers, D., Raghuram, P., & Tincknell, E. (2004). *The practice of cultural studies*. London: Sage.

Jung, C. (1959). Psychology of the transference. In V. S. de Laszlo (Ed.), *The basic writings of C. G. Jung* (pp. 398–429). New York: Modern Library.

Kazan, E. (1988). *A life*. New York: Alfred A. Knopf.

Kendall, G., & Wickham, G. (1999). *Using Foucault's methods*. London: Sage.

LaFountain, M. J. (1989). Foucault and Dr. Ruth. *Critical Studies in Mass Communication, 6*(2), 123–137.

Lamarche, S. R. (2005). *Tainos y Caribes*. San Juan, Puerto Rico: Editorial Punto y Coma.

Lasswell, H. D. (1927/1971). *Propaganda technique in World War I*. Cambridge. MIT Press.

Mali, J. (1992). *The rehabilitation of myth: Vico's New Science*. New York: Cambridge University Press.

Mather, C. (1866/1970). Wonders of the invisible world. In Samuel G. Drake (Ed.), *The witchcraft delusion in New England* (vol. 1, pp. 1–247). New York: Burt Franklin.

Melville, H. (1851/1957). *Moby Dick or the whale*. New York: Holt, Rinehart and Winston.

Miller, A. (1953). *The crucible*. New York: Penguin.

Miller, A. (1987). *Timebends*. New York: Grove Press.

Mills, S. (2003). *Michel Foucault*. New York: Routledge.

Mouffe, C. (2000). *The democratic paradox*. London: Verso.

Mouffe, C. (2005). *On the political*. London: Routledge.

Ono, K. A., & Sloop, J. M. (1992). Commitment to *telos*—a sustained critical rhetoric. *Communication Monographs, 59*, 48–60.

Ono, K. A., & Sloop, J. M. (2002). *Shifting borders: Rhetoric, immigration, and California's proposition 187*. Philadelphia: Temple University Press.

Osborn, M. (1967). Archetypal metaphor in rhetoric: The light-dark family. *Quarterly Journal of Speech, 53*(2), 115–126.

O'Shaughnessy, N. J. (2004). *Politics and propaganda: Weapons of mass seduction*. Ann Arbor: University of Michigan Press.

Owen, D. (1999). Orientation and Enlightenment: An essay on critique and genealogy. In S. Ashenden & D. Owen (Eds.), *Foucault contra Habermas: Recasting the dialogue between genealogy and critical theory* (pp. 21–44). London: Sage.

Pané, Fr. R. (1988). *Relación de las antiguedades de los indios*, J. J. Arrom (Ed.). México: Siglo XXI.

Prado, C. G. (2000). *Starting with Foucault: An introduction to genealogy*. Boulder, CO: Westview Press.

Ransom, J. S. (1997). *Foucault's discipline: The politics of subjectivity*. Durham: Duke University Press.

Roberts-Miller, P. (1999). *Voices in the wilderness: Public discourse and the paradox of Puritan rhetoric*. Tuscaloosa: University of Alabama.

Rosenau, P. M. (1992). *Postmodernism and the social sciences: Insights, inroads, and intrusions*. Princeton, NJ: Princeton University Press.

Rouse, I. (1992). *The Taínos: Rise and decline of the people who greeted Columbus*. New Haven: Yale University Press.

Rushing, J. H., & Frentz, T. S. (1995). *Projecting the shadow: The cyborg hero in American film*. Chicago: University of Chicago Press.

Russell, S. (2001). Witchcraft, genealogy, Foucault. *British Journal of Sociology, 52*(1), 121–137.

Schaeffer, J. D. (1990). *Sensus communis: Vico, rhetoric, and the limits of relativism*. Durham: Duke University Press.

Schrift, A. D. (1990). *Nietzsche and the question of interpretation: Between hermeneutics and deconstruction*. New York: Routledge.

Simons, J. (1995). *Foucault and the political*. London: Routledge.

Sloop, J. M. (2004). *Disciplining gender: Rhetorics of sex identity in contemporary culture*. Amherst: University of Massachusetts Press.

Splichal, S. (2006). In search of a strong European public sphere: Some critical observations on publicness and the (European) public sphere. *Media, Culture and Society, 25*(5): 695–714.

Starkey, M. L. (1949/1989). *The devil in Massachusetts: A modern enquiry into the Salem witch trials*. New York: Anchor Books.

Stormer, N. (2004). Articulation: A working paper on rhetoric and *taxis*. *Quarterly Journal of Speech, 90*(3), 257–284.

Turner, G. (1996). *British cultural studies: An introduction* (2nd ed.). New York: Routledge.

Upham, C. W. (1867/1971). *Salem witchcraft* (Vol. 2). Williamstown, MA: Corner House Publishers.

Vaughan, A. T., & Clark, E. W. (Eds.). (1702/1981). *Puritans among the Indians: Accounts of captivity and redemption, 1676–1724*. Cambridge, MA: Harvard University Press.

Venn, C. (2007). Cultural theory, biopolitics, and the question of power. *Theory, Culture & Society, 24*(3), 111–124.

Vico, G. (1744/1999). *New science* (D. March, Trans.). London: Penguin Books.

Visker, R. (1995). *Michel Foucault: Genealogy as critique* (Chris Turner, Trans.). London: Verso.

Von Franz, M.-L. (1991). *Dreams*. Boston: Shambhala.

Von Franz, M.-L. (1968). The process of individuation. In C. Jung. (Ed.), *Man and his symbols* (pp. 157–254). New York: Laurel Editions.

Von Hendy, A. (2002). *The modern construction of myth*. Bloomington: Indiana University Press.

Wallis, J. (2005). *God's politics*. New York: HarperSanFrancisco.

Wendt, R. F. (1996). Answers to the gaze: A genealogical poaching of resistances. *Quarterly Journal of Speech, 82*(3), 251–273.

White, H. (1976). The tropics of history: The deep structure of the *New Science*. In G. Tagliacozzo & D. P. Verene (Eds.), *Giambattista Vico's science of humanity* (pp. 65–85). Baltimore: The Johns Hopkins University Press.

Wink, W. (1998). *The powers that be: Theology for a new millennium*. New York: Galilee Doubleday.

Winkler, C. K. (2006). *In the name of terrorism: Presidents on political violence in the post-World War II era*. Albany: State University of New York.

Ziegler, J. A. (2007). The story behind an organizational list: A genealogy of Wildland Firefighters' 10 Standard Fire Orders. *Communication Monographs, 74*(4), 415–442.

VI
NETWORK AND DELIBERATION ANALYSIS

17

Methods for Analyzing and Measuring Group Deliberation

Laura W. Black
School of Communication Studies
Ohio University

Stephanie Burkhalter
Department of Politics
Humboldt State University

John Gastil
Department of Communication
University of Washington

Jennifer Stromer-Galley
Department of Communication
University of Albany–SUNY

In a chapter on deliberative democratic theory written for the *Annual Review of Political Science*, Chambers (2003) wrote that "deliberative democratic theory has moved beyond the 'theoretical statement' stage and into the 'working theory' stage." If that was true in 2003, it is even truer now. The authors of this chapter have focused their research on how deliberative democracy works in practice; specifically, each of us has asked whether the ideals of democratic theory are realized in group settings that are designed for deliberation. What motivates us is a sense that group discourse about important public issues, whether public policy topics or jury decision-making in trials, constitutes an important component of democracy. As empirical researchers, however, we, like many others interested in this subject, continue to ask if, how, and why democracy is enhanced by actual deliberative discussion.

The ideals of deliberative democracy are numerous. The basic theoretical argument goes something like this: through political talk in manageable groups (i.e., not too large), citizens who adhere to the norms of reciprocity and equal respect will build a stronger community through learning about others' views and increasing their own political knowledge or sophistication. Deliberative talk leads to more reflective and refined political judgment than individualized processing of information. Engagement in the process of deliberative discussion could lead to increased investments in civic life and enhance legitimacy in decision-making (Barber, 1984; Benhabib, 1996; Bohman, 1996; Cohen, 1989, 1997; Dryzek, 1990, 2000; Habermas, 1984, 1987; Fishkin, 1991, 1995; Gastil, 1993; Gutmann & Thompson, 1996; Warren, 1992). There is an implied—some would say unrealistic—positive feedback loop within deliberative theory: the more citizens deliberate, the more informed, participatory, and respectful of others they will become (Burkhalter, Gastil, & Kelshaw, 2002).

In light of deliberative theory's claims about the potential benefits of deliberative discussion, in a 2005 review of empirical work on deliberation Ryfe asked "Does deliberative democracy work?" In their recent study of public deliberation, Jacobs, Cook, and Delli-Carpini (2009, p. 21) assert that "few areas of American public life have received as little actual on-the-ground study as citizen deliberation." Indeed, supporters and skeptics of deliberation have called for increased empirical research of the process as it is used in small groups (Delli-Carpini, Cook, & Jacobs, 2004; Fung, 2007; Gastil, 2008; Jacobs et al., 2009; Levine, Fung, & Gastil, 2005; Rosenberg, 2005, 2006). Such empirical research is a challenge because, as Ryfe (2005, p. 49) maintains, "deliberation is a difficult and relatively rare form of communication." Further, the empirical research community has not agreed on a definition of deliberation. As Burkhalter, Gastil, and Kelshaw (2002, p. 399) have noted, public deliberation has been loosely defined "to encompass the legislative process in the United States (Bessette, 1994), an unrealized form of citizen politics (Barber, 1984), or even existing media practices (Page, 1996)." Despite wide-ranging enthusiasm for the process and a proliferation of practical deliberative projects in western democracies, there exists no universally accepted—or even conventionally adopted—definition of small group public deliberation, let alone a consistent set of empirical measures derived from such a definition (see Burkhalter et al., 2002; Delli-Carpini et al., Jacobs et al., 2009; 2004; Stromer-Galley 2007).

In the absence of a consistent definition of small group public deliberation, researchers have drawn on diverse literatures to create research designs aimed at empirically capturing aspects of deliberation. In this chapter, we discuss examples of research that operationalize normative conceptions of democratic deliberative theory to gauge the deliberativeness of small group discussion. Rather than providing an extended review of empirical studies, we aim simply to make the wider community of deliberation scholars aware of a range of approaches to measurement currently in use.[1]

We begin with a brief explanation of a model of small group deliberation proposed by Burkhalter et al. (2002) and elaborated on by Gastil and Black (2008) that has provided a basis for measures in some of these studies. In our subsequent discussion of measures of deliberation, we divide them into two main types: those that directly measure aspects of a theoretical definition of deliberation (direct measures), and those that attempt to measure deliberation by studying variables that can be seen as indicators of deliberative processes (indirect measures). In the conclusion, we argue that a more rapid advance in deliberation research requires a more consistent definition and corresponding operationalization of small group deliberation. Measures must also take into account different forms and settings of deliberation and reflect that there will be variation in levels of deliberation depending on the different types. Empirical research of small group deliberation remains in its early stages, and we expect that future studies will refine considerably the measures that we review herein.

A MODEL OF SMALL GROUP PUBLIC DELIBERATION

Burkhalter et al. (2002) provide a conceptual definition and theoretical model of public deliberation in small groups that we think is a good starting point for the development of reliable measures that could be widely used to expand the body of empirical research on deliberation.[2] Their model defines ideal small group deliberation as "a combination of careful problem analysis and an egalitarian process in which participants have adequate speaking opportunities and engage in attentive listening or dialogue that bridges divergent ways of speaking and knowing" (p. 398). An innovation of this model is that group discussion is seen as more or less deliberative depending on how deliberative norms are put into practice and how participants respond to those norms. The basic norms of deliberation entail individualized and group analysis of the political issue under discussion (for example, a policy problem and its potential public solutions), careful consideration of information, provision of sufficient opportunities for participants to speak, and recognition of and respect for—though not necessarily agreement with—participants' different points of view and approaches to the issue. Recognition of and respect for different points of view should take into account diverse ways of speaking and understanding among participants.

Burkhalter et al.'s (2002) model identifies deliberative norms as potentially measurable discussion conditions that, if met, could produce certain outcomes. These outcomes include mainly post-deliberation changes among the participants, such as reinforcing deliberative habits, the discovery of previously unrecognized shared values and identities, an increased sense of democratic citizenship (or community identification), increased analytic and communicative skills necessary for political reasoning, and increased feelings of political efficacy. Contextual characteristics, such as motivation to deliberate and the perceived potential for common ground, will influence the group's ability to deliberate well. The more motivated and invested in the process the participants are, the more successful the deliberation will be.

In recent work, Gastil and Black (2008) build on Burkhalter et al.'s (2002) conceptualization to give a more detailed model of the ideal analytic and social processes involved in public deliberation. As they describe it, deliberation's analytic processes include building an information base, prioritizing key values, identifying solutions, weighing solutions, and making the best decision possible (if the situation calls for a decision). The social processes include ensuring equal and adequate speaking opportunities to group members, demonstrating mutual comprehension of one another's perspectives, adequately considering the views of other participants, and demonstrating respect for one another.[3]

That general definition captures a wide range of deliberative practices, the most popular of which bring citizens together for focused face-to-face (or online) discussion of a given public problem. Whether formally organized as Citizen Juries (Smith & Wales, 2000), Citizen Assemblies (Warren & Pearse, 2008), Deliberative Polls (Fishkin & Luskin, 1999), or any other number of specific processes, these events feature the exchange of policy-relevant information and expertise, personal testimony, and varying combinations of facilitated small group dialogue, discussion, and/or debate. Unlike focus groups, which tend to include a sample of people with shared demographic attributes, deliberative forums bring together people from a wide range of backgrounds and experiences to present a public forum in which diverse perspectives can be brought to the table (Jacobs et al., 2009). The experiences of practitioners (i.e., those who actually design and orchestrate deliberative events) suggests that these processes vary in the degree to which they actually *achieve* deliberation (Gastil & Levine, 2005). But, as explained below, there exists no agreement on how to systematically assess the deliberative quality of such events.

Moving from Theory to Measurement

The study of group deliberation is challenging, to say the least, which is one reason why the empirical literature of such a popular idea has not fully blossomed already. The definitions advanced in Burkhalter et al. (2002) and Gastil and Black (2008) provide concepts that can be operationalized in empirical studies to examine deliberative processes and consequences. However, because the conceptual foundation of democratic deliberation is fundamentally normative, it is difficult to precisely determine a threshold level that variables must meet in order for group discussion to count as being deliberative (Chambers, 2003; Cohen, 1989; Gastil, 2008; Mendelberg, 2002). One of the main research questions for empirical study, then, is: When is group discussion deliberative (i.e., reflective of the norms of deliberative theory)? Further, if a threshold of deliberation can be determined through high-quality measures, how does one distinguish the varying degrees of deliberativeness (e.g., low, medium, and high levels of deliberation)?

There are a number of challenges inherent in studying group deliberation that are similar to those faced by other group researchers. For example, researchers looking at group deliberation face methodological issues such as interdependence of data and difficulty in getting enough groups together for study to achieve adequate statistical power (cf. Poole, Keyton, & Frey, 1999). One choice that researchers need to make when examining deliberation in small groups is to determine the unit of analysis most appropriate for their study. Three distinct units of analysis that are common in deliberative studies are the individual, the group, and units of discourse. Research examining deliberation at the level of the individual typically will measure changes in outcome variables assumed to be influenced by deliberative processes such as political knowledge, attitudes, or efficacy (cf., Craig, Niemi, & Silver, 1990; Fishkin & Luskin, 1999; Gastil, Black, Deess, & Leighter, 2008; Jacobs et al., 2009; Morrell, 2005). This approach is useful for under-standing how the experience of deliberation can influence group members' outlook, information level, and subsequent behavior.

Studies that examine deliberation at the group level typically focus on measuring group outcomes such as decision quality (Sulkin & Simon, 2001), conflict management (Black, 2006), or changes to individual-level outcomes noted above. When measuring these changes at the group level, researchers could choose to aggregate or average individual scores and compare those scores across groups, which can provide information about how much group members moved while allowing comparisons across groups (cf. Gastil, Black, & Moscovitz, 2008; Gastil & Dillard, 1999). However, these tactics could mask potentially important intergroup differences. To address this issue, researchers can choose to provide group-level data by displaying the range of scores within particular groups.

The final level of analysis that receives close attention by deliberative researchers is the unit of discourse. Research that focuses on units of discourse includes close, systematic attention to the communication that occurs during the deliberative discussion. Examples of such units include speaking turns, thought units, stories, evidence, responses, and arguments (cf. Dutwin, 2003; Hart & Jarvis, 1999; Holzinger, 2001; Ryfe, 2006; Stromer-Galley, 2007). These units are explained more fully below in our review of particular studies. Research that uses discourse categories as a unit of analysis is most appropriate for answering questions about how the deliberative discussion works and what kinds of communication people engage in when they are brought together to deliberate.

MEASURES OF DELIBERATION

In the following sections, we discuss studies that have attempted to measure deliberation directly and indirectly. Those that measure deliberation directly examine the deliberative discussion itself to determine the extent to which the discussion corresponds to theoretical conceptions of deliberation. Studies using indirect measures assess deliberation based on either antecedents (for example, by measuring the extent to which conditions necessary for deliberation are met) or outcomes of a deliberative discussion (for example, by comparing pre-discussion and post-discussion survey responses of participants). The strengths and limitations of each of these approaches are discussed below.

Direct Measurement

The most common direct measurement of deliberation in small groups is what we call discussion analysis, which includes a range of methods used to systematically evaluate the communication engaged in during a deliberative discussion. Another common method used for the direct study of deliberation is to ask participants for their own assessments of the deliberative process. This is typically done through post-deliberation surveys or interviews in which respondents reflect on their experience as a participant and answer questions about the deliberative quality of the discussion. The final direct approach we review is the case study.

Discussion Analysis   Discussion analysis involves attempts to directly measure aspects of deliberation by systematically examining the communication that occurs during a deliberative meeting. This typically involves analyzing records of the interaction as it is preserved in a transcript or video recording of a face-to-face meeting, or in the verbatim, automatically generated record of an online discussion.

Within the discussion analytic method, there are both micro-analytic and macro-analytic approaches. Micro analysis involves assessing the deliberative quality of discussion discourse through closely analyzing the content of people's comments during the deliberation. Methods used for a micro-analytic approach include content analysis and discourse analysis. By contrast, the macro-analytic approach asks coders to make summary judgments of the discussion as a whole. We call this a macro-analytic approach because, although it attends to the quality of the deliberative discourse, it is not as closely tied to individual speaking turns and each group member's contribution to the discussion.

Micro-Analytic Approaches.   An increasingly common approach to studying political deliberations is to analyze the content of the discussions. Krippendorff (2004) defines this type of analysis as "a research technique for making replicable and valid inferences from texts . . . to the contexts of their use" (p. 18). An essential assumption of content analysis is that texts (in this case, *deliberative discussions*) are meaningful but that meaning is often not fixed. In some cases, the researcher is counting the number of times a speaker speaks, or the number of words that are uttered. Such counts are fixed and "objective" in that all reasonable analysts can agree that they see the same number of words or utterances. Most content analysis, however, focuses on elements of the content where meaning is not fixed. That is, meaning is not found or identified in the manifest features of texts, but rather is interpreted by analysts and by participants in the deliberation. Moreover, context and purpose matters, since meaning is derived from the context in which the communication act occurs (Krippendorff, 2004).

Thus, micro-analysts of deliberations face the daunting task of investigating elements of the deliberation in the face of unfixed or loosely fixed meaning. Put another way, analysts who content analyze deliberations should not enter into the analysis with a view that the content analysis measures "the deliberation," since there are many aspects to the deliberation, only some of which will be captured by the content analysis that is conducted. Moreover, there are often multiple ways to interpret the same elements within a deliberative event. As a result, content analysis poses challenges to scholars who aim to analyze aspects of the deliberation with an eye towards validity and reliability.

For the content analysis to be reliable, it must be done in such a way that the measurement "responds to the same phenomenon in the same way regardless of the circumstances of its implementation" (Krippendorff, 2004, p. 211). The accepted approach for achieving a reliable measure is first to develop a codebook, which records the sets of definitions and operationalizations of the categories or elements of the deliberation to be analyzed. Second, two or more analysts are trained to analyze the deliberation by applying the rules from the codebook.[4] Third, the researcher assesses how much agreement the coders have when analyzing the text. The greater the agreement that exists between the coders, the more reliable the coding scheme is likely to be (for descriptions of content analysis measurement techniques see Krippendorff, 2004, and Neundorf, 2002).

Intercoder reliability, however, does not guarantee construct validity. Validity in the context of content analysis focuses on how close the measure approximates the theoretical concept. It is possible that two coders can apply the rules of the codebook reliably to an element of a deliberation yet not actually capture the phenomenon of interest. Thus, deliberation analysts must be very careful in crafting the definitions and measurements that comprise the codebook to ensure that they are doing their best to capture accurately the concepts of interest.

In application, content analysis has been used to analyze many different aspects of group deliberation. The range of possibilities includes, for example, the topics raised and the equality of participation (Dutwin, 2003; Gastil, 1993), the balance of opinions (Barabas, 2004), the types of evidence provided by deliberators (Steenbergen, Bachtiger, Sporndli, & Steiner, 2003), argument-based discussion versus bargaining (Holzinger, 2001), the frequency of personal narratives (Dutwin, 2002), the use of identity statements in argumentation (O'Doherty & Davidson, 2010), the climate of the deliberative group's opinion (Price, Nir, & Cappella, 2006), the use of arguments based on shared values and interests (Carroll, 2002), the values, goals, and concerns of deliberators (Hawkins & O'Doherty, 2010), and even the overall quality of deliberations (Stromer-Galley, 2007). Other deliberative measures have been developed for analysis of media discourse (e.g., Gerhards, 1997; Page, 1996) but could potentially be adapted to analysis of deliberative groups.

Content analysis schemes that have been developed to assess deliberation typically begin with categories based on political theory and measure the extent to which these categories occur in the actual talk of participants. For example, Hart and Jarvis (1999) analyze the communication that occurred during small group meetings in the 1996 National Issues Convention. Their analytic scheme is based on features of political thought drawn from a number of democratic theorists— coalition formation, integrative complexity, rational action, social constructionism, and civic republicanism. In their analysis they argue that the pattern derived from these categories as they are seen in the participants' discussion presents an image of participants' "political model" that characterizes them as distinctively American (p. 64).

There are a few content analytic studies of deliberation that are noteworthy in their presentation of coding schemes that can be used for other deliberative forums. One is the Discourse Quality Index (DQI), developed by Jurg Steiner and his colleagues (Steiner, forthcoming; Steiner, Bachtiger, Sporndli, & Steenbergen, 2004; Steenbergen et al., 2003) and used in their study of deliberation in the British Parliament. The DQI is a coding scheme developed from Habermas' (1987, 1995) notion of discourse ethics. Steenbergen et al. (2003) argue that high-quality (i.e., deliberative) discourse should ideally be open to participation, require assertions to be justified, consider the common good, embody respect for all participants, include constructive politics, and require authenticity or honesty. They translate these theoretical constructs into a content analytic coding scheme, which they use to code speakers' "demands" about what should be done (p. 27) during political speeches in parliamentary deliberations.

The DQI identifies several categorical variables for measurement: participation (normal participation or interruption), levels of justification given for arguments (none, inferior, qualified, or superior justification), the content of justification given, respect for groups of people (none, implicit, or explicit), respect for counterarguments (counterarguments ignored, degraded, neutrally included, or valued), and constructive politics or consensus-building (positional politics, alternative proposal, or mediating proposal). Steenbergen et al. (2003) show that the DQI is a reliable measure, and several of their items (those measuring how people justified their arguments and the extent to which speakers demonstrated respect toward other groups) were highly correlated, and the authors argue that they could be used to create a scale to measure the quality of deliberative discourse.

A second noteworthy content analysis study comes from Dutwin (2003), who investigated participation levels within a deliberative context and assessed whether prior political conversations or political sophistication better prepares participants to engage in deliberation. Dutwin counted the number of times participants spoke and the number of words they produced as well as whether participants produced arguments when they spoke. Dutwin developed a codebook, which included a clear definition and operationalization of "argument." His trained coders achieved high levels of intercoder agreement, thereby ensuring a satisfactory level of reliability for each of the coded elements.

The content analysis allowed Dutwin (2003) to examine whether demographic characteristics such as age, gender, and education levels were correlated with the production of arguments during deliberation. The results suggested that individuals who were likely to engage in political conversations in their daily lives were more likely to produce arguments during the deliberations. Moreover, Dutwin found a fairly balanced amount of participation during the deliberations. Men, for example, did not appear to produce more arguments than women.

Content analysis has its limitations. Perhaps the biggest reason systematic content analysis is not conducted more frequently is the time and effort involved. Dutwin (2003) reported that the coding took approximately 100 hours, not counting coder training or the development of the codebook itself. A deliberation content coding project reported by Stromer-Galley (2007) took approximately two months to develop, an additional 40 hours for training the coder, and then almost six months to do the coding. Part of the reason for such a lengthy process was that 23 groups were included in that project, and each group produced approximately 40 pages of written transcripts. The substantial amount of text that deliberation projects produce can be daunting. For Dutwin's (2003) project, court reporters were hired to create transcripts of the deliberations on the fly. This approach to creating transcripts is quite novel. The benefits include a near-instant transcript of the discussions. Drawbacks include the possibility of an inaccurate transcript, given the challenge of transcribing people who speak over each other, and the cost of hiring transcribers. Most projects do not have such financial resources. Instead, projects record the deliberations and subsequently transcribe the results, which also entail considerable costs. Audio quality problems can make transcription difficult, as can the presence of multiple voices on a single audio track.[5]

Moreover, there is risk in putting forth the effort to develop a codebook and train coders, only to discover that the coders cannot get sufficiently acceptable levels of agreement that would serve as the basis for statistical analysis. Published articles rarely include their failures, and we expect that some undiscovered efforts to directly measure deliberation have failed to reach our attention, let alone achieve publication, owing to this difficulty. An unpublished project by the fourth author of this chapter, for instance, attempted to code expressions of disagreement in an online deliberation but found that the coders could not agree as to what counted as an expression of disagreement. Because meaning is not in the text but is constructed in the moment of interaction (Krippendorff, 2004), two reasonable people can construct an interaction and interpret it differently. It is possible, then, that months of time can be spent without any useable data to show for it.

In such a situation, it is possible to shift the analysis away from the systematic counting of elements in a deliberation to a more interpretive thematic approach to analyzing the deliberations. Ryfe (2006), for example, analyzed five National Issues Forums and discovered that a primary form of reasoning was storytelling. He analyzed the role that facilitation plays in promoting narrative as a form of reasoning. He also speculated on why storytelling is such a prominent aspect of the deliberations' content. Similar works (Black, 2008; Hendriks, 2005; Polletta, 2006; Polletta & Lee, 2006) examine storytelling as important aspects of deliberation and argue that personal stories are important discursive resources that participants draw on during deliberative discussion. Such interpretive analysis, although less common than systematic content analysis, is a useful approach to analyzing what comprises a deliberation. Interpretive analysis is even more effective when situated as part of a case study, a method discussed later in this chapter.

Another type of micro-level analysis focuses on the interactions and the discursive processes involved in the deliberation. Whereas content analysis measures aspects of participants' contributions according to a predetermined coding scheme and typically analyzes data quantitatively, discourse analysts take a more qualitative approach to examining the communication that occurs in a deliberative meeting turn by turn. Discourse analytic approaches focus on interaction by examining *how* people are communicating with each other. Some of the predominant traditions in discourse analysis include conversation analysis, the ethnography of communication, and critical discourse analysis (for an overview of discourse analysis, see Jaworski & Coupland, 1999).

There is a growing body of discourse analytic work in the larger field of political communication that might be relevant to deliberation scholars (e.g., Townsend, 2006; Tracy, 2007; and the 2009 special issue of the *International Journal of Public Participation* called "The Practice of Public Meetings"), but very little research has been conducted to directly measure aspects of deliberation in this way. In a recent reflection on the challenges of qualitative approaches to studying deliberation, Haug and Teune (2008) provide a general framework for engaging in "comparative participant observation" (p. 6) across multiple groups. These authors argue that participant observation is a good way to gain access to and build understanding of deliberative discourse. However, researchers who wish to study multiple groups and compare findings across cases must deal with issues of reliability similar to those faced by content analysts as described above.

Haug and Teune (2008) provide a framework to guide how participant observers record field notes that facilitate reliable comparison across cases. First, they ask researchers to focus most attention on "controversial discussion about a conflictual issue" (Haug & Teune, 2008, p. 9), which helps narrow the focus of the observations. Next, they ask observers to create three types of documents: (1) a "group portrait" that describes the overall impression of the group, which is completed at the end of the researcher's observation, (2) a "session report" that serves as a description of a particular meeting, and (3) "controversy protocols," which researchers fill out for each controversy that occurred during the session they observed (Haug & Teune, 2008, p. 23). At the end of the observation period, each group will have one group portrait, multiple session reports (one for each meeting), and multiple controversy protocols (some number corresponding to however many controversies were observed for each session). Formalizing the field notes in this way addresses concerns about reliability by enabling researchers to make appropriate comparisons across cases.

Another example of a discourse analytic approach to deliberation is Black's (2006) investigation into how deliberative group members tell and respond to personal stories during disagreements. Black qualitatively analyzed the communication of two groups involved in an online deliberative forum to explore and describe interactive patterns related to storytelling, collective identity, and conflict. She discerned four distinct types of stories, each with a different discursive function. She posited that the different types of stories drew on different ideas about the storyteller's identity and connection to the group, and that group members' use of different types of stories would likely lead to different conflict management strategies.

Some systematic content analysis borrows heavily from discourse analysis to help construct coding categories. Black (2006) uses her findings from the qualitative study of storytelling in online deliberative forums to create a coding scheme to assess the extent to which different types of stories told by participants generated response patterns that led to different conflict management outcomes. Coders were trained to assess aspects of the stories themselves, but also looked at the responses to stories to assess aspects of interaction such as agreement, use of collective identity statements, and conflict management. Similarly, Stromer-Galley (2007) used existing research on expressions of agreement and disagreement in content analysis (see, for example, Pomerantz, 1984). She also approached the coding of the deliberation from the perspective of an interaction. Coders were trained to analyze the deliberation by looking at the thought expressed in the context of what preceded it.

The discourse analytic approach allows researchers to pay close attention to the actual communication that occurred and discern the patterns and meanings that seem most relevant to the case at hand. The drawback to such an approach is that because it is quite time-consuming and typically involves paying close attention to a small number of groups, the generalizability of the research findings is limited. However, translating the findings of a discourse analytic study into a content analysis coding scheme allows researchers to examine a much greater number of instances and test hypotheses that could not have been adequately addressed with smaller-scale, qualitative, discourse analytic studies.

Macro-Analytic Approaches.   The methods and measures of the studies discussed so far have all operated at a micro-analytic level by focusing on the communication at a rather small unit of analysis (i.e., the speaking turn, argument, thought unit, story, or response). In contrast, a macro-analytic approach to discussion analysis takes a step back to view the conversation as a whole. In this kind of content analysis, coders are trained to look at the transcript overall and make a summary judgment about the quality of the deliberation that occurred. As with micro-level content analysis, coders must be well trained in the concepts and coding rules, and need to reach an acceptable level of intercoder reliability.

Gastil, Black, and Moscovitz (2008) take this approach by asking coders to read transcripts of group discussions and rate the discussions on six dimensions of deliberation, which they based on the conceptual definition given by Burkhalter et al. (2002). For example, to assess the deliberative dimension of consideration, coders gave each discussion a score between 1 ("strongly disagree") and 7 ("strongly agree") in response to the statement, "The group carefully considered what each participant had to say." In this study, the six dimensions were combined to give each discussion an overall rating of its level of deliberation, as assessed by trained observers. In another example, Black, Welser, DeGroot, and Cosley (2008) operationalized Gastil and Black's (2008) definition to assess deliberation in some of Wikipedia's policy-making discussions. To supplement a more micro-level content analytic coding scheme that was used to evaluate each discussion post, coders were trained to read the discussion thread as a whole and rate how well it embodied the analytic and social processes of deliberation.

The macro-level approach does not provide the detailed information about deliberation that is available through micro-level discussion analysis. However, it gives researchers more of a bird's eye view of the interaction, and may be able to capture important aspects of the interaction that are not evident by studying each individual comment separately. Both of the studies reviewed here use global ratings to supplement other measures, such as micro-level content analysis or self- reports from group discussion participants. For example, Black et al. (2008) combine the findings of their content analysis with social network analysis to describe both the content and structure of deliberative discussion.

Combining measures allows researchers to examine deliberation in a multifaceted way by providing details of the interaction, a global rating of the session overall, and the perspectives of the participants themselves. A challenge of a multi-level approach is that different approaches to measurement may yield different conclusions, and results from different measures may not be strongly correlated with one another. As Gastil et al. (2008) note, a lack of association among measures indicates that "a great challenge faces those who hope to operationally define deliberation in a way that is meaningful for participants, practitioners, and researchers alike" (p. 39).

Participant Assessments   Another way to directly assess aspects of deliberation is to ask the participants themselves to comment on their experiences. Rather than closely examining the content of the meetings, participant assessment methods give the deliberators a chance to reflect on their experience with the discussion. Although it is not based on the researcher's firsthand observation of the meeting, we categorize participant assessment as a direct measure of deliberation because the questions posed to participants are carefully crafted to closely correspond with theoretical definitions of deliberation such as level of respect among participants, relative equality of speaking opportunities, and consideration and comprehension of diverse points of view during the discussion. Researchers typically ask participants to do their assessment through survey questionnaires after completing their discussions (e.g., Gastil, Black, Deess, & Leighter, 2008; Halvorsen, 2001; Reykowski, 2006). In lieu of surveys, in-depth interviews are more typically used as part of a more intensive case study (e.g., Grogan & Gusmano, 2005; Mansbridge, 1980), so the focus here is on questionnaire-based assessments.

One of the most recent efforts to measure deliberation by post-discussion survey is Nabatchi's (2007) doctoral dissertation on deliberative meetings. Given no consensus definition to work from, she inductively constructed a reliable ten-item scale dubbed the Deliberative Quality Index. Study participants agreed/disagreed with items concerning a range of issues, such as consensus ("Participants worked toward consensus agreement on the issues"), the policies discussed ("A variety of policy alternatives were explored"), values ("The discussions identified shared values in the community"), and consideration ("The discussions helped me consider other sides of the issues"). The items also included measures of perceived context (diversity), process (equal speaking turns), and outcomes (changing one's opinion). In the end, the index did not prove predictive of changes in participants' political efficacy, though Nabatchi (2007) speculated that this may have been due to limited variance in her Deliberation Quality Index, an issue we return to in the concluding section of this chapter.

Compared to Nabatchi's (2007) wide-ranging set of survey items, Gastil (2006) tried to hit on a single, key element of deliberation. His single-item scale measuring participant assessments of public meetings on the activities of Los Alamos Laboratories read,

> Sometimes public meetings or group discussions are dominated by people who take up all the meeting time and don't let others speak. In general, were the public meetings you attended dominated by people favorable toward the Lab, dominated by people unfavorable toward the Lab, or did no group dominate the meeting?

A *deliberative* public meeting was one where participants reported that no group dominated the meeting. (This is analogous to, and was inspired by, the sharp distinction Page [1996] and

Zaller [1992] make between balanced and one-sided elite debate in media.) Gastil (2006) found that such meetings appeared to yield greater relevant knowledge gains than those meetings that were dominated by one side or the other.

Measures like these may achieve reliability but have limited construct validity as full-fledged indicators of the process of group deliberation. Neither focuses exclusively on the quality of the interaction, and Gastil's (2006) measure would be unable to distinguish a balanced deliberative forum from what was merely a fair fight, albeit an acrimonious and counter-productive affair.

A more promising attempt at participant self-assessment was conducted by Gastil and Sawyer (2004). This unpublished study was unusual in that its primary purpose was to establish the convergent validity of participant and observer assessments of deliberation. The researchers assembled 106 undergraduates into 15 groups, each of which discussed a proposed state law concerning sexual harassment in high schools. Three different measures of deliberation were undertaken: (1) the participants themselves completed a survey including 49 post-discussion assessment items; (2) the forum moderators, all graduate students in a deliberation seminar, completed a six-item assessment after the discussion; and (3) other undergraduates were given 15 minutes of training, then sent to observe the discussion in three-person teams, completing the same six-item assessment aided only by a tally sheet they had used during the discussion to record deliberative moments.

Simplifying the presentation of results in Gastil and Sawyer (2004), three aspects of deliberation were measured using these instruments: the rigorousness of the analytic process (Rigor); the degree to which participants understood each other and considered one another's arguments (Listening); and the equality of participant speaking opportunities (Equality).[6] For the participant measures, these were three multi-item scales, all with sufficient reliability (minimum alpha = .84), whereas for the moderators and observers, the scales were combinations of their smaller pool of rating items. All individual scores and ratings were then averaged to create three sets of group-level deliberation ratings—one set for the participants, one for the observers, and one for the forum moderator.

Table 17.1 shows the associations among these nine ratings. Given the small sample size ($N = 15$), only a few of the associations were statistically significant, but there were clear indications that for each measurement approach, the different dimensions were positively related.

TABLE 17.1
Correlations among Observer, Moderator, and Participant Ratings of Analytic Rigor, Careful Listening, and Equality of Speaking Opportunities

		Observer Ratings			Moderator Ratings			Participant Ratings	
		Rigor	Listen	Equal	Rigor	Listen	Equal	Rigor	Listen
Observer Ratings	Listening	.30							
	Equality	.09	.25						
Moderator Ratings	Rigor	.17	−.11	−.15					
	Listening	.09	.04	−.11	.33				
	Equality	−.02	.31	.56*	−.22	.17			
Participant Ratings	Rigor	−.20	.44*	.39	−.20	−.25	.07		
	Listening	−.09	.71**	.07	−.36	−.04	.30	.44*	
	Equality	.24	.72**	−.28	−.09	−.02	.06	.28	.40+

Note: For one-tailed alpha, ** $p < .001$, * $p < .05$, + $p < .10$. $N = 15$.

The three participant ratings were moderately correlated (avg. $r = .37$). For both moderator and observer ratings, the Listening scale was modestly correlated with both Rigor and Equality (avg. $r = .26$). Moderators and observers, however, did *not* have a clear positive association between Rigor and Equality (with the correlation trending negative in the case of moderator ratings).

Comparing deliberative dimensions across the three measurement approaches, other patterns also appeared. In the case of Rigor, there was little agreement across methods, with moderators and observers giving positively related Rigor scores ($r = .17$) and both having identically negative associations with participants' self-assessed Rigor scores ($rs = -.20$). Moderators and observers were in even stronger agreement on Equality scores ($r = .56$) and did not have clear associations with participant ratings. In the case of Listening, however, moderators' scores had no association with observers' or participants' scores, whereas observers' and participants' scores had a very high association ($r = .71$).

This last association is related to the only remaining important correlations across methods and measures. The Listening score from observers' post-deliberation assessments was predictive of *all three* participant scores, including the aforementioned correlation, plus average participant scores on Equality ($r = .72$) and Rigor ($r = .44$).[7]

In sum, Gastil and Sawyer's (2004) study suggests that participants' assessments of their deliberative experience can differ considerably from equivalent ratings made by forum moderators or trained observers. There is at least some degree of correspondence, however, between participants' assessments and those of neutral observers from a similar background.[8]

Case Study Integration   The final method that we categorize as a direct measure of deliberation is what we call the integrated case study. The case study utilizes both direct observation of interaction and participant assessments to measure aspects of deliberation that were present in the group. Case studies typically involve prolonged engagement with the group being studied as the researcher engages in participant observation of the group meetings over time.

Mansbridge (1980) provides an early example of an integrated case study of deliberation. Her study of New England town meetings and a nonprofit public health organization provide detailed descriptions of the deliberative processes and the structural conditions that help facilitate deliberation. Like other integrated case studies of deliberation (e.g., Edwards, Hindmarsh, Mercer, & Rowland, 2008; Gastil, 1993; Grogan & Gusmano, 2005; Karpowitz & Mansbridge, 2005; Mendelberg & Oleske, 2000; Nishizawa, 2005; Wilson, Payne, & Smith, 2003), Mansbridge uses a combination of research methods to provide a rich description of the sites studied and explicate their implications for deliberative theory.

Some recent examples of case studies of deliberation include Tracy's (2010) investigation of school board meetings in Colorado, Ryfe's (2007) study of a town he calls "Civicville," Hartz-Karp's research on forums held in Western Australia (2007), and Polletta's (2006, 2008; Polletta & Lee, 2006) extensive study of Listening to the City, AmericaSpeak's 21st Century Town Meeting held in NYC after 9/11. (For more information on this kind of forum, see Lukensmeyer, Goldman, & Brigham, 2005.) All these prototypical case studies share a deep engagement with the site of their study, which is partially evidenced by the fact that each followed the groups in question for several years. Another prominent feature of integrated case studies is the use of multiple methods. Ryfe (2007) combines ethnographic observation with in-depth interviews and analysis of newspaper coverage. Polletta's (2006, 2008) methods include observation, interviews, and content analysis of both face-to-face and online discussions. Gastil's (1993) study involved participant observation, video and transcript analysis, participant questionnaires, and in-depth interviews during which discussants watched a videotaped portion of their meetings to prompt reflection on critical junctures in their deliberations.

Occasionally, deliberative scholars find themselves acting in dual roles, both as a researcher and also as a consultant or facilitator for a deliberative group. For instance, in addition to interviewing forum participants after the meetings, Polletta (2008) served on the steering committee for one of the organizations she studied. She also "worked as a facilitator, helped to plan the workshops and to synthesize ideas generated in them for the draft visions, and interviewed organizers" (p. 6). Similarly, Hartz-Karp (2007) served as a consultant to the organization hosting the forums she studied. This dual role of researcher and consultant/facilitator can be tricky because there is potential for conflict between the goals and expectations of these two roles. Hartz-Karp describes herself as "walking a tightrope" between the roles and states: "Naturally it is not possible for me to be completely objective in analyzing a process I had a large share in devising and executing. However, failing to report on the work in which I was involved would constitute a waste of years of experience and hard-won insight" (p. 8). In these situations, the integrated case study approach can take on a kind of action research paradigm (e.g., Frey & Carragee, 2007) because it involves collaborating with practitioners to address a particular social issue as well as addressing research questions of interest to scholars.

INDIRECT MEASUREMENT

The research discussed above presents models for directly measuring aspects of deliberation through focusing close attention to the processes involved in deliberation. In contrast, many scholars measure deliberation *indirectly* by looking for indicators that deliberation might occur or has occurred. Indirect measures are often used when the antecedents or outcomes of the deliberation are the best (or only) data available to be measured.

For example, in cases of real-world institutionalized small group deliberation, such as congressional committee deliberation, researchers may not have access to the actual deliberation or even to the participants. In jury deliberations, researchers may have access to participants after the deliberative meetings—but not to the content of the meetings themselves. These are valuable examples of regularized deliberation, but because of institutional and practical limits, one may be able to know only if the conditions for deliberation have been satisfied such that the group is likely to have deliberated.

Antecedents

Some groups within established governmental institutions routinely claim to have deliberated before making consequential decisions, whether weighing the merits of a proposed administrative rule change or a resolution to go to war. Frequently, however, such deliberations are not available to researchers to observe, or may be too prohibitive for most researchers to access. Burkhalter (2007) took on the task of examining the conditions for deliberation present in six instances of congressional lawmaking. Some of the conditions for deliberation are enshrined in the U.S. House of Representatives through what is called the "regular order"; however, as Burkhalter found, this regular order is often ignored, along with consideration of diverse views in venues such as legislative hearings. Burkhalter demonstrated that when the majority party's public message on a piece of legislation was important, the likelihood that deliberation occurred on the legislation declined. The likelihood that deliberation occurred was measured by how much the conditions for deliberation were met in each case.

More commonly, when the subject is public meetings where participants can share their points of view, researchers simply assume a form of deliberation has occurred (Mendelberg & Oleske, 2000). It is thus a taken-for-granted background variable, without any measured variance across observations. This approach has also been taken in studies that ascribe deliberative discussions to conversations that occur in the circumstance of a carefully designed, and typically professionally facilitated, public forum, such as in studies of National Issues Forums (e.g., Gastil, 2004; Gastil & Dillard, 1999; Ryfe, 2006) and Deliberative Polls (Fishkin & Luskin, 1999; Luskin, Fishkin, & Jowell, 2002; Sturgis, Roberts, & Allum, 2005).

Experimental researchers set up structural conditions that they believe sufficiently model the presence or absence of one or more deliberative features, then compare the results between deliberative and non-deliberative experimental subgroups. Thus, Morrell (2005) compared an argument-oriented group (i.e., one that exchanges arguments, as in a parliamentary debate) against one that was agreement-oriented (i.e., encouraging participants to seek intersubjectivity and convergent preferences). Sulkin and Simon (2001) reduced the question even further, simply labeling communicative interaction under experimental conditions as deliberative and comparing it against the circumstances under which participants cannot talk with each other. In this extreme case, deliberation is simply redefined as merely the opportunity to communicate, surely the minimal structural condition under which deliberation *could* take place.

More promising is the approach taken by Reykowski (2006), which compared three experimental conditions—minimal conditions for deliberation, introduction of deliberative norms, and support for deliberative norms. In the first condition, the facilitator simply advised the participants at the outset to stay on topic, not offend, and give everyone the chance to speak. In the second, the facilitator introduced a more complete and detailed set of deliberative norms (not unlike those in Burkhalter et al., 2002), which were also given in writing to each participant. The third condition added active intervention by the facilitator, as necessary, to reiterate and reinforce those norms. Unfortunately, post hoc analysis of the discussions revealed that the experimental conditions were "not very successful in differentiating the conditions of the debates," with all groups showing "some forms of deliberative functioning" (p. 344).

A straightforward drawback to the indirect method of measuring deliberation is that the researcher can only make conclusions regarding the presence or absence of antecedents and cannot speak definitively on whether deliberation actually occurred, let alone *how* it occurred. Nevertheless, in measuring the conditions for deliberation, researchers can make suggestions regarding aspects of a group's process that need to be adjusted to make it more likely that the group discussion will be deliberative. This is important when government-sponsored groups that deliberate behind closed doors or at different moments in time regarding the same matter claim that they have "deliberated" about different policy options or action items in an effort to provide some legitimacy to the group's ultimate decision.

Outcomes

An outcome-oriented approach conventionally uses surveys questionnaires, but instead of asking participants to comment on the deliberative process, the instruments are designed to measure variables that assume high-quality deliberations. Muhlberger's (2007) review of the literature shows that participants in deliberative forums demonstrate increased political knowledge and political reasoning, as well as an increased sense of citizenship. These variables have been measured by a range of studies, which typically use pre- and post-deliberation surveys to compare levels within variables.[9] Gastil, Deess, Weiser, and Meade's (2008) study of the civic impact of jury deliberation contrasts the post-service civic experiences of those jurors who had the chance to deliberate in the jury room with those who sat in the jury box during the trial but were dismissed without having the chance to deliberate together.

One way to determine whether individuals' political knowledge has increased as the result of a deliberative discussion is to ask participants specific questions about relevant political topics immediately after they engage in group discussions. Fishkin and colleagues use this approach in Deliberative Polls, by comparing forum participants' knowledge to the general level of political knowledge in a control group that did not deliberate (Fishkin & Luskin, 1999; Luskin, Fishkin, & Jowell, 2002).

A related measure of political knowledge is what Cappella, Price, and Nir (2002) call "argument repertoire." These authors argue that "those who can identify multiple explanations with genuine evidence for them, counterarguments to their own explanations, and a resolution in favor of their own explanation are at the highest levels of knowledge about the issue under discussion" (p. 275). Cappella and colleagues. measure participants' ability to articulate their own opinions about a political topic as well as opinions and arguments given by others. They find that argument repertoire is a good indicator of participation in deliberative conversation, and also that deliberation can lead to an increase in one's argument repertoire. (For another variant of the argument repertoire approach, see Lustick & Miodownik, 2000.)

Similarly, political attitudes can be measured by asking topical questions about the extent to which participants agree with statements about a relevant topic such as "the United States should continue to engage in military cooperation with other nations to address trouble spots in the world" (Fishkin & Luskin, 1999, p. 24). Studies that investigate attitude change (e.g., Gastil, Black, Deess, & Leighter, 2008; Gastil & Dillard, 1999; Sturgis, Robers, & Allum, 2005) use a pre- and post-forum design to examine the extent to which participating in deliberative forums changes participants' attitudes about political topics.

Another outcome of deliberation that is often studied is political efficacy, which is the degree to which an individual feels confident that he or she can effectively carry out political action. Craig, Niemi, and Silver (1990) present a measure of efficacy that has been taken up by deliberation scholars to examine the extent to which deliberating with fellow citizens influences one's level of political efficacy (e.g., Fishkin & Luskin, 1999; Gastil, Black, Deess, & Leighter, 2008; Morrell, 2005).

Some measures used by deliberation scholars that are relevant to a sense of citizenship include interest in politics (Verba, Schlozman, & Brady, 1995), along with political identity, trust in fellow citizens, and trust in governmental institutions (Gastil, Black, Deese, & Leighter, 2008; Muhlberger, 2005, 2007). Survey items developed to measure these variables assess different aspects of participants' sense of identity and responsibility as citizens, which can be influenced by participating in deliberative discussion.

Part of the positive feedback loop embedded in the Burkhalter et al. (2002) model is that participating in deliberation can influence participants' future civic habits. One such habit is voting. In a series of studies, Gastil and colleagues (Gastil, Deess, Weiser, & Meade, 2008) found that criminal jury service increased participants' future voting rates when they had the opportunity to deliberate (as compared to those empanelled jurors designated as alternates or had their trials end before the deliberation phase had begun). This line of research makes a noteworthy methodological contribution to deliberative research by combining questionnaire data from jurors with corresponding individual voter turnout histories, which are publicly available. Most deliberative studies that examine outcomes rely solely on survey measures, but the jury studies show that secondary data can be used to supplement primary research techniques.

A final outcome-based approach steps back to the deliberation itself by focusing on the correspondence between participants' pre- and post-deliberation support for different reasons and policies. Niemeyer (2006) takes this approach in studying the shifting bases of citizens' policy judgments in events like Citizen Juries. In Niemeyer's view, "complete preference agreement should only occur where there is also concurrence at the level of reasons" and "disagreement at the level of preferences should reflect a similar level of disagreement at the underlying level of reasons" (p. 9). Thus, Niemeyer reviews deliberative case studies and finds evidence that deliberation has occurred owing to the stronger correspondence between participants' reasons and preferences *after* their discussions than existed beforehand.

Indirectly measuring deliberation through survey questionnaires that assess the effects of deliberation has a number of benefits. The methods and measures associated with survey research are well established and surveys can be given to a large number of participants. Such large samples make it possible for researchers to investigate a number of hypotheses related to deliberation and present generalizable conclusions. A liability of this approach is that researchers need to be cautious not to assert that a variable, such as attitude change, is both an indicator of and also caused by deliberation. Moreover, there cannot be an automatic assumption that deliberation produces the range of outcomes we highlight here, and it is possible that any number of outcomes could arise from unmeasured attributes of the participants or result from communicative acts that fall short of what would be considered deliberation. At the very least, studies relying exclusively on outcome-based measures of deliberation will not be helpful in assessing the impact of deliberation on those same outcomes, lest they be subject to a tautological fallacy.

SUMMARY AND RECOMMENDATIONS

Without an agreed upon definition and corresponding measures of deliberation, questions arise regarding whether or not small group deliberation actually achieves the normative conditions and outcomes that democratic deliberative theory imagines (Levine et al., 2005; Rosenberg, 2005). The lack of agreement on a uniform definition of deliberation from which reliable empirical measures can be derived has already had an impact on the burgeoning field of empirical studies of public deliberation. For example, some empirical observers relying on early conceptualizations of ideal public deliberation articulated by theorists like Habermas (1984) and Cohen (1997) have found actual public deliberations to fall quite short of the normative vision (Mendelberg, 2002; Mendelberg & Oleske, 2000; Rosenberg, 2006; Sanders, 1997; Sturgis et al., 2005; Sulkin & Simon, 2001).

A goal of Gastil and Black's (2008) project was to distinguish between different types of public deliberation, with group-based deliberation being the best-known variant. Further, deliberation researchers should acknowledge that all types of organized small group public deliberation are not alike: It is quite possible that different, ostensibly deliberative designs will achieve varying levels of deliberation, both within and between different designs. In other words, there is surely a different kind of discussion at a National Issues Forum, as compared to a Deliberative Poll, as compared to a criminal jury or town meeting. Moreover, there is surely considerable variation in the deliberative quality of different events that are all billed as National Issues Forums.

To take just one example, the pitfalls of unstructured discussion have led most deliberation practitioners to conclude that to have a chance at meeting predictions derived from normative democratic deliberative theory, small group deliberation should be structured to include a trained facilitator to orient the group around deliberative norms (Levine et al., 2005). As Ryfe (2006) maintains, facilitation establishes norms and encourages participants to adhere to them. Practitioners who have been involved in overseeing or facilitating deliberative projects seem to agree that groups need facilitation to reach deliberative outcomes (Guttman, 2007; Mansbridge et al., 2006). Reykowski (2006) demonstrated that the mere presence of a neutral facilitator who articulates even minimal deliberative norms can help groups achieve at least a modicum of deliberation. Yet even in the midst of this agreement, there are different views of what the facilitator should do to structure the discussion, and there remain those who eschew the idea of facilitation altogether.[10]

As Guttmann (2007, p. 417) notes, "there are profound differences in the way different [deliberative] initiatives conceive the normative stipulations" of deliberative democratic theory. Fung (2007) urges researchers to create uniform conceptual definitions and empirical expectations for theories of democracy because, from the standpoint of democratic theory, it is important to test deliberative theory to understand when different practices and institutional designs may promote or undermine democratic principles. In addition, we should avoid holding deliberative democracy to an absolute standard of perfection, something not expected of other regularized forms of political participation (e.g., voting, writing a letter to a member of Congress, expressing one's opinion at a city council meeting). Grimes (2008) may be right that even "imperfect" processes may deliver the civic benefits theorists ascribe to deliberation, but the larger point is to let go of the idea that a deliberative discussion will fully meet the ideal requirements when grounding deliberative theory in empirical observation.

All this is to say that the degree of deliberation that occurs in group meetings surely *varies*, probably to large degrees if we begin studying the wider range of group practices beyond the most carefully constructed deliberative venues and events. If we are to effectively measure group deliberation in the future, we believe that studies must take into account the different dimensions of the deliberative process and whether the norms of deliberation are explicitly established and how well they are adhered to in deliberative discussion.

In Table 17.2, we summarize the pros and cons among the different measurement approaches we have reviewed. The table makes plain that a single approach to measuring deliberation would likely impoverish the field, as each method has a significant pitfall. At the same time, most methods have a compelling advantage that makes them a good candidate for a deliberation

TABLE 17.2
Principal Benefits and Limitations of Different Approaches to Measuring Group Deliberation

Measurement	Principal Benefits	Principal Limitations
Direct Measures		
Content analysis	Close attention to the content of the deliberation. Can include large sample.	Time consuming and can be hard to obtain intercoder reliability.
Discourse analysis	Close attention to interaction, patterns that are relevant to the group.	Small sample limits generalizability.
Global ratings	Integrated assessment of deliberation.	Glosses over distinctions among different facets of deliberation.
Participant surveys	Systematic assessment by the prospective deliberators themselves	Subject to self-report biases and desire to please event organizers or researchers.
In-depth participant interviews	Learn about deliberation in participants' own language	Difficult to compare experiences across individuals and groups.
Integrated case study	Integrates the strengths of different measures. Prolonged engagement provides rich detail.	Time consuming and complicates comparison across different groups.
Indirect Measures		
Antecedents/conditions	Ease of comparison across contexts and wide availability of data.	No knowledge of actual content or process of discussion.
Consequences	Focuses on those outcomes of deliberation that often originally justified its use.	Unable to assess independently the impact of deliberation.

measurement toolkit. The lone exception, we believe, is using outcome measures as an indicator of deliberation, a move that renders research unable to test whether those same indicators are, in fact, regular outcomes of deliberation. The research record to date shows that deliberation, like virtually every other civic tonic, delivers some but not all of the goods the most optimistic theorists have imagined (Delli-Carpini et al., 2004; Mendelberg, 2002; Ryfe, 2005).

What is needed is a range of measurement techniques suited to different purposes. On the one hand, we believe the case study approach will always be the best approach for intensive study of specific deliberative events and venues. This is really an umbrella approach, which can incorporate participant observation, in-depth interviews, and even formal content analysis and surveys. As a means of simultaneously making micro- and macro-level observations about deliberative process in all its complexity, we expect the case study approach to be most fruitful as a generative mechanism, pushing forward deliberative theory.

For empirical verification of the theory's claims, larger samples will be required. These, in turn, will make case studies, along with intensive content and discourse analyses, impractical. In these cases, we believe global observer ratings and participant surveys will be necessary. The survey instruments to date have not been sufficiently road tested, which will entail validating them against more intensive case study techniques and across a range of deliberative contexts.

The Gastil and Sawyer (2004) study illustrates just one part of this process—comparing participant evaluations against those of neutral observers.[11] Much more validation work needs to be done, and publication outlets like the *Journal of Public Deliberation* and *Communication Methods and Measures*, along with the wider community of deliberation scholars, will welcome any such undertaking.

We also wish to stress the potential value of developing short-form versions of any participant assessment tool. Many of the surveys described herein used reliable multi-item scales, but practitioners convening deliberative events may often be willing to sacrifice formal scale reliability to keep their post-discussion survey short. If, for example, a researcher wanted to add regular measures to the surveys produced by the National Issues Forums, it is unlikely that more than a pair of questions could be accommodated, given the existing purposes and logistic constraints of the existing survey. Thus, a long- and short-form version of any measure would be ideal.

At the same time, we believe that researchers should continue to think of deliberation as having distinct dimensions, which we doubt can be reduced to any single-dimensional measure. Given the practical challenges faced by anyone undertaking research on deliberative groups, it may be prudent for researchers to choose to focus their study on the analytic rigor of a deliberative process, on the egalitarian nature of relations among participants, on the degree of respect shown during discussion, or one other element of the process, rather than on all simultaneously. The latter approach sacrifices conceptual and measurement precisions, which is particularly costly if it turns out that different aspects of deliberation prove to be associated with different deliberative outcomes.

As for the approach that simply inventories the antecedents or structural conditions of deliberation, we believe that particular variants of this approach have value and that this orientation has done the field a favor. The very fact that researchers have carried out fruitful studies using this method should highlight the fact that certain conditions are *very* conducive to deliberation. This becomes a problem when researchers look for variations in deliberative quality among already well-constructed groups, as was noted in Nabatchi's (2007) study of elaborate deliberative designs and even Reykowski's (2006) experimental designs. After all, a variable is only useful for testing when one can generate sufficient variance. Those who take the structural antecedent approach to measuring deliberation—and those who assume certain groups were sufficiently deliberative by virtue of their circumstances—appear to have at least some sound basis for their research designs.

Nonetheless, we hope that there is a way of better formalizing the antecedent approach, such that one can assess the deliberative potential of a wide range of groups using similar criteria. One method might be to assess the degree to which deliberative norms, as articulated by Burkhalter et al. (2002) or others, are reflected by institutional features of the group or embraced by persons with any degree of process authority. Institutional features might range from formal group by-laws to printed posters put on the wall of a meeting venue, and persons with process authority would range from strong facilitators to the members themselves in an egalitarian discussion.

These recommendations regarding the approaches discussed in this chapter should help scholars advance the study of deliberation, and they should also help practitioners systematize their program evaluations. Working together, deliberative researchers and civic reformers might even use methods like these to bridge the gap between formal academic studies and the more practically oriented field studies that so rarely appear in scholarly journals. Ultimately, we must bring these strands together if we are to honestly and completely assess the value of public deliberation as a means of advancing the democratic project.

NOTES

1. Good reviews include Delli-Carpini et al. (2004), Mendelberg (2002), and Ryfe (2005). The online *Journal of Public Deliberation* is a good resource for examples of empirical studies of deliberation.
2. This is perhaps not surprising since two of the authors of this chapter collaborated to develop the model!
3. Gastil and Black (2008) and Gastil (2008) demonstrate how this definition can be extended meaningfully to characterize deliberative practices beyond the small group setting, from dyadic conversations to governments, media systems, electoral processes, and societies.
4. Increasingly, researchers are trying to automate analysis of texts using computer software. Such efforts have a long history, even within the field of communication (e.g., Rod Hart's DICTION program, www.dictionsoftware.com), which has even been applied in a deliberative context (Hart & Jarvis, 1999). To date, however, none of these computer-analytic approaches have proven adept at measuring deliberation directly.
5. For example, the Virtual Agra project (Muhlberger, 2005) that provided the deliberations that Stromer-Galley content analyzed had both a face-to-face and an online condition; due to poor audio quality in the face-to-face groups, transcripts could not be made.
6. These roughly correspond to the elements of Burkhalter et al.'s (2002) definition of deliberation, and its Listening and Equality elements parallel Reykowski's (2006) Deliberative Functioning Scale, a multi-item participant assessment instrument.
7. The observers' Listening score was based on responses to two items: "Discussion participants were able to comprehend the ideas expressed by one another" and "Generally, the group did NOT really consider what participants had to say" (reversed). Answers were recorded on a five-point scale, with the five points defined as Strongly Disagree, Disagree, Neutral, Agree, and Strongly Agree.
8. As an indicator of convergent validity, the participant ratings were also strongly associated with an independent participant assessment that combined measures of overall satisfaction, perceived fairness, and group effectiveness (Gastil & Sawyer, 2004, p. 16).
9. Most of these parallel the outcomes hypothesized in Burkhalter et al. (2002), which makes their definition of deliberation particularly apt for considering this parallel set of outcome-based proxy measures for deliberation.
10. For a sense of the range of different deliberative practices, see the National Coalition on Dialogue and Deliberation (www.thataway.org). David Mathews, president of the Kettering Foundation, which began

the National Issues Forums program, has on more than one occasion publicly inveighed against the idea of "facilitating" a public forum.
11. That study also compared participant surveys with forum moderator assessments. In retrospect, it is likely that the cognitive burden of even minimally moderating a forum is too great to expect reliable deliberation ratings from the facilitators themselves.

REFERENCES

Barabas, J. (2004). How deliberation affects policy opinions. *American Political Science Review, 98*, 687–701.

Barber, B. (1984). *Strong democracy: Participatory politics for a new age.* Berkeley: University of California Press.

Benhabib, S. (1996). Toward a deliberative model of democratic legitimacy. In S. Benhabib (Ed.), *Democracy and difference: Contesting the boundaries of the political* (pp. 67–94). Princeton, NJ: Princeton University Press.

Bessette, J. (1994). *The mild voice of reason.* Chicago: University of Chicago Press.

Black, L. W. (2006). *Deliberation, difference, and the story: How storytelling manages identity and conflict in deliberative groups.* Unpublished doctoral dissertation, Department of Communication, University of Washington, Seattle.

Black, L. W. (2008). Deliberation, storytelling, and dialogic moments. *Communication Theory, 18*, 93–116.

Black, L. W., Welser, H. T., DeGroot, J., & Cosley, D. (2008, May). *"Wikipedia is not a democracy": Deliberation and policy making in an online community.* Paper presented at the annual meeting of the International Communication Association. Montreal, Canada.

Bohman, J. (1996). *Public deliberation: Pluralism, complexity, and democracy.* Cambridge, MA: MIT Press.

Burkhalter, S., Gastil, J., & Kelshaw, T. (2002). A conceptual definition and theoretical model of public deliberation in small face-to-face groups. *Communication Theory, 12*, 398–422.

Carroll, C. (2002). *Deliberation in the House of Representatives: The impact of preference misrepresentation and orthodox preferences.* Unpublished doctoral dissertation, Department of Political Science, Emory University, Atlanta, GA.

Chambers, S. (2003). Deliberative democratic theory. *Annual Review of Political Science, 6*, 307–326.

Cohen, J. (1989). Deliberation and democratic legitimacy. In P. Pettit & A. Hamlin, *The good polity* (pp. 17–34). New York: Basil Blackwell.

Cohen, J. (1997). Deliberation and democracy legitimacy. In J. Bohman & W. Rehg. (Eds.), *Deliberative democracy: Essays on reason and politics* (pp. 67–91). Cambridge, MA: MIT Press.

Craig, S. C., Niemi, R. G., & Silver, G. E. (1990). Political efficacy and trust: A report on the NES pilot study items. *Political Behavior, 12*, 289–314.

Delli-Carpini, M. X., Cook, F. L., & Jacobs, L. R. (2004). Public deliberation, discursive participation, and citizen engagement: A review of the empirical literature. *Annual Review of Political Science, 7*, 315–344.

Dryzek, J. (1990). *Discursive democracy: Politics, policy and political science.* Cambridge, MA: Harvard University Press.

Dryzek, J. (2000). *Deliberative democracy and beyond: Liberals, critics, contestation.* Oxford: Oxford University Press.

Dutwin, D. (2002). *Can people talk politics? A study of deliberative democracy.* Unpublished doctoral dissertation, Annenberg School for Communication, University of Pennsylvania, Philadelphia.

Dutwin, D. (2003). The character of deliberation: Equality, argument, and the formation of public opinion. *International Journal of Public Opinion Research, 15*, 239–264.

Edwards, P. B., Hindmarsh, R., Mercer, M. B., & Rowland, A. (2008). A three-stage evaluation of a deliberative event on climate change and transforming energy. *Journal of Public Deliberation, 4*(1), Article 6. Retrieved from http://services.bepress.com/jpd/vol4/iss1/art6.

Frey, L. R., & Carragee, K. M. (2007). *Communication activism, vol. 1: Communication for social change.* Cresskill, NJ: Hampton Press.

Fishkin, J. (1991). *Democracy and deliberation: New directions for democratic reform.* New Haven, CT: Yale University Press.

Fishkin, J. (1995). *The voice of the people: Public opinion and democracy.* New Haven, CT: Yale University Press.

Fishkin, J. S., & Luskin, R. C. (1999). Bringing deliberation to the democratic dialogue. In M. McCombs & A. Reynolds (Eds.), *The poll with a human face: The National Issues Convention experiment in political communication* (pp. 3–38). Mahwah, NJ: Lawrence Erlbaum.

Fung, A. (2007). Democratic theory and political science: A pragmatic method of constructive engagement. *American Political Science Review, 101,* 443–458.

Gastil, J. (1993). *Democracy in small groups: Participation, decision making, and communication.* Philadelphia, PA: New Society Publishers.

Gastil, J. (2004). Adult civic education through the National Issues Forums: Developing democratic habits and dispositions through public deliberation. *Adult Education Quarterly, 54,* 308–328.

Gastil, J. (2006). How balanced discussion shapes knowledge, public perceptions, and attitudes: A case study of deliberation on the Los Alamos National Laboratory. *Journal of Public Deliberation, 2,* 1–39.

Gastil, J. (2008). *Political communication and deliberation.* Thousand Oaks, CA: Sage.

Gastil, J., & Black, L. W. (2008). Public deliberation as an organizing principle for political communication research. *Journal of Public Deliberation, 4,* Article 3. Retrieved from http://services.bepress.com/jpd/vol4/iss1/art3.

Gastil, J., Black, L. W., Deess, P., & Leighter, J. (2008). From group member to democratic citizen: How deliberating with fellow jurors reshapes civic attitudes. *Human Communication Research, 35,* 137–169.

Gastil, J., Black, L. W., & Moscovitz, K. (2008). Ideology, attitude change, and deliberation in small face-to-face groups. *Political Communication, 25,* 23–46.

Gastil, J., Deess, E. P., Weiser, P., & Meade, J. (2008). Jury service and electoral participation: A test of the participation hypothesis. *Journal of Politics, 70,* 351–367.

Gastil, J., & Dillard, J. P. (1999). The aims, methods, and effects of deliberative civic education through the National Issues Forums. *Communication Education, 48,* 1–14.

Gastil, J., & Levine, P. (Eds.). (2005). *The deliberative democracy handbook: Strategies for effective civic engagement in the 21st century.* San Francisco: Jossey-Bass.

Gastil, J., & Sawyer, K. (2004, February). When process matters: An exploration of different approaches to operationalizing public deliberation. Paper presented at the annual meeting of the Western States Communication Association, Albuquerque, NM.

Gerhards, J. (1997). Diskursive vs liberale Öffentlichkeit: Eine empirische Auseinandersetzung mit Jürgen Habermas. *Kölner Zeitschrift für Soziologie und Sozialpsychologie 49*(1), 1–34.

Grimes, M. F. (2008). The civic benefits of imperfect deliberation. *Journal of Public Deliberation, 4*(1), Article 7. Retrieved from http://services.bepress.com/jpd/vol4/iss1/art7.

Grogan, C. M., & Gusmano, M. K. (2005). Deliberative democracy in theory and practice: Connecticut's Medicaid managed care council. *State Politics and Policy Quarterly, 5,* 126–146.

Gutmann, A., & Thompson, D. (1996). *Democracy and disagreement.* Cambridge, MA: Harvard University Press.

Guttman, N. (2007). Bringing the mountain to the public: Dilemmas and contradictions in the procedures of public deliberation initiatives that aim to get ordinary citizens to deliberate policy issues. *Communication Theory, 17,* 411–438.

Habermas, J. (1984). *The theory of communicative action, vol.1* (T. McCarthy, Trans.). Boston: Beacon Press.

Habermas, J. (1987). *The theory of communicative action, vol.2* (T. McCarthy, Trans.). Boston: Beacon Press.

Habermas, J. (1995). Reconciliation through the public use of reason: Remarks on John Rawls's political liberalism. *Journal of Philosophy, 92,* 109–131.

Halvorsen, K. E. (2001). Assessing public participation techniques for comfort, convenience, satisfaction, and deliberation. *Environmental Management, 28,* 179–186.

Hart, R., & Jarvis, S. (1999). We the people: The contours of lay political discourse. In M. McCombs, & A. Reynolds (Eds.), *The poll with a human face: The National Issues Convention experiment in political communication* (pp. 59–84). Mahwah, NJ: Lawrence Erlbaum.

Hartz-Karp, J. (2007). Understanding deliberativeness: Bridging theory and practice. *International Journal of Public Participation, 1*(2). Retrieved from http://www.iap2.org.

Haug, C., & Teune, S. (2008). Identifying deliberation in social movement assemblies: Challenges of comparative participant observation. *Journal of Public Deliberation, 4*, Article 8. Retrieved from http://services.bepress.com/jpd/vol4/iss1/art8.

Hawkins, A. K., & O'Doherty, K. (2010). Biobank governance: A lesson in trust. *New Genetics and Society, 29*(3), 1–17.

Hendriks, C. M. (2005). Participatory storylines and their influence on deliberative forums. *Policy Sciences, 38*, 1–20.

Holzinger, K. (2001). Verhandeln statt Argumentieren oder Verhandeln durch Argumentieren? Eine empirische Analyse auf der Basis der Sprechakttheorie. *Politische Vierteljahresschrift, 42*, 414–446.

Jacobs, L. R., Cook, F. L., & Delli-Carpini, M. (2009). *Talking together: Public deliberation and political participation in America*. Chicago, IL: University of Chicago Press.

Jaworski, A., & Coupland, N. (Eds.). (1999). *The discourse reader*. New York: Routledge.

Karpowitz, C. F., & Mansbridge, J. (2005). Disagreement and consensus: The importance of dynamic updating in public deliberation. In J. Gastil, & P. Levine (Eds.), *The deliberative democracy handbook* (pp. 237–253). San Francisco, CA: Jossey-Bass.

Krippendorff, K. (2004). *Content analysis: An introduction to its methodology* (2nd ed.). New York: Sage.

Levine, P., Fung, A., & Gastil, J. (2005). Future directions for public deliberation. *Journal of Public Deliberation, 1*, Article 3. Retrieved from http://services.bepress.com/jpd/vol1/iss1/art3.

Lukensmeyer, C. J., Goldman, J., & Brigham, S. (2005). A town meeting for the twenty-first century. In J. Gastil & P. Levine (Eds.), *The deliberative democracy handbook: Strategies for effective civic engagement in the 21st century* (pp. 154–163). San Francisco: Jossey-Bass.

Luskin, R. C., Fishkin, J. S., & Jowell, R. (2002). Considered opinions: Deliberative polling in Britain. *British Journal of Political Science, 32*, 455–487.

Lustick, I. A., & Miodownik, D. (2000). Deliberative democracy and public discourse: The agent-based argument repertoire model. *Complexity, 5*(4), 13–30.

Mansbridge, J. (1980). *Beyond adversary democracy*. New York: Basic Books.

Mansbridge, J., Hartz-Karp, J., Amengual, M., & Gastil, J. (2006). Norms of deliberation: An inductive study. *Journal of Public Deliberation, 2*, Article 7. Retrieved from http://services.bepress.com/jpd/vol2/iss1/art7.

Mendelberg, T. (2002). The deliberative citizen: Theory and evidence. In M. X. Delli-Carpini, L. Huddy, & R. Shapiro (Eds.), *Research in micropolitics: Political decision-making, deliberation, and participation* (Vol. 6, pp. 151–193). Greenwich, CT: JAI Press.

Mendelberg, T., & Oleske, J. (2000). Race and public deliberation. *Political Communication, 17*, 169–191.

Morrell, M. E. (2005). Deliberation, democratic decision-making and internal political efficacy. *Political Behavior, 27*, 49–69.

Muhlberger, P. (2005). The Virtual Agora Project: A research design for studying democratic deliberation, *Journalof Public Deliberation, 1*, Article 5. Retrieved from http://services.bepress.com/jpd/vol1/iss1/art5.

Muhlberger, P. (2007). *Report to the Deliberative Democracy Consortium: Building a deliberation measurement toolbox* (Version 2). Retrieved from http://www.geocities.com/pmuhl78/DDCReport.pdf.

Nabatchi, T. (2007). *Deliberative democracy; The effects of participation on political efficacy*. Unpublished doctoral dissertation, School of Public and Environmental Affairs, Indiana University, Bloomington, IN.

Neuendorf, K. A. (2002). *The content analysis guidebook*. Thousand Oaks, CA: Sage.

Niemeyer, S. (2006). *Intersubjective rationality: Measuring deliberative quality*. Paper presented to the Political Science Seminar at Australian National University. Retrieved fromhttp://deliberativedemocracy.anu.edu.au/People/Niemeyer.htm.

Nishizawa, M. (2005). Citizen deliberations on science and technology and their social environments: Case study of the Japanese consensus conference on GM crops. *Science and Public Policy, 32*, 479–489.

O'Doherty, K. C., & Davidson, H. J. (2010). Subject positioning and deliberative democracy: Understanding social processes underlying deliberation. *Journal for the Theory of Social Behaviour, 40*, 224–245.

Page, B. I. (1996). *Who deliberates? Mass media in modern democracy*. Chicago: University of Chicago Press.

Polletta, F. (2006). *It was like a fever: Storytelling in protest and politics*. Chicago: University of Chicago Press.

Polletta, F. (2008). Just talk: Political deliberation after 9/11. *Journal of Public Deliberation, 4*, Article 2. Retrieved from http://services.bepress.com/jpd/vol4/iss1/art2.

Polletta, F., & Lee, J. (2006). Is storytelling good for democracy? Rhetoric in public deliberation after 9/11. *American Sociological Review*, *71*, 699–723.

Pomerantz, A. M. (1984). Agreeing and disagreeing with assessments: Some features of preferred/ dispreferred turn shapes. In J. M. Atkinson & J. Heritage (Eds.), *Structures of social action: Studies in conversation analysis* (pp. 57–101). Cambridge: Cambridge University Press.

Poole, M. S., Keyton, J., & Frey, L. R. (1999). Group communication methodology: Issues and considerations. In L. R. Frey (Ed.), *The handbook of group communication theory and research* (pp. 92–112). Thousand Oaks, CA: Sage.

Price, V., Nir, L., & Cappella, J. N. (2006). Normative and informational influences in online political discussion. *Communication Theory*, *16*, 47–74.

Reykowski, J. (2006). Deliberative democracy and "human nature": An empirical approach. *Political Psychology*, *27*, 323–346.

Rosenberg, S. W. (2005). The empirical study of deliberative democracy: Setting a research agenda. *Acta Politica*, *40*, 212–224.

Rosenberg, S. W. (2006). *An empirical study of types of democratic deliberation: The limits and potential of citizen participation.* Paper presented at the annual meeting of the American Political Science Association, Philadelphia, PA.

Ryfe, D. M. (2005). Does deliberative democracy work? *Annual Review of Political Science*, *8*, 49–71.

Ryfe, D. M. (2006). Narrative and deliberation in small group forums. *Journal of Applied Communication Research*, *34*, 72–93.

Ryfe, D. M. (2007). Toward a sociology of deliberation. *Journal of Public Deliberation*, *3*, Article 3. Retrieved from http://services.bepress.com/jpd/vol3/iss1/art3.

Sanders, L. M. (1997). Against deliberation. *Political Theory*, *25*, 347–376.

Smith, G., & Wales, C. (2000). Citizens' juries and deliberative democracy. *Political Studies*, *48*, 51–65.

Steenbergen, M. R., Bachtiger, A., Sporndli, M., & Steiner, J. (2003). Measuring political deliberation: A discourse quality index. *Comparative European Politics*, *1*, 21–48.

Steiner, J. (Forthcoming). *The foundation of deliberative democracy: Empirical research and normative implications.* Cambridge, UK: Cambridge University Press.

Steiner, J., Bachtiger, A., Sporndli, M., & Steenbergen, M. R. (2004). *Deliberative politics in action: Analyzing parliamentary discourse.* Cambridge, UK: Cambridge University Press.

Stromer-Galley, J. (2007). Measuring deliberation's content: A coding scheme. *Journal of Public Deliberation*, *3*, Article 12. Retrieved from http://services.bepress.com/jpd/vol3/iss1/art12.

Sturgis, P., Roberts, C., & Allum, N. (2005). A different take on the deliberative poll—Information, deliberation, and attitude constraint. *Public Opinion Quarterly*, *69*, 30–65.

Sulkin, T., & Simon, A. (2001). Habermas in the lab: An experimental investigation of the effects of deliberation. *Political Psychology*, *22*, 809–826.

Townsend, R. (2006). Widening the circumference of scene: Local, politics, local metaphysics. *K.B. Journal*, *2*(2), Article 7. Retrieved from http://kbjournal.org/townsend.

Tracy, K. (2007). The discourse of crisis in public meetings: Case study of a school district's multimillion dollar error. *Journal of Applied Communication Research*, *35*, 418–441.

Tracy, K. (2010). *Challenges of ordinary democracy: A case study in deliberation and dissent.* University Park, PA: The Pennsylvania State University Press.

Verba, S., Schlozman, K. L., & Brady, H. E. (1995). *Voice and equality: Civic voluntarism in American politics.* Cambridge, MA: Harvard University Press.

Warren, M. (1992). Democratic theory and self-transformation. *American Political Science Review*, *90*, 46–60.

Warren, M., & Pearse, H. (Eds.). (2008). *Designing deliberative democracy: The British Columbia Citizens' Assembly.* Cambridge: Cambridge University Press.

Wilson, R. W., Payne, M., & Smith, E. (2003). Does discussion enhance rationality? *Journal of the American Planning Association*, *69*, 354–367.

Zaller, J. R. (1992). *The nature and origins of mass opinion.* Cambridge: Cambridge University Press.

18

Porous Networks and Overlapping Contexts

Methodological Challenges in the Study of Social Communication and Political Behavior

Scott D. McClurg
Department of Political Science
Southern Illinois University

The distinguishing characteristic of social communication research is the presumption that citizens are influenced by the environments in which they reside. In contrast to political communication research originating from rationalistic or psychological perspectives, it takes as the fundamental subject of inquiry how environments vary and the consequences this holds for citizens, either as individuals or groups. A significant line of research within this subfield focuses specifically on *communication networks*, which encompass the information available to citizens from formal and informal social units, including interpersonal networks, geographic contexts, religious institutions, the workplace, and other social conglomerates.[1]

Despite having origins stretching at least as far back as Berelson et al.'s (1954) landmark analyses in Elmira, NY, social communication research was not "in vogue" throughout much of the twentieth century.[2] Nevertheless, social communication research is moving again to the forefront of the disciplines of political science and communication. Consequently, there is good reason to consider and assess the methodological challenges facing this promising area of inquiry. In this chapter, I focus on three research design issues that are of particular note in social communication research: (1) choosing among levels of analysis, (2) trade-offs between depth and breadth in sampling environments, and (3) difficulties in demonstrating causality.[3] Though by no means exhaustive, this list serves as a starting point for a broader discussion about how the unique assumptions of social communication research pose specific inferential challenges and affect the advancement of knowledge.

After defining the key terms in this field of study, I outline each problem, discuss its consequences, and offer advice for moving forward. My thesis throughout this discussion is that social communication researchers should prioritize measuring independent variables with as much depth as possible at multiple levels of analysis. As the discussion below makes clear, this has implications for other methodological issues, including case selection, statistical analysis, and the ability to draw externally valid conclusions. In broad terms, my justification is that even under favorable conditions it is difficult to draw conclusions across a variety of social environments simultaneously. Consequently, greater attention should be given to better understanding specific environments, the theoretical properties of those environments, and the potential relationships among them. This in turn requires careful and deep measurement of those environments that is built on strong, theoretically motivated concepts. Heeding this advice encourages attention to social diversity, development of models that are more attendant to this diversity, and recognition of inherent theoretical ambiguities underlying complex social effects.

ENVIRONMENTS FOR SOCIAL COMMUNICATION: NETWORKS AND CONTEXTS

Conceptual development is an intellectual task that falls in between theory building and methodology (Adcock & Collier, 2001; Chaffee, 1991; Collier & Mahon, 1993; Gerring, 2001) and is therefore a crucial element of understanding research challenges. For this chapter I focus specifically on two types of social communication environments: networks and contexts. In general terms, *social network* research examines interpersonal communication, while *contextual* research investigates the relationship between people and social groups more generally.[4]

Social Networks

Definition.   The key definitional element of a social network is the presence of identifiable relationships between people where conversations create opportunities for the transfer of politically relevant information, such as pertinent political facts, general perspectives on politics, political norms and mores, and so on. Analytically speaking, this means that work in this vein often focuses on such questions as how frequently people talk about politics and what political content those conversations involve. Issues addressed by this research include whether people recognize political differences between themselves and others and the consequences such relationships hold for political behavior (Finifter, 1974; Huckfeldt, Johnson, & Sprague, 2004, 2002; Huckfeldt, Mendez, & Osborn, 2004; Leighley, 1990; McClurg, 2006a, 2006b; Mutz, 2006; Mutz & Martin, 2001; Price, Cappella, & Nir, 2002; Walsh, 2004).

Another stream of network analyses investigates how the structure of social relationships influences information flows between people. Stated differently, the interest here is in how the substance of relationships between people—familial, professional, socially hierarchical—is related to information exchange and influence. Along these lines, some researchers examine how social isomorphism in terms of race, class, income, education, and gender affects acquisition of information and eventual political behaviors (e.g., Brickell, Huckfeldt, & Sprague, 1988; Djupe, Sohkey, & Gilbert, 2007; Levine, 2005; Mendez & Osborne, 2005). Others focus on levels of intimacy between parties in a social relationship, such as filial ties and/or the somewhat more amorphous concept of "closeness," which refers to a respondent's personal estimate of relationship intimacy (Huckfeldt & Sprague, 1991; Kenny, 1994). Finally, there is the idea of social tie strength identified by Grannovetter (1973), which focuses on how integrated one specific discussion partner is with other people in a network. Of particular interest in political communication research is how tie strength influences exposure to diverse viewpoints (Huckfeldt, Johnson, & Sprague, 2004) and the capacity for collective action stemming from social capital (Coleman, 1988; Putnam, 2000).

Types of Social Networks.   As these examples suggest, social network studies encompass a diverse set of substantive questions. Accordingly, a variety of strategies are employed to identify networks and measure their properties. To help categorize this diversity as much as possible, I use a typology that classifies networks along two dimensions: (1) completeness, which refers to how extensively networks are identified and mapped out; and (2) permanence, which refers to the nature of the relationships between people in a network. Figure 18.1 provides a visual representation of this conceptual space, showing illustrative studies at different points in that space. This figure demonstrates how a wide variety of communication environments—from protests to school reform organizations to families—can be usefully studied from a network perspective. With this general conceptual space in mind, it is helpful to explain each dimension in greater detail.

Completeness. At one extreme of the completeness dimension is research examining only parts of an identifiable network, typically through the eyes of a single individual. The most common approach in this vein is the study of *ego-centric networks*, where social relationships are defined in terms of a particular person (the ego) and the people with whom she has discussions (the alters). Defining networks in this manner is particularly useful for large sample surveys because it enables use of "name generators"—survey questions asking people for the names of family, friends, and acquaintances—to identify a respondent's immediate discussion partners (Burt, 1985, 1984; Huckfeldt & Sprague, 1995; Marsden, 1987). Such survey questions elicit *partial network data*, meaning that they are only capturing a specific slice of the respondent's relationships.

At the other end of the completeness spectrum is research investigating "whole" networks, where the analyst typically identifies a specific and bounded social organization (formal or informal) and then measures *all* of the relationships within it.[5] Rather than relying on an ego's identification of relevant network partners, then, the goal here is to identify all of the people within a network and then find which links exist from the set of all possible interactions (Scott, 2000). Studies in this vein typically focus on network structure rather than individual behavior as the unit of analysis (but see Lazer et al. 2007). As such, the nature of the research question often changes from one of individual influence to understanding information flows and group dynamics.

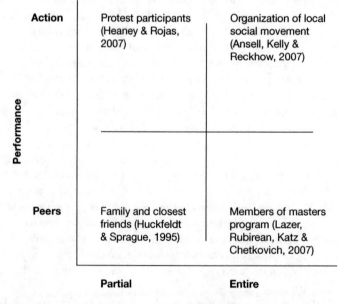

FIGURE 18.1 Conceptual mapping of social network types, with examples.

Permanence.   As anyone who has changed jobs, moved, or engaged in political action knows, interpersonal relationships vary in terms of length and intensity over time. And, we are undoubtedly influenced in different ways by the variety of relationships that we have (e.g., a boss versus a spouse). Consequently, networks can be usefully distinguished on the permanence of the relationships. At one end of this dimension are *peer networks*, more often than not the subject of social communication research on politics. Here the relationships are relatively enduring because they are with spouses, family members, and long-term acquaintances.[6] At the other end are less stable and typically more functional networks. Referred to as *action networks*, these are relationships that arise in response to particular stimuli and then later dissipate.[7] Included here are temporary social groupings, such as classes and/or working groups, and purpose driven networks that people consult *because* of their particular expertise or situation.

Peer and action networks can be distinguished on the basis of how people enter and exit them. While peer networks are less likely to be selected on the basis of criteria relevant to political analysis, action networks are more likely to be selected *because* of political factors. Analysts should be cognizant of selection processes in both cases, but the types of investigation will clearly vary by network type. For example, studies of a network that people join as they enter a social movement should be far more cognizant of the formation process than a study of how one's parents influence your political views, if only because you can choose your friends but not your parents.

Social Contexts

Definition.   Social communication research is also interested in *contextual effects*. While social network research focuses on specific and observable patterns of human interaction, contextual research thinks of social communication through the lens of citizens reacting to information from or about groups of people (e.g., religious institutions, workplaces, fraternal organizations, neighborhoods, and so forth). Although these social contexts are groups where social interaction *can*—but does not necessarily—occur, contextual research does not focus only on observable conversations between people. Instead, the focus is on the relationship between individuals and *aggregations of people*. As such, it is a more difficult-to-define concept than the social network. To provide traction, I define social contexts as specific and identifiable social spaces (i.e., they have real physical or social boundaries) from which citizens can receive politically relevant information. What matters with specific contexts, then, are their social and political properties and how people are (or are not) influenced by those properties. Thus, when we speak of a social context effect we are referring to how people are influenced by its compositional properties, such as the level of education or political attitudes of people in the context.

Excluding social interaction as the principal element defining contextual effects leads to an important question: Given that people live in multiple contexts, how are they influenced by them? For example, if someone moved from a highly Republican neighborhood into a highly Democratic one, what influence would this new environmental context have on that person's political behavior— and why? A common model of contextual effects is based on work by McPhee (1963) and elaborated by Huckfeldt and Sprague (1995). In this model, contexts influence citizens by probabilistically determining the range of people with whom they will have social interactions. In other words, contexts matter to the extent they influence social networks. Building on our example, this means that when someone moves to a Democratic neighborhood they are more likely to have conversations and make friends that provide information supportive of voting Democratic than what they experienced in their old Republican neighborhood. This approach has two important advantages: (1) it provides a concrete conceptual model for thinking about contextual effects, and (2) it creates unity between the contextual and network approaches to studying social communication effects.

However, as the above discussion implies, this may be an overly restrictive way to think about "contextual effects."[8] If we were to take such an approach it would restrict the field of social communication to only those areas where networks and contexts overlap. Yet there are many ways that people may be influenced by contexts even in the absence of a network effect. An obvious alternative to social networks, particularly to communication scholars, are the news media (Mutz, 1998). Less obvious are low-level cues, such as personal observations, that lead people to make inferences about their contexts. Along these lines Huckfeldt and Sprague (1992) find that people's judgments about the political leanings of their neighborhoods are in part influenced by the political signs displayed nearby. Similarly, Baybeck and McClurg (2005) find that residents know much about their neighborhoods (e.g., how educated they are relative to their neighbors) that is *not* a function of belonging to neighborhood organizations or reading the local newspaper. Whatever the case, analysts ought to consider which types of causal mechanisms are relevant to the *type of context* they are examining and gather appropriate information for sorting through different causal mechanisms. Contextual effects need not be seen simply as equivalent to network effects; while the two concepts overlap in reality, they are not necessarily the same.

Types of Social Contexts.   Setting aside the question of the causal mechanisms linking contexts to political behavior, we still need a framework for delineating between types of social contexts. The most important issue in this regard involves defining *contextual boundaries*. To identify the universe of different contexts and to measure the properties of individual contexts, the boundaries that delineate among separate contexts must be clearly identified. Potential ambiguities in this process are nicely illustrated by the idea of "neighborhood effects." Deciding that people on one street, for example, are "in" the neighborhood while others in adjacent locations are not is a necessary part of studying the influence of neighborhood contexts. However, these kinds of determinations clearly involve judgment calls.

Two convenient methods are typically used for delineating contextual boundaries. The first, and most common approach in my experience, is use of readily-available geographic boundaries (Brown, 1981; Huckfeldt, 1996; Johnston, Jones, Propper, & Burgess, 2007; Putnam,1966; Wright, 1977). These are convenient because they are widely accepted as meaningful and allow for clear delineation of contexts by reference to physical space. For instance, when voters refer to their county as a social context, the lines of demarcation are generally clearer than when they refer to their neighborhoods instead. But though such boundaries may be more clearly understood, they are, to a significant degree, arbitrary, or at least based on criteria that are irrelevant to contextual theories. When analysts want to understand how people respond to their neighbors, it is unclear what should guide their choice from the menu of geographic options. Is a census block group the appropriate choice? Or, should it be the city? Unfortunately, the necessities of gathering data mean that such ambiguities are often built into the social communication research process.

A second way of defining contexts is with organizational boundaries, the paradigmatic examples here being churches and workplaces (e.g., Djupe & Gilbert, 2006; Huckfeldt, Plutzer, & Sprague, 1993; Mutz & Mondak, 2006). As with geographic boundaries, using formal membership organizations to delineate among contexts is convenient. Not only are referents like "churches" and "workplaces" substantively interesting, it is also relatively clear who is "in" and who is "out" of the context. Unlike geographic contexts, the boundaries of formal social units are *not* arbitrarily drawn. Yet this strength also involves tradeoffs, the most important being that because the boundaries are meaningful to average people, self-selection into the context is an even more acute concern. Additionally, these contexts are typically seen as unique and/or specialized, thereby limiting how widely conclusions drawn from them are believed to extend to other contexts.

METHODOLOGICAL ISSUES: CHOOSING A LEVEL OF ANALYSIS

Problem

The first methodological choice facing any scholar testing a social communication hypothesis regards the appropriate level of analysis to measure an environmental effect. Level of analysis problems outside political communication research typically center on appropriate measurement of dependent variables (e.g., to avoid the ecological inference fallacy), but the aggregate characteristic of most *independent variables* in political communication research means that important choices are to be made there as well. Almost any social communication hypothesis could be formulated in such a way as to be tested across a variety of networks and contexts. But which one of those social environments is the most appropriate unit of analysis? In some situations the decision is not daunting because the substantive question narrows analytical choices, such as studies of family or marital influence on voting behavior (Brickell, Huckfeldt, & Sprague, 1988; Stoker & Jennings, 2005; Zuckerman, Fitzgerald, & Dasovic, 2005). Yet theoretical expectations are often not sufficiently precise to make the choice obvious.

Take, for example, the question of how racial context affects white voter attitudes toward African Americans. Key (1949) argued that whites would be more hostile to blacks in those areas where "racial threat"—measured by the proportion of blacks in a particular county—was at its highest. While Key's argument is straightforward, the countervailing question of whether the proportion of minorities in a white person's immediate locale makes them *more* tolerant is also plausible (Branton & Jones, 2005; Giles & Buckner, 1993, 1996; Giles & Hertz, 1994; Oliver & Mendelberg, 2000; Voss, 1996a, 1996b). In short, the problem is that the results *depend upon* the contextual unit employed. As Baybeck's (2006) analysis of survey and census data from St. Louis and Indianapolis shows, the impact of racial context on behavior differs when the unit of analysis for the independent variable is the census block group compared to when it is the municipality in which people reside. Although both contexts are reasonable choices, the fact that the results *depend upon* the choice demonstrates the underlying problem—the environmental level of analysis issue can be among the most significant research design choices a researcher makes.

Implications

Ignoring the unit of analysis problem can lead to a variety of substantive misunderstandings, the first of which is that study findings are unresponsive to the choice of environment.[9] *Choices about which networks and/or contexts to analyze are meaningful because they prioritize certain types of theoretical links between social environments and political behavior.* If we were to believe, for example, that racially charged political debate is the source of racial hostility between whites and blacks, then it would be inappropriate to choose neighborhoods or networks as the unit of analysis. In the case of the former, neighborhoods are not meaningful arenas of political debate. In the case of the latter, it is possible that political debate occurs between acquaintances but these discussions are unlikely to be a function of cross-race interaction on account of racial isomorphism in interpersonal networks. Instead, it would make far more sense to focus on social diversity within governing boundaries like municipalities, political districts, and the like, as those are the units that constrain political debate through election campaigns and policy.

A second, related issue is that social communication effects may be incorrectly treated as constant across multiple levels of analysis. This raises the issue of *causal heterogeneity*, where the effect of one independent variable depends at least in part on how it combines with other independent variables to influence the dependent variable or outcome of interest.[10] For example,

McClurg (2006b) shows that political disagreement in social networks demobilizes people who are *also* in the political minority in their neighborhood, whereas it has *no effect* for people who are in the neighborhood majority (see Djupe & Gilbert, 2009, for an application of this idea to religious institutions). Because citizens are less likely to make the sorts of distinctions between social environments that scholars make to ensure a tractable empirical analysis, scholars should be cognizant that empirical conclusions are vulnerable to change when additional levels of analysis are incorporated. Indeed, the possibility of cross-environmental heterogeneity is what makes social communication research interesting. Yet most studies look at a slice of social life, so analysts should be sensitive to unexplored heterogeneity in causal parameters.

A final point to make is that level of analysis problems may arise simply because environments are chosen as a matter of convenience rather than for theoretically driven reasons. Even though many social communication hypotheses are not precise enough to provide clear expectations across different networks and contexts, the lack of precision does not imply that certain environments cannot be ruled out as inappropriate for a specific research question. If the research hypothesis suggests that face-to-face interaction is necessary for social communication effects, then using a neighborhood or church context to measure the social environment is less appropriate than peer networks, as considerable variation exists among individuals in how much face-to-face interaction occurs in these settings. Likewise, if the research hypothesis suggests that behavior depends upon social diversity, a network study is unlikely to be meaningful if it focuses on core networks rather than the extended network because core networks tend to be socially, economically, racially, and politically homogenous.

Advice

Ideally, the best way to address levels of analysis questions is straightforward—rely on theory. Yet advancement in this area is limited by the absence of conceptual development that distinguishes among the multitude of social environments and their theoretical properties. Huckfeldt and Sprague (1995) provide a solid foundation for thinking about mechanisms linking aggregate social contexts to networks, while Books and Prysby (1991) discuss issues of causality in some detail for aggregate social contexts. Yet there is very little work that either expands upon these beginnings or empirically explores important conceptual distinctions, such as what causal mechanisms prevail in different social environments (but see Djupe, Gilbert, & Sohkey, 2007; Huckfeldt, Johnson, & Sprague, 2004; McClurg, 2006b). To help alleviate these concerns, future research should try to rule in and out different causal mechanisms linking social environments to political behavior.

In lieu of more refined conceptual definitions that can guide choices about appropriate units of analysis, it may be beneficial to test the robustness of the assumptions underlying social communication research designs with data. In a paradigmatic example, Branton and Jones (2005) show that the joint effect of racial and socioeconomic context on political attitudes holds across *multiple geographic contexts*, simultaneously building some support for a claim of generality and providing hard evidence on the scope of that claim.

METHODOLOGICAL ISSUES: SAMPLING

Problem

The second methodological choice in social communication research regards sampling. Here, two related issues arise. The first is the selection of environmental cases on which to gather data, an important choice because random sampling is unavailable as a method at the aggregate level; the second is how many different types of social units (*between* unit sampling) to select versus how much information to gather about each unit that is in the data set (*within* unit sampling). While the substance of research questions may again provide guidance in dealing with sampling issues, these two issues create a natural tension between breadth and depth of analysis that is fundamental to social communication research. In essence, the wider variety and larger number of environments—be they networks or contexts—that are measured, the less that can be learned about any specific environment. The end result of this tension is that, even with tremendous resources, original data collection will struggle to have a deep and generalizable understanding of any social communication effect.

To understand the problems, first consider the contrasting case of a random sample survey. All social scientists understand that survey samples need to be comprised of respondents who have been selected in a manner that is independent from the study itself lest they incur selection bias.[11] Likewise, social scientists recognize that estimates of relationships between any two individual-level characteristics are less certain when based on a handful of observations then when based on thousands (e.g., Gill 1999). Accordingly, good survey researchers draw large random samples of individuals from well-defined populations in order to avoid selection bias and statistical ineffi-ciency, while maximizing the ability to make generalizable statements about the population.

Yet to use this kind of procedure, it is necessary to have a well-defined population *and* a large number of observations within that population. Unfortunately, the questions pursued in social communication research usually make it difficult to match these conditions, especially when multiple individuals are embedded within a single environment.[12] When referring to a single type of environment, for example a specific type of network or context, not only is there rarely a well-defined list of component parts from which to sample, but the underlying "population" of environmental units may not be large enough to make random sampling useful. At the same time, it is often impractical to gather information on *all* environmental units. This means that analysts are usually given two choices when trying to determine how much information to gather within the environment: "some" or "all," with the second option involving fewer individual-units per social communication environment.

While this suggests that choosing "some" environments for analysis must be done pur-posively, there is a second sampling decision involved regarding *how many* environments to include in a study. Whether the goal is to examine as many neighborhoods, churches, or types of network relationships as possible, larger environmental sample sizes in a study (either per individual or across all individuals) comes at the price of reduced information on any specific environment itself.

Huckfeldt and Sprague (1995) illustrate these kinds of tradeoffs in their study of how neighborhoods affect political behavior. To measure their independent variable—neighborhood political composition—it was necessary to aggregate survey responses within each neighborhood. In doing so, the authors not only had to decide how many individuals to select per neighborhood (they settled on about 100), but also identify the specific neighborhoods in which to conduct the surveys (they settled on 16). While it was possible to randomly select *within* neighborhoods to avoid *systematic* measurement error, the amount of imprecision in their measurements (i.e., *unsystematic* measurement error) was a direct function of the neighborhood sample size; thus, their ability to draw conclusions about how neighborhoods influence behavior has uncertain generalizability.[13]

At its most basic level, these sampling concerns mean that social communication research—and likely political communication research more generally—has a *built-in* trade off between good measurement of the independent variables and generalizability of the sample. For a political psychologist who uses survey data, the main concerns with measurement have little to do with external validity of the population except to the degree that respondents self-select out of surveys and experiments. By contrast, any study of a social network or context will have to decide whether it is more important to examine multiple environments or understand the environments that can be measured with greater depth. At the same time, this work must *still be concerned* with the same self-selection problems faced by other researchers.

Implications

What consequences do these sampling problems hold for social communication research? By accepting that "context matters," findings are inherently contingent on the particular group of people included in an analysis; gains in external validity across and within environments depend particularly on environmental sampling decisions. Keep in mind that this is not a *flaw* of social communication research per se, but rather a reflection of the complexity caused by the multiple, overlapping social environments that surround people in the modern world.

Drawing on this perspective, one implication of the sampling problem is that social communication researchers must make *purposive* decisions about *what* to observe. In this sense, research in this area starkly differs from volumes of other research on political behavior that effectively employs random sampling strategies. But as noted above, what environments to include in a study and what component parts of those environments to include in the analysis are not decisions that can be readily solved with random sampling. This potentially introduces researcher-induced selection bias into social communication data. The last codicil—that the bias is a function of investigator choices—not only distinguishes it from selection biases induced by the behavior of respondents (see below), but highlights a potentially serious problem for social communication research. Although all research is likely affected to some degree by researcher bias, particularly with regard to the questions that get asked, there are techniques for reducing bias from the sample selection process. Almost by definition, these concerns are more acute in social communication research.

A second implication is that these sampling issues may lead scholars to simply ignore the unique issues involved in environment sampling, instead randomly sampling individuals and relying either on their perceptions of the environment or using external information (e.g., census data) as a measure of the context. In my opinion, while both strategies can yield some useful information on social communication effects, neither is satisfactory as a panacea for sampling concerns.

First, let us consider an approach that only measures the context through citizen perceptions. Understanding people's beliefs about social environments is clearly a necessary part of research in this area and does avoid tricky issues of sampling on both independent and dependent variables simultaneously. Yet people's perceptions of their environments are not entirely accurate because they are partly a projection of individual characteristics (Baybeck & McClurg, 2005; Huckfeldt & Sprague, 1988, 1992; Mutz & Martin, 2001). And while we should study such perceptual errors, ignoring the actual social communication environment means we are only focused on the individual side of the equation. This is akin to ignoring supply to only study demand in economics in that we would only be examining part of the environmental process (people's views of the environment) and overlooking the role of the informational supply (the composition of the environment). Such a one-sided approach would completely reshape the core questions of the field into ones of social psychology with less emphasis on communication and information exposure. As defined earlier, network and context research necessarily cares about *both* processes.

What about using aggregate data to measure contexts and linking them to a random sample of individuals? Are there drawbacks to this approach? As with studies relying only on perceptions, such an approach has some merit as *one among many* because it would provide good information across environments. However, limited within-context sampling would mean that estimates of the associated causal effect would be limited. At its most basic level, the problem is obvious—if we only had one person per county, the variability around estimates of county-level effects would be much larger than if we had 1,000 people per county. It would be very difficult to hold much confidence in such a result as the standard errors would be based on cross-individual variance when what we care about are the within-context, cross-individual variance. Additionally, this kind of approach is naturally limited to only certain types of questions—those for which aggregate data are available—which are not necessarily motivated by theoretical concerns.

Advice

My initial inclination when writing about environment sampling and the trade-offs it necessitates is to suggest throwing your hands up in the air, if only because they seem so overwhelming. My second inclination is to advocate sticking as closely as possible to previous practices, largely because that would speed the accumulation of knowledge which these types of problems generally retard. Instead, I will advocate giving priority to the *within-environment* criterion in social communication research. The one thread running through this discussion is that generalizability is not only difficult to achieve, but if over-emphasized leads to strategies that are in the long run not likely to facilitate the accumulation of knowledge.

Accordingly, my primary piece of advice for gathering new data is to focus first and foremost on defining what specific type of network or context is appropriate and then gathering sufficient observations within that social unit for measuring it accurately. Then—and only then—should attention be given to thinking about how many different environments in which to gather data. Although this certainly prioritizes sampling for the purpose of measurement at the expense of external validity, it will enrich the details about *how* social environments structure individual behavior. The justification for this advice is simply that trying to measure environments broadly (but shallowly) is futile—no matter how hard you try, the outcome is unlikely to capture most interesting social phenomenon well enough to make it worth the extra purchase in external validity.

In pursuit of deep, rich measurement of social units, we need not simply and uncritically default to standard techniques such as the important matters name generator (i.e., a question asking respondents to name people with whom they discuss important matters) or hierarchically stratified samples for gathering contextual data. Instead, special priority should be given to developing new and creative strategies appropriate for a wider variety of units. For example, scholars interested in how disagreement influences attitudes might consider manipulating discussion environments and group composition in focus groups to gain theoretical control over properties of the environment (Druckman & Nelson, 2003; Fishkin, 1997). Similarly, contextual researchers might consider purposively choosing contextual units to maximize variation in key independent variables, much in the way that comparative politics scholars choose nations to provide maximum empirical leverage from a handful of cases. Indeed, paying closer attention to strategies developed in the fields of comparative politics and communication where large-N research is frequently not plausible may hold some of the best advice for dealing with purposeful selection of environmental cases for inclusion in analysis.

Although these suggestions in essence mean that knowledge will be more diffuse in the area of social communication than in some other fields of study, it is faithful to fundamental theoretical issues addressing how individual behavior is influenced by social groupings, including networks and contexts. If taken seriously, this advice points to the inevitability of there being only a handful of purposefully chosen environments included in any particular study that are thoroughly measured and representative of social diversity, but not necessarily generalizable to some well-defined population of social units.

METHODOLOGICAL ISSUES: ESTABLISHING INTERNAL VALIDITY

Problem

While it is by no means true that all social communication scholarship is based on a belief that the environment has a direct and coercive impact on individuals, questions of causality remain at the center of the field. The question of whether social environments have causal effects is nicely stated by Michael Laver in his review of *A Social Logic of Politics*, an edited volume by Alan Zuckerman. While complimentary of the book, Laver (2005, p. 933) writes that,

> There is, of course, always the potential for selection bias . . . in survey evidence on "network contacts" of respondents. It seems at least plausible that those explicitly named by respondents as people with whom they discuss politics may be a biased selection of those with whom politics is actually discussed—contacts who are more similar in views or more persuasive, perhaps.

Consequently, social communication researchers who are interested in causal effects face serious challenges to establish causality that are difficult to parse because the characteristics of social environments are tough to disentangle from individual characteristics that drive people into different environments.[14] Social communication processes—like most political phenomena—are inherently endogenous, with social aggregates influencing individuals and then evolving as those individuals make decisions that influence the environment. Given that there is feedback between people within networks and contexts, these processes may even be of *specific* empirical and theoretical interest.[15]

Comparing social communication research designs with classical experimental designs clarifies the problem. If we want to use an experiment to know whether a context or network is the perpetrator of a social science "whodunit," we would have to meet at least two minimal conditions: (1) random assignment of individuals to environments, and (2) control over the environmental stimulus. Starting with the first condition, we could circumvent many of the problems with establishing causality because we could rule out any *individual-level* explanations were it possible to randomly assign people to networks, neighborhoods, churches, and so on. Doing so would allow us to isolate environmental factors as explanations of behavior; such control is, of course, the principal strength of experiments.

The second condition, however, is also important and likely overlooked. Consider the hypothetical example in Figure 18.2, which plots two possible relationships between how neighborhood partisanship (represented by the X-axis) is related to the probability an individual participates in politics (represented by the Y-axis). In both cases we can see that there is a parabolic relationship, with participation highest in more competitive neighborhoods and lower in uncompetitive contexts where there is a significant advantage for one party over the other. The main difference between the two curves is in the strength of the neighborhood effect. In an experimental situation, the ability to control the size of partisan divisions within the neighborhood would allow us to accurately distinguish between the two situations. In short, it would facilitate a more accurate estimate of the *true causal effect*. However, because of the processes by which people select neighborhoods, *real observable contexts* rarely reach out to these extremes, limiting

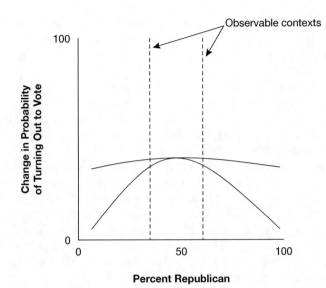

FIGURE 18.2 Importance of controlling environmental stimuli.

what can be examined as causal effects. Once sampling variability is introduced, researchers might be unable to detect all but the strongest environmental effects. Our ability to discern the strength of causal effects will be constrained by selection processes.

Implications

One vexing consequence of these internal validity problems is the difficulty of empirically distinguishing between true social communication effects and the processes by which individuals are exposed to communication in the first place. Whether we are looking at religious institutions, the workplace, friendship circles, or any other *social* environment, people typically exercise some control over both their entry into that social environment and the types of information available to them therein. Moreover, the reasons for *selecting* those contexts and receiving specific information may be strongly correlated with the individual's beliefs, especially with respect to politics.[16] Such problems are similar to issues of selective communication that are commonly recognized in research with a mass communication orientation, where people have considerable control over what messages they see—or do not see—in a modern media environment (e.g., Slater, 2007; Stroud, 2007).

For example, if a young urban professional votes in most elections and identifies as a Democrat, the desire to avoid conflict with her family and friends as well as the need for social support might lead to intentionally limiting discussions with Republicans. If we then observe that her network or neighborhood is highly Democratic, we still do not know whether she chose that environment because it was Democratic, whether she has developed Democratic preferences due to its partisan bias, or even if the environment plays an important role in *sustaining* her original preference.

It is important to recognize that this is not a problem of analytical technique, but one of theory and data. There are well-established statistical methods for dealing with different types of selection bias, such as the Heckman selection model and seemingly unrelated modeling techniques (Heckman, 1976; see King, 1989, chapter 9, for an overview of this class of statistical models).

Yet such statistical methods only provide purchase when variables are available which independently predict the selection process, something that is very hard to come by in social communication research *because* of the presumption that politics and social interaction are intertwined (Kenny, 1992, 1994).

The second consequence is possible reciprocal causation. As with the case of selection bias, the root concern here is that estimates of social communication effects are not exact because of the underlying data generating process. Assuming for a moment that no selection effect is likely present—for example, if we were studying employee–supervisor relationships and their impact on politics—serious questions about the direction and strength of the causal impact would still exist. If the employee donates money to a specific presidential candidate, as does her supervisor, is it because the boss has persuaded her to make that donation in lieu of facing professional setbacks? Such an argument gets raised frequently in discussions of campaign reform. However, it is equally possible that it is the employee, anxious to demonstrate her political perspicacity, who explains to her supervisor the importance of making the contribution in order to advance the company's interests. It is also possible that *both* processes are acting simultaneously to produce the behavior of interest. Another possibility is that there are no social effects at all, with only individual characteristics driving behavior.

The problem faced by social communication scholars in distinguishing between a communication effect and reciprocal causation, as suggested above, is again that most potential observations that can be made would constitute evidence for *either* explanation. Moreover, in-depth probing of the parties to the interaction would not provide the necessary answers; in short, a procedure equivalent to "process tracing" in qualitative research would not help. Why? Even if the boss were influenced by his employee, a number of other variables might produce in him the impression that he was not—gender differences, status differences, and so forth. And, again, the variables necessary for properly identifying statistical models of simultaneity are difficult to find.

Advice

There are three ways to establish validity for causal claims in social communication research. The most obvious, but to some degree least useful, is use of advanced statistical techniques. As noted above, adequate statistical techniques exist for demonstrating causality. For either selection bias or simultaneity problems, these techniques require the analyst to identify variables that independently predict values of both the dependent variable and the social environment under investigation. For example, we could potentially model the type of neighborhood that someone chooses as a function of its distance from the workplace, property values, and the quality of the schools. Each of these variables would be independent of most political outcomes and behaviors of interest, such as willingness to participate or vote choice. Likewise, we might estimate variation in those dependent variables with information on family background, career choice, and campaign stimuli.

Unfortunately, such solutions are frequently intractable and impractical, as social communication theory is underdeveloped with respect to selection processes and reciprocal causation. Even assuming that a theory is sufficiently specified to identify good exogenous variables to model processes that confound causality, introducing such variables into the data collection process would further restrict the depth of information that can be collected about the social environments themselves. For these reasons, statistical solutions often provide only imprecise and rough estimates about causal effects, implying that a certain amount of circumspection should be employed when using these methods.

A second approach to establishing causality is to use creative analytic strategies. In particular, there are natural variations in real-world data that might allow us to build at least a circumstantial case against some threats to internal validity. For example, people cannot choose their parents and siblings on the basis of politics, but could potentially structure the extent of their interaction and political discussion as a consequence of political views. Analysts who have enough information to parse their data into groups of relations who interact frequently and infrequently can re-estimate causal models and compare parameter estimates in order to obtain some sense of how much of an effect selection processes have on estimates.

While this approach ultimately relies on the creativity of individual scholars, it also has natural limitations that even the most creative among us must consider. To use a trial metaphor, this approach is akin to building a circumstantial case. It is not as definitive as DNA evidence but builds towards a guilty verdict. Additionally, the fact that such an approach requires the parsing of data increases the chances that sampling error is responsible for null findings. In other words, the utility of such strategies is positively correlated with the number of observations. As most widely available data sets for analyzing social communication have fewer than 1,500 observations, split-sample analytic strategies become unworkable very quickly.

A final way to tackle these questions is through the use of innovative research designs that explicitly tackle internal validity problems. Some of the most promising efforts in this regard use field and natural experiments. For example, Klofstad (2007) examines naturally evolving roommate effects among college freshmen. Since students are randomly assigned to dorms, he reasons that any change in their political behavior from the start of a fall term to its end is caused by the level of political discussion that occurs between roommates. Similarly, Nickerson (2008) shows that the spouses of people contacted in a traditional voting experiment are much more likely to vote than the spouses of a group that was *not* contacted. Though this is not definitive evidence of a social communication effect per se, one can reasonably argue that the social tie is responsible.

These two examples show the power of clever research designs for establishing strong inferences about the impact of social environments on political behavior. However, these designs are not only difficult to specify and execute, they are also not equally useful for all types of problems. While we can find situations where we can adequately randomize the stimulus (as in Nickerson, 2008) or where assignment to new environments is independent of social content (as in Klofstad, 2007), there is a limited array of environments in which these situations occur. And, unfortunately, these situations may be unique and not necessarily of broad interest. For example, Nickerson's research cannot speak to the influence of friends, congregationalists, and so on without an extensive survey of all parties involved. This would significantly increase the practical costs and problems of this kind of research, while also adding in survey stimuli as plausible alternative explanations for political outcomes. Moreover, Klofstad was restricted to a study of college freshman, a clearly unique population when it comes to how open they are to persuasion. Nevertheless, these "shortcomings" show why we need *more* of these kinds of designs rather than fewer, as they hold promise for building evidence in a wide variety of environments about causal effects of social communication.

As should be evident from this discussion, there is no one way for avoiding problems in making causal inferences. And while each approach is helpful, none holds out the promise for solving these problems "once and for good" in the field of social communication. This again suggests that healthy progress in the subfield of social communication depends deeply on the use of multiple methods and the slow accumulation of evidence and knowledge, rather than a single set of methodological solutions to resolve causal validity issues.

CONCLUSION

As interest in the study of social communication effects grows, increasing energy is being devoted to gathering new data for exploring the multitude of contexts and networks surrounding typical citizens. While we should be enthusiastic about such efforts, the desire to advance knowledge should not overwhelm a sober understanding of the challenges facing researchers in this area. Whereas most political behavior research can make good use of fundamental methodological principles to gather data on the basis of the dependent process being studied, those scholars interested in understanding how social systems influence citizens must also be cognizant of how they gather information on those systems. While traditional dependent variable-driven data can be used, it is suboptimal because it is not driven by the core questions of social communication research, which generally center on whether and to what extent individual behavior is a function of social forces that are beyond the individual's control.

In summary, this chapter has advocated an in-depth understanding of specific contexts to more effectively assess social communication effects. Undue concern for capturing the multiple social influences surrounding people will lead to research designs that are unfocused, lacking depth of measurement, and ultimately unable to satisfy a desire to broadly understand the nature of social communication processes. Rather than attempt to resolve all the issues raised in this chapter in a single study, it seems far more prudent to embrace the incremental nature of this research program, in large part because it reflects the slow and incremental nature of social influence itself.

NOTES

1. For the remainder of this chapter, I use the term "political communication" to refer to the broader array of subjects covered in this volume and "social communication" to refer specifically to research that focuses on political communication within networks, groups, and contexts.
2. Zuckerman (2005) provides an excellent overview of the lineage of socially oriented political analysis.
3. Please note that this chapter focuses on research design issues in communication rather than on issues of statistical modeling, as these are addressed elsewhere in this volume (see chapters 22–24).
4. I leave the term *environment* intentionally undefined even though it is frequently used in this literature, especially to encompass the general notion of external influences on people. I do this for two reasons. First, because political communication research is generally interested in such external influences, nearly all research in this area is concerned with the environments that operate upon individuals. Second, to the extent that it could be distinguished from a context or network, not every environment is necessarily a source of *social* communication. Accordingly, I use the term in this chapter to refer broadly to any type of social conglomerate that might be a source of socially supplied and politically relevant information.

    There are also layers of social interaction that may exist *between* networks and contexts—e.g., small groups—that have some properties of both. For example, membership in small groups clearly involves conversation and personal interaction. At the same time, the relationships between individuals may not constitute the entire influence of the group. A nice example of this work can be seen in Djupe & Gilbert (2009). An extended discussion of methodological issues can be found in Chapter 17 by Black, Burkhalter, Gastil, & Stromer-Galley, this volume.
5. Of course, different people—nodes—in the network can in a strict sense be perceived of as "egos" and "alters." Similarly, the individuals that constitute the basis of whole network studies are undoubtedly also in other networks as well, implying that "completeness" of a network is not a property of people but of a social grouping or organization. Thus, this approach is distinguished by a focus on networks as holistic phenomena and focuses on different issues than ego-centric studies, such as the presence of "holes" in a network that might disrupt communication (Burt, 1985).

6. There is some question as to whether people even have "peer networks" that are politically meaningful because they either self select into expert networks or only talk to people with whom they already share political views. While little evidence addresses this specific question, Klofstadt, McClurg, and Rolfe (2007) find that survey-based name generators tend to produce very similar networks, regardless of whether they ask people to identify "most important matters" or "political matters," implying that many people have a core set of relationships which they consult for a wide array of matters rather than specialized friendships that exist for political purposes. Nevertheless, this area is ripe for additional research.

7. The distinction between peer and action networks is not hard and fast, as relationships that originally form in response to some external stimulus—such as the need for community action—may in fact evolve into lasting relationships.

8. Even advocates of this model do not suggest that contextual influences only operate through social networks (Huckfeldt & Sprague, 1995). The fluidity of learning effects reinforces two points underlying the discussion in this chapter. First, there are multiple levels of social reality that may operate simultaneously upon individuals, complicating level of analysis questions in research designs. Second, these different levels of social reality are not necessarily equivalent to each other in their composition and consequences (Huckfeldt, Plutzer, & Sprague, 1993; Huckfeldt & Sprague, 1988).

9. In geography this methodological concern is known as the *modifiable areal unit* problem, though it is expanded here to include not just the appropriate geographic context but the choice of types of networks and contexts as well.

10. Ragin (2000) provides an excellent and broad discussion of causal heterogeneity. A discussion more germane to this chapter is Iversen's (1991) arguments about cross-level effects in contextual analysis.

11. For example, if we want to study the relationship between standardized test scores and performance in graduate school, we would have to account for the fact that people with low scores do not gain admission into graduate school in the first place (e.g., King, 1989, chapter 9).

12. There are some exceptions to this kind of statement, for example, using clustered sampling designs where aggregate units are randomly selected—but these designs are not always viable for studies of specific contexts for which sampling frames are not available.

13. Their example also illustrates the first set of sampling concerns as they had to systematically choose from among all South Bend neighborhoods a subset within which they would conduct their random samples. Among the many choices they made, they decided to focus on predominantly white neighborhoods (1995, p. 37). While the choices they made were all reasonable or done out of necessity, it illustrates the difficulties of coming up with a study that was generalizable even to South Bend.

14. Note that this is a different type of selection bias than the one discussed in the section on sampling as this represents a *substantive* process, rather than a *methodological* one.

15. See Mark Buchanan's *The Social Atom* (2007) for a popularized account of how positive and negative feedback are central to understanding social phenomena.

16. The degree to which selection and communication processes correlate is not constant across all environments. For example, most people don't attend church or take a job for political reasons, while they may in fact choose friends on this basis.

REFERENCES

Adcock, R., & Collier, D. (2001). Measurement validity: A shared standard for qualitative and quantitative research. *American Political Science Review, 95*, 529–546.

Ansell, C., Kelly, A., & Reckhow, S. (2007). One man's reform is another man's hostile takeover: Using network leverage to identify opportunities in Oakland school reform. Paper presented at the Annual Meeting of the American Political Science Association, Chicago, IL.

Baybeck, B. (2006). Sorting out the competing effects of context. *Journal of Politics, 68*, 386–396.

Baybeck, B., & McClurg, S. D. (2005). What do they know and how do they know it? An examination of citizen awareness of context. *American Politics Research, 33*(4), 492–520.

Berelson, B. R., Lazarsfeld, P. F., & McPhee, W. N. (1954). *Voting: A study of opinion formation in a presidential campaign.* Chicago, IL: University of Chicago Press.

Books, J. W., & Prysby, C. L. (1991). *Political behavior and the local context.* New York: Praeger Press.

Branton, R. P., & Jones, B. S. (2005). Reexaming racial attitudes: The conditional relationship between diversity and socioeconomic environment. *American Journal of Political Science, 49,* 359–372.

Brickell, B., Huckfeldt, R., & Sprague, J. (1988). *Gender effects on political discussion: The political networks of men and women.* Paper presented at the annual meeting of the Midwest Political Science Association, Chicago, IL.

Brown, T. A. (1981). On contextual change and partisan attitudes. *British Journal of Political Science, 11,* 427–448.

Burt, R. S. (1984). Network items and the General Social Survey. *Social Networks, 6,* 293–339.

Burt, R. S. (1985). General Social Survey network items. *Connections, 8,* 119–123.

Chaffee, S. H. (1991). *Communication concepts 1: Explication.* Newbury Park, CA: Sage.

Coleman, J. S. (1988). Social capital in the creation of human capital. *American Journal of Sociology, 94*(Supplement), S95–S120.

Collier, D., & Mahon, J., Jr. (1993). Conceptual "stretching" revisited: Adapting categories in comparative politics. *American Political Science Review, 87*(4), 845–55.

Djupe, P. A., & Gilbert, C. P. (2006). The resourceful believer: Generating civic skills in church. *Journal of Politics, 68*(1): 116–127.

Djupe, P. A., & Gilbert, C. P. (2009). *The political influence of churches.* New York: Cambridge University Press.

Djupe, P. A., Sohkey, A. E., & Gilbert, C. P. (2007). Present but not accounted for? Gender differences in civic resource acquisition. *American Journal of Political Science, 51*(4), 906–920.

Druckman, J. N., & Nelson, K. R. (2003). Framing and deliberation: How citizens' conversations limit elite influence. *American Journal of Political Science, 47*(4), 729–745.

Fishkin, J. C. (1997). *Voice of the people: Public opinion and democracy.* New Haven, CT: Yale University Press.

Finifter, A. (1974). The friendship group as a protective environment for political deviants. *American Political Science Review, 68*(2), 607–625.

Gerring, J. (2001). *Social science methodology: A critical framework.* New York: Cambridge University Press.

Giles, M. W., & Buckner, M. A. (1993). David Duke and black threat: An old hypothesis revisited. *Journal of Politics, 55*(3), 702–713.

Giles, M. W., & Buckner, M. A. (1996). Comment. *Journal of Politics, 58*(4), 1171–1181.

Giles, M. W., & Hertz, K. (1994). Racial threat and partisan identification. *American Political Science Review, 88*(2), 317–326.

Gill, J. (1999). The insignificance of null hypothesis testing. *Political Research Quarterly, 52*(3), 647–674.

Granovetter, M. S. (1973). The strength of weak ties. *American Journal of Sociology, 78*(6), 1360–1380.

Heaney, M. T., & Rojas, F. (2007). Partisans, nonpartisans, and the antiwar movement in the United States. *American Politics Research, 35*(4), 431–464.

Heckman, J. J. (1976). The common structure of statistical models of truncation, sample selection and limited dependent variables, and a simple estimator for such models. *Annals of Economic and Social Measurement, 5,* 475–492.

Huckfeldt, R., Johnson, P. E., & Sprague, J. (2002). Political environments, political dynamics, and the survival of disagreement. *Journal of Politics, 64*(1), 1–21.

Huckfeldt, R., Johnson, P. E., & Sprague, J. (2004). *Political disagreement: The survival of diverse opinions within communication networks.* Cambridge: Cambridge University Press.

Huckfeldt, R., Morehouse Mendez, J., & Osborn, T. 2004. Disagreement, ambivalence, and engagement: The political consequences of heterogeneous networks. *Political Psychology, 25*(1), 65–95.

Huckfeldt, R., Plutzer, E., & Sprague, J. (1993). Alternative contexts of political behavior: Churches, neighborhoods, and individuals. *Journal of Politics, 55*(2), 365–381.

Huckfeldt, R., & Sprague, J. (1988). Choice, social structure, and political information: The information coercion of minorities. *American Journal of Political Science, 32*(2), 467–482.

Huckfeldt, R., & Sprague, J. (1991). Discussant effects on vote choice: Intimacy, structure, and interdependence. *Journal of Politics, 53*, 122–158.

Huckfeldt, R., & Sprague, J. (1992). Political parties and electoral mobilization: Political structure, social structure, and the party canvas. *American Political Science Review, 86*, 70–86.

Huckfeldt, R., & Sprague, J. (1995). *Citizens, politics, and social communication: Information and influence in an election campaign.* New York: Cambridge University Press.

Iversen, G. R. (1991). *Contextual analysis.* London: Sage.

Johnston, R., Jones, K., Propper, C., & Burgess, S. (2007). Region, local context, and voting in the 1997 general election in Britain. *American Journal of Political Science, 51*(3), 6450–6454.

Kenny, C. (1992). Political participation and effects for the social environment. *American Journal of Political Science, 36*, 259–267.

Kenny, C. (1994). The microenvironment of attitude change. *Journal of Politics, 56*(3), 715–728.

Key, Jr., V. O. (1949). *Southern politics.* New York: Alfred A. Knopf.

King, G. (1989). *Unifying political methodology: The likelihood theory of statistical inference.* Cambridge: Cambridge University Press.

Klofstad, C. A. (2007). Talk leads to recruitment: How discussions about politics and current events increase civic participation. *Political Research Quarterly, 60*(2), 180–191.

Klofstad, C., McClurg, S. D., & Rolfe, M. (2007). Measurement of political discussion networks: A comparison of two "name generator" procedures. Unpublished manuscript.

Laver, M. (2005). Book review of *The social logic of politics. Perspectives on Politics, 3*(4), 933–934.

Lazer, D., Rubineau, B., Katz, N., & Chetkovich, C. (2007). *Networks and political attitudes: Structure, influence, and co-evolution.* Paper presented at the annual meeting of the American Political Science Association, Chicago, IL.

Leighley, J. E. (1990). Social interaction and contextual influences on political participation. *American Politics Quarterly, 18*(4), 459–475.

Levine, J. (2005). Choosing alone? The social network basis of modern political choice. In A. S. Zuckerman (Ed.), *The social logic of politics* (pp. 132–151). Philadelphia, PA: Temple University Press.

Marsden, P. V. (1987). Core discussion networks of Americans. *American Sociological Review, 52*, 122–131.

Mendez, J., & Osborn, T. (2005). *Artificial intelligence? Women, knowledge, and political discussion.* Paper presented at the annual meeting of the American Political Science Association, Washington, DC.

McClurg, S. D. (2006a). The electoral relevance of political talk: Examining disagreement and expertise effects in social networks on political participation. *American Journal of Political Science, 50*(3), 737–754.

McClurg, S. D. (2006b). Political disagreement in context: The conditional effect of neighborhood context, disagreement, and political talk on electoral participation. *Political Behavior, 28*, 349–366.

McPhee, W. N. (1963). *Formal theories of mass behavior.* New York: MacMillan.

Mutz, D. C. (1998). *Impersonal influence: How perceptions of mass collectives affect political attitudes.* Cambridge: Cambridge University Press.

Mutz, D. C. (2006). *Hearing the other side: Deliberative versus participatory democracy.* Cambridge: Cambridge University Press.

Mutz, D. C., & Martin, P. S. (2001). Facilitating communication across lines of political difference. *American Political Science Review, 95*(1), 71–114.

Mutz, D. C., & Mondak, J. J. (2006). The workplace as a context for cross-cutting political discourse. *Journal of Politics, 68*(1), 140–156.

Nickerson, D. (2008). Is voting contagious? Evidence from two field experiments. *American Political Science Review, 102*, 49–57.

Oliver, J. E., & Mendleberg, T. (2000). Reconsidering the environmental determinants of white racial attitudes. *American Journal of Political Science, 44*(3), 574–589.

Price, V., Cappella, J. N., & Nir, L. (2002). Does disagreement contribute to more deliberative opinion? *Political Communication, 19*(1), 95–112.

Putnam, R. D. (1966). Political attitudes and the local community. *American Political Science Review, 60*, 640–654.

Putnam, R. D. (2000). *Bowling alone: The collapse and revival of American community.* New York: Simon & Schuster.

Ragin, C. C. (2000). *Fuzzy-set social science.* Chicago: University of Chicago Press.

Scott, J. (2000). *Social network analysis: A handbook* (2nd ed.). London: Sage.

Slater, M. D. (2007). Reinforcing spirals: The mutual influence of media selectivity and media effects and their impact on individual behavior and social identity. *Communication Theory, 17*(3), 281–303.

Stoker, L., & Jennings, M. K. (2005). Political similarity and influence between husbands and wives. In Alan S. Zuckerman (Ed.), *The social logic of politics* (pp. 51–74). Philadelphia: Temple University Press.

Stroud, N. J. (2007). Media effects, selective exposure, and *Fahrenheit 9/11. Political Communication, 24*(4), 415–432.

Voss, D. S. (1996a). Beyond racial thread: Failure of an old hypothesis in the New South. *Journal of Politics, 58*(4), 1156–1170.

Voss, D. S. (1996b). Familiarity doesn't breed contempt: A rejoinder to "comment." *Journal of Politics, 58*(4), 1181–1183.

Walsh, K. K. (2004). *Talking about politics: Informal groups and social identity in American life.* Chicago: University of Chicago Press.

Wright, G. C., Jr. (1977). Contextual models of electoral behavior: The southern Wallace vote. *American Political Science Review, 71,* 497–508.

Zuckerman, A. S. (2005). Returning to the social logic of politics. In A. S. Zuckerman (Ed.), *The social logic of politics.* Philadelphia: Temple University Press.

Zuckerman, A. S., Fitzgerald, J., & Dasovic, J. (2005). Do couples support the same political parties? Sometimes: Evidence from British and German household panel surveys. In A. S. Zuckerman (Ed.), *The social logic of politics* (pp. 75–94). Philadelphia: Temple University Press.

VII
COMPARATIVE POLITICAL COMMUNICATION

19

Mediatization of Politics

Toward a Conceptual Framework for Comparative Research

Jesper Strömbäck
Department of Journalism
Mid Sweden University

Mediatization has been described as a meta-process on par with other large-scale social changes such as globalization and individualization (Krotz, 2007, 2009). As such, mediatization represents a long-term trend that affects all parts of society, including politics (Mazzoleni, 2008a), everyday life and identity formation (Hjarvard, 2009), and religion (Hoover, 2009). It is only recently, however, that scholars have sought to develop a deeper conceptual understanding of mediatization and the related concept of mediation. Both concepts are still casually invoked more than they are properly defined or employed analytically in programmatic research. This is unfortunate, not least since the concept of mediatization has the potential to integrate different strands of political communication theory and research and offers a framework for comparative research.

Against this background, the purpose of this chapter is to survey the literature on the mediatization of politics, and to present a conceptual framework to guide further empirical and comparative research on the mediatization of politics.[1] The chapter ends with a discussion of approaches for investigating mediatization.

MEDIATIZATION, MEDIALIZATION, AND MEDIATION

At heart, mediatization refers to a social change process in which media have become increasingly influential (Hjarvard, 2008; Lundby, 2009a, 2009b; Mazzoleni, 2008a, 2008b; Strömbäck, 2008). However, it is not the only concept being used in this regard. Related concepts include *medialization* (Asp & Esaiasson, 1996), *mediation* (Altheide & Snow, 1988), and *mediazation* (Thompson, 1995).

Among these, the two most established concepts are mediatization and mediation. The former appears to be favored by scholars from continental Europe (Hjarvard, 2008; Kepplinger, 2002; Lundby, 2009a, 2009b; Mazzoleni & Schulz, 1999; Schulz, 2004), whereas British and U.S. scholars appear to favor the term mediation (Altheide & Snow, 1988; Couldry, 2008; Davis, 2007; Livingstone, 2009; Silverstone, 2007). To some extent these varied usages follow from different understandings of the terms, but in some cases (Altheide & Snow, 1988) the terms are explicitly perceived as synonymous.

Following Mazzoleni (2008a) and others, I would, however, argue that mediation and mediatization should not be conceptualized as synonymous. To begin with, mediation has at least two meanings. On the one hand, mediation refers to the rather neutral act of transmitting messages through various media channels (Mazzoleni, 2008a). On the other hand, when scholars such as Altheide and Snow (1988), Nimmo and Combs (1983), and Silverstone (2007) have used the term, they have usually referred to the much broader "overall effect of media institutions existing in contemporary societies, the overall difference that media make by being there in our social world" (Couldry, 2008, p. 379). In this latter respect, the influence that media wield in shaping social and political processes is anything but neutral. Using "mediation" to denote both meanings makes the term more ambiguous, less precise, and, hence, less useful (Strömbäck & Esser, 2009).

For these reasons, mediation and mediatization should not be understood as synonymous concepts (Lundby, 2009a, 2009b; Mazzoleni, 2008a; Strömbäck, 2008). Instead, mediation should be reserved for describing the rather neutral act of communicating through different media, as opposed to reconfiguring the whole of political life around media practices, technologies, and institutions. Mediated politics, then, describes a situation where the media have become both the most important source of information about politics and society, superseding face-to-face communication, and the primary channel of communication between political actors and citizens (Bennett & Entman, 2001; Strömbäck & Esser, 2009). In this sense, the mediation of politics is a necessary prerequisite for the mediatization of politics.

MEDIATIZATION AS A THEORY OF MEDIA INFLUENCE

Although the concept of mediatization has come into more common use in political communication research only recently, the term itself dates back to the reorganization of the German states by Napoleon in the early nineteenth century (Livingstone, 2009; Lundby, 2009b). In that context, mediatization referred to "the subsumption of one monarchy into another monarchy in such a way that the ruler of the annexed state keeps his or her sovereign title and, sometimes, a measure of local power" (in Livingstone, 2009, p. 6).

Although mediatization in the original sense did not have anything to do with the media, from the beginning it was used to refer to a *process* where some parts of society increase their *influence* at the expense of others. This is also reflected in various contemporary definitions. Asp and Esaiasson (1996), for example, write that mediatization is a process "in which there is a development toward increasing media influence" (pp. 80–81). Similarly, Mazzoleni (2008b, p. 3053) notes, "the concept of 'mediatization of society' indicates an extension of the influence of the media into all societal spheres," while Hjarvard (2008, p. 113) defines mediatization as "the process whereby society to an increasing degree is submitted to, or becomes dependent on, the media and their logic." With respect to the mediatization of politics specifically, Mazzoleni and Schulz (1999, p. 250) furthermore write that, "To characterize politics as being mediatized goes beyond a mere description of system requirements. Mediatized politics is politics that has lost its autonomy, has become dependent in its central functions on mass media, and is continuously shaped by interactions with mass media."

In this context, mass media should be understood not only as single media organizations, formats, or outlets, even though these aspects are important. Rather, mass media should be understood as an ever-present social and cultural system of production and dissemination of symbols, signs, messages, meanings, and values. The media should be regarded, then, as a system or an institution (Cook, 2005;

Sparrow, 1999). Different media organizations and their formats, operations, practices, genres, and contents constitute the building blocks of this system, yet the sum is greater than its individual parts, and the norms that govern the media taken overall are often more important than what distinguishes one form of media from another (Altheide & Snow, 1979; Hjarvard, 2008; Mazzoleni, 2008b; Nimmo & Combs, 1983). This is particularly the case with respect to news media.

Stated differently, mediatization denotes a process where media organizations form a system and function as a social institution in their own right, *independent* although *interdependent* on other social and political systems and institutions such as parliaments or political parties (Altheide & Snow, 1988; Cook, 2005; Hjarvard, 2008; Mazzoleni, 2008b; Sparrow, 1999; Strömbäck, 2008). Within the media system, there are hierarchies, with some media playing a more important role in shaping the overall media logic than others. For example, during the past several decades, television has arguably been the most influential medium in politics and other sectors of society. Although some believe the Internet will change this, thus far, the Net has supplemented rather than replaced the dominant media logic (Schulz, 2004), and television still constitutes the most influential medium (Grabe & Bucy, 2009).

MEDIA DEPENDENCE

What makes the media important is not only that they have come to constitute an increasingly independent societal system, but also that they serve as "an omnipresent symbolic environment creating an essential part of the societal definitions of reality" (Schulz, 2004, p. 93). Hence, media permeate all spheres of contemporary societies and have become the most important source of information and communication about matters beyond everyday face-to-face experiences. Graber (2005, p. 274) has thus noted that "media do more than depict the political environment; they *are* the political environment." Silverstone (2007, p. 5) similarly asserts that, "the media are becoming environmental."

The notion of media providing the ecological context for social processes and actors highlights the impracticability of separating "media" from "society" and our everyday experiences, as well as delineating "politics" from "political communication." As Lippmann (1922/1997) observed about 90 years ago, the media are creating a pseudo-environment that ultimately becomes more real to individual citizens than reality as such, if only because it is the only "reality" we have ready access to. In a similar vein, Nimmo and Combs (1983, p. 8) observed that media create a "fantasy reality," where

> A *fantasy* is a credible picture of the world that is created when one interprets mediated experiences as the way things are and takes for granted the authenticity of the mediated reality without checking against alternative, perhaps contradictory, realities so long as the fantasy offers dramatic proof for one's expectations.

The more people depend upon media for information that is used to form impressions of and opinions about societal processes, events, and issues, the more susceptible they are to media influence, and the more difficult it becomes to separate what people think and feel from the media-created pseudo-environment. As again noted by Silverstone (2007, p. 51), one can make the case that in a mediated world "there is no difference between being and appearance, just as there is no longer a significant difference between the world as it appears on the screen and the world that is lived."

If people are guided by their social constructions of reality, then these social constructions are heavily shaped by the media's social constructions. Ample evidence of this can be found in research on the media's ability to influence audiences through, for example, the processes of agenda setting, framing, priming, and cultivation.

At the same time, a proper understanding of the media's influence *on society* requires more than estimating effects on individual perceptions and opinions. Conventional effects theories and methodologies depend on a causal logic in which it is possible to make a distinction between dependent and independent variables (Schulz, 2004). They also assume that media effects largely follow from the content of media messages. From the perspective of mediatization theory, media content, however, cannot be isolated from media formats and grammar (Altheide & Snow, 1979, 1988, 1991). Furthermore, the ubiquity and omnipresence of media make it virtually impossible to compartmentalize media experiences from life experiences, just as media institutions cannot be conceived of as being separate from other social, political, or cultural processes. Conventional media effects theories also fail to recognize the reciprocal effects of the media on the subjects and processes of media coverage (Kepplinger, 2007), how social actors beyond "the audience in general," for example politicians, use and are affected by the media (Davis, 2007), and how social actors accommodate themselves to the media.

While conventional media effect theories are important, they are thus also insufficient for a full understanding of media influence. As a concept, mediatization "both transcends and includes media effects" (Schulz, 2004, p. 90).

This does not mean that it is impossible to get at a greater understanding of the mediatization of society, or of politics more specifically. As suggested by Schulz (2004, pp. 88–90), at least four processes of social change arising from media-driven transformations can be identified: extension, substitution, amalgamation, and accommodation.

First, media *extend* human communication capabilities across both space and time (McLuhan, 1964). Second, media and communication technologies "partly or completely *substitute* social activities and social institutions and thus change their character" (Schulz 2004, p. 88). Activities that formerly required face-to-face interaction or a physical presence can now be accomplished or experienced through media use (Bucy & Gregson, 2001). Third, media activities *merge* and mingle with non-media activities or processes, thus making it difficult to separate media from these other activities and processes. Similarly, information gained from media merges and mingles with information gained through interpersonal communication or experiences. As this happens, "the media's definition of reality amalgamates with the social definition of reality" (Schulz, 2004, p. 89). Fourth, as media become increasingly important, social actors must alter their behaviors to *accommodate* the media's logic and standards of newsworthiness (Schulz, 2004). In addition to these four processes, one should add *creation* (Strömbäck & Esser, 2009). Not only do media produce their own products and programs, the importance of media makes other social actors *create* pseudo-events (Boorstin, 1962) with the main purpose of attracting media coverage.

Thus, five social change processes that flow from mediatization are extension, substitution, amalgamation, accommodation, and creation. These affect society from the individual to the institutional level. In each case, it is our media dependence that lends and perpetuates their influence.

Summing up, the first important aspect of the mediatization of politics is thus the degree to which politics has become mediated; that is, the degree to which people depend on the media for information about political and social matters.

THE MEDIA AS INSTITUTION AND SYSTEM

In addition to being understood as a social and cultural system or institution (Cook, 2005; Sparrow, 1999), media organizations should be recognized as increasingly independent from, although also interdependent on, other social and political institutions (Hjarvard, 2008; Mazzoleni, 2008b; Meyer, 2002; Strömbäck, 2008). This is not to deny that there are variances across different media, but from the perspective of mediatization theory, the similarities or commonalities are more important than the differences.

At heart, institutions consist of formal and informal norms and procedures that provide a framework through which humans act and interact (Sparrow, 1999). Institutions can also be described as patterns of social behavior, identifiable across organizations that form them. Institutions are furthermore recognized as such, both by those on the inside and on the outside. As noted by Cook (2005, p. 70–71):

> The rules and procedures that constitute institutions are understood as the quasi-natural way to get things done. As such, they endure over time and extend over space, and are widely recognized both within the organizations that constitute the institutions as well as from outside as all performing similar jobs that occupy a central place in the society and polity.

From this perspective, the news media form an institution partly because people within as well as without think about media organizations as independent entities, distinguishable from yet reliant on other institutions or spheres, partly because the news media are characterized by certain common norms, procedures, and practices. The fact that different news media follow similar news production practices and adhere to similar criteria of newsworthiness (Cook, 2005; Shoemaker & Cohen, 2006; Sparrow, 1999), and that journalists hold similar, though not identical, journalistic role conceptions across news organizations (Weaver et al., 2007), contributes to the understanding of media as an institution. In fact, the whole notion of the media as a "fourth estate" presupposes that news organizations in particular form an institution separate from other institutions.

Historically, and in some countries this is still the case, media were considered to be part of and subsumed by the political system. As long as this is the case they cannot form an institution in their own right (Hallin & Mancini, 2004). In such cases, it is more relevant to speak of a *politicization* of the media than of a *mediatization* of politics.

This points towards mediatization as a dual process, where media organizations have not only acquired the status of an independent institution, but where they have also become increasingly integrated in the operations of other social and political institutions (Hjarvard, 2008). Increasing autonomy thus becomes a prerequisite for the media's independent influence over other social and political institutions, and hence *their* increasing dependence on the media. Sparrow (1999, p. 9–10) thus regards the media as an institution partly because "the production of news by the media—indeed, often their simple presence—provides a regular and persisting framework by which and within other political actors operate." And he continues:

> As an institution, the news media constrain the choice sets of these other political actors; that is, they structure—that is, guide and limit—the actions of those working in the three formal branches of government, in public administration, and at various stages or parts of the political process. The news media thereby exert important effects on other political actors. . . .

As long as the media act as mouthpieces for other institutions, they might have influence on their audiences, but in such cases the influence does not originate with and should not be assigned to them. Only when news organizations have attained a significant independence from other social and political institutions do they exercise influence over these institutions. Only then is it correct to assign influence to the media. And only then must other social and political institutions adapt to the media and their logic.

Granted, the degree to which the media form an institution largely autonomous from other political institutions varies across time as well as countries and different political and media systems (Hallin & Mancini, 2004). Conversely, the degree to which different political institutions are dependent on the media is variable, not constant. Nevertheless, the discussion about the news media as an institution suggests that the second important aspect of the mediatization of politics is the degree to which the media have become separate and independent from political institutions.

MEDIATIZATION AND MEDIA LOGIC

An important part of conceptualizing news media as an institution is the observation that different media share highly similar norms and practices. Although television news is different from newspaper or radio news, the standards of newsworthiness do not differ significantly across news media (Schudson, 2003; Shoemaker & Reese, 1996). To the extent that there are differences across media channels, they can be largely attributed to different presentation formats and delivery platforms. Thus, such differences stem mainly from media organizations themselves.

In this context, the notion of media logic is highly relevant (Brants & Praag, 2006; Hjarvard, 2008; Mazzoleni, 2008c). As suggested by Schrott (2009, p. 42), "the core of mediatization consists in the mechanism of the institutionalization of media logic in other societal subsystems. In these subsystems, media logic competes with established guidelines and influences on the actions of individuals."

Altheide and Snow (1979, p. 10) first proposed the concept of media logic. Media logic, they argued,

> consists of a form of communication; the process through which media present and transmit information. Elements of this form include the various media and the formats used by these media. Format consists, in part, of how material is organized, the style in which it is presented, the focus or emphasis on particular characteristics of behavior, and the grammar of media communication. Format becomes a framework or a perspective that is used to present as well as interpret phenomena.

Media logic can be understood as a particular way of interpreting and covering social, cultural, and political phenomena. According to the theory, the various media formats, production processes, and routines, as well as the need for compelling stories, shape how the media interpret and cover public affairs. News organizations favor stories that include conflict, for instance, since conflict lends itself to dramatic storytelling. The need for stories that are dramatic and capable of capturing audience attention might also help explain the propensity of news media to focus on scandals (Thompson, 2000), to frame politics as a horse race or strategic game rather than issue debates (Patterson, 1993), and the media's quest for compelling visuals (Grabe & Bucy, 2009).

The growth of the information society turned information scarcity into information surplus (Hernes, 1978). This rendered attention a strategic resource and commodity, and created an urgent need for the news media to both reduce information complexity and produce compelling news stories. To this end, scholars have observed that the media have developed storytelling techniques such as simplification, polarization, dramatization, personalization, visualization, and stereotyping, as well as particular ways of framing the news (Asp, 1986; Bennett, 2003; Hernes, 1978). In each of these cases, media content is "molded by a format logic" (Altheide & Snow, 1988, p. 201), where format considerations come first and content concerns second; this, together with media production routines, guide both the selection and production of news and shape the standards of newsworthiness. The media's own formats and needs, then, take precedence over other considerations.

There is an important exception, however. As most media are run as commercial businesses in fierce competition with each other for audience attention and advertising revenue, what might be called commercial logic is instrumental in shaping media logic. Media logic thus both follows from and is adapted to commercial logic (Hamilton, 2004; McManus, 1994), although it should not be reduced to commercial logic alone (Hjarvard, 2008). Hence, if media logic is conceived of as an engine of mediatization, then commercialization is crucially important in shaping media logic.

Having said this, some have questioned the concept of media logic (Hepp, 2009; Lundby, 2009c). One reason is that the focus on media formats easily lends itself to technological determinism. Lundby (2009c) also notes that it would be more appropriate to talk about media *logics*, in the plural, and stresses that concepts such as *format* and *form* do not give the social and interactional character of media enough consideration.

While these limitations should be recognized, I would argue that it is not necessary to abandon the concept of media logic. Media logic does not necessarily denote technological determinism, and is convenient shorthand for summarizing various media characteristics that might influence both media themselves and their products and other social actors. However, I would also suggest a somewhat different definition of media logic, to address some of the critique of the concept and to focus on the news media specifically. Hence, I would define *news media logic* as follows:

> News media logic refers to the institutional, technological, and sociological characteristics of the news media, including their format characteristics, production and dissemination routines, norms, and needs, standards of newsworthiness, and to the formal and informal rules that govern news media.

Having said this, what is more important in the context of the mediatization of politics is that news media logic can be conceived of as distinct from political logic (Mazzoleni, 1987; Meyer, 2002; Strömbäck, 2008). Thus, the concept has a value not only in itself but also as a means to contrast whether the news media are guided by their own logic and needs or by the logic and needs of political institutions and actors (Bucy & D'Angelo, 2004).

POLITICAL LOGIC

Although the concept of *political logic* is less developed than that of media logic, at the heart of any conceptualization is that politics ultimately is about collective and authoritative decision-making and implementation of political decisions. More precisely, at least six dimensions of politics can be identified (Strömbäck & Esser, 2009):

- The *power allocation* dimension, which includes the processes of and rules governing the distribution and allocation of political power.
- The *policy* dimension, which includes the processes of and rules governing how problems that require political solutions are defined and framed, and of finding solutions for politically defined problems.
- The *partisan* dimension, which includes the efforts to win partisan advantages.
- The *deliberation* dimension, which includes the processes of and rules governing political deliberation, bargaining and consensus building, and of reaching authoritative decisions.

- The *implementation* dimension, which includes the processes of and rules governing the implementation of political decisions.
- The *accountability* dimension, which includes the processes of and rules governing the monitoring of political decision-making and implementation, the allocation of political responsibility, and of holding those responsible accountable.

In each of these cases, the rules governing the processes that political actors must consider or adhere to can be formal or informal. In some cases, the formal rules are more important than the informal ones, while in other cases the informal rules may take precedence. In either event, politics is about who has the right to make authoritative decisions and policies for solving problems that require political decisions.

Equally important is the communication aspect of politics, and that media communication is an integral part of all the dimensions that form what politics is about. Political actors, located within political institutions, consequently need to take the media into consideration, and the media might independently intervene in all the processes and dimensions that form politics—just like media actors, located within media institutions, need to take politics into consideration while political actors might intervene to shape media policies and content (Blumler & Gurevitch, 1995).

This situation creates tension and conflicts between news media logic and political logic, both with respect to how the media cover politics and in political communication and governing processes (Mazzoleni, 1987; Meyer, 2002; Semetko et al., 1991; Strömbäck & Esser, 2009).

According to this reasoning, political processes and the media practices that are now central to them can be governed *mainly* by either news media logic or political logic (Meyer, 2002; Strömbäck, 2008). In the former case, the requirements of the media take center stage and shape the means by which political communication and governing is played out by political actors, covered by the media, and understood by the people. In the latter case, the needs of the political system take center stage and shape how political communication is played out, covered, and understood. Here, what is important for people to know, as interpreted mainly by political actors and institutions, takes precedence. Media are perceived as political or democratic institutions, with some kind of obligation to assist in making democracy work (Ferree et al., 2002; Strömbäck, 2005). In the former case, media are mainly perceived as commercial business with no particular obligation apart from catering to the wants and needs of their audiences and advertisers. The tendency here is for commercial imperatives to take precedence (Croteau & Hoynes, 2001; McManus, 1994; Hamilton, 2004).

In practice there are, of course, many gray areas between politics and political communication governed by either news media logic or political logic, and the relationship between media and politics should be understood as interdependent and interactional. Nevertheless, for analytical purposes the distinction might be helpful, as it enables empirical investigations of the extent to which politics, across time, countries, or political institutions has become mediatized.

Building on the notion of media and politics involved in an interactive relationship, the influence of news media and their logic can be located and empirically investigated in at least two broad domains: first, in news coverage of politics and society, and second, in the priorities, attitudes, and behaviors of political institutions and actors.

MEDIA INFLUENCE OVER MEDIA CONTENT . . .

Given the centrality of media to politics, political actors are continuously involved in efforts to shape news coverage of political and current affairs. At the same time, media personnel do not want to be reduced to passive carriers of political actors' messages. They view it as their responsibility to act as a watchdog and make their own decisions regarding what to cover and how to cover newsworthy events (Blumler & Gurevitch, 1995; Schudson, 2003). While journalists are necessarily dependent on their sources for information that can be transformed into news (Bennett, 2003; Berkowitz, 2009; Reich, 2009), they struggle to maintain their independence and control over media content. At the same time, sources are dependent on media for access to publicity and for the opportunity to communicate to important mass publics.

Whether journalists or their sources have the most power in this "negotiation of newsworthiness" (Cook, 2005) is a contested issue. What is consequential in this context, however, is that news media content can be governed mainly either by the characteristics and needs of the media—or the wants and needs of political actors and institutions. In the former case, news media logic is decisive for how the media cover social and political affairs, whereas in the latter case political logic is decisive. This suggests that the third important aspect of the mediatization of politics is the degree to which *news media content* is governed mainly by news media logic as opposed to political logic.

. . . AND OVER POLITICAL INSTITUTIONS AND ACTORS

The more dependent political institutions and actors are on public opinion, and the greater their need to influence public opinion, the greater their dependence on, and hence their need to influence, the news media and news coverage. For political institutions and actors, this raises the question of how to influence news coverage when journalists highly value their independence from politics.

One strategy is to leverage the advantage political actors retain with respect to the access to information that might be transformed into news (Bennett, 2003; Gans, 1980). Another strategy is through increased efforts at agenda-building and news management (Palmer, 2000; Semetko et al., 1991). A third strategy is to make the media and their potential reactions and coverage an important consideration in all political processes, from the selection of issues to promote, policies to pursue, and people to appoint or nominate, to the way campaigns are run (Kernell, 2007; Skewes, 2007).

Underlying these and other strategies is the insight that the surest way to influence media coverage is through efforts to define and then meet the news organizations' needs and logic, including the media's interest in and need for exclusive information, news that is dramatic or unexpected, compelling visuals, or stories with conflict, or events which lend themselves to well-known storytelling techniques.

By providing such "information subsidies" (Gandy, 1982), political actors make it easier and more attractive for the media to cover particular issues or events. "Permanent campaigning" can also be perceived as an example of how political actors need to take the media into consideration on an everyday basis (Blumenthal, 1980), while the strategy of "going public" (Kernell, 2007) also recognizes how central the media are to governing—and not only campaigning—processes. As Cook (2005, p. 162) has noted with reference to the United States, "all political actors in Washington are now using publicity as part of their strategies for governing and to a greater extent than they were twenty or thirty years ago."

To influence the news, political actors must devote ever more resources to manage the tasks of news management. And yet success may come at a price—the adaptation to or adoption of media logic. As Cook (2005, p. 163) has observed, "politicians may then win the daily battles with the news media, by getting into the news as they wish, but end up losing the war, as standards of newsworthiness begin to become prime criteria to evaluate issues, policies, and politics."

What this suggests is that political institutions and actors, just like the press itself, can be governed mainly by either news media logic or political logic. The more political institutions and actors adapt to the news media, and the more attention and resources they devote to activities designed to influence the news, the more political institutions and actors are governed by media logic as opposed to political logic.

MEDIATIZATION OF POLITICS AS A FOUR-DIMENSIONAL CONCEPT

This analysis suggests that the mediatization of politics is a multidimensional concept where at least four distinct yet interrelated dimensions can be identified (Strömbäck, 2008; Strömbäck & Esser, 2009). The first dimension is concerned with the degree to which the media constitute the most important or dominant source of information and communication. The second dimension is concerned with the degree to which media have become independent of other social, in particular political, institutions. The third dimension is concerned with media content—most importantly, news—and the degree to which media content is governed by media logic or political logic. The fourth dimension focuses on political actors and the degree to which they are governed by media logic or political logic. These four dimensions are depicted as a series of continua in Figure 19.1.

According to this framework, these four dimensions together determine the degree to which politics in a particular setting is mediatized. Although depicted as separate, these dimensions are highly related to each other. More precisely, mediatization along the second dimension should be perceived as a prerequisite for the third and fourth dimensions, while mediatization along the first, second, and third dimension is likely a prerequisite for the fourth dimension. The relationships between the four dimensions are depicted visually in Figure 19.2.

Presumably, it is only when media are highly independent of political institutions that media content is mainly governed by media logic as opposed to political logic. When this occurs, and news media remain the most important source of information, political actors feel the need and pressure to adapt to media logic.

Nevertheless, the understanding of mediatization of politics as a four-dimensional concept should facilitate empirical research on the degree to which politics has, in fact, become mediatized

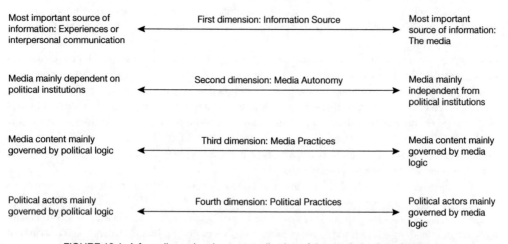

FIGURE 19.1 A four-dimensional conceptualization of the mediatization of politics.

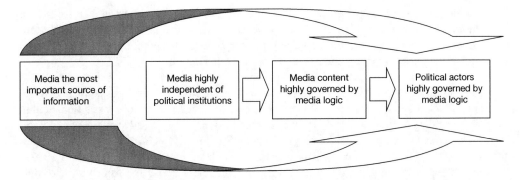

FIGURE 19.2 Relationship between the four dimensions of the mediatization of politics.

across different countries. This conceptualization of mediatization also has the potential to integrate different strands of theory and research in political communication, as discussed below.

MEDIATIZATION AS AN INTEGRATIVE CONCEPT

Throughout this chapter I have argued that mediatization is a process-oriented concept about increasing media influence. In elaborating the above dimensions, I also argued that the news media should be understood as an institution; thus, this conceptualization of mediatization incorporates an institutional perspective (Cook, 2005; Sparrow, 1999). It also incorporates the theory of media logic (Altheide & Snow, 1979).

There are, however, several other concepts and theories that also fit into this conceptualization of mediatization. One of those is the concept of the discretionary power of the media, suggested by Semetko and colleagues (1991). As they explain (p. 3), the discretionary power of news concerns "the extent to which the media are capable of playing a formative role in shaping the agenda of election campaigns, and with the forces that enable them to play such a role or limit their performance of it." Closely related is the concept of media interventionism (Esser, 2008), where high interventionism is likely to be found in journalistic cultures characterized by what Semetko et al. (1991) label a "pragmatic" as opposed to "sacerdotal" approach to politics.

In the accounts of Esser (2008), as well as Blumler and Gurevitch (1995), Gurevitch and Blumler (2004), and Pfetsch (2004), media cultures and political (communication) cultures are of great importance, and these are likely to mediate the extent to which politics has become mediatized. Broadly, political culture refers to unwritten norms and expectations within political communication processes and the relationships between political actors, media actors, and the citizenry (Blumler & Gurevitch, 1995; Gurevitch & Blumler, 2004; Pfetsch, 2004). Political communication culture can be conceived of as a subdimension of political culture, or as defined by Pfetsch (2004, p. 348), "the empirically observable orientations of actors in the system of production of political messages towards specific objects of political communication, which determine the manner in which political actors and media actors communicate in relation to their common political public."

Media culture, finally, refers to how media organizations and journalists orient themselves toward political actors and institutions on the one hand and their audiences and the market on the other, to role conceptions that journalists have, and to how journalists value news and what standards of newsworthiness they apply (Blumler & Gurevitch, 1995; Esser, 2008; Gurevitch & Blumler, 2004; Hanitzsch, 2007; Pfetsch, 2004; Semetko et al., 1991).

All these cultures are partly shaped by different media and political communication systems, as highlighted by Hallin and Mancini (2004) in their analysis of media systems among Western democracies and their identification of three different models of media and politics: a liberal model, polarized pluralist model, and democratic corporatist model.

Which model a particular country belongs to is likely to have an impact on the degree to which politics has become mediatized, and the same is true of media cultures as well as political cultures and political communication cultures. There might also be differences across institutions within countries, depending on the extent to which they are shielded from or exposed to public opinion, and across issues, depending on whether a policy monopoly (Sparrow, 1999) is in place; that is, whether an issue belongs to the sphere of consensus, deviance, or of legitimate controversy (Hallin, 1986).

Thus, there are presumably a host of factors, highlighted in other strands of political communication research, which might shape the degree to which politics in a particular setting has become mediatized. These factors could and should be integrated in further empirical research.

Other research relevant for understanding the mediatization of politics include, to mention a few examples, research showing increasing media negativity and an increasing focus on the framing of politics as a strategic game (Patterson, 1993; Strömbäck & Kaid, 2008). Both media negativity and the framing of politics as a strategic game can be considered indicators of mediatization along the third dimension. The same is true of evidence of shrinking soundbites, a more interpretive journalistic style, and other measures of media interventionism (Esser, 2008; Hallin, 1992) such as visual bias (Grabe & Bucy, 2009) and meta-coverage (Esser & D'Angelo, 2003). Even theory and research on how media affect people's political participation (Bucy & Gregson, 2001) can be perceived as one aspect of mediatization. Permanent campaigning and going public as a governing strategy could likewise be considered indicators of mediatization along the fourth dimension, as could evidence that political actors have increased the attention and resources devoted to news management. In these and other cases, there is variance both across and within countries, which can help guide further research on the antecedents of mediatization.

Thus, the conceptual framework suggested here should not be interpreted as suggesting that politics everywhere has become mediatized—or that it has become equally mediatized cross-nationally. This is ultimately an empirical question, where it might be possible to identify different phases of mediatization (Strömbäck, 2008).

DISCUSSION AND CONCLUSIONS

The mediatization of politics is a process of increasing media influence in all aspects of politics. The more mediatized politics has become, the more important news organizations become for opinion formation, the more news content is governed by media logic, and the more political institutions and actors take media into continuous consideration and adapt to, or adopt, media logic. Thus, it is reasonable to conceive of mediatization as a meta-process (Krotz, 2007, 2009). From such a perspective, further theorizing about the mediatization of politics could help bridge the differences between different strands of research and integrate seemingly disparate theories and findings into a whole that might help scholars gain a fuller understanding of the media's impact on political processes.

To this end, this chapter has surveyed the literature and suggested a framework that might be used to guide further research on the mediatization of politics. According to this framework, mediatization is a multi-dimensional concept where at least four dimensions can be identified. The first dimension is concerned with the degree to which the media constitute the most important source of information and channel of communication. The second dimension is concerned with the degree to which media have become independent of other social, in particular political, institutions. The third dimension is concerned with the degree to which media content is governed by media logic or political logic. And the fourth dimension focuses on political institutions and actors and the degree to which they are governed by media logic or political logic. Importantly, all four dimensions should be regarded as continua—a matter of degree as opposed to a question of whether politics has become mediatized or not.

Ultimately, though, the degree of mediatization is an empirical question. More studies are thus needed with respect to the linkages between mediatization and other theories of political communication; the antecedents, manifestations, and consequences of mediatization; variations across time and countries; and, ultimately, how and to what extent media shape and reshape politics (Strömbäck & Esser, 2009).

Preferably, further research should be comparative across both time and countries. While the ideal would be research that investigated mediatization along all four dimensions both longitudinally and comparatively across countries, investigations of mediatization along any of the four dimensions would also further our knowledge, providing that such research compares across either time or countries.

As noted by Pfetsch and Esser (2004, p. 7), comparative research "lives up to the rule that 'every observation is without significance if it is not compared with other observations.'" This is true with respect to comparisons across both time and space. It is only through comparisons across *time* that it is possible to investigate the process of mediatization, and it is only through comparisons across *space* that it is possible to investigate variations in the degree to which politics in different countries has become mediatized—and what factors have an impact on the mediatization of politics along any or all of the four dimensions.

Thus, if we want to understand both the process of mediatization and the forces that facilitate or inhibit its realization, then comparative research across these lines is essential. Fortunately, it should not be exceedingly complicated to investigate the first three dimensions of mediatization comparatively across time or countries. In many cases there are available statistics that reveal the importance of the media as a source of information; further research on the degree to which media are independent of political institutions can also draw upon existing research and historical–institutional analyses; and through content analyses it is possible to investigate across time or countries the degree to which media content is governed by media logic.

The most problematic dimension to investigate comparatively is probably the fourth dimension, as there is a dearth of longitudinal data about the degree to which political actors in different countries, past and present, are governed by media logic. Note, however, that problematic does not mean impossible. Through elite surveys of journalists and political actors it would, for example, be possible to investigate differences across countries, and by extending such surveys into the future, longitudinal data could also be obtained. Through memoirs, previous research, and other documents it would also be possible to go back in time and investigate changes longitudinally. Further work in this area may reliably uncover variations across time or space with respect to the degree to which political actors are governed by media logic.

Much remains to be done with the mediatization of politics. In this respect, it is hoped that the framework suggested here will increase our understanding of and serve as a springboard for further theoretical analyses as well as conceptually driven empirical research on the mediatization of politics across time and space.

NOTE

1. The author would like to thank Erik Bucy and Gianpietro Mazzoleni for their very useful and important comments and suggestions on an earlier draft of this chapter.

REFERENCES

Altheide, D. L., & Snow, R. P. (1979). *Media logic.* Beverly Hills: Sage.

Altheide, D. L., & Snow, R. P. (1988). Toward a theory of mediation. In J. A. Anderson (Ed.), *Communication Yearbook 11* (pp. 194–223). Newbury Park, CA: Sage.

Altheide, D. L., & Snow, R. P. (1991). *Media worlds in the postjournalism era.* New York: Aldine de Gruyter.

Asp, K. (1986). *Mäktiga massmedier. Studier i politisk opinionsbildning.* Stockholm: Akademilitteratur.

Asp, K., & Esaiasson, P. (1996). The modernization of Swedish campaigns: Individualization, professionalization, and medialization. In D. L. Swanson & P. Mancini (Eds.), *Politics, media, and modern democracy: An international study of innovations in electoral campaigning and their consequences* (pp. 73–90). Westport, CT: Praeger.

Bennett, W. L. (2003). *News: The politics of illusion* (5th ed.). New York: Longman.

Bennett, W. L., & Entman, R. M. (Eds.). (2001). *Mediated politics: Communication in the future of democracy.* New York: Cambridge University Press.

Berkowitz, D. A. (2009). Reporters and their sources. In K. Wahl-Jorgensen & T. Hanitzsch (Eds.), *The handbook of journalism studies* (pp. 102–115). New York: Routledge.

Blumenthal, S. (1980). *The permanent campaign: Inside the world of elite political operatives.* Boston, MA: Beacon Press.

Blumler, J. G., & Gurevitch, M. (1995). *The crisis of public communication.* London: Routledge.

Boorstin, D. J. (1962). *The image: A guide to pseudo-events in America.* New York: Harper Colophon.

Brants, K., & van Praag, P. (2006). Signs of media logic. Half a century of political communication in the Netherlands. *Javnost–The Public, 13*(1), 25–40.

Bucy, E. P., & D'Angelo, P. (2004). Democratic realism, neoconservatism, and the normative underpinnings of political communication research. *Mass Communication & Society, 7*(1), 3–28.

Bucy, E. P., & Gregson, K. S. (2001). Media participation. A legitimizing mechanism of mass democracy. *New Media & Society, 3*(3), 357–380.

Cook, T. E. (2005). *Governing with the news. The news media as a political institution* (2nd ed.). Chicago: University of Chicago Press.

Couldry, N. (2008). Mediatization or mediation? Alternative understandings of the emergent space of digital storytelling. *New Media & Society, 10*(3), 373–391.

Croteau, D., & Hoynes, W. (2001). *The business of media: Corporate media and the public interest.* Thousand Oaks, CA: Pine Forge Press.

Davis, A. (2007). *The mediation of power: A critical introduction.* London: Routledge.

Esser, F. (2008). Dimensions of political news cultures: Sound bite and image bite news in France, Germany, Great Britain, and the United States. *International Journal of Press/Politics, 13*(4), 401–428.

Esser, F., & D'Angelo, P. (2003). Framing the press and the publicity process. A content analysis of meta-coverage in campaign 2000 network news. *American Behavioral Scientist, 46*(5), 617–641.

Ferree, M. M., Gamson, W. A., Gerhards, Jurgen, & Rucht, Dieter. (2002). Four models of the public sphere in modern democracies. *Theory and Society, 31*(3), 289–324.

Gandy, O. H. (1982). *Beyond agenda setting: Information subsidies and public policy.* Norwood: Ablex.

Gans, H. J. (1980). *Deciding what's news. A study of CBS Evening News, NBC Nightly News, Newsweek and Time.* New York: Vintage.

Grabe, M. E., & Bucy, E. P. (2009). *Image bite politics. News and the visual framing of elections.* New York: Oxford University Press.

Graber, D. (2005). *Mass media and American politics* (7th ed.). Washington, DC: CQ Press.

Gurevitch, M., & Blumler, J. G. (2004). State of the art of comparative political communication research: Poised for maturity? In F. Esser & B. Pfetsch (Eds.), *Comparing political communication. Theories, cases, and challenges* (pp. 325–343). New York: Cambridge University Press.

Hallin, D. C. (1986). *The "uncensored war": The media and Vietnam.* Berkeley: University of California Press.

Hallin, D. C. (1992). Sound bite news: Television coverage of elections, 1968–1988. *Journal of Communication, 42*(2), 5–24.

Hallin, D. C., & Mancini, P. (2004). *Comparing media systems: Three models of media and politics.* New York: Cambridge University Press.

Hamilton, J. T. (2004). *All the news that's fit to sell: How the market transforms information into news.* Princeton, NJ: Princeton University Press.

Hanitzsch, T. (2007). Deconstructing journalism culture. Toward a universal theory. *Comunication Theory, 17*(4), 367–385.

Hepp, A. (2009). Differentiation: Mediatization and cultural change. In K. Lundby (Ed.), *Mediatization: Concepts, changes, consequences* (pp. 139–157). New York: Peter Lang.

Hernes, G. (1978). Det mediavridde samfunn. In G. Hernes (Ed.), *Forhandlingsøkonomi og blandadministrasjon* (pp. 181–195). Oslo: Universitetsførlaget.

Hjarvard, S. (2008). The mediatization of society: A theory of the media as agents of social and cultural change. *Nordicom Review, 29*(2), 105–134.

Hjarvard, S. (2009). Soft individualism: Media and the changing social character. In K. Lundby (Ed.), *Mediatization: Concepts, changes, consequences* (pp. 159–177). New York: Peter Lang.

Hoover, S. M. (2009). Complexities: The case of religious cultures. In K. Lundby (Ed.), *Mediatization: Concepts, changes, consequences* (pp. 123–138). New York: Peter Lang.

Kepplinger, H. M. (2002). Mediatization of politics: Theory and data. *Journal of Communication, 52*(4), pp. 972–986.

Kepplinger, H. M. (2007). Reciprocal effects: Toward a theory of mass media effects on decision makers. *Harvard International Journal of Press/Politics, 12*(2), 3–23.

Kernell, S. (2007). *Going public: New strategies of presidential leadership* (4th ed.). Washington, DC: CQ Press.

Krotz, F. (2007). The meta-process of "mediatization" as a conceptual frame. *Global Media and Communication, 3*(3), 256–260.

Krotz, F. (2009). Mediatization: A concept with which to grasp media and societal change. In K. Lundby (Ed.), *Mediatization: Concepts, changes, consequences* (pp. 21–40). New York: Peter Lang.

Lippmann, W. (1997). *Public opinion.* New York: The Free Press.

Livingstone, S. (2009). On the mediation of everything. *Journal of Communication, 59*(1), 1–18.

Lundby, K. (Ed.). (2009a). *Mediatization: Concepts, changes, consequences.* New York: Peter Lang.

Lundby, K. (2009b). Introduction: "Mediatization" as key. In K. Lundby (Ed.), *Mediatization: Concepts, changes, consequences* (pp. 1–18). New York: Peter Lang.

Lundby, K. (2009c). Media logic: Looking for social interaction. In K. Lundby (Ed.), *Mediatization: Concepts, changes, consequences* (pp. 101–119). New York: Peter Lang.

Mazzoleni, G. (1987). Media logic and party logic in campaign coverage: The Italian general election of 1983. *European Journal of Communication, 2*(1), 81–103.

Mazzoleni, G. (2008a). Mediatization of politics. In W. Donsbach (Ed.), *The international encyclopedia of communication* (pp. 3047–3051). Malden, MA: Blackwell.

Mazzoleni, G. (2008b). Mediatization of society. In W. Donsbach (Ed.), *The international encyclopedia of communication* (pp. 3052–3055). Malden, MA: Blackwell.

Mazzoleni, G. (2008c). Media logic. In W. Donsbach (Ed.), *The international encyclopedia of communication* (pp. 2930–2932). Malden, MA: Blackwell.

Mazzoleni, G., & Schulz, W. (1999). Mediatization of politics: A challenge for democracy? *Political Communication, 16*(3), 247–261.

McLuhan, M. (1964). *Understanding media: The extensions of man.* New York: McGraw-Hill.

McManus, J. H. (1994). *Market-driven journalism: Let the citizen beware?* Thousand Oaks, CA: Sage.

Meyer, T. (2002). *Media democracy: How the media colonize politics.* Cambridge: Polity.

Nimmo, D., & Combs, J. E. (1983). *Mediated political realities.* New York: Longman.

Palmer, J. (2000). *Spinning into control. News values and source strategies.* London: Leicester University Press.

Patterson, T. E. (1993). *Out of order.* New York: Vintage.

Pfetsch, B. (2004). From political culture to political communications culture: A Theoretical approach to comparative analysis. In F. Esser & B. Pfetsch (Eds.), *Comparing political communication: Cases, theories, challenges* (pp. 344–366). New York: Cambridge University Press.

Pfetsch, B., & Esser, F. (2004). Comparing political communication: Reorientations in a changing world. In F. Esser & B. Pfetsch (Eds.), *Comparing political communication: Cases, theories, challenges* (pp. 3–22). New York: Cambridge University Press.

Reich, Z. (2009). *Sourcing the news*. Cresskill: Hampton Press.

Schrott, A. (2009). Dimensions: Catch-all label or technical term. In K. Lundby (Ed.), *Mediatization: Concepts, changes, consequences* (pp. 41–61). New York: Peter Lang.

Schudson, M. (2003). *The sociology of news*. New York: W. W. Norton.

Schulz, W. (2004). Reconstructing mediatization as an analytical concept. *European Journal of Communication, 19*(1), 87–101.

Semetko, H. A., Blumler, J. G., Gurevitch, M., & Weaver, D. H. (1991). *The formation of campaign agendas: A comparative analysis of party and media roles in recent American and British elections*. Hillsdale: Lawrence Erlbaum.

Shoemaker, P. J., & Cohen, A. (2006). *News around the world: Content, practitioners, and the public*. New York: Routledge.

Shoemaker, P. J., & Reese, S. D. (1996). *Mediating the message: Theories of influences on mass media content* (2nd ed.). New York: Longman.

Silverstone, R. (2007). *Media and morality: On the rise of the mediapolis*. Cambridge: Polity.

Skewes, E. A. (2007). *Message control: How news is made on the presidential campaign trail*. Lanham, MD: Rowman & Littlefield.

Sparrow, B. H. (1999). *Uncertain guardians: The news media as a political institution*. Baltimore: Johns Hopkins University Press.

Strömbäck, J. (2005). In search of a standard: Four models of democracy and their normative implications for journalism. *Journalism Studies, 6*(3), 331–345.

Strömbäck, J. (2008). Four phases of mediatization: An analysis of the mediatization of politics. *International Journal of Press/Politics, 13*(3), 228–246.

Strömbäck, J., & Esser, F. (2009). Shaping politics: Mediatization and media interventionism. In K. Lundby (Ed.), *Mediatization: Concepts, changes, consequences* (pp. 205–223). New York: Peter Lang.

Strömbäck, J., & Kaid, L. L. (Eds.). (2008). *Handbook of election news coverage around the world*. New York: Routledge.

Thompson, J. B. (1995). *The media and modernity: A social theory of the media*. Stanford: Stanford University Press.

Thompson, J. B. (2000). *Political scandal: Power and visibility in the media age*. Cambridge: Polity.

Weaver, D. H., Beam, R. A., Brownlee, B. J., Voakes, P. S., & Wilhoit, G. C. (2007). *The American journalist in the 21st century: U.S. news people at the dawn of a new millenium*. Mahwah, NJ: Lawrence Erlbaum.

20

International Applications of Agenda-Setting Theory's Acapulco Typology

Maxwell E. McCombs
School of Journalism
University of Texas–Austin

Salma Ghanem
College of Communication and Fine Arts
Central Michigan University

Federico Rey Lennon
Institute of Social Communication, Journalism, and Advertising
Catholic University, Argentina

R. Warwick Blood
Faculty of Communication and International Studies
University of Canberra, Australia

Yi-Ning (Katherine) Chen
Department of Advertising
National Chengchi University, Taiwan

Hyun Ban
Department of Mass Communication
University of Incheon, Korea

The Chapel Hill study is well known as both the theoretical and empirical origin of agenda-setting theory. To a considerable degree, however, this study conducted by McCombs and Shaw (1972) during the 1968 U.S. presidential election also set the methodological agenda for a significant proportion of the hundreds of empirical studies that have followed. Although the Chapel Hill study design was not the first mass communication research study to use content analysis and survey research in tandem, it was the study that brought this combination of research methods to center stage in investigating cognitive effects.

To test agenda setting's theoretical proposition that the pattern of coverage for public issues in the news influences the public's perception of what are the most important issues of the day, a survey asked a sample of randomly selected undecided voters in Chapel Hill to name what they thought were the key issues of the day, regardless of what the candidates were saying. The issues named in this survey were ranked according to the percentage of voters naming each one to yield a description of the public agenda. Concurrent with this survey, the nine major news sources used by these voters—five newspapers (both local and national), two television networks, and two news magazines—were content analyzed. The rank order of issues on the media agenda was determined by the number of news stories devoted to each issue. Then, the rank orders of this set of issues on the media agenda and public agenda were compared using Spearman's *rho*. The high degree of correspondence found between these two agendas of public issues was the opening gambit in the empirical evidence for agenda-setting effects.

Moving beyond the limited span of the 1968 Chapel Hill study, subsequent studies, also based on the tandem use of content analysis and survey research, found agenda-setting effects among general population samples of voters during the 1972 and 1976 U.S. presidential elections (Shaw & McCombs, 1977; Weaver et al., 1981). Outside election settings, dozens of other studies based on this same methodological combination have found agenda-setting effects of news coverage in both national and local studies in the United States (Funkhouser, 1973; Palmgreen & Clarke, 1977; Smith, 1987; Wanta & Hu, 1994) as well as in such diverse international settings as Spain, Japan, and Argentina (Canel, Llamas, & Rey, 1996; Casermeiro de Pereson, 2003; Rey, 1998; Takeshita, 1993). A meta-analysis of 90 empirical studies found a mean correlation of +.53, with most agenda-setting effects about six points above or below the mean (Wanta & Ghanem, 2000). And as agenda-setting research expanded to a second level of news media influence on the public, attribute agenda setting, this methodological combination of content analysis and survey research has been used in a variety of settings ranging from the attributes of political candidates in the United States and Taiwan (Becker & McCombs, 1978; King, 1997) to the attributes of such public issues as the environment (Cohen, 1975) and the economy (Benton & Frazier, 1976) in non-election settings.

This move away from the limited effects model to investigations of news media cognitive effects had wider impact. Blumler (1981) proposed a pathway to bridge the epistemological gap between U.S. quantitative agenda-setting research and more qualitative models investigating news in the U.K., Europe, and elsewhere. While noting Chaffee's (1978) comment that agenda-setting was one of the best two or three research ideas in the field, Blumler (1981) argued that it had been pursued only in a truncated version up to that point, that is, an almost exclusive focus on the media content/audience interface. For Blumler, a fuller theory would also encompass the impact of the social system on media institutions, especially on journalists and editors, and investigate those political and interest groups that constantly strived to manipulate public opinion by influencing journalists and editors. And in the decade that followed, numerous studies on the "social construction" of news pursued the question of who sets the media's agenda. (See, for example, Semetko, Blumler, Gurevitch, and Weaver's (1991) comparative study on the news coverage of British and U.S. national elections.) Some of this research explicitly follows the agenda-setting tradition and some represents the coming together of agenda-setting theory and the venerable sociology of news tradition (McCombs, 2004, Chapter 7). Kwansah-Aidoo's (2001) African study discussed below is one of the few examples that follow the qualitative approach linking both of these approaches.

Altogether, in the forty-plus years since the seminal Chapel Hill study, agenda-setting theory has expanded to encompass five distinct stages. Beyond basic agenda-setting effects of the media agenda on the public agenda that are grounded in agendas of public issues and other "objects" are second-level agenda-setting effects or the transfer of the salience of the attributes of those objects from one agenda to another. These attributes can be the qualities of public figures, as already noted in some of the examples cited above, or the attributes of issues or other objects. The 1972 presidential election study of agenda-setting effects also introduced a third theoretical stage, the psychological variables that explicate the process of agenda-setting. And as noted, the early 1980s introduced a fourth stage, the influences shaping the media agenda. Most recently, scholars have begun mapping a fifth stage, the implications of first- and second-level agenda-setting effects for attitudes, opinions, and behavior. This is a somewhat ironic development because it was the conventional wisdom of the 1950s and 1960s that the mass media had few, if any, effects on attitudes and opinions that led scholars to turn their attention to agenda-setting and other cognitive effects of the media.

THE ACAPULCO TYPOLOGY

Over time, a number of tactical variations have evolved in research practice for investigating these agenda-setting effects. A four-part typology summarizing these perspectives is frequently referred to as the Acapulco typology because McCombs initially presented it in Acapulco, Mexico, at the invitation of International Communication Association president-elect Everett Rogers. The Acapulco typology is defined by two dichotomous dimensions. The first dimension considers the focus of attention, which can be on the entire set of items that define an agenda, or can be narrowed to one particular item on the agenda. The second dimension distinguishes two ways of measuring the salience of items on the agenda, either aggregate measures describing an entire population or measures that describe individual responses.

Type I studies encompass the entire agenda and use aggregate measures of the population to establish the salience of these items. The original Chapel Hill study took this perspective, as did the subsequent national population studies during the 1972 and 1976 U.S. presidential elections. This perspective, drawing upon both survey research and content analysis to obtain aggregate measures of the media and public agenda, also is reflected in the variety of U.S. and international

	Measure of Public Salience	
	Aggregate data	Individual data
Focus of attention		
Entire agenda	Type I	Type II
	Competition	*Automaton*
		(null/abandoned)
Single item on agenda	Type III	Type IV
	Natural History	*Cognitive Portrait*

FIGURE 20.1 The Acapulco typology: Four perspectives on agenda setting.

examples cited above for nonelection studies of basic agenda-setting effects. This frequently employed design also is reflected in the examples cited above for attribute agenda-setting effects. The name frequently applied to this perspective is "Competition" because it examines an array of issues or other items that are competing for positions on the agenda.

Type II designs are similar to all these agenda-setting studies with their focus on the entire agenda of items, but shift their focus to the agenda of each individual. In other words, rather than an aggregate measure of the rank order of items on the public agenda, the focus here is on how each individual ranks a set of issues. However, when individuals are asked to rank order a series of issues, there is little evidence of any correspondence at all between those individual rankings and the rank order of those same issues in the news media (McLeod, Becker, & Byrnes, 1974). This perspective is labeled "Automaton" because of its unflattering view of human behavior. An individual seldom, if ever, reproduces to any significant degree the entire agenda of the media. Due to the lack of supporting evidence for this perspective, Type II designs have been abandoned.

Type III designs narrow their focus to a single item on the agenda, but similar to Type I studies use aggregate measures to establish the salience of these items. Typically, in line with Type I designs, the measures of salience include the total number of news stories about the item and the percentage of the public citing an issue as the most important problem facing the country. However, in contrast to most Type I designs that measure media and public salience at one or, at most, a few points in time, this perspective is named "Natural History" because the focus typically is on the degree of correspondence between the media agenda and the public agenda for a single item over a longer period of time. A prime example of this widely employed perspective is Winter and Eyal's (1981) study of the civil rights issue over a 23-year period. Other examples include a series of 41-month investigations of eleven individual issues in the U.S. during the 1980s (Eaton, 1989), investigations spanning eight years for eight individual issues in the city of Louisville (Smith, 1987), and a week-by-week analysis for the entire year of 1986 for 16 individual issues in Germany (Brosius & Kepplinger, 1990).

Type IV designs focus on the individual, as does Type II, but narrow their observations to the salience of a single agenda item. The research grounded in this perspective, which is named "Cognitive Portrait," is more diverse methodologically than the research based on the other three perspectives of the Acapulco typology. Some of the research follows the methodological tradition of those perspectives and is grounded in content analysis and survey research. However, a considerable portion of the Type IV research is based on laboratory experimentation where the independent variable is an explicit measure (or set of measures) of individual attention to mass media messages and the dependent variable is the salience of a single object or attribute on an individual's agenda.

Takeshita and Mikami's (1995) simultaneous investigation of attention to an object and comprehension of its attributes, the first and second levels of agenda-setting, during the 1993 Japanese general election illustrates this departure from the traditional content analysis/survey research design. Their content analysis of two major national newspapers and three TV networks found that political reform accounted for more than 80% of the issue coverage. This finding clearly precluded any meaningful rank ordering of the issues on the media agenda (eliminating the use of a Type I approach) and their survey was a single observation of the voter population (eliminating the use of a Type III approach).

In most studies based on Type I or III designs, a major assumption behind the comparisons of the media agenda and the public agenda is that the agenda-setting effects reflected in the correspondence between the salience of items on these agendas result from exposure to the mass media. In Takeshita and Mikami's study of the Japanese election, the behavior linking these two agendas was explicitly measured. Combining measures of exposure and political interest to yield an index of attentiveness to political news, support was found for the proposition that the salience of the dominant media issue, political reform, among members of the public was positively correlated with their level of attentiveness to political news. Moving to the second level of agenda-setting, the fact that both TV news and the newspapers mentioned system-related aspects of reform twice as often as ethics-related aspects created counterbalanced expectations about the attribute agenda-setting roles of the news media. Both hypotheses were supported. For the ethics-related aspect of political reform, the correlations with attentiveness to political news were nearly zero in contrast to the significant correlations for the system-related aspect of political reform.

This model, in which the independent variable is individual attention to the mass media and the dependent variable is the salience of an item on an individual's agenda, also is found in laboratory experiments. The extensive exploration of agenda-setting effects on a wide range of issues reported in Iyengar and Kinder's *News That Matters* (1987) employed numerous variations of this exposure–salience design. And experimental studies using this basic design to study the agenda-setting effects of new Internet media include Wang's (2000) study of racism and Althaus and Tewskbury's (2002) study of international issues. Also at the first level of agenda-setting, Miller (2007) used this design to study the potential role of two mediating variables, accessibility and emotion, on the salience of crime. She found support for the role of emotions, but not accessibility, as mediators of agenda-setting effects. At the second level of agenda-setting, Kiousis, Bantimaroudis, and Ban (1999) employed this experimental design to study attribute agenda-setting effects on the images of political candidates.

AN INTERNATIONAL PERSPECTIVE

Beyond the diversity of methodological perspectives in the research on the agenda-setting role of the mass media, an additional strength is its international scope. Agenda-setting research has moved geographically far beyond its origins four decades ago in Chapel Hill, North Carolina. There are numerous studies in Europe stretching from Spain to Sweden and east to Turkey and the Middle East, on the Pacific Rim from Japan and Korea to China and Taiwan, and on across the world to Australia and South America. Agenda-setting effects have been documented across a vast array of political and cultural settings around the world, leading to the axiom that these communication phenomena can occur in any setting with a reasonably open media system and reasonably open political system. By a reasonably open media system, we mean one not under government control or the dominance of a political party. By a reasonably open political system, we mean a political setting where elections matter and determine the course of government. Further explication of these general definitions of open systems can advance the international scope of agenda-setting theory. At the aggregate nation-state level, there are a number of comprehensive indices on the degree of openness around the world. For example, the venerable Freedom House (www.freedomhouse.org) offers the advantage of annual international reports on both the levels of press freedom and freedom in regard to political and civil rights. There are detailed quantitative Freedom in the World annual reports from 1972 to the present covering 208 countries and territories, and detailed quantitative Freedom of the Press annual reports from 1980 to the present covering 195 countries and territories.

Although numerous countries fit generally into the open media/open political system category, many countries reflect a mixed situation, especially in regard to the various news media. For example, in the 1994 mayoral election in Taipei, King (1997) found significant attribute agenda-setting effects for two major daily newspapers, but no effects at all for the three Taipei television stations. Voters were well aware that the stations were under the domination of the government and long-ruling KMT political party. In other words, the newspapers reflected an open media system; the television stations, a closed media system.

The central question in this chapter is whether the methodological variations in this international evidence for the agenda-setting role of the media are effectively universal, reflecting an invisible college of scholars worldwide whose research follows similar methodological patterns, or whether there are significant regional differences in the methodological preferences of agenda-setting researchers.

To answer this question, an international team of agenda-setting scholars comes together in this chapter to assess the accumulated literature, a team that brings a diversity of cultural perspectives to this task. Warwick Blood, who is from Australia, earned his PhD at Syracuse University in the United States. He is now in Canberra. Hyun Ban, who is from Korea, completed his PhD at the University of Texas at Austin. He is now in Incheon. Yi-Ning Chen, who is from Taiwan, completed her PhD at the University of Texas at Austin. She is now in Taipei. Salma Ghanem, who is from Egypt, earned her PhD at the University of Texas at Austin and is now at the Central Michigan University. Federico Rey Lennon, who is from Argentina, completed his PhD at the University of Navarra in Spain. He is now in Buenos Aires. Maxwell McCombs, an American who is a co-founder of the agenda-setting tradition, is in Austin.

The task undertaken by this international team was a comprehensive review of the research designs found in agenda-setting research around the world. Because these studies now number in the hundreds and because there is no extant sampling frame listing all these studies, the sample of studies examined by our team is largely grounded in the knowledge of each team member about their part of the world and its accumulated research on agenda-setting.

AGENDA SETTING AROUND THE WORLD

Western Europe

The large body of European research on agenda-setting greatly favors Type III designs with their focus on a single issue. In recent years this may be the result of major continental issues—European unification, the Euro, immigration, and persistent unemployment issues. But the trend is more long standing, perhaps the response of European scholars to the multitude of political parties and the plethora of issues on their agendas. However, there is significant Type I research. In Spain, for example, Lopez-Escbobar, Llamas, and McCombs (1998) documented increasing consensus about the agenda of public issues with increased newspaper reading and TV news viewing. Taking agenda-setting research to the local level in Spain, Canel, Llamas, and Rey (1996) investigated the most important problems in the city of Pamplona.

Among the many Type III studies, two in particular introduce important nuances into agenda-setting theory. Schönbach and Semetko (1992) found that interest in political news on television was positively associated with an increase in the salience of environmental problems—a traditional agenda-setting effect—while exposure to a national tabloid was negatively associated with the salience of problems in assimilating the former East Germany—an agenda-deflating effect.

Focusing on the issue of European integration, Peter (2003) found that the agenda-setting effects of EU coverage on television were contingent upon the nature of elite opinion. The more EU stories people watched in countries in which political elites disagreed about European integration, the more important they considered European integration. However, in countries where elite opinion about integration was consensual, this pattern of agenda-setting effects was absent. Political conflict as a contingent condition for agenda-setting effects on public issues also was found by Auh (1977a, 1977b) in a U.S. Senate race. It is important to distinguish these findings about conflict as a contingent condition for agenda-setting effects from Zaller's (1992) well known models about one-sided and two-sided information flows in which media influence is greatest when elites are united and the flow is largely one-sided. The distinction is in the nature of the influence of the news media—their impact on the direction of public opinion (Zaller) versus their impact on the salience of issues among the public (Auh and Peter). For additional discussion of this distinction in agenda-setting research, see McCombs (2004, Chapter 8).

Agenda-setting effects have been extensively documented across western and northern Europe. In recent years, research has begun to appear in the former communist countries of eastern Europe. Fewer studies have been done in southern Europe with the major exception of Spain.

Eurasia and Africa

Moving east, both first- and second-level agenda-setting effects have been investigated in Turkey with Type I designs. At the second level, Yuksel (2003) found evidence of significant newspaper influence on Turkish voters' images of candidates for Parliament. And reflecting the expansion of agenda-setting research into domains beyond public affairs, Gorpe and Yuksel (2007) found traditional first-level effects of news coverage on the reputations of major business corporations.

Using a Type I design in Egypt, Mohamed (2006) found a high degree of correspondence between the aggregate media agenda and the public's issue agenda. Further comparisons of an Egyptian national newspaper and an opposition newspaper with their audience's agendas found a significant correlation between the opposition newspaper's agenda and that of its readers. Little correspondence was found between the government newspaper agenda and that of its readers. And Al-Haqeel and Melkote (1995) found that Saudi Arabian media were very effective in influencing the salience of international issues on the public's agenda.

These findings from the Middle East again reflect the mixed media systems discussed earlier in regard to the conditions for the appearance of agenda-setting effects. The Egyptian situation is analogous to the divide between newspapers and television in Taiwan. And, arguably, Saudi audiences perceive the international news agenda to be open and the domestic news agenda to be dominated by the government.

In Ghana, using a qualitative version of a Type III design, Kwansah-Aidoo (2001) concluded that the media influenced the environmental agenda of the public in that African country. This creative multi-method qualitative approach, which combined focus groups, in-depth personal interviews, and document analysis, sets a major precedent for more broad-based investigations of the agenda-setting process. Even the highly quantitative designs summarized by the Acapulco Typology rely upon strategic open-ended questions, such as the "most important problem" (MIP) question, as the foundation for much of their data. Extending the research methodology into other qualitative areas is a logical expansion of the research tradition in every part of the world.

The agenda-setting tradition is young in this part of the world and greatly favors Type I investigations. More Type III and Type IV studies are needed to broaden our knowledge of how agenda-setting works in these societies.

Australia

Most communication research here follows the qualitative tradition of British and European media studies. Consequently, there has been less interest in agenda-setting theory and only a few quantitative agenda-setting studies. Gadir (1982) presents evidence from a Type I design for agenda-setting effects that result from the activation and deactivation of issues on the larger issue agenda. The sudden reemergence of a dormant issue (e.g., defense) may be more significant than the "permanent" higher salience of another issue (e.g., inflation). Also using a Type I design, Denemark (2002) examined the agenda-setting effects of television news among Australian voters stratified by differing levels of political interest and awareness. Voters with moderate levels of political interest were the only group demonstrating significant agenda-setting effects.

Using a Type III design, Brown and Deegan (1998) drew on agenda-setting and legitimacy theories to investigate the relationship between the print media's attention to an industry's environmental performance and the subsequent environmental disclosures in companies' annual reports. Environmental disclosures in annual reports were related to Australian newspaper coverage for the majority of industries, evidence that business elites, not just the general public, can reflect the agenda-setting influence of newspapers. The growing interest in agenda-setting theory around the world for investigations of corporate reputations and other aspects of business and public relations is likely to stimulate a greater volume of this research in the future.

South America

Although a tradition of empirical agenda-setting research in South America largely dates from the 1990s, there already is a rich accumulation of election studies reminiscent of the inaugural work in the United States. Rey Lennon (1998) and Casermeiro de Pereson (2003) used Type I designs to study the agenda-setting effects of newspapers and television news during legislative elections in the Buenos Aires metropolitan area. Both sets of evidence suggest considerable media impact on the public's issue agenda in these elections. In Chile, a national study of the 1999 presidential election based on a Type I analysis of the relationships among three issue agendas—the public agenda, media agenda (both TV and daily newspapers), and the political advertising agenda— found the strongest correspondence between the advertising and public agendas (Dussaillant, 2005). And in an innovative application of agenda-setting theory using a Type I design, Casermeiro de Pereson, De La Torre, and Téramo (2007) found significant media influence on the images of Pope John Paul II and the Argentine bishops, but not on general perceptions of Catholic clergy or Catholics. This is another example of the recent trend in agenda-setting research to expand into domains beyond public affairs.

Examining the issue of unemployment in a middle-sized Argentine city, Monteiro's (2006) Type III study found significant effects for local prime time TV news at both the first and second levels of agenda-setting. Using a Type III design focusing the analysis on each of five presidential candidates during Argentina's 2003 presidential election, Yang (2006) reported significant correlations between media attention and the level of popular support for two of the candidates, including the candidate who won the election.

The lack of Type IV studies, notably controlled laboratory experiments, undoubtedly reflects the relative newness of quantitative research among any significant number of Latin American scholars. Communication research in Latin America is primarily grounded in the qualitative approaches of Europe.

East Asia

The scholars of East Asia, particularly Japan, Korea, and Taiwan, are a major faculty in the invisible college of agenda-setting researchers. Over the past 20 years or so, they have produced a large volume of research. In line with the origins of agenda-setting research in the United States, a significant number of these studies are election studies based on Type I designs. In Taiwan, this extensive body of research covers both presidential elections (Han, 2000; Wang, 1999) and the key Taipei mayoral elections (Chen, 2001, 2004; King, 1997; Li & King, 1996). In Japan and Korea, Type I election studies also examine both news and advertising (Kawakami, 1999) as well more recently, the Internet and online news sources (Ku, 2002; Lee, 2007). There also is a substantial body of nonelection Type I research ranging from traditional news coverage (Iwabuchi, 1986) and online journalism (Joe & Kim, 2004) to corporate reputations (Cha, 2004).

Type III studies include advertising (Tokinoya, 1983) as well as traditional Type III studies focused on specific issues. The issues investigated range widely from that perennial subject on issue agendas around the world, the economy (Lee, Shim, & Park, 2007), to specific aspects of the economy, the bubble in Korean real estate prices (Choi & Ban, 2006) to AIDS (Hsu, 1999) and the U.S.–Taiwan relationship (Guo, 1980).

Recent Type IV studies examined the environment (Lee, Yoo, & McCombs, 2007) and the issue of nuclear waste (Ban, Choi, & Shin, 2004). More specifically, Ban, Choi, & Shin's (2004) experiment documented the successful transfer of the media's attribute agenda for nuclear waste to the public's agenda of these attributes in terms of both their cognitive and affective dimensions. Similarly, Lee, Yoo, and McCombs's (2007) experiment involving the issue of global warming found that the media boost the salience of the audience's perceived affective attributes better than substantive attributes salience. These rigorous experimental investigations not only document second-level agenda-setting effects, they expand and enhance our knowledge about agenda-setting effects found in Type I and Type III studies. In that regard, these studies establish an important precedent for Type IV studies in other parts of the world and further comparative research on the similarity (or differences) in agenda-setting effects across cultures.

CONCLUSION

The existence of these varied perspectives on agenda-setting phenomena, especially an abundance of evidence based on Type I and III designs, strengthens the degree of confidence that we can have in our knowledge about these media effects. Beyond the fact that these two perspectives dominate the research on agenda-setting, there are significant variations by geographic region. Western Europe, in particular, stands out because of the large number of Type III studies done there examining the influence of news media on particular public issues. South America and East Asia largely mirror the pattern found in the United States, particularly early emphasis on the Type I design first used in the Chapel Hill election study, but increasingly complemented by a wealth of Type III studies on single issues. In Australia, Turkey, and the Middle East, where agenda-setting is a young research tradition, the emphasis not surprisingly is on Type I designs. Of course, this emphasis worldwide has been enhanced in recent years by the use of Type I designs to study attribute agenda setting.

Type I designs provide useful, comprehensive descriptions of the rich, ever-changing, mix of mass media content and public opinion at particular points in time. This perspective strives to describe the world as it is. Type III designs yield useful descriptions of the natural history of a single issue, but at the expense of the larger social context in which this issue exists. Nevertheless, knowledge about the dynamics of a single issue over an extended period of time is highly useful for understanding how the process of agenda-setting works. Type IV designs, which are a newer approach in the methodological repertoire of agenda-setting researchers, also make valuable contributions to our understanding of the dynamics of agenda setting. From a theoretical viewpoint, evidence generated by Type III and IV designs is absolutely necessary to the detailed explication of agenda-setting theory that will explain how and why this phenomenon occurs. But the ultimate goal of agenda-setting theory returns us to Type I studies, a comprehensive view of mass communication and public opinion in the life of each community and nation.

Beyond the empirical testing of agenda-setting effects, it is significant that the phrases *agenda-setting, media agenda,* and *public agenda* now are commonly part of political and social discourse worldwide. Politicians, editors, journalists, and, at times, various publics use these phrases as a way of describing or explaining social and political processes in their own words.

REFERENCES

Al-Haqeel, A., & Melkote, S. (1995). International agenda-setting effects of Saudi Arabian media: A case study. *Gazette, 55,* 17–37.

Althaus, S. L., & Tewksbury, D. (2002). Agenda setting and the "new" news. *Communication Research, 29,* 180–207.

Auh, T. S. (1977a). *Issue conflict and mass media agenda setting.* Unpublished doctoral dissertation, School of Journalism, Indiana University, Bloomington.

Auh, T. S. (1977b). *Issue conflict and mass media agenda-setting during the Bayh-Lugar senatorial campaign of 1974.* Paper presented at the annual meeting of the Association for Education in Journalism, Madison, Wisconsin.

Ban, H., Choi, W. S., & Shin, S. H. (2004). News attributes and the second-level agenda setting study: Coverage of the nuclear waste storage facility in Wido. *Korean Journal of Communication and Information Studies, 25,* 65–102.

Becker, L., & McCombs, M. (1978). The role of the press in determining voter reactions to presidential primaries. *Human Communication Research, 4,* 301–307.

Benton, M., & Frazier, J. P. (1976). The agenda-setting function of the mass media at three levels of "Information holding." *Communication Research, 3,* 261–274.

Blumler, J. (1981). Mass communication research in Europe: Some origins and prospects. In G. C. Wilhoit and H de Bock (Eds.), *Mass communication review yearbook* (Vol. 2, pp. 37–49). Beverly Hills, CA: Sage.

Brosius, H.-B., & Kepplinger, H. M. (1990). The agenda-setting function of television news: Static and dynamic views. *Communication Research, 17,* 183–211.

Brown, N., & Deegan, C. (1998). The public disclosure of environmental performance information—A dual test of media agenda setting theory and legitimacy theory. *Accounting and Business Research, 29,* 21–41.

Canel, M. J., Llamas, J. P., & Rey, F. (1996). El primer nivel del efecto agenda setting en la informacion local: Los "problemas mas importantes" de la ciudad de Pamplona. *Communicacion y Sociedad, 9,* 17–38.

Casermeiro de Pereson, A. (2003). *Los medios en las elecciones. Agenda setting en la ciudad de Buenos Aires.* Buenos Aires: EDUCA.

Casermeiro de Pereson, A., De La Torre, L., & Teramo, T. (2007). *La imagen de la Iglesia Catolica en la Argentina.* World Association of Public Opinion Research (WAPOR), Colonia del Sacramento, Uruguay.

Cha, H. W. (2004). Agenda-setting effects of mass media on corporate reputations by public involvement and media credibility. *Korean Journal of Journalism and Communication Studies, 48*(6), 274–304.

Chaffee, S. (1978). Review of the book, *The emergence of American political issues: The agenda-setting function of the press. Political Communication Review, 3*(1), 25–28.

Chen, Y. N. (2001).The relationships between attack news against the presidential candidates and voters' support in the Taiwanese presidential election in 2000. *Mass Communication Research, 69,* 113–140.

Chen, Y. N. (2004). Agenda setting in the 2002 Taipei mayoral election: Evolution of the image and issue agenda. *Mass Communication Research, 81,* 125–162.

Choi, W. S., & Ban, H. (2006). The study of agenda-setting effect model on public opinion and behavior: Coverage of bubble real estate prices and government policies. *Korean Journal of Journalism and Communication Studies, 50*(1), 406–435.

Cohen, D. (1975). A report on a nonelection agenda-setting study. Paper presented at the annual meeting of the Association for Education in Journalism, Ottawa, Canada.

Denemark, D. (2002). Television effects and voter decision-making in Australia: A reexamination of the Converse model. *British Journal of Political Science, 32*(4), 663–691.

Dussaillant, P. (2005). *Medios y elecciones. La elección presidencial de 1999.* Santiago: Centro de Estudios Bicentenario.

Eaton, H., Jr. (1989). Agenda setting with bi-weekly data on content of three national media. *Journalism Quarterly, 66,* 942–948.

Funkhouser, G. R. (1973). The issues of the sixties. *Public Opinion Quarterly, 37,* 62–75.

Gadir, Simon. (1982, November). The rise and fall of public issues. *Media Information Australia, 26,* 13–23.

Gorpe, S., & Yuksel, E. (2007). *Media content and Corporate Reputation Survey 2006 in Turkey: A first-level agenda-setting study.* 5th International Symposium, Communication in the Millennium: A Dialogue between Turkish and American Scholars. Bloomington, Indiana.

Guo, Y. D. (1980). The agenda setting function of news media: A study on university students' perception of the US–Taiwan relationship. *Mass Communication Research, 25,* 1–59.

Han, C. H. (2000). *The agenda setting effects of the Internet in the 2000 presidential election in Taiwan.* Unpublished master's thesis. Shih-Hsin University, Taiwan.

Hsu, M. L. (1999). Issue agenda and source setting of AIDS news in Taiwan. *Mass Communication Research, 58,* 171–199.

Iwabuchi. (1986). Issue coverage and issue acquiring: Testing the agenda setting effects. *Journal of Keio University, 33,* 75–94.

Iyengar, S., & Kinder, D. (1987). *News that matters.* Chicago: University of Chicago Press.

Joe, S. S., & Kim, Y. J. (2004). A comparative study of online journalism in relation to agenda-setting function. *Korean Journal of Journalism and Communication Studies, 48,* 302–330.

Kawakami, K. (1999). The agenda setting function of news media and political advertising in the 1996 presidential election. *The Meji Gakuin Law Review, 66,* 157–178.

King, P. (1997). The press, candidate images, and voter perceptions. In M. E. McCombs, D. L. Shaw, & D. Weaver (Eds.), *Communication and democracy: Exploring the intellectual frontiers in agenda setting* (pp. 29–40). Mahwah, NJ: Lawrence Erlbaum.

Kiousis, S., Bantimaroudis, P., & Ban, H. (1999). Candidate image attributes: Experiments on the substantive dimension of second-level agenda setting. *Communication Research, 26*(4), 414–428.

Ku, G. T. (2002). The impact of website campaigning on traditional news media and public agenda: Based on agenda-setting. *Korean Journal of Journalism and Communication Studies, 46*(4), 46–75.

Kwansah-Aidoo, K. (2001). The appeal of qualitative methods to traditional agenda-setting research: An example from West Africa, *Gazette, 63,* 521–537.

Lee, D. H. (2007). A comparative study on the agenda setting effects of portal news and newspapers. *Korean Journal of Journalism and Communication Studies, 51*(3), 328–357.

Lee, W. S., Shim, J. C., & Park, Y. S. (2007). A time series analysis of the reciprocal agenda-setting relationships running among economic news, the state of the economy, consumer expectations, and consumer behaviors. *Korean Journal of Journalism and Communication Studies, 51*(4), 280–309.

Lee, G. H., Yoo, C. Y., & McCombs, M. (2007). The second level agenda-setting effects of environment issue: Regarding competing attributes in global warming issue. *Korean Journal of Journalism and Communication Studies, 51*(2), 153–180.

Li, Y. C., & King, P. T. (1996).Second level of image agenda setting in the 1994 Taipei mayor election. *Public Opinion Research Quarterly, 197,* 141–174.

Lopez-Escobar, E., Llamas, J. P., & McCombs, M. (1998). Agenda setting and community consensus: First and second-level effects. *International Journal of Public Opinion Research, 10*(4), 355–348.

McCombs, M. (2004). *Setting the agenda: The mass media and public opinion.* Cambridge: Polity Press.

McCombs, M., & Shaw, D. (1972). The agenda-setting function of mass media. *Public Opinion Quarterly, 36,* 176–187.

McLeod, J., Becker, L., & Byrnes, J. E. (1974). Another look at the agenda-setting function of the press. *Communication Research, 1,* 131–166.

Miller, J. (2007). Examining the mediators of agenda setting: A new experimental paradigm reveals the role of emotions. *Political Psychology, 28,* 689–717.

Mohamed, H. (2006). *Agenda-setting in a quasi-democratic country: A case study of Egypt.* 7th International Media Tenor Agenda Setting Conference. Bonn, Germany.

Monteiro, R. (2006). *La agenda setting en la televisión. Teorías, perspectivas y estudio de caso.* Río Cuarto, Argentina: Universidad Nacional de Río Cuarto.

Palmgreen, P., & Clarke, P. (1977). Agenda setting with local and national issues. *Communication Research, 4,* 435–452.

Peter, J. (2003). Country characteristics as contingent conditions of agenda setting: The moderating influence of polarized elite opinion. *Communication Research, 30,* 683–712.

Rey Lennon, F. (1998). *Argentina: Elecciones 1997. Los diarios y la campaña electoral.* Buenos Aires: The Freedom Forum y Universidad Austral.

Schönbach, K., & Semetko, H. A. (1992). Agenda setting, agenda-reinforcing or agenda-deflating? A study of the 1990 German national election. *Journalism Quarterly, 69,* 837–846.

Semetko, H., Blumler, J., Gurevitch, M., & Weaver, D. (1991). *The formation of campaign agendas: A comparative analysis of party and media roles in recent American and British elections.* Hillsdale, NJ: Lawrence Erlbaum.

Shaw, D., & McCombs, M. (Eds.). (1977). *The emergence of American political issues: The agenda-setting function of the press.* St. Paul, MN: West.

Smith, K. (1987). Newspaper coverage and public concern about community issues. *Journalism Monographs, 101,* 1–34.

Takeshita, T. (1993). Agenda-setting effects of the press in a Japanese local election. *Studies of Broadcasting, 29,* 193–216.

Takeshita, T., & Mikami, S. (1995). How did mass media influence the voters' choice in the 1993 general election in Japan? *Keio Communication Review, 17,* 27–41.

Tokinoya, H. (1983). Agenda-setting function of advertising. *Proceedings of Jyosei,* 16, 75–87.

Wang, T. L. (2000). Agenda-setting online: An experiment testing the effects of hyperlinks in online newspapers. *Southwestern Mass Communication Journal, 15*(2), 59–70.

Wang, T. T. (1999). *The image agenda setting-effect of the press in the 1996 presidential election in Taiwan.* Unpublished master's thesis, National Chengchi University, Taiwan.

Wanta, W., & Ghanem, S. (2000). Effects of agenda-setting. In J. Bryant & R. Carveth (Eds.), *Meta-analyses of media effects.* Mahwah, NJ: Lawrence Erlbaum.

Wanta, W., & Hu, Y. (1994). Time-lag differences in the agenda-setting process: An examination of five news media. *International Journal of Public Opinion Research, 6*(3), 225–240.

Weaver, D., Graber, D., McCombs, M., & Eyal, C. (1981). *Media agenda setting in a presidential election: Issues, images and interest.* New York: Praeger.

Winter, J., & Eyal, C. (1981). Agenda setting for the civil rights issue. *Public Opinion Quarterly, 45,* 376–383.

Yang, K. (2006). *Media coverage of establishment and non-establishment candidates in Argentina's 2003 presidential election.* Unpublished doctoral dissertation, Ohio State University.

Yuksel, E. (2003). *A second level agenda-setting study in the Turkish parliamentary elections.* 1st International Symposium, Communication in the Millennium: A Dialogue between Turkish and American Scholars. Austin, Texas.

Zaller, J. (1992). *The nature and origins of mass opinion.* New York: Cambridge University Press.

21

Political Communication across the World

Methodological Issues Involved in International Comparisons

Christina Holtz-Bacha
Department of Communication Studies
University of Erlangen–Nürnberg, Germany

Lynda Lee Kaid
Department of Telecommunication
University of Florida

Political communication refers to the communication sent out by or taking place among political actors: the messages of the political system and its individual parts to either the media or directly to the citizens and the politically relevant offerings of the media. A major part of research into political communication deals with election campaigns which present unique occasions for studying the strategies and effects of political communication. Because in elections the (re)distribution of power is at stake, insights into the mechanisms of communication processes during election campaigns is what usually most interests the political actors themselves. However, election campaigns are specific times of the political process and findings from respective studies do not necessarily apply to political communication in general.

Although the U.S. context has clearly dominated research on political communication, international political communication represents a central frontier necessary to advance our understanding of democratic processes. Methodological issues in international political communication research are derived from research that occurs in contexts outside the United States or in directly comparative international contexts. This chapter addresses examples of qualitative and quantitative research issues in both contexts, and some methodological issues that are not unique to either qualitative or quantitative research paradigms.

Regardless of the context or specific approach, the application of research methods to international political communication questions requires objectivity which can be difficult to establish and determine when multiple settings and researchers are involved. Regardless of research training and methodological background, individual researchers bring their own experiences and prejudices to any research project. One advantage of multi-country research teams is the ability to spread and diversify these experiences in ways that can enrich, rather than limit or restrict, research outcomes.

Political communication processes are influenced by both political and communication factors. Therefore, in addition to the specific object of a study, political communication research must take into account background factors deriving from the political system and the media/communication system. These variables differ from country to country, hinder or foster political communication, and thus can explain differences in the findings from replications or comparisons across countries. The role that communication plays for the political system in general or for a certain political event, how messages are designed and received, depends on the political system (democracies at different stages, presidential or parliamentary system, candidate or party system), the electoral system (majoritarian or proportional), the regulatory environment, cultural traditions, media system (role of public service versus private broadcasting), and the degree of professionalization of political actors (politicians, consultants, journalists).

CLASSIFICATIONS OF POLITICAL, MEDIA, AND CULTURAL SYSTEMS

Of tremendous value to researchers seeking to find ways of replicating and comparing political communication across countries have been the development of accepted standards for classifying and comparing the central features of political systems. For instance, countries have been classified according to the nature of their political and voting system (Reynold, Reilly, & Ellis, 2005–2006). Norris (2002) has also demonstrated that there is considerable variation in how political parties are regulated, funded, and allowed to pay for their campaign communication costs (Norris, 2002).

An early way of classifying philosophies of government/media interplay was the breakdown of press systems into authoritarian, libertarian, communist, and social responsibility models (Siebert, Peterson, & Schamm, 1956). Hallin and Mancini (2004) have provided a structure for analyzing the relationship between the government and press, classifying various Western democracies as Liberal, Democratic Corporatist, or Polarized Pluralism. These models account for four dimensions: (1) the development of media markets, (2) amount of political parallelism linking media and political parties or other political participants, (3) journalistic professionalism, and (4) the extent of state intervention in the media system. The Freedom House rates countries according to the level of press freedom they enjoy and classifies each as free, partly free, or not free (Freedom House, 2007).

Just as important as government-press philosophy, the operation of political communication within a society has a great deal to do with the legal and regulatory environment within which it operates. The evolution of public versus commercial broadcasting (Gunther & Mughan, 2000), for instance, as well as the development of dual systems of broadcasting (Holtz-Bacha, 1991) have affected the conduct of political communication. As Holtz-Bacha (2004c) points out, there have been substantial changes in the operation of public and commercial broadcasting in Europe in recent decades, and there is little doubt that the European Union's centralization of media regulation will have increasing implications for political communication.

Differences in political cultures represent another recurring concern in replications and comparisons of political communication research within and across countries and regions (Pfetsch, 2004). Almond and Verba's (1963) original conception of political culture referred to the understanding of the norms and values of the citizens of a state or region, and their comparative study provided broad and generalized distinctions among ideal types of political culture, distinguishing between parochial, subject, and participant orientations to culture. Hofstede's dimensions of political culture have provided ways of understanding communication in terms of power distance, uncertainty avoidance, individualism, masculinity, and long-term/short-term orientation in various cultures (Hofstede, 2001). Such classifications provide meaningful ways of helping political communication scholars analyze and compare various aspects of political communication among countries since, as Strömbäck and Kaid (2008) maintain, political systems, media systems, journalistic norms and values, style and character of campaigning, and voter characteristics all matter.

The methodological issues that involve these media and political system differences are not trivial ones. Beyond their obvious importance for understanding how political communication operates in varying settings and contexts, such differences are also important in making sampling decisions. The comparison of many countries often leads to a loss in detail. The researcher therefore has to decide whether the advantage lies in the inclusion of many countries or whether a restriction to only a small number of countries which can then be analyzed in more detail better serves the research interest. One question is left open, namely, whether political communication and electoral communication in particular, should and can be studied in nondemocratic regimes where power is not contested. Free competition among political actors and a free media system may be regarded as a *sine qua non* of political communication. In order to take into account its one-sided and coercive nature, political communication in a nondemocratic system is often called propaganda. In any case, the differences of structures and processes of political communication seem to make it difficult to compare democracies and nondemocratic systems. This is, of course, particularly true in relation to electoral communication, but the failure to tolerate competing viewpoints also makes it difficult to compare political leadership styles and the interactions between government and citizens in the everyday governing process of nondemocratic governments.

ISSUES IN RESEARCH ACROSS COUNTRIES

As political communication began to develop as a unique field of study in the middle of the last century, the first research projects with international focus could be found in the single country context. Holtz-Bacha (2004c) points out that these first advances came in Britain and Germany. Enterprising researchers in Great Britain used survey research techniques to analyze the role of communication in the 1959 and 1964 British General Elections (Blumler & McQuail, 1968; Trenaman & McQuail, 1961). In the 1970s in Germany, Elisabeth Noelle-Neumann began to develop her theory of public opinion, the "spiral of silence" (Noelle-Neumann, 1980). This early research in Europe was characterized by its focus on election communication, which continues to dominate international political communication research (Franklin, 1995; Holtz-Bacha, 2004c; Scammell, 1995; Schulz, 1997; Neveu, 1998; Wring, 1999).

Different approaches have been taken for cross-national research. Some publications are compilations of single-country studies on a certain topic and, preferably, follow the same structure. If readers are not left alone to draw conclusions on similarities and differences themselves, these are often discussed in a summary chapter. Other comparative studies compare political and media phenomena according to certain criteria. However, comparative research in the strictest sense applies the same instrument for the study of the same event or issue (cf., Holtz-Bacha, 2004a). The latter approach has major advantages. Harmonization of the research object and the research method allows for the best possible comparability. Although a plethora of individual studies has accumulated that tests or applies specific aspects of political communication in various national or region contexts, the most interesting international political communication research is research that applies theory and findings in comparative contexts. The obvious goal and challenge in comparative work is generalizability which can contribute to theory building. To achieve acceptable levels of generalizability, political communication researchers engaged in comparative research must deal with unique problems related to study design and sampling.

Study designs and methods are often compromised by the inability to develop consistent methodologies and data-gathering techniques across countries. Of critical importance in study design and sampling for comparative studies is the determination of countries or regions for analysis. Quantitative research lives on large numbers. It is therefore one of the major short-comings of cross-national research that the number of cases is limited where the unit of analysis is a country. Across five continents, there are almost 200 countries in the world. Depending on the particular research question, the researcher interested in international comparisons will select either a few countries (if the objective of the study is a detailed in-depth analysis) or all countries of a certain category (if the study seeks to make a statement about the occurrence of specific variables in countries that have a common characteristic, e.g., established democracies, African countries, and so on). If, however, the aim is to assess the state of a certain characteristic of, for instance, the media systems across the globe, a study will try to include all countries of the world and to be as complete as possible.

In practice, it is often difficult to apply ideal sampling techniques when using country as the unit of analysis in comparative research. While theoretically driven selection is desirable and researchers often seek groups of "most different" or "most similar" countries, inevitably access and convenience are often driving forces in the selection of cases (Wirth & Kolb, 2004). In election research in particular, it is often difficult to develop sets of countries whose elections occur in similar time and circumstance necessary to rule out the potential effect of other variables. The variation in election cycles and timing often make comparability very difficult. For instance, since the middle of the twentieth century, the United States and France held their presidential elections in the same year only once (1988), and thus this single incident provided an ideal time to compare political communication content and effects (Kaid, Gerstlé, & Sanders, 1991). European Parliamentary elections also provide a good research setting because similarity of time of election allows holding many other variables constant, but this advantage must be balanced against the election's classification as a "second-order" interntional election, which reduces public involvement and interest (Holtz-Bacha, 2004b).

Political communication research in international and comparative contexts also faces unique challenges relation to measurement and data analysis. In the remainder of this chapter, we consider these issues in relation to four specific topics in political communication: news exposure and coverage of political events, public opinion, political advertising, and political debates.

ISSUES IN COMPARATIVE NEWS EXPOSURE AND COVERAGE

Studies of news exposure and coverage of political events, particularly elections, has received considerable attention from political communication researchers. Most common are studies and descriptions of individual countries. Many publications compile single-country chapters on a common topic and along the same structure and then discuss differences and similarities in con-clusion. Examples of this approach include the multi-national studies of European Parliamentary elections (Blumler, 1983; Cayrol, 1991; Hallin & Mancini, 1984, 1992; Maier & Maier, 2007; Schulz & Blumler, 1994) and other groupings of country-specific election coverage (DeVreese, 2003b; Lange & Ward, 2004; Rössler, 2004; Semetko, Blumler, Gurevitch, & Weaver, 1991; Strömbäck & Kaid, 2009). A joint United States–French team attempted a more detailed comparative approach to the 1988 presidential elections in both countries (Kaid, Gerstlé, & Sanders, 1991), and researchers have compared the United States, Sweden, Spain, Germany, and Britain (Esser, 2000; Esser & D'Angelo, 2006; Esser, Reinemann, & Fan, 2001; Strömbäck & Dimitrova, 2006; Strömbäck & Luengo, 2006; Strömbäck & Shehata, 2007). Most of these studies lack any formal comparability of method or measurement. However, Semetko, who has been a leader in advancing comparative media use and effects research, successfully adapted survey data to compare media use and effects in the 1988 French and U.S. presidential elections (Semetko & Borquez, 1991).

Agenda setting research is a bright spot in these scenarios of comparative news studies. Since McCombs and Shaw (1972) first proclaimed that the issues covered by the media set the agenda of issues considered salient by the public, agenda-setting researchers have been able to apply the relatively simple methodology to media and public responses in many countries using similar method and measurement approaches (Weaver, McCombs, & Shaw, 2004). Agenda setting researchers generally use an open-ended question on issue importance when surveying the public and construct an agenda of issues covered by the media using content analysis. Evidence for the transfer of media salience to the public agenda has been validated for Germany (Brettschneider, 1994; Brosius & Kepplinger, 1990, 1992, 1995; Eichhorn, 1996; Huegel, Degenhardt, & Weiss, 1992; Mathes & Pfetsch, 1991; Schoenbach & Semetko, 1992), Israel (First, 1997), Italy (Mandelli, 1996; Semetko & Mandelli, 1997), Japan (Mikami, Takeshita, Nakada, & Kawabata, 1995; Ogawa, 2001; Takeshita, 1997), Hong Kong (Willnat & Zhu, 1996), Spain (McCombs, Lopez-Escobar, & Llamas, 2000), and Taiwan (King, 1997).

Methodological clarity has not been so easy to achieve in many other aspects of international research on news exposure and coverage. Researchers continue to have difficulties adopting and applying consistent and replicable measures of media use and exposure. Althaus and Tewksbury (2007) have recently reviewed some of the issues involved in media use measures used by the American National Election Studies, including questions about self-report reliability and measuring minutes versus days and other question time-reference issues (hours per day, days per week, typical days, typical weeks). They note that questions that ask respondents to report the "days in the past week" they are exposed to particular news media have proven unreliable (Bartels, 1993; Chang & Krosnick, 2003; Price, 1993). The proliferation of news media and alternative format programming has also complicated the measurement of exposure, both in the United States and other countries. Political media habits of young citizens are particularly difficult to measure as these groups have turned increasingly to alternative media formats for their political information (Zukin, Keeter, Andolina, & Delli-Carpini, 2006).

For these and other reasons, Althaus and Tewksbury (2007) reinforce the need, noted by other political communication researchers, to increase predictive power by measuring both attention and exposure to news (Chaffee & Schleuder, 1986; Drew & Weaver, 1990; Eveland, Shah, & Kwak, 2003) and broadening study of the campaign environment to include Internet, radio, and interpersonal media as well as newspapers and television. The need for broader and more comprehensive measures is essential when working cross-culturally because of the differing role played by the various media outside the United States. For instance, around the world, radio remains a more universally available medium than television and, although the Internet is becoming widely available in China, it is still subject to political censorship by the government.

News measurement is also affected by the concentration of political viewpoints in some areas of the world. For instance, the newspaper industry in the United States has been decreasing in political influence, and newspapers are no longer representative of opposing political views within geographic areas. One newspaper reader in Washington, D.C. will be exposed to about the same information as another newspaper reader in that city, as both will likely be consumers of *The*

Washington Post. However, one newspaper reader in London may be a reader of *The London Times* or the *Daily Telegraph* (both conservative leaning papers), whereas another reader may be getting very different information from reliance on the Labour-loyal *Daily Mirror.* Likewise, a reader of the Paris *Liberation* would receive a very left-leaning political view of events, in opposition to a reader of *Le Figaro* (right-leaning). Thus, media use measures outside the United States may require more differentiation of specific outlets, rather than just among media types in order to capture a true picture of a respondent's media exposure (Schmitt-Beck, 2004).

In addition to measuring exposure and media use in comparable ways, international news coverage research suffers from a lack of consistency in definitions and application of categories used in content analysis of news coverage. Many researchers have attempted to examine coverage patterns in individual countries, and some have made comparisons, but they have been hampered by a lack of common definitions and coding systems for fundamental concepts like "horserace" or "strategy" journalism (Kaid & Strömbäck, 2008).

These issues are compounded, of course, by the uneven political system, media system, and governmental regulation processes at work in various countries. In Russia, for instance, new press freedoms have not been realized as fully as once hoped, and content analysis of television election news continues to reveal political bias in coverage of the ruling party and little acknowledgement or willingness to legitimize the positions of the opposition (Oates & Roselle, 2000). Similar problems have been uncovered in other countries formerly in the Eastern bloc, making it difficult for researchers to measure accurately the amount of bias in coverage.

Research grounded in framing theory has also been hampered by a failure of researchers to adopt common definitions of framing patterns, making cross-national comparisons difficult. However, some real progress has been made in recent years by the development of types of frames that can and have been successfully applied across different types of content, different issues, and different countries. Good examples of such frame categories include the identification of generic frames such as conflict, human interest, and economic consequences (Semetko & Valkenburg, 2000), the development of episodic and thematic framing categories (Iyengar, 1991), and the distinction between frames as either ambiguous or substantive (Williams & Kaid, 2006, 2009; Williams et al., 2008). DeVreese (2003a; DeVreese & Boomgarden, 2003) has also successfully argued for the application of valence (negativity vs. positivity). Other generic frames which can be applied across countries have also emerged. Particularly useful have been the frames detailing political consequences (Kaid et al., 2005) and frames that have captured meta-communication or self-reflexive media coverage (Dimitrova, Kaid, Williams, & Trammell, 2005; Esser, 2000; Esser & D'Angelo, 2006; Esser, Reinemann, & Fan, 2001; Williams, 2008). The continued development of broad and generic frames is important, since as De Vreese (2003a) points out, analyzing generic news frames in different cultures facilitates the linkage between universally applicable frames and those that are unique to specific cultures.

News coverage analysis across countries also faces obvious challenges of language translation and equivalence (Wirth & Kolb, 2004). Even assuming the ability to use native speakers of a language as coders when multiple languages are involved, there are other important issues that may relate to translation and measurement. However, when comparing the amount of coverage in English with other languages, it may be important to remember also that space occupied in a written or printed text may not lend itself to equivalent measurement with Asian languages. For instance, column inches occupied or word totals, commonly used as measures of newspaper stories in English, do not work for Asian languages. Because Asian languages employ symbols that may represent concepts and relationships, rather than individual words, a Japanese newspaper story that says the same thing as an English language newspaper story may take up much less physical space on a page than the equivalent English language story.

The ability to make comparisons across countries also depends upon the degree of equivalence in journalistic values and professionalism (Donsbach & Patterson, 2004). Journalists in some countries are intertwined with the parties and government and do not function as independent or objective evaluators. In some cases, differences in journalistic norms and professionalism among countries, as well as differences in language structures and organization, may account for differences in news presentation (Peter & DeVreese, 2003; Weaver, McCombs, & Shaw, 2004). Such differences may even lead to different news story structures which make it difficult for researchers to compare news coverage equivalence. For instance, in the English language journalistic objectivity is embedded in journalistic traditions and norms and is often said to be exemplified in the "inverted pyramid" style of journalistic writing, whereby the most important information is provided first in a hard news story and then followed by other details. However, the selection of what goes first (is most important) can also be a value-laden assessment that may differ among cultures. Many languages use the headline/lead synopsis format, but it is common in French and some other languages to provide background information and setting with an interpretive orientation first, leading to different interpretations of a story (Thomson, White, & Kitley, 2008). Such situations may also have implications for sampling and unit of analysis decisions (i.e., using headlines or first pages for story coding or selection, as opposed to the entirety of a story as continued to subsequent pages).

METHODOLOGICAL ISSUES IN INTERNATIONAL PUBLIC OPINION RESEARCH

Communication scholars are interested not only in how media and interpersonal communication present political issues and events, but also in how that communication may affect the development of public opinion, including citizen knowledge levels and attitudes toward political leaders, issues, and events. Public opinion research across cultures raises many difficult issues. In some parts of the world, Asia for instance, it is often not possible to gather public opinion data at all. As Willnat and Aw (2004, p. 480) point out, "the restricted freedom to conduct political communication studies in Asia is compounded by the small research community, the often limited financial and institutional support, and the size and quality of research infrastructure and personnel."

Even in areas where public opinion polling is permitted, cultural and political norms may limit the applicability and interpretation of results. Measurement of public opinion related to the "spiral of silence" theory presents good examples of this problem. Developed originally in Germany (Noelle-Neumann, 1980; Noelle-Neumann & Petersen, 2004), the spiral of silence theory asserts that citizens who feel their opinions run counter to those of the majority do not express their opinions out of a fear of isolation. While efforts have been made to test the spiral of silence theory outside Germany (Glynn, Hayes, & Shanahan, 1997), empirical testing across cultures has been difficult (Salmon & Glynn, 1996). For one thing, it seems likely that the willingness to conform to a majority view and the fear of isolation from speaking out has cultural aspects that may determine the applicability of the theory in different cultures (Scheufele & Moy, 2000). In Japan, for instance, as with other Asian cultures, citizens tend to be socially cohesive and the expression of political views of any kind is not likely due to the desire to avoid open confrontations (Ito, 2000). Spencer and Croucher (2008) attributed differences in French and Spanish respondents' willingness to speak up about ETA terrorism to cultural differences. Spanish citizens holding a minority view were more fearful of isolation from the perceived majority view than were French citizens. Hofstede's (2001) dimensions of cultural behavior are relevant here, since a collectivistic society would probably be much more likely to exhibit spiral of silence behavior, but these same predispositions might make measurement scenarios difficult (Perry & Gonzenbach, 2000).

A related issue has centered on the best way to measure a respondent's willingness to speak up or risk isolation. Some research scenarios have relied on the presentation of hypothetical situations, which Noelle-Neumann and Petersen (2004) argue do not present a sufficiently compelling context to trigger the fear of isolation. They suggest that the issue involved must be one that resides in the context of strong moral opinions that the respondent perceives as creating a strong opinion climate, and thus a strong threat of isolation. Scheufele, Shanahan, and Lee (2001) have, in fact, found experimental verification of the superiority of real versus hypothetical situations for demonstrating the spiral of silence theory. Hayes, Glynn, and Shanahan (2005) developed a "willingness to self-censor" scale to measure the degree of fear of speaking up, but the scale has not been tested across cultures. Liu (2006) attempted to solve the cross-national scenario problem by using "an unspecified controversial issue" and measuring an individual's reactions in both a minority and majority context.

MEASURING POLITICAL ADVERTISING ACROSS CULTURES

The last three decades have seen a growing interest in comparing styles and effects of political advertising across countries. Political advertising is a means through which parties and candidates present themselves to the electorate, primarily through the mass media. Political ads only appear in systems where the distribution of political power is contested and determined in elections and in which parties or candidates compete with each other. Since the 1950s, in the United States, ever increasing amounts of money have gone into TV ads, devouring large percentages of campaign budgets (Devlin, 2005; Kaid, 2004b). The popularity of ads in the U.S. and the fact that the decision about the design and contents of ads can be decided directly by the candidates and parties without the risk of their messages being changed or commented upon by journalists (as is the case in the so-called free media), has attracted politicians everywhere (Plasser, 2002). The spread of political advertising has been one of the signs attributable to what has been described by Mancini and Swanson (1996, p. 4) as "Americanization," a process by which "democracies around the world [are] becoming more and more Americanized as candidates, political parties, and news media take cues from their counterparts in the United States."

However, countries differ considerably in the role television advertising plays in electoral campaigns. There are many countries that do not have electoral TV advertising at all, either because it is prohibited or because political actors (parties, candidates) agree not to use this kind of advertising channel for their campaigns. In many countries, political broadcast slots are allocated free to qualified parties or candidates. Restrictions on broadcast time, whether provided free or offered for purchase, abound. Many countries only permit political advertising during election campaigns, usually during the so-called *hot* campaign phase, which may be the last four to six weeks before Election Day. Countries may also limit the amount of money parties are allowed to spend for their campaign or, specifically, for ads; some have released detailed provisions for the contents of electoral broadcasts. Any study of political advertising in an internationally comparative perspective must take into account the differences in political structures and processes, in political culture, and in the organization of the media (cf. Hallin & Mancini, 2004; Swanson & Mancini, 1996). These variables and their specific interrelations provide for a distinctive national background against which the regulations for political advertising, the role of television spots in campaign strategies, and findings about effects of political advertising must be interpreted.

Comparing Political Advertising Styles and Content

Given the differences in political and media system variables, a first consideration in comparisons of political advertising style and content across countries must be a consensus on the object to be studied and whether it is at all comparable across countries. In fact, for political ads on TV, differences start at the level of terminology. In the United States, the usual term is ads. Electoral ads are thus equated with commercial ads and therefore also referred to as "paid media" since time must be purchased and the electoral broadcasts are therefore usually quite short. In other countries, particularly in those where broadcast time cannot be purchased, researchers tend to avoid the term ads. In Western European countries where public broadcasting has long dominated the market and where the public service philosophy is still present, parties and candidates are usually provided with free broadcasting time to be used for their advertising. Compared to the United States, free time segments are often, and in some cases considerably, longer. Researchers from these countries often shrink back from calling the electoral spots *ads* and instead use the term *political electoral broadcasts* (e.g., PEBs in the United Kingdom), *polispots* (Greece), or, in the English translation of the Italian term, *independently produced political messages* (Italy). However, if a country allows electoral advertising on public service broadcasting and on commercial broadcasting, as, for instance, in Germany, it still remains an open question whether the broadcasts on both public and private commercial systems are indeed that much different. In fact, German parties tend to use the same ad for both broadcasting systems and only shorten it for broadcasting on commercial television.

Another consideration is the determination of who is responsible for the advertising, to whom or what entity the message can be attributed. The political system and the electoral system go hand-in-hand with the role of parties. In this respect, the United States is an exceptional case in which candidates, parties, independent interest groups, and even individual citizens may sponsor ads which are generally directed in favor of or in opposition to a specific candidate. In the United States the candidate orientation has led to a decline of parties. Elsewhere, the parties remain in a dominant role. This is definitely the case for parliamentary elections. In spite of trends towards personalization and a focus on individual candidates, campaigning overwhelmingly lies in the hands of parties (Holtz-Bacha & Kaid, 2006, p. 7). The strong role parties play in most political systems is also indicated by the fact that, even in presidential elections, sponsorship of television advertising does not lie with the candidates everywhere. In many countries, TV ads are regarded as serving the information needs of voters, facilitating the formation of electoral preferences, and broadcast time is therefore provided free during elections.

The electoral system of a country naturally has a major impact on campaign strategies and thus on the design of electoral advertising (cf. Roper, Holtz-Bacha, & Mazzoleni, 2004). Strategies will vary according to the number and size of parties running in a race, their relation to each other (e.g., single-party or coalition governments) and thresholds that parties have to overcome in order to be represented in the parliament. Where parties are provided with free broadcast time but not on a strictly equal basis, the strength of a party in earlier elections is often taken as a criterion for a graded allocation (Holtz-Bacha & Kaid, 2006).

Despite these differences in political and media systems, researchers have had some success in comparing the style and content of ads across culture. *Videostyle*, originally developed to describe the verbal, nonverbal, and production characteristics used by American candidates to present themselves through political advertising (Kaid & Davidson, 1986; Kaid & Johnston, 2001), has been adapted and applied to describe political broadcasts in a number of countries in Europe, Asia, and Latin America (Carlson, 2001; Hodess, Tedesco, & Kaid, 2000; Holtz-Bacha, Kaid, & Johnston, 1994; Holtz-Bacha & Kaid, 1993, 1995; Johnston, 1991; Kaid, Gerstlé, &

Sanders, 1991; Kaid & Holtz-Bacha, 1995; Kaid & Tedesco, 1993; Lee, Tak, & Kaid, 1998; Tak, Kaid, & Lee, 1997). Through such analysis, researchers have been able to compare across countries the differences and similarities in political advertising emphasis on specific issues, on candidate qualities, on production styles, on negative versus positive content, in how frequently candidates speak for themselves in their ads, and other content aspects. Researchers have used other methods to study ads from different perspectives. For instance, Griffin and Kagan (1996) compared how candidates and parties in the United States and Israel used visual and mythic techniques in political ads to communicate cultural identities, and Chang (2000) compared cross-cultural aspects of U.S. and Taiwanese campaign spots.

While videostyle has been successfully adapted to measure style and effects of ads across countries, problems with its application have been encountered. One important difficulty has been the identification of the proper unit of analysis for content analysis of television spots across countries. Videostyle, as originally developed, used the entire spot as the unit of analysis, and all categories related to verbal, nonverbal, and production characteristics of U.S. ads were applied to each individual spot in its entirety. If content involved more than one aspect of a category, coders were instructed to record the one that was "dominant." Since most U.S. ads are short (30 seconds or less), this was usually not difficult, and high intercoder reliability was usually achieved with this coding system. However, as mentioned above, many other countries use ad lengths that are much longer than the U.S. model, often as long as five, ten or fifteen minutes. In such situations, much more content can be and is conveyed, and it is sometimes difficult to determine a single, dominant characteristic to meet the demands of videostyle's category assignment. For instance, a five-minute ad may discuss many more issues, may use combinations of production techniques for visual interest, and may involve many different speakers with different characteristics. In such situations, coding the spot as a single unit of analysis may be very difficult, even misleading, and can lead to low intercoder reliability.

One solution to this problem, successfully employed by Holtz-Bacha (2000; Esser, Holtz-Bacha, & Lessinger, 2008), has been to divide an ad into smaller units or scenes (defined as a continuum of place, time, action, personnel, or format) and code each unit individually. Because the length of an individual scene is determined on the basis of the visual part of the spot, minor differences easily occur and can also provide for insufficient intercoder reliability. Lee and Benoit (2004) resolved the problem when comparing U.S. and Korean ads by using the *theme* as the unit of analysis, thus coding every theme in each spot as a separate unit. Thus, the unit of analysis to which categories are applied in such content analysis varies along a continuum from a very literal and explicit unit of content (a whole spot) to a more implicit or latent unit of content (a theme). Of course, the problem with using units that tend toward the latent end of this continuum is that it may make it difficult to draw conclusions and make comparisons that can be useful across countries and cultures.

Measuring Effects of Political Advertising across Countries

Fewer attempts have been made to measure the effects of political advertising across countries. Political and media system differences obviously play a role here as well. One difficulty in making such comparisons is the lack of uniform methods for measuring effects. Knowledge effects often require specialized instruments that must be adapted to different electoral situations, although some studies have been successful in using generic scales that ask respondents to self-report how much they have learned from exposure to particular campaigns or specific campaign messages. Such measures can be used in survey or experimental settings.

Measures of candidate image or personal qualities also offer possibilities for measuring advertising effects across countries. One clear goal of most electoral advertising, regardless of country or culture, is to enhance the favorable image of a party or its candidate and/or to diminish positive evaluation of the opposing candidate or party. Semantic scales provide a useful mechanism for such measures and have proven adaptable across countries. For instance, an image evaluation scale originally developed for use in the United States (Kaid, 2004a; Kaid & Hirsch, 1973; Sanders & Pace, 1977) has been successfully used in a variety of countries in Europe, Asia, and Latin America. This twelve-item scale was developed to represent candidate characteristics based on the original measurement scales developed to measure semantic meaning by Osgood, Suci, and Tannenbaum (1957) and derived also by McCroskey (1966) to measure source credibility. The scale generally achieves high reliability even when transferred and applied across countries. The scale has been used to measure candidate images and make comparisons of favorable and unfavorable reactions to candidates in the United States (Kaid & Chanslor, 2004), France (Gagnere & Kaid, 2006, Kaid, 1991; Kaid & Gagnere, 2006), Germany (Kaid & Holtz-Bacha, 1993a, 1993b; Kaid & Tedesco, 1999a), Italy (Mazzoleni & Roper, 1995), Poland (Cwalina & Falkowski, 2000), Romania (Miron, Marinescu, & McKinnon, 1999), Britain (Kaid & Holtz-Bacha, 2006), and to make comparisons across a number of these countries (Cwalina, Falkowski & Kaid, 2000, 2005; Kaid, 1999; Kaid & Holtz-Bacha, 2006).

A few problems have arisen with use of the scale across countries, illustrating issues that are important to consider when attempting to transfer measurement items across countries. First, of course, is the difficulty of achieving precise and comparable translations of the adjective pairs used in the scale. For instance, in Romania the term for *competent* worked better than the translation of *qualified* (Miron, Marinescu, & McKinnon, 1999). A second consideration has been the direction of the scoring for the adjective pairs. While honest is always more positive than dishonest and qualified is always superior to unqualified, regardless of country or culture, some concepts in the scale are more subtle and invoke less uniform positive/negative reactions across cultures. One example is aggressive–unaggressive. In the United States aggressiveness, when displayed by politicians in pursuit of policies and viewpoints, is generally considered a positive trait. However, in Germany, particularly after the tragedies of the World Wars in the twentieth century, aggressiveness in politics is often viewed with suspicion and negativity. Although this is not universally true for all Germans or all Americans, the scoring of the positive and negative directions must frequently be reversed. Researchers must be constantly on guard for such situations when attempting to make transfers of language and rating scales across cultures.

One way to deal with the problem of measuring advertising effects across cultures is to adopt a system of measuring effects that is not affected by language differences. ADSAM, based on Lang's (1985) Self-Assessment Manikin Scales, has been employed to measure emotional responses to advertising messages across cultures. The nonverbal system of measurement assesses responses to visual representations of the three components of emotion: Pleasure, which measures the positive/negative aspect of feelings; Arousal, which represents intensity or involvement of feelings; and Dominance, which relates to the extent that one feels empowered (Morris, 1995). Levels of each of the three emotional components are depicted by visual symbols that require no translation.[1]

MEASURING POLITICAL DEBATES ACROSS CULTURES

The expansion of televised debates in many democratic systems has also been a growing feature of mediated campaigning. Since the earliest television debates in the United States in 1960, debates have evolved into an almost institutionalized element of the U.S. campaigns, not just at the presidential level but at all levels of government. Other countries, including France, Germany, South Korea, Canada, Australia, New Zealand, and Israel have adopted various forms of mediated debates that have attracted the interest of scholars (Baker & Norpoth, 1981; Blais & Boyer, 1996; Coleman, 2000; Faas & Maier, 2004; Kang & Hoon, 1999; Legavre, 1991; Maurer, 2007; Maurer & Reinemann, 2003; Schrott, 1990); however, as McKinney and Carlin (2004) note, very few researchers have attempted comparisons of debates in a cross-national context. Exceptions are a comparative study of the 1980 U.S. and West German debates (Schrott, 1984), an analysis of the U.S. presidential and Greek prime minister debates in 2000 (Matsaganis & Weingarten, 2001), discussion of debates in Sweden and the United States (Asard & Gronbeck, 2000), and a comparison of event and production factors in the 1988 U.S. and French campaign debates (Downs, 1991). However, none of these studies used the same methodological approaches that allowed for comparisons across countries.

Benoit, who has applied his functional classification system to U.S. debates, has also applied the same system to debates in the Ukraine (Benoit & Klyukovski, 2006), and used the system to compare debates in the United States with South Korea (Lee & Benoit, 2005) and Israel (Benoit & Sheafer, 2006). The researchers, using functional theory for cross-cultural purposes, argue that this classification system is transferable across cultures because the concepts (acclaim, attack, defend) are simple, and can be easily operationalized and defined across languages and cultures (Benoit & Sheafer, 2006). However, even with simple concepts such as those in functional theory, cultural aspects of some countries may not lend themselves to universal application, as Isotalus (2008) has pointed out in relation to debates in Finland.

Another method that has been used to measure responses to debates and shows promise for use in international research is the real-time-response (RTR) or continuous dial response system (Maier, Maier, Maurer, Reinemann, & Meyer, 2009). Originally called "program analyzers" or "perception analyzers," continuous response technology was developed by Lazarsfeld and Stanton (Levy, 1982; Millard, 1992) to evaluate radio programs. The current technology employs various handheld devices on which respondents register their immediate responses to programming as they see or hear it, allowing researchers to pinpoint with precision the aspects of a candidate's message that register the most favorable responses from voters. Campaign consultants use these devices to "instantaneously monitor respondents' thoughts" in relation to campaign messages (Malone, 1988, p. 34).

In the United States, researchers have used these devices most often to track voter reactions to debates (Bystrom, Roper, Gobetz, Massey, & Beall, 1991; McKinnon & Tedesco, 1999; McKinnon, Tedesco, & Kaid, 1993; Steeper, 1978) and political advertising (Biocca, 1991; Kaid, 1994, 1996, 2008; Kaid & Tedesco, 1999b; Tedesco, 2002). Outside the United States, German researchers have productively employed similar technology to measure moment-to-moment responses to political messages. Detailed studies of debates in Germany have allowed researchers to pinpoint the success and failure of positive and negative comments, identify emotional appeals that are received favorably by the audience, and determine the specific issues where candidates have been able to impress audiences and convey their views to voters (Maier, 2007; Maier & Faas, 2004; Maier, Maurer, Reinemann, & Faas, 2006; Maurer, 2006; Maurer & Reinemann, 2004). Applications of the computer response technology have also been applied to measure responses to political ads in Germany (Kaid, 1996; Maier & Maier, 2007). Since these devices work similarly from one culture to another, registering automatic responses that do not require explicit semantic input, they may be particularly useful in making comparisons across cultures. The same may be true for technological measures that record psychophysiological responses (galvanic skin response, brain imaging, heart rate, facial muscle activation, eye-tracking) to media messages with political content (see Chapter 27, this volume).

CONCLUSION

Many other research areas in political communication confront problems similar to those discussed above. Some of these have long traditions of international and comparative research. Diffusion of innovation researchers, for instance, have dealt with and tested research in numerous countries, and the international context is integral to work in this area (Rogers, 1995). A key concept in diffusion, opinion leadership, has been widely used, and measures testing its validity and reliability have been developed across countries and languages (Nisbet, 2006).

Other approaches to studying political communication across and within different countries have been developing, and these often rely on differing research traditions that characterize research in various parts of the world. For instance, in recent decades the growth of quantitative methods for analyzing political language has characterized American approaches to political rhetoric, campaigns, debates, and ads, aided by application of sophisticated computerized word and language analysis (Coleman & Manna, 2007; Hart, 1984; Hart & Jarvis, 1997). On the flip side, European traditions have favored more qualitative and interpretive approaches to political language analysis (Young, Bourne, & Younane, 2007). Political language researchers on both sides of the Atlantic have been aided by the increased availability of digital formats of recordings and transcripts, online media databases, and scanners that have made international research more feasible, efficient, accurate, and less time-bound (Young, Bourne, & Younane, 2007).

Many other methodological challenges certainly confront researchers who are willing to take them on. The analysis and interpretation of visual and nonverbal communication across cultures, for instance, presents many challenges (Graber, 2004; Wirth & Kolb, 2004). Researchers who have been successful in confronting such issues have generally benefited from the formation of international research teams, since involving colleagues from countries with "local" expertise may help to avoid misinterpretations and produce more robust findings and accurate insights.

NOTE

1. The ADSAM visual measures (see Lang, 1985; Morris, 1995). The first row represents Pleasure (from high to low), the second row indicates Arousal (from high to low), and the third row represents Dominance (from low to high). More information about the use of these scales for measuring emotional reactions across cultures can be found at http://www.adsam.com.

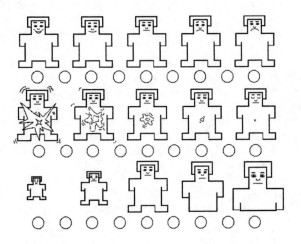

REFERENCES

Almond, G. A., & Verba, S. (1963). *The civic culture: Political attitudes and democracy in five nations.* Princeton, NJ: Princeton University Press.

Althaus, S. L., & Tewksbury, D. H. (2007, May 2). *Toward a new generation of media use measures for the ANES.* Report to the Board of Overseers, American National Election Studies. Retrieved April 23, 2008, from http://www.electionstudies.org/resources/papers/Pilot2006/nes011903.pdf.

Asard, E., & Gronbeck, B. E. (2000). Televised party leader and presidential candidate debates in Sweden and the United States. In T. A. Holihan (Ed.), *Argument at century's end: Reflecting on the past and envisioning the future* (pp. 394–402). Annandale, VA: National Communication Association.

Baker, K. L., & Norpoth, H. (1981). Candidates on television: The 1972 electoral debates in West Germany. *Public Opinion Quarterly, 45,* 329–345.

Bartels, L. M. (1993). Messages received: The political impact of media exposure. *American Political Science Review, 87*(2), 267–285.

Benoit, W. L., & Klyukovski, A. A. (2006). A functional analysis of 2004 Ukrainian presidential debates. *Argumentation, 20* (2), 209–225.

Benoit, W. L., & Sheafer, T. (2006). Functional theory and political discourse: Televised debates in Israel and the United States. *Journalism & Mass Communication Quarterly, 83*(2), 281–297.

Biocca, F. (1991). Models of a successful and unsuccessful ad: An exploratory analysis. In F. Biocca (Ed.), *Television and political advertising, vol. 1: Psychological Processes* (pp. 91–122). Hillsdale, NJ: Lawrence Erlbaum.

Blais, A., & Boyer, M. M. (1996). Assessing the impact of televised debates: The case of the 1988 Canadian election. *British Journal of Political Science, 26,* 143–164.

Blumler, J. G. (Ed.). (1983). *Communicating to voters. Television in the first European parliamentary elections.* London: Sage.

Blumler, J. G., & McQuail, D. (1968). *Television in politics.* London: Faber and Faber.

Brettschneider, F. (1994). Agenda setting. Forschungsstand und politische konsequenzen. In M. Jaeckel & P. Winterhoff-Spurk (Eds.), *Politik und medien: Analysen zur entwicklung der politischen kommunikation* (pp. 211–229). Berlin: Vistas.

Brosius, H.-B., & Kepplinger, H. M. (1990). The agenda-setting function of television: Static and dynamic views. *Communication Research, 17,* 183–211.

Brosius, H.-B., & Kepplinger, H. M. (1992). Linear and nonlinear models of agenda setting in television. *Journal of Broadcasting & Electronic Media, 36,* 5–24.

Brosius, H.-B., & Kepplinger, H. M. (1995). Killer and victim issues: Issue competition in the agenda-setting process of German television. *International Journal of Public Opinion Research, 7,* 211–231.

Bystrom, D., Roper, C., Gobetz, R., Massey, T., & Beall, C. (1991). The effects of a televised gubernatorial debate. *Political Communication Review, 16,* 57–80.

Carlson, T. (2001). Gender and political advertising across cultures. *European Journal of Communication, 16,* 131–154.

Cayrol, R. (1991). European elections and the pre-electoral period: Media use and campaign evaluations. *European Journal of Political Research, 19,* 17–29.

Chaffee, S. H., & Schleuder, J. (1986). Measurement and effects of attention to media news. *Human Communication Research, 13,* 76–107.

Chang, C. (2000). Political advertising in Taiwan and the U.S.: A cross-cultural comparison of the 1996 presidential election campaigns. *Asian Journal of Communication, 10,* 1–17.

Chang, L., & Krosnick, J. A. (2003). Measuring the frequency of regular behaviors: Comparing the "typical week" to the "past week." *Sociological Methodology, 33,* 55–80.

Coleman, J. J., & Manna, P. (2007). Above the fray? The use of party system references in presidential rhetoric. *Presidential Studies Quarterly, 37,* 399–426.

Coleman, S. (Ed.). (2000). *Televised election debates: International perspectives.* New York: St. Martin's Press.

Cwalina, W. & Falkowski, A. (2000). Psychological mechanisms of political persuasion: The influence of political advertising on voting behaviour. *Polish Psychological Bulletin, 31*(3), 203–222.

Cwalina, W., Falkowski, A., & Kaid, L. L. (2000). Role of advertising in forming the image of politicians: Comparative analysis of Poland, France, and Germany. *Media Psychology, 2*, 119–146.

Cwalina, W., Falkowski, A., & Kaid, L. L. (2005). Advertising and the image of politicians in evolving and established democracies: Comparative study of the Polish and U.S. presidential elections in 2000. *Journal of Political Marketing, 4*(2/3), 29–54.

Devlin, L. P. (2005, October). Contrasts in presidential campaign commercials of 2004. *American Behavioral Scientist, 49*, 279–313.

de Vreese, C. (2003a, April). Communicating Europe. Paper produced by the Next Generation Democracy: Legitimacy in Network Europe Project. London: Foreign Policy Center. Retrieved May 4, 2005, from http://fpc.org.uk/publications/73.

de Vreese, C. H. (2003b). Television reporting of second-order elections. *Journalism Studies, 4*(2), 183–198.

de Vreese, C. H., & Boomgarden, H. (2003, May). *Valenced news frames. Linking content analysis and experimental evidence on the support for the EU.* Paper presented at the annual meeting of the International Communication Association, San Diego, CA.

Dimitrova, D. V., Kaid, L. L., Williams, A. P., & Trammell, K. D. (2005). War on the Web: The immediate news framing of Gulf War II. *Harvard International Journal of Press/Politics, 10*, 22–24.

Donsbach, W., & Patterson, T. E. (2004). Political news journalism: Partisanship, professionalization, and political roles in five countries. In F. Esser & B. Pfetsch (Eds.), *Comparing political communication: Theories, cases and challenges* (pp. 251–270). Cambridge: Cambridge University Press.

Downs, V. C. (1991). The debate about debates: Production and event factors in the 1988 broadcast debates in France and the United States. In L. L. Kaid, J. Gerstlé, & K. Sanders (Eds.), *Mediated politics in two cultures: Presidential campaigning in the United States and France* (pp. 184–193). New York: Praeger.

Drew, D., & Weaver, D. (1990). Media attention, media exposure, and media effects. *Journalism Quarterly, 67*, 740–748.

Eichhorn, W. (1996). *Agenda-setting prozesse: Eine theoretische analyse individueller und gesellschaftlicher themenstrukturierung.* Munich: Reinhard Fischer.

Esser, F. (2000). Tabloidization of news: A comparative analysis of Anglo-American and German press journalism. *European Journal of Communication, 14*, 291–324.

Esser, F., & D'Angelo, P. (2006). Framing the press and the publicity process in U.S., British, and German general election campaigns: A comparative study of metacoverage. *Harvard International Journal of Press/Politics, 11*(3), 44–66.

Esser, F., Holtz-Bacha, C., & Lessinger, E.-M. (2008). A low-key affair: German parties' TV advertising. In L. L. Kaid (Ed.), *The EU expansion: Communicating shared sovereignty in the parliamentary elections* (pp. 65–84). New York: Peter Lang.

Esser, F., Reinemann, C., & Fan, D. (2001). Spin doctors in the United States, Great Britain, and Germany: Metacommunication about media manipulation. *Harvard International Journal of Press/Politics, 6*(1), 16–45.

Eveland, W. R. Jr., Shah, D. V., & Kwak, N. (2003). Assessing causality in the cognitive mediation model: A panel study of motivations, information processing, and learning during campaign 2000. *Communication Research, 30*, 359–386.

Faas, T., & Maier, J. (2004). Chancellor candidates in the 2002 televised debates. *German Politics, 13*, 300–316.

First, A. (1997). Television and the construction of social reality: An Israeli case study. In M. McCombs, D. L. Shaw, & D. Weaver (Eds.), *Communication and democracy* (pp. 41–50). Mahwah, NJ: Lawrence Erlbaum.

Franklin, B. (1995). Political communication scholarship in Britain. *Political Communication, 12*, 223–238.

Freedom House. (2007). *Global press freedom 2007: Growing threats to media independence.* Washington, DC: Freedom House. Retrieved September 8, 2007, from http://www.freedomhouse.org/uploads/fop/2007/pfscharts.pdf.

Gagnere, N., & Kaid, L. L. (2006). Political broadcasting in the 2002 French presidential election: Appeals and effects for young voters. In A. Schorr & S. Seltmann (Eds.), *Changing media markets in Europe and abroad: New ways of handling information and entertainment content* (pp. 3–22). New York/Lengerich: Pabst Science Publishers.

Glynn, C. J., Hayes, A. F., & Shanahan, J. (1997). Perceived support for one's opinions and willingness to speak out: A meta-analysis of survey studies on the "spiral of silence." *Public Opinion Quarterly, 61,* 457–463.

Graber, D. A. (2004). Methodological developments in research. In L. L. Kaid (Ed.), *Handbook of political communication research* (pp. 45–67). Mahwah, NJ: Lawrence Erlbaum.

Griffin, M., & Kagan, S. (1996). Picturing culture in political spots: 1992 campaigns in Israel and the United States. *Political Communication, 13,* 43–61.

Gunther, R., & Mughan, A. (Eds.). (2000). *Democracy and the media. A comparative perspective.* Cambridge: Cambridge University Press.

Hallin, D., & Mancini, P. (1984). Speaking of the president: Political structure and representational form in the U.S. and Italian television news. *Theory and Society, 13,* 829–850.

Hallin, D., & Mancini, P. (1992). The summit as media event: The Reagan/Gorbachev meetings on U.S., Italian, and Soviet television. In J. G. Blumler, J. M. McLeod, & K. E. Rosengren (Eds.), *Comparatively speaking: Communication and culture across space and time* (pp. 121–139). Newbury Park, CA: Sage.

Hallin, D. C., & Mancini, P. (2004). *Comparing media systems. Three models of media and politics.* Cambridge: Cambridge University Press.

Hart, R. P. (1984). *Verbal style and the presidency.* New York: Academic Press.

Hart, R. P., & Jarvis, S. E. (1997). Political debate: Forms, styles, and media. *American Behavioral Scientist, 40,* 1095–1122.

Hayes, A. F., Glynn, C. J., & Shanahan, J. (2005). Validating the willingness to self censor scale: Individual differences in the effect of the climate of opinion on opinion expression. *International Journal of Public Opinion Research, 17*(4), 443–455.

Hodess, R., Tedesco, J. C., & Kaid, L. L. (2000). British Party Election Broadcasts: A comparison of 1992 and 1997. *Harvard Journal of International Press/Politics, 5*(4), 55–70.

Hofstede, G. (2001). *Culture and organizations: Comparing values, behaviors and organizations across nations* (2nd ed.). Thousand Oaks, CA: Sage.

Holtz-Bacha, C. (1991). The road to commercialization: From public monopoly to a dual broadcasting system in Germany. *European Journal of Communication, 6,* 223–233.

Holtz-Bacha, C. (2000). *Wahlwerbung als politische kultur: Partienspots im fernsehen 1957–1998.* Wiesbaden: Westdeutscher Verlag.

Holtz-Bacha, C. (2004a). Germany: The "German Model" and its intricacies. In J. Roper, C. Holtz-Bacha, & G. Mazzoleni; *The politics of representation: Election campaigning and proportional representation* (pp. 9–27). New York: Peter Lang.

Holtz-Bacha, C. (2004b). Political campaign communication: Conditional convergence of modern media elections. In F. Esser & B. Pfetsch (Eds.), *Comparing political communication: Theories, cases and challenges* (pp. 213–230). Cambridge: Cambridge University Press.

Holtz-Bacha, C. (2004c). Political communication research abroad: Europe. In L. L. Kaid (Ed.), *The handbook of political communication research* (pp. 463–477). Mahwah, NJ: Lawrence Erlbaum.

Holtz-Bacha, C., & Kaid, L. L. (1993). Wahlspots im Fernsehen: Eine Analyse der Parteienwerbung zur Bundestagwahl 1990. In C. Holtz-Bacha & L. L. Kaid (Eds.), *Die Massenmedien im Wahlkampf* (pp. 46–71). Opladen, Germany: Westdeutscher Verlag.

Holtz-Bacha, C., & Kaid, L. L. (1995). Television spots in German national elections: Content and effects. In L. L. Kaid & C. Holtz-Bacha (Eds.), *Political advertising in Western democracies* (pp. 61–88). Thousand Oaks, CA: Sage.

Holtz-Bacha, C., & Kaid, L. L. (2006). Political advertising in international comparison. In L. L. Kaid & C. Holtz-Bacha (Eds.), *The Sage handbook of political advertising* (pp. 3–13). Thousand Oaks, CA: Sage.

Holtz-Bacha, C., Kaid, L. L., & Johnston, A. (1994). Political television advertising in Western democracies: A comparison of campaign broadcasts in the U.S., Germany and France. *Political Communication, 11*, 67–80.

Huegel, R., Degenhardt, W., & Weiss, H.-J. (1992). Strukturgleichungsmodelle für die analyse des agenda setting-prozesses. In W. Schulz (Ed.), *Medienwirkungen einflüsse von presse, radio und fernsehen auf individuum und gesellschaft* (pp. 143–159). Weinheim: VCH Verlagsgesellschaft.

Isotalus, P. (2008, May). *Agreement and disagreement in focus: Cultural perspective on televised election debates.* Paper presented at the annual meeting of the International Communication Association Convention, Montreal, Canada.

Ito, Y. (2000). What causes the similarities and differences among the social sciences in different cultures? Focusing on Japan and the West. *Asian Journal of Communication, 10*, 93–123.

Iyengar, S. (1991). *Is anyone responsible?* Chicago: University of Chicago Press.

Johnston, A. (1991). Political broadcasts: An analysis of form, content, and style in presidential communications. In L. L. Kaid, J. Gerstlé, & K. R. Sanders (Eds.), *Mediated politics in two cultures: Presidential campaigning in the United States and France* (pp. 59–72). New York: Praeger.

Kaid, L. L. (1991). The effects of television broadcasts on perceptions of political candidates in the United States and France. In L. L. Kaid, J. Gerstlé, & K. Sanders (Eds.). *Mediated politics in two cultures: Presidential campaigning in the United States and France* (pp. 247–260). New York: Praeger.

Kaid, L. L. (1994). Political advertising in the 1992 campaign. In R. E. Denton, Jr. (Ed.), *The 1992 presidential campaign: A communication perspective* (pp. 111–127). Westport, CT: Praeger.

Kaid, L. L. (1996). "Und dann, auf der wahlparty . . ." Reaktionen auf wahlwerbespots: Computergestützte messungen. In C. Holtz-Bacha & L. L. Kaid (Eds.), *Wahlen und Wahlkampf in den Medien* (pp. 178–224). Opladen, Germany: Westdeutscher Verlag.

Kaid, L. L. (1999). Comparing and contrasting the styles and effects of political advertising in European democracies. In L. L. Kaid (Ed.), *Television and politics in evolving European democracies* (pp. 219–236). Commack, NJ: NovaScience Publishers.

Kaid, L. L. (2004a). Measuring candidate images with semantic differentials. In K. L. Hacker (Ed.), *Presidential candidate images* (pp. 231–236). Westport, CT: Praeger.

Kaid, L. L. (2004b). Political advertising. In L. L. Kaid (Ed.), *The handbook of political communication research* (pp. 155–202). Mahwah, NJ: Lawrence Erlbaum.

Kaid, L. L. (2009). Immediate responses to political television spots in U.S. elections: Registering responses to advertising content. In J. Maier, M. Maier, M. Maurer, C. Reinemann, & V. Meyer (Eds.), *Real-time response measurement in the social sciences.* Frankfurt: Peter Lang.

Kaid, L. L., & Chanslor, M. (2004). The effects of political advertising on candidate images. In K. L. Hacker (Ed.), *Presidential candidate images* (pp. 133–150). Westport, CT: Praeger.

Kaid, L. L., & Davidson, J. (1986). Elements of videostyle: Candidate presentation through television advertising. In L. L. Kaid, D. Nimmo, & K. R. Sanders (Eds.), *New perspectives on political advertising* (pp. 184–209). Carbondale, IL: Southern Illinois University Press.

Kaid, L. L., & Gagnere, N. (2006). Election broadcasts in France. In L. L. Kaid & C. Holtz-Bacha (Eds.), *The Sage handbook of political advertising* (pp. 37–61). Thousand Oaks, CA: Sage.

Kaid, L. L., Gerstlé, J., & Sanders, K. R. (Eds.). (1991). *Mediated politics in two cultures: Presidential campaigning in the United States and France.* New York: Praeger.

Kaid, L. L., & Hirsch, R. O. (1973). Selective exposure and candidate image: A field study over time. *Central States Speech Journal, 24*, 48–51.

Kaid, L. L., & Holtz-Bacha, C. (1993a). Audience reactions to televised political programs: An experimental study of the 1990 German national election. *European Journal of Communication, 8*, 77–99.

Kaid, L. L., & Holtz-Bacha, C. (1993b). Die beurteilung von wahlspots im fernsehen: Ein experiment mit teilnehmen in den alten und neuen bundesländern. In C. Holtz Bacha & L. L. Kaid (Eds.), *Die massenmedien im wahlkampf* (pp. 185–207). Opladen, Germany: Westdeutscher Verlag.

Kaid, L. L., & Holtz-Bacha, C. (Eds.). (1995). *Political advertising in Western democracies.* Thousand Oaks, CA: Sage.

Kaid, L. L. & Holtz-Bacha, C. (2006). Television advertising and democratic systems around the world: A comparison of videostyle content and effects. In L. L. Kaid & C. Holtz-Bacha (Eds.), *The Sage handbook of political advertising* (pp. 445–457). Thousand Oaks, CA: Sage Publications.

Kaid, L. L., & Johnston, A. (2001). *Videostyle in presidential campaigns*. Westport, CT: Praeger/ Greenwood.

Kaid, L. L., Postelnicu, M., Landreville, K. D., Williams, A. P., Hostrup-Larsen, C., Urriste, S., Fernandes, J., Yun, H. J., & Bagley, A. (2005). Campaigning in the new Europe: News media presentations of the 2004 European Union Parliamentary elections. In C. Holtz-Bacha (Ed.), *Europawahl 2004: Massenmedien im Europawahlkampf* (pp. 228–251). Wiesbaden, Germany: VS Verlag für Sozialwissenschaften.

Kaid, L. L., & Strömbäck, J. (2008). Election news coverage around the world: A comparative perspective. In J. Strömbäck & L. L. Kaid (Eds.), *The handbook of election news coverage around the world* (pp. 419–429). New York: Routledge.

Kaid, L. L., & Tedesco, J. C. (1993). A comparison of political television advertising from the 1992 British and American campaigns. *Informatologia, 25*, 1–12.

Kaid, L. L., & Tedesco, J. (1999a). Die arbeit am image: Kanzlerkandidaten in der wahlwerbung. Die rezeption der fernsehspots von SPD und CDU. In C. Holtz-Bacha (Ed.), *Wahlkampf in den medien— Wahlkampf mit den medien* (pp. 218–241). Opladen, Germany: Westdeutscher Verlag.

Kaid, L. L., & Tedesco, T. (1999b). Tracking voter reactions to television advertising. In L. L. Kaid & D. G. Bystrom (Eds.), *The electronic election: Perspectives on the 1996 campaign communication* (pp. 233–245). Mahwah, NJ: Lawrence Erlbaum.

Kang, W. T., & Hoon, J. (1999). The 1997 presidential election in South Korea. *Electoral Studies, 18*, 2–13.

King, P. (1997). The press, candidate images, and voter perceptions. In M. McCombs, D. L. Shaw, & D. Weaver (Eds.), *Communication and democracy* (pp. 29–40). Mahwah, NJ: Lawrence Erlbaum.

Lang, P.J. (1985). *The cognitive psychology of emotion: Anxiety and the anxiety disorders*. Hillsdale, NJ: Laurence Erlbaum.

Lange, B.-P., & Ward, D. (Eds.) (2004). *The media and elections: A handbook and comparative study*. Mahwah, NJ: Lawrence Erlbaum.

Lee, C., & Benoit, W. L. (2004). A functional analysis of presidential television spots: A comparison of Korean and American ads. *Communication Quarterly, 52*(1), 68–79.

Lee, C., & Benoit, W. L. (2005). A functional analysis of the 2002 Korean presidential debates. *Asian Journal of Communication, 15*(2), 115–132.

Lee, S., Tak, J., & Kaid, L. L. (1998). Americanization of Korean political advertising: A comparative perspective on televised political spots in the 1992 presidential campaign. *Asian Journal of Communication, 8*(1), 73–86.

Legavre, J.-P. (1991). Face to face: The 1988 French debates. In L. L. Kaid, J. Gerstlé, & K. Sanders (Eds.), *Mediated politics in two cultures: Presidential campaigning in the United States and France* (pp. 173–181). New York: Praeger.

Levy, M. R. (1982). The Lazarsfeld-Stanton Program Analyzer: An historical note. *Journal of Communication, 32*(4), 30–38.

Liu, J. (2006, July). *A cross-national and double-sided test of "spiral of silence" theory: Culture, governmental form and personality*. Paper presented at the annual meeting of the International Communication Association Meeting, Dresden, Germany. Retrieved April 11, 2008, from http://www.allacademic.com/ meta/p91582.index.html.

Maier, J. (2007). Erfolgreiche überzeugungsarbeit urteile über den debattensieger und die veränderung der kanzlerpräferenz. In M. Maurer, C. Reinemann, J. Maier, & M. Maier (Eds.), *Schröder gegen Merkel: Wahrnehmung und wirkung des TV-duells im ost-west-vergleich* (pp. 91–109). Wiesbaden: VS Verlag für Sozialwissenschaften.

Maier, J., & Faas, T. (2004). Debattenwahrnehmung und kandidatenorientierung: Eine analyse vom real-time-response und paneldaten zu den fernsehduellen im bundestagwahlkampf 2002. *Zeitschrift für Medienpsychologie, 16*, 26–35.

Maier, J., & Maier, M. (2007). Audience reactions to negative campaign spots in the 2005 German national elections: The case of two ads called "The Ball." *Human Communication, 10*(3), 329–344.

Maier, J., Maier, M., Maurer, M., Reinemann, C., & Meyer, V. (Eds.). (2009). *Real-time response measurement in the social sciences.* Frankfurt: Peter Lang.

Maier, J., Maurer, M., Reinemann, C., & Faas, T. (2006). Reliability and validity of real-time response measurement: A comparison of two studies of a televised debate in Germany. *International Journal of Public Opinion Research, 19,* 53–73.

Maier, M., & Maier, J. (2008). News coverage of EU Parliamentary elections. In J. Strömbäck & L. L. Kaid (Eds.), *The handbook of election news coverage around the world* (pp. 401–418). New York: Routledge.

Malone, M. (1988). The evolution of electronic data collection: The perception analyzer. In J. Swerdlow (Ed.), *Media technology and the vote: A sourcebook* (pp. 31–36). Boulder, CO: Westview Press.

Mancini, P., & Swanson, D. L. (1996). Politics, media, and modern democracy: Introduction. In D. L. Swanson & P. Mancini (Eds.), *Politics, media, and modern democracy: An international study of innovations in electoral campaigning and their consequences* (pp. 1–26). Westport, CT: Praeger.

Mandelli, A. (1996). *Agenda-setting of public sentiments: Bringing values into the concept.* Paper presented at the annual meeting of the World Association for Public Opinion Research, Salt Lake City, Utah.

Mathes, R., & Pfetsch, B. (1991). The role of the alternative press in the agenda-building process: Spill-over effects and media opinion leadership. *European Journal of Communication, 6,* 33–62.

Matsaganis, M., & Weingarten, C. (2001). The 2000 U.S. presidential debate versus the 2000 Greek prime minister debate. *American Behavioral Scientist, 44,* 2398–2409.

Maurer, M. (2006). Learning versus knowing: Effects of misinformation in televised debates. *Communication Research, 33*(6), 489–506.

Maurer, M. (2007). Themen, argumente, rhetorische strategien: Die inhalte des TV-duelles. In M. Maurer, C. Reinemann, J. Maier, & M. Maier (Eds.), *Schröder gegen Merkel: Wahrnehmung und wirkung des TV-duells im ost-west-vergleich* (pp. 33–52). Wiesbaden: VS Verlag für Sozialwissenschaften.

Maurer, M., & Reinemann, C. (2003). *Schröder gegen Stoiber: Nutzung, wahrnehmung und wirkung der TV-duelle* [Schroeder vs. Stoiber. Uses, perceptions and effects of the televised debates]. Wiesbaden, Germany: Westdeutscher Verlag.

Mauer, M., & Reinemann, C. E. (2004, May). *The power of emotionally packaged commonplaces. Short-term effects and post-debate consequences of different rhetorical strategies in televised political debates.* Paper presented at the annual meeting of the International Communication Association, New Orleans, LA.

Mazzoleni, G., & Roper, C. S. (1995). The presentation of Italian candidates and parties in television advertising. In L. L. Kaid & C. Holtz-Bacha (Eds.), *Political advertising in Western democracies* (pp. 89–108). Thousand Oaks, CA: Sage.

McCombs, M., Lopez-Escobar, E., & Llamas, J. P. (2000). Setting the agenda of attributes in the 1996 Spanish general election. *Journal of Communication, 50*(2), 77–92.

McCombs, M. E., & Shaw, D. L. (1972). The agenda-setting function of mass media. *Public Opinion Quarterly, 36,* 176–185.

McCroskey, J. (1966, March). Scales for the measurement of ethos. *Speech Monographs, 33,* 65–72.

McKinney, M. S., & Carlin, D. B. (2004). Political campaign debates. In L. L. Kaid (Ed.), *Handbook of political communication research* (pp. 203–234). Mahwah, NJ: Lawrence Erlbaum.

McKinnon, L. M., & Tedesco, J. C. (1999). The influence of medium and media commentary on presidential debates effects. In L. L. Kaid & D. G. Bystrom (Eds.), *The electronic election: Perspectives on the 1996 campaign communication* (pp. 191–206). Mahwah, NJ: Lawrence Erlbaum.

McKinnon, L. M., Tedesco, J. C., & Kaid, L. L. (1993). The third 1992 presidential debate: Channel and commentary effects. *Argumentation and Advocacy, 30,* 106–118.

Mikami, S., Takeshita, T., Nakada, M., & Kawabata, M. (1995). Media coverage and public awareness of environmental issues in Japan. *Gazette, 54,* 209–226.

Millard, W. J. (1992). A history of handsets for direct measurement of audience responses. *International Journal of Public Opinion Research, 4,* 1–17.

Miron, D., Marinescu, V., & McKinnon, L. M. (1999). Romanian elections and the evolution of political television. In L. L. Kaid (Ed.), *Television and politics in evolving European democracies* (pp. 85–111). Commack, NY: NovaScience Publishers.

Morris, J. D. (1995). SAM: The self-assessment manikin. An efficient cross-cultural measurement of emotional response. *Journal of Advertising Research, 35,* 63–68.

Neveu, E. (1998). Media and politics in French political science. *European Journal of Political Research, 33,* 439–458.

Nisbet, E. C. (2006). The engagement model of opinion leadership: Testing validity within a European context. *International Journal of Public Opinion Research, 18*(1), 3–30.

Noelle-Neumann, E. (1980). *Die schweigespirale—Unsere soziale haut.* Munich: Piper.

Noelle-Neumann, E., & Petersen, T. (2004). The spiral of silence and the social nature of man. In L. L. Kaid (Ed.), *The handbook of political communication research* (pp. 339–354). Mahwah, NJ: Lawrence Erlbaum.

Norris, P. (2002). Campaign communications. In L. LeDuc, R. G. Niemi & P. Norris (Eds.), *Comparing democracies 2: New challenges in the study of elections and voting* (pp. 127–147). London: Sage.

Oates, S., & Roselle, L. (2000). Russian elections and TV news: Comparison of campaign news on state-controlled and commercial television channels. *Harvard International Journal of Press/Politics, 5*(2), 30–51.

Ogawa, T. (2001). Framing and agenda setting function. *Keio Communication Review, 23,* 71–80.

Osgood, C. E., Suci, G. J., & Tannenbaum, P. H. (1957). *The measurement of meaning.* Urbana, IL: University of Illinois Press.

Perry, S. D., & Gonzenbach, W. J. (2000). Inhibiting speech through exemplar distribution: Can we predict a spiral of silence? *Journal of Broadcasting and Electronic Media, 44*(2), 268–281.

Peter, J., & de Vreese, C. H. (2003). Agenda rich, agenda poor: A cross-national comparative investigation of nominal and thematic public agenda diversity. *International Journal of Public Opinion Research, 15,* 44–64.

Pfetsch, B. (2004). From political culture to political communication culture: A theoretical approach to comparative analysis. In F. Esser & B. Pfetsch (Eds.), *Comparing political communication: Theories, cases and challenges* (pp. 344–366). Cambridge: Cambridge University Press.

Plasser, F., with Plasser, G. (2002). *Global political campaigning: A worldwide analysis of campaign professionals and their practices.* Westport, CT: Praeger.

Price, V. (1993). The impact of varying reference periods in survey questions about media use. *Journalism Quarterly, 70,* 615–627.

Reynolds, A., Reilly, B., & Ellis, A. (2005–2006*). Electoral system design: The new international IDEA handbook.* Stockholm: IDEA-International.

Rogers, E. (1995). *The diffusion of innovations* (4th ed.). New York: Free Press.

Roper, J., Holtz-Bacha, C., & Mazzoleni, G. (2004). *The politics of representation. Election campaigning and proportional representation.* New York: Peter Lang.

Rössler, P. (2004). Political communication messages: Pictures of our world on television news. In F. Esser & B. Pfetsch (Eds.), *Comparing political communication: Theories, cases and challenges* (pp. 271–292). Cambridge: Cambridge University Press.

Salmon, C. T., & Glynn, C. J. (1996). Spiral of silence: Communication and public opinion as social control. In M. B. Salwen & D. W. Stacks (Eds.), *An integrated approach to communication theory and research* (pp. 165–180). Mahwah, NJ: Lawrence Erlbaum.

Sanders, K. R., & Pace, T. J. (1977). The influence of speech communication on the image of a political candidate: "Limited effects" revisited. In B. Ruben (Ed.), *Communication yearbook I* (pp. 465–474). New Brunswick, NJ: Transaction Press.

Scammell, M. (1995). *Designer politics. How elections are won.* Basingstoke, England: Macmillan.

Scheufele, D., & Moy, P. (2000). Twenty-five years of the spiral of silence: A conceptual review and empirical outlook. *International Journal of Public Opinion Research, 12*(1), 3–28.

Scheufele, D. A., Shanahan, J., & Lee, E. (2001). Real talk: Manipulating the dependent variable in spiral of silence research. *Communication Research, 28*(3), 304–324.

Schmitt-Beck, R. (2004). Political communication effects: The impact of mass media and personal communication on voting. In F. Esser & B. Pfetsch (Eds.), *Comparing political communication: Theories, cases, and challenges* (pp. 293–322). Cambridge: Cambridge University Press.

Schoenbach, K., & Semetko, H. A. (1992). Agenda-setting, agenda-reinforcing or agenda-deflating? A study of the 1990 German national election. *Journalism and Mass Communication Quarterly, 69*, 837–846.

Schrott, P. R. (1994) The content and consequences of the 1980 televised debates in West Germany and the United States. Unpublished manuscript. State University of New York, Stony Brook.

Schrott, P. R. (1990). Electoral consequences of "winning" televised campaign debates. *Public Opinion Quarterly, 54*, 567–585.

Schulz, W. (1997). Political communication scholarship in Germany. *Political Communication, 14*, 113–146.

Schulz, W., & Blumler, J. G. (1994). Die bedeutung der kampagnen für das Europa-engagement der bürger: Eine mehr-ebenen-analyse. In O. Niedermayer & H. Schmitt (Eds.), *Wahlen und Europäische Einigung* (pp. 199–223). Opladen: Westdeutscher Verlag.

Semetko, H. A., Blumler, J. G., Gurevitch, M., & Weaver, D. H. (1991). *The formation of campaign agendas: A comparative analysis of party and media roles in recent American and British elections.* Hillsdale, NJ: Lawrence Erlbaum.

Semetko, H. A., & Borquez, J. (1991). Audiences for election communication in France and the United States: Media use and candidate evaluations. In L. L. Kaid, J. Gerstlé, & K. Sanders (Eds.), *Mediated politics in two cultures: Presidential campaigning in the United States and France* (pp. 223–245). New York: Praeger.

Semetko, H. A., & Mandelli, A. (1997). Setting the agenda for cross-national research: Bringing values into the concept. In M. McCombs, D. L. Shaw, & D. Weaver (Eds.), *Communication and democracy* (pp. 195–207). Mahwah, NJ: Lawrence Erlbaum.

Semetko, H. A., & Valkenburg, P. M. (2000). Framing European politics: A content analysis of press and television news. *Journal of Communication, 50*(2), 93–109.

Siebert, F. S., Peterson, T., & Schramm, W. (1956). *Four theories of the press.* Champaign, IL: University of Illinois Press.

Spencer, A. T., & Croucher, S. M. (2008, April 1). Basque nationalism and the spiral of silence: An analysis of public perceptions of ETA in Spain and France. *International Communication Gazette, 70*(2), 137–153.

Steeper, F. T. (1978). Public responses to Gerald Ford's statement on Eastern Europe in the second debate. In G. F. Bishop, R. G. Meadow, & M. Jackson-Beeck (Eds.), *The presidential debates: Media, electoral, and policy perspectives* (pp. 81–101). New York: Praeger.

Strömbäck, J., & Dimitrova, D. V. (2006). Political and media systems matter: A comparison of election news coverage in Sweden and the United States. *Harvard International Journal of Press/Politics, 11*(4), 131–147.

Strömbäck, J., & Kaid, L. L. (2008). A framework for comparing election news coverage around the world. In J. Strömbäck & L. L. Kaid (Eds.), *The handbook of election news coverage around the world* (pp. 1–18). New York: Routledge.

Strömbäck, J., & Luengo, Ó. G. (2006, June). Framing and election news coverage in Spain and Sweden. Paper presented to the 4th International Symposium on Communication in the Millenium, Eskisehir, Turkey.

Strömbäck, J., & Shehata, A. (2007). Structural bias in British and Swedish election news coverage. A comparative study. *Journalism Studies, 8*, 798–812.

Swanson, D. L., & Mancini, P. (Eds.). (1996). *Politics, media, and modern democracy: An international study of innovations in electoral campaigning and their consequences.* Westport, CT: Praeger.

Tak, J., Kaid, L. L., & Lee, S. (1997). A cross-cultural study of political advertising in the United States and Korea. *Communication Research, 24*, 413–430.

Takeshita, T. (1997). Exploring the media's roles in defining reality: From issue-agenda setting to attribute-agenda setting. In M. McCombs, D. L. Shaw, & D. Weaver (Eds.), *Communication and democracy* (pp. 15–27). Mahwah, NJ: Lawrence Erlbaum.

Tedesco, J. C. (2002). Televised political advertising effects: Evaluating responses during the 2000 Robb-Allen senatorial election. *Journal of Advertising, 31*(1), 37–48.

Thomson, E. A., White, P. R. R., & Kitley, P. (2008). "Objectivity" and "hard news" reporting across cultures. *Journalism Studies, 9*(2), 212–228.

Trenaman, J., & McQuail, D. (1961). *Television and the political image: A study of the impact of television on the 1959 General Election*. London: Methuen.

Weaver, D., McCombs, M., & Shaw, D. L. (2004). Agenda-setting research: Issues, attributes and influences. In L. L. Kaid (Ed.), *The handbook of political communication research* (pp. 257–282). Mahwah, NJ: Lawrence Erlbaum.

Williams, A. P. (2008). Strategy-process metacommunication framing during Operation Iraqi Freedom. *Business Research Yearbook, XV*, 227–231.

Williams, A. P., & Kaid, L. L. (2006). Media framing of the European Parliamentary elections: A view from the United States. In M. Maier & J. Tenscher (Eds.) *Campaigning in Europe—Campaigning for Europe: Political parties, campaigns, mass media, and the European Parliament elections 2004* (pp. 295–304). London, England: LIT Publishers.

Williams, A. P., & Kaid, L. L. (2009). Framing the new EU: U.S. media portrayals of the 2004 European Union expansion and parliamentary elections. *Journal of Political Marketing, 8*, 70–79.

Williams, A. P., Kaid, L. L., Landreville, K., Fernandes, J., Yun, H. J., Bagley, A., & Urriste, S. (2008). The representation of European Union elections in news media coverage around the world. In L. L. Kaid (Ed.), *The EU expansion: Communicating shared sovereignty in the parliamentary elections* (pp. 153–173). New York: Peter Lang.

Willnat, L., & Aw, A. (2004). Political communication in Asia: Challenges and opportunities. In L. L. Kaid (Ed.), *Handbook of political communication research* (pp. 155–202). Mahwah, NJ: Lawrence Erlbaum.

Willnat, L., & Zhu, J. H. (1996). Newspaper coverage and public opinion in Hong Kong: A time-series analysis of media priming. *Political Communication, 13*, 231–246.

Wirth, W., & Kolb, S. (2004). Designs and methods of comparative political communication research. In F. Esser & B. Pfetsch (Eds.), *Comparing political communication: Theories, cases, and challenges* (pp. 87–111). Cambridge: Cambridge University Press.

Wring, D. (1999). The marketing colonization of political campaigning. In B. I. Newman (Ed.), *Handbook of political marketing* (pp. 41–54). Thousand Oaks, CA: Sage.

Young, S., Bourne, S., & Younane, S. (2007). Contemporary political communications: Audiences, politicians, and the media in international research. *Sociology Compass, 1*(1), 41–59.

Zukin, C., Keeter, S., Andolina, K. J., & Delli-Carpini, M. X. (2006). *A new engagement? Political participation, civic life, and the changing American citizen*. New York: Oxford University Press.

VIII
STATISTICAL TECHNIQUES

22

Expanding the Use of Structural Equation Modeling (SEM) in Political Communication

R. Lance Holbert
School of Communication
The Ohio State University

Heather L. LaMarre
School of Journalism & Mass Communication
University of Minnesota

There are several definitions for structural equation modeling (SEM) and most of these definitions are field-specific (e.g., Byrne, 2001; Hoyle, 1995; Kaplan, 2000; Kline, 2005; Schumacker & Lomax, 2004). However, the most concise definition of SEM can be found in Klem (2000), who states, "In its most general form, SEM can be viewed as a combination of path analysis and factor analysis" (p. 227). The path analysis side focuses more specifically on the testing of simultaneous equations and the origins of this portion of SEM can be found in the fields of econometrics and genetics. The factor analysis side is comprised of restricted (i.e., confirmatory) factor analysis and stems from work completed in psychology and, more specifically, psychometrics (Kaplan, 2000). The origins of the technique are more in measurement than in the testing of structural relationships between variables (see Haggland, 2001), but Joreskog was instrumental in linking the two seemingly disparate techniques into a single analytical procedure we now call SEM (Kline, 2005).

Political communication has been a leading proponent of the use of SEM within the communication sciences. The use of this particular analytical tool can be found throughout the political communication literature, especially in recent years (e.g., Eveland, Hayes, Shah, & Kwak, 2005; Holbert, 2005a, 2005b; Shah & Scheufele, 2006). As with the use of any analytical tool, a specific field of study tends to emphasize certain aspects of a technique while undervaluing other aspects of that same tool. Over time, certain patterns of implementation become common-place, serving to solidify a particular way of approaching a given analytical procedure. As one surveys the use of a particular analytical procedure (e.g., multiple regression) across different fields of study, it becomes evident that a certain degree of provinciality can develop from one field to another (e.g., dominant use of all-entry multiple regression in one field versus stepwise regression in another field). The differentiation in use may be due to varied research questions being addressed across disciplines, but may also simply evolve as a result of nothing more than a "this is the way we have always done it" mentality.

Clearly, there is differentiation in the use of SEM across a range of social scientific fields. If we think of SEM in terms of branding, then there are two dominant dimensions of the brand (measurement and structure). Some fields tend to think of SEM as a tool to study measurement (e.g., psychology; see MacCallum & Austin, 2000), while other fields are more likely to associate SEM with the assessment of relationships between variables (latent or observed; e.g., communication; see Holbert & Stephenson, 2002). Still other fields reflect a healthy balance between the study of measurement and structural relationships (e.g., marketing and consumer research; see Baumgartner & Homburg, 1996). The fields that tend to emphasize the measurement component of SEM were the earlier adopters of the technique, when SEM began as a tool for the study of measurement, whereas those fields that tend to associate SEM with the testing of structural relationships between variables were late adopters of the innovation, once the testing of structural relationships became more fully integrated with the study of measurement. In short, different fields approach the multi-faceted tool of SEM from unique perspectives, with each perspective reflective of a different balance between the factor analysis and path analysis aspects of the technique.

The flexibility of SEM as an analytical tool is the attribute which has led to its current breadth and depth of use across the social sciences, but this flexibility needs to be recognized as a double-edged sword. Greater diversity means that it can be of value to a wider range of interests intended to address a broad range of research questions. However, diversity can also lead to the tool being used in a limited manner by one field, while being used in an altogether different, but still limited, manner by another field—while still retaining value within both fields. As unique within-field uses of the technique develop over time, there comes an inability of any one field to utilize SEM to its full potential. While no one use of SEM may be incorrect in theory (although its implementation may be deeply flawed; see Holbert & Stepehnson, 2002), there is still a failure to employ SEM in a manner that allows researchers to obtain maximum benefit.

As a result, it is important for any field to constantly reacquaint itself with the latest advances in the use of important analytical techniques. This is especially true for a multivariate tool like SEM since it is constantly evolving and expanding in terms of how it is used and the types of questions it can address (Kline, 2005). The goal of this chapter is to introduce a series of arguments that speak to ways in which political communication scholarship can expand its use of SEM. Political communication researchers need to remain abreast of the latest advances in the use of SEM in order to utilize the technique to its full potential. The list of topics offered in this chapter is by no means exhaustive, but it represent uses of SEM that have become commonplace in other social scientific fields. The only way to reduce the provincial use of a particular analytical technique within a field of research is to constantly infuse researchers with new ways of looking at the technique. The ultimate purpose of this chapter is to get political communication researchers to step beyond their own individualized use of SEM to more fully utilize the technique as a whole.

The chapter focuses on three distinct areas: measurement, specification, and estimation/ evaluation. Given that political communication scholarship utilizes SEM overwhelmingly for the purposes of studying structural relationships between variables (observed or latent) and not the internal measurement structures of various constructs, there are many points that can be raised just concerning measurement models. As for the broader process of model building in SEM, it is common to divide that process into the specification, estimation, and evaluation phases (see Hoyle,

1995). The specification phase concerns the formation of the model, while the estimation and evaluation phases are concerned with the testing and interpretation of the model, respectively. Four issues are raised in each of the three areas (measurement, specification, and estimation/evaluation).

MEASUREMENT

SEM originated with the study of measurement (Jöreskog, 1967). Jöreskog linked previous works by Lawley on maximum likelihood (ML) and restricted factor analysis to create the SEM-based technique of confirmatory factor analysis (CFA) that is common to all major SEM programs (i.e., LISREL, EQS, AMOS; see Jöreskog & Lawley, 1968). Levine (2005) has stressed a need for communication researchers in general to conduct more CFAs. Indeed, the following quote from Blalock (1979) applies well to the field of political communication: "The most serious and important problems that require our immediate and concerted attention are those of conceptualization and measurement, which have for too long been neglected" (p. 382). With this in mind, we review how the CFA envelope is being pushed in the SEM literature in the belief that a general awareness of the technique's versatility will best achieve the goal of increasing the frequency of SEM-based CFAs in political communication research.

Higher-Order Factor Structures

Even more surprising than the scant use of SEM-based CFAs in political communication research is the complete dearth of testing of higher-order factor structures (cf. Kohring & Matthes, 2007). More than 50 years of social scientific research has argued for the existence of higher-order factor structures (e.g., Thurstone, 1947). SEM allows not only for the direct assessment of a set of lower-order factors, but also the existence of one or more higher-order factors (see Holbert & Stephenson, 2008, for a detailed discussion). Higher-order factor structures reflect the fact that "the latent variables directly influencing the observable variables may be influenced by other latent variables that need not have direct effects on the observable variables" (Bollen, 1989, pp. 313–314). Political communication scholarship has been explicit in pointing to potential higher-order factor structures (e.g., Hullett, Louden, & Mitra, 2003). However, there has been little direct empirical assessment of higher-order measurement models. To gain a broader understanding of underlying measurement structures it is imperative for the field to begin a more systematic assessment of higher-order factor structures.

Research from other disciplines routinely tests higher-order factor structures (e.g., Cheung, 2000; Kaplan & Elliott, 1997; Russell & Cutrona, 1991). However, it is important to recognize that the movement toward the testing of higher-order factor structures reflects a subtle shift away from testing a pure measurement model. Inherent to the establishment of a higher-order factor is the testing of causal associations between latent variables. Thus, higher-order factor models can been viewed as a bridge between the testing of pure measurement models and what have come to be defined as hybrid models that simultaneously test measurement and structural associations within a single model.

Multitrait-Multimethod (MTMM) Matrix Models

Campbell and Fiske (1959) were the first researchers to create a measurement model that allows for the simultaneous assessment of the convergent and discriminant validity of a scale of items. An MTMM matrix model is described by Kenny and Kashy (1992) as follows:

... this matrix involves factorially combining a set of traits with a set of measurement methods. This factorial combination of traits and methods allows an examination of variance that is due to traits, variance that is due to methods, and unique or error variance. (p. 165)

The variance associated with traits concerns the discriminant validity of a scale, while the variance associated with method allows for an assessment of convergent validity. MTMM matrix models provide a sophisticated, efficient means by which to improve the discipline's assessment of measurement models (see Benoit & Holbert, 2008).

Political communication scholars value convergent and discriminant validity in their measurement, so expanded use of MTMM matrix models could serve the discipline well. For example, a researcher interested in the study of communication-oriented political socialization patterns among students entering their college experience (e.g., Klofstad, 2007) would want to know trait characteristics of incoming freshman, which could be assessed with a series of self-report measures (e.g., internal political self-efficacy, political ideology, level of political discussion). A researcher could collect these self-report measures, but then increase the number of methods used by asking a parent to rate their child on the various scales and get a close friend to do the same (see Byrant, 2000, for other multiple method approaches). This approach to establishing multiple methods is akin to MTMM matrix data collected in education, where a student will offer self-report data but the researcher will also collect data on teacher and school aide perceptions of individual students (e.g., Boruch, Larkin, Wolins, & MacKinney, 1970). The validity of the student self-report data can be judged relative to the responses offered by other individuals as distinct methods. The validity of self-report measures is constantly up for debate within the field, but one way to reduce the uncertainty that may exist with these types of measures is to collect MTMM matrix data for the purposes of assessing the ability of multiple methods to converge on a single construct.

Semiconfirmatory Factor Analysis

Political communication researchers are familiar with exploratory factor analysis and confirmatory factor analysis, although the latter is not employed nearly as often as the former (see Holbert & Stephenson, 2008). However, the field is less aware of a third factor analysis avenue, semiconfirmatory factor analysis, which represents a mix of the first two techniques. McDonald (2005) points out that there are instances when a researcher is able to test a set of theoretically driven relationships between multiple observable variables and a set of latent constructs, but additional items are then added to the mix of well-established items to generate increased factorial complexity in the measurement model. McDonald (2005) points out that this scenario represents an analysis that is "clearly partially confirmatory and partially exploratory" (p. 165).

Space constraints do not allow us to detail the steps necessary for a factor analysis of this kind (see McDonald, 2005, for examples of the use of the semiconfirmatory factor analysis technique). However, we wish to articulate that conducting a traditional restricted factor analysis (i.e., confirmatory factor analysis) with elements of an unrestricted factor analysis (i.e., exploratory factor analysis) allows a researcher "to see if anything has been missed" in a purely confirmatory model. In short, the introduction of new items to a previously established factor structure has the ability to alter the underlying factor structure in significant ways, ways that may not be anticipated. Attempting to fit any new items into an existing factor structure may lead to masking the true measurement structure of a given set of data. Performing parallel confirmatory and exploratory factor analyses under the auspices of semiconfirmatory factor analysis increases the likelihood that the true measurement structure will become evident. We do not anticipate the use of semi-confirmatory factor analysis to become commonplace in the communication sciences any time soon, especially since confirmatory factor analyses have yet to be conducted with sufficient regularity. However, there may be instances when a semiconfirmatory factor analysis may be the best option for a researcher. We simply wish to make this technique known to the discipline in the hope that it will one day be employed with increased frequency when appropriate.

Dichotomous Data

One limitation to the use of traditional forms of data reduction (e.g., exploratory factor analysis, principle components analysis) is a general inability to study dichotomous variables (Bryant & Yarnold, 1995). This is an unfortunate matter given the prevalence of dichotomous measures in communication and other social scientific disciplines (Hipp & Bollen, 2003). Item response theory (IRT) models, which were developed at about the same time as structural equation models, are most typically used for the study of measurement issues related to dichotomous variables (Lord & Novick, 1968). However, research has been completed by SEM scholars on the similarities that exist between IRT and SEM, allowing researchers to "formulate and evaluate IRT measurement models within the broader SEM framework" (Glöckner-Rist & Hoijtink, 2003, p. 546). In short, analytical techniques are now available that allow researchers to incorporate the use of dichotomous data in confirmatory factor analyses.

Political communication researchers can look to a number of sources to better understand the proper means by which to introduce dichotomous data into a structural equation model (e.g., Muthén, 1984; Olsson, 1979). Researchers will have to become familiar with relationship coefficients not commonly utilized in the communication sciences (e.g., polychoric correlations, tetrachoric correlations). However, some SEM software packages can aid researchers in the formation of data matrices that best match the use of dichotomous data. For example, PRELIS, a companion software package for LISREL created for the purpose of data preparation, will create tetrachoric correlation-based matrices. Also, various software packages like EQS will default to the employment of tetrachoric correlations when analyzing relationships among dichotomous variables. In short, popular SEM software packages are already ahead of the communication sciences in allowing for the possibility of using dichotomous data in SEM-based confirmatory factor analysis models. The onus thus does not fall entirely on the researcher, which may aid in the use of dichotomous variables in communication-based confirmatory factor analyses (e.g., Holbert et al., 2005).

SPECIFICATION

Researchers seeking to employ SEM to test relationships between a combination of observed and latent variables must perform a series of tasks that establish a solid foundation by which a theoretical model can be estimated and evaluated. The analytical steps that unfold prior to the actual testing of a model have come to be defined as the specification phase of SEM. This phase involves making determinations about the type of model that can be tested based on the data collected, establishing the potential structure for a model based on the research questions and/or hypotheses posed, estimating the statistical power embodied within a given structural model, and engaging in data screening to best allow the dataset in question to adhere to the assumptions of the statistical theory that serves as the basis for SEM analyses. As with other areas of SEM, there are specification matters that require clarification relative to the use of this multivariate technique. There are also a series of specification issues that reflect recent advancements in the use of SEM. Offered in the following sections are several specification advancements that may be of special interest to political communication researchers.

Power Estimation

Estimating statistical power is exponentially more difficult in SEM than in ANOVA or other well-known statistical techniques given the large number of parameters in a traditional structural equation model (Kaplan, 1995). Satorra and Saris (1985) first created a labor intensive method by which to estimate power in structural equation models, but Satorra (1989) later clarified the fact that the univariate LM tests provided by the major SEM software packages can be used as a quick and simple test of statistical power. A univariate LM test is a one-degree-of-freedom noncentrality parameter. As a result, these tests can be compared to a χ^2 distribution table to assess the power required to estimate a given parameter (the square of the t-values in LISREL and the W statistics in EQS can be used in the same manner for those paths that have been established as free). The use of modification indices only allows for an assessment of a model's statistical power *after* the model has been estimated. However, it would be ideal for researchers to perform power estimation *a priori* to the estimation and evaluation of a structural equation model.

Muthén and Muthén (2002) argue for the use of Monte Carlo simulation for the purposes of estimating the power of the hypothesized structural equation model prior to testing the model against real data. The fact of the matter is that the statistical power of a structural model depends on a seemingly endless number of factors. Just a few highlighted by Muthén and Muthén include the size of the model, the strength (small, medium, and large) of associations between variables in the model, and the respective reliabilities of the latent constructs. Basically, power needs to be assessed on a case-by-case basis with SEM given that "there is no rule of thumb that applies to all cases" when addressing the ever popular question, "What sample size do I need for my study?" (p. 599). Interestingly, these researchers find that the existence of nonnormality in CFA measurement models is a greater deterrent to achieving adequate levels of statistical power than the presence of missing data. Monte Carlo simulations allow a researcher to create controlled environments to ascertain the performance of a given statistic. Given the breadth of influences that can affect the statistical power of a structural equation model, Monte Carlo simulation provides the best means by which to tailor a power analysis to the combination of considerations that are unique to a specific research endeavor.

Specifying Interaction Terms

A historically fatal flaw of SEM analyses has been researchers' inability to establish a standard technique by which to assess possible interaction effects between latent variables in a single structural equation model (Schumaker & Marcoulides, 1998). Three techniques, all retaining their inherent strengths and weaknesses, have become commonplace in recent SEM literature. Schumaker and Marcoulides (1998) define these techniques as: multiple-group, product indicant, and nonlinear. The multiple-group approach is suitable when the moderator variable is discrete and categorical. Basically, a multi-group model is tested and a specific parameter estimate is compared across groups to assess changes in effect size. The more cumbersome product indicant procedure is used when the moderator variable is a multiple-indicator latent variable. A new latent interaction variable is created within the model by multiplying pairs of observed variables that are indicators of the respective latent constructs involved in forming the interaction. There are multiple ways by which to form the latent product-indicant variable, either using all indicators to form the new observable variables or using a sample of observable items (the latter is used when the original latent variables consist of a large number of items). The nonlinear technique replaces the traditional linear estimate with a nonlinear estimate (i.e., squared, cubic, quadratic). Schumaker and Marcoulides (1998) detail the strengths and limitations of each procedure.

Recent advances made by Jöreskog (2000) concerning the estimation of latent variable scores has allowed for a fourth, relatively sophisticated, technique for testing interactions in latent variable structural equation models. The latent variable score approach to interaction modeling is detailed in full by Schumaker (2002), and the means by which to computed latent variable scores in LISREL is outlined in Jöreskog et al. (1999). The computing of latent variable scores in LISREL is similar to estimating factor scores in exploratory factor analysis (e.g., Lawley & Maxwell, 1971). This technique yields a single latent construct that generates a relatively simple model structure when compared to the latent interaction variables typically created with the product indicant approach. Schumaker (2002) finds the latent variable score approach "easier to implement" than the product indicant method. In addition, "the latent variable approach also has utility when testing more complex structural equation interaction models" (p. 49). Given that political communication scholars using SEM have not to our knowledge employed the technique for testing interaction effects, the field has been given the rare opportunity to leapfrog over many disciplines that are still employing relatively cumbersome techniques for analyzing moderator variables in structural equation models. The introduction of interaction effects in SEM through the use of the latent variable score approach would represent a major methodological advancement in our view.

Multi-Level Models

Political communication is a variable field. As a result, the theoretical questions of greatest interest to the discipline are often inherently multi-level concerns (Pan & McLeod, 1991). Translating these theoretical concerns to SEM analyses, the issue of specification in multi-level models becomes obvious.

Communication scholars can run multi-level models in SPSS using a variety of Advanced Models commands (see Leyland, 2004). However, multi-level modeling has become part of the purview of SEM as well. In addition, new statistical techniques like Hierarchical Linear Modeling (HLM) have been created specifically for testing multi-level models (Raudenbush & Bryk, 2002). Just as the widespread use of longitudinal data has brought a range of analytical procedures that have evolved beyond SEM, so too has the introduction of multi-level modeling introduced new modeling procedures. Communication scholars need to be aware of the multitude of possibilities available to them for analyzing multi-level models. Most recently, Wendorf (2002) conducted an analytical comparison of SEM and HLM to test similar multi-level models. Wendorf found the HLM and SEM techniques "offered nearly identical parameter estimates and standard errors, thus leading to identical conclusions about the data" (p. 136). However, he also found that "SEM offers more flexibility in terms of model specification" (p. 136). In short, the jury remains out in terms of employing SEM versus HLM for the purposes of testing a multi-level model. At this point, we would recommend that the field not jump head first into the use of HLM for multi-level modeling if SEM has the possibility of offering some clear advantages over the relatively fledgling HLM technique.

Multiple-Sample/Multiple-Group Models

As mentioned in our discussion of different techniques for testing interactions in SEM, a question that often arises is whether a given parameter estimate varies across groups. This question has led to advancements in the study of multiple-sample or multiple-group models (e.g., Holbert & Hansen, 2008). However, the comparative study of groups does not pertain just to differences in individual parameter estimates. Multiple-sample/multiple-group models can also be used to assess whether there are broader competing model structures across groups (Bollen, 1989). Most multi-group modeling works under an assumption of broader model equivalence across groups, and then proceeds with the establishment of equality constraints assessed via a change in the χ^2-distributed test statistic to determine whether there are differences in path estimates across groups. The existence of a difference across groups would signal that the group variable serves as a moderator in the path estimate that connects an independent variable to a dependent variable (i.e., multiple groups moderator test).

Political communication scholars should not be too quick to assume equivalence of model structures across groups. Cheung, Leung, and Au (2006) argue that this point is particularly relevant to the study of cross-cultural research. There are several examples of cross-cultural studies that reveal a general lack of model equivalence across national groups (e.g., Byrne & Campbell, 1999; Poortinga, 1989). In short, it is important that communication researchers not assume model equivalency across groups and jump into the testing of equality constraints for individual parameter estimates prematurely. The study of multiple-sample/multiple-group models should be approached as a two-level process. First, it is important to test broader model equivalency. Second, once model equivalency has been established, then researchers can confidently proceed and test the equality of parameter estimates across groups.

ESTIMATION AND EVALUATION

Once issues related to measurement and specification have been addressed, researchers are faced with a series of important choices about how to estimate the model as well as how to evaluate and present the model. Estimation has been called the "first logical step" that follows specification (Chou & Bentler, 1990, p. 37), and these decisions have critical implications for the evaluation of a structural equation model. While estimation issues are fairly straightforward (covariance versus correlation matrixes, partial versus full information estimators), model evaluation is somewhat more complex. Researchers must address concerns about sample size, multivariate normality, and goodness-of-fit statistics, issues at the forefront of estimation and evaluation for essentially every structural model. Most issues pertaining to estimation and evaluation, sans goodness of fit, have benefited from some stability in recent years. The challenge is for political communication scholars to take advantage of that stability and tread into waters that remain unexplored. As a means of moving in that direction, we address both familiar and unexplored terrain in more detail, beginning with clarification of issues pertaining to estimation and evaluation.

Replication and Cross-Validation

There exist two valid, yet underutilized, techniques to offset the criticism of post hoc modification: validation and cross-validation. To validate a model implies that a researcher replicates the model (including the post hoc modifications) with a new sample. Should the model be replicated with the new sample, there is some justification for post hoc modification to the original sample that may have implications for theory development or refinement. In addition to validation (replication), a second option for testing post hoc modifications is cross-validation. How one cross-validates a model depends on the size of one's sample. If sample size is large, researchers can randomly split the sample into two smaller samples. Following Maruyuma (1998), "if datasets are large enough, then samples should be split, with one half used to examine plausibility of a model and perhaps even subtly refine it using modifications to the model that do not change the critical components and are conceptually defensible, and with the second half held to fit the model from the first half" (p. 199).

When samples are not large enough to split, one can consult the expected cross-validation index (ECVI) developed by Browne and Cudeck (1993). The ECVI represents the discrepancy between the model tested with the existing sample and a model that would be tested with a new sample. According to MacCallum (1995), "if the model ECVI is lower than that of the saturated ECVI (where all model parameters are estimated), then the model shows good fit. The model ECVI should be closer to saturated ECVI than the ECVI for the independence model."

The ECVI has rarely appeared in SEM articles in political communication. The reasons are threefold. First, there exists no "cutoff" value that scholars use as benchmarks with other fit indexes. However, smaller values of ECVI are preferred. Second, the ECVI is not available in all software packages. Third, any hand computation of the ECVI is likely to take effort and few have taken on the challenge (including the authors of this chapter) (see Browne & Cudeck, 1993). Nonetheless, for political communication researchers who make modifications to their original hypothesized model, the reporting of ECVI with small samples, or alternatively splitting larger samples for replication, would serve the discipline well. This evidence would be valuable for ascertaining the usefulness of post hoc model modifications and definitely lend credibility to the literature.

Testing Competing Models

In the previous discussion about modifying indexes, one element merits additional elaboration. In addition to providing evidence of cross validation, we find that positing and then testing alternative models, as described by Jöreskog (1993), a very attractive procedure all too rarely employed in political communication research. Testing multiple theoretical models, sometimes referred to as a critical test, is a scientifically rigorous but exciting alternative that should be made better use of by political communication scholars. In political communication there exists a handful of theories that offer competing theoretical explanations and outcomes. SEM would allow researchers to test, refine, and potentially develop new communication theory by conducting critical tests in SEM.

An exemplary test of competing models using SEM can be found in Eveland et al. (2005). Eveland and colleagues detail the need to properly address a core causal issue of the relationship between media use and political knowledge. A series of competing structural equation models were offered by the researchers, allowing for definitive directional claims to be made that media use produces knowledge more so than knowledge produces political mass communication consumption. The testing of competing models to address core causal concerns within an area of research is but one example of how this particular SEM technique can aid the field.

Decomposition of Effects

In considering how to best understand political communication processes, we agree with Cudeck and Henly (1991), who stated that "A model is a descriptive device. It can summarize a large amount of data or provide a way to operationalize a complex behavioral process that is intriguing but incompletely understood" (1991, p. 517). Indeed, as has been argued before, researchers using SEM have not fully considered political communication as a *process* which can be better understood by considering both direct *and* indirect effects (Holbert & Stephenson, 2003). To the contrary, a substantial amount of political communication research has focused only on direct effects, neglecting the important assumption that communication can work indirectly through other variables. By not assessing indirect effects, the discipline is systematically underestimating the overall influence of communication in a number of contexts. By extracting measurement, the effects—both indirect and direct—will be less likely to be attenuated. Decomposing the effects reveals a much more complete understanding of communication as a process and moves the discipline beyond the study of direct effects alone.

To illustrate, consider a study by McLeod, Scheufele, and Moy (1999) on the influence of newspaper public affairs use, television public affairs use, and interpersonal communication on institutional versus nontraditional forms of political participation. The structural models are fairly complex, therefore we extracted one example from their institutional participation model to illustrate the utility of examining media's indirect influence. McLeod and colleagues (1999) determined that political interest in local politics directly influences institutionalized political participation. The direct effect is .21. Yet, political interest further influenced institutionalized participation indirectly through TV hard news consumption, interpersonal discussion, and newspaper hard news consumption. Hence, after examining the *indirect* effect of political interest through both mass media and interpersonal channels, the total effect on political participation increases to .35. This total effect is almost double what an analysis of only the direct effect would produce. Moreover, the study sheds light on the relations among the mass media and interpersonal channels in a political context. A review of their model shows that TV hard news use influences newspaper hard news use both directly and indirectly through interpersonal discussion. Hence, various forms of communication can act as mediators of one another in a given model. Their conclusions are far richer as a result of examining both the direct and indirect effects of media use and interpersonal communication in political participation.

Two-Staged Least Squares Estimation

However, there exist alternative estimators that afford a different set of advantages to full information estimators, such as generalized least squares (GLS), which are generally regarded as more restrictive in their assumptions (Oczkowski, 2002). Two-stage least squares (2SLS) estimation is a noniterative, partial/limited estimation technique (Bollen, 2001) designed for continuous variables. 2SLS is appropriate for use in SEM when a predictor variable is related both to the criterion variable but also to its error or disturbance term. The error or disturbance term may also be correlated with the predictor variable's error term. As a result of these relationships, the structural model is no longer unidirectional, or recursive, but instead it is now a nonrecursive (and fairly complex) model (Bollen, 1996a). "Nonrecursive models contain reciprocal causation, feedback loops, or they have correlated disturbances" (Bollen, 1989, p. 83). When such relationships exist in a structural model, but are not specified, the path coefficient is likely to be over- or underestimated and therefore will portray an inaccurate relationship between the variables.

To compensate for these nonrecursive relationships, researchers must replace the problematic predictor variable with an *instrumental variable*. The instrumental variable must (a) be highly correlated with the original predictor variable, but (b) not have a reciprocal relationship with the criterion variable or its error or disturbance term. According to Bollen (1996b), the 2SLS estimator is an instrumental variable estimator that "uses the instrumental variables to find a consistent estimator of the coefficient of the original explanatory" or predictor variable (p. 110). When more than one replacement is available, the 2SLS estimator "forms the optimal combination of IVs [instrumental variables] when more than one IV is available" (p. 110). Clearly, the use of 2SLS requires careful consideration of not only distributional but also theoretical properties of measured variables.

There exist multiple 2SLS estimators. Jöreskog (1983) applied 2SLS to confirmatory factor analysis while Jöreskog and Sörbom (1996) used 2SLS estimation to generate start values in LISREL. Lance, Cornwell, and Mulaik's (1988) version uses maximum likelihood for the measurement model and then applies 2SLS to the structural model. More recent work on 2SLS, however, can be solely applied to structural parameters, allows correlated errors, is free of asymptotical distributional properties, and can be used to estimate interactions (see Bollen, 1996b, 2001; Bollen & Paxton, 1998). Oczkowski (2002) provides a comparison of 2SLS to ML estimators, specifically noting that 2SLS maintains relaxed distributional properties, is a limited information estimator and thereby isolates specification error to a single equation, is robust to medium deviations from normality (Brown, 1990), and tends to perform better with smaller samples (Bollen, 1996b). Bollen and Biesanz (2002) note that the 2SLS estimator "does not require that the observed variables come from normal distributions, and it is less sensitive to specification errors than are the full information estimators" (p. 568).

For political communication, 2SLS estimators could be appropriate for scale development (Oczkowski, 2002) or estimating nonlinear interactions (Bollen & Paxton, 1998). Additionally, 2SLS can be used to estimate a model that presents a complex set of relationships between variables, for example, within organizations where recursive relationships are very likely to exist. To the best of our knowledge, 2SLS estimators have yet to be used for SEM in political communication research, although they clearly afford some advantages.

CONCLUSION

The points outlined in this chapter focus on specific aspects of SEM that have not been widely employed in political communication, but which may be of vital importance as the field continues to advance in the areas of measurement development and testing of relationships between constructs. Some techniques have been around for several decades but have not made their way into the political communication literature with any consistency (e.g., MTMM matrix models, multiple group models). Still other techniques represent relatively new advancements in the use of SEM (e.g., semi-confirmatory factor analysis, latent variable score interaction modeling). Other procedures speak to the heart of SEM as a confirmatory technique (e.g., testing competing models). No matter the case, increased exploration of these varied SEM techniques would serve to advance the field immeasurably.

SEM should be treated as but one analytical tool in the political communication researcher's analytical tool box. SEM is a highly flexible technique that can take on a variety of analyses but should be not been seen as the optimal means by which to address every research question. It is easy for researchers in any field to get lost in the models they are testing, but there needs to be recognition that other analytical tools may offer more utility when addressing a certain set of research questions. While this chapter has called for expanded use of SEM in some very specific ways, there are no set boundaries as to what SEM can and cannot do as a multivariate technique. These boundaries are continuously evolving, so it is important for political communication researchers to remain vigilant with regards to the latest uses of the technique to stay current with how it may best suit the field's needs.

REFERENCES

Baumgartner, H., & Homburg, C. (1996). Applications of structural equation modeling in marketing and consumer research: A review. *International Journal of Research in Marketing, 13*, 139–161.

Benoit, W. L., & Holbert, R. L. (2008). Conducting communication research at methodological intersections: Replication, multiple quantitative methods, and bridging the quantitative–qualitative divide. *Journal of Communication, 58*, 615–628.

Blalock, H. M., Jr. (1979). Measurement and conceptualization problems: The major obstacle to integrating theory and research. *American Sociological Review, 44*, 370–390.

Bollen, K. A. (1989). *Structural equations with latent variables*. New York: John Wiley & Sons.

Bollen, K. A. (1996a). A limited-information estimator for LISREL models with and without heteroscedastic errors. In G. Marcoulides & R. Schumacker (Eds.), *Advanced structural equation modeling techniques* (pp. 227–241). Mahwah, NJ: Lawrence Erlbaum.

Bollen, K. A. (1996b). An alternative two stage least squares (2SLS) estimator for latent variable equations. *Psychometrika, 61*, 109–121.

Bollen, K. A. (2001). Two-stage least squares and latent variable models: Simultaneous estimation and robustness to misspecifications. In R. Cudeck, S. Du Toit, & D. Sorbom (Eds.), *Structural equation modeling: Present and future* (pp. 119–138). Lincolnwood, IL: Scientific Software.

Bollen, K. A., & Biesanz, J. C. (2002). A note on a two-stage least squares estimator for higher-order factor analyses. *Sociological Methods and Research, 30*, 568–579.

Bollen, K., & Paxton, P. (1998). Interactions of latent variables in structural equation models. *Structural equation modeling, 5*, 267–293.

Boruch, R. F., Larkin, J. D., Wolins, L., & Mackinney, A. C. (1970). Alternative methods of analysis: Multitrait-multimethod data. *Educational and Psychological Measurement, 30*, 833–853.

Brown, R. L. (1990). The robustness of 2SLS estimation of a non-normally distributed confirmatory factor analysis model. *Multivariate Behavioral Research, 25*(4), 455–466.

Browne, M. W., & Cudeck, R. (1993). Alternative ways of assessing model fit. In K. A. Bollen & J. S. Long (Eds.), *Testing structural equation models* (pp. 136–162). Thousand Oaks, CA: Sage.

Bryant, F. B. (2000). Assessing the validity of measurement. In L. G. Grimm & P. R. Yarnold (Eds.), *Reading and understanding more multivariate statistics* (pp. 99–146). Washington, DC: American Psychological Association.

Bryant, F. B., & Yarnold, P. R. (1995). Principle-components analysis, and exploratory and confirmatory factor analysis. In L. G. Grimm & P. R. Yarnold (Eds.), *Reading and understanding multivariate statistics* (pp. 99–136). Washington, DC: American Psychological Association.

Byrne, B. M. (2001). *Structural equation modeling with AMOS: Basic concepts, applications, and programming*. Mahwah, NJ: Lawrence Erlbaum.

Byrne, B. M., & Campbell, T. L. (1999). Cross-cultural comparisons and the presumption of equivalent measurement and theoretical structure: A look beneath the surface. *Journal of Cross-Cultural Psychology, 30*, 555–574.

Campbell, D. T., & Fiske, D. W. (1959). Convergent and discriminant validation by the multitrait-multimethod matrix. *Psychological Bulletin, 56*, 81–105.

Cheung, D. (2000). Evidence of a single second-order factor in student ratings of teaching effectiveness. *Structural Equation Modeling, 7*, 442–460.

Cheung, M. W. L., Leung, K., & Au, K. (2006). Evaluating multilevel models in cross-cultural research: An illustration with social axioms. *Journal of Cross-Cultural Psychology, 37*(5), 522–541.

Chou, C. P., & Bentler, P. M. (1990). Model modification in covariance structure modeling: A comparison among likelihood ratio, LaGrange multiplier, and Wald tests. *Multivariate Behavioral Research, 25*, 115–136.

Cudeck, R., & Henly, S. J. (1991). Multiplicative models and MTMM matrices. *Journal of Educational Statistics, 13*, 131–147.

Eveland, W. P., Hayes, A. F., Shah, D. V., & Kwak, N. (2005). Understanding the relationship between communication and political knowledge: A model comparison approach using panel data. *Political Communication, 22*, 423–446.

Glöckner-Rist, A., & Hoijtink, H. (2003). The best of both worlds: Factor analysis of dichotomous data using item response theory and structural equation modeling. *Structural Equation Modeling, 10*, 544–565.

Haggland, G. (2001). Milestones in the history of factor analysis. In R. Cudeck, S. DuToit, & D. Sorbom (Eds.), *Structural equation modeling: Present and future* (pp. 11–38). Chicago: Scientific Software International.

Hipp, J. R., & Bollen, K. A. (2003). Model fit in structural equation models with censored, ordinal, and dichotomous variables: Testing vanishing tetrads. *Sociological Methodology, 33*, 267–305.

Holbert, R. L. (2005a). Television news viewing, governmental scope, and postmaterialist spending: Assessing partisan differences in mediation-based processes of influence. *Journal of Broadcasting & Electronic Media, 49*, 416–434.

Holbert, R. L. (2005b). Intramedia mediation: The cumulative and complementary effects of news media use. *Political Communication, 22*, 447–462.

Holbert, R. L., & Hansen, G. J. (2008). Stepping beyond message specificity in the study of emotion as mediator and inter-emotion associations across attitude objects: *Fahrenheit 9/11*, anger, and debate superiority. *Media Psychology, 11*, 98–118.

Holbert, R. L., & Stephenson, M. T. (2002). Structural equation modeling in the communication sciences, 1995–2000. *Human Communication Research, 28*, 531–551.

Holbert, R. L., & Stephenson, M. T. (2003). The importance of analyzing indirect effects in media effects research: Testing for mediation in structural equation modeling. *Journal of Broadcasting & Electronic Media, 47*, 553–569.

Holbert, R. L., & Stephenson, M. T. (2008). Commentary on the uses and misuses of structural equation modeling in communication research. In A. F. Hayes, M. D. Slater, & L. B. Snyder (Eds.), *The Sage handbook of advanced data analysis methods for communication research* (pp. 185–218). Thousand Oaks, CA: Sage.

Holbert, R. L., Tschida, D. A., Dixon, M., Cherry, K., Steuber, K., & Airne, D. (2005). The *West Wing* and depictions of the American presidency: Expanding the theoretical and empirical domains of framing in political communication. *Communication Quarterly, 53*, 505–522.

Hoyle, R. H. (Ed.). *Structural equation modeling: Concepts, issues, and applications.* Thousand Oaks, CA: Sage Publications.

Hullett, C. R., Louden, A. D., & Mitra, A. (2003). Emotion and political cognition: A test of bipolar, two-dimensional, and discrete models of emotion in predicting involvement and learning. *Communication Monographs, 70*, 250–263.

Jöreskog, K. G. (1967). Some contributions to maximum likelihood factor analysis. *Psychometrika, 32*, 443–482.

Jöreskog, K. G. (1983). Factor analysis as an error-in-variables model. In H. Wainer & S. Messick (Eds.), *Principles of modern psychological measurement* (pp. 185–196). Hillsdale, NJ: Lawrence Erlbaum.

Jöreskog, K. G. (1993). Testing structural equation models. In K. A. Bollen & J. S. Long (Eds.), *Testing structural equation models* (pp. 294–316). Newbury Park, CA: Sage.

Jöreskog, K. G. (2000, July 10). *Latent variable scores and their uses.* SSI technical report retrieved July 4, 2010, from http://www.ssicentral.com/lisrel/techdocs/lvscores.pdf

Jöreskog, K. G., & Lawley, D. N. (1968). New methods in maximum likelihood factor analysis. *British Journal of Mathematical and Statistical Psychology, 21*, 85–96.

Jöreskog, K. G., & Sörbom, D. (1996). *LISREL 8: User's reference guide.* Chicago: Scientific Software.

Jörsekog, K., Sörbom, D., du Toit, S., & du Toit, M. (1999). *LISREL 8: New statistical features.* Chicago: Scientific Software.

Kaplan, D. (1995). Statistical power in structural equation modeling. In R. Hoyle (Ed). *Structural equation modeling: Concepts, issues, and applications* (pp. 100–117). Thousand Oaks, CA: Sage.

Kaplan, D. (2000). *Structural equation modeling: Foundations and extensions.* Thousand Oaks, CA: Sage.

Kaplan, D., & Elliott. P. R. (1997) A model-based approach to validating education indicators using multilevel structural equation modeling. *Journal of Educational and Behavioral Statistics, 22*, 323–348.

Kenny, D. A., & Kashy, D. A. (1992). Analysis of the multitrait-multimethod matrix by confirmatory factor analysis. *Psychological Bulletin, 112*, 165–172.

Klem, L. (2000). Structural equation modeling. In L. G. Grimm & P. Yarnold (Eds.), *Reading and understanding MORE multivariate statistics* (pp. 227–260). Washington, DC: American Psychological Association.

Kline, R. B. (2005). *Principles and practice of structural equation modeling* (2nd ed.). New York: Guilford.

Klofstad, C. A. (2007). Talk leads to recruitment: How discussions about politics and current events increase civic participation. *Political Research Quarterly, 60*, 180–191.

Kohring, M., & Matthes, J. (2007). Trust in news media: Development and validation of a multidimensional scale. *Communication Research, 34*, 231–252.

Lance, C. E., Cornwell, J. M., & Mulaik, S. (1988). Limited information parameter estimates for latent or mixed manifest and latent variable models. *Multivariate Behavior Research, 23*, 155–167.

Lawley, D. N., & Maxwell, A. E. (1971). *Factor analysis as a statistical method.* London: Butterworth.

Levine, T. R. (2005). Confirmatory factor analysis and scale validation in communication research. *Communication Research Reports, 22*, 335–338.

Leyland, A. H. (2004, August). *A review of multilevel modeling in SPSS.* Unpublished manuscript. Retrieved July 4, 2010, from http://stat.gamma.rug.nl/snijders/reviewspss.pdf.

Lord, F. M., & Novick, M. R. (1968). *Statistical theories of mental test scores.* Reading, MA: Addison-Welsey.

MacCallum, R. C. (1995). Model specification: Procedures, strategies, and related issues. In R. H. Hoyle (Ed.), *Structural equation modeling: Concepts, issues, and applications* (pp. 16–36). Thousand Oaks, CA: Sage.

MacCallum, R. C., & Austin, J. T. (2000). Applications of structural equation modeling in psychological research. *Annual Review of Psychology, 51*, 201–226.

Maruyama, G. M. (1998). *Basics of structural equation modeling.* Thousand Oaks, CA: Sage.

McDonald, R. P. (2005). Semiconfirmatory factor analysis: The example of anxiety and depression. *Structural Equation Modeling, 12*, 163–172.

McLeod, J. M., Scheufele, D. A., & Moy, P. (1999). Community, communication, and participation: The role of mass media and interpersonal discussion in local political participation. *Political Communication, 16*, 315–336.

Muthén, B. (1984). A general structural equation model with dichotomous, ordered categorical, and continuous latent variable indicators. *Psychometrika, 49*, 115–132.

Muthén, L. K., & Muthén, B. O. (2002). How to use a Monte Carlo study to decide on sample size and determine power. *Structural Equation Modeling, 9*, 599–620.

Oczkowski, E. (2002). Discriminating between measurement scales using non-nested tests and 2SLS: Monte Carlo evidence. *Structural Equation Modeling, 9*, 103–125.

Olsson, U. (1979). Maximum likelihood estimation of the polychoric correlation coefficient. *Psychometrika, 44*, 443–460.

Pan, Z., & McLeod, J. M. (1991). Multilevel analysis in mass communication research. *Communication Research, 18*, 140–173.

Poortinga, Y. H. (1989). Equivalence of cross-cultural data: An overview of basic issues. *International Journal of Psychology, 24*, 737–756.

Raudenbush, S. W., & Bryk, A. S. (2002). *Hierarchical linear models: Applications and data analysis methods.* Thousand Oaks, CA: Sage.

Russell, D., & Cutrona, C. E. (1991). Social support, stress, and depressive symptoms among the elderly: Test of a process model. *Psychology and Aging, 6*, 190–201.

Satorra, A. (1989). Alternative test criteria in covariance structure analysis: A unified approach. *Psychometrika, 54*, 131–151.

Satorra, A., & Saris, W. E. (1985). The power of the likelihood ratio test in covariance structure analysis. *Psychometrika, 50*, 83–90.

Schumacker, R. E. (2002). Latent variable interaction modeling. *Structural Equation Modeling, 9*, 40–54.

Schumacker, R. E., & Lomax, R. G. (2004). *A beginner's guide to structural equation modeling* (2nd ed.). Mahwah, NJ: Lawrence Erlbaum.

Schumacker, R. E., & Marcoulides, G. A. (1998). *Interaction and nonlinear effects in structure equation modeling*. Mahwah, NJ: Lawrence Erlbaum.

Shah, D. V., & Scheufele, D. A. (2006). Explicating opinion leadership: Nonpolitical dispositions, information consumption, and civic participation. *Political Communication, 23,* 1–22.

Thurstone, L. L. (1947). *Multiple-factor analysis*. Chicago: University of Chicago Press.

Wendorf, C. A. (2002). Comparisons of structural equation modeling and hierarchical linear modeling approaches to couples' data. *Structural Equation Modeling, 9,* 126–140.

23

Mediation and the Estimation of Indirect Effects in Political Communication Research

Andrew F. Hayes
School of Communication
The Ohio State University

Kristopher J. Preacher
Department of Psychology
University of Kansas

Teresa A. Myers
School of Communication
The Ohio State University

Much research in the communication and political science fields—political communication research being no exception—seeks to establish the extent to which certain communication-related variables (e.g., exposure to political debates, the tone of news coverage about politicians, or the diversity in opinions of those with whom one talks about politics) have effects on various political outcomes (e.g., evaluation of candidates running for office, political cynicism, or participation in the political process). To be sure, studies to establish or refute the existence of effects are important. But studies, and the investigators who conduct them, are usually much more impressive and helpful in advancing our understanding when they go further by establishing not only *whether or not* an effect exists or *how large* that effect is, but also *why* that effect exists. What is the process at work that produces an association between political discussion and participation, or between exposure to political debates and political cynicism, or between the tone of news coverage and evaluation of candidates running for public office? For example, is it that frequent political talk exposes one to more diverse viewpoints, which in turn makes one feel confused or less confident in one's beliefs, which in turn translates into a reduced likelihood of converting those beliefs into political action? Or might frequent talk increase one's sense that one can make a difference in the outcomes of the political process, spawning greater participation in that process?

Questions about mechanisms or process invoke the concept of *mediation*, the topic of this chapter. We say that the effect of some independent variable X on outcome variable Y is *mediated by M* if M is causally situated between X and Y such that changes in X cause changes in M, which in turn cause changes in Y. The most basic mediation model one can test takes the form in Figure 23.1 panel A. In this model, X's effect on Y occurs both *directly* (the link directly from X to Y) as well as *indirectly*, through X's effect on mediator variable M, which then affects Y. Of course, other more complicated mediation models are possible and no doubt are at work in political communication processes. Figure 23.1 Panel B, for instance, depicts a model in which X's effect is transmitted indirectly through multiple mediators. An extension of this model allows the mediators to affect each other, as in Figure 23.1 Panel C. Many such models can be constructed by linking variables in a sequence of causal associations together.

Quantifying and testing indirect effects is the focus of this chapter. After first briefly reviewing some recent examples of published research in political communication focused on testing questions about mediation, we describe how indirect effects are typically quantified and how inferences about their magnitudes are made. Although there are many methods that can be used to estimate the paths in these models, we focus on the use of ordinary least squares (OLS) regression and structural equation modeling (SEM), as these are the methods most likely to be familiar to the reader. Similarly, there are many methods that have been discussed in the literature for making statistical inferences about indirect effects, but we focus largely on those few that are implemented in existing computing packages, so as to reduce the computational burden on those interested in applying the material described in this chapter in their own research.

Throughout this chapter, we will use the terms "mediation" and "indirect effect" loosely and somewhat interchangeably, although there is some debate in the literature over whether or not it is legitimate to do so (Mathieu & Taylor, 2006). Implied in the definition of mediation provided above is that X and Y are associated. That is, an effect that doesn't exist (what we will call the "total effect" below) can't be said to be mediated. For this reason, it is not uncommon for investigators to ignore

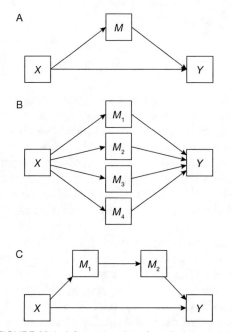

FIGURE 23.1 A few examples of mediation models.

the possibility of an indirect effect of X on Y through one or more intervening variables in the absence of an association between X and Y. This is a practice we do not endorse, for it is possible for X to indirectly affect Y in the absence of compelling evidence of an association between X and Y, especially in models that involve more than one intervening variable. Regardless, there is general agreement among experts in this area that a nonzero indirect effect in the direction consistent with the proposed mediation process is a necessary condition for a claim of mediation. For this reason, understanding how to quantify and test indirect effects is important for researchers interested in testing mediation hypotheses. Mathieu and Taylor (2006, pp. 1037–1039) dwell at some length on the distinction between an indirect effect and mediation, and their discussion is worth reading.

Before beginning, we want to emphasize that questions about mediation and indirect effects are ultimately questions about causality, and in the absence of a research design that affords a causal conclusion, confidence in one's causal inferences must necessarily be tempered. Ideally, the proposed causal agent (labeled X in Figure 23.1) is experimentally manipulated or, if not, can at least be known to be causally prior to its presumed effect (on M and Y). In many studies in the published literature that include tests of mediation, including the examples in this chapter, the correct temporal sequencing of cause and effect cannot be established except through theoretical or logical argument. Although it is true that there is no substitute for a good theory, causal theories cannot be definitively supported empirically unless the conditions of causality have been established by good research design. The methods we describe in this chapter are based on mathematical operations involving indices of association. But as there are many explanations for association between variables in a mediation model (such as spuriousness; cf. MacKinnon, Krull, and Lockwood, 2000), in the absence of design that allows for confident cause–effect inference, the methods described here can be used to assess only whether the evidence is consistent with a mediation process. This should come as no surprise and is no different from any statistical method, as inferences are products of the mind more than products of math. Use your analysis to inform your thinking rather than as a substitute for thinking. A good overview of the criteria for establishing causality and the sticky philosophical debates to which the concept of "cause" give rise can be found in Davis (1985) or Holland (1986).

MEDIATION IN RECENT POLITICAL COMMUNICATION RESEARCH

Political communication scholars have devoted considerable empirical attention to understanding how mass and interpersonal communication exert their effects on various political outcomes. Keum and colleagues (2004), for instance, explored how the use of news (televised and print) and exposure to various forms of televised entertainment (dramas, sitcoms, and talk shows) are linked to civic participation, such as volunteering and participating in community meetings. They tested a model in which the use of news and entertainment television affects participation through their influence on concerns and behavior pertaining to achieving social status and environmental degradation. They found that both news and entertainment media have both direct and indirect effects on participation, with increased exposure actually prompting both social status-oriented consumerism and concerns about the environment, which in turn both prompt greater participation. Relatedly, Holbert (2005a) examined the effects of television news viewing on attitudes about government spending on social programs, testing the hypothesis that the use of televised news exerts its influence on such attitudes by changing perceptions of the role of government in society. Indeed it does, although the strength of this effect differs as a function of party identification. According to Holbrook and Hill (2005), exposure to certain kinds of television shows can affect evaluations of political leaders by changing the salience or chronic accessibility of social issues pertaining to the themes portrayed in those shows. Using experimental and cross-sectional survey data, they find that exposure to crime dramas makes crime a more salient problem facing the nation, which in turn influences how the president is evaluated. In the realm of interpersonal communication, Eveland (2004) examines the mechanisms through which political discussion can increase political knowledge. His results support a mediated relationship in which interpersonal discussion about politics increases political knowledge through the cognitive elaboration of political information such discussion produces, which in turn facilitates greater knowledge acquisition.

These studies show that communication's effects on political outcomes (such as knowledge and attitudes) frequently are mediated. But communication-related variables have also been conceptualized and empirically studied as mediators of the effects of other variables. For example, Gidengil and Everitt (2003) show that the effect of the sex of a political leader on the public's evaluations of the leader occurs in part through the tone of the news coverage about politicians. Specifically, they found that journalists more frequently use negative or aggressive verbs in their coverage of female compared to male politicians, and this tonal difference contributes to differences in individuals' evaluations of those politicians, with females being perceived more negatively as a result of these differences in tone of coverage. Holbert, Shah, and Kwak (2003) report that exposure to three types of prime-time television programming (traditional dramas, progressive dramas, and situational comedies) mediates the effects of demographic variables on opinions about women's rights issues. That is, some of the differences in opinions that we see between people who differ in education, age, or sex is attributable to differences in their selection of entertainment television, which tends to portray women in certain ways. Other examples of communication as mediator include Pinkleton and Austin's (2001) study of political disaffection and Eveland's (2001) cognitive mediation model of learning from the news.

Although there are many studies in the field of political communication which place communication squarely in the role of independent or mediating variable, relatively few studies focus on communication as the ultimate outcome of interest. One notable exception is Sellers and Schaffner's (2007) analysis of media coverage of the U.S. Senate. They found that the way politicians structured events (such as press conferences) impacted the interest journalists found in the event, which then influenced the amount of coverage the event received. Therefore, news coverage of a U.S. senator was influenced by the extent to which a senator could structure an event that captured the attention and interest of journalists. Another example is Stroud's (2007) study of the determinants of political discussion. She found that an individual's attitude toward President G. W. Bush predicted whether or not they viewed the film *Fahrenheit 9/11* (communication as mediator), which in turn purportedly affected frequency of political discussion (communication as outcome).

Stroud's *Fahrenheit 9/11* study is an example of one in which communication variables play multiple roles, as both mediator (i.e., selective exposure to certain media content) and outcome (frequency of political talk). So, too, is Eveland's (2001) cognitive mediation model of learning, frequently applied to political contexts, in which motivations to use certain forms of news media (an independent variable) affect attention to news (a mediator), which in turn affects how much one learns. We would also expect there to be a feedback loop or "cycle," whereby communication (e.g., exposure to campaign advertisements) has certain effects on noncommunication variables (e.g., political cynicism) which, in turn, affect communication-related variables (e.g., interest in campaign news and selective avoidance of political advertisements). Alternatively, a communication-related outcome could function as a mediator of a communication outcome to follow, as in Holbert's (2005b) intermedia mediation model of political engagement and learning. Although such cyclical processes no doubt are at work in the world (cf. Slater, 2007), the extra empirical demands they require result in relatively few such studies in the literature. Regardless, as the above discussion makes clear, the study of mediation, mechanism, and process in one form or another is alive and well in the field of political communication.

PARSING THE TOTAL EFFECT INTO DIRECT AND INDIRECT COMPONENTS

One of the fundamental rules of path analysis is that a variable's effect, such as the effect of X on Y, can be mathematically partitioned into various components by tracing the paths between the two variables in a path diagram (as in Figure 23.1). In this section we will focus on those components of a path diagram directly pertinent to mediation analysis—the *total effect* of X on Y, the *indirect effect(s)* of X on Y through one or more mediators, and the *direct* effect of X on Y. We will illustrate the computation of these effects using data provided to us by William Eveland from an investigation of the cognitive mediation model of learning from the news (Eveland, 2001). This model proposes that people learn more through the media when they are motivated to attend to and deeply process the information in a way that facilitates learning. The data we use are from a sample of residents of Madison, Wisconsin, and nearby communities in 1985. Responses to various questions were aggregated to form indices quantifying the constructs central to the cognitive mediation model: *surveillance gratifications* (motivation to acquire information from the media about politics), *attention to news* (the extent to which respondents are exposed to and, when so exposed, focus their attention on news about national government and politics), *elaborative processing* (the extent to which respondents report thinking about things they've heard about in the news), and knowledge of recent events in politics and national and international affairs. For details on measurement, see Eveland (2001).

Simple Mediation Model

Figure 23.2 illustrates the *simple mediation model*, in which X transmits its effect on Y through a single mediator variable M. The tracing rules of path analysis tell us that the effect of X on Y in

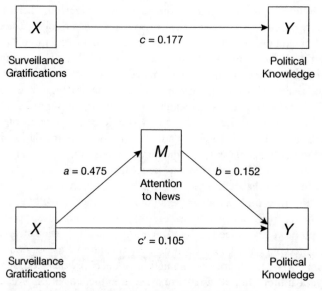

FIGURE 23.2 A simple mediation model.

this model can be partitioned into components by tracing the paths along which one can travel in the diagram to get from X to Y while never moving in a direction opposite to the direction of presumed causal flow. The direction of causal flow is denoted in a path diagram by the direction of the arrow.

The various effects in a mediation model that we discuss here can be estimated in a number of different ways. The simplest approach is through a set of OLS regression models. A more general approach that could be applied to simple models such as this as well as more complicated models would involve the use of an SEM program such as EQS, AMOS, LISREL, or Mplus, among others. An illustration of the use of SEM will be provided later. Unless we say otherwise, all effects in this chapter are estimated using OLS regression. Although any statistical software that can conduct regression could be used, we used a set of macros described by Preacher and Hayes (2004, 2008b) written for SPSS and SAS, which provide all the necessary information while simultaneously providing various inferential statistics for testing hypotheses about the indirect effects that we discuss later in this chapter.

The total effect of X on Y in any causal diagram is quantified quite simply as the regression coefficient in a model predicting Y from X, denoted in Figure 23.2 as c. This total effect in a simple mediation model can be partitioned into two components. The direct effect of X on Y is the c' path in Figure 23.2, quantified as the unstandardized regression weight for X in a model predicting Y from *both* X and M. It quantifies how two cases which differ by one measurement unit on X but which are equal on M (i.e., adjusting or controlling for M) are expected to differ on Y. The second component is the indirect effect of X on Y through M, which consists of the product of the a and b paths in Figure 23.2. The a path is the regression weight in a model estimating M from X, and the b path is the partial regression weight for M in a model estimating Y from both X and M. In a model with only observed (rather than latent) variables, the direct and indirect effects of X sum to produce the total effect of X. That is, $c = c' + ab$. Simple algebraic manipulation shows that the indirect effect is the difference between the total and direct effect, $ab = c - c'$. So the indirect effect quantifies the change in the effect of X on Y after controlling for M's effect on Y.[1]

Using the Eveland (2001) data, we estimated the direct, indirect, and total effects of surveillance gratifications (X) on political knowledge (Y), with attention to news (M) as the proposed mediator. The first step is to estimate the total effect of surveillance gratifications on knowledge, derived by regressing political knowledge on surveillance gratifications. In these data, $c = 0.177$ (see Appendix 23.1 for the output from the SPSS version of the macro that we used to estimate the effects we discuss here, and Table 23.1 for a summary of these effects). So two people who differ by one unit in their surveillance gratifications are estimated to differ by 0.177 units in their political knowledge. Although these data come from a correlational design, a very liberal causal interpretation would be that if we could move people upward one unit on the gratifications scale, we would expect that their political knowledge would increase by 0.177 units on the knowledge scale.

According to the model in Figure 23.2, some of the change in political knowledge that we would expect to occur by increasing a person's surveillance gratification would occur by changing his or her attention to news, which in turn would affect how much that person learns. This is the indirect effect of gratification on knowledge through attention. But some of the effect of surveillance on knowledge is direct, occurring either without the aid of attention, or through some other mechanism not included in this simple mediation model. Just how much of this effect of X on Y is direct and how much is indirect through attention to news?

To answer this question, we must estimate the direct and indirect effects. The indirect effect of surveillance gratifications on political knowledge is estimated as the product of the effect of surveillance gratifications on attention (a) and the effect of attention on political knowledge (b).

TABLE 23.1
Path Coefficients and Indirect Effects for Three Mediation Models (Standard Errors in Parentheses)

	Path Coefficients			Indirect Effects			
	to Knowlege (K)	to Attention (A)	to Elaboration (E)	Estimate	Sobel Z	Symmetric 95%CI	Bootstrap 95% CI†
Model 1 (Figure 23.2)							
from Surveillance (S)	.105 (.035)	.475 (.058)					
from Attention (A)	.152 (.027)						
S→A→K				.072 (.016)	4.651	.042, .103	.042, .107†
Model 2 (Figure 23.3)							
from Surveillance (S)	.086 (.034)	.475 (.058)	.280 (.057)				
from Attention (A)	.126 (.027)						
from Elaboration (E)	.108 (.027)						
Total				.090 (.017)	5.311	.057, .123	.062, .129
Specific: S→A→K				.060 (.015)	4.064	.031, .089	.033, .094
Specific: S→E→K				.030 (.010)	3.080	.010, .050	.013, .056
Model 3 (Figure 23.4)							
from Surveillance	.087 (.034)	.475 (.058)	.167(.059)				
from Attention	.126 (.027)		.238(.046)				
from Elaboration	.108 (.027)						
Total				.090 (.017)	5.318	.057, .123	.058, .127
Specific: S→A→K				.060 (.015)	4.069	.031, .089	.030, .096
Specific: S→E→K				.018 (.008)	2.290	.002, .034	.005, .039
Specific: S→A→E→K				.012 (.004)	2.942	.004, .020	.005, .024

Total Effect = 0.177 (0.033) † Percentile CIs for Model 1 (from Preacher & Hayes, 2004) and BC CIs for models 2 (from Preacher & Hayes, 2008b) and 3 (Mplus)

The former is the regression weight estimating attention from just surveillance gratifications. Here, $a = 0.475$. The latter is the regression weight for attention in a model estimating political knowledge from both attention and surveillance gratifications. In these data, $b = 0.152$. When multiplied together, the indirect effect of surveillance gratifications on knowledge through attention is $ab = (0.475)(0.152) = 0.072$. The direct effect of surveillance gratifications comes out of the same model used to derive b, as it is the regression coefficient for surveillance gratifications controlling for attention to news. We found that $c' = 0.105$. Notice that, as promised, the total effect equals the sum of the direct and indirect effects: $0.177 = 0.105 + 0.072$.

Combining all this information, we can say that of the 0.177 unit difference in knowledge attributable to a unit difference in surveillance gratifications (the total effect), 0.072 of it is the result of the effect of gratification on attention, which in turn influences knowledge. The remaining 0.105 is direct, spurious, or attributable to other indirect effects not explicitly modeled.

An interesting question is how much of a variable's effect is due to a mediation process and how much of it is due to some other process. There is no universally agreed-upon approach to answering this question. One approach is to calculate the ratio of the indirect effect to the total effect, i.e., ab/c. In this example, this quantity is $0.072/0.177 = 0.407$. This *proportion of total effect that is mediated* measure can be interpreted to mean that 40.7% of the total effect of surveillance gratifications on political knowledge is due to its indirect effect through attention to news. An alternative proposal is to calculate the *ratio of the indirect effect to the direct effect*, i.e., ab/c'. Here, this ratio is $0.072/0.105 = 0.686$, meaning that the indirect effect through attention is about 68.6% of the size of the direct effect. Although these ratios make sense, they can be problematic in some situations. The proportion of total effect that is a mediated measure is not constrained to lie between 0 and 1 because, paradoxical as it may seem, it actually is possible for the indirect effect to be larger than the total effect or for the indirect effect and direct effect to have different signs, producing a negative proportion. The ratio of the indirect to direct effect also can be negative, or may involve division by 0 or by a very small number, which in turn produces impossible or ambiguous estimates. See Preacher and Hayes (2008a) and Hayes (2009) for a discussion of effect size measures for mediation effects.

Single-Step Multiple Mediator Model

Of course, X may and often does exert its effect indirectly on some outcome Y through multiple mediators. Figure 23.3 is an example of one type of such a model, the *single-step multiple mediator model*. Although there are several mediators in this model, no mediator causally affects another mediator, so it requires stepping through only a single mediator to get to Y (and hence the name, "single-step" model). Path c' is the direct effect of X on Y, as in the simple mediation model, defined as the regression weight for X in a model estimating Y from X and all k of the proposed mediator variables ($k = 2$ in Figure 23.3). But now there are multiple paths from X to Y through the set of mediators, each referred to as a *specific indirect effect*. The specific indirect effect of X on Y through M_i is the product of the a and b paths linking X, M_i, and Y. For example, the specific indirect effect of X on Y through M_1 is $a_1 b_1$, where a_1 is the weight for X in a model estimating M_1 from X, and b_1 is the weight for M_1 in a model estimating Y from X and all k M variables. In a single-step multiple mediator model, the *total indirect effect* of X on Y is the sum of the k specific indirect effects:

$$\text{total indirect effect of } X \text{ on } Y = \sum_{i=1}^{k} a_i b_i \tag{1}$$

As in the simple mediation model, the total effect, c, is the sum of the direct and indirect effects:

$$c = c' + \sum_{i=1}^{k} a_i b_i \qquad (2)$$

Simple algebra shows that the difference between the total and direct effect of X on Y, $c - c'$, is equal to the total indirect effect.

To illustrate, we extend the earlier example examining the direct and indirect effects of surveillance gratifications on political knowledge by adding an additional proposed mediator from the cognitive mediation model—elaboration—while retaining attention to news as a mediator variable. Here we use an SPSS macro described by Preacher and Hayes (2008b) to estimate the effects (see Appendix 23.2 for the output), although a series of OLS regressions could be conducted using any statistical program capable of doing regression, as could an SEM program such as Mplus, AMOS, EQS, or LISREL. But not all programs will produce the inferential tests we prefer, described in the next section.

The total effect is unchanged by the inclusion of additional mediators in the model. It remains $c = 0.177$. But now there are two indirect effects through which surveillance gratifications is proposed to exert its effect on political knowledge—the specific indirect effect through attention, and the specific indirect effect through elaboration. Arbitrarily labeling attention to news M_1 and elaboration M_2, to estimate these specific indirect effects we estimate a_1 and a_2, the paths from surveillance gratifications to attention and elaboration, respectively. The first path, a_1, is the same as the estimate from the simple mediation model, as this is still derived from a regression of attention on surveillance gratifications: $a_1 = 0.475$. The path from surveillance to elaboration is estimated by regressing elaboration on only surveillance gratifications: $a_2 = 0.280$. The b_1 and b_2 paths are derived from a model simultaneously predicting political knowledge from attention,

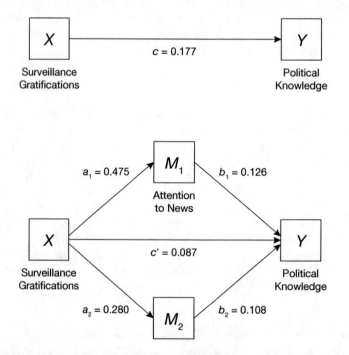

FIGURE 23.3 A single-step multiple mediator model with two proposed mediators. Not pictured is the covariance between the mediator residuals, rending this a saturated model.

elaboration, and surveillance gratifications. In these data, $b_1 = 0.126$ and $b_2 = 0.108$. Multiplying the corresponding a and b paths together yields the specific indirect effects of interest. For attention, $a_1 b_1 = (0.475)(0.126) = 0.060$, and for elaboration, $a_2 b_2 = (0.280)(0.108) = 0.030$. Summing the specific indirect effects yields the total indirect effect: $0.060 + 0.030 = 0.090$. Finally, the direct effect of elaboration comes from the same model used to estimate b_1 and b_2. It is the regression weight for surveillance gratifications in the model of knowledge, controlling for attention and elaboration: $c' = 0.087$. From equation (2), observe that the total effect is indeed equal to the sum of the direct effect and the two specific indirect effects (or, equivalently, the direct effect plus the total indirect effect): $0.177 = 0.087 + 0.060 + 0.030$.

In many instances, the single-step multiple mediator model is a much more realistic model of a process than is the simple mediation model, as effects often function through multiple mediators. When this is so and the investigator fails to include all the mediators that might be at work producing an effect, the simple mediation model can produce estimates of indirect effects that are statistically biased, in the same way that leaving an important variable out of a regression model related to one or more of the predictors and the outcome can bias the regression coefficient for those predictors. Indeed, it could be argued that direct effects in principle don't exist—that any direct effect that exists in a simple mediator model probably is itself mediated in some way, and the inclusion of another mediator in the model would likely shrink that direct effect toward zero. Thus, investigators should be open to investigating simultaneous indirect effects through multiple mediators. Furthermore, by doing so, it is possible to test for differences in the size of indirect effects through different mediators, as we discuss later.

Multiple-Step Multiple Mediator Model

This procedure for the partitioning of total effects into direct and indirect components also applies when mediators are allowed to causally affect other mediators. Figure 23.4 illustrates such a *multiple-step multiple mediator* model. Observe that, unlike the single-step multiple mediator model in Figure 23.3, this model has a path between two mediators, from M_1 to M_2. Using the tracing rule, four effects of X on Y can be identified—three specific indirect effects and one direct effect. The direct effect of X on Y, path c', is the weight for X in a model estimating Y from X, M_1, and M_2. The first specific indirect effect progresses only through M_1 and is defined as the product of the a_1 and b_1 paths, where the a_1 path is the weight for X in a model predicting M_1 from X and the b_1 path is the weight for M_1 in a model estimating Y from X, M_1, and M_2. The second specific indirect effect progresses through M_2 only. This effect is defined as the product of a_2 and b_2, where a_2 is the weight for X in a model predicting M_2 from X and M_1, and b_2 is the weight for M_2 in a model predicting Y from X, M_1, and M_2. The third specific indirect effect progresses first through M_1 and then through M_2 before ending at Y and is quantified as the product of a_1, a_3, and b_2, where a_3 is the regression weight for M_1 in a model predicting M_2 from M_1 and X, and a_1 and b_2 are defined as previously. These three specific indirect effects, when added together, define the total indirect effect of X on Y:

$$\text{Total indirect effect of } X \text{ on } Y = a_1 b_1 + a_2 b_2 + a_1 a_3 b_2 \tag{3}$$

and the total effect, c, is, as always, the sum of the direct and indirect effects:

$$c = c' + a_1 b_1 + a_2 b_2 + a_1 a_3 b_2 \tag{4}$$

Again, simple algebra shows that the total indirect effect is simply the difference between the total and direct effects: $c - c'$.

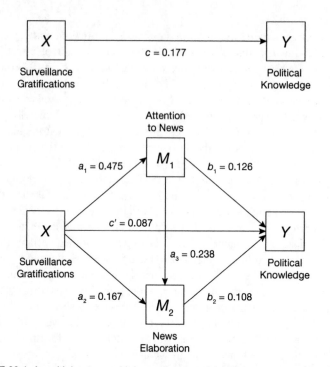

FIGURE 23.4 A multiple-step multiple mediator model with two proposed mediators.

Using the Eveland (2001) data, we estimated the direct and indirect effects for the full cognitive mediation model using both Mplus and SPSS. Mplus is also capable of doing all the inferential tests we soon discuss. Although SEM programs can be useful because they allow the investigator to analyze structural relations between latent variables and also provide measures of model fit, in this example the model is saturated so fit is necessarily perfect, and we use only observed variables, so these advantages of SEM do not exist here. Note that we could have estimated the coefficients in this model using any OLS regression program and then either used a different program for the inferential tests or conducted some of those tests by hand. Having said that, some of the inferential statistics we advocate later cannot be hand-calculated at all or, if they can, only with considerable effort with high potential for mistakes. For models of this variety, Mplus is our platform of choice, but others could be used. The estimates for this model can be found in Table 23.1 and Figure 23.4, and relevant Mplus and SPSS output can be found in Appendices 23.3 and 23.4, respectively.

Because the total effect of surveillance gratifications on political knowledge is not a function of the proposed mediators, the total effect remains $c = 0.177$. To derive the direct and indirect effects, we estimate all the path coefficients in the model simultaneously. The path from surveillance gratifications is estimated from a model predicting attention from just surveillance gratifications. As in all prior models, $a_1 = 0.475$. The path from surveillance gratifications to elaboration, a_2, is estimated by predicting elaboration from both surveillance gratifications and attention. Here, $a_2 = 0.167$. The model of elaboration also provides a_3, the path from attention to elaboration: $a_3 = 0.238$. All that remains for calculating indirect effects are the paths from the proposed mediators to the outcome. These are derived by predicting knowledge from both attention and elaboration while controlling for surveillance gratifications. Our model yields $b_1 = 0.126$ and $b_2 = 0.108$, respectively. The coefficient for surveillance gratifications in this model is c', the direct effect. In these data, $c' = 0.087$. Combining all this information yields the total and specific indirect effects of surveillance gratifications. The specific indirect effect through attention only is $a_1b_1 = (0.475)(0.126) = 0.060$. The specific indirect effect through elaboration only is $a_2b_2 = (0.167)(0.108) = 0.018$. The specific indirect effect through both attention and elaboration is $a_1a_3b_2 = (0.475)(0.238)(0.108) = 0.012$. Adding up the specific indirect effects yields the total indirect effect of surveillance gratifications on political knowledge: $0.060 + 0.018 + 0.012 = 0.090$. Notice that as discussed earlier, the total effect is equal to the sum of the direct effect plus all the indirect effects: $0.177 = 0.087 + 0.060 + 0.018 + 0.012$.

STATISTICAL INFERENCE ABOUT MEDIATION AND INDIRECT EFFECTS

In the prior section we explained the parsing of a total effect into direct and indirect components. To this point, our discussion of these effects has been a purely descriptive one—quantifying how changes in X are related to changes in Y directly and indirectly through one or more mediators. Of course, these estimates are subject to sampling error, given that the participants who participated in the study were a random sample from the community in which data collection occurred. Of interest is whether the effects observed give us reason to believe that they represent a property of the population sampled rather than merely the vagaries of sampling error, i.e., "chance." That is, is there evidence in the analysis that some kind of mediation process is at work in the population? We now shift to an inferential focus by discussing three popular ways of making inferences about mediation and indirect effects. These are by no means the only methods that are available, but we focus on these three because they are fairly easy to conduct and are implemented in several computing packages. For discussions of available inferential methods, see MacKinnon (2008) and Preacher and Hayes (2008a).

Causal Steps Approach

The causal steps procedure is the most widely implemented procedure for testing a mediation hypothesis (Baron & Kenny, 1986; Hyman, 1955). The popularity of this approach is no doubt due in part to how easy it is to understand and implement. In essence, the causal steps procedure requires the investigator to conduct a set of hypothesis tests for each link in a path diagram. A failure to reject one or more of the null hypotheses leads one to claim an absence of evidence of mediation.

Applied to a simple mediation model as in Figure 23.2, the causal steps approach first asks whether there is evidence of an effect to be mediated. That is, is the total effect of X on Y (i.e., path c in Figure 23.2) statistically significant? If not, the investigator cannot claim mediation, as an effect that does not exist cannot be mediated, and further testing stops. Presuming that there is evidence of a relationship between X and Y, the investigator then tests for evidence that X is related to M (path a in Figure 23.2). Again, in the absence of a statistically significant relationship in a model predicting M from X, testing for mediation stops and the investigator claims no mediation effect. However, if this condition is met, the investigator then asks whether M is significantly related to Y after controlling for X (path b in Figure 23.2). If not, the investigator claims no mediation. If b is significant, then the investigator examines the relative size of c and the partial effect of X on Y controlling for M (path c' in Figure 23.2). If all effects are in the direction consistent with the proposed mediation process, c' will typically be closer to zero than c is. If c' is not statistically significant, the investigator claims that M completely mediates the effect of X on Y. But if c' remains significant but closer to zero than c, then this supports a claim of partial mediation—that some but not all of the effect of X on Y is carried through M.

The causal steps procedure can, in principle, be applied to more complicated mediation models involving multiple mediators. The investigator can test each specific effect in a path diagram with multiple mediators by conducting a hypothesis test for each step in the path. If all links are significant and the pattern of the total and direct effects of X on Y is consistent with a reduction in the effect of X after accounting for the proposed mediator or mediators, this suggests mediation is at work through that mediator or mediators. However, problems arise when indirect effects work in opposite directions. In such a situation, c (the total effect of X on Y) may not even be statistically significant. For this reason, we do not believe that a significant total effect should be a prerequisite to testing for indirect effects using any of the methods we discuss in this chapter. This is an important point worth stressing again. Investigators should not condition the hunt for indirect effects on a significant total effect, for it is possible for an indirect effect to exist in the absence of compelling evidence of a total effect (see Hayes, 2009, for a more detailed discussion and a concrete example).

In spite of its popularity—one might say even *dominance* in the research literature—we cannot advocate the routine use of the causal steps approach. There are two primary reasons for our position on this. First, the causal steps approach does not rely on an estimate of the indirect effect, which is ultimately what carries information about X's effect on Y through one or more intervening variables. Thus, this method encourages researchers to not think about effect size, and it does not allow for the construction of a confidence interval for the indirect effect to acknowledge the uncertainty in the estimation process. Second, it relies on a series of hypothesis tests which requires the investigator to think in categorical terms about each step of the model. Either an effect exists or not, and if any of the criteria are not met, the investigator is left with nothing. There would be nothing inherently wrong with this if the causal steps procedure led the investigator to the correct conclusion given the data available. But, unfortunately, the causal steps procedure is among the *lowest* in power among tests of the effect of intervening variables in causal models (MacKinnon, Lockwood, Hoffman, West, & Sheets, 2002; MacKinnon, Lockwood, & Williams, 2004).

Product of Coefficients Approach

Unlike the causal steps approach, the product of coefficients approach acknowledges that the investigator has an estimate of an indirect effect—the product of estimates of the paths linking X to Y through a specific mediator variable M—and inferences about the indirect effects and mediation are based on that estimate. Like any statistic, the product of these regression coefficients (ab) has a sampling distribution. And, like any sampling distribution, the sampling distribution of ab has a standard deviation. The standard deviation of the sampling distribution of ab—also known as the *standard error* of ab—can be estimated and used for hypothesis testing and the construction of confidence intervals for the indirect effect. Typically, the investigator would be interested in testing the null hypothesis that the population indirect effect is equal to zero. Rejection of the null hypothesis implies that there is an indirect effect of X on Y through a given mediator M. This procedure is popularly known as the *Sobel test* (after Sobel, 1982). Alternatively, the investigator could construct a confidence interval for the population value of ab and make inferences about its size (including whether zero is a plausible value for the indirect effect).

There are numerous formulae circulating for how to estimate the standard error of ab that applies to single-step simple and multiple mediator models. The formula implemented in the Preacher and Hayes (2004) macro used in the simple mediation model above is

$$s_{ab} = \sqrt{b^2 s_a^2 + a^2 s_b^2 + s_a^2 s_b^2} \tag{5}$$

where a^2 and b^2 are the squares of the estimates for the paths from X to M and M to Y, respectively, and s_a^2 and s_b^2 are the squared standard errors of those path coefficients. An alternative formula subtracts $s_a^2 s_b^2$ under the radical in (5) rather than adding it, and another omits the $s_a^2 s_b^2$ term altogether (see, e.g., Goodman, 1960). In practice, the difference between these approaches is small and it usually matters little which formula is used. How to best estimate the standard error is a moot question when using bootstrapping, the approach we ultimately favor and discuss later.

Once the standard error is estimated, the ratio of the indirect effect to its standard error (typically denoted as Z) is used as a test statistic for testing the null hypothesis that the population indirect effect is zero. The p-value for this ratio is derived in reference to the standard normal distribution, as this approach assumes that the sampling distribution of ab is normal. Alternatively, a 95% confidence interval (CI) for the indirect effect can be derived in the usual way, as

$$95\% \text{ CI} = ab \pm 1.96 s_{ab} \tag{6}$$

If 0 is not in the confidence interval, one can claim that there is evidence of an indirect effect linking X and Y through that mediator with 95% confidence. Confidence intervals for different levels of confidence can be used by substituting the appropriate critical value in equation (6) for the desired confidence (e.g., 2.57 for 99% confidence).

We illustrate this procedure for the two specific indirect effects in the single-step multiple mediator model above. Recall in that model that attention to news (M_1) and elaboration (M_2) were proposed mediators of the relationship between surveillance gratifications (X) and political knowledge (Y). To four significant digits (see Appendix 23.2), the two estimates were $a_1 b_1 = 0.0599$ (for attention to news) and $a_2 b_2 = 0.0302$ (for elaboration). Using the standard errors for the paths shown in the output in Appendix 23.2,

$$s_{a_1 b_1} = \sqrt{(0.1261)^2 (0.0578)^2 + (0.4750)^2 (0.0271)^2 + (0.0578)^2 (0.0271)^2} = 0.0149 \tag{7}$$

$$Z_{a_1 b_1} = \frac{0.0599}{0.0149} = 4.0201, p < .001 \tag{8}$$

$$95\% \text{ CI} = 0.0599 \pm 1.96(0.0149) = 0.0301 \text{ to } 0.0891 \tag{9}$$

and

$$s_{a_2 b_2} = \sqrt{(0.1081)^2 (0.0571)^2 + (0.2796)^2 (0.0274)^2 + (0.0571)^2 (0.0274)^2} = 0.0099 \tag{10}$$

$$Z_{a_2 b_2} = \frac{0.0302}{0.0099} = 3.0505, p < .002 \tag{11}$$

$$95\% \text{ CI} = 0.0302 \pm 1.96(0.0099) = 0.0108 \text{ to } 0.0496 \tag{12}$$

For both specific indirect effects, we can reject the null hypothesis of no indirect effect through that mediator. These results are very close to those displayed in Appendix 23.2, differing as a result of rounding error produced by hand computation. In practice, there would be no need to implement these procedures by hand, as the macros we use here and SEM programs such as Mplus will do the computations for you.

Standard Errors in a Multiple-Step Multiple Mediator Model. The formula in equation (5) is used to compute the standard error of a single-step indirect effect in models containing one or more mediators. However, what about the standard error for the multiple-step $X \rightarrow M_1 \rightarrow M_2 \rightarrow Y$ indirect effect $(a_1 a_3 b_2)$? This term, after all, is the product of *three* regression weights, so the formula becomes somewhat more complicated. Taylor, MacKinnon, and Tein (2008; see also Fletcher, 2006) derive the standard error of $a_1 a_3 b_2$ as:

$$s_{a_1 a_3 b_2} = \sqrt{a_1^2 a_3^2 s_{b_2}^2 + a_1^2 b_2^2 s_{a_3}^2 + a_3^2 b_2^2 s_{a_1}^2 + a_1^2 s_{a_3}^2 s_{b_2}^2 + a_3^2 s_{a_1}^2 s_{b_2}^2 + b_2^2 s_{a_1}^2 s_{a_3}^2 + s_{a_1}^2 s_{a_3}^2 s_{b_2}^2} \tag{13}$$

As before, once the standard error is estimated, the ratio of the indirect effect to $s_{a_1 a_3 b_2}$ is used as a test statistic for testing the null hypothesis that this specific indirect effect is zero in the population. In our running example, the standard error equates to 0.0042, as the reader may verify in Appendix 23.3. Because the specific indirect effect $a_1 a_3 b_2 = .0122$,

$$Z_{a_1 a_2 b_3} = \frac{0.0122}{0.0042} = 2.903, p < .004 \tag{14}$$

which differs from Table 23.1 and Appendix 23.3 only as a result of rounding error produced by hand computation. We conclude that the specific indirect effect through M_1 and M_2 is statistically significant.

Standard Errors for the Total Indirect Effect. Thus far we have discussed inferences for specific indirect effects. But in models with multiple mediators, there is also a total indirect effect, which we noted earlier is equal to the sum of the specific indirect effects. Using a similar logic as described above, it is possible to construct confidence intervals or test hypotheses about the total indirect effect by estimating its standard error. These computations are somewhat complex and generally done by a computer, so we don't discuss them here. See Fletcher (2006), MacKinnon (2000), and Preacher and Hayes (2008b) for guidance. Most SEM programs, as well as our SPSS and SAS macro for multiple mediator models (for single-step multiple mediator models; Preacher & Hayes, 2008b) provide standard errors for the total indirect effect. For example, in Appendix 23.2, the estimated standard error for the total indirect effect is 0.0170. The ratio of the total indirect effect to its standard error is $Z = 0.0901/0.0170 = 5.3106$, $p < .001$ and a 95% confidence interval for the total indirect effect is $0.0901 \pm 1.96(0.0170) = 0.0568$ to 0.1234.

Bootstrapping

The product of coefficients approach purchases power over the causal steps approach by focusing specifically on the estimate of the indirect effect rather than the use of multiple hypothesis tests for making inferences about a sequence of relations. Nevertheless, the product of coefficients approach suffers from one major limitation which leads us to prefer an alternative approach. The product of coefficients approach relies on the assumption of a normally distributed sampling distribution of the indirect effect. This assumption was used to justify the standard normal distribution as the reference distribution for generating a *p*-value, as well as for the construction of a symmetric interval estimate for the population indirect effect. By *symmetric*, we mean that the distance between the point estimate (the value of *ab* in the sample) and upper bound of an interval estimate of the indirect effect is the same as the distance between the point estimate and the lower bound. A less serious limitation of this method is that it also relies on a standard error formula based on mathematical theory that is itself based on certain assumptions. Furthermore, there are several standard error formulas for the indirect effect, and it is not clear whether one or the other is best in a given situation.

The problem with assumptions is that they are not always justified or met, and in this case, we know that the assumption of a normally distributed sampling distribution for the indirect effect simply is not justified, at least not in small samples (Bollen & Stine, 1990). Instead, it is skewed and kurtotic. Although this distribution approaches normality with increasingly larger samples, it is difficult to know in a particular application whether this assumption is reasonable, making it hard to justify the use of the normal distribution as the reference distribution for generating a p-value for the Sobel test. Furthermore, it means that a confidence interval, if it accurately reflected the asymmetric of the sampling distribution of the indirect effect, would not and should not be symmetric. That is, the distances between the upper and lower bounds of a confidence interval and the point estimate should differ.

Although researchers have been satisfied to rely on assumptions about the shape of distributions throughout the history of statistics and its application to real data problems, in modern times it is not necessary to rely on obsolete assumptions known to be incorrect. An alternative method for making inferences about indirect effects exists that does not rely on the normality assumption: *bootstrapping*. Bootstrapping is a member of the category of statistical methods sometimes called *resampling methods*, in that it relies on the repeated sampling of the data set to empirically estimate properties of the sampling distribution of a statistic. The resampling of the data set allows the investigator to relax many of the assumptions that ordinary inferential statistics require. A few decades ago, bootstrapping was nice in theory but somewhat difficult to implement in practice because of the computing power it requires. But desktop computing power has increased substantially since the invention of bootstrapping and, as a result, this approach to statistical inference has gained in popularity. New applications of the method are appearing in the empirical journals regularly. There are numerous books and journal articles that describe bootstrapping (e.g., Boos, 2003; Efron & Tibshirani, 1993; Stine, 1989), and we encourage the reader to explore this fascinating method in greater detail. In the interest of space, here we focus on the application of bootstrapping to the problem at hand—making inferences about the size of indirect effects in the kinds of mediation models discussed in this chapter.

As with all statistical methods, bootstrapping starts with a sample of size n from some population of interest. With bootstrapping, this sample is treated as a pseudopopulation that represents the population from which the sample was derived. More specifically, bootstrapping assumes that the data set with n cases that the investigator has available represents, in a sense, the population in miniature—that the distributions of the variables measured (i.e., the relative frequency of various observed measurements) are fairly similar to the distributions that would have been observed had the entire population been available for measurement. With this construal of the sample as a pseudopopulation, bootstrapping requires that the investigator take a simple random sample of size n from the original sample *with replacement*, meaning that when a case is randomly drawn to be included in the new sample, that case is put back to potentially be redrawn in that same sample. In this "resample" of size n from the original sample (which, remember, is also of size n) the coefficients of the model are estimated and recorded. So, for instance, for a simple mediation model, the investigator estimates the a and b paths in this resample of the original sample. This process is then repeated by taking a new resample of size n, again from the original sample, and a and b are estimated again. Of course, the two values of a in these two resamples will differ from each other, as will the two values of b, just as a and b would differ from sample to sample when sampling from the full population. This process is repeated a total of k times, with k at least 1,000, although the larger the k the better. After k resamples, k estimates of *a* and *b* and, therefore, the product of *a* and *b* are available. This distribution of *k* values of *ab*, each estimated in a resample of size *n* from the original sample, represents an empirical approximation of the sampling distribution of the indirect effect of *X* on *Y* through *M* when taking a sample of size *n* from the full population. It is this empirically derived representation of the sampling distribution that is used for making inferences about the indirect effect.

Observe that this method can be used to make inferences about all of the effects in a mediation model—direct, specific indirect, total indirect. Furthermore, it can be used for mediation models of any complexity. For instance, in a single-step multiple mediation model, one can simultaneously generate a bootstrap approximation of the sampling distribution for each of the specific indirect effects by calculating (for a two-mediator model) a_1b_1 and a_2b_2 in each of the *k* resamples. Or in a multiple-step multiple mediator model as in Figure 23.4, the sampling distribution of the indirect effect of *X* on *Y* through M_1 and M_2 can be estimated *k* times by estimating $a_1a_3b_2$ (along with a_1b_1 and a_2b_2) in each resample. Indeed, bootstrapping can be used to estimate the sampling distribution of nearly any statistic one might want to compute.

Before describing how these *k* estimates of an indirect effect can be used to our advantage, let us pause and contemplate the elegance of this method. Traditionally, statistical methods rely on various statistical theories about the behavior of a statistic, such as the Central Limit Theorem, when sampling from a population. By relying on theory, all that is needed is a single sample in order to make inferences about the population from which the sample was derived. But applications that rely on statistical theories often make assumptions, such as assumptions about the shape of the sampling distribution of the statistic. Bootstrapping eliminates the need for such assumptions about the shape of the sampling distribution because it relies on an empirical approximation of the sampling distribution by mimicking the sampling process. When bootstrapping, each case in the original sample is construed as an exemplar or representative of all units in the population like it. This is why any case that is resampled is put back into the pool to be potentially redrawn when building each resample. In other words, if "John" happened to be included in the original sample, John is used to represent all the other people just like John in the population who could have been included in the sample but happened not to be. Thus, John could show up several times (or never) in a single resample, just like many people just like John could have ended up in the original sample but perhaps were not. By mimicking the sampling process in this way, bootstrapping empirically approximates the sampling distribution of the indirect effect when taking a random sample of size *n* from a larger population.

So what do we do with these *k* estimates of an indirect effect once they are calculated? There are many applications. For example, one could calculate the standard deviation of the *k* estimates and use this as the standard error in the Sobel test rather than the standard error based on a theoretical formula (of which there are several, as described above). This would yield a "bootstrap Sobel test" of sorts. Indeed, the SPSS outputs in Appendices 23.1 and 23.2 provide the standard deviation of the bootstrap sampling distribution of the indirect effect (under "S.E." in the "Bootstrap Results" section), as do some SEM programs that bootstrap. But if the *p*-value is generated using the standard normal distribution, this does not eliminate the very problem that leads us to prefer bootstrapping in the first place, in that it still relies on the assumption of a normally distributed sampling distribution of the indirect effect. So we do not recommend a bootstrap-based Sobel test.

Instead, we recommend the use of bootstrap confidence intervals for making inferences about indirect effects. A bootstrap confidence interval for the indirect effect is constructed by sorting the distribution of *k* indirect effect estimates from low to high and then finding the estimates in this sorted distribution that define the LL = $(k / 100)(50 – \delta / 2)$th and UL = $[(k / 100) (\delta / 2) + 1]$th position in this list, where δ is the desired confidence level for the interval. The estimate in the

LLth position is the lower limit of the confidence interval, and the estimate in the ULth position is the upper limit. For instance, for a $\delta = 95\%$ confidence interval based on 5000 bootstrap samples, LL = (5000 / 100)(50–95/2) = 125 and UL = (5000 / 100)(50 + 95/2) + 1 = 4876. So the lower and upper limits of the confidence interval are the 125th and 4876th estimates in the list, respectively. Although this sounds obtuse when described formally, this procedure does nothing other than delineate the inner $\delta\%$ of the sampling distribution of the indirect effect. In other words, the indirect effect estimate in the LLth and ULth positions cut off the lower and upper $0.5(100-\delta)\%$ of the sampling distribution from the rest of the distribution. Typically, the lower and upper limits of the confidence interval will not be equidistant from the point estimate of the indirect obtained in the original sample because the empirical approximation of the sampling distribution of the indirect effect will usually be skewed. As a result, a bootstrap confidence interval is sometimes called an *asymmetric* interval estimate.

The approach we just described is known as the *percentile bootstrap*, and it is the method implemented in our SPSS and SAS macros for simple mediation models (Preacher & Hayes, 2004) and SPSS for multiple-step multiple mediator models of the form in Figure 23.4 (see Appendix 23.4). As can be seen in Appendix 23.1, based on 5000 bootstrap samples, the 95% confidence interval for the indirect effect of surveillance gratifications on knowledge through attention to news is 0.0422 to 0.1072 (note that a 99% CI is also provided in the output). As zero is not in this interval, we can say with 95% confidence that the "true" indirect effect is positive. Technically, we cannot say that we are rejecting the null hypothesis that the indirect effect is zero at a 0.05 level of significance because this is not really a null hypothesis test as a hypothesis test is formally defined. Nevertheless, our substantive conclusion is that the indirect effect is probably not zero. It is likely to be somewhere between about 0.042 and 0.107, with the obtained indirect effect of 0.072 being a sensible point estimate. Notice that, as promised, the confidence interval is asymmetric; the upper and lower bounds of the confidence interval are not the same distance from the point estimate of 0.072, reflecting the skew in the sampling distribution of the indirect effect.

Bootstrap confidence intervals can be made more accurate through the use of bias correction or through bias correction and acceleration, yielding a *bias corrected* (BC) or *bias corrected and accelerated* (BCa) confidence interval. These adjustments defy nonmathematical explanation, so we refer the reader elsewhere for the details (Efron, 1987; Efron & Tibshirani, 1993). Suffice it to say that they adjust the upper and lower limits of the interval estimate so as to produce intervals that are more likely to contain the true indirect effect without changing the level of confidence. Neither adjustment is clearly superior to the other, and in practice it makes little difference whether BC or BCa limits are used, although one or the other is generally preferred to percentile bootstrap intervals. Mplus has implemented both percentile and BC bootstrap confidence intervals but prints only 95% and 99% intervals. In Appendix 23.3, BC confidence intervals are printed for all three indirect effects and the total effect in the multiple-step multiple mediator model corresponding to the cognitive mediation model. As can be seen, for all these indirect effects, the 95% BC confidence intervals do not contain zero, suggesting evidence for a positive indirect effect for each and every indirect path from surveillance gratifications to political knowledge. Our SPSS and SAS macros for single-step multiple mediator models allow the user to specify which among all three methods to calculate, including all three at once if desired, and the user can specify any level of desired confidence. In Appendix 23.2, bias corrected and accelerated confidence intervals are displayed for the two specific indirect effects in that model as well as the total indirect effect. Again, all are positive.

We believe bootstrapping is the most sensible approach to assessing the size of indirect effects. It makes no assumptions about the shape of the sampling distribution. It does not require the investigator to think about each step in a causal sequence in dichotomous terms (i.e., significant or not). And given that it does not rely on the computation of a standard error, it is immune to problems that can arise when the assumptions associated with the use of a standard error are not met. When combined, these properties of bootstrapping are no doubt what accounts for the findings from various simulations that bootstrapping has greater statistical power than the product of coefficients strategy for detecting indirect effects when they are present (Briggs, 2006; MacKinnon et al., 2002, 2004; Williams & MacKinnon, 2008).

Having said this, at the same time we do not want to overstate our case. In many instances, the choice of which method to use will matter little in terms of substantive findings, as was the case in the analyses presented above. This would tend to be true in large samples or when effects are large enough to be detected with power near 1. But researchers often do not have the luxury of large samples or the kinds of sample sizes that make inferential tests a mere formality. In those situations, the choice of method can make a difference. When given the choice, bootstrapping is our preferred method.

Comparing Specific Indirect Effects

An indirect effect is free of the scale of measurement of the mediator or mediators in the model. That is, the indirect effect quantifies how much Y is expected to change on the Y measurement scale through M as X changes by one unit on the X measurement scale, irrespective of the scale of the mediator or mediators that the causal influence passes through (see Preacher & Hayes, 2008b, for an informal proof of this point). Therefore, it is possible to make meaningful comparisons, both descriptive and inferential, between the sizes of indirect effects in models with more than one mediator. For example, in the single-step multiple mediator model described earlier, is the indirect effect of surveillance gratifications on political knowledge larger through attention to news or elaboration of news content?

To answer such a question, all that is necessary is a quantification of the difference between specific indirect effects and either an estimate of the standard error of the sampling distribution of the difference or, alternatively, the ability to bootstrap that sampling distribution. Mplus, LISREL, and our SPSS and SAS macros for multiple mediator models provide standard errors for pairwise comparisons between specific indirect effects as well as the ability to bootstrap the sampling distribution of the difference. Notice in Appendix 23.2, for example, the lines of the output that read "C1." These lines provide the difference between the specific indirect effect of surveillance on knowledge through attention and through elaboration (i.e., $a_1 b_1 - a_2 b_2$), including the standard error for this difference as well as a Z and p-value for testing the null hypothesis of no difference. A bootstrap 95% CI is also provided in the bootstrap section of the output. Both of these approaches point to the same conclusion—that there is no evidence that these specific indirect effects differ from each other in size. Preacher and Hayes (2008b) provide Mplus and LISREL code for conducting comparisons between indirect effects in those SEM programs, and MacKinnon (2000) describes simple and complex contrasts between specific indirect effects.

MEDIATION IN MORE COMPLEX MODELS

The mediation models we have described to this point all have been variations on the same theme. Simply put, there is an effect of X on Y that needs explaining, and the models we have described represent different hypotheses about the means by which X exerts its influence on Y. The researcher may posit one mediator to explain the effect, or even two or more mediators acting in tandem in a variety of ways (see Figures 23.1, 23.3, and 23.4 for simple examples). As causal models go, these are relatively simple ones. But such simple causal models are rarely sufficient to describe and explain the complexity of social phenomena and causal processes that are the focus of much communication research.

The basic mediation model may be (and has been) extended in a number of ways. We have already described a few alternative methods of testing mediation hypotheses; there are many more that we did not discuss, and these issues are currently being debated, studied, and resolved in an extensive methodological literature (see, e.g., MacKinnon, 2008; MacKinnon et al., 2002, 2004). Mediation modeling has also been extended to accommodate nonnormal data (Finch, West, & MacKinnon, 1997), binary data (Huang, Sivaganesan, Succop, & Goodman, 2004; Li, Schneider, & Bennett, 2007; MacKinnon, Lockwood, Brown, Wang, & Hoffman, 2007), multilevel or hierarchical data (Bauer, Preacher, & Gil, 2006; Kenny, Korchmaros, & Bolger, 2003), and survival data (Tein & MacKinnon, 2003). New models and ways of thinking about mediation have been proposed (Cole & Maxwell, 2003; Collins, Graham, & Flaherty, 1998). The variety and complexity of models that may be proposed is enormous. We have scarcely scraped the surface, and much is yet to be discovered.

In the sections that follow, we describe extensions of the basic mediation model that may be of particular interest to political communication scientists. Specifically, we address the interface and combination of mediation and moderation effects, and mediation models for longitudinal data. Finally, we emphasize the value of including covariates and (whenever possible) using latent variable models to provide unbiased effects.

Moderated Mediation and Mediated Moderation

Moderation (or interaction) effects are common in political communication research. Moderation occurs when the effect of X on Y depends on a moderator variable W. For example, Scheufele (2002) hypothesized (and found) that the impact of people's exposure to hard news content (X) on political participation (Y) would be moderated by interpersonal discussion about politics (W). Moderation hypotheses like this are usually tested by including the product term XW (along with conditional terms X and W) as a predictor of Y in a regression or SEM context. If the coefficient for XW is statistically significant, then W is said to moderate the effect of X on Y, and further plotting and exploration are often warranted (Aiken & West, 1991; Bauer & Curran, 2005; Hayes & Matthes, 2009).

It is not difficult to imagine scenarios in which a moderation effect is itself hypothesized to be mediated by some intervening variable M. Likewise, it is simple to imagine scenarios in which a mediation effect is thought to be moderated by some variable W. Such effects are called, respectively, *mediated moderation* and *moderated mediation*, and statistical methods exist to assess these processes.

Mediated moderation hypotheses are becoming increasingly common in political communication research. For example, Scheufele (2002) hypothesized that the interactive effect of hard news exposure and political discussion on political participation would be mediated by political knowledge (M). Mediated moderation is particularly easy to assess. Say we have demonstrated an interaction effect of X and W predicting Y. That is, the effect of X may be of a different magnitude, or even a different sign, for different values of W. This effect must somehow find its way to Y, and it is not unreasonable to suppose that it does so via a mediator M. The researcher would specify a model in which X and W interact in predicting M, which in turn may predict Y. If the interaction slope of XW on Y is denoted a_3, and the effect of M on Y (controlling for X, W, and XW) is denoted b, then the mediated moderation effect is simply $a_3 b$. The significance of this effect may be determined by any of the methods we described earlier, although we particularly recommend using bootstrap confidence intervals. The SPSS and SAS macros provided for multiple mediator models (Preacher & Hayes, 2008b) can be used to assess such effects. Only one mediator is involved, but the macros permit the inclusion of X and W as covariates, with XW serving as the primary predictor.

Mediation processes may also be moderated. For example, Holbert (2005b) tests a moderated mediation hypothesis showing that the indirect path from TV news viewing to attitudes about government involvement in social issues via perceptions of the government's role is different for Democrats, Republicans, and Independents. This analysis was accomplished using multiple-group SEM, but the moderator variable (political affiliation in this example) may be continuous or categorical. Moderated mediation is somewhat more difficult to assess than mediated moderation, but methods exist (Edwards & Lambert, 2007; Preacher, Rucker, & Hayes, 2007). The basic idea is to specify one's model as a path model and consider which path or paths are expected, on the basis of theory, to be moderated by one or more potential moderator variables. Product terms are then entered into the model in the appropriate places, which will differ from situation to situation. Once the model is estimated, the researcher can plot, and explore the significance of, *conditional indirect effects*—that is, indirect effects at specific values of the moderator(s) that are of key theoretical interest. Preacher et al. (2007) provide an SPSS macro that considerably eases the burden on researchers.

Mediation in Longitudinal Studies

Mediation models are causal models. One implication of a simple mediation model is that if case i's X value were changed in some fashion, then case i's M value would change as a result, and this change in M would in turn cause case i's Y value to change. In the examples used throughout this chapter, such a strong causal interpretation is hard to justify in spite of the statistical evidence because there has been no measurement of change and no manipulation of one or more of the proposed causal agents. Instead, claims of mediation in the examples described thus far have been based on a cross-sectional or between-persons argument—that people who differ in X also differ on M as a result of those differences in X, which in turn produce differences between those people in Y. Longitudinal designs, where X, M, and Y are measured repeatedly at set intervals, allow for the actual assessment of change over time, and this can give the researcher much greater confidence in a mediation claim when it can be substantiated that difference is actually related to the specified variables.

There is a growing literature on the testing of mediation when the variables in the proposed causal system are measured over time. One approach is the use of the standard cross-lagged panel design. For example, to examine the indirect effect of negative political advertisements (X) on political participation (Y) through its effects on political cynicism (M), an investigator could measure these three variables at three or more times during an election season, preferably with roughly equally spaced intervals that are appropriately timed given the causal process being studied. With such a design, indirect effects can be calculated as the product of the effect of ad exposure at time 1 on political cynicism at time 2 and the effect of political cynicism at time 2 on political participation at time 3 all while controlling for temporal stability in the variables over time as well as direct effects between ad exposure and participation that reach across time. In such a design, change is operationalized somewhat loosely as being either higher or lower on the outcome variable than would be expected given the prior measurement on that variable and other variables in the model. There are many assumptions that one must make when using such an approach to the analysis of mediation, and there are still alternative explanations that can account for indirect effects in such models. Careful thought must go into the planning of a longitudinal design such as this. For guidance, we recommend Cole and Maxwell (2003), Little, Preacher, Selig, and Card (2007), and Maxwell and Cole (2007).

An exciting alternative for assessing mediation in longitudinal studies is the use of *parallel process latent growth curve modeling*. Latent growth curve modeling is typically conducted using SEM. With at least three repeated measurements of each variable, latent growth curve modeling capitalizes on regularity in the fluctuation in measurement of each case over time to quantify that case's "latent change" per unit of time on that variable, or "latent growth" as it more typically called. The mean latent growth parameters (e.g., intercept and slope) estimated from the data can then be linked together in a structural model to assess mediation. In Figure 23.5 we present one way of setting up such a model, although there are many ways that the parameters can be linked together, depending on various substantive, theoretical, or statistical considerations. This model includes several indirect effects of X on Y through M. One indirect effect, $a_0 b_0$, quantifies the influence of baseline X (π_{X0}) on baseline Y (π_{Y0}) through baseline M (π_{X0}). A second indirect effect, $a_1 b_1$, quantifies the extent to which change in X (π_{X1}) predicts change in M (π_{M0}) which in turn predicts change in Y (π_{Y1}). But observe as well that baseline X could influence the extent to which M changes, which in turn could influence change in Y. This indirect effect of X on Y through M is quantified as $a_2 b_1$. Finally, this model also allows for the possibility that baseline X could

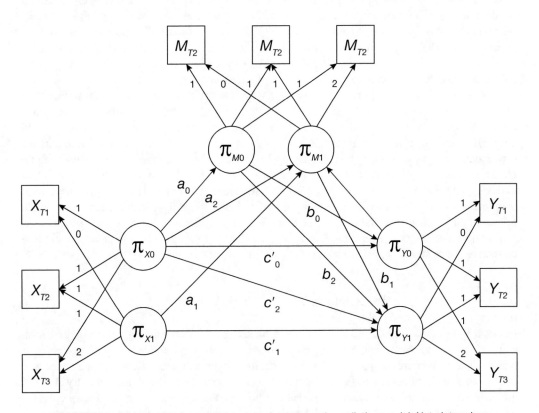

FIGURE 23.5 An example of a parallel process latent growth mediation model. Not pictured are correlations between intercept and slope residuals (within M and Y), the correlation between X intercept and slope, and intercorrelations between indicator residuals within time.

influence baseline M, which in turn influences change in Y, quantified as a_0b_2. The parallel process model for assessing mediation shows great promise when experimental manipulation of X is not possible, but measurement over time is. Simons-Morton, Chen, Abroms, and Haynie (2004) present an application in a health communication context, but to our knowledge, this method has never been used in a political communication study. Cheong, MacKinnon, and Khoo (2003) discuss a form of the parallel process growth curve model where X is experimentally manipulated at time 1 whereas M and Y are measured longitudinally over three occasions. In such a design, it is possible to assess whether the experimental manipulation changes the latent change trajectory for the proposed mediator and whether that change in turn is related to latent change in the outcome.

Models with Covariates or Latent Variables

Thus far we have neglected to acknowledge that many models that political communication researchers would be interested in testing would include numerous statistical controls. For instance, it is common to estimate the paths in a mediation model after first partialing out demographic variables such as sex, education, income, age, and so forth. The basic logic of the methods described here do not need modification to handle covariates. One version of our SPSS and SAS macros (Preacher & Hayes, 2008b) for multiple mediators, as well as the one for moderated mediation (Preacher et al., 2007) allows for the inclusion of covariates under the assumption that all covariates are partialed out of all mediators and the outcome. When an SEM program such as Mplus is used, the inclusion of covariates is accomplished quite simply by including directional paths from the covariates to whatever variable in the model the investigator desires, and all direct and indirect effect estimates, standard errors, and confidence intervals (bootstrapped or otherwise) will be correctly calculated after statistical adjustment for the control variables.

In all examples we have presented in this chapter, the variables linked in causal sequence in each model were treated as observed variables. Doing so greatly simplifies our discussion and also allows the use of the various macros we have produced for popular platforms such as SPSS and SAS. Of course, with few exceptions, it is usually not so much the observed measurements we care about, but rather the latent variables that give rise to the observed measurements. Fortunately, all the methods we have discussed can be used to test mediation hypotheses involving latent variables, although doing so requires the use of structural equation modeling rather than any of the macros we have described. An advantage of going latent is that it typically reduces one source of bias in the estimation of indirect effects that we have not acknowledged—measurement error. Mplus provides all the features the user will need to implement these methods, including bootstrapping of structural paths and estimation of indirect effects.

RECOMMENDING FURTHER READING

In this chapter we have discussed the application of basic principles in the estimation of mediation and indirect effects to political communication research. Out of necessity, we have glossed over many interesting controversies as well as important extensions. It is our hope that the discussion above has stimulated readers to further explore the vast literature on this topic and to try some of the methods we describe here and others that can be found elsewhere. For a good starting place, we recommend MacKinnon (2008), which promises to be the seminal treatment of the analysis of mediation. In it you will find examples of mediation analyses in many different fields, as well as valuable guidance on how to conduct mediation analyses using data from numerous research designs. Additional good and brief treatments include Frazier, Tix, and Barron (2004), MacKinnon, Fairchild, and Fritz (2007), Mathieu, DeShon, and Bergh (2008), Preacher and Hayes (2008a), and Shrout and Bolger (2002).

APPENDIX 23.1

The computer output below comes from the SPSS version of the simple mediation macro described in Preacher and Hayes (2004). In this example, X is surveillance gratifications, M is attention to news, and Y is political knowledge.

```
sobel y = know/x = grats/m = newsattn/boot = 5000.
```

Run MATRIX procedure:

DIRECT AND TOTAL EFFECTS

	Coeff	s.e.	t	Sig(two)	
b(YX)	.1767	.0333	5.3003	.0000	← c path
b(MX)	.4750	.0578	8.2137	.0000	← a path
b(YM.X)	.1518	.0267	5.6852	.0000	← b path
b(YX.M)	.1046	.0346	3.0229	.0027	← c′ path

INDIRECT EFFECT AND SIGNIFICANCE USING NORMAL DISTRIBUTION

	Value	s.e.	LL 95 CI	UL 95 CI	Z	Sig(two)	
Sobel	.0721	.0155	.0417	.1025	4.6514	.0000	← ab

BOOTSTRAP RESULTS FOR INDIRECT EFFECT

	Mean	s.e.	LL 95 CI	UL 95 CI	LL 99 CI	UL 99 CI	
Effect	.0721	.0165	.0422	.1072	.0352	.1195	← ab

SAMPLE SIZE
   437

NUMBER OF BOOTSTRAP RESAMPLES
   5000

95% bootstrap confidence interval for indirect effect

− − − − − END MATRIX − − − − −

APPENDIX 23.2

The computer output below comes from the SPSS version of the mediation macro described in Preacher and Hayes (2008b). We recommend this macro even for simple mediation models, as it has more options than the Preacher and Hayes (2004) macro.

```
INDIRECT y=know/x=grats/m = newsattn elab/contrast = 1
/normal = 1/bca = 1/boot = 5000.
```

Run MATRIX procedure:
Dependent, Independent, and Proposed Mediator Variables:
DV   =   know
IV   =   grats
MEDS   =   newsattn
           elab

Sample size
       437

IV to Mediators (a paths)

	Coeff	se	t	p	
newsattn	.4750	.0578	8.2137	.0000	← a_1 path
elab	.2796	.0571	4.8977	.0000	← a_2 path

Direct Effects of Mediators on DV (b paths)

	Coeff	se	t	p	
newsattn	.1261	.0271	4.6586	.0000	← b_1 path
elab	.1081	.0274	3.9452	.0001	← b_2 path

Total Effect of IV on DV (c path)

	Coeff	se	t	p	
grats	.1767	.0333	5.3003	.0000	← c path

Direct Effect of IV on DV (c' path)

	Coeff	se	t	p	
grats	.0866	.0343	2.5215	.0120	← c' path

Model Summary for DV Model

R-sq	Adj R-sq	F	df1	df2	p
.1561	.1503	26.6989	3.0000	433.0000	.0000

****

NORMAL THEORY TESTS FOR INDIRECT EFFECTS

Indirect Effects of IV on DV through Proposed Mediators (ab paths)

	Effect	se	Z	p	
TOTAL	.0901	.0170	5.3106	.0000	← $a_1b_1 + a_2b_2$
newsattn	.0599	.0147	4.0639	.0000	← a_1b_1
elab	.0302	.0098	3.0802	.0021	← a_2b_2
C1	.0296	.0184	1.6092	.1076	← $a_1b_1 - a_2b_2$

****

BOOTSTRAP RESULTS FOR INDIRECT EFFECTS

Indirect Effects of IV on DV through Proposed Mediators (ab paths)

	Data	Boot	Bias	SE
TOTAL	.0901	.0902	.0001	.0177
newsattn	.0599	.0599	.0000	.0164
elab	.0302	.0304	.0001	.0109
C1	.0296	.0295	−.0001	.0215

Bias Corrected and Accelerated Confidence Intervals

	Lower	Upper	
TOTAL	.0565	.1256	**95% BCA bootstrap confidence interval for indirect effect**
newsattn	.0306	.0959	←
elab	.0123	.0560	**CI for difference between specific indirect effects**
C1	−.0117	.0725	←

****

Level of Confidence for Confidence Intervals: 95
Number of Bootstrap Resamples: 5000

****

INDIRECT EFFECT CONTRAST DEFINITIONS: Ind_Eff1 MINUS Ind_Eff2

Contrast	IndEff_1	IndEff_2
C1	newsattn	elab

− − − − − END MATRIX − − − − −

APPENDIX 23.3

Mplus code and output for the multiple-step multiple mediator model discussed in the text. The exclamation points in the code denote comments and should be removed to implement boot-strapping and to obtain bias-corrected confidence intervals for the indirect effects.

```
TITLE:    Multiple Step Multiple Mediator Model
DATA:
          FILE IS C:\CMM1985.dat;
          FORMAT IS free;
VARIABLE:
          NAMES ARE elab grats newsattn know;
          USEVARIABLES elab grats newsattn know;
ANALYSIS:
! BOOTSTRAP = 5000;
MODEL:
      newsattn ON grats;
      elab on grats newsattn;
      know ON newsattn elab grats;
MODEL INDIRECT:
      know IND newsattn grats;
      know IND elab grats;
      know IND elab newsattn grats;
OUTPUT:
! CINTERVAL(BCBOOTSTRAP);
```

MODEL RESULTS

	Estimate	S.E.	Est./S.E.	Two-Tailed P-Value	
NEWSATTN ON					
GRATS	0.475	0.058	8.236	0.000	← a_1 path
ELAB ON					
GRATS	0.167	0.059	2.805	0.005	← a_2 path
NEWSATTN	0.238	0.046	5.190	0.000	← a_3 path
KNOW ON					
NEWSATTN	0.126	0.027	4.680	0.000	← b_1 path
ELAB	0.108	0.027	3.963	0.000	← b_2 path
GRATS	0.087	0.034	2.529	0.011	← c' path
Intercepts					
KNOW	−0.398	0.121	−3.291	0.001	
NEWSATTN	0.892	0.170	5.237	0.000	
ELAB	2.691	0.168	15.991	0.000	

```
Residual
 Variances
   KNOW           0.100    0.007     14.782      0.000
   NEWSATTN       0.336    0.023     14.782      0.000
   ELAB           0.308    0.021     14.782      0.000
```

TOTAL INDIRECT, SPECIFIC INDIRECT EFFECTS

	Estimate	S.E.	Est./S.E.	Two-Tailed P-Value

Effects from GRATS to KNOW

Sum of
indirect   0.090   0.017   5.318   0.000   ← $a_1b_1 + a_2b_2 + a_1a_3b_2$

Specific indirect

KNOW
NEWSATTN
GRATS   0.060   0.015   4.069   0.000   ← a_1b_1

KNOW
ELAB
GRATS   0.018   0.008   2.290   0.022   ← a_2b_2

KNOW
ELAB
NEWSATTN
GRATS   0.012   0.004   2.942   0.003   ← $a_1a_3b_2$

The sections of the output below are from a rerunning of the model by requesting bootstrapping and bias corrected confidence intervals. This is accomplished by removing the exclamation points "!" from the lines in the code above.

CONFIDENCE INTERVALS OF TOTAL, TOTAL INDIRECT, SPECIFIC INDIRECT, AND DIRECT EFFECTS

	Lower .5%	Lower 2.5%	Estimate	Upper 2.5%	Upper .5%

Effects from GRATS to KNOW

Sum of
indirect   0.047   0.058   0.090   0.127   0.140

```
Specific indirect
KNOW
NEWSATTN
GRATS         0.023        0.030        0.060        0.096        0.108

KNOW
ELAB
GRATS         0.002        0.005        0.018        0.039        0.047


KNOW
ELAB
NEWSATTN
GRATS         0.003        0.005        0.012        0.024        0.028
```

95% BC bootstrap confidence interval for indirect effect

APPENDIX 23.4

SPSS output from the MEDTHREE macro for estimating paths in a multiple-step multiple mediator model as discussed in the text. The macro and instructions on its use can be downloaded from http://www.comm.ohio-state.edu/ahayes/macros.htm.

MEDTHREE y = know/x = grats/m1 = newsattn/m2 = reflect/boot = 5000.

— — — — — — — — — — — — — — — — —

Run MATRIX procedure:

```
VARIABLES IN MEDIATION MODEL
   Y     know
   X     grats
   M1    newsattn
   M2    elab
```

```
DESCRIPTIVES STATISTICS AND PEARSON CORRELATIONS
             Mean       SD       know      grats    newsattn      elab
know        .5435     .3451    1.0000     .2463      .3277       .2807
grats      2.9134     .4810     .2463    1.0000      .3664       .2286
newsattn   2.2769     .6235     .3277     .3664     1.0000       .3021
elab       3.7185     .5883     .2807     .2286      .3021      1.0000
```

SAMPLE SIZE: 437

Model Path Estimates

		Coeff	SE	t	p
a1	:	.4750	.0578	8.2137	.0000
a2	:	.1666	.0596	2.7944	.0054
a3	:	.2379	.0460	5.1734	.0000
b1	:	.1261	.0271	4.6586	.0000
b2	:	.1081	.0274	3.9452	.0001
c	:	.1767	.0333	5.3003	.0000
c¢	:	.0866	.0343	2.5215	.0120

Indirect Effects (with bootstrap 95%CI and standard errors)

		Effect	LL95%CI	UL95%CI	BootSE
Total	:	.0901	.0575	.1262	.0177
M1	:	.0599	.0299	.0928	.0163
M2	:	.0180	.0038	.0371	.0086
M1&M2	:	.0122	.0043	.0225	.0047

— — — — — — — — — — — — — — — —NOTES— — — — — — — — — — — — — — — —

Number of Bootstrap Samples: 5000

NOTE

1. In all examples, our discussion is based on estimates of the direct, indirect, and total effects derived using available data rather than on population values of these effects. We discuss inference from the estimates to population values in a later section of this chapter.

REFERENCES

Aiken, I. S., & West, S. G. (1991). *Multiple regression: Testing and interpreting interactions*. Newbury Park, CA: Sage.

Baron, R. M., & Kenny, D. A. (1986). The moderator-mediator variable distinction in social psychological research: Conceptual, strategic, and statistical considerations. *Journal of Personality and Social Psychology, 51*(6), 1173–1182.

Bauer, D. J., Preacher, K. J., & Gil, K. M. (2006). Conceptualizing and testing random indirect effects and moderated mediation in multilevel models: New procedures and recommendations. *Psychological Methods, 11*, 142–163.

Bauer, D. J., & Curran, P. J. (2005). Probing interactions in fixed and multilevel regression: Inferential and graphical techniques. *Multivariate Behavioral Research, 40*, 373–400.

Bollen, K. A., & Stine, R. (1990). Direct and indirect effects: Classical and bootstrap estimates of variability. *Sociological Methodology, 20*, 115–140.

Boos, D. D. (2003). Introduction to the bootstrap world. *Statistical Science, 18*, 168–174.

Briggs, N. E. (2006). *Estimation of the standard error and confidence interval of the indirect effect in multiple mediator models*. Unpublished doctoral dissertation, Ohio State University, Columbus, OH.

Cheong, J., MacKinnon, D. P., & Khoo, S. T. (2003). Investigation of meditational processes using parallel process latent growth modeling. *Structural Equation Modeling, 10*, 238–262.

Cole, D. A., & Maxwell, S. E. (2003). Testing meditational models with longitudinal data: Questions and tips in the use of structural equation modeling. *Journal of Abnormal Psychology, 112*, 558–577.

Collins, L. M., Graham, J. W., & Flaherty, B. P. (1998). An alternative framework for defining mediation. *Multivariate Behavioral Research, 33*, 295–312.

Davis, J. A. (1985). *The logic of causal order.* Newbury Park, CA: Sage.

Edwards, J. R., & Lambert, L. S. (2007). Methods for integrating moderation and mediation: A general path analytical framework using moderated path analysis. *Psychological Methods, 12*, 1–22.

Efron, B. (1987). Better bootstrap confidence intervals. *Journal of the American Statistical Association, 82*, 171–185.

Efron, B., & Tibshirani, R. (1993). *An introduction to the bootstrap.* New York: Chapman & Hall.

Eveland, W. P., Jr. (2001). The cognitive mediation model of learning from the news: Evidence from nonelection, off-year election, and presidential election contexts. *Communication Research, 28*, 571–601.

Eveland, W. P., Jr. (2004). The effect of political discussion in producing informed citizens: The roles of information, motivation, and elaboration. *Political Communication, 21*, 177–193.

Finch, J., West, S. G., & MacKinnon, D. P. (1997) Effects on non-normality on mediated effect estimates. *Structural Equation Modeling, 4*, 87–107.

Fletcher, T. D. (2006, August). *Methods and approaches to assessing distal mediation.* Paper presented at the 66th annual meeting of the Academy of Management, Atlanta, GA.

Frazier, P. A., Tix, A. P., & Barron, K. E. (2004). Testing moderator and mediator effects in counseling psychology research. *Journal of Counseling Psychology, 51*, 115–134.

Gidengil, E., & Everitt, J. (2003). Talking tough: Gender and reported speech in campaign news coverage. *Political Communication, 20*, 209–233.

Goodman, L. A. (1960). On the exact variance of products. *Journal of the American Statistical Association, 55*, 708–713.

Hayes, A. F. (2009). Beyond Baron and Kenny: Statistical mediation analysis in the new millennium. *Communication Monographs, 76*, 408–420.

Hayes, A. F., & Matthes, J. (2009). Computational procedures for probing interactions in OLS and logistic regression: SPSS and SAS implementations. *Behavior Research Methods, 41*, 924–936.

Holbert, R. L. (2005a). Television news viewing, governmental scope, and postmaterialist spending: Assessing mediation by partisanship. *Journal of Broadcasting and Electronic Media, 49*, 416–434.

Holbert, R. L. (2005b). Intramedia mediation: The cumulative and complementary effects of news media use. *Political Communication, 22*, 447–462.

Holbert, R. L., Shah, D. V., Kwak, N. (2003). Political implications of primetime drama and sitcom use: Genres of representation and opinions concerning women's rights. *Journal of Communication, 53*, 45–60.

Holbrook, R. A., & Hill, T. G. (2005). Agenda-setting and priming in primetime television: Crime dramas as political cues. *Political Communication, 22*, 277–295.

Holland, P. W. (1986). Statistics and causal inference. *Journal of the American Statistical Association, 81*, 945–960.

Huang, B., Sivaganesan, S., Succop, P., & Goodman, E. (2004). Statistical assessment of mediational effects for logistic mediational models. *Statistics in Medicine, 23*, 2713–2728.

Hyman, H. H. (1955). *Survey design and analysis.* New York: The Free Press

Kenny, D. A., Korchmaros, J. D., & Bolger, N. (2003). Lower level mediation in multilevel models. *Psychological Methods, 8*, 115–128.

Keum, H., Devanathan, N., Deshpand, S., Nelson, M. R., & Shah, D. V. (2004). The citizen-consumer: Media effects at the intersection of consumer and civic culture. *Political Communication, 21*(3), 369–391.

Li, Y., Schneider, J. A., & Bennett, D. A. (2007). Estimation of the mediation effect with a binary mediator. *Statistics in Medicine, 26*, 3398–3414.

Little, T. D., Preacher, K. J., Selig, J. P., & Card, N. A. (2007). New developments in latent variable panel analyses of longitudinal data. *International Journal of Behavioral Development, 31*, 357–365.

MacKinnon, D. P. (2000). Contrasts in multiple mediator models. In J. S. Rose, L. Chassin, C. C. Presson, & S. S. Sherman (Eds.), *Multivariate applications in substance use research* (pp. 141–160). Mahwah, NJ: Lawrence Erlbaum.

MacKinnon, D. P. (2008). *Introduction to statistical mediation analysis.* New York: Lawrence Erlbaum.

MacKinnon, D. P., Fairchild, A. J., & Fritz, M. S. (2007). Mediation analysis. *Annual Review of Psychology, 58,* 593–614.

MacKinnon, D. P., Krull, J. L., & Lockwood, C. (2000). Equivalence of the mediation, confounding, and suppression effect. *Prevention Science, 1,* 173–181.

MacKinnon, D. P., Lockwood, C. M., Brown, C. H., Wang, W., & Hoffman, J. M. (2007). The intermediate endpoint effect in logistic and probit regression. *Clinical Trials, 4,* 499–513.

MacKinnon, D. P., Lockwood, C. M., Hoffman, J. M., West, S. G., & Sheets, V. (2002). A comparison of methods to test mediation and other intervening variable effects. *Psychological Methods, 7,* 83–104.

MacKinnon, D. P., Lockwood, C. M., & Williams, J. (2004). Confidence limits for the indirect effect: Distribution of the product and resampling methods. *Multivariate Behavioral Research, 39,* 99–128.

Mathieu, J. E., DeShon, R. P., & Bergh, D. D. (2008). Mediation inferences in organizational research: Then, now, and beyond. *Organizational Research Methods, 11,* 202–223.

Mathieu, J. E., & Taylor, S. R. (2006). Clarifying conditions and decision points for mediational type inferences in organizational behavior. *Journal of Organizational Behavior, 27,* 1031–1056.

Maxwell, D. E., & Cole, D. A. (2007). Bias in cross-sectional analyses of longitudinal mediation. *Psychological Methods, 12,* 23–44.

Pinkleton, B. E., & Austin, E. W. (2001). Individual motivations, perceived media importance, and political disaffection. *Political Communication, 18,* 321–334.

Preacher, K. J., & Hayes, A. F. (2004). SPSS and SAS procedures for estimating indirect effects in simple mediation models. *Behavior Research Methods, Instruments, and Computers, 36,* 717–731.

Preacher, K. J., & Hayes, A. F. (2008a). Contemporary approaches to assessing mediation in communication research. In A. F. Hayes, M. D. Slater, & L. B. Snyder (Eds.), *The SAGE sourcebook of advanced data analysis methods for communication research* (pp. 13–54). Thousand Oaks, CA: Sage.

Preacher, K. J., & Hayes, A. F. (2008b). Asymptotic and resampling strategies for assessing and comparing indirect effects in multiple mediator models. *Behavior Research Methods, 40,* 879–891.

Preacher, K. J., Rucker, D. D., & Hayes, A. F. (2007). Assessing moderated mediation hypotheses: Theory, methods, and prescriptions. *Multivariate Behavioral Research, 42,* 185–227.

Scheufele, D. A. (2002). Examining differential gains from mass media and their implications for participatory behavior. *Communication Research, 29,* 46–65.

Sellers, P. J., & Schaffner, B. F. (2007). Winning coverage in the U.S. Senate. *Political Communication, 24,* 377–391.

Shrout, P. E. & Bolger, N. (2002). Mediation in experimental and nonexperimental studies: New procedures and recommendations. *Psychological Methods, 7*(4), 422–445.

Simons-Morton, B., Chen, R., Abroms, L., & Haynie, D. L. (2004). Latent growth curve analyses of peer and parent influences on smoking progression among early adolescents. *Health Psychology, 23,* 612–621.

Slater, M. D. (2007). Reinforcing spirals: The mutual influence of media selectivity and media effects and their impact on individual behavior and social identity. *Communication Theory, 17,* 281–303.

Sobel, M. E. (1982). Asymptotic confidence intervals for indirect effects in structural equation models. *Sociological Methodology, 13,* 290–312.

Stine, R. (1989). An introduction to bootstrap methods. *Sociological Methods and Research, 18,* 243–291.

Stroud, N. J. (2007). Media effects, selective exposure, and *Fahrenheit 9/11. Political Communication, 24,* 415–432.

Taylor, A. B., MacKinnon, D. P., & Tein, J.-Y. (2008). Tests of the three-path mediated effect. *Organizational Research Methods, 11,* 241–269.

Tein, J.-Y., & MacKinnon, D. P. (2003). Estimating mediated effects with survival data. In H. Yanai, A. O. Rikkyo, K. Shigemasu, Y. Kano, & J. J. Meulman (Eds.), *New developments on psychometrics* (pp. 405–412). Tokyo, Japan: Springer-Verlag Tokyo Inc.

Williams, J., & MacKinnon, D. P. (2008). Resampling and distribution of the product methods for testing indirect effects in complex models. *Structural Equation Modeling, 15,* 23–51.

24

Time Series Analysis and the Study of Political Communication

Jennifer Jerit
Department of Political Science
Florida State University

Adam F. Simon
Department of Political Science
Yale University

In *Public Opinion and American Democracy*, V. O. Key (1961) described popular government as a "two-way flow of communications." In one direction, information flows from citizens to elites, as individuals convey their preferences to public officials. In the other, communication travels from political parties, interest groups, and the mass media to ordinary people. The most obvious example is electoral campaigns, when candidates compete for the support of voters through political advertisements, news coverage, speeches, online communications, and a host of other information modalities. But communication also occurs between elections as partisan elites turn to issues of governance and policy making. Indeed, it is difficult to conceive of election campaigns or policy debates as anything other than a sequence of unfolding and interrelated messages.

In many cases, how a policy debate or campaign process unfolds *over time* is essential to understanding the eventual outcome. We believe that researchers can improve their understanding of such phenomena by using a method that accounts for this dynamic aspect of communication and persuasion. Toward this end, this chapter examines how researchers have used time series analysis in the study of political communication. Despite the strengths of this method, time series analysis is not the field's modal technique. But that is part of what motivates our focus here. Whether geared toward campaigning or governing, political communication is, at its core, a dynamic phenomenon that plays out over time.

Our purpose is not to teach readers how to *do* time series analysis.[1] Instead, we seek to provide a sense for how one might use this technique to better answer political communication questions. We begin by describing what time series data look like and what one does, generally speaking, with this type of data. We then describe some of the most commonly used time series techniques in political communication research. Next, we consider the strengths and limitations of this mode of analysis and compare it to other empirical approaches. We conclude with some thoughts on how future research might use time series analysis to explore enduring topics in the field.

WHAT IS A TIME SERIES?

A time series is a sequence of observations dispersed over time. Some examples from the field of political communication include daily measures of the audience for campaign ads throughout an election (Beltran, 2007), the amount of weekly broadcast time devoted to crime on the nightly news (Edwards & Wood, 1999), or the annual number of presidential speeches (Powell, 1999). To conduct time series analysis, each observation should be an interval-level measurement of the process and the observations should be *evenly* spaced. Minor violations of these requirements are permissible (McCleary & Hay, 1980, p. 21). For example, the time between observations in a monthly series usually is 30 days, but this value can range from 28 to 31. On occasion, the only information available is an *intermittent* time series. This would be the case, for example, if a researcher had public opinion data from surveys administered in 1985, 1990, 1992, 1995, and 2000. Fortunately, there are techniques for transforming intermittent time series into an evenly spaced series that can be analyzed (see Stimson, 1999).[2]

Irrespective of what the observations represent, a time series generally is thought of as a particular realization of some underlying stochastic (i.e., random) process and, in time series analysis, the researcher seeks to make inferences about that process. In this sense, the relationship between realization and process in time series is "analogous to the relationship between *sample* and *population* in cross-sectional analysis" (McCleary & Hay, 1980, p. 30, emphasis original). Wooldridge (2006, p. 343) elaborates on this idea: "When we collect a time series dataset, we obtain one possible outcome, or realization, of the stochastic process . . . The set of all possible realizations of a time series plays the role of the population in cross-sectional analysis. The sample size for a time series dataset is the number of time periods over which we observe the variables of interest." (For a related discussion, see Chapter 2, this volume, on panel designs.)

Time series data are different from cross-sectional data, another, arguably more common, type of data used by political communication researchers. Whereas a time series consists of time-ordered observations on some variable of interest (e.g., the number of speeches) for the same unit of analysis (e.g., U.S. presidents), cross-sectional datasets consist of observations on a series of variables at the same point in time across many units of analysis, such as survey respondents (Ostrom, 1978).[3] The differences between cross-sectional and time series data are important for understanding why special methods have developed for time series data. More to the point, when observations are ordered in time, one of the central assumptions of OLS (ordinary least squares) regression—that the errors are uncorrelated—is likely to be violated. This leads to the problem of autocorrelation, a topic we return to below.

As with survey data generally, both time series and cross-sectional data are nonexperimental; that is, the data are not subject to the control of the researcher. Naturally, this lack of control makes it more difficult, though not impossible, to make statements about causal relationships. Experimental data come in many varieties, but "the common attribute in all experiments is control over the treatment" (Shadish, Cook, & Campbell, 2002, p. 12). When combined with random assignment to treatment and control conditions, the experimenter is able to make stronger inferences about the causal relationship among the variables of interest. We return to the strengths and weaknesses of the various modes of analysis in political communication research below.

WHAT IS TIME SERIES ANALYSIS?

Time series analysis accounts for the fact that data points taken over time may have an internal structure, such as a trend, seasonal variation, or autocorrelation.[4] Like other analytical approaches, in time series analysis the researcher assumes that the data consist of a systematic pattern and random noise (or error). Most time series analysis techniques involve some form of "picking apart" the series or decomposing it into its main components to better understand the underlying forces that produced the observations. The preceding reference to time series analysis *techniques* is deliberate. There is no single time series model; there are, instead, a variety of techniques and approaches, some of which have yet to be applied in political communication research. Some of the more common uses of time series analysis are described below.

Regardless of the particular model or approach employed, the first step in nearly any time series analysis is to determine whether the data are stationary. To be stationary, a series must have a constant mean and variance (i.e., the mean and variance do not change over time). A non-stationary series, by contrast, is one that trends, either up or down. Take, for example, newspaper readership since the mid-twentieth century, which evidences a downward trend over time. Because a trend denotes *systematic* change in the level of a series, it can lead to the problem of spurious regression. More specifically, two series that are trending in the same direction may appear to be related to one another (e.g., there is a high R^2), but this often is due to the presence of a third factor, such as a linear time trend. Thus, what appears to be a statistical relationship actually is spurious. It also has been shown that standard t- and F-testing procedures are invalid when one nonstationary series is regressed on another.

Several tests exist for stationarity (e.g., Dickey-Fuller, Augmented Dickey-Fuller, Phillips-Perron, the KPSS test), most of which are available in statistical software packages.[5] In many cases, differencing a series once (by subtracting each datum in a series from its predecessor) will remove a trend. Differencing entails some trade-offs, discussed later, but its primary virtue is that it highlights "the interesting portion of the variation in the systematic component" of one's data (King, 1989, p. 181).[6]

CURRENT PRACTICES IN POLITICAL COMMUNICATION RESEARCH

Scholars have used a variety of time series methods in political communication research. Here we summarize the most commonly used techniques: Regression Analyses with Time Series Data, Vector Autoregression and Granger Causality, and Autoregressive Integrated Moving Average (ARIMA) modeling. We close the section by discussing some of the newer techniques used by researchers in other disciplines.

Regression Analyses with Time Series Data

Ordinarily, the researcher who conducts a time series analysis is interested in the relationship between variables that are paired at different times—for instance, how public opinion at time t is related to media coverage in some previous period (e.g., t-1), or how support for a candidate in the current period is related to past support as well as to recent campaign advertising and campaign events. As such, one of the most common uses of time series in political communication research involves some version of the following general model:

$$Y_t = \alpha + \gamma_1 Y_{t-1} + \beta_0 X_t + \beta_1 X_{t-1} + \ldots + u_t \qquad (1)$$

Equation (1) represents an Autoregressive Distributed Lag (or ADL) Model (Charemza & Deadman, 1997). The term "autoregressive" refers to the fact that lagged values of Y appear as a regressor. The term "distributed" refers to the fact that the effect of X may be spread over multiple time periods (e.g., t-1, t-2, and so on).[7]

At least ten different models can be derived from the general model in Equation (1). We highlight a few of them here (with simplified models containing one or two covariates) and refer the reader to Appendix 24.1 for the complete list. The idea behind this approach is to write a general time series model and then test restrictions that represent specific dynamic relationships (e.g., by restraining certain coefficients to equal 0). For this reason the strategy is sometimes referred to as general-to-specific modeling (Charemza & Deadman, 1997).

The simplest variant of Equation (1) is called the "static regression" because there are no lagged terms in the model (i.e., $\gamma_1 = \beta_1 = 0$). This formulation implies that the dependent variable responds immediately to changes in the value of the explanatory variable(s). Such a model would be appropriate if we thought, for example, that campaign advertising (or some other form of political communication) at time t had its full effect on public opinion in that same period. While some political communication effects may indeed be immediate, in most cases the static regression will be a poor approximation for many of the processes we are interested in (but see Powell, 1999). Static regression also has limitations when it comes to establishing the direction of causality between two series.

Another variant of Equation (1) is a model that includes a lagged measure of the dependent variable along with an array of exogenous variables (i.e., X terms) measured at time t (i.e., = $Y_t = \alpha + \gamma_1 Y_{t-1} + \beta_0 X_t + \ldots + u_t$ with β_1 from Equation [1] set to 0). This specification is used when there is reason to expect inertia in the outcome measure (i.e., the value of the dependent variable in the current period does not deviate far from its value in the previous period). Aggregate public opinion generally has this property (Erikson, MacKuen, & Stimson, 2002; Page & Shapiro, 1992). Thus, many studies that examine change in public opinion as a function of media coverage, elite rhetoric, and related factors employ a lagged dependent variable (e.g., Beltran, 2007; Geer, 2006; Kelleher & Wolak, 2006; Page, Shapiro, & Dempsey, 1987).[8] This particular model still presumes that Y responds immediately to changes in X, which may be a limitation if we expect a certain amount of time to pass before the effect of X is felt on Y.

In this case, the "dead-start" model may be more appropriate. As the name implies, this model contains lagged information only (i.e., β_0 in Equation [1] is set to zero). Contrary to the two preceding models, this formulation does *not* imply that the dependent variable responds immediately to changes in the independent variable(s); instead, the model presumes that it takes time for one variable to affect another.[9] Such a scenario is especially likely in political communication studies (e.g., Brosius & Kepplinger, 1990; Jerit, 2008; Kepplinger et al., 1989). Even in the age of the 24-hour news cycle, it may take several days for rhetoric, campaign ads, or other forms of political information to diffuse through media outlets and conversation circles (e.g., Katz & Lazarsfeld, 1955; Mutz & Mondak, 2006).[10]

It is not our intention, though, to promote one model over another. As the name of this approach suggests, researchers should first estimate a general model and then test the various restrictions that are suggested by their theory (De Boef & Luke, 2008). The simplest way to test whether a restriction is valid is to conduct a t-test or F-test (e.g., Gujarati, 1995; Kennedy, 1998; Wooldridge, 2006).[11]

At this point, it is worth mentioning some of the special issues that arise when conducting regression on time series data. As noted earlier, one of the central assumptions of OLS regression is that the errors are uncorrelated—or that, "the disturbance term relating to any observation is not influenced by the disturbance term relating to any other observation" (Gujarati, 1995, p. 401). This assumption is likely to be violated in most time series data. If it is, OLS estimates are still unbiased and consistent but they are no longer efficient (i.e., practically speaking, it will be harder to achieve statistical significance). It therefore becomes important to test for autocorrelation when estimating Equation (1) or any of its variants. A common test is the Durbin–Watson test; however, it only detects first-order autocorrelation and cannot be used when there is a lagged dependent variable in the model. Fortunately, there are several tests that detect higher-order autocorrelation and can be used in models with endogenous variables. These include Durbin's alternative test, the Breusch–Godfrey test, and the Box–Ljung Q test.

If autocorrelation is present, the researcher may resort to generalized least squares (if the form of the autocorrelation is known) or related techniques such as the Cochrane–Orcutt or Prais–Winsten methods (Gujarati, 1995; Wooldridge, 2006).[12] Another way to address autocorrelation is to include a lagged dependent variable in the model as a regressor. Not only does this rid the residuals of serial correlation, but many scholars also see a compelling theoretical reason to include a lagged dependent variable in their models. Indeed, Keele and Kelly (2006) argue that this practice captures "a type of dynamic that frequently occurs in politics" (p. 188). Whenever the researcher expects there to be inertia in the outcome measure, a lagged dependent variable specification can be useful. To return to the example of aggregate public opinion, one of the strongest predictors of public opinion on an issue is its own past values. Changes in aggregate opinion, when they occur, reflect measured movements in response to real-world events, attention to media coverage, and the argument and counter-argument of major policy debates, among other factors. In such instances, the phenomena of interest to political communication scholars seem likely to require a lagged dependent variable in the model specification.[13]

When it comes to estimating models with lags of the X terms ("distributed lag models"), several considerations come into play. First of all, it is not always possible to accurately specify the amount of time it takes X to affect Y. Moreover, few social science theories are specific enough to offer clear guidance when it comes to the question of how many lags to include. Second, when multiple lags are included, they are likely to be highly correlated, making it difficult to obtain precise estimates. Depending on the number of observations, researchers also may find themselves left with very few degrees of freedom. This broad class of issues has led to the development of models that put restrictions on the coefficients in distributed lag specifications, such as Koyck and Almon lag models (Gujarati, 1995; Wooldridge, 2006; for applications, see Kellstedt, 2000; Rudolph & Evans, 2005).

The models described so far have used stationary series as their starting point. But some scholars criticize the practice of differencing to yield a stationary series on the grounds that all the long-run information in the data is lost.[14] From this standpoint, an integrated (i.e., nonstationary) series is not a "problem" in need of correction; such series reflect the fact that many features of our political system (public opinion, the policy making process, etc.) change slowly.[15] When two (or more) series are thought to exhibit an *equilibrium* relationship, changes to one series should result in short- *and* long-term changes in the other. Put somewhat differently, the dependent variable will exhibit short-term changes in response to changes in the independent variable(s) but it will also experience a period of re-equilibration (hence, the observed long-term effect).[16] In this situation, an error correction model (ECM) may be appropriate. Like the previous models, the ECM can be derived from the general formulation in Equation (1) (see the appendix for details).

Although the explicit accounting for long- and short-term change would seem to make this an attractive model for political communication researchers, ECMs have not been widely used (for notable exceptions, see Jenkins, 1999; Lebo & Cassino, 2007).[17] This is a lost opportunity, for the parameters of an ECM—e.g., the rate of return to equilibrium—can convey substantively important information. For example, Jenkins (1999) examined the relationship between the density of media coverage of Canada's Reform party and voting intention in the 1993 election. His analysis showed that there was an immediate increase in voting intention in favor of the Reform party when the party received a larger share of television coverage, and that it took roughly four days for voting intentions to return to their equilibrium level. More generally, there may be particular topics in political communication research that lend themselves to this type of modeling. To provide another illustration, the journalistic norm to remain balanced may produce an equilibrium relationship between positive and negative arguments during a policy debate.[18] Taken as a whole, the general-to-specific modeling framework allows researchers to test different theoretical possibilities in a systematic way.

Vector Autoregression and Granger Causality

Unlike the models we have described so far, in which there are endogenous and exogenous variables, in Vector Autoregression (VAR) models all the variables are treated as endogenous. Thus, in VAR, the current value of each variable is regressed on the lagged values of all the other variables in the analysis (see Brandt & Williams, 2007). As an illustration, consider the following representation of a VAR system from Simon and Jerit's (2008) analysis of the relationship between elite rhetoric and news coverage on partial-birth abortion. The system has three variables, denoting news content, editorial content, and elite statements in the *Congressional Record*. In this study, three lags of each variable were included in the analysis, producing the following model:

$$News_t = \delta + \sum_{j=1}^{3} \phi_j News_{t-j} + \sum_{j=1}^{3} \tau_j Elites_{t-j} + \sum_{j=1}^{3} \rho_j Editorials_{t-j} + u_{1t} \qquad (2)$$

$$Editorials_t = \varphi + \sum_{j=1}^{3} \xi_j Editorials_{t-j} + \sum_{j=1}^{3} \psi_j News_{t-j} + \sum_{j=1}^{3} \lambda_j Elites_{t-j} + u_{2t} \qquad (3)$$

$$Elites_t = \alpha + \sum_{j=1}^{3} \beta_j Elites_{t-j} + \sum_{j=1}^{3} \gamma_j News_{t-j} + \sum_{j=1}^{3} \omega_j Editorials_{t-j} + u_{3t} \qquad (4)$$

The u's are stochastic error terms, commonly referred to as "impulses" or "innovations."[19]

There are many reasons one might consider using VAR in political communication research. Although some prominent models of the public opinion formation process assume a top-down (i.e., elite driven) model (e.g., Fan, 1988; Zaller, 1992), other researchers view elite behavior as endogenous and highly responsive to public opinion (e.g., Carsey, 2001; Erikson et al., 2002; Jacobs & Shapiro, 2000). Thus, VAR is an appropriate modeling choice for those who view the behavior of partisan elites, the mass media, and public opinion as interconnected. Indeed, from this standpoint, endogeneity is not a methodological nuisance; rather, it is "the critical substantive feature" of democratic politics (Box-Steffensmeier, Darmofal, & Farrell, 2008, 2). Not too surprisingly, VAR is a commonly used technique for analyzing time-series data (for recent applications, see Bartels, 1996; Blood & Phillips, 1995; Edwards & Wood, 1999; Wood, Owens, & Durham, 2005; Wu, Stevenson, Chen, & Güner, 2002).

Coefficients from a VAR are difficult to interpret, so estimation of the model usually is combined with two types of post-estimation analyses. First, causality can be assessed through Granger causality tests (see Gujarati, 1995, pp. 620–621). A measure X is said to "Granger cause" a measure Y if Y can be better predicted from past values of X and Y together than the past values of Y alone (Freeman, 1983). In practice, VAR modelers test hypotheses by assessing the joint statistical significance of the coefficients on blocks of variables with an F-test. These tests indicate whether the inclusion of a set of variables improves the prediction of the corresponding dependent variable.[20] Returning to the above example, Simon and Jerit (2007) report that pro-ban rhetoric in congressional discourse significantly predicts such rhetoric in news content, even after controlling for the effect of previous news coverage. In other words, the set of coefficients on *News* and *Elites* in Equation (2) was significantly different from zero while the set of coefficients on *Editorials* was not. Simon and Jerit also found that congressional discourse is largely exogenous, influenced only by its own past values (only the set of coefficients on *Elites* was significant in the third equation; the coefficients for *News* and *Editorials* were insignificant).

A second tool used in VAR is simulations (called "impulse response functions" or "moving average response"), which examines how a change in one series influences the other variables in the VAR system. This is particularly useful for examining how responsive each series is to changes in the others and estimating the duration of these effects.[21]

VAR models have been described as "parsimonious approximations of the true data generation process" (Wood et al., 2005, p. 635), but this approach has certain disadvantages. One of the biggest challenges involves selecting the appropriate lag length. The conclusions drawn from VAR analyses can be "sensitive to the choice of lag length and the number of included variables, for neither of which there is an agreed-upon choice mechanism" (Kennedy, 1998, p. 174). One widely used method of selecting the appropriate number of lags is to choose the length that minimizes either the Akaike (AIC) or Bayesian (BIC) information criterion (see Lütkepohl, 1993, for an introduction to this topic). Nevertheless, if one's model has a several variables and/or lags, this will consume a lot of degrees of freedom.[22]

Autoregressive Integrated Moving Average (ARIMA) Modeling and Intervention Analysis

A final technique employed by political communication researchers is ARIMA modeling. This method came into fashion in economics when researchers realized that simple, atheoretical models could outperform complex structural models of the economy. Unlike the regression models described earlier, in which Y_t is explained by the regressors X_{t-1}, X_{t-2}, and so on, this type of modeling is premised on the idea that when analyzing the stochastic properties of a time series, the analyst should "*let the data speak for themselves*" (Gujarati, 1995, p. 735, emphasis original). In other words, Y_t is explained only in terms of its own past values along with current and past errors.[23]

As with time series more generally, the goal in ARIMA modeling is to "identify and estimate a statistical model which can be interpreted as having generated the sample data" (Porkorny, 1987, p. 343). Autoregressive (AR) and Moving Average (MA) are two different mechanisms in that regard. We say that Y_t is AR(1), or first-order autoregressive, if the value of Y at time t depends on its value in the previous time period and a random error term. In the general case, Y_t is a pth-order autoregressive process (i.e., AR(p)), represented by p lags of Y and an error term. A moving average (MA) process, on the other hand, is a linear combination of white noise error terms, which can be MA(1), MA(2), . . ., MA(q). After establishing that Y_t is stationary (or differencing it d times to become stationary), the analyst "identifies" a time series by examining the lags of the series and determining the order of p and q.[24] ARIMA modeling is intended to be iterative: the researcher identifies, estimates, and then diagnoses his or her model by examining the residuals (McCleary & Hay, 1980). The process continues until the researcher establishes that the residuals are white noise, containing no further information (for applications, see Gonzenbach, 1992; Romer, 2006).[25]

Intervention analysis (or interrupted time series) also makes use of ARIMA models. Here, the researcher examines the influence of an exogenous "intervention" on a time series. This approach has been used to understand how campaign events affect vote intention (e.g., Shaw, 1999b; Shelley & Hwang, 1991), as well as how certain focusing events, such as congressional hearings (Wood & Doan, 2003) or presidential speeches (Peake & Eshbaugh-Soha, 2008) influence the governmental agenda. The general form taken by these models is presented below:

$$Y_t = F(I_t) + N_t \qquad (5)$$

where $f(I_t)$ represents the intervention component (or transfer function) and N_t denotes the noise component of an ARIMA model.[26] The intervention component can be represented in a variety of ways. This allows the researcher to model events that are either gradual or abrupt in their onset, and either temporary or permanent in their effects. In their treatment of transfer functions, McCleary and Hay (1980) develop a "simple theory of impact" (see Figure 24.1) that may serve as a template for political communication researchers (also see Mills, 1990).

In each cell of Figure 24.1, the *x*-axis corresponds to time and the *y*-axis represents the magnitude of the effect of an intervention. Four distinct types of effects are possible, depending on the onset and duration of the intervention. Consider the top-left cell in Figure 24.1, which shows an intervention that has a gradual but permanent effect. This pattern seems to approximate the introduction and diffusion of television, as described by Prior (2007). The bottom-left cell illustrates an intervention with an immediate and permanent effect. This model specification might be appropriate for political events that occur over a short period of time and are covered by all of the major news outlets, such as nominating conventions or scandals (Shaw, 1999b). With the exception of dramatic events such as the September 11 attacks, most political events probably do not have a lasting effect on public opinion, which means that either of the two right-most cells may be more appropriate for political communication researchers. The top-right cell seems especially useful for studying the effects of social influence, which can take days to materialize and then subside over time (e.g., Katz & Lazarsfeld, 1955). By contrast, the bottom-right cell might be more

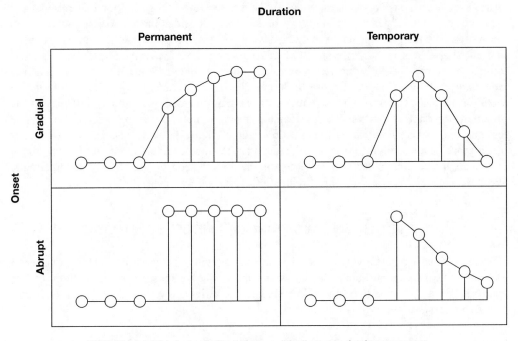

FIGURE 24.1 Typology of effects from political communication processes.
Adapted from McCleary & Hay (1980).

suitable for understanding rally-around-the-flag events, which often have an immediate, though transitory, effect on public opinion (e.g., Callaghan & Virtanen, 1993; Mueller, 1973).

With this framework, scholars can develop and test theories about the influence of media coverage, campaign events, political rhetoric, advertising, and other communication processes. As was the case with the general-to-specific modeling approach, transfer functions permit researchers to test a rich array of theoretical arguments.

Areas for Future Research

We close our discussion of time series applications by noting two areas of research that are common in political science but have yet to find wide application in political communication research. The first concerns the concept of *fractional* integration. To this point, we have distinguished between series that are integrated (or non-stationary) and those that are integrated of order 0 (or stationary). But time series scholars note that many series—especially those common in political science—are *fractionally* integrated (Box-Steffensmeier & Tomlinson, 2000; Lebo, Walker, & Clarke, 2000; also see DeBoef & Granato, 1997). When one models a series with fractional integration, I(d), the value of d can be any value between 0 and 1 (i.e., the analyst is not forced into modeling a series as either stationary or integrated). Fractional integration is appropriate when one has data that aggregate heterogeneous microprocesses—as would be the case if a scholar using aggregate public opinion data believed that sophisticates and non-sophisticates engage in different styles of information processing (e.g., Box-Steffensmeier et al. 2008). Likewise, macropartisanship may be fractionally integrated if particular subpopulations (e.g., strong versus weak partisans) exhibit distinct types of behavior or respond differently to political events (Box-Steffensmeier & Smith, 1996; Lebo et al., 2000).

The second topic concerns time series *variance* models. Most scholars performing time series analysis focus on modeling the mean of the series. But there are a host of important statistical and substantive issues related to the variance of a series. Consider presidential approval as an illustration. The typical approach to studying presidential approval focuses on modeling the mean of the series—that is, identifying variables that account for shifts in average presidential approval ratings over time. Recently, however, scholars have attempted to account for the changing *magnitude* of these shifts (e.g., Gronke & Brehm, 2002). One of the findings to emerge from this research is that the *volatility* of presidential approval has increased over time—a finding that has important implications for presidential leadership and the strategic behavior of political elites. The lesson, then, is that political communication scholars should ask themselves whether their theoretical arguments imply changes in the mean or the variance of a time series. This approach falls under the heading of autoregressive conditional heteroskedasticity (ARCH) models (Engle, 1982; for applications, see Gronke & Brehm, 2002; Maestas & Preuhs, 2000).

STRENGTHS AND LIMITATIONS OF TIME SERIES ANALYSIS

Having provided a general overview of what time series analysis consists of and how it has been used in political communication research, we now consider the strengths and limitations of this approach. We also discuss the kinds of knowledge time series analysis produces relative to other forms of analysis.

Estimating Causal Effects

An important element in most accounts of causality is the notion of temporal precedence, or the idea that the cause comes before the effect in time (for a summary, see Cook & Campbell, 1979). Because time series analysis respects the ordering of data in time, it would seem to have several advantages when it comes to understanding causal relationships. Having information on the timing of the independent and dependent measures, and being able to establish that an elite message (or some other form of political communication) *precedes* opinion or some other outcome measure is potent evidence for a causal relationship. Contrast this with cross-sectional data, where all variables, independent and dependent, are measured at the same point in time. While theory or common sense may dictate one causal ordering over another, it can be difficult to establish the direction of causality between variables with cross-sectional data.[27]

Time series analysis may have an advantage when it comes to the sequencing of observations, but the use of time series data is no different from cross-sectional data when it comes to problems related to omitted variables or spurious causation. That is, simply knowing that elite messages preceded opinion change does not establish that elite rhetoric was the *cause* of the opinion change. Elites and masses might both be responding to some other factor, such as real-world events. What's more, scholars have observed that, "many of these time-varying omitted factors may be difficult or impossible to measure and control for" (Gabel & Scheve, 2007, p. 1015).[28]

When it comes to making causal inferences, both time series and cross-sectional studies are inferior to experiments. Laboratory and survey-based experiments remove the problem of omitted variable bias through the random assignment to treatment and control conditions (see Chapter 8, this volume). Because the manipulation is under the control of the researcher, it is, by definition, exogenous. This means that any differences across conditions on the outcome measure can be attributed to the manipulation. Greater internal validity comes at a price, however. Both laboratory and survey-based experiments expose people to communication-relevant treatments (e.g., arguments, frames, campaign commercials) in a sterile environment—i.e., one that is free of the distractions and competing messages that often exist in the natural world. This problem is compounded if the manipulation itself is artificially strong (Kinder, 2007). Time series analysis, on the other hand, makes use of data that capture people in real time, after they have been exposed to actual political stimuli. In most instances, then, the treatments have a high degree of external validity.

Time series analysis is at a disadvantage, however, when it comes to breaking down the psychological processes underlying mass survey results—especially in comparison to laboratory or survey-based experiments. Describing this as the advantage of *analytic decomposition*, Kinder and Palfrey (1993) write: "Experimenters need not wait for natural processes to provide crucial tests and telling comparisons: they can create them on their own" (p. 15). This control has several advantages: it allows the researcher to examine the effects of incremental changes to a stimulus over a series of studies (e.g., Iyengar & Kinder, 1987). It also makes it possible to examine how relationships change in the presence or absence of other variables, so that the researcher can examine the conditions under which certain relationships hold (McDermott, 2002). In a similar way, small *N* research, such as in-depth interviews and focus groups (e.g., Chong, 1993; Gamson, 1992; Graber, 1993), can provide a window into the intricacies of people's political reasoning and has revealed such thought processes to be more sophisticated than originally assumed.

Generating Knowledge about Political Communication Processes

In addition to providing a unique type of analytical leverage relative to some of the other techniques used by political communication researchers, whether cross-sectional surveys, in-depth interviews, or laboratory experiments, time series analysis produces a different kind of knowledge. Time series analysis informs us about the relationship between variables over time and therefore sheds light on the action-reaction dynamic that is fundamental to many political communication processes. In that sense, there is an isomorphism between method and object of study that is absent in many other approaches (but see Lau & Redlawsk, 2006). To date, most time series applications in the field of political communication lack an emphasis on psychological processes. However, there is nothing inherent in the time series approach that prevents a focus on psychological processes. For example, Mutz (2007) has reported time series data on skin conductance level for subjects viewing political discussions at different camera angles. Chong (1996) presents a dynamic model of framing effects that could, in theory, be tested with a time series model.

In addition to their other advantages, many of the time series techniques discussed here (e.g., VAR, error correction modeling) generate information about the duration or persistence of effects—information that is difficult, if not impossible, to recover from single-shot studies. Thus, research using time series can explore how responsive people are to elite and media messages— how quickly an initial response can be observed—as well as how long those effects last.[29] Being able to characterize how the citizenry responds to strategic efforts of political elites (and vice versa) is essential for evaluating the health of a representative democracy.

For time series analysis to live up to its full potential, however, researchers must be sensitive to the unit of time implied by their theory. When the time intervals in one's data are large (say, years), but theory leads us to expect effects that occur at shorter intervals (e.g., months or weeks), no time series model will do an adequate job of approximating the underlying process (Freeman, 1989). However, as many of the applications in this chapter demonstrate, it is possible to find rich data coded at the monthly, weekly, and even daily level. Another concern has to do with the quality of the underlying data in political communication time series. Just as time series analysis loses many of its advantages when the time intervals are overly large, it lacks analytical power when communications data are coarsely coded. Fortunately, researchers today can go beyond "big message" indicators such as story counts (e.g., Althaus & Kim, 2006). The availability of online archives and automated content analysis programs makes it possible to create detailed measures of media coverage and elite rhetoric (for perspectives on content analysis techniques, see the chapters in Part IV, this volume). By taking advantage of these resources, researchers will be able to expand our knowledge about enduring topics in the field.

CONCLUSION

In a recent review of the field, Graber (2004) characterized political communication scholars as studying "the salient characteristics of the originators of political messages, the form and substance of messages, the impact that various types of communication channels leave on the messages that flow through their networks, and, ultimately the impact of the messages of political processes at individual and societal levels" (p. 46). The time series techniques described here can help shed light on many of these topics. Indeed, when it comes to questions about the inter-relationship between the mass media, political elites, and public opinion, these techniques seem uniquely qualified to handle nonrecursive relationships that play out over time. As the preceding discussion implies, however, this method has strengths *and* limitations. Perhaps the most compelling research design is one that combines time series analysis with other techniques, eliminating threats to causal inference by harnessing the distinctive strengths of different methods.

APPENDIX 24.1

Our treatment of the general-to-specific modeling approach follows from Charemza and Deadman (1997, pp. 58–62). Consider a simple ADL(1) model with one explanatory variable:

$$Y_t = \alpha + \gamma_1 Y_{t-1} + \beta_0 X_t + \beta_1 X_{t-1} + \ldots + u_t$$

Restrictions on this general model lead to ten common economic models, described below. Any number of restrictions may yield other models that can be applied in political communication research.

1. Static Regression $\qquad\qquad\qquad\qquad\qquad\qquad\quad \gamma_1 = \beta_1 = 0$
2. First-order autoregressive process $\qquad\qquad\qquad \beta_0 = \beta_1 = 0$
3. Leading indicator equation $\qquad\qquad\qquad\qquad \gamma_1 = \beta_0 = 0$
4. Equation in first differences $\qquad\qquad\qquad\qquad \gamma_1 = 1, \beta_0 = -\beta_1$
5. First-order finite distributed lag equation $\qquad \gamma_1 = 0$
6. Partial adjustment equation $\qquad\qquad\qquad\qquad \beta_1 = 0$
7. Dead-start model (lagged information only) $\qquad \beta_0 = 0$
8. Proportional response model $\qquad\qquad\qquad\qquad \beta_0 = -\lambda_1$
    (The explanatory variables are X_{t-1} and $Y_{t-1} - X_{t-1}$)
9. Error correction model $\qquad\qquad\qquad\qquad\qquad \gamma_1 - 1 = -(\beta_0 + \beta_1)$
10. Common factor restriction $\qquad\qquad\qquad\qquad\quad \beta_1 = -\lambda_1 * \beta_0$

(The coefficient of autocovariance, ρ, replaces λ_1)

NOTES

1. For introductions to the topic, see Enders (2004), Charemza and Deadman (1997), McCleary and Hay (1980), or an econometrics textbook.
2. Additionally, an event process can be aggregated into a time series (for example, a time series of monthly veto threats). Special methods are often required, however, when there is temporal dependence in count data (Brandt, Williams, Fordham, & Pollins, 2000).
3. Time series cross-sectional (TSCS) data contain information about multiple units (e.g., countries, states) over time. Because this kind of data is uncommon in political communication research, we will not discuss models for TSCS data (for introductions to this topic, see Beck & Katz, 1995; Stimson, 1985; for applications, see Brandenburg, 2004; Shaw, 1999a).
4. However, King (1989) writes that, "data with time series properties need not have been collected over time in a series" (p. 162). Serial correlation also can occur across space. That's because people's opinions and behaviors are influenced by their social context (e.g., their neighborhood, interpersonal networks, or workplace). See McClurg (Chapter 18, this volume) for a discussion of these topics.
5. Mean stationarity can also be examined visually, with a correlogram (e.g., Romer, 2006).
6. If a series is nonstationary in its variance and mean, one should first log the series and then difference it. This "fixes" the problem of nonconstant variance without seeking to explain the source of the volatility. In an approach we describe later, the researcher can identify variables that account for changes in the variance of a series.
7. Technically, Equation (1) represents an ADL (1,1) model because there is a single lag of both Y and X. ADL (k) designates an autoregressive distributed lag model containing lags for all the variables up to the level of k. For ADL models with an unequal number of lags, the following notation is used: ADL $(k_1, k_2, k_3, \ldots, k_m)$.

8. Naturally, inertia also may characterize the behavior of political elites. For example, Wood, Owens, and Durham (2005) contend that presidential rhetoric is habitual (i.e., current presidential rhetoric on the economy is influenced by past presidential rhetoric on the economy).

9. Romer (2006) calls this a "lag-lead relationship" (p. 223).

10. See Gujarati (1995) for a discussion of the psychological, technical, and institutional reasons for including lags in a model (pp. 589–560).

11. Charemza and Deadman (1997) also discuss tests for nonlinear restrictions (e.g., likelihood ratio, Wald, and Lagrange multiplier tests).

12. Newey–West standard errors are consistent in the presence of autocorrelation. With this approach, one need not know the form of the autocorrelation.

13. This modeling choice is not without costs, however. Most notably, the use of lagged endogenous variables violates the assumption that the explanatory variables are non-stochastic. This can lead to biased coefficient estimates (Achen, 2000). See Keele and Kelly (2006) for an excellent discussion of when lagged dependent variables are appropriate.

14. This can be seen by recalling the definition of differencing ($\Delta Y = Y_t - Y_{t-1}$). Each time point in a differenced series should be seen not as the *level* of the series at time t, but the *change* from t-1 to t (Durr, 1993).

15. Durr (1993) describes an integrated time series as "one for which the value of any given point in time may be expressed as the sum of all past disturbances" (p. 163). Such series drift in one direction for an extended period of time before changing course. When a series must be differenced once to become stationary, it is "integrated of order 1," or I(1). A stationary series is, by definition, I(0). Practically speaking, this means that nothing needs to be done to the series to make it stationary.

16. In this context, the phrase "equilibrium relationship" has a very specific meaning. If two variables are individually I(1) but their linear combination is I(0), they are said to be "cointegrated." As Kennedy (1998) observes, "the cointegrating combination is interpreted as an equilibrium relationship" (p. 270).

17. Several interesting applications exist in the field of political science. See, for example, Barabas (2006), Durr (1993), Krause (1997), or Lebo and Moore (2003).

18. One recent study (De Boef & Luke, 2008) argues that the error correction model need not be restricted to cointegrated series and that the error correction model is appropriate for use on stationary data.

19. Contemporaneous measures can also be included in a VAR system (Enders, 2004).

20. Granger causality tests can be employed in any time series context and do not necessarily have to be accompanied with VAR (e.g., Althaus, 2003; Jenkins, 1999; Kellstedt, 2000, 2003).

21. In practice, it is necessary to specify a causal chain (i.e., order the variables) when doing these simulations. See Freeman, Williams, and Lin (1989, pp. 846–847) for discussion on this point.

22. A second complication with the use of VAR models is that stationarity remains a contested issue. There is considerable debate regarding whether the variables in a VAR system should be jointly stationary (Gujarati, 1995). Because transforming a subset of variables may lead to difficulties of interpretation (e.g., King, 1989, pp. 181–182), some time series scholars recommend working in levels (i.e., with data that are not differenced). However, critics of that approach note the potential for spurious relationships. Many of the applications noted above contain discussions of this issue (for example, see Wood et al., 2005, p. 635, note 7).

23. ARIMA models are called atheoretic because they cannot be derived from any economic theory. This approach is commonly used in forecasting, and also is referred to as the Box–Jenkins method, named after the statisticians George Box and Gwilym Jenkins. We focus on univariate ARIMA models and refer readers interested in learning more about multivariate ARIMA to McCleary and Hay (1980).

24. Here, one uses the autocorrelation function (ACF) and partial autocorrelation function (PACF), and the resulting correlogram.

25. The distinction between ARIMA (p, d, q) models and the regression models described earlier is somewhat artificial. If anything, the distinction amounts to a difference in modeling style rather than substance. ARIMA models are identified empirically, whereas other times series models are identified theoretically (see McCleary & Hay, 1980, p. 269, for a discussion).

26. See Shadish, Cook, and Campbell (2002) for a general treatment of interrupted time series.

27. For example, does media use lead to greater levels of knowledge or are knowledgeable people more likely to use the media? There are techniques for dealing with endogeneity and related problems in cross-sectional data (e.g., selection), but that is outside the scope of our discussion.
28. Gabel and Scheve (2007) mention another problem, one that seems especially acute for communication researchers seeking to use time series analysis, which is that "elites may appear to lead opinion simply because they correctly anticipate changes in opinion rather than cause them" (p. 1015). Finally, some argue that there is "theoretical ambiguity" in the time series approach because different processes can be mathematically equivalent (King, 1989). For example, a lagged dependent variable is often used as a proxy for a set of lagged independent variables with geometrically declining coefficients (e.g., Kellstedt, 2000, 2003).
29. See De Boef and Luke (2008) for guidance on how to calculate various quantities of interest, such as short- and long-term effects, as well as mean and median lag lengths.

REFERENCES

Achen, C. H. (2000, July). *Why lagged dependent variables can suppress the explanatory power of other independent variables*. Proceedings of the annual meeting of Political Methodology, Los Angeles, CA.

Althaus, S. L. (2003). *Collective preferences in democratic politics: Opinion surveys and the will of the people*. New York: Cambridge University Press.

Althaus, S., & Kim, Y. M. (2006). Priming effects in complex information environments: Reassessing the impact of news discourse on presidential approval. *Journal of Politics, 68*(4), 960–979.

Barabas, J. (2006). Rational exuberance: The stock market and public support for social security privatization. *Journal of Politics, 68*, 50–61.

Bartels, L. M. (1996). *Politicians and the press: Who leads, who follows?* Paper presented at the annual meeting of the American Political Science Association, San Francisco, CA.

Beck, N., & Katz, J. N. (1995). What to do (and not to do) with time-series cross-section data. *American Political Science Review, 89*(3), 634–647.

Beltran, U. (2007). The combined effect of advertising and news coverage in the Mexican presidential campaign of 2000. *Political Communication, 24*(1), 37–63.

Blood, D. J., & Phillips, P. C. B. (1995). Recession headline news, consumer sentiment, the state of the economy and presidential popularity: A time series analysis 1989–1993. *International Journal of Public Opinion Research, 7*, 2–22.

Box-Steffensmeier, J. M., Darmofal, D., & Farrell, C. A. (2008). *The aggregate dynamics of campaigns*. Working paper, Department of Political Science, The Ohio State University, Columbus, Ohio.

Box-Steffensmeier, J. M., & Smith, R. M. (1996). The dynamics of aggregate partisanship. *American Political Science Review, 90*(3), 567–580.

Box-Steffensmeier, J. M., & Tomlinson, A. R. (2000). Fractional integration methods in political science. *Electoral Studies, 19*, 63–76.

Brandenburg, H. (2004). Who follows whom? The impact of parties on media agenda formation in the 1997 British general election campaign. *Harvard International Journal of Press/Politics, 7*(3), 34–54.

Brandt, P. T., & Williams, J. T. (2007). *Multiple time series models*. Thousand Oaks, CA: Sage.

Brandt, P. T., Williams, J. T., Fordham, B. O., & Pollins, B. (2000). Dynamic modeling for persistent event-count time series. *American Journal of Political Science, 44*(4), 823–844.

Brosius, H. B., & Kepplinger, H. M. (1990). The agenda-setting function of television news. *Communication Research, 17*(2), 183–211.

Callaghan, K. T., & Virtanen, S. (1993). Revised models of the "rally phenomenon": The case of the Carter presidency. *Journal of Politics, 55*(3), 756–764.

Carsey, T. M. (2001). *Campaign dynamics: The race for governor*. Ann Arbor: University of Michigan Press.

Charemza, W.W., & Deadman, D. F. (1997). *New directions in econometric practice* (2nd ed.). Aldershot: Edward Elgar.

Chong, D. (1993). How people think, reason, and feel about rights and liberties. *American Journal of Political Science, 37*, 867–899.

Chong, D. (1996). Creating common frames of reference on political issues. In D. C. Mutz, P. Sniderman, & R. A. Brody (Eds.), *Political persuasion and attitude change* (pp. 195–224). Ann Arbor: University of Michigan Press.

Cook, T. D., & Campbell, D. T. (1979). *Quasi-experimentation: Design and analysis issues for field settings.* New York: Houghton Mifflin.

DeBoef, S., & Granato, J. (1997). Near-integrated data and the analysis of political relationships. *American Journal of Political Science, 41*(2), 619–640.

DeBoef, S., & Luke, K. (2008). Taking time seriously. *American Journal of Political Science, 52*(1), 184–200.

Durr, R. H. (1993). What moves policy sentiment? *American Political Science Review, 87*(1), 158–170.

Edwards, G. C., & Wood, B. D. (1999). Who influences whom? The president, Congress, and the media. *American Political Science Review, 93*(2), 327–344.

Enders, W. (2004). *Applied econometric time-series* (2nd ed.). New York: John Wiley & Sons.

Engle, R. F. (1982). Autoregressive conditional heteroscedasticity with estimates of the variance of United Kingdom inflation. *Econometrica, 50*(4), 987–1007.

Erikson, R. S., MacKuen, M. B., & Stimson, J. A. (2002). *The macro polity.* New York: Cambridge University Press.

Fan, D. P. (1988). *Predictions of public opinion from the mass media: Computer content analysis and mathematical modeling.* New York: Greenwood Press.

Freeman, J. R. (1983). Granger causality and the time series analysis of political relationships. *American Journal of Political Science, 27*, 327–358.

Freeman, J. R. (1989). Systematic sampling, temporal aggregation, and the study of political relationships. *Political Analysis, 1*, 61–98.

Freeman, J. R., Williams, J. T., & Lin, T. (1989). Vector autoregression and the study of politics. *American Journal of Political Science, 33*(4), 842–877.

Gabel, M., & Scheve, K. (2007). Estimating the effect of elite communication on public opinion using instrumental variables. *American Journal of Political Science, 51*(4), 1013–1028.

Gamson, W. A. (1992). *Talking politics.* New York: Cambridge University Press.

Geer, J. G. (2006). *In defense of negativity: Attack ads in presidential campaigns.* Chicago: University of Chicago Press.

Gozenbach, W. J. (1992). A time-series analysis of the drug issue, 1985–1990: The press, the president, and public opinion. *International Journal of Public Opinion Research, 4*(2), 126–147.

Graber, D. A. (1993). *Processing the news: How people tame the information tide* (3rd ed.). Lanhan, MD: University Press of America.

Graber, D. A. (2004). Methodological developments in political communication research. In L. L. Kaid (Ed.), *Handbook of political communications research* (pp. 45–67), Mahwah, NJ: Lawrence Erlbaum.

Gronke, P. I,, & Brehm, J. (2002). History, heterogeneity, and presidential approval: A modified ARCH approach. *Electoral Studies, 21*, 425–452.

Gujarati, D. N. (1995). *Basic econometrics.* New York: McGraw-Hill.

Iyengar, S., & Kinder, D. (1987). *News that matters.* Chicago: University of Chicago Press.

Jacobs, L. C., & Shapiro, R. Y. (2000). *Politicians don't pander: Political manipulation and the loss of democratic responsiveness.* Chicago: University of Chicago Press.

Jenkins, R. W. (1999) How much is too much? Media attention and popular support for an insurgent party, *Political Communication, 16*(4), 429–445.

Jerit, J. (2008). Issue framing and engagement: Rhetorical strategy in public policy debates. *Political Behavior, 30*, 1–24.

Katz, E., & Lazarsfeld, P. F. (1955). *Personal influence.* Glencoe, IL: Free Press.

Keele, L., & Kelly, N. J. (2006). Dynamic models for dynamic theories: The ins and outs of lagged dependent variables. *Political Analysis, 14*, 186–205.

Kelleher, C. A., & Wolak, J. (2006). Priming presidential approval: The conditionality of issue effects. *Political Behavior, 28*, 193–210.

Kellstedt, P. M. (2000). Media framing and the dynamics of racial policy preferences. *American Journal of Political Science, 44*(2), 245–260.

Kellstedt, P. M. (2003). *The mass media and the dynamics of American racial attitudes.* New York: Cambridge University Press.

Kennedy, P. (1998). *A guide to econometrics* (4th ed.). Cambridge, MA: MIT Press.

Kepplinger, H. M., Donsbach, W., Brosius, H. B., & Staab, J. F. (1989). Media tone and public opinion: A longitudinal study of media coverage and public opinion on Chancellor Kohl. *International Journal of Public Opinion Research, 1*(4), 326–342.

Key, Jr., V. O. (1961). *Public opinion and American democracy.* New York: Alfred A. Knopf.

Kinder, D. R. (2007). Curmudgeonly advice. *Journal of Communication, 57*, 155–162.

Kinder, D. R., & Palfrey, T. R. (Eds.). (1993). *Experimental foundations of political science.* Ann Arbor: University of Michigan Press.

King, G. (1989). *Unifying political methodology: The likelihood theory of statistical inference.* New York: Cambridge University Press.

Krause, G. A. (1997). Voters, information heterogeneity, and the dynamics of aggregate economic expectations. *American Journal of Political Science, 41*(4), 1170–1200.

Lau, R., & Redlawsk, D. (2006). *How voters decide.* New York: Cambridge University Press.

Lebo, M. J., & Cassino, D. (2007). The aggregated consequences of motivated reasoning and the dynamics of partisan presidential approval. *Political Psychology, 28*(6), 719–746.

Lebo, M. J., & Moore, W. H. (2003). Dynamic foreign policy behavior. *Journal of Conflict Resolution, 47*(1), 13–32.

Lebo, M. J., Walker, R. W., & Clarke, H. D. (2000). You must remember this: Dealing with long memory in political analysis. *Electoral Studies, 19*, 31–48.

Lütkepohl, H. (1993). *Introduction to multiple time series* (2nd ed.). New York: Springer.

Maestas, C., & Preuhs, R. R. (2000). Modeling volatility in political time series. *Electoral Studies, 19*, 95–110.

McCleary, R., & Hay, R. A. (1980). *Applied time series analysis for the social sciences.* Beverly Hills, CA: Sage.

McDermott, R. (2002). Experimental methods in political science. *Annual Review of Political Science, 5*, 31–61.

Mills, T. C. (1990). *Time series techniques for economists.* New York: Cambridge University Press.

Mueller, J. E. (1973). *War, presidents, and public opinion.* New York: John Wiley & Sons.

Mutz, D.C. (2007). Effects of "in your face" television discourse on perceptions of a legitimate opposition. *American Political Science Review, 101*, 621–636.

Mutz, D. C., & Mondak, J. J. (2006). The workplace as a context of cross-cutting political discourse. *Journal of Politics, 68*, 140–55.

Ostrom, C. W. (1978). *Time series analysis: Regression techniques.* Beverly Hills, CA: Sage.

Page, B. I., & Shapiro, R. Y. (1992). *The rational public: Fifty years of trends in American policy preferences.* Chicago: University of Chicago Press.

Page, B. I., Shapiro, R. Y., & Dempsey, G. R. (1987). What moves public opinion? *American Political Science Review, 81*, 23–44.

Peake, J. S., Eshbaugh-Soha, M. (2008). The agenda-setting impact of major presidential TV addresses. *Political Communication, 25*(2), 113–137.

Porkorny, M. (1987). *An introduction to econometrics.* New York: Basil Blackwell.

Powell, R. J. (1999). "Going public" revisited: Presidential speechmaking and the bargaining setting in Congress. *Congress & the Presidency, 26*(2), 153–170.

Prior, M. (2007). *Post-broadcast democracy: How media choice increases inequality in political involvement and polarizes elections.* New York: Cambridge University Press.

Romer, D. (2006). Time series models. In D. Romer, K. Kenski, K. Winneg, C. Adasiewizc, & K. H. Jamieson, *Capturing campaigning dynamics 2000 & 2004: The National Annenberg Election Survey* (pp. 165–243). Philadelphia: University of Pennsylvania Press.

Rudolph, T. J., & Evans, J. (2005). Political trust, ideology, and public support for government spending. *American Journal of Political Science, 49*(3), 660–671.

Shadish, W. R., Cook, T. D., & Campbell, D. T. (2002). *Experimental and quasi-experimental designs for generalized causal inference.* New York: Houghton Mifflin.

Shaw, D. R. (1999a). The effect of TV ads and candidate appearances on statewide presidential votes, 1988–1996. *American Political Science Review, 93*(2), 345–361.

Shaw, D. R. (1999b). A study of presidential campaign event effects from 1952–1992. *Journal of Politics, 61*(2), 387–422.

Shelley II, M. C., & Hwang, H. (1991). The mass media and public opinion polls in the 1988 presidential election: Trends, accuracy, consistency, and events. *American Politics Quarterly, 19*(1), 59–79.

Simon, A. F., & Jerit, J. (2007). Toward a theory relating political discourse, media, and public opinion. *Journal of Communication, 57,* 254–271.

Stimson, J. A. (1985). Regression in space and time: A statistical essay. *American Journal of Political Science, 29*(4), 914–947.

Stimson, J. A. (1999). *Public opinion in America: Moods, cycles, and swings* (2nd ed.). Boulder, CO: Westview Press.

Wood, B. D., & Doan, A. (2003). The politics of problem definition: Applying and testing threshold models. *American Journal of Political Science, 47*(4), 640–653.

Wood, B. D., Owens, C. T., & Durham, B. M. (2005). Presidential rhetoric and the economy. *Journal of Politics, 67*(3), 627–645.

Wooldridge, J. M. (2006). *Introductory econometrics: A modern approach* (3rd ed.). Mason, OH: South-Western.

Wu, H. D., Stevenson, R. L., Chen, H. C., & Güner, Z. N. (2002). The conditioned impact of recession news: A time-series analysis of economic communications in the United States, 1987–1996. *International Journal of Public Opinion Research, 14*(1), 19–36.

Zaller, J. R. (1992). *The nature and origins of mass opinion.* New York: Cambridge University Press.

IX
MEASUREMENT

25

Concept Explication in the Internet Age
The Case of Political Interactivity

S. Shyam Sundar
Media Effects Research Laboratory
College of Communications
The Pennsylvania State University

Saraswathi Bellur
Media Effects Research Laboratory
College of Communications
The Pennsylvania State University

Mass communication research as a scholarly endeavor came of age in the latter half of the twentieth century, fueled by an interest in the uses and effects of newspapers and television, the two dominant media of the time. It is little wonder then that most concepts in the literature are explicated and theorized in a manner that reflects the traditional media-effects paradigm of a powerful, centralized medium received by a generally passive audience. Scholars tend to characterize media offerings in terms of content (e.g., news vs. entertainment, national vs. local news) and audience activity in terms of usage. The latter has been particularly keenly explicated, with researchers differentiating between "exposure" and "attention" (McLeod & Pan, 2005) *en route* to devising sophisticated measures for capturing audience members' engagement with public affairs information in the media (Chaffee & Schleuder, 1986).

When the Internet became a major vehicle of mass communication in the late 1990s, many researchers directly imported these measures to the context of the new medium. Large surveys conducted by the Pew Charitable Trusts on a regular basis employed simplistic questions such as "Do you ever use the Internet to look online for news or information about politics or the upcoming campaigns?" to measure Internet use. More recent surveys have attempted to achieve greater precision by asking questions pertaining to reading blogs and bulletin boards when online. But, the overall emphasis is on "reading" the Internet. That is to say, most researchers seem to be assuming that simple exposure to various Internet venues of public affairs information—online news sites, blogs, search engines—is predictive of a wide variety of social and behavioral effects, ranging from political knowledge to civic engagement. A spurt of linear models and structural equation modeling betrays an outlook among communication researchers that assumes media variables as antecedents on the left-hand side and psychological outcomes as effects on the right-hand side of a causes-and-effects equation.

Driven by a larger question about the influence of the Internet on democracy, political communication scholars have sought to measure the relative role of this medium in determining such outcome variables as deliberation and voting decision. Self-reported measures of "Internet use" have been used to test arguments about both utopian and dystopian effects (DiMaggio, Hargittai, Neuman, & Robinson, 2001; Foot & Schneider, 2002; Hacker, 1996; Stromer-Galley & Foot, 2002) of the Internet. Over the years, such measures have yielded data that support both claims (Howcroft, 1999; Katz & Rice, 2002), thus raising questions about their measurement validity.

There are two problems to conceptualizing Internet use in this way. First, it assumes that users can clearly differentiate between Internet and other sources from which they obtain public-affairs information—not quite tenable in this day and age of media convergence where online content overlaps with many traditional media as well as interpersonal sources. For example, many online users watch TV news clips on cable and broadcast news websites and read newspaper stories forwarded from both local and national newspaper site by e-mail. Therefore, "the Internet" is unlikely to be a psychologically distinct source, as evident in the "I read somewhere that" phenomenon described by Sundar (1998). Second, the Internet as a media source is not as monolithic as traditional media—not just because there are many, many more channels of information (which would be analogous to variety in newspaper and television outlets), but because there are many *layers* of sources within the larger medium (websites, blogs, e-mail, bots, other users) that are known to affect users' perception of information (Sundar & Nass, 2001). Therefore, while individuals are able to distinguish between different sources of information while using the Internet, they may not see the Internet itself as a distinct media source.

AFFORDANCE, NOT USE

One solution to the problem of conceptualizing the Internet as a monolithic source is to splinter the concept of "Internet use" into use of different destinations on the Internet, such as blogs, bulletin-boards, websites and so on. But, this would imply a certain uniformity of content within a given vehicle. Thanks to the rise of Web 2.0 and widespread generation of content by users, we cannot safely make this assumption. In traditional media, the gatekeeping task was performed by journalistic professionals who adhered to industry-wide norms of writing, reporting, and editing, leading to certain degree of uniformity of content. On the Internet, gatekeeping is not a privilege held by a few but an *affordance* available to many.

In fact, this notion of affordance permeates almost all aspects of the Internet. The concept of "Internet use" may well be an indication of the degree to which the "affordances" offered by the medium are used. The concept of affordances is rooted in perceptual psychology, with Gibson (1977, 1986) arguing that visual stimuli in our environment suggest how to interact with them. For example, a chair invites the user to sit down, the round shape of a softball implies that this object is meant for throwing or catching, and so on. Gibson saw affordances as "actionable properties between the world and an actor" (Norman, 1999, p. 39). For example, blogs afford the reading of public affairs and opinion information as if from a newspaper. In addition, they afford the possibility of browsing archived posts, commenting on someone's post, linking it to other online sources of information, inviting other "readers" to online blogs inhabited by likeminded others, and so on.

Given the wide variety of user actions made possible by the new affordances of the Internet, the concept of "use" has expanded. More generally, while use of traditional media means perusing content produced by those media, Internet use should be understood as referring to the ways in which respondents engage the features of the medium. That is, traditional media use is content-oriented while Internet use is affordance-oriented.

Therefore, we recommend conceptualizing Internet use in terms of relevant affordances. We say "relevant" because different affordances will be relevant for different study contexts. For example, a study exploring the role of blogs in political communication may define use in terms of reading blog entries, reading blog comments, following debates, writing comments, blog-rolling, track-backs, and so on. These features afford different functions, and their differential use may predict the degree of user engagement within the blogosphere. A set of similar features may be combined to form higher-order affordances, such as agency-enhancing affordances and community-building affordances (Stavrositu & Sundar, 2008). Alternatively, a study exploring the impact of candidate websites may be interested in the degree to which the site's architecture afforded a satisfying exploration of the candidate's accomplishments and actions. Here, the navigability affordance of the site would be more relevant than the ones discussed in the context of blogs. For example, when Bucy and Affe (2006) investigated whether online newspapers led to political engagement and involvement, they examined so-called "civic affordances" (p. 236) by tallying the various opportunities for user interaction, and found that nearly two-thirds of metropolitan newspaper websites analyzed offered some form of *user-to-system* interaction and over half provided some opportunities for *human* interaction (see Stromer-Galley, 2000).

THE TWO FACES OF AFFORDANCES

According to Gibson (1986), the mere existence of a technological feature in a medium does not make it an affordance. To qualify as an affordance, a given feature has to be relevant to the user and visually suggestive of the intended use and/or other actions. Most modern technologies lack uniformity of use. They have different uses for different purposes and users. As Holbert (2004) points out, each individual develops a unique "medium-specific, sensori-motor schema" (p. 112) based not only on the medium's physical characteristics but also on one's usage of the medium and physiological profile relative to others. Such schemata is said to influence the meanings that users extract from content. But, more fundamentally, they can shape the user's stance toward the technology. How users engage the affordance may depend a great deal upon how they perceive it (Sundar, 2008b). Human–computer interaction researchers such as Norman (1999) claim that an affordance is an action possibility perceived by the user and therefore exists in the "interaction" between the technology and the user. Although Gibson (1986) saw affordances as a relationship between the environment and the person, he still maintained that affordances could objectively exist without being visible or cognizant to a user and as a result possess little functional value. Norman (1999) suggests a separation between "real affordances" (invariant properties of the system) and "perceived affordances" (what the user perceives as being possible to do with the system) in designing products and interfaces.

For the positivist, this poses a challenge in terms of locating a given affordance. Where does it belong—in the medium or in the user? The "interactivity debate" between those espousing the structural approach and those following the perceptual approach is a good example of this conceptual problem. Bucy (2004) favors a subjective user-centered definition of interactivity instead of an objective technological one so that we can capture variance across users in their experience of the affordance. Sundar (2004) claims that the experience of interactivity is a behavioral effect, not a defining feature, and that in order to build knowledge about media effects, we would need to vary attributes of the technology instead of merely observing perceptual variations among users.

In some ways, this is the difference between the *potential* of an affordance and *realization* of the affordance. The former is offered by the technology of the medium while the latter places the onus on the user. The best way to account for both these aspects of affordances is to treat them as distinct concepts—"available interactivity" and "perceived interactivity" for example. The former is ontological in that it exists in the media interface and may be manipulated in experiments to take on ordinal values (e.g., low, medium, and high) while the latter is psychological, measured on continuous scales via self-report questionnaires administered to users of the media interface in question.

As Tao and Bucy (2007) observe, media stimuli employed in experimental research fall into two categories of variables, *media attributes* (or inherent message features) and *psychological states* (e.g., emotions, perceptions, cognitions, evaluations). They treat the former as independent variables and the latter as mediator variables. In an experiment that manipulated interactivity as a media attribute, they found that the existence of interactive tasks on a news website predicted site credibility, and this effect was fully mediated by perceived interactivity (the psychological state that was measured by a five-point, single-item measure of self-reported interactivity as experienced by the user). Song and Bucy (2007, p. 32) make a conceptual and operational distinction between objective aspects of interactivity embedded in media systems and perceptual interactivity, which is psychologically realized and experienced by users. They found that *perceived* interactivity mediated the effect of *objective* interactivity in a gubernatorial website on attitude toward the website, content, and the political sponsor (candidate) of the site. Such findings empirically demonstrate the importance of taking into account both the ontological and psychological aspects of media affordances.

PERCEPTION DOES NOT MEAN USE

We must recognize, however, that the perceptual side of affordances is not always borne out of use. For example, respondents in the above-mentioned study may produce high scores on measures of perceived interactivity even without actually trying out the interactivity features embedded in the site. Sometimes, the existence of an affordance is richly suggestive. For example, interactivity features that call for user interaction may lead to a perception that this is a "cold" site (i.e., one requiring heightened user engagement) even though the user arrived at it with a "hot media" (McLuhan, 1964) mindset during a bout of casual browsing. Likewise, a site that has a lot of multimedia features may give users the impression that it is full of "rich media" because of the *promise* of extending one's "perceptual bandwidth" (Reeves & Nass, 2000) and not because the user actually downloaded the video or operated the real-time camera available through the site. To qualify McLuhan (1964), we can say that "media affordances are the message," for they alter our perceptions of the nature of user activity offered by the medium.

These perceptions may either directly lead to evaluative responses on survey questionnaires or serve to frame the ways in which the user engages the medium. In the latter case, users' perceptions grow out of their actual use of the affordance in question. Here, the affordance is given a test run, so to speak, and its resulting performance would likely influence perceptions. For example, a high-end interactive feature on a website, say a 360-degree view of the convention floor on the Democratic Party's site, may be perceived as more interactive (or user friendly) on a high-bandwidth Internet connection compared to accessing it with a low-bandwidth connection. Such perceptions are based on actual *use* of the affordance, not simply on its existence.

In sum, the functionality proffered by an affordance can be psychologically meaningful, not only in its actual operation (assessed by respondents based on their actual use of the functionality), but also by its sheer presence. The way the feature is marketed to users and their cognitive realization of its potential could well cue positive impressions of the affordance. We therefore recommend distinguishing between perceptions arising from actual use versus those based on meanings attached to the mere existence of an affordance. For example, questionnaire items could be designed to discriminate between the two: "Did you notice the chat function on the site?" versus "Did you use the chat feature?" or even "Did you chat with other supporters of the candidate through the site?"

WHERE DOES INTERNET USE BELONG?

All these dichotomies surrounding affordances (ontological vs. psychological; use vs. perception) bring to the fore the truly interactive nature of Web-based media. Unlike traditional media, where the concept of "use" was primarily an audience variable, Internet use implicates both the medium and the user. In fact, a case can be made for the involvement of other elements of traditional communication models, such as source and message. For example, Sundar and Nass (2001) have shown how the agency affordance of Web-based media allows for differential perception of information based on who or what is identified as the source of that information. The agency affordance in technologies such as blogs allow both blog creators and blog readers to serve as agents (or sources) of information. When viewed in terms of traditional transmission models of communication, both the sender and the receiver could be construed as a "source of communication" due to this affordance. What this implies for the explication of networked media is that the affordance of agency may have to be conceptualized differently depending on whether the agent is a sender or receiver of communication, i.e., agency as a source feature (e.g., how often do you read Daily Kos?) is quite distinct from agency as a receiver feature (e.g., how often do you comment on the Daily Kos blog?).

That said, not all affordances of the Internet medium have multiple loci when mapped onto traditional communication models. Modality, for example, is clearly associated with the medium, as is navigability. Of course, being affordances, these have their ontological existence in the medium and a perceptual counterpart residing in the user. As we suggested earlier, it would be prudent to distinguish the two by labeling the latter differently (e.g., perceived modality and navigability respectively). If receiver, as the locus of a given affordance, is handled in this way, then the choices for locating any given affordance are the three remaining elements common to most communication models: source, medium, and message. The ontological component of most affordances can be located in one or more of these elements. If a particular affordance is manifested in more than one, then it would be necessary to label it with a modifier identifying its locus. In the sections that follow, we illustrate this with the particularly complicated concept of interactivity, which could exist in all three elements.

But, before we get into that, a word about the need for invoking traditional communication models in an era where a variety of new media have called them into question. Much of the theorizing in media effects, most especially political communication, is based on the assumption of such linear models. Instead of abandoning this rich body of research, a pragmatic solution would be to view the various elements of linear models as vehicles for delivering the new affordances offered by the Internet. In this way, we preserve the theoretical frameworks governing classic theories in the field while examining their operation in the current media climate. A second reason for relying on transmission models is methodological—considerable advances in concept explication (Chaffee, 1991; McLeod & Pan, 2005), scale development, and statistical modeling methods can be leveraged for conceptualizing and operationalizing new affordances of the Internet without having to commission a paradigm change by way of nonlinear formulations. While Internet-based communications, as a whole, may not be adequately captured by traditional models, we believe that the affordances of Internet technology can be rigorously examined with a linear framework.

THE CASE OF POLITICAL INTERACTIVITY

> The history books will likely reflect that 2008 is the campaign of voter-generated content—when ordinary people seize the moment and use the increasingly powerful tools at their fingertips to create and spread information without any help from the campaigns.
>
> —Graff, 2007

In the spring of 2008, the official campaign websites of the front-runners in the 2008 presidential race—Clinton, Obama, and McCain—revealed a striking similarity: They all started with an online sign-up form urging visitors to create an account that would allow them to actively participate in the campaign process. Would this opportunity to receive personalized campaign information right into one's mailbox be considered an interactive experience? These sites also included prominent links for making donations, allowing voters to directly contribute to the fundraising efforts. Would having a say on matters that form a key aspect of political campaigns, such as fundraising, evoke in users a sense of heightened interactivity? Some sites also provided a short video clip featuring the candidate's welcome message or a recent televised public appearance. Does this opportunity for viewing the candidates live in action translate into a more interactive experience than merely reading about them?

Either as a part of the official campaign website or as a separate entity on its own, another unmistakable part of the technological ensemble of online political campaigns today are election blogs. Blogs have been powerful in not only mobilizing support but also in enabling voters to create and share content with each other and their party ideologues. Would this form of voter empowerment constitute greater levels of interactivity? To further bolster group interactions, all the candidates maintained a presence on popular social networking communities such as MySpace and Facebook, along with added multimedia capabilities on sites like YouTube, Digg.com, and Flickr. The official campaign websites also possessed some e-commerce functionalities in the form of online stores, where voters could purchase all types of campaign gear and products such as clothing, bumper stickers, signs and posters, and much more to avow their allegiance. Then, does turning netizens into consumers online make it a highly interactive political experience?

A question that emerges from the trends noted above is, What exactly does political interactivity constitute? Is it a gestalt of the several highly involving experiences described above? Is it a sum of several interactive affordances that create the larger whole of greater political engagement? When questions like these arise about a much-touted concept, the answer is a rigorous exercise in explication so that the scholarly community is clear on its meaning, for purposes of operationalization in empirical research.

EXPLICATING INTERACTIVITY

There have been several attempts at explicating the concept of interactivity (Bucy, 2004; Kiousis, 2002; Sundar, 2004; Bucy & Tao, 2007) and yet the need for further meaning and empirical analysis continues. While most early attempts at defining the concept were limited to identifying dimensions and creating typologies, what interactivity does as a variable and how it achieves its effects have not been studied systematically (Bucy, 2004). Previous definitions and measures of the concept have noted three main approaches—message-based, structural, and perceptual. Bucy and Tao (2007) argue that limitations of current theorizing about the concept of interactivity are mainly due to testing of incomplete conceptual models. In the message-centered approach, the outcomes most relevant to media effects (cognition, affect, and behavior) are not always accounted for. In the structural approach, the user's subjective experience is often overlooked, and in the perceptual approach, the causal mechanisms (technological features) that evoke user perceptions in the first place are not overtly modeled or measured. Additionally, researchers (Bucy & Tao, 2007; Sundar, 2004) have noted that the concept of interactivity and its effects cannot be comprehensively studied with simple two-variable (cause–effect) models but instead should account for several moderating and mediating influences that affect the relationship between interactivity and its effects (see also Chapter 23, this volume).

But before testing complex models of moderation and mediation, the core concept of interactivity still needs to be understood. Further, every attempt in trying to theoretically grasp and measure the concept requires the need to be sensitive to the particular communication context in which it is being studied and hence calls for renewed meaning and empirical analysis with specific examples in the chosen domain, be it political communication, e-commerce, or health campaigns, among many others. The goal of this explication is to analyze and synthesize the meaning and measurement of interactivity, with particular reference to the domain of political communication.

THEORETICAL DEFINITIONS

As Bucy and Gregson (2001) note, regular political *activity* is different from political *interactivity*. Political activity in traditional media involved very limited audience participation. However, the authors contend that new media have tremendously modified the "participatory landscape" (p. 358). They define online political interactivity as the "broader range of citizen actions that can take place online" and the "psychological feeling of being engaged with the political system" (p. 358). Defined at a macro level, Hacker (1996) notes that political interactivity allows citizens to "interact, discuss, debate and argue about political matters." The objective of such political interactivity is "co-creation of political perceptions and policies." Under such communication contexts, interactants in a communication process are said to "work together to ask questions, find answers and formulate policies and actions" (Hacker, 1996, p. 228). In the context of interactive television (namely, call-in shows), researchers (Bucy & Newhagen, 1999; Newhagen 1994) have defined perceived interactivity as a sense of "system responsiveness" (Bucy & Gregson, 2001, p. 366) experienced at an individual, subjective level, irrespective of whether an outside observer considers such an experience to be interactive or not.

Stromer-Galley (2004) considers political interactivity an "increase in horizontal communication among people and an increase in vertical communication between people and political elites" (p. 114). In her earlier work, Stromer-Galley (2000) distinguishes between two forms of interactions—*human interaction* as transactions between people via technology, and *media interaction* as transactions between people and the medium—arguing that political leaders embrace a façade of heightened interaction by choosing *media interaction* over *human interaction*. She defines computer-mediated *human interaction* as "prolonged interaction between two or more people through the channel of a computer network" and claims "communication is interactive when there is a high degree of responsiveness and reflexivity" (p. 117). The author also notes that in highly interactive situations, the receiver is able to take on the role of the sender. She conceptualizes *media interaction* as the interactive nature of the medium itself, and the "ease with which people can control the medium to make it provide the information they want" (p. 118).

McMillan (2002) reviews several theoretical perspectives in interpersonal, organizational and public relations literature to articulate a user-centered definition of interactivity. She proposes two dimensions to create four different types of online interactivity. The two dimensions include "level of receiver control" (comprising high or low values) and "direction of communication" (comprising one-way or two-way), leading to a typology of cyber-interactivity with four different categories—*monologue, feedback, responsive dialogue,* and *mutual discourse.* Of the four categories, the author argues that *mutual discourse* is the most interactive as it involves two-way communication and greater symmetry in the level of control between sender and receiver.

Sundar (2007) conceptualizes interactivity as a versatile technological variable that can act as a *source, medium,* or *message* feature. He argues that no matter in what form the variable is construed, interactivity serves to enhance user involvement with content. The remainder of this explication will employ this tripartite model to illustrate how a new media concept can be associated with different elements of traditional communication models, leading to vastly different conceptions and operationalizations.

Interactivity as a Source Feature

In treating interactivity as a source feature, Sundar (2007) conceptualizes it as the *ability of an individual to manipulate the source of information or interaction.* This view adopts a user-centered approach but with a critical difference. While in most user-centered approaches interactivity is seen as a perceptual variable (perceived interactivity) situated in the subjective, individual experiences (minds) of users (Bucy & Newhagen 1999; McMillan, 2002; McMillan & Hwang, 2002), Sundar (2008a) adopts an agentic perspective where, at high levels of interactivity, an individual is vested with the power and opportunity to switch from being a receiver to being the sender. This view is akin to Steuer's (1992) definition of interactivity, which considers interactivity as "the extent to which users can participate in modifying the form and content of a mediated environment in real-time" (p. 84). Bucy and Gregson (2001) propose a similar notion of source-based interactivity when they recognize the potential of new media that "allows the user to select the message delivery method" (p. 366). However, these authors still treat interactivity as a perceptual variable. But, in the source view of Sundar (2007), level of interactivity translates into the degree to which the technology enables the user to serve as a source or sender of communication (Sundar & Nass, 2001), regardless of how it is perceived by the user.

Interactivity as a Medium Feature

Drawing upon prior empirical work (Sundar, Kalyanaraman, & Brown, 2003), Sundar (2007) integrates the feature-based (McMillan, 2002) and interactivity-as-product (Stromer-Galley, 2004) approaches into the *medium* view of interactivity, where *the greater the capacity for interactions afforded by an interface or medium, the higher the level of interactivity.* Interactivity as a medium feature is based on the notion of perceptual bandwidth (Reeves & Nass, 2000), which takes into account the amount and type of sensory channels involved in an interaction, as a sign of greater user engagement. Thus, in this approach, the number and types of multimodal features (Oviatt, Coulston & Lunsford, 2004; Sundar 2000), such as text, pictures, audio, video, gaze, and gestures, create a cumulative experience. Further, the *medium* view of interactivity could also be conceptualized as a Human Computer Interaction (HCI) approach to interactivity or, as Stromer-Galley (2004) observes, interactivity-as-product, where a "set of technological features allows users to interact with the interface or system itself" (p. 391), as opposed to interactivity-as-process, which looks at interactivity between people.

Interactivity as a Message Feature

As a message feature, interactivity is conceptualized as *the degree of contingency in a communication exchange*. This view is rooted in one of the earliest conceptualizations of interactivity by Rafaeli (1988), who defined it as "an expression of the extent that in a given series of communication exchanges, any third (or later) transmission (or message) is related to the degree to which previous exchanges referred to even earlier transmissions" (p.111). In a similar vein, Ha and James (1998) define interactivity as "the extent to which the communicator and the audience respond to, or are willing to facilitate, each other's communication needs" (p. 461). Sundar et al. (2003) observe that this contingency approach to interactivity adopts a more behavioral (rather than perceptual) view because each message exchange is systematically contingent upon previous, current, and future user action. Message exchange is considered noninteractive if a receiver and sender are communicating independently, without any form of mutual acknowledgement of each other. If a receiver simply responds to a query by the sender, the exchange becomes reactive. However, if subsequent message exchanges between the receiver and sender refer to message elements present in initial messages in an iterative fashion, then the message exchange is considered to be interactive.

EMPIRICAL ANALYSIS

In attempts to operationalize the concept, several dimensions of interactivity have been identified by scholars (Downes & McMillan, 2000; Heeter, 1989). Most dimensions noted by Heeter (1989), such as complexity of choice available, effort that users must exert, responsiveness of the system to the user, monitoring of information use (system tracking user activity), or ease of adding information could be categorized under medium-based or HCI view of interactivity (Hoffman & Novak, 1996). On the other hand, most dimensions noted by Downes and McMillan (2000), such as direction of communication, timing flexibility, sense of place, level of control, responsiveness, and perceived purpose of communication, can be categorized under the person-to-person or CMC view of interactivity. Although several such dimensions exist, very few studies have operationalized these dimensions in ways that facilitate empirical testing.

Based on broad theoretical classifications of interactivity as either a technological feature or perceptual feature, there are two distinct groupings under which operationalizations of interactivity fall—measures that treat interactivity as (1) an independent or causal variable associated with functional features of technology that can be *manipulated* (Sundar, Hesser, Kalyanaraman, & Brown, 1998; Sundar, Kalyanaraman, & Brown, 2003), or (2) measures of interactivity as a process (mediator) variable or outcome (dependent) variable, where interactivity is *measured* in the form of self-reported "perceived interactivity" (Bucy, 2004; Bucy & Newhagen, 1999; Kalyanaraman & Sundar, 2006; McMillan & Hwang, 2002; Sundar & Kim, 2005).

Manipulating Actual Interactivity

As noted earlier, locating interactivity as an affordance within linear communication models has been a challenge to scholars because the concept can be situated in all the elements of the model—source, medium, message, and receiver. As a way to partially address this issue, this section on empirical analysis will examine ways in which interactivity can be operationalized in both ways—first, as a variable that exists ontologically, lending itself to various forms of experimental manipulation, and second, as a psychological counterpart of technological affordances, assuming the form of perceived interactivity in the minds of the user/receiver. We will first look at the ways in which source, medium, and message features of interactivity have been manipulated and tested for effects as an antecedent variable.

Interactivity as a Source Feature

When studied as a source attribute (Sundar & Nass, 2001), interactivity has been operationalized as different nominal source categories—editors, computers, other users, and the self—with increasing levels of source-ness (the ability to gatekeep information), implying higher levels of interactivity. In this approach, the ability of a receiver to customize information by essentially *becoming* the source is considered the highest level of interactivity engendered by new media. Stromer-Galley (2000), in her examination of political websites during the 1996 presidential campaign, described Bob Dole's site as a good example of high interactivity because users were able to customize the site to reflect a particular issue that was personally important. Information on the website could also be customized to suit different tastes. Users could download campaign desktops and screensavers, as well as send "I support Dole" e-postcards to other users. Further, at the end of every posted issue position, a 10-point rating scale was presented to visitors seeking their feedback about the importance of the issue in the campaign, thus allowing users to voice their opinions and prioritize information on their own terms. Even though these operationalizations of interactivity reflect a medium-oriented or attributes-based approach, seen from Sundar's (2007) source-interactivity notion discussed above, it was the ability of the users to customize (and act as sources) that made Dole's website truly interactive.

Interactivity as a Medium Feature

In studies that have adopted the medium-based view (McMillan, 2002; Sundar et al., 2003; Sundar & Kim, 2005), interactivity has been operationalized as multi-modal affordances or features offered by the medium, also termed the "bells and whistles" approach (Sundar, 2007). Examples include content analyses by scholars like Massey and Levy (1999), who operationalized interactivity as the presence (or absence) of features on interfaces such as e-mail links, hyperlinks, feedback forms, and chat rooms (see also Stromer-Galley, 2000). In her content analysis of political websites, Kamarck (1999) coded only those features that allowed users some opportunity to engage in a dialogue with candidate or campaign staff as fully interactive. These operationalizations fall under the medium-based (HCI) or interactivity-as-product view (Stromer-Galley, 2004), or more generally, interactivity-as-a-medium feature.

Research on political websites has shown that higher levels of interactivity tend to positively influence perceptions of the candidates and their campaigns (Ahern & Stromer-Galley, 2000; Sundar et al., 1998). In this domain, Sundar et al. (1998) operationalized the *medium* view of interactivity in terms of the number of hyperlinks and presence of feedback forms in an ordinal fashion. Thus, low, medium, and high interactivity versions of a political candidate's website were created, where the low version of the website had no hyperlinks. While the medium-level version allowed participants to click on some hyperlinks to access information, the high-level interactivity version allowed participants to send e-mail directly to the political candidate (Sundar et al., 1998).

Interactivity as a Message Feature

The message or contingency approach to interactivity has been operationalized in several different ways. Since the main focus or unit of analysis in this approach tends to be individual message exchanges, this view is more common in the literature pertaining to computer-mediated inter-personal communication (Walther, Anderson, & Park, 1994). Under this view, interactivity has been operationalized as the degree of reciprocity between sender and receiver, degree of responsiveness or self-disclosure, and coherence of discussion (Stromer-Galley, 2000).

In a mass-communication context, Sundar et al. (2003) operationalized the *message* contingency view of interactivity by fragmenting website information into hierarchical layers accessible by hyperlinks. In the low-level interactive version of the website, all the information about the candidate and his campaign issues were presented in one single webpage. In the medium-level interactive version, an additional layer of information was provided where issues were broken down into various headings, and clicking on these headings took users to a more detailed description of campaign issues. In the high-level interactive version, after participants had entered the site by clicking on the main heading (or hyperlink), they were presented with more subheadings and links to access different aspects of an issue. In this manner, each clicking activity and subsequent message output was made to be contingent upon prior click activity, operationalizing Rafaeli's (1988) message contingency view via affordances situated in a medium.

A completely different example of interactivity as a message feature can be found in a study by Welch and Fulla (2005) that assessed citizen-bureaucrat interactions on such dimensions as content sophistication, dialogue complexity, response commitment, and feedback. In their study, *content sophistication* was operationalized as complexity, choice of information, and the ease with which citizens could access such information. *Feedback opportunity* was operationalized as the ease of providing response and the type and number of feedback opportunities. The greater the feedback opportunities through synchronous (chat) and asynchronous (e-mail and bulletin boards) features, the higher the levels of presumed interactivity. Further, *dialogue complexity* was operationalized as the frequency of threaded two-way communication between bureaucrats and citizens, and the appropriateness of feedback exchanged in such interactions. Finally, *response commitment* was measured as the frequency and speed of response sent by the bureaucrat to the citizen. The authors found that heightened interactivity leads to a greater sense of community where citizens and governments can occupy the same "interlocutory space" (p. 232) to engender positive outcomes.

Similarities and Differences

Two common elements that run through all the above definitions is that interactivity is treated as something that is central to new media technology and involves some form of active user engagement with the medium, message, and source elements present in the communication process. It could be argued that these theoretical and operational definitions differ along their principal object of interest or the unit of analysis—as in the specific factors they examine and where (or in whom) those factors are situated. Some are seen as message (or content) factors; others are seen as user-centered factors—or they are considered to be technical (structural or medium related) factors (Kiousis, 2002). When seen together, they reflect Sundar's (2007) tripartite conceptualization of *medium-*, *source-*, and *message*-based interactivity.

MEASURING PERCEIVED INTERACTIVITY

Thus far we have examined interactivity as an ontological, rather than as a psychological, variable. The purpose of this section is to explicate the latter, in the form of "perceived interactivity." As Bucy and Tao (2007) argue, scholars preoccupied with the structure of interactivity have identified various dimensions to capture the specific technological attributes that define interactivity (Ha & James, 1998; Heeter, 1989; Jensen, 1998; Steuer, 1992), but have failed to explain why certain technological attributes lead to specific interactive outcomes. The objective presence of interactivity in technological interfaces does not always ensure the subjective experience of interactivity, without considering actual use of technology. The MAIN (Modality–Agency–Interactivity–Navigability) model proposed by Sundar (2008b) offers one explanation for the gap between interactivity features embedded in technological interfaces and resultant interactivity by users, by invoking the notion of cognitive heuristics. The advantage of this heuristics-based approach is that one can measure interactivity without necessarily severing ties with some of the key technological features that *enable* interactivity. Specific interactive features of an interface, say for example, related hyperlinks in a website, will trigger a heuristic, such as a sense of connectedness, and this quick judgment about the connectedness afforded by the interface will further influence how a user will evaluate both the system and the content presented through it. The central argument of the MAIN model is that users employ evaluative rules of thumb (or "heuristics") through which they make theoretical connections between (a) interactivity cues that objectively exists in an interface, and (b) psychological evaluations of the objects possessing these cues, for example, assessments of credibility of both the content and the medium. The MAIN model covers four different types of affordances (modality, agency, interactivity, and navigability), but we focus here on the specific affordance of interactivity for this discussion.

Using the definition of interactivity as a set of technological affordances that heighten the sense of interaction via source, medium, and message features (Sundar 2007), this section explores the possibility of creating a scale that can capture the psychological realizations (or instantiations) of specific interactive affordances in the minds of the user. More specifically, in the context of carrying out an empirical explication of perceived interactivity, we will examine ways in which the abstract concept of interactivity can be pinned down to its real-world referents, which will lend themselves to various forms of measurement. Thus, at first, system features that trigger cognitive heuristics will be used to understand how users psychologically experience interactivity. And second, we capture that experience with the help of measurement scales widely used in the psychology and communication literature.

The eventual goal would be to construct a scale of perceived interactivity consisting of items that signify the operation of specific heuristics underlying user perceptions of interactivity. Apart from the heuristics identified in the MAIN model, some of the existing measures of interactivity can also be grouped under source, medium, and message dimensions of perceived interactivity (see Table 25.1). Since this chapter focuses more on the process of explication and not empirical assessment, we will address but will not be able to test the reliability and validity concerns that inevitably arise in such a hypothetical scale-construction process.

Understanding Heuristics in the Context of Political Interactivity

This section explains interactivity-related heuristics identified in the MAIN model, along with examples of how these heuristics can be operationalized in the context of political interactivity. Our fundamental thesis is that affordances do not exist as structural characteristics alone but possess cues that trigger perceptions in the form of quick evaluations (which we call heuristics) about the intentions behind their creation and perceived consequences. Heuristics do not always lead to heuristic processing. In fact, they are often well-rehearsed generalizations that can act as important analytical tools for systematic processing of underlying information. They may be invoked by the users' actual experience of an interactive interface (e.g., a website) or by the user perceiving a certain action possibility in the interface without even using it directly.

TABLE 25.1
Conceptual Dimensions of Perceived Interactivity

Dimension 1 *Source Interactivity*	Dimension 2 *Medium Interactivity*	Dimension 3 *Message Interactivity*
• Control over the medium (Stromer-Galley, 2000) • Active listeners and callers (Newhagen, 1994) • Level of receiver control (McMillan, 2002) • Choice (Ha & James, 1998) • Feature-enabled user control (Jensen, 1998) • Activity heuristic (Sundar, 2008b) • Choice heuristic (Sundar, 2008b) • Control heuristic (Sundar, 2008b) • Own-ness heuristic (Sundar, 2008b)	• System responsiveness (Newhagen, 1994) • Connectedness and reciprocity (Ha & James, 1998) • Responsiveness and reflexivity (Stromer-Galley, 2000) • Customized and timely feedback (Straubhaar & LaRose, 1997) • Speed (or delay) in system response (McMillan & Hwang, 2002) • Engagement with the system (McMillan & Hwang, 2002) • Embedded & experienced interactivity (Song & Bucy, 2007) • Media attribute or psychological state (Tao & Bucy, 2007) • Perceived and real affordances (Bucy & Affe, 2006) • Interaction heuristic (Sundar, 2008b) • Responsiveness heuristic (Sundar, 2008b)	• Responsiveness (Rafaeli, 1988) • Real-time participation (Steuer, 1992) • Playfulness (Ha & James, 1998) • Direction of communication—one or two-way (McMillan, 2002) • Sense of place and time sensitivity (McMillan & Downes, 2000) • Two-way communication (Liu & Shrum, 2002; McMillan & Hwang, 2002) • Concurrent communication (McMillan & Hwang, 2002) • Real-time conversation (McMillan & Hwang, 2002) • Message contingency (Sundar, Kalyanaraman, & Brown, 2003) • Telepresence heuristic (Sundar, 2008b) • Flow heuristic (Sundar, 2008b)

Dividing the term interactivity into the two dimensions of interaction and activity, Sundar (2008b) identifies some of the indicators that represent the concept via the following heuristics. The *activity* heuristic refers to the users' immediate judgment that more activity is possible in this venue than in traditional media. If this judgment is operationalized as the amount of resultant activity—for instance, the number of times a visitor clicks on a campaign website's available features—then interactivity can be measured as a continuous variable. Interactivity can also be operationalized as a cue that triggers the *interaction* heuristic, whereby the medium provides affordances that seek specific user input, for instance, dialog boxes that open up on a website or online polls and surveys that presumably serve to enhance a feeling of user interaction with both medium and content. The *responsiveness* heuristic, which is triggered when a system responds to users on a continual basis, goes beyond interaction and captures the contingency aspect of interactivity (Rafaeli, 1988) that is inherent in threaded interactions. While these heuristics have been theorized as effects resulting from the design and manipulation of interactive features embedded in an interface (Sundar, 2008b), our current interest in treating them as manifestations of *perceived interactivity* requires us to examine the perceptual consequences of the triggering of these heuristics, when users feel that the interface offers them opportunities to participate actively, interact, engage with a responsive system, and so on. Measures of perceived interactivity would ideally tap into heuristics in two ways—(1) by directly measuring user perceptions about the intention and usefulness of the affordance at hand, and (2) by tracking behaviors logically arising from such perceptions (e.g., clicking actions, participation in online forums, and so on).

Coming back to specific interactivity heuristics identified by Sundar (2008b), the *choice* heuristic is involved when users perceive *variety* and *level of detail* in the information presented to them, often resulting from the presence of multiple options (drop-down lists), tabbed menus, layered links, and so on. The effects of choice tend to transfer over to another powerful judgment, the *control* heuristic, which is triggered when users feel empowered because they are put in charge of their own interactive experience. These two heuristics, *choice* and *control*, can be critical in political websites where visitors, especially "netizens" who are politically savvy (Sundar et al., 1998), appreciate information and features that they can customize or make their own. Since traditional media are saturated with an overdose of information, particularly during election years and campaigns, source-based interactivity that aids users to pick and choose the amount and type of issues (based on relevance and usefulness) could result in favorable outcomes and assessments of a political party. Source-based interactivity can be operationalized in ways that aid customization (entailing both choice and control), for instance, by allowing users to create a blog where they can exchange ideas and debate issues with fellow citizens online.

Telepresence as a heuristic is activated when users perceive that an interface offers possibilities of real-time interactions (Liu & Shrum, 2002; McMillan & Hwang, 2002; Steuer, 1992) that could transport them to a different world. This could happen in the form of virtual townhall meetings or debates where citizens may lose their sense of time and space and feel part of a wider national audience. Recent instances of YouTube debates are a case in point (Glover, 2007). The *flow* heuristic based on Csikzentmihalyi's (1990) work, could also be operationalized as a sense of playfulness (Ha & James, 1998) that a user experiences while interacting with the system (or another user). The facility to create political caricatures and cartoons and other online features that would allow users to creatively explore what and how they want to process messages could elicit this heuristic. In this manner, different interactive cues present in interfaces trigger different cognitive heuristics about the political site and its content. The operation of these heuristics can be psychologically measured by way of questionnaire items related to the perception of interactivity in the three loci of source, medium, and message. Table 25.2 provides an example of items pertaining to perceived interactivity, when operationalized in terms of interactivity related heuristics under each dimension of source, medium, and message. These measures are, of course, representative and do not exhaustively capture each of the heuristics. Further, they constitute just the heuristic-based measures of perceived interactivity. Measures based on other conceptualizations of perceived interactivity, listed under the three dimensions of Table 25.1, ought to be tested for their correspondence with these heuristics-based measures to empirically validate our grouping.

Unit of Analysis and Levels of Measurement

A principal aim of concept explication is to narrow down the concept to a form in which it can be easily identified and measured. Thus, if one adopts the structural approach by looking at specific interactive features present in a technological medium, such as hyperlinks and feedback forms, then the presence of such features or affordances on the homepage or other sections of a website constitute the unit of analysis, treated mostly as categorical variables. If the object of study happens to be contingent message exchanges that could occur in an interactive chat forum, then the unit of analysis would be the messages being exchanged. If, on the other hand, the intention were to measure perceptions of interactivity in the minds of users, then the unit of analysis would be individual users.

The interactivity-related heuristics from the MAIN model discussed in Table 25.2 lend themselves to different levels of measurement. On the one hand, they can be treated as categorical

TABLE 25.2
Items for Measuring Perceived Interactivity via Heuristics

Perceived Interactivity as a Source Feature

Activity Heuristic
– I was able to perform a lot of actions on the website.
– The website had a lot of things in it to keep me active.

Control Heuristic
– I took action to control what I wanted to see (or avoid) on the website.
– I felt like I had a lot of control over the flow of information on the website.

Choice Heuristic
– I believe the website offered me several choices while browsing it.
- I had many things to choose from when I browsed the website.

Own-ness heuristic
– I could customize the site to make it my own.
– The website is a good reflection of who I am.

Perceived Interactivity as a Medium Feature

Responsiveness heuristic
– I felt as if the system was constantly responding to my needs.
– I felt as if the system could understand what I was trying to do.

Interaction heuristic
– I felt like I was involved in an actual conversation with the system (or another user).
– The interface asked for my input at every stage of the interaction.

Perceived Interactivity as a Message Feature

Contingency Heuristic
– I felt as if the information on the website was well connected with one another.
– The messages I received on the website were based on my previous inputs.

Telepresence Heuristic
– I felt like I was in the same place as the person with whom I was interacting.
– I felt immersed in the campaign while browsing the website.

Flow Heuristic
– Once I started to browse, I did not feel like stopping the activity.
– The site offered good features that could engage and encourage me to keep browsing.

variables and tracked for their presence (availability in the medium) and use (actual user activity) or lack thereof. If these heuristics are operationalized in such a manner where they account for the presence and use of *more than one* affordance at a time, then they could be aggregated and measured via ordinal categories of high, medium, and low values. These heuristics can also be measured on a continuous scale to obtain psychological experiences of these technological affordances in the minds of the user with the help of summated rating scales designed to capture user perceptions or actions indicating the operation of the heuristics.

For a concept explication to be useful, the meaning analysis ought to be followed by empirical analysis involving the formation of a scale on which individuals can be located by assigning them specific scores or values based on their responses (McLeod & Pan, 2005). The process of generating items that comprise a scale and grouping them under certain indices could be driven by basic hypotheses that act as guidelines to deductively direct the grouping of certain indicators together to build models, which can be tested later with inductive, data-driven approaches.

Reliability and Validity

In his guidelines to scale development, specifically with respect to generating items, DeVellis (2003) emphasizes the importance of collecting a large number of items that can be included in the scale. This would mean drawing a subset of items from a theoretically infinite pool of all possible items that exist, and the larger the number of items, the greater the reliability. Once the items under each dimension are generated, the next step is to check all the indicators for their reliability, mainly their internal consistency. Cronbach's alpha measures provide a good assessment of the unidimensionality of an index or the homogeneity of the items that fall under a certain dimension (DeVellis, 2003; McLeod & Pan, 2005).

Further, as McLeod and Pan (2005) note, assessments of reliability should complement evaluations of content validity. That is, as the item-generation procedure of scale development progresses, researchers should check whether the addition or deletion of more items sacrifices content validity for the sake of higher reliability, or whether an acceptable reliability coefficient would allow for the inclusion of additional items, which might enhance content validity. Further, since Cronbach's alpha strengthens when the items within an index are positively correlated to one another, grouping dimensions that share a similar conceptual and operational meaning will not only make the scale more reliable, but also more valid by including items that are an integral part of the concept.

CONCLUSION

Our goal with this chapter has been to shed light on some of the challenges that await researchers while explicating variables that are unique to Web-based communication, and demonstrate ways to overcome them without having to forego either traditional communication models or the rich explication paradigms established by communication scholars (Chaffee, 1991; McLeod & Pan, 2005).

Concept explications have a directorial function to them by offering several guidelines for future research. After a concept has been removed from its abstract realm by rigorous meaning analyses and has been construed in a form that can be observed and measured in the empirical domain, it offers researchers much-needed specificity and clarity to measure the effects of the variable that they have explicated. In the case of our example, explicating the concept of interactivity offers several such guidelines:

a. First, instead of blanket conceptualizations of Internet use, researchers ought to identify the specific aspects of online media that are relevant to their study context when designing their survey or experiment.
b. The degree of specificity brought about from the explication exercise urges researchers to contextualize Internet use in terms of explicit and relevant affordances offered by the medium.
c. After recognizing the affordance of interest, researchers should decide whether they are interested in the technological or psychological aspect of the affordance. If technological, then an explication would be helpful in isolating and (potentially) manipulating the affordance in an experimental study. If psychological, then the explication will determine measures for tapping into user experience of the affordance, in both experimental and survey contexts.

d. The next task is to situate the affordance in one or more elements (source, medium, message) of traditional communication models, and perform a separate explication of the concept for each element.

e. If primarily interested in the technological aspect, care should be taken to operationalize the concept within a given element of the model (e.g., specify a low, medium, and high *source* interactivity variable that is distinct from a low, medium, and high *medium* interactivity variable, which is distinct from a low, medium, and high *message* interactivity variable).

f. If primarily interested in the psychological aspect and in employing the concept as a mediating or dependent variable, care should be taken to differentiate between those items that measure the perceived affordance from a source perspective and those that measure it from a medium- or message-based perspective.

g. Care should also be exercised to distinguish between the perceived presence of the affordance versus *actual use* of the affordance by users, in order to understand the process by which users attach meaning to the affordance or feature in question.

h. User interpretations of website features can be understood in terms of both questionnaire measures of perception as well as action and unobtrusive measures of user activity with the system that tap into the operation of cognitive heuristics triggered by affordances.

i. These heuristics can be critical not only in shaping the psychological construal of affordances but also in explaining the process by which affordances shape social and behavioral outcomes of interest to Web-based communication.

NOTE

This research was supported by the National Science Foundation (NSF) via Standard Grant No. IIS-0916944 awarded to the first author and by the Korea Science and Engineering Foundation under the WCU (World Class University) program at the Department of Interaction Science, Sungkyunkwan University, Seoul, South Korea (Grant No. R31-2008-000-10062-0).

REFERENCES

Ahern, R. K., & Stromer-Galley, J. (2000, June). *The interaction effect: An experimental study of high and low interactivity political websites.* Paper presented at the annual meeting of the International Communication Association, Acapulco, Mexico.

Bucy, E. P. (2004). Interactivity in society: Locating an elusive concept. *The Information Society, 20,* 373–383.

Bucy, E. P., & Affe, R. B. (2006). The contributions of Net news to cyberdemocracy: Civic affordances of major metropolitan newspaper sites. In X. Li (Ed.), *Internet newspapers: The making of a mainstream medium* (pp. 227–242). Mahwah, NJ: Lawrence Erlbaum.

Bucy, E. P., & Gregson, K. S. (2001). Media participation: A legitimizing mechanism of mass democracy. *New Media and Society, 3*(3), 357–380.

Bucy, E. P., & Newhagen, J. E. (1999). The micro- and macrodrama of politics on television: Effects of media format on candidate evaluations. *Journal of Broadcasting & Electronic Media, 43*(2), 193–210.

Bucy, E. P., & Tao, C. C. (2007). The mediated moderation model of interactivity. *Media Psychology, 9*(3), 647–672.

Chaffee, S. H. (1991). *Communication concepts 1: Explication.* Newbury Park, CA: Sage.

Chaffee, S. H., & Schleuder, J. (1986). Measurement and effects of attention to media news. *Human Communication Research, 13*(1), 76–107.

Csikszentmihalyi, M. (1990). *Flow: The psychology of optimal experience.* New York: Harper & Row.

DeVellis, R. F. (2003). *Scale development: Theory and applications.* Thousand Oaks, CA: Sage.

DiMaggio, P., Hargittai, E., Neuman, W. R., & Robinson, J. P. (2001). Social implications of the Internet. *Annual Review of Sociology, 27,* 307–336.

Downes, E. J., & McMillan, S. J. (2000). Defining interactivity: A qualitative identification of key dimensions. *New Media and Society, 2*(2), 157–179.

Foot, K. A., & Scheider, S. M. (2002). Online action in campaign 2000: An exploratory analysis of the U.S. political web sphere. *Journal of Broadcasting & Electronic Media, 46*(2), 222–244.

Gibson, J. J. (1977). The theory of affordances. In R. Shaw & J. Bransford (Eds.), *Perceiving, acting and knowing: Toward an ecological psychology.* Hillsdale, NJ: Lawrence Erlbaum.

Gibson, J. J. (1986). *The ecological approach to visual perception.* Hillsdale, NJ: Lawrence Erlbaum.

Glover, K. D. (2007). Scoring debate points. *National Journal, 39*(30), 62.

Graff, M. (2007). *The first campaign: Globalization, the web, and the race for the White House.* New York: Farrar Straus & Giroux.

Ha, L., & James, E. L. (1998). Interactivity reexamined: A baseline analysis of early business web sites. *Journal of Broadcasting & Electronic Media, 42*(4), 457–474.

Hacker, K. L. (1996). Missing links in the evolution of electronic democratization. *Media, Culture & Society, 18,* 213–232.

Heeter, C. (1989). Implications of new interactive technologies for conceptualizing communication. In J. Salvaggio & J. Bryant (Eds.), *Media in the information age: Emerging patterns of adoption and consumer use* (pp. 217–235). Hillsdale, NJ: Lawrence Erlbaum.

Hoffman, D. L., & Novak, T. P. (1996). Marketing in hypermedia computer-mediated environments: Conceptual foundations. *Journal of Marketing, 60,* 50–68.

Holbert, R. L. (2004). An embodied approach to the study of media forms: Introducing a social scientific component to medium theory. *Explorations in Media Ecology, 3*(2), 101–120.

Howcroft, D. (1999). The hyperbolic age of information: An empirical study of Internet usage. *Information, Communication & Society, 2*(3), 277–299.

Jensen, J. F. (1998). Interactivity: Tracking a new concept in media and communication studies. *Nordicom Review, 19*(1), 185–204.

Kalyanaraman, S., & Sundar, S. S. (2006). The psychological appeal of personalized online content in web portals: Does customization affect attitudes and behavior? *Journal of Communication, 56,* 110–132.

Kamarck, E. C. (1999). Campaigning on the Internet in the elections of 1998. In E. C. Kamarck & J. S. Nye (Eds.), *Democracy.com? Governance in a networked world* (pp. 99–123). Hollis, NH: Hollis Publishing.

Katz, J. E., & Rice, R. E. (2002). Project Syntopia: Social consequences of Internet use. *IT & Society, 1*(1), 166–179.

Kiousis, S. (2002). Interactivity: A concept explication. *New Media and Society, 4*(3), 355–383.

Liu, Y., & Shrum, L. J. (2002). What is interactivity and is it always such a good thing? Implications of definition, person, and situation for the influence of interactivity on advertising effectiveness. *Journal of Advertising, 31*(4), 53–64.

Massey, B. L., & Levy, M. R. (1999). Interactive online journalism at English-language Web newspapers in Asia. *Gazette, 61*(6), 523–538.

McLeod, J. M., & Pan, Z. (2005). Concept explication and theory construction. In S. Dunwoody, L. B. Becker, D. M. McLeod, & G. M. Kosicki (Eds.), *The evolution of key mass communication concepts* (pp. 13–76). Cresskill, NJ: Hampton Press.

McLuhan, M. (1964). *Understanding media: The extensions of man.* New York: McGraw Hill.

McMillan, S., & Downes, E. J. (2000). Defining interactivity: A qualitative identification of key dimensions. *New Media and Society, 2*(2), 157–179.

McMillan, S. J. (2002). A four-part model of cyber-interactivity: Some cyber-places are more interactive than others. *New Media and Society, 4,* 271–291.

McMillan, S. J., & Hwang, J. S. (2002). Measures of perceived interactivity: An exploration of the role of direction, user control, and time in shaping perceptions of interactivity. *Journal of Advertising, 31*(3), 29–42.

Newhagen, J. E. (1994). Self-efficacy and call-in political television show use. *Communication Research*, *21*(3), 366–379.

Norman, D. A. (1999). Affordance, conventions, and design. *Interactions*, *6*(3), 38–42.

Oviatt, S., Coulston, R., & Lunsford, R. (2004). When do we interact multimodally? Cognitive load and multimodal communication patterns. *Proceedings of the 6th International Conference on Multimodal Interfaces (ACM)*, 129–136.

Rafaeli, S. (1988). Interactivity: From new media to communication. In R. P. Hawkins, J. M. Wiemann, & S. Pingree (Eds.), *Advancing communication science: Merging mass and interpersonal processes* (pp. 110–134). Newbury Park, CA: Sage.

Reeves, B., & Nass, C. (2000). Perceptual bandwidth. *Communications of the ACM*, *43*(3), 65–70.

Song, I., & Bucy, E. P. (2007) Interactivity and political attitude formation: A mediation model of online information processing. *Journal of Information Technology and Politics*, *4*(2), 29–61.

Stavrositu, C., & Sundar, S. S. (2008). Can blogs empower women? Designing agency-enhancing and community-building interfaces. *Proceedings of the Conference on Human Factors in Computing Systems (ACM SIGCHI)*, *26*, 2781–2786.

Steuer, J. (1992). Defining virtual reality: Dimensions determining telepresence. *Journal of Communication*, *42*, 73–93.

Stromer-Galley, J. (2000). Online interaction and why candidates avoid it. *Journal of Communication*, *50*(4), 111–132.

Stromer-Galley, J. (2004). Interactivity-as-product and interactivity-as-process. *The Information Society*, *20*(5), 391–394.

Stromer-Galley, J., & Foot, K. A. (2002). Citizen perceptions of online interactivity and implications for political campaign communication. *Journal of Computer-Mediated Communication*, *8*(1). Retrieved July 4, 2010, from http://jcmc.indiana.edu/vol8/issue1/stromerandfoot.html.

Straubhaar, J., & LaRose, R. (1997). *Communications media in the information society* (rev. 1st ed.). Belmont, CA: Wadsworth Publishing.

Sundar, S. S. (1998). Effect of source attribution on perception of online news stories. *Journalism & Mass Communication Quarterly*, *75*(1), 55–68.

Sundar, S. S. (2000). Multimedia effects on processing and perception of online news: A study of picture, audio, and video downloads. *Journalism & Mass Communication Quarterly*, *77*(3), 480–499.

Sundar, S. S. (2004). Theorizing interactivity's effects. *The Information Society*, *20*, 385–389.

Sundar, S. S. (2007). Social psychology of interactivity in human-website interaction. In A. N. Joinson, K. Y. A. McKenna, T. Postmes, & U.-D. Reips (Eds.), *The Oxford handbook of Internet psychology* (pp. 89–104). Oxford: Oxford University Press.

Sundar, S. S. (2008a). Self as source: Agency and customization in interactive media. In E. Konijn, S. Utz, M. Tanis, & S. Barnes (Eds.), *Mediated interpersonal communication* (pp. 58–74). New York: Routledge.

Sundar, S. S. (2008b). The MAIN model: A heuristic approach to understanding technology effects on credibility. In M. J. Metzger & A. J. Flanagin (Eds.), *Digital, media, youth, and credibility* (pp. 72–100). Cambridge, MA: MIT Press.

Sundar, S. S., Hesser, K., Kalyanaraman, S., & Brown, J. (1998, July). *The effect of website interactivity on political persuasion*. Paper presented at the 21st General Assembly and Scientific Conference of the International Association for Media and Communication Research, Glasgow, UK.

Sundar, S. S., Kalyanaraman, S., & Brown, J. (2003). Explicating website interactivity: Impression formation effects in political campaign sites. *Communication Research*, *30*(1), 30–59.

Sundar, S. S., & Kim, J. (2005). Interactivity and persuasion: Influencing attitudes with information and involvement. *Journal of Interactive Advertising*, *5*(2), 6–29.

Sundar, S. S., & Nass, C. (2000). Source orientation in human-computer interaction: Programmer, networker, or independent social actor. *Communication Research*, *27*(6), 683–703.

Sundar, S. S., & Nass, C. (2001). Conceptualizing sources in online news. *Journal of Communication*, *51*(1), 52–72.

Tao, C.-C., & Bucy, E. P. (2007). Conceptualizing media stimuli in experimental research: Psychological versus attribute-based definitions. *Human Communication Research*, *33*(4), 397–426.

Walther, J. B., Anderson, J. F., & Park, D. W. (1994). Interpersonal effects in computer-mediated interaction: A meta-analysis of social and antisocial communication. *Communication Research*, *21*(4), 460–487.

Welch, E. W., & Fulla, S. (2005). Virtual interactivity between government and citizens: The Chicago Police Department's citizen ICAM application demonstration case. *Political Communication*, *22*(2), 215–236.

26

Beyond Self-Report

Using Latency to Respond to Model the Question Answering Process on Web-Based Public Opinion Surveys

John E. Newhagen
Philip Merrill College of Journalism
University of Maryland

This chapter proposes that measuring the time it takes survey respondents to answer a question can be a valuable tool in opening the black box of the response formation process. Measuring latency to respond time, it will be argued, offers a deeper understanding of processes typically relegated to the status of functional artifacts of self-report, such as social desirability biasing, to the status of theoretically interesting mental processes. An important caveat to add to this discussion is that the technique described to capture latency data is practical, inexpensive, and accessible for most researchers using Web-based surveys. The question "Did you vote in the last presidential election?" is the focus of the study because a substantial social desirability biasing effect has been repeatedly verified for it. Drawing from the information processing paradigm, the project tests the idea that respondents engaged in social desirability biasing will take longer to respond to questions than those who are not. This is important because the voting question is frequently used as a filter to identify likely voters in upcoming elections. Eliminating respondents who misreport voting is critical to making accurate predictions about the outcome of elections for both proprietary and media-sponsored polls. Further analysis of response latency data taken from four waves of Web-administered cross-sectional surveys administered over a five-year period shows biasing takes place on a much larger set of survey questions than previously recognized. Thus, using response latency suggests social desirability biasing is more than an annoying methodological artifact and should be integrated into a larger theory of the answer generation process in survey research. Further, social desirability may be but one example of how self-report surveys can be augmented by the latency to respond measure.

Probability sample surveying is the mother's milk of American public opinion research. Its results are surpassed in importance only by actual election outcomes. A well-executed national survey with 1,200 to 1,400 respondents generates results with an error margin of about 3% most of the time.[1] The survey has been the backbone of attitude and opinion research for over a half century because, so the story goes, the methodology can generate meaningful data by sampling a large population that is geographically dispersed, a claim other quantitative methods cannot make.

However, as useful as surveying might be, this methodology has historically been limited by data that are bound to respondent self-report. This is not news. Presser (1990) points out that a discussion of the limits of self-report takes place in survey research about every 10 years. Nisbett and Wilson (1977) detailed many of the limits of self-report in their seminal article on the topic over 30 years ago. Research has documented a raft of artifacts linked to self-report, including satisficing (the tendency for respondents to go the positive end of a scale), acquiescing (the tendency of respondents to go to the middle, or neutral, part of a scale when questions are overly complex), and social desirability biasing (the tendency of respondents to give what they believe to be a normatively acceptable answer even though it does not truly reflect their behavior or opinion) (Krosnick et al., 2002). An important aspect underlying the discussion of such artifacts is the assumption that a "real" or "true" answer exists, if only the question could be worded in just the right way. However, framing the problem in this context tends to focus on epistemological issues relating to the measurement process rather than searching for the cognitive processes at the root of the discrepancy. Simply put, attempts to rework the instrument without addressing the limits of what a respondent can verbally report "black boxes" or obscures the answer generation process. Making adjustments to the instrument might make sense in some cases, such as satisficing or acquiescing, but are problematic for others, such as social desirability biasing, where more complex processes involving opinion and attitude expression come into play.

Social desirability biasing has been recognized as a problem on attitude and opinion surveys for half a century (see Crowne & Marlowe, 1960). The phenomenon is much like the weather: survey researchers talk a lot about it but haven't been able to do much to change it. The bias can lead to either over- or underreporting. Questions about illicit drug use, smoking, abortion, and income are examples of topics where underreporting has been detected in validation studies (Tourangeau, Rips, & Rasinski, 2000). Voting and attending religious services figure among questions where overreporting takes place (Schaeffer, 2000). A common thread that runs through the social desirability biasing literature is that most of the topics discussed deal with behaviors that can be externally validated. However, validation may prove problematic when dealing with the generation of attitudes, beliefs, and even memories, where direct external evidence does not exist.

The question "Did you vote in the last presidential election?" has been the focus of a great deal of attention owing to the disparity between actual turnout, more or less 50% for contemporary national presidential elections, and typical survey results, where about 70 to 80% of respondents reporting saying they voted. Also, voting can be verified at the level of the individual respondent, albeit with considerable effort and resources. While Presser (1990) details some reasons why the disparity between turnout and survey results may be inflated, he admits that "over reporting has been detected in virtually every validation study" (p. 1). Also, the social norm is apparent; voting is "the right thing to do." School children are socialized into the notion that voting is part of their civic responsibility in a liberal democracy. Come voting day "I Voted" stickers proliferate.[2] This disparity has important practical implications as well; both practitioners and academics rely heavily on this question as a filter in pre-election surveys to identify likely voters in order to make predictions.[3]

THE EMOTIONAL DIMENSION OF SOCIAL DESIRABILITY

Two interrelated processes cited most frequently as causes for social desirability biasing are respondent concerns about confidentiality and embarrassment. It stands to reason that confidentially would be a serious concern for a fairly small universe of questions dealing with illegal or antisocial behaviors, such as marijuana use, that could result in stiff sanctions against the respondent if results were disclosed. However, typically the questions on opinion surveys suggest only a loss of face or embarrassment if respondents feel they do not measure up to what they believe prevailing social norms are. Krosnick (1999) defines the problem as a bias in reports intended to present a socially desirable self image to one's interviewer. Paulhus (1990) divides the scale created by Crowne and Marlow (1960), which offers "fake good" alternatives to statements with pro-social outcomes, into two groups: impression management and self-deception. Impression management has to do with putting a good face forward to the interviewer, while self-deception has to do with maintaining one's self-image. Social desirability biasing questions typically fall into the latter category.

An important component of this process that is not usually addressed is whether the respondent is intentionally giving false data. From an ethical perspective this would constitute lying, or the conscious misrepresentation of what the perpetrator knows to be the truth. This assumption is implicitly embedded in much of the discussion of effect. However, many important cognitive processes take place below conscious awareness and beyond the ability of the respondent to verbalize them. An important example is the assignment of emotion to a mental construct when forming an attitude. Evidence suggests primitive emotions such as fear are hard wired into the central nervous system and generated thoughtlessly (Plutchik, 1989). Automatic preconscious emotional response to danger makes sense from a functional perspective, where adaptive behavior based on limited information in real time is critical for survival (Frijda, 1986). Thus, habitual marijuana users may answer "no" to questions addressing the topic without ever consciously contemplating their response if they elicit fear of incarceration. However, questions on public opinion or political surveys typically do not evoke this level of arousal. More often, questions subject to a social desirability biasing deal with violation of social norms that hold the threat of only mild sanction, and evoke embarrassment (Tourangeau et al., 2000).

Embarrassment stands out from fear because it is a learned emotion and the sanction involved is usually comparatively mild. A case might be made that because embarrassment is learned and dependent on social context, respondents must be consciously aware of their circumstance in order to bias their answers to prosocial questions. However, Ekman and Davidson (1994) use embarrassment as an example of an emotion that becomes so highly over-learned it appears to be fully integrated into the central nervous system, even though it is dependent on social context. If this is the case, social desirability biasing may be activated in the complete absence of a social agent, such a survey interviewer. The embarrassment aroused by normatively laden questions could take place even on self-administered surveys. Krosnick (1999) points out that lying is a routine part of human behavior, citing research that shows most people lie at least once each day. Such routine lying might be called *lies of convenience*, such "I love your new hairdo," and is mainly intended to grease the wheels of social harmony. He concludes that social desirability bias is a process of self-deception that may occur below the respondent's conscious awareness. He proposes that the process be labeled the "misconstrual of fact," rather than lying, thus avoiding the implication of conscious awareness and moral misdeed.

THE ROLE OF INDIRECT MEASURES IN CAPTURING SOCIAL DESIRABILITY BIASING

A number of efforts have attempted to either limit or at least quantify social desirability biasing within the framework of self-report. For instance, the use of a "bogus pipeline," which leads respondents to believe interviewers have more information about them than they really do, elicits more truthful responses (Krosnick, 1999). One of the most notable attempts to capture biasing through self-report has been the Crowne–Marlowe Social Desirability Scale (Crowne & Marlowe, 1960), where respondents are offered "fake good" alternatives to statements with prosocial outcomes such as: "No matter who I am talking to, I am always a good listener"; "It is sometimes hard for me to go on with my work if I am not encouraged"; "I can remember 'playing sick' to get out of something."

However, if biasing is driven by an emotional heuristic outside conscious awareness, respondents cannot be expected to render introspective data about its effects, no matter how clever the question might be. This turns attention to indirect measures of emotion and cognition.

Latency Measures.   Latency to respond is a widely accepted laboratory measure of mental effort based on the simple premise that longer response times indicate increased mental effort. The assumption underlying the latency measure is that the stronger the links between the nodes in the associative networks that make up memories and attitudes, the more they are accessible and readily recalled. For instance, the measure has been used extensively to assess memory for visual information in television research (for example, see Newhagen & Reeves, 1991, 1992). Latency to respond has also been used as a measure of attitude strength (Bassili, 2000). Fazio, Williams, and Powell (2000) view an attitude as an association in memory between an object and a summary evaluation of that object. Thus, the idea has generally been accepted that the longer it takes subjects or respondents to respond to a cue, the more mental effort they exert. Feinstein (2000) compared self-report to response latency for estimates of certainty. He found latency to be significantly more reliable and less prone to conscious censure than self-report.

But how would biasing driven by social desirability figure into this mechanism? Consider the question "Did you vote in the last presidential election?" Respondents who truly voted would carry out a simple memory search and check off the appropriate response rapidly. In such a case the object (voting) and the attitude (voting is part of a person's civic duty) would be closely bound. Similarly, respondents who did not vote and had no qualms about the fact would be expected to answer the question rapidly. For the non-repentant nonvoter, the object (not voting) and the attitude (my vote doesn't count) also would be tightly bound and response would be fast. In either case no significant underlying emotional turmoil would be elicited by the question. But what about respondents who did not vote but hold the attitude that it is a social responsibility? This poses a special problem for the object-attitude matching process described by Fazio. Festinger (1957) pointed out a half-century ago that when a person confronts internal inconsistency between behavior and attitude there is "psychological discomfort" (p. 2). If the consequences of the mismatch are grave, such as smoking cigarettes in the face of evidence that the practice can be deadly, the emotion will be fear. Festinger, using this same example of smoking, suggests three options to resolve the dissonance: either to change the object to match the attitude, to avoid information about the attitude, or to "rationalize" the object.

One important condition both he and students of social desirability biasing do not consider is the possibility that the mismatch may activate an emotion-bound heuristic that simply modifies memory. In the example given above, where the mismatch is significant and the consequences are grave enough to generate a state of fear in the individual, such modification would not be adaptive; the outcome would be to ignore a true threat. However, if the consequences of the mismatch were mild, say in the range of simple social discomfort, the emotion would be embarrassment and the notion of automatic memory modification would appear much more adaptive. Krosnick (1999) points out that this may be a very common strategy used to avoid socially awkward situations. Frankly put, this is the strategy of telling people what they want to hear when it is socially convenient, even though it might not be the absolute truth. The strategy is perfectly adaptive to the situation in the sense that the problem is resolved without making any concrete adjustment to either object or attitude; life goes on. The unique thing about such a heuristic is that while it may be going on near or below the limen of conscious awareness, it still takes mental effort that should be detectable by the latency measure. If this is the case with the voting question, then why not suppose it could be the case across a broad range of other typical public opinion survey items probing respondents' political dispositions and attitudes?

THE PROCESS OF CONVENIENT LYING: MODELING AND MEASURING THE "MISCONSTRUAL OF FACT"

Because it is so normatively charged and sacred to democracy, the voting question begs for a description of the underlying processes that go into answer generation. Figure 26.1 details the components of a response to a simple dichotomous question, such as "Did you vote in the recent presidential election?" Time estimates, based on five waves of data taken across four years, are included for each component. The actual mechanics of the program used to collect the data are explained in Appendix 26.1, but suffice it to say that the respondent has to read a question, think about it, and use the computer mouse to answer. This process is made up of the following components:[4]

- *Somatic processing*: This component is largely made up of the motor and sensory effort needed to move the mouse around the screen and click it. It may vary according to variations in acuity with a mouse and keyboard, but is essentially constant within respondents. One or two "training" questions not used in the analysis can be included at the very beginning of the survey to give the respondent a chance to practice the answering task. The somatic component normally requires from 1000 to 1500 milliseconds (ms), or 1 to 1.5 seconds, to respond to a dichotomous item.
- *Meaning processing*: The time measured during this part of the process reflects mental effort. While the processes named here are not exhaustive, they do reflect important components of survey taking. Online, the survey respondent must read the text. Meaning is extracted from the question and serves as a cue for memory search and evaluation. Finally, an answer must be generated. The entire process takes about 1500 to 6000 ms for a dichotomous question. Text processing, or reading speed, should be constant within respondents. What does vary is the time it takes to generate answers. Social desirability biasing can account for up to 4000 ms of meaning processing depending on the magnitude of the discrepancy between respondents' perception of social norms and their relationship to them.

It is important to recognize that the stages of meaning generation, text recognition, recall, and answer production are neither linear nor independent. A key assumption within the information processing paradigm is that such processes are distributed throughout the respondent's cognitive apparatus and may be taking place concurrently (see Rumelhart & McClelland, 1986). Thus, the idea has to be considered that social desirability biasing may begin *during* text recognition and recall, in addition to playing an important role in answer generation. Given this very real possibility, premised on the assumption of parallel processing, there are important methodological considerations for researchers to consider. For instance, nearly all of the work looking at latency as a measure of social desirability biasing on surveys administered by telephone begin measuring latency at some point *after* the interviewer reads the question (Bassili, 2000). If respondents begin biasing answers even as they hear the question read to them, then the issue of when to start the latency clock may need to be rethought.

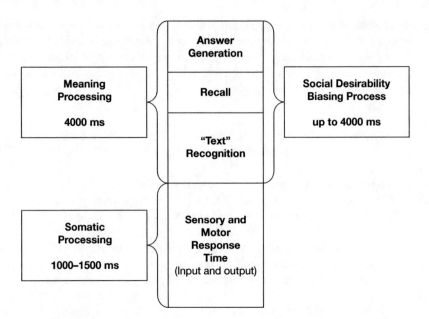

FIGURE 26.1 Components of answering a dichotomous Internet survey question.

Curiously, neither experimental psychology nor survey research has considered the implications of latency in the measurement of truth telling. For instance the National Research Council (2003) lists functional magnetic resonance imaging (fMRI), positron emission tomography (PET), electroencephalogram (EEG), and other event-related potentials including infrared detection of facial blushing as alternatives to the traditional physiological measures associated with polygraph tests in its compressive text on the subject of lie detection—but not latency to respond. In the wake of the terrorist attacks of September 11, 2001, serious efforts have taken place to do just that, to use sophisticated implicit measures of stress and other psychophysiological indicators to screen travelers at airports in real time (Frank, 2008). However, latency to respond has not been part of that project either.

A growing body of research has shown that the length of time it takes a person to make a judgment can be used to gauge evaluations, such as evaluations of estimates of levels of certainty in rule-based expert systems (Feinstein, 2000), and such data have been shown to be more reliable and valid than self-report. A cottage industry known as *neuromarketing* now employs the tools of psychophysiology, such as electromyography (EMG) and brain scanning in the domain of political consulting (Gellene, 2008). It has, however, been largely confined to experimental settings where only a few subjects at a time are tested. Ekman and O'Sullivan (1991) have demonstrated in the laboratory that measuring changes in a subject's facial musculature can detect lying through the use of EMG data. But the use of the experimental apparatus necessary to collect such data is impractical outside the laboratory. Krosnick (1999) suggests reaction time as an alternative. A recent inventory of consultants using cognitive measures found just one example of a firm, Virginia-based TargetPoint, that employs latency to respond measures on Web surveys (Gellene, 2008). The consultants at TargetPoint interpret faster latency times to indicate stronger convictions, a conclusion more or less in accord with the discussion here.

In sum, using latency measures to supplement standard opinion survey self-report questions prompts the following questions:

- Can respondents who say "yes" to the question "Did you vote in the last presidential election?" be differentiated according to the veracity of their response based on how long it takes them to generate a response?
- If latency can be used to reasonably define groups of respondents who said they voted into "fast" and "slow" response groups, will that differentiation predict outcomes on Crowne–Marlowe Social Desirability Scale items?
- If latency scores are used to separate respondents who said they voted into two groups, will adjustment reveal possible biasing among other normatively loaded questions, such as media usage and political self efficacy?

DEMONSTRATING LATENCY TO RESPOND TO WEB-BASED SURVEY QUESTIONS

Sampling

Data for this project were collected by snowball sampling, a procedure implemented by using known members of the target population and then asking them to recruit other members of that population and so on (Babbie, 1998). This strategy was used as the most resource efficient way to recruit respondents who have Internet access.[5] A careful comparison with recent American National Election Study (ANES) data, the gold standard among public opinion researchers, shows that respondents in this study compare favorably on key variables. Table 26.1 shows a comparison between data taken during waves 4 and 5, NES data from 2003, and NES data for Internet users only taken in 2000.

Respondents were recruited by students in public opinion research methods courses. Students were expected to recruit 10 respondents each as a course requirement. They were instructed not to recruit other students or media professionals and were encouraged to recruit as diverse a group as possible across such demographic variables as age, gender, education, and income. Many students recruited members of their extended families. Also, it was not unusual for relatives of a student to recruit within their workplace or among their friends. While respondents remained anonymous, they were issued identification numbers to register online and complete the survey. Recruiters were then able to check the list of completed questionnaires with respondent identification numbers to determine a response rate, which was 74% across all years and waves of the study.

The Instrument

Five waves of data collection were taken between 1999 and 2003 ($N = 2189$).[6] Respondents were asked to answer questions related to the best-documented case of social desirability biasing— over-reporting of voting. Questionnaire items also probed political attitudes, behaviors, and political self efficacy, as well as media exposure and demographic variables. The last two waves also included selected questions from Crowne and Marlowe's (1960) social desirability scale. It is one of the most commonly employed scales used to measure an individual's need for approval. As originally developed, this measure contained 33 true–false items that describe both acceptable but improbable behaviors, as well as those deemed unacceptable but probable.

TABLE 26.1
Demographic Data Comparison between Waves 4 and 5 and National Election Study Data

Comparison of Voting, Mass Media Use, and Demographics

	Online Latency Study[a] (N = 701)	National Election Studies 2000[b] (N = 1807)	National Election Studies 2000 Internet Users[c] (N = 973)
Did you vote in 2000?	Yes = 74.9 No = 25.1	Yes = 76.1 No = 23.9	Yes = 82.5 No = 17.5
Watch Local News	M = 3.47 Std. Dev. = 1.17	M = 3.28 Std. Dev. = 2.86	M = 2.83 Std. Dev. = 2.75
Watch National News	M = 3.06 Std. Dev. = 1.28	M = 3.29 Std. Dev. = 2.8	M = 3.12 Std. Dev. = 2.7
Read Newspaper	M = 3.14 Std. Dev. = 1.44	M = 3.44 Std. Dev. = 2.9	M = 3.56 Std. Dev. = 2.85
Age	M ≅ 35 years M = 3.17 Std. Dev. = 1.28	M = 47.2 years Std. Dev. = 16.96	M = 43.4 years Std. Dev. = 14.5
Education	M ≅ College graduate M = 5.04 Std. Dev. = 1.28	M ≅ More than high school diploma M = 4.29 Std. Dev. = 1.69	M ≅ Two-year college degree M = 4.86 Std. Dev. = 1.49
Household Income	M ≅ $70,000 M = 3.7 Std. Dev. = 2.1	M ≅ $50,000 M = 6.76 Std. Dev. = 3.75	M ≅ $35,000 M = 5.62 Std. Dev. = 3.36
Gender	Female = 55.1 Male = 44.9	Female = 43.7 Male = 56.3	Female = 54.1 Male = 45.9
Marital Status	Married = 51 Not Married = 48.9	Married = 52.1 Not Married = 47.9	Married = 60.2 Not Married = 39.8

Notes:
[a] Media scales: 1= Never, 2 = Rarely, 3 = Sometimes, 4 = Frequently, 5 = All the time
[b] Media scales: How many times per week?
[c] Internet access for NES 2000: Yes = 62.6%; No = 37.4%

COMPARING SELF-REPORT TO LATENCY SCORES

Differentiating Respondents by Latency Scores

The first step in the analysis looked at self-report and latency scores for the question "Did you vote in the last presidential election?[7] A total of 74.9% of respondents reported voting, while national turnout was actually just above 50%, indicating some 25% of respondents may have been misreporting their voting behavior.[8] The percentage of respondents claiming to have voted in this study closely parallels (within 2%) results from recent ANES data based on national probability sampling (Newhagen, 2004). While the 25–75 split is common in contemporary ANES data sets, year 2000 data were especially interesting because they continued to show voting at a rate 25% higher than national turnout despite attempts to word the voting question in such a way as to allow respondents to say without embarrassment that they did not vote.[9]

For the analysis, respondents who said they voted were divided into two groups, those who responded to the questions rapidly and those who responded slowly. The break point in latency scores among those who said they voted was set such that the "fast" group represented 50% of the total sample and the "slow" group represented 25% of the total sample. This tactic is based on the assumption, proposed earlier, that accurate responses would be faster than inaccurate responses and intended to reflect the disparity between actual turnout and self-reported data typical to most public opinion surveys. The remaining 25% of the sample was made up of those who said they did *not* vote. Analysis of variance revealed a significant difference between latency scores across self-reported voting adjusted for latency, $F(2, 610) = 6.98$, $p < .001$. Figure 26.2 shows that scores for "fast" voters ($M = 2401$ ms, $SD = 764$ ms) was nearly identical to the scores for non-voters ($M = 2403$ ms, $SD = 797$ ms), while the "slow" voters scored 200 ms above either of those groups ($M = 2664$ ms, $SD = 644$ ms).

The similarity in both central tendency and variance for "fast" voters and non-voters—and the dissimilarity of "slow" voters with those two groups—is critical to the assumption that latency can be used to differentiate among true voters and misreporting respondents. There simply was no analog group of "slow" nonvoters similar to the "slow" group who said they voted. This similarity between "fast" respondents who said they voted and non-voters is striking and supports the argument advanced here. That is, setting the cumulative percentage of respondents at 50%,

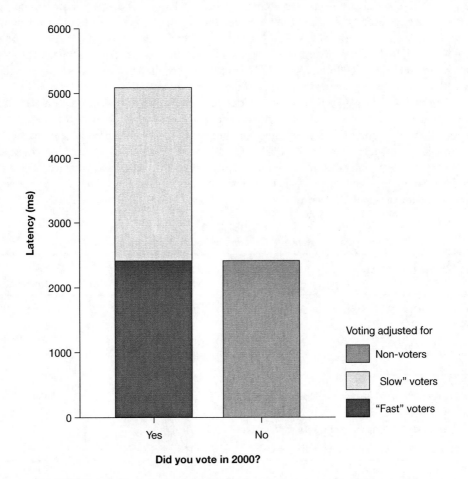

FIGURE 26.2 Self-reported voting adjusted for latency in response to the question: "Did you vote in the last presidential election?"

the actual turnout in the previous election, generated virtually identical latency scores for both voters and non-voters, as was earlier suggested should be the case.

Latency and Crowne–Marlowe Scale Items.   The next step in the analysis was to test whether self-reported voting adjusted for latency could predict outcomes on selected Crowne–Marlowe Social Desirability Scale items. The six items asking questions about prosocial behaviors, similar to questions on a typical political survey, were selected, with three measuring image maintenance and three measuring self-deception.[10] Table 26.2 shows the statistical associations between the Crowne–Marlowe Social Desirability Scale items and self-reported voting adjusted for latency; three of the six tests were significant using the chi-square statistic. However, results from all six comparisons were in the predicted direction, with "slow" voters more likely to give "fake good," responses, that is, questions worded to invite misreporting of prosocial behaviors. Application of a sign test yielded a significant association at $p < .05$.[11]

When latency to respond data were compared to the Crowne–Marlowe items, all six tests were statistically significant. "Slow" voters took longer to answer Crown–Marlowe items than either of the other two groups ("fast" voters and non-voters). For example, this was the case for the relationship between self-reported voting adjusted for latency and agreement with the statement "There have been times when I felt like rebelling against people in authority even though I knew they were right," $F(2, 671) = 11.49, p < .001$. "Slow" voters took longer ($M = 8668$ ms, $SD = 4460$ ms) to the Crown–Marlowe items than either "fast" voters ($M = 6896$ ms, $SD = 4460$ ms) or non-voters ($M = 6276$ ms, $SD = 3749$ ms). In each of the six tests, "slow" voters took at least 1000 ms longer to respond than either of the other two groups.

Thus, while analysis of self-report data alone predicted respondent outcomes only at chance levels, both a sign test of self-report responses and analysis of variance of latency data support the idea that self-reported voting adjusted for latency can be used to predict outcomes on the Crown–Marlowe Social Desirability Scale. Those who were slow to say they had voted also tended to give the socially desirable answer to Crown–Marlowe items and were slower than the other two voting groups to respond. This analysis further supports the value of using latency to respond data to enhance self-report.

TABLE 26.2
Self-Report and Latency to Respond to Social Desirability Scale Items

Social Desirability Scale Item[a]	Chi-square Test for Self-Reported "Fake Good" Answers	F test for Latency Scores
It is sometimes hard for me to go on with my work if I am not encouraged.	.001*	.006*
On occasion, I have had doubts about my ability to succeed in life.	.007*	.005*
I sometimes feel resentful when I don't get my way.	.2	.001*
There have been times when I felt like rebelling against people in authority even though I knew they were right.	.5	.001*
No matter who I am talking to, I'm always a good listener.	.4	.001*
I can remember "playing sick" to get out of something.	.001*	.019*

Notes:
*$p < .05$
[a] Respondents were asked the extent to which they agreed or disagreed with the statements.

Further analysis showed some intriguing associations between latency to respond to the voting question and both political self-efficacy and news media use, revealing possible social desirability biasing among those questions that has not been previously considered.[12]

Political Self-Efficacy.   Political self-efficacy is the respondents' sense of being able to cope with and operate effectively within the political system and is distinct from judgments about the performance of the system itself. A battery of six questions, including such items as "I feel that I have a pretty good understanding of the important political issues facing our country," and "I consider myself to be well qualified to participate in politics," were included (for an explanation of the efficacy items used in this study, see Craig, Niemi, & Silver, 1990). Figure 26.3 shows that self-report for both "fast" and "slow" voters' scores were nearly identical—and well above the scores of non-voters. On the other hand, Figure 26.4 shows "fast" voters and non-voters took a nearly identical amount of time to respond to the question, while "slow" voters took a full second (1000 ms) longer than either of those groups. Looking at the latency data for this question and comparing it to self-report shows a clear trend toward social desirability biasing that would not be obvious by looking at self-report alone. This trend persisted across all of the other five efficacy variables.

These results are in line with the notion that, as with voting, our society promotes active citizen involvement in the political system and that reporting high political self-efficacy would be socially desirable.

News Media Use.   The same trend found for self-efficacy responses appeared for news media usage questions. Here, the social norm would be that citizens should monitor news to keep well informed about current events. Data show that "slow" voters scored at about the same level

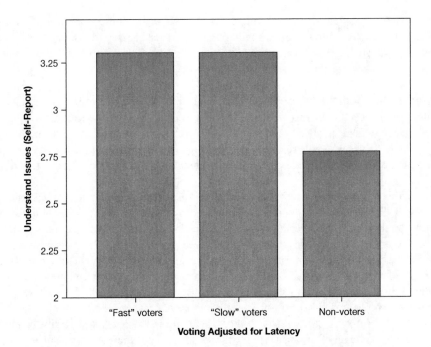

FIGURE 26.3 Issue understanding adjusted for latency in response

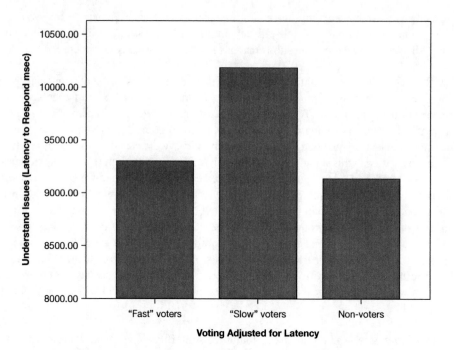

FIGURE 26.4 Latency to respond to understand issues by voting, adjusted for latency.

as "fast" voters, and well above non-voters, on the self-report item probing television news (Figure 26.5). However, "slow" voters again took a full second longer to respond to the question than either "fast" voters or non-voters (Figure 26.6). As with the self-efficacy battery, this trend persisted across other news media usage questions.

Gender and Marital Status. Despite the evident response bias to the voting and media usage items, the question remains whether there is a category of factual questions with no social desirability component at all. If such a category of questions exists, the list might include demographic variables where there is less social incentive to misrepresent reality, such as income, but not others where there is some plausible perceptual benefit, such as age, gender, and marital status.

To test this notion, latency scores for the gender question were compared to voting adjusted for latency. As it turned out, respondents who were slow to say "yes" to the voting question also were considerably slower answering the gender question (for both males and females). On the other hand, there was no significant difference between voting adjusted for latency and latency scores for the marital status question. This might suggest that the gender question causes respondents to think about related issues that have been prominent in the contemporary political and cultural discourse. Gay rights and women's rights do represent two issues where there is a consistently significant division in opinion among survey respondents, sometimes called the "cultural divide" (Fiorina, 2005). Thus, respondents prone to social desirability biasing may expend additional mental effort answering what appears to be a straightforward question simply because it evokes consideration of collateral issues that do have socially correct responses.

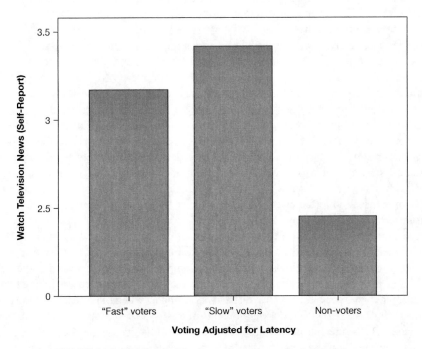

FIGURE 26.5 Watch television news by voting, adjusted for latency.

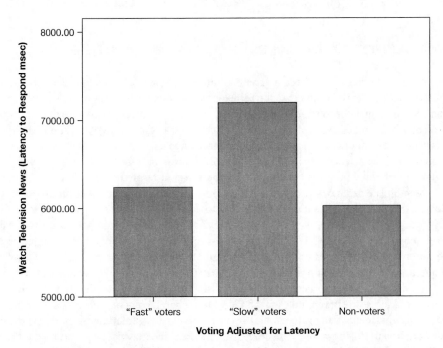

FIGURE 26.6 Watch television news latency by voting, adjusted for latency.

Interaction Effects.   Finally, examining the complexity of current affairs news coverage associated with defining events in national politics shows how latency to respond can reveal interactions between factors that would not be apparent looking solely at self-report data.

The interaction analysis was performed by comparing data from three waves of this project. The first wave was taken near the end of former president Bill Clinton's second term in office. At that time the topic dominating the news was his affair with intern Monica Lewinsky. While the Washington press corps seemed obsessed with the scandal, given the amount of attention it gave to the topic, public opinion polls showed most people were not that interested in the issue or persuaded by the coverage (or they clearly distinguished between the president's private life and public performance in office). Clinton's job performance rating thus remained high. The second wave was administered in the wake of the 2000 presidential election between George W. Bush and Al Gore. That election also received a great deal of news coverage, as recounts dragged on for weeks with the decision about who won the election finally being decided in court. Finally, a third wave of data was collected one week after the terror attacks of September 11, 2001, an event that consumed the American consciousness.

A case can be made that the Clinton wave constituted an era of low news complexity, the Bush–Gore election represented an era of moderate news complexity, and the September 11 attacks a moment of extreme news complexity. Comparing latency scores for the variables reported here, including political self-efficacy and media use, revealed an interesting set of interactions, where the social desirability effect was strongest when the intensity of the news was either low or moderate. However, during moments of crisis, latency scores converged, especially for media use. These interactions suggest even "slow" voters meet what they see as their civic obligation to pay attention to events during times of crisis, and answer questions about media with a clear conscience because they are engaged as citizens. They are, however, prone to bias their responses to social norms in less stressful moments. These interactions were not detected based solely on self-report. A full discussion of these results can be found in Newhagen (2002).

INSIDE THE BLACK BOX OF SURVEY QUESTION RESPONSE

Social desirability biasing has been a perennial thorn in the side of survey research because by its very nature it frequently yields inaccurate responses to questions central to political communication. While all manner of strategies have been employed to arrest or correct the problem in the context of self-report, such as wording response sets in a way that removes the stigma from socially incorrect answers, none have really been widely accepted as a remedy. Other alternatives require deception, such as manipulating respondents' self impression with a "bogus pipeline" (Paulhus, 1990). The technique involves telling subjects their responses are being monitored by a machine or a polygraph (lie detector), resulting in more truthful answers. Electrodes and wires connected to participants, which represent a reliable means to detect the truth, are not actually real. Krosnick (1999) suggests alternatives such as psychophysiological measures that could more directly measure cognitive processes, but his suggestions require elaborate equipment suited for small-scale experiments in a laboratory setting and would not be feasible in the context of a survey. He also questions the validity of post hoc statistical techniques, such as response weighting.[13]

The analysis presented here tests a fairly simple alternative to detect social desirability biasing—looking at the time it takes respondents to respond to survey questions. Findings for the voting question, media usage items, and news complexity interactions support the notion that latency can be a useful measure for detecting respondents who may not be reporting their behaviors or attitudes accurately. Identifying this group can have important practical and theoretical applications. Political pollsters hoping to predict election outcomes, for instance, rely heavily on the voting question and others similar to it as filter questions to identify "likely voters." (For the *Washington Post*'s complete list of filter questions, see Morin, 2004.)

Clinical psychology has contributed a substantial body of research about social desirability biasing based on the Minnesota Multiphasic Personality Inventory (MMPI), an instrument that has been used in industry for decades to evaluate the psychological fitness of potential employees (for example, see Holden, 1995). An obvious weakness of the instrument is the concern that applicants may be consciously misreporting to appear as desirable as possible to potential employers. However, biasing on public opinion and political surveys has to be seen as distinct from the kind of conscious deception employed by devious MMPI takers. The stakes and sanctions are just not as high and, consequently, the underlying process driving the biasing may be different as well. This leads to a discussion about consideration of the limits of self-report and the advantages of indirect measures of mental effort.

Buying into latency as a viable methodological tool for detecting, and controlling for, social desirability biasing rests on important theoretical assumptions about question answering that sometimes range beyond the usual boundaries of conversations about the topic. One proposition the data reported here suggest is that social desirability biasing is not confined to a narrow range of question topics where there are obvious issues of respondent embarrassment. In fact, traces of biasing were found on many variables in this project. Even questions as straightforward as respondent gender are not immune.

An alternative explanation might be that all these data reveal is simply that some people take longer to answer questions than others. But that only makes the issue more problematic. A careful examination of self-reported voting adjusted for latency shows that the latency distributions for "fast" voters and non-voters are remarkably similar, while the scores for "slow" voters are uniquely distinct from them. Slow response is more than a cognitive style—it stands out as a prominent feature of responses among a subset of respondents who reported they did vote, but does not show up among those who said they did not. There is a wealth of literature in political communication and psychology elaborating the importance of schematic complexity in cognition (for examples see Collins & Loftus, 1988; Fiske, 1986; Garramone, Steele, & Pinkleton, 1991; Lau, 1986; McGuire, 1990). A basic assumption in the information processing model of communication is that cognitive complexity engenders effort which takes time that can be measured. Schematic models of memory and attitude propose that two factors should be taken into account concerning memory retrieval or attitude generation—both the complexity of the schema and strength of the associations within them. Thus, information from simple schema should be readily available. This scenario could represent political schema for many non-voters who do not attend to the political ecology much. Even when schematic complexity increases, if between-node connections are strong, retrieval should still be rapid. This describes Converse's (1964) "ideologues," respondents who have well-formed and complex ideological frameworks available to process political information.

But what about respondents driven by loosely bound schema relating to specific issues, such as gun control, or temporal circumstances, such as the state of the economy? Information processing theory would predict that this group will generally take longer to respond to many of the topics that appear on public opinion or political surveys because they have not completely thought certain issues through. It could be further posited that this group not only takes longer, but output from such a belief system would be more likely to depend on reference to external norms. This group would thus be more apt to give socially desirable responses on nearly any topic. Long processing times dependent on searches for baseline social norms may also run the risk of having emotional states, such as guilt or embarrassment, coloring answers because they would evoke more complex answer generation processes than a straightforward memory search. This group can be thought of as "ruminators," or respondents who expend more mental effort and therefore more time assessing attitude and opinion schema. They represent upwards of one-third of all survey respondents, a percentage that roughly maps onto Converse's model for people who attend to the political landscape with much rigor.

This elevates social desirability biasing from the status of a methodological nuisance to a theoretically driven aspect of the question answering process, and must be regarded as such in the interpretation of survey results generally. Such a realization could change the discourse about survey research fairly dramatically. If we know, for instance, that some respondents systematically over-report reading newspapers, the problem goes beyond simply how to control statistical error. Bartels (1993), for instance, argues that measurement error of self-reported media exposure is likely to be substantial in magnitude, unpredictable in direction, and prone to bias correlations with political opinions. He proposes that ordinary least squares statistics may underestimate the overall effects of television news as much as 50%.

If society assigns more value to some news media than it does to others (e.g., newspaper reading over television viewing, and news content of any kind over entertainment fare) and a group of respondents understands that norm but does not comply with it, the upshot is likely to produce systematic response bias on surveys. This predicament goes well beyond questions about voting. Addressing the so-called weak effects problem in political communication research not only requires recognition of statistical artifacts arising from favored methodologies but also a focus on the implications of noncompliance to social and political norms in opinion and attitude measurement.

Perhaps respondents who know what the norm is but do not comply with it are really giving us the right answers; it may be that we're asking the *wrong questions*. What would the response pattern and latency scores to the question "Should people like me vote?" look like in comparison to asking if respondents actually do vote?

APPENDIX 26.1

Capturing Latency to Respond Data on a Web-Based Survey

The main difference between basic HTML files and software used to recover data in an online survey is the inclusion of a number of small executable programs written in the Java computer programming language. The data for this project were recovered within the server's CGI file system in the same way utilized by many server-based data recovery programs. The following sequence of events took place during an interview session:

- First, respondents were recruited for participation in a Web-based survey study. Upon accessing the URL supplied by the recruiter, respondents were shown a page asking if they could see a clock on their screen. This operation determined if the respondent's computer had a browser plug-in installed capable of reading the Java program language used to recover latency times. If the clock (based on a Java applet) appeared, the respondent was instructed to click on a "continue" button. If the clock did not appear, the respondent was prompted to click on a link taking them to a site where the necessary Java plug-in could be downloaded for free. After that they were asked to continue.
- To continue, respondents were required to enter a recruiter identification number and an anonymous respondent identification number supplied by the recruiter, which were recorded for bookkeeping purposes.

- Upon proceeding, the respondent's Web browser activated an HTML file with an applet embedded in it for each question on the survey. These applets loaded on the respondent's computers and ran in the background while the session took place.
- Respondents then saw a brief introductory page. At the bottom of the page they were instructed to click on a "continue" button. By clicking the continue button, the applets corresponding to the first question would execute, displaying the text of the question and a vertically aligned response set with a radio button adjacent to each answer.
- To answer, respondents clicked on the appropriate radio button, followed by clicking on a link at the bottom of the page saying "next." An applet computed and stored the time it took, in milliseconds, from the moment the question first appeared until the "next" button was selected. The applet also recorded a numeric value corresponding to the item on the response set selected by the respondent.

This sequence was repeated for each question in the survey. At the very end of the survey the respondent clicked a "submit" button, at which time the latency and self-report data from each applet was transferred to a unique file on the survey server. This process made the latency time-keeping function local to the respondent's computer and insulated it from variance in network performance.

Data for each respondent were later concatenated into a tab-delimited master file that was readable by the SPSS statistics program.

The mechanics of the HTML portion of the project should be well within the expertise of an intermediate level Web designer. The creation of the applets required an experienced Java programmer. In addition, the templates for response sets of various lengths had to be created, along with library files and other supporting programs on the survey server. The cost of this portion of the program development is relatively modest and represents a one-time expense. Once the system is up and running the principle investigator or trained assistant should be able to manage data collection with no further programming costs.

NOTES

1. Only a few hundred votes separated George W. Bush and Al Gore in Florida's tabulation of the 2000 presidential election. Election officials admitted that up to 6% of actual ballots in that critical state were either miscounted, or went completely uncounted. In the wake of recounts and court challenges, some went so far as to suggest survey data were a more accurate predictor of political preference than the election itself. Since then a number of elections for Congress and other high offices have had similarly close results.
2. Why aren't there "I Didn't Vote" stickers? This is not just a flippant observation because boycotting the polls or casting null or mutilated ballots in rigged elections is not uncommon elsewhere in the world.
3. The degree to which self-report invites social desirability can be seen if the bank of all seven filter questions used in *Washington Post/ABC News* polls is examined. At least six of the seven questions invite normative bias in the same way the voting question does because they suggest socially desirable outcomes. Those questions are: "Are you registered to vote?," "Do you intend to vote?," "Did you vote in the last election?," "How interested are you in the presidential campaign?," respondent age, whether the respondent was old enough to vote in the previous election, and "Do you know the location of your polling place?" (Morin, 2004).
4. While the technologies of administration, such as the telephone or the Web, undoubtedly affect latency times, answer generation is driven by the same dynamics of the underlying core cognitive processes.
5. Some public opinion researchers maintain that only data generated by a random probability sample can be generalized to the full population. This position, however, has stymied the development of otherwise important Web-based research for both practical and epistemological reasons. One important

epistemological issue those supporting this position have yet to come to grips with is how to identify what constitutes the universe, or population of Internet users. It is not infinite, but it is large enough, or so vast and mutable, as to seem so. Even if it was possible to accurately delimit the population, this still begs the question of how to draw a sample. Some projects claim sample integrity by culling respondents from random samples collected by telephone or other means and then sampling from the subset of those who say they have Internet access—or can be provided with online access (see Chapter 8, this volume). This approach has two weaknesses: First, the claim that the "sample within the sample" represents a random variable is statistically specious; second, this removes Internet survey research from the grasp of investigators who do not have access to such a data pool to draw from. This is an important issue because it has limited the reporting of important research done on the Internet in a palpable way, and represents an issue the survey research community must grapple with sooner or later. The implications of these issues are beyond the scope of this chapter but warrant further discussion.

6. Wave 1: October, 1999, $N = 746$; Wave 2: April 2001, $N = 586$; Wave 3: December 2001, $N = 156$; Wave 4: March 2002, $N = 340$; Wave 5: October 2003, $N = 361$.

7. In the first wave this referred to the 1996 election and in subsequent waves it referred to the 2000 election. The 2003 wave included six items from the Crowne–Marlowe scale.

8. The idea that respondents in this project might have been extraordinarily engaged citizens and actually voted at a rate 25% above the actual turnout is highly unlikely given the fact data were collected across a four-year period and that such overreporting is typical on opinion surveys and has been documented to be an artifact of social desirability biasing.

9. For details, see the NES codebook, available at http://www.electionstudies.org.

10. Those items were: It is sometimes hard for me to go on with my work if I am not encouraged; On occasion, I have had doubts about my ability to succeed in life; Sometimes I feel I don't get my way; There have been times when I felt like rebelling against people in authority even though I knew they were right; No matter who I am talking to I am always a good listener; I can remember "playing sick" to get out of something.

11. The sign test represents a coarse index of association. When it is significant while other statistical tests are not, as was the case with the chi-square tests reported here, the use of an alternative measure, such as latency to respond, may be appropriate.

12. All relationships reported in this section were statistically significant at least at $p < .05$.

13. The technique gives the responses from a segment of a sample more (or less) weight than would be generated by individual scores. It has been criticized on the grounds that the discrepancy of over- or underrepresentation may be systematic and that the weighting process only exacerbates differences from a "true" probability sample, rather than rectifying them.

REFERENCES

Babbie, E. (1998). *The practice of social research* (8th ed.). Belmont, CA: Wadsworth.

Bartels, L. M. (1993). Messages received: The political impact of media exposure. *American Political Science Review, 87*(2), 267–284.

Bassili, J. N. (2000). Reflections on response latency measurement in telephone surveys. *Political Psychology, 21*(1), 1–5.

Collins, A., & Loftus, E. (1988). A spreading-activation theory of semantic processing. In A. Collins & E. Smith (Eds.), *Readings in cognitive science: A perspective from psychology and artificial intelligence* (pp. 126–136). San Mateo, CA: Morgan Kaufmann.

Converse, P. (1964). The nature of belief systems in mass publics. In D. Apter (Ed.), *Ideology and discontent* (pp. 206–261). New York: The Free Press.

Craig, S., Niemi, R., & Silver, G. (1990). Political efficacy and trust: A report on the NES pilot study items. *Political Behavior, 12*(3), 289–314.

Crowne, D. P., & Marlowe, D. (1960). A new scale of social desirability independent of psychopathology. *Journal of Consulting Psychology, 24*(4), 349–354.

Ekman, P., & Davidson, R. J. (1994). *The nature of emotion: Fundamental questions*. New York: Oxford University Press.

Ekman, P., & O'Sullivan, M. (1991). Who can catch a liar? *American Psychologist, 46*(9), 913–920.

Fazio, R. H., Williams, C. J., & Powell, M. C. (2000). Measuring associative strength: Category-item associations and their activation from memory. *Political Psychology, 21*(1), 7–25.

Feinstein, J. L. (2000). Comparing response latency and self-report methods for estimating levels of certainty in knowledge elicitation for rule-based expert systems. *Expert System, 17*(5), 217–225.

Festinger, L. (1957). *A theory of cognitive dissonance*. Stanford CA: Stanford University Press.

Fiorina, M. P. (2005). *Culture war? The myth of a polarized America* (2nd ed.). New York: Pearson Longman.

Fiske, S. (1986). Schema-based versus piecemeal politics: A patchwork quilt, but not a blanket, of evidence. In R. R. Lau & D. O. Sears (Eds.), *The 19th annual Carnegie symposium on cognition: Political cognition* (pp. 41–53). Hillsdale, NJ: Lawrence Erlbaum Associates.

Frank, M. (2008, July). *Thinking about lying and lying about thinking*. Paper presented at the National Communication Association conference, Communication and Social Cognition: Methods and Measures for Communication and Cognition Research, College Park, MD.

Frijda, N. (1986). *The emotions*. Cambridge: Cambridge University Press.

Garramone, G., Steele, M., & Pinkleton, B. (1991). The role of cognitive schemata in determining candidate characteristic effects. In F. Biocca (Ed.), *Television and political advertising, vol. 1: Psychological processes* (pp. 311–328). Hillslade, NJ: Lawrence Erlbaum Associates.

Gellene, D. (2008, February 10). Getting inside voters' minds. *Los Angeles Times*, p. A22.

Holden, R. R. (1995). Response latency detection of fakers on personnel tests. *Canadian Journal of Behavioral Science, 27*(3), 343–355.

Krosnick, J. A. (1999). Maximizing questionnaire quality. In J. P. Robinson, P. R. Shaver, & L. S. Wrightsman (Eds.), *Measures of political attitudes* (pp. 37–57). San Diego, CA: Academic Press.

Krosnick, J. A., Holbrook, A. L., Berent, M. K., Carson, R. T., Hanemann, W. M., Koop, R. J., et al. (2002). The impact of "no opinion" response options on data quality: Non-attitude reduction or an invitation to satisfice? *Public Opinion Quarterly, 66*, 371–403.

Lau, R. (1986). Political schemata, candidate evaluations, and voting behavior. In R. Lau & D. Sears (Eds.), *The 19th annual Carnegie symposium on cognition: Political cognition* (pp. 95–126). Hillsdale, NJ: Lawrence Erlbaum Associates.

McGuire, W. (1990). Dynamic operations of thought systems. *American Psychologist, 45*(4), 504–512.

Morin, R. (2004, October 24). Probable voters: How polls are made, swayed. *Washington Post*, p. A07.

National Research Council. (2003). *The polygraph and lie detection*. Washington, DC: The National Academies Press.

Newhagen, J. E. (1994). Self efficacy and call-in political television show use. *Communication Research, 21*(3), 366–379.

Newhagen, J. E. (2002, July). The impact of news ecology complexity on social desirability biases in a Web-based survey. Paper presented to the annual meeting of the International Communication Association, Information Systems Division, Seoul, South Korea.

Newhagen, J. E. (2004, May). The role of mental effort in social desirability biasing. Paper presented to the annual meeting of the International Communication Association, Information Systems Division, New Orleans, LA.

Newhagen, J. E., & Reeves, B. (1991). Responses for negative political advertising: A study of the 1988 presidential election. In F. Biocca (Ed.), *Television and political advertising, vol. 1: Psychological processes*. Hillsdale, NJ: Lawrence Erlbaum Associates.

Newhagen, J. E., & Reeves, B. (1992). This evening's bad news: Effects of compelling negative television news images on memory. *Journal of Communication, 42*(2), 25–41.

Nisbett, R., & Wilson, T. (1977). Telling more than we can know: Verbal reports on mental processes. *Psychological Review, 84*(3), 231–259.

Paulhus, D. L. (1990). Measurement and control of response bias. In J. P. Robinson, P. R. Shaver, & L. S. Wrightsman (Eds.), *Measures of personality and social psychological attitudes* (pp. 17–24). San Diego, CA: Academic Press.

Plutchik, R. (1989). Measuring emotions and their derivatives. In R. Plutchik & H. Kellerman (Eds.), *Emotion: Theory, research, and experience, Vol. 4* (pp. 1–35). San Diego, CA: Academic Press.

Presser, S. (1990). Can changes in context reduce vote over reporting in surveys? *Public Opinion Quarterly, 54*, 586–593.

Rumelhart, D., & McClelland, P. (1986). *Parallel distributed processing: Explorations in the microstructure of cognition.* Cambridge, MA: MIT Press.

Schaeffer, N. C. (2000). Asking questions about threatening topics: A selective overview. In A. Stone, S. Jaylan, S. Turkkan, A. Christine, J. Bachrach, B. Jared, B. Jobe, H. S. Kurtzman, & V. S. Cain (Eds.), *The science of self-report: Implications for research and practice* (pp. 105–121). Mahwah, NJ: Lawrence Erlbaum Associates.

Tourangeau, R., Rips, L. J., & Rasinski, D. (2000). *The psychology of survey response.* Cambridge: Cambridge University Press.

27

What the Body Can Tell Us About Politics

The Use of Psychophysiological Measures in Political Communication Research

Erik P. Bucy

Department of Advertising
Texas Tech University

Samuel D. Bradley

Department of Advertising
Texas Tech University

In recent years political communication has experienced a growth of new methods and analytical techniques that are bringing increased sophistication, precision, and rigor to the study of political phenomena. Psychophysiological measurement has been employed for some time in psychology but has been slowly gaining ground in political communication and political psychology. Although currently under-utilized, psychophysiology is a promising method that provides direct measures of citizen response—responses to political content *during* exposure as opposed to cognitively filtered self-reports after the fact—that is gradually gaining acceptance in the field. Employed in political communication research since the early 1980s (see Lanzetta, Sullivan, Masters, & McHugo, 1985), physiological measurement has recently been utilized in studies of viewer responses to political debates (Mutz & Reeves, 2005), negative political advertising (Bradley, Angelini, & Lee, 2007), still photographs of candidate faces (Kaplan, Freedman, & Iacoboni, 2007), and televised leader displays (Bucy & Bradley, 2004).

The most common psychophysiological techniques include measures of heart rate (an indicator of attention), skin conductance (an indicator of arousal), facial muscle activation, or EMG (a measure used for assessing emotional valence), and the startle reflex (an index of aversive or negative activation). In their study of presidential expressions and viewer emotion, Bucy and Bradley (2004) employed a variety of physiological measures to show how counter-empathic responses to televised leader displays—positive reactions to negative expressive displays and negative reactions to positive displays—may be evoked in political communication by considering the associated news context. In a test of televised incivility on political trust, Mutz and Reeves (2005) found that uncivil debate exchanges elicited higher levels of physiological arousal over time than civil exchanges. The memorable quality of negative ads, namely their arousingness and aversiveness, has also been validated through the use of psychophysiological measures (Bradley, Angelini, & Lee, 2007). In their brain imaging study, Kaplan and colleagues found that political attitudes can guide the activation of emotional systems in the brain and influence the regulation of emotional responses to opposing candidates (Kaplan, Freedman, & Iacoboni, 2007).

Depending upon the research question, there are two general advantages to using physiological over other outcome measures, particularly self-report questionnaires. The first is the ability to capture viewer or participant responses in real time, and with a high degree of precision. Since the body's signals are sampled electronically (at a rate of 20 or more times per second), researchers are able to pinpoint exactly when an effect occurred—what particular aspect of a candidate's voice, message, expressive display, or delivery impacted potential voters. Readings of participant responses are taken during exposure, not after. The second advantage is the indirect nature of the measures. Since they do not rely upon participant self-reflections, they are less subject to social desirability biases, prior attitudes, or cognitive consistency pressures; if an effect occurs, it generally happens without the interference of ideological orientations, what participants feel they *should* say, or efforts to maintain a consistent outlook or self-image. Because they largely occur automatically in response to media stimuli and outside conscious awareness, physiological measurements are often considered more accurate evidence of actual media influence.

Psychophysiological measurement thus has great relevance to political communication, where elections—especially close contests—often turn on perceived competence or other heuristic source cues rather than close scrutiny of policy positions. Since physiological measures take the form of bodily signals, they should be approached and used differently than participant self-reports or verbal responses to political messages. Rather than yielding "thoughtful" answers or replies to questions that are carefully contemplated (and sometimes strategically answered) by study participants, psychophysiological data may indicate how much mental effort viewers dedicate to a particular message or stimulus, the direction of emotional response at the time of exposure, or the state of action readiness or arousal that a political communication may place different viewers in. In the case of fMRI or brain imaging techniques, also considered a type of psychophysiological recording (Stern, Ray, & Quigley, 2001), specific regions of the brain that are engaged during message processing may be identified. Hence, psychophysiological measures are particularly useful for studying political information processing.

The following sections review the biological basis of information processing (particularly of political visuals), which is important to understand when considering the use of psychophysiological measurement because responses occur largely outside conscious awareness. But just because physiological responses are not consciously recognized by subjects does not mean they have no influence or political significance. To the contrary, they form the cognitive and emotional basis of political evaluation and decision making, including the neurological processes that drive social and political behavior (see Fowler & Schreiber, 2008). Next, we describe the most common psychophysiological measures employed in political communication research, explaining their basic operation, appropriate use, and kinds of insights they facilitate. To illustrate the benefits of using psychophysiology, we present a case study involving negative political advertising. Lastly, we provide an overview of the lab apparatus necessary to conduct this unique and precise brand of research.

THE BIOLOGICAL BASIS OF POLITICAL INFORMATION PROCESSING

Contrary to the preferences of political theorists for a rationally engaged public that relies on reason and deliberation to make informed decisions, much of political experience and citizen decision making is relegated to the intuitive domain of "gut feelings" and emotional responding—areas that physiological recording techniques are particularly well suited to measure. As becomes evident through a brief consideration of neuroscientific principles, the speed with which the human mind processes certain types of information determines whether a given evaluation, sentiment, or political thought is available for conscious use by even the most aware citizens.

Processing Speed

In his time scale of human action, Newell (1990) describes different bands or levels of information processing and their corresponding units of time. At the lowest and fastest level is the biological band that accounts for operations among organelles or structures *within* cells, as well as neuronal activity or synapse firings *between* cells. Whereas organelles perform their work on the order of microseconds (i.e., millionths of a second), neurons have a characteristic operation time of about a millisecond (i.e., one one-thousandth of a second). Up a level, but still within the biological band, are neural circuits, which provide the means through which the nervous system connects to and controls bodily systems. Neural circuits, including those that drive visual perception, operate on the order of tens of milliseconds (i.e., ten one-thousandths of a second), but still outside conscious awareness.

Though biological processes serve as the foundation for human thought and action, politically relevant responses operate at a much higher level of abstraction and take place within what Newell refers to as the cognitive and rational bands of consciousness—self-aware activities that are orders of magnitude higher on the time scale of human action, which occur between 10^{-1} and 10^4 seconds, than events within the biological band, which occur between 10^{-4} and 10^{-2} seconds (Newell, 1990, p. 122). The cognitive band addresses issues of comprehension and decision, followed by implementation and movement. Up a level from that, the rational band facilitates goal-oriented behavior and what is classically called "reason." Interactions with the environment that evoke cognitive considerations take place on the order of seconds, whereas considerations within the rational band may play out over minutes or hours. Above both of these levels is the social band of human activity, in which political processes occur, unfolding over days, weeks, or months (Newell, 1990).

The precise degree of correspondence between psychophysiological measures and cognitive processes has been contested for some time (for an overview, see Cacioppo & Tassinary, 1990; Lang, 1994a; Potter & Bolls, in press). With regard to dynamic symbol processing, in other words political stimuli broadcast via the mass media, Newhagen (2004) asserts that meaning "will *always* be created at a level of analysis just below the particular level where it emerges and becomes apparent" (p. 398). That is, elaborate mental processes that constitute "rationality" rest upon more basic cognitive operations while cognition emerges from neurological events at the biological level. Stimulus-driven or bottom-up processing is particularly salient when mismatches occur between internal states and environmental developments, or expected and observed events, that prompt greater attentiveness and increased motivation for learning (Marcus, Neuman, & MacKuen, 2000, p. 57). In Marcus et al.'s affective intelligence model, disruptions to habitual routines, especially those perceived as threatening, elicit anxiety and feelings of uneasiness, activating the surveillance system of emotion that signals the need to look for solutions to novel circumstances (see also Gray, 1987).

Earlier debates over whether emotional reactions precede cognition have been superseded by findings in cognitive neuroscience that show sensory information can reach emotional brain centers before continuing on to cortical regions for further processing (Damasio, 1994; LeDoux, 1996). Libet and colleagues have estimated that it takes about half a second, or 500 milliseconds, for the brain to represent sensory data (i.e., sight, sound, smell, touch, taste) in consciousness (Libet et al., 1991). However, affective responses and even visual recognition occur much faster. Once a facial image is presented for viewing, for example, perception of that image *as a face* occurs approximately 47 milliseconds after exposure (Watanabe, Kakigi, Koyama, & Kirino, 1999), the equivalent of about two frames of video or one-twentieth of a second. By this time, sensory information from the optic nerve has already traveled through the thalamus to the limbic region of the brain, particularly the amygdala, "where the emotional import of the incoming sensory streams can be determined" (Marcus, Neuman, & MacKuen, 2000, p. 37). A second pathway, from the thalamus to the "higher" brain regions, including the visual, somatosensory, motor, and prefrontal cortices, supports conscious awareness or knowable feelings and appraisals (see LeDoux, 1996; Mishkin & Appenzeller, 1987).

The two pathways by which sensory data travel to different neurological regions process information at vastly different speeds. The thalamo-amygdala pathway to the limbic region yields appraisals in less than half the time it takes for sensory data to become consciously available via the cortical pathway (Marcus, Neuman, & MacKuen, 2000, p. 37). Thus, the body may begin to mobilize for fight or flight, or basic emotional assessments may place a person in a state of action readiness, before the mind realizes what is happening and makes a conscious decision to act. Physiological measures are capable of reliably capturing these impulses whereas self-report is not; even if research participants have some inkling as to their interior motivational states, they may not be willing to acknowledge and disclose their fears, aggressive responses, revulsion, or other tendencies that seem unbecoming.

As is evident by the delay between basic emotional assessments and conscious awareness of environmental developments, the brain is built to anticipate likely occurrences, which it accomplishes by calling up memories and templates from past experience to continuously make predictions about the future (Barry, 2005, p. 57). This principle applies to perceptual as well as motivational systems. "What we see is not what is on the retina at any given instant," Gazzaniga (1998, p. 75) explains, "but is a prediction of what will be there." The brain's anticipatory and emotional design is evolutionary advantageous because in critical situations resources must be mobilized without the delay involved in making cognitive appraisals.

The next section reviews the most common physiological measures employed in political communication research, including skin conductance, heart rate, and facial electromyography. A brief overview of brain imaging studies of political stimuli is also offered since neuroscientists over the past decade have begun to identify the neural processes and specific brain regions associated with political evaluation.

SKIN CONDUCTANCE

Perhaps the most straightforward physiological measure available to political communication researchers is electrodermal activity (EDA), typically measured as skin conductance. Electrodermal activity refers specifically to activation of the eccrine sweat glands, which are innervated by the sympathetic branch of the autonomic nervous system (ANS). When under stress or preparing to take action, the sympathetic nervous system, which aids in the control of most of the body's internal organs, becomes engaged and mobilizes the body's resources. Eccrine sweat glands, which are concentrated in the palms of the hands and the soles of the feet, are of particular interest to psychophysiologists because they "respond primarily to 'psychic' stimulation, whereas other sweat glands respond more to increases in temperature" (Stern, Ray, & Quigley, 2001, p. 209). Although we cannot be certain as to the evolutionary origin and precise purpose of this perspiration, many researchers believe that increased sweating at time of activity or anxiety allows humans to better grip with their hands and have better traction with their feet, perhaps in preparation for fighting or fleeing from a threat.

An increase in electrodermal activity can be measured with sensors placed on the palm of the hands. Thankfully, few situations are intense enough for eccrine gland perspiration to visibly wet the palm. Instead, most electrodermal activity never reaches the surface of the skin. However, increased subcutaneous moisture nonetheless changes the electrical conductivity of the skin. Although there are multiple ways to measure this activity, the most common method is to run a small current (usually 0.5 volt) between two sensors placed on the palm. As physiological arousal increases, sweating increases and the signal can more easily pass between the sensors (measured in µSiemens).

Physiological arousal has been associated with numerous constructs over the previous century. Perhaps most reliably, arousal has been strongly associated with becoming energized and preparing for action. Both of these outcomes are of interest to political communication researchers. In recent years, skin conductance has been used to measure responses to negative political advertising (Bradley, Angelini, & Lee, 2007), appropriateness of leader responses (Bucy & Bradley, 2004), and political incivility (Mutz, 2007; Mutz & Reeves, 2005). Mutz's studies on televised incivility are notable as much for what they found as where they appeared—in *American Political Science Review*, the leading journal in political science. In her study of aggressive, or "in your face" television discourse, Mutz (2007) found that uncivil political discussion combined with a close-up camera perspective was significantly more physiologically arousing to viewers than a civil version of the same discussion; civil discussions shown with a medium shot length were least arousing. Though perhaps more memorable, the uncivil, close-up segments also caused audiences to view oppositional perspectives as less credible and legitimate than they would have otherwise.

HEART RATE

The effects of almost any communication begin with attention. If one fails to attend to a message, then the content is almost assuredly not perceived, and hence there can be no basis for causal claims about effects. For many researchers, therefore, attention marks an important step in understanding how citizens encode, interpret, and ultimately are affected by political communication. However, human attention—especially in response to a complex stimulus such as a mediated message—has proven difficult to measure. The relationship between attention and heart rate is not particularly intuitive. A slowing heart rate, for instance, can either indicate increased attention to a compelling stimulus or point to a decrease in emotional arousal. Moreover, attention may be allocated briefly, as is the case with phasic attention to sudden changes in the environment, or tonically, over the longer-term, in response to increased concentration, vigilance, or mental effort.

The human heart is regulated by two branches of the autonomic nervous system. Both the sympathetic and parasympathetic divisions govern the rate of contraction and relaxation of cardiac muscle fibers. Because of this dual control, "autonomic arousal may result in a speeding up or a slowing down of the heart depending on what a person is doing" (Lang, 1994a, p. 100).

Parasympathetic activation, which is associated with rest and contemplation, leads to a slowing heart rate or cardiac deceleration. Parasympathetic arousal causes the heart to slow down and is associated with attention (Lang, 1994a). Conversely, the sympathetic nervous system is associated with action, exertion, and emotional arousal and leads to cardiac acceleration. These dual innervations of the heart lead to difficulties in interpreting cardiac data. At any given moment, the heart may be decelerating due to an *increase* in parasympathetic activation, a *decrease* in sympathetic activation, or both.

The relationship between heart rate and the dual innervations of the sympathetic and parasympathetic nervous systems is a perennial topic among psychophysiological researchers (see Lang, 1994a; Ravaja, 2004). One take on this is to look at simultaneous data of heart rate and respiration to measure what is known as respiratory sinus arrhythmia (RSA), a naturally occurring variation in heart rate due to respiration. Heart rate increases as an individual inhales and decreases during exhale. RSA is a purer index of parasympathetic activity and is therefore a superior measure of controlled attention than simple heart rate. Research has shown that sustained attention has been demonstrated to decrease RSA; however, the benefit of RSA must be weighed against the increased difficulty in measuring respiration and interpreting the data.

Recent work has demonstrated that RSA can be reliably estimated from the inter-beat interval (or IBI) using computer software. This is preferable to actually measuring respiration simply for the fact that respiration need not be measured separately (Allen, Chambers, & Towers, 2007).

FACIAL ELECTROMYOGRAPHY

By measuring skin conductance and heart rate, researchers can ascertain a fair amount about audience behavior, including how much attention is being paid to a message and how energized or aroused a message makes someone feel. But if only using these measures, emotional valence or the direction of that response—whether positive or negative—goes unmeasured. And how viewers respond to political stimuli, whether negative advertising, critical news coverage, or contentious exchanges from televised debates, merits research attention. When compared to neutral messages, both pleasant messages and unpleasant messages elicit greater arousal; however, arousal alone cannot reliably distinguish between the two. Oftentimes, favorable or unfavorable reactions may be the *key* variable of interest for a political campaign or political communication researcher. Among the range of physiological measures that are available, facial electromyography, or EMG, most directly facilitates covert measurement of emotional response.

Facial EMG accomplishes this task by measuring electrical activity over muscle groups associated with frowning and smiling. Two facets of emotional response make EMG superior to manual facial coding (i.e., observations of facial expressions) and self-reports of felt emotion. First, through the use of electrode sensors and bioamplifiers, EMG can reliably measure facial muscle activation by recording muscle contractions that are too slight to visibly observe. Even trained observers would completely miss most instances of facial muscle activation, which are too subtle to move the skin, and assume the viewer was feeling no emotion at all. The second, related, benefit is that subtle emotional responses are not always available for conscious introspection. Media audiences and study participants sometimes cannot say if they are starting to feel positive or negative about a particular message or candidate—or are sometimes unwilling to admit when they are. For these reasons, facial EMG can provide a powerful window into emotional response.

In communication research, EMG is typically measured over three sites. The first site, *corrugator supercilli*, is located above the nose and draws the brow down in a characteristic frown. Muscle activity in this group is associated with negative emotion. The second site, *zygomaticus major*, is located in the cheek and draws up the corners of the mouth in a smile. Together with *corrugator supercilli*, this is the most commonly measured form of EMG in communications research. However, there also is a reason to measure activity over the *orbicularis occuli*, which draws up the outside corner of the eye during a smile. Unlike *zygomaticus major*, the *orbicularis occuli* muscle group is not under voluntary control. Thus, one can easily fake a polite or social smile by drawing up the corners of the mouth. Only genuine smiles draw up the corners of the eye.

In addition to emotional valence, facial EMG can be used to measure an aversive response known as the eyeblink startle reflex. Most readers have been startled at some point in their lives and are thus aware of the reflex; however, few probably have been aware of their own involuntary eyeblink when startled. The *orbicularis oculli* muscle group is involved in the eyeblink, and EMG sensors over this site can record the magnitude of the response. The magnitude of this startle reflex can index emotion or attention depending upon the nature of the stimulus and other procedural details. For a complex stimulus, such as a televised political advertisement, the startle reflex reliably indexes emotional responding. However, recent research has demonstrated that the emotional response appears to overwhelm the attentional response for complex stimuli, suggesting that the startle reflex may be better suited for measuring emotional responses to television (Bradley, Maxian, Wise, & Freeman, 2008).

TRACING THE SIGNAL

Proper collection and analysis of psychophysiological data requires a thorough understanding of underlying bodily processes and a firm grasp of procedural issues, from affixing electrodes on the surface of the skin to storing and analyzing the data via computer. First, the signal must be acquired from the skin by a transducer. Although clinical researchers often take physiological measurements below the surface of the skin with invasive procedures, this is uncommon in communication research. For most of the measures described here, the signal is transduced using a surface electrode sensor. These are relatively low-cost and can be purchased from a number of vendors, such as In Vivo Metric (see http://www.invivometric.com).

A word of caution about using electrodes attached to a human subject to collect data: because a small electrical current passes through the subject on the way to being amplified, there is a small risk of electrical shock. Training, education, and safety awareness are critical to the successful operation of any psychophysiology lab. While the electrical environment of the lab is at least as safe as a modern home or office and ordinarily poses little threat of shock, "there are important implications for the treatment of the subject, particularly concerning grounding" (Stern, Ray, & Quigley, 2001, p. 70). Erring on the side of safety is always preferable to taking any unnecessary risks. Many labs, for example, suspend data collection during active thunderstorms to eliminate any risk from the remote possibility of a direct lightning strike. Review of any proposed research by an Institutional Review Board and human subjects committee is, of course, necessary and desirable before any psychophysiological data recording can proceed. For primers on lab safety, consult authoritative references on psychophysiological research (e.g., Cacioppo, Tassinary, & Berntson, 2007; Stern, Ray, & Quigley, 2001) as well as professional associations with established reputations, such as the Society for Psychophysiological Research (see https://www.sprweb.org/teaching/index.cfm).

Typically, sensors are not applied directly to the skin but are instead affixed with a double-sided adhesive collar. The collar is then attached to the skin. These sensors are often coated with a thin layer of silver/silver-chloride, which is especially well suited to pick up biological potentials. A conductance medium is also needed when placing sensors in touch with the skin. An electrode paste or gel is commonly used to fill the cup-shaped sensors. The gel then actually touches the skin and passes the signal to the sensor surface. Adhesive collars and conductance gels are widely available from companies such as Discount Disposables (see http://www.discount disposables.com). Before applying the sensor, the subject's skin is typically abraded to ensure a proper signal. Electrode prep pads containing alcohol and pumice are often used for this. However, researchers are urged to consult safety guidelines (e.g., Greene, Turetsky, & Kohler, 2000) before abrading skin to prevent health risks.

After the signal is transduced, it must be amplified and filtered. Sensor wires affixed to the participant are usually plugged into an electrode cable, which in turn connects to a bioamplifier in a control room, technology cart, or flexible workspace. Physiological signals are then amplified and filtered for unwanted noise. A major problem with physiological data collection is 60 Hz interference, as every plugged-in electrical device in North America cycles at 60 Hz, or 60 cycles per second (in Europe devices cycle at 50 Hz). Although it is possible to shield experimental participants with a Faraday cage, this is expensive and inconvenient. Instead, most commercial bioamplifiers have a notch filter that automatically removes any signal frequencies near 60 Hz. Most filters also have a bandpass filter that allows the researcher to filter signals both below and above a specified frequency range. This allows researchers to collect—or pass—only those frequencies related to the signal of interest and filter out any other nuisance frequencies.

Other signal conditioning techniques are available but are beyond the scope of this chapter. Both EMG and EEG data typically receive additional treatment, and interested researchers are invited to consult physiological handbooks and research primers for further guidance in this area (see, for example, Cacioppo, Tassinary, & Berntson, 2007; Lang, 1994b; Potter & Bolls, in press; Stern, Ray, & Quigley, 2001). After amplification and filtering, the signal must then be converted from an analog (waveform) format into a discrete digital signal. This is accomplished by the aptly named analog-to-digital converter. These can be purchased as part of a system of amplifiers and filters or separately from vendors, such as Scientific Solutions (see http://www.labmaster.com). Finally, the data are routed from the analog-to-digital converter into a PC or Macintosh computer. A variety of software packages are available to process the data. Most users simply purchase the proprietary software offered by the bioamplifier manufacturer.

LOOKING AT THE BRAIN

Perusing recent issues of journals in psychology, cognitive neuroscience, and psychophysiology reveals the increasing attention that brain imaging is receiving across disciplines. Journals such as *Brain Research, NeuroImage, Psychophysiology*, and *Human Brain Mapping* routinely publish fMRI-based studies of neurological response, as do a growing number of other scholarly publications, including those addressing the emerging field of neuroeconomics. Discussions about neuroscience are also making their way into mainline political science journals (e.g., Hibbing & Smith, 2007; McDermott, 2004). Marco Iacoboni and colleagues at UCLA's Brain Research Institute have begun to publish brain imaging studies involving political stimuli (Kaplan, Freedman, & Iacoboni, 2007), as have David Amodio and colleagues at NYU (Amodio, Jost, Master, & Yee, 2007). Darren Schreiber of UC San Diego's Political Science department (who worked with Iacoboni at UCLA) moderates an informative listserv on neuropolitics that summarizes brain imaging research relevant to politics (see http://dss.ucsd.edu/mailman/listinfo/neuropolitics).

Although in some ways brain research represents the "state of the art" in scientific investigation, it is not yet entirely clear how imaging studies will improve our understanding of political communication beyond locating regions of the brain where political stimuli are most heavily processed. The oldest measure of brain activity is the electroencephalogram (EEG), which uses scalp recordings to capture the electrical activity of the brain. Neurons in the brain fire at reliable frequencies (e.g., alpha, beta, gamma), and the activity in each of these frequency ranges has been correlated with certain cognitive functions. For example, controlled attention to an external stimulus is associated with a decrease in alpha waves, a phenomenon known as alpha blocking. Despite the decades-old existence of EEG as a measure of brain activity, it is almost nonexistent in communication research (for a rare exception, see Reeves et al., 1985).

The application of brain imaging techniques, such as PET scanning and fMRI (functional magnetic resonance imaging), to political questions and evaluative processes has attracted growing interest in recent years (e.g., Amodio et al., 2007; Fowler & Schreiber, 2008; Kaplan, Freedman, & Iacoboni, 2007; Lieberman, Schreiber, & Ochsner, 2003; Schreiber et al., 2009). While these measures are helpful when employed in well-designed studies executed by properly trained scientists, much work in brain imaging remains speculative. Because imaging techniques produce colorful images that correspond to increased blood flood and oxygenation in certain brain regions, these studies are often reported in the popular press as definitive proof not just of brain activity but of specific voter tendencies and ideological differences (e.g., Begley, 2007; Iacoboni et al., 2007). Unfortunately, journalists—and sometimes researchers themselves—fail to communicate the nuances of interpreting brain imagining studies and make overreaching claims. At times these misrepresentations are severe enough to lead prominent scientists to publicly refute hastily drawn conclusions (e.g., Aron et al., 2007).

A key limitation of current imaging techniques is their inability to capture distributed processing. The human brain represents an amalgamation of billions of neurons and trillions of connections between neurons. Indeed, the brain's wiring is likely the most distributed network in the natural world. As a result, information processing is distributed across different regions of the brain rather than remaining confined to localized areas (as, for instance, the way food moves through the digestive system in distinct stages). Since brain imaging techniques concentrate on aggregate activity, imaging techniques largely miss distributed processing—an important and informative aspect of cognitive functioning—and may over-concentrate attention on a particular brain region. As Lieberman, Schreiber, and Ochsner (2003) rightly observe, "functional imaging—or any neuroscience technique, for that matter—should not be seen as providing a readout of what 'really' is going on in the mind" (p. 692). Instead, as with any psychophysiological measure, fMRI should be used in conjunction with converging evidence from other data sources and studies to identify recurring patterns of response.

> Consider the researcher who wants to identify the neural bases of political attitudes and finds that the amygdala is activated when participants express such attitudes. Does this mean that the amygdala is the political attitude center of the brain? This is clearly the wrong conclusion to reach, for at least two important reasons. First, cognitive neuroscience research has shown that any given brain structure may participate in many kinds of behavior . . . Second, even seemingly simple forms of behavior and cognition depend on networks of interacting brain structures. Just as there is no single language "organ" in the brain, neither will there be a single political organ in the brain. Instead, studies are likely to reveal distributed patterns of activation across networks of brain structures, each of which may carry out a computation integral to the behavioral whole. (Lieberman, Schreiber, & Ochsner, 2003, pp. 695–696)

Brain imagery is a compelling data collection technique that holds much promise for political communication research, but caution is urged in throwing participants into an expensive research "magnet" and showing them any and every stimulus available without the guidance of a solid theoretical rationale—and a thorough understanding of brain functioning. Indeed, research in this area is likely to be most productive when collaborations occur between political communication researchers and cognitive neuroscientists.

NEGATIVE ADVERTISING AND PSYCHOPHYSIOLOGY: A CASE STUDY

At the level of observable political behaviors, such as public affairs media use, voting in elections, or donating to worthy causes, self-report data often prove misleading and are subject to social desirability biasing where respondents over-report socially valued behaviors. Psychologically, however, self-report is one of the few windows we have into the workings of the human mind. Although conscious thought often operates in ignorance of a person's underlying motives, it is the only form of introspection available. In order to demonstrate the utility of psychophysiological measures as a reliable indicator of internal mental and emotional states, recorded signals should at a minimum be compared to self-reports.

To make a case for psychophysiology, we illustrate a situation where psychophysiological measures uncovered a difference that self-report was unable to find, and present physiological data that show no signs of statistical difference despite a large difference in self-reported responses. In each case, the self-report data point to social desirability biasing because they reflect what most researchers—and participants themselves—believe they should report *normatively*. Physiological data, on the other hand, reflect what should be happening *psychologically*. (The origins of psychophysiological measurement are rooted in lie detection, after all.) Taken together, these results suggest that psychophysiology can help reveal cases where social desirability leads to both Type I and Type II error, that is, finding significance where it doesn't exist and not finding it where it does.

In one of the first applications of psychophysiology to political communication, Lanzetta and colleagues at Dartmouth College investigated the basis of Ronald Reagan's political appeal using a combination of self-report and physiological measures (Lanzetta et al., 1985). Democrats, they found, evaluated televised appearances of Reagan negatively but their EMG responses indicated positive affect—something they were not willing to consciously admit. Democratic voters, after all, were not *supposed* to feel positively about images of the smiling Republican president, and this finding showed up in the self-report data. However, the human face is a potent vehicle for emotional communication and one of the best documented effects of facial-processing research is the tendency of observers to spontaneously mimic the expressive display of the person being observed, a response known as facial mimicry (see Laird et al., 1994).

In the Dartmouth studies, participants exhibited increased zygomatic muscle activation in response to the jovial, reassuring president, just at they had smiled back at other genuinely happy people their entire lives (whether Reagan was actually being sincere and not just performing the role of "happy warrior" is another matter entirely). Ideology and partisanship clouded these participants' self-reports, and the physiological data showed that conscious introspection obscured the true nature of the emotional response—positive feelings in the face of ideological disagreement.

The findings from this compelling study showed that physiological measures were capable of detecting a favorable emotional response toward a political figure when viewers were not willing (or able) to admit one. But do psychophysiological measures always tell a different story than participant self-reports, and will they fail to find significant differences when social desirability pressures create them in self-report data? To examine these questions, we performed a secondary analysis on data collected for another project, a study of the emotional, motivational, and memory effects of negative political advertising (Bradley, Angelini, & Lee, 2007).

For the study, we showed college students positive, moderate, and negative political advertisements for George W. Bush and Al Gore. The data were collected after the 2000 election but well before the 2004 primary season. Before physiological data were collected, participants indicated their affective orientations toward Bush and Gore on a pre-experiment questionnaire that included a 0–100 feeling thermometer. After each political advertisement, participants were asked to self-report their emotional responses consistent with the repeated measures design of the study. While participants viewed the ads, psychophysiological measurements were recorded.

The literature on emotion and psychophysiology suggests that unpleasant stimuli will evoke negative feelings and pleasant stimuli positive emotion. Consequently, personal attacks will make viewers respond negatively. Indeed, photographs of *physical* attacks elicit powerful negative responses (Bradley, Codispoti, Cuthbert, & Lang, 2001). Negative advertisements represent a type of verbal aggression and, although we would expect responses to be less intense than to depictions of physical aggression, "attack ads"—whether of the opponent's character, voting record, or policy stand—should nevertheless elicit negative psychological responses in viewers. Indeed, we have long known this to be the case from previous research (see Lang, 1988; Newhagen & Reeves, 1988) and the original study offered further confirmation (Bradley, Angelini, & Lee, 2007).

For the original analysis, the feeling thermometer data served merely as a type of control: negative ads elicited aversive responses in viewers, and this effect did not differ as a function of political attitudes. This is exactly as the psychophysiological literature would predict. Except in the case of neural damage or psychopathy, unpleasant stimuli elicit negative responses even when viewers are positively disposed to the source of the unpleasantness. However, the question remains whether this felt negativity manifests consciously. The physiological data showed no interaction between ad sponsorship and participants' political preferences. For both Bush supporters and Gore supporters, negative ads from one's *own* candidate produced as much aversive activation or negative emotional responding as the opponent's. But would viewers be willing to admit this at the level of self-report—or even have access to their own negative feelings?

To examine this question, we made fuller use of the feeling thermometer data. Not surprising for a college campus, the average rating was higher for Gore ($M = 59.06$) than for Bush ($M = 49.13$). A median split was performed for each candidate, and participants were considered to be Bush or Gore supporters if they were above the median for one candidate and below the median for the other. Participants who were above or below the median for *both* candidates were considered nonpartisan. Although these groupings were somewhat arbitrary, they resulted in approximately equal groups (59 nonpartisans, 62 Gore supporters, and 73 Bush supporters).

So did attack ads elicit an equal amount of negativity in all groups, as they did in the physiological analysis? The answer is no. Ads for preferred candidates did not result in as much self-reported negative emotion as ads sponsored by the opponent. Interestingly, this was not the case solely for negative ads. Participants responded to the opponent's ads, whether positive, negative, or moderate, more negatively across the board. Not only did the supported candidate's ads receive a positive reaction regardless of their emotional tone, even the opponent's positive ads elicited negative responses. Turning to the nonpartisans, however, there were no significant differences between ads for Gore or Bush. Also for nonpartisans, the negative ads for each candidate evoked more self-reported negativity than the moderate and positive ads. Nonpartisans, therefore, seemed to be responding more to the content of the ads themselves, whereas supporters seemed to report their feelings toward the candidates based on partisan leanings rather than ad content. Figure 27.1 summarizes this analysis.

Taken together, these analyses illustrate the capacity of psychophysiological measurement to further our understanding of political phenomena. Democratic identifiers in the original Dartmouth studies were unwilling to admit that Reagan made them feel positively, despite the

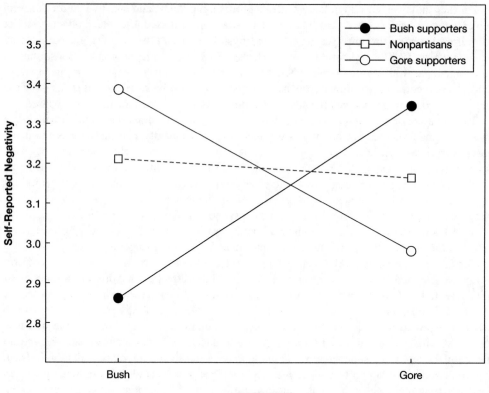

FIGURE 27.1 Effects of partisanship and ad sponsorship on self-reported negativity.

significant EMG ratings. Our secondary analysis of responses to political advertising showed no difference among political supporters in terms of facial muscle activation—positive and negative ads reliably evoked similar responses in all groups. However, in the case of self-report, cognitive consistency pressures made it difficult for partisans to admit that their preferred candidate evoked any negative feelings whatsoever. No matter what the actual emotional tone and content of the ad, viewers reported less negativity for ads by their preferred candidate and more in response to ads from the opponent. The exceptions were the nonpartisans who, without as much investment in their political commitments, appeared to be fair observers.

Overall, then, the psychophysiological data appear to have captured responses to the *messages themselves*, whereas participant self-report data seem to have captured responses to the *source* of the messages. Such self-report findings are not terribly interesting or insightful—they do not tell us why some Gore supporters, for instance, may have ended up voting for Bush in the 2000 election. But the physiology data point to a more nuanced explanation.

EQUIPPING THE PSYCHOPHYSIOLOGY LAB

Setting up a psychophysiology lab can range from a few thousand dollars to more than $3 million for an fMRI machine. Due to their cost, fMRI machines (known as research "magnets" by practitioners) are generally purchased by institutions rather than individual researchers or even departments, and access to them is generally funded through large research grants. Typically, a start-up budget of $30,000 or more can fund a reasonably well-equipped psychophysiology lab, covering the cost of the physiological recording equipment, bioamplifiers, filters, personal computers, and software. Part of the budget may also include a widescreen television for viewing stimuli and a comfortable chair for subjects to sit in while participating in experimental studies.

Assuming some access to research space, a variety of configurations are available. Perhaps the most affordable units on the market are those sold by BIOPAC (see http://www.biopac.com), which offers a starter system for well under $5,000. This system typically can collect two channels of data and includes bioamplifiers, filters, and electrode cables. Many studies designed to measure heart rate and skin conductance could operate with the starter system and a Windows or Macintosh computer. One or both of the channels also could be used to collect EMG data. For researchers looking for an entry-level system, BIOPAC is probably a good choice. BIOPAC also offers far more complex—and expensive—systems for researchers looking to collect heart rate, skin conductance, EMG, and EEG data.

More elaborate set-ups may require more control and flexibility than the BIOPAC system easily allows. Psychophysiology labs at several research universities, including Indiana, Ohio State, Alabama, Washington State, Missouri, and Texas Tech use equipment from Coulbourn Instruments (see http://www.coulbourn.com). Although custom estimates are generated for each potential client on a case-by-case basis, multiple-channel Coulbourn systems have recently ranged in price from $10,000 to $15,000. However, a system designed solely to collect only heart rate and skin conductance data would be much cheaper. Coulbourn also offers a noise generator that creates the acoustic startle probe for startle reflex studies. Of course, for multiple units designed to collect data from multiple subjects simultaneously, the cost rises accordingly.

The cost also rapidly increases if a research team desires a more complex apparatus, such as a dense array of EEG sensors (64, 128, or 256 sensors covering the scalp) for collecting brain wave data. These systems can easily cost more than $100,000. Electrical Geodesics (see http://www.egi.com) offers such systems for both the PC and Macintosh platforms. These systems typically are not for the start-up researcher. Instead, investigators using these types of systems typically have graduate or post-doctoral experience in a lab using a dense array EEG unit. Even so, novice psychophysiologists should not shy away from such systems if their research questions require access to brain wave data and they are able to secure adequate funding. Most companies provide some training, and Electrical Geodesics offers an annual summer institute to familiarize research clients with EEG and ERP methodology.

DISCUSSION

As reviewed briefly in this chapter, psychophysiology has much to offer the field of political communication research. In addition to measuring direct response to media content or political stimuli, as opposed to participants' after-the-fact assessments of emotional response or cognitive effort, physiological recording techniques enable researchers to more fully consider the complete person. Whereas paper and pencil questionnaires tap psychological responses within the cognitive and rational bands of awareness (cf. Newell, 1990), psychophysiology operates within both of these levels *and* captures what happens at the biological band of experience beginning within tens of milliseconds upon exposure. What happens cognitively and emotionally between, say, 50 and 500 milliseconds (that is, between .05 and .5 seconds) can be quite consequential—but invisible to conventional measurement techniques and, for the most part, out of the realm of conscious awareness, and therefore self-report.

As Marcus and colleagues have noted in their work on the affective intelligence model, the temporal dimension of response is important to consider in studying political phenomena. Affective processes arise very early as new information and sensory streams reach the brain, cycle far more rapidly and frequently than consciousness can manage, and are influential in shaping behavior and many aspects of conscious thought and action, including attention and modes of decision making (Marcus, Neuman, & MacKuen, 2000). Rather than functioning as a separate system, affect works *in conjunction* with cognition by shaping consciousness and regulating when we rely on automatic systems to govern our evaluations and behavior (see Bargh & Chartrand, 1999) towards, among other things, developments in the political landscape.

Sampled at a rate of 20 times per second or more, psychophysiological measurement offers precision data. Yet it is also quite flexible and widely applicable to a range of different research conditions. Physiological measures are capable of assessing such diverse outcomes as attention, arousal, emotional response, and cognitive effort allocated to a particular stimulus—or segment within a media message. Moveover, they can be applied across a broad array of political communication content domains, including news reports, political advertisements, televised political debates, clips of nonverbal leader displays, and even audio recordings of political speeches or statements. Because they are capable of capturing participant responses at a level below conscious awareness, physiological measures are particularly well-suited for studies testing viewer reactions to nonverbal communication that have influence but often go unrecognized by members of the news audience and research community alike (see Bucy, 2010; Stewart, Salter, & Mehu, Chapter 10, this volume). Having access to such findings, and previously unobserved citizen responses, could shed considerable new light on political communication processes and effects.

Despite a 25-year history, the application of psychophysiology remains underutilized in political communication and related fields like political psychology. Since many of the field's major findings and theories are based on self-report measures (whether from surveys, experiments, or even focus groups) that are subject to social desirability biasing and cognitive consistency pressures, it may be worth revisiting some core concepts to assess how well they stand up to psychophysiological validation. Not every area of research will be amenable to this kind of testing, but examining such perennial topics as framing, priming, and political knowledge from a visual perspective could very well lend itself to physiological investigation. Physiology may be employed not just to challenge established theories but to extend conceptual understandings beyond conclusions dependent on self-awareness. Research into the psychological underpinnings of emotion suggests, for instance, that negative compelling images have lasting effects, cognitively engaging audiences and impacting memory in ways in which viewers are not always consciously aware. Television messages seem to reflexively activate underlying motivational systems associated with approach and avoidance and these emotional systems are involved in the allocation of cognitive resources designed to contend with both opportunities and threats (Hutchinson & Bradley, 2009).

These and similar findings from studies of viewer information processing could find interesting application to political advertising, televised leader reactions to difficult or crisis situations, or any number of topics that are an enduring part of the political communication landscape.

REFERENCES

Allen, J. J. B., Chambers, A. S., & Towers, D. N. (2007). The many metrics of cardiac chronotropy: A pragmatic primer and a brief comparison of metrics. *Biological Psychology, 74*, 243–262.

Amodio, D. M., Jost, J. T., Master, S. L., & Yee, C. M. (2007). Neurocognitive correlates of liberalism and conservatism. *Nature Neuroscience, 10*(10), 1246–1247.

Aron, A., Badre, D., Brett, M., Cacioppo, J. T., Chambers, C., Cools, R., et al. (2007, November 14). Letter: Politics and the brain. *New York Times*.

Bargh, J. A., & Chartrand, T. L. (1999). The unbearable automaticity of being. *American Psychologist, 54*(7), 462–479.

Barry, A. M. (2005). Perception theory. In K. Smith, S. Moriarty, G. Barbatsis, & K. Kenney (Eds.), *Handbook of visual communication* (pp. 45–62). Mahwah, NJ: Lawrence Erlbaum.

Begley, S. (2007, September 9). Red brain, blue brain: Politics and gray matter. Lab Notes blog. *Newsweek* online. Retrieved from http://blog.newsweek.com/blogs/labnotes/archive/2007/09/09/red-brain-blue-brain-politics-and-gray-matter.aspx.

Bradley, M. M., Codispoti, M., Cuthbert, B. N., & Lang, P. J. (2001). Emotion and motivation I: Defensive and appetitive reactions in picture processing. *Emotion, 1*, 276–298.

Bradley, S. D., Angelini, J. R., & Lee, S. (2007). Psychophysiological and memory effects of negative political ads: Aversive, arousing, and well-remembered. *Journal of Advertising, 36*(4), 115–127.

Bradley, S. D., Maxian, W., Wise, W. T., & Freeman, J. D. (2008). Emotion trumps attention: Using prepulse startle probe methodology to assess cognitive processing of television. *Communication Methods and Measures, 2*(4), 313–322.

Bucy, E. P. (2010). Nonverbal communication, emotion, and political evaluation. In E. Konijn, K. Koveling, & C. von Scheve (Eds.), *Handbook of emotions and mass media* (pp. 195–220). New York: Routledge.

Bucy, E. P., & Bradley, S. D. (2004). Presidential expression and viewer emotion: Counterempathic responses to televised leader displays. *Social Science Information, 43*, 59–94.

Cacioppo, J. T., & Tassinary, L. G. (1990). Inferring psychological significance from physiological signals. *American Psychologist, 45*(1), 16–28.

Cacioppo, J. T., Tassinary, L. G., & Berntson, G. G. (Eds.) (2007). *Handbook of psychophysiology* (3rd ed.). New York: Cambridge University Press.

Damasio, A. R. (1994). *Descartes' error: Emotion, reason and the human brain*. New York: G. P. Putnam's Sons.

Fowler, J. H., & Schreiber, D. (2008, November 7). Biology, politics, and the emerging science of human nature. *Science, 322*, 912–914.

Gazzaniga, M. S. (1998). *The mind's past*. Berkeley: University of California Press.

Gray, J. A. (1987). *The psychology of fear and stress* (2nd ed.). Cambridge: Cambridge University Press.

Greene, W. A., Turetsky, B., & Kohler, C. (2000). General laboratory safety. In J. T. Cacioppo, L. G. Tassinary, & G. G. Berntson (Eds.), *Handbook of psychophysiology* (2nd ed., pp. 951–977). Cambridge: Cambridge University Press.

Hibbing, J. R., & Smith, K. B. (2007). The biology of political behavior: An introduction. *The Annals of the American Academy of Political and Social Science, 614*, 6–14.

Hutchinson, D., & Bradley, S. D. (2009). Memory for images intense enough to draw an administration's attention: Television and the "war on terror." *Politics and the Life Sciences, 28*(1), 31–47.

Iacoboni, M., Freedman, J., Kaplan, J., Jamieson, K. H., Freedman, T., Knapp, B., et al. (2007, November 11). This is your brain on politics. *New York Times*.

Kaplan, J. T., Freedman, J., & Iacoboni, M. (2007). Us versus them: Political attitudes and party affiliation influence neural response to faces of presidential candidates. *Neuropsychologia, 45*, 55–64.

Laird, I. D., Alibozak, T., Davainis, D., Deignan, K., Fontanella, K., Hong, I., Levy, I., & Pacheco, C. (1994). Individual differences in the effects of spontaneous mimicry on emotional contagion. *Motivation and Emotion, 18*, 231–247.

Lang, A. N. (1988). Emotion, formal features, and memory for televised political advertisements. In F. Biocca (Ed.), *Television and political advertising, Vol. 1: Psychological processes* (pp. 221–243). Hillsdale, NJ: Lawrence Erlbaum.

Lang, A. N. (1994a). What can the heart tell us about thinking? In A. N. Lang (Ed.), *Measuring psychological responses to media messages* (pp. 99–111). Hillsdale, NJ: Lawrence Erlbaum.

Lang, A. N. (Ed.) (1994b). *Measuring psychological responses to media messages*. Hillsdale, NJ: Lawrence Erlbaum.

Lanzetta, J. T., Sullivan, D. G., Masters, R. D., McHugo, G. J. (1985). Emotional and cognitive responses to televised images of political leaders. In S. Kraus & R. M. Perloff (Eds.), *Mass media and political thought: An information-processing approach* (pp. 85–116). Beverly Hills: Sage.

LeDoux, J. (1996). *The emotional brain: The mysterious underpinnings of emotional life*. New York: Simon & Schuster.

Libet, B., Pearl, D. K., Morledge, D., Gleason, C. A., Morledge, Y., & Barbaro, N. (1991). Control of the transition from sensory detection to sensory awareness in man by the duration of a thalamic stimulus. *Brain, 114*, 1731–1757.

Lieberman, M. D., Schreiber, D., & Ochsner, K. N. (2003). Is political cognition like riding a bicycle? How cognitive neuroscience can inform research on political thinking. *Political Psychology, 24*(4), 681–704.

Marcus, G. E., Neuman, W. R., & MacKuen, M. (2000). *Affective intelligence and political judgment*. Chicago: University of Chicago Press.

McDermott, R. (2004). The feeling of rationality: The meaning of neuroscientific advances for political science. *Perspectives on Politics, 2*(4), 691–706.

Mishkin, M., & Appenzeller, T. (1987). The anatomy of memory. *Scientific American, 256*, 80–89.

Mutz, D. C. (2007). Effects of "in-your-face" television discourse on perceptions of a legitimate opposition. *American Political Science Review, 101*, 621–635.

Mutz, D. C., & Reeves, B. (2005). The new videomalaise: Effects of televised incivility on political trust. *American Political Science Review, 99*, 1–14.

Newell, A. (1990). *Unified theories of cognition*. Cambridge, MA: Harvard University Press.

Newhagen, J. E. (2004). Interactivity, dynamic symbol processing, and the emergence of content in human communication. *The Information Society, 20*, 395–400.

Newhagen, J. E., & Reeves, B. (1988). Emotion and memory responses for negative political advertising: A study of television commercials used in the 1988 presidential election. In F. Biocca (Ed.), *Television and political advertising, vol. 1: Psychological processes* (pp. 197–220). Hillsdale, NJ: Lawrence Erlbaum.

Potter, R. F. & Bolls, P. D. (in press). *Psychophysiological measures and meaning: Cognitive and emotional processing of media*. New York: Routledge.

Ravaja, N. (2004). Contributions of psychophysiology to media research: Review and recommendations. *Media Psychology, 6*, 193–235.

Reeves, B., Thorson, E., Rothschild, M., McDonald, D., Hirsch, J., & Goldstein, R. (1985). Attention to television: Intrastimulus effects of movement and scene changes on alpha variation over time. *International Journal of Neuroscience, 25*, 241–255.

Schreiber, D. M., Simmons, A. N., Dawes, C. T., Flagan, T., Fowler, J. H., & Paulus, M. P. (2009, September). *Red brain, blue brain: Evaluative processes differ in Democrats and Republicans*. Paper presented to the annual meeting of the American Political Science Association, Toronto, Canada.

Stern, R. M., Ray, W. J., & Quigley, K. S. (2001). *Psychophysiological recording* (2nd ed.). New York: Oxford University Press.

Watanabe, S., Kakigi, R., Koyama, S., & Kirino, E. (1999). Human face perception traced by magneto- and electro-encephalography. *Cognitive Brain Research, 8*(2), 125–142.

CONCLUSION

28

Looking Back and Looking Forward

Observations on the Role of Research Methods in the Rapidly Evolving Field of Political Communication

Gerald M. Kosicki
School of Communication
The Ohio State University

Douglas M. McLeod
School of Journalism and Mass Communication
University of Wisconsin–Madison

Jack M. McLeod
School of Journalism and Mass Communication
University of Wisconsin–Madison

We focus on the methods of political communication research to understand their role in advancing theory and knowledge. We address the adequacy and inadequacies of current methodological practices and the extent to which they are able to capture current developments in political communication. Though many of our comments apply to communication research in general, we embed our discussion in the context of political communication. In addition to the unique aspects imposed by this context detailed below, political communication provides a topic domain in which research questions raise matters of real-world significance and broad macro-social implications. Indeed, political communication, both mass and interpersonal, is at the very heart of fundamental democratic processes. Thus, research questions and the methods used to answer them play important roles in understanding how our political system works, as well as in revealing where it is broken.

There are a number of important reasons for focusing attention on the role of methods in research. Choices regarding methods should be made with regard to the nature of the research questions. It is important to choose the right tools for the job. Choices regarding methods also have implications for what the answers to these questions are likely to be. Different tools will produce different outcomes. In political communication research, there are several reasons why the implications of such choices are likely to be particularly acute. The questions that political communication researchers deal with have consequences that may affect leadership, policies, and democratic processes involving the lives of hundreds of millions of people. They inherently involve not just empirical questions about *what is*, but also normative questions about *what ought to be*. Moreover, political processes examined by political communication researchers tend to be publicly visible and intuitively meaningful to the media. This means that the products of political communication research are likely to have broad exposure and incur additional scrutiny. All of this puts extra pressure on producing high-integrity research that tackles meaningful questions. Moreover, it places an additional burden on researchers to make the answers to such research questions accessible to policymakers, media, and the public, which may become increasingly difficult as researchers develop more advanced, technically sophisticated methods.

The importance of political communication research has been underscored by growing threats to the quality of mass-mediated political information, as well as a fundamental transformation of communication media as a result of changes in the technological infrastructure. While the need for public information is universally regarded as crucial to democratic processes in theory, it is not always regarded as such in practice. Not only are news media often castigated by various political interests, they suffer from questions about their economic viability in a media environment that emphasizes profitability, not the needs of citizens and communities. Out of concern for profit, news media tend to popularize and trivialize the news in favor of the mass appeal of infotainment. Newspapers, the traditional standard bearer of political information, are facing severe challenges, as most local newspapers are on life-support systems. Some have shut down completely. Those that are still publishing have cut back on staff and are replacing experienced journalists with younger, less expensive workers. These trends curtail the media's ability to cover news adequately and thereby weaken the content available to audiences. Local TV news also faces dwindling resources. As a result, high-quality information regarding the events and issues that pertain to local communities is becoming a scarce resource. It is imperative that researchers scrutinize such change and document what is being lost in the process. At the same time, technological innovations in the media infrastructure offer new information conduits and opportunities for public engagement. These are just some of the fundamental changes that are accentuating the significance of political communication research at the end of the first decade of the twenty-first century.

The potential of mass communication research to make such important contributions has been increased by significant innovations in research methods and analysis procedures. One way to get a sense of how far the field of political communication has come in terms of methodological practices is to consider what this book might have looked like had it been written thirty-five years ago. Arguably, the contemporary political communication field began with the publication of Chaffee's (1975) *Political Communication: Issues and Strategies for Research.* To begin with, as we have detailed above, the landscape of political communication and the nature of political communication research have changed markedly. The expanding boundaries of political communication, along with technological and methodological advancements, have fostered growth in long-established methods and the development of new modes of inquiry.

Of course, thirty-five years ago such a book would have included chapters on surveys, experiments, and content analyses as the most prominent modes of communication inquiry. However, the content of these chapters would be quite different. In terms of survey research, serious interviews were done in person with an interviewer going to a respondent's house. Panel designs were uncommon; rolling cross-sectional surveys were not practiced; and online surveys didn't exist. The chapters on experimental methodology would have been different too. Again, online experiments didn't exist, and response latency measures were not commonly practiced in political communication research. Though one-shot experiments were, and still are, the norm today, few researchers were discussing, much less practicing, long-term experimental designs. Experiments in the earlier era tended to concentrate on end-state behaviors and did not include processes in between. Content analysis was only beginning to make the move from the realm of text into that of visuals. Framing analysis had yet to make the significant leap from qualitative textual analysis to systematic content analysis. Computers occupied large rooms in far-away buildings, not desktops. Computer-assisted content analysis was just beginning.

Not only would the chapters for the most common modes of inquiry be different thirty-five years ago, many of the other chapters of this book pertaining to other modes of inquiry would not have existed at all. Meta-analysis was not practiced as a systematic approach to synthesizing literature. Discourse analysis was only beginning to make its mark on political communication research. Focus group techniques were only practiced in applied political communication research. Rhetorical analyses operated in the separate disciplinary universe of rhetoric. Deliberation, as the focus of political communication research, and the methods used to study it, had yet to appear on the scene. Network analysis had yet to migrate from the discipline of sociology to the context of political communication research. This would have been prior to the developments in electronic communication technology (e.g., the Internet, social networking Web sites, user-created content) that have underscored the importance of the expanding communication networks to contemporary political processes. European and American political communication scholars were only beginning to connect and the dialogue on comparative research was scarce. Statistical techniques such as SEM, HLM, and time-series analysis were still on the horizon. Moreover, researchers were only beginning to consider the influence of mediating and moderating variables, and few were performing the type of data analyses that reveal their influence. Physiological measurement was just starting to make its way into communication research, largely in the contexts of media violence and pornography research. Indeed, this book would have been very different if written thirty-five years ago.

The recent growth in research technology and methods offers considerable reason for optimism regarding the potential contributions of political communication research. However, to go forward blindly, without considering key questions regarding the role of methods, their potential and pitfalls, is not wise. This chapter considers a number of interrelated issues to assess the role that research methods play in the development of theory and knowledge of political communication processes. We begin by examining the synergistic relationship between theory and research as it applies to communication research in general. We expand this discussion by considering the context of political communication as it provides unique opportunities and challenges for researchers in this area. We also consider the institutional constraints that impinge upon the practice of communication research. Next, we examine current research practices in political communication research, pointing out the vast change in the research landscape that has occurred over the past thirty-five years, and then discuss some of the issues that are likely to drive change in the near and long-term future of political communication research. We then identify some of the pitfalls that continue to hamper research in this field. Finally, we identify promising new avenues for future research.

SYNERGY OF THEORY AND METHOD

The primary goal of social scientific inquiry is to create theories that explain how things work in the social world. Understanding how things work has a variety of practical benefits including being able to make predictions of future outcomes and being able to identify and rectify problems when things are not working up to expectations. Understanding our world also suggests that we can improve the conditions of human existence. Our ability to accomplish these goals is predicated on developing and improving our theoretical explanations by subjecting them to empirical testing. The empirical testing of scientific explanations is where theory and method work hand in hand toward the advancement of science.

In the logic of science (see McLeod & Tichenor, 2001), all theoretical explanations are considered tentative. They are the best fitting explanations for empirical observations at a given point in time. They must be continually put to the test by making new observations, which may lead to modifications, extensions, or even outright rejections of existing theory when a competing theory provides a more adequate and parsimonious account of such observations. One important process in the evolution of theoretical explanations is the derivation of hypotheses for empirical testing. Putting theoretically derived hypotheses to the test is where methods come into play. The availability of research methods that are capable of validly testing hypotheses is crucial to the advancement of scientific knowledge.

To adequately test theoretical explanations, methods must provide systematic and objective procedures for making observations and analyzing results. Researchers must strive to identify and eliminate potential sources of bias that would compromise the ability to isolate the relationships specified in the hypotheses in question. They must also accept observations that challenge or even falsify a proposed explanation. One of the most exciting occurrences in research is when observations defy conventional wisdom, motivating the search for new and better explanations. This highlights an important principle of scientific research: Explanations are never proven, though they may be falsified when they don't fit with existing observations.

Theoretical explanations involve establishing causal relationships between variables. Here, scientific methods are crucial in evaluating the three conditions of causality (Cook & Campbell, 1979). Toward that end, researchers must apply methods that permit (1) the observation of covariational relationships between the concepts involved in the explanation; (2) the establishment of time-order in such relationships such that the presumed cause precedes the presumed effect; and (3) the investigation of the possibility that the relationship in question is not the product of some other variable or set of variables. To accomplish this, researchers must often employ advanced multivariate techniques (e.g., structural equation modeling) and multi-observation research designs (e.g., panel surveys) that can account for the impact of antecedent variables external to the relationship that might contribute to the appearance of spurious relationships. Similarly, such methods can reveal the existence of suppressor variables that mask our ability to observe such relationships. They may also help to unveil more complex, multivariate relationships that include the influence of mediating and moderating factors that ultimately contribute to more sophisticated theoretical explanations.

A rigorous approach to the application of research methods is important in a number of respects. The detailed specification of research procedures is an important step in the process of peer review. By laying bare the methodological procedures used for inquiry, researchers can facilitate the peer review process, which is a necessary safeguard against bias and logical flaws that inhibit the valid testing of theory. Such practices also enable the important process of replication, by which other researchers can make additional observations. Replication is important to establishing the scope and vigor of a scientific explanation. An additional benefit of detailed specification of procedures is that it contributes to the standardization of methodological practices that are important to consistent measurement. Quality measurement is fundamental for programmatic inquiry and the accumulation of knowledge.

The development of rigorous, sophisticated methods is essential to the evolution of more elaborate and powerful explanations that produce a more comprehensive understanding of the

social world. Concurrently, the development of more complex theories may motivate developments of new, more sophisticated methods and techniques. The progress of theory and research
does truly reflect their mutually synergistic nature. This point about the reciprocal relationship
between theory and data has been made regularly over the years. Mills (1959) referred famously
to the notion of "crafting theories." By this he meant the development of research programs
simultaneously improving the fit between theory and methods. As described, one fits theory to the
data as produced using certain methods. Methods are refined to illuminate certain theoretical
issues, and so on (for other important statements of this issue, see Hage, 1972; King, Keohane, &
Verba, 1994; McLeod & Pan, 2005; Reynolds, 1971; Stinchcombe, 2005).

Of course, there are some drawbacks to systematic inquiry. For example, the standardization
of method can be dysfunctional if the approach is inherently flawed or limited. Theory can be
hampered by concepts that are poorly defined, labeled, or measured, flaws which are compounded
when those practices are replicated by standardization or the desire to make research comparable.
Perhaps even more troubling is the situation in which the nature of inquiry is circumscribed by
the demands of systematic inquiry. The fact is, some questions lend themselves to scientific
investigation more readily than others. For example, the concept of news bias, which is quite
prevalent in discussions in academic, political, and popular circles, is notoriously difficult to
operationalize systematically. It is important to recognize that difficulty of measurement is not the
same as saying it is not a relevant or useful concept for constructing explanations. But it does
mean that researchers may shy away from it because of its problematic operationalization and
inherently normative nature. Techniques long associated with evaluation research might be most
appropriately adapted for this purpose.

In political communication, there may be other hurdles beyond those posed by constructing
adequate conceptual and operational definitions that hinder scientific inquiry. Some important
political processes may be difficult to study due to limitations imposed by institutional review
boards charged with protecting human subjects (e.g., obedience to authority) or by the challenges
of obtaining data (e.g., the viral flow of rumor and innuendo about political candidates spread
person to person over the Internet during a political campaign, which may be difficult to obtain,
as would evidence of its impact).

To keep political communication research relevant, researchers must continually strive
toward theoretical and methodological advances. This need is underscored by the importance of
keeping up with the dizzying pace of "real world" changes in media economics and communication technologies (e.g., the disintegration of newspapers and the growth of the Internet),
government and political strategies (e.g., the sophistication of disinformation and propagation of
political and economic myths), and structural changes in societies, communities, and families.

Political communication researchers must ask whether our current methods and practices are
capable of capturing the impact of new media and the diversification of our information landscape,
which is fostering the growing sophistication of political communication messages. The influence
of political communication is no longer simply about the influence of political messages, crafted
by elite power holders and disseminated through traditional mass media and mainstream news
organizations. It includes communication that takes place through a wide variety of mass and
interpersonal channels (and channels that represent hybrids thereof). It includes a diverse array of
activities that might be classified as canvassing, organizing, talking, and deliberating. It includes
the activities of organizations such as AmericaSpeaks.org, and MoveOn.org. It includes online
and in-person forums such as 21st Century Town Meetings and other variations on deliberative
polling. It includes viral marketing and stealth campaigns. It includes activities that take place in
the workplace, churches, online chat rooms, and blogosphere. We could certainly go on, but
suffice it to say that new political communication innovations continually emerge.

To keep up with change, researchers must keep several principles in mind. Theoretical questions must match pragmatic realities. Methods must be suited to answering theoretical questions and must provide a valid test of existing explanations. Methods must be selected for their ability to answer the research questions at hand, not by the pull of methodological fetishism. Methods must be capable of communicating answers to relevant audiences, be those academic, policy stakeholders, or members of the public. Researchers must be vigilant and innovative if political communication research is going to play a relevant, if not leading, role in these political processes. Can research keep up with the rapid innovations in real-world practices? Can we even keep up with the research that is being done by private and political interests, whose research is not only better funded, but whose results are proprietary? The answers to these questions will determine the place of political communication in society for the coming decades.

THE CONTEXT OF POLITICAL COMMUNICATION

Although there is an emerging perspective in communication that development of theory is an end in itself and that theory should transcend topical areas of application, there are unique aspects of the political communication terrain that need to be considered if research is to have social significance and relevance in the contemporary world of politics and policy. The institutions that provide political information (i.e., news organizations) are businesses that seek profits, but the quality of the information they provide is important for the smooth functioning of democratic institutions. As much recent, careful scholarship in history makes clear, representative democracy and democratic institutions and norms did not evolve until systems of literacy, public discussion, and popular communication developed with sufficient rigor to support such a role by the people (e.g., Knights, 1994; Raymond, 1996; Starr, 2004; Zaret, 2000). Media provide certain materials from which people learn about the world outside their own experiences, form impressions of the relative importance of various topics, make judgments about candidates and issues, and form opinions about the issues of the day. Such expectations have fostered the creation of a vast normative literature on media goals and performance.

Normative theories can offer useful suggestions for research programs into topics about the quality of public communication and what the public thinks, feels, and learns about political life as a result of media experiences. This has become particularly important in recent years as campaigns have grown increasingly contentious and controversial. Campaign consultants have become more adept at manipulating news frames and more skillful at obfuscating the truth and distorting reality. This has led observers to raise significant questions of fairness, accuracy, quality, and representativeness that strike at the heart of the political system in that the quality of democratic decision making depends to a large degree on the amount and type of information that voters use in learning about the choices and deciding their own preferences. Given the importance of such topics, it is surprising that relatively few studies attempt to deal explicitly with the normative values that are applied to voting decisions (e.g., Lau & Redlawsk, 2006).

In the United States, traditional news media, particularly newspapers, were organized around local communities and metropolitan areas, leading to a less centralized media system than many other nations. Various macroeconomic trends, including the rise of the Internet, have begun to threaten the economic viability of these local news media, and early in 2009 the nation experienced the failure of several large newspaper firms. Others adopted online-only business models, dropping their printed versions. The information environment of local communities has suffered. Advertising revenue has shifted to Google and other news aggregators and away from organizations that actually produce the news (Edmonds, 2009). Newspapers rely on subscription and single-copy sales for revenue, which is undercut by content available free online. Newspaper advertising revenue has also declined in response to the emergence of such websites as Craigslist.com (for classified advertising), Monster.com (for career ads), and numerous others for real estate and automobiles. Similar issues affect local television stations, resulting in dramatic cuts in resources available to local television news operations. There is scholarly disagreement about attributing the problems of newspapers to the Internet per se. For example, Meyer (2004) acknowledges online competition but argues that newspapers have been declining for decades and need to take steps to increase their social influence and overall quality relative to other competitors. Whatever the reasons for newspaper decline, few viable online competitors have surfaced in the realm of local news. These trends pose long-term challenges to American democratic traditions since they undercut the information base that citizens use to keep abreast of developments and interact with their neighbors and others toward common political goals. This suggests the need for political communication researchers to focus on subnational levels such as regions, states, and communities.

Campaign Contexts

Political campaigns at the national level are highly visible and important contexts for political communication research. To some extent, political communication may be over-identified with campaign studies to the point that many people think the two are synonymous terms. This reflects a very narrow view of the political process. Campaigns are also unique to times and places and may be over-studied in terms of their ability to provide platforms upon which to build general theories of political communication. The focus on campaign coverage may also downplay the important role of political communication in day-to-day governance.

Non-campaign Contexts

The more normal media coverage of politics between election campaigns may actually have more to do with what most people think and believe about politics than campaign coverage. Media generally cover the activities of government officials outside election contexts, along with routine coverage of a variety of issues. Matters such as the economy, crime, poverty, racial tensions, and the general state of social equality are matters that social scientists write about. Many of these reports become the basis of news reporting and commentary in the printed and televised media. In recent years, media competition and declining standards have led to the coverage of politics as a "freak show" (Halperin & Harris, 2006). Such coverage tends to focus on party-based conflict and negativity, often featuring personal and cultural attacks rather than policy differences. The freak show generally undervalues goals of helping citizens make informed judgments on policy issues and encourages identity politics grounded in cultural issues. The role of audiences in such a news system is that of consumers satisfying preferences for interesting bits of entertainment, not citizens, who require very different kinds of information about a wider range of topics than might be of interest to people in their role as consumers.

Governance and Communication

Elections are often won by candidates who are adept at mastering the art and science of campaigns. Such communication talents and tools are now increasingly being adapted to problems of governance, leading to the notion of governance as a type of "permanent campaign" in which governments assume responsibility for waging political-style campaigns to pass or rebuff certain legislation, or to build support for important government policies or appointments. The idea of governance as a permanent campaign also suggests that the process of governing has imported the tools and norms of campaigns, along with the focus on polling, use of advertisements and publicity tours desiqred to sell policies to the public. Travel exposes the campaign to local media markets in hopes of attracting free media exposure both nationally and locally. Such trends emphasize the need for research in times when elections are not the focus.

During the inter-election periods, routine news coverage informs popular understanding of the key issues facing the nation and the world. News workers choose to cover stories that fit their definitions of news and fulfill other requirements of their medium. Television often is drawn to stories that have visual elements that are believed to make for compelling viewing. Some narratives are important but are difficult to tell in short sound bites and brief news stories. This includes important trend stories such as the increasing disparity of income between the haves and have-nots, tax policy, or the growing indebtedness of families, businesses, and other institutions. These important, but difficult-to-tell, stories typically do not get much attention outside selected high-quality media until they become part of a major crisis in which action cannot be postponed (e.g., Graetz & Shapiro, 2005; Jones & Williams, 2008; Klein, 2008). Crises are usually not the best venues for extended democratic deliberation of alternative solutions.

The problems of domestic politics are not the only ones that tend to be ignored. International news is increasingly given short-shrift due to the expenses of maintaining news bureaus around the world. Moreover, when international news is reported, it is typically covered from an American point of view with an eye toward how it affects U.S. domestic political dramas. In an increasingly interconnected and interdependent world, such problems regarding international news are discordant notes.

Changes in political parties are also making the system more open and less predictable. When candidates raise their own campaign funds, they may become relatively independent of party control. Particularly in certain regions of the country, extremism may be facilitated when congressional districts are gerrymandered to produce safe seats such that candidates don't fear opposition parties. In fact, in many congressional districts the gravest threat to an incumbent is often fear of being challenged by a more extreme member of his or her own party.

Politicians operate in an environment of growing sophistication and complexity. As a result, political communication of all kinds and at all levels is growing more sophisticated. This means, among other things, a more central role for political communication research in guiding message development, and finding and targeting voters. Campaign officials understand the importance of location, whether it relates to certain battleground states, key swing districts of competitive states, or the types of neighborhoods where supporters are likely to be found.

Changing Communication Technology

Politics is carried out today in a multimedia environment that operates 24/7 and includes online and traditional media supplemented by entertainment shows as well as more typical venues such as news and political talk programs. Traditional media remain powerful and continue to have large audiences, but patterns of use suggest that national network news, newspapers, and other traditional news venues are heavily weighted toward older citizens. Younger voters are more likely to be reached online and through various entertainment venues.

The Obama campaign of 2008 will be studied by political communication scholars for years to come due to its ability to use the Internet in flexible ways for fundraising, organizing locating supporters, and communicating directly to voters and supporters through email, embedded videos, and text messaging, among other communication technologies. A key feature of the Obama campaign's communication efforts was investment in an open, easy-to-use platform that supporters could add to as they wanted. Popular artists and entertainers created materials that were sold or shared widely online at sites such as www.dipdive.com and YouTube.

Other new forms of communication are proliferating and exerting their influence on the political world. Some blogs are gaining large followings, particularly among politically partisan and interested individuals. The Internet does lower the barrier to publishing, however, and many talented people are able to comment, collate, and report on news in ways they were not able to before. Among blogs that became well known during the 2008 election was FiveThirtyEight.com, a comprehensive site for election-related polling that gained notice for its very accurate final prediction of the popular vote in the election using weighted averages of national polling data.

Various other forms of news and information are evolving, some increasingly populated by newly unemployed professional journalists. Popular forms of online communication include the so-called "crowd-sourced" wiki outlets written by volunteers (Howe, 2008). These range in scope from international (e.g., OhMyNews.org, wikinews.org) to intensely local (MadisonCommons.org). In addition, some American cities are now served by nonprofit news corporations. These are often collections of former newspaper reporters and editors who have created local online organizations to report news and information for their communities. Financial support varies, but often they accept donations and try to sell online ads. Other forms of nonprofit news are supported by foundations and universities.

Whether at the local, state, or national level, new forms of communication are producing new types of news and new venues for campaigning, organizing, and even governing. Most political communication research is focused on national and international issues and topics and this remains important. But, it is noteworthy that there is tremendous activity at local levels that is quite consequential and is tied to interesting theories about community and community organization (e.g., Gastil & Levine, 2005; Leighninger, 2006).

INSTITUTIONAL CONSTRAINTS SHAPING POLITICAL COMMUNICATION RESEARCH

In discussing the role of method in political communication research, it is important to consider the institutions that shape the methods and practices of researchers. First, researchers are subjected to the requisites of their respective universities, colleges, schools, and departments. The demands of productivity for promotion and tenure typically push researchers toward methods that yield volume over quality. The pressures to produce research in volume often lead researchers to ask questions and select methods that produce results quickly, which may lead to play-it-safe strategies that have a high likelihood of return and to the avoidance of research designs capable of capturing long-term processes. As communication lacks the strong, institutionalized survey research tradition of political science subfields, such as American politics and political behavior, researchers may opt for the efficiency of experimental methods over survey research methods, which often require more time and resources to conduct.

In an era of dwindling resources, researchers are facing added pressure to compete for external funding. This pressure may move the field in directions that are potentially fundable through grants from governments and foundations, which will likely shape the nature of the research questions asked as well as methods used. Government-funded projects may steer researchers clear of criticizing the status quo and may narrow the research focus. Private foundations may also have an axe to grind, or an agenda to promote, shaping what they are willing to fund. The competition for research dollars may lead researchers to safe, mainstream proposals emphasizing traditional concepts and methods.

In choosing methods, researchers must also consider constraints imposed by their institution's human subjects institutional review boards. Beyond the necessary hassles presented by IRBs, their largest impact on political communication research may be in hampering the ability to do "firehouse" research in response to sudden events in the political communication environment (e.g., the 9/11 terrorist attacks, major campaign developments, and so on). Such bureaucratic structures make it harder to make timely contributions on current public issues. This leaves the field somewhat dependent on the public polls and other commercial sources of public opinion data that operate in a less regulated environment than academic research.

Professional disciplines and fields of inquiry exert their influence on research as well. They provide norms, standards of practice, and a set of rules for playing the game that shapes methods and research. Many of these conformity pressures exert a positive influence by setting standards that protect the quality and integrity of research. However, conformity can induce homogeneity that, if taken too far, can limit theoretical growth in the discipline. Moreover, growing workloads and demands on professional time that researchers are facing may further reinforce the practice of short-sighted, quick-and-dirty research.

There may also be a bias toward accepting inherent personality traits as explanations of phenomena. This thinking mistakes descriptions for explanations. Such "explanations" inhibit the consideration of what processes might change the political outcome and unwittingly encourage the readers to "blame the victim," that is, the citizen, instead of the system.

Finally, the journals and publishers of the field shape methodological choices. The journals of the discipline of communication are dominated by an editorial philosophy, manifested through the approach taken by editors and reviewers, that seems to privilege psychological-level theories over sociological-level theories. Given the relative imbalance in the output of journals, particularly those that publish political communication research, it would seem that there is a disciplinary norm that maintains that if theory does not involve cognitive processes, it is accorded second-class status. As young researchers observe this imbalance, they are likely to opt for theory and methods that replicate that imbalance. In the peer review process, there may be countervailing forces at work. On one hand, reviewers may favor research that has a proven track record to accord it legitimacy and thereby may be more amenable to publishing similar research in the future. This may lead reviewers to reject theory and methods that are novel or innovative. On the other hand, when reviewers fail to understand novel theories or advanced techniques, they may not detect the flaws and thereby give it a free pass. The Sokal Affair provides an extreme example: David Sokal, an NYU physics professor, published a paper ("Transgressing the Boundaries: Toward a Transformative Hermeneutics of Quantum Gravity") in the journal *Social Text* that was admittedly nonsense dressed up in academic jargon.

The practices and conventions of journals pose further limitations on the scientific endeavor by omitting necessary details for replication in the interest of conserving journal space. However, a key part of any kind of rigorous scientific project is replication (Altman & King, 2006; King, 1995, 2007). Although replication may be more talked about than done, it is a key element of the system of checks on scientific accuracy and integrity. Providing for replication is an important safeguard built into scientific culture. For replication to be possible, data and analysis practices need to be carefully preserved and documented. This will enable other researchers to reanalyze the data and check the results. Scientists owe the community sufficient details of research procedures, such as sampling information, question wording, treatment of missing data, variable recoding, index construction, and data analysis, to permit replication. Journals often omit some or even all of this information such that researchers may need to seek other means of sharing data and providing key information, perhaps by posting it to websites. The Dataverse Network Project (King, 2007) attempts to fill this void as well as to achieve a number of other goals related to archiving and research replication. Dataverse is an ambitious effort to promulgate data citation standards and create scholarly recognition for those who produce or organize data, as well as facilitate the archiving of data and analysis from entire projects. The creative and methodological skills needed for the creation of high-quality data is a significant scholarly achievement in its own right that deserves credit. Unfortunately, such efforts have been devalued in contemporary academic life. The communication research community and indeed the entire social scientific research community would benefit from widespread participation in the Dataverse project and embracing the values that motivate its creation. For special issues related to replication in communication studies, see Benoit and Holbert (2008).

MODES OF INQUIRY AND INSIGHTS YIELDED

Political communication researchers have a variety of tools at their disposal. Traditionally, the subfield has been dominated by survey research, experiments, and content analyses. However, there are a variety of other approaches, both quantitative and qualitative, that contribute to our knowledge of political communication processes, including discourse analysis, network analysis, meta-analysis, rhetorical analysis, ethnography, and participant observation, several of which are elaborated on in preceding chapters in this book. In addition to these research tools, there are approaches to political communication (e.g., historical, legal, and political economy) that also make important contributions. There have been important developments in recent years in each of these areas, but beyond that, there is an encouraging trend toward designing research that combines these methods to yield significant insights.

In this section, we will focus our discussion on recent developments involving the most common tools of political communication research (i.e., surveys, experiments, and content analyses), particularly as they have adapted to the changing conditions in which they are applied (e.g., the increasing costs and falling response rates of public opinion surveys).

Survey Research

Survey research thrives in political communication and survey tools remain fundamental to many priority questions that animate the discipline. In recent years attempts have been made to broaden the American National Election Studies (ANES) series and incorporate more variables related to mass communication and new forms of communication technology. The ANES project, since its move to Stanford University, has attempted to incorporate many new ideas and capabilities into the venerable time series. One example is a partnership with the National Longitudinal Survey series in which adolescents are asked about political attitudes and behaviors, including their use of mass media. This will likely enable a series of advances in the understanding of socialization to politics. Recently, the ANES has adopted a general openness to methodological, conceptual, and administrative advancements that has not been seen in many years.

The National Annenberg Election Study (NAES) at the University of Pennsylvania has taken a different path to survey innovation. The NAES uses a system of independent samples known as rolling cross-sections taken at fixed intervals over an entire presidential election season to better understand the dynamics of public opinion and its relationship to communication. Hallmarks of the NAES include extremely large sample sizes (around 100,000 respondents in both the 2000 and 2004 election cycles) to facilitate close examination of the dynamics of the campaign as well as impacts of geography and other spatially oriented phenomena such as political advertising within media markets. (For a comparison of the ANES and NAES, see Chapter 6, this volume.)

Far more extensive use of survey research by political communication scholars originates with public polls—studies undertaken without formal hypotheses but which ask about current political and social issues. Large-scale, good-quality public policy polling is performed by a large number of foundations, public policy centers, and media organizations. Examples include the various centers supported by the Pew Foundation, such as the Pew Research Center for the People & the Press, and the Pew Internet & American Life projects. Data from such projects are often made widely available for secondary analysis. Other leading examples include the Public Policy Institute of California (PPIC), and the Program on International Policy Attitudes (PIPA) at the University of Maryland. Major polling firms such as Gallup also routinely ask questions for public dissemination, but more frequently major polling firms associated with media polls release a steady stream of public opinion data about current events and politics into the public realm. Some high quality media polls active in the 2008 election cycle included the New York Times-CBS Poll, the Washington Post-ABC News Poll, AP/Ipsos Poll, and the Time Magazine/Abt SRBI Public Affairs poll, among others. Another major, but somewhat underused, source of data about elections is the National Election Pool exit poll conducted for the major media by Edison Media Research and Mitofsky International.

All of these surveys share a common purpose, which is to present accurate, representative snapshots in time of the opinions, knowledge base, and political and demographic characteristics of populations. Survey research remains the way that social scientists examine characteristics of populations and test relevant hypotheses. This unique quality—the ability to represent populations based on a randomly chosen sample—is important in political communication research. Advances in sampling, question construction, survey administration, and analysis have turned survey research into a complex specialty that could scarcely be imagined three decades ago.

The Total Survey Error (TSE) approach represents the new science of survey research that emerged from the insight by Groves (1989) that disciplinary discussions of research errors often obscured as much as they illuminated. This prompted Groves to formulate a theory of sampling and non-sampling errors as they relate to survey research, incorporating work from psychometrics, sampling statistics, and econometrics. TSE also focuses attention on the costs of errors and the various attempts to reduce them. TSE is a unified theory of the types of errors that occur in sampling and non-sampling contexts of survey research and includes principles for weighing the costs and benefits of various strategies to eliminate or reduce those errors.

A key principle of the TSE approach is the standardization of the diverse language of errors that has resulted from the interdisciplinary nature of survey research. All surveys are subject to various types of errors. Coverage error results from problems with the sampling frame or other issues that arise from situations in which some eligible elements of the population are not eligible for inclusion in the sample. Non-response error results from failing to collect data from all elements of the sample. Sampling error occurs because we gather data from samples, not entire heterogeneous populations. Measurement error arises from inaccuracies in recording survey responses. Measurement error has a number of sources, including interviewer effects, respondents' inability to answer the questions accurately, survey question construction techniques, mode of data collection (e.g., face-to-face, telephone, Internet, mail, mixed mode), among others well known in the psychometric literature. The TSE approach helps illuminate the administrative features of surveys such as interviewer training, sample design, size of sample, call-back rules, and ways of handling refusals and partial completions in terms of their effects on errors. Some errors are actually the result of attempts to control others. For example, the aggressive use of techniques to reduce non-response may result in larger measurement errors for certain key variables (Groves, 1989). Finding the right balance of techniques for each project is the payoff of the TSE approach (Weisberg, 2005).

Despite the cost–benefit analysis of the TSE, funding survey research projects is expensive and large grants are required. This feature of survey projects may work against certain types of theoretical innovation on large-scale surveys in that the funders and principal investigators tend to be highly risk averse. Smaller population projects conducted at a local or regional level are often excluded from national and international journals. This pursuit of national "quality" data tends to reduce innovation and risk-taking. In recent years some investigators have chosen to pursue their research by using large data sets assembled through the use of Internet-based data collection in which self-selected samples are used. This undercuts the main benefit of survey research— its ability to represent populations of interests. Such samples also may yield questionable relationships among the key variables of interest.

Another limitation of survey design is that the limits of expense and respondent attention may reduce the number of items that investigators feel comfortable asking. In response, investigators often try to eliminate seemingly "redundant" questions that are used in multi-item indexes to measure complex constructs. A cost-effective alternative is to rely on concepts often measured by a single item and validated by face validity. However, this discourages creative and scientifically more valid approaches to question construction.

Fortunately a number of data archives for quality survey data exist and increasing attention is being paid to such matters, even in the case of historical data sets (e.g., Berinsky, 2006). The ICPSR at the University of Michigan and the Roper Center at the University of Connecticut are two large survey data archives that have vast holdings of contemporary and historically significant survey data from the United States and around the world. International survey data sets can often be found at the UK Data Archive (UKDA) at the University of Essex. In addition, the Odum Institute for Research in the Social Sciences at the University of North Carolina has a large and growing collection of state polls and other significant public opinion resources. The Dataverse Network Project mentioned above is a particularly useful effort.

New Technology and Survey Research. Widespread telephone penetration made the transition from in-person surveys to telephone surveys occur very rapidly in the United States a generation ago. Computer Assisted Telephone Interviewing is now the standard for many serious purposes in and out of academic and government research circles. This regime is under challenge due to the rapid conversion to wireless telephones now under way in the United States and the rest of the world. Surveys of cellular telephone users are complex and difficult for a number of reasons, but they are doable and increasingly important due to the growing proportion of cell-only households. Research on the issues raised by cell phone surveying has been burgeoning (e.g., Lavrakas, Shuttles, Steeh, & Fienberg, 2007).

Internet technology, Voice-over-IP telephones, advances in survey software, and database technology are also creating new opportunities for sophisticated survey capabilities. Web-based surveying is inexpensive but limited to those who have Internet access and whose contact information appears on a list of some kind that can be sampled. Some scientifically valid and representative online surveys can be done with randomly sampled panels such as those by Knowledge Networks of Menlo Park, CA. Knowledge Networks has innovated a scientifically valid approach that has been recognized by the National Science Foundation for use in an ongoing original data collection project known as TESS—Timesharing Experiments in the Social Sciences.

Easy-to-use web-based technology also creates dangers for survey research. Some investigators who are unmindful of respondent burden and the criteria for effective survey research, namely, the representativeness of populations, are tempted to obtain large population lists and instead of sampling and following up many times with reluctant respondents, just send email invitations to huge numbers of list members. Mass mailings combined with aggressive incentives for quickly responding can generate thousands of completed questionnaires within hours, although the response rate and representativeness are low. Reviewers for high-quality academic journals who were vigilant in their gatekeeping to control this behavior would reinforce high standards by rejecting this approach, but too often these practices slide through the reviewing system.

Experimental Approaches

Along with the emphasis on cognitive concepts and theories, experimental procedures have become quite common in political communication over the past decade. This is generally a welcome development in that well-controlled laboratory experiments can help sort out various communication processes and resolve issues of causal relations. The tight control of subjects, communication, and conditions of communication, along with the measurement of dependent variables makes this so. Typical experiments conducted in political communication may rely on college students majoring in communication or political science who receive some course credit for their participation. Besides the rather artificial nature of the experience, experimentalists often employ long sets of complex constructs (question batteries) that do not necessarily translate well to real-world settings.

The logic of experiments is suffused with careful control of every experience in the lab and so it is not surprising that the experimental community often insists on tight standardization of measures for ascertaining particular concepts. This logic often leads to an intolerance of variations. This has the effect of limiting publication opportunities for those who try new or varied measurement strategies. This is a particular concern when the standardized concepts are not the main focus of the study. It remains the case, however, that the strongest experiments are those that impose the fewest assumptions in estimating the effect.

Technology is also transforming the experimental paradigm. Suites of computer programs can readily be used to create standardized questionnaires and for capturing the answers in a database. These programs can be used to control a great many aspects of a typical experiment as well as facilitate the standardized display of video or other visual elements.

Experimental approaches, of course, are thriving in the contexts of survey research where entire literatures are now being built on question experiments integrated into population surveys. These are facilitated by survey software that automatically chooses the version of the question-naire appropriate for each respondent. It can also rotate or even randomize the order of elements of an individual question, response options, the order of the questions, or even whole sections of questions within the questionnaire. When variations in such orders are observed it is important that such order effects be controlled by routinely varying these elements of the questionnaire. This is another example of the way that new methodological practices raised the bar on rigorous professional standards through research.

Although they have not been used much in political communication, randomized social policy experiments are generally the gold standard for program evaluation. Typical randomized experiments (using between-subjects designs) divide the initial group of subjects into treatment and control groups. Randomization assures equivalence at the start of the experiment. Subsequent differences observed between the groups are then attributed to the effects of the treatment. Government programs are often evaluated by studying the recipients before and after the treatment conditions, or more typically after. Beneficiaries of programs are often chosen on the basis of need, and so group membership is confounded with the treatment such that improvements may be due to factors other than the experimental treatment. Randomized social policy experiments, in contrast, employ procedures that eliminate this problem.

One form of field experiment becoming popular in political communication is the so-called deliberative poll and its many variations. As envisioned by Fishkin (1996), the deliberative poll begins with a random sample of community members, who are presented with background information about a topic, issue, or candidate. Sometimes they are exposed to experts or detailed lessons about a topic. The participants then break into discussion groups. The process of explaining one's position and listening to others is thought to be helpful in forming or reforming considered opinions on an issue. Considered opinions are those formed under sufficient information and opportunity to deliberate about the topic and are believed to be of higher quality in the sense that they are based on a person's true values and therefore substantive knowledge base, and more resistant to change. Finally, participants' opinions are assessed and compared to the pretest when they were recruited into the process. Differences are typically reported between the before–after answers. As specified by Fishkin, deliberative polls are not true experiments in that they lack any sort of control group. Arguably they should have two control groups since there are two sources of influence—the background information and the deliberation. Despite their technical limitations, deliberative polls and comparable interventions by organizations such as AmericaSpeaks.org, the National Issues Forum Institute, Public Agenda, and others, are used regularly as demonstration projects in applied political communication settings. In some cases such methods have been empowered by policymakers to actually make real policy decisions. For example, a group convened by AmericaSpeaks in New York City scuttled a developer's initial plan for rebuilding the site of the World Trade Center. There are, of course, various flaws and limitations pointed out by critics (see Newport, 2004; Sanders, 1997).

Content Analysis

There have been numerous advancements in information access and the techniques of content analysis research in recent years. First, the Internet has served to increase potential access to content. Most news organizations now post content online and often permit users to search for past content. Most research universities now have access to news archives such as Lexis/ Nexis so that researchers can access material for content analysis. Significant technological advancements in the storage and retrieval of news content greatly expand the potential for content analysis research on not just print media, but web pages, news transcripts, and even video of news broadcasts (see Chapters 12–14, this volume).

The development of computer-aided content analysis and latent semantic analysis have simplified the laborious procedures of traditional content analysis. Moreover, the procedures of contiguity analyses, the examination of beyond-chance or below-chance co-occurrence of pairs of themes/frames, can now examine the extent to which political actors differ in their use of verbs and adjectives associated with them. These developments have expanded opportunities to go beyond the description of content, which plagued early content analysis research.

Technologies such as Google Analytics permit content analysis researchers to track raw exposure to content of interest on the Web by tracking visitors to various websites. Given the recent expansion in the technological capabilities of content analysis research, it is ironic that its prominence in the political communication literature has somewhat declined in recent years.

ON THE PITFALLS OF METHODS

Methodological Choices

Despite the tremendous growth in methodological techniques and data analysis procedures, researchers continue to face many potential pitfalls. In their exuberance to apply state-of-the-art analysis techniques and procedures, some researchers exhibit a tendency to hide behind method by elevating methodological sophistication over theoretical substance. Readers should resist the temptation to be impressed by the complexity of methods of analysis without regard to the theoretical questions they address. While sophisticated analysis tools can yield important insights and unveil complex relationships, they can also make mountains out of molehills. In short, judicious methodological choices must take into account the theoretical questions they are designed to answer. It must be noted that the focus on new methods as a hammer and all research problems as nails was also true at the birth of the contemporary communication discipline a half-century ago. Early communication researchers tended to believe that factor analysis and the semantic differential would be the golden keys to making the discipline respectable.

Advanced data analysis techniques can obfuscate important findings for readers who are not trained in advanced statistics. Sometimes, simple techniques are sufficient and may be more accessible to a broader audience. Of course, technical sophistication is not the only factor that can make research inaccessible. The broader impact of research can also be hampered by impenetrable language and by arcane questions devoid of practical implications. By making research inaccessible to the media, public, and policymakers, researchers limit its impact thereby stifling its ability to create positive change in our political processes.

Theory should drive methods, not the other way around. The expediency of one-shot surveys and experiments leads to another methodological drawback, the emphasis on short-term rather than long-term effects (but see Chapter 11, this volume). This may be reinforced by the constraints of tenure demands and lack of sufficient resources, both of which may discourage researchers from engaging in research designs that are capable of revealing long-term effects. As such, our knowledge of media effects and other agents that affect long-term processes like political socialization is limited. Similarly, professional and resource constraints may steer researchers away from addressing novel and important questions in favor of asking routine and mundane questions that are more likely to pay off. Statistical techniques such as data mining and boot-strapping techniques pose a danger of putting methods in the driver's seat, generating knowledge but not necessarily building theory. Putting methods first can also lead to the condition of *methodological myopia*, in which the method is adopted as the starting point for research and research questions are subsequently extrapolated. For instance, some researchers may be wedded to a particular method and pro-ceed by asking what can we do with it. When method is the starting point, research questions may be constrained to the point of being mundane. Similarly, researchers working with secondary data sets may ask the question of what can we do with the data. Such approaches are unlikely to produce theoretically meaningful research. When methodological myopia is prevalent within a discipline, theoretical growth is inhibited and knowledge stagnates. For example, for many decades political communication research was dominated by survey methodology. As researchers have begun to adopt other methods, knowledge and indeed theory, have blossomed. Compatible sentiments have been voiced by Holbert (2005) who has stressed a "back to basics" approach. By maintaining a focus on careful explication and measurement of key theoretical concepts such as media exposure and attention, the discipline will be less likely to veer off course.

Measurement Problems

The ubiquity of research methods courses in the dozens of communication doctoral programs that have emerged in the past 50 years should have made measurement problems of political communication concepts unproblematic or nonexistent by now. This is not the case. As the field has grown in recent years, along with the diversity of sources of political information, research concepts have grown in number and complexity. This growth, unfortunately, has not been accompanied by sustained attention to improving measurement of existing concepts and systematic development of new concepts appropriate to changing communication technologies and contexts. Publication and other rewards of academic research seem to come more from producing significant findings than from analyses of measurement difficulties in the field. Selection of indicators of key communication concepts appears to be made on an ad hoc basis of reliability and "what works" rather than a thoughtful consideration of the role that these concepts play in the theoretical connections to their antecedents or effects. Because *alpha*, the criterion for reliability, mandates at *least* three items, it is not surprising that a large proportion of indices in political communication have exactly three indicators.

Inattention to measurement development has led to contradictory findings for concepts that have the same labels but different indicators in the various studies making them incomparable. The selection of familiar marketable labels for research concepts that have varied meanings and measures has added to the confusion. Involvement is a prime example of such a vague concept with multiple affective, cognitive, behavioral meanings. The growing complexity of modern political communication models has led researchers to include as many variables as possible in sample surveys. Other researchers may subsequently select a few of these indicators to represent complex multidimensional concepts originally measured with multiple items. This can result not only in the underestimation of effect size, but also in content validity problems in tapping certain dimensions or facets of a concept over others.

Research concepts are the building blocks of our knowledge. As such, they deserve more careful attention through meaning analysis and empirical explication. Though we lack space to explain these procedures here, we recommend McLeod and Pan (2005) for a more complete treatment. The concept *media use* illustrates the measurement problems of political communication research. In public discourse and in some academic publications various effects (most often negative) are ascribed to what "the media" do, leaving all details ambiguous. In much of political communication research, media use is extended only to the frequency of use (e.g., days per week) either of a given medium in general or of some specific type of content within a medium. For most research questions, frequency of use of a medium has produced only weak or null findings. Despite validity research showing that *attention* to news content is more strongly related to political knowledge than news exposure measures, particularly for television (Chaffee & Schleuder, 1986; McLeod & McDonald, 1985), advice to include both measures has been largely ignored. Explication from meaning analyses suggested an additional dimension of media use in going beyond what is used to examine audience reports on how news content is processed (Kosicki, Amor, & McLeod, 1987). Explication via empirical analyses reveals patterns of influence of reflective integrative news processing on knowledge and participation that is distinct from those of frequency and attention, thus recommending a broadening of measurement of media use that includes strategies of how audiences process news.

Moreover, the measurement of media effects has largely failed to distinguish between the impact of "dosage" and "potency." That is, media effects are both a product of the amount of exposure and the nature of the specific content to which one is exposed. To continue this medical analogy, dosage and potency may have differential effects depending on the characteristics of the recipient (e.g., age, education, gender). There are cohort effects that complicate the normal evolution of media use patterns over time. For example, given the diverse but seemingly irregular use of new and traditional media among the current cohort of young adults, it is essential for political communication researchers to develop new models for assessing the dosage and potency of exposure to sources of political information, including those that operate through mass, non-traditional, and interpersonal channels. This includes the post-data collection disaggregation of indices to further pinpoint what is influencing what, for whom, and why. But researchers need to go beyond assessing the *what* in political communication to also consider questions that concern *how*—how do different audience members process the information they are exposed to and how does this condition the nature of media effects? Toward this end, researchers should explicate the salient styles of media use and processing, which take on vastly different characteristics across different audience cohorts.

The development of new communication technologies (e.g., blogs, wikis, user-created content) pose huge challenges for the measurement of media use in our dynamic new media environment. This is further complicated by the concomitant change in the nature of the information content being provided. For example, we might hypothesize that the information gained through the use of these new communication technologies contains more by way of conclusions than about the facts upon which these conclusions are based. Clearly, the challenges to measurement that are imposed by the changing media environment are almost as vast as the new body of research questions that it has generated.

Respondent Burnout

Respondent burnout is a danger that plagues social science. Whether it is the general public who have been over-targeted by surveys from marketing researchers and social scientists alike, or college students who are besieged by requests to participate in experiments, there is growing fatigue and cynicism toward social science research. Such burnout and irritation is further compounded by the length of surveys driven by the necessities of multi-purposing data collections, high-quality measurement, and advanced data analysis. This problem produces such symptoms as diminishing response rates that may compromise generalizability and the erosion of data quality as respondents skip questions or answer them haphazardly. Social scientists can do their part to remedy the problem by limiting their data collections to reasonable numbers justified by the research problem and not by how many respondents they can get. This is a particular issue when online data collection methods are used. Institutional review boards have an important role in being vigilant in questioning the need for large samples and curbing abuses.

Data Analysis Pitfalls

There are many pitfalls when it comes to analyzing data. For instance, a common methodological mistake is to infer causality from correlational data. The most commonly used correlation-based statistical procedures demonstrate only one of the three necessary conditions for causality—the association between the two variables in question. They do not address the other two conditions—time order and the absence of third variables that pose alternative explanations. The fact that correlational data do not establish time order between cause and effect leaves interpretation vulnerable to the possibility that the presumed effect is actually the cause and vice versa. Correlational analyses do little to alleviate *endogeneity*, the possibility that both variables have a reciprocal influence on each other. Time-based designs, such as panel surveys, can be useful for establishing evidence of causal relationships, but only if we have selected the appropriate time intervals for the variables in question. In designing panel studies, these intervals are usually based on expedience and intuition rather than on theoretical and methodological justifications. The success of panel designs depends in part on substantial changes in the presumed causal variable (e.g., changes in campaign intensity, or the pace of events). Structural equation modeling (SEM) can help establish causal evidence as well, but its ability to establish causality is predicated on sound pre-established theory and when paired with panel data where the same respondents are interviewed at two or more points in time. In terms of ruling out the possibility of spurious relationships that are the result of a common antecedent or intervening variable, SEM can help by evaluating such relationships. But again, solid theorizing is necessary to identify potential third variables to rule out the possibility that they might account for the correlation in question. Of course, we can never be sure that we have identified all of the potentially relevant variables. Controlled experiments are typically the method of choice for establishing causal relationships because of their potential to hold third variables constant. However, not all causal variables avail themselves to experimental manipulation and experiments often impose artificial conditions that limit the external generalizability of findings. One strategy may be to combine methods in order to capitalize on the advantages of each as well as to triangulate findings. This is more possible than ever before due to platforms such as TESS and Knowledge Networks which can display all sorts of stimuli to random samples of subjects (see Chapter 8, this volume).

Another common analysis mistake occurs when researchers equate significance with meaningfulness. A relationship may be statistically significant, but this does not mean that the results indicate an important relationship that informs real-world decisions. This points to the dangers of large sample sizes when they are not justified by need for subgroup analysis or some similar theoretically guided purpose. On the one hand, large sample sizes are considered desirable in that they help researchers find significant results; however, they may also lead researchers to make false inferences when conclusions translate into gross over-generalizations about the importance of relationships between variables. This is why it is desirable for researchers to contemplate the issue of what constitutes a meaningful difference before collecting data so that power analyses can be conducted to determine the optimal sample size.

Another problem stems from the tendency of researchers to ignore null findings. There is a natural tendency to want to find significant results in order to publish research. In the process, researchers may engage in data mining, fishing expeditions, and post hoc theorizing, or they may also ignore lots of nonsignificant findings that might be important in falsifying theories. Thus researchers may be complicit in a confirmation bias that allows weak theories to persist, which is compounded by journals that prioritize significant results. It may be appropriate in certain cases to try to resolve null or surprising findings (or to clarify predicted findings) after hypothesis testing by disaggregating indices to identify which items in the independent variable are associated with which items in the dependent variable. Such procedures may provide a more sensitive account of the processes at work.

Generalizability Problems

Finally, methodological choices may invoke generalizability problems. Some are unique to communication, such as the practice of publishing "surveys" of intact groups such as large classes and treating them as if they were a population sample of college students. This is mainly a reviewer and journal gatekeeping problem that does not occur in most other flagship social science journals. Other generalizability issues occur in that much of the experimental research in political communication uses student samples and examines phenomena in an artificial setting. This is typically justified in psychology by the assumption that mental processes are invariant across individuals. But investigators should be more careful when dealing with other types of concepts. While such laboratory research may be essential to establishing internally valid estimates of causal relationships, it may also limit the relevance of the findings to real-world applications. In many situations, results from student sample experiments may provide an adequate approximation of the relationships observed in random samples of the larger population, but it is crucial for researchers to periodically replicate experiments for representative samples of the population.

Moreover, multiple methodological approaches may be used to triangulate findings to satisfy concerns about both internal and external validity. It is also worth repeating that in order for replication to assist in the resolution of such research dilemmas, researchers need to share methodological information, data, and analysis procedures in sufficient detail.

THE FUTURE OF METHODS, DATA, AND ANALYSIS

We may not have to worry as much about the future of political communication methods per se as we do knowing what to do about the immediate future that so rapidly descends upon us. Vast changes over the past thirty-five years, in communication technology and media economics, generational values and lifestyles, and political governance and campaign strategies, have forced upon us the necessity of rethinking what we study and how we do research on politics. The rise of the Internet and the growth of cable and satellite networks has contributed to the decline in audience sizes of traditional print and broadcast news media. Recent youth cohorts have adopted the Internet more readily than older adults but have shown much less interest in traditional news media than did earlier cohorts (see Tewksbury, Weaver, & Maddex, 2001). This results in markedly aging audiences for traditional news media that have been recognized as being strong promoters of civic engagement. As such, the rapidly shifting media landscape raises extremely important issues for political communication research.

Reactions to the rise of the Internet have varied from seeing it as the potential savior of democracy to being a blot on the political landscape. Replicating the early debates about television effects, much of the controversy surrounding the Internet has centered on inherent physical characteristics of the medium, its accessibility, or costs to disadvantaged groups. The first effects studies tended to measure Internet use as days per week or average daily time online rather than as frequency of exposure to news or other relevant public affairs content. Although more recent research has included measures of attention as well as exposure to public affairs content online, it has become apparent that the measurement of Internet content use, particularly among the crucial youth cohort, is a far more complex matter than is assessing the use of such content for traditional news sources.

Internet news use is distinctive in a least five ways. First, Internet news use has not yet reached the levels of habitual regularity historically or even recently found for newspaper reading in any age group (McLeod, Shah, Hess, & Lee, 2009). Second, Internet news use coincides with other online uses often making political learning incidental to other outcomes. Third, learning from the Internet tends to be a part of information seeking from a number of other media sources and through exchange of information within interpersonal networks (Jenkins, 2006). Fourth, Internet news consumption among younger citizens constitutes multitasking, characterized by the simultaneous use (with alternating attention) of multiple media and sometimes face-to-face conversations that could impede learning. Finally, despite the modest dosage levels and fluctuating attention to content, the potency in terms of strength of Internet news effects among younger users is considerably greater than that for older adults. Considering its complexity, the measurement of Internet news use deserves careful explication and development of new ways of assessing the processes, sequences, and strategies directing its use among various audiences.

Future research is likely to progress by broadening the scope of research models to connect the daily lives of average citizens, their use of mediated and interpersonal communication, and their participation as citizens. The assumptions underlying the argument for a broader model is that both the processes of media content selection by audiences and the processes of transformation into political action have been underrepresented in political communication theory and research. The separation of audience analysis and effects research several decades ago led effects researchers to relegate social structural variables as mere locators and to the statistical demotion of demographic influences on audiences. A recent approach outlined by McLeod, Kosicki, and McLeod (2002) takes the form of an O-S-O-R model where the first O is pre-exposure orientations, which direct the effects of social structural influences on communication behavior. As such, they represent the sense-making efforts of citizens to connect their daily "life-world" activities with the expectations of distant political and economic institutions. Examples of pre-exposure orientations as mediators are empirical lay theories about how the world operates in terms of predictability and possibility for change, and normative theories about what the world or community ought to become. The second O represents post-exposure orientations, communication processes (e.g., issue discussion), and cognitive structures (e.g., factual knowledge) that mediate by connecting and transforming information gained from media use (S) into various forms of political participation (R). Simple factual knowledge is a good mediator of structural and communication effects on low-effort behaviors such as voting, but growing evidence of the effects of attentive media use, classroom civics learning, and service learning on civic participation suggests the desirability of measuring more complex forms of knowledge when investigating stronger forms of civic engagement (Shah, Kwak, Schmierbach, & Zubric, 2004; Sotirovic & McLeod, 2004).

Structural equation modeling (SEM) is the best way to study mediation in complex models (e.g., Holbert & Stephenson, 2003). The LISREL version of SEM provides essential information on indices of overall model fit, identifies poorly fitting paths, and coefficients dividing the impact of each predictor variable into its direct, indirect, and total effects on each predicted subsequent variable. Mediation is indicated by the extent to which the mediating variable reduces the unmediated direct effect of a path between an antecedent and dependent variable to its direct effect and produces an indirect effect for that path. Indirect effects tend to be undervalued because they are the product of two coefficients, but they should be appreciated as providing a potentially better explanation of why the antecedent variable affects the dependent variable. Mediation analyses of public affairs media use also provide convincing evidence of its political effects. In the 2004 ANES presidential election survey, a block of five campaign media use variables mediated 59% of the variance in knowledge and 86% of variance for campaign participation accounted for by a block of demographic and structural variables (McLeod, 2007).

Future progress can be expected in correcting the longstanding problem of imbalance in the dominance of individual-level research and its lack of connection to macro-level scholarship. Progress was made possible by multilevel modeling (MLM), a set of statistical models that overcome the earlier problems of non-independence of variance between levels of OLS regression models by analyzing the variance of two or more levels simultaneously (e.g., between communities, neighborhoods, and individuals within them) (Bryk & Raudenbush, 1987). After some delay, these models have begun to appear in political communication and other fields within the discipline (Slater, Snyder, & Hayes, 2006). Most of the communication multilevel examples have come in the form of contextual analyses less formally initiated with the research program of Tichenor, Donohue, and Olien (1973). Contexts can be defined as properties of macro-units that operate as constraints, shaping individual-level behavior (or other lower-level phenomena) through incentives, or discouraging behaviors through deterrents or sanctions.

More elaborate discussion of opportunities and problems of multi-level research can be found elsewhere (McLeod, Kosicki, & McLeod, 2009; Slater et al., 2006), but two general problems can be mentioned: Which macro-levels to choose? And, what macro-variables to use? The choice of levels should be determined by theory and research, suggesting the one most likely to impinge on key concepts at the individual or sub-macro level. Unfortunately, the availability of data sets and comparable measures may lead to a less than optimal choice.

The development of computer programs connecting statistical data for macro units, such as census units of social data, precincts, or congressional district of voting data, and markets for media data, have alleviated the problem of unit selection somewhat. In choosing macro-level variables, the earliest communication applications of MLM have tended to use simple aggregation of individual-level analytical variables, most often the key independent or dependent variables of the study, rather than developing relational variables between units or global variables uniquely appropriate to the particular macro level (Lazarsfeld, 1958). In specifying macro variables it is necessary to use theory at both macro and micro levels to select variables at each level, ideally generating corresponding theoretical statements at each level. Other "level" areas within communication—intercultural, organizational, interpersonal—may be sources of useful concepts and theories unfamiliar to political communication researchers. Given the large differences in size of the largest macro units such as nations and the smallest such as individuals, it may be necessary to develop auxiliary cross-level theories of the processes by which the constraints at the macro level reach the micro level, either as direct influences on the levels of micro independent variables or as interactions with them in generating effects. The result of careful explication of macro-to-micro processes is likely to be the specification of concepts and relationships at one or more intermediate meso levels. These might be community or discussion network levels, for example.

We should view multilevel research as part of the broader area of comparative research where comparisons are made not only of space as in our examples above, but also in terms of time in modeling multiple historical periods, election campaigns, stages, or cohorts across the life cycle. Changes over time may involve changes in different macro level units as well as individuals at the micro level. Finally, we must acknowledge that our discussion of multilevel research has been confined to the macro-to-micro influence of structuration processes that dominate theoretical concerns to the neglect of less theorized micro-to-macro influence processes of human agency that are of no less importance (Giddens, 1986).

New resources and tools are rapidly becoming available that can assist with this agenda. Social scientists are in the midst of unparalleled development of a new research infrastructure for data collection, archiving, analysis, and reporting of results thanks to the open-source software movement. The use of open-source software, created by the research community for its own customizable use, is growing rapidly. A powerful aspect of the open source movement is that it facilitates the unification of certain teaching, research, and publication goals. The open-source software community has created invaluable research tools and made them available worldwide for free. The operating system Linux with distributions such as Ubuntu and Red Hat, and the OpenOffice productivity suite, are among the best known. These are free alternatives that attempt to replace and extend the functions of Microsoft Windows and Office. Free Web server software created by Apache Software Foundation, for example, reportedly powers a high proportion of the world's Web servers. Mozilla Software Foundation has created the popular open-source Web browsers Firefox and Chrome. Open source software is created and maintained by volunteers and typically distributed free online (e.g., Lessig, 2005). Updates are routinely made available for active projects.

The world of scientific statistical software has been enriched by an open-source project known as R, which maintains a software platform that scholars can use to create new statistics. As new social scientific tests and procedures are published in journals, source code is often made available to implement the routines in R. In this way, scholars can have a place to operationalize their latest ideas and make them immediately available to their students to use for free. R thus facilitates teaching and publication. Social statistics is now taught at a number of leading institutions using bundles of R programs such as Zelig (Imai, King, & Lau, 2009), a suite of statistical routines in a common format that rivals the basic functions of SPSS, SAS, and Stata, commonly used commercial social statistics programs. Hundreds of R applications exist and are accessible through a worldwide network of servers hosted by major universities. This network is known as the Comprehensive R Archive Network (CRAN). Although some see R as an alternative to SPSS, the makers of SPSS have created an SPSS-R Integration Package that is available free from SPSS. R is particularly known for its impressive capabilities for graphing data as well as mapping and various forms of spatial analysis. Gelman and Hill (2007) wrote a leading text on MLM that develops numerous examples created in the syntax of R's multilevel module as well as the open-source program BUGS. A recent research monograph on voting and polarization provides extensive examples in the use of open-source MLM, graphics, and replication across time and data sets (Gelman, 2008).

Open-source projects are also active in many other areas of interest to political communication methodologists. LimeSurvey is a project dedicated to developing and maintaining survey software. It has a long list of features and is available in more than fifty languages. Content analysis is facilitated by an R program called ReadMe (Hopkins & King, 2008). Geographic analysis, spatial analysis, and mapping are implemented in programs known as GeoDA, R-Geo, and others (Bivand, Pebesma, & Gomez-Rubio, 2008).

More than a half-century ago, Coombs (1953) noted a significant dilemma of social science data analysis—that standard and commonly used data analysis techniques required ratio or interval data, while most social science variables tended to be measured at nominal or interval levels. Weisberg (2005) revisited the issue, noting that many researchers simply ignored the issue and treated ordinal data as interval. Some scholars worked on ways to more correctly reflect the proper interval for the ordinal categories. He noted a second solution would be to improve social science measurement, a project generally endorsed by Hage (1972). Instead of settling for ordinal measures, scholars might attempt to improve their measurements up to interval data. Weisberg (2005) argued that a better solution would be to become more innovative in terms of inventing more statistics for use with ordinal and nominal data, and noted that there was indeed, even in the early 1980s, very real progress with this, although the knowledge was not as diffused as it needed to be. Over the past quarter-century there has been substantial progress in the development of analysis tools specifically geared to nominal and ordinal data, and a number of leading software programs today allow users to define the level of measurement as part of the variable definitions so as to ensure the correct statistics are always calculated (e.g., Sall, Creighton, & Lehman, 2007; Joreskog & Sorbom, 1996).

One unmistakable data analysis trend of recent years is a substantial effort across many social science disciplines of focusing on the correct form of statistical test to match the nature of the data. Unlike the political science literature where such matters are closely attended to, communication scholars are often less concerned, perhaps feeling that the tests and routines they are used to using are sufficiently robust. However, in recent years, many new tests have been created to increase the technical precision of analyses and make them more defensible to the larger social science community. This is of particular concern with the use of weighted survey data. R helps solve this problem by making new statistical tests readily available to the research community and eliminating the cost of specialized software.

Another area of basic data analysis that needs attention is dealing with weighted survey data. Most high-quality survey research now produced is released with a complex series of sample-based weights. These are an important part of the random digit dialing sampling process and make important corrections for the probability of selecting a given respondent in a multi-member household. Weights also represent the number of unique telephone numbers that ring in the house and on which an interview could be completed. Corrections for such variables are essential. Most weighting systems also attempt to re-weight the sample to match population characteristics for a given area as ascertained by the census, Current Population Survey, American Community Survey, or some similar standard. There is increasing recognition that analyzing data containing such weights is potentially problematic for software not explicitly designed to handle them. In fact, many popular and widely used software packages do not accommodate sample weighting schemes without special additional software. Ignoring this issue can produce incorrect standard errors for many statistical tests, typically in the direction of creating standard errors that are too small, thus inflating many tests of statistical significance. Statistical software packages such as WesVar, Sudaan, and Stata build in such capabilities. SPSS requires the addition of a special software module called Complex Samples when using weighted data. Software built by Project R can handle many types of complex weighting (Lumley, 2004).

A final issue related to the precision of data analysis is the increased attention deserved by the problem of missing data. When working with large data sets, many analysts are content to simply use listwise deletion of missing cases. While this yields a complete data set to work with, depending on the number of variables, the total number of cases can drop significantly, thus raising questions about the representativeness of the remaining cases. Preferable solutions involve some means of managing missing data on the independent variable side, most preferably by multiple imputation or modeling. Although the basics of these procedures were worked out decades ago (e.g., Rubin, 1987), it is now recognized that not all imputation methods are equally sound and some produce less bias in certain situations. Communication scholars have also been slow to adopt these methods, often preferring to use listwise deletion or simple systems incorporated into SPSS such as mean substitution or other procedures in which cases are retained pairwise. A variety of programs are now available to assist with the analysis imputation of missing data, including an R program called Amelia II (Honaker, King, & Blackwell, 2009).

The Prospects for a Computational Social Science

Social scientists across a range of disciplines have been investigating macro communication behavior by exploiting the traces left by our society's use of new communication technologies and other types of public activities. Each digital transaction leaves a record that can be compiled to provide snapshots or dynamic records of individual and macro behavior. Lazer and colleagues (2009) argue that the time is right for the development of a "computational social science" in which these types of records would be collected and analyzed to improve our understanding of human interactions in the new technology-rich world. For political communication, this might involve analyzing elements of the Internet for traces of what people are saying to whom and how they are doing it on social networking sites, blogs, and through emails. This could be helpful in understanding the spread of rumors, certain types of perceptions, and the spread of activation of individuals. Computational social science holds great promise, particularly with respect to a range of macro phenomena including media use. As this literature gains traction and techniques for data gathering and analysis become more widely known, this is likely to be a promising area of research.

Measuring media use is a perennially important topic in political communication and the study of media effects, but the problem has grown dramatically more complicated with the proliferation of media opportunities, times of day, and the wide range of material present on the Internet. Attempts in the commercial research world to measure television audiences accurately suggest that these problems are very complex and not readily resolvable. Take the example of a typical network program. It might air on the network at 9 p.m., but many people set their digital video recorders to record the program. How many of them do that is certainly relevant, as is how many people actually watch the program over the next few hours or days. These additional viewings can add substantially to the viewership of a program. People can now also watch some programs streamed online, or download them after paying a fee on iTunes or another digital pay service. Deciding the relevant cutoffs and aggregating these disparate sources of data is necessary for an accurate measurement of audiences. Transferring these concerns to survey research or media use diaries for research purposes causes a substantial increase in complexity.

The proliferation of media opportunities also raises questions about the practice of multitasking with multiple media and other activities. Many measurements of aggregated media use, particularly within certain age ranges, are highly inflated because of research decisions to allow people to say they are Web surfing or texting while watching television, listening to music, reading, or doing other things. A great deal of basic research is necessary to sort out exactly what people are doing and with what impacts. Given the complexity of the problem, this is not going to be resolved easily. Any hopes the research community has of integrating content and audience data in studying media effects must begin with resolving basic, complex issues of media use and attention. These are important micro issues in terms of the psychological processes involved in understanding the true meaning of multitasking and measuring population-based measures of media use that are fundamental to understanding macro effects of communication.

Those scholars hoping for a golden age of computational social science are counting, at least in part, on being able to mine metadata about activities such as Internet searches, patterns of email traffic, text message networks, and similar information with other traces of mass behavior. At this stage, it is unclear how the legal, ethical, and privacy considerations involved in such massive data-gathering efforts will be resolved and whether the payoffs might be worth the effort. As communication phenomena continue to evolve, it is certain that researchers will be challenged to keep pace.

REFERENCES

Altman, M., & King, G. (2006). A proposed standard for the scholarly citation of quantitative data. Harvard University: Institute for Quantitative Social Science. Retrieved April 1, 2009, from http://gking. harvard.edu.

Benoit, W. L., & Holbert, R. L. (2008). Conducting communication research at methodological intersections: Replication, multiple quantitative methods, and bridging the quantitative-qualitative divide. *Journal of Communication, 58*, 615–628.

Berinsky, A. (2006). Public opinion in the 1930s and 1940s: The analysis of quota controlled sample survey data. *Public Opinion Quarterly, 70*, 530–564.

Bivand, R. S., Pebesma, E. J., & Gomez-Rubio, V. (2008). *Applied spatial data analysis with R*. New York: Springer.

Bryk, A. S., & Raudenbush, S. W. (1987). Application of hierarchical linear-models to assessing change. *Psychological Bulletin, 10*, 147–158.

Chaffee, S. H. (Ed.). (1975). *Political communication: Issues and strategies for research*. Beverly Hills, CA: Sage Publications.

Chaffee, S. H., & Schleuder, J. (1986). Measurement and effects of attention to media news. *Human Communication Research, 13*, 76–107.

Coombs, C. (1953). *A theory of data*. New York: John Wiley.

Cook, T. D., & Campbell, D. T. (1979). *Quasi-experimentation: Design and analysis issues for field studies*. Boston: Houghton-Mifflin.

Edmonds, R. (2009). *The state of the news media, 2009*. Pew Project for Excellence in Journalism. Retrieved April 1, 2009, from http://www.stateofthenewsmedia.org/2009/index.htm.

Fishkin, J. S. (1996). *The voice of the people: Public opinion and democracy*. New Haven: Yale University Press.

Gastil, J., & Levine, P. (2005). *The deliberative democracy handbook: Strategies for effective civic engagement in the 21st century*. San Francisco: Jossey-Bass.

Gelman, A. (2008). *Red state, blue state, rich state, poor state: Why Americans vote the way they do*. Princeton, NJ: Princeton University Press.

Gelman, A., & Hill, J. (2007). *Data analysis using regression and multilevel/hierarchical models*. New York: Cambridge University Press.

Giddens, A. (1986). *The constitution of society: Outline of the theory of structuration*. Cambridge: Polity Press.

Graetz, M. J., & Shapiro, I. (2005). *Death by a thousand cuts: The fight over taxing inherited wealth*. Princeton: Princeton University Press.

Groves, R. M. (1989). *Survey errors and survey costs*. New York: John Wiley & Sons.

Hage, J. (1972). *Techniques and problems of theory construction in sociology*. New York: John Wiley & Sons.

Halperin, M., & Harris, J. F. (2006). *The way to win: Taking the White House in 2008*. New York: Random House.

Holbert, R. L. (2005). Back to basics: Revisiting, resolving and expanding some of the fundamental issues of political communication research. *Political Communication, 22*, 511–514.

Holbert, R. L., & Stephenson, M. T. (2003). The importance of analyzing indirect effects in media effects research: Testing for mediation in structural equation modeling. *Journal of Broadcasting & Electronic Media, 47*, 553–569.

Honaker, J., King, G., & Blackwell, M. (2009). *Amelia II: A program for missing data*. Retrieved February 24, 2009, from http://gking.harvard.edu/amelia/.

Hopkins, D., & King, G. (2008). *A method of automated nonparametric content analysis for social science*. Retrieved February 21, 2009, from http://gking.harvard.edu/readme/.

Howe, J. (2008). *Crowdsourcing*. New York: Crown Business.

Imai, K., King, G., & Lau, O. (2009). *Zelig: Everyone's statistical software*. Retrieved February 21, 2009, from http://gking.harvard.edu/zelig/docs/index.html.

Jenkins, H. (2006). *Convergence culture: Where old and new media collide*. New York: New York University Press.

Jones, B. D., & Williams, W. (2008). *The politics of bad ideas: The great tax cut delusion and the decline of good government in America*. New York: Pearson Longman.

Joreskog, K. G., & Sorbom, D. (1996). *Prelis 2: User's reference guide*. Chicago: Scientific Software International.

King, G. (1995). Replication, replication. *PS: Political Science and Politics, 28*, 443–99.

King, G. (2007). An introduction to the Dataverse Network as an infrastructure for data sharing. *Sociological Methods & Research, 36*(2), 173–199.

King, G., Keohane, R. O., Verba, S. (1994). *Designing social inquiry*. Princeton, NJ: Princeton University Press.

Klein, N. (2008). *Shock doctrine: The rise of disaster capitalism*. New York: Picador.

Knights, M. (1994). *Politics and opinion in crisis, 1678–81*. Cambridge: Cambridge University Press.

Kosicki, G. M., Amor, D. L., & McLeod, J. M. (1987). Processing strategies for mass media information: Selecting, integrating, and making sense of the news. Paper presented at the annual meeting of International Communication Association, Montreal, Canada.

Lau, R., & Redlawsk, D. (2006). *How voters decide: Information processing during election campaigns*. Cambridge: Cambridge University Press.

Lavrakas, P. J., Shuttles, C. D., Steeh, C., & Fienberg, H. (2007). The state of surveying cell phone numbers in the United States. *Public Opinion Quarterly, 71*, 840–854.

Lazarsfeld, P. F. (1958). Evidence and inference in social research. In D. Lerner (Ed.), *Evidence and inference* (pp. 107–135). New York: Free Press.

Lazer, D., et al. (2009). Computational social science. *Science, 323*, 721–723.

Leighninger, M. (2006). *The next form of democracy*. Nashville: Vanderbilt University Press.

Lessig, L. (2005). *Free culture: The nature and future of creativity*. New York: Penguin.

Lumley, T. (2004). Analysis of complex survey samples. *Journal of Statistical Software, 9*, 1–19.

McLeod, D. M., & Tichenor, P. J. (2001). The logic of social and behavioral science. In G. H. Stempel III & B. H. Westley (Eds.), *Research methods in mass communication* (3rd ed.). Englewood Cliffs, NJ: Prentice-Hall.

McLeod, D. M., Kosicki, G. M., & McLeod, J. M. (2002). Resurveying the boundaries of political communication effects. In J. Bryant & D. Zillmann (Eds.), *Media effects: Advances in theory and research* (2nd ed., pp. 215–267). Hillsdale, NJ: Lawrence Erlbaum.

McLeod, J. M. (2007, August). Using mediation analysis to develop explanations of communication processes and effects. Paper presented at Sungkyunkwan University, Seoul, South Korea.

McLeod, J. M., Kosicki, G. M., & McLeod, D. M. (2009). Levels of analysis and communication science. In C. Berger, M. Roloff, & D. Roskos-Ewoldsen (Eds.), *The handbook of communication science* (2nd ed., pp. 183–200). Thousand Oaks, CA: Sage.

McLeod, J. M., & McDonald, D. G. (1985). Beyond simple exposure: Media orientations and their impact on political processes. *Communication Research, 12*, 3–33.

McLeod, J. M., & Pan, Z. (2005). Concept explication and theory construction. In S. Dunwoody, L. B. Becker, D. M. McLeod, & G. M. Kosicki (Eds.), *The evolution of key mass communication concepts* (pp. 13–76). Cresskill, NJ: Hampton Press.

McLeod, J. M., Shah, D. V., Hess, D. E., & Lee, N.-J. (2009). Communication and education: Creating communication competence for socialization into public life. In L. R. Sherrod, C. A. Flanagan, and J. Torney-Purta (Eds.), *Handbook of research on civic engagement in youth*. New York: Wiley.

Meyer, P. (2004). *The vanishing newspaper: Saving journalism in the information age*. Columbia, MO: University of Missouri Press.

Mills, C. W. (1959). *The sociological imagination*. New York: Oxford University Press.

Newport, F. (2004). *Polling matters: Why leaders must listen to the voice of the people*. New York: Warner Books.

Raymond, J. (1996). *The invention of the newspaper: English newsbooks 1641–1649*. Oxford: Oxford University Press.

Reynolds, P. D. (1971). *A primer in theory construction*. Indianapolis: Bobbs-Merrill.

Rubin, D. B. (1987). *Multiple imputation for nonresponse in surveys*. Hoboken, NJ: John Wiley & Sons.

Sall, J., Creighton, L., & Lehman, A. (2007). *JMP Start Statistics: A guide to statistics and data analysis using JMP* (4th ed.). Cary, NC: SAS Publishing.

Sanders, L. (1997). Against deliberation. *Political Theory, 25*(3), 347–376.

Shah, D. V., Kwak, N., Schmierbach, M., & Zubric, J. (2004). The interplay of news frames on cognitive complexity. *Human Communication Research, 30*, 102–120.

Slater, M. D., Snyder, L., & Hayes, A. F. (2006). Thinking and modeling at multiple levels: The potential contribution of multilevel modeling to communication theory and research. *Human Communication Research, 32*, 375–384.

Sotirovic, M., & McLeod, J. M. (2004). Knowledge as understanding: The information processing approach to political learning. In L. Kaid (Ed.), *Handbook of political communication research* (pp. 357–394). Mahwah, NJ: Lawrence Erlbuam.

Starr, P. (2004). *The creation of the media: Political origins of modern communications*. New York: Basic Books.

Stinchcombe, A. L. (2005). *The logic of social research*. Chicago: University of Chicago Press.

Tewksbury, D., Weaver, A. J. & Maddex, B. D. (2001). Accidentally informed: Incidental news exposure on the World Wide Web. *Journalism & Mass Communication Quarterly, 78*, 533–554.

Tichenor, P. J., Donohue, G. A., & Olien, C. N. (1973). Mass communication research: Evolution of a structural model. *Journalism Quarterly, 50*, 419–426.

Weisberg, H. F. (2005). *The total survey error approach: A guide to the new science of survey research*. Chicago: University of Chicago Press.

Zaret, D. (2000). *Origins of democratic culture: Printing, petitions, and the public sphere in early modern England*. Princeton: Princeton University Press.

Index

Abroms, L. 456
Abu Ghraib prisoner abuse scandal 42, 201, 246, 248, 252, 254, 259, 261, 313
Acapulco Typology 10, 385–7, 389
Achen, C. H. 194
ADSAM visual measures 405, 407–8
advertising, political: agenda setting 390; comparative research 402–5; content analysis 274; deceptive 46; experiments 131–2, 135–6, 137, 138–9; exposure 130–1; memory of 130; meta-analysis 120–1; NAES 101; physiological responses to 534–6; viewers' reactions 135–6, 137, 138
Affe, R. B. 487
affinity displays 170–2, 174, 181, 214–18, 224
affordances 486–8, 489, 496, 500–1
agenda setting 10, 200, 383–94; Acapulco Typology 385–7, 389; Chapel Hill study 383–4, 385; comparative research 387–91, 399; content analysis 268, 271, 274; cross-sectional surveys 34–5; media influence 201, 369–70; NAES 102
agonistic displays 169, 172–3, 174, 180
Ahn, T. K. 155
Al-Haqeel, A. 389
Allen, M. 119
Allport, G. 56
Almond, G. A. 396
Althaus, S. L. 64, 103, 104, 106, 387, 399
Altheide, D. L. 367, 368, 372
Ambady, N. 184
ambivalence 67, 88–9, 194, 233
American National Election Studies (ANES) 5, 96–113, 511, 512, 553; future of 108–10; institutions 106; issues and evaluations 105–6; media use 63, 102–5, 399, 563; origins 97–8; overreporting 60–1; panel data 20, 99–100; research design 35, 98–9; secondary analysis 6, 81, 84, 88; strengths and weaknesses 28–31; television news 203n2
Americanization 402
Amodio, D. 532
An, C. 196–7
Andersen, R. 315
Anger-Elfenbein, H. 184
Ansolabehere, S. 130, 131, 136–8, 141, 150
Antonakis, J. 183

archetypes 302, 314
Argentina 390
"argument repertoire" 89–90, 337
Arntfield, M. 304
Aronson, E. 198, 201, 202
Asp, K. 368
associational juxtaposition 214
attention 27, 63, 91–2, 399, 485, 558; agenda setting 385, 386; indirect effects 438, 439–45, 447, 452, 457; measurement of 529; television viewing 90–1
attitudes 55, 56–7, 72, 526; deliberation 337; four-stage model 58; framing 239, 240, 241–2, 244, 248; instability 194; racial 351; response latency 508; satisficing model 59; strength of 66–7, 84
attrition 28, 31, 39, 99
Au, K. 426
Auh, T. S. 389
Austin, E. W. 437
Australia 389–90, 391, 405
authenticity 87, 91–2, 233
autocorrelation 467, 469–70
autonomic nervous system (ANS) 528, 529–30
autoregressive conditional heteroskedasticity (ARCH) models 474
Autoregressive Distributed Lag (ADL) model 468, 477
Autoregressive Integrated Moving Average (ARIMA) modeling 472–4, 478n23, 478n25
Averill, J. R. 86
Aw, A. 401

Babbie, E. 200
backward telescoping 66
Ban, H. 387, 391
Bantamaroudis, P. 387
Bartels, L. M. 520
Battaglini, M. 155
Baum, M. A. 61–2, 85
Baxter, L. A. 200
Baybeck, B. 350, 351
Bechtel, A. 84–5
Beckmann, M. N. 150
Behr, R. L. 34–5
Benjamin, D. J. 182

570

Bennett, S. E. 56
Benoit, W. L. 119, 271, 274, 275, 404, 406
Berelson, B. 20, 269, 346
Bernstein, R. 60
bias 58, 451, 547; experiments 129, 139; media 119–20, 186, 254, 400; newscasters' facial expressions 175; rolling cross-sectional surveys 47–50; selection 354, 356, 357–8; social desirability 60, 63–4, 505–11, 514–16, 518–20, 534; visual 210
Biesanz, J. C. 429
Bin Laden, Osama 315
biopolitics 108–9
Bishop, G. F. 56, 57, 65
Black, L. W. 325, 330–1, 338, 341n3
Blais, A. 49
Blalock, H. M., Jr. 421
blogs 486, 487, 489, 551
Bloor, M. 292
Blumler, J. 384
"bogus pipeline" procedure 67, 507, 518
Bollen, K. A. 428–9
Bone, P. F. 156
Books, J. W. 352
bootstrapping 11, 448–52, 457, 459, 558
Bracken, C. C. 268
Bradburn, N. 65
Brader, T. 151, 153–4, 200
Bradley, S. D. 177, 525
Brady, H. E. 49, 52n4, 53n15
brain 526, 527–8, 532–4
Branton, R. P. 352
Breslaw, E. G. 309
Brody, R. A. 22
Brown, N. 390
Browne, M. W. 427
Bryant, J. 120
Bryman, A. 82, 83
Bucy, E. P. 4, 177, 179, 184, 288, 291–2, 296, 487, 488, 490–2, 495–6, 525
Buhr, T. A. 150
Burkhalter, S. 324–5, 331, 335, 337, 341, 341n6, 341n9
Bush, George H. W.: facial displays 175; negative campaigning 287; public opinion 92; visual framing 219, 220, 221, 223, 225–6, 232
Bush, George W. 44, 46, 88, 91, 133–4; Abramoff ethics scandal 136; affinity displays 224; election controversy 246, 248, 252, 254, 259, 261, 518, 521n1; *Fahrenheit 9/11* film 197, 437; focus groups 287; media frames 238; NAES 100, 105, 106; negative campaigning 219, 287; physiological responses to 535; rhetoric of evil 300, 303, 304, 315; selective exposure 135; televised speeches 171; visual framing 216, 217, 223, 229–31

Cacioppo, J. T. 56

campaign messages 34, 121, 129–30, 212, 270
Campbell, A. 97
Campbell, David 301
Campbell, Donald T. 198, 199, 200–1, 203n1, 203n3, 421
Canache, D. 66
Canada 35, 405, 470–1
Canel, M. J. 388
Cannell, C. 58
Caplan, S. E. 197
Cappella, J. N. 87, 89, 337
Carlin, D. 289
Carlsmith, J. M. 198
Carroll, J. S. 156
Carter, D. F. 82, 83
Carter, Jimmy 174, 175, 210
cascading outcome approach 195, 197
case studies 334–5, 339, 340
Casermeiro de Pereson, A. 390
Casey, M. A. 292–3
casinos 247, 248, 252, 260, 261
causal steps approach 445–6
causality: data analysis pitfalls 560–1; experiments 52n2, 129–31, 200, 561; Granger causality tests 471; heterogeneity 351–2; mediation and indirect effects 436; panel studies 23–4, 32, 39; proximate causation 167, 186n4; rolling cross-sectional surveys 51; scientific methods 546; social communication research 356–7, 358–9; time-series analysis 475; ultimate causation 167, 186n4
celebrities 218, 224
cell phones 70–1, 555
Chadha, A. 60
Chaffee, S. H. 63, 91–2, 544
Chaiken, S. 56
Chambers, S. 323
Chang, C. 404
Chapel Hill study 383–4, 385
Chen, R. 456
Cheong, J. 456
Cheung, M. W. L. 426
children, images with 216, 224
Chile 390
China 399
Chirac, Jacques 176
Choi, W. S. 391
Chong, D. 476
Cialdini, R. B. 156
citizenship 325, 336, 337
Clark, A. 70
Clinton, Bill: casual style 218–19; facial displays 175, 177, 182, 210; focus groups 287, 288; Lewinsky scandal 241, 516–18; unexpected events 44; visual framing 216, 217, 223, 225–9, 232–3
Clinton, Hillary 44, 102, 490
coding process: computer-aided coding 8, 234;

content analysis 272; deliberation 328, 329, 330–1; focus groups 292; framing 241, 250–1, 262n14; visual framing 222–3

cognitive appraisal 180–1

cognitive mediation model of learning 437, 438, 442

Cohen, J. 338

Cole, D. A. 24

Combs, J. E. 368, 369

commercial logic 373

comparative research 10, 13, 395–416, 545; agenda setting 387–91, 399; mediatization 379; multiple-sample/multiple-group models 426; news exposure and coverage 398–401; political advertising 402–5; political debates 405–6; public opinion 401–2

compassion 213, 214–18, 224, 226–30, 233

Computer Assisted Personal Interviewing (CAPI) 98

computer content analysis 274–7, 341n4, 545, 557

Condit, C. M. 301, 305–6

confidentiality 506–7

confirmatory factor analysis (CFA) 421, 422–3, 424

Congress 57, 104, 106, 107–8

Conrad, F. G. 71–2

constructivist approach 287

content analysis 7–8, 268–79, 557; agenda setting 384, 386; categories for 270–1; coding process 272; computer 274–7, 341n4, 545, 557; definitions of 268–70; deliberation 327, 328, 329, 330–1, 339; facial displays 178–9; focus groups 291–2; framing 240–1, 243–61; mediatization 379; panel studies 20, 28, 32n1; reliability 273; sampling texts 271–2; validity 274, 275, 328; visuals 209–37, 545

contexts 349–50, 360, 548–51; context effects 62, 68, 69, 70; level of analysis 351, 352; sampling 354; validity 356

convenience samples 272

conversation analysis 292, 330

Converse, J. M. 56, 57, 65, 97, 194, 519

Conway, M. T. 234

Cook, T. D. 203n1

Cook, T. E. 371, 375

Coombs, C. 565

Cooperative Campaign Analysis Project (CCAP) 108

Corker, Bob 136

Cornwell, J. M. 429

Cosley, D. 331

Cotton, J. 135

Couper, M. P. 71–2

covariates 456

Craig, S. C. 337

creativity 81–2, 86–8, 92

Crète, J. 49

critical tests 427

cross-sectional surveys 4, 5, 19, 23; costs 27, 28; limitations 34–5; "rally-round-the-flag" effect 22; repeated cross-section design 38, 39, 42, 44–5, 46, 51; see also rolling cross-sectional surveys

Crosstalk project 287–8, 290

cross-validation 426–7

Croucher, S. M. 401

Crowne, D. P. 507–8, 511, 514

The Crucible (Miller) 304, 307, 314, 315

Csikszentmihalyi, M. 498

Cudeck, R. 427–8

culture 396–7, 401–2

Curtin, R. 53n16

Czilli, E. J. 87, 89

D'Alessio, D. 119

Dalgas, O. 183

Dalrymple, K. E. 84

Damasio, A. R. 186n5

Daniel, S. H. 303

Dartmouth group 166, 168, 170, 174, 176, 178–9, 182, 184, 534, 535–6

Darwin, C. 169, 171, 172, 180

data: data analysis trends 565; Dataverse Network Project 552–3; dichotomous 423; focus groups 291–3; meta-analysis 117, 118; missing 566; rolling cross-sectional surveys 46; social communication research 354–5, 359, 360; time-series analysis 467–8, 476; weighted survey data 565–6

Davidson, D. K. 214

Davidson, R. J. 507

De La Torre, L. 390

De Vreese, C. H. 261n3, 400

debates: ANES 103; comparative research 405–6; content analysis 270; facial displays 175; focus groups 289, 290; honesty ratings 45; meta-analysis 119; multi-stage experiments 196, 197; secondary analysis 84

Deegan, C. 390

Deess, E. P. 336

DeGroot, J. 331

deliberation 9, 323–45, 545; antecedents 335–6, 339, 340–1; case study integration 334–5, 339, 340; discussion analysis 327–32; model of 324–6; outcomes 336–8, 339, 340; participant assessments 327, 332–4, 339, 340; political logic 373

deliberative polls 556–7

Deliberative Quality Index 332

Delli Carpini, M. X. 61, 288, 292, 341n1

democracy, deliberative 323–4, 339

Democrats: "argument repertoire" 90; content analysis 275–6; debates 270; media bias 119–20; news preferences 104, 143; online experiments 141; physiological responses to Reagan 534, 535–6; viewers' reactions to

advertising 136, 138; visual framing 223, 232, 233
demonology 303–4, 311
Denemark, D. 389–90
Deshpand, S. 436
Devanathan, N. 436
Dever, J. A. 72
Devil 303–4, 306–12, 313, 314–15, 316
DeVillis, R. F. 500
diffusion of innovation 407
Dillman, D. 65, 72
discourse 8–9, 304–5, 326, 328–9
discourse analysis 292, 330–1, 339, 545
Discourse Quality Index (DQI) 328–9
diversity 286, 347, 352, 356
Doan, K. 159
Dole, Bob: debate with Mondale 187n7; visual framing 214, 215, 220–1, 223, 228–9, 232–3; website of 494
dominance 169, 172–3, 176, 177, 183, 186n6, 210, 408
donations 153
Dovidio, J. F. 166
Downes, E. J. 493
dress 214, 224–5, 232
"drop-in" samples 139–41
Duff, B. 61
Dukakis, Michael 92, 130, 225, 231, 287
Durr, R. H. 478n15
Dutwin, D. 329
dynamic information board 153

Eagly, A. H. 56
East Asia 390–1
Eco, U. 315
ecological fallacy 47
Edelman, M. J. 233
Edwards, G. C. 22
effectiveness 87, 89–91
Egypt 389
Ehlen, J. & P. 71
Eibl-Eibesfeldt, I. 170–1, 172
Ekman, P. 169, 172, 173, 179–80, 507, 510
election campaigns: agenda setting 383–4, 390; attention to 27, 49–50; candidate traits 42–3, 44; candidate websites 490; communication flows/processes 395, 466; comparative research 398; contentious nature of 548; contexts 549; facial displays 165–6, 178–9; focus groups 287–8, 290; media influence on 52n1, 470–1; meta-analysis 122–3; panel studies 25, 28–31; re-interviewing bias 39–40; repeated cross-section design 38; rolling cross-sectional surveys 40–2, 46; secondary analysis 84; selective exposure 135; tracking polls 38; unexpected events 43–4; visuals 209–37; *see also* American National Election Studies; National Annenberg Election Studies; negative

campaigning; presidential candidates; voting behavior
electoral systems 403
electrodermal activity (EDA) 528–9
electroencephalogram (EEG) 510, 532, 533, 537
elites 241–2, 388–9, 475, 476
Ellen, P. S. 156
Ellyson, S. L. 166
embarrassment 507, 508, 519
emotions: agenda setting 387; brain activation 526, 528; facial displays 169, 174, 176–7, 180, 184, 187n8, 187n10; facial electromyography 530–1; focus groups 288; psychological underpinnings 538; responses to advertising messages 405; survey responses 507
Engell, A. D. 183
Entman, R. M. 211
environmental issues 391
equality 306
error: measurement 194, 456, 520, 554; media exposure 64; memory 130; meta-analysis 115, 116; multiple-step multiple mediator model 448; product of coefficients approach 446–7; question wording 66; questionnaire design 68; reducing 65–8; sampling 47–8, 445, 554; self-reports 152; Total Survey Error approach 554; Web-based surveys 71, 72; weighted survey data 565–6; *see also* bias
error correction model (ECM) 470
Esaiasson, P. 368
Esser, F. 379
estimation 11, 420–1, 424, 426–9
ethical issues 124–5, 294, 507, 567
ethnographic trap 116–17
ethology 7, 168–70, 176, 178, 186
Europe: agenda setting 388–9, 391; broadcasting systems 396; comparative research 398; European Social Survey 88; political advertising 403; qualitative language analysis 407
evaluation 11, 420–1, 426–9
Evans, H. K. 4
Eveland, W. P., Jr. 23, 84, 87, 91–2, 198, 427, 437, 438, 439, 444
Everitt, J. 437
evil 300–1, 302–5, 312, 315
evolutionary psychology 132, 165, 166–7, 173, 178
Exline, R. V. 174, 175
expectancy value model 239
expected cross-validation index (ECVI) 427
experimental realism 198, 199, 200
experimental studies 6–7, 109, 129–48, 149, 475, 544–5, 556–7; agenda setting 386, 387, 391; causality 52n2, 129–31, 561; expressed preferences 7, 150–2, 154–6, 160–1; facial displays 173–8, 180–1, 183–4; facial similarity as political cue 132–4, 146n3; generalizability 136–44, 561; institutional constraints 551;

Internet use 500; long-term effects 7; methodological issues 167–8; multi-stage 194–205; quasi-experiments 25, 27; racial cues in news coverage 132, 133; research participants 177–8, 184–5; respondent burnout 560; revealed preferences 152–4, 160; scripts 156–60, 161; selective exposure 134–5; short-term effects 558; social communication research 359; viewers' reactions to advertising 135–6, 137, 138

exposure 62–4, 91–2, 130–1, 485, 558; comparative research 398–401; selective 134–5; television 436–7

expressed preferences 149, 150–2, 154–6, 157, 158, 160–1

Eyal, C. 386

eyes 173, 181

Fabius, Laurent 176

faces 165–93; anger/threat 172–3, 182, 210; automatic analysis 184; cognitive processing 528; ethological approach 168–70; evolutionary questions 166–7; facial attractiveness 182–3, 187n12; facial similarity 132–4, 146n3; fear/submission 173, 182, 210; future research 178–85; happiness/reassurance 170–1, 182, 210; methodological issues 167–8; primate comparisons 170, 172; sadness/appeasement 171–2, 182, 210; viewer responses to nonverbal leader displays 173–8

face-to-face surveys 69, 72, 98, 108

Facial Action Coding System (FAC) 179–80, 184

facial electromyography (EMG) 177, 183–4, 510, 530–1, 532, 534, 535–6

Fahrenheit 9/11 197, 437

fairness 119, 120, 123

false attribution 44–5

family images 216, 224, 231

Fan, D. P. 87, 92

favorability ratings 39, 90

Fazio, R. H. 202, 508

fear 116–17, 173, 180, 181, 182, 187n9, 210

"feeling thermometers" 44–5, 88, 91, 105, 111n22, 176, 535

Feinstein, Dianne 131

Feinstein, J. L. 508

Feldman, L. 81, 87, 90

Feldman, S. 57

Fenske, M. 304

Fern, E. F. 293

Ferris, A. L. 271–2

Festinger, L. 508

Fico, F. G. 269, 275

"file-drawer" model 56

Fishkin, J. 337, 556, 557

Fiske, D. W. 421

focus groups 8–9, 283–99, 545; contrast with deliberation 325; data analysis 291–3; definition and overview 283–6; ethical considerations 294; history of 286; number of participants 285; practical concerns 290–1; strengths and limitations 293; uses of 286–9

Ford, Gerald 174, 175

Ford, Harold Jr. 136, 137

forward telescoping 66

Foucault, M. 302, 305

four-stage model 58–9, 68

Fowler, J. H. 152, 153

Fox News 105, 120, 135, 142–3

fractional integration 474

framing 8, 238–67, 545; coding process 250–1, 262n14; comparative research 400; definition of 239–40; effects of 241–2; identification of 240–1, 249–50; media influence 369–70; NAES 102; physiological measures 538; racial issues 107; selection of issues 243–8; sources and articles 248–9; time periods 248; visual 211, 212–34, 249

France 398–9, 400, 401, 405, 406

free speech 240, 244, 257, 260

Frentz, T. S. 315–16

Friedman, H. S. 165–6, 175

Friesen, W. V. 179

Fulla, S. 495

Fung, A. 339

Gabel, M. 479n28

Gadir, S. 389

Gallup 38, 70, 554

Gamson, W. 240, 287, 289

Garland, M. W. 52n9

Gastil, J. 324, 325, 331–4, 336, 338, 340, 341n3

Gaudet, H. 20

gay marriage 244–8, 249, 252, 253, 254, 258, 261

gaze 173, 181

Gazzaniga, M. S. 528

Geer, J. G. 274

Gelman, A. 52n1, 565

gender: ideographic approach 306; negative media coverage of women 437; online experiments 141; response latency 512, 516; sexual harassment 244; survey responses 66

genealogy 301, 303, 304–6, 316

General Social Survey (GSS) 81, 84, 107, 108, 110n2

generalizability 47, 200, 201, 561; comparative research 398; deliberation 331, 338; experiments 129, 136–44, 145; facial displays 178; focus groups 292–3; meta-analysis 117; scripts 161; social communication research 353, 355, 356

genetics 108–9

Germany 388, 397, 399, 401, 403, 405, 406

Ghana 389

Gibson, J. J. 486, 487

Gidengil, E. 437

Giuliani, Rudy 102
Glick, J. A. 284
global warming 245, 248, 252, 254, 257–8, 261
Glynn, C. 151, 402
Gore, Al 45, 88, 91, 210; casual style 218–19; election controversy 246, 248, 252, 254, 259, 261, 518, 521n1; physiological responses to 535; selective exposure 135; visual framing of 213, 214, 215, 223, 229–30, 232, 233
Gorpe, S. 389
governance 549–50
Graber, D. A. 72, 85, 209, 288, 292, 369, 476
Graff, M. 490
Grammer, K. 171
Grandjean, D. 169
Granger causality tests 471
Grannovetter, M. S. 347
Great Britain 397, 399, 400, 403, 405
Greece 403, 406
Greenberg, B. S. 271–2
Gregson, K. S. 491, 492
Grice, H. P. 57
Griffin, M. 404
Grimes, M. F. 339
group interaction 284, 289, 326, 360n4
Groves, R. M. 554
Guba, E. 293
guessing 66
Gutmann, N. 339

Ha, L. 493
Habermas, J. 328, 338
Hacker, K. L. 491
Hage, J. 565
Haider-Markel, D. P. 84
Hallin, D. C. 396
Hanmer, M. J. 61
Hansen, G. J. 119, 197, 275
Harris Interactive 72
Hart, R. P. 276, 328
Hartz-Karp, J. 334, 335
hate group rallies 240, 244, 247, 248, 252, 254, 260, 261
Haug, C. 330
Hay, R. A. 473
Hayes, A. F. 23, 402, 439, 442, 446, 452, 457, 458
Haynie, D. L. 456
heart rate 529–30
Heeter, C. 493
Henly, S. J. 427–8
Hershey, M. 102
Hess, V. 91
Hetherington, M. J. 84
heuristics 58, 62, 496–8, 499, 501
Hierarchical Linear Modeling (HLM) 425
higher-order factor structures 421
Hill, J. 565
Hill, T. G. 436–7

Hispanics 46, 70
Hjarvard, S. 368
Hofstede, G. 396–7, 401
Holbert, R. L. 23, 84–5, 87, 89, 197, 202, 436–7, 454, 487, 558
Holbrook, R. A. 436–7
Holbrook, T. M. 52n1, 97
Hollander, B. A. 120, 284
Holsti, R. R. 269
Holtz-Bacha, C. 396, 397
Hong Kong 399
Horton, Willie 130
Houston, D. A. 159
Hovland, C. 130, 131
Huckfeldt, R. 155, 349, 350, 352, 353
Huffington, Arianna 70
Huge, M. 151
Hughes, R. T. 300
Human Computer Interaction (HCI) 492, 493
Hyman, H. H. 82
hypothesis testing 546, 561

Iacoboni, M. 532
ideal candidates 213–18, 223–4, 226–8, 230, 232
ideodynamic model 92
ideographic approach 306
"image bites" approach 209, 210–12
image evaluation 404–5
immigration 151, 153–4, 246–7, 248, 252, 254, 259, 261, 306
Implicit Association Test (IAT) 109
indirect effects 428, 435–6, 563; bootstrapping 448–52; causal steps approach 445–6; longitudinal studies 454–6; moderation 453–4; multiple-step multiple mediator model 443–5, 448, 451, 460–3; product of coefficients approach 446–8; simple mediation model 438–41, 457, 458; single-step multiple mediator model 441–3, 450, 451, 452
information processing 288, 509–10, 519, 526, 527–8, 533
inoculation 196–7
institutions: ANES/NAES 106; democratic 548; institutional constraints 551–3; mediatization 370–2, 375–6, 378–9
intelligent design 244–8, 252, 254, 255–7, 258, 261
interactivity 12, 486, 487–8, 490–501
interdisciplinary research 10, 109
international research 13, 395–416; agenda setting 10, 384, 387–91; news exposure and coverage 398–401; political advertising 402–5; political debates 405–6; public opinion 401–2
Internet 64, 123, 160, 369, 399, 485–504, 550–1, 566–7; affordances 486–8, 489, 500–1; ANES 103; content analysis 557; experiments 129, 134, 135–6, 139–44; impact on mainstream media 548–9, 562; interactivity 12, 486, 487–8, 490–501; NAES 104; perceptions 488–9;

response latency in online surveys 510, 511–18, 520–1; revealed preferences 153; rolling cross-sectional surveys 41–2; sampling issues 521n5; secondary analysis 84–5; subject recruitment 185; Web-based surveys 12, 31, 71–2, 108, 555
intervention analysis 472–4
interviews: ANES 98; Computer Assisted Telephone Interviewing 555; face-to-face surveys 69; NAES 100; normative structure 57; open-ended 289; re-interviewing bias 39–40; rolling cross-sectional surveys 35, 40–2, 46, 47
Iraq War 42, 43, 136, 238, 312
Israel 399, 404, 405, 406
Issue Ownership theory 275
Italy 399, 403, 405
item response theory (IRT) 423
Iyengar, S. 34–5, 130–1, 136–8, 141, 150, 160, 196, 199–202, 387

James, E. L. 493
Jamieson, K. H. 46, 91, 97, 274, 288
Japan 386, 390–1, 399, 401
Jarvis, S. 328
Jenkins, R. W. 470
Jerit, J. 262n6, 471–2
Johnston, R. 49, 52n4, 53n15, 97, 274
Jones, B. S. 352
Jöreskog, K. 419, 421, 425, 427, 429
Joslyn, M. R. 84
journalistic values 401
journals 4, 23, 85, 532, 552, 555
juries 336, 337
Just, M. R. 287–8, 292

Kagan, S. 404
Kaid, L. L. 214, 274, 288–9, 290, 397
Kam, C. D. 153
Kamarck, E. C. 494
Kaplan, J. T. 526
Kaplan, Marty 233
Karp, J. A. 52n9
Kashy, D. A. 421–2
Kazan, Elia 306–7, 316n2
Keele, L. 470
Keeter, S. 61, 70–1
Kellstedt, P. M. 107, 241
Kelly, N. J. 470
Kelshaw, T. 324
Kendall, P. 289
Kennedy, C. 70
Kennedy, P. 478n16
Kenny, D. A. 421–2
Kenski, K. 39, 46, 84
Kerry, John 42–4, 46, 133–4, 197; NAES 100, 101, 105; negative campaigning against 121, 219, 230, 287; visual framing 211, 216, 218, 220, 223, 231, 232–3

Keum, H. 436
Key, V. O., Jr. 351, 466
Khoo, S. T. 456
Kiecolt, K. J. 81
Kinder, D. R. 196, 199–200, 201–2, 213, 387, 475
King, G. 52n1, 477n4
King, P. 387
Kiousis, S. 81, 84, 387
Klein, J. 225, 229, 230
Klem, L. 419
Klofstad, C. A. 359, 361n6
knowledge, political 24, 26, 61–2, 72; ANES/NAES 105; civic engagement 563; deliberation 337; focus groups 284, 288; meta-analysis 122, 124; news media 22–3, 104; physiological measures 538; political debates 119; political discussion 437; secondary analysis 89; smoothing bias 49; structural equation modeling 427; surveillance gratifications 438, 439–45, 447, 452, 457; time-series analysis 475–6
Knowledge Networks 72, 144, 555, 561
Korea 390–1, 404, 405, 406
Kosicki, G. M. 562–3
Krippendorff, K. 269, 327
Kroes, E. P. 151
Krosnick, J. A. 59, 65, 67, 97, 507, 508, 510, 518
Krueger, R. A. 291, 292–3, 295
Krupnikov, Y. 150, 155, 156
Ku Klux Klan 247, 252, 254, 260
Kwak, N. 23, 85, 198, 437
Kwansah-Aidoo, K. 384, 389

Lacy, S. 269, 275
LaMarre, H. 84
Lance, C. E. 429
Landreville, K. 84
language: comparative research 400, 401; myths 301; political 287; quantitative analysis 407
Lasswell, H. D. 315
latent content 273, 275, 276
latent growth curve modeling 455–6
latent variable approach 424–5, 456
latent-composite modeling 89
Latin America 390, 391
Lau, R. 120, 153
laughter 186n4
Laver, M. 356
Lazarsfeld, P. F. 20, 134, 284, 286, 406
Lazer, D. 566
leaders: facial attractiveness 182–3, 187n12; facial displays 168–9, 173–8, 183, 185, 210; negative media coverage of women leaders 437; physiological responses to 525–6, 534–6; see also presidential candidates
Lee, C. 404
Lee, E. 402
Lee, G. H. 391

Leshner, G. 152
Leung, K. 426
Levine, A. S. 153, 154, 158
Levine, T. R. 421
Levy, M. R. 494
Lieberman, M. D. 533
Lincoln, Y. 293
linear models 489, 493
Lippmann, W. 369
LISREL 424, 425, 429, 442, 563
Liu, J. 402
Liu, Y. 84
Llamas, J. P. 388
Lockhart, Joe 211
Lombard, M. 268
longitudinal studies 19, 454–6
Lopez-Escobar, E. 388
Lorenz, B. 171
Lucaites, J. L. 301, 305–6
Lundby, K. 373
Lunney, C. 151
Luntz, Frank 287, 294
Lupia, A. 97

MacKinnon, D. P. 448, 456
macro-analytic approaches 327, 331–2
mail surveys 31, 68–9
MAIN (Modality-Agency-Interactivity-Navigability) model 496, 498
Mancini, P. 396, 402
manifest content 273, 275
Mansbridge, J. J. 334
Marcoulides, G. A. 424–5
Marcus, G. E. 527, 538
marketing 286, 291
Marlowe, D. 507–8, 511, 514
Marsh, A. A. 184
Martin, L. L. 58
Maruyuma, G. M. 427
mass appeal 218, 224, 226, 227, 230, 231
Massey, B. L. 494
Masters, R. D. 174, 175, 181
Mather, Cotton 311
Maxwell, S. E. 24
Mazzoleni, G. 368
McCain, John 102, 315, 490
McCarthyism 304, 306
McCleary, R. 473
McClure, R. D. 61
McClurg, S. D. 350, 352, 361n6
McCombs, M. 81, 84, 383, 385, 388, 391, 399
McDermott, R. 288
McDonald, M. P. 84
McDonald, R. P. 422
McHale, J. P. 271
McKinney, M. 288–9, 290
McLeod, D. M. 562–3
McLeod, J. M. 428, 500, 559, 562–3

McLuhan, M. 488
McMillan, S. J. 491–2, 493
McPhee, W. N. 349
Meade, J. 336
meaning 284, 287, 327, 329, 509–10, 527
measurement 11–12; deliberation 324, 325, 326–38, 339–40; error 194, 456, 520, 554; facial displays 176, 178–80, 183–4; indirect effects 452; interactivity 12, 495–500; Internet use 485–6; media use 62–4, 559–60, 566–7; panel studies 26, 30, 31; political knowledge 62; problems 558–60; psychophysiological 12–13, 525–40; social communication research 346–7; social desirability bias 507–9; structural equation modeling 420, 421–3
media 52n1, 72–3, 130, 544, 548; agenda setting 34–5, 383–4, 385, 386–7, 388–91, 399; ANES 99, 102–5, 106, 399, 563; bias 186, 254; changing technology 550–1; Congressional Elections Study 107; debates 270; exposure 91–2, 130–1, 485, 558; "face time" 166; focus groups 288, 289, 296; frames 238–67; influence over content 374–5; influence over political actors 375–6, 379; institutions 370–2; interactivity 491; measurement problems 559–60, 566–7; mediatization 367–82; meta-analysis 119–20; multi-stage experiments 196; NAES 102, 104–5; negative coverage of women leaders 437; non-campaign coverage 549, 550; panel studies 27, 31, 102; political knowledge 22–3, 61–2, 89; political logic 374; political perceptions 121–2; political systems 396; polls 38; public scrutiny 185–6; racial issues 107, 132, 133; "rally-round-the-flag" effect 22; reinforcing spirals system approach 197–8; secondary analysis 85, 91–2; self-selected audiences 145; simple mediation model 438–41; surveys 62–4; time-related effects 23, 25; voting behavior 470–1; *see also* Internet; news media; newspapers; television
mediation 11, 367–8, 434–65, 545, 563; bootstrapping 448–52; causal steps approach 445–6; concept of 367–8; interactivity 491; intramedia 23; longitudinal studies 454–6; moderated 453–4; multiple-step multiple mediator model 443–5, 448, 451, 460–3; panel studies 22; product of coefficients approach 446–8; simple mediation model 457, 458; single-step multiple mediator model 441–3, 450, 451, 452
mediatization 10, 367–82; content 374–5; as four-dimensional concept 376–7, 378–9; institutions 370–2, 376, 378–9; as integrative concept 377–8; media dependence 369–70; media logic 372–3, 376, 377, 378; political actors 375–6, 379; political logic 373–4, 376
Melkote, S. 389
Melville, H. 300

memory 56, 66, 130, 508, 519
Mendelberg, T. 341n1
Merton, R. 284, 286, 289
Messaris, P. 214
meta-analysis 6, 114–26, 545; advertising 120–1; agenda setting 384; description of technique 115–16; future implications 122–3; limitations of 116–18, 123; news coverage 119–20; political debates 119; political perceptions 121–2; regulatory bodies 123–4
metaphor 302, 303, 312–14
methods 4, 13, 167–8, 543–4; choice of 557–8; content analysis 271; data analysis pitfalls 560–1; deliberation 326; focus groups 289; future research 562–7; generalizability 561; international research 395; measurement problems 558–60; repeated cross-section design 38, 39; respondent burnout 560; rolling cross-sectional surveys 35–7; theory and 545–8; *see also* experimental studies; panel studies; statistical analysis; surveys
Meyer, P. 549
micro-analytic approaches 327–31
Middle East 389, 391
midterm studies 107, 110n5
Mikami, S. 386
Milgram, S. 201–2
Miller, Arthur 304, 306–7, 308, 310, 312, 314, 315
Miller, J. 387
Miller, P. 58
Miller, W. 97
Mills, C. W. 547
Mindich, D. 287
Minnesota Multiphasic Personality Inventory (MMPI) 518–19
Miron, D. 120
mise-en-scène 214
Mitchell, L. 290
moderation effects 453–4, 491, 545
Modigliani, A. 240
Mohamed, H. 389
Mokrzycki, M. 70
Mondak, J. J. 66
Mondale, Walter 174, 175, 182, 187n7
Monte Carlo simulations 424
Monteiro, R. 390
Montjoy, R. 60
Mook, D. G. 201, 202
Moore, D. W. 24
Moore, Michael 70, 197
Morgan, D. L. 285, 286, 293
Moriarty, S. E. 214
Morrell, M. E. 336
Morris, D. 170
Morrison, D. E. 293, 294
Mortensen, S. 197
Morton, R. 155
Moscovitz, K. 331

Moy, P. 87, 91, 428
Mueller, J. 22
Muhlberger, P. 151, 336
Mulaik, S. 429
Mullen, B. 175
multilevel research 13, 331–2, 425, 563–4, 565
multiple-sample/multiple-group models 426
multi-stage experimental designs 194–205; external validity 200–2; realism 198–200; types of approach 195–8
multitrait-multimethod (MTMM) matrix models 421–2
mundane realism 136–9, 198, 199–200
"mushiness index" 67
Muskie, Edmund 171
Muthén, B. O. & L. K. 424
Mutz, D. 91, 97, 476, 526, 529
myth 300–20; evil 303–4; literalization of metaphors 312–14; political piety 301–2; rhetorical genealogy 304–6, 316; Salem witch hunts 306–14, 316

Nabatchi, T. 332, 340
Nader, Ralph 223
Nass, C. 489
Nathan, L. E. 81
National Annenberg Election Studies (NAES) 5, 47, 96–113; future of 108–10; institutions 106; issues and evaluations 105–6; media use 23, 63, 104–5; number of interviews 46; origins 97–8; panel data 39, 101–2; RCS design 35–7, 40–2, 51, 100–1, 102, 553; response rate 53n17; secondary analysis 6, 81, 84, 88–91; time-series data 46; voting behavior 60
National Issues Forums 329–30, 336, 338, 340
Native Americans 46, 53n14, 307, 309, 311, 314–15
negative campaigning 120–1, 155, 156, 219, 225, 228, 230; content analysis 274; experiments 131–2; focus groups 287; physiological responses to 529, 534–6
neighborhood effects 349, 350, 353, 356–7
Nelson, M. R. 436
networks 9–10, 104, 346, 347–9, 360n5, 361n6, 545; level of analysis 351, 352; sampling 354; validity 356
neuromarketing 510
New Zealand 35, 405
Newell, A. 527
Newhagen, J. E. 177, 288, 291–2, 296, 527
news media 52n1, 90–1, 130, 234n1, 428; agenda setting 201, 383–4, 386–7, 388–91; aging audiences 562; ANES 103–4, 203n2; bias 547; challenges to 544, 548–9; changing technology 550–1; civic participation relationship 436; comparative research 398–401; content analysis 268, 272; contextual effects 350; exposure 63–4, 398–401; facial expressions 165–6, 175;

frames 238–67; image bite analysis of political visuals 209–37; international news 550; measurement problems 520, 559–60; mediatization 371, 372–3, 374–6, 378; meta-analysis 119–20; moderation effects 453–4; multi-stage experiments 196; NAES 102; newsworthiness 122, 375, 377; non-campaign coverage 549, 550; online 141–3, 487, 488, 562; panel studies 27, 31; political knowledge 22–3, 89; racial cues 132, 133; "rally-round-the-flag" effect 22; realism 199–200; response latency 512, 515–16, 517; time-related effects 23, 25; Vanderbilt Archive 111n25; young people 287

newspapers 212, 428; agenda setting 386–7, 389, 390; ANES 103; challenges to 544, 548–9; comparative research 399–400; content analysis 272; endorsements 124–5; framing 249; measurement error 520; panel studies 27; Republican bias 119; response latency 512; secondary analysis 89

Nickerson, D. 359

Niemeyer, S. 337–8

Niemi, R. G. 337

Nimmo, D. 368, 369

Nir, L. 87, 88–90, 337

Nisbet, E. C. 87, 88

Nisbett, R. 506

Noelle-Neumann, E. 397, 402

"nonattitudes" 55, 56–7, 66, 72, 194

non-probability panel designs 31

nonverbal communication 69, 166, 169, 181; news visuals 210; physiological measures 538; viewer responses to leader displays 7, 173–8; *see also* faces

Norman, D. A. 487

norms: deliberation 325, 336, 338, 341; social desirability bias 507, 518, 519

Norris, P. 396

novelty 86, 87, 88–9

Obama, Barack 44, 102, 211, 490, 550

Ochsner, K. N. 533

Oczkowski, E. 429

Oksenberg, L. 58

Oldendick, R. W. 56

Online Commons 99

ontogenetic development 167, 168, 186n4

Oosterhof, N. N. 183

open media systems 387

open-source software 564–5

ordinariness 218–19, 224–5, 226, 227, 230–2, 233

ordinary least squares (OLS) 90, 435, 439, 442, 444, 467, 469, 520, 563

Osborn, M. 302

O'Shaughnessy, N. J. 315

O-S-O-R model 562–3

O'Sullivan, M. 510

Otherness 307, 311, 312

overreporting 60–1, 151–2, 155, 506

Page, B. I. 332

Palagi, E. 169

Palfrey, T. 155, 475

Palin, Sarah 214

Pan, Z. 500, 559

Pané, Fray Ramón 309, 311

panel studies 4–5, 19–33, 39–40, 46, 560; ANES 99–100; definition of 19; design considerations 23–7; inherent limitations 27–8, 31, 32; integration of data with other sources 27; mediation 454; NAES 101–2; non-probability 31; past and present research 20; political knowledge 22–3; "rally-round-the-flag" effect 22; respondent conditioning 47; strengths and weaknesses 28–31; value of 20–2

parallel process latent growth curve modeling 455–6

Park, W. 61

participant assessments 327, 332–4, 339, 340

participant observation 289, 330, 333, 334

party conventions 39

Patriot Act 245, 248, 250, 252, 254, 257, 261

patriotism 22, 214, 226

Patterson, M. L. 174, 182

Patterson, T. E. 61

Paulhus, D. L. 507

perceptions 121–2, 497

Perot, Ross 223

personality 109, 111n27, 187n11, 552; Congressional Elections Study 107–8; content analysis 271; facial appearance 183; ideal candidate 213; Minnesota Multiphasic Personality Inventory 518–19; trait variables 26

Peter, J. 388

Petersen, T. 402

Petrocik, J. R. 275

Petrova, P. K. 156

Petty, R. E. 56

Pew Center for the People and the Press 63, 64, 554

Pfau, M. 196–7

Pfetsch, B. 377, 379

phylogenetic roots 167, 168, 186n4

physiological measures 12–13, 108, 406, 510, 525–40, 545; brain research 532–4; facial electromyography 177, 183–4, 510, 530–1, 532, 534, 535–6; heart rate 529–30; information processing 527–8; laboratories 536–7; sensors 531–2; skin conductance 528–9

Pinkleton, B. E. 437

Poland 405

policy analysis 118, 124

Polimetrix 108, 144

political culture 377, 396–7, 402

political logic 373–4

political participation 120, 122, 153, 378, 428; *see also* voting behavior
political science 6, 96, 129
political systems 378, 387, 396, 397, 403
politicization of the media 371
Polletta, F. 334–5
polls 70, 552, 553–4; deliberative 556–7; ideodynamic model 92; repeated cross-section design 38; *see also* public opinion
Popovich, M. N. 214
populations 46, 288, 449, 450
populist campaigners 218–20, 224–33
Powell, M. C. 508
power asymmetry hypothesis 181
power estimation 424
Preacher, K. J. 439, 442, 446, 452, 454, 457, 458
preferences 7, 149–64; costs 155–6, 160–1; expressed 149, 150–2, 154–6, 157, 158, 160–1; revealed 149–50, 152–4, 160, 161; scripts 156–60, 161
presidential candidates: ANES 105–6; black 48; content analysis 275–6; facial attractiveness 182–3; facial similarity of voters 132–4, 146n3; focus groups 287; image evaluation scale 405; media coverage 120; NAES 91, 105; newscasters' facial expressions 175; personal qualities 271; physiological responses to 525–6, 534–6; political debates 119; political knowledge 61; "rally-round-the-flag" effect 22; rhetoric 302, 303; traits 42–3, 44–5; visuals of 209–10; websites of 490, 494
press freedom 387, 396, 400
Presser, S. 53n16, 56, 65, 506
Preuschoft, S. 172
Price, J. S. 171, 186n6
Price, V. 87, 89–90, 102, 337
primates 169, 170, 172
priming 24, 102, 196, 200, 369–70, 538
Prior, M. 63, 72, 103, 473
privacy issues 294, 567
problem-oriented research 202, 203n4
product of coefficients approach 446–8
propaganda 397
protocols: "controversy" 330; focus groups 291, 295–6
proximate causation 167, 168, 186n4
Prysby, C. L. 352
psychological realism 198, 200
psychology 129, 172–3, 242, 496
psychophysiology 12–13, 176, 178, 510, 525–40; brain research 532–4; facial electromyography 177, 183–4, 510, 530–1, 532, 534, 535–6; heart rate 529–30; information processing 527–8; laboratories 536–7; sensors 531–2; skin conductance 528–9
public meetings 332, 335–6
public opinion 552; agenda setting 389; comparative research 401–2; framing 241, 242,

243, 254–5; ideodynamic model 92; intervention analysis 473–4; time-series analysis 469, 470, 475; *see also* polls
Public Opinion Quarterly (POQ) 84
Puritanism 301, 307, 309, 311–12, 314
purposive sampling 272
Putnam, R. D. 81

quasi-experiments 25, 27
question wording 65–7, 68
questionnaire design 67–8

R software platform 564–5, 566
racial issues: facial displays 184–5; framing 107, 241; Internet users 140–1; media coverage 132; racial harassment 244; readiness for black president 48; voter attitudes 351
radio 103, 104, 399
Rafaeli, S. 493, 495
Rafferty, A. 72
"rally-round-the-flag" effect 22, 473–4
randomization 195–6, 271–2, 353, 521n5, 556
Randomized Response Technique 67
Reagan, Ronald: facial displays 174, 175, 176, 182, 210; focus groups 287; image-based messaging 211; physiological responses to 534, 535–6; rhetoric 303
realism 136–9, 198–200
real-time-response (RTR) 406
reassurance 170–1, 176, 179, 181, 182, 183, 187n9, 210
Redlawsk, D. 153
Reeves, B. 526
regression analysis 468–71
regulatory bodies 123–4
reinforcing spirals system approach 195, 197–8
re-interviewing bias 39–40
reliability 500, 559; content analysis 8, 273, 277; deliberation 327–8, 333; facial displays 176; framing 250, 251, 260–1; intercoder 8, 241, 272, 273, 277; participant observation 330; secondary analysis 90
religion 224, 244, 256–7; piety 302; Puritanism 301, 307, 309, 311–12, 314
repeated cross-section design 38, 39, 42, 44–5, 46, 51
replicates 35–6, 42, 46, 47, 51
replication 13, 109, 200, 426–7, 546, 552, 561
Republicans: "argument repertoire" 90; content analysis 275–6; debates 270; media bias 119–20; news preferences 104, 105, 135, 142–3; online experiments 141; viewers' reactions to advertising 136, 138; visual framing 223, 231, 232, 233
Research Subject Volunteer Program (RSVP) 185
respiration 530
respondent burnout 560
respondent conditioning 47

response latency 12, 99, 505, 510–20; capturing 520–1; facial displays 176, 183; information processing 509; sampling 511; social desirability bias 508
response rates: ANES 101; face-to-face surveys 69; NAES 53n17, 101; rolling cross-sectional surveys 50–1, 53n16
revealed preferences 149–50, 152–4, 160, 161
Rey, F. 388
Rey Lennon, F. 390
Reykowski, J. 336, 338, 340, 341n6
rhetoric 9, 300, 301, 302–3, 545; evil 303–4, 305, 315; genealogy 304–6, 316
Riffe, D. 269, 275
Roberts-Miller, P. 311–12, 316n4
Rolfe, M. 361n6
rolling cross-sectional (RCS) surveys 5, 34–54, 553; challenges 47–51; data aggregation 46; methodology 35–7; minimal conditioning 47; NAES 40–2, 100–1, 102; populations and subpopulations 46; prevention of false attribution 44–5; repeated cross-section design 38; temporal heterogeneity 42–4; unexpected events 43–4
Romania 405
Roper Center 108
Rosenau, P. M. 301
Rove, Karl 229, 230, 233
Rovner, I. B. 120
Rushing, J. H. 315–16
Russia 400
Ryan, J. B. 155
Ryfe, D. 324, 329–30, 334, 338, 341n1

Said, C. P. 183
Salem witch hunts 303–4, 306–14, 315, 316
Salter, F. K. 168, 169, 170, 181
same-sex marriage 244–8, 249, 252, 253, 254, 258, 261
sampling: ANES 98; bootstrapping 449–50; comparative research 398; content analysis 271–2; error 47–8, 445, 554; experiments 129, 139, 143–4; meta-analysis 117; NAES 100; optimal sample size 561; random 521n5; snowball 511; social communication research 352–6, 359; structural equation modeling 427; visual frames 222
Saris, W. E. 424
satisficing model 59, 65
Satorra, A. 424
Saudi Arabia 389
Sawyer, K. 333–4, 340
Sawyer, R. K. 86–7
Schaffner, B. F. 437
Scherer, K. 169
Scheufele, D. A. 84, 87, 91–2, 402, 428, 453
Scheve, K. 479n28
Schiefenhovel, W. 171

Schjelderup-Ebbe, T. 186n6
Schleidt, M. 171
Schleuder, J. 63, 91–2
Schönbach, K. 388
Schreiber, D. 532, 533
Schrott, A. 372
Schubert, J. 182–3
Schulz, W. 368, 369, 370
Schumaker, R. E. 424–5
Schuman, H. 56
Schwarz, N. 65
scripts 154, 156–60, 161
Sears, D. O. 177–8, 187n11
secondary analysis 5–6, 81–95; authenticity 91–2; benefits of 82; creativity 86–8; definition of 82; effectiveness 89–91; limitations of 83; novelty 88–9; panel studies 31
self-administered surveys 68–9, 72
self-efficacy 337, 515
Sellers, P. J. 437
Semetko, H. A. 377, 388, 399
semiconfirmatory factor analysis 422–3
sensitization 26, 39–40
sequential implementation approach 195, 196–7
Shadish, W. R. 203n1, 203n3
Shah, D. V. 23, 85, 198, 241, 436, 437
Shanahan, J. 402
Shapiro, J. M. 182
Shaw, D. 383, 399
Sheldon, R. J. 151
Shin, S. H. 391
Shrum, Bob 229, 231, 233
Siegelman, L. 120
Silver, G. E. 337
Silverstone, R. 368, 369
Simon, A. F. 160, 336, 471–2
Simons-Morton, B. 456
Simonton, D. K. 86
Singer, E. 53n16
Slater, M. D. 197–8
Sloman, L. 171, 186n6
smiles 169–70, 171, 181, 530–1, 534
Smith, J. L. 84
Smith, S. L. 272–3
Smith, S. W. 271–2
smoothing techniques 48–50
Sniderman, P. 108
Snow, R. P. 368, 372
Snyder-Duch, J. 268
Sobel test 446, 450
social communication research 9–10, 346–64; contexts 349–50; level of analysis 351–2; networks 347–9; sampling 352–6, 359; validity 356–9
social contexts 349–50, 360; level of analysis 351, 352; sampling 354; validity 356
social desirability bias 60, 63–4, 505–11, 514–16, 518–20, 534

social networks 9–10, 104, 346, 347–9, 360n5, 361n6; level of analysis 351, 352; sampling 354; validity 356
Social Security 240, 244, 246, 248, 252, 254, 258–9, 261
software: computer content analysis 8, 274–7; experimental studies 6–7; focus group data analysis 292; indirect effects 439; open-source 564–5; physiological data 532; questionnaire design 556; structural equation modeling 423; weighted data 566
Sokal, David 552
Song, I. 488
Sörbom, D. 429
South America 390, 391
Spain 388, 399, 401
Sparrow, B. H. 371
specification 11, 420–1, 423–6
Spencer, A. T. 401
"spiral of silence" theory 397, 401–2
split samples 100
Sprague, J. 349, 350, 352, 353
standardization 546, 547, 556
Stanley, J. C. 199, 200–1, 203n3
Starkey, M. 306
state variables 26–7
statesmanship 213–14, 223–4, 226, 227, 228, 230
statistical analysis 11, 13, 545, 558; content analysis 269; indirect effects 445–52; meta-analysis 115, 116; multilevel modeling 563–4; open-source software 564–5; selection bias 357–8; weighted survey data 565–6; *see also* structural equation modeling
statistical significance 445–6, 561
Steenbergen, M. R. 328–9
Stephenson, M. T. 202
Steuer, J. 492
Stewart, L. E. 187n11
Stokes, D. 97
Stormer, N. 301
storytelling 329–30, 372, 550
Strack, F. 58
Strömbäck, J. 397
Stromer-Galley, J. 151, 329, 331, 341n5, 491, 492, 494
Stroud, N. J. 46, 84, 437
structural equation modeling (SEM) 11, 419–33, 560, 563; bootstrapping 450; covariates 456; definition of 419; estimation and evaluation 426–9; facial displays 183; indirect effects 428, 435, 439, 442, 444, 447, 448, 452; latent growth curve modeling 455; measurement 421–3; meta-analysis 116; secondary analysis 89; specification 423–6
Sudman, S. 65
Suhay, E. 151
Sulkin, T. 336
Sundar, S. S. 486–7, 489, 492–8

sure losers 220–2, 225, 227, 229–33
surveillance gratifications 438, 439–45, 447, 452, 457
surveys 4, 55–77, 544, 553–5; agenda setting 383–4; attitudes 56–7; cell phones 70–1; deliberation 332, 336–8, 339, 340; face-to-face 69, 72, 98, 108; four-stage model 58–9, 68; generalizability 561; information processing 509–10; Internet use 485, 500; media use 62–4; mixed-mode 72; open-source software 565; panel data 4–5, 19–33; political knowledge 61–2; probability sample 505–6, 521n5; question wording 65–7, 68; questionnaire design 67–8, 556; respondent burnout 560; response latency 505, 511–21; sampling 353–4; satisficing model 59; self-administered 68–9, 72; short-term effects 558; social desirability bias 505, 506–9, 510, 511, 514–16, 518–20; telephone 69, 72; voting intention and behavior 60–1; weaknesses 130; Web-based 12, 31, 71–2, 108, 555; weighted data 565–6; *see also* panel studies; rolling cross-sectional surveys
Swanson, D. 212, 402
sweat (skin conductance) 528–9
Sweden 399, 406
Swenson, T. 22

Taiwan 387, 390, 399, 404
Takeshita, T. 386
Tao, C.-C. 488, 490, 495–6
Taylor, A. B. 448
technology 550–1, 562, 566–7; content analysis 557; experiments 129, 139–44, 145, 556; measurement of media use 560; survey research 555; *see also* Internet; software
Tedesco, J. 288–9, 290
Tein, J.-Y. 448
telephone surveys 35–7, 40–1, 50–1, 52n10, 69, 72, 555
television 8, 130, 369, 428, 544; agenda setting 386–7, 388, 390; ANES 103, 203n2; broadcasting systems 396; civic participation 436; exposure 63, 64, 436–7; facial displays 185; local 549; measurement problems 566; moderation effects 454; multi-stage experiments 196; NAES 100, 104; panel studies 27, 31; physiological responses 525–6, 529, 538; political advertising 402, 403; political debates 405–6; response latency 512, 517; secondary analysis 89, 90–1; spots 270, 271; storytelling 550; visual framing 212
temporal heterogeneity 42–3
temporary accessibility 24
Téramo, T. 390
terrorism 303, 306, 312
Teune, S. 330
Tewksbury, D. H. 64, 103, 104, 387, 399
theory 4–5, 13, 352, 545–8, 558

Thorson, E. 152
ticket-splitting 52n9
time-series analysis (TSA) 11, 466–82; ARIMA models 472–4; definition of 467–8; future research 474; regression analysis 468–71; rolling cross-sectional surveys 46, 47–8, 51; strengths and limitations 474–6; Vector Autoregression 471–2
Time-sharing Experiments for the Social Sciences (TESS) 6–7, 108, 109, 555, 561
Tims, A. 87, 92
Tinbergen, N. 167, 178
Tituba 307–11, 312
Todorov, A. 182, 183
Tompson, T. 70
Total Survey Error (TSE) approach 554
Tourangeau, R. 58–9, 68, 71–2
tracking polls 38
trait variables 26
truthfulness 57
Tuchfarber, A. J. 56
Turkey 389, 391
two-stage least squares (2SLS) estimation 428–9

Ukraine 406
ultimate causation 167, 186n4
underreporting 506
United States, comparative research 398–9, 402, 404, 405, 406
units of analysis: comparative research 398; deliberation 326, 331; focus groups 291–2, 293; interactivity 495, 498–9; multilevel modeling 563–4; social communication research 346, 351–2; visuals 404
Upham, C. W. 307, 311

Valentino, N. A. 150, 151, 153
validation 426–7
validity 167–8, 203n1, 203n4, 561; content analysis 8, 274, 275, 328; deliberation 332, 333; ecological 178; facial displays 176; focus groups 285, 292; interactivity 500; measurement problems 559; multi-stage experiments 196, 197, 200–2; multitrait-multimethod matrix models 421–2; predictive 144; realism 198–9; respondent conditioning 47; secondary analysis 90; social communication research 356–9; time-series analysis 475
Valliant, R. 72
Van Hooff, J. 172
Vavreck, L. 130
Vector Autoregression (VAR) 471–2, 478n22
Verba, S. 396
Verser, R. M. 119

Vico, Giambattista 301–2, 303
Videostyle 403–4
visuals 7–8, 209–37, 249, 270, 545; comparative research 404; content analysis 276–7; ideal candidates 213–18, 223–4, 226–8, 230, 232; populist campaigners 218–20, 224–33; sampling procedures 222; sure losers 220–2, 225, 227, 229–33
volunteering 154, 157–8
Von Franz, M.-L. 312, 313, 314
voter turnout 120, 145, 150–2, 155, 159
voting behavior 60–1, 212, 470–1; deliberation 337; expressed preferences 150–2, 154; political debates 119; response latency 508, 511–20; social desirability bias 505, 506, 509, 511, 514–16, 518–20

Wagner, M. W. 91
Wang, T. L. 387
Wansink, B. 65
Washingtonpost.com 141–3
Way, B. M. 175
Weisberg, H. F. 59, 72, 565
Weiser, P. 336
Welch, E. W. 495
Welser, H. T. 331
Wendorf, C. A. 425
White, H. 302
White, I. K. 61
Williams, B. 288, 292
Williams, C. J. 508
Willnat, L. 401
Wilson, Pete 131
Wilson, T. 506
Winneg, K. 46
Winter, J. 386
Wisconsin Advertising Project 101, 107
Wooldridge, J. M. 467
Wu, H. D. 84–5

Xenos, M.. 91

Yang, K. 390
Yankelovich, D. 67
Yoo, C. Y. 391
Young, D. G. 81, 85, 87, 90
young people 46, 70–1; focus groups 287; Internet use 562; online experiments 141; voter turnout 145
Yuksel, E. 389

Zaller, J. 57, 102, 105, 108, 194, 243, 254, 332, 388–9
Zanna, M. P. 202
Zogby International 70